Bibl. Alcove

BBC MUSIC LIBRARY CATALOGUES

ORCHESTRAL CATALOGUE

BBC MUSIC LIBRARY

ORCHESTRAL CATALOGUE
IV
COMPOSERS S—Z

edited by

Sheila Compton

BRITISH BROADCASTING CORPORATION

1982

Published by the
British Broadcasting Corporation
35 Marylebone High Street
London W1M 4AA

First published 1982
© British Broadcasting Corporation 1982
ISBN 0 563 12478 4 (complete set)
0 563 20123 1 (volume 4)

Printed in England by Imediaprint Limited

CONTENTS

S., J.A.   see   SCHMIERER, Johann Abraham

SAAR, Louis Victor (1868-1937)

AUS DER KANADISCHEN ALPENWELT: 4 impressions
   1. Pastorale   3. The Glacier
   2. Lake Emerald   4. Where the waters meet
                         φ   2+picc.2+ca.2+bcl.2/4341/timp/hp/str   17'   Leuckart   Misc 1104
OLD GERMAN MASTERS: suite, arr
   1. Overture (Georg Philipp Telemann)
   2. Minuet   (Friedrich Wilhelm Marpurg)
   3. Jig   (Johann Mattheson)
   4. Fantasy (Gottlieb Georg Muffat)
   5. Fugue   (Johann Pachelbel)
                         φ   str   Schirmer   1516

SAAR, R.W.

SCHUBERTIANA: selection, arr
   orch F.Adlington   PC   2020/0210/timp.perc/str   Paxton   6128

SAARENPAA, Toivo

2 FINNISCHE VOLKSLIEDER: suite, op.32
   1. Tuoll' on man kultani (My love is far away)   2. En voi sua unhoittas (I cannot forget thee)
                         φ   str   Edn Musica (Finland)   19486

SABATA, Victor de   see   DE SABATA, Victor

SABOL, Andrew

LOVERS MADE MEN: masque (Ben Jonson)
   Arranged and adapted from compositions by Nicholas Lanier, Alphonso Ferrabosco and their
   contemporaries   φ   str (3.0.1.1.[1])/cont   Brown University Press,1963   Misc 6355

SACCHINI, Antonio (Maria Gaspero Gioacchino)(1730-1786)

L'AMORE SOLDATO: comic opera
   Songs from Act III
      1. Poverina disperata, in F   3. Deh t'invola, in E
      2. Bel piacer, in B♭   4. Piano un po', in A
                         φ   0200/2000/str/cont   Bremner,1778   Misc 1683
ASTARTO: pasticcio
   Extracts
      Questo vano, in E♭   φ   2202/2000/str   Bremner,1776   Misc 2452
CHIMÈNE, or Le Cid: tragédie lyrique
                         φ   2202/2000/timp/str   Sacchini,1784   Misc 3996
La COLONIE: comic opera (French version of 'L'Isola d'amore')
                         φ   0200/2000/str   Enouville,1777   Misc 3997
La CONTADINA IN CORTE: opera
   Favourite songs
      1. Questo ch'io serbo, in E   3. Mi permetta, Signorina, in F
      2. Cara addio, in B♭
                         φ   0200/2000/str/cont(hpsd)   W.Napier,1777   Misc 1683
      No.1 only   φ   str/cont   (W.Napier,1777)   27074 +
      No.2 only   φ   0201/2000/str/cont   (W.Napier,1777)   27074 +

SACCHINI, Antonio (cont)

CRESO: opera
  Favourite songs
    1. Overture   8. Se al genitor: aria in D
    2. Se un'alma amante: aria in C   9. Tergi il pianto: aria in Bb
    3. Poveri affetti: aria in Bb   10. Di che pieta: aria in A
    4. Ah, mio cor: aria in Eb   11. Parto, più non: duet in Bb
    5. Sò che fedele: aria in E   Tu confuso: recit
    6. Quest'alma: aria in C   12. Che mora: aria in Eb
    7. Mi lachera: aria in A   Ecco mi: recit
       Nami che ascolto: recit
                        ∅   2202/2000/str/cont(hpsd)   Preston,c.1785   Misc 1548
       No.4 only   ∅   2000/2000/str   (Preston)   22797 +
DIDONE: pasticcio
  Favourite songs
    1. Son Regina, in Bb   3. Infelice, in E
    2. Ah, tu piangi: aria in Eb   4. Parto è ver: duet in A
       Ah, se il mio amor: recit   Placati idolo mio: recit
                        ∅   2200/2000/str/cont   Bremner,1775   Misc 3001
       Nos 1, 2 & 3 only ∅ 2200/2000/str/cont   Bremner,1786   Misc 1683
ENEA E LAVINIA: opera
  Favourite songs
    1. Rasserena i tuoi: aria in F   3. Serene tornate: aria in E
    2. Non più le vie: aria in G (with chorus)   4. Incerto è mio core, in Bb
                        ∅   2102/2000/str/cont(hpsd)   Napier,c.1780   Misc 57
EVELINA, or Arvire et Evelina: opera
  Complete (completed by J.B.Rey)
                        ∅   2222/2230/timp/str   Imbault,1788   Misc 5470
L'ISOLA D'AMORE: opera (see also 'La COLONIE')
    Intermezzi à quattro voci   ∅   0200/2000/str/cont   Bremner,1776   Misc 1877
LUCIO VERO: opera
  Favourite songs
    1. Overture (pf arr)   3. Se non avete: aria in Bb
    2. Se il cara bene: aria in C   4. Se mi rende: aria in F
                        ∅   0200/2000/str   Bremner,1773   Misc 2416
MITRIDATE: opera
  Favourite songs
    1. Senza di te ben mio: duet in Bb   4. Io parto ben mio, in F
    2. Care luci, in E   5. Resta in pace, in A
    3. Adorate mio speranza, in A
       Dove, ah i dove: recit
                        ∅   2000/2000/str/cont   Bremner,1781   Misc 1683
OEDIPE À COLONE: opera
  Complete   Imbault,1789   Misc 3425
  Overture
    ed A.de Almeida   ∅   0200/2000/timp/str   Heugel,1961   23592
    arr Rhené-Baton   ∅   0200/2000/timp/str   4'   Eschig   14392
L'OLYMPIADE, or Le Triomphe de l'amité
  Complete   ∅   2222/2200/str   d'Enouville,1777 Misc 3448
RENAUD: tragédie lyrique
  Complete   ∅   2202/2200/str   Sacchini,1783   Misc 3424
                        ∅   2202/2200/str   (Sacchini,1783) 26863
RINALDO: opera (Revised version of 'Armida')
  Favourite songs
    1. Se tu sequir, in A   4. Ah Rinaldo: duet in G min   7. Non partir bell: aria in Eb
    2. Torni la pace, in E   5. Dolce speme I, in C   Infelicei: recit
    3. Calma, calma, in Eb   6. Dolce speme II, in G   8. Cara saro: duet in D
                        ∅   2200/2000/str/cont   Bremner,1780   Misc 1683

SACCHINI, Antonio (cont)

SEMIRAMIDE: opera
   Overture
      arr A.Carse   φ   0202/2200/timp/str   4'   Augener,1953   20995 B
SON REGINA: aria
   in Bb   φ   0200/2000/str   Donaueschingen [MS 1702]   22056 Negs only
SOFONISBA: pasticcio see   VENTO, Mattia: SOFONISBA - pasticcio by M.Vento, G.Maio & A.Sacchini

SACHSEN-WEIMAR, Johann Ernst, Herzog von   see   JOHANN ERNST

SACKMAN, Nicholas

DOUBLES, for percussion & 2 instrumental groups
                           φ   Group I: 1(picc)1+ca.0.ssx.0/1100/mba(2timbales)
                               Group II: 1(picc)10.Ebcl.tsx.0/1010/vib(3tdm)
                               perc: African slotted dms.crot.2timbales.3dm   (Composer)   Misc 9528
ELLIPSIS for chamber orch (1976)
                           φ   1(afl)01(Ebcl)ssx(tsx)0/1200/
                               timp.3perc(African slitdms.cgas.cbells.mba.
                               tamb.timbales.tomtoms.wdchimes.vib.xyl)/
                               hp.prpf.org.pf/str   (Composer)   Misc 9583

SADERO, Geni

IN MEZO AL MAR: song
   in C, arr R.Chignell   φ   2121/2220/timp.perc/hp/str/chorus   (Sadero)   MS 839
   in Bb   2121/2220/timp.perc/hp/str   (Sadero)   MS 2392
TARANTELLA NAPOLITANA: song
   in E min, arr Catalinet   φ   1+picc.222/4230/perc/hp/str   (Chappell)   TO 1799

SAENGAR, G.

JACQUITA, op.106, no.2
   arr Roberts   PC   1121/2210/timp.perc/org/str   C.Fischer   1289

SAEVERUD, Harald (1897-

CANTO OSTINATO, op.9   φ   2+picc.2(ca)2(bcl)2/4331/timp.perc.tamtam/
                               cel.hp/str   9'   Norsk Musikforlag   Misc 110
CONCERTO for piano & orch, op.31
                           φ   3222/4200/timp.perc/str   Composer   Misc 3286 B
DEN SISTE BÄ'NLÄT (Her last cradle-song), op.22a, no.3
                           φ   str   Musikk-Huset,1953   23092
DIVERTIMENTO, no.1, op.13   φ   str   Norsk   Misc 2968
GALDRESLÄTTEN: Danza sinfonica con passacaglia, op.20
                           φ   2(picc)22(bcl)2/4231/timp.perc/hp/str   7'45"-9'   Musikk-Huset   Misc 3693
KJEMPEVISE-SLÄTTEN (Canto rivoltoso), op.22a, no.5
                           φ   2+picc.222/4331/timp.perc/hp/str   6'   Musikk-Huset   20100
PEER GYNT: incidental music, op.28
   Excerpts
      1. The Devil's five-hop   7. Anitra
      2. Bridal dance   8. Solveig sings
      3. The threatener   9. Grave Hymn
      4. Dovretroll jog   10. Twinnan
      5. Hymn against the Boyg   11. Here is my Empire!
      6. Mixed company   12. Sleep my precious, my darling boy
                           φ   2(2picc)2(ca)2+bcl.2ssx.2[+cbsn]/4331/timp.perc.
                               bells.tpbell.cast.cym.bdm.mildm.sdm.maracas.siren.
                               tomtom.xyl/hp.pf/str/S-solo.chorus   Musikk-Huset,1950   Misc 3694 +

SAEVERUD, Harald (cont)

RONDO AMOROSO, op.14, no.7 (from 'Seven pianoforte pieces')
                        ∅   0101/0000/str   4'10"   Norsk,1940   23005
SINFONIA DOLOROSA, op.19   ∅   3(picc)222(cbsn)/4331/timp/hp/str   12'05"-14'   Norsk   Misc 2969
SYLJETONE, op.14a, no.2 (Il fermaglio rusticano)
                        ∅   0.picc.111/0000/hp/str   2'30"   Norsk   Misc 2967

SAFRANEK, V.F.

DON QUIXOTE: suite
   1. A Spanish village   3. Dulcinea
   2. Sancho Panza   4. Don Quixote
                        PC   1121/2210/timp.perc/str   C.Fischer   6527

SAFRONI, Arnold

IMPERIAL ECHOES: march
   arr D.Bowden   PC   212.3sx.1/2230/perc/str   2'50"   Boosey & H   20260
       see also MILITARY BAND CATALOGUE
SAMOAN LOVE WALTZ: divertissement
   arr Middleton   PC   1121/2230/perc/str   Boosey,1927   20377

SAGER, Sidney

The MOONSTONE: music for BBC Bristol drama production
                        ∅   01(ca)1(bcl)0/ptimp.tabla/vln.vlc   Composer MS:BBC   MS 31791

SAILER, George

MAYP' EIN'H NYXTA: Greek National march
   arr Seredy   PC   112.2sx.1/2210/perc/bjo/str   Apollo   19276

SAINT-GEORGE, G.

CORONATION MARCH   PC   2222/4231/timp.perc/str   Boosey   13988
RÉVEIL DU PRINTEMPS (Spring's awakening)
                        ∅   2(picc)222/2210/timp/str   Woolhouse   Misc 914
SUITE, op.20, in D
   1. Preludio   3. Aria   5. Passepied
   2. Allemand   4. Bourrée   6. Giga
                        ∅   2222/2200/timp/str   (Woolhouse)   12899

SAINT-GEORGE, Joseph Boulogne Chevalier de (1739-1799)

SINFONIA CONCERTANTE, op.13, in G
   reconstr B.S.Brook   ∅   2vln-soli.str   in La Symphonie Française.Univ de Paris   MRL
   reconstr & cadenzas by J.-P.Paillard
                        ∅   2vln-soli.str   Costallat,1966   26404 *

ST HELIER, Ivy

COAL BLACK MAMMY: song
   in Eb & G   PC   2121/0220/perc/pf/str   (FD & H)   LM G 4290
FOLLOW YVETTE: song (interpolated in 'The Street singer', by Fraser-Simson)
   in Ab, arr R.Tilsley   ∅   1+picc.222/4230/timp.perc/str   1'30"   (AH & C)   22446

SAINT MARTINI, Giovanni Battista   see   SAMMARTINI, Giovanni Battista

ST QUENTIN, E

FORGET ALL YOUR TROUBLES: song
   in D, arr de Groot   org.pf/str   K.Prowse   18207

SAINT-SAËNS, Charles Camille (1835-1921)

AFRICA: fantasie for piano & orch, op.89
                    φ   2222/2230/timp.perc/str   10'-12'   Durand   2746 B +
ALGÉRIENNE see SUITE ALGÉRIENNE
ALLEGRO APPASSIONATO for cello & orch, op.43
                    φ   2222/2000/str   4'   Durand   14690
ALLEGRO APPASSIONATO for piano & orch, op.70
                    φ   2222/2200/str   4'   Durand,1905   20476
ANDROMAQUE: incidental music
   Overture   φ   2(picc)222/2230/timp.perc/str   8'   Durand   2824
   Prelude to Act IV   φ   2222/2230/str   5'   Durand   11535
ASCANIO: opera
   Complete   φ   3(picc)222+cbsn/40.3cnt.31/timp.perc/
                        hca/str   23'   Durand   6296 B

   Ballet suite
     1. Entrée du maître de jeux (Introduction)
     2. Vénus, Junon et Pallas (Danse ancienne)
     3. Diane, dryades et naïades (Gavotte)
     4. Bacchus et les bacchantes (Bacchanale)
     5. Apparition de Phoebus et des muses
     6. Évocation de l'amour par Phoebus
     7. L'Amour fait apparaître Psyché (Adagio)
     8. Ensemble des déesses avec les muses, les nymphes et les bacchantes
     9. Variation pour la flûte
    10. Le dragon des Hespérides apporte la pomme d'or
    11. Final-valse
       Nos 1-6 only   PC   1121/2210/timp.perc/str   8'   Durand   3559
       Nos 7-11 only   PC   1121/2210/timp.perc/str   9'   Durand   3560
       Nos 7 & 9 only
         arr Taffanel   PC   2222/2000/hp/str   Durand   7681 B
L'ASSASSINAT DU DUC DE GUISE: incidental music, op.128
   Introduction & 5 tableaux   1111/1000/str   Durand   4786
Les BARBARES: opera
   Overture   φ   2+picc.2+ca.2+bcl.2+cbsn/4431/timp.perc/
                        2hp/str   Durand   7851
CAPRICE ANDALOUS for violin & orch, op.122
                    φ   2222/2230/timp/[hp]/str   Durand   15395
Le CARNAVAL DES ANIMAUX: grande fantaisie zoologique [Ogden Nash narration available from Ref. Lib B.H.]
   1. Introduction et marche royale du lion   8. Personnages à longues oreilles
   2. Poules et coqs   9. Le coucou au fond des bois
   3. Hémiones   10. Volière
   4. Tortues   11. Pianistes
   5. L'Éléphant   12. Fossiles
   6. Kangourous   13. Le cygne
   7. Aquarium   14. Final   (2793 + Cmv Ds
     Complete   φ   1(picc)010/0000/hca.xyl/2pf/str   Durand   (Ewa Fm Gn
       ed M.Pommer   φ   1(picc)010/0000/hca.xyl/2pf/str   24'   Peters,1973   Misc 8372
        No.13 only
         arr Vidal   φ   0000/2000/hp.pf/str   2'30"   Durand   745 C

SAINT-SAËNS, Charles Camille (cont)

CHANSON D'ANCÊTRE for Baritone solo, chorus & orch, op.53, no.2 (No.2 of 2 pieces from Victor Hugo's
    'L'Art d'être grandpère')
    in Eb   ø   2222/2230/timp.perc/str   Durand   658

La CLOCHE, arr H.Mouton from 'Les Cloches du soir', op.85
               PC 1010/0000/str   Durand   3542

COELI ENARRANT (The Heavens declare)(Psalm 19), for SSATBarB soli, chorus & orch, op.42
              ø   2+picc.222/4230/timp/1[+]hp.org/str   Durand   Misc 1846
              ø   2+picc.222/4230/timp/1[+]hp.org/str   Novello   27017

CONCERTI
   Cello & orch
      No.1, op.33, in A min ø   2222/2200/timp/str   17'-20'30"   Durand   4811 + Awa Dm E
                           ø   2222/2200/timp/str   Eulenburg,1969 Misc 8746
      No.2, op.119, in D min ø   2222/4200/timp/str   Durand   15390
   Piano & orch
      No.1, op.17, in D   ø   2222/4200/timp/str   28'   Durand   27047
      No.2, op.22, in G min ø   2222/2200/timp.perc/str   20'30"-23'   Durand   4823 Dn +
      No.3, op.29, in Eb   ø   2222/2230/timp/str   28'   Durand   15391
      No.4, op.44, in C min ø   2222/2230/timp/str   23'-25'   Durand   7735 Amv Cn
      No.5, op.103, in F   ø   2+picc.222/4230/timp.perc/str 30'   Durand   5153
   Violin & orch
      No.1, op.20, in A   ø   2222/2200/timp/str   10'   Hamelle   3514 B
      No.2, op.85, in C   ø   2222/2230/timp/hp/str   14'   Durand   15747
      No.3, op.61, in B min ø   2(picc)222/2230/timp/str   28'   Durand   6158 Amv Cn

CORONATION MARCH, op.117   ø   2+picc.222+cbsn/4431/timp.perc.bells/
                               2hp/str   8'   Durand   4784

DANSE MACABRE: symphonic poem, op.40
              ø   2+picc.222/4231/timp.perc.xyl/hp/str 7'   Durand   4205 Amv Cs En
   arr H.Carr   ø   2121/2230/timp.perc/str   (Durand) TO 1170 **
   arr H.Mouton   PC 1(picc)221/2210/timp.perc/str   Durand   844 Dwa
   arr Moses-Tobani PC 1+picc.222/4231/timp/hp/str   C.Fischer (Durand) 2585
   Song version   ø   2222/2000/timp.tri/vln-solo.str   Durand   Misc 1203

DÉJANIRE: opera
   Prélude et cortège from act IV
              ø   1+picc.222/233[1]/timp.perc/hp/str   Durand   7844 B
             PC 1121/2210/timp.perc/str   Durand   6440

Le DÉLUGE: oratorio, op.45
   Complete   ø   2+picc.222/42.2cnt.30/timp.perc/hp/str   Durand   15392
   Prélude   Durand   6664 B
     arr M.Tobani, rev Seredy PC 2222/4230/str   C.Fischer 1855

ÉTIENNE MARCEL: opera
   Selection, arr H.Mouton PC 2(picc)222/2230/timp.perc/str   Durand   5466
   Suite
      1. Entrée des écoliers et des ribaudes (1'45")   4. Valse   (4'30")
      2. Musette guerrière   (2')   5. Entrée des bohémiens et bohémiennes (1'30")
      3. Pavane   (1'30")   6. Final   (2'30")
       Complete   ø   2+picc.222/4230/timp.perc/str   17'   Durand   7286 B
        arr H.Mouton PC 1121/2210/timp.perc/str   Durand   7297 & 7292
       No.3 only   ø   2202/0000/pf/str   Durand   4785 B
       No.4 only
        arr O.Messager ø   2+picc.222/4230/timp.perc/str   Durand   Misc 280

La FIANCÉE DU TIMBALIER (The Kettledrummer's betrothed): ballad for voice & orch, op.82
   in Eb   ø   2+picc.222/42.2cnt.31/timp.perc/hp/str   Durand   4206 B

La FOI: incidental music
   3 tableaux   ø   2+picc.2(ca)22/4330/timp.perc/2hp/str 16'   Durand   5734

SAINT-SAËNS, Charles Camille (cont)

GAVOTTE, op.23	φ	2222/2030/timp/pf/str	3'	Durand	4789 B
HAVANAISE, for violin & orch, op.83					
	φ	2222/2200/timp/str	9'15"-11'30"	Durand	7399 Amv B
HENRY VIII: opera					
Selections					
arr H.Mouton	PC	2(picc)222/2230/timp.perc/str		Durand	3549
arr Roques	PC	2(picc)222/0231/timp.perc/hp/str		Durand	8868
Suite of ballet music					

    1. Introduction et entrée des clans (4'30")   4. Danse de la gipsy (2')
    2. Idylle écossaise   (4')   5. Scherzetto
    3. La fête du Houblon   6. Gigue et final (4')

Complete					
arr M.Tobani	PC	2(picc)222/4230/timp.perc/str		C.Fischer	2304-5
Nos 1, 2, 4 & 6	φ	2+picc.2+ca.2(Fcl)+bcl.2/42.2cnt.31/timp.perc/			
		2hp/str		Durand	7877 Cn
Nos 1, 2, 4 & 6					
arr H.Mouton	PC	2(picc)121/2210/timp.perc/str		Durand	2241 B
No.5 only	φ	2222/4030/2hp/str		Durand	10240
No.4 only					
arr H.Mouton	PC	1(picc)121/2210/timp.perc/str		Durand	5244
Extracts					
Entr'acte to Act II	φ	3011/4000/hp/str		Durand	8429
Marche du Synode from Act III					
	φ	2+picc.2+ca.2+bcl.2+cbsn/4331/timp.perc/str		Durand	7484
Menuet de la Reine Anne	PC	1100/0000/hp.[pf]/str		Durand	4617
HYMNE À VICTOR HUGO, op.69	φ	2+picc.222+cbsn.[sarr]/42.2cnt.31/timp.perc/			
		hp/str/[chorus]		Durand	4698
INTRODUCTION ET RONDO CAPRICCIOSO, for violin & orch, op.28					
	φ	2222/2200/timp/str	9'30"	Durand	4207 Amv B
arr H.Mouton	PC	112+bcl.1/2200/timp/str		Durand	7728
JAVOTTE: ballet					
Suite	φ	2+picc.222/4431/timp.perc/hp/str	8'-9'30"	Durand	8271
arr H.Mouton	PC	2(picc)222/2230/timp.perc/str		Durand	4208
La JEUNESSE D'HERCULE: symphonic poem, op.50					
	φ	2+picc.222/42.buglehorn.2cnt.31/timp.perc/			
		hp/str	16'-18'	Durand	4208 Amv B
arr H.Mouton	PC	2121/2210/timp.perc/str		Durand	5401
JOTA ARAGONESA, op.64	φ	2+picc.222/42.2cnt.31/timp.perc/hp/str	4'	Durand	8268 B
arr H.Mouton	PC	1111/2210/timp.perc/str		Durand	5400
The JOUSTING OF KING JOHN see Les PAS D'ARMES					
MARCHE DU COURONNEMENT see CORONATION MARCH					
MARCHE HÉROÏQUE, op.34	φ	2+picc.222/4231/timp.perc/hp/str	7'-8'	Durand	4705 Amv B
arr H.Mouton	PC	1(picc)121/2210/timp.perc/str		Durand	854 B
arr Roberts	PC	2+picc.222/4231/timp.perc/hp/str		C.Fischer	7108
MARCHE RÉLIGIEUSE, op.107					
arr Branga	PC	1121/2210/str	6'	Durand	10019
MESSE SOLENNELLE for chorus, organ & orch, op.4					
	φ	20.2ca.00/0230/2org/str		Durand	Misc 2290
MESSE, op.54 see REQUIEM					
MORCEAU DE CONCERT for harp & orch, op.154					
	φ	2222/2200/timp/str		Durand	8335
MORCEAU DE CONCERT for horn & orch, op.94					
	φ	2222/0030/timp/str		Durand	15393
	φ	2222/0030/timp/str		Durand	Misc 9533
MORCEAU DE CONCERT for violin & orch, op.62					
	φ	2222/2200/timp/str	15'	Durand	15394

SAINT-SAËNS, Charles Camille (cont)

La MUSE ET LE POÈTE, for violin, cello & orch, op.132					
	φ	2222/2230/timp/hp/str		Durand	8112
Les NOCES DE PROMÉTHÉE: cantata, op.19					
	φ	2+picc.2+ca.2+bcl.3sx.2+cbsn/433+cbtuba.0/ timp.perc/2hp/str		Maho	Misc 1445
La NUIT for Soprano solo, female chorus & orch					
	φ	2222/4000/hp/str		Durand	Misc 2168
Une NUIT À LISBONNE: barcarolle for orch, op.63					
	φ	1111/2000/hp.pf/str	3'50"-5'20"	Durand	7379 C
NUIT PERSANE, for soli, chorus & orch					
Part 1 La Solitaire					
Prélude	La brise				
La solitaire	La fuite				
Part 2 La Vallée de l'union					
Prélude	Au cimetière				
Les cygnes					
Part 3 Fleurs de sang					
Prélude	Sabre en main				
Part 4 Songe d'opium					
Prélude	Tournoiement				
	φ	32+ca.22/42.2cnt.30/timp.perc/hp/str		Durand,1892	Misc 651 B
ODELETTE for flute & orch, op.162					
	φ	0202/0000/str	14'	Durand,1920	21262
ORIENT ET OCCIDENT: march	φ	2+picc.2+ca.2+bcl.2+cbsn/4331/timp.perc/str		Durand	4303 B
OUVERTURE DE FÊTE, op.133	φ	2+picc.2+ca.2+bcl.2+cbsn/4431/timp.perc/ 2hp/str	8'	Durand	4699
OVERTURE TO AN UNFINISHED COMIC OPERA					
	φ	2222/2220/str	5'30"	Durand	4317
PARYSATIS: incidental music					
Suite	φ	3(picc)3(ca)2+bcl.3+cbsn/4431/timp.perc/ 4hp/str	7'	Durand	7855 B
arr H.Mouton	PC	1121/2210/timp.perc/str		Durand	3558 B
Les PAS D'ARMES DU ROI JEAN: ballade					
in F min	φ	2(picc)222/2200/timp/str		Durand	15676
PHAÉTON: symphonic poem, op.39	φ	2(2picc)+picc.222+cbsn/4231/timp.perc/ 2hp/str	8'-8'30"	Durand	6213 + Amv Cn
arr H.Mouton	PC	1(picc)121/2210/timp.perc/str	9'30"	Durand	843 C
PHRYNÉ: opera					
Introduction to Act II	φ	2222/2000/str	4'	Durand	5175 B
La PRINCESSE JAUNE: opera in one act, op.30					
Complete (without overture)	φ	2222/4030/timp.perc/hp/str		(Durand)	Misc 4496
Overture	φ	2(picc)2(ca)22/4230/timp.perc/hp/str	6'	Durand	7223 B
arr H.Mouton	PC	1121/2210/timp.perc/str		Durand	794 Bp C
PROSERPINE: opera					
Entr'acte	φ	2+picc.1+ca.22/4231/timp.perc/str	3'	Durand	8571
Pavane	φ	1010/0000/str(no cb)		Durand	5054
RAPSODIE BRETONNE, op.7 bis	φ	21+ca.22/4230/str	23'	Durand	4319 B
RAPSODIE D'AUVERGNE, for piano & orch, op.73					
	φ	2+picc.222/4230/timp.perc/str		Durand	5891
REQUIEM, for SATB soli, chorus & orch, op.54					
	φ	42+2ca.04/4000/4hp.2org/str 4tbn from near organ added MS pts: 2cl 2tpt		Durand,1878	25550
RIGAUDON, op.93, no.2	φPC	2222/2210/timp/str	3'	Durand	4788 B

<u>SAINT-SAËNS, Charles Camille</u> (cont)

ROMANCES
Flute & orch, op.37	∅	1222/4200/timp/str		Durand	20475
Horn & orch, op.36	∅	2121/0000/str	5'	Durand	4209 +
Violin & orch, op.48	∅	1111/2000/**str**		Durand	14761

ROMANCE SANS PAROLES
arr Turlet	PC	1121/2000/str	Joubert	3585 B

RONDO CAPRICCIOSO
18 bars only (used as signature tune for programme 'String song')
	2hp/vln-solo.str/chorus	Durand	LM G 5945

Le ROUET D'OMPHALE: symphonic poem, op.31   En)
	∅	2+picc.222+cbsn/4230/timp.perc/hp/str	8'30"-10'15"	Durand	4210 + As Bmv Dwa)
arr Moses-Tobani	PC	2(picc)222/4230/timp.perc/hp/str		C.Fischer	1856 B
arr H.Mouton	PC	1(picc)121/2210/timp.perc/str		Durand	9922 B

SAMSON ET DALILA: opera, op.47
Complete	∅	3(picc)2+ca.2+bcl.2+cbsn/42.2cnt.31.oph/timp.perc.		
		glock.tamtam/2hp/str	Durand	Misc 794 C

Act II, Sc.3 (without the aria 'Mon coeur s'ouvre')
(orig keys), arr H.Carr	∅	21+ca.22/4230/str	(Durand)	TO 1174 **

Selections
arr Luigini	∅	2(picc)222/4231/timp.perc.glock/hp/str	9'30"-13'	Durand	5903 B
arr M.Moses-Tobani (op.425)					
	PC	1222/2210/timp.perc/str		C.Fischer	2301
arr H.Mouton	PC	2121/2210/timp.perc/str		Durand	11288
arr E.Tavan	PC	2222/2231/timp.perc/str		Durand	741 Bwa

Extracts
Amour! viens aider (O love from thy power): aria
Samson, recherchant (Tonight, seeking hither): recit
in A♭ (orig)	∅	32+ca.22/4000/timp.perc/str	4'30"	Durand	7866 C
in A♭, arr H.Carr	∅	21+ca.21/2230/timp.perc/str		(Durand)	TO 1201 & 7866 **
in A♭, arr G.Stacey		pf/str		(Durand)	LM G 3785
Bacchanale	∅	3(picc)2+ca.2+bcl.2+cbsn/42.2cnt.31/timp.perc/			
		2hp.pf/str	6'-7'30"	Durand	4359 C
arr H.Mouton	PC	1121/2210/timp.perc/str		Durand	6905 B

Danse des prêtresses de Dagon
	∅	2222/4200/timp.perc/hp/str	2'15"-3'	Durand	4311 C
arr H.Mouton	PC	1121/2000/timp/str		Durand	6297

Mon coeur s'ouvre à ta voix (Softly awakes my heart): aria from Act II, Sc.3
in D♭ (orig)	∅	22+ca.2+bcl.2/4230/timp/hp/str	Durand	7261 Amv D
in D♭, arr S.Robinson	∅	21+ca.22/4230/timp/hp/str	(Durand)	TO 448
in D♭ & D, arr G.Stacey		pf/str	(Durand)	LM G 3270
in B♭	∅	21+ca.22/2130/timp/hp/str	(Durand)	MLO 1803
arr H.Mouton (non-voca)				
	PC	1121/2000/str	Durand	743 B

Printemps qui commence (Fair spring is returning): aria
in E (orig)	∅	2222/4000/hp/str	Durand	7262 Amv C
in E & F, arr G.Stacey		pf/str	(Durand)	LM G 3585
orch H.Mouton (non-vocal)				
	PC	1121/2000/str	Durand	423

Voici le printemps nous portant des fleurs (Fair spring smiles again): chorus of Philistine
maidens
in A (orig)	∅	2000/2000/hp/str	4'25"	Durand	1684
in A, arr S.Robinson	∅	2222/4000/hp/str		(Durand)	TO 533
SARABANDE, op.93, no.1	∅	str	15'	Durand	2655 Amv B
SERENADE, op.15	∅PC	20.ca.20/2000/hp/str	4'-5'	Choudens	2638

SAINT-SAËNS, Charles Camille (cont)

La SPLENDEUR VIDE, op.26, no.2 (orig voice & pf)
    arr H.Mouton   PC 1121/2000/str   5'   Durand   3189
SUITES
    op.16
        1. Prélude   3. Gavotte   5. Tarantelle
        2. Sérénade   4. Romance
          arr F.Salabert   PC 1(picc)121/2230/timp/str   Salabert   9646
    op.49, in D
        1. Prélude   3. Gavotte   5. Tarantelle
        2. Sarabande   4. Romance
                     φ 22(ca)22/2200/timp/str   20'-23'   Durand   5733 B
SUITE ALGÉRIENNE, op.60
    1. Prélude   3. Rêverie du soir
    2. Rhapsodie Mauresque   4. Marche militaire française
    Complete   φ 2+picc.222/42.2cnt.31/timp.perc/str   18'45"-20'30"   Durand   11276
    No.2 only
        arr H.Mouton   PC 1121/2230/timp.perc/str   Durand   8261
    No.3 only
        arr H.Mouton   PC 1021/2000/str   Durand   1506 C
    No.4 only
        arr H.Mouton   PC 2(picc)121/2230/timp.perc/str   Durand   855 Cwe
SYMPHONIES
    No.1, op.2, in E♭ (1853)   φ 2+picc.2(ca)2+bcl.2/42.2cnt.2sxhn.30/timp.perc/
                                   4hp/str   31'   Durand   5731
    No.2, op.55, in A min (1859) φ 2+picc.2(ca)22/2200/timp/str   23'-25'   Durand   5732 +
        Adagio & Prestissimo (2nd & 4th mvts) only
        arr Roberts   PC 1(picc)121/2210/timp/org/str   C.Fischer   2010
    No.3, op.78, in C min (Organ symphony)(1886)
                         φ 3(picc)2+ca.2+bcl.2+cbsn/4331/timp.perc/
                            org.pf/str   30'-36'   Durand   5504 +
    in A (c.1850)
        ed J.Martinon   φ 2222/2200/timp/str   Eds Françaises,1974 Misc 8800
TARANTELLE for flute, clarinet & orch, op.6
                      φ 0.picc.202/2220/timp/str   6'-7'   Durand   5728
    arr Roth   PC 0212/0210/timp/str   C.Fischer   1869
Le TIMBRE D'ARGENT (The Magic harp): opera
    Overture   φ 2+picc.222/4230/timp.perc/hp/str   8'   Choudens   4445
    Selection
        arr Labis   PC 2(picc)121/2230/timp.perc/hp/str   Choudens   6611 B
    Extracts
        Valse Vénétienne   φ 2+picc.222/4230/timp.perc/hp/str   5'   Choudens   4446
WEDDING CAKE: caprice-valse for piano & orch, op.76
                      φ str   6'-7'   Durand   6055 Dni

SAINTON, Philip (1891-1968)

The ISLAND: symphonic poem   φ 3(picc)2+ca.22/4331/timp.perc/str   17'30"   Lengnick   Misc 2905 B
SÉRÉNADE FANTASTIQUE, for oboe & strings
                      φ str   11'30"   Chester,1952 Misc 3710 C

SAINTON-DOLBY, Charlotte (1821-1885)

BONNIE DUNDEE, attrib
    arr R.Barsotti   PC 1+picc.12.4sx.2/4230/perc/str   Boosey & H   21039 B
    arr M.L.Lake   PC 1+picc.12.2sx.1/2210/perc/str   C.Fischer   19720

SAITON, Wataru

MARASON (Marathon)
    arr M.Saunders (1961)   ∮   001.sx.0/0220/timp.perc.vib/cel.gtr.pf/
                                      vln.vlc.cb   Arranger MS:BBC   MS 31335 + ∮ only

SALABERT, Francis (1844-1946)

Les AIRS DE FRAGSON: selection, arr
                              PC   112.2sx.1/2230/perc/bjo/str   Salabert   12122
Les AIRS DE MAURICE CHEVALIER: selection, arr
                              PC   212.3sx.1/2230/perc/str   Salabert   11918
Les AIRS DE POLIN: selection, arr
                              PC   1(picc)12.3sx.1/2230/perc/str   Salabert   12366
Les AIRS DU POILU: selection of French marches, arr
                              PC   112.sx.1/2230/timp.perc/str   Salabert   12223
AU TEMPS DES FIACRES: selection of popular melodies, arr
                              PC   112.3sx.1/2230/perc/bjo/str   Salabert   8032
COMTE OBLIGADO: selection of songs from the operetta by Raoul Moretti, arr
                              PC   1(picc)121/2230/timp.perc/str   Salabert   12456
FOX-COCKTAIL: selection of old American hit-tunes, arr
                              PC   112.3sx.1/2230/perc/bjo/str   Salabert   13115
GAI SOUPER CHEZ SUPPÉ: selection, arr
                              PC   112.3sx.1/2230/timp.perc/str   Salabert   13115
Le MASQUE DE BEETHOVEN: selection from the works of Beethoven, arr
                              PC   1121/2230/timp/str   Salabert   12035
2 MENUETS, arr
    1. Menuet from 'Don Juan' (Mozart)   2. Menuet from 'Castor et Pollux' (Rameau)
                              PC   1110/0110/timp/str   Salabert   12050
PADILLA SELECTION, arr   PC   112.3sx.1/2230/perc/bjo/str   Salabert   9948
PROMENADE À L'ÉXPOSITION DE 1900, arr
                              PC   112.3sx.0/2230/perc/bjo/str   Salabert   12645
SÉRÉNADE FLORENTINE, for violin & strings, by J.Francheschi & F.Salabert
                              PC   str   Salabert   12501
Les SOURIRES DU DIVIN MOZART: selection, arr
                              PC   1121/2230/timp.perc/str   Salabert   12049
SOUVENIRS DES TROIS STRAUSS, arr
                              ∮PC 112.sx.1/0130/timp.perc/str   Salabert   13646
Le TOUR DU MONDE EN 80 AIRS, arr
                              PC   1(picc)12.3sx.1/2230/timp.perc/bjo/str   Salabert   12448
YANKEE DOODLE, arr   PC   1(picc)221/223[1]/timp.perc/str   Salabert   3816

SALGADO, Luis Humbert

QUENAS Y RONDADORES: Danza Vernacular no.2
                    ∮   2+picc.222/2220/timp.perc/str   BBC   Misc 2199

SALIERI, Antonio (1750-1825)

AXUR RE D'ORMUZ: opera
    Overture (Sinfonia)
        rev N.Negrotti   ∮   2222/2200/timp.perc/str   Carisch   25581
    Act III, Sc.2, 5 & 6   2222/2200/perc/str   (BBC)   19708
    Extracts
        Rüfe mir bald das Volk: aria from the orig version
            in C   ∮   0111/0200/str   [B.M.Add.16118 P.26089]   Misc 3209 B

SALIERI, Antonio (cont)

CONCERTO for flute, oboe & orch, in C
   ed R.Sabatini   φ   0001/2200/str   Doblinger,1963   23949
   ed J.Wojciechowski (Critical edn)
                           φ   0001/2200/str   Litolff,1962/Peters   Misc 6809

Les DANAÏDES: opera
  Complete   φ   2222/2220/timp/str   Des Lauriers [1784]   Misc 2126
  Overture
    ed P.Spada   φ   2222/2230/timp/str   10'   Boccaccini & S,1978   Misc 10429
La GROTTA DI TROFONIO: opera
  Sinfonia
    rev G.Piccioli   2222/0200/timp/str   Carisch,1961   Misc 5536
  Extracts
    Nello stato conjugate: aria in G from Sc. 9
                    φ   2202/2200/timp/str   [B.M.H.340]   19798 & mf 35
      Spiriti invisibili: aria in D min from Sc.10
                    φ   2202/2200/timp/str   [B.M.H.340]   19798 & mf 35
JUSTORUM ANIMAE: Offertorium für Allerheilgen, for chorus & orch, in A
  ed K.Rouland   0201/0020/str   Böhm [1952?]   21143
PALMIRA REGINA DI PERSIA: opera
  Overture
    ed P.Spada   φ   2221/2200/timp/str   8'   Boccaccini & S,1978   Misc 10456
La SECCHIA RAPITA: opera
  Overture
    ed A.Braga   φ   1+picc.222/2200/timp/str   8'   Curci,1960   Misc 8276
SINFONIA in D (Veneziane)
  rev R.Sabatini   φ   0200/2000/str   9'   Ricordi,1961   25139
SINFONIA in D (Giorno onomastico)
  rev R.Sabatini   φ   2202/2200/timp/str   19'   Ricordi,1961   25587
TARARE: opera (early version of 'AXUR RE D'ORMUZ')
  Danse, transcr Q.Maganini   φ   str   Aff Mus Corp   16376
VARIATIONS on 'La Follia de Spagna' (1815)
                         φ   2222/2230/timp.perc/hp/str   17'   Boccaccini & S,1978   Misc 10032

SALLINEN, Aulis (1935-

MAUERMUSIK 1962   φ   2(picc)+afl.22+bcl.1+cbsn/3221/str   Fazer,1969   Misc 7676
VARIATIONS for cello & orch φ   2(picc)12(bcl)1/1111/timp.perc.bells.mba/
                               hp/str   (Finnish Mus Inf Centre)   Misc 7682
VARIATIONS SUR MALLARMÉ (1967) φ   2(picc)22(bcl)2(cbsn)/4311/timp.perc(glock.mba)/
                               cel.hp.pf/str   [Composer]   Misc 8921

SALMENHAARA, Erkki (1941-

SYMPHONY no.2 (1963-6)   φ   2222/4220/timp.perc.mba/cel/str   Yleisradio,1966   Misc 6418

SALMHOFER, Franz

FAIRGROUND POLKA (Rummelplatz) PC 3222/4320/perc/str   Weinberger   20276

SALOMÉ, Théodore (1834-1896)

MARCHE FRANÇAISE, op.39   φ   1+picc.121/2230/timp.perc/str   Lemoine   9824 B

SALOMON, Karl (1897-

PARTITA FOR STRINGS
  1. Jerba   2. Burla   3. Aria   4. Theme & Variations
                              ∅   str
                                                          Hargail   Misc 3089

SALTER, J.

ROSA, REIZENDE ROSA: song
   in D, arr Greenbaum   ∅   2(picc)11.3sx.1/2230/perc/gtr/str
                                                       (Wiener Boheme)   MS 2317

SALTER, Lionel (1914-

The BARNSTORMERS: radio show
   Complete
       arr P.Akister, including the following songs:-
         Please don't forget me: song
             in F   ∅   1131/0000/pf/str
         We're playing "East Lynne": song
             in Eb   ∅   1131/0220/perc/pf-solo/str
         No more arties for me: song
             in D   ∅   1130/0000/pf-solo/str
         Good morning Mr. Sun: song
             in Bb   ∅   1131/0220/perc/pf/str
         Julia: song
             in F   ∅   1131/0220/perc/pf/str
         To be or not to be in love: song
             in F   ∅   1131/0220/perc/pf/str   BBC   Var MS 23832
The CUCKOO: traditional song, arr
                                    1121/1000/str   BBC   TO 1518
I'M THE OLDEST JUVENILE IN LONDON: song
   in Eb, arr B.Berlin   ∅   2121/0000/perc/hp/str   BBC   TO 556
MR. DITCHWATER'S CHRISTMAS (The Barsley Pantomime), by L.Salter & F.Curzon
                              ∅   112+bcl.1/2220/timp/hp.pf/str   BBC   MS 30174
ONS HÉMÉCHT: Luxemburg National Hymn, in C
                              ∅   1111/2110/str   BBC   2032
The SCHOOL FOR SCANDAL: radio production arranged from music by Sheridan's contemporaries
                              ∅   1101/2000/str   Arranger MS:BBC   MS 31596 +
SKYE BOAT SONG: Scottish song, arr
   in G   ∅   2222/2030/str   BBC   TO 1580
   in G   ∅   2222/2030/timp/hp/str   BBC   TO 1581
SWINTON MAY SONG: traditional song, arr
                              ∅   1121/2000/hp/str   BBC   TO 1519

SALVADOREZ, A.

La SORRENTINA
   Overture
       arr W.H.Myddleton   PC   2+picc.222/2230/timp.perc/str
                                                          Lafleur   8159

SALVAYRE, Gaston (Gervais Bernard)(1847-1916)

Le BRAVO
   Overture   ∅   2(picc)222/4431/timp.perc/str
                                                          Lemoine   11770
SUITE ESPAGNOLE
   1. Alla Zingara   3. Sérénade burlesque
   2. Aragonaise lente   4. Marche Bohémienne
                              ∅   2(picc)222/42.2cnt.31/timp.perc/hp/str
                                                          Choudens   15045

SALVIUCCI, Giovanni (1907-1937)

SINFONIA DA CAMERA for 17 instruments
                    φ   1111/1100/str   15'-19'   Ricordi   Misc 2792

SALZEDO, Leonard (1921-

CONCERTO for harpsichord & strings (1968)
                    φ   str   Lopés,1969   Misc 8646
LADIONOS (Four Sephardic Impressions for orch), op.55
    1. Ferial Morisco (Moorish Fair)(3'35")   3. Canción en la noche (Song in the night)(3'10")
    2. Fado (Portugese Work song) (4')   4. Baile (Dance)   (4'35")
                    φ   2222/4220/timp.perc/hp/str   Lopés,1962(H)   PL 335
WITCH BOY: ballet
    3 Dances
        1. Dance of the Witch Boy   2. Dance of Love   3. Square Dance
                    φ   2222/4331/timp.perc/hp.pf/str   FD & H,1958   Misc 5303 C

        Square Dance
            arr H.Dexter   PC 2121/2230/timp.perc/hp/str   FD & H,1959   23193

SAMARAKOON, Ananda

CEYLON: National Anthem (Namō Namō Mathā)(adopted 1952)
    arr G.French   φ   21+ca.22/2230/timp.perc/str   Blandford   25224 +

SAMAZEUILH, Gustave (Marie Victor Fernand)(1877-1967)

DIVERTISSEMENT ET MUSETTE   φ   1111/1000/str(no cb)   Durand   3391

SAMEHTINI, Maurits

Le DRAPEAU: marche militaire   PC 1+picc.221/2220/perc/str   3'   Byst (de Wolfe) 11432

SAMINSKY, Lazare (1882-1959)

AUSONIA (Italian pages), op.30
    Fanfare - inscription "To the genius of Ausonia"
    1. Il pensieroso   3. Campo di fiori
    2. Venezia   4. Oda romana
                    φ   2222/4200/perc/hp.pf(cel)/str   18'   Senart   Misc 1802
LITANIES DES FEMMES, for voice & orch, op.34
                    φ   201(bcl)0/1000/perc/pf(cel)/str   Senart   Misc 1800
SYMPHONIES
    No.2, op.19 (Symphonie des sommets)
                    φ   3(picc)2+ca.2+bcl.2+cbsn/4331/timp.perc/
                         2hp.pf/str   Senart   Misc 1801
    No.3, op.30 (Symphonie des mers)
                    φ   3(picc)2+ca.2+bcl.2+cbsn/4331/timp.perc/pf(cel).2hp/
                         str   Universal,1926 Misc 3189 B
VÉNISE: poème sérénade for chamber orchestra, op.36
                    φ   2010/1000/perc/pf(cel)/str   Senart   Misc 1799

SAMMARTINI, Giovanni Battista (1698-1775)

see JENKINS, N & CHURGIN, B: Thematic catalogue of the works of G.B.Sammartini.   Harvard U.P., 1976
     The numbers prefixed 'J' refer to entries in this book

N.B. There is considerable confusion about the attributions of the Sammartini (Sanmartini)
      brothers' music

6 CONCERTI GROSSI for 2 violins & strings, op.6, arr F.Barsanti from various symphonies, trios etc by
     G.B.Sammartini

No.1, in G		str		Walsh [1750]	21595
ed S.Cooper	∅	str		OUP,1976	Misc 9072
No.2, in A		str		Walsh [1750]	21595
No.3, in E		str		Walsh [1750]	21595
No.4, in A		str		Walsh [1750]	21595
No.5, in D		str		Walsh [1750]	21595
No.6, in A		str		Walsh [1750]	21595

CONCERTI
   Violin & orch, J.69, in C

ed N.Jenkins	∅	str/cont(hpsd)	Eulenburg,1956	22148

CONCERTINI
   in G

ed N.Jenkins	str	Grahl,1952	26008

MAGNIFICAT, for SATB soli, chorus & orch
   in B♭

ed N.Jenkins	∅	0200/0200/hpsd/str	Eulenburg,1957	22147

MEMET: opera
   Overture, in C

ed B.Churgin	∅	str	Harvard UP,1968	MRL

SYMPHONIES
   J. 2, in C

ed Torrefranca	∅	0202/2000/timp/str		Carisch	Misc 1789

   J. 4, in C

ed E.Bonelli	∅	0000/2000/str	7'	Zanibon,1956	25556

   J. 7, in C

ed B.Churgin	∅	str	Harvard UP,1968	MRL

   J. 9, in C min

ed B.Churgin	∅	str	Harvard UP,1968	MRL

   J.14, in D

ed B.Churgin	∅	str	Harvard UP,1968	MRL

   J.15, in D

ed B.Churgin	∅	str	Harvard UP,1968	MRL
ed R.Sondheimer	∅	str/cont(pf)	Bernoulli	Misc 2184 C

   J.18, in D (Overture to L'Olimpiade by B.Galuppi)

ed R.Lupi	∅	0200/2000/str	Carisch,1956	26300

   J.23, in D min

ed B.Churgin	∅	str(no vla)	Harvard UP,1968	MRL

   J.32, in F

ed B.Churgin	∅	str	Harvard UP,1968	MRL
ed N.Jenkins	∅	str/cont(hpsd)	Grahl,1953	21704

   J.33, in F

ed A.Bernard	∅	0000/2000/str/cont	(Grahl)	19659
ed B.Churgin	∅	0000/2000/str	Harvard UP,1968	MRL

   J.34, in F

ed B.Churgin	∅	str	Harvard UP,1968	MRL

   J.35, in F

ed B.Churgin	∅	str	Harvard UP,1968	MRL

   J.36, in F

ed B.Churgin	∅	str	Harvard UP,1968	MRL

SAMMARTINI, Giovanni Battista (cont)

SYMPHONIES (cont)
    J.37, in F
        ed B.Churgin   ∅   str   Harvard UP,1968   MRL
    J.38, in F
        ed B.Churgin   ∅   str (no vla)   Harvard UP,1968   MRL
    J.39, in G
        ed B.Churgin   ∅   str   Harvard UP,1968   MRL
        ed N.Jenkins   ∅   str/cont(hpsd)   Eulenburg,1956   22054
        ed L.de la Laurencie   ∅   str   in Inventoire....Fonds Blancheton,vol 2.E.Droz,1930-31   MRL
    J.59, in G min
        ed B.Churgin   ∅   str   Harvard UP,1968   MRL
    J.64, in A
        ed B.Churgin   ∅   str (no vla)   Harvard UP,1968   MRL
    J.65, in A
        ed B.Churgin   ∅   str   Harvard UP,1968   MRL
    J.66, in B♭
        ed B.Churgin (versions A & B)
                                ∅   str   Harvard UP,1968   MRL
    J.67, in B♭
        ed B.Churgin   ∅   str   Harvard UP,1968   MRL
    J.68, in B♭
        ed B.Churgin   ∅   str   Harvard UP,1968   MRL

SAMMARTINI, Giuseppe (1693-?1750)

CANTO AMOROSO
    arr Elman, orch J.Bürger   PC   1111/1110/timp.perc/str   3'30"   Schott   2586 B
    arr Kaiser, orch Wurmser, with title 'An old Italian love song'
                                2131/2000/hp/str   4'15"   (Schott)   TO 1075
CONCERTI
    Harpsichord (or organ)
        No.1, in A
            ed H.Illy   ∅   2vln/cont   Bärenreiter,1971   25284
    Recorder (Descant)
            ed J.Brinckmann   ∅   str/cont (real W.Mohr)   Schott,1959   23540
    Strings
        in E♭
            ed A.Carse   ∅   str   7'15"   Augener,1952   20544 B
    Violins & orch   see   CONCERTI GROSSI, op.8
CONCERTI GROSSI
    op.5: 6 Concerti grossi for string quartet & orch, arr from the sonatas for 2 violins & continuo, op.3
        No.1, in E min   str/cont   Walsh [1750]   26163 & 22802
        No.2, in B♭   str/cont   Walsh [1750]   26163 & 22802
        No.3, in G min   str/cont   Walsh [1750]   26163 & 22802
        No.4, in A min   str/cont   Walsh [1750]   26163 & 22802
        No.5, in C min   str/cont   Walsh [1750]   26163 & 22802
        No.6, in G min   str/cont   Walsh [1750]   26163 & 22802
    op.8: 6 Concerti grossi for 2 violins, cello & orch
        No.1, in G min   str/cont   Walsh [1750]   22802
        No.2, in A   str/cont   Walsh [1750]   22802
        No.3, in E min   str/cont   Walsh [1750]   22802
        No.4, in C   0100/0000/str   Walsh [1750]   22802
        No.5, in G min   0100/0000/str   Walsh [1750]   22802
        No.6, in A   0100/0000/str   Walsh [1750]   22802
    op.11
        No.4, in D min
            arr S.Beck   ∅   str   Music Press NY   19157

SAMMARTINI, Giuseppe (cont)

PASTORALE
   arr Martucci   ø   2202/2000/str   Ricordi   Misc 2752
SONATA, op.3, no.9
   Aria (Adagio)
      arr Gui   ø   str   Universal   1206

SAMMONS, Albert (1886-1957)

An ANGEL'S SONG, op.21
   arr A.Lotter   PC 1121/2110/timp.perc/str   Hawkes   3205
LITTLE COLUMBINE (Entr'acte), op.22
                   PC 1121/2230/timp/str   2'30"-3'30"   Hawkes   9351

SAMMUT, Robert

INNU MALTI: National Anthem of Malta (adopted 1941)
   arr G.French   ø   2222/2230/timp.perc/str   Arranger/Blandford   25207 +

SAMPSON, Godfrey (1903-1949)

SUITE FOR STRING ORCHESTRA
   1. Chaconne   3. Finale
   2. Passacaglia and scherzo
                   ø   str   13'   Novello,1949   Misc 1351 B

SAMUEL, Gerhard (1924-

LOOKING AT ORPHEUS LOOKING (1970/71)
                   ø   4444/4431/perc.bells.crot.glock.vib.xyl/hp.ehpsd.eorg/
                      str   Belwin Mills,1974   Misc 8419
REQUIEM FOR SURVIVORS: "and suddenly it's evening" (1973/74)
                   ø   4(4picc)44(bcl.,tsx)4(cbsn)/0431/5perc(timp.bells.
                      crot.flex.glock.2gro.mba.3tamtam.thermos.vib.washboard)/
                      hp/str   18'   Belwin Mills,1976   Misc 9440

SAMUEL, Harold (1879-1937)

DIAPHENIA: song
   in F, arr D.Darlow   ø   3222/2230/perc/hp/str   (Boosey)   TO 1535
JOGGIN' ALONG THE HIGHWAY: song
   in D, arr Jaxon   PC 1121/2220/perc/str   AH & C   3840
   in D, arr G.French   ø   0010/0000/gtr/str   (AH & C)   LM G 9712
The TOP OF THE HILL: song
   in D, arr Jaxon   PC 1121/2220/perc/str   AH & C   626

SAMUEL-ROUSSEAU   see   ROUSSEAU, Marcel Samuel

SAMUELS, A

POPPY, by A.Samuels & S.Jones
   Selection, arr H.M.Higgs   PC 2(picc)122/2230/perc/str   Chappell   3295 B

SANDBERGER, Adolf (1864-1943)

KÖNIGS-MARSCH, op.21	∅	2+picc.222+cbsn/4331/timp.perc/hp/str	Schmid	Misc 929
RICCIO: symphonic prologue, op.16				
	∅	3(picc)2+ca.2+bcl.2+cbsn/4331/timp.perc.tamtam/		
		hp/str	Breitkopf	Misc 855
VIOLA: symphonic poem, op.17	∅	3(picc)2+ca.2+bcl.2+cbsn/4331/timp.perc/		
		hp/str	Schmid	Misc 927

SANDBY, Herman (1881-1965)

AFTENSTEMNING (At twilight)	∅	0000/4000/str	Skandinavisk	Misc 2442
BERCEUSE		[hp]/str	Borup,1935	Misc 3446 B
EFTERAARSSANG (Autumn song)	∅	2(picc)222/4200/str	Skandinavisk	Misc 2534 B
ISLANDSK FOLKEVISE (Icelandic folksong), arr				
	∅	hp/str	Hansen,1938	Misc 1493
NORWEGIAN BRIDAL MARCH	∅	str	C.Fischer	13379
SOLO-STYKKE, for double bass & strings				
	∅	str	Skandinavisk	Misc 2443
SONG OF VERMLAND: Swedish folksong				
	∅	str	C.Fischer	13378
VALRAVNEN: Danish folksong, arr				
	∅	hp/str	Hansen	Misc 382
VED STRANDBREDDEN (On the sea shore)				
	∅	3(picc)2+ca.2+bcl.2/4331/timp/hp.[pf]/str	Borup	Misc 2441
VINTERSANG	∅	2222/2200/str	Borup,1941	Misc 3409

SANDERS, Geo H.

SELECTION OF HEBREW MELODIES	PC	112.sx.1/2210/timp.perc/str	G.Schirmer	8716

SANDERS, J.

SOUTHOLOGY, arr Savino	∅PC	112.3sx.1/1210/timp.perc/bjo/str	Robbins	11329

SANDERS, Robert Levine (1906-1974)

SATURDAY NIGHT				
Barn dance	∅	3(picc)222/4331/timp.perc/str	C.Fischer	15424

SANDERS, Scott

ON THE ROAD TO ANYWHERE: march	PC	112.2sx.1/2230/perc/str	FD & H	4505

SANDERSON, James

HAIL TO THE CHIEF				
arr M.L.Lake	PC	1+picc.12.2sx.1/2210/perc/str	C.Fischer	19720

SANDERSON, Wilfred (1878-1935)

AFTER LONG ABSENCE: song					
in A♭, arr A.Franzel	∅	1110/0000/perc/acdn.hp.pf/str		(Boosey)	LM A 654
AS I SIT HERE REMEMBERING YOU: song					
in D		1111/1110/perc/str		(Boosey)	LM G 4386
in E♭, arr G.Stacey		pf/str		(Boosey)	LM G 5193
in E♭, arr J.Turner	∅	1110/1000/hp/str		(Boosey)	LM G 9087
in F, arr S.Robinson	∅	2121/2230/timp/hp/str	3'05"	(Boosey)	TO 6

SANDERSON, Wilfred (cont)

BEYOND THE DAWN: song
in C, arr Myddleton	PC	2222/2200/timp.perc/str		Boosey	3647 C
in E, arr F.Cramer		[hp].pf/str		(Boosey)	LM G 5479
in Bb		1111/0110/str		(Siddell)	17262

A BLACKBIRD'S SONG
in Eb, arr Jaxon	PC	1121/2230/timp.perc/str		Boosey	12568

BREAK O' DAY: song
in C, arr Dyck	∅PC	1020/0210/timp.perc/str		Boosey	17087 +
in D		1010/0110/str		(Siddell)	17088
in Bb		1121/2210/timp.perc/str		(Boosey)	MS 30111

BRISE D'ÉTÉ
arr Hickling	PC	1121/2210/hp.org.[pf]/str	4'	Leonard, Gould & B	10607 B

CAPTAIN MAC: song
in D, arr E.Griffiths		pf/str		(Boosey)	LM G 6650

CHARM ME ASLEEP (To Music): song
in C, arr G.Stacey		pf/str		(Boosey)	LM G 3474

The COMPANY SERGEANT MAJOR: song
in C, arr Van Dyck	PC	1121/2220/timp.perc/str		Boosey	267

DEVONSHIRE CREAM & CIDER: song
in C & D, arr S.Baynes	PC	2122/2230/timp.perc/str		Boosey	3641 + Ap B
in C, arr E.Griffiths		pf/str		(Boosey)	LM G 7405
in D, arr J.O.Turner	∅	1110/1000/hp/str		(Boosey)	LM G 7511

DRAKE GOES WEST: song
in C, arr E.Griffiths		pf/str		(Boosey)	LM G 5456
in C & D, arr G.Stacey		1010/0000/pf/str		(Boosey)	LM G 3130
in D, arr H.Carr	∅	2121/2230/perc/hp/str		(Boosey)	TO 896 +
in D, arr J.Turner	∅	1110/1000/hp/str		(Boosey)	LM G 8554
in D, arr Van Dyck	SC	2222/2330/perc/str		Boosey	2401 Ap
in G, arr Zalva	PC	2121/2230/timp.perc/str	3'15"	Boosey	18769 +

EASTER FLOWERS: song
in Bb, arr J.O.Turner	∅	1110/1000/hp/str		(Boosey)	LM G 7513

FRIEND O' MINE: song
in F, G, Ab & C, arr H.Carr '	∅	2121/2230/perc/hp/str	2'55"	(Boosey)	TO 22
in Ab & G, arr G.Stacey		pf/str		(Boosey)	LM G 3293
in Ab, arr G.Stacey		1010/0000/pf/str		(Boosey)	LM G 3746
in Ab, arr Van Dyck	PC	1121/2210/timp/str	3'	Boosey	3652 B
in Ab, arr G.Zalva	PC	112.4sx.1/2330/timp.perc/str		Boosey & H	19510
in A, arr B.Thompson	∅	1110/1000/hp/str		(Boosey)	LM G 7516

The GLORY OF THE SEA: song
in C, arr Van Dyck	PC	1121/2220/timp.perc/str		Boosey	3651 Ap C
in Bb		str		(Siddell)	17115

GOD THAT MADEST EARTH AND HEAVEN: song
arr A.Schmid (non-vocal)		2222/2230/timp/str		Boosey, 1905	17260

HARLEQUIN: song
in B min, arr S.Baynes	∅PC	2122/2230/timp.perc/str/chorus	3'	Boosey	3650 B

The HILLS OF DONEGAL: song
in A, arr Van Dyck	PC	1(picc)121/2210/timp/str		Boosey	3426 Ap C
in C, arr F.Cramer		acdn.pf/str		(Boosey)	LM G 7484
in C, arr F.Hartley	PC	1010/0000/str		Boosey & H	16870

LAND OF DELIGHT: song
in D		1121/2210/timp/str		(Siddell)	17999

LAUGHING CAVALIER: song
in A min & Bb min, arr H.Carr					
	∅	2121/2230/perc/hp/str	3'30"	(Boosey)	TO 41
in Bb min, arr G.Stacey		pf/str		(Boosey)	LM G 3099

SANDERSON, Wilfred (cont)

LOOKING FOR YOU: entr'acte
  arr S.Baynes   PC 212.3sx.2/2220/timp.perc/bjo/str   Boosey & H   10385

MY DEAR SOUL: song

in A♭ & B♭, arr G.Stacey		pf/str		(Boosey)	LM G 4442
in B♭, arr S.Baynes	PC	2122/2330/perc/str		Boosey	3882 Ap
in B♭, arr G.Stacey		1010/0000/pf/str		(Boosey)	LM G 3665
in B♭, arr J.Turner	∅	1110/1000/hp/str		(Boosey)	LM G 8551
in B♭, arr L.Wurmser	∅	21+ca.22/4000/cel.hp/str		(Boosey)	TO 1407

NIGHTINGALE OF JUNE: song
  in E♭, arr S.Baynes   PC 2122/2230/timp.perc/str   Boosey   3642 B

ONE MORNING VERY EARLY: song

in F, arr C.Watters	∅	pf/str		(Boosey)	LM G 10056
in G, arr D.Darlow	∅	3222/4030/perc/hp/str	3'25"	(Boosey)	TO 1513

PASS EVERYMAN: song
  in A   1111/2210/timp.perc/str   (Siddell)   18308

RUSSET AND GOLD: song cycle
  1. Haymaker's dance   3. Russet maids
  2. Shepherds gay   4. Come dance at our wedding
    orch & arr S.Baynes   PC 2(picc)122/2230/timp.perc/str   Boosey   7754

SANDERSON'S SONGS: selection, arr S.Baynes
                        PC 212.3sx.1/2230/timp.perc/str   Boosey & H   11228

SERENATA   PC 1121/2210/timp.perc/org/str   Leonard, Gould & B   10426

SHIPMATES O' MINE: song

in G	PC	1121/2210/timp/str	3'	Boosey	2312 Ap C
in G, arr G.Stacey		[hp].[org].pf/str		(Boosey)	LM G 5476
in G, arr G.Zalva	PC	112.4sx.1/2230/timp.perc/str		Boosey	18767
in A♭, F & G (3 settings), arr H.Carr					
	∅	2121/2230/timp.perc/hp/str	3'25"	(Boosey)	TO 373

SPRING'S AWAKENING: song

in A	1121/2310/perc/str	Boosey	3649 Ap
in A, orch J.Buerger	2121/2230/timp.perc/hp/str	(Boosey)	MS 2641
arr G.Williams	1121/2210/timp.perc.glock/hp/str/Soprano solo.chorus	Boosey & H	MLO 132

SUSAN IS HER NAME, O: song
  in G, arr A.Franzel   1010/0000/str   (Boosey)   LM G 3713

UNTIL: song

in D♭, arr A.Franzel as duet	∅	1110/0000/perc/hp.pf/str	(Boosey)	LM A 624
in E♭	PC	1111/2210/timp/str	Boosey	16882
in E♭, arr M.Saunders	∅	1110/1000/hp/str	(Boosey)	LM G 7560
in F		1111/2210/str	Boosey,1913	17273
in F	PC	1111/2210/timp/str	Boosey	3648 B
in F	∅PC	1111/1210/timp/str	Boosey	16505
in F & G, arr H.Carr	∅	2121/2230/timp.perc/hp/str	(Boosey)	TO 372
in F, arr G.Stacey		pf/str	(Boosey)	LM A 131
in F & G, arr G.Stacey		1110/0000/perc/acdn.hp/str	(Boosey)	LM A 131
in G, arr G.Stacey		1111/2210/perc/str	(Boosey)	LM G 5695
in G, arr G.Williams for Tenor solo, chorus & orch				
	∅	1121/2210/timp.perc/hp/str	Boosey & H	MLO 127
paraphrase on song, arr H.Wood				
	PC	222.3sx.2/2230/timp/str	Boosey & H	11791 Ap

UP FROM SOMERSET: song

in C	PC	1(picc)222/2120/timp.perc/str	Boosey	2783 Bp D
in D♭, arr G.Stacey		pf/str	(Boosey)	LM G 3230
in D		2+picc.222/4230/timp.perc/str	(Boosey)	21355

SANDERSON, Wilfred (cont)

VALLEY OF LAUGHTER: song
    in D min, arr J.Turner   ø 1110/1000/hp/str   (Boosey & H)   LM G 8548
    in E♭   1222/2220/timp/str   (Siddell)   17239
    in F   PC 1(picc)222/2220/timp/str   3'   Boosey   3776 Ap B
The VOYAGERS: duet
    in D min, arr J.Turner   ø 1110/1000/hp/str   (Boosey & H)   LM G 8548
YOU ALONG O' ME: song
    in A, arr G.Stacey   pf/str   (Boosey)   LM G 3148

SANDEY, Bob

IMAGE   see   GLENN, Joe: IMAGE

SANDFORD, Arthur

CALYPSO   ø 1020/0210/timp/hp.pf/str   Composer   19188
EARLY ONE MORNING, arr   2121/2220/perc/pf/str   Arranger   WE 345
SUR LE PONT D'AVIGNON: traditional song, arr
    in A♭, for chorus & orch   ø 2121/0000/hp/str   Arranger   LM G 5069
TROTTIE TRUE   ø 2121/0220/timp.perc/str   Composer MS:BBC   MS 31084

SANDRÉ, Gustave

BERCEUSE DE PHILIS (17th century air), arr
                       ø str   Schott   9335
SERENADE for strings, op.24 ø str   Breitkopf   27039

SANFORD, Harold

VICTOR HERBERT FAVORITES: selection, arr
                      PC 1(picc)12.3sx.1/2210/timp.perc/str   9'15"   Witmark   14939 B

SANITA, Giovanni

SABOR FLAMENCO
    arr I.Sutherland   ø 2(picc)121/2220/perc/hp.pf/str   2'15"   Senlac Music   25803

SANMARTINI   see   SAMMARTINI, Giovanni Battista   and   SAMMARTINI, Giuseppe

SANS-SOUCI, Gertrude

WHEN SONG IS SWEET
    in G, arr J.O.Turner   ø 1110/1000/hp/str   (Harris)   LM G 7543

SANSOM, C.

MUSIC FOR AN IMAGINARY BALLET, for jazz/rock sextet & orch (1974-76)
                       ø 3(afl,picc)3(ca)3(E♭cl,bcl)3(cbsn)/4441/
                          3perc(timp.cbells.crot.glock.gro.mba.tamtam)/
                          2hp.pf(cel)/str (12.12.10.10.8)
                          sextet: 000.ssx(tsx)0/0010/egtr.bgtr.epf/
                          kit   23'   Universal,1976   Misc 9448

SANTOLIQUIDO, Francesco (1883-1971)

ACQUARELLI: symphonic suite
  1. La mattina nel bosco   3. Vespro
  2. Nevica   4. Festa notturna
           ø 2+picc.2+ca.2+bcl.3/4331/timp.perc/hp/str 14'   Ricordi,1922   Misc 564
L'ULTIMA VISIONE DI CASSANDRA: cantata for Soprano solo, fv-chorus & orch
           ø 2222/4240/timp/hp/str   Forlives,1921   Misc 9283

SANTORO, Claudio (1919-

3 ABSTRAÇÕES (1966)   ø str   Jobert,1969   Misc 8139
INTERAÇÕES ASSINTÓTICAS (1969) ø 3(picc)3(ca)3(Dcl)+bcl.3(cbsn)/4431/timp.perc.
                              bells.cbells.glock.3gong.mba.tamtam.vib.xyl/
                              cel.hp.pf/str   8'   Jobert,1971   Misc 8437
INTERMITENCIAS II, for piano and chamber orch (1967)
           ø 1111/1110/2perc.glock.vib.xyl/str(1.1.1.1.1)/
             elec   6'30"   Jobert,1969   Misc 8629 B

SANTOS, Artur

8 CANCOES POPULARES PORTUGEUESAS
  Extracts
    1. Sete anos que andei na guerra   7. Santa Luzia
    5. Oh! que calma   8. A Marcela
    6. Boina - Boina!
           ø 2+picc.2+ca.22+cbsn/4331/timp.perc/hp/str   BBC   4557

SANTOS, Pablo

CIELITO LINDO (O lonely moon): Mexican serenade
  in D, arr Leslie & Cowlrick PC 112.3sx.1/2210/perc/gtr/str   2'15"   Ricordi   11032
  in C, arr A.Franzel   ø 1110/0000/perc/hp.pf/str   (Ricordi)   LM A 608

SAPIYEVSKI, Jerzy (1945-

MORPHEUS for wind symphony orch (1974)
           ø 2+picc.112+cbsn/5521/timp.3perc.mba.2tamtam/
             hp (min wind strength given)   9'   Peters,1975   Misc 9079
SUMMER OVERTURE (1975)   ø 2+picc.32+bcl.3/5331/timp.perc.mba.tamtam/
             hp/str   10'   Mercury,1977   26245

SARACINI, Claudio (also known as Il PALUSI)(1586-16??)

CRISTO SMARRITO (Lamento della Madonna), for solo voice, mv-chorus & orch
  ed V.Frazzi   ø 2222/3230/hp/str   De Santis,1937   Misc 4352

SÁRAI, Tibor (1919-

MUSICA PER 45 CORDE (1971)   ø str(6.-.2.2.1)   11'   Ed Musica,1972 Misc 8135
SYMPHONIES
  No.1 (1968)   ø 2(picc)222/4331/timp/str   Ed Musica,1969 Misc 7135
  No.2 (1972/73)   ø 2(picc)+afl.222/4230/str/S-solo 18'   Ed Musica,1976 Misc 9296

SARASATE, Pablo de (1844 1908)

La CHASSE (Morceau caractéristique), for violin & orch, op.44
           ∅   2222/4230/timp.perc/str   Zimmermann,1901   26531

L'ESPRIT FOLLET, for violin & orch, op.48
           ∅   2222/2000/timp/str   Zimmermann,1908   Misc 4312

FANTAISIE on Mozart's 'Zauberflöte', for violin & orch, op.54
           ∅   2222/2000/timp/hp/str   7'   Zimmermann   26532

INTRODUCTION ET CAPRICE JOTA: Spanish dances, for violin & orch, op.41
           ∅   2222/2230/timp/str   7'   Zimmermann   Misc 2278

INTRODUCTION ET TARANTELLE, for violin & orch, op.43
           ∅   2222/2200/timp.perc/str   5'-7'   Zimmermann,1900   Misc 2174

JOTA NAVARRA: Spanish dance, op.22, no.2
           PC   1121/2210/timp.perc/str   4'30"-6'   Simrock   11679 B
           ∅   2(picc)121/2230/timp.perc/str   (Simrock)   15783

JOTA DE PAMPLONA, for violin & orch, op.50
           ∅   2222/2230/timp.perc/str   7'   Zimmermann,1904   26530

NAVARRA, for 2 violins & orch, op.33
           ∅   2222/2230/timp.perc/str   Simrock   11423

NOCTURNE - SERENADE, for violin & orch, op.45
           ∅   2222/2000/[hp]/str   5'   Zimmermann,1901   26526

Le RÊVE, for violin & orch, op.53
           ∅   2222/2000/timp/hp/str   9'   Zimmermann   Misc 4315

ROMANZA ANDALUZA, op.22, no.1
   arr Leopold   ∅PC 1121/2210/timp/str   3'40"-4'40"   Simrock   10083

SPANISH DANCE, op.26, no.2, in C
           PC   1121/2210/timp.perc/str   5'30"   Simrock   2791 B

ZIGEUNERWEISEN (Gipsy airs), for violin & orch, op.20
           ∅   2222/2200/timp.perc/str   10'30"   Senff   5155 B +

SARGEANT, J.

BLOW, BLOW THOU WINTER WIND: song
   in C min   2122/2220/timp/str   (Boosey)   17889
   in C min, arr F.Cramer   pf/str   (Boosey)   LM G 4379
   in B♭ min, arr J.Turner   ∅   1110/1000/hp/str   (Boosey)   LM G 9302

WATCHMAN, WHAT OF THE NIGHT?: duet
   in C, arr G.Williams for Tenor & Bass soli, TTBB chorus & orch
           ∅   1121/2220/timp/hp/str   Boosey & H   MLO 119
   in F, arr E.Griffiths   ∅   hp.mustel-org.org/str   or   pf/str   (Boosey)   LM G 5458
   arr S.Herbert for violin & cello (2 brass instruments) & orch
           PC   1121/2230/perc/str   Boosey   13194

SARGENT, Malcolm (1895-1967)

NOCTURNE from Quartet in D by A.Borodin, arr for string orch
           ∅   str   Boosey & H   19295 An D

SÁRKÖZY, István (1920-

CONCERTO GROSSO (1943)(revised as RICORDANZE I)
           ∅   2+picc.222/4321/timp/str   15'30"   Ed Musica,1972   Misc 8405

RICORDANZE I   see   CONCERTO GROSSO

SINFONIA CONCERTANTE for clarinet & orch   incl)
   1st version (1963)   ∅   str (12.0.4.4.4)   22'-24'   Ed Musica,1965   Misc 9091 solo)
   2nd version (1964)   ∅   3(picc)2+ca.22+cbsn/0000/str (12.0.4.4.4)   22'-24'   Ed Musica,1965   Misc 9182

SARNO, G.

CONCERTO for piano, organ & orch [c.1972]
                              ⌀ 000.4sx.0/2020/str   25'   (Composer)   Misc 7857

SARONY, Leslie

FOLLOW THE PLOUGH: song
   in C & D   PC   1110/0000/str   (Feldman)   LM G 4876
SILVER WINGS
   Far away: song
      Refrain only, in A♭, arr B.Berlin
                              ⌀ 2020/0000/str   (Chappell)   TO 929

SARRI, Domenico   see   SARRO, Domenico

SARRO (SARRI), Domenico (1679-1744)

ARSACE: opera (1718)
   Complete facsimile of contemporary Ms (I Mc MS Noseda G.11)
                              ⌀ 1201/0.2cor-dc.000/str/cont   Garland,1978   MRL facs
DIDONE ABBANDONATA: opera (1724)
   Extracts
      Ardi per me fedele: aria for Soprano solo & orch. Facsimile of contemporary Ms (I Nc 31-3-12)
         in D (orig)   ⌀   str/cont   in Analecta Mus 16/2.Arno Volk,1976   BRL

SARSFIELD, Michael

The THIRD MAN: film
   The Casanova melody
      orch G.Zalva   PC   str   Chappell,1950   20281

SARTI, Giuseppe (1729-1802)

FRA I DUE LITIGANTI IL TERZO GODE
   Complete   ⌀   220[1]/2200/str   (H-Bn Ms.mus.OE-4) mf 413-4
   Extracts
      Un giardinier par mio: aria & rondo (No.19
      Ed io dovrò esser: recit
         in G (orig)   ⌀   0200/2000/str   (H-Bn Ms.mus.OE-4) 27093
      Non potrò del caro bene: aria (No.20)
      Ahime, dove m'inoltre: recit
         in E♭ (orig)   ⌀   2201/2000/str   (H-Bn Ms.mus.OE-4) 27092
GIULIO SABINO: opera
   Extracts
      Lungi dal caro bene (Far from my love): song
         in F   1121/2000/str   (Siddell)   17878
MARCIA LUGUBRE
   arr Dent   0201/2000/str   Arranger   19707

SARTORIO, Antonio (c.1620-1680)

L'ADÉLAÏDE: opera
   Complete
      Facsimile of contemporary MS (I:Vnm MS It.IV,380)
                              ⌀ 0000/0200/str/cont   Garland,1978   MRL facs
   Overture
      arr Bethan   ⌀   str   Nagel   19487

SARYAN, L.

SCENES for orchestra
   Introduction   Dawn   Drinking song   Scherzo   Finale
                  ∅   2(picc)222/3320/timp.perc/hp/str   Russian SM,1956   Misc 8172

SÁS, Andrés (1900-1967)

3 ESTAMPAS PERUANAS
   No.1 'Himno y danza'   ∅   3+picc.2+ca.2+bcl.2+cbsn/4331/timp.perc.sbells/
                                  cel.2hp/str   BBC   12004

SASONKIN, Manus

SYMPHONY op.4 (1949-54)   ∅   2(picc)222/4231/timp.perc/str   (Composer)   Misc 10093

SATIE, Erik (1866-1925)

La BELLE EXCENTRIQUE: fantasy for dance
   Mystérieux baiser dans l'oeil
      arr W.Kaufmann for 'Eiffel Tower'
                  ∅   1021/1110/perc/pf/str   Arranger MS:BBC   MS 20425
GENEVIÈVE DE BRABANT: music for a puppet-play, for Soprano & Baritone soli, chorus & small
      orch (orig voices & pf)(1899)
   orch R.Désormière (1926)   ∅   1121/20.cnt.10/2perc/str(3.2.2.1.1)   Universal,1939/1958   Misc 9014
5 GRIMACES for 'A Midsummer Nights Dream' (op.post)
                  ∅   3(picc)2+ca.22+cbsn/2331/timp.perc/str   Universal,1929   Misc 3834
3 GNOSSIENNES   see   2 PRÉLUDES POSTHUMES ET UNE GNOSSIENNE
3 GYMNOPÉDIES (orig pf)
   Nos 1 & 3
      orch C.Debussy   ∅   2100/4000/perc/2hp/str   6'35"   Baudoux   7858 B
   Nos 1 & 3
      orch C.Debussy, ed P.Dickinson (Score also includes pf version of nos 1, 2 & 3)
                  ∅   2100/4000/perc/2hp/str   Eulenburg,1980   Misc 10502
   No.2
      orch H.Murrill   ∅   2100/4000/str   3'15"-4'25"   Arranger   19711
JACK IN THE BOX: music for a pantomime (op.posth.)
   1. Prélude (2'30")   2. Entr'acte (1'30")   3. Final (2')
                  ∅   2(picc)222/2200/timp.perc/str   6'   Universal   Misc 781
PARADE: ballet réaliste
   Choral   Petite fille Américaine   Final
   Prélude du Rideau rouge   Acrobates   Suite au 'Prélude du Rideau rouge'
   Prestidigitateur Chinois
                  ∅   2+picc.2+ca.2+E♭cl.2/22.cnt.31/timp.perc.bouteillophone.
                      lottery wheel.tamtam.typewriter.water-splash.xyl/hp.org/str   Salabert   Misc 5330 E
3 PETITES PIÈCES MONTÉES
   1. De l'enfance de Pantagruel (Rêverie)   3. Jeux de Gargantuo (Coin de polka)
   2. Marche de Cocagne (Démarche)
      arr H.Mouton   ∅   1111/1210/perc/str   5'35"   Ed de la Sirène   5199 B
PRÉLUDE DE LA PORTE HEROIQUE DE CIEL: drame ésotérique (orig pf)
   orch & arr R.Manuel   32+ca.23/4331/timp.perc/cel.hp.org/str   4'10"   BBC   19334
2 PRÉLUDES POSTHUMES et Une GNOSSIENNE (orig pf), arr & orch F.Poulenc   8'
   1. Fête en l'honneur d'une jeune démoiselle
                  ∅   2202/2120/str
   2. Prélude du Nazaréen   ∅   01+ca.22/2220/hp/str
   3. Gnossienne   ∅   1112/2000/str
   Complete   ∅   22(ca)22/2220/hp/str   Rt Lerolle,1949/Salabert   Misc 4171
SOCRATE: symphonic drama   ∅   11+ca.11/1100/timp/hp/str   28'-37'   Eschig,1950   Misc 3248

SATS, Ilya (1875-1912)

The BLUEBIRD (Der Blaue Vogel)(L'Oiseau Bleu): suite for SSAA chorus & orch
   1. Traum und der Weihnachtsbaum
   2. Licht.   Die Fee.   Die Uhr.   Tanz der Uhr
   3. Marsch
   4. Im Lande der Erinnerung (Grossvater und Grossmutter) Abschied
   5. Die Zeit
   6. Lied der Mütter
   7. Licht und Marsch
      arr R.Glière (Russian & German texts)
                         φ   3(picc)2+ca.2(bcl)2/4331/timp.perc.bells.tamtam.xyl/
                             cel.hp.pf/str   Ed Russe,1913   Misc 3005
DANCE OF THE SATYRS (Danse de chèvre pieds)
      arr R.Glière   φ   2+picc.2+ca.2+bcl.2+cbsn/4331/timp.perc.xyl/
                             str   8'-10'
                                                                                     Ed Russe de Musique   Misc 1355
MISERERE VALSE
      arr R.Glière   φ   21+ca.22/4231/timp.perc/str
                                                                                     Jurgenson   2244

SATZ, Ilja   see   SATS, Ilya

SAUGUET, Henri (1901-

La SOLITUDE: rêverie symphonique (1958)
                         φ   1111/1100/perc/pf/str   Heugel,1960   Misc 6088
VARIATION sur un thème de l'opéra 'Camille' par André Campra
                         φ   2222/2200/timp.perc/hp/str   Salabert   Misc 4163
La VOYANTE: cantata for Soprano & orch
   1. Cartomancie   3. Chiromancie
   2. Astrologie
                         φ   1111/0100/perc/str   16'50"   Lyrebird   19061 +

SAUKA, Michael Fred P.

MLUNGU DALITSANI MALAWI (O God bless Malawi): National Anthem of Malawi (adopted 1964)
      arr G.French   φ   2222/2230/timp.perc/str   Arranger/Gvt Malawi   25208 +

SAUNDERS, Max (1903-

BLOW THE WIND SOUTHERLY: traditional song, arr
   in F   φ   hp/str   (Curwen)   LM G 8589
A COTSWOLD PASTORAL, for oboe & orch
                         φ   str   Composer MS:BBC   MS 20441
DIVERSIONS FOR STRINGS
   1. Praeludium   3. Serenata
   2. Sempre Pizzicato   4. Burlesca
                         φ   str   11'35"   Mozart Edn,1964   LM G 9386
FANTASIA ON NATIONAL AIRS   φ   2121/0000/cel.hp/str   (Arcadia)   Misc 6429
The GENTLE MAIDEN: traditional song, arr
   in F   φ   hp/str   Cramer   LM G 8281
GOD'S GENTRY: radio production (1953)
                         φ   1000/0000/ctina.hp/str   Composer MS:BBC   MS 30599
The HEART OF ENGLAND: song
   in Eb, arr K.Warner   φ   1010/0000/pf/str   (Paxton)   LM G 3528
HOGMANAY NIGHT
   in Bb, orch M.Saunders (orig arr H.Hopekirk)
                         φ   hp/str   (Chappell,1965)   24366 +

SAUNDERS, Max (cont)

The HUNTING OF THE SNARK: radio production (1952)
                           1121/0010/timp.perc/pf/str   Composer MS:BBC   MS 30580
INTERLUDIUM for string orch   ∅   str   7'30"   Ricordi,1954   Misc 4332 F
JOSHUA FIT DE BATTLE OB JERICO: Negro spiritual
    in C min, arr M.Saunders & L.Brown
                         ∅   2121/2230/perc/gtr.hp.pf/str   (Curwen)   LM G 10180
The JUMBLIES AND THE DONG: radio production
                         ∅   1121/0010/timp.perc/hp.pf/str   Composer MS:BBC   MS 30799
KANIKANI (A Maori dance)   ∅   2121/0000/perc/hp/str   Mozart Edn   LM G 11296
LEADINGS THROUGH: country dance from Sibford, Oxfordshire (as used as signature tune for radio
      feature 'Leslie Baily's logbook')
                         ∅   2+picc.222/4231/timp.perc/hp/str   Arranger MS:BBC   MS 30608
The LITTLE BEGGARS: radio feature (1956)
                         ∅   1121/0110/perc/hp/str/chorus
       Stereophonic version material
                         ∅   1001/0100/timp.perc/acdn.hp/cb   Composer MS:BBC   MS 31171
The LOCUST: A Maori folk song, arr
    in E min   ∅   2222/4230/timp.perc/hp/str   Arranger   22966 +
MEMORIES OF FRED ASTAIRE AND GINGER ROGERS: vocal selection, arr (1954)
                       ∅   2222/4230/timp.perc.glock.vib.wdbl/
                             str/chorus   Arranger   21845 +
OLD KING COLE, arr   2121/2220/perc/cel.pf/str   4'10"   Arranger   WE 365
5 POEMS, by Vachel Lindsay, for reciter & orch
    1. The Santa-Fe Trail   4. How Samson bore away the Gates of Gaza
    2. General Booth enters into Heaven   5. The Congo
    3. Daniel
                         ∅   1121/0110/perc/gtr.pf/cb   Arranger   MS 31276 ∅ only
PURGATORY: radio production (1960)
                         ∅   1121/1000/timp.cym.vib.xyl/hp/str   Composer MS:BBC   MS 31355 ∅ only
TE IWI MAORI: Maori suite   ∅   1121/2220/perc/cel.hp.pf/str   Arranger   MS 8452

SAURET, Émile (1852-1920)

CONCERTO for violin & orch, op.26
                       2222/4230/timp/str   Breitkopf   9861
RAPSODIE RUSSE for violin & orch, op.32
                       ∅   2222/2200/timp/str   Kistner   Misc 761
RAPSODIE SUÉDOISE for violin & orch, op.59
                       ∅   2222/4200/timp.perc/str   Forberg,1898   Misc 779

SAVASTA, G.

IN SOUTHERN SEAS: waltz   PC   1122/2230.euph/perc/str   Hawkes   928

SAVASTA, Jean

NIPPY: Rag intermezzo   PC   1121/2230/perc/str   Salabert   15687
POPULARITÉ: march   PC   1(picc)110/0110/perc/str   Salabert   5640
The PRESIDENT'S MARCH   PC   1(picc)222/2231/perc/str   Salabert   5639
VIOLET'S SISTER   PC   1121/2231/timp.perc/str   Salabert   5649

SAVILE, Jeremy (fl.1651-65)

HERE'S A HEALTH UNTO HIS MAJESTY: song
    in G♭, arr S.Herbert   PC   1132/2330/perc/str   Boosey   8082 B
    arr Barsotti   PC   1+picc.12.4sx.2/4230/perc/str   Boosey & H   21039 B
      see also   DOCKER, Robert: SALUTE TO THE QUEEN

SAVINO, Domenico

EARL CARROLL VANITIES (6th edn.): selection
	PC 1121/2210/timp.perc/str		Robbins	7758
FIREFLIES: intermezzo-patrol	PC 112.2sx.1/2220/perc/str	3'	Chappell	16556
INTERLUDE	PC 112.3sx.1/2210/timp.perc/hp/str	4'30"	Robbins	11395
MARCHE ORIENTALE	∅PC 212.3sx.1/2230/timp.perc/str	3'30"	Robbins	11781
MARCHE SYMPHONIQUE	∅ 112.3sx.1/2210/timp.perc.xyl/str	3'45"	Robbins	11396
	PC 112.3sx.1/2210/perc/str		Robbins	13312
MITZI: intermezzo	∅PC 112.3sx.1/2210/timp.perc/pf/str	3'30"	Robbins	11397 Bp

Une PAROLE D'AMOUR
  arr Berge   PC   1121/2210/timp.perc/str   G Schirmer   3613

SHANGHAI GESTURE: Chinese episode
                          ∅   1121/2230/timp.perc/str   5'45"-6'15"   Robbins   11459

STUDY IN BLUE: composition in the modern idiom
                          PC   112.3sx.1/2210/timp.perc/bjo.gtr.pf/str   Robbins   11326

SAXTON, Robert

REFLECTIONS OF NARZISS AND GOLDMUND for harp, piano (cel) & 2 chamber groups (1975)
                    ∅   1: 1(afl)00.asx.0/0110/vla
                        2: 0110/1000/vla.vlc.cb   13'   Chester/Hansen,1977   Misc 9517

SAY, Jack

FANTASIA ALL' ONGARESE, arr   PC   2221/2210/timp.perc/str   7'   Schott,1951   20243

SAYER, Michael

The YELLOW IRIS: incidental music to play by Agatha Christie
                    ∅   000.2sx.0/0210/perc/hp.pf   Composer MS:BBC   MS 5454 ∅ only

SAYERS, Henry J.

TA-RA-RA BOOM-DEE-AY: song
  in F   ∅   1121/2220/perc/str   (FD & H)   MS 559 ∅ only
  Concert novelty arrangement, arr H.Dexter
                          PC   2(picc)121/2230/timp.perc/hp/str   FD & H,1958   23202

SCALERO, Rosario

SUITE, op.20
  1. Choral prelude   3. Finale
  2. Variations on a theme by R.Schumann, op.68, no.2
                          ∅   str   Breitkopf   9659

SCARLATTI, Alessandro (1660-1725)

see   PAGANO, R. & BIANCHI, L.: Alessandro Scarlatti: Catalogo generale delle opere a cura di
      G.Rostirolla.   Turin: Edizioni RAI Radiotelevisione Italiana, 1972
      The Operas of Alessandro Scarlatti, edited D.J.Grout.   Harvard: Harvard UP. 1974-

AGAR ET ISMAELE ESILIATI (Hager and Ishmael sent into exile)
  ed L.Bianchi   ∅   str/cont   De Santis,1965 CW 2   MRL
AUDI FILIA: Gradual for St. Cecilia's Day, 1720, for SSA soli, SSATB chorus & orch
  ed J.Steele   ∅   020[1]/0000/org/str   Novello   Ch Lib 12336
BELLA MADRE DE' FIORI: cantata for Soprano solo & orch, in D min (orig)
                          ∅   str(no vla)/cont   Nazionalmusik   26456 *

SCARLATTI, Alessandro (cont)

CANTATA PASTORALE PER LA NATIVITÀ DI NOSTRO GESÙ CRISTO (Christmas cantata) 'O di Betlemme povertà',
    for Soprano solo & orch
                              ɸ   str/cont   (GB-Lbl Add.14165)   27098
    transcr E.J.Dent (see also CM 54466)
                              ɸ   str/cont/vocal pts   [B.M.] (Dent)   22623 +

CONCERTO for harpsichord (or organ) & orch, in C min (attrib)
    arr L.Salter   ɸ   str(no vla)   OUP,1969   Misc 7034

6 CONCERTI GROSSI
    No.1, in F min   No.3, in F   No.5, in D min
    No.2, in C min   No.4, in G min   No.6, in E
      Complete   str   Benjamin Cooke,1740   23387
      No.1 only
        arr W.Upmeyer   ɸ   str   Vieweg,1952   20736
      No.2 only
        ed H.Carr   ɸ   str   [BBC]   5900
        arr W.Upmeyer   ɸ   str   Vieweg,1952   20736
      No.3 only
        arr Lenzewski   ɸ   str/cont(hpsd)   Vieweg   10028
        arr F.M.Napolitano ɸ   str/cont(hpsd)   7'   Zanibon,1956   25558
      No.6 only
        rev R.Fasano   ɸ   str/cont(hpsd)   9'   Ricordi,1959   23158 +

CREDO CONCERTATO for SATB soli, chorus & orch
    rev J.Napoli   PC 0202/2000/str   Curci,1960   Misc 7851

Il DAVID (Davidis pugna et victoria): Oratorio for SATB soli, double chorus & orch (1700)
    ed L.Bianchi   ɸ   str/cont   De Santis,1969.CW 5   MRL
      see also   CHORAL CATALOGUE

EST DIES TROPHEI: motet for SATB soli, chorus & orch
    ed M.Martens   ɸ   str(no vla)/cont(bsn)   9'
                                                   Brooklyn College/Leeds Mus,1961   24815

Il GIARDINO DI AMORE: serenata
    Sinfonia
      ed M.Talbot   ɸ   0000/0100/str(no vla)/cont(lute)   Musica Rara,1973   25572

La GRISELDA: opera in 3 acts
    ed D.Grout   ɸ   2200/2200/str/cont   in Music 9; The Operas of
                                                   A.Scarlatti III.Harvard Publications   MRL
    ed B.Trowell   ɸ   1.2rec.201/2200/timp/hpsd/str/cont(vlc)   [BBC]   24696 +
    arr A.Bernard for radio production
                              ɸ   1200/1120/2hpsd/str   Arranger MS:BBC   MS 30203

La GIUDITTA (Judith)(di Napoli): oratorio for 5 solo voices & orch
    ed L.Bianchi   ɸ   2000/0100/str/cont   De Santis,1964.CW 1   MRL

La GIUDITTA (Judith)(di Cambridge): oratorio for 3 solo voices & orch
    ed L.Bianchi   ɸ   str/cont   De Santis,1966.CW 3   MRL

INNO A S.CECILIA, for SAT soli, chorus & orch (1720)
    rev E.Gubitosi   ɸ   org/str   Curci,1962   Misc 7862

LIFE'S A DREAM: radio feature, music from the works of A.Scarlatti
                              ɸ   1001/0200/str   Arranger MS:BBC   MS 30067

MARCO ATTILIO REGOLO: opera
    ed D.Grout   ɸ   0201/0.2cor-dc.0.2cntto.00/str/cont   in Music 8; The Operas of
                                                   A.Scarlatti II.Harvard Publications   MRL

Il MITRIDATE EUPATORE: tragedy in 3 acts, reconstructed & orch by G.Piccioli
                              ɸ   22(ca)02/2200/timp/hpsd/str
                                  On stage: 0202/0400/timp/org   Curci   Misc 7865
    Sinfonia
      ed G.Piccioli   ɸ   2202/2200/timp/str/cont   Curci,1953   Misc 8989 B

SCARLATTI, Alessandro (cont)

NACQUI A' SOSPIRI E AL PIANTO: cantata for Soprano solo & orch, in E min (orig)
          ø str(no vla)/cont
                       Nazionalmusic 26456 *
NELL' SILENTIO COMMUNE: cantata for Soprano solo & orch
 ed R.Halton   ø str/cont
                         (Editor)   26963
O CESSATE DE PIAGARMI: song
 in E min   str   (Siddell)   18138
OLIMPIA: cantata de camera a voce con instrumenti
 Overture   ø str/cont   in Geschichte der Ouvertüre by H.Botstiber.Breitkopf BRL
Il PRIMO OMICIDIO (The first murder): oratorio for SSAATB soli & orch (1707)
 ed L.Bianchi   ø str/cont   De Santis,1968.CW 4 MRL
La PRINCIPESSA FEDELE (The faithful princess): opera
 ed D.Grout   ø 0000/0100/str/cont   in Music 9; The Operas of
                     A.Scarlatti IV Harvard Publications MRL
La ROSAURA: opera (1690)
 Complete
  ed R.Eitner   OS   Breitkopf.PAPTM 14 MRL
 Act 3 only (Act 1 & 2, all material on hire from Opera Integra)
          ø str/cont   (GB-Lbm Add.14167) Misc 8902
ST.CECILIA MASS, for SSATB soli, chorus & orch (1720)
 ed J.Steele   ø org/str   Novello,1968 Ch Lib
ST.JOHN PASSION (Passio D.N. Jesu Christis secundum Johannem), for SSB soli, with ST from choir,
 chorus & orch (c.1680)
 ed E.Hanley   ø str/cont   Yale University,1955 Misc 4741
 rev E.Gubitosi   ø str/cont   Curci,1961 Misc 7860
SAN FILIPPO NERI (St. Philip Neri): oratorio for S.Mz.AT soli, chorus & orch
 ed R.Giazotto & G.Piccioli PS 0000/0100/str/cont   50'   Curci,1960 Misc 7845
SANTA TEODOSIA: oratorio
 Overture
  arr A.Carse   ø str   2'30"   Augener 12670
SEDECIA RÉ DI GERUSALEMME: oratorio for SSATB soli, chorus & orch (1706)
 Complete
  rev G.Guerrini   ø 0202/2200/timp/str/cont   60'   Curci,1962 Misc 7852
 Overture   ø str/cont   in Geschichte der Ouvertüre by H.Botstiber.Breitkopf BRL
 Suite: Introduction, Aria & Finale
  rev G.Guerrini   ø 0202/2200/timp/str/cont   Curci,1960 Misc 7863
SENTO NEL CORE: song
 in A♭, arr G.Williams ø str   Arranger MS:BBC MS 30025
12 SINFONIE DI CONCERTO GROSSO
 No.1, in F
  arr R.Meylan   ø 2000/0000/str/cont(hpsd)   6'50" Bärenreiter,1954 21500
 No.2, in D
  arr R.Meylan   ø 1000/0100/str/cont(hpsd)   Bärenreiter,1957 22454
 No.3, in D min
  arr L.Ring   ø 0.tblrec.000/0000/str/cont(hpsd)   Schott,1955 21474 B
 No.4, in E min
  arr R.Meylan   ø 1100/0000/str/cont(hpsd)   14'   Bärenreiter,1950 20203
 No.5, in D min
  arr R.Meylan   ø 2000/0000/str/cont(hpsd)   Bärenreiter,1954 21616
 No.12, in C min
  arr R.Meylan   ø 1000/0000/str/cont(hpsd)   Bärenreiter,1960 23298
7 SONATAS for flute & strings
 No.1, in D (7'50")   No.4, in A min (9'15")   No.7, in G min (7'45")
 No.2, in A min (11'50") No.5, in A (7'25")
 No.3, in C min (8'45") No.6, in D (7'50")
 Complete
  ed L.Bettarini   ø str(no vla)/cont   Nazionalmusic,1969 Misc 9495
 No.4 only
  arr A.Casella   ø str/cont(hpsd)   9'   Ricordi,1959 Misc 5423

SCARLATTI, Alessandro (cont)

La STATIRA: opera (1690)
  ed L.Friend   φ   str   [GB-Lbm Add.22103]   Misc 7252 B
SU LE SPONDE DEL TEBRO: cantata
  arr B.Paumgartner   φ   0000/01[=ob]00/2vln.vlc.[cb]   18'   W.Müller,1956   23078
SUITE OF PIECES, arr M.Esposito
  1. Toccata   2. Aria   3. Minuetto   4. Giga
                           φ   str   OUP   6331 Ds
TELEMACO: opera (1718)
  Complete (Facs of autograph MS: A Wn MS 16487)
                           φ   0201/2100/str/cont   Garland,1978   MRL facs
II TIGRANE: opera (1715)
  Sinfonia, Danze & Finale
    ed G.Piccioli   φ   0200/2200/str/cont   12'   Curci,1960   Misc 7850
II TRIONFO DELL' ONORE (The Triumph of Virtue): opera
  Complete (English version by Geoffrey Dunn)
    arr S.Robinson   φ   02+ca.02/0000/str   [BBC]   19393
  Extracts
    Vi par: aria for Soprano solo & orch
      in F (orig), ed R.Strohm
                           φ   str/cont   in Analecta Mus 16/II.Arno Volk,1976   BRL φ only
TU ES PETRUS: motet for 2 choruses, organ & orch
  ed G.Piccioli   φ   0000/0100/org/str   20'   Curci,1960   Misc 6566 B
TURNO ARICINO: opera (1720)
  Extracts
    Perchè più strugg d'amor: aria fro Soprano solo & orch
      in A (orig), ed R.Strohm
                           φ   str/cont   in Analecta Mus 16/II.Arno Volk,1976   BRL φ only
Le VIOLETTE: canzone
  in Bb   2202/0000/str   2'   [BBC]   20723
  in Bb   str   [Siddell]   18136
  in G   str   [Siddell]   18137

SCARLATTI, Domenico (1685-1757)

see   KIRKPATRICK, R: Domenico Scarlatti.   Princeton: Princeton UP,1953.   The numbers prefixed 'K'
        refer to entries in this book

AMOR D'UN OMBRA   see   NARCISO
ANDANTINO E FUGA DEL GATTO (Cat's Fugue), orch Limenta from harpsichord sonatas, K.220 & K.30
                           φ   1122/2210/timp.perc/hp/str   Carisch   Misc 1383 B
  see also 5 SONATAS
BURLESCA, orch Elkan from harpsichord sonata, K.450
                           φ   str   Elkan-Vogel   12291
CAPRICCIO, arr L.Bridgewater from harpsichord sonata, K.20
                               pf/str   3'   Universal   16381
CONCERTI
  Oboe & strings
    No.1, in G
      arr Bryan   φ   str   15'   Chester   Misc 2963 B
  Organ & strings
    arr G.F.Malipiero from a sonata
                           φ   str   6'30"   Universal   Misc 9164 B

SCARLATTI, Domenico (cont)

CONCERTI (cont)

12 Concerti, arr C.Avison from 2 books of lessons for the harpsichord, with additional slow
    movements from MS solo pieces

No.1, in A	No.4, in A min	No.7, in G min	No.10, in D
No.2, in G	No.5, in D min	No.8, in E min	No.11, in G
No.3, in D min	No.6, in D	No.9, in A min	No.12, in D min

Complete		2vln-soli.str	R.Denson,1744	21340
No.2 only	∅	2vln-soli.str/cont	(R.Denson,1744)	26977 +
No.5 only	∅	2vln-soli.str/cont	(R.Denson,1744)	26973 +
No.6 only	∅	2vln-soli.str	(R.Denson)	22326 +
No.11 only	∅	2vln-soli.str	(R.Denson)	22818 +

The GOOD HUMOURED LADIES: a choreographic comedy

Suite, arr Tommasini	∅	2222/4200/timp.perc/hpsd/str	11'-15'	Chester	4211 + C

L'HEURE GALANTE: suite arr L.Ward from the harpsichord sonata, K.366

	PC	2222/2110/str	10'	Boosey & H	16360 B

NARCISO: opera (formerly 'Amor d'un ombra')(see also SINFONIAS)
                                                mf 160 &)

Complete	∅	1202/2000/hpsd/str	(Hamburg Staats Univ Bibl)	Misc 5415 +)

Extracts

   Vieni o cara: aria

in A, ed L.Salter	∅	hpsd/str	5'10"	[B.N.H 315]	22336 +

PASTORALE, arr L.Bridgewater from harpsichord sonata, K.9

		pf/str	4'30"	Universal	16381

4 PIECES, arr M.Esposito

1. Prélude (K. 69)	3. Pastorale (K. 9)
2. Siciliana (K.446)	4. Scherzo (K.525)

	∅	[1001]/0000/[timp]/str	10'	OUP	6070 Cwa

SALVE REGINA, for Mezzo soprano solo & orch

ed R.Ewerhart	∅	str/cont	Arno Volk,1960	25034
rev E.Gubitosi	∅	str/cont	Curci,1962	Misc 7861

SCARLATTI: suite for orch, arr R.Selvaggi from the harpsichord sonatas of D.Scarlatti

	∅	2+picc.222/4300/timp.perc.xyl/cel.hp.pf/str	Universal	Misc 1527

SCARLATTI SUITE, for piano & strings, arr F.Swinstead from the harpsichord sonatas of D.Scarlatti

	∅	str	Novello	11363 Bwa

SCARLATTIANA see CASELLA, A: SCARLATTIANA: Divertimento

SERENATA FOR FOUR VOICES (Spring; Summer; Autumn; Winter), for S.Mz.TB soli, chorus & orch

ed R.Fasano	∅	1000/2200/hpsd/str	50'	Ricordi,1965	Misc 6433

SINFONIAS

  in G (F-Pc)

ed R.Meylan	∅	0100/0000/str/cont	Leuckart,1969	Misc 7343

  in G (F-Pc)

ed R.Meylan	∅	0100/0000/str/cont	Leuckart,1969	Misc 7343

  in Bb (F-Pc)

ed R.Meylan	∅	0100/0000/str/cont	Leuckart,1969	Misc 7343

  in Bb (Overture)

ed R.Leppard)	∅	0200/0000/str/cont	(F-Pc Res.2634)	Misc 6785 C

5 SONATAS, arr Bonelli from harpsichord sonatas

1. Grave (K. 90)(3'55")	4. Siciliana (K.446)
2. Minuetto (K.259)(4'15")	5. Fuga del gatto (K.30)(2'55")
3. Bourrée (K.377)(3')	

	∅	str	Zanibon	19459

SUITE for flute & strings, arr A.Benjamin from harpsichord sonatas

1. Introduzione e allegro maestoso (K.217)	3. Allegretto (K.181)
2. Allegro (K.180)	4. Andante (K.481)

	∅	str	21'30"	Boosey & H	18748

SCARLATTI, Domenico (cont)

SUITE for strings, arr J.Harrison from harpsichord sonatas
   1. Praeludium (K.430)   2. Sarabande (K.8)   3. Capriccio (K.20)
                             ø   str   9'-11'45"   Novello   5443 Cs Dn Ewe

TE DEUM, for double chorus & orch
   rev E.Gubitosi, orch M.Ràpalo
                             ø   0200/0200/org/str   Curci   Misc 7856

TEMPO DI BALLO (arr from harpsichord sonata in D, K.430)
   arr L.Bridgewater   pf/str   3'30"   Universal   16383
   arr J.A.Westrup   ø   str   OUP   10699
   arr J.A.Westrup   ø   0111/1000 [=str orch]   OUP   10696

TETIDE IN SCIRO: opera (1712)
   Extracts
      Alla pendola prigione: aria (Achilles)
                     ø   str/cont(pf)   Polish SM,1966   24640
      Atterrato, fulminato: aria (Achilles)
                     ø   str/cont(pf)   Polish SM,1966   24640
      Digli ch'ho un'alma in petto: aria (Achilles)
                     ø   str/cont(pf)   Polish SM,1966   24640
      Gusto il nèttare: aria (Achilles)
                     ø   str/cont(pf)   Polish SM,1966   24640
      Impara a compatir: aria (Likomedes)
                     ø   str/cont(pf)   Polish SM,1966   24639
      Quando Troia vinta cada: aria (Achilles)
                     ø   str/cont(pf)   Polish SM,1966   24640
      Saprò ben il petto opporre: aria (Achilles)
                     ø   str/cont(pf)   Polish SM,1966   24640
      Se non vedo quei bei lumi: aria (Likomedes)
                     ø   str/cont(pf)   Polish SM,1966   24639
      Se vuoi d'alloro cinger la chioma: aria (Ulisses)
                     ø   str/cont(pf)   Polish SM,1966   24639
      Son tuo figlio: aria (Achilles)
                     ø   str/cont(pf)   Polish SM,1966   24640

TOCCATA, BOURRÉE & GIGUE arr A.Casella from the harpsichord sonatas
   Toccata (K.13)   Bourrée (K.377)   Gigue (K.96)
                     ø   2112/2100/perc.xyl/str   Senart   Misc 1087 B

SCASSOLA, A.

ANDANTE APPASSIONATA   PC   2122/2000/str   Gregh   5978
AUBADE À MIMI (Song to Mimi at dawn)
                       PC   2222/2230/timp.perc/str   Salabert   5606 B
BRITANNICUS   PC   2222/2230/timp.perc/str   Salabert   5594
DOLCE PRIMAVERA: intermezzo campestre
                       PC   1121/2210/timp/str   Augusta (Turin) 12060
The LITTLE GEISHA: intermezzo
   arr Beltramo   PC   1121/2210/timp.perc/str   Rahter   12154
NUITS PARISIENNES: waltz   PC   2(picc)221/2230/perc/str   Salabert   5613
PASTORALE: suite   øPC   2222/4230/timp.perc/str   Salabert   12721 **
   1. Fête villageoise   3. Rêverie
   2. À la source   4. Cortège rustique
                     øPC   2222/4230/timp.perc/str   Salabert   12721 **
PAVANE (danse style ancien) PC   2212/2000/timp.perc/hp/str   3'15"   Salabert   5647 B
QUO VADIS: overture   PC   2222/2230/timp.perc/hp/str   Salabert   5696
Le RETOUR D'ULYSSE: symphonic poem
                       PC   2222/2230/timp.perc/hp/str   Moulin   10643

SCASSOLA, A (cont)

SWISS AIRS: suite, arr
1. Marche Bernoise
2. Helvétie (Naegeli)
3. La Patrie (Zoellner)
4. Le Drapeau (Lauer)
5. À mon pays (Baumgartner)
6. Sempach (Wehrli)
7. Ranz des vaches de la Gruyère
8. Salut amis!
9. Au Grütli
10. Ce que j'aime
11. Marche des amourins

12. Canton de Vaud si beau (Caurtat)
13. Le Rhin suisse (Stunz)
14. Armons-nous
15. Hymne Vaudois
16. Les Alpes (Leib)
17. La Diane
18. La retraite
19. Cantique suisse Zwyssig)
20. Roulez, tambours! (Amiel)
21. O monts indépendents! (Carey)

	VS	1221/2230/timp.perc/str		Foetisch	6425
THERMIDOR: overture	PC	2222/2230/timp.perc/str		Moulin	5964

SCHAEFERS, Anton

CONCERTO for oboe & orch, op.20

	∅	2(picc)022/2210/timp.perc/str	22'	Bote & B,1955	Misc 5401

SCHAEFER, Dirk (1873-1931)

SUITE PASTORALE, op.8, in E	∅	2+picc.2+ca.2+bcl.2/4231/timp.perc/hp/str		Alsbach	896

SCHAEFFER, H.

Die POST AM WALDE, for cornet & orch
  arr Zoeller

	PC	1121/2210/timp/str		C.Fischer	1286

SCHAFER, R.Murray (1933-

ADIEU ROBERT SCHUMANN, for Soprano solo, tape & orch (1976)

	∅	2222/2220/2perc(timp.Japanese bell tree.amsll bell. bgos.sizzle-cym.glock.gro.tamtam.[tin sheet]. tomtoms.xyl)/pf/str	18'-20'	Universal,1980	Misc 10105
CANZONI FOR PRISONERS (1962)	∅	2+picc.2+ca.2+bcl.2+cbsn/4331/timp.5perc(bgo. chimes.glock.gong.Provençal dm.tamtam.tomtoms. tpbl.vib.whip.wdbl.xyl)/cel.hp.pf/str	18'	Berandol,1977	Misc 9554
EAST (1972)	∅	2(picc)222/2200/1perc(crot.5gongs.tamtam)/ str	8'15"	Universal,1977	Misc 9479

LUSTRO
    Part 1: Divan i shams i Tabriz for 7 singers, electronic sounds & orch (1969)

	∅	3(2picc)2+ca.2+bcl.2+cbsn/4331/timp.4perc(anv. bells.bicycle wheel.bgos.chain.glock.gongs.tamb. tamtams.tomtoms.tpbells.tpbl.vib.wdlb.xyl)/Horg/ str/2S(2crots)2A(crots.cym.tri)2T(cym.tri) Bar(crots)-soli/tape	23'	Universal,1977	Misc 9579

    Part 1a: Divan I Shams I Tabriz for 7 singers & orch (1969)

	∅	on stage: 0000.cbsn/0000/4perc(timp.bells. bicycle wheel.chain.glock.gongs.tamtam. tpbells[=gongs].vib.xyl/Horg			
		in auditorium: 3(2picc)2+ca.22/4331/hp/elec/str/ SSAATTBar-soli (vocalists play perc. incl crot.finger-cyms)		Universal,1977	Misc 9477 B

SCHAFER, R.Murray (cont)

LUSTRO (cont)
   Part 2: Beyond the Great Gate of Light for 8 singers & orch
                        ϕ   on stage: 0000.cbsn/0000/4perc(timp.
                                          bells.bicycle wheel.chain.glock.
                                        gongs.tamtam.tpbells[=gongs].vib.xyl)
                          in auditorium:
                                        3(2picc)2+ca.22/4331/hp/elec/str/
                                        SSMzAATTBar-soli(vocalists play perc.
                                        incl.crot.finger cyms.small brass
                                        chimes   14'30"-15' Universal,1977   Misc 9478 B

...NO LONGER THAN TEN (10) MINUTES (1970)
                        ϕ   3(2picc)33(bcl)3(cbsn)/4331/timp.4perc(anv.
                            bells.bgo.chimes.crot.glock.gongs.Japanese
                            tree bell.mrc.tamb.tamtam.tpbl.vib)/hp/
                            str(16.12.10.9.1)   10'   Doblinger,1977   Misc 9547

NORTH/WHITE (1973)
                        ϕ   4(4picc)444[+2cbsn]/6441/6perc (3anv.chain.
                            2oildm.tamtam.timp [also several unconventional
                            devices: see score for details])/hp.pf/
                            str(22.20.16.15.10)   Universal,1980   Misc 10072

PATRIA I (The Characteristics Man): theatre work tor voices & orch
                        ϕ   1(picc)11.asx.1/2331/timp.perc.bells.bgos.congas.
                            metal-dms.glock.gongs.gro.metal-objects.tamtam.
                            vib.whip.xba/acdn.egtr.eorg/vln.vla.vlc.cb 84'   Berandol,1978   Misc 10433

SON OF HELDENLEBEN for tape & orch
                        ϕ   3(picc:afl)2+ca.1+Ebcl+bcl.2+cbsn/4331/
                            5[=6](timp.perc.bells.glock.vib.xyl[=mba, or both])/
                            hp.pf/str(min.12.12.8.8.6)   10'35"   Universal,1976   Misc 8783 B

THRENODY for youth choir, youth orchestra, 5 narrators & electronic music
                        ϕ   3(2picc)2(ca)32/4341/timp.perc.bells.glock.xyl/
                            hp.pf/str/elec   17'   Berandol,1970   Misc 7562

TRAIN, for youth string orchestra & percussion, with optional wind (1976)
                        ϕ   timp.perc(bgos.brakedrums[=anv.radiator caps].
                            chimes.claves.crots[=bells].glock.metal tubes.
                            sleighbells[=wrist bells].tamb.tamtam[=gong].
                            tin sheet.tomtoms.tpbl.vib[=mtl]wdbl.xyls)/
                            hp [=pf, or both]/str(whistles)   Berandol,1977   Misc 9605

UNTITLED COMPOSITION FOR ORCHESTRA
   No.1 (1963)   ϕ   1111/1110/cel[=glock]/str   4'   Berandol,1977   Misc 9542
   No.2 (1963)   ϕ   1+2picc.2+ca.2+bcl.2+cbsn/3431/5perc(timp.
                            bgo.glock.mba.xyl)/hp.pf(cel)/str   3'15"   Berandol,1977   Misc 9529

SCHÄFFER, Boguslaw

COLLAGE (1964)
                        ϕ   2+picc.2+ca.1+Ebcl.ssx.asx.2/3220/perc.tomtoms.vib/
                            cel.gtr.hp.pf/str(4.0.2.2.2)   Polish SM,1972   Misc 8877

SCHAFFRATH, Christoph

CONCERTO for harpsichord & strings, in Bb
   ed K.Louwenaar   ϕ   str   A-R Ed.,1977   Misc 9654

SCHARWENKA, Philipp (1847-1917)

ARKADISCHE SUITE (Arcadian suite), op.76
  1. Frühlingsfeier ländliches Fest   3. Schäfers Liebesklage und Ständchen
  2. Damon and Daphne   4. Brautzug und Hochzeitsfeier
                          ø   2+picc.222/4230/timp.perc/str   Breitkopf   3595
FRÜHLINGSWOGEN: symphonic poem, op.87
                          ø   2+picc.222/4231/timp/hp/str   Scharwenka (C.Simon,Berlin)   Misc 2484
FÜR DIE JUGEND (For the young), op.71
  Nos.1, 3 & 4 only, arr Burger ø str   Breitkopf   8164
2 POLNISCHE VOLKSTÄNZE, op.20   ø 2+picc.222/2200/timp/str   10'-14'   André   7194
SYMPHONIA BREVIS, op.115, in Eb ø 2222/4330/timp/str   Breitkopf   Misc 1500 B
TRAUM UND WIRKLICHKEIT: tone poem, op.92
                          ø   2+picc.222+cbsn/4331/timp.perc/hp/str
WALD-UND BERGGEISTER: intermezzo, op.37
                          øPC 2+picc.222/4200/timp/str   14'   Breitkopf   9857

SCHARWENKA, Xavier (1850-1924)

À LA HONGROISE, op.43, no.6
  arr Gillet   ø   2(picc)121/2210/perc/str   4'30"-5'   G.Schirmer   9707
ANDANTE RELIGIOSO, op.46 ø   hp.org/str   Augener   7103
CONCERTI
  Piano & orch
    No.1, op.32, in Bb min ø 2(picc)222/2230/timp/pf/str   30'30"   Praeger & M   Misc 1841
    No.2, op.56, in C   ø 2222/4230/timp/str   30'   Breitkopf   16896
    No.3, op.80, in C# min ø 2222/4230/timp/str   30'   Breitkopf   Misc 1481
MATASWINTHA: opera
  Overture   ø   2+picc.2+ca.2+bcl.2+cbsn/4331/timp.perc/
                              hp/str   Breitkopf   6864

  Extracts
    King Witichi's wooing episode
                          ø   2+picc.2+ca.2+bcl.2+cbsn/4331/timp.perc/
                              hp/str   Breitkopf   4475 B

POLISH DANCE, op.3, no.1
  arr Geehl   PC 1+picc.222/2230/timp.perc/str   Augener   13761
  arr Kling   øPC 1+picc.222/4230/timp.perc/str   3'-4'45"   Breitkopf   3775
  arr Roermeister   PC 1121/2210/timp.perc/str   Ditson   6918
SPANISH SERENADE   PC 1121/2210/perc/str   9'   J.Church   8474
SWEDISH PROCESSIONAL MARCH
  arr O.Langey   PC 1121/2210/perc/str   G.Schirmer   9702
SYMPHONY, op.60, in C min ø   2(picc)222/4230/timp.perc/str   Breitkopf   Misc 1839

SCHAT, Peter (1935-

ENTELÈCHIE 1 for 5 instrumental groups
                          ø   Group 1: 1001/0100/4vln
                              Group 2: 0010/0100/3vla
                              Group 3: hp/cb
                              Group 4: 5vlc
                              Group 5: 0101/0000/perc.vib   Donemus,1961   Misc 6874
HOUDINI SYMPHONY for SMzTB soli, chorus & orch, op.25b (1976)
                          ø   3(picc)3(ca)34(cbsn)/43(Dtpt)40/5perc(timp.bells.
                              glock.2mba.bmba.tamtam)/steel band(4 players)/
                              2hp/str   35'   Donemus,1976   Misc 10076

SCHAT, Peter (cont)

MONKEY SUBDUES THE WHITE BONE DEMON (Aap verslaat de Knekelgeest): cartoon opera, op.28 (1980)
　　　　　　　ø   1111/1000/perc.wood-chimes.crot.mba/
　　　　　　　　　　hpsd/str   Donemus,1980   Misc 10431
TO YOU, for solo voice, chorus & ensemble (1972)
　　　　　　　ø   6gtr.3bgtr.2org.4pf/tapes.elec   Donemus,1972   Misc 8647

SCHAUSS, Ernst

FESTLICHES PRÄLUDIUM (Festival Prelude)
　　　　　　　ø   2222/2221/timp.perc/hp.org/str   Afa Verlag,1932   Misc 96 B

SCHEDLICH, David (1607-1687)

HERZEN UND TROSTSPRUCK, for Tenor & strings
　　ed H.Federhofer   ø   str/cont   Akad Verlag Graz,1955   Misc 4535
NUN LOB' MEIN SEEL: psalm 103, for SAB voices & strings
　　ed H.Federhofer   ø   str/cont   Akad Verlag Graz,1955   Misc 4535
NUNMEHR HAT SICH GEENDET, for SAB voices &.strings
　　ed H.Federhofer   ø   str/cont   Akad Verlag Graz,1955   Misc 4535
SYMBOLUM, for SAB voices & continuo
　　ed H.Federhofer   ø   cont   Akad Verlag Graz,1955   Misc 4535

SCHEDRIN, R.K.   see   SHCHEDRIN, R.K.

SCHEIDT, Samuel (1587-1654)

COMPLETE WORKS

Samuel Scheidt's Werke, ed G.Harms & C.Mahrenholz.   Ugrino, 1923-

For complete instrumental works, see   CHAMBER CATALOGUE, or COMPLETE WORKS

ALAMANDE à 4 voci (Cantus XVI)
　　arr Seiber   ø   str   [Ugrino.CW 2]   19366 #
CANTIONEM-GALLICANI: canzon à 5 voci (Cantus XXVII)
　　arr Seiber   ø   str   [Ugrino.CW 3]   19363 #
COURANT DOLOROSA à 4 voci (Cantus IX)
　　arr Seiber   ø   str   [Ugrino.CW 2]   19365 #
COURANT à 4 voci (Cantus XIII)   str/cont   [Ugrino.CW 2]   20343 #
COURANT à 5 voci (Cantus XXIII)
　　arr Seiber   ø   str   [Ugrino.CW 2]   19361 #
ERBARM DICH MEIN
　　arr Redlich   ø   0002/0000/org/vla-dg.vla.2vlc.cb   Arranger   19177
GALLIARD à 4 voci (Cantus VII)
　　arr Seiber   ø   str   [Ugrino.CW 2]   19367 #
IN DULCI JUBILO (Cantiones sacrae No.VI), for double chorus, in C
　　arr Seiber   ø   0220/00.2cnt.00   [Ugrino.CW 4]   19241 #
O DOMINE JESU CHRISTE (Cantiones sacrae No.VI)
　　arr Seiber   ø   str   [Ugrino.CW 4]   19358 #
O LITTLE ONE SWEET: Christmas carol
　　3 arrangements from Oxford book of carols by Stanton, Bach & M.Shaw, arr W.K.Stanton
　　　　　　　　　　ø   str   OUP   18987 #
O NACHBAR ROLAND à 5 voci (Cantus XXVIII 'Lord Willobie')
　　arr Seiber   ø   str   [Ugrino.CW 3]   19364 #
PADUAN à 4 voci (Cantus V)
　　arr Seiber   ø   str   [Ugrino.CW 2]   19362 #
QUARITE PRIMUM (Cantiones sacrae No.XXXIV)
　　arr Seiber   ø   str   [Ugrino.CW 4]   19359 #

SCHEIFFELHUT, Jakob (1647-1709)

LIEBLICHEN FRÜHLINGS-ANFANG: suite no.7
 1. Praeludium   3. Courante   5. Sarabande   7. Gigue
 2. Allemande   4. Ballo   6. Aria
    arr Moser   φ   hpsd/str   Vieweg   10183

SCHEIN, Johann Hermann (1586-1630)

COMPLETE WORKS

Johann Hermann Scheins Sämtliche Werke, ed A.Prüfer. Leipzig: Breitkopf & H, 1901-23. 7 vols   MRL
Johann Hermann Schein: Neue Ausgabe Sämtlicher Werke. Kassel: Bärenreiter,1963-   MRL

BANCHETTO MUSICALE (<u>see also</u> CHAMBER MUSIC CATALOGUE)
  Suite no.1 (Padoana, Gagliarda, Courante, Allemande & Tripla)
    arr N.Stone   φ   str   6'50"   Arranger   19463
    arr A.Schering   φ   str   Kahnt   Misc 622 B
  Suite no.3 (Padouana, Gagliarda, Courante, Allemande & Tripla)
    ed D.Krickeberg   2vln.2vla.vlc.[cb] (or 5 wind)   Bärenreiter,1967   CM 55068
  Suite no.5 (Padouana, Gagliarda, Courante, Allemande & Tripla)
    ed D.Krickeberg   2vln.2vla.vlc.[cb] (or 5 wind)   Bärenreiter,1967   CM 55068
  Suite no.7 (Padouana, Gagliarda, Courante, Allemande, Tripla)
    ed D.Krickeberg   2vln.2vla.vlc.[cb] (or 5 wind)   Bärenreiter,1967   CM 55068
  Suite no.8 (1617)
    arr A.Prüfer   φ   str/cont   Breitkopf,1903   Misc 4146
  Suite no.10 (Padouana à 5, Gagliarda à 5, Courante à 5, Allemande à 4, Tripla à 4)
                          φ   str/cont   10'40"   (Breitkopf.CW 1)   24163 +
    arr A.Prüfer   OS instruments not specified   Breitkopf,1903   Misc 4147
  Suite no.14
    arr A.Prüfer   OS instruments not specified   Breitkopf,1903   Misc 4148
  Suite no.19 (Allemande & Tripla)
    arr A.Prüfer   OS instruments not specified   Breitkopf,1903   Misc 4149
    arr A.Prüfer   φ   str/cont   Breitkopf,1901.CW 1   25570 + & MRL
CANZON (5-voice fugue)   PS str   Breitkopf   Misc 4145
CANZON e INTRADA
  arr G.Lenzewski   φ   str   Vieweg   10253
MACH DICH AUF, WERDE LICHT: sacred conerto for Soprano & Bass (or Baritone) soli, SST[-A]TB chorus,
  organ & strings, in G min
                          φ   1011/0030/hpsd.org/vln.cb   BBC   19317
  ed D.Krüger   φ   org/str   Harmonia-Uitgave,1966   Misc 6375
MARIA, GEGRÜSSET SEIST DU HOLDSELIGE: dialogue, for Soprano & Tenor soli, SATTTB chorus & orch
  transcr N.Stone   φ   0000/0240/org/str   BBC   19316 +
  ed A.Prüfer   φ   0001/0240/org/vlc   BBC   19138
SELIGPREISUNGEN (The Beatitudes), for SSTTB voices & orch, in G min
  real N.Stone   φ   1111/0230/str   BBC   19384
SIEHE, DAS IST MEIN KNECHT, in G min
                          φ   1001/0000/org/vln   BBC   19263
UNS IST EIN KIND GEBOREN, à 5, in G min
                          φ   1001/0010/org/vln.cb   BBC   19315
VATER UNSER, DER DU BIST IM HIMMEL, for Contralto & Tenor soli, chorus & orch
  ed A.Prüfer   φ   0001/0000/org/str   (Breitkopf.CW 7)   25159 +

SCHEINPFLUG, Paul (1875-1937)

OVERTURE to a Shakespeare comedy, op.15
        φ   3(picc)2(ca)+ca.3+Dcl+bcl.3(cbsn)/4331/
            timp.perc.glock/str   Heinrichshofen,1908   Misc 893

SCHEINPFLUG, Paul (cont)

Ein SOMMERTAGEBUCH: suite
   1. Ausfahrt   3. Kleine Balletszene
   2. Nachtgang am Meer   4. Fahnen über einer Stadt
                      ⌀   2(picc)121/3210/timp.perc.glock/hp/str   Wrede,1938   Misc 1995

SCHELLE, Johann (1648-1701)

BARMHERZIG UND GNÄDIG IST DER HERR: cantata for SSATB soli, SSATB chorus & orch
   ed A.Schering   ⌀   0001/0000/str/cont(org)   Breitkopf,1918.DDT 58-59   MRL
LOBE DEN HERRN, MEINE SEELE: cantata for SSATB soli, double SSATB chorus & orch
   ed A.Schering   ⌀   0001/00.4clno[=4tpt].2cntto[=2cl].30/timp/
                               str/cont(org)   Breitkopf,1918.DDT 58-59   MRL
VOM HIMMEL HOCH: actus musicus for Christmas, for Soprano & Tenor soli, SSATTB chorus & orch
   ed & arr F.Wanek   ⌀   0200/0230/str/cont   28'   Schott,1969   Misc 10331
VOM HIMMEL KAM: cantata for SSATB soli, SSATB chorus & orch
   ed A.Schering   ⌀   0000/00.2clno.2cntto.20/timp/str.vltta/
                               cont(org)   Breitkopf,1918.DDT 58-59   MRL

SCHELLING, Ernest (1876-1939)

IMPRESSIONS FROM AN ARTIST'S LIFE: symphonic variations for piano & orch
                      ⌀   3(picc)2+ca.2+bcl.2+cbsn/4331/timp.perc.
                          glock.xyl/2hp.org.pf/str   Leuckart   13412
LÉGENDES SYMPHONIQUES   ⌀   2+picc.2+ca.22+cbsn/4230/timp/hp/str   23'   G.Schirmer   4433
MOROCCO: symphonic tableau   ⌀   2+picc.2+ca.3(bcl)+Dcl.2+cbsn/4431/
                               timp.perc.glock.tamtam.xyl/cel.2hp.pf/str 20'   C.Fischer Misc 2139
SUITE FANTASTIQUE, for piano & orch, op.7
   1. Allegro marziale   3. Intermezzo
   2. Molto vivace   4. Virginia reel
                      ⌀   2+picc.2+ca.2+bcl.2+cbsn/4231/timp.perc/
                          hp/str   24'30"-30'   Rahter   6034
A VICTORY BALL: fantasy (to the memory of an American soldier)
                      ⌀   3(picc)2+ca.2+bcl.2+cbsn/4431/timp.perc/
                          2hp.org/str   25'   Leuckart   13421

SCHENJCHIN, Alexander Alexejewitsch (1890-1944)

SOMMERFÄDEN (Fil de la Vierge): musical sketch, op.2
                      ⌀   32+ca.2+bcl.3/4001/cel.hp/str   Jurgenson [1913] Misc 9243

SCHENK, Aegidius (1719-1780)

MASS for SATB soli, chorus & orch, in C
   ed E.Benczik   ⌀   0000/0200/timp/vln/cont(org)   Akademische Druck,1980   Misc 10100

SCHENK, J.DECKER   see   DECKER-SCHENK, J.

SCHENK, Johann (1753-1836)

CONCERTO for harp & orch, in Eb (1788)
   ed & cadenzas by P.Angerer   ⌀   0202/2200/timp/str   Doblinger,1977   26423 *
Der DORFBARBIER: Singspiel
   arr R.Haas   ⌀   2222/2200/timp/str   Universal,1927.DTÖ 66   MRL

SCHERBER, Martin (1908?-

SYMPHONIES
No.1, in D min (1938)	φ	2+picc.222/4331/timp/str		H.Bosannek,1971	Misc 7716
No.2, in F min (1951-2)	φ	3(picc)2+ca.2+bcl.2+cbsn/4331/timp/str	60'	H.Bosannek,1973	Misc 8497

SCHERCHEN-HSIAO, Tona (1938-

BIEN (Mutations)(1973)	φ	0010/1110/2perc(ptimp.bell.bgos.conga.crot. Chinese cym.Tibetan cyms.Chinese dm.3gong. gro.2tamtam.3tomtom.vib.xyl)/pf(Chinese cym)/ 2vln.vla.vlc.cb	20'	Universal,1974	Misc 9862
OEIL DE CHAT I	φ	4444/4441/timp.perc.bell.clv/str		(Composer,1978)	Misc 1777

SCHERTZINGER, Victor

KISS THE BOYS GOOD-BYE: musical play					
Selection, arr G.Zalva	PC	112.3sx.1/2220/timp.perc/str		Victoria	16678
The LOVE PARADE: film					
Selections					
arr C.Grey	PC	1(picc)11.3sx.1/2210/timp.perc/str		C.Connelly	5456
arr R.Hanmer	φ	212.4sx.1/2330/timp.perc/hp.pf/str		(C.Connelly)	18660 Ap
Extracts					
Dream lover: song					
in D, arr G.Stacey		pf/str		(C.Connelly)	LM G 3258
in F, arr Chappelle	PC	1131/0230/perc/str		(C.Connelly)	LM G 4423
in F, arr P.Hope	φ	2222/4030/perc/hp/str		(C.Connelly)	23820
in F, arr R.Green	φ	1110/1000/perc/gtr.hp.pf/str		(C.Connelly)	LM G 8526
orch & arr R.Green (non-vocal)					
	φ	2222/4230/timp.perc/hp.pf/str		(C.Connelly)	18461
March of the grenadiers: song					
in F, arr J.Beaver for chorus & orch					
	φ	2(picc)121/2230/timp.perc/hp/str		(BBC)	TO 45
in A♭, arr R.Docker	φ	2140/2330/perc/hp.pf/str		(C.Connelly)	LM J 2304
orch & arr C.Shadwell (non-vocal)					
	PC	101.3sx.0/0210/perc/str		C.Connelly	15905 Ap
My love parade: song					
in C, arr H.Carr	φ	2122/2230/perc/hp/str		(C.Connelly)	TO 749
MARCHÉTA: song of old Mexico					
in F, arr M.Mackie		1130/1320/perc/str		(Chappell)	LM G 4565
ONE NIGHT OF LOVE: film					
One night of love: song					
in F, arr B.Berlin for SATB voices & orch					
	φ	2121/2230/perc/hp/str	3'20"	(Chappell)	TO 1010
in F & G, arr G.Stacey		pf/str(no vla)		(Sterling)	LM G 3244
in G, arr S.Andrews	φ	hp.pf/str		(Chappell)	MS 20372
in G, A♭ & F, arr P.Cardew					
	φ	2222/4330/timp.perc/hp/str		(Chappell)	18476 +
in A♭, arr B.Berlin		2121/2230/perc/hp/str		(Sterling)	LM G 4419
ROAD TO SINGAPORE: film					
Moon and the willow tree: song					
in G, arr B.Berlin	φ	111.3sx.1/2220/timp.perc/gtr/str		(Victoria)	TO 225
ROBIN HOOD					
March					
arr H.M.Higgs	PC	1(picc)121/2220/perc/str		Chappell	1438

SCHETTINO, V.S.

JUAREZ: march
  arr A.Winter   PC 1(picc)22.2sx.2/2230.euph/timp.perc/str   Hawkes   118

SCHIASSI, Gaetano Maria

PASTORALE per il Santissimo Natale di nostro Signr Jesu (Christmas Symphony)
  ed W.Upmeyer   φ str/[cont(hpsd=org)]   Vieweg   25579
  4th mvt only (Andante)
    ed A.Hoffmann   φ str/cont   Nagel,1963 25541

SCHIBLER, Armin (1920-

CONCERTINI
  Cello & strings, op.64   φ str   Eulenburg,1961 Misc 5718
  Clarinet & strings, op.49 φ str   Eulenburg,1957 Misc 5717 B
FANTASIE for viola & orch, op.15
                   φ 1011/2000/timp/str   (Composer)   19105

SCHICKELE, Peter (1935-

CELEBRATION WITH BELLS, for orch
                   φ 21[=2]3+[bcl].[asx].[tsx].1+[cbsn]/2[=4]33[=2]1/
                      timp.3perc(gong)/str   Elkan-Vogel,1976 Misc 9070

SCHIERBECK, Poul (1888-1949)

The CHINESE FLUTE, for voice & orch, op.10
                   φ 2222/4231/perc.bells.tamtam/cel.hp/str   Hansen,1952 Misc 3154 B
FÊTE GALANTE: opera, op.25
  Overture   φ 2222/4231/timp.perc.glock/str   Dania,1941   Misc 6515

SCHIERER, J.A.   see   SCHMIERER, J.A.

SCHIFRIN, Lalo (1932-

The EAGLE HAS LANDED: film
  March
    arr I.Sutherland   φ 2(picc)2(ca)2(bcl)2/4331/timp.2perc(Kit)/
                      hp.pf/str   (ATV)   26902
VARIANTS on a madrigal by Gesualdo (lo pur respiro), for large chamber ensemble (1965)
                   φ 0.afl.111/11[=cnt]11/timp.4perc.bells.glock.mba.
                      vib.xyl/hp.hpsd(pf,cel)/str-4tet   18'   AMP,1974   Misc 8519

SCHILLINGER, Joseph (1895-1943)

MARCH OF THE ORIENT, op.11
  ed A.Shaw   φ 2+picc.2+ca.2+bcl.2+cbsn/6[=4]331/timp.perc.
                    bells.xyl/2hp/str   Leeds Music Corp,USA Misc 2907 B

SCHILLINGS, Max (1868-1933)

CONCERTI
  Violin & orch, op.25, in A min
                      3(picc)2+ca.2(bcl)2/4331/timp.perc/hp/str   Simrock,1910 26295 *
Das HEXENLIED (The witch song): musical recitation, op.15
                 φ 3(picc)2+ca.2+bcl.2+cbsn/4331/timp.perc/
                      hp/str   Forberg   7377

SCHILLINGS, Max (cont)

INGEWALDE: opera
  Prelude to Act II   ∅   32+ca.2+bcl.2/4331/timp.perc/hp/str   6'   J.Schuberth   11909
KÖNIG OEDIPUS: symphonic prologue, op.11
                               ∅   32+ca.23/4331/timp.perc.tamtam/str   Bote & B   Misc 440
MEERGRUSS (Thalatta)   see   2 SYMPHONIC FANTASIES, op.6, no.1
Der PFEIFERTAG: opera, op.10
  Introduction to Act III   ∅   3(picc)2+ca.22+cbsn/4331/timp.perc/str
                                   On stage: 0000/0220   Bote & B   9631
SEEMORGEN   see   2 SYMPHONIC FANTASIES, op.6, no.2
2 SYMPHONIC FANTASIES, op.6
  No.1: Meergruss (Thalatta) ∅   32+ca.2+bcl.3/4331/timp.perc/hp/str   Furstner   14816
  No.2: Seemorgen   ∅   3(picc)2+ca.2+bcl.3/4331/timp.perc/hp/str   Furstner   14817
TANZ DER BLUMEN (Dance of the flowers)
                               ∅   2222/3000/hp/str   Heinrichshofen Misc 852 C
Ein ZWIEGESPRÄCH: tone poem for violin, cello & small orch, op.8
                               ∅   2222/4200/perc/[hp]/str   Ries & E   Misc 1738

SCHIRA, Francesco (1809-1883)

NICCOLÒ DE LAPI: opera
  Extracts
    La Bella mea: aria
        in E   2222/4230.oph/timp.perc/str   (Siddell)   17882
SOGNAI   PC   2222/2230.euph/timp.perc/hp/str   Hawkes   910

SCHIRMANN, Alexander

SASCHINKA: potpourri of Russian Gipsy songs & dances, arr A.Schirmann & R.Ralf
                               2(picc)12.sx.1/2210/timp.perc/str   13'   Roehr   11479

SCHISKE, Karl Hubert Rudolf (1916-1969)

CONCERTO for piano & orch, op.11 (1938/39)
                               ∅   2(picc)222/4331/timp.perc/str   19'   Doblinger,1978 Misc 9667
SYMPHONY no.1, op.16   ∅   2+picc.222/4331/timp.perc/str   Doblinger,1970 Misc 7466
SYNTHESE for 4 groups of 4 instruments, op.47 (1958)
                               ∅   1111/2110/4perc(pf.xyl)/str(1.0.1.1.1.)   Universal,1976 Misc 9271

SCHJELDERUP, Gerhard (1859-1933)

NORWEGIAN SUITE
  1. Night on the mountain lake   4a. Festive music
  2. Bridal march   4b. Dawn of day
  3. In the old church

A SUMMER NIGHT ON THE FIORD ∅   2(picc)2(ca)22/4200/timp.perc/hp.org/str   25'   Tischer & J   10574
                             ∅   2+picc.222/2000/str   Bote & B   Misc 2266

SCHLESINGER, Sebastian B.

MARCHE DES ENFANTS
  arr Gervasio   ∅   2222/4230/perc/str   Hofmeister   11571

SCHLÖGEL, Ludwig

SELECTION FROM OPERAS BY JOHANN STRAUSS (ii)
                          PC   2(picc)222/42.flg.30/timp.perc.glock.zither/
                               hp/str   18'30"   Cranz   7063

SCHLÖGER, Matthaeus (1722-1766)

PARTITA in B♭
     ed K.Horwitz & K.Riedel   ∅   str(no vla)/cont   Artaria,1908.DTÖ 31   MRL

SCHMALSTICH, Clemens

FASCHING (Carnival), op.75
     1. Ouverture   4. Liebesduett
     2. Harlekins Ständchen   5. Finale (Maskeneinzug)
     3. Pierette
                              ∅   3(picc)222/4331/timp.perc.glock/cel.hp/str 26'   Birnbach   10913
MUSIKALISCHES KUNTERBUNT: selection, arr
     Part I   PC 2(picc)121/2210/timp.perc/hp.org/str   Bote & B   10115

SCHMELING, Martin

Ein ABEND IN ARANJUEZ: suite
     1. Serenade   2. Spanischer Tanz
         arr Korke   PC 2222/2230/timp.perc/str   Bosworth   957
Ein ABEND IN TOLEDO: suite
     1. Serenade   2. Spanischer Tanz
         arr Korke   PC 1+picc.222/4230/timp.perc/str   Bosworth   958
         arr Chignell   str   (Bosworth)   MS 3002
SOLDIERS LIFE: march   ∅PC 2+picc.22.2sx.2/4231/perc/hp/str   2'35"   Bosworth   9

SCHMELZER, Johann Heinrich (ca.1620-1680)

ARIE CON LA MATTACINA
     ed P.Nettl   ∅   str/cont   Universal,1921.DTÖ 56   MRL
BALDRACCA: ballet music (1679)
     1. Von schwäbischen Mädeln   3. Di saltalori
     2. Von schwäbischen Bauern
         ed P.Nettl   ∅   str/cont   Universal,1921.DTÖ 56   MRL
2 BALLETTI (1670)
     1. Di zingari   2. Di matti
         ed P.Nettl   ∅   str/cont   Universal,1921.DTÖ 56   MRL
BALLETTI à 4 (Pastorella)
     ed P.Nettl   ∅   str/cont   Universal,1921.DTÖ 56   MRL
BALLETTO in C (1670)
     1. Intrada   3. Borea (Bourée)
     2. Balletto   4. Sarabande
         ed R.Minter   ∅   0001/01[=2]30/str/cont(real J.Madden)   Musica Rara,1977   26413 *
BALLETTO DI CENTAURI, NINFE E SALVATICI per la festa a Schönbrunn (1674)
     ed P.Nettl   ∅   0.3piffari.001/00.2cntto.30/str/cont   Universal,1921.DTÖ 56   MRL
BALLETTO DI SPIRITELLI
     ed P.Nettl   ∅   0001/00.2cntto[=2vla piffarato]00/
                                    vln piffarato.str/cont   Universal,1921.DTÖ 56   MRL
CRESO: ballet music (1678)
     1. Di spoglia di pagagi   3. Di capitani
     2. Di ginochi di Giunone   4. Di 7 pianeti
         ed P.Bettl   ∅   str/cont   Universal,1921.DTÖ 56   MRL
FECHTSCHULE
     ed P.Nettl   ∅   str/cont   Universal,1921.DTÖ 56   MRL
La LATERNA DI DIOGENE: ballet music (1674)
     1. Balletto di capitani   2. Balletto di filosofi
         ed P.Nettl   ∅   str/cont   Universal,1921.DTÖ 56   MRL

SCHMELTZER, Johann Heinrich (cont)

MASS: Missa nuptialis, for SSATTB soli, SSATTB chorus & orch
    ed G.Adler   ø   0000/0400/str/cont   Artaria,1918.DTÖ 49   MRL
NETTUNO E FLORA FESTEGGIANTI: ballet music (1669)
    ed P.Nettl   ø   0000/0200/str/cont   Universal,1921.DTÖ 56   MRL
II POMO D'ORO: ballet music (1667)
    ed P.Nettl   ø   str/cont   Universal,1921.DTÖ 56   MRL
SERENATA CON ALTRE ARIE (1669)
    ed P.Nettl   ø   str/cont   Universal,1921.DTÖ 56   MRL
SONATA CON ARIE ZU DER KAISERLICHEN SERENADA (1672)
    ed P.Nettl   ø   0000/0300/[timp]/str/cont   Universal,1921.DTÖ 56   MRL

SCHMID, Adolf (1868-1958)

FROM THE DAYS OF GEORGE WASHINGTON: suite, arr
    1. Introduction   7. Quick march (Band march)
    2. The President's march   8. Successful campaign
    3. Washington's march   9. Brandywine quick step
    4. General Burgoyne's march   10. Yankee Doodle (Original version)
    5. Washington's march (at the battle of Trenton)   11. Yankee Doodle (Modern version)
    6. Roslyn castle   12. Finale (Apotheosis)
                        PC 2(picc)22[3sx].2/4230/timp.perc/str   G.Schirmer   12646 B
JOSEPH AND HIS BRETHREN: suite
    1. Prelude   2. Caravan dance   3. Bacchanalian dance
                      PC 2(picc)2(ca)22/423[1]/timp.perc/hp/str   Hawkes   1898
                      ø   2(picc)2(ca)22/423[1]/timp.perc/
                         hp/str (ø - no.3 only)   Hawkes   15767
RUSSIAN BOATMEN SONG, arr   PC 21+ca.22/4230/timp.perc/hp/str   Lafleur   912

SCHMIDEK, Kurt

DIVERTISSEMENT, op.48
    1. Overtüre   2. Sarabande   3. Rondeau
                   ø   0200/2000/str   16'   Doblinger,1971   Misc 7694

SCHMIDT, Christfried

MEIN GOTT, WARUM HAST DU MICH VERLASSEN: psalm 22, for Soprano & Baritone, chorus & ensemble (1970)
                  ø   2(picc:afl)02(bcl)0/0220/2(perc.bells.vib.xyl)/
                    org/2vln.2vlc   15'   Moeck Verlag,1974 Misc 8626

SCHMIDT, Franz (1874-1939)

Das BUCH MIT SIEBEN SIEGELN: oratorio
                  ø   2+picc.2+ca.2+bcl(Dcl).2+cbsn/4331/
                    timp.perc.tamtam.xyl/str   120'   Universal   Misc 4111 B
CONCERTANTE VARIATIONEN on a theme by Beethoven, for piano (left hand) & orch
    Version for 2 hands, arr F.Wührer
                  ø   2222/4230/timp.perc/str   26'   Universal   Misc 3828
CONCERTO for piano (left hand) & orch, in Eb
    Version for 2 hands, arr F.Wührer
                  ø   2222/4200/timp/str   38'   Universal   Misc 3829
NOTRE DAME: opera
    Entr'acte & Carnival music   ø   2+picc.222+cbsn/4330/timp.perc.tamtam/
                    2hp/str   Universal   Misc 1217

SCHMIDT, Franz (cont)

SYMPHONY no.2, in E♭ (1911-13)
   ed K.Trötzmüller (Critical edn)
                          φ   3+picc.2+ca.3+E♭cl+bcl.2+cbsn/8431/timp.perc/
                              str   50'   Universal,1914/72   Misc 7806
VARIATIONEN ÜBER EIN HUNSARENLIED
                          φ   22+ca.2+E♭cl.2/4331/timp.perc.tamtam/str   Universal   Misc 1164

SCHMIDT, R.

MEDITATION on the Prelude in C min by J.S.Bach (No.2 from 48 Preludes & Fugues of Bach)
                          φ   str   Arranger   3283

SCHMIERER, Johann Abraham (1661-1719)

SUITES à 4
   No.1, in D min
      1. Overture   5. Ballet
      2. Entrée   6. Gigue
      3. Passacaille   7. Gavotte
      4. Minuet   8. Rondeau
                          φ   4-pt ensemble/cont   Bärenreiter,1974   26134 *
   No.2, in F
      1. Overture   5. Minuet
      2. Allemande   6. Gavotte
      3. Rondeau   7. Gigue
      4. Bourée   8. Plainte
                          φ   4-pt ensemble/cont   Bärenreiter,1974   26134 *
ZODIACUS: 6 suites for optional harpsichord & stringed instruments
   ed E.von Werra, rev H.J.Moser
                          φ   str   Breitkopf,1958.DDT 10   MRL

SCHMIKERER, Johann Abraham   see   SCHMIERER, Johann Abraham

SCHMITT, Florent (1870-1958)

see   L'Oeuvre de Florent Schmitt, ed Y.Hucher. Durand, 1960

ANTOINE ET CLÉOPATRE: incidental music, op.69
   Suite no.?
      1. Nuit au palais de la Reine
      2. Orgie et danses
      3. Le Tombeau de Cléopatre
                          φ   2(picc)2+ca.2(E♭cl)+bcl.2+cbsn/4331/timp.perc/
                              cel.hp/str   20'   Durand   Misc 2095
CANCUNIK: suite, op.79
   1. Lied-Nocturne
   2. Scherzo-Tarantelle
                          φ   1+picc.222(cbsn)/4231/timp.perc/2hp/str 10'   Durand   13613
CHANSON À BERCER for violin (or cello) & orch, op.19, no.1
                          PS 1111/0000/str   Hamelle,1909   25236
CHANT ÉLÉGIAQUE for cello & orch, op.24
                          φ   2(picc)1+ca.22.[sarr]/4231/timp.perc/hp/str   Durand   6012
DANSE D'ABISAG, op.75   φ   1+picc.1+ca.22+[cbsn]/4231/timp.perc/
                              2[=1]hp/str   Durand,1925   Misc 2552

SCHMITT, Florent (cont)

FEUILLETS DE VOYAGE: suite, op.26
   1. Sérénade   4. Berceuse
   2. Le retour à l'endroit familier   5. Marche burlesque
   3. Danse britannique

∅	2+picc.2(ca)22+cbsn/4231/timp.perc/hp/str	15'-17'	Durand	Misc 1662

GLOIRE AU SEIGNEUR!: psalm 48 for Soprano solo, chorus, organ & orch, op.38
∅	3(picc)3(ca)3(bcl)3+cbsn/4331/		
	timp.perc.glock.tamtam/2hp.org/str	Mathot,1922	Misc 3560

JANIANA: symphony for strings, op.101
∅	str	Durand	Misc 2371

LÉGENDE, for saxophone (or viola) & orch, op.66
∅	2+picc.2+ca.2+bcl.2+cbsn/4331/timp.perc/cel.hp/		
	str	Durand	4620

LIED ET SCHERZO, for horn & wind ensemble, op.54
∅	1+picc.1+ca.22/1000	Durand	19460

MUSIQUES FORAINES, op.22
   1. Harlequinade   4. Les éléphants servants
   2. Boniment de clowns   5. La pythonisse
   3. Beautiful Fathma   6. Chevaux
PC	1(picc)121/2231/timp.perc/hp/str	Salabert	1906

MUSIQUES INTIMES, op.16
   1. Aux Rochers de Naye   4. La promenade au Lido
   2. Sur le chemin désert   5. Dans la forêt ensoleillée   (1'45")
   3. Silence Troublé   6. Chanson des feuilles   (1'15")
PC1121/1100/hmn/str		Heugel	11559

PSALM 48 see GLOIRE AU SEIGNEUR!
3 RAPSODIES, op.53
1. Viennoise	∅	2+picc.222.sarr/4231/timp.perc/hp/str	8'	Durand	13964
2. Polonaise	∅	2+picc.1+ca.22+cbsn/4231/timp.perc		
		cel.2hp/str		Durand	13965
3. Française	∅	2+picc.222+[cbsn]/4231/time.perc.[glock]/		
		[2hp]/str		Durand	13862

REFLETS D'ALLEMAGNE: suite, op.28
   1. Nuremberg   2. Dresden   3. Werder   4. Munich
∅	2+picc.222/2231/timp.perc/hp/str	Mathot,1906	21024

RÊVE AU BORD DE L'EAU, for violin (or cello) & orch, op.19, no.4
PS	1111/0000/hp/str	Hamelle,1919	25235

RONDE BURLESQUE, op.78
∅	2+picc.222+cbsn/4231/timp.perc.xyl/		
	cel.2hp/str	Heugel	13368

SALAMMBO: film music, op.76
  Suite no.1
     1. Le palais silencieux   2. Au gycécée
∅	2+picc.2+ca.2+bcl.2+cbsn/4331/timp.perc.tamtam.xyl/		
	cel.2hp/str	Durand	Misc 2463

SOIRS: 8 short pieces for small orch, op.5
   1. En rêvant (2'12")   4. Après l'été (strings)   7. Un soir (3'45")
   2. Spleen (strings)   5. Parfum exotique   8. Églogue
   3. Gaiety   6. Sur l'onde (4'30")
∅	1(picc)111/0000/timp.perc/hp[=pf]/str	Durand	9716
No.4 only	∅	str	Durand	21033

SUITE SANS ESPRIT DE SUITE, op.89
   1. Majeza   4. Thrène
   2. Charmille   5. Bronx
   3. Pécorée de Calabre
∅	2(picc)2(ca)22/2220/hp/str or		
	3(picc)3(ca)2+bcl.2+cbsn/4331/timp.perc.bells.tamtam/		
	cel.2hp/str	Durand	Misc 702

SCHMITT, Florent (cont)

SYMPHONIE CONCERTANTE for piano & orch, op.82

       ø 2+picc.2+ca.2+bcl.2+cbsn/4331/timp.perc/
        cel.2[=1]hp/str   Durand   Misc 1360

SYMPHONY no.2, op.137 ø 2+picc.2+ca.2+bcl.2+cbsn/4331/timp.perc.
        tamtam.xyl/cel.2hp/str   25' Durand,1959 Misc 5312

La TRAGÉDIE DE SALOMÉ: ballet, op.50

       ø 2+picc.2+ca.2+bcl.3.sarr/4331/timp.perc.glock/
        cel.2hp/str/voice pt in 2nd mvt 28' Durand   8506

SCHMITT, Joseph (1734-1791)

SYMPHONY, op.1, in D   0200/2000/str   Hummel   19140

SCHNABEL, Artur (1882-1951)

SYMPHONY no.1   ø 3(2picc)333(cbsn)/4330/timp.perc/cel/str Adler,NY Misc 2404

SCHNEIDER, Bobby

AM SILBERSEE (By the silver sea): serenade
 arr Zimmer   PC 2222/4230/timp/str   6'   Huhn   12126

SCHNEIDER, Hans

LEHAR IN 3/4 TAKT (Waltzing with Lehar): selection of waltzes
       PC 2222/4230/perc/hp/str   Glocken 20404

TANZENDE OPERATTENSTERNE: selection of operetta waltzes, arr
       PC 2122/4230/timp.perc/acdn.hp/str   Weinberger 19672

WALTZING WITH ZELLER: selection of waltzes
       PC 2222/4230/timp.perc/acdn.hp/str   Weinberger,1952 20783

SCHNEITZHOFFER, Jean-Madeleine (1785-1852)

La SYLPHIDE: ballet in 2 acts (1832)

       ø 2+picc.222/4430.spt/timp.perc/str   (Composer:F-Po) Misc 6730 & mf 298

SCHNITTKE, Alfred (1934-

CONCERTI
 Oboe, harp & strings (1971) ø str   Universal,1972 Misc 9999
 Violin & orch, no.3 (1978) ø 2(picc)1+ca.2(Ebcl)+bcl.1+cbsn/2110/
        vln.vla.vlc.cb   28' Universal,1979 Misc 10465

CONCERTO GROSSO for 2 violins, harpsichord (or piano) & strings (1976-7)
       ø str(6.6.4.4.1)   Russian SM Misc 10092

GOGOL SUITE
 1. Overture   5. Ferdinando VIII
 2. Chichikov's childhood 6. Clerks
 3. Portrait   7. Ball
 4. Greatcoat   8. Testimony
       ø 1(picc)1(ca)2(Ebcl:bcl)1(cbsn)/2111/timp.perc.
        bells.flex.glock.rattle.tamtam.whistle.xyl/
        cel.bgtr.egtr.hpsd.org.pf/str   (Boosey & H) 26881 +

SYMPHONY no.2 (St.Florian)(1980)

       ø 4(2picc:afl)4(ca:ob-d'a)3(Ebcl)+bcl.4(cbsn)/4441/
        timp.perc.bells.glock.3gong.mba.3tamtam.vib/
        cel.bgtr.egtr.2hp.hpsd.org.pf/str(12.12.8.8.8)/
        ACtTB chorus   55' Universal,1980 Misc 10551

SCHOBERT, Johann (1720-1767)

CONCERTI
 Harpsichord & orch
  No.2, op.12, in E♭
   ed H.Riemann   ø 2[=2ob]000/[2]000/str/cont(hpsd)   Breitkopf,1909.DDT 39 MRL
  No.5, op.19, in G
   ed H.Riemann   ø 2[=2ob]000/2000/str   Breitkopf,1909.DDT 39 MRL

SCHOECK, Othmar (1886-1957)

CONCERTI
 Horn & strings, op.65 ø str   18' Boosey & H,1952 Misc 3849 B
 Violin & orch, op.21, in B♭ (quasi una fantasia)
        ø 2222/2200/timp/str   Hug Misc 7827
ELEGY: song cycle from poems by Lenau & Eichendorff, for voice & small orch, op.36
        ø 11(ca)2(bcl)0/1000/timp.tamtam/pf/str   Breitkopf Misc 3548 B
GASELEN: song cycle for voice & ensemble, op.38
        1(picc)10.bcl.0/0100/perc/pf   17' Breitkopf 54128
NOTTURNO, for voice & string quartet, op.47
        ø str   Universal 52094
SERENADE for small orch, op.1 ø 1111/1000/str   Hug,1907 23625
SOMMERNACHT: pastorales intermezzo, op.58
        ø str   13'20"-17' Hug,1956 Misc 4990 B
SUITE for strings, op.59, in A♭ ø str   Universal Misc 2786 B

SCHOEMAKER, Maurice (1890-1964)

FEU D'ARTIFICE: symphonic poem ø 22+ca.2+E♭cl+bcl.2+cbsn/4331/timp.perc.xyl/
        str   Schott,1932 Misc 2514
Les ROIS MAGES   ø 2222/2220/timp.perc.vib/str   Buyst 14454

SCHOENBERG, Arnold (1874-1951)

see RUFER, Joseph: A.Schoenberg - Catalogue of Compositions. London: Faber & Faber
COMPLETE WORKS

Arnold Schönberg: Sämtliche Werke, ed J.Rufer & others. Mainz: Schott/Vienna: Universal, 1966- MRL
ALLE, WELCHE DICH SUCHEN see LIEDER: 4 Lieder, op.22, no.2
BEGLEITUNGSMUSIK ZU EINER LICHTSPIELSZENE: film music threatening danger, fear & catastophe, op.34
        ø 2(picc)121/2210/timp.perc.tamtam.xyl/
        pf/str   7'46"-9' Heinrichshofen Misc 844 B
CONCERTI
 Cello & orch, in D (after concerto for harpsichord by M.G.Monn)
        ø 2(picc)222/2210/timp.perc.glock.xyl/
        cel.hp/str   17'30" G.Schirmer Misc 1634 B
  ed N.Kokkinis   ø 2(picc)222/2210/timp.perc.glock.tamtam.xyl/
        cel[=pf].hp/str Schott/Universal,1976.CW (III) VII/27 MRL
 Piano & orch, op.42 ø 2(picc)222/4231/timp.perc.xyl/pf/str 19'30"-28'G.Schirmer,1944 Misc 5150 D
  ed T.Okuljar   ø 2(picc)222/4231/timp.perc.glock.tamtam.xyl/
        str   Schott/Universal,1975,CW IV/A/15 MRL
 String quartet & orch, in B♭(freely transcribed after concerto grosso, op.6, no.7 by G.F.Handel)
        ø 2(picc)222/2210/timp.perc.glock.xyl/
        hp.pf/str   27' G.Schirmer,1935/63 Misc 6979
  ed N.Kokkinis   ø 2(picc)222/2210/timp.perc.glock.xyl/
        hp.pf/str   Schott/Universal,1976.CW (III) VII/27 MRL

SCHOENBERG, Arnold (cont)

CONCERTI (cont)
Violin & orch,	∅	3(picc)31+E♭cl+bcl.3/4331/timp.perc.glock.xyl/			
		str	29'	G.Schirmer	Misc 2948 C
ed T.Okuljar	∅	3(picc)31+E♭cl+bcl.3/4331/timp.perc.glock.			
		tamtam.xyl/str	Schott/Universal,1975,CW IV/A/15		MRL

Der ERSTE PSALM, op.50c, for speaker, chorus & orch <u>see</u> MODERNE PSALMEN
ERWARTUNG: monodrama for voice & orch, op.17
	∅	2(picc+picc.4(ca)3+Dcl+bcl.3+cbsn/4341/			
		timp.perc.glock.tamtam.xyl/str	28'55"-35'	Universal	Misc 845 B

Die GLÜCKLICHE HAND: drama with music, op.18
	∅	3(picc)+picc.3+ca.3+Dcl+bcl.3+cbsn/4341/		
		timp.perc.glock.tamtam.xyl/cel.hp/str	Universal,1916/7	Misc 2531 B

GURRELIEDER, for soli, chorus & orch
  Part I (62'20")   Part II (5'15")   Part III (44')
Complete	∅	8(4picc)5(2ca)7(2E♭cl:2bcl)3+2cbsn/		
		10(4wtuba)6+btpt.71/timp.perc.xyl/		
		cel.4hp/str	Universal,1920/48	Misc 986 D

    Extracts
      Lied der Waldtaube (Song of the wood dove)
arr for small orch	∅	1+picc.1+ca.2(E♭cl)+bcl.1+cbsn/2000/hmn.pf/		
		str	Universal	Misc 863

Die JAKOBSLEITER (Jacob's Ladder): oratorio for soli, chorus & orch (unfinished)(1917-22)
	∅	3(picc)+picc.3+ca.3+E♭cl.+bcl.3+cbsn/4331/timp.perc		
		glock.xyl/cel.hp.pf/str	[BBC,1965]	Misc 6130 E
orch W.Zillig, rev R.Stephan	∅	3(picc)+picc.3+ca.3+E♭cl+bcl.3+cbsn/4331/timp.perc.		
		glock.tamtam.wmc.xyl/cel.hp.pf/str		
		Separate group: 03+ca.1+bcl.0/0300/cel.2hmn.hp.mand/		
		11 solo-vln		
		Off stage: 0000/4320/2hmn/12 solo vln	Belmont,1980	Misc 10466

KAMMERSYMPHONIEN
  No.1 for 15 solo instruments, op.9, in E
	∅	11+ca.1+Dcl+bcl.1+cbsn/2000/str-(2.-1.1.1.)	21'55"	Universal,1912	Misc 804 C
Orch version, op.9b	∅	0.picc.2+ca.1+E♭cl+bcl.2+cbsn/3230/str	26'	Schirmer,1963	Misc 5814 C
ed C.M.Schmidt (early version)					
	∅	1(picc)1+ca.1+E♭cl+bcl.1+cbsn/2000/			
		str(2.-.1.1.1)	Schott/Universal,1976.CW IV/11,1		MRL
ed C.M.Schmidt, with sketches,	fragments & notes				
	∅	1(picc)1+ca.1+E♭cl+bcl.1+cbsn/2000/			
		str(2.-.1.1.1)	Schott/Universal,1976.CW IV/11,2		MRL
No.2, op.38	∅	2(picc)2(ca)22/2200/str	20'-21'15"G.Schirmer,1962		21632 + **
ed C.M.Schmidt, with sketches, fragments & notes					
	∅	2('picc)2(2ca)22/2200/str(1.1.1.1.1)	Schott/Universal,1976.CW IV/11,2		MRL

KOL NIDRE, for narrator & chorus (6-8S.6A.6T.6B) & orch, op.39
	∅	2(picc)11+E♭cl+bcl.1/2221/timp.perc.bell.xyl/		
		str	Bomart Music Pub	Misc 3992
ed J-L.Monod	∅	2(picc)11+E♭cl+bcl.1/2221/timp.perc.bell.flex.		
		xyl/str	Boelke-Bomart,1967	Misc 8875
ed J.Rufer & C.M.Schmidt	∅	2(2picc)11+E♭cl+bcl.1/2221/timp.perc.flex.		
		glock.tamtam.xyl/str(6-9.3-5.3-4.3-4.2-3)		
			Schott/Universal,1975.CW V/A/19	MRL

LIEDER
  6 Lieder, op.8
1. Natur	∅	22(ca)1+bcl.2/4231/hp/str	Universal,1913	Misc 3183 B
2. Das Wappenschild	∅	2+picc.333(cbsn)/4330/timp.perc/str	Universal,1913	Misc 3184 B
3. Sehnsucht	∅	21+ca.1+bcl.2/4000/str	Universal,1913	Misc 3185 B
4. Nie ward ich, Herrin, müd				
	∅	32+ca.2+bcl.2+cbsn/4331/timp/str	Universal,1913	Misc 3186 B
5. Voll jener Süsse	∅	32+ca.2+bcl.2+cbsn/4331/timp/str	Universal,1913	Misc 3187 B
6. Wenn Vöglein klagen	∅	3(picc)2+ca.2+bcl.2+cbsn/4231/str	Universal,1913	Misc 3188 B

SCHOENBERG, Arnold (cont)

LIEDER (cont)
    4 Lieder for voice & orch, op.22
      1. Seraphita   3. Mach mich zum Wächter deiner Weiten
      2. Alle, welche dich suchen   4. Vorgefühle
                    φ 4(picc)3(ca)+ca.6(3bcl:cbcl)+Dcl.3+cbsn/4131/
                      timp.perc.tamtam.xyl/hp/str   13'   Universal,1917   Misc 1654 D

MACH MICH ZUM WÄCHTER DEINER WEITEN see LIEDER: 4 Lieder, op.22, no.3
MODERNE PSALMEN (Psalm no.1: O, Du mein Gott), for speaker, chorus & orch
    ed R.Kolisch, with facs of sketches & text
                    φ 2+picc.2+ca.1+E♭cl+bcl.2/2210/perc/str   Schott,1956   Misc 4753 E
    ed J.Rufer & C.M.Schmidt   φ 2(picc)2(ca)1+E♭cl+bcl.2/2210/bdm.glock.tamtam/
                      str(8.-.4.4.4)   Schott/Universal,1975.CW V/A/19   MRL
MOSES UND ARON: opera (Acts 1 & 2 only - act 3 not composed)
    Complete   φ 3(picc)3(ca)2+E♭cl+bcl.2+cbsn/4331/timp.perc.
                      bells.flex.gong.xyl/cel.gtr.hp.2mand.pf/str
                                      G.Schoenberg (Schott),1958   Misc 5024 B
      ed C.M.Schmidt, with sketches & fragments
                    φ 3(3picc)3+ca.3(E♭cl)+bcl.3(cbsn)/4331/
                      timp.perc.hbells of determinate & indeterminate
                      pitch (high & low).flex.glock.rattle.tamtam.xyl/
                      cel.2hp.2mand.pf/str
                      On stage: 00.ca.00/1200/instrs to double chorus lines
                      Offstage: 1+picc.100/1020/timp.perc.sbells.gongs/
                              2gtr.2-4mand.pf   Schott/Universal,1977-80.CW III/8,1 & 2   MRL
    Extracts
      Der Tanz um das Goldene Kalb, for SATTBar soli, chorus & orch
                SS 3(3picc)3(ca)4(E♭cl:bcl)2+cbsn/4331/timp.perc.
                      bells.glock.gong.xyl/cel.gtr.hp.2mand.pf/
                      str   Ars Viva   Misc 3506

NATUR see LIEDER: 6 Lieder, op.8, no.1
NIE WARD ICH, HERRIN, MÜD see LIEDER: 6 Lieder, op.8, no.4
O, DU MEIN GOTT see MODERNE PSALMEN
ORCHESTERSTÜCKE
    3 Orchesterstücke (Drei kleine Stücke für Kammerorchester)(No.3 unfinished), without opus (1910)
                    φ 1111/1000/cel.org[=hmn]/str(1.1.1.1.1)   G.Schoenberg   Misc 6238 +
      with facsimile of orig score
                    φ 1111/1000/cel.org[=hmn]/str(1.1.1.1.1)   Belmont Mus,1962   25219 C
    5 Orchesterstücke, op.16
      1. Vorgefühle (Premonitions)   2'15"
      2. Vergangenes (Yesteryears)   5'45"
      3. Farben (Colours)(Summer morning by a lake)   3'50"
      4. Peripetie (Peripetia)   2'
      5. Das obligate Rezitativ (The obligatory recitative)   3'35"
      Original version   φ 3(picc)+picc.3+ca.3+bcl.3+cbsn/6341/
                      timp.perc.tamtam.xyl/cel.hp/str   Peters,1912   Misc 3196 D
      Original version, revised edn
                    φ 3(picc)+picc.3+ca.3+bcl+cbcl.3+cbsn/6341/
                      timp.perc.tamtam.xyl/cel.hp/str   Peters,1922/Eulenburg   Misc 6075
      1949 revised version   φ 3(picc)+picc.2+ca.2+E♭cl+bcl.2+cbsn/4331/
                      timp.perc.tamtam.xyl/cel.hp/str   17'25"   Peters,1952(H)   PL 465
        ed P.Boulez   φ 3(picc)+picc.2+ca.2+E♭cl+bcl.2+cbsn/4331/
                      timp.perc.tamtam.xyl/cel.hp/str   17'25"
                                    Henmar Press,1952/Peters(H)   PL 435 Amv
      1973 version (Collation of all existent sources of op.16)
        ed R.Hofmann   φ 3(picc)+picc.2+ca.2+E♭cl+bcl.2+cbsn/4331/
                      timp.perc.xyl/cel.hp/str   Henmar Press,1952/Peters,1973   Misc 8532

SCHOENBERG, Arnold (cont)

PELLÉAS AND MÉLISANDE: symphonic poem, op.5
                                    φ   3+picc.3+ca.3+Ebcl+bcl.3+cbsn/8451/
                                         timp.perc.glock/2hp/str   42'50"-45'   Universal   13034

PIANO QUINTET by J.Brahms, op.25, in G min, orch A.Schoenberg
     ed R.Stephan   φ   3(3picc)3(ca)2(cbcl)+Ebcl.3(cbsn)/4331/
                                         timp.perc.glock.xyl/str   Schott/Universal,1972.CW (II) VII/26   MRL

PIERROT LUNAIRE, for voice & orch, op.21
     1. Mondestrunken   8. Nacht (Passacaglia)   15. Heimweh
     2. Colombine   9. Gebet an Pierrot   16. Gemeinheit
     3. Der Dandy   10. Raub   17. Parodie
     4. Eine blasse Wäscherin   11. Rote Messe   18. Der Mondfleck
     5. Valse de Chopin   12. Galgenlied   19. Serenade
     6. Madonna   13. Enthauptung   20. Heimfahrt (Barcarole)
     7. Der kranke Mond   14. Die Kreuze   21. O alter Duft
                                    φ   1(picc)01(bcl)0/0000/pf/str   40'   Universal   Misc 1988 B

PRELUDE TO A 'GENESIS' SUITE, for chorus & orch, op.44 (1945)
     ed C.M.Schmidt & J.Rufer   φ   3(picc)3(ca)3(bcl)2+cbsn/4331/timp.perc.
                                         glock.tamb.tamtam.xyl/cel.hp/str   Schott/Universal,1975.CW V/A/19   MRL
     Bars 55-83 only   PS   only   [BBC]   Misc 5610 B

SEHNSUCHT see LIEDER: 6 Lieder, op.8, no.3
SERAPHITA see LIEDER: 4 Lieder, op.22, no.1
SONGS see LIEDER
SUITE for string orch, in G (1934)
     1. Overture   2. Adagio   3. Minuet   4. Gavotte   5. Gigue
                                    φ   str   Schirmer,1935   Misc 1630 B
SUITE, op.29 see CHAMBER CATALOGUE
A SURVIVOR FROM WARSAW, for narrator, mv-chorus & orch, op.46
                                    φ   2+picc.222/4331/timp.perc/hp/str   6'22"-8'   (Bomart)   20266 + # Amv
     ed C.M.Schmidt & J.Rufer   φ   3(picc)222/4331/timp.perc.bells.cast.
                                         glock.tamb.tamtam.xyl/hp/
                                         str(10.10.6.6.6)   Schott/Universal,1975.CW V/A/19   MRL
     1947 rev version
        ed J-L.Monod   φ   2(2picc)222/4331/timp.perc.bells.xyl/
                                         hp/str   Boelke-Bomart,1974   Misc 8531
     Newly rev J-L.Monod   φ   2(2picc)222/4331/timp.perc.bells.tamtam.xyl/
                                         hp/str   Boelke-Bomart,1979   Misc 10001

SYMPHONIES see KAMMERSYMPHONIEN
THEME & VARIATIONS, op.43
     op.43a, for symphonic wind band
                                    φ   2+picc.23+Ebcl+acl+bcl.2asx.tsx.barsx.2/
                                         43.2cnt.2flg.31.bar.euph.btuba/timp.perc.
                                         glock.xyl/cb   Schirmer   MB 4547
     op.43b, for orch   φ   2+picc.2+ca.2+bcl.2+cbsn/4331/timp.perc.bells.
                                         glock.xyl/str   11'35"-14'   Schirmer   Misc 3003 B
VARIATIONS, op.31   φ   4(2picc)4(ca)4(Ebcl)+bcl.4(cbsn)/4341/timp.perc.
                                         flex.glock.tamtam.xyl/cel.hp/str   20'-22'30" Universal   Misc 843 E
VERKLÄRTE NACHT (Enchanted Night), op.4 (orig 2vln.2vla.2vlc), arr for string orch 1913, rev 1943
                                    φ   str   AMP,1943   Misc 9038
                                    φ   str   28'30"-30'15" Universal   13488
VOLL JENER SÜSSE see LIEDER: 6 Lieder, op.8, no.5
VON HEUTE AUF MORGEN: opera in one act, op.32
     Complete   φ   2(picc)2(ca)2+Ebcl+bcl.2sx.1+cbsn/2231/
                                         timp.perc.flex.glock.tamtam.xyl/
                                         gtr.hp.mand.pf(cel)/str   B.Balan   Misc 2581 B
        ed R.Hoffmann & W.Bittinger
                                    φ   2+picc.2(ca)2+Ebcl+bcl.ssx(asx).barsx(tsx).2(cbsn)/
                                         2231/timp.perc.cast.flex.glock.tamtam/gtr.hp.mand.pf/
                                         str(8-10(1.2.3.solo)8-10.6-8(1.2.3.solo)
                                         6-8(1.2.3.solo)6-8(1.2.3.solo)) Schott/Universal,1974.CW III/7   MRL

SCHOENBERG, Arnold (cont)

VON HEUTE AUF MORGEN (cont)
   Text & sketches for act 1, ed G.Neuwirth   Schott/Universal,1972.CW III/7,1   MRL
   Bars 1-452, & 453-1131, ed G.Neuwirth & T.Okuljar from orig MS   Schott/Universal,1974.CW III/7,2   MRL
VORGEFÜHLE see LIEDER: 4 Lieder, op.22, no.4
Das WAPPENSCHILD see LIEDER; 6 Lieder, op.8, no.2
WENN VÖGLEIN KLAGEN see LIEDER: 6 Lieder, op.8, no.6

SCHOENFELD, Henry (1857-1936)

CHARACTERISTIC SUITE, op.15
   1. Allegretto con moto e grazioso   3. Menuetto
   2. Marcio fantastico (Southern Negro life)   4. Rondo
                   φ   str   Summy   9302

SCHOLL, John

SPRINGTIME IN HOLLAND: musical pl by J.Scholl & L.P.Altar
   Extracts
      The Girl on the little blue plate: song
         in Eb   PC 111.2sx.1/2210/perc/gtr/str   Feldman   13505

SCHOLLUM, Robert (1913-

GESPRÄCHE (Conversations): 4 pieces for chamber orch, op.62
                 φ   0200/2000/pf/str   20'   Doblinger,1960   Misc 8138
KONTRASTE: variations for orch, op.56
                 φ   2+picc.222/4331/timp.perc.glock.xyl/
                    str   10'   Doblinger,1960   Misc 7216
SYMPHONY no.2 (Istrianische), op.60
                 φ   2+picc.222+cbsn/4331/timp.perc.glock.xyl/
                    cel.hp/str   Doblinger,1970   Misc 7465
TOCCATA in 5 parts, op.59 (1958)
                 φ   str   15'   Doblinger,1961   Misc 7218

SCHOLZ, Robert

ORCHESTRAL SUITE no.1
   Andante & allegro (scherzo) φ 2(picc)2(ca)2(bcl)1/2310/timp.perc/
                              cel.pf/str
                                     M & H Publications,1946   Misc 2646

SCHONBERGER, John

WHISPERING: song
   in Eb, arr E.Griffiths   φ 1121/2230/perc/hp.pf/str   (K.Prowse)   LM G 4428

SCHÖNHERR, Max (1903-

BAUERNMUSI' AUS ÖSTERREICH (Austrian peasant dances), op.14
   1. Hochzeitsmarsch (2'55")   5. Sautanz   (1'25")
   2. Schuhplattler (2'15")   6. Zwoaschritt   (1'50")
   3. G'strampfter   (1'45")   7. Veitscher Ochsengalopp (6'15")
   4. Steirischer   (4'35")
                 φ   2(picc)2[-1](ca)22[-1]/4[-2]230/perc.glock.xyl/   (PL 299 &
                    hp/str   20'   Universal,1936   (Misc 1767

SCHÖNHERR, Max (cont)

CARILLON: a little overture   PC 2222/2220/timp.perc/hp/str   4'30"   Bosworth,1959   23100
FLUGS UMI: Austian barn dance, op.26
   arr L.Weninger   PC 2(picc)222/4330/timp.perc/hp/str   6'   Zimmermann   14495
KURPARKZAUBER: concert waltz   PC 2(picc)222/4230/timp.perc/hp/str   8'   H.Pero   23063
MILLOCKER-MELODIEN see MILLÖCKER, Karl: MILLÖCKER-MELODIEN
PERPETUUM MOBILE, op.29 (after a violin study by R.Kreutzer)
                                ø   2(picc)2[=1](ca)22[=1]/4[=2]23[=1]0/
                                    timp.perc/[hp]/str   5'   Universal   Misc 1979
RÁKÓCZY: Hungarian march, arr   PC 1+picc.22.3sx.2/4231/timp.perc/hmn[=acdn]/
                                    str   Krenn (Bosworth) 22917 B
4 STÜCKE
   1. Präludium (6')   3. Scherzo (6'15")
   2. Notturno (7'25")   4. Epilog (3'10")
                                ø   str   (Composer)   Misc 7312
TÄNZE AUS ÖSTERREICH, op.25
   1. Hochzeitsmarsch aus Ebensee   (5')   5. Schleifer   (1'05")
   2. Guggu-Polka   (1'05") 6. Polsterltanz aus Ischl (3'45")
   3. Bandltanz und Tiroler Plattler aus Brixlegg (2') 7. Die sieben Sprünge (2'05")
   4. Salzburger Schustertanz   (2')   8. Bauerngalopp   (3')
                                ø   2222/4230/timp.perc/hp/str   20'   Doblinger   21009
TÄNZE AUS SALZBURG (Dances from Salzburg)
                                ø   1121/2000/timp.perc/hp/str   7'   Universal,1961   Misc 6331
WIENER-FIAKER-HUMOR, for chorus & orch
   1. Fiaker-G'stanzeln   3. Loblied auf den Wiener Fiaker
   2. Altes Fiakerlied   4. Neues Fiakerlied
                                PC 0021/0000/[acdn].[gtr].hp/str   Bosworth,1956   23997
WIENER TAGEBUCH (Vienna Diary): suite
   1. Fahnen am Ring (Banners in the Ring street)   (2'15")
   2. Kursalon-Promenade (Kurpark Promenade)   (4')
   3. Abends in der Vorstadt (Evening in the suburbs)(2'30")
   4. Kabarett-Finale (Revue-Finale)   (2')
                                PC 2(picc)222/4230/timp.perc/[acdn].hp/str   Doblinger/Arcadia,1961 24139-40
WIENER OPERETTEN: potpourri for Soprano & Tenor soli (added chorus arr A.Masters) & orch, arr
                                PC 2222/4230/timp.perc/hp/str   (Vienna Radio)   22900 +

SCHRAMMEL, Johann (1850-1893)

ALLÉGRESSE (Lusti' und Fidel): waltz, op.133
                                PC 1121/2210/perc/str   Cranz Odeon   8514
DORNBACHER-HETZ (Tally-Ho): march, op.97
                                PC 1121/2230/perc/str   Cranz   7060
Les GARDES NOBLES: march   PC 1+picc.222/2230.euph/perc/str   Hawkes   3177
WIEN-BERLIN: march, op.100   PC 1121/2210/perc/str   Cranz   7062
WIEN BLEIBT WIEN: march   PC 1121/22.cnt.30/perc/str   Cranz   7057
   arr A.Winter   PC 1(picc)12.3sx.1/2230/perc/str   Boosey & H   10536
WIEN KÜNSTLER-MARSCH, op.111   PC 0.picc.121/2210/perc/str   Cranz   7061

SCHREIER-BOTTERO

The SONG OF THE ROSE (Tango des roses)
                                PC 101.3sx.0/0000/acdn.bjo/str   Ricordi   16551 **

SCHREINER, Adolf

BLÜTHENKRANZ (Musical blossoms): selection of famous melodies by C.M.Weber, arr A.Schreiner &
        L.Weninger for oboe, trumpet & orch
                        PC 2(picc)222/4230/perc/str   Benjamin   474
OPERN-ALBUM: selection by A.Schreiner & M.Rhode
                        PC 1+picc.222/4230/timp.perc/str   Apollo Verlag   12474
Der POSTILLON VON LONJUMEAU: fantasy on themes from the opera by A.Adam
                        PC 2(picc)222/4231/perc/str   Benjamin   16938
SCHUMANN-ALBUM: selection arr from the works of R.Schumann for oboe, clarinet & orch
    arr Hohenstein   PC 2222/4231/timp.perc/str   15'   Benjamin   477
SLAVISCHE FANTASIE: selection
    arr L.Weninger   PC 2(picc)222/4231/timp.perc/str   10'   Benjamin   1678
VON GLUCK BIS R.WAGNER: chronological potopourri
                        PC 2(picc)222/4230/perc/str   8'45"-12'   Benjamin   473

SCHREKER, Franz (1878-1934)

Der GEBURTSTAG DER INFANTIN: ballet
    Suite   ∅   2+picc.2+ca.2+bcl.2+cbsn/4331/timp.perc.
                           bells.glock.tamtam.xyl/cel.4gtr.4hp.4mand/
                           str   30'   Universal,1923   Misc 2253
5 GESÄNGE for mezzo soprano (or Baritone) & orch
    1. Ich frag' nach dir jedwede Morgensonne   4. Sie sind so schön
    2. Dies aber kann mein Sehnen   5. Einst gibt ein Tag
    3. Die Dunkelheit
                       ∅   222.bthn.2/2110/perc./cel.2hp./str   20'   Universal   Misc 3190 B
Die GEZEICHNETEN (The Branded): opera (see also VORSPIEL ZU EINEM DRAMA)
    Acts 1-3   ∅   3+picc.3+ca.4(Ebcl.bthn)+bcl.2+cbsn/6431+btuba/
                           timp.perc.bells.glock.xyl/cel.2hp.pf/str   Universal,1916   Misc 1465-7
INTERMEZZO, op.8   ∅   str   Bosworth   11509
KAMMERSYMPHONIE for 23 solo instruments
                       ∅   1111/1110/timp.perc/cel.hmn.hp.pf/str 30'   Universal,1922   Misc 806
4 KLEINE STÜCKE, for large orch
    1. Timoroso   3. Incalzando
    2. Violente   4. Gradevole
                       ∅   2+picc.3(ca)2+bcl.sx.3+cbsn/4331/timp.perc.
                           glock.xyl/2hp.pf/str   Heinrichshofen,1930   Misc 827
6 KLEINE STÜCKE for chamber orch
    1. Präludium   4. Fughette
    2. Marcia   5. Intermezzo
    3. Canon   6. Capriccio
                       ∅   1(picc)1+ca.1+bcl.sx.1+cbsn/2121/timp.perc.
                           glock.xyl/cel.hp.pf/str   20'   Universal [1929]   Misc 3924
SCHWANNENGESANG for chorus & orch, op.11
                       ∅   22+ca.2+bcl.2+cbsn/4230/timp.perc.glock/
                           str   12'   Universal   Misc 2693
TANZSPIEL
    Menuett & Gavotte PC 1121/2210/timp.perc/str   6'   Universal   15671
VORSPIEL ZU EINEM DRAMA (used as prelude to 'Die Gezeichneten')
                       ∅   4(picc)3+ca.4(Ebcl)+bcl.2+cbsn/4431/timp.perc.
                           bells.glock.tamtam.xyl/cel.2hp.pf/str   Universal,1914   Misc 2692

SCHRØDER, Walther

REBILD BAKKER (Rebild National Park): Danish rhapsody, op.15
                       ∅   2+picc.22+ca.22/4231/timp.perc/cel.hp/str   Skandinavisk Forlag,1947   Misc 2535 C

SCHUBERT, Ferdinand (1794-1859)

REQUIEM (Deutsches Requiem), for STB soli, chorus & small orch, op.9, in G min (1828)
    ed O.Biba   φ 0000/2020/timp/org/str   Coppenrath [1978?]   Misc 9677
TANTUM ERGO, op.5
   No.1, in B♭ for chorus & orch   No.2, in B♭, for chorus & orch
     ed L.Dité   VS 0200/2200/timp/org/str   Doblinger,1947   21358

SCHUBERT, Franz (1797-1828)

see DEUTSCH, Otto: Franz Schubert Thematisches Verzeichnis in chronologischer Folge von Otto
      Erich Deutsch. 2nd edition, edited Werner Aderhold. Kassel: Bärenreiter, 1978. The
      numbers prefixed 'D' refer to entries in this book.

COMPLETE WORKS

F.Schuberts Werke: Kritisch durchgesehene Gesamtausgabe, ed E.Mandyczewski, J.Brahms & others
Leipzig: Breitkopf & H, 1884-97. Reprinted 1964-9
F.Schubert. Neue Ausgabe Sämtlicher Werke, ed W.Dürr, A.Feil, C.Landon & others

ADAGIO AND RONDO CONCERTANTE, for piano & strings (orig for pf-4tet), D.487
    ed A.Orel   φ str   14'   Edn Pacific,1955   23505
ADIEU (Lebe wohl): song (attrib to Schubert; composed by A.H.von Weyrauch), D.app.1
    in E♭, arr M.Tobani   PC 2222/2210/str   C.Fischer   11060
    in E♭, arr C.Clarke for duet & orch
                       1121/2200/pf/str   BBC   TV MS 130
    arr for cornet & orch   PC 1122/2200/str   Hawkes   6481
ADRAST: unfinished opera, D.137 (fragments)
                     φ 2222/2230/timp/str   Breitkopf.CW 15/7   MRL
ALFONSO UND ESTRELLA: opera in 3 acts, D.732
    Complete   φ 2+picc.222/4230/timp.perc/hp/str   Breitkopf.CW 15/5   MRL
    Overture (also used for ROSAMUNDE)
                     φ 2222/2230/timp/str   6'30"   Breitkopf   7234 Amv Cn Dwa
      ed A.de Almeida   φ 2222/2230/timp/str   Heugel,1962   23660
      arr A.Oelschlegel PC 1121/2210/timp/str   Cranz (Odeon)   3496
      arr A.Winter   PC 2222/4230/timp/str   Boosey & H   13135 Bwa
    Selection of vocal excerpts

1. Still noch decket: introduction (No.1)	11. Herrlich auf des Berges: aria (No.21)
2. Sei mir gegrüsst: aria (No.2)	12. Introduction (No.23)
3. Zur Jagd: chorus & aria (No.7)	13. Hörst du rufen: duet (No.24)
4. Verweile, O Prinzessin: recit & aria (No.8)	14. Du wirst mir: duet (No.25)
5. Jagib, vernimm mein Flehen: duet (No.9)	15. Doch nun werde: duet (No.27)
6. Glänzende Waffe: finale (No.10)	16. Wehe, meines Vaters: duet & chorus (No.29)
7. O sing' mir: recit & aria (No.11)	17. Was geht hier: recit & ensemble (No.31)
8. Freundlich bist du: duet (No.14)	18. Kein Geist: duet (No.33)
9. Könnt ich ewig: aria (No.15)	19. Die Schwerter hoch geschwungen: finale
10. Stille, Freunde: chorus & ensemble (No.17)	

                     φ 2+picc.222/4230/timp.perc/hp/str   [Breitkopf.CW 15/5]   19570
ALLEGRETTO QUASI ANDANTINO (from Sonata in A min for piano, D.537)
    arr L.Weninger   PC 1121/2210/timp/hp/str   10'   Benjamin   1041
Die ALLMACHT (Great is Jehovah, our Lord): song, D.852
    in C (orig), arr Mottl φ 2222/4331/timp/hp/str   5'   Breitkopf   17561
    in C, arr F.Liszt (G.376), for Tenor solo, chorus & orch
                     φ 2222/4231/timp/hp.org/str   Schuberth   14450 B
     in G   φ 2222/4231/timp/hp/str   (Siddell)   17563
     in A   φ 2222/4231/timp/hp/str   (Siddell)   17562

SCHUBERT, Franz (cont)

AM GEBURTSTAGE DES KAISERS   see   CANTATAS: Am Geburtstage des Kaisers
AM MEER   see   SCHWANENGESANG
AM TAGE ALLER SEELEN (Litanei auf das Fest Aller Seelen): song, D.343
   in G (orig E♭)   ∅   str   (Siddell)   18332
AN DIE MUSIK (To Music): song, D.547
   in D (orig), arr M.Reger   ∅   1111/2000/timp/str   2'30"   Breitkopf   16666 B
   in D & D♭, arr G.Stacey   PC   str   (Augener)   LM G 3714
AN SCHWAGER KRONOS: song, D.369
   orch J.Brahms   ∅   2222/2200/timp/str   OUP,1953   25711
AN SYLVIA (Who is Sylvia?): song, D.891
   in A (orig)   1121/2000/str   3'30"   (BBC)   18257
   in A, arr G.Stacey   pf/str   (Wood)   LM G 3136
   in B♭   1111/2000/pf/str   (Augener)   LM G 4254
   arr Baron   PC   1121/2210/timp/str   Schirmer   4440
ANDANTE (From Octet in F for strings & wind instruments, D.803)
   arr L.Weninger   PC   1111/2110/timp/pf/str   Benjamin   1048
AUF DEM WASSER ZU SINGEN (The Water Song), D.774
   in A♭ (orig)   ∅   1020/2000/str   (Siddell)   17498
   in F   ∅   1020/2000/str   (BBC)   17497
AUFENTHALT   see   SCHWANENGESANG
AUFLÖSUNG: song, D.807
   in G (orig), arr L.Wurmser   ∅   2222/4200/timp/str   BBC/Arranger   TO 1561
AUGUSTE JAM COELESTIUM: duet for Soprano & Tenor soli & orch, D.488
   in G (orig)   ∅   0202/0000/str   (Breitkopf)   23678 +
   ed K.Pfannhauser   ∅   0202/0000/str/cont(org)   Doblinger,1947 26001
AVE MARIA (Ellens Gesang III): song D.839
   in B♭ (orig)   1122/2000/str   (Siddell)   18002 +
   in B♭ & A, arr G.Stacey   PC   str   (Chappell)   LM G 3162
   in G   1122/2000/hp/str   (Paxton)   24019
   in A♭, arr D.Edge, orch C.Groves for chorus & orch
                                  ∅   1131/0220/hp/str   (BBC)   TO 900
   in A♭, arr Winter/McCarthy   PC   2222/4230/perc/str   (Boosey)   LM G 10417
   in A, arr S.Torch   ∅   21+ca.22/4030/hp.pf/str   (BBC)   24146 +
   arr Cathcart   PC   2222/2230.euph/timp.perc/pf/str   Lafleur   1151
   arr Kleinecke   ∅   vln.vlc-soli.str   (Kramer)   23818 +
   arr L.Weninger   PC   2222/4231/timp/str   Benjamin   12773
   arr A.Winter   PC   2222/4231/timp/org/str   6'30"   Boosey & H   11806
   arr Wilhelmj, orch J.Buerger
                                  ∅   2121/2030/hp/vln-solo.str   (Schott)   MS 6983
Die BEIDEN FREUNDE VON SALAMANKA   see   Die FREUNDE VON SALAMANKA
BERCEUSE, D.527   see   SCHLAFLIED
Die BÜRGSCHAFT: opera in 3 acts (act 3 incomplete), D.435
   Fragments   ∅   2222/2230/timp.perc/str   Breitkopf.CW 15/7 MRL
CANTATAS
   Am Geburtstage des Kaisers (Steig empor, umblüht von Segen), for SATB soli, chorus & orch, D.748
                                  ∅   2222/2200/timp/str   Breitkopf.CW 17   MRL
   Kantate zu Ehren Joseph Spendou's (Da liegt er, **Starr**), for soli, chorus & orch, D.472
                                  ∅   0202/2200/timp/str   Breitkopf.CW 17   MRL
   Lazarus, or Die Feier der Auferstehung (La Solennita della Risurrezione): Easter
      cantata (fragments), for SSSTTB soli, chorus & orch, D.689
                                  ∅   2222/2030/str   Breitkopf.CW 17   MRL
                                  ∅   2222/2[2]30/[timp]/[hp]/str   (Breitkopf.CW 17) 25529
    Extracts
      So schlummert auf Rosen: Jemima's aria
                                  ∅   2020/0000/str   (Breitkopf.CW 17) Misc 8980
   Namensfeier (Erhabner! Verehrter Freund der Jugend), for STB soli, STB chorus & orch, D.294
                                  ∅   0202/2000/str   Breitkopf.CW 17   MRL

SCHUBERT, Franz (cont)

CHANSON D'AMOUR (Lilac Time): musical play. arr Berté, H   see   BERTÉ, H: CHANSON D'AMOUR
CLAUDINE VON VILLA BELLA: singspiel in 3 acts (Unfinished - Act 1 only), D.239

Complete	φ	2222/2200/timp/str		Breitkopf.CW 15/7	MRL
	φ	2222/2200/timp.perc/str		[BBC]	26535
without overture	φ	2222/2000/timp/str		(Breitkopf.CW 15/7)	Misc 8195 B +
Overture	φ	2222/2200/timp/str	7'45"	(Breitkopf)	12056 #

CONCERTO for violin & orch (Conzertstück), D.345, in D

	φ	0200/0200/timp/str		Breitkopf.CW 21 supp	MRL
	φ	0200/0200/timp/str		Breitkopf	13058

The CONSPIRATORS   see   Die VERSCHWORENEN
DA LIEGT ER, STARR   see   CANTATAS: Kantata zu Ehren Joseph Spendou's
DANSES ALLEMANDES   see   DEUTSCHE TÄNZE
DEATH AND THE MAIDEN   see   Der TOD UND DAS MÄDCHEN
DEUTSCHE MESSE, D.872   see   MASSES
DEUTSCHE TÄNZE (see also CHAMBER CATALOGUE)

D.90: 5 German dances with coda & 7 trios

No.1, in C	No.3, in D	No.5, in C
No.2, in G	No.4, in F	

	φ	str	11'	Breitkopf.CW 2	MRL
	φ	str [=str-4tet]		Broude	20656
arr K.Geiringer	φ	str		Music Press	Misc 2633

D.783: 16 German dances & 2 écossaises [no.2.= D.781, no.1] (orig for pf)
arr Flitner in Suite 'Welcome Spring', for chorus & orch (includes 1 valse sentimentale from
         D.779)

1. Tönet ihr Lieder	7. Nun end ich der Zweifel
2. Am Waldes Rand	8. Hoch wogen die Pulse
3. Komm, oh komm	9. Thauperlen sie schwimmen
4. Wie die Kranke	10. Auf lasset die Jubelfanfaren
5. Warte nur	11. Wie mit Sehnen
6. Verliebtes Schmachten	

	φ	2222/4230/timp.perc/str	Hug	12679

Excerpts from 'Welcome Spring', arr as part songs

1. Welcome thrice welcome (No.1)	(1')
2. How sweet to wander neath the trees (No.2)	(1'15")
3. I'm in no hurry to marry (No.5)	(0'40")
4. When gallant lovers come a-wooing (No.6)	(0'45")
5. Tender music all inviting (No.11)	(1'30")

	φ	2222/2230/timp.perc/str	(BBC)	TO 1116 **

arr F.Salabert

No.1, in D	No.4, in C
No.2, in Bb	No.5, in C
No.3, in G	No.6, in F

	PC	1121/2230/timp.perc/str	Salabert	10830

D.820: 6 German Dances (orig for pf)

No.1, in Ab	No.4, in Bb
No.2, in Ab	No.5, in Bb
No.3, in Ab	No.6, in Bb

arr Webern	φ	2222/2000/str	8'	Universal	11486 + Amv B

Suite, arr Heissler

1. in C (D.790, no.1)	5. in G (D.969, no.4)
2, in A (D.969, no 2	6. in Eb (D.790, no.12)
3. in A min (D.783, no.10)	7. in G (D.783, no.12)
4. in D (D.790, no.3)	

	φ	1+picc.222/2200/timp/str	7'	Brockhaus	8155

SCHUBERT, Franz (cont)

DEUTSCHE TÄNZE (cont)
  Suite, orch Herbeck
    1. in Ab (Trauer-Walzer)(D.365, no.2)   7. in C min (D.779, no.23)
    2. in Ab (D.799, no.34)   8. in B (D.734, no.14)
    3. in C (D.783, no.12)   9. in G (D.783, no.11)
    4. in A min (D.783, no.10)   10. in D (D.734, no.5)
    5. in F (D.790, no.10)   11. in A (D.779, no.13)
    6. in Bb (D.146, no.11)(Trio)   12. in G (D.734, no.9)
          φ   2+picc.111/2100/str   Cranz   15344

  Suite No.1, orch Herbeck
    Introduction
    1. in D (D.783, no.2)   6. in Eb (D.783. no.8)
    2. in Bb (D.783, no.3)   7. in C (D.734, no.8)
    3. in G (D.734, no.1)   8. in F min (D.783, no.14)
    4. in B min (D.783, no.5)   9. in Ab (D.783, no.15)
    5. in Bb (D.783, no.7)   10. in G (D.783, no.4)
          φ   2+picc.111/2100/str   Cranz   15578

  Suite No.2, orch Herbeck
    Introduction
    1. in C (D.779, no.17)   6. in D (D.790, no.3)
    2. in A min (D.779, no.31)   7. in Ab (D.790, no.11)
    3. in G (D.145, nos 11 & 15)   8. in E (D.790, no.12)
    4. in Eb (D.924, no.2)   9. in G (D.779, no.4)
    5. in C (D.783, no.9)(Wiedersehen-Deutscher)   10. in G (D.734, no.4)
          φ   1+picc.111/2100/str   Cranz   15579

DIVERTISSEMENT À LA HONGROISE, D.818, in G min (orig pf-duet)
  orch V.Mortari   φ 2(picc)222/2200/timp.perc/str   18'   Ricordi,1955   Misc 9730
  Andante Marcia (Marche à la hongroise); Allegretto
    arr Grohmann   PC 1(picc)121/2210/perc/str   Cranz   3487
  Andante & Allegretto
    arr Erdmannsdorfer   φ 2+picc.222/4331/timp.perc/str   Furstner   Misc 1852
  Marcia (Marche à la Hongroise)
    arr Bordier   φ 2222/4230/perc/str   Richault   8643
    arr Liszt (S.363, no.1) φ 2222/4231/timp.perc/str   Furstner   8149

Der DOPPELGANGER see SCHWANENGESANG

Das DREIMÄDERLHAUS: musical play, arr Berté, see BERTÉ, H: Das DREIMÄDERLHAUS

DU BIST DIE RUH (Kehr ein bei mir): song, D.776
  in Eb (orig), arr M.Reger   φ 2122/2000/timp/str   Breitkopf 18000
  arr L.Weninger   PC 2222/4231/timp/str   4'   Benjamin 12773

DU LIEBST MICH NICHT (Thou lov'st me not): song, D.756b
  in A min (orig), arr L.Wurmser
          φ 0222/4000/str   (Arranger) TO 1558

Der EINSAME (The Recluse): song, D.800
  in G (orig), arr L.Wurmser   φ 2222/2200/str   (Arranger) TO 1559

ELLENS GESANG I   see RASTE KRIEGER
ELLENS GESANG III see AVE MARIA

ERLKÖNIG (The Earl King): song, D.328
  in G min (orig), arr F.Liszt (S.375, no.4)
          φ 2222/2200/timp/hp/str   Forberg   17508 B

  Liszt transcription, arr Roberts
          PC 1121/2210/timp.perc/str   4'   Fischer   11061 B
  in D min   2222/2200/timp/hp/str   (Siddell) 17507
  in E min   2222/0030/timp/str   (OUP)   TO 604
  in E min   2222/2200/timp/hp/str   (Siddell) 17506
  in F min, arr Tobani   PC 2222/2210/timp.perc/str   C.Fischer 11060
  orch H.Berlioz   φ 22+ca.22/3200/timp/str   Breitkopf Misc 2889
  arr O.Langey   PC 2222/2210.euph/timp.perc/hp/str   Lafleur   1331
  arr J.Offenbach   PC 1121/2100/str   Costallat 5803
  arr F.Salabert   PC 1111/2210/timp/str   Salabert   5608

SCHUBERT, Franz (cont)

The FAITHFUL SENTINAL   see   Der VIERJÄHRIGE POSTEN
FANTASIA, D.940, in F min (orig for pf-duet)
    arr F.Mottl   ∅   2+picc.222/4230/timp.perc/hp/str   18'   Schott   7336
    arr Rudorff   PC 2222/4230/timp/str   Simrock   9800
Die FEIER DER AUFERSTEHUNG   see   CANTATAS: Lazarus
FERNANDO: Singspiel in 1 act, D.220
                          ∅   2222/2230/timp/str   Breitkopf.CW 15/2   MRL

FIERABRAS: heroic opera, D.796
  Complete   ∅   2+picc.222/4230/timp/str   Breitkopf.CW 15/6   MRL
  Critical edition, ed J.N.Fuchs
                          ∅   2+picc.222/4230/perc/str
                              Off stage: 0000/2200/perc
                              Stage band: 0222/2230   Breitkopf,1886/Dover,1964 Misc 7283 C
  Overture   ∅   2222/4230/timp/str   8'-9'   Breitkopf   7217 Amv Cwa
                          ∅   2222/4230/timp/str   Eulenburg,1964   Misc 6038 B
    arr Piercy   PC 2222/2230/timp/str   Boosey   36
Die FORELLE (The Trout): song, D.550
    arr F.Salabert   PC 1110/0110/timp/str   Salabert   12596
Die FREUNDE VON SALAMANKA: singspiel, D.326
  Complete   ∅   2222/2200/timp/str   Breitkopf.CW 15/2   MRL
  Overture   ∅   2222/2200/timp/str   6'   (Breitkopf) 10071 B
  3 excerpts
    1. Einsam schleich' ich durch die Zimmer: aria for Soprano solo & orch (No.4)
    2. Lebensmuth und frische Kühlung: trio for SSS soli & orch (No.5
    3. Gelagert unter'm hellem Dach der Bäume: duet for Soprano & Tenor soli & orch (No.12)
                          ∅   2202/2000/str   (Breitkopf.CW 15/2)   Misc 8194 B +
FRÜHLINGSGLAUBE: song, D.686
    arr L.Weninger   PC 1010/0110/perc/str   Benjamin   10468
    see also   LIEDER-SUITE
GALOP, D.925   see   GRAZER GALOPP
GEHEIMES (My Secret): song, D.719
    orch J.Brahms   ∅   0000/1000/str   OUP   25711
GESANG DER GEISTER ÜBER DEN WASSERN, for mv-chorus & string orch, D.714
    in C (orig)   ∅   str(vla & II, vlc I & II, cb)   10'30"-12'30" Breitkopf   9728
    in C   ∅   str(vla I & II, vlc I & II, cb)   Breitkopf.CW 16   MRL
GESÄNGE ZUR FEIER DES HEILIGEN OPFERS DER MESSE   see   MASSES: Deutsche Messe
GLAUBE, HOFFNUNG UND LIEBE (Gott! lass die Glocke): song for SATTBB chorus & wind instruments, D.954
    in Bb (orig)   ∅   0222/2020/[pf]   (Breitkopf) 23073 #
    in Bb   ∅   0222/0202/[pf]   Breitkopf.CW 17   MRL
Der GONDELFAHRER: quartet for TTBB voices & orch, D.809 (orig TTBB & pf)
    in C (orig), arr G.Hausmann ∅ 2022/2000/timp/str   Spina   14157
GOTT IN DER NATUR: song for SSAA soli & pf, D.757
    arr Bülow for fv-chorus & orch
                              2222/2200/timp/str   Schreiber   Misc 1849 B
GOTT IST MEIN HIRT (The Lord is my Shepherd): psalm 23, D.705 (orig SSAA voices & pf)
    [arr]   ∅   2021/2211/timp.perc/str   (Siddell)   18107
GRADUALE (Benedictus es, Domine) for chorus, orch & orch, D.184, in C
                          ∅   0220/0230/timp/org/str   Breitkopf.CW 14/5   MRL
                              02[=cl]00/0210/timp/org/str   Diabelli,1844 21151
Der GRAF VON GLEICHEN: opera - unfinished
  Extracts
    Morgengesang im Walde, for mv-chorus & orch, D.918
      arr J.Herbeck   ∅PS 0222/2000/str   Cranz   Misc 2717
GRAND DUO (Sonata in C for piano duet), D.812   see   SYMPHONIES: Symphony in C

SCHUBERT, Franz (cont)

GRAND MARCHE HÉROÏQUE   see   MARCHES
GRAND RONDO, D.951, in A (orig for piano duet)
   transcr L.Weiner   2222/2230/timp/str   12'   Hungarian SM,1961   Misc 5646
GRÄZER GALOPP, D.925 (orig pf)
   transcr V.Tausky   PC 1+picc.222/2230/timp.perc/str   Dix,1950   20821 C
GREAT IS JEHOVAH   see   Die ALLMACHT
GRETCHEN AM SPINNRADE (Marguerite at the Spinning Wheel): song, D.118 (from Goethe's Faust)
   in D min (orig), arr F.Liszt (S.375, no.2)
                          ∅ 2222/2000/timp/hp/str   Forberg   17859
   arr O.Langey   PC 2222/2230/timp/str   3'30"   Lafleur   11038
   arr J.Offenbach   PC 1121/2100/timp/str   Costallat   1050
GRUPPE AUS DEM TARTARUS: song, D.583
   orch J.Brahms   ∅ 2222+cbsn/2230/timp/str   [BBC]   Misc 3860
   orch J.Brahms, ed O.Deutsch for chorus & orch
                          ∅ 2222+cbsn/2230/timp/str   OUP,1937   14318
HARK, HARK, THE LARK   see   2 SERENADES, no.2
Der HÄUSLICHE KRIEG   see   Die VERSCHWORENEN
HEIDENRÖSLEIN (Red rose): song, D.257
   in Eb (orig G), arr G.Stacey
                          PC 1010/0000/pf/str   (K.Prowse)   LM A 40
HEROISCHER MARSCH   see   MARCHES
Die HIRT AUF DEM FELSEN (The Shepherd on the rock): song for Soprano, clarinet & orch, D.965 (orig
      soprano, clarinet and piano)
   in Bb (orig)   1111/2200/str   (Siddell)   18266
   in Bb, arr Catalinet   ∅ 2002/2000/str   (Arranger)   TO 1729
   in Bb, arr Halliwell   ∅ 1111/2010/str   9'15"-11'30"   Kahnt   13896
   in Bb, arr Reinecke   ∅ 2212/4000/str   10'30"   Kahnt   8244
HORCH, HORCH, DIE LERCH   see   2 SERENADES, no.2
HYMNE   see   HYMNUS AN DEN HEILIGEN GEIST, D.964
HYMNUS AN DEN HEILIGEN GEIST (Herr, unser Gott), for TTBB soli, TTBB chorus & wind instruments, D.964
   in C (orig)   ∅ 0222/2230   (Breitkopf)   22286 + #
   in C   ∅ 0222/2230   Breitkopf.CW 16   MRL
IM ABENDROT (At Sunset): song, D.799
   in Ab (orig), arr M.Reger   ∅ 1122/2000/timp/str   Breitkopf,1914   24331
   in Ab, arr L.Wurmser   ∅ 2222/2230/timp/str   (Arranger)   TO 1560
IM FRÜHLING (In Spring): song, D.882
   in G (orig), arr L.Wurmser   ∅ 2222/2000/str   (Arranger)   TO 1557
IM WALDE: song, D.708   see   WALDESNACHT
IMPROMPTU, D.899, no.1, in C min (orig for pf)
   arr Scholz   2222/0000/str   Rieter-Biedermann   10866
INTENDE VOCI   see   OFFERTORIA, D.963
INVOCATION (2nd mvt (Adagio) from octet, D.803, in F
   arr Wolf   PC 1020/0210/timp.perc/str   Schott   7146
Die JUNGE NONNE: song, D.828
   in F (orig), arr F.Liszt (S.375, no.1)
                          ∅ 2222/2000/timp/hp/str   4'   Forberg   20451 B
Eine KLEINE TRAUERMUSIK for wind instruments
                          ∅ 0022+cbsn/2020   Breitkopf   20612
                             0022+cbsn/2020   Breitkopf   52644
KONZERTSTÜCKE for violin & orch   see   CONCERTI for violin & orch, D.345, in D
KYRIES
   D.31, to a Mass in D min for chorus & orch (1812)
                          ∅ 1202/0200/timp/org/str   Breitkopf.CW 14/14   MRL
   D.49, to a Mass in D min for chorus & orch (1813)
                          ∅ 0202/0230/timp/org/str   Breitkopf.CW 14/15   MRL
   D.66, in F for chorus & orch ∅ 0202/0200/timp/org/str   Breitkopf.CW 14/16   MRL

SCHUBERT, Franz (cont)

LAZARUS see CANTATAS: Lazarus
Der LEIERMANN (The Organ Man): song, D.911, no.24 see WINTERREISE
LIED DER MIGNON, D.877 (from 'Gesänge aus Wilhelm Meister')
  in Bb (orig B), arr F.Liszt (S.375, no.3)
| | | ϕ | 2121/2000/str | | Forberg | 17860 |

LIEDER-SUITE, arr L.Artok
  1. Am Meer (D.957, no.12)(from 'Schwanengesang')   3. Frühlingsglaube (D.686)
  2. Ständchen (D.957, no.4)

| | | PC | 1121/2210/timp.perc/str | | Schott | 9622 |

LILAC TIME: musical play, arr Clutsam from the works of Schubert see CLUTSAM: LILAC TIME
LITANEI, D.343 see AM TAGE ALLER SEELEN
MAGNIFICAT, for SATB soli, chorus & orch, D.486, in C (1816)

		ϕ	0202/0200/timp/org/str		Breitkopf.CW 14/11	MRL
		ϕ	0202/0200/timp/org/str		(Breitkopf.CW 14/11)	24938 + #
ed O.Biba		ϕ	020[2]/0200/timp/org/str		Alfred Coppenrath,1977	Misc 9559

MARCHES
  D.733: 3 Marches militaires (orig pf-duet)
    No.1, in D   [arr]

			4(2picc)4(ca)3+bcl.2+cbsn/4441/timp.perc.			
			glock/str		Zimmermann	Misc 780
arr L.Damrosch		ϕ	2+picc.222/4331/timp.perc/str		G.Schirmer	16451
arr Guiraud		ϕ	1+picc.222/4231/timp.perc/str	4'-5'	Durand	4212 Amv Cs Dn E
arr Myddleton		PC	2(picc)222/2230/timp.perc/str		Lafleur	351 Cp Dwa

    No.2, in G

arr Kleinecke			pf/str		Kramer	Misc 2201
arr Oelschlegel		PC	1121/2210/perc/str		Cranz	3574
arr A.Winter		ϕ	222.3sx.2/4231/timp.perc/str		Boosey & H	15267
arr A.Winter		PC	222.2sx.2/2231/timp.perc/str		Boosey & H	16745

    No.3, in Eb

| arr Oelschlegel | | PC | 1(picc)121/2210/timp.perc/str | | Cranz | 3575 |

  D.818, no.2: Marche à la hongroise see DIVERTISSEMENT À LA HONGROISE
  D.819: 6 Grandes marches & trios (orig for pf-duet)
    No.2: Grande marche héroïque, in G min

| arr J.Bürger | | ϕ | 1111/1120/timp.perc/str | | Arranger MS:BBC | MS 6029 |
| arr R.Ochs | | ϕ | 2222/2230/timp.perc/str | | Ries & E | 14704 |

    No.3: Grande marche héroïque, in B min

| | | PC | 1121/2210/timp.perc/str | | Cranz | 3481 |
| arr J.Bürger | | ϕ | 2121/2230/timp.perc/str | | Arranger MS:BBC | MS 6028 |

    arr F.Liszt (S.363, no.1)

| | | ϕ | 2+picc.222/4231/timp.perc/str | | Furstner | 8146 |

    No.5: Trauer Marsch, in Eb min
      arr F.Liszt (S.363, no.4)

| | | ϕ | 2222/4231/timp/str | | Furstner | 8147 |

  D.885: Grande marche héroïque, in A min (orig for pf-duet)

| arr O.Bach | | ϕ | 2222/4230/timp.perc/str | | Schott | 4802 |

  D.886: 2 marches caractéristiques, in C (orig for pf-duet)
    No.1: Reiter Marsch
      arr F.Liszt (S.363, no.3)

| | | ϕ | 2+picc.222/4231/timp/str | 7'30" | Furstner | 8148 |

    Liszt transcription, arr L.Weninger

| | | PC | 2222/4231/timp/str | | Benjamin | 7619 |

MARGUERITE AT THE SPINNING WHEEL see GRETCHEN AM SPINNRADE
MASSES
  D.105: No.1, in F, for SATB soli, chorus & orch
    Complete, with alternative 'Dona Nobis Pacem' & 'Quonim'

| | | ϕ | 0222/2230/timp/org/str | | Breitkopf.CW 13/1 | MRL |

SCHUBERT, Franz (cont)

MASSES (cont)
   D.167: No.2, in G, for STB soli, chorus & orch (1815)

	∅	org/str	26'	Breitkopf.CW 13/1	MRL
	∅	org/str		(Breitkopf.CW 13/1)	20785 + # B

   D.324: No.3, in B♭, for SATB soli, chorus & orch (1815)

∅	0202/0200/timp/org/str		Breitkopf.CW 13/1	MRL
∅	0202/0200/timp/org/str		(Breitkopf.CW 13/1)	19222 #

   D.452: No.4, in C, for SATB soli, chorus & orch (1816)
     Complete, with alternative 'Benedictus'

∅	0[2=2cl]00/0[2]00/[timp]/org/str		Breitkopf.CW 13/1	MRL
∅	0[2=2cl]00/0[2]00/[timp]/org/str		(Breitkopf.CW 13/1)	23831 + #
ed L.Dité	0200/2200/timp/org/str		Weinberger,1949	20413

     Cum Sancto Spiritu: extract from the Gloria
      in E (orig)   1222/2230/timp/str   (BBC)   MS 20397

   D.678: No.5, in A♭, for SATB soli, chorus & orch (1819-1822)
     First version
       ed D.Finke-Hecklinger ∅ 1222/2230/timp/org/str   Bärenreiter,1980.NSA 1/3a MRL
     Second version
       ed D.Finke-Hecklinger ∅ 1222/2230/timp/org/str   Bärenreiter,1980.NSA 1/3b MRL
      With alternative 'Cu Sancto Spiritu' & 'Osanna'

∅	1222/2230/timp/org/str	50'	Breitkopf.CW 13/2	MRL
∅	1222/2230/timp/org/str		Breitkopf	21337 +

   D.872: Deutsche Messe (Gesänge zur Feier des Heiligen Opfers der Messe, with Appendix, Das
      Gebet des Herrn), for chorus, wind instruments & organ (1826-27)

∅	0222/2030/org/[cb]		Breitkopf.CW 13/2	MRL
∅	0222/2230/timp		Robitscheck	20278
∅	0222/2030/org/[cb]		Doblinger,1977	26344

     ed F.Burkhart for mv-chorus & orch

∅	0000/2020/timp		Doblinger,1977	Misc 9560

   D.950: No.6, in E♭, for SATB soli, chorus & orch (1828)

∅	0222/2230/timp/org/str	57'30"	Breitkopf.CW 13/2	MRL
∅	0222/2230/timp/str		Breitkopf	20421

MEMNON: song, D.541
  orch J.Brahms   ∅ 2222/4000/str   OUP,1933   25711

MIGNON'S SONG <u>see</u> LIED DER MIGNON
MILITARY MARCHES <u>see</u> MARCHES
MINUETS

   D.2d; 6 Minuets & Trios (1811)
     1st edition
       No.1, in C (orig pf - D.995)   No.3, in D
       No.2, in F (orig pf - D.995)
         ed C.Landon   ∅ [2]222/2100   Bärenreiter,1970 CM 54637
       No.4, in C   No.6, in B♭
       No.5, in D
         arr A.Weinmann, ed C.Landon
            ∅ 1122/2000 (with orig pf draft) Bärenreiter,1970 CM 54640

   D.86, in D

∅	str	1'45"	Breitkopf	6862
∅	str		Breitkopf.CW 2	MRL

   D.89: 5 Minuets with 6 trios
     No.1, in C   No.2, in F   No.3, in D min   No.4, in G   No.5, in C

∅	str		Breitkopf	8530
∅	str		Breitkopf.CW 2	MRL

   D.894: Minuet in B min (from Sonata (Fantasia) in G for piano)
     arr E.Guiraud   PC 2222/2000/str   Durand   3896 B

SCHUBERT, Franz (cont)

MIRJAMS SIEGESGESANG (Miriam's song of triumph): song for Soprano solo, chorus & orch, D.942
    orch F.Lachner   φ 2222/2230/timp/str   Senff [c.1869]   Misc 7729
    orch F.Mottl   φ 2222+cbsn/4331/timp.perc/hp/str   Breitkopf   16983
6 MOMENTS MUSICAUX, D.780 (orig for pf)
    No.3, in F min   PC 1120/0100/perc/str   1'45"   Lafleur   883 Ap Cwe
      arr Ascher   PC 1(picc)121/2211/perc/str   Ascher   8002
      arr M.Guiraud (Impromptu Hongroise)
                    PC 2222/2000/str   Durand   8160 B
      arr Haensch   PC 1010/0110/timp.perc/str   Roehr   13020
      arr Moses   PC 1121/2210/perc/str   C.Fischer   1991
      arr C.Woodhouse   φ str   2'   Hawkes   8668 Bwe
      arr Zandonai   φ str   (Ricordi)   TO 51
    No.4, in C# min
      arr A.Lotter   pf/str   4'   Boosey & H   6997
MORGENGESANG IM WALDE   see   Der GRAF VON GLEICHEN
NACHT UND TRÄUME: song, D.827
    in C (orig B), arr L.Wurmser 0022+cbsn/0230/str   2'30"   (Arranger)   TO 1562
    orch F.Hartley   str   (BBC)   TV MS 130
NACHTGESANG IM WALDE, for TTBB soli & 4 horns, D.913
                    φ 4hn   Breitkopf   CM 57391
NACHTSTÜCK : song, D.672
    in C min (orig), arr L.Wurmser
                    φ 2222/2030/hp/str   (Arranger)   TO 1556
NAMENSFEIER CANTATE   see   CANTATAS
OCTET, D.803, in F
    Andante only
      arr L.Weninger   PC 1111/2110/timp/pf/str   Benjamin   1048
    Invocation only
      arr Wolf   PC 1020/0210/timp.perc/str   Schott   7146
    Scherzo & minuet only
      arr Barnards   PC 1110/0110/timp/str   Junne   7252
OFFERTORIA
    D. 27 (Salve Regina), for Soprano & orch, in F
      ed F.Kosch   φ 002[=ob]0/2000/org/str   [Strache]   22324
    D.106 (Salve Regina), for Tenor solo, organ & orch, in Bb
                    φ 0202/2000/org/str   Breitkopf.CW 14/9 MRL
                    φ 0202/2000/org/str   (Breitkopf)   17197 +
    D.136 (Totus in corde), for Soprano or Tenor solo, clarinet or violin concertante & orch, in C
                    φ 2010/2000/org/str   Breitkopf.CW 14/1 MRL
                    φ 2010/2000/org/str   (Breitkopf)   19515 +
      ed K.Pfannhauser   2010/2000/str/cont(org)   Doblinger,1947 26001 **
    D.181 (Tres Sunt), for chorus & orch, in A min
                    φ 0222/0030/org/str   Breitkopf.CW 14/4 MRL
    D.223 (Salve Regina), for Soprano & orch, in F
                    φ 0022/2000/org/str   6'30"   (Breitkopf)   19516 +
                    φ 0022/2000/org/str   Breitkopf.CW 14/2 MRL
                      0022/2000/org/vlns.cb   Diabelli   19881
    D.676 (Salve Regina), for Soprano & strings, in A
                    φ str   Breitkopf.CW 14/3 MRL
                    φ str   (Breitkopf)   18798 B +
                    φ str   Kneusslin,1956 Misc 7715
      ed K.Pfannhauser   str/cont(org)   Doblinger,1947 26001
    D.963 (Intende voci), for Tenor solo, chorus & orch, in Bb
                    φ 0122/2030/str   Breitkopf.CW 21 supp MRL
                      0122/2030/str   Breitkopf   23321
      arr Friedlaender   φ 0122/2030/str   Peters [1890] Misc 1609 B

SCHUBERT, Franz (cont)

OVERTURES
 D. 4 see Der TEUFEL ALS HYDRAULICUS
 D. 8, in C min (orig for strings)
  1st version
   ed E.Hess   φ str   Litolff/Peters,1970 Misc 7383
  2nd version
   ed E.Hess   str   Litolff/Peters,1948 26373
   orch W.Hofmann φ 1021/2000/str   Litolff/Peters,1970 25102
 D. 11, in B♭ see Der SPIEGELRITTER
 D. 12, in D   φ 2222/2230/timp/str   Breitkopf.CW 21 supp MRL
          φ 2222/2230/timp/str   Breitkopf Misc 1165 B
 D. 26, in D   φ 2222/2230/timp/str   Breitkopf.CW 2 MRL
          φ 2222/2230/timp/str 7'-9' Breitkopf 10052
   arr Sabec-el-Cher PC 1110/0210/timp/str   Schaper 7242
 D.470, in B♭   φ 0202/2200/timp/str   Breitkopf.CW 2 MRL
          φ 0202/2200/timp/str 6'-7' Breitkopf 11900
   arr Piercy   PC 2222/2230/timp/str   Boosey 3519 Bwa
 D.556, in D   φ 2222/2000/timp/str   Breitkopf.CW 2 MRL
          φ 2222/2000/timp/str 7' Breitkopf 10409 +
 D.590: Overture in the Italian style, in D
          φ 2222/2200/timp/str 6'30"-9' Breitkopf.CW 2 MRL
          φ 2222/2200/timp/str   Breitkopf 6285 + Amv Dwa
 D.591: Overture in the Italian style, in C
          φ 2222/2200/timp/str 7' Breitkopf.CW 2 MRL
          φ 2222/2200/timp/str   Breitkopf 6815 Amv Bs Cn ▌
   arr Atzler   PC 1121/2210/timp/str   Cranz 1616
 D.648, in E min   φ 2222/4230/timp/str 6'15" Breitkopf.CW 2 MRL
          φ 2222/4230/timp/str   Breitkopf 8322 C
   arr Wallner   PC 1110/0210/timp/str   Bote & B 7126
 D.675, in F (orig for pf duet)
   arr Stillman-Kelly (Romantic Overture)
          φ 2+picc.222/4230/timp/str 6'45"-8' Ditson 8929

POLONAISES
 D.580, for violin & small orch, in B♭
   ed Deutsch   φ 0202/2000/str   Strache 21986
 D.824: 6 Polonaises (orig for pf-duet)
   No.1, in D min
    arr Kasanli   φ 2121/2210/timp/str   Zimmermann 6429 B
POTPOURRI OF SCHUBERT WALTZES, arr J.Buerger
          φ 2(picc)121/2230/timp.perc/hp/str 10'30"-12' BBC MS 3149
PSALM 23 see GOTT IST MEIN HIRT
RASTE KRIEGER (Ellens Gesang I), D.837 (orig voice & pf)
 [arr]   φ 2021/2211/timp.perc/str   (Siddell) 18107
REITER MARSCH see MARCHES
REQUIEM, D.453, in C min. Fragment completed for performance by P.Reinhard Van Hoorickx, for SATB
   voices & orch   φ 0222/2000/str   P.R.von Hoorickx,1967 Misc 6725 B
ROMANTIC OVERTURE see OVERTURES, D.675
RONDO for violin & string orch, D.438, in A
          φ str   12'-14'
                  Breitkopf.CW 21 supp MRL
          φ str   Breitkopf 14237 +
 see also GRAND RONDO, D.951, in A
RONDO BRILLANT, D.895 (orig vln & pf)
 arr A.Wilhelmj   φ 2222/4230/timp.perc.tamb/str (Arranger) Misc 9707

SCHUBERT, Franz (cont)

ROSAMUNDE FÜRSTIN VON CYPERN: incidental music, D.979
  Complete (includes overture to 'Alfonso und Estrella')
                          ø 2222/4230/timp/str   Breitkopf.CW 15/4   MRL
                          ø 2222/4230/timp/str   Breitkopf   Misc 1495
  Overture see Die ZAUBERHARFE and ALFONSO UND ESTRELLA
  Ballet music and entr'actes
    2 Ballets
      D.797, no.2, in B min (Act 2)
      D.797, no.9, in G (Act 4)
                    ø 2222/2230/timp/str   Breitkopf   4213 Amv Fn
        arr R.Douglas   PC 2222/2230/timp.perc/str   Boosey & H   20363
    2 Entr'actes
      D.797, no.1, in B min (Act 1)
      D.797, no.5, in B♭ (Act 3)
                    ø 2222/2230/timp/str   Spina [1867]   8869 An
        arr A.Winter   PC 2222/2230/timp/str   Hawkes   9474 D
    2 Entr'actes and 2 Ballets
      Entr'acte, D.797, no.1, in B min (Act 1)
      Entr'acte, D.797, no.5, in B♭ (Act 3)
      Ballet, D.797, no.2, in B min (Act 2)
      Ballet, D.797, no.9, in G (Act 4)
        arr L.Weninger   PC 2222/4230/timp/str   Benjamin   480 B
    3 Entr'actes
      D.797, no.1, in B min (Act 1)(9'20")
      D.797, no.3a, in D (Act 2) (3')
      D.797, no.5, in B♭ (Act 3) (7'40")
                    ø 2222/2230/timp/str   20'   Breitkopf   4214 Amv Bs En

    Extracts
    Hier auf   Fluren: chorus of shepherds, D.797, no.7
      in B♭ (orig)   ø 2222/2000/str   (Breitkopf)   19170 +
    In der Tiefe wohnt das Licht (Far beyond all mortal ken): chorus of spirits, D.797, no.4
      in D (orig)   ø 0000/3030/mv-chorus   Novello   7599 +
      in D   0000/3030   (Breitkopf)   Misc 4814 B +
    Shepherds melody, D.797, no.6
                    ø 0202/2000   (Breitkopf)   Misc 4815 B +
                    ø 2002/2000/str   Novello   19170
    Der Vollmond strahlt (The full moon rises): romance, D.797, no.3b
      in F min (orig)   ø 0222/2000/str vla.vlc)   (Siddell)   17857
      in F min   ø 2222/2000/str   Novello   19170 +
    Wie lebt sich's so fröhlich (How merry is life): chorus of huntsmen, D.797, no.8
      in D (orig)   ø 2222/4000/str   Novello   19537
RÜDIGERS HEIMKEHR: sketches for an opera 'Rüdiger', D.791
  arr J.Berbeck for Tenor solo, mv-chorus & orch
                    PS 2222/2230/timp/str   Spina   Misc 2716
SALVE REGINA, D.27, D.106, D.223 and D.676   see   OFFERTORIA
SCHERZO AND MINUET (from Octet, D.803)
  arr Barnards   PC 1110/0110/timp/str   Junne   7252
2 SCHERZI
  No.1, in A♭ (from unfinished piano sonata in C)
    Completed & arr G.Bush   ø 2222/2200/timp/str   Elkin,1967   Misc 7442
  No.2, in B min (from unfinished symphony in B min), D.759
    Completed & arr G.Bush   ø 2222/2230/timp/str   Elkin,1967   Misc 7442
SCHLAFE, SCHLAFE, HOLDER, SÜSSER KNABE see WIEGENLIED
SCHLAFLIED (Schlummerlied): Es mahnt der Wald, D.527
  arr F.Salabert   PC 1110/0110/timp/str   7'-8'   Salabert   10833

SCHUBERT, Franz (cont)

Die SCHÖNE MÜLLERIN: song cycle, D.795
  Das Wandern: song (D.795, no.1)
    arr & orch M.Lubbock   ø 1021/0100/pf/str   Arranger MS.BBC MS 30785
    orch F.Hartley   1111/2000/str   BBC TV MS 130
  Ungeduld (Impatience): song (D.795, no.7)   (LM G 3265 &
    in A (orig), arr G.Stacey   1020/0000/acdn.pf/str [=pf/str]   (Paxton) (LM A 21
    in A♭   1111/2000/str   2'   (Siddell) 18260
    in A♭   1011/2000/str   (BBC) MS 6135

SCHUBERT SELECTIONS
  arr Fetrás, op.205   PC 1121/4210/timp/str   Benjamin 3819
  arr Finck (Selection of waltzes)
                    PC 2(picc)222/2230/timp.perc/str   AH & C 5988
  arr Finck (Schubertiana)   PC 2(picc)222/2230/timp. erc/hp/str 14'   Hawkes 8168
  arr Foulds   PC 2122/223[1]/timp.perc/str 11'-13'45" Bosworth 11415 C
  arr Roberts (Selection of songs)
                    PC 1121/2210/timp.perc/str   C.Fischer 10965
  arr Saar and Adlington (Schubertiana)
                    PC 2020/0210/timp.perc/str   Paxton 6128
  arr Urbach   PC 2222/4230/perc/str   Wrede 9342

SCHWANENGESANG: song cycle, D.957
  Am Meer (By the sea): song (D.957, no.12)
    in C (orig)   ø 0021/2000/str   (Siddell) 18263
    arr L.Weninger   PC 1010/0110/timp.perc/str   Benjamin 10468
    arr Altendorf for trombone or saxophone & orch
                    PC 2222/2210/timp.perc/str   Schaper 10834
    arr Boettger for trombone & orch
                    PC 1121/2210/str   C.Fischer 1286 B
      see also LIEDER-SUITE
  Aufenthalt (My dwelling place): song (D.957, no.5)
    in C# min (orig E min) PC 1121/2110/str   (Siddell) 18259
  Der Doppelgänger (The Shadow): song (D.957, no.13)
    in G min (orig B min)   0021/2110/str   (Siddell) 18265
  Ständchen (Serenade): Leise flehen: song (D.957, no.4)
    in D min (orig), arr B.Orr
                   ø str   (Arranger) LM G 9027
    in D min, arr S.Robinson ø 2222/4010/hp/str   (Arranger) TO 1390
    in D min, arr G.Stacey   1010/0000/pf/str   (Schott) LM A 91
    in D min & B min, arr G.Stacey
                      pf/str   (Walsh) LM G 3621
                  PC 1121/22.cnt.10/timp.perc/str   Cranz 3671
    arr for trombone & orch   1120/2000/str   C.Fischer 11054
    arr Boettger for cornet, trombone & orch
                    PC 1121/2210/str   C.Fischer 1286 B
    arr Morrow for cornet & orch
                    ø 2222/2010/str   3'45"   Hawkes 5282
    arr J.Offenbach   PC 1121/2200/timp/str   Costallat 682
    arr L.Weninger   PC 1010/0110/timp.perc/str   Benjamin 499
      see also LIEDER-SUITE   and 2 SERENADES

SEHNSUCHT (Der Lerche wolkennahe Lieder)(Longing): song, D.516
  in C (orig)   1121/2210/str   (Siddell) 18262

2 SERENADES
  1. Ständchen (Leise flehen meine Lieder), D.957, no.4
  2. Horch, horch, die Lerch (Hark, Hark the Lark): song, D.889
                  PC 1121/2210/timp/hp/str   Cranz 3671
    arr L.Weninger   PC 1010/0110/timp/str   Benjamin 499

SCHUBERT, Franz (cont)

2 SERENADES (cont)
   No.2 only: Hark, Hark the Lark

in C (orig)		1222/2000/str	2'50"	(Siddell)	18264
in C, arr G.Stacey		1010/0000/pf/str		(Arranger)	LM G 71
in Bb, orch Hartley		1121/2000/hp/str		(BBC)	TV MS 43

The SHEPHERD ON THE ROCK   see   Die HIRT AUF DEM FELSEN
SINFONIE (Sonata in C (Grand Duo) for pf duet), D.812   see   SYMPHONIES: Symphony in C
SOIRÉES DE VIENNE: valses caprices, transcr F.Liszt for piano (S.427)

orch J.Dvorzak	PC	1121/2210/timp.perc/str	5'50"	Oertel	8154

La SOLENNITA DELLA RISURREZIONE   see   CANTATAS: Lazarus
SONATA, D.812, in C   see   SYMPHONIES: Symphony in C
Der SPIEGELRITTER: operetta (unfinished), D.11 - 1 act only

Fragments	ϕ	2222/2200/timp/str		Breitkopf.CW 15/7	MRL
Overture, in Bb	ϕ	2222/2200/timp/str		Breitkopf	Misc 1166 B
	ϕ	2222/2200/timp/str		Breitkopf.CW 21 supp	MRL

STABAT MATER, for chorus & orch, D.175, in G min

	ϕ	0222/0030/str/cont(org)		Breitkopf.CW 14/12	Misc 4495 C & MRL
arr A.Schmid	ϕ	[0222]/00[3]0/org/str		Böhm,1955	21706

STABAT MATER (Jesus Christus schwebt am Kreuze), for soli,chorus & orch, D.383, in F

	ϕ	2202+cbsn/2030/str		Breitkopf.CW 14/13	21792 + & MRL

STÄNDCHEN: Horch, horch die Lerch   see   2 SERENADES
STÄNDCHEN: Leise flehen   see   SCHWANENGESANG
STÄNDCHEN (Notturno): Zögernd leise, D.920
   Version A for Contralto solo, TTBB chorus & orch, D.920a

arr F.Mottl	ϕ	2222/4000/str		Breitkopf	Misc 2377

   Version B for Contralto solo, SSAA chorus & orch, D.920b

arr F.Mottl	PS	only		Breitkopf	Misc 3052
arr Reinecke	ϕ	2022/2000/str		Spina	Misc 1847
in F, arr V.Tausky	ϕ	2222/3000/hp/str		(Novello)	TO 1806

SULEIKA'S ERSTER GESANG: Was bedeutet die Bewegung, D.720

in B min (orig), arr F.Mottl	ϕ	2222/2000/str		Breitkopf [1898]	20674

SULEIKA'S ZWEITER GESANG: Ach, um deine feuchten Schwingen, D.717

	ϕ	2222/2000/str		Breitkopf [1898]	20675

SYMPHONIES

No.1, D.82, in D	ϕ	1222/2200/timp/str	26'-28'30"	Breitkopf	5253 + Amv Bn C
	ϕ	1222/2200/timp/str		Breitkopf.CW 1/1	MRL
ed A.Feil & C.Landon	ϕ	1222/2200/timp/str		Bärenreiter,1977.NSA 5/1	MRL
arr Piercy	PC	2222/2230/timp/org/str		Boosey	2113
Minuet only					
arr R.Mayes	ϕ	2222/2220/timp/pf/str		J.Williams,1961	24630
No.2, D.125, in Bb	ϕ	2222/2200/timp/str	22'45"-26'30"	Breitkopf	4983 + Amv Cn Ds
	ϕ	2222/2200/timp/str		Breitkopf.CW 1/1	MRL
ed A.Feil & C.Landon	ϕ	2222/2200/timp/str		Bärenreiter,1977.NSA 5/1	MRL
Menuetto only					
arr K.Simpson	ϕ	pf/str(no vla)		Ashdown,1937	26084
No.3, D.200, in D	ϕ	2222/2200/timp/str	21'-26'	Breitkopf	4215 + Amv Bn Dwe
	ϕ	2222/2200/timp/str		Breitkopf.CW 1/1	MRL
ed A.Feil & C.Landon	ϕ	2222/2200/timp/str		Bärenreiter,1977.NSA 5/1	MRL
No.4, D.417, in C min 'The Tragic'					
	ϕ	2222/4200/timp/str	26'30"-27'	Breitkopf	4216 Amv Bs Fwe
	ϕ	2222/4200/timp/str		Breitkopf.CW 1/1	MRL
ed R.Schwarz	ϕ	2222/4200/timp/str		Breitkopf	22709 Amv
2nd mvt only					
arr Piercy	PC	2222/2230/timp/org/str		Boosey	2678
Finale (Allegro)					
Rejected section, real & orch B.Newbould					
	ϕ	2222/4200/timp/str		(Editor)	26932

SCHUBERT, Franz (cont)

SYMPHONIES (cont)
No.5, D.458, in Bb 'Symphony without trumpets & drums'   (5762 Amv Bs Cn
                  φ   1202/2000/str   24'30"-27'   Breitkopf   (Ewa Hwe
                  φ   2202/2000/str   Breitkopf.CW 1/2   MRL

    2nd mvt only
        arr Piercy   PC 1121/2210/timp/org/str   Boosey   2672
No.6, D.589, in C 'Little Symphony in C'   (4217 + Amv Bn
                  φ   2222/2200/timp/str   26'30"-30'   Breitkopf   (Dwa Es
                  φ   2222/2200/timp/str   Breitkopf.CW 1/2   MRL
No.7, D.729, in E (sketch only)
    Facsimile sketches φ 2222/4230/timp/str   (GB-Lcm)   Misc 4469 & mf 54
    real B.Newbould   φ 2222/4230/timp/str   (Editor,1978) Misc 9536 B
    Completed Weingartner φ 2222/4230/timp/str   Universal Misc 588 B
No.8, D.759, in B min 'Unfinished Symphony'   (4219 Amv Bs Cn
                  φ   2222/2230/timp/str   22'30"-25'   Breitkopf   (Fwa Gwe
                  φ   2222/2230/timp/str   Breitkopf.CW 1/2   MRL
        arr Myddleton PC 2222/2230.euph/timp/str   Lafleur   146 B
        Scherzo in B min, completed by G.Abraham
                  φ   2222/2230/timp/str   6'40"   OUP,1971   Misc 7636
No.9, D.944, in C 'Great Symphony in C' (formerly no.7, also no.8)   (4218 + Amv Bs
                  φ   2222/2230/timp/str   47'45"-50'   Breitkopf   (Cwe Dn Fwa
                  φ   2222/2230/timp/str   Breitkopf.CW 1/2   MRL
        arr Oelschlegel PC 1121/2210/str   Cranz   1554
D.2b, in D (?1811)
    Fragment of 1st mvt, real & orch B.Newbould
                  φ   2222/2230/timp/str   (Editor)   26933
Fragments of unfinished symphonies
    D.615, in D
        Openings of 1st & 4th mvts, real & orch B.Newbould
                  φ   2222/2200/timp/str   (Editor)   26769
        Facsimile of piano score   Bärenreiter,1978   MRL
    D.708a, in D
        Openings of 1st, 2nd & 4th mvts, and 3rd mvt (Scherzo) complete, real &
          orch B.Newbould
                  φ   2222/2200/timp/str   (Editor)   26770
        Facsimile of piano score   Bärenreiter,1978   MRL facs
    D.936a, in D
        Opening (2 versions) & closing sections of 1st mvt, complete 2nd mvt & complete 3rd
          mvt (Scherzo), real & orch B.Newbould
                  φ   2222/2230/timp/str   (Editor)   26771
                  φ   2222/2230/timp/str   (Editor)   26900
        Facsimile of piano score   Bärenreiter,1978   MRL facs
    Symphony in C, orch Joachim from sonata 'Grand Duo, D.812, in C for piano duet
                  φ   2+picc.222/4230/timp/str   Cranz   19619
TANTUM ERGO
    D.460, in C for chorus & orch
                  φ   0200/0200/timp/org/str   Breitkopf.CW 14/7   MRL
        ed L.Dité   0200/2200/timp/org/str   Doblinger,1947   21358
    D.461, in C for soli, chorus & orch
                  φ   0200/0200/timp/org/str (also org reduction) Universal,1935   Misc 4564
    D.730, in Bb for soli, chorus & orch
        ed K.Rouland   2222/2220/timp/str   Böhm   21142
    D.739, in C for chorus & orch
                  φ   02[=2cl]00/0200/timp/org/str   Breitkopf Misc 458 B
                  φ   02[=2cl]00/0200/timp/org/str   Breitkopf.CW 14/6   MRL
        ed K.Rouland   2222/2220/timp/str   Böhm   21142

SCHUBERT, Franz (cont)

TANTUM ERGO (cont)
   D.750, in D for chorus & orch
                            ϕ 2202/0220/timp/org/str   Breitkopf.CW 14/8   MRL
     ed K.Rouland   2222/2220/timp/org/str   Böhm   21142
   D.962, in E♭ for SATB soli, chorus & orch (1828)
                            ϕ 0222/2230/timp/str   Breitkopf   25492 +
                            ϕ 0222/20.2clnó.30/timp/str   Breitkopf.CW 21 supp   MRL
Der TEUFEL ALS HYDRAULICUS: overture, D.4
                            ϕ 2021/2000/str   3'30"-6'   Breitkopf   9058
                            ϕ 2021/2000/str   Breitkopf.CW 2   MRL
Des TEUFELS LUSTSCHLOSS: opera in 3 acts, D.84
   Complete   ϕ 2222/2230/timp/str   Breitkopf.CW 15/1   MRL
   Extracts
      Hab' ich dich wieder: duet for Soprano & Tenor soli & orch (No.21)
                            ϕ 1222/2200/str   Breitkopf,1888   Misc 8192 B
      Ich lach', ich wein': trio for STB soli & orch (No.22)
                            ϕ 1222/2000/str   Breitkopf,1888   Misc 8192 B
      Welcher Frevel! So sind die Menschen: aria for Soprano solo & orch (No.7)
                            ϕ 1200/2000/str   Breitkopf,1888   Misc 8192 B
      Wohin zwei Liebende sich retten: aria for Soprano solo & orch (No.4)
                            ϕ 0202/2000/str   Breitkopf,1888   Misc 8192 B
THEKLA (eine Geisterstimme): song 'Wo ich sei und wo mich hingewendet, D.595
   in C# min, arr F.Mottl   ϕ 21+ca.22/2000/hp/str   Breitkopf,1896   24833
Der TOD UND DAS MÄDCHEN: song, D.531
   in D min (orig)   ϕ 0.122/1000/timp/str   2'45"   Breitkopf   18018
TOTUS IN CORDE, D.136 see OFFERTORIA, D.136
TRAUER MARSCH see MARCHES
TRES SUNT, D.181 see OFFERTORIA, D.181
The TROUT see Die FORELLE
Dem UNENDLICHEN: song, D.291b
   in D♭ (orig E♭), arr F.Mottl ϕ 3222/4231/timp/2hp/str   Breitkopf   19941
UNGARISCHER MARSCH see DIVERTISSEMENT À LA HONGROISE
UNGEDULD see Die SCHÖNE MÜLLERIN
VALSES SENTIMENTALES, arr L.Blech.   Arrangements of D.365, nos 1, 14 & 36; D.145, no.2; D.783, no.2;
    D.779, no.13 (Not Schubert's 'Valses sentimentales')
                            ϕ 21+ca.22/2000/timp.perc/str   Breitkopf,1958   22661
VARIATIONS, D.813, in A♭ (orig pf duet)
   orch Gouvy   ϕ 2222/4200/timp/str   Rieter-Biedermann   Misc 979
   orch Simon   ϕ 2222/2200/timp/str   Ringbuchhandlung   14394
Die VERSCHWORENEN (Der Häusliche Krieg)(The Conspirators): singspiel in one act, D.787
   Complete   ϕ 2222/2200/timp/str   Breitkopf.CW 15/3   MRL
                            ϕ 2222/2230/timp/str   [NP-MS ca 1870]   Misc 3755
     English translation by G.Barker & H.Trevelyan
                          ϕ 2222/2230/timp/str   Breitkopf & H   21572 + #
   Overture
     Compiled by Hermann   ϕ 2222/2210/timp/str   Tischer & J   15541
     Completed by F.Racek (from autograph score)
                        ϕ 2222/2200/timp/str   Doblinger,1964   24198
   Extracts
     Ich schleiche bang: romance
       in F min (orig), for Soprano solo & orch
                          0022/0000/str   (Breitkopf)   23276
Der VIERJÄHRIGE POSTEN (The Faithful Sentinel): singspiel in 1 act, D.190
   Complete   ϕ 2222/2200/timp/str   Breitkopf.CW 15/2   MRL
   Overture   ϕ 2222/2200/timp/str   7'   (Breitkopf)   11296 +
     rev A. de Almeida   ϕ 2222/2200/timp/str   Heugel,1965   24943

SCHUBERT, Franz (cont)

WALDESNACHT (Im Walde): song, D.708
  in E♭ (orig E), arr F.Mottl ∮ 2222/2230/timp/hp/str   (Schott)   20450
WALTZES
    4 Waltzes, arr H.Perry
      No.1, D.969, no.5, in A min   No.3, D.146, no.16, in F
      No.2, D.783, no.1, in A   No.4, D.366, no. 9, in B
                    ∮ 1121/2210/timp.perc/pf/str   Boosey & H   Misc 3528 B
    5 Waltzes, arr H.Perry
      No.1, D.969, no. 1, in C   No.4, D.779, no.12, in D
      No.2, D.783, no.10, in A min   No.5, D.365, no. 7, in A♭
      No.3, D.783, no.16, in F
                    ∮ 112.2sx.1/2210/timp.perc/pf/str   Hawkes,1942 21661
WANDERER FANTASIA: fantasia, D.760, in C (orig for pf)
  arr F.Liszt (S.366)   ∮ 2222/2230/timp/str   17'-22'   Cranz   8855 Amv Cs
Der WANDERER: 'Ich komme vom Gebirge her': song, D.493
  in E (orig)   2222/2000/str   (BBC)   18258
  in F   PC 1121/2210/perc/str   Cranz   6080
Das WANDERN see Die SCHÖNE MÜLLERIN
WELCOME SPRING see DEUTSCHE TÄNZE, D.783
WHO IS SYLVIA? see AN SYLVIA
WIEGENLIED: 'Schlafe, schlafe, holder, süsser Knabe': song, D.498
  in A♭ (orig), arr F.Mottl   ∮ 1010/0000/str   Breitkopf,1898 24832
  arr F.Salabert as La jeune mère (non-vocal)
                      PC 1110/0110/timp/str   Salabert   10833
    arr Walther for horn & strings
                    ∮ str   Breitkopf   6883
WIENER TÄNZE, including D.365, D.779, D.783 & D.969
  arr M.Schönherr   PC 2222/2230/timp.perc/acdn.hp/str Bosworth,1957 22673
WINTERREISE: song cycle, D.911
  Der Leiermann: song, D.911, no.24
    in F min   PC 1121/2000/pf/str(vlc.cb)   (Siddell) 18261
    arr F.Salabert   PC 1110/0110/timp/str   Salabert   12051
Die ZAUBERHARFE: musical play in 3 acts, D.644
  Complete   ∮ 2222/4230/timp/2hp/str   Breitkopf.CW 15/4 MRL
               ∮ 2222/4230/timp/2hp/str   Bärenreiter,1975.NSA 2/4 MRL
  Overture (also used as overture to 'Rosamunde')   (4459 Amv Ds
               ∮ 2222/4230/timp/str   Breitkopf (En Gwa
    arr Evans   PC 2222/2230.euph/timp/str   Hawkes   585 D
    arr H.Perry   ∮ 2222/4230/timp/str   Boosey & H 19142
  Extracts
    Chorus of Genii for fv-chorus & orch (No.9)
      in B♭ (orig)   ∮ 2222/2000/2hp/str   (Breitkopf) 21216 +
    Chorus of Knights for mv-chorus & orch (No.7)
      in B♭ (orig)   ∮ 0222/2230/timp   (Breitkopf) 21215 +
Das ZAUBERGLÖCKEN (La Clochette): opera comique in 2 acts by Hérold. 2 items interpolated by
  F.Schubert (D.723)
  1. Aria   2. Duet
               ∮ 2+picc.222/4200/timp.perc/str   Breitkopf.CW 15/7 MRL
ZÖGERND LEISE see STÄNDCHEN (Notturno): Zögernd leise, D.920
Der ZWERG: song, D.771
  in A min (orig), arr A.Nikisch
               ∮ 222+bcl.2/4220/timp/str   (Breitkopf) 21754
Die ZWILLINGSBRÜDER: Singspiel in 1 act, D.647
  Complete   ∮ 2222/2200/timp/str   Breitkopf.CW 15/3 MRL
  Overture   ∮ 2222/2200/timp/str   3'45"-4'15" Breitkopf 10593 +
               PC 2222/4230/timp.perc/str   Oertel   7770
  Extracts
    Der Vater mag wohl immer Kind: aria (Lieschen)(No.3)
      in G (orig)   ∮ 2222/2000/str   5'40"   (BBC)   19079

SCHUBERT, Franz (1808-1878)

Die BIENE (L'Abeille), op.13, no.9
  arr E.Griffiths for violin & orch
                              φ   2222/4000/timp/hp/str   1'30"   [BBC]   18369

SCHUBERT, Joseph (1757-1837)

CONCERTI
  Viola & orch, in C
    ed K.Schultz-Hauser   φ   0200/2000/str   25'   Schott,1967   Misc 6657

SCHUBERT, Manfred (1937-

CONCERTI   (incl
  Clarinet & orch (1971)   φ   2(picc)000/2231/timp.2perc.vib/pf/str   22'   DVfM,1974   Misc 8665(solo
DANCE STUDIES for small orch (1965)
                              φ   2(picc)1(ca)2(E♭cl:bcl).asx.1/1110
                                   timp.2perc(cbells.tamb.tamtam.tomtom.
                                   wooden beater.xyl)/pf/str   15'   DVfM,1971   Misc 9617
HOMMAGE A RUDOLF WAGNER-REGENY: concertante meditations on themes of the composer, for
    harp & orch (1972)
                              φ   perc/bells.claves.crot.tamtam.3tomtom.vib)/   (incl
                                   cel/str(7.-.3.2.1)   DVfM,1980   Misc 10455 (solo

SCHULE, Bernard

SERENADE for strings, op.5   φ   str   Rt Lerolle,1949 Misc 3101

SCHULLER, Gunther (1925-

AMERICAN TRIPTYCH (A study in textures)
                              φ   3(picc)3(ca)3(bcl)3(cbsn)/4331/timp.perc.
                                   glock.tamtam.vib/hp/str   AMP,1966   Misc 6614
CONCERTINO for jazz quartet and orch
  1.   φ   jazz 4-tet: vib.pf.perc.cb
                                   orch   : 2(picc)222/2320/timp.perc/str   19'   MJQ Music,1961   Misc 5676
CONTOURS
  1. Entrata   3. Partita   5. Chiusa
  2. Capriccio   4. Lamento
                              φ   1(picc)11(E♭cl)+bcl.1/1110/perc.glock.xyl/hp/str   Schott,1960   Misc 5325
COUNTRY DANCE MUSIC: a collection of fiddle tunes, arr
  1. Larry)'Gaff   7. On the road to Boston
  2. Miller's Reel   8. Silver and gold two-step
  3. Steamboat waltz   9. Balkan hills Schottische
  4. Devil's Dream   10. Over the waves (Sabre las Olas: J.Rosas)
  5. Fischer's Hornpipe (J.C.Fischer) 11. Money Musk
  6. Flop-eared Mule
                              φ   5(2picc)000/0000/perc(spoons.washboard.xyl)/
                                   acdn.5gtr(2bjo)pf/9vln.3cb   Margun,1976   Misc 9467
DRAMATIC OVERTURE (1951)   φ   3(2picc)3+ca.2+E♭cl+bcl.2+cbsn/4331/timp.perc.
                                   glock.2tamtam.xyl/cel.2hp.pf/str   10'   AMP,1979   Misc 10018
JOURNEY INTO JAZZ, for narrator, jazz ensemble & small orch
                              φ   jazz ensemble: 000.2sx.0/0100/perc/cb
                                   orch: 1111/1100/perc/hp/str   AMP,1967   Misc 7091
The POWER WITHIN US: narrative oratoria for narrator, Baritone sole, chorus & orch (1971
                              φ   3(3picc)2+ca.2+bcl.3(cbsn)/4331/timp.5perc(bells.
                                   cel.claves.sizzle cym.glock.gong.gro.mrc.mba.tamtam.
                                   3tomtom.vib)/hp.org.pf/str   25'   AMP,1978   Misc 9863

SCHULLER, Gunther (cont)

4 SOUNDSCAPES (Hudson Valley Reminiscences)(1975)
   1. A day on the river (Homage to Ives)   3. Peace and plenty (After Innes)
   2. Nocturnal diversions   4. Scherzo fantastique (After Irving)
                 φ   3(picc:afl)[+picc]2+ca.2+bcl.2+cbsn/4331/
                    timp.perc.bells.glock.gong.mba.tamtam.vib/
                    hp.2pf(cel)/str   AMP,1978   Misc 10363
SPECTRA (1958)   φ   2+picc+afl.3(ca)+ca.2+Ebcl+bcl.2+cbsn/43+Dtpt.31/
                    timp.perc.glock/hp/str   25'   Schott,1964   Misc 7916
7 STUDIES ON THEMES OF PAUL KLEE
    1. Antique harmonies   5. Arab village
    2. Abstract trio   6. An eerie moment
    3. Little blue devil   7. Pastorale
    4. The twittering-machine
               φ   3(2picc)2+ca.2+bcl.2+cbsn/4331/timp.perc.
                    glock.vib/hp.pf/str   Universal,1962   Misc 5691
SYMPHONY FOR BRASS & PERCUSSION, op.16 (1969-50)
        φ   0000/4632.bar/timp.perc   18'   Malcolm Music,1959   25955

SCHULTZ, Johann Abraham   see   SCHULZ, Johann Abraham

SCHULTZ, Svend (1913-

SERENADE for string orch   φ   str   Hansen   Misc 2329 B
STORSTRØMSBROEN (The Storstroem Bridge): symphonic vision
        φ   2(picc)121/2211/timp.perc/str Samfundst til Udgivelse/Edn Dania,1951   Misc 7350

SCHULTZE, Norbert (1911-

GELIEBTES LEBEN: intermezzo for optional Contralto (or Baritone) solo & orch
                   φ   2(picc)2(ca)2(bcl)2/3210/glock/cel.hp/str   N.Schultze,1954   25277
LILLI MARLENE: song by N.Schultze, T.Connor & H.Leip
   in C, arr G.Williams   φ   2131/2231/perc/pf/str   (P.Maurice)   MS 20073

SCHULTZE-BIESANTZ, C

SYMPHONISCHE TONGEDICHTE
    1. Glucksritter (Knight-errant)   3. Marche humoristique
    2. Patheticon
           PC 2+picc.2(2ca)20/0010/str   Litolff   12413 **

SCHULZ (Schultz), Johann Abraham Peter (1747-1800)

HØSTGILDET: overture (1790)
   ed K.Clausen & P.Fledelius   φ   2202/2200/str   Engstrøm & Sødring,1947   26009
The LAST HOUR OF THE YEAR (Des Jahres letzte Stunde)(Am Sylvester-abend)
   arr M.L.Lake   PC 1+picc.12.2sx.1/2210/perc/str   C.Fischer   19720
WE PLOUGH THE FIELDS AND SCATTER: hymn
   arr H.Perry   PC 1121/0000/timp.perc/org/str   Hawkes   4970

SCHUMAN, William (1910-

AMARYLLIS: variants for strings on an Old English Song (adaptation of parts of Concerto on
    Old English Rounds)
               φ   str   Merion,1975/77   Misc 9294
AMERICAN FESTIVAL OVERTURE   φ   3(picc)2+ca.2+bcl.2+[cbsn]/4331/timp.perc.xyl/
                     str   7'45"   G.Schirmer   Misc 2904

SCHUMAN, William (cont)

CONCERTO ON OLD ENGLISH ROUNDS, for viola, fv-chorus & orch (1973)
  1. Amaryllis - Introduction & variations   3b. Come follow me
  2. Great Tom is cast   4. Combinations
  3a. Who'll buy my roses   5. Amaryllis - Recapitulation

	φ 3(picc)2+ca.2+bcl.2+cbsn/4331/bells/str	40'	Merion Mus,1975	Misc 9295
CONCERTO for violin & orch	φ 3(picc)2+ca.3+bcl.2+cbsn/4331/timp.perc/ str	26'-32'25"Merion Mus,1960		Misc 5496
CREDENDUM (Article of Faith)	φ 4(2picc)3+ca.3+E♭cl+bcl.3+cbsn/6432/ timp.perc/pf/str	18'	Merion Mus,1956	Misc 4782
JUDITH: choreographic poem	φ 2+picc.2+ca.2+bcl.2+cbsn /4231/ pf/str	24'	G.Schirmer,1950	Misc 3275

NEW ENGLAND TRIPTYCH: 3 pieces for orchestra after William Billings
  1. Be glad then, America   3. Chester
  2. When Jesus wept

	φ 3(picc)2+ca.2+E♭cl+bcl.2/4331/timp.perc/str	13'	Merion Mus	Misc 4781

NEWSREEL: suite
  1. Horse race   4. Monkeys at the Zoo
  2. Fashion show   5. Parade
  3. Tribal dance

	φ 3(picc)+picc.2+ca.3+E♭cl+bcl.3sx.2+cbsn/4331/ timp.perc/pf/str		G.Schirmer	12518
The ORCHESTRA SONG	φ 1+picc.11+[bcl]1/4331/timp.perc.bells.vib.xyl/ str	3'30"	Merion Mus,1964	Misc 6063
PRAYER IN TIME OF WAR	φ 3(picc)2+ca.2+bcl.2/4331/timp.perc/str	15'	G.Schirmer,1958	Misc 3078

SYMPHONIES

No.4	φ 33+ca.3+E♭cl+bcl.3+cbsn/4331/timp.perc.glock.xyl/ str	25'	G.Schirmer	Misc 3119
No.5: symphony for strings (1943)	φ str	17'30"-22'	G.Schirmer	Misc 2297
No.6 (1948)	φ 32+ca.2+bcl.2+cbsn/4331/timp.perc.bells/ str	28'	G.Schirmer,1952	Misc 3742 B
No.7	φ 4[=3](2picc)3[=2]+ca.3[=2]+[E♭cl]+bcl.3[=2]/ 6[=4]3[=3]32+[ttuba]/timp.perc.bells.glock.xyl/ pf/str	30'	Merion Mus,1962	Misc 5672
No.8	φ 4(2picc)3[=2]+ca.3[=2]+bcl.3[=2]+cbsn/6441/ timp.perc.bells.glock.tamtam.vib.xyl/ 2hp.pf/str	30'	Merion Mus,1966	Misc 6033
No.10 (American Muse)	φ 4(2picc)3+ca.3+E♭cl+bcl.3+cbsn/6441/timp.4perc(bells. crot.glock.vib.xyl)/cel.hp.pf/str	30'	Merion Mus,1977	Misc 9508

UNDERTOW: choreographic episodes for orchestra

	φ 3(2picc)2+ca.33/4231/timp.perc.bells.tamtam/ pf/str		G.Schirmer,1945	Misc 3760

The YOUNG DEAD SOLDIERS: lamentation for Soprano solo, horn & orch

	φ 02+ca.22/0000/str(0.0.4.4.1)	15'	Merion Mus,1976	Misc 9069 B

SCHUMANN, Carl

TANZ-SUITE, op.21
  1. March   4. Polka (Rheinländer)
  2. Pastorale   5. Galopp
  3. Waltzer

	φ str		Merseburger	10422

SCHUMANN, Georg (1866-1952)

AMOR UND PSYCHE, op.3
    Extracts
        Tanz der Nymphen und Satyr

ø	2+picc.222/4230/timp.perc/str	4'45"	Breitkopf	8815

IM RINGEN UM EIN IDEAL: symphonic poem, op.66

ø	3(picc)3(ca)32+cbsn/4331/timp.perc/hp/str		Leuckart,1914	Misc 816

LIEBESFRÜHLING: overture, op.28

ø	2+picc.222+cbsn/42.cnt.31/timp.perc/str		Breitkopf	9730

SYMPHONY, op.42, in F min

ø	2+picc.2+ca.2+bcl.2+cbsn/4231/timp/hp/str	38'	Leuckart,1905	Misc 776

VARIATIONEN UND DOPPELFUGE über ein lustiges Thema, op.30

ø	2+picc.223+cbsn/4231/timp.perc/hp/str	17'	Hofmeister	Misc 1083

VARIATIONEN UND FUGE über ein Thema von J.S.Bach, op.59

ø	32+ca.32+cbsn/4331/timp.perc/hp/str		Ries & E,1914	Misc 817

VARIATIONEN UND GIGUE über ein Thema von Handel, op.72

ø	2+picc.22+bcl.2+cbsn/4331/timp.perc/2hp/str	30'	Schlessinger,1925	Misc 775

ZUR CARNEVALSZEIT: suite
    1. Allegro   3. Humoreske: presto
    2. Andantino marcato

ø	2+picc.222+cbsn/4231/timp.perc/hp/str		Hofmeister	11615

SCHUMANN, Robert (1810-1856)

COMPLETE WORKS

Robert Schumann: Werke, ed C.Schumann, J.Brahms & others. Leipzig: Breitkopf & H, 1881-93

ABENDLIED, op.85, no.12 see ALBUM FÜR DIE JUGEND, op.85
ADVENTLIED for Soprano solo, SATTBB chorus & orch, op.71
    ed C.Schumann

ø	2222/4230/timp/str		Breitkopf,1882	25211
ø	2222/4200/timp/str		Breitkopf	Misc 2373

    ed C.Schumann

ø	2222/4200/timp/str		Breitkopf & H.CW 9/2	MRL

ALBUM FÜR DIE JUGEND, op.68 (orig for piano)
    Suite no.1, arr H.Mouton
        1. Fröhlicher Landmann (The merry peasant)(No.10)   3. Mai, lieber Mai (No.13)
        2. Volksliedchen (No.9)   4. Fremder Mann (No.29)

øPC	1121/2200/timp/str		Durand	3188 B

    Suite no.2, arr H.Mouton
        1. Ländliches Lied (No.20)   3. Intermezzo (No.26)
        2. Frühlingsgesang (No.15)   4. Kriegslied (No.31)

PC	1121/2210/timp/str		Durand	3608

    Nachklänge aus dem Theater (No.25)
        arr F.Salabert   PC   1110/0210/timp/str

		Salabert	11934

ALBUM FÜR DIE JUGEND, op.85 (2nd Album for the Young)(orig for pf duet)
    Suite, arr Müller-Reuter
        1. Gespenstermärchen (No.11)   3. Am Springbrunnen (No.9)
        2. Abendlied (No.12)

ø	22(ca)22/4200/timp.perc/str		Rieter-Biedermann	4881

    Abendlied (No.12)

	str		C.F.Schmidt	14636
	str		Cranz	14594

        arr Svendsen

ø	str	3'15"-4'	Warmuth	4355 B

        arr C.Saint-Saëns

ø	2022/2000/str	2'	Durand	5130 B

    Am Springbrunnen (No.9)
        arr Rudorff for violin & orch

ø	2222/2200/timp/str	3'	Bote & B	4951

        arr W.Goehr, orch L.Wurmser

ø	2222/2230/timp.perc/cel.hp/str		BBC	TO 1554

SCHUMANN, Robert (cont)

ALBUM FÜR DIE JUGEND (cont)
   Gartenmelodie (No.3)
      arr Rudorff for violin & orch

	ø	0022/2000/str	2'	Bote & B	4957
arr F.P.	ø	str		J.Williams	2842 B

   see also 3 SONGS, arr Ritter

AM SPRINGBRUNNEN, op.85, no.9 see ALBUM FÜR DIE JUGEND, op.85

ANDANTE CANTABILE from piano quartet, op.47
   arr O.Langey

	PC	1121/2210/timp/str	G.Schirmer	2520

ARIA from sonata for piano, no.1, op.11
   arr A.Vecsey   PC 1121/2200/timp.perc/str   G.Schirmer   12644

AUFSCHWUNG (Soaring), op.12, no.2 (from 'Fantasiestücke, orig for pf)
   arr Baron   PC 1121/2210/timp/str   G.Schirmer   3900

Die BEIDEN GRENADIERE: song, op.49, no.1

in G min (orig), arr Blech	ø	1(picc)1+ca.22/2210/timp.perc/str	Süddeutscher Musikverlag,1902		11508 B
in G min, arr J.Meloy	ø	str		BBC	LM G 10832
in C min, arr Lewis	PC	2221/2210/timp/str		C.Fischer	5875
in C min, arr G.Stacey		pf/str		(Augener)	LM G 3589
in A min	PC	1222/2230/timp.perc/str		Schirmer	5845
in A min, arr Pitt	ø	2121/2130/timp.perc/hp/str	4'	BBC	11785

   in B♭, arr G.Williams for Baritone & orch

	ø	1121/2210/perc/hp/str	Arranger	MLO 301

BEIM ABSCHIED ZU SINGEN, for SATB soli, chorus & orch, op.84

ed C.Schumann	øPS	2222/2200	Breitkopf,1887	25210
ed C.Schumann	ø	2222/2200	Breitkopf & H.CW 9/3	MRL

BILDER AUS OSTEN (Oriental Pictures): 6 impromptus, op.66 (orig for pf duet)

arr Hermann	ø	str		Kistner & S	6117
arr Reinecke	ø	2+picc.222/2200/timp.perc/str	20'	Kistner & S	6076

Die BRAUT VON MESSINA: overture, op.100

	ø	2+picc.222/2230/timp/str	8'15"-9'15"	Breitkopf	8444
	ø	2+picc.222/2230/timp/str		Breitkopf & H.CW 2	MRL
arr Grohmann	PC	1(picc)121/2210/timp/str		Cranz (Odeon)	5792

CARNAVAL: ballet by Fokine, op.9, orch Rimsky-Korsakov, Glazunov etc

1. Préambule	12. Chopin
2. Pierrot	13. Estrella
3. Arlequin	14. Reconnaissance
4. Valse noble	15. Pantalon et Colombine
5. Eusebius	16. Valse Allemande
6. Florestan	17. Paganini
7. Coquette	18. Aveu
8. Replique	19. Promenade
9. Papillons	20. Pause
10. A.S.C.H-S.C.H.A	21. Marche des "Davidsbündler" contre les Philistins
11. Chiarina	

ed & rev S.Robinson	ø	3(picc)222/4231/timp.perc.bells.vib/hp/str	(BBC,1964)	23345 + & mf 204
arr G.Jacob		vlns & vlcs for use with material from		
		Sadlers Wells	[BBC]	19505
arr R.Chignell	ø	2222/4230/perc/cel.hp/str	Arranger	MS 4897
arr Konstantinov	ø	2+picc.2(ca)22/4231/timp.perc/cel.hp.pf/str	Hawkes,1936	Misc 3754
Arlequin				
arr R.Douglas	ø	1+picc.222/4100/timp.perc/hp/str	Arranger	MS 30092
Pierrot				
arr R.Douglas	ø	2222/4230/timp.perc/hp/str	Arranger	MS 30092
Valse noble				
arr F.Salabert	PC	1110/0110/timp/str	Salabert	10837

SCHUMANN, Robert (cont)

CARNIVAL FANTASY, orch A.Collins from CARNAVAL, op.9
     φ 1(picc)1[=2]21[=2]/2[=4]23[1]/timp.perc.glock/
      [cel].hp/str   (K.Prowse) 26141

CONCERT ALLEGRO MIT INTRODUCTION, op.134 <u>see</u> INTRODUCTION AND ALLEGRO, op.134

CONCERT!
 Cello & orch
  op.129, in A min   φ 2222/2200/timp/str   21'-22'30" Breitkopf 9524 + Amv Cn
   ed C.Schumann   φ 2222/2200/timp/str   Breitkopf & H.CW 3 MRL
   orch D.Shostakovitch φ 2(picc)222/4200/timp/hp/str   Russian SM,1966 Misc 6424
 Piano & orch
  op.54, in A min   φ 2222/2200/timp/str   28'-31' Breitkopf 4704 Amv Ds En
   ed C.Schumann   φ 2222/2200/timp/str   Breitkopf & H.CW 3 MRL
   rev A.Dörffel   φ 2222/2200/timp/str   Universal/Peters Misc 6808
    2nd mvt only: intermezzo
     arr H.Finck PC 2121/2230/timp/hp/str   Hawkes 7638
 Violin & orch
  in C <u>see</u> FANTASY for violin & orch, op.113
  in D min   φ 2222/2200/timp/str   32'-35'30" Schott Misc 1103

CONCERTSTÜCK for 4 horns & orch, op.86
     φ 2+picc.222/2230/timp/str   19'30"-21' Breitkopf 7964

DEIN ANGESICHT, op.127, no.2 <u>see</u> 2 SONGS, arr Selmer
Der DICHTER SPRICHT <u>see</u> KINDERSCENEN, op.15
DREAMING <u>see</u> KINDERSZENEN: Träumerei
ELFE, op.124, no.17 <u>see</u> 3 PIECES, arr Urban
ENDE VOM LIED, op.12, no.8 (from 'Fantasiestücke' - orig for pf)
 arr A.Wood   PC 2121/2230/timp.perc/str   AH & C 2700 B

ER, DER HERRLICHSTE: song <u>see</u> FRAUENLIEBE UND -LEBEN: song cycle
ÉTUDES SYMPHONIQUES EN FORME DE VARIATIONS, op.13 (orig for pf)
 arr Kes   φ 2(picc)2+ca.2+bcl.2+cbsn/4231/timp/hp/
     str   Simrock 10803

FAHRENDE MUSIKANTEN (Strolling wandering musicians): operetta based on Schumann's music, by Doebber
 Selection   PC 2(picc)222/4230/timp.perc/hp/str   Drei Masken 12576

FANTASIESTÜCKE, op.73 (orig cl & pf)
 arr Brown   φ pf/str   Stainer & B 9210

FANTASY for violin & orch, op.131, in C
 ed C.Schumann   φ 2222/2200/timp/str   Breitkopf & H.CW 3 MRL & 21225 + #

FAUST: scenes from Goethe's Faust, for solo voices, chorus & orch
 Complete   φ 2+picc.222/4231/timp/hp/str 130' Breitkopf 9904
  ed C.Schumann φ 2+picc.222/4231/timp/hp/str   Brietkopf & H.CW 9/18 MRL
  rev Bargiel φ 2+picc.222/4231/timp/hp/str   Peters Misc 768
 Overture   φ 2222/4230/timp/str 6' Breitkopf 5678
  ed C.Schumann φ 2222/4230/timp/str   Breitkopf & H.CW 2 MRL

FESTIVAL OVERTURE on the 'Rheinweinlied', for chorus & orch, op.123
     φ 2222/4230/timp/str 8' Breitkopf 6130
 ed C.Schumann φ 2222/4230/timp/str   Breitkopf & H.CW 2 MRL
 arr Margis-Berger PC 1222/2210/timp.perc/str   C.Fischer 1278

8 FRAUENCHORE (8 songs for female choir), arr H.Pfitzner
 1. Klosterfräulein, op.69, no.3   5. Jäger Wohlgemuth, op.91, no.2
 2. Waldmädchen, op.69, no.2   6. Der Wassermann, op.91, no.3
 3. Die Kapelle, op.69, no.6   7. Meerfey, op.69, no.5
 4. Soldatenbraut, op.69, no.4   8. Spruch, op.114, no.3
     φ 2(2picc)2+ca.2+bcl.3/4331/timp/hp.org/str 32' Universal,1910 Misc 3191 B

FRAUENLIEBE UND -LEBEN: song cycle, op.42 (orig voice & pf)
 No.2: Er, der Herrlichste
  arr F.Salabert (Délire d'amour)
     PC 1121/2210/timp/str   Salabert 5335

SCHUMANN, Robert (cont)

6 FUGUES ON THE NAME BACH for organ or pedal piano, op.60
  No.1, orch with introduction by Filson Young
                          ø   3(picc)2+ca.2+bcl.2+cbsn/4331/timp.perc/
                               hp/str   Arranger   27046
GARTENMELODIE, op.85, no.3   see   ALBUM FÜR DIE JUGEND, op.85
GENOVEVA: opera, op.81
  Complete   ø   2+picc.222/4231/timp/str
                               Offstage: 0.2picc.020/3410/TB chorus   Peters   Misc 1615
    ed C.Schumann   ø   2+picc.222/4231/timp/str   Breitkopf & H.CW 9/3   MRL
  Overture   ø   2222/4230/timp/str.   8'30"   Breitkopf   4220 Amv Cn D
                         ø   2222/4230/timp/str   Eulenburg   Misc 7213 Am Bs
    ed C.Schumann   ø   2222/4230/timp/str   Breitkopf & H.CW 2   MRL
    arr Oelschlegel   PC   1121/2210/perc/str   Cranz (Odeon)   3494
Das GLÜCK VON EDENHALL: ballade for Tenor & Bass soli, TTB chorus & orch, op.143
                         ø   2222/4331/timp.perc/str   Breitkopf   25551
                         ø   2222/4331/timp.perc/str   Breitkopf & H.CW 9/14   MRL
The GOLDEN TOY: musical play, arr Herbert Griffiths from music of Schumann
  Selection   PC   2(picc)222/4230/timp.perc/hp/str   9'   AH & C   11713 C
  Extracts
    An Elephant never forgets: song (based on 'Fröhlicher Landmann', op.68, no.10)
      in Eb, orch B.Berlin   ø   2121/2230/perc/str   (AH & C)   TO 898
    Evening song (based on 'Schlummerlied', op.124, op.16)
      in Eb   0100/0000/pf/2vln.vlc   (AH & C)   MS 2267
    Hope will lead you: song (based on op.68, no.30)
      in Eb   PC   str   (AH & C)   MS 2266
    Moonlight night: song (based on 'Mondnacht', op.39, no.5)
      in Db   PC   0100/0000/vlns.vlc   (AH & C)   MS 2265
A HAUNTED PLACE   see   VERRUFENE STELLE
HERMANN UND DOROTHEA: overture, op.136
                         ø   2+picc.222/2200/perc/str   8'   Breitkopf   10435
    ed C.Schumann   ø   2+picc.222/2200/perc/str   Breitkopf & H.CW 2   MRL
    arr Grohmann   PC   1(picc)121/2210/perc/str   Cranz (Odeon)   6632
INTRODUCTION AND ALLEGRO for piano & orch, op.134
                         ø   2222/2210/timp/str   13'   Breitkopf   4859
    ed C.Schumann   ø   2222/2210/timp/str   Breitkopf & H.CW 3   MRL
INTRODUCTION AND ALLEGRO APPASSIONATO (Concertstück) for piano & orch, op.92, in G
                         ø   2222/2200/timp/str   14'-16'30"   Breitkopf   4694 Amv Cn +
                         ø   2222/2200/timp/str   Eulenburg,1968   Misc 7019
    ed C.Schumann   ø   2222/2200/timp/str   Breitkopf & H.CW 3   MRL
JÄGER WOHLGEMUT, op.91, no.2   see   8 FRAUENCHÖRE, arr Pfitzner
JULIUS CAESAR: overture, op.128
                         ø   1+picc.222/4231/timp/str   9'   Breitkopf   7360
                         ø   1+picc.222/4231/timp/str   Breitkopf & H.CW 2   MRL
Die KAPELLE, op.69, no.6   see   8 FRAUENCHÖRE, arr Pfitzner
KINDERSZENEN (Scenes from childhood), op.15 (orig for pf)
  1. Von fremden Ländern   8. Am Camin
  2. Curiose Geschichte   9. Ritter vom Steckenpferd
  3. Hasche-Mann   10. Fast zu ernst
  4. Bittendes Kind   11. Fürchtenmachen
  5. Glückes genug   12. Kind im Einschlummern
  6. Wichtige Begebenheit   13. Der Dichter spricht
  7. Träumerei
  Complete
    arr Godard   ø   str   Durand   10292

SCHUMANN, Robert (cont)

KINDERSZENEN (cont)

Der Dichter spricht					
arr F.Salabert	PC	1110/0110/timp/str		Salabert	10837
Träumerei	PC	str		C.F.Schmidt	14636
	PC	str		Cranz	14594
arr Herbeck	∅	0000/1000/str	2'30"-4'	Breitkopf	6942
arr Urich	PC	0010/1000/str		Lafleur	1150
arr G.Walter		hp/6vlc.2cb		Arranger	TO 1705
arr C.Woodhouse	∅	str		Hawkes	8656
arr Zandonai		hp/str		Ricordi	Misc 3618

    <u>see also</u>   SCHUMANN SUITE, arr Clark

KLOSTERFRÄULEIN, op.69, no.3 <u>see</u>   8 FRAUENCHÖRE, arr Pfitzner

Der KÖNIGSSOHN for T.2Bar.B soli, chorus & orch, op.116

ed C.Schumann	∅	2+picc.222/4431/timp.perc/str	Breitkopf & H.CW 9/10	MRL

MANFRED: incidental music, op.115

Complete					
ed C.Schumann	∅	2+picc.222/4331/timp.perc/str		Breitkopf	Misc 1616
ed C.Schumann	∅	2+picc.222/4331/timp.perc/str		Breitkopf & H.CW 9/9	MRL
	∅	2+picc.2(ca)22/4331/timp.perc/hp/str		Peters	Misc 2956
Overture	∅	2222/4330/timp/str	11'30"-13'	Breitkopf	4221 Amv Dn
ed C.Schumann	∅	2222/4330/timp/str		Breitkopf & H.CW 2	MRL
ed R.Schwarz	∅	2222/4330/timp/str		Breitkopf	23013 Amv
arr Oelschlegel	PC	1121/2210/timp/str		Cranz (Odeon)	3493 B
Excerpts					

    1. Entr'acte (No.5)   3. Rufung der Alpenfee (No.6)
    2. Alpenkuhreigen (No.4)

	∅	22(ca)22/2100/hp/str	8'	Durand	4318

MARCHE FUNÈBRE: 2nd mvt from piano quintet, op.44

arr Godard	∅	2222/4231/timp.perc/2hp/str	8'	Durand	8161

MÄRCHENBILDER: 4 pieces, op.113 (orig for vla & pf)

arr Erdmannsdorfer	∅	2222/2000/timp/str	Raabe & Plothow	Misc 1021 B

MASS for chorus & orch, op.147

ed C.Schumann	∅	2222/2230/timp/org/str	Breitkopf & H.CW 9/16	MRL

MATROSENLIED: song <u>see</u>   3 SONGS, arr Ritter

MEERFEY, op.69, no.5 <u>see</u>   8 FRAUENCHÖRE, arr Pfitzner

MONDNACHT: song, op.39, no.5

arr E.Jacque		0100/0000/str	Enoch	7857
arr F.Salabert	PC	1121/2210/timp/str	Salabert	5607

NACHKLÄNGE AUS DEM THEATER, op.68, no.25 <u>see</u>   ALBUM FÜR DIE JUGEND, op.68

NACHTLIED, for chorus & orch, op.108

ed C.Schumann	∅	2222/2210/timp/str	Breitkopf & H.CW 9/7	MRL

NEUJAHRSLIED, for chorus & orch, op.44

	∅	2222/2240/timp/str	Breitkopf	Misc 3757
ed C.Schumann	∅	2222/2240/timp/str	Breitkopf & H.CW 9	MRL

NORDISCHES LIED: song <u>see</u>   3 SONGS, arr Ritter

NOVELETTE, op.21, no.7, in E (orig for pf)

arr L.Salter	2222/4231/timp/hp/str	Arranger	TO 1640

OVERTURE, SCHERZO AND FINALE, op.52

	∅	2222/22[3]0/timp/str	16'-19'	Breitkopf	8135 + Amv B
ed C.Schumann	∅	2222/22[3]0/timp/str	Breitkopf & H.CW 2	MRL

PAPILLONS, op.2 (orig for pf)

arr & orch L.Lucas	∅	1121/0210/perc/pf/str	(Arranger)	TV MS 280

Das PARADIES UND DIE PERI, for S[=Tr]Mz.AT.Bar.B soli, chorus & orch, op.50

Complete	∅	2+picc.222/4230.oph/timp.perc/hp/str	Breitkopf	Misc 2148
ed C.Schumann	∅	2+picc.222/4230.oph/timp.perc/hp/str	Breitkopf & H.CW 9/1	MRL
Overture	∅	2222/4230/timp.perc/hp/str	Peters	Misc 1614

SCHUMANN, Robert (cont)

3 PIÉCES, arr Urban
    1. Schlummerlied, op.124, no.16 (from 'Albumblätter')
    2. Provenzalisches Lied, op.139, no.4 (from 'Des Sängers Fluch')
    3. Elfe, op.124, no.17 (from 'Albumblätter')
                    ⌀   2222/2000/str   Fürstner   7427 **
The POET SPEAKS: suite of pieces by Schumann, arr G.Vinter
    1. The poet speaks (Scenes of childhood, op.15, no.13)
    2. Eusebius (Carnaval, op.9)
    3. Pantalon et Columbine (Carnaval, op.9)
    4. Aveu (Carnaval, op.9)
    5. Why? (Phantasiestücke, op.12)
    6. Album leaf, op.99
    7. Chopin (Carnaval, op.9)
    8. Quite happy (Scenes of Childhood, op.15, no.5)
    9. Coda (Scenes of Childhood, op.15, no.13)
                    PC   0010/0000/hp/str   Hawkes,1959   23095
REQUIEM for chorus & orch, op.148
                    ⌀   2222/2230/timp/str   Breitkopf   Misc 2147
                    ⌀   2222/2230/timp/str   Breitkopf & H.CW 9/17   MRL
REQUIEM FOR MIGNON, for SSAAB soli, chorus & orch
                    ⌀   2222/2230/timp/hp/str   (Breitkopf,1881)   23470
                    ⌀   2222/2230/timp/hp/str   Breitkopf & H.CW 9/6   MRL
3 REVOLUTIONARY SONGS for 2 Tenors, 2 Basses & wind instruments
    1. Zu den Waffen   3. Freiheitssang
    2. Schwartz-Rot-Gold
                    ⌀   1+picc.244/4220.spt/timp   BBC   19101
Der ROSE PILGERFAHRT, for SSATB soli, chorus & orch, op.112
    1. Die Frühlingslüfte   13. Von dem Greis geleitet
    2. Johannis war gekommen   14. Bald hat das neue Töchterlein
    3. Elfenreigen   15. Bist du im Wald gewandelt
    4. Und wie sie sangen   16. Im Wald, gelehnt am Stamme
    5. So sangen sie, da dämmert's schon 17. Der Abendschlummer
    6. Bin ein armes Waisenkind   18. O sel'ge Zeit
    7. Es war der Rose   19. Wer kommt am Sonntagsmorgen
    8. Wie Blätter am Baum'   20. Ei Mühle, liebe Mühle
    9. Die letzte Scholl' hinunter rollt 21. Was klingen denn
    10. Gebet (Dank, Herr)   22. Im Hause des Müllers
    11. Ins Haus des Totengräbers   23. Und wie ein Jahr
    12. Zwischen grünen Bäumen   24. Röslein
                    ⌀   2222/4230/timp/str   Kistner   20434
    ed C.Schumann   ⌀   2222/4230/timp/str   Breitkopf & H.CW 9/8   MRL
Des SÄNGERS FLUCH, for SATTB soli, chorus & orch, op.139
    1. Es stand in alten Zeiten   8. Nicht diese wilden
    2. Die Stunde ist gekommen   9. Des Frühling kündet
    3. Schon steh'n die beiden Sänger 10. Kamt ihr hier her
    4. Provencalisches Lied   11. Fangt an! Lausche, Jungfrau
    5. Wie schlägt der Greis die Saiten 12. Und wie vom Sturm zerstoben
    6. Genug des Frühlings   13. Weh euch, ihr stolzen Hallen
    7. Ballade (In der hohen Hall')   14. Alte hat's gerufen
                    ⌀   2222/4231/timp/str   Breitkopf   Misc 3758 B
    ed C.Schumann   ⌀   2222/4231/timp/str   Breitkopf & H.CW 9/12   MRL

SCHUMANN, Robert (cont)

SCHLUMMERLIED, op.124, no.16 (from 'Albumblätter')(orig for pf)
    arr P.Carroll, orch G.Stacey, in E♭
                            1110/0000/perc/acdn.pf/str   4'   (Boosey)   LM A 670
    arr Kleinecke for piano & strings
                            pf/str   Kramer   Misc 2204
    arr Rutter   PC 1122/2210.euph/str   Hawkes   971 B
    arr C.Woodhouse   ø   str   Boosey & H   11711 B
      see also 3 PIÈCES, arr Urban
SCHLUSSLIED, op.25, no.26. see   2 SONGS, arr Selmer
SCHUMANN SELECTIONS
    arr Roberts: selection of Schumann songs
                   PC 1121/2210/timp.perc/str   C.Fischer   10966
    arr Schreiner (Schumann Album)
      revised & arr Hohenstein   PC 2222/4230/timp.perc/str   15'   Benjamin   477
    arr Urbach (Frühlingstau auf Schumanns Grab)
                   PC 2222/4230/perc/str   Wrede   9470
SCHUMANN SUITE, arr Clark
    1. Soldiers' march, op.68, no.2 (from 'Album für die Jugend')
    2. Curious story, op.15, no.2 (from 'Kinderszenen')
    3. The Merry farmer, op.68, no.10 (from 'Album für die Jugend')
    4. Träumerei, op.15, no.7 (from 'Kinderszenen')
    5. Little romance, op.68, no.19 (from 'Album für die Jugend')
    6. Hunting song, op.68, no.7 (from 'Album für die Jugend')
                  ø   112.3sx.1/2210/timp.perc/str   G.Schirmer   5300
SCHUMANN SUITE, arr O.Langey
    1. Allegro pomposo   3. Allegretto
    2. Andantino
                   PC 1121/2210/timp.perc/str   C.Fischer   1537
4 SKIZZEN FÜR DEN PEDAL-FLÜGEL, op.58
    arr Chevillard   ø   2222/4230/timp.perc/str   Durand   4586
SOARING, op.12, no.2 see   AUFSCHWUNG
SOLDATENBRAUT, op.69, no.4   see   8 FRAUENCHÖRE, arr Pfitzner
2 SONGS, arr Selmer,(op.26)
    1. Dein Angesicht, op.126, no.2   2. Schlusslied, op.25, no.26 (from 'Myrthen')
                  ø   0000/2000/timp/str   Constantin   5449
3 SONGS, arr Ritter from 1st and 2nd Albums for the Young (Album für die Jugend)
    1. Matrosenlied (Sailor's song), op.68, no.37   3. Trauer (Mourning), op.85, no.6
    2. Nordisches Lied (Northern song), op.68, no.42
                       str   Hawkes   4581
SPANISCHE LIEBESLIEDER, op.138 (orig for voices & pf)
    1. Vorspiel   6. Intermezzo
    2. Lied   7. Lied
    3. Lied   8. Lied
    4. Duett   9. Duett
    5. Romanze   10. Quartett
    arr R.Chignell   ø   2222/4230/timp.perc/hp/str   (Breitkopf)   MS 5512
SPANISCHES LIEDERSPIEL (Spanish cantata), op.74 (orig for voices & pf)
    1. Erste Begegnung (Von dem Rosenbusch)   6. Melancholie
    2. Intermezzo (Und schläfst du mein Mädchen)   7. Geständniss
    3. Liebesgram (Dereinst, dereinst)   8. Botschaft
    4. In der Nacht   9. Ich bin geliebt
    5. Es ist verrathen
    arr Hermann   ø   str   Kahnt   8049
SPRUCH, op.114, no.3   see   8 FRAUENCHÖRE, arr Pfitzner

SCHUMANN, Robert (cont)

STÜCK IM VOLKSTON, op.102, no.2 (orig for cello & pf)
   arr Urban   ø 0010/1000/hp/str   Raabe & P   10678
SYMPHONIES

No.1, op.38, in B♭ ('Spring' Symphony)(1841)					(4230 Amv Cn
	ø	2222/4230/timp.perc/str	28'-32'	Breitkopf	(Es + Fwa
ed C.Schumann	ø	2222/4230/timp.perc/str		Breitkopf & H.CW 1	MRL
ed R.Schwarz	ø	2222/4230/timp.perc/str		Breitkopf	22158 Amv
arr A.Dörffel	ø	2222/4230/timp.perc/str		Peters	Misc 2144
arr G.Mahler	ø	2222/4230/timp.perc/str		Universal	19182
arr A.Oelschlegel	PC	1121/2210/timp/str		Cranz	1557
Facsimile edn - Lib of Congress, Washington D.C.					
	ø	2222/4230/timp.perc/str		R.O.Lehman Foundation,1967	Misc 6663
No.2, op.61, in C (1845-6)	ø	2222/2230/timp/str	34'-38'15"	Breitkopf	4222 + Bmv Cn
ed C.Schumann	ø	2222/2230/timp/str		Breitkopf & H.CW 1	MRL
ed R.Schwartz	ø	2222/4230/timp/str		Breitkopf	22719 Amv +
arr A.Dörffel	ø	2222/2230/timp/str		Peters	Misc 2248
arr G.Mahler	ø	2222/2230/timp/str		Universal	19183
arr A.Oelschlegel	PC	1121/2210/timp/str		Cranz	1556
arr F.Weingartner	ø	2222/2230/timp/str		Breitkopf	7228 Amv
No.3, op.97, in E♭ ('Rhenish' Symphony)(1851)					
	ø	2222/4230/timp/str	31'-32'30"	Breitkopf	4223
ed C.Schumann	ø	2222/4230/timp/str		Breitkopf & H.CW 1	MRL
ed R.Schwarz	ø	2222/4230/timp.perc/str		Breitkopf	22765
arr A.Dörffel	ø	2222/4230/timp/str		Peters	Misc 76
arr G.Mahler	ø	2222/2200/timp/str		Universal	19184
arr A.Oelschlegel	PC	1121/2210/timp/str		Cranz	1555
No.4, op.120, in D min (Composed 1841 as no.2; rev 1851 as no.4)					
1st version (1841)	ø	2222/4230/timp/str		Breitkopf	15750
2nd version (1851)	ø	2222/4230/timp/str	27'-32'30"	Breitkopf	4224 + Amv Cn Dwa
ed C.Schumann	ø	2222/4230/timp/str		Breitkopf & H.CW 1	MRL
ed R.Schwarz	ø	2222/4230/timp/str		Breitkopf	22773 Amv +
arr A.Dörffel	ø	2222/4230/timp/str		Peters	Misc 2247
arr G.Mahler	ø	2222/4230/timp/str		Kalmus	19185
Romance only					
arr A.Leschetitsky	PC	1121/2110/str		Benjamin	1066
op.7, in G min (Jugendsymphonie)(1832)					
Revised version					
ed M.Andreae	ø	2222/2230/timp/str		Peters,1972	Misc 8035
1st & 2nd mvts only	ø	2222/2230/timp/str		BBC	Misc 7313 +

TALISMANE: song, op.25, no.8 (from song cycle 'Myrthen')
  in C (orig)   ø 0000/2221/(no str)/chorus   Hampe   11089
TRAUER: song see 3 SONGS, arr Ritter
TRÄUMEREI see KINDERSZENEN
The TWO GRENADIERS see Die BEIDEN GRENADIERE
VALSE NOBLE see CARNAVAL, op.9
VERRUFENE STELLE (A haunted place, op.82, no.4 (from 'Waldszenen' orig for piano)
   arr Hely-Hutchinson   ø 21+ca.1+bcl.2/2200/timp/str   Arranger   5884
VERZWEIFLE NICHT IM SCHMERZENSTHAL: motet for double male voice chorus & orch, op.93
                  ø 2222/2230/timp/[org]/str   Breitkopf & H.CW 9/4   MRL
VOM PAGEN UND DER KÖNIGSTOCHTER: 4 ballades for solo voices, chorus & orch, op.140
                  ø 2+picc.222/4231/timp/hp/str   Breitkopf   Misc 3533
WALDMÄDCHEN, op.69, no.2 see 8 FRAUENCHÖRE, arr Pfitzner
WARUM?,op.12, no.3 (from 'Fantasiestücke' orig for pf)
   arr Dumont   PC 1121/2100/str   C.Fischer   1262 +
   arr Wood   PC 2121/2230/timp/str   2'15"   AH & C   1777

SCHUMANN, Robert (cont)

Der WASSERMANN, op.91, no.3   see   8 FRAUENCHÖRE, arr Pfitzner
   arr Grädener for chorus & orch
                         ⌀   2+picc.222/2000/perc/hp/str   Rieter-Biedermann   Misc 1219 B
      arr Grädener   2222/2000/perc/hp/str   Arranger   TO 1693
      arr Gevaert for duet or chorus & orch
                         PC 1+picc.222/2210/perc/str   Durand   19690

SCHÜRMANN, Georg Caspar (c.1672-1751)

LUDOVICUS PIUS: opera
   Complete
      ed H.Sommer   ⌀   str/cont   Breitkopf/Broude.PAPTM 17   MRL

SCHURMANN, Gerard (1928-

ATTACK AND CELEBRATION (1971)   ⌀   2(picc)2(ca)22/4231/timp.perc.bells.glock.tamtam/
                                    hp/str   8'   Novello,1973   Misc 8108
CONCERT!
   Piano & orch (1972/3)   ⌀   2(picc)2(ca)22/4231/timp.3perc.glock.vib.xyl/
                                str   29'   Novello,1975   Misc 8633
   Violin & orch (1978)   ⌀   2(picc)2(ca)2(bcl)2/4231/timp.perc.claves.
                                glock.tamtam.vib.xyl/cel.hp/str   30'   Novello,1979   Misc 10021
CHUENCH'I (The Spirit of Spring): song cycle for Soprano (or Tenor) solo & orch (1967)
   1. New Corn   5. Look at that libble bay of the Ch'i
   2. Plucking the Rushes   6. Self-abandonment
   3. Shang Yai   7. At the end of Spring
   4. Flowers and moonlight on the Spring River
                            ⌀   3(2picc)2(ca)22/4230/timp.perc.bells.glock.
                                vib.xyl/cel.hp/str   18'   Fairfield,1967   Misc 6752
6 STUDIES OF FRANCIS BACON (1968)
   1. Figures in a landscape   4. Crucifixion
   2. Popes   5. George and the bicycle
   3. Isabel   6. Self-portrait
                            ⌀   3(3picc)3(ca)3(Ebcl:bcl)2+cbsn/4431/timp.perc.bells.
                                crot.glock.2gong.2tamtam.vib.xyl/pf(cel)/
                                str   30'-32'   Novello,1970   Misc 7078
VARIANTS for small orch (1970) ⌀   1(picc)2(ca)02/2000/str   16'   Novello,1970/72   Misc 7595 E

SCHUSTER, Josef (1748-1812)

SINFONIA CONCERTATA in C
   ed W.Jerger   ⌀   020[1]/2000/str/cont   Doblinger,1975   26111

SCHÜTZ, Heinrich (1585-1672)

COMPLETE WORKS

Heinrich Schütz sämtliche Werke, ed P.Spitta. Leipzig: Breitkopf & Härtel, 1885- 18 vols
(abbreviated CW)
Heinrich Schütz: Neue Ausgabe sämtlicher Werke. Kassel: Bärenreiter, 1955- (abbreviated NSA)   MRL
STUTTGARTER SCHÜTZ-AUSGABE. Heinrich Schütz sämtliche Werke nach den Quellen neu herausgegeben   MRL
von Günter Graulich unter Mitarbeit von Paul Horn. Stuttgart: Hänsler, 1971- (abbreviated SSA)

N.B. Many of the works of H.Schütz have instruments doubling a vocal line, or are for a small
     instrumental ensemble. These will be found listed in the Chamber Catalogue. Where
     individual editors have specified a larger ensemble, those editions are listed below.

SCHÜTZ, Heinrich (cont)

ALLELUJA, LOBET DEN HERREN: Psalm 150, for SSAATTBB soli, SSAAATBB chorus & instruments, SWV 38
    ed B.Lam   ∅   1(rec)002/0240/2vln.vla/cont   Editor/CW 3   19830 +
    ed P.Steinitz   ∅   0000/00.4cntto[=fl+3vln]4[=2tbn+2bsn]/
                        cont(org)   OUP,1978   Ch Lib 17570
AUF DICH, HERR, TRAUE ICH: Psalm 7, for SSAATTBB soli, chorus & instruments, SWV 462
    ed W.Breig   ∅   0000/00.cntto.30/org/2vln.vla   Bärenreiter,1970.NSA 27/1   MRL
AUFERSTEHUNGS-HISTORIE   see   HISTORIA VON DER AUFERSTEHUNG JESU CHRISTI
CHRISTMAS ORATORIO   see   HISTORIA VON DER GEBURT JESU CHRISTI
DOMINI EST TERRA (Psalm 24): anthem for 2 solo quartets or semi-choruses (SATB/SATB), 13 obbligato
    instruments, two or three ripieno choirs (SATB/SATB/SSATTB) and continuo, SWV 476
    ed W.Breig   ∅   0005/00.2cntto.40/2vln/cont(vlc.cb)   Bärenreiter,1970.NSA 27/1   MRL
    ed G.Graulich   ∅   00.2ca.05/00.2cntto[=2tpt]40/org/str/
                        cont(2vln.2cb)   Hänssler,1969.SSA 20   25227 & MRL
ES GING EIN SÄMANN, for SSAATTBB soli, chorus & instruments, SWV 408
    ed P.Spitta   ∅   0001/0000/2vln/cont   (Breitkopf.CW 2)   19794
    ed B.Lam (transposed 3rd higher)
                    ∅   0001/0130/2vln.2vlc/cont(cb)   Editor/CW 2   19887
    ed H.Hoffmann (transposed 3rd higher)
                    ∅   org/2vln.vlne/cont(org)   Bärenreiter,1958   23431
GELOBET SEIST DU, HERR, DU GOTT UNSRER VÄTER (Gesang der drei Männer im feurigen Ofen): motet for
    double SSATB chorus, wind, optional strings, & continuo, SWV 448
    ed C.Gottwald   ∅   0000/00.2cntto.30/[str]/cont   Hänssler,1964   Misc 5937
GESANG DER DREI MÄNNER IM FEURIGEN OFEN   see   GELOBET SEIST DU, HERR, DU GOTT UNSRER VÄTER
Der GOTT ABRAHAMS, for ATB soli, chorus & instruments, SWV Anh.3   (Ch Lib 13541 -
    ed G.Graulich & P.Horn   ∅   0000/0030/2vln/cont   Hänssler,1967   (∅ only
HERR GOTT, DICH LOBEN WIR, for double chorus & instruments, SWV 472
    ed K.Ameln, C.Mahrenholz & W.Thomas
                    ∅   0000/02[4]0/timp/org/vlns[=cntti]   Vandenhoeck & Ruprecht   Misc 10488
HERR, UNSER HERRSCHER: Psalm 8, for SAATB soli,chorus & instruments, SWV 449
    ed W.Breig   ∅   0000/00.cntto.40/org/vln   Bärenreiter,1970.CW 27/1   MRL
HISTORIA VON DER AUFERSTEHUNG JESU CHRISTI (Resurrection History), for SSSAATT.Bar.B soli,
    SSATTB chorus & instruments, SWV 50
    rev F.Stein   ∅   4vla-d'g[=vln.vla.vlc.cb]/cont   Eulenburg   Misc 1189
    arr W.S.Huber   ∅   4vla-d'g[=vln.vla.vlc.cb]/cont   Bärenreiter,1956   21758
    transposed tone higher ∅   2vla.2vlc.cb/cont(vocal pts)   (Breitkopf.CW 1)   18923
HISTORIA VON DER GEBURT JESU CHRISTI (Weihnachts-oratorium): Christmas oratorio for STB soli, chorus
    & instruments, SWV 435
      arr A.Schering   ∅   2001/0220/str/cont   46'   Breitkopf   14626
      arr F.Schöneich   ∅   2001/0220/str/cont   43'   Bärenreiter,1955   21759
      arr F.Stein   ∅   2001/0220/str/cont   60'   Eulenburg,1935   22052
    Overture & No.19 only
      ed & real P.Steinitz   0001/0020/str   BBC   24676
ICH DANKE DEM HERRN: Psalm 111, for 4 choruses & instruments, SWV 34
    ed W.Ehmann   ∅   SSSSAABB instruments/cont   Bärenreiter.NSA 24   MRL
    ed R.Norrington   ∅   00.2ca.00/0440/2org/4vln.2vla.2vlc.cb/
                        cont(2vlc.2cb)   Editor/CW 2   25240 +
ICH HEBE MEINE AUGEN AUF: Psalm 121, for 2 choruses & instruments, SWV 31
    ed W.Ehmann   ∅   SSAATTBB instruments/cont   Bärenreiter.NSA 24   MRL
IST NICHT EPHRAIM MEIN THEURER SOHN, for 4 choruses & instruments, SWV 40
    ed J.E.Gardiner   ∅   0000/0240/cont(vlc.cb)   Editor/CW 3   24704
    ed E.H.Meyer   ∅   0000/0150/cont   Editor/CW 3   19267 +
MAGNIFICAT: 'Magnificat anima mea', for 3 choruses & instruments, SWV 468
    ed E.H.Meyer   ∅   0000/0030/2vln/cont   Editor/CW 18   19777
    see also   MEINE SEELE ERHEBT DEN HERREN (German magnificat)

SCHÜTZ, Heinrich (cont)

MEIN SOIIN, WARUM HAST DU UNS DAS GETHAN (Der zwölfjährige Jesus im Tempel), for SAB soli, chorus
       & instruments, SWV 401

    ed C.Backers   φ   2vln/cont   Harmonia-Uitgave,1958   Misc 5923
    ed A.Hänlein   2vln/cont   Breitkopf   20681
    ed G.de Mauny   φ   0000/0130/2vln.2vla.vlc.cb   Editor/CW 10   19383
    ed & real P.Steinitz   φ   2vln/cont (other doubling wind instruments &
                              org ad lib)
                                                           OUP,1962   Misc 5553

MEINE SEELE ERHEBT DEN HERREN: Magnificat for Soprano solo & instruments, SWV 344
    ed H.W.Shaw   φ   2000/0220/2vln/cont(vlc.cb)   Editor/CW 7   19823

MEISTER, WIR WISSEN DASS DU WAHRHAFTIG BIST, for SSATB soli, chorus & instruments, SWV 414
    ed R.Holle   φ   0001/0000/org/vln.vlne (other doubling
                                  instruments ad lib)
                                               Bärenreiter,1955   Misc 4450

NUN LOB, MEIN SEEL, DEN HERREN: Psalm 103, for 4 choruses, organ & instruments, SWV 41
    ed W.Ehmann; continuo ed W.Bittinger
                      φ   0000/03.4cntti.20/str(vln.1.2.3[=vla-d'g 1 or vla 1].
                          vla 1[=vln 3 or vla-d'g 1].vla 2[=vla-d'g 2].vlne.
                          vlc.cb)
                                               Bärenreiter,1963   Misc 5920
                                                                  (Ch Lib 13610

O BONE JESU, FILI MARIAE, for SSAATB chorus & strings, SWV 471
    ed G.Graulich & P.Horn   φ   str   Hänssler,1967   (φ only

PSALM   8   see   HERR, UNSER HERRSCHER
PSALM 24   see   DOMINI EST TERRA
PSALM 103   see   NUN LOB,MEIN SEEL, DEN HERREN
PSALM 111   see   ICH DANKE DEM HERRN
PSALM 121   see   ICH HEBE MEINE AUGEN AUF

SAUL, WAS VERFOLGST DU MICH, for SSATBB soli, SSAATTBB chorus & instruments, SWV 415
    ed A.Goldsbrough   φ   2vln.vlc.cb/cont   Editor/CW 11   19266
    ed G.Graulich & P.Horn   φ   2vln/cont (other doubling instruments ad lib)   Hänssler,1969   Misc 5938

SEI GEGRÜSST MARIA, for Soprano & Contralto soli, SSATB chorus & instruments, SWV 333, in C
    ed N.Stone (in C & D - 2sets)
                      φ   org/2vln.2vla.2vlc   Editor/CW 6   19382 +
    ed K.Ameln, C.Mahrenholz & W.Thomas
                      φ   4vln[=2vln+2vla].vlc.cb/cont   Vandenhoeck & Ruprecht   27028 *
    arr â ed W.Ehmann (in D)   φ   str/cont   Bärenreiter,1959   23389

Die SIEBEN WORTE JESU CHRISTI AM KREUZ (Seven Last Words from the Cross), for SAATTB soli,
    chorus & instruments, SWV 478
                   org/2vln.2vla.vlc/cont(cb)   (Breitkopf.CW 1)   19103
    rev F.Stein; cont real H.Hoffman
                      φ   org/vln.2vla.2vlc.cb (or org/3vla.cb)   Eulenburg   23779

SUMITE PSALMUM: motet for SSATB soli, chorus & instruments, SWV Anh.9
    ed. C.Engelbrecht   φ   0000/0020/2vln/cont   Bärenreiter,1959   Misc 5490 B

VENI SANCTI SPIRITUS: anthem for SSATTTB soli, 4 choruses of 16 voices, instruments & cont, SWV 475
                    φ   1001/00.4cntti.30/3vln.vla.vlc.cb/cont   Hänssler,1967   25928

ZION SPRICHT DER HERR HAT MICH VERLASSEN, for S.Mz.T.Bar soli, chorus & instruments, SWV 46
    ed J.E.Gardiner   φ   0001/0340/cont   Editor/CW 3   25268 +

Der ZWÖLFJÄHRIGE JESUS IM TEMPEL   see   MEIN SOHN, WARUM HAST DU UNS DAS GETHAN

SCHUYT,Nico (1922-

DISCORSI, DISCORSI (1979)   φ   1[=2](picc)00.ssx.asx.barsx.tsx.0/131+2btbn.1/
                                pf
                                                    Donemus,1979   Misc 10150

SCHWANDT, W

DREAM A LITTLE DREAM OF ME   see   KAHN, G: DREAM A LITTLE DREAM OF ME

SCHWANTER, Joseph

AND THE MOUNTAINS RISING NOWHERE (1977)
                          ⌀   6(4picc)4(2ca)(4glasses)24/4441/timp.5perc(bells.
                              bell tree.crot.2glock.watergong.mba.2tamtam.timb.
                              11tomtom.2vib.2xyl)/amppf/cb
                              (Players also have to sing and whistle)   11'   Helicon,1977   Misc 9779

SCHWARTZ,Arthur (1900-

The BAND WAGON: revue
   Selection, arr F.Rapley   PC   21+ca.2.3sx.1/2230/timp.perc/hp/str   6'30"   Chappell   21115 Cp D
   Extracts
      Dancing in the dark: song
         arr R.Farnon for fv-chorus & orch, with rhythm section
                          ⌀   22(ca)22/0331/rhythm-sdm.mrc.gtr.bgtr.pf/
                              timp.glock/cel.hp/str/chorus pts   (Chappell)   26832
         arr Tilsley (non-vocal)
                          ⌀   2222/4230/timp.perc/hp/str   (Chappell)   22383 +
      That's entertainment: song
         in C, arr R.Docker   ⌀   2222/4330/perc/hp.pf/str   (Chappell)   23023
         arr P.Knight for orch with rhythm section
                          ⌀   2(2picc)2(ca)22/4331/rhythm-kit.bgtr.gtr/
                              timp.perc.glock.vib.xyl/cel(pf).hp/str   (Chappell)   26741
FOLLOW THE SUN: film
   Extracts
      Love is a dancing thing: song
         in E♭, arr R.Burston   ⌀   2121/2230/perc/hp/str   (Chappell)   TO 528
         arr J.Byfield (non-vocal)
                          ⌀   2222/4230/timp.perc/hp/str   (Chappell)   22265 +
FUNNY SIDE UP: revue
   Extracts
      Terribly attractive: song
         in E♭, arr R.Hanmer   ⌀   2222/4230/timp.perc/hp.pf/str   (Chappell)   20894
HERE COMES THE BRIDE
   Selection, arr Jones   PC   2122/2230/perc/str   Chappell   493 Ap
The HOUSE THAT JACK BUILT: musical play
   Extracts
      She's such a comfort to me: song
         in E♭, arr H.Carr & M.Lubbock
                          ⌀   2121/2230/perc/hp/str   (Chappell)   TO 524
I GUESS I'LL HAVE TO CHANGE MY PLAN: song
   in C, arr M.Mackie   ⌀   2222/4000/timp/hp.pf/str   (Chappell)   21803
I'LL BUY YOU A STAR: song
   in E♭, arr A.Fones   ⌀   1110/1000/gtr.hp.pf/str   (Chappell)   LM G 7892
STOP PRESS: revue
   Extracts
      You and the night and the music: song
         Refrain only, in D min, arr A.Yates
                          ⌀   1132/0220/timp.perc/pf/str   (Chappell)   22261 +
         in A min, arr A.Masters, for baritone solo, chorus & orch
                          ⌀   22(ca)22/4330/timp.perc/hp.pf(cel)/str   (Chappell)   23767 +

SCHWARTZ, Elliot (1936-

TEXTURE   ⌀   1111/1110/str [soli or orch]   7'30"   Broude,1967   Misc 8731

SCHWARTZ, Jean (1878-1956)

GOOD-BYE, VIRGINIA: song
   in Eb, arr Stodden   PC 1121/2210/timp.perc/str   Feldman   16710
PUSH AND GO: revue
   Extracts
      Chinatown, my Chinatown: song
         in C, arr M.Mackie   ø 2131/2230/timp.perc/hp.pf/str   (FD & H)   18553

SCHWARTZ, Phil

KNICK KNOCKS RAG
   arr Zamecnik   PC 1121/2210/perc/str   Sam Fox   11881

SCHWEMMER, Heinrich (1621-1696)

MEINE STUND' IST KOMMEN, for Soprano solo & strings
                 ø str   Akademische Verlag,Graz,1955   Misc 4535
MÜH UND ARBEIT IST DAS LEBEN, for Soprano solo & strings
                 ø str   Akademische Verlag,Graz,1955   Misc 4535
VICTORIA, PLAUDITE COELITES: motet (1689), for SSATB chorus & orch
   ed M.Seiffert   ø 0001/00.2clno.2cnt.20/timp/org/str   Breitkopf.DDTB 6/1   MRL

SCHWERTSIK, Kurt

CONCERTO for violin & orch, op.31 (Romanzen im Schwarztinten-Ton und in der geblümten Paradies-Weis)
                ø 1+picc.12(Ebcl:bcl)2/2101/timp.perc.bells.mba/
                  hp/str   20'   Boosey & H,1978   Misc 9950
DRACULAS HAUS- UND HOFMUSIK: symphony for string orch
                ø str   12'   Doblinger,1970   Misc 7467
MUSIK VOM MUTTERLAND MU   ø 111+bcl.0/1010/perc/vln.vla.vlc.cb   13'30"   Doblinger,1974   Misc 8591 B

SCHWINDEL, Friedrich (1737-1786)(Schwindl)

SYMPHONY in F
   arr A.Carse   ø 02[=fl]00/2000/hp[=hp]str   11'   Augener,1937   21245

SCHYTTE, Ludvig (1848-1909)

BERCEUSE, for clarinet & orch, op.26, no.7
   arr S.Robinson   ø 2121/2000/str   (Hansen)   MS 5607
PANTOMIMES, op.30
   1. Introduction   5. Columbine
   2. Pierrot   6. Harlequin
   3. Cassander   7. Gelsomino
   4. Polichinel   8. Finale
      arr Müller-Berghaus   ø 2+picc.2+ca.2+bcl.2/4231/timp.perc/hp/str   Simon   7649
SPRINGTANZ: Norwegian peasants' dance, op.79, no.1
   arr Bernarde   PC 1121/2210/perc/str   Simrock   10783 B

SCIARRINO, Salvatore (1947-

CLAIR DE LUNE, for piano & orch (1976)
                ø 2222/2200/timp/str(6.0.2.2.2)   Ricordi,1976   Misc 9140
...DA UN DIVERTIMENTO (1968-70) ø 1111/1000/str(2.-.1.1.1)   Ricordi,1971   Misc 8157
DI ZEFIRO E PAN: Poemetto for 10 wind instruments (1976)
                ø 2222/2000   5'   Ricordi   Misc 9373

SCIARRINO, Salvatore (cont)

GRANDE SONATA DA CAMERA   ∅   1+picc+afl.11+bcl.1/2220/2perc(plate-bell.
                                        tamtam.vib)/cel.hp.pf/str(2.0.2.2.1)   10'   Ricordi,1972   Misc 9447
ROMANZA, for viola d'amore & orch
                                   ∅   2+afl.2+ca.2+bcl.2+cbsn/4440/timp.perc.plate-bell.
                                        steel plate.tamtam.vib.xba/cel.hp.2pf/str   Ricordi,1973   Misc 9775
RONDO, for flute solo & orch   ∅   0200/2000/str(6.-.2.2.1)   Ricordi,1973   Misc 8158
VARIAZIONI, for cello & orch   ∅   2+afl.2+ca.2+bcl.2+cbsn/4331/5perc(timp.
                                        bells.2gro.mba.metal blocks.plate bell.
                                        steel plate.tamtam.vib)/str(12.8.6.6.4[+])   17'   Ricordi,1974   Misc 9432

SCONTRINO, Antonio (1850-1922)

SINFONIA MARINARESCA   ∅   3(picc)+picc.2+ca.2+bcl.2/4441/timp/hp/str   34'30"Carisch & Jänichen   Misc 1369 B

SCOTT, Bennett

BY THE SIDE OF THE ZUYDER ZEE: song
   in C   PC   1(picc)121/2220/perc/str   (Feldman)   LM G 5142
   in C & Bb   PC   1121/2210/perc/str   Feldman   18651
   in Bb   PC   1(picc)121/2220/timp.perc/str   (Feldman)   MS 78 (∅ only)
   in Bb   1121/2220/str   (Feldman)   MS 4825
CHEERIO! SAILOR BOY HOW DO?: song
   in D, arr Baker   PC   1121/2210/perc/str   Star Music Pub Co   10666
I DON'T CARE WHAT BECOMES OF ME: song
   in Eb   ∅   2121/2230/perc/pf/str   (Feldman)   MS 859
IF I SHOULD PLANT A TINY SEED OF LOVE: song
   in Bb, arr J.Neat   PC   1111/2210/timp.perc/str   Feldman   16583
IT'S A DIFFERENT GIRL AGAIN: song
   in Bb   ∅   2121/2220/timp.perc/str   (FD & H)   MS 82 (∅ only)
The SEVEN STEP: "Come do the seven"
   arr Lucas   PC   112.3sx.2/2230/timp.perc/2bjo/str   Chappell   9434
SHIP AHOY: song
   in F   1131/0220/perc/pf/str   (Feldman)   LM G 5155
   in G   PC   1131/0220/perc/pf/str   (Feldman)   MS 30273
SOMEBODY'S SAILOR BOY: song
   in C   ∅   2121/2220/perc/str   (AH & C)   MS 134
TAKE ME BACK TO DEAR OLD BLIGHTY: song by B.Scott, F.Godfrey & A.J.Mills
   in Bb, arr Baker   PC   1121/2210/perc/str   Star Music Pub Co   10264

SCOTT, Charles Kennedy (1876-1965)

EVERYMAN; a music mystery play (1916-17, rev 1940)
                                   ∅PS 1(picc)2(ob-d'a)+ca.2(bcl)3/0131/perc.bells/
                                        hmn.hp.org/str(min.5.4.3.3.4)   (Composer)   26117 +

SCOTT, Clement

NOW IS THE HOUR (Haere Ra); Maori song of farewell
   in G   PC   112.3sx.1/0320/perc/gtr/str   Paling (K.Prowse)   18973

SCOTT, Cyril (1879-1970)

AUBADE, op.77   ∅   3(picc)2+ca.2+bcl.2/4231/timp.perc/
                                        2hp/str   18'   Schott   Misc 787
BLACKBIRD'S SONG: song
   in F, arr A.Franzel   ∅   1110/0000/acdn.pf/str   (Elkin)   LM A 653
   in F, arr J.Turner   ∅   1110/1000/hp/str   (Elkin)   LM G 9268

SCOTT, Cyril (cont)

CHERRY RIPE, arr

arr L.Artock	PC	1121/2210/timp.perc/str	3'	Schott	7609 C
arr R.King	PC	str		Schott	19253

CONCERTI

Piano & orch	∅	2122/0000/timp.perc.tamtam/hp/str	26'30"	Schott	Misc 846

3 DANCES (orig Symphony no.2)
  1. Gavotte   3. English dance
  2. Eastern dance

arr A.Schmid	PC	2(picc)121/2230/timp.perc/str		Boosey	1393 Cwa

DANSE NÈGRE

arr Newman	PC	2111/2110/timp.perc/cel.hp/str	2'	Elkin	9912 B

EARLY ONE MORNING: poem for piano & orch

Revised edition	∅	22(ca)23/4030/timp.perc/hp/str	16'	Boosey & H, 1962	Misc 5696

INTERMEZZO

arr Howard		pf/str	Elkin	7320

LOTUS LAND, op.47, no.1

arr Bridgewater		pf/str	Elkin	3311
arr Newman	∅	2(picc)1+ca.22/4111/timp.perc/cel.hp/str	Elkin	12579

LULLABY: song

in D♭, arr G.Stacey		pf/str	(Elkin)	LM G 3557
orch Dexter	PC	[1]0[1]0/0000/[gtr]/str	K.Prowse	20189

NOËL: Christmas overture

	∅	3(picc)2+ca.2+bcl.2+cbsn/4331/timp.perc.bell.xyl/ org.pf/str	16'15"	Schott	Misc 1013 B

2 PASSACAGLIAS on Irish themes

	∅	4(picc)3+ca.4+bcl.4+cbsn/6431/timp.perc.glock. tamtam.xyl/cel.2hp.org.pf/str	13'	Schott	Misc 851
No.1 only, arr Howard		pf/str		Elkin	12272

2 PIERROT PIECES
  1. Lento (4')   2. Allegro (Pierrot gai)(3'30")

arr Coppersmith	∅	str	7'30"	Boosey & H	15570

RHAPSODIE ARABESQUE

	1000/0000/hp/str		(Elkin)	18644

SONG FROM THE EAST, op.54, no.2

arr Newman	∅	2(picc)1(ca)22/2100/perc/cel.hp/str	Elkin	10496
arr Newman	PC	2(picc)1(ca)22/2100/perc/cel.hp/str	Elkin	2996

SOUVENIR DE VIENNE

arr Austin	∅	2022/2210/timp.perc/str	3'	Elkin	13615
arr Austin	PC	2022/2210/timp.perc/str		Elkin	2587

SUITE no.1, for strings
  1. Silver threads among the gold   3. Oh, dear what can the matter be
  2. Long, long ago

	∅	str	7'30"-10'	Boosey & H	9913 B

SUMMER GARDENS: suite
  1. Reverie in the rose garden   3. Raindrops
  2. Where the bee sucks

	∅	1111/1000/perc/hp/str	5'30"-8'	Schott	13234
	PC	1111/1000/perc/hp/str		Schott	16950

VESPERALE, op.40, no.2

arr H.Carr	∅	str	4'	(Elkin)	TO 1293
arr Howard		pf/str		Elkin	12270
arr Newman	PC	1121/2110/bells/cel/str		Elkin	9912 B

WATER-WAGTAIL, op.71, no.3

arr Newman	∅	2(picc)2(ca)22/2100/perc/cel.hp/str	2'45"	Elkin	10496
arr Newman	∅	2(picc)2(ca)22/2100/perc/cel.hp/str		Elkin	2996

SCOTT, Harold

THANK GOD FOR THE MIDDLE CLASSES: song
    Refrain only, in A, arr M.Mackie
                        ∅   1121/2210/timp.perc/hp.pf/str   (Reynolds)   22136

SCOTT, J.Sebastian

CORYDON'S ROUND: suite
    1. His joyous task: allegro (2'20")   4. Lament: poco adagio   (2'30")
    2. His love: andante   (1'45")   5. His pastime: allegro ben moderato (2'30")
    3. His jest: allegro   (2'30")
                        PC str   11'45"   Hawkes,1953   20973

SCOTT, Lady John Douglas (Alicia A.Spottiswoode)(1810-1900)

ANNIE LAURIE: song
    in C, arr Clark   PC 1121/2210/timp/str   G.Schirmer   9704
    in C, arr Lehmann   ∅   1121/0000/str   (Siddell)   17949
    in C, arr Lehmann   0000/0110/timp/str   (Siddell)   17950
    in D   1121/2210/timp.perc/str   (Siddell)   17952
    in Bb, arr Lehmann   1010/0110/timp/str   (Siddell)   17951
    Non-vocal arrangements
    arr Barsotti   PC 1+picc.12.4sx.2/4230/perc/str   Boosey & H   21039 B
    arr de Witt   PC 1121/2210/perc/str   C.Fischer   5922
    arr M.L.Lake   PC 1+picc.12.2sx.1/2210/perc/str   C.Fischer   19720
    arr Hartley   PC str   2'15"   Bosworth   9276
    arr A.Winter   PC 1222/2230/perc/str   Hawkes   7977
THINK ON ME: song
    in C,arr Moffatt, orch R.Douglas
                        ∅   2121/2120/hp/str   3'   Arranger MS:BBC MS 6265
    in Eb, arr G.Stacey   ∅   1100/1000/perc/gtr.hp.org.pf/str   (Paterson)   LM G 4477
    in Eb & F, arr G.Williams ∅ 1121/2210/hp/str   (Paterson)   MLO 318
    in Ab & Gb, arr G.Stacey   00[1]0/0000/pf/str   (Paterson)   LM G 3747

SCOTT, Maurice

FRIENDS AND NEIGHBOURS: song by M.Scott & M.Lockyer
    in G, arr J.Muston   ∅   2221/4230/timp.perc/hp.pf/str   (Southern)   18515
I'VE GOT RINGS ON MY FINGERS: song
    in G, arr H.Carruthers ∅   2121/0220/timp.perc/str   (FD & H)   MS 20396
A NICE QUIET DAY, or The Postman's Holiday: song
    in G, orch A.Collins   ∅   1121/2230/perc/str   (FD & H)   MS 6367

SCOTT-GATTY, Alfred (1847-1918)

BENDEMEER'S STREAM: Irish folk-song, arr
    in Ab, arr E.Griffiths ∅   2222/4230/timp.perc/hp/str   (Boosey & H)   22870 +
BUT IT IS SO: plantation song
    in G, arr S.Robinson   ∅   str   (Boosey)   MS 5609
CLICK CLACK: plantation song
    in C, arr R.Chignell & Woodgate
                        ∅   1121/2230/perc/str   (Boosey)   MS 449
DANCE AND SONG (from 'Plantation Songs')
    arr S.Robinson   ∅   bjo/str   (Boosey)   MS 5624
DING DONG DING
    in E min, arr R.Chignell ∅ str   (Boosey)   MS 4923

SCOTT-GATTY, Alfred (cont)

DIS OLE NIGGER: plantation song
   in G, arr R.Chignell   φ   bjo/str   (Boosey)   MS 4927
DOWN BY DAT RIBBER: plantation song
   in F, arr R.Chignell   φ   str   (Boosey)   MS 4925
GOOD NIGHT (Shine, shine moon): plantation song
   in B♭, arr S.Robinson   φ   1121/2210/timp/bjo/str   (Boosey)   MS 5631
   in B♭, arr L.Woodgate for soli & chorus
                  φ   1121/2230/perc/str   (Boosey)   MS 449
   in B♭, arr L.Wurmser for chorus & orch
                  φ   222+bcl.2/4230/perc/cel.hp/str   (Boosey)   TO 1545
De LADY MOON: plantation song
   in C, orch A.Collins (duet)   φ   1021/2000/hp/str   (Boosey)   MS 6325
   in D, arr R.Chignell (duet)   φ   bjo/str   (Boosey)   MS 4926
De LECTURE: plantation song
   in G, arr S.Robinson   φ   str   (Boosey)   MS 5627
De NEW YEAR: plantation song
   in F, arr R.Chignell for Baritone solo, chorus & orch
                  φ   bjo/str   (Boosey)   MS 4924
De OLE BANJO: plantation song
   in E♭, arr S.Robinson   φ   1121/2210/org/str   (Boosey)   MS 5622
   in E♭, arr L.Woodgate for soli & chorus
                  φ   1121/2230/perc/str   (Boosey)   MS 449
OUR DINAH: plantation song
   in G, arr R.Chignell for Baritone solo, chorus & orch
                  φ   str   (Boosey)   MS 5621
De RINGTAIL'D COON: plantation song
   in A, arr S.Robinson   φ   str   (Boosey)   MS 5557
ROTHESAY BAY: song, arr A.Scott-Gatty & P.Cardew
   in F   φ   110.4sx.0/2320/perc/gtr.hp.pf/str [Arrangers]   LM J 2251
WHO DID?: plantation song
   in G, arr R.Chignell for solo voice, chorus & orch
                                          (Boosey)   MS 5557

SCOTT-WOOD, George

CARNIVAL OF BACCHUS: suite
   1. Amontillado (Spanish sherry)   3. Tokay (Hungarian czardas)
   2. Moselle (German)   4. Champagne (Galop - French)
     arr R.Hanmer   PC   2121/2230/timp.perc/acdn.hp/str   FD & H,1951   20459 Ap
The FLYING SCOTSMAN
     arr R.Hanmer   PC   212.4sx.1/2320/timp.perc/acdn.gtr/str   Liber-Southern,1951   21540
The LAUGHING SEINE (La Seine qui rit)
     arr P.Hope   PC   2121/2230/perc.glock/gtr.hp/str   Metro Mus   MLO 708
LONDON CAPRICE
     arr J.Muston   PC   1121/2220/timp.perc/hp/str   I.Dash   19312
SERENADE TO EVENING
     arr J.Muston   PC   1121/2220/timp/hp/str   I.Dash   19340
SHY SERENADE   PC   1111/2210/timp.perc/str   4'   L.Wright   15339 B
SONG WITHOUT WORDS   PC   112.3sx.1/2320/timp.perc/str   L.Wright   3699

SCOTTO

La PETITE TONKINOISE   see   CHRISTINÉ, H: La PETITE TONKINOISE

SCOTTO, Vincent

SOUS LES PONTS DE PARIS: waltz PC 1121/2230/perc/str   Delormel   15319

SCRIABIN, Aleksandr Nikolayevich (1872-1915)

CONCERTO for piano & orch, op.20, in F# min

	∅	2222/4200/timp/str	23'-27'	Belaieff	8487
MAZURKA					
arr L.Artok	PC	1121/2210/timp/str	2'	Schott	7595 B
The POEM OF ECSTASY, op.54	∅	3+picc.3+ca.3+bcl.3+cbsn/8531/timp.perc/ cel.2hp.org/str	20'-25'	Belaieff	4225
	∅	3+picc.3+ca.3+bcl.3+cbsn/8531/timp.perc.glock/ cel.2hp.org/str		Russian SM,1975	Misc 8909
POEM, op.32, no.2 (orig for pf)					
arr Q.Maganini	PC	1121/1210/timp/str		Ed Musicus	16525
arr Q.Maganini	PC	1+picc.222/2220/timp/str		Ed Musicus	14658
POEM TRAGIQUE					
arr J.Lanchbery	∅	3222/4231/timp.perc/hp/str		Mozart Edn	LM G 11483
PRELUDE, op.11, no.5, in D					
arr Q.Maganini	∅	1121/2110/timp.perc/str		Ed Musicus	16540
PROMETHEUS: The Poem of Fire, op.60					
	∅	3+picc.3+ca.3+bcl.3+cbsn/8531/timp.perc/ cel.2hp.org.pf/str/[chorus]	18'-22'	Ed Musicus	11252
RÊVERIE, op.24	PC	2222/4231/timp/str	4'	Belaieff	4226
SYMPHONIES					
No.1, op.26, in E	∅	3(picc)232/4331/timp.perc/hp/str/[chorus]	45'	Belaieff	4227
	∅	3(picc)232/4331/timp.bells/hp/str/ Mz.T soli.SSATBB chorus		Russian SM,1971	Misc 7722
No.2, op.29, in C min	∅	3(picc)232/4331/timp.perc/str	40'-50'	Belaieff	4228 B +
No.3, op.43, in C (The Divine Poem)					
	∅	3+picc.3+ca.3+bcl.3+cbsn/8531/timp.perc/ 2hp/str	38'-42'	Belaieff	4229

SCULL, Harold T.

ÉVEILLE DE L'AMOUR (Love's awakening)

arr J.Engleman	PC	112.2sx.1/2230/timp.perc/org/str		Bosworth	18791
SOLEMN PRELUDE, op.76	∅	org/str	6'	Augener,1940	Misc 4183

SCULTHORPE, Peter Joshua (1929-

IRKANDA IV, for violin, strings & percussion (solo can be leader from front desk)(1961)

	∅	1perc(bdm.tomtom[=sdm].gong.large cym. small cym.tri)/str	12'	Faber,1967	Misc 6781 E
LAMENT FOR STRINGS (1976)	∅	str	10'	Faber,1978	Misc 9669
MUSIC FOR JAPAN (1970)	∅	2[=3=2+picc]222/4431/timp.3perc(bgos.claves. crot.gro.mrc.tamtam.timb)/str	12'	Faber,1979	Misc 9935

PORT ESSINGTON (1977)

1. Prologue: The Bush
2. Theme & Variations: The Settlement
3. Phantasy: Unrest
4. Nocturnal: Estrangement
5. Arietta: Farewell
6. Epilogue: The Bush

	∅	str	14'30"	Faber,1980	Misc 10231
SUN MUSIC					
I (1965)	∅	0000/4331/timp.perc.bells/str	10'	Faber,1966	Misc 6398 E
II (1969)	∅	2+picc.222/4231/timp.perc/str	6'	Faber,1973	Misc 8282
III (1967)	∅	2+picc.222/3220/timp.perc.bells.vib/str	13'	Faber,1973	Misc 7989
IV (1967)	∅	2222/4231/timp.perc.bells/str	9'	Faber,1973	Misc 8328 C

SEARLE, Humphrey (1915-

ALIVE AND WELL AND LIVING IN LONDON: radio production (1971)
                ∅   1(picc)111/1110/timp.perc/vln.vla.vlc.cb   Composer MS:BBC   MS 31681
ANTONY AND CLEOPATRA: incidental music to radio production
                ∅   2(picc)1+ca.10/2220/timp.perc/cim.hp/str/
                   voices   Composer MS:BBC   MS 31514 +
BLOOMSDAY: radio production (1961)
                   1(picc)110/0110/timp.perc/acdn.hp/2vln.vla.
                   vlc.cb   Composer MS:BBC   MS 31342
The CAVE AND THE GRAIL: radio production
                   111.asx.1/1110/perc/cel[=pf]/str   Composer MS:BBC   MS 31279
CONCERTANTE for piano, strings & percussion, op.24
                ∅   perc/pf/str   5'   Ars Viva,1954   Misc 4317
CONTEMPLATIONS for Mezzo-Soprano solo & orch, op.66 (1975)
                ∅   2222/2200/timp.perc.glock/hpsd/str   20'   Faber   Misc 10214 B
The DEATH OF ANTON WEBERN: radio production (1971)
                ∅   0010/1010/timp.perc.glock/gtr.hp.mand/
                   str-4tet   Composer MS:BBC   MS 31686
The DEVIL'S JIG (Dr. Faustus), op.69: radio opera (1977)
                ∅   2+2picc.2(ca)2.sx.2/4331/2timp.2perc(bells.
                   cast.glock.mba.tamtams.tomtoms.vib.whip.xyl)/
                   cel.hp.hpsd.org.pf/str/speaker   Composer MS:BBC   MS 31779
DR. FAUSTUS: radio production (1970)
                ∅   1(picc)111/1110/timp.perc.glock.vib/
                   cel.org.pf/str 5-tet   Composer MS:BBC   MS 31674
DON JUAN IN HELL: radio production by H.Searle & others
                ∅   1(picc)01(bcl)1(cbsn)/1100/1perc/org/
                   2vln.vlc.cb   Composer MS:BBC   MS 31768 ∅ only
ENGLAND'S HARROWING: radio production
   Part 1: Trafalgar   Part 2: Waterloo
                ∅   1111/1110/timp.perc/str   Composer MS:BBC   MS 31328
The FOUNDLING: radio production (rev 1965)
                   1(picc)1(heck)1(sx)1(cbsn)/2220/timp.perc/
                   hp.org/str/chorus   Composer MS:BBC   MS 31261 +
A GENTLE CREATURE: radio feature (1961)
                ∅   1(picc)110/1110/timp.perc.glock.vib.xyl/
                   gtr/str   Composer MS:BBC   MS 31353
The GOLDEN FLEECE: radio production (1962)
                ∅   111.Ebsx.1/1110/timp.perc/str/soli.chorus   Composer MS:BBC   MS 31377 +
The GUILT OF KING POLYCRATES: radio production
                   1111/2210/timp.perc/hp/str   Composer MS:BBC   MS 31305
GULLIVER'S TRAVELS: incidental music for radio drama production
                ∅   2000/0211/timp.perc.bell.glock.tabor.tamtam.
                   vib.xyl/hpsd/2vln.cb   (Composer,1980)   MS 31797
HAMLET: incidental music to radio production
                ∅   1111/1210/perc/cel(pf)/str   Composer MS:BBC   MS 31555 +
JERUSALEM: radio production (1970)
                ∅   2(2picc)2(ca)2(bcl)2(cbsn)/2221/timp.perc.glock.
                   tamtam.vib.xyl/cim.pf/2vln.vla.vlc.cb/T-solo.chorus Composer MS:BBC   MS 31662
KUBLA KHAN, for Tenor solo, chorus, electronics & orch, op.60 (1975)
                ∅   2(2picc)22(bcl)2(cbsn)/4231/4(timp.perc.bells.
                   glock.vib)/cim.hp.org.pf(cel)/str   16'   Faber,1975   Misc 5796
LABYRINTH, op.56 (1971)   ∅   3(3picc.afl)33(Ebcl.bcl.asx)2+cbsn/4331/
                   timp.5perc.bells.cbell.crot.acym.glock.mba.vib.xyl/
                   hp.org.pf/str   CML,1975/Faber,1971   Misc 8700 B
A LONELY PLACE IN A DARK WOOD: radio production (1967)
                ∅   1(picc)111/1110/perc.xyl/vln.vla.vlc.cb   Composer MS:BBC   MS 31609 +

SEARLE, Humphrey (cont)

The MARRIAGE: radio production (1969)
     ø 1(picc)100/0210/timp.perc.bells.vib.xyl/
      org/vln.vla/voices   Composer MS:BBC MS 31648

The MASQUE OF FALSEHOOD: radio production
     ø 111.asx.0/1100/timp/hp/str   Composer MS:BBC MS 31222 +

The MASTER BUILDER: radio production (1967)
     ø 1(picc)111/1110/perc.glock.vib/
      2vln.vla.vlc   Composer MS:BBC MS 31599 +

NIGHT MUSIC for chamber orch, op.2
     ø 1(picc)11(bcl)1/1110/timp/str 9'-13'30" J.Williams Misc 2648 C

NIGHT THOUGHTS: radio production (1955)
      111.tsx.1/1220/timp.perc/pf/str   Composer MS:BBC MS 31086

The NOSEBAG: radio production ø 1010/1110/timp.perc/gtr/vln.vlc.cb/voice Composer MS:BBC MS 31542 +

The PALLINGHAM DEPRESSION: radio production (1969)
     ø 1(picc)110/1110/perc.vib.xyl/vln.vla.vlc Composer MS:BBC MS 31639

POEM, for 22 strings, op.18 ø str   12' J.Williams,1960 Misc 5266 E

SINFONIETTA, op.49 (1969) ø 1(picc)111/1000/vln.vla.vlc.cb Faber,1970/CML,1972 Misc 8046

SYMPHONIES
 No.1, op.23 (1953) ø 2(picc)22(bcl)2(cbsn)/4231/timp.perc/str 25' Ars Viva,1958 Misc 5043
 No.2, op.33   ø 2(picc)222/4231/timp.perc.tamtam/str 20' Schott,1959 Misc 5172 B
 No.3, op.36 (1959) ø 2(picc)2(ca.barob.heck)2(bcl)2(cbsn)/4231/
          timp/str   18'45" Schott   Misc 7392
 No.5, op.43   ø 2(picc)2(ca)2(bcl)2(cbsn)/4231/timp.perc.
          glock.tamtam.vib.xyl/cel.hp.pf/str 20' Schott,1966 Misc 6587

WHO AM I NOW?: radio production (1975)
     ø 1010/0100/timp.perc/str(3.0.2.2.1) Composer MS:BBC MS 31741 ø only

SEAVER, F.

SOLOMON LEVI
 in Bb, arr R.Chignell for chorus & orch
     ø 2222/2220/perc/str   Arranger MS:BBC MS 5523
 arr M.L.Lake   PC 1+picc.12.2sx.1/2210/perc/str C.Fischer 19720

SEBASTIANI, Johann (1622-1683)

PASSION according to St. Matthew, for SATTB chorus & orch
 ed F.Zelle, rev H.J.Moser ø org/str/cont   Breitkopf,1958.DDT 17 MRL

ŠEBEK, Gabriel

2 BULGARIAN DANCES, op. 7 ø 2(picc)222/4230/timp.perc/str   Urbanek 2087
BULGARIAN WAR MARCH, op.29 PC 1+picc.122/3230/perc/str   Zimmerman 10120
IN THE SOUDAN (A Dervish chorus), op.45
     PC 2222/2230/perc/str   Hawkes 2911 B
SHOUMI MARITZA: former National Anthem of Bulgaria
     PC 2(picc)222/4230/timp.perc/str   Breitkopf 14305
     PC 2(picc)222/4231/timp.perc/str   Benjamin 16363
 arr M.L.Lake   PC 112.2sx.1/2210/perc/str   C.Fischer 19720

SECCHI

LOVE ME OR NOT: song, arr A.L.
 in E, orch L.Wurmser ø 21+ca.22/4200/hp/str   4' (Boosey) TO 1568

SEELIG, Paul Johann (1876-1944)

MAHA TCHAY: Siamese hymn	∅	2222/4231/timp.perc.bells/hp/str		Hug	Misc 828 B
NINA-NINI: overture	∅	2(picc)222/4230/timp.perc/str		Hug	Misc 850 B
RHAPSODIE JAVANAISE	∅	22(ca)22/4230/timp.perc.tamtam/str		Matatani	Misc 1510

SEGERSTAM, Leif (1944-

7 RED MOVEMENTS: suite
    No.4 only - Nocturne   ∅   2+picc.1+ca.1+bcl.2/2320/timp.perc(cel.glock.tamtam)/
                           hp/str   3'   Fazer,1977   Misc 9632

SEIBER, Mátyás (1905-1960)(see also MATHIS, G.S.)

ARABIAN MUSIC: suite of 6 pieces
    1. Taksirn Saba   4. Tahmila Biyati I
    2. Bashraf Nahawand   5. Tahmila Biyati II
    3. Bashraf Huzar Kan   6. Samaiz Nahawand
               ∅   1000/0000/perc/2gtr/vln.vlc   Composer MS:BBC   MS 8424

BESARDO SUITES   (PL 576 Ani &
   No.1 (1940)   ∅ 2(picc)222/2220/timp.perc/str   16'   Augener,1952   (Misc 3028 B
   No.2 (1942)   ∅ str   14'   Schott,1950   Misc 3292
The CHRISTMAS CHILD: radio production (1948)
               ∅   1120/2100/perc/str   Composer MS:BBC   MS 30270
CHRISTMAS CRACKERS: radio production (1950)
                  0100/1110/perc/str   Composer MS:BBC   MS 30414
ELEGIE for viola & small orch ∅ 1(picc)11+bcl.1/2300/timp.perc/str 8'   Schott,1958   Misc 5044 B
FANTASIA CONCERTANTE for violin & strings
               ∅ str   22'   Ars Viva,1959 Misc 5237 B
FAUST: incidental music for radio play for Counter-tenor solo, boys' chorus & orch
               ∅   3+picc.rec.1+ca.2+bcl.sx.0/4331/timp.perc/
                  acdn.cel.hp.org/str   Composer MS:BBC   MS 30326
FAUST: choral suite for Soprano & Tenor soli, chorus & orch
                  2(picc)2(ca)2(bcl)0.cbsn/4331/timp.perc/
                  hp/str   Composer(H)   PL 240
FOR THE TIME BEING: a Christmas oratorio
               ∅   1+picc.1+ca.2+bcl.sx.0/2310/timp.perc/
                  acdn.bjo/str   Composer   20767
FÜR DICH, MEIN SCHATZ, arr ∅ 0010/0210/perc/str   Arranger MS:BBC MS 8326
3 HUNGARIAN FOLKSONGS, for women's chorus & orch
   1. The handsome butcher, in G   3. The old woman, in C
   2. Apple, apple, in E min
               ∅   2221/2320/perc/str   Composer   TO 1778
IMPROVISATIONS for jazz band & symphony orchestra, by M.Seiber & J.Dankworth
               ∅   Jazz band: 000.ssx.0/0440/perc/pf/cb
                  Orch: 2(picc)22(bcl)2/4331/timp.perc.tomtoms.
                        vib.xyl/hp/str   11'   Schott,1961   Misc 5559 B

INDIAN FANTASY no.1 "Mohana"	∅	1100/0000/timp.mba.xyl/gtr.hpsd/str	4'45"	Composer MS:BBC	MS 20272
2 JAZZOLETTES	∅	000.2sx.0/0110/perc/pf		Hansen,1958	22613
JOHNNY MINER: radio production	∅	112+bcl.0/0100/timp.perc/acdn.gtr.hp/str		Composer MS:BBC	MS 30199
LILLIBURLERO, arr	∅	2(picc)222/4231/timp.perc/str		Arranger MS:BBC	MS 20064

MORDVIN LULLABY for Contralto solo & chamber orch
   in F# min, arr Clements for chorus & orch
               ∅   2100/0000/cel.hp/str   Composer   TO 1381
NORTH COUNTRY LULLABY for Contralto solo, women's chorus & orch
   in B min   ∅   1120/0000/tri/hp/str   Composer   TO 1788
NOTTURNO for horn & strings   ∅ str   8'   Schott,1951   Misc 3580 B

SEIBER, Mátyás (cont)

OLD SCOTTISH AIR, arr for violin & orch
                         φ   hp[=pf]/str   FD & H,1954   23106
ON LEAVE, arr for Contralto solo, women's chorus & orch
                         φ   1121/2230/hp/str   Composer   TO 1309
PARTISAN SONG   φ   2(picc)222/4231/timp.perc/str   Arranger MS:BBC   MS 20472
PASTORALE AND BURLESQUE, for flute & strings
                         φ   str   6'30"   Schott   Misc 2364 C
The SAGA OF GRETTIR THE STRONG: radio production
                         φ   11+ca.21/1211/perc/hp/str   Composer MS:BBC   MS 30040
The STAR WE FOLLOW: radio programme (1955)
                             212+2bcl.1/3210/timp.perc/hp.om.pf/str   Composer MS:BBC   MS 31091 +
The STORY OF THE BALLET: radio production.   Medley of extracts from various ballets
                         φ   2(picc)222/4200/timp.perc.glock/cel.hp/
                             str/chorus   Arranger MS:BBC   MS 8242
SUR LE PONT D'AVIGNON   φ   2222/4231/timp.perc/str   Arranger MS:BBC   MS 20470
TIME HATH BROUGHT ME HITHER (May 1953)
                         ·   1000/1200/timp.perc/hpsd.lute.pf.virginals/
                             str   Composer MS:BBC   MS 30602
A VILLAGE GREEN   see   GOEHR, Walter: TRAVEL MUSIC
WHY DOESN'T HE TELL HER: Ukrainian folk song, arr for women's chorus & orch
    in A   φ   1+picc.121/2230/perc/str   Composer   TO 1310

SEITZ, Ernest (1893-

The WORLD IS WAITING FOR THE SUNRISE: song
    in C,   arr H.Carr   φ   2121/2230/timp.perc/hp/str   (Chappell)   TO 567
    in Bb, arr H.Carr   2121/2130/perc/hp/str   (Chappell)   LM G 5698

SEITZ, Friedrich

CONCERTO for violin & orch, op.15, in D
                             str   Laudy   2984

SEIXAS, José Antonio Carlos (1704-1742)

CONCERTO à 4 for harpsichord & strings, in A
    rev P.Salzmann   φ   str/cont   Gulbenkian Fdn,1960.Portugaliae Musica XV   25250 & MRL
OVERTURE 1a, in D (Abertura 1a)
    rev & real P.Salzmann φ   0200/2200/timp/hpsd/str   Gulbenkian Fdn,1969.Portugaliae Musica XVI   25259 & MRL
SINFONIA in Bb
    rev P.Salzmann   φ   str/cont(hpsd)   Gulbenkian Fdn 1969.Portugaliae Musica XVII   25258 & MRL

SEKACZ, Ilona

The RAMSHACKLE COMPANY: music for BBC radio drama production (1981)
                         φ   001(bcl)0/0110/perc.kib.vib/gtr.kantele.pf   (Composer)   MS 31810
TOM JONES: music for BBC radio drama production (1981)
                         φ   1(picc)111/1100/hpsd/vln   Composer MS:BBC   MS 31812

SEKLES, Bernhard (1872-1934)

Der DYBUK, op.35   φ   3(picc)2+ca.3(bcl)3(cbsn)/4331/timp.perc.tamtam/
                             hp/str   Schott   Misc 2088
SERENADE for 11 solo instruments, op.14
                         φ   1111/1000/hp/str   Rahter   Misc 1473

SELLE, Thomas (1599-1663)

ST. JOHN PASSION for SAATTB soli, SAATTB chorus & instruments
                    ∅   0002[=1+tbn]/0000/3vln[=3fl=2cntto+vla]vlc.cb
                        (Alternative combinations of instruments
                        ad lib)   Möseler   25676

SELLENICK, A.

MARCHE INDIENNE
    arr Petiot   PC 2+picc.22.4sx.2/2230/timp.perc/cel/str   Leduc   10541

SELMER, Johan Peter (1844-1910)

L'ANNÉE TERRIBLE: scène funèbre, op.4
                    ∅   2+picc.222/42.2cnt.31/timp.perc/hp/str   Hansen   Misc 461
CARNIVAL IN FLANDERS (Karneval i Flandern), op.32
                    ∅   2+picc.222/4231/timp.perc/str   Constantin   5453
IN DEN BERGEN: Norwegian fantasy, op.35
                    ∅   2+picc.222/4231/timp/str   Fritzsch   Misc 2283
NORDISCHER FESTZUG, op.11   ∅ 2+picc.222/4331/timp.perc/str   Warmuth   9413 B
PROMETHEUS: symphonic poem, op.50
                    ∅   2+picc.222/4331/timp.perc.bells/hp/str   Fritzsch   Misc 2279
2 SONGS OF SCHUMANN, arr,op.26
    1. Dein Angesicht, op.127, no.2   2. Schlusslied, op.25, no.26 (from 'Myrthen')
                    ∅   0000/2000/timp/str   Constantin   5449

SELVAGGI, Rito

SCARLATTI SUITE, arr from the harpsichord sonatas of Domenico Scarlatti
    1. Fuga del gatto   4. Marcia dei soldatini
    2. Notturno   5. Scherzo festivo
    3. Menuetto
                    ∅   2+picc.222/4300/timp.perc.bells.xyl/cel.hp.pf/
                        str   Universal   Misc 1527

SELVELLI, Aug G.

EI VATAN EI UMMI: former National Anthem of Turkey
                    PC 2(picc)222/4231/timp.perc/str   Benjamin   16363 +

SEMINI, C.F.

DIVERTIMENTO   ∅   2(picc)2(ca)22/3330/timp.perc/cel.pf/str   Curci,1960   Misc 8243

SEMLER, Paul

ALHAMBRA: caprice espagnole
    arr V.Nemeti   PC 1+picc.121/4230/timp.perc/str   Bosworth   3526 B

SEMMLER, A.

The ODYSSEY OF RUNYON JONES: incidental music
                    ∅   1121/2000/timp.perc/hp.pf/str   Composer MS:BBC MS 20123

SEMPRINI, A.

HISPANIA (Spanish rhapsody): medley, arr
     φ 2222/4231/timp.perc/hp/str   (UME) 23843 +
MEDITERRANEAN CONCERTO
 Extract (used as signature tune for Semprini programme)
     φ 2222/4230/timp.perc/hp/str   Composer 22968
 Themes, arr R.Binge PC 2222/4330/timp.perc/hp/str 3'30" AH & C,1950 19970
NEAPOLITAN: medley of Italian songs for piano & orch, arr
     φ 2222/4231/timp.perc/hp/str   BBC 23861 +

SENAILLÉ, J.B.

INTRODUCTION & ALLEGRO SPIRITOSO, for bassoon & orch
 arr J.M.Evans   φ 0200/2000/str   (Arranger) 26907

SENGER, Rudolf

BALLETT-SUITE, arr from music of Offenbach, orch H.J.Vieth
 1. Marsch   7. Bolero
 2. Angelus   8. Cavatine
 3. Polka   9. Menuett
 4. Zweitanz   10. Lamento (Burleske)
 5. Walzer   11. Ländler
 6. Burleskes Ständchen 12. Finale and Rondo
     φ 2(picc)2(ca)22/42.cnt.31/timp.perc.vib.xyl/
      gtr.hp.mand/cel/str   Bote & B Misc 643 C

SENSTIUS, Kai

CONCERTINO for flute & orch, op.5, in G
     φ 0111/1000/str   Kistner Misc 1560

SENTIS, José

MALAGA: valse expagnole
 arr F.Salabert   PC 112.sx.1/2230/perc/str   Salabert 689

SEREBRIER, José

COLORES MAGICOS: variations for harp & chamber orch (1971)
     φ 2(2picc)000/2211/[timp].perc/[cel].pf/str 12' Peer Int,1971 Misc 7685
TWELVE PLUS TWELVE, for wind & percussion (1969)
     φ 2+picc.2+ca.2+bcl.2+cbsn/4332/6perc(timp.
      cel.tamtam.vib.xyl)   12' Peters,1969 Misc 9158

SERLY, Tibor

LAMENT for strings   φ str   Southern Music,1963 Misc 6118
VARIATIONS ON A THEME OF ZOLTÁN KODÁLY see KODÁLY, Zoltan: VARIATIONS ON A THEME OF ZOLTÁN KODÁLY

SEROCKI, Kazimierz (1922-1981)

AD LIBITUM: 5 pieces for orch (1977)
     φ 3(picc)3(ca)3(bcl)3/4330/timp.3perc(bells.bgos.
      gongs.gro.mbn.mrcs.rattle.tamb.tamtam.tomtoms.
      tplbl.viv.whip.xyl)/cel.2hp.pf/
      str(24.-10.8.6)   16'-18' Moeck,1978 Misc 9670

SEROCKI, Kazimierz (cont)

AUGEN DER LUFE   see   EYES OF AIR
CONCERTO ALLA CADENZA for 6 recorders & orch (1974)

	φ timp.2perc(bells.bgos.gong.gro.mbn.mrc. rattle.tamb.tomtoms.tplbl.vib.whip.xba)/ cel.hp.hpsd.pf/str(20.-.6.4.3)	14'-16'	Moeck,1976	Misc 9574
CONCERTO for trombone & orch φ	3(picc)222/4300/timp.perc/str	20'	Polish SM,1956	Misc 8007

CONTINUUM: sextet for percussion (1965-6)

	φ timp.perc.bells.4cbells.16acym.2glock. mba.9Siamese gongs.6tamtam.3vib.2xba	13'	Moeck,1968	CM 54795
DRAMATIC STORY (1968-70) φ	4(4picc)2+ca.4(bcl)3(cbsn)/4331/timp.perc bells.glock.gong.mba.tamtam.vib.xba/ 2hp.pf/str		Moeck,1972	Misc 8026

EPISODES for strings & 3 percussion groups

	φ timp.perc.gong.tamtam/str	11'	Polish SM,1961	Misc 6524

EYES OF AIR (Augen der Luft): song cycle for Soprano solo & orch

1. Spotkanie   3. Chwila   5. Wieczor
2. Bez   4. Sciezka

	φ 2+2picc.04(bcl)0/4321/timp.perc.glock.mba. vib.xyl/gtr.2hp/str	12'	Moeck,1963	Misc 6497

FANTASIA ELEGIACA for organ & orch (1971/72)

	φ 3030/4330/3perc(timp.bells.kglock[=cel].mba. vib.xba/2hp.pf/str(24.0.6.6.6)	15' Moeck/Polish SM,1973		Misc 9011 (incl (org pt

FORTE E PIANO for 2 pianos & orch (1967)

	φ 3(3picc)1+ca.3(bcl).asx.tsx.1/4431/4perc(timp. bells.bgos.glock.kglock.gong.mbn.rattle.tamtam. tomtoms.vib.whip.xba(/hp/str(24.-.10.8.6)(2cb must be 5 stringed)	11'-12'		
		Moeck/Polish SM,1969		Misc 9844

FRESKI SYMFONICZNE   see   SYMPHONIC FRESCOES
GLEICHNISSE: 4 movements for Soprano solo & chamber & orch

1. Ich verkaufte Früchte (Sprzedawałam owoce)   2'50"
2. Das Licht in der Gartenlaube (Swiatło wogrodowej altanie) 2'25"
3. Nachts das Wort (W nocy słowo nic)   3'10"
4. Rascheln Tautropfen fallen (Szelest spaajyą krople rosy) 2'45"

	φ 1(picc)+afl.01+bcl.asx.0/0000/2perc.bells.mba.vib/ cel.2hp/6vln.3vla.3vlc	11'10"-13'	Moeck,1970	Misc 7858

HEART OF THE NIGHT: song cycle for Baritone solo & orch (1956)

1. Noc (Night)   4. Sanie (The Sleigh)
2. Epistoła do Zakochanych (Epistle to lovers)   5. Księzyc (The moon)
3. Spotkanie z Matka (Meeting with my mother)

	φ 3(picc)03(bcl)2/2000/perc.bells.mbn.xyl/ cel.gtr.2hp.mand/str		Polish SM,1959	Misc 7560
IMPROMPTU FANTASQUE (1973) φ	0.6rec.000/0000/2perc(bells.glock.mbn.xba)/ 3[=6]gtr.3[=6]mand.pf	9'-11'		
			Moeck/Polish SM,1975	Misc 9009
MUSICA CONCERTANTE (1958) φ	0.picc.00.bcl.sx.0/0100/perc.bells.mbn.vib/ 2hp/str	15'	Polish SM,1960	Misc 7441

NIOBE, for 2 reciters, chorus & orch (1966)

	φ 4(2picc)04(bcl)0/4400/perc.bells.vib.mba.xba/ 2hp.pf/str	13'	Moeck,1967	Misc 7482
SEGMENTI (1960/1 φ	1(picc)11+bcl.sx.1/11.Ebcnt.sxhn.01/timp.perc. bells.glock.gongs.mba.tamtam.vib.xyl/egtr.emand. hp.phsd(cel).pf/str	7'	Moeck,1962	Misc 6525

SERCE NOCY   see   HEART OF THE NIGHT
SINFONIETTA for double string orchestra

	φ str	13'55"	Polish SM,1957	Misc 4796 B

SEROCKI, Kazimierz (cont)

SYMPHONIC FRESCOES (Freski symfoniczne)(1963-4)
	φ	4(4picc)4(ca)4(bcl)4/6441/timp.perc.cbells.		
		glock.mba.vib.xyl[=xba]gtr.2hp.mand.2pf/str 11'40"	Polish SM,1966	Misc 6386

SYMPHONIES
No.1 (1952)	φ	4(2picc)23(E♭cl)+bcl.2/6431/timp.perc.bells.		
		xyl/pf/str	Polish SM,1954	Misc 3525
No.2 (Symphony of Song), for Soprano & Baritone soli, chorus & orch				
	φ	3(picc)2+ca.3(bcl)2+cbsn/4331/6perc(timp.		
		bells.mbn.vib.xyl)/hp.pf(cel)/str(14.12.10.8.6		
		or 16.14.12.10.8) 23'	Polish SM,1970	Misc 9169

SEROV, Aleksandr Nikolayevich (1820-1871)

COSSACK DANCE   φ 2+picc.2+ca.23/4231/timp.perc/str   Universal   1924

SERRADELL, N.

La GOLONDRINA (The Swallow)
in F, arr E.Griffiths		pf/str	(Ditson)	LM G 7062
arr M.L.Lake	PC	1+picc.12.2sx.1/2210/perc/str	C.Fischer	19720
arr G.Melachrino	φ	2121/2000/hp/str (also contains alternative		
		orchestration) 3'	(BBC)	24750

SERRALLONGA, Juan   see   GERHARD, Roberto

SESSIONS, Roger (1896-

The BLACK MASKERS: incidental music
1. Dance (Scene 1)	3. Dirge (Scene 4)			
2. Scene (Scene 3)	4. Finale (Scene 5)			
	φ	3(picc,bfl)3(ca)2+E♭cl+bcl.2+cbsn/4431/		
		timp.perc.tamtam.xyl/pf/str 22'	Cos Cob Press,1932	Misc 1482 C

New enlarged version (1923)
1. Dance (Scene 1)	3. Dirge (Scene 4)			
1a.Romualdo's song (Optional	4. Finale (Scene 5)			
2. Scene (Scene 3)				
	φ	3(picc:bfl)3(ca)2+E♭cl+bcl.2+cbsn/4431/timp.		
		perc.tamtam.xyl/pf/str/[S solo in No.1a] 26'	E.B.Marks,1963	Misc 8387

CONCERTI
Piano & orch	φ	2+picc.2+ca.2+bcl.2+cbsn/4231/timp.perc.		
		xyl/pf/str	[BBC]	Misc 6199
Violin & orch (1935)	φ	3(picc,afl)2(ca)+ca.3(E♭cl,acl,bthn)+bcl.2+cbsn/		
		4220/timp.perc/str 35'	E.B.Marks,1937	Misc 6438 B

IDYLL OF THEOCRITUS   for Soprano solo & orch
	φ	21+ca.1+bcl.2/4231/timp.perc/cel.hp/str 42'	E.B.Marks,1957	Misc 5057

SYMPHONIES
No.1 (1927)	φ	3(picc)3(ca)2+E♭cl+bcl.2+cbsn/4431/timp.perc		
		bells.xyl/pf/str	Cos Cob Press	Misc 835
No.2 (1946)	φ	0.picc.2+ca.2+bcl.2/4331/timp.perc.xyl/		
		pf/str 24'-30'	(G.Schirmer)	21342 +
No.3 (1957)	φ	2(picc)+picc.2+ca.2+E♭cl+bcl.2+cbsn/4231/		
		timp.perc.tamtam.vib.xyl/cel.hp/str 32'	E.B.Marks,1957	Misc 5776
No.4 (1958)	φ	0.picc.2+ca.2+E♭cl+bcl.2+cbsn/4331/timp.perc.		
		vib.xyl/hp.pf(cel)/str 24'	E.B.Marks,1963	Misc 6668 B
No.7 (1967)	φ	2+picc.2+ca.2+E♭cl+bcl.2+cbsn/4331/timp.perc.		
		(Chinese dm.glock.mba.vib.xyl)/hp.pf/str 20'	Merion Mus,1977	Misc 9527

ŠESTÁK, Zdeněk (1925-

SYMPHONY no.2 (1970)   ∅   4(4picc)3(3ca)3(E♭cl)+bcl.2+cbsn/6441/timp.perc.
                                   bells.gong/cel.hp.pf/str(18.16.12.10.8)   36'   Czech SM,1975   Misc 10444

SETER, Mordecai (1916-

JERUSALEM: symphony for chorus, brass & strings
                              ∅   0000/4441/str(no vln)   Israel MI,1970   Misc 9407 B
MIDNIGHT VIGIL, for Tenor solo, 3 choruses & orch
                              ∅   2(picc)+picc.2+ca.32+cbsn/4231/timp.perc.
                                   bells.glock.vib.xyl/cel.hp.pf/str   40'   Israel MI,1962   Misc 5843 B
RICERCAR, for violin, viola, cello & strings (1956)
                              ∅   str(no cb)   19'   Israel MI,1968   Misc 6751
SABBATH CANTATA, for SATB soli, double chorus & strings (1940)
                              ∅   str   31'   Israel MI,1955   Misc 6116

SÉVERAC, Déodat de (1873-1921)

Le COEUR DU MOULIN: opera
   Fête des vendanges: ballet music
                              ∅   3(2picc)2+ca.23/4440/timp.perc/2hp/str   Ed Mutuelle   14724

SEVERNE, Paul

MAYTIME: song
   in D, arr F.Cramer   1110/0000/hp.pf/str   (L.Wright)   LM G 4926

SEYFRIED, Ignaz von (1776-1841)

OX MINUET (often attrib to Haydn)
      arr L.Artok   PC 2222/2210/timp/str   Schott   10348
      arr S.Baynes   PC 2122/2230/timp/str   Boosey   6241 B

SEYNES, Georges de

PAGES D'ORCHESTRE: suite
   1. Près du rouet   2. Idylle aux champs   3. Heure d'automne
                              ∅   2222/2230/timp.perc/hp/str   Costallat   11607

SGAMBATI, Giovanni (1841-1914)

BERCEUSE-RÊVERIE, op.42, no.2
   orch J.Massenet   ∅   20.ca.11/1000/timp/hp/str   Schott   Misc 1822
CONCERTO for piano & orch, op.15 (also known as op.10), in G min
                              ∅   22(ca)22/4231/timp/str   Schott   Misc 1691
TE DEUM LAUDAMUS: andante solenne, for organ & orch, op.28 (also known as op.21)
                              ∅   22+ca.22/4231/timp/[org]/str   Schott   Misc 1629

SGATBERONI, Johann Anton (c.1708-1795)

CONCERTI
   Harpsichord & strings
      in G
         ed H.Federhofer & G.M.Schmeiser
                              ∅   str(no vlas)   Akad.Dr.Verl,1972 Misc 7824
      in A
         ed H.Federhofer & G.M.Schmeiser
                              ∅   str   Akad.Dr.Verl,1972 Misc 7824

SGRIZZI, Luciano (1910-

ENGLISH SUITE: suite based on English virginal music
                    ⌀   2+picc.2+ca.22/4231/timp.perc/pf/str   14'   Universal,1956   Misc 4650
SINFONIETTA ROCOCO for small orch
                    ⌀   1111/0000/str   13'   Oertel,1957   Misc 4745
SUITE NAPOLETANA for chamber orch
                    ⌀   1111/0000/str   Zerboni,1953   Misc 4212
VIOTTIANA: divertimento for small orch
                    ⌀   2(picc)111/2210/timp.perc/str   18'   Zerboni,1954   Misc 4217 B

SHADWELL, Charles

DOWN WITH THE CURTAIN: march
    arr R.Hanmer   PC 112.4sx.1/2320/perc/str   AH & C   18831 B
LULWORTH COVE
    arr G.Zalva   PC 2121/2230/timp/str   4'30"   Chappell   14093 Bp Cwe
WILL O' THE WISP   PC 1121/2210/perc/str   Liber   6165

SHANNON, J.R.

THAT'S AN IRISH LULLABY: song
    in E♭   ⌀   2222/4230/timp.perc/hp.pf/str   (Feldman)   17944

SHAPEY, Ralph (1921-

TESTAMENT TO MAN: trilogy for orch (1959)
    No.3 only - Rituals   ⌀   2+picc.2+ca.2+bcl.asx.tsx.barsx.2+cbsn/3221/
                              timp.4perc(anvil.cbell.gong.iron.tomtom.wdbl.xyl)/
                              pf/str   12'30"   Presser,1978   Misc 9690

SHAPIRO, Dan

FOLLOW THE GIRLS: musical comedy   see   CHARIG, Philip: FOLLOW THE GIRLS

SHAPORIN, Yuri Aleksandrovich (1889-1966)

The FLEA (Blokha): humourous suite, op.8
                    ⌀   2+2picc.02+E♭cl.21/2210/timp.perc.bells.
                        tamtam.xyl/2adomre.2tdomre.2hca.pf/cb   Russian SM,1935   Misc 1191 B
ON THE FIELD OF KULIKOVO: symphonic cantata for solo voices, chorus & orch
    Prologue   (12'30")   5. Now strikes the hour: chorus (8'30")
    1. Cavatina   (5')   6. The mother: lullaby   (4')
    2. While Mamai: chorus (11')   7. Our freedom: chorus   (4')
    3. Dimitri Donskoi: aria (3'30")   Epilogue   (10')
    4. Ballade of the Vitez (5'45")
                    ⌀   3(picc)3(ca)3(bcl)3(cbsn)/6341/timp.perc.
                        bells.tamtam/cel.2hp/str
                        Offstage: 0000/0600   Russian SM,1946   Misc 2382
SAGA OF THE BATTLE FOR THE RUSSIAN LAND: oratorio for Mz.TB soli, chorus & orch
                    ⌀   2+picc.2+ca.3(bcl)2+cbsn/4442/timp.perc.tamtam/
                        2hp/str   Soviet Composer,1969 Misc 7125
SYMPHONY for chorus & orch, op.11
                    ⌀   3(picc)+picc.4(ca)3(E♭cl)+bcl.4(cbsn)/4341/
                        timp.perc.glock.tamtam/cel.2hp.pf/str
                        banda: 83.4cnt.43.2bar   Russian SM,1972   Misc 7948

SHARAN, Shiva

JANA GANA MANA: National anthem of India (traditional), arr
          ø   2222/4230/timp.perc/hp[=pf]/str   Music Board Calcutta   Misc 3224

SHARP, Cecil J. (1859-1924)

ADMIRAL BENBOW: Somerset folksong, arr
                1010/0100/pf/str   (Novello)   MS 4496
ARGEERS: country dance, arr
  arr G.Williams   ø   1121/2110/perc/str   Arranger MS:BBC   MR 7074
BACCA PIPES JIG (6 variants)
  orch G.Williams   ø   1111/2120/perc/str   (Novello)   MS 7352
BEAUTIFUL NANCY: Gloucestershire folksong, arr
  in G min, orch G.Williams   ø   1111/1000/str   Arranger MS:BBC   MS 7689
BRENNAN ON THE MOOR: Somerset folksong, arr
  in D   1010/0100/str   (Novello)   MS 4493
BRISK YOUNG WIDOW: Somerset folksong, arr
  in C   ø   1120/1000/hp/str   (BBC)   LM G 10922
  in Bb, arr G.Williams   ø   1111/1000/timp.perc/str   (Novello)   MS 7688
CHAPS OF COCAIGNY: Somerset folksong, arr
  in E min, orch G.Williams   ø   1111/0000/str   (Novello)   MS 8197
The COASTS OF HIGH BARBARY, arr
  in Bb   1010/0100/str   (Novello)   MS 4494
DUKE OF MARLBOROUGH: Somerset folksong, arr
  in C, orch G.Williams   ø   1111/2100/perc/str   (Novello)   MS 7072
FAREWELL, NANCY: Somerset folksong, arr
  in G, orch G.Williams   ø   1111/2000/str   (Novello)   MS 6136
GEORDIE: Somerset folksong, arr
  in A min, orch G.Williams   ø   0111/1000/str   (Novello)   MS 6869
HIGH BARBARY   see   The COASTS OF HIGH BARBARY
I'M SEVENTEEN COME SUNDAY: Somerset folksong, arr
  in G   1010/0100/str   (Novello)   MS 4492
IN BRUTON TOWN: Somerset folksong, arr
  in E min   ø   1112/1000/timp/str   (Novello)   MS 6871
The LITTLE TURTLE DOVE: Somerset folksong, arr
  in C   1010/0100/str   (Novello)   MS 4495
LOWLANDS LOW: Cornish chantey, arr
  in Bb   1010/0100/str   (Novello)   MS 4497
MORRIS DANCE TUNES
  Selection arr C.Sharp, orch J.Buerger
          ø   2(picc)121/2230/timp.perc.tabor/hp/str   (Novello)   MS 6659
  Sets 1 & 2, collected C.Sharp & H.C.Macilwaine, arr G.Holst   see   HOLST, Gustav: MORRIS DANCE
    TUNES
OH, NO JOHN: folksong, arr
  in G, orch S.Prokofiev   ø   2021/0000/timp/cel/str   (Novello)   26864 +
  in A & G, orch J.Bürger ø   2121/1000/hp/str   2'15"   (Novello)   MS 6333
The ROBBER: folksong, arr
  in Bb min, orch C.Groves   ø   2121/2000/hp/str   (Arranger)   TO 1144
The WATCHET SAILOR: Somerset folksong, arr
  in C   1010/0100/str   (Novello)   MS 4500
WILLIAM TAYLOR: Somerset folksong, arr
  in D   1010/0100/str   (Novello)   MS 4498

SHARP, Vernon Latham

DEAREST OF ALL: song
  in C & F, arr G.Stacey   1010/0000/pf/str   (L.Wright)   LM G 3525
  in Eb, arr E.Griffiths   PC   101.2sx.0/0210/perc/str   L.Wright   18632 Ap
  in G, arr G.Williams   pf/str   Arranger MS:BBC   MS 20354

SHARP, Vernon Latham (cont)

SERENADE TO HAPPINESS: song
   in C, arr G.Stacey   1010/0000/pf/str   (L.Wright)   LM G 3672

SHARPE, Cedric (1891-

HOLYROOD SUITE
   1. Ruffs and laces: gavotte   3. Lute song: ariette
   2. Monsieur le Marquis: sarabande   4. Kitchen boys' dance: gigue
                  PC 1121/0100/timp.perc/str   Cramer   12516
POMPADOUR: suite
   1. Menuet pompeux   3. Gavotte gracieuse
   2. Air à danser (La Romanesca)   4. Tambourin et musette
      arr H.Bath   PC 2(picc)222/2230/timp.perc/hp/str   Liber   7494

SHARPE, Evelyn

DEVON: suite
   1. Barnstaple (Fairings)   3. Exeter (Twilight in the cloisters)
   2. Brixham (The witches' cave)   4. Cockington (Harvesters' dance)
      arr Walker   PC 1(picc)121/2210/perc/str   Cramer   6251 B
ESSEX: suite
   1. Mark's Gate (The mill wheel)   3. Alphamstone (The old forge)
   2. Waltham Abbey (From the belfry tower)   4. Little Dunmow (Country dance)
      arr Walker   PC 2(picc)2(ca)21/2210/timp.perc/cel.[hp].org/
                    str   Cramer   716
HAMPSHIRE: suite
   1. Boscombe (At Fisherman's Walk)   3. Beaulieu (The mill pond)
   2. Portsmouth (Saturday night)   4. Aldershot (On parade)
                  PC 1121/2210/timp.perc/str   Cramer   4931 B
IN OLD QUEBEC   PC 2121/2000/perc/str   2'30" Leonard Gould & B   12520
TALES FROM TOYLAND: suite
   1. The humming toy   3. March of the toy soldiers
   2. The three-legged bear   4. The fan dance
      arr Hickling   PC 1121/2210/perc/str   Leonard Gould & B   6256
The WAYSIDE CROSS   PC 1121/2210/timp/str   Cramer   721
WHEN THE GREAT RED DAWN IS SHINING: song
   in G   PC 1121/2230.euph/perc/str   Cramer   10363
   in A♭, arr H.Carr   ∅ 2121/2230/timp/hp/str   3'15"   (Cramer)   TO 256
   in B♭, arr J.Turner for SATB voices
                ∅ 1110/1000/hp/str   (Cramer)   LM G 9054
WHEN THE WORLD WAS A GARDEN OF LOVE: song
   in C   1010/0210/str   Cramer,1921   18168
WHERE THE MILESTONES END: song
   in G   1020/0010/timp.perc/str   Cramer,1918   18204

SHARPLES, Winston

GULLIVER'S TRAVELS, by W.Sharples, L.Robin, R.Rainger & S.Timberg
   Selection, arr G.Zalva   PC 1(picc)12.3sx.1/2220/timp.perc/str   Victoria   16235 B

SHAW, Artie

CONCERTO for clarinet & orch
   arr A.Bristov   ∅ 000.4sx.0/0330/perc/gtr.hp.pf/str   (C.Connelly)   TV 1381

SHAW, Geoffrey (1879-1943)

HOW FAR IS IT TO BETHLEHEM?: song
   in D min, arr J.O.Turner   ∅   111+bcl.0/1000/vib/cel.hp/str   (Novello)   LM G 10982
MERRY CHRISTMAS: song
   in C, arr Redman   str   Composer   WE 38
The SNOW LIES THICK: song
   in G, arr Redman   str   Composer   WE 37

SHAW, Martin (1875-1958)

CUCKOO: song
   in B♭   ∅   1121/0000/tri/str   1'   (Curwen)   TO 942
   in G, arr S.Robinson   pf/str   (Curwen)   MS 5673
EASTER CAROL
   in C, arr H.Carr   ∅   3222/4230/timp.perc/hp/str   1'30"   (Curwen)   18411
The FIRST NOWELL: carol, arr
   in D, arr W.K.Stanton   ∅   str   OUP   16688
GENTLE JESUS MEEK AND MILD
   arr Perry   PC   1121/0000/timp.perc/org/str   Hawkes   4970
HILLS OF THE NORTH REJOICE: hymn
   in E♭, arr S.Robinson   str   Arranger MS:BBC   MS 5677
I KNOW A BANK: song
   in B♭   1111/0000/str   1'30"   (Cramer)   TO 1790
   in F   ∅   1121/2000/cel[=vib].hp/str   (Cramer)   Misc 4363
   in F, arr J.Byfield   ∅   acdn.pf/str   (Cramer)   LM G 7890
OLD CLOTHES AND FINE CLOTHES: song
   in B♭, arr F.Cramer   pf/str   (Cramer)   LM G 4914
   in B♭, arr S.Robinson   ∅   2+picc.222/4231/bells.glock/str   (Cramer)   20061
REJOICE AND BE MERRY: carol, arr
   in G, arr W.K.Stanton   ∅   str   OUP   16457
WITH A VOICE OF SINGING: anthem for female voices & orch
   in C, orch T.Widdicombe   2222/4230/timp.perc/hp/str   (Curwen)   22643 +

SHAW, Robert (1916-

SET DOWN SERVANT: Negro spiritual, arr
   in A min, orch P.Hope   ∅   0002/4230/timp.perc/str   (Shawnee Press N.Y)   22787 +

SHAYNE, Gloria   see   REGNEY, Noel

SHCHEDRIN, Rodion Konstantinovich (1932-

CHAMBER SUITE (1961)
   1. Prelude   3. Amoroso   5. Finale
   2. Intermezzo   4. Cadenza & Fuga
                          ∅   acdn.hp/20vln.2cb   Russian SM,1976   Misc 9422
The CHIMES (Zvony)(1967): 2nd concerto for symphony orch
                          ∅   3(2picc)24(2bcl)2/4440/timp.perc.bells.tamtam/
                              pf(cel)/str   10'   Leeds (Canada)   Misc 7288 B
                          ∅   3(2picc)24(2bcl)2/4440/timp.perc.bells.tamtam/
                              pf(cel)/str   Russian SM,1972   Misc 7747
CONCERTI
   Piano & orch
     No.1   ∅   2+picc.2+ca.2+bcl.2/4331/timp.perc.glock.xyl/
                              hp/str   Russian SM,1959   Misc 6819
     No.2 (1966)   ∅   2+picc.222/4330/timp.perc.bells.vib/
                              jazz perc/str   Russian SM,1970   Misc 7298
   Symphony orch   see   The CHIMES
                         NAUGHTY LIMERICKS

SHCHEDRIN, Rodion Konstantinovich (cont)

The LITTLE HUMPBACKED HORSE: ballet (1955)
   Suite no.2
      1. Dance with balalaikas
      2. The brothers on the night watch
      3. Scherzino
      4. The firebird's feather
      5. The white mare gives Ivan the little humpbacked horse
      6. Duettino of Ivan and the Tsar-maid
      7. The Tsar waits for the Tsar-maid
      8. Adagietto
      9. Ivan at the bottom of the ocean
     10. Bathing in the boilers
     11. Girls' round dance and quadrille

	∅ 3(2picc)2+ca.3(E♭cl:bcl)2+cbsn/4331/timp.perc. bells.vib.xyl/cel.claviolina.2hp.pf/str	Russian SM,1968	Misc 6820

NAUGHTY LIMERICKS: concerto for orch (1963)

	∅ 2+picc.2+ca.3(bcl)2+cbsn/4440/timp.perc/ hp.pf/str	Russian SM,1971	Misc 7594

NOT LOVE ALONE: lyrical opera in 3 acts with epilogue (1961)

	∅ 3(picc)2+ca.3(bcl)2+cbsn/4331/timp.perc.glock. [klaxon].tamtam.xyl/cel.hp.pf/str Stageband: 0020/2201/perc/[bal]	Soviet Composer,1976	Misc 9397

SYMPHONIC FANFARES (Festive Overture)(1967)

	∅ 2+picc.222/4331/timp.perc/str	Russian SM,1970	Misc 7253

SYMPHONIES
   No.1 (1958)

	∅ 3(picc)2+ca.3(E♭cl:bcl)2+cbsn/4331/timp.perc. sbells.tamtam.whip/2[=1]hp.pf(cel)/str	Russian SM,1973	Misc 10353

   No.2 (25 preludes for orch)(1962-5)

	∅ 2(2picc)+picc.2(ca)+ca.2[=3]+E♭cl+bcl.2+cbsn/ 4441/timp.perc.bell.tamtam.xyl/hp.2pf/str	Russian SM,1969	Misc 6994

SHCHERBACHEV, Nikolai Vladimirovich (1853-?)

2 IDYLLES
   1. L'étoile du berger: tableau pastoral   2. En passant l'eau: scherzino

	∅ 2+picc.1+ca.22/4000/timp.perc/hp/str	Belaieff	6135
SÉRÉNADE, op.33	∅ 2+picc.222/4000/hp/str	Belaieff	6127

SHCHERBACHEV, Vladimir Vasilyevich (1889-1952)

L'ORAGE (The Thunderstorm): suite from the film
   1. Fanfares: les marchands s'amusent; l'orgue de barbarie; le Gostiny Dvor; l'arrivée de Boris
   2. Barbe et Koudriache
   3. Catherine
   4. Fête populaire
   5. Romance sentimentale
   6. Le boulevard; les grossacs à la promenade; rencontre de Catherine et Boris
   7. Les angoisses de Catherine; à l'église; souffrances de Catherine; l'orage

	∅ 3(picc)2+ca.3(E♭cl,bcl)3(cbsn)/4331/timp.perc. bells.tamtam.xyl/hp/str		Russian SM,1937	Misc 773 B
SYMPHONY no.1, op.5, in C min	∅ 3(picc)+bfl.2+ca.3+bcl.2+cbsn/4331/timp.perc/ 2hp/str	30'	Russian SM	13415

SHEBALIN, Vissarion Yakovlevich (1902-1963)

BALLET SUITE
   1. Introduction and waltz   5. Gavotte
   2. Nocturne   6. Slow waltz
   3. Dance of the maidens   7. Galop
   4. Adagio
      orch L.Feigin

∅	2+picc.2+ca.2+bcl.2+cbsn/4331/timp.perc.bells.xyl/ cel.hp/str	Russian SM,1973	Misc 8200

CONCERTI
   Horn & small orch, op.14, no.2

∅	2222/0210/timp.perc.xyl/hp/str	Russian SM,1960	Misc 5310

   Violin & strings, op.14, no.1

∅	str	Russian SM,1960	Misc 6786 B

DANCE TUNE
   orch V.Smirnova, arr V.Blok

∅	sdm.glock.tamb.tri.xyl/2acdn.5-pt bal.ensemble. 4-pt domre ensemble.kgusli	Russian SM,1962	Misc 1371

GLINKA: film
   3 Pieces from the film music, orch V.Smirnova, arr V.Blok
      Quadrille   Waltz   Kontrdans

∅	sdm.cym.glock/2acdn.5-pt bal ensemble. 4-pt domre ensemble.kgusli	Russian SM,1962	Misc 1371

MEDITATION
   orch V.Smirnova for orch of Russian folk instruments

∅	glock/2acdn.5-pt bal ensemble.4-pt domre ensemble. kgusli	Russian SM,1962	Misc 1371

SINFONIETTA for symphony orch
   Andante only
     orch A.Toninim for orch of Russian folk instruments, arr V.Blok

∅	cym.bdm/2acdn.5-pt bal ensemble.4-pt domre ensemble. kgusli	Russian SM,1962	Misc 1371

SYMPHONIES
   No.1, op.6, in F min (1925)

∅	3(picc)2+ca.2+bcl.2+cbsn/6331/timp.perc. bells.tamtam/str	Russian SM,1932	Misc 1826

   No.5, op.56, in C (1962)

∅	2+picc.2+ca.2+bcl.2+cbsn/4331/timp.perc/ cel.hp/str	Russian SM,1965	Misc 6756

The TAMING OF THE SHREW: opera, op.46

∅	2(picc)222/4231/timp.perc.bells.tamtam/ hp/str	Russian SM,1963	Misc 5886

SHELLEY, Harry Rowe

DANCE OF THE EGYPTIAN MAIDENS

arr O.Langey	PC	1121/2210/timp.perc/str	G.Schirmer	2614

FUJI-KO: Japanese intermezzo

arr Kiefert	PC	1121/2210/timp.perc/str	G.Schirmer	2614

HARK! HARK! MY SOUL, for Soprano solo, chorus & orch

in A♭	VS	1010/0100/org/str	Curwen	6680

The SNAKE CHARMER: oriental picture

arr A.Schmid	PC	1121/2210/timp.perc/str	G.Schirmer	2537

SHEPHERD, Arthur (1880-

HORIZONS: 4 Western pieces
   1. Westward   3. The old Chisholm trail
   2. The lone prairee   4. Canyons

∅	3+picc.2+ca.2+bcl.sx.2+cbsn/44.Dtpt.31/timp.perc glock.tamtam/cel.2hp.org.pf/str	Juilliard,1929	Misc 774

SHERIFF, Noam (1935-

MUSIC FOR WOODWINDS, TROMBONE, PIANO & BASS (1961)
ϕ 3(picc,afl)2+ca.2+bcl.2+cbsn/0010/pf/cb   16'   Israel MI,1962   Misc 7351

SHERMAN, Al

NO, NO, A THOUSAND TIMES NO: song by A.Sherman, A.Lewis & A.Silver
    in F, arr R.Redman   LS   1110/0210/perc/str   (FD & H)   LM G 4980

SHERMAN, Richard M.

The HAPPIEST MILLIONAIRE: film, music by R.M.Sherman & R.B.Sherman
    Extracts
        What's wrong with that: song for SATB voices & orch
                        ϕ 2(2picc)222/4331/timp.perc.glock.vib.xyl/
                             hp.pf(cel)/str   (Wonderland)   24698 +
MARY POPPINS: film, music by R.M.Sherman & R.B.Sherman
    Selections
        arr A.F.Fones   PC   1+picc.121/2230/perc/gtr.hp/str   4'25"
                                                        Disney/Wonderland,1965   24186 Cp
        Selection A for Soprano solo, chorus & orch, arr P.Hope & S.Torch
            1. Oh, a spoonful of sugar   3. Supercalifragilisticexpialidocious
            2. Let's go fly a kite   4. Reprise - Oh, a spoonful of sugar
                        ϕ 2(picc)222/4330/timp.perc.vib.xyl/cel.hp.pf/
                             str   (Walt Disney Music,1965)   24298 +
        Selection B for Soprano solo, chorus & orch, arr P.Hope & S.Torch
            1. Oh, a spoonful of sugar   3. Supercalifragilisticexpialidocious
            2. Chim, chim, cheree   4. Reprise - Oh, a spoonful of sugar
                        ϕ 2(picc)222/4331/timp.perc.glock.vib/hp.pf(cel)/
                             str   (Walt Disney Music,1965)   24297 +
The SLIPPER AND THE ROSE (The Story of Cinderella)
    Selection, arr N.Ingham ϕ 2(2picc,2afl)2+[ca].22/4331/timp.perc.glock.
                             vib.xyl/bgtr.gtr.hp.pf(cel,hpsd)/str   8'50"   (Noel Gay)   26105 B

SHERWIN, P.Manning (1903-

MUSIC FOR ROMANCE: song (from MAGYAR MELODY by G.Posford & Grün)
    in D & E♭, arr G.Stacey   VS   perc/str   (Chappell)   LM G 3420
    arr G.Posford (signature tune for programme 'Music for Romance')
                        ϕ 2222/4330/timp.perc/hp/str   Composer   TO 875
A NIGHTINGALE SANG IN BERKELEY SQUARE (from NEW FACES)
    in A♭ & E♭, arr J.Beaver ϕ 2121/2230/perc/hp/str   (P.Maurice)   TO 240
    arr P.Hope ϕ 2(picc)2(ca)22/4230/timp.glock.vib/cel.hp/
                             str   (P.Maurice)   26784
    arr A.Roper ϕ 2130/2230/perc(glock.kit.vib)/
                             gtr.hp[=pf(cel)]/str   P.Maurice   MLO 70
    arr Spoliansky   gtr.hp/perc.vib/str   Arranger MS:BBC   MS 20171
    arr N.Richardson for violin & orch
                        ϕ 1(picc)010/1000/perc/gtr.hp.pf/str   (P.Maurice)   25253
SOMETHING IN THE AIR: musical comedy
    Complete
        arr L.Ephraim ϕ 004(4sx)0/0320/perc/hp.2pf/str   (L.Ephraim)   21351 Awe
UNDER THE COUNTER
    Extracts
        The moment I saw you: song
            in D♭, arr R.Docker ϕ 21+ca.22/4030/perc/hp.pf(cel)/str   (P.Maurice)   24433 +
            in F, arr M.Mackie ϕ 2131/2000/timp.perc/hp.pf/str   (P.Maurice)   18534
WHO'S TAKING YOU HOME TO-NIGHT?: song
    in F, arr M.Mackie ϕ 2131/2230/timp.perc/hp.pf/str   (FD & H)   18574

SHIELD, William (1748-1829)

I AM A FRIAR OF ORDERS GREY: song attrib W.Shield _see_ REEVES, William: I AM A FRIAR OF
    ORDERS GREY

OLD TOWLER: song
  arr J.Desmond   PC 1222/2230.euph/perc/str   Hawkes   2682

ON BY THE SPUR: song
  in D   0201/2200/str   (Siddell)   17945

The PLOUGHBOY: song
  in F & G, arr B.Britten for Baritone & orch
                ø 0.picc.000/0000/str   (Boosey)   23406 +

ROSINA: comic opera
  Overture
    ed R.Fiske   ø 1+picc.222/2000/str   (Editor)   Misc 10382
  Extracts
    I've kissed and I've prattled: duet
      in A   ø 2001/0000/str   (GB-Lbl Add.Ms.33815)   27088
    Light as thistledown: song
      in C   ø 0202/2000/str   (GB-Lbm G.363 (17))   22144 +
    When William at eve: song
      in D   ø 2001/0000/str   (GB-Lbl Add.Ms 33815)   27087

The WCLF: song (from 'The Castle of Andalusia')
  in D   øLS 1022/4210/timp/str   BBC   23904 Awa +

SHIELDS, Ren

The NEW ALADDIN
  Extracts
    Waltz me around again, Willie: song
      in B♭   PC 2121/2220/perc/pf/str   (Feldman)   MS 137
      in A, arr H.Carr (refrain only)
               ø 2121/2230/perc/hp/str   (Feldman)   TO 1180

SHIFRIN, Seymour

CHAMBER SYMPHONY   ø 102+bcl.0/2020/str   20'   Peters,1960   Misc 5472 B

3 PIECES FOR ORCHESTRA (1958) ø 3(picc)3(ca)3(bcl)2+cbsn/4331/timp.perc.glock.xyl/
                          cel.hp/str   18'   Peters,1959   Misc 5474

SHILKRET, Nat.

CHANTE D'AMOUR, by N.Shilkret & A.Grechaninov
  arr Schoenfeld   PC 1121/2210/timp/str   Chappell   10695

WEE BIT O' HEART: Scottish episode
  arr Roberts   PC 1121/2210/timp.perc/str   C.Fischer   6692

SHIPLEY, Edward

NOCTURNE (1974)   ø str(min 8.0.3.2.1)   Fentone,1976   Misc 9028

THRENI (1973)(Previously entitled 'Sonata for strings')
                  ø str(min 11.0.4.3.2)   Fentone,1976   Misc 9029

SHIRLEY, Lilian

UNTIL WE MEET AGAIN: song
  in A♭, arr Weaver   PC 2222/2440/timp.perc/str   L.Wright   16883

SHISHIDO, Mutsuo

CONCERTI
    Piano & orch
        No.2 (1975)   φ   3(3picc)333/4331/4perc(2ptimp.bells.3cbell.4bgo.
                                 conga.Chinese-cym.glock.gro.hi-hat.mrc.mba.rattle.
                                 tamtam.3tomtom.vib.whip.xyl)/cel.hp/
                                 str(12.12.10.8.6)(3cbs must be 5-stringed)   Neue Musik,1978   Misc 10337

SHISHOV, Ivan P.

10 FOLK SONGS (Volkslieder)
    1. Buryat song   6. A Chuvash joke song
    2. Song from the Altai   7. A lullaby from the Kursk District
    3. Song of the Goldish maiden   8. A Goldish partisan song
    4. Song of the young communists (from Yakutsk)   9. Song of the Siberian Young communists
    5. Moldavian Lullaby   10. Tochfi (A man's name) A Tartar
                          φ   2222/2000/perc/str   Russian SM,1932   10024

SHLONSKY, Verdina

GLÜHENDE RÄTSEL for Mezzo-soprano (or Baritone) solo & chamber orch
                          φ   11+ca.11/1100/timp.perc(tamtam.vib)/
                              cel.pf/str(no vlns)   (Composer,1977)   Misc 9563

SHORT, E.P.

GOBLIN'S FROLIC: humoresque
    arr Engleman   PC   1(picc)12.2sx.1/2230/timp.perc/str   Bosworth   8341

SHOSTAKOVICH, Dmitri Dmitriyevich (1906-1975)

BALLET SUITE no.1 (1949) [published as op.84]
    1. Valse lyrique   4. Polka
    2. Dance   5. Valse-badinage
    3. Romance   6. Galop
                          φ   2(picc)121/3221/timp.perc.glock.vib.xyl/
                              cel.pf/str   Russian SM,1950   24106 +
BELINSKI (Vissarion Belinski): film music, op.85 (1950)
    Suite
        1. Overture   5. Song without words
        2. Melancholy little song, for chorus & orch   6. Scene
        3. Strength of the Nation, for TB chorus & orch   7. Finale
        4. Intermezzo
                          φ   2+picc.332+cbsn/4331/timp.perc.bells.
                              tamtam.xyl/hp/str   Russian SM,1960   Misc 5679 B
The BOLT (Der Bolzen): ballet, op.27 (1930/31)
    Satirical dance (polka)
        transcr Q.Maganini φ   1(picc)121/2210/timp.perc/str   Aff Mus Corp,1940   16415
CHAMBER SYMPHONY see SYMPHONIES: Chamber Symphony, op.110 bis, in C
CONCERTI
    Cello & orch
        No.1, op.107, in E♭ (1959)
            ed L.Atovmyan   φ   2(picc)222(cbsn)/1000/timp/cel/str   29'   Russian SM,1960/61   24709 +
            ed L.Roth   φ   2(picc)222(cbsn)/1000/timp/cel/str   MCA/Leeds,1966   Misc 9073
        No.2, op.126   φ   1+picc.223(cbsn)/2000/timp.perc.xyl/2hp/str
                                                                            Boosey & H/Anglo Soviet,1968   Misc 6775
                          φ   1+picc.223(cbsn)/2000/timp.perc.xyl/2hp/
                              str   30'   Russian SM,1970   Misc 7428

SHOSTAKOVICH, Dmitri Dmitriyevich (cont)

CONCERT! (cont)
  Piano & orch
    No.2, op.102, in F (1956/7)

	ø	2+picc.222/4000/timp.perc/str	19'25"	Russian SM,1957	24281
	ø	2+picc.222/4000/timp.perc/str		Leeds Mus, 1957	Misc 6074

  Piano, Trumpet & strings
    op.35, in C min (1933)   ø str   19'-24' Russian SM,1934   12771

  Violin & orch
    No.1, op.77, in A min (1947-8)(Revised 1955 as op.99)
      Revised version   ø 3(picc)3(ca)3(bcl)3(cbsn)/4001/timp.perc/
                            cel.2hp/str   33'-36'30"   PL 406 &   )
                                            Anglo-Soviet/Russian SM,1957 Misc 4774 C)
      No.2, op.129, in C# min ø 1+picc.222+cbsn/4000/timp.perc/str 29'
                                             Boosey & H/Anglo-Soviet,1968 Misc 6776
                      ø 1+picc.222+cbsn/4000/timp.perc/str   Russian SM,1970 Misc 7414

The EXECUTION OF STEPHAN RAZIN: poem for Bass solo, chorus & orch, op.119
                      ø 2+picc.2+ca.2+Ebcl+bcl.2+cbsn/4331/
                           timp.perc.bells.xyl/cel.hp.pf/str   Russian SM,1966 Misc 6417

FESTIVAL (HOLIDAY) OVERTURE, op.96 (1954)
                      ø 2+picc.332+cbsn/4331/timp.perc/str   Russian SM,1955 21904 + An B

FIRST ECHELON: film music
  11 fragments [published as op.99](1956)

1. Overture	7. Intermezzo
2. The Train	8. Waltz
3. Song of Youth, for chorus & orch	9. Song-Maidens' sweetness, for SA chorus & orch
4. The Field	10. Fire
5. Evening Landscape	11. New Settlers
6. The Quarry	

                      ø 2+picc.33.3sx.2+cbsn/4331/timp.perc.bells.
                         tamtam.vib.xyl/cel.hp.pf/str   Russian SM,1962 Misc 5775

FIVE DAYS AND FIVE NIGHTS (Dresden Art Gallery): film
  Suite

1. Introduction	4. Interlude
2. Dresden in Ruins	5. Finale
3. Liberated Dresden	

                      ø 2+picc.332+cbsn/4331/timp.perc.bells/
                         hp.pf/str   Russian SM,1970 Misc 7427

The GADFLY (Die Pferdebremse): film music, op.97 (1955)
  Suite

1. Overture	7. Introduction (1'50")
2. Contradance	8. Romance
3. Folk feast (2'40")	9. Intermezzo
4. Interlude	10. Nocturne (3'20")
5. Waltz - 'Barrel-organ' (2')	11. Scene
6. Galop (1'55")	12. Finale

                      ø 2+picc.33(3sx)3(cbsn)/4431/timp.perc.bells.
                       tamtam.xyl/cel.hp.pf/str   Russian SM,1960 Misc 5513 C
      No.3 only   2+picc.13+bcl.1/4331/hp/str (Material copied   (PL 429 - ø
                       & adapted for use by the Radio Orchestra) Russian SM/Boosey(H) (Misc 5513

The GOLDEN AGE (Das Goldene Zeitalter/L'Age D'Or): ballet, op.22 (1929/30)
  Suite

1. Introduction	3. Polka
2. Adagio	4. Dance

                      ø 1+picc.1+ca.1+Ebcl+bcl.1+cbsn/4431.bar/timp.perc.
                         tamtam.xyl/hmn/str   Russian SM,1935 13782 B +
      No.3 only
        arr Q.Maganini PC 1(picc)1+ca.22/2220/perc.xyl/str   2' Edn Musicus,1944 16378
      No.4 only
        arr C.Waters   PC 2(picc)121/2230/timp.perc.xyl/acdn.hp/str Anglo-Soviet,1957/Boosey 22672 B

SHOSTAKOVICH, Dmitri Dmitriyevich (cont)

The GOLDEN MOUNTAINS (The Golden Hills/Goldene Berge/Les Monts D'Or
   Suite
      1. Introduction   4. Intermezzo
      2. Valse   5. Marche funèbre
      3. Fugue   6. Finale
                ø   2+picc.2+ca.2+bcl.3sx.2+cbsn/4842/timp.perc.
                   bells.xyl/gtr.2hp.org/str   Russian SM,1935   Misc 1710 B
HAMLET: incidental music to the play, op.32 (1931-32)
   Suite, op.32a
      1. Introduction & night patrol   8. The banquet
      2. Funeral march   9. Ophelia's song
      3. Fanfare & dance music   10. Cradle song
      4. Longing   11. Requiem
      5. The strolling players   12. The tournament
      6. Procession   13. Fortinbras march
      7. Musical pantomime
               øPC 1111/2211/timp.perc/str   (Russian SM,1960)   23635 +
   2 Fragments from 2nd series
      1. Pantomime   2. Fortinbras march
       arr N.Rakov   PC 1111/2211/timp.perc/hmn/str   Russian SM,1936   18964 +
HAMLET: incidental music to the film, op.116
   Suite, op.116a
      1. Introduction   5. Scene of the poisoning
      2. Ball at the palace   6. The arrival and scene of the players
      3. The Ghost   7. The duel and death of Hamlet
      4. In the garden
                ø   2+picc.222/4331/timp.perc.bells.tamtam/
                   hp.pf/str   Russian SM,1968   Misc 7005
        No.8 only   2+picc.222/4231/timp.perc.tamtam.whip/str   (Russian SM)   26670 + #
6 JAPANESE SONGS for Tenor solo & orch, op.21 (1928-32)
               ø   2+picc.22+E♭cl+bcl.2+cbsn/4331/timp.perc.glock.
                   tamtam.xyl/2hp/str   (Boosey & H)   26774
KATERINA IZMAILOVA: opera, op.114 (1963)(Revised version of Lady Macbeth of Mtsensk, op.29)
               ø   2(picc,afl)+picc.2+ca.2+E♭cl+bcl.2+cbsn/4331/
                   timp.perc.glock.xyl/cel.2hp/str   Russian SM,1965   Misc 6313
LADY MACBETH OF MTSENSK: opera, op.29 (1930-32)   see also KATERINA IZMAILOVA
   3 fragments
      1. Burying the corpse in the cellar   3. The drunks at the wedding
      2. The ghost disappears
       arr Q.Maganini   ø   2+picc.2+ca.22/4231/timp.perc/str   Edn Musicus,1940   16439
MAXIM: fragments from the film trilogy, for chorus & orch, with optional brass band, op.50a
   arr L.Atovmyan   ø   2+picc.34(bcl)+E♭cl.2+cbsn/4331/timp.perc.
                   glock.xyl/2hp/str   Russian SM,1961   Misc 6421
MY DEAR FATHERLAND (Otchizna): oratorio for reciter, STB soli, SSATTB chorus & orch, op.63
               ø   1+picc.222/3331/timp.perc.bells/[balalaika].pf/
                   str   Russian SM,1972   Misc 7886
NEW BABYLON: suite from film music, op.18
      1. War   4. Operetta
      2. Paris   5. Paris has stood for centuries
      3. The siege of Paris   6. Versailles
                ø   1111/2110/3perc(timp.flex.tamtam.xyl)/
                   pf/str   50'   Russian SM,1976   Misc 9096
The NOSE: opera, op.15 (1927/28)
   Overture
       arr Q.Maganini   PC 0.picc.121/1210/perc/pf/str   2'30" Edn Musicus,1940   16450
   Act 1   percussion pts only   BBC   25453

SHOSTAKOVICH, Dmitri Dmitriyevich (cont)

The NOSE (cont)
Suite for Tenor & Bass soli & orch, op.15a
1. Overture   5. Ivan's song
2. Kovalyov's aria   6. Kovalyov's monlogue
3. Entr'acte I   7. Galop
4. Entr'acte II

∅	1(picc)1(ca)1(bcl)1(cbsn)/1110/perc.bells.		
	tamtam.xyl/2hp/str	(Universal)	Misc 5546 B +

OCTOBER: symphonic poem, op.131 [also published as op.132](1967)

∅	2+picc.2+ca.32+cbsn/4331/timp.perc/str	Russian SM,1969	Misc 7122 B
∅	2+picc.2+ca.32+cbsn/4331/timp.perc/str	Peters	Misc 7122

OCTOBER SYMPHONY   see   SYMPHONIES: No.2
OVER THE HOMELAND THE SUN SHINES (Über unserer Heimat scheint die Sonne): cantata for SA children's
voices, chorus & orch, op.90

∅	2+picc.332/4331/timp.perc.bells.tamtam/		
	hp/str		
	Off-stage: 0000/0330	Russian SM,1963	Misc 4324

OVERTURE on Russina and Kirghiz folk themes, op.115

∅	2+picc.222+cbsn/4231/timp.perc/str	Russian SM,1967	Misc 6590 B

2 PIECES, op.11

1. Prelude (1924)	∅	str	9'30"	Russian SM,1928	10164
rev & ed Q.Maganini	∅	str		Edn Musicus	15126
2. Scherzo (1925)	∅	str	4'	Russian SM,1928	10164

PLIASKA (Dance for wind orch)
orch M.Vakhutinsky

∅	[1][1]3[=2]+E♭cl.0/2[=1]2[=1].2cnt.3[=2].2E♭atbn.		
	3[=2]B♭ttbn.1+bar/perc	Russian SM,1971	25329

POEM OF WORK, for chorus & orch ∅ 2+picc.222/4331/timp.perc/hp/str   Russian SM,1956   Misc 7014
PRELUDE in E♭ min [orig for piano, op.34, no.14]
arr L.Stokowski   ∅ 32+ca.33+cbsn/4441/timp.perc/hp/str   Broude,1947   20660
8 PRELUDES for piano & orch (from "24 Preludes for piano, op.34"), arr M.Kalemen
1. (orig no. 7), in A   5. (orig no.14), in E♭ min
2. (orig no.10), in C# min   6. (orig no.24), in D min
3. (orig no.22), in G min   7. (orig no.17), in A♭
4. (orig no. 8), in F# min   8. (orig no. 5), in D

∅	1111/1110/pf(cel)/str	Litolff/Peters,1971	Misc 7604

SALUTE TO LIFE (Song of Youth): Soviet song

in G, arr L.Isaacs	∅	3222/2100/perc/hp/str	Arranger	13006
arr L.Isaacs		3122/2100/perc/hp/str	Arranger MS:BBC	MS 1546

SONG OF THE FORESTS (Song of the woods/Das Lied von den Wäldern): oratorio for Tenor & Bass soli,
boys' chorus, chorus & orch, op.81

Original Russian text	∅	3(picc)2+ca.32/4991/timp.perc.bells/2hp/str	Russian SM,1950	Misc 3948

With slightly different Russian text from 1950 edn

∅	3(picc)2+ca.32/4991/timp.perc.bells/2hp/str	Russian SM,1962	Misc 6690

SYMPHONIES
No.1, op.10, in F min (1924/25)

∅	3222/4331/timp.perc/pf/str	27'45"-33'30" Russian SM	12830 B +

No.2, op.14 'October Symphony' (Symphonic Prologue,1927)

∅	2+picc.222/4331/timp.perc.bells/str/chorus	Russian SM,1927	16990 +

No.3, op.20 'First of May' (1929/30)

∅	2+picc.222/4231/timp.perc.bells.tamtam.xyl/		
	str/chorus	30' Russian SM,1932	12955

No.4, op.43 (1935/36)

∅	4+2picc.4(ca)4+E♭cl+bcl.3+cbsn/8432/2timp.perc.		
	bells.tamtam.xyl/cel.2hp/str	Russian SM,1962	23839 +

SHOSTAKOVICH, Dmitri Dmitriyevich (cont)

SYMPHONIES
    No.5, op.47, in D min (1937)   2+picc.22+E♭cl.2+cbsn/4331/timp.perc.bells.tamtam.xyl/
                                          2[-1]hp.pf(cel)/str   Boosey & H/(Russian SM)(H)   PL 685 An
                                  ∅   2+picc.2+E♭cl.22+cbsn/4331/timp.perc.bells.tamtam.xyl/
                                          2[-1]hp.pf(cel)/str   Russian SM   24009 Amv
        2nd mvt (Scherzo) only
            transcr Q.Maganini   ∅   2222/4331/timp.perc.xyl/hp/str   Edn Musicus,1942   2882
    No.6, op.54, in B min (1937)
                                  ∅   2+picc.2+ca.3(E♭cl)+bcl.3(cbsn)/4331/
                                          timp.perc.tamtam.xyl/str   32'50"-35'15"Anglo-Soviet   Misc 2888 B
                                  ∅   2+picc.2+ca.3(E♭cl)+bcl.3(cbsn)/4331/
                                          timp.perc.tamtam.xyl/str   Russian SM,1962/68   Misc 917 D
    No.7, op.60, in C 'Leningrad Symphony' (1941)
                                  ∅   3(picc,bfl)2+ca.3(E♭cl)+bcl.2+cbsn/8661/
                                          timp.perc.tamtam.xyl/2hp.pf/str   72'   Russian SM,1942   Misc 2193 C
                                  ∅   3(picc,bfl)2+ca.3(E♭cl)+bcl.2+cbsn/8661/
                                          timp.perc.tamtam.xyl/2hp.pf/str   Peters   Misc ?770
    No.8, op.65, in C min (1943)
                                  ∅   4(2picc)2+ca.2+E♭cl+bcl.3(cbsn)/4331/
                                          timp.perc.tamtam.xyl/str   Breitkopf,1947   21435 +
                                  ∅   4(2picc)2+ca.2+E♭cl+bcl.3(cbsn)/4331/
                                          timp.perc.tamtam.xyl/str   52'-64'15"Russian SM,1946   Misc 1287
    No.9, op.70, in E♭ (1945)   ∅   2+picc.222/4231/timp.perc/str   22'-36'   Breitkopf,1947   21434 +
    No.10, op.93, in E min (1953)
                                  ∅   2(picc)+picc.3(ca)2+E♭cl.2+cbsn/4331/
                                          timp.perc.tamtam.xyl/str   52'   Russian SM,1964   23980 Cwe +
    No.11, op.103, in G min 'The Year of 1905' (1957)
        ed L.Atovmyan   ∅   3(picc)3(ca)3(bcl)3(cbsn)/4331/
                                          timp.perc.bells.xyl/cel.hp/str   53'30"-63'30"
                                                                                        Russian SM,1958   23343 + Cwe
    No.12, op.112 'The Year of 1917' (1961)
                                  ∅   3(picc)333(cbsn)/4331/timp.perc.tamtam/
                                          str   34'-38'30" Breitkopf   24039
                                  ∅   3(picc)333(cbsn)/4331/timp.perc.tamtam/
                                          str   Russian SM,1961/64   Misc 5759 B
    No.13, op.113 (Babi Yar)(1962)
                                  ∅   2+picc.3(ca)3(E♭cl,bcl)3(cbsn)/4331/timp.perc.
                                          bells.glock.xyl/cel.2[-4]hp/str/
                                          B-solo.mv-chorus   56'   Leeds Mus,1970   Misc 7382
                                  ∅   2+picc.3(ca)3(E♭cl,bcl)3(cbsn)/4331/timp.perc.
                                          bells.glock.xyl/cel.2[-4]hp/str/
                                          B-solo.mv-chorus   Russian SM,1971   Misc 7721
    No.14, op.135   ∅   0000/0000/perc.bells.tomtoms.vib.whip.xyl/
                                          cel/str(10.-.4.3.2)(cbs must be 5-stringed)/   (Misc 7717 &
                                          Soprano & Bass soli   Russian SM,1971   (PL 605 Amv
    No.15, op.141, in A   ∅   2+picc.222/4231/timp.perc.tamtam.glock.vib/
                                          cel/str (30.12.12.10)   Anglo-Soviet,1972   Misc 8156
                                  ∅   2+picc.222/4231/timp.perc.glock.tamtam.vib.xyl/
                                          cel/str(30.12.12.10)   Russian SM,1972   Misc 8162
    Chamber Symphony, op.110 bis, in C min, arr R.Barshai from quartet for strings, no.8, op.110
                                  ∅   str   Peters,1967   Misc 7812
The UNFORGETTABLE YEAR OF 1919 (Das unvergessliche Jahr 1919): film music, op.89 (1951)
    Suite, op.89a
        1. Introduction   5. The storming of Krasnaya Gorka (The Red Hill)
        2. Romance - Shibayev's meeting with Katya   6. Interlude
        3. Scene from the sea battle   7. Finale
        4. Scherzo
                                  ∅   3(picc)332+cbsn/4661/timp.perc.bells.tamtam.xyl/
                                          cel.hp.pf/str   Russian SM,1955   Misc 5255

SHOSTAKOVICH, Dmitri Dmitriyevich (cont)

WALTZ no.1
    arr C.Waters   PC 1+picc.121/2230/timp.perc.bells.xyl/hp/str 3'30"   Hawkes,1960   24669
A YEAR IS LIKE A LIFETIME: film music, op.120
    Suite, ed L.Atovmyan

1. Overture	5. Scene (A little waltz)
2. Barricades	6. Battle
3. Interlude	7. Finale
4. Farewell (Monologue)	

                  ø 2+picc.222/4331/timp.perc.bell/str   Russian SM,1970 Misc 7299
The YOUNG GUARD (Die junge Garde): film music, op.75
    Suite (fragments)

1. Introduction	5. Song of young guardsmen
2. By the river	6. Death of the heroes
3. Scherzo	7. Apotheosis
4. Turbulent night	

                  ø 3(picc)2(ca)3(E♭cl)2+cbsn/4661/timp.perc/
                     str   Russian SM,1954 Misc 5972

SHRIMPTON, Bert

WHO'S IN FRONT?: song for voice & orch
                  PC 1121/2220/perc/str   Composer MS:BBC MS 20492

SHTERICH, E.

WALTZ on a theme from Weber's 'Oberon'
    orch M.I.Glinka, ed G.V.Kirkor
                  ø 1020/2110/timp/str   Russian SM,1968.CW 18   MRL

SHULDHAM SHAW, Patrick

The CRYSTAL SPRING, arr for voice & small orch
    in G   1110/0000/str   Arranger   WE 19
GOWER WASSAIL SONG, arr for Tenor & orch
    in D min   1121/0000/str   Arranger   WE 16
The HOLLY AND THE IVY, arr for voice & small orch
    in G   1111/0000/str   Arranger   WE 20
4 SOMERSET FOLK SONGS, arr for Tenor & orch

1. I'm seventeen come Sunday, in F# min	3. Heave away, my Johnny, in B
2. O waly, waly, in B	4. The apple tree wassail, in A

                    1+picc.120/0000/str   Arranger   WE 17

SHULMAN, Alan (1915-

THRENODY   ø   str   5'30"   Tetra,1974 Misc 8481

SIBELIUS, Jean (1865-1957)

ANDANTE FESTIVO   ø   str   5'   Westerlund   18839
ARIOSO, for voice & strings, op.3
                  ø   str   Southern Mus Co,1960 23382
AUTREFOIS (Scène pastorale) see 3 PIECES, op.96
AUTUMN NIGHT (Herbstabend): song, op.38, no.1
    in B min   ø 022+bcl.2+cbsn/4030/perc/hp/str   Breitkopf,1906-7 20478 +
The BARD: tone poem, op.64 ø 222+bcl.2/4231/timp.perc/hp/str 6'30"-7'30" Breitkopf   8205 C

SIBELIUS, Jean (cont)

BELSHAZZAR'S FEAST: incidental music, op.51
   1. Oriental procession   3. Night music
   2. Solitude   4. Khadra's dance

	⏀	2(picc)120/2000/perc/str		Schlesinger	1323 Bni
arr Pagel	PC	2(picc)120/2110/timp.perc/str		Schlesinger	13986

BLACK ROSES (Roses funèbres): song, op.36, no.1
   in B♭ min, orch L.Wurmser   ⏀ 21+ca.2+bcl.2/4231/timp/hp/str   (Breitkopf)   20074

CANZONETTA, op.62a   ⏀ str   Breitkopf   1325 Bwa

The CAPTIVE QUEEN, for chorus & orch, op.48
                      ⏀ 2(picc)21+bcl.1/4230/timp.perc/str   Schlesinger   15381

CONCERTO for violin & orch, op.47, in D min
                      ⏀ 2222/4230/timp/str   30'-34'15" Schlesinger   6200 + Amv B

DANCE INTERMEZZO <u>see</u> 2 PIECES for orch, op.45
The DRYADS   <u>see</u> 2 PIECES for orch, op.45

EVERYMAN (Jedermann): incidental music, op.83
                      ⏀ 2121/2200/timp.perc/org.pf/str   (Finnish Radio Helsinki,1955)   21752 +

The FERRYMAN'S BRIDES: Finnish ballade for voice & orch, op.33
                      ⏀ 2222/4230/timp.perc/str   11'-12' Breitkopf   19544

FINLANDIA: tone poem, op.26   (4232 Amv Es

	⏀	2222/4331/timp.perc/str	6'30"-9'	Breitkopf	(Fn Gwa
arr Humiston	PC	1121/2210/timp/org/str		Breitkopf	735 Cp D

   arr G.Vinter for combined orch & military band
                      ⏀ 2222/4230/perc/str/full mil band   (Breitkopf)   23263 +

FROM THE NORTH
   arr Bauer & Schmid   ⏀ 222.2sx.2/4331/timp.perc/hp/str   G.Schirmer   5007

HUMORESQUES for violin & orch

No.1, op.87, no.1	⏀	2222/2000/timp/str	3'30"	W.Hansen,1923/42	19044
	⏀	2222/2000/timp/str		W.Hansen,1923/42	Misc 2890 B
No.2, op.87, no.2	⏀	0000/2000/timp/str	2'40"	W.Hansen,1923/42	19988
	⏀	0000/2000/timp/str		W.Hansen,1923/42	Misc 2890 B
No.3, op.89, no.1					
ed & rev J.A.Burt	⏀	str		W.Hansen,1923	19989
ed & rev J.A.Burt	⏀	str		W.Hansen,1923/42	Misc 2891 B
No.4, op.89, no.2					
ed & rev J.A.Burt	⏀	str		W.Hansen,1923	19990
ed & rev J.A.Burt	⏀	str		W.Hansen,1923/42	Misc 2891 B
No.5, op.89, no.3					
ed & rev J.A.Burt	⏀	2022/0000/str		W.Hansen,1923	19991
ed & rev J.A.Burt	⏀	2022/0000/str		W.Hansen,1923/42	Misc 2891
No.6, op.89, no.4					
ed & rev J.A.Burt	⏀	2002/0000/str		W.Hansen,1923	16922
ed & rev J.A.Burt	⏀	2002/0000/str		W.Hansen,1923/42	Misc 2891

IN MEMORIAM: funeral march, op.59
                      ⏀ 22+ca.2+bcl.2+cbsn/4331/timp.perc/str   8'15" Breitkopf   4486 +

KARELIA: incidental music, op.10
   Overture   ⏀ 2+picc.222/4331/timp.perc/str   7'-8'30" Breitkopf   5765
   Suite, op.11
      1. Intermezzo   2. Ballad   3. Alla marcia   (4781 + Amv Bs
                      ⏀ 2+picc.2+ca.22/4331/timp.perc/str   14'30"-16' Breitkopf   (Cn F
   No. 1 only
      arr R.Hanmer   PC 2121/2230/timp.perc/acdn.gtr.hp/str   Breitkopf,1960   23721

KING CHRISTIAN II: incidental music, op.27
   Suite
      1. Nocturne   3. Serenade
      2. Élégie and musette   4. Ballade (Entr'acte no.3)
                      ⏀ 2(2picc)222/4230/timp.perc/str   25'-26' Breitkopf   7273 Amv C

SIBELIUS, Jean (cont)

KING CHRISTIAN II (cont)
   Suite, arr Roberts
     1. Élégie, musette & menuet   3. Serenade
     2. Nocturne   4. Ballade

	PC	2222/4230/timp.perc/str		C.Fischer	7382

KULLERVO: symphonic poem for Soprano & Baritone soli, mv-chorus & orch, op.7 (1892)
   Part 1: Introduction — 15'
   Part 2: Kullervo's youth (Kullervos ungdom) — 14'50"
   Part 3: Kullervo and his sister (Kullervo och hans suster) — 27'50"
   Part 4: Kullervo goes to war (Kullervo tägar it till strid) — 11'45"
   Part 5: Kullervo's death (Kullervos död) — 12'45"

	⌀ 2(picc)2+ca.2(bcl)2/4331/timp.perc/str	83'20"	(Breitkopf,1961)	Misc 6212
Parts 3-5 only	⌀ 2(picc)2+ca.2(bcl)2/4331/timp.perc/str		(Breitkopf,1961)	mf 273

KUOLEMA: incidental music   see VALSE TRISTE

LADY OF SHALOTT: ballet music arr G.Jacob from music of Sibelius
   Introduction   5. Allegro moderato, agitato
   1. The Iris   6. Vivace
   2. The Birch tree   6a. Poco lento
   3. Novelette   7. Vivace
   4. Poco lento   8. Andantino

⌀ 2121/2210/timp.perc/hp/str	16'45"	G.Jacob	20690

LEMMINKÄINEN LEGENDS, op.22
   No.1 Lemminkäinen & the Maidens of Saari

⌀ 2222/4330/timp.perc/str	15'30"	Breitkopf,1954	21544 +
⌀ 2222/4330/timp.perc/str		Russian SM,1960	Misc 7044

   No.2 The Swan of Tuonela

⌀ 01+ca.0.bcl.2/4030/timp.perc/hp/str	7'30"-9'30"	Breitkopf	4235 Amv Cs D
⌀ 01+ca.0.bcl.2/4030/timp.perc/hp/str		Russian SM,1960	Misc 7044

   No.3 Lemminkäinen in Tuonela

⌀ 21+ca.1+bcl.2/4330/perc/str	14'30"	Breitkopf,1954	21545 +
⌀ 21+ca.1+bcl.2/4330/perc/str		Russian SM,1960	Misc 7044

   No.4 The Return of Lemminkäinen

⌀ 0.2picc.222/4331/timp.perc/str	5'45"-6'30"	Breitkopf	4382 Amv Cs
⌀ 0.2picc.222/4331/timp.perc/str		Russian SM,1960	Misc 7044

LUONNOTAR: tone poem for Soprano solo & orch, op.70

⌀ 2(2picc)22+bcl.2/4230/timp/2hp/str	10'	Breitkopf,1981	Misc 10432

MARCH OF THE FINNISH INFANTRY, op.91a

⌀ 222+bcl.2/4330/timp.perc/str		Breitkopf	9176

NIGHT-RIDE AND SUNRISE: symphonic poem, op.55

⌀ 2+picc.22+bcl.2+cbsn/4231/timp.perc/str	20'	Schlesinger	5196 B

The OCEANIDES (Aallottaret): symphonic poem, op.73

⌀ 2+picc.2+ca.2+bcl.2+cbsn/4330/timp.perc/2hp/str	8'30"-9'45"	Breitkopf	5754 Amv B

ONWARD, YE PEOPLES! processional

PC 1121/2210/timp/str		Galaxy	6533

ORCHESTRAL SUITE, arr Hermann from 8 short pieces for piano, op.99
   1. Pièce humoristique (no.1)   4. Moment de valse (no.7)
   2. Impromptu (no.4)   5. Petite marche (no.8)
   3. Couplet (no.5)

PC 1110/0110/timp.perc/str		Fazer	12790

PAN AND ECHO: dance intermezzo, op.53

⌀ 2(picc)222/4230/timp.perc/str	5'	Schlesinger	5523 B

PELLÉAS ET MÉLISANDE: incidental music, op.46
   1. At the Castle Gate (3'30")   6. Pastorale (2'15")
   2. Mélisande (4')   7. Mélisande at the spinning-wheel (2'30")
   3. On the seashore   8. Entr'acte (2'45")
   4. A Spring in the park (2')   9. The Death of Mélisande (6')
   5. The three blind sisters

⌀ 1(picc)1(ca)22/2000/timp.perc/str		Schlesinger	1327 B

SIBELIUS, Jean (cont)

2 PIECES for orch, op.45
  1. The Dryads: tone picture   ∅ 2+picc.22+bcl.2/4331/perc/str   Breitkopf   5766 B
  2. Dance intermezzo   ∅ 2122/4200/t mp.perc/hp/str   3'-5'   Breitkopf   4494 Dwa
2 PIECES for violin (or cello) & orch, op.77
  1. Laetare anima mea
     ed J.Burt   ∅ 2020/2000/2timp/hp/str   Hansen,1972   Misc 9518
  2. Devotion (Ab imo pectore)
     ed J.Burt   ∅ 2022/4030/str   Hansen,1923   Misc 9519
3 PIECES, op.96
  1. Valse lyrique   ∅ 2222/4230/timp.perc/str   5'   Hansen   14241 B
  2. Autrefois (Scène pastorale)
                    ∅ 2022/2000/timp/str   Hansen   5986
  3. Valse chevaleresque ∅ 2222/4230/timp.perc/str   Hansen   4628
     arr Hansen   PC 1010/0110/timp.perc/str   3'30"   Hansen   4605 B
POHJOLA'S DAUGHTER: symphonic fantasia, op.49
                    ∅ 2+picc.2+ca.2+bcl.2+cbsn/42.2cnt.31/timp/
                        hp/str   12'25"   Schlesinger 5550 + Amv B
RAKASTAVA (The Lover/Der Libende/Den älskande): suite, op.14
  1. Rakastava, the lover   3. Goodnight, my beloved, farewell
  2. The way of the lover
                    ∅ timp.tri/str   Breitkopf   5774 C +
The RETURN OF LEMMINKÄINEN   see LEMMIMKÄINEN LEGENDS
ROMANCES
  op.24, no.9 (from 10 Pieces for piano)
    arr Roberts   PC 1121/2210/timp.perc/str   C.Fischer   1879
    arr Schmeling   PC 1110/0110/timp/pf/str   Breitkopf   11620
  op.42, in C   ∅ str   4'45"-6'15"   Breitkopf   1324 Cn Dwa
  Violin (or cello) & orch, op.78, no.2
                    PC 1110/0110/timp.perc/str   Hansen   4603 B
RONDINO, op.68, no.1 (orig for piano)
  arr Eber   PC 1121/2210/timp.perc/str   Universal   11234
En SAGA: tone poem, op.9
  Orig version (1892)   ∅ 2(picc)222/4331/perc/str   21'20"   (Misc 6073 &
                                           (Helsingfors Stadorkester) (mf 238
  Revised version (1901) ∅ 2(picc)222/4331/perc/str   17'30"-20' Breitkopf   4231 + Amv Cs Dn
SCARAMOUCHE: pantomime, op.71
  Scène d'amour   PC 1010/0110/timp.perc/str   Hansen   3765 B
SCÈNES HISTORIQUES
  1st suite, op.25
    1. All' overtura (20')   3. Festivo (6'30")
    2. Scène   (22'30")
                  ∅ 2+picc.222/4330/timp.perc/str   Breitkopf   7351 B
  2nd suite, op.66
    1. The Chase (Overture)(6'15")   3. At the draw-bridge (6')
    2. Love song   (4'30")
                  ∅ 2+picc.222/4330/timp.perc/str   Breitkopf   7364 Amv
       No. 1 only   ∅ 2222/4000/timp/str   Breitkopf   11533 B
SCOUT MARCH, op.91b   ∅ 2222/4331/timp/str   Hansen   5147
2 SERENADES for violin & orch, op.69
No.1   ∅ 2222/4000/timp/str   7'   Breitkopf   11322
No.2   ∅ 2222/4000/timp.perc/str   7'45"   Breitkopf   11321
SNÖFRID: recitation with chorus & orch, op.29
                  ∅ 2(2picc)11+bcl.1/2310/timp.perc/str 10'30"   Hansen,1929   Misc 2798 B

SIBELIUS, Jean (cont)

SONG OF THE ATHENIANS, for boys' and men's voices, horn septet and percussion, op.31a
		∅	0000/00.3cnt.01.althn.thn.euph/bdm.cym.tri		Breitkopf	18100
arr M.Parantainen		∅	0030/0001.althn.thn.euph		BBC	MB 4351
SPRING SONG (Vårsång), op.16		∅	2(2picc)222/4331/timp.perc/str	8'45"-12'	Breitkopf	4233 B

Der STURM   see   The TEMPEST

SUITE CHAMPÈTRE, op.98b
  1. Pièce caractèristique   3. Danse
  2. Mélodie élégiaque   ∅   str   Hansen,1923   6952 Bwe

SUITE MIGNONNE, op.98a
  1. Petit scène   3. Épilogue
  2. Polka
| | | ∅ | 2000/0000/str | 7'30" | Chappell | 1599 B |

SWAN OF TUONELA   see   LEMMINKÄINEN LEGENDS, no.2

SWANWHITE (Swanehvit): incidental music, op.54
  1. The peacock   (3'45")   5. The Prince alone
  2. The harp   (3')   6. Swanwhite and the Prince
  3. The maiden with the roses (2'-3')   7. Song of praise
  4. Listen, the robin sings   (4'45")
| | | ∅ | 2222/4000/timp.perc/hp/str | | Schlesinger | 5551 Amv Bs |

SYMPHONIES
No.1, op.39, in E min	∅	2(2picc)222/4331/timp.perc/hp/str	33'30"-39'	Breitkopf	4236 + Amv Cn
No.2, op.43, in D	∅	2222/4331/timp/str	40'30"	Breitkopf	5862 + Amv Bwa)
					Cs Dn E
No.3, op.52, in C	∅	2222/4230/timp/str	27'15"-29'	Schlesinger	8971 Amv Cs +
No.4, op.63, in A min	∅	2222/4230/timp.perc/str	32'43"-36'	Breitkopf	7827 Cs
No.5, op.82, in E♭	∅	2222/4330/timp/str	27'-34'	Hansen	8946 Amv Cs Dn)
					Ewe +)
No.6, op.104, in D min	∅	222+bcl.2/4330/timp/hp/str	26'30"-27'30"	Hirsch	8960 Amv Cs
No.7, op.105, in C	∅	2(2picc)222/4330/timp/str	18'30"-22'	Hansen	8874 Amv Cn
	∅	2(2picc)222/4330/timp/str		Hansen(H)	PL 292 As

TAPIOLA: symphonic poem, op.112
| | | ∅ | 32+ca.2+bcl.2+cbsn/4330/timp/str | 15'-19'30" | Breitkopf | 7106 Amv Cwe + |

The TEMPEST: incidental music, op.109
  Overture   ∅   2(picc)21+E♭cl+bcl.2/4331/timp.perc/str   5'30"   Hansen   Misc 1734 D
  Suite no.1
    1. The oak-tree   (3'30")   6. Scène   (1'30")
    2. Humoreske   (1')   7. Berceuse   (2'45")
    3. Caliban's song (1'30")   8. Entr'acte
    4. The harvesters   9. The storm (9'30")
    5. Canon   (1'30")
| | | ∅ | 2+picc.22+E♭cl+bcl.2/4331/timp.perc/hp/str | | Hansen | 19440 |

  Suite no.2
    1. Chorus of winds   (3'30")   5. Songs 1 and 2
    2. Intermezzo   (2'30")   6. Miranda   (2')
    3. Dance of the Nymphs (2')   7. The Naiads   (1')
    4. Prospero   (1'30")   8. Dance episode
| | | ∅ | 222(bcl)2/4000/timp.perc/str | | Hansen,1929 | Misc 1736 E |

  Extracts
    Where the bee sucks
      in E   ∅   2102/0000/str   1'15"   (Hansen)   21543

The TRYST: song, op.37, no.5
| in E♭, orch L.Wurmser | ∅ | 21+ca.1+bcl.2/4231/timp/hp/str | 3' | (Breitkopf) | 20073 |
| in D♭, orch F.Cramer | | pf/str | | (Brit & Cont) | LM G 4628 |

SIBELIUS, Jean (cont)

VALSE CHEVALERESQUE   see   3 PIECES, op.96
VALSE LYRIQUE   see   3 PIECES, op.96
VALSE ROMANTIQUE, op.62b   ∅   2020/2000/timp/str   Breitkopf,1911   23759
VALSE TRISTE from Kuolema, op.44   (4239 Bs Cmv Dn
                              ∅   1010/2000/timp/str   5'   Breitkopf   (Ewe Fni Hm
    arr P.Henneberg   PC 1121/20.2cnt.10/timp/str   Breitkopf,1917   755
    arr B.Thompson   ∅   31+ca.22/4230/timp/hp/str   (Argo)   Misc 6135

SIBELLA, Gabriele

La GIROMETTA (Who has fashioned the tiny slippers/Chi t'ha fatto quelle scarpete): song
    in F, arr A.Franzel   ∅   1110/0000/perc/hp.pf/str   (Schirmer)   LM A 626
    in G, arr P.Hope   ∅   2(picc)122/2000/perc/hp/str   (Chappell)   24077 +

SIBOLD, J.H.

GEMS OF IRELAND: selection, arr PC   2222/2230.euph/timp.perc/str   Lafleur   2236 B
GEMS OF SCOTLAND: selection, arr
    arr E.Reyloff   PC 1222/2230.euph/perc/str   Lafleur   8472

SICARD

The PRESIDENT OF THE UNITED STATES: march
    arr Goldman & Smith   VS 112.4sx.1/2230/perc/str   G.Schirmer   3852

SICILIANOS, Yorgo

SYNTHÈSE (Synthesis), for strings & percussion, op.21 (1962)
                              ∅   timp.3perc(glock.tamtam.xyl)/2str orch (each
                                  8.7.6.5.4 [-9.8.7.6.5]   (Composer)   Misc 9163

SIDAY, Eric

The FOUNTAIN   pf/str   Goodwin & T   7861 B

SIEBERT, Edrich

OVER.THE STICKS
    Version used for opening music for 'Mid-Day Music Hall' until 8.1.62, & differs from printed
    version   PC 1121/2320/timp.perc/str   (AH & C)   23565 Ap

SIEBERT, Friedrich

AHRENSBURGER POLONAISE   ∅   2(picc)222/4231/timp.perc/hp/str   5'   Eulenburg,1965   Misc 6543
RONDO for orchestra   ∅   2222/4230/timp.perc/hp/str   Eulenburg,1953   Misc 4303 B
SCHERZETTO for horn & strings ∅   str   3'30"   Eulenburg,1963   Misc 6544
SCHERZO for large orch   ∅   2222/4231/timp.perc/str   7'   Ahn & Simrock,1955   Misc 6545
SERENADE no.1
    Präludium   Menuett   Rondo
                              ∅   str   12'   Heinrichshofen   19042
SILESIAN FOLK SONG: variations for string orch
                              ∅   str   4'30"   Wrede,1953   Misc 3902
STÄNDCHEN   ∅   2222/4230/timp.perc/hp/str   5'   R.Maul   3653
TANZ DER REISBEAUERN (Rice-planters' dance)
                              ∅   2222/4231/timp.perc/hp/str   Eulenburg,1962   Misc 6546
TARANTELLA MALAGUENA   PC 1120/0110/timp.perc/acdn/str   4'   Hohner,1952   20649

SIECZYŃSKI, Rudolf

VIENNA, CITY OF MY DREAMS Wien, du Stadt meiner Träume): song, op.1
 in G, arr J.Brown   ø 1131/2220/perc/hp/str   (AH & C) LM G 4761
 in G, arr Sadek   PC 2(picc)222/4330/timp.perc/hp/str   Robitschek 9060 + Ap
 in G, arr M.Schönherr for chorus & orch
  17 bars only, used as signature tune for programme 'Vienna rhapsody'
          ø 2220/0000/perc/hp/str   Arranger/AH & C 23837 +
 in A, arr P.Hope   ø 2222/4230/timp.glock/hp/str   (Robitschek) 25932 +
 arr W.R.Collins as waltz PC 112.3sx.1/2230/timp.perc/bjo/str   AH & C 8508 B
 version used as signature tune for programme 'Vienna, City of my Dreams'
          ø 2222/4330/timp.perc/hp.pf/str   BBC TO 875

SIEDE, Ludwig

AM LAGERFEUER: characteristic piece, op.50
          PC 2222/4231/perc/str   14'   Benjamin 11749
BALLET-SUITE
 1. Introduction   3. Schottisch
 2. Valse   4. Intermezzo grotesque
  arr Wilke   PC 1(picc)121/2230/timp.perc/str   Scheithauer 2816
CHINESISCHE STRASSENSERENADE: characteristic piece
          PC 1+picc.222/4230/perc/str   11'   Westphal 10685
INDISCHE GAUKLER   PC 1+picc.222/4230/perc/str   Westphal 7535
KARNEVAL: suite
 1. Introduction   4. Valse
 2. Pierette tänzt   5. Finale
 3. Serenade
  arr Wilke   PC 2(2picc)222/4231/timp.perc/hp/str   Birnbach 9350
LEUCHTKÄFERCHENS HOCHZEIT, op.227
          PC 1222/2210/perc/hp/str   6'   Benjamin 4536
LIEBESRAUSCH: waltz-intermezzo, op.143
          PC 1121/2210/perc/str   Schott 11958
Ein NAGERSTELLDICHEIN   PC 1+picc.222/4230/perc/str   Westphal 6799
Le PETIT CHAT   PC 1121/2230/perc/str   3'   Salabert 7888
La PETITE PAGODE   PC 1(picc)121/2230/timp.perc/str 2'30" Salabert 5479
Ein SCHÄFERSTUNDCHEN, op.69 PC 1+picc.222/4230/timp.perc/str   Wrede 16909
STÄNDCHEN (In shönen Lenz)
 arr Wilke   PC 1121/2230/timp.perc/str   Scheithauer Musikverlag 7715
UNTER DEM HALBMOND: Turkish intermezzo, op.52
          PC 2(picc)222/2230/perc/str   Westphal 6859
WENN DIE SONNE LACHT: waltz
 arr Wilke   PC 1121/2210/timp.perc/str   Scheithauer 7536
Die WICHTELMÄNNCHEN: intermezzo, op.155
          PC 1121/2210/perc/str   Birnbach 11961

SIEGL, Otto (1896-

LYRISCHE TANZMUSIK, op.82 ø 2222/2100/timp/[pf]/str   17'   Universal Misc 500
SINFONIETTA, op.63   ø str   Filser 4933

SIEGMEISTER, Elie (1909-

5 FANTASIES OF THE THEATER (1967)
 1. Beckett   3. Brecht   5. O'Casey
 2. Ionesco   4. Pirandello
          ø 2(2picc)2(ca)2(E♭cl)+bcl.2(cbsn)/4331/timp.perc.glock.
           vib.xyl/hp.pf/str   12'   MCA Mus.,1971 Misc 7611

SIEGMEISTER, Elie

LONESOME HOLLOW   ∅   2(picc)2(ca)2(E♭cl)2/4220/timp.perc.glock/
                                      hp[=pf]/str   7'   Fischer,1977   Misc 9802
OZARK SET, for orch
    1. Morning in the hills   3. Lazy afternoon
    2. Camp meeting   4. Saturday night
                                  ∅   2(picc)2(ca)22/4331/timp.perc.xyl/str   E.B.Marks Mus Corp,1944   Misc 5622
SHADOWS AND LIGHT (Homage to five paintings)
    1. Night ship (Albert Ryder)   4. Blind woman arranging flowers (Edgar Degas)
    2. All around the fish (Paul Klee)   5. Starry night (Vincent Van Gogh)
    3. The Great Parade (Fernand Leger)
                                  ∅   2(picc)2(ca)2(E♭cl,bcl)2(cbsn)/4331/timp.4perc(bells.
                                      cbells.bgos.crot.glock.ratchet.timb.2tomtom.xyl/
                                      cel.hp.pf/str   18'   Fischer,1977   Misc 9803
SYMPHONY no.5 (Visions of Time) ∅   2(2picc)2(ca)2+bcl.2(cbsn)/4331/timp.4perc(bells.
                                      cbell.2bgo.crot.glock.mrc.tamtam.vib.xyl)/hp.pf/
                                      str   17'30"   Fischer,1978   Misc 9870
WESTERN SUITE (1945)
    1. Prairie Morning (5'30")   4. Buckaroo (3'15")
    2. Round-up   (2'30")   5. Riding Home (4'15")
    3. Night-herding   (4')
                                  ∅   2(picc)2(ca)4(E♭cl,bcl)2/4331/timp.perc.bells.xyl/
                                      str   19'30"   MCA Mus,1948/71   Misc 7610

SIEP, W.F.

ALT-HOLLÄNDISCHE BAUERNTÄNZE: selection, op.2
                    PC 1+picc.122/2230/timp.perc/str   Alsbach   11241

SIGLER, Maurice

SHE SHALL HAVE MUSIC: selection of melodies from the film by M.Sigler, A.Goodhart & A.Hoffman
    arr Terry   PC 111.3sx.1/2210/timp.perc/bjo.gtr/str   Cinephonic   13504
SQUIBS: selection of melodies from the film by M.Sigler, A.Goodhart & A.Hoffman
    arr C.Connelly   PC 111.3sx.1/2210/timp.perc/bjo.gtr/str   Cinephonic   13167
THIS'LL MAKE YOU WHISTLE: musical show by M.Sigler, A.Goodhart & A.Hoffman
    Extracts
        I'm in a dancing mood: song
            in E♭, arr C.Mackerras ∅   21+ca.22/4230/timp.perc/hp.pf/str   (Cinephonic)   21948

SIGNORELLI, F. & MALNECK, M.   see   MALNECK, M.

SIGNORINI, A.Ricci

BALLATA E DANZA   ∅   1+picc.111/4230/timp.perc/hp/str   Carisch   Misc 1810
FINALE FARSESCO
    Version for full orchestra   ∅   2+picc.22.sx.2/4240/timp.perc.bells.xyl/
                                      hp/str   Carisch   Misc 276
    Version for small orchestra   ∅   112.sx.1/0000/bells.xyl/str   Carisch   Misc 690
3 IMPRESSIONI da 'A Regoledo' for small orchestra
    1. Montanine che cantano   3. Montanine che danzano
    2. Mulattieri in cammino   ∅   1+picc.121/0000/perc/str   Carisch   Misc 613
PRELUDIO AGRESTE for small orchestra
                                  ∅   0100/1000/bells/cel/str   Carisch   Misc 642
SERENATA RUSTICA for small orchestra
                                  ∅   1010/1000/hp/str   Carisch   Misc 642

SIKORSKI, Kazimierz (1895-

JESZCZE POLSKA NIE ZGINEŁA (Dombrowski anthem): National Anthem of Poland, revised Sikorski
  orch Maklakeivicz   PC 2121/2210/timp.perc/str   Polish SM   21659 +
SYMPHONIC ALLEGRO (1946)   ∅ 2+picc.2+ca.2+bcl.2+cbsn/4331/timp.perc.tamtam/
                         str   15'   Polish SM,1948   Misc 2759 C

SIKORSKI, Tomasz (1939-

HOLZWEGE (1972)   ∅ 0122/4131/bells/str   6'30"   Polish SM,1974   Misc 8823
INNE GŁOSY (Other voices), for wind & percussion
                  ∅ 0444/4440/10perc(bells.4 Japanese gongs)   13'   Polish SM,1977   Misc 9388
MUZYKA Z ODDALI (Music from afar), for chorus & ensemble (1974)
                  ∅ 0000/4420/1perc(bells)/pf   10'   Polish SM   Misc 8913
SICKNESS UNTO DEATH (Choroba na śmierć), for reciter & instruments (1976)
                  ∅ 0000/4400/2pf   11'15"-12'15"
                                                      Polish SM,1981   Misc 10538
VOX HUMANA, for chorus & orch (1971)
                  ∅ 0000/4440/4gong.4tamtam/2pf   10'-14'   Polish SM,1973   Misc 8824

SILBERTA, Rheá

YOHRZEIT (In memoriam): song
  in D min, arr G.Stacey   pf/str   (Huntzinger)   LM G 3614

SILCHER, F. (1789-1860)

Die LORELEY
  arr E.Ascher   PC 1121/2210/perc/str   E.Ascher   8014
  arr M.L.Lake   PC 112.2sx.1/2210/perc/str   C.Fischer   19720

SILÉSU, Lao

LOVE HERE IS MY HEART (Mon coeur est pour toi): song
  in E   PC 2222/2230/timp/hp/str   AH & C   3923
  in E, arr B.Berlin   ∅ 2121/2220/timp.perc/hp/str   (AH & C)   TO 638
  in G & F   2222/2230/perc/hp/str   (AH & C)   LM G 4406
  in G & F, arr G.Stacey   pf/str   (AH & C)   LM G 3302
  arr R.Docker (non-vocal) ∅ 20.ca.20/0000/glock.vib/hp/str   (Ascherberg)   23342 +
  arr for cornet (or cello) & orch
                  PC 2222/2230/timp/hp/str   AH & C   3923 B
Un PEU D'AMOUR (A little love, al little kiss): song
  in E♭   2101/2230/timp/str   (Chappell)   TO 62
  in F & C   2121/2230/perc/str   (Chappell)   LM G 3849
  in F, arr J.Turner   ∅ 1110/1000/hp/str   (Chappell)   LM G 9273
  non-vocal arrangement   PC 2222/2230/timp/str   4'   Chappell   18424
  arr R.Green   ∅ 2222/4230/timp.perc/hp/str   (Chappell)   18424
SÉRÉNADE PASSIONNÉE, for violin & orch
                  PC 1122/2230/timp/cel/str   Chappell   5695 Bp C
SERENATA
  arr H.M.Higgs   PC 1(picc)121/2230.euph/timp.perc/hp/str   Chappell   9814
STAR OF MY LIFE: song
  in D   org.pf/str   Chappell,1918   18201

SILVA, C.A.

SAN LORENZO MARCH: National march of Argentine
                  PC 2(picc)222/4220/str   Benjamin   16364

SILVA, Francisco Manoel da (1795-1865)

OUVIRAM DA YPIRANGA: National Anthem of Brazil
	PC	2(picc)222/4220/str		Benjamin	16364
	PC	2(picc)222/4230/timp.perc/str		Breitkopf	14305
orch L.Miguez		2+picc.222/4231/timp.perc/str		Brazilian Consulate	Misc 2122
arr E.Pereira	∅	pf/str		Brazilian Embassy	16374 B
arr F.Salabert	PC	1(picc)221/2231/timp.perc/str	.	Salabert	3816
arr G.Williams	∅	2222/4231/timp.perc/str		Arranger	16323

SILVA, Jesus Bermaudez (Daniel ZAMUDIO)

CUENTO DE HADAS	∅	2222/2000/timp/str	3'15"	Composer	11188 +
DANZA TIPICA	∅	2+picc.2+ca.2+bcl.2/4331/timp.perc/hp/str	5'15"-6'15"	Composer	11191
MARCHA TRIUNFAL	∅	2+picc.222/2230/timp.perc/str	4'15"	Composer	11187

SILVER, Abner

NO, NO, A THOUSAND TIMES NO: song by A.Silver, A.Sherman & A.Lewis
in F, arr R.Redman	1110/0210/perc/str	(FD & H)	LM G 4980

SILVER, Bassett

The HAPPY HIKER
arr S.Crooke	PC 1121/2210/perc/str	P.Maurice	19450

SILVESTER, E.

QUE SABE NADIE: song
in D♭, arr M.Mackie	∅ 112+bcl.1/0220/dms/acdn.gtr.pf/str	Arranger	MS 20222

SILVESTRI, Constantin (1913-1969)

BIHOR DANCES, op.4, no.1 (1929)	∅	2[(picc)]222/3220/timp/pf[=hp]/str	(Novello)	Misc 9955

3 PIECES for string orch, op.4, no.2
1930 revised version	∅	str	Novello,1966	Misc 6428
1950 revised version		str	Roumanian SM	22160

PRAELUDIUM ET FUGA (Toccata), op.17, no.2
∅ 3+picc.2+ca.2+bcl.2+cbsn/4431/timp.perc.glock.			
tamtam.xyl/cel.hp.pf/str	8'	Salabert,1959	Misc 5331

SIMON, Anton

DANSE DE BAYADÈRES: fantasie, op.34
∅ 2+picc.222/4231/timp.perc/hp/str	(Jurgenson)	6889

La REVUE DE NUIT: symphonic poem, op.36
∅ 2+picc.222+cbsn/42.2cnt.31/timp.perc/str	Jurgenson	14630

SIMON, Ernst (1850-1916)

FRÖHLICHE CHRISTNACHT, by E.Simon & P.Korke
PC 1010/0110/timp.perc/str	Bosworth	2226 B

SIMONETTI, Achille (1857-1928)

MADRIGALE	PC 2101/1000/str	3'	Ricordi	507
ROMANZA for violin & orch	PC 0022/2000/str	3'30"	Ricordi	10023
RONDE JOYEUSE	str		Ricordi	12093
VALSE LOINTAINE	str		Ricordi	12485

SIMONOT, Jacque

SUITE DES DANSES ROYALES (arr from the film 'Marie Antoinette')
   1. Menuet (1'20")   2. Passacaille (2')   3. Gavotte (1'40")
            ø   2222/1000/hp/str   Edn Méridian,1956   22321

SIMONS, Moises

PEANUT VENDOR
   arr G.Langford (used as signature tune for programme 'Southern Serenade')
                    1010/0100/perc.latin/acdn.gtr.pf/str   L.Wright   LM Lib

SIMONS, Netty

BUCKEYE HAS WINGS, for any number of players, with optional dancer(s) and projections (1971)
                    OS no specified instrumentation   Merion,1975   CM 55992
PUDDINTAME, for any number of players and narrator
                    OS no specified instrumentation   Merion,1974   CM 55991

SIMONSEN, Rudolf (1889-1947)

SYMPHONIES
   No.1, in C min
      1. Der Kampf gegen die Knechtschaft   2. Die Verheissung
              ø 2(picc)222/4231/timp/str   Raabe & P   Misc 765
   No.2 'Hellas'
      1. Die Orestie   3. Die Siegesgöttin Pallas Athene
      2. Einsamkeit von den Tempeln
              ø 2(picc)2(ca)22/4231/timp/str   Raàbe & P   Misc 777

SIMPSON, Jack

ON ANOTHER TRACK, for xylophone & orch
   arr F.Stewart   PC 111.4sx.1/0220/perc/gtr/str   Premier Drum Co   18617
RED HEARTS, by J.Simpson & F.G.Charrosin
                  PC 111.4sx.1/0220/perc.xyl/gtr/str   Premier Drum Co   18617

SIMPSON, Robert (1921-

ALLEGRO DECISO, for strings (arr from Quartet for strings, no.3)
              ø str   11'   Lengnick,1958   23405
SYMPHONIES
   No.1 (1951)   ø 3(picc)222+cbsn/4331/timp/str   25'   Lengnick,1956   Misc 4678 C
   No.2 (1955-6)   ø 2222/2200/timp/str   26'-29' Lengnick,1958   •Misc 9052 B
   No.3 (1962)   ø 3(3picc)222+cbsn/4231/timp.perc/str   33'   Lengnick/CML,1972   Misc 8043
   No.4 (1970-72)   ø 3(3picc)222+cbsn/42+2Dtpt.31/timp.perc/str 47'   Lengnick,1973   Misc 8208
   No.5   ø 3(picc)32+bcl.2+cbsn/4432/2timp.perc/str   Composer   mf 403

SIMPSON, Thomas (c. 1582-c.1630)

BALLETT 'La mia Salome' (Pavana)
   arr G.Lenzewski   ø str   Vieweg   10254

SIMS, Lee

ISLE O' MAYE
   arr Grofe   PC 1(picc)12.4sx.1/2320/timp.perc/gtr.hp/
                    str   K.Prowse   16386

SIMSON, Harold Fraser   see   FRASER-SIMSON, Harold

SINDICI, Orestes

O GLORIA INMARCESIBLE: National Anthem of Colombia
	∅	2+picc.222/4331/perc/str		Colombian Ministry	Misc 3743
	PC	2(picc)222/4220/str		Benjamin	16364
	PC	2(picc)222/4230/timp.perc/str		Breitkopf	14305
arr M.L.Lake	PC	112.2sx.1/2210/perc/str		C.Fischer	19720

SINDING, Christian (1856-1941)

AT EVENTIDE, op.110, no.6	PC	1122/2110/timp/str			Simrock	3028
CONCERTI						
Piano & orch						
Op.6, in D♭	∅	2222/4231/timp/str	36'		Hansen	5450
Violin & orch						
Op.45, in A	∅	2222/4200/timp/str	19'		Hansen	8459
Op.60, in D	∅	2222/4200/timp/hp/str			Forberg	Misc 760 B
ÉPISODES CHEVALERESQUES, op.35	∅	2+2picc.232+cbsn/4331/timp.perc/hp/str			Peters	8588
EVENING HARMONIES (Abendstimmung), for violin & orch, op.120						
	∅	2222/4000/timp/hp/str			Breitkopf	Misc 1024
JANE GREY: ballad, op.109, no.3, in F min						
	∅	1122/2000/timp/str			Breitkopf,1911	21529
LEGEND, for violin & orch, op.46						
	∅	2222/4200/timp/hp/str			Hansen	Misc 2176
MARCHE GROTESQUE, op.32, no.1						
arr Klugeschied	PC	1(picc)222/4231/timp.perc/str	3'		Peters	8806
arr Lindemann	PC	2(picc)222(cbsn)/2230/timp.perc/str			Peters	9189
MY HOME (An die Heimat), for chorus & orch						
	∅	2122/2210/timp/str			Forberg	Misc 2771
RONDO INFINITO, op.42	∅	3(picc)222/4331/timp.perc/str			Hansen	4324
RUSTLE OF SPRING, op.32, no.3 (orig pf solo)						
arr Dexter for piano & orch	PC	1121/2230/timp/hp/str	2'30"		Peters	20350
orch & arr R.Docker for piano & orch						
	∅	2(picc)1+ca.22/4330/timp.perc/hp/str	2'		(Peters)	25098 +
arr Stitt	∅	2222/4231/timp.perc/hp/str			Peters	8527 B
arr A.Wilkinson	∅	31+ca.22/4230/timp.perc/hp/str			Arranger	24255
arr C.Woodhouse	PC	2222/4231/timp.perc/hp/str			Hawkes	14669 Bwe
[arr]	PC	1121/22.cnt.10/timp/pf/str			Peters	31 C
SUITE for violin & orch, op.10, in A min						
	∅	2222/2000/hp/str			Peters	2789
SYMPHONIES						
No.1, op.21, in D min	∅	2+picc.222/4331/timp/str	32'15"		Peters	9534
No.2, op.83, in D	∅	3(picc)222/4331/timp.perc/str			Simrock	2440
No.3, op.121, in F		3(picc)222/4331/timp.perc/str	35'		Peters	2807
VALSES						
Op.59, no.3, in G						
arr Hansen	PC	1010/0110/timp.perc/str			Hansen	3772 B
Op.59, no.6, in A♭						
arr Hansen	PC	1010/0110/timp.perc/str			Hansen	11225

SINGER, Lou

OH MY LOVE - OH MY HEART: song by L.Singer, L.Wagner & J.Eaton
| in G, arr Bob Sharpe | ∅ | 1110/0000/hp.pf/str | | | (Feldman) | LM G 8876 |

SINIGAGLIA, Leone (1868-1944)

Le BARUFFE CHIOZZOTTE: overture, op.32					(4240 Amv Cn
	∅	2+picc.222/4230/timp.perc/str		Breitkopf	(Ds Ewa +
BERCEUSE DE L'ENFANT JÉSUS					
in G, arr L.Lucas	∅	hp/str		(Ricordi)	21065
2 CHARACTERSTÜCKE, op.35					
1. Regenlied 2. Étude-caprice					
	∅	str		Breitkopf	4242 B
CONCERTO for violin & orch, op.20, in A					
	∅	2222/4200/timp/str		Breitkopf	Misc 2586
DANZE PIEMONTESI, op.31					
No.1	∅	2+picc.222/4200/timp/hp/str	8'	Breitkopf	5656 Cwa
arr Schmeling	PC	1110/0110/str		Breitkopf	11621
No.2	∅	2+picc.222/4230/timp.perc/str	6'30"	Breitkopf	5657 Amv Cwa
ÉTUDE DE CONCERT, op.5	∅	str		Irbanek	8896
HUMORESKE for cello & orch, op.16, no.2					
	∅	2+picc.222/4200/timp/str		Rahter	24853
PIEMONTE: symphonic suite, op.36					
1. Per campi e boschi 3. In montibus sanctis					
2. Un Balletto rustico 4. Carnevale piemontese					
	∅	2+picc.2+ca.22/4230/timp.perc/hp/str		Breitkopf	4241 Amv B
RAPSODIA PIEMONTESE for violin & orch, op.26					
	∅	2222/4200/timp/str		Breitkopf	5120
ROMANZE for cello & orch, op.16, no.1					
	PS	2122/4000/timp/str		Rahter	24852
ROMANZE for violin & orch, op.29					
	∅	2222/4000/timp/str		Breitkopf	Misc 2419
RONDO for violin & orch, op.42	∅	1111/2100/perc/pf/str	6'	Breitkopf	Misc 1160 B
SCHERZO, op.8	∅	str		Ricordi	8157

SINOPOLI, Giuseppe (1946-

SOUVENIRS À LA MÉMOIRE, for SS.Ct-soli & orch (1974)					
	∅	2(picc.afl)2(ca)2(E♭cl.bcl)1/1110/			
		3perc(anvils.bells.cbells.church bells.			
		congas.crot.glock.gongs.log drums.mba.tamtams.			
		2[=1]vib/cel.hp.hpsd.pf/str(1.1.1.1.1)	35'	Ricordi,1974	Misc 9435
TOMBEAU D'AMOUR	∅	4(4picc,afl)44(E♭cl.2bcl)+cbcl.4(2cbsn)/			
		6(2wtuba)431/timp.perc(bells.cbells.crot.			
		7gongs.mba.plate-bells.vib.xyl)/2cel(2pf).2hp/			
		str(14.12.10.8.6)	20'	Ricordi,1975	Misc 9522

SIRED, L.

JUNE RÊVERIE	PC	112.3sx.1/2210/perc/str	Cosmo Mus	19833

SIRMAY, Albert (1880-1967)

The GIRL ON THE FILM: musical play by A.Sirmay, W.Bredschneider & W.Kollo				
Selection, arr H.M.Higgs	PC	2(picc)122/2230.euph/timp.perc/str	Chappell	2091
Extracts				
In Bond Street: march				
arr H.M.Higgs	PC	1+picc.121/2230.euph/perc/str	Chappell	3060
LADY MARY: musical play				
Complete				
arr L.Ephraim		1121/2210/timp.perc/cel.hp/str	(L.Ephraim)	21577 Awe
Selection, arr H.M.Higgs	PC	1+picc.122/2230/timp.perc/cel.hp/str	Chappell	5982

SIRMAY, Albert (cont)

PRINCESS CHARMING: musical play by A.Sirmay, R.Bennett, J.Waller & H.Ruby
   Selection, arr H.M.Higgs   PC 2122/2230/timp.perc/cel.hp/str   Chappell   6884 C
   Extracts
      Swords and Sabres: song (R.Bennett), for Tenor & Bass soli, chorus & orch
        in C min, arr P.Cardew   ϕ 2(picc)121/2230/timp.perc/hp.pf/str   (Chappell)   22937

ŠÍSTEK, Vijtěch

SLAVONIC SCHERZO
   arr Lotter   ϕ str   Boosey & H   13897 B

SISSLE, Noble

SHUFFLE ALONG: musical show by N.Sissle & E.Blake
   Selection, arr Brockton   PC 1121/2210/perc/str   Witmark   14223
   Extracts
     I'm just wild about Harry: song
       in D, arr B.Berlin   ϕ 2121/2000/perc/str   (Feldman)   TO 963

SITSKY, Larry (1934-
APPARITIONS (1966)   ϕ 2120/2221/timp.perc.glock.xyl/pf-duet/str   7'   Boosey & H,1975 Misc 8730

SITT, Hans (1850-1922)

CONCERTSTÜCK for viola & orch, op.46, in G min
                ϕ 2222/2230/timp/str   Eulenburg   27015
CRADLE SONG, op.48, no.1   ϕ str   Bosworth   7765
GAVOTTE, op.48, no.2   str   Bosworth   6389

SKALKA, Max

DOBRA-DOBRA, by M.Skalka & F.Stahl
   arr P.Fenoulhet   PC 112.3sx.1/2230/perc/str   3'   Bosworth,1952   21231

SKALKOTTAS, Nicos (1904-1949)

ANDANTE SOSTENUTO for solo piano, wind instruments, timpani & percussion
        ϕ 1(picc)1+ca.11+cbsn/1111/timp.perc/str   18'   Universal,1954   Misc 4242 C

CONCERTINI
   Oboe & strings (orig ob & pf)(1961)
      orch P.Guarino   ϕ str   20'   (Composer)   Misc 7433 B
   2 pianos & orch (1935)   ϕ 2222+cbsn/2211/timp.perc/str   14'   Universal,1969   Misc 7159
GREEK DANCES
   Set 1
     1. Peloponnisiakes (Ser. I/3) (3'30")   4. Hostianos (Ser. III/1)(2'30")
     2. Eporotikos 1   (Ser. I/4) (2')   5. Klefikos (Ser. III/3)(2'20")
     3. Eporotikos 2   (Ser. III/2)(3')
           ϕ 2(picc)222+cbsn/4331/timp.perc/str   12'-14' Universal,1953/4 Misc 4385 B

   Set 2
     6. Peloponnisiakos (Ser. II/12)(2')   9. Mavro Yemeni   (Ser II/6)(2'30")
     7. Arkadikos   (Ser III/10)(2'20")   10. O Choros tou Zalonyou (Ser. I/9)(2'15")
     8. Thessalikos   (Ser. I/12)(1'20")   11. Vlachikos   (Ser. II/5)(2'45")
           ϕ 2(picc)222+cbsn/4331/timp.perc/str   Universal,1965   Misc 6177
LARGO SINFONICO   Auto-positives of 2hp parts & strings only   [Composer]   25170 +

SKALKOTTAS, Nicos (cont)

LITTLE SUITE for strings   ∅   str   7'-8'15" Universal,1953   Misc 3926
The RETURN OF ULYSSES (Die Heimkehr des Odysseus): overture to an unwritten opera
   [Provisional edn. - uncorrected blueprints]
                                  ∅   3(3picc)3+ca.2+Dcl+bcl.2+cbsn/
                                      4.2bthn.3.cnt.3+cbtbn.1/
                                      timp.perc.glock.vib/cel.hp/str   M.Skalkottas.1951 Misc 6080
10 SKETCHES for strings   ∅   str   19'   Universal   Misc 4150 C
SYMPHONIC SUITE no.2
   1. Ouverture Concertante   4. Largo-Sinfonico
   2. Toccata   5. Thema con variazioni
   3. Promenaden-Marsch   6. Finale (Perpetuo)
   Nos 1 & 3 only   ∅   2(picc)+picc.2+ca.2+bcl.2+cbsn/4331/
                                      timp.perc.glock.vib.xyl/cel.hp/str   (Kalmus)   Misc 6889-90

SKELLY, J.P.

OLD RUSTIC BRIDGE BY THE MILL: song
   in G   PC   1121/2220/str   Composer MS:BBC   MS 4826
   in Ab   1121/2220/pf/str   BBC   LM G 5205

SKELTON, A.

The ULLSWATER PACK: song
   in Bb, arr Normon   ∅   1110/1000/perc/hp/str   Arranger MS:BBC   MS 30362

ŠKERJANC, Lucijan (1900-1973)

PRELUDIO for string orch   ∅   str   Universal   Misc 1923
SYMPHONY no.5   ∅   2+picc.22+bcl.2/4331/timp.perc.bells/str   Chester   Misc 3197

SKINNER, James Scott (1843-1927)

SELECTION OF SCOTTISH AIRS, arr
   arr R.Chignell   ∅   1121/2220/perc/str   Arranger MS:BBC   MS 5522

SKÖLD, Sven

SJÖGRENS-ELANGER: selection arr from music of Emil Sjögren
                                 PC   2222/2210/timp.perc/str   Gehrmans   12083 B

SKÖLD, Yngve (1899-

FESTPOLONÄS, for military band   ∅   2(picc)03+Ebcl.0/44.2cnt.2thn.30.bar/
                                      timp.perc/cb   Ed Suecia   MB 4569
2 PIECES for small orch, op.42a
   1. Siciliano (5')   2. Gavotte (5')
                                 ∅   1121/2200/str   Ed Suecia   26399 *

SKORZENY, Fritz

CONCERTO for oboe (1955)   ∅   hp/str   20'   Doblinger,1965   Misc 6154

ŠKROUP, František (1801-1862)

KDE DOMOV MŮJ? (Where is my home?): Part 1 of National Anthem of Czechoslavakia

Part 1 only	PC	2(picc)222/4231/timp.perc/str	Benjamin	16363 +
arr M.L.Lake	PC	112.2sx.1/2210/perc/str	C.Fischer	19720

Complete anthem, including Part 2 (NAD TATROU SA BLYSKA - traditional)

	PC	2(picc)222/4230/timp.perc/str	Breitkopf	14305
arr A.Franzel	∅	2121/2230/timp.perc/hp/str	Arranger MS:BBC	MS 20142 +
arr A.Franzel	∅	2222/4331/timp.perc/hp/str	Arranger	19637
arr J.Flegl for orchestra	PC	1+picc.222/4230/timp.perc/str	Urbanek	9760
arr J.Flegl for chorus & orch				
	PC	1121/2220/timp.perc/str	Urbanek	10812

SKROWACZEWSKI, Stanislaw (1923-

MUZYKA NOCA (Musique dans la nuit): symphonic variations (1952)

	∅	2(2picc)2(ca)2(sx)2/4231/timp.bells/hp.pf/ str	22'	Polish SM,1958	Misc 7349
SYMPHONY, op.25	∅	str	9'	Polish SM,1956	Misc 4810

SKRYABIN, Aleksandr   see   SCRIABIN, Aleksandr

SLACK, Roy (1912-

TOO MANY CLARINETS: mini suite for 3 (or 6, or 9) clarinets & strings

	PC	str	K.Prowse	25845 Ap

SLADE, Julian (1930-

The DUENNA

orch J.O.Turner & B.Couzens	∅	1011/0000/timp.perc/hp.hpsd[=pf]/str/ SATB voices	Composer MS:BBC	MS 31510

FREE AS AIR: musical play

Selection, arr L.Young	PC	2(picc)121/2320/timp.perc/gtr.hp/str	7'	FD & H,1957	22342

Extracts

I'm up early: song				
in F, arr P.Cardew	∅	2222/4230/timp.perc/hp/str	(FD & H)	22681 +
Let the grass grow: song for soli, mv-chorus & orch				
in Eb, arr P.Cardew	∅	2222/4230/timp.perc/hp.pf/str	(FD & H)	22743

SALAD DAYS: musical play

Selection, arr L.Young	PC	212.4sx.1/2320/timp.perc/str	FD & H ,1954	21516 B

Extracts

I sit in the sun: song				
in Ab, arr R.Green		hp.org.pf/str	(FD & H)	LM G 10162
in Bb, arr L.Young	∅	1110/0000/hp.pf/str	(FD & H)	LM G 7008
Oh, look at me: song				
in Eb, arr L.Young	∅	1110/0000/hp.pf/str	(FD & H)	LM G 7117
in G, arr P.Cardew for chorus & orch				
	∅	2222/4230/timp.perc/hp.pf str	(FD & H)	22869 +

SLANEY, Ivor

La CUNA (The Cradle), by I.Slaney & D.Whistler

	PC	2121/2220/cast.hp/str	2'15"	B.Wood,1958	22861 Ap
An EDWARDIAN ENTR'ACTE	PC	1121/0000/timp.perc/cel.pf/str		B.Wood,1957	22977 Cs
GEORGIAN RUMBA	PC	2121/2220/perc/hp/str	2'30"	B.Wood,1956	21969 Cp

SLANEY, Ivor (cont)

HI FIDDLE DIDDLE	ø cel/str		FD & H,1953	21120

3 IRISH JIGS
   1. Cork Road   2. Donegal Fair   3. Barndoor jig

	PC 2121/2230/timp.perc/hp/str	3'	Metro Music,1956	22114 Bp Cni

3 IRISH REELS
   1. Young Charlie   2. Antrim fiddlers   3. Ulster market

	PC 2122/2220/timp.perc/hp/str		Metro Music,1950	22087
REVEILLE FOR TOY SOLDIERS	PC 2121/2210/perc/str	2'30"	B.Wood,1952	19768 B
The SWANEE WHISTLER	PC 2121/2220/timp.perc/str	2'30"	B.Wood,1959	22877 Cs
WHISTLING WALLABY	PC 2121/2220/perc/str		·B.Wood,1954	21749

SLATER, Walter L.

PICCOLO PIC: humoresque for piccolo & orch
   arr Roberts

PC 0121/2210/timp.perc/str	C.Fischer	11103

SLATTER, J.W.

MELODY MAZE: selection	PC 2121/2230/perc/str	Duff Steward	2953 B

SLAUGHTER, Walter (1860-1908)

BLUE-BELL IN FAIRYLAND: musical play
   Selection   PC 2(picc)121/2210/perc/str   Hawkes   16775
   Extracts
      Dreamland: song
         in F (refrain only)   str   (FD & H)   TO 271
The DEAR HOMELAND: song
   in D, arr G.Stacey   pf/str   (Cramer)   LM G 5819
   in F, arr J.O.Turner   ø 1110/1000/hp/str   (Cramer)   LM G 7547
GENTLEMAN JOE: musical play
   Extracts
      In my 'ansom: song
         in D, arr H.Carr   ø 2121/2230/perc/str   (AH & C)   TO 1054
MARJORIE: comic opera
   Extracts
      In the still silent night: song
         in G, arr C.Groves   ø 2121/2000/str   BBC   TO 1074

SLAVENSKI, Josip (1896-1955)

BALKANOPHONIA: suite, op.10
   1. Serbian dance   3b.Roumainian dance
   2a.Albanian song   4. My song (reminiscences of my string quartet)
   2b.Turkish dervish dance   5. Bulgarian dance
   3a.Greek song

ø 2(picc)2(ca)22/4230/timp.perc/hp/str	Schott	Misc 2013

SLAVICKY, Klement (1910-

MORAVIAN DANCE FANTASIAS for orchestra

ø 2+picc.222/4330/perc/hp/str	24'	Artia,1954	Misc 4151

SLONIMSKY, Serge (1932-

FESTIVE MUSIC for balalaika, Russian spoons & orch
                    ø   2+picc.222/4231/timp.3perc(bells.glock.tamtam.xyl)/
                        cel.2hp/str   Russian SM,1978   Misc 9750

SLOTHOUWER, Jochem

Il RITORNO D'ORFEO for cello, harp & strings (1977)
                    ø   str   Donemus,1978   Misc 10175

SMALLEY, Roger (1943-

STRATA for 15 solo strings (1970-71)
                    ø   str(10.2.2.1)   Faber,1971   25580
VARIATIONS for strings   ø   str   8'   Faber,1969   Misc 7031

SMAREGLIA, Antonio (1854-1929)

The VASSAL OF SZIGETH: opera
  Extracts
    Ballet music   ø   2+picc.22+bcl.2/42.2cnt.31/timp.perc/str   J.Weinberger   15060

SMART, Henry (1813-1879)

ALL HAIL THE POWER OF JESU'S NAME: hymn. Tune St. Leonards
  in C, arr D.Godfrey   PC 2222/4230/timp.perc/str   Chappell   2867
FESTIVE MARCH, in D
  arr H.M.Higgs   PC 2222/4231/timp/str   Novello   5434
MOONGLADE
  arr Crooke   PC 2121/2210/perc/hp/str   Dix   19071

SMART, Thomas (1776-1867)

The FORSAKEN MAID: song
  in F, arrJ.Buerger   ø   2121/2000/tri/str   (Boosey)   MS 5893

SMETANA, Bedřich (1824-1884)

ALLA POLKA see FROM MY LIFE
The BARTERED BRIDE (Prodaná nevěsta): opera
  Complete   2+picc.222/4230/timp.perc/str   Bote & B/Artia   22175 +
    (Score lacks Act II, no.17 & Act III, nos.28-35)
                  ø   2+picc.222/4230/timp/str   Bote & B   Misc 3239
  Act III only   ø   2222/4230/timp/str   (Bote & B)   TO 1101
  Overture   ø   2+picc.222/4230/timp/str   6'45"-7'30"   Bote & B   4293 Amv Cwe Ds)
                                                                           En)
    arr Grohmann   PC 1(picc)121/2210/timp/str   Cranz   3492
    arr Winter   ø   0020/2100/str   Boosey & H   14435
  Selections
    arr Fetrás   PC 2(2picc)222/4230/timp.perc/hp/str   Benjamin   5249
    arr Kovarovic   incomplete set, no ø   Bote & B   4398
    arr Kraus-Haensch PC 2(picc)22.3sx.2/4230/timp/str   13'   Bosworth   13604
    arr B.Leopold   PC 22(ca)22/4230/timp.perc/str   Edn Continental   16000
    March, arr from themes from the opera
                  PC 1222/2230.euph/perc/str   3'   Boosey   309

SMETANA, Bedrich (cont)

The BARTERED BRIDE (cont)
  Suite, arr A.Lotter
    1. Overture; village scene; lvoe duet and opening chorus   (4')
    2. Jenik's aria and Dance of the villagers   (5')
    3. Sextet   (3')
    4. March of the clowns; teasing duet and Dance of the clowns (3'30")

	PC 2+picc.222/4230/timp.perc/str	16'-19'	Boosey & H	11985 Bp Cwe

  Suite of three dances
    1. Polka (4'15")   3. Dance of the clowns (3'30")
    2. Furiant (2'30")

				Dwe E +)
arr Riesenfeld	⌀ 2+picc.222/4230/timp.perc/str		G.Schirmer	2559 Bmv Cn)
arr Wolf	PC 2(picc)222/2230/timp.perc/str		Schott	10379 B

  Extracts

Dance of the clowns	⌀ 2+picc.222/4230/timp.perc/str	4'30"	Bote & B	22380
arr Wood	PC 2(picc)222/2230/perc/str		Paxton	14553 Bm D
Furiant	⌀ 2+picc.222/4230/timp.perc/str		Bote & B	22377

    Just a word with you (Nuže, milý chasníku...): duet

in G	2222/4000/timp/str		(Smetana Soc,1934)	24112 (⌀ - 22175)

    Our dream of love how fair: aria (Marenka)
    Ah bitterness: recit

in A♭ (orig)	⌀ 2222/2000/str		BBC	11507
in A♭	2222/2000/str		Bote & B	23401
in B♭, arr E.Griffiths	pf/str		(Boosey & H)	LM G 6451
Polka	⌀ 2+picc.222/4230/timp.perc/str		Bote & B	22378 +

    Stay awhile here: sextet

arr A.Lotter(non-vocal) PC str			Hawkes	2627

    Though a Mother (Jatke matka): duet (Act 1, nos 4 & 5)
    Lastly how can I account (Konačně je celá): recit

	⌀ 2222/2000/str		(Bote & B)	26119

BAYADER GALOP see GALOP BAJADEREK
BLANÌK see MÁ VLAST
BOHEMIAN POLKA

orch D.Darlow	⌀ 3(picc)222/4231/perc/hp/str		BBC	TO 1548

The BRANDENBURGERS IN BOHEMIA (Braniboři v Cochàch): opera
  Complete

ed F.Bartoš	⌀ 2+picc.22(bcl)2/4231/timp.perc/str		Czech SM,1952	Misc 4396
Selection, arr B.Leopold	PC 2222/2231/timp.perc/str		Springer	4960

CARNIVAL OF PRAGUE (Pražský Karneval)(1883)

ed F.Bartoš	⌀ 2+picc.222/4431/timp.perc/str	5'05"	Czech SM,1965	Misc 9403
ed F.Bartoš	⌀ 2+picc.222/4431/timp.perc/str		Foerster	Misc 784

CEREMONIAL PRELUDE see FESTIVE OVERTURE, in C
DALIBOR: opera

Complete	⌀ 2+picc.222/4231/timp.perc/hp/str			
	Offstage: 0000/04[-8] 131/bells		Czech SM,1945	Misc 2332 C
Selection, arr L.Weninger	PC 2222/4231/timp.perc/hp/str	16'	Benjamin	5290

  Extracts
    Act 2, Scene 1 (Complete scene)
      Rough, tough, but the world is jolly: chorus
      I know that song well: duet
      Yes truly the world is jolly: chorus

				(⌀ Misc
	2222/4231/timp.perc/str		(Czech SM)	24367 + (2332

    Entr'acte & entrance of King Vladislav (non-vocal)

	⌀ 2(picc)333/4230/timp.perc/hp/str		Weinberger	9536
arr K.T.Grohmann	PC 1(picc)121/2210/timp.perc/hp/str		Cranz	3479
Fanfare (from overture)	⌀ 0000/4331/timp		BBC	11036

SMETANA, Bedrich (cont)

DALIBOR (cont)
    Extracts (cont)
        I know that song well (Dle této písně poznávám): duet (Act II)
            in A (orig)   2222/4230/timp/str   (Czech SM)   24367 + (2332   (∅ Misc
        Love of a woman.. (Vzoly o-dolal jsemčvozraku)(Dalibor's narration & exit)
            translated C.Hassall   2222/4231/timp.perc/hp/str   (Czech SM,1945)   22897 +
        Rough, tough, but the world is jolly (Ba, nejveselejší je tento svět): drinking song
            (with introduction), for TB chorus & orch (Act II)   (∅ Misc
            in A (orig)   2222/4231/timp.perc/str   (Czech SM)   24367 + (2332)
            in A   ∅   2222/4231/timp.perc/str   (Czech SM)   22469
        Yes, truly the world is jolly (Ba, nejveselejší je tento svět), for TB soli, mv-chorus &
            orch (Act II)(reprise of previous item)   (∅ Misc
            in A (orig)   2+picc.222/4231/timp.perc/str   (Czech SM)   24367 + (2332
    see also MORAVIAN MEMORY
The DEVIL'S WALL (Certova Stěna): opera (1882)
                              ∅   2+picc.222/4230/timp.perc/hp/str
                                   Offstage: 0000/0200   Czech SM,1959   Misc 5813
DOKTOR FAUST: overture   ∅   0000/2010/perc/pf/str   Czech SM,1951   Misc 3421 C
                                   0000/2010/timp.perc/str   BBC   19111
FANFARE for Shakespeare's 'Richard III'
    ed F.Bartoš   ∅   0000/4230/timp   Czech SM,1951   Misc 3421 C
FARMYARD FROLIC: Czech polka (based on piano work), arr Grün
                             PC   2(picc)121/2230/timp.perc/hp/str   2'45"   Hawkes,1952   20570
FESTIVE OVERTURE (Slavností Předehra), in C
                             PC   2(picc)222/4231/timp/str   Barvitius   13627
FESTIVE OVERTURE (Vélka Předehra), op.4, in D
    1st version (1848-49)
        ed F.Bartoš   ∅   2+picc.222/4331/timp.perc/str   Czech SM,1962   Misc 5828
FESTIVE SYMPHONY   see   TRIUMPH SYMPHONY
The FISHERMAN (Rybář)(1869)
    ed F.Bartoš   ∅   hmn.hp/str   Czech SM,1951   Misc 3421 C
FROM BOHEMIAS FIELDS AND WOODS   see   MÁ VLAST
FROM MY LIFE (Z méno života): string quartet no.1, in E min, arr G.Szell for orch
    1. Allegro vivo appassionata   3. Largo sostenuto
    2. Allegro moderato alla polka   4. Vivace
                             ∅   2+picc.222/4231/timp.perc.tamtam/hp/str   Boosey & H   2198
        2nd mvt (Alla polka) only
            arr O.Langey   ∅   1121/2210/timp.perc/str   G.Schirmer   14453
            arr O.Langey   PC   1121/2210/timp.perc/str   G.Schirmer   3764
FURIANT [orig no.1 of Czech Dances, Set 2, for piano]
    orch A.Waldenmaier   ∅   2+picc.222/4330/timp.perc.glock/hp/str   Mozart Edn,1976(H) PL 604 Ani
GALOP BAJADEREK (Kvapík Bajadér)(1842)
                             ∅   2+picc.224/4220/timp.perc/str   Czech SM   P 12416
    ed F.Bartoš   ∅   2+picc.242/4220/timp.perc/str   Czech SM,1962   Misc 5828
GAUDEAMUS: march for the Prague University Legion, 1848 (orig for piano)
    arr B.Leopold   PC   2222/4231/timp.perc/str   Edn Continental   12377
HAAKON JARL: symphonic poem ∅   2+picc.22+bcl.2/4231/timp.perc/hp/str   16'30"   Simrock   2457
HOMAGE TO SMETANA, arr B.Grün from the music of Smetana
    1. Furiant   (2'30")   4. Nocturne (3')
    2. Folk song (2'50")   5. Galop   (3')
    3. Polka   (2'45")
                             ∅   2+picc.222/4230/timp.perc/hp/str   14'   BBC   20089
JUBEL OUVERTÜRE   see   FESTIVE OVERTURE

SMETANA, Bedřich (cont)

The KISS (Hubička): opera

Complete	φ	2+picc.222/4230/timp.perc/str		Czech SM,1942	Misc 4026
Overture	φ	2+picc.222/4230/timp.perc/str	6'15"	Weinberger	4472 Bs
arr K.T.Grohmann	PC	1(picc)121/2210/timp.perc/str		Cranz	6258
Selection, arr B.Leopold	PC	2(picc)222/4230/timp.perc/str		Edn Continental	12354

Extracts
   Lullaby

arr A.Lotter	PC	str		Hawkes	2627

   see also SLAVONIC LULLABY

LIBUSE'S JUDGEMENT (Libušin Soud): tone poem (1869)

ed F.Bartoš	φ	2222/4230/timp/str		Czech SM,1951	Misc 3421 C

LIBUSSA (Libuše): opera

Complete	φ	2+picc.222/4431/timp.perc/hp/str			
		Offstage: 0000/04+btpt.00		Czech SM,1949	Misc 3462 B
Overture	φ	2+picc.222/4431/timp.perc/str	9'45"	Weinberger	9537 Amv
arr K.T.Grohmann	PC	1(picc)121/2210/timp.perc/str	6'	Cranz	6163

Extracts

Fanfare from overture	φ	0000/4431/timp		Edn Continental	13470

   Však, nechť se stane: aria
   Český národ: chorus

in D (orig)	φ	2222/4340/timp.perc/str		BBC	11117

MÁ VLAST (My Country): cycle of symphonic poems

1. Vyšehrad	φ	2+picc.222/4231/timp.perc/2hp/str		Urbanek	2958
rev J.Clapham (1975)	φ	2+picc.222/4231/timp.perc/2hp/str		Eulenburg,1976	Misc 9067
2. Vltava (Moldau)	φ	2+picc.222/4231/timp.perc/hp/str	10'30"-12'45"		(6634 Amv Bs C Dn
				Urbanek	(Ewe +
rev W.Zemanek (1914)	φ	2+picc.222/4231/timp.perc/hp/str		Eulenburg	Misc 6160
arr O.Haensch	PC	2322/4230/timp/str		Benjamin	4532
arr A.Lotter	PC	2(picc)222/4231/timp.perc/cel.hp/str	9'30"-10'15"	Hawkes	1247 B
3. Šárka	φ	2+picc.222/4231/timp.perc/str	9'20"-10'50"	Urbanek	2419 + Amv Bs C
rev W.Zemanek	φ	2+picc.222/4231/timp.perc/str		Eulenburg	Misc 6161
4. From Bohemia's fiels and woods (Z českych luhů a hájů)					
	φ	2+picc.222/4231/timp.perc/str	11'-13'15"	Urbanek	7663 +
rev J.Clapham	φ	2+picc.222/4231/timp.2perc/str		Eulenburg,1967	Misc 9068
arr O.Langey	PC	1(picc)121/2210/timp/str		G.Schirmer	2506 B
5. Tábor	φ	2+picc.222/4231/timp.perc/str	12'-13'15"	Urbanek	8107 +
rev J.Clapham (1975)	φ	2+picc.222/4231/timp.perc/str		Eulenburg,1976	Misc 9066
6. Blaník	φ	2+picc.222/4231/timp.perc/str		Urbanek	8106 Amv Bs C
rev J.Clapham (1975)	φ	2+picc.222/4231/timp.perc/str		Eulenburg,1976	Misc 9311

MEDITABITUR IN MANDATIS (Offertorium à la Händel), for chorus & orch (1846)

ed J.Plavec		0000/2000/org/str		Czech SM,1956	Ch Lib

MOLDAU   see   MÁ VLAST: Vltava
MY COUNTRY   see   MÁ VLAST
OFFERTORIA   see   1. MEDITABITUR IN MANDATIS   2. SCAPULIS SUIS
OLDRICH AND BOZENA: overture

ed F.Bartoš	φ	0020/2200/timp/str		Czech SM,1951	Misc 3421 C

OVERTURE in C (Solemn Overture)(1868)

ed F.Bartoš	φ	2+picc.222/4231/timp.perc/str		Czech SM,1951	Misc 3421 C

OVERTURE II in A (1842)

	PC	1(picc)121/2210/timp.perc/str		Edn Continental	10181

The PEASANT WOMAN (Venkovanka): polka (1879)

ed F.Bartoš	φ	2+picc.222/4231/timp.perc/str		Czech SM,1951	Misc 3421 C

POLKA in F

arr M.Seiber	PC	2222/2230/timp.perc/str	3'	Schott	16829 B

POLKA DANCE

arr & orch D.Darlow	φ	3222/4231/perc/hp/str		Arranger	TO 1549

SMETANA, Bedrich (cont)

PRAGUE CARNIVAL see CARNIVAL OF PRAGUE
RICHARD III: symphonic poem   ∅ 2+picc.222/4231/timp.perc/hp/str   13'   Simrock   9414 B
   ed F.Bartoš & K.Solc   ∅ 2+picc.222/4231/timp.perc/hp/str   Czech SM,1958 Misc 9404
ŠÁRKA see MÁ VLAST
SCAPULIS SUIS: offertory for SATB soli & orch
   ed J.Plavec   0000/2000/org/str   Czech SM,1951 Ch Lib
The SECRET (Tajemství): opera
   Complete
      ed F.Bartoš   ∅ 2222/4230/timp.bells/gtr/str   Czech SM   Misc 4353
   Overture   ∅ 2222/4230/timp/str   5'30"-7'30" Weinberger   7902 B
      arr B.Leopold   PC 1110/0110/timp/str   Edn Continental 10231 B
SLAVONIC LULLABY: Czech folk tune. arr Grün (based on theme from 'The Kiss')
                                   PC 2(picc)121/2230/timp.perc/hp/str   3'   Hawkes,1952   20572
SMETANA'S LEGACY: selection, arr O.Urbach from the music of Smetana
                                   PC 2222/4230/perc/str   Wrede   9425
SOLEMN MARCH FOR SHAKESPEARE CELEBRATIONS see MARCH FOR THE SHAKESPEARE FESTIVAL
SOLEMN OVERTURE see OVERTURE in C
SONG OF THE CZECHS (Česká Píseň)(Jan z Hvězdy): cantata for double chorus & orch (Final version (1878)
   ed J.Plavac   ∅ 2222/4231/timp.perc/str   Czech SM,1965 Ch Lib
TÁBOR see MÁ VLAST
TO OUR GIRLS (To our lassies)(Našim děvám)(orig for piano)
   Polka, in D, arr Labsky   PC 322.2sx.1/2011/timp.perc/str   2'45"   Barvitius   12793
TRIUMPHAL SYMPHONY (Festive Symphony)(Slavostni symfonie), op.6
                                   ∅ 2222/4230/timp.perc/str   BBC   Misc 1893
   ed F.Bartoš   ∅ 2+picc.222/4231/timp.perc/str   Czech SM,1955 Misc 7171
      Scerzo & Trio only   2222/4200/timp.perc/str   BBC   23201 +
The TWO WIDOWS (Dve vdevy): opera
   Complete   ∅ 2222/4230/timp.perc/str   Czech SM   Misc 3461
   Overture   2222/4230/timp/str   6'30"   (Czech SM)   20559
   Selections
      Polka, arr B.Leopold on melodies from the opera
                                   ∅ 2222/4230/perc/str   3'   (Continental) 12378
   Extracts
      Ballet music   ∅ 2222/4230/timp.perc/str   Bote & B   8050 B
      Entr'acte (Act 2)   2222/4220/timp/str   2'30"   (Czech SM)   20560
      We can no longer doubt it (Nbní pochybností více): duet for 2 Sopranos (Act 2)
         in E   2222/4200/timp/str   (Czech SM)   23828 +
      With God's blessing comes the golden harvest (Musí nás mit... Pán buh rád): final chorus &
         polka   2222/4230/timp.perc/str   (Czech SM)   20561
      see also VILLAGE HOP-HOP
VALSES, arr B.Leopold   PC 1121/2210/perc/str   Czech SM   1746
VILLAGE HOP-HOP: Czech galopade, arr Grün (based on theme from 'The Two Widows')
                                   PC 2(picc)121/2230/timp.perc/hp/str   3'   Hawkes,1952   20569 Ani
VLTAVA (Moldau) see MÁ VLAST
VYSEHRAD see MÁ VLAST
WALLENSTEIN'S CAMP (Valdštýndv Tabor)(Wallensteins Lager): symphonic poem, op.14
   ed F.Bartoš   ∅ 2+picc.222/4431/timp.perc/str   15'30"   Czech SM,1956 Misc 6777 B
   March only   ∅ 3222/4431/timp.perc/str   5'   BBC   TO 1661
WEDDING SCENES (Svatební scény)(orig for piano)
   1. Wedding procession (Svatebná průved)(4')
   2. The Betrothed (Zenich a nevesta)   (2'45")
   3. Wedding day (Svatební vesself)   (5'15")
      arr O.Haensch   ∅ 2(picc)222/4231/timp.perc/hp/str   Benjamin   15533
      arr O.Haensch   PC 2(picc)222/4231/timp.perc/hp/str   Benjamin   5288

SMITH, Alice Mary (1839-1884)

O THAT WE TWO WERE MAYING: song
  in Ab   PC str   Ricordi   1718

SMITH, Clay

AMERICA ANSWERS THE CALL: song by C.Smith, R.P.Weston & L.Bert
   in F, arr H.Carr   φ   2121/2230/perc/hp/str   (FD & H)   TO 899
CHEEP: revue by C.Smith, R.P.Weston & B.Lee
  Extracts
      Good-bye Madam Fashion: song
          in G, arr H.Carr   φ   2121/2230/perc/hp/str   (FD & H)   TO 945
      I shall see you to-night: song
          in G, arr H.Carr   φ   2121/2000/perc/hp/str   (FD & H)   TO 535
      Where did that one go: song
          in C, arr M.Lubbock   φ   2121/2230/perc/hp/str   (FD & H)   TO 536
SOMEBODY'S COMING TO TEA: song by C.Smith, R.P.Weston & B.Lee
   in Ab, arr B.Berlin   φ   2121/2220/perc/hp/str   BBC   TO 643

SMITH, Colin

HAYMAKER'S HOLIDAY
   arr A.Fones   PC 1121/2230/perc/str   Gay,1951   20275
LOOKING AROUND
   arr B.Campbell   PC 2121/2230/perc/hp/str   2'45"   Chappell,1951 20647 Cp

SMITH, Eric

JACK ASHORE: nautical march
   arr Barsotti   PC 222.3sx.1/0230/perc/str   Bosworth   9794

SMITH, F.S.Breville-   see   BREVILLE-SMITH, F.S.

SMITH, H.Elliott

The DRUMMER'S BIRTHDAY   PC 0.picc.222/2230/perc/str   Hawkes   2877 Ap C
The PIG AND WHISTLE: march   PC 1121/2230/timp/str   Hawkes   1932

SMITH, John Christopher (1712-1795)

The FAIRIES: opera
  Overture
      ed R.Graves   φ   0[2]00/0[1]00/str/cont   7'30"   OUP,1972   25649
  Extracts
      Ye spotted snakes: aria for Soprano solo & orch
                               φ   1000/0000/str/cont   (Walsh,1755)   Misc 10068
GIDEON: oratorio compiled from the works of G.F.Handel (1769)   see   HANDEL, G.F: GIDEON
TERAMINTA: opera, attrib J.C.Smith   see STANLEY, John: TERAMINTA

SMITH, John Stafford (1750-1836)

The STAR-SPANGLED BANNER: National Anthem of the United States of America (melody from 'To
      Anacreon in heaven', attrib J.S.Smith; formerly attrib Samuel Arnold)
                               PC 2(picc)222/4230/timp.perc/str   Breitkopf   14305
                               PC 2(picc)222/4220/str   Benjamin   16364
                               φ   2222/4231/timp.perc/str   BBC   19653
   arr F.M.Collinson   φ   1121/2220/hp/str   Arranger MS:BBC MS 30863
   arr Fitz-Gerald   PC 1222/2230.euph/perc/str   Hawkes   1841
   arr M.L.Lake   PC 112.2sx.1/2210/perc/str   C.Fischer   19720
   arr F.Salabert   PC 1(picc)221/223[1]/timp.perc/str   Salabert   3816

SMITH, Kenneth Leslie   see   LESLIE-SMITH, Kenneth

SMITH, Malcolm

AQUARIUS SELECTION, arr for chorus & orch
    1. Jesus Christ Superstar (A.Lloyd-Webber)   3. Aquarius   (G.McDermot)
    2. I don't know how   (A.Lloyd-Webber)   4. Day by day (G.McDermot)
                 ϕ 21+ca.1+bcl.2/4331/timp.2perc(kit.vib)/
                  bgtr.hp.pf/str   Arranger   26443 **

SMITH, Nicholls

IT COSTS SO LITTLE, ny N.Smith & Ritter
                  ϕ 001.2sx.0/0100/perc/gtr.pf/str   (L.Wright)   MS 1518 Ap

SMITH, Roger

LANDMARKS OF EARLY AMERICAN MUSIC 1760-1800: a collection of 32 compositions compiled, edited &
    arranged for orchestra, band or smaller instrumental groups by Richard Franks Goldman &
    Roger Smith
                  ϕ 112.4sx.1/2230/perc/str   Schirmer,1943   3852

SMITH, Seymour

The SPIDER AND THE FLY: song
    in D, arr H.Carr ϕ 2121/2230/timp.perc/str   2'30"
                                        (Beale, Stuttard & Co)   MS 30149
    in D, arr A.Franzel as duet ϕ 1110/0000/perc/hp.pf/str   (Beale, Stuttard & Co)   LM A 622
    in D, orch P.Ryan ϕ 1121/2220/str   (Beale, Stuttard & Co)   MS 5114

SMITH, Sidney

FOR YOU: song
    in F, arr R.Chignell ϕ 2222/2230/timp/str   Arranger MS:BBC   MS 4944

SMITH, Vere

The GROTESQUE: selection of popular songs, arr H.M.Higgs
                PC   2(picc)122/2230.euph/timp.perc/str   Chappell   2900

SMITH, Wilson G.

AT THE BAL MASQUÉ: suite
    1. Mélodie érotique (Pierrot's confession)   3. Danse exotique
    2. Promenade (Harlequin and Columbine)   4. Pierrot's sadness
       arr Zamecnik   PC   1121/2210/timp.perc/str   Sam Fox   14254

SMITH-BRINDLE, R.   see   BRINDLE, Reginald Smith

SMITH-MASTERS, Anthony B.

The DYNASTS: radio production (1951)
                22+ca.22/4231/timp.perc/cel.hp/str   Composer MS:BBC   MS 30431
The FELLOWSHIP OF THE RING: radio production
                ϕ 2+picc+bfl.1+ca.11+cbsn/2330/timp.perc/
                  hp/str   Composer MS:BBC   MS 31081 +

SMITH-MASTERS, Anthony B (cont)

FIRST HALF CENTURY: radio programme of the years 1945-1950
                  φ   2+picc.222+cbsn/4331/timp.perc/str   Composer MS:BBC   MS 30393

The FLOOD: radio production 9.9.77
                  φ   1(picc,afl)01(E♭cl,bcl)/0100/timp/vlc   Composer MS:BBC   MS 31773

LOVE AND FRIENDSHIP: radio production (1953)
                  φ   1101/2000/str   Composer MS:BBC   MS 30657

The STREETS OF POMPEII: radio feature (1952)
                  φ   0010/2230/perc/str   Composer MS:BBC   MS 30534

The TOWER OF HUNGER: radio production
                  φ   1222/0230/timp   Composer MS:BBC   MS 30560

SMYTH, Dame Ethel (1858-1944)

ANACREONTIC ODE for Mezzo-soprano or Baritone solo & chamber orch
                  φ   1000/0000/perc/hp/str   4'30"-5'15"   Novello   52379

The BOATSWAIN'S MATE: opera
  Overture   φ   2222/4230/timp.perc/str   6'15"   Composer   TO 1646 φ only
  Extracts
    Mrs Water's aria
      in F   φ   21+ca.21/3020/hp/str   Composer   TO 1723, φ only

CHRYSILLA, for Mezzo-soprano, or Baritone, solo & chamber orch
                  φ   1000/0000/tri/hp/str   4'15"   Novello   52380

The DANCE, for Mezzo-soprano, or Baritone, solo & chamber orch
                  φ   1000/0000/perc/hp/str   5'15"-6'   Novello   52378

FÊTE GALANTE: opera
  Extracts
    Madrigal
      in G   0101/1000/hp/str   3'50"   Composer   TO 605

2 INTERLINKED FRENCH FOLK MELODIES (arr from 'Entente Cordiale')
                  φ   1111/2100/timp.perc/hp/str   OUP   14316 Bmv C

The MARCH OF THE WOMEN   φ   1111/2120/timp.perc/str   Breitkopf   14612
  arr F.Collinson   φ   1021/1210/perc/hp/str   Arranger MS:BBC MS 20436

ODELETTE for Mezzo-soprano, or Baritone, solo & chamber orch
                  φ   1000/0000/perc/hp/str   5'-6'   Novello   52377

The WRECKERS: opera
  Overture   φ   2(picc)+picc.2+ca.2+bcl.2+cbsn/4231/timp.perc/
                      hp/str   9'-10'   Curwen   2144 Amv B
  Extracts
    On the cliffs of Cornwall: prelude to Act 3   9'
                  φ   2+picc.2+ca.2+bcl.2+cbsn/4231/timp.perc/
                      hp/str   Curwen   2210 Amv B

SNELL, Gordon

HANDS ACROSS THE SKY: opera for 3 voices by G.Snell & A.Hopkins
                  φ   1111/1000/perc/pf/str   (Composers,1959) 22965 & mf 149

SNODGRASS, Louise

LONDON GIRL: song
  in B min, arr G.Stacey   [1]0[1]0/0000/pf/str   (Cramer)   LM G 3655

SNOEK, I.

ARÉVELK: Armenian rhapsody, no.4, op.112
               PC 2+picc.1+ca.22/4231/timp.perc/hp/str   Yves   12024

SNOEK, I.(cont)

VARDAVAR: Armenian rhapsody, no.3, op.107
                              P.C 2222/4231/timp.perc/str   Miran   4579
Le VIEUX BARDE (The old singer): caprice for double bass & orch, op.122
                                    str   Yves   8350

SNYDER, Ted

THAT MYSTERIOUS RAG: characteristic rag
    arr Schulz   PC 1121/2210/perc/str   Feldman   10948
YIDDLE ON YOUR FIDDLE, by T.Snyder & I.Berlin
    arr Schulz   PC 0.picc.010/0210/timp/str   Snyder   11006

SOCOR, Matei

TE SLÁVIM, ROMÂNIE (We glorify thee, Romania): National Anthem of Romania (adopted 1953)
    arr G.French   ∅ 2222/2230/timp.perc/str   Arranger/Blandford   25513 +
    arr N.Fulton   ∅ 2222/4330/timp.perc/str   Arranger/Blandford   24113 +

SÖDERMAN, Johann August (1832-1876)

JUNGFRAU VON ORLEANS (Joan of Arc): overture
                         ∅ 2(picc)222/4231/timp.perc/str   7'   Hirsch   12255
    arr Borch   PC 2(picc)222/4231/timp.perc/str   Schirmer   2634 B

SOHAL, Naresh

ASHT PRAHAR for orch   ∅ 3(2picc,afl)2+ca.2(asx)2+cbsn/4331/timp.3(perc.
                              bells.crot.glock.mba.2tamtam.vib.xyl)/
                              2hp.pf(cel.[dulcitone])/str/S-solo   25'   Novello,1976   Misc 9077 B

SOKOLOV, Nikolai Aleksandrovich (1859-1922)

La CARESSANTE: polka, op.38 ∅ str   Belaieff   8033
2 CHORUSES for female voices & orch, op.12
    1. Deux roses   2. La fée de l'été
                         ∅ 2+picc.22+bcl.2/4000/timp.bells/hp/str   Belaieff   Misc 2763
ELEGY, op.4   ∅ 2222/4200/timp/str   8'15"   Belaieff   5287
IN A GONDOLA   ∅ 2222/4200/timp/str   Belaieff   5287
ISLAMIC CHANT   ∅ 2222/4200/timp/str   Belaieff   5287
    arr A.Schmid   PC 2(picc)12.2sx.1/2210/timp.perc/hp/str   G.Schirmer   8810
Le ROSSIGNOL S'EST TU (The silent nightingale), op.1, no.4
    arr O.Rudd   PC 1121/2200/timp.perc/str   Enoch   11979
SERENADE on a children's song (after the quintet, op.3)
                         ∅ str   Belaieff   10222 B
SERENADE, no.2, op.23   ∅ str   4'   Belaieff   8029
VARIATION on a Russian theme: variation no.5 for 'Variations on a Russian theme' by various composers
                         ∅ 2+picc.222/4231/timp.perc/hp/str   Belaieff,1903 8973
Les VENDREDIS: polka by N.Sokolov, A.Glazunov & A.Lyadov
                         ∅ str   4'25"   Belaieff   8614 Bn Cwe D
The WILD SWANS: ballet
    Suite, op.40a
        1. Introduction   6. Adagio
        2. Polka   7. Danse des bouffons
        3. Valse caprice   8. Danse orientale
        4. Scène et danse des sorcières   9. Mazurka
        5. Pastorale
                         ∅ 3(picc)222/4231/timp.perc/hp/str   Belaieff   5587

SOLAL, Martial

STRESS, by M.Solal & M.Constant see   CONSTANT, Marius: STRESS

SOLER, Antonio (1729-1783)

CONGREGANTE Y FESTERO, for Soprano & Tenor soli, SSAT & SATB choruses & orch
     ed F.Marvin   ∅   str/cont   Universal,1967   VS 14080
CONTRADANZA DE COLEGIO, for Soprano solo, chorus & orch
     ed F.Marvin   ∅.   str/cont   Universal,1967   VS 14082
DE UN MAESTRO DE CAPILLA, for Soprano & Contralto (or Baritone) soli, SSAT chorus & orch
     ed F.Marvin   ∅   str/cont   Universal,1967   VS 14077
En PIÉLAGOS INMENSOS, for 2 Soprano soli, SSAT & SATB choruses & orch
     ed F.Marvin   ∅   1000/0200/str/cont(org)   Universal,1967   VS 14078
SALVE REGINA, for Soprano solo, chorus & orch
     ed F.Marvin   ∅   str/cont   Universal,1970   VS 14081
STABAT MATER, for SSB soli & orch
     ed F.Marvin   ∅   str/cont   Universal,1970   VS 14079

SOLER, Josep (1935-

The SOLAR CYCLE   ∅   2+picc.2+ca.2+bcl.2+cbsn/4331/timp.perc.bells.
                                        glock.mba.2vib.xyl/hp.org.pf/str   Seesaw Music,1968   Misc 8671

SOLOMON, Edward (1855-1895)

The NAUTCH GIRL: comic opera
     Selection, arr C.Godfrey   PC   2(picc)222/2230.euph/timp.perc/str   Chappell   559
     Extracts
        When all the world was bright: song
            in B, arr H.Carr   ∅   2121/2230/timp.perc/hp/str   (Chappell)   TO 386
The RED HUSSAR: comic opera
     Selection, arr C.Godfrey   PC   2(picc)222/2230.euph/timp.perc/str   Metzler   2620
SEE ME DANCE: polka arrangement of G.Grossmith's song 'See me dance the polka'
                                   ∅   1+picc.22.sx.2/2230.euph/perc/str   Reynolds   1492

SOMERS, Debroy

BATTLE DRESS: regimental march medley
                                 PC   112.4sx.1/2330/perc/str   Boosey & H   16767 B
CAVALCADE OF MARTIAL SONGS: selection by D.Somers & H.Nicholls
                                      1[1]1.3sx.[1]/[2]210/perc/gtr/str   L.Wright   12636 Ap
CHILDHOOD MEMORIES: selection PC   112.3sx.1/2220/perc/hp/str   K.Prowse   6683 Ap B
ERINALIA: Irish waltz medley   PC   111.3sx.1/2210/perc/2bjo/str   Chappell   11705 Ap
FANTASIA: selection from the Walt Disney film
                                 PC   112.3sx.1/2220/perc/hp/str   Chappell   16720 B
FOR THE FORCES: an Empire medley
                                 PC   101.4sx.0/0320/timp.perc/bjo.gtr/str Chappell,1940   20903
HUNGARIAN MEDLEY by D.Somers & F.E.Bentley
                                      111.3sx.1/2210/perc.bjo/str   6'30" L.Wright   9168 Atvc
OPERAS IN RHYTHM: selection from Bizet's 'Carmen' and Gounod's 'Faust'
                                 PC   1(picc)11.3sx.1/2220/perc/bjo/str   Chappell   12637
POEM: arrangement of extract from op.39 of Fibich
                                 PC   112.2sx.1/2210/timp.perc/2bjo/str   K.Prowse   1721 Bni
SAVOY AMERICAN MEDLEY   PC   111.3sx.1/2210/perc/bjo/str   L.Wright   2345
SAVOY CHRISTMAS MEDLEY   PC   112.4sx.1/2210/perc/bjo/str   K.Prowse   3281 Atvc Bp Dp E
SAVOY COMMUNITY MEDLEY   PC   112.4sx.1/1210/perc/3bjo/str   K.Prowse   8737 Ap

SOMERS, Debroy (cont)

SAVOY ENGLISH MEDLEY	PC	111.4sx.1/2320/perc/bjo.gtr/str		L.Wright	5296 Atvc Cp
SAVOY HUNTING MEDLEY	PC	102.3sx.1/2210/perc/bjo/str		K.Prowse	8736 Atvc Cp
arr W.Goehr, orch L.Wurmser	φ	2222/4330/timp/str		BBC	TO 1554 φ only
SAVOY IRISH MEDLEY	PC	112.3sx.1/2320/perc/gtr/str		L.Wright	6017 Ap Btvc CniD
SAVOY MEDLEY OF MEDLEYS	PC	112.3sx.1/2210/perc/bjo/str		L.Wright	1858 Ap B
SAVOY MEDLEY OF MINSTREL SONGS (based on songs by Stephen Foster)					
	PC	112.4sx.1/2320/perc/gtr/str		K.Prowse	16456 Atvc C
SAVOY MEDLEY OF SOLDIER SONGS	PC	112.4sx.1/2320/perc/gtr/str		K.Prowse	16454
SAVOY RUSSIAN MEDLEY	PC	111.3sx.1/2210/timp.perc/2bjo/str		K.Prowse	3571
SAVOY SCOTTISH MEDLEY	PC	112.3sx.1/2210/perc/bjo/str		L.Wright	3181 Ap Ctvc
SAVOY SOUTHERN MEDLEY	PC	000.3sx.0/0210/perc/bjo:gtr/str		FD & H	15478
SAVOY WELSH MEDLEY	PC	112.4sx.1/2210/perc/bjo/str		L.Wright	1859 B
SEA SONGS: selection	PC	1(picc)12.3sx.1/2210/perc/bjo/str		K.Prowse	7781 A Bpc
THIS ENGLAND: selection of traditional airs					
	PC	1(picc)11.3sx.1/2220/perc/str		Cinephonic	14163 Ap
VALSE MEMORIES: selection	PC	101.3sx.1/2210/timp.perc/str		K.Prowse	6308 Ap

SOMERS, Harry Stewart (1925-

MOVEMENT FOR ORCHESTRA	φ	2222/3331/timp.perc/hp/str	10'	Ricordi,1964	Misc 5964
NORTH COUNTRY: 4 movements for strings orch					
	φ	str		B.M.I.Canada,1960	Misc 5439

SOMERSET, Henry Vene Fitzroy (1898-

A SONG OF SLEEP					
in F	φ	1111/1000/timp.perc/hp/str		BBC	MS 4634
arr E.Griffiths	φ	2121/2220/timp/hp/str		(Ricordi)	MS 4634 φ only
arr H.Finck for cornet solo & orch					
	PC	2122/2000/timp/str		Ricordi	895

SOMERVELL, Arthur (1863-1937)

AIR, in C	φ	str		J.Williams	9354
The BARGAIN: 'My true love hath a heart': song					
in C, arr G.Stacey		pf/str	2'30"	(W.Rogers)	LM G 3592
CONCERTO for violin & orch, in G min					
	φ	2222/3231/timp/str	34'-36'30"	Boosey	Misc 1207
CROSSING THE BAR: song					
in A♭, arr R.Chignell	φ	2222/4231/timp.perc/hp/str		(Ashdown)	MS 4908
The GENTLE MAIDEN: Irish song, arr					
in D♭, E♭ & F, orch S.Robinson					
	φ	31+ca.1+bcl.2/4000/str		(Cramer)	20332
HELEN OF KIRKCONNELL	PC	2+picc.222/4231/timp/str		Novello	3185
IN ARCADY: suite					
1. Introduction 4. Sunset					
2. In the woods 5. Gipsies					
3. Fairy rings					
	φ	2022/2000/str	15'30"	Stanley Lucas	953
IN SUMMERTIME ON BREDON: song see A SHROPSHIRE LAD					
JENNY JONES: song					
in D, arr H.Carr	φ	2121/2230/perc/hp/str		(Boosey)	TO 39

SOMERVELL, Arthur (cont)

LOVE IN SPRING-TIME: song cycle
   Young love lies sleeping
      in G, arr F.Cramer   pf/str   3'   (Boosey)   LM G 4667
        in Bb   φ 1110/0000/str   (Boosey)   MLO 579
        in Bb & B, arr S.Robinson φ 2121/2000/hp/str   (Boosey)   TO 944
LOVELIEST OF TREES: song <u>see</u> A SHROPSHIRE LAD
The LOVING HEART: incidental music
   6 dances
     1. Sarabande   4. Pavane
     2. Pantomime   5. Passepied
     3. Two gavottes   6. Jig
                      φ str   Augener   2942
MAUD: song cycle
   Birds in the high Hall-garden
      in Ab, arr J.Beaver   φ 1121/0210/hp.pf/str   (Boosey)   MS 13560
      in Ab, arr Gill   φ 1030/0020/perc/cel/str   (Boosey)   MS 15177
   Come into the garden Maud
      in G, arr G.Stacey   1110/0000/perc/acdn.hp.pf/str   (Boosey)   LM A 684
   She came to the village church
      in D min, arr L.Wurmser φ 31+ca.22/2000/str   1'30"   (Boosey)   TO 1814
   A Voice by the cedar tree
      in F, arr L.Wurmser   φ 3222/4230/timp.perc/hp/str 3'45"   (Boosey)   TO 1815
MENTRA GWEN <u>see</u> VENTURE, GWEN
The PASSION OF CHRIST: oratorio
   Praise to the holiest in the height
     arr H.Perry   PC 1121/0000/timp.perc/org/str   Hawkes   4970
PRETTY POLLY OLIVER: traditional song, arr
   in Eb, arr H.Carr   φ 2121/2230/timp.perc/hp/str   (Cramer)   TO 825
SHEPHERD'S CRADLE SONG
   in Eb, G & A   str   (Siddell)   17886
   in F   φ str   Mathias & Strickland 17885 +
   in G, F & A, arr F.Bye φ 1121/1000/str   Ashdown   MLO 197
A SHROPSHIRE LAD: song cycle
   In summertime on Bredon
      in B, arr F.Cramer   pf/str   (Boosey & H) LM G 4534
   Loveliest of trees
      in E, arr H.Carr   φ 2121/2230/timp/hp/str   2'15"   (Boosey)   TO 630
The SNOWY-BREASTED PEARL: Irish song, arr
   in E, arr S.Robinson   φ 3222/4000/hp/str   (Cramer)   20331
SYMPHONY in D min (Thalassa) φ 22+ca.22+cbsn/4231/timp.perc/str   Boosey   2182
The TWA SISTERS OF BINNARIE: song, arr
   in C, orch F.Bye   φ 1121/2210/hp/str   (Boosey)   MLO 490
The VALE OF CLWYD: Welsh song, arr
   in F min, arr H.Carr   φ 0222/4231/timp.perc/hp/str 2'45"   (Boosey)   20366
VENTURE, GWEN (Mentra Gwen): Welsh song, arr
   in A, arr H.Carr   φ 2121/2230/perc/hp/str   (Boosey)   TO 90
YOUNG APRIL: overture (1910) φ 2222+cbsn/4231/timp/str   Composer,1910 Misc 10117
YOUNG LOVE LIES SLEEPING: song <u>see</u> LOVE IN SPRING-TIME

SOMERVILLE, Reginald

4 FANCIES: suite   PC 1121/2230/timp/str   Hawkes   4717 B
The HONEY BEE   PC 1121/2230/timp/str   AH & C   3655
The KNIGHT ERRANT   PC 1121/2230/timp/str   Hawkes   10135 B
3 LIGHT PIECES
   1. Bagatelle   2. Melody   3. Valse
                   PC 2222/2230/timp.perc/str   Hawkes   820 Bni

SOMERVILLE, Reginald (cont)

SABOT DANCE	PC	1121/2230/perc/str	Hawkes	1459
SOUVENIR D'AUTREFOIS	PC	2222/2230/timp/str	Hawkes	1431

SOMMER, Vladimir (1921-

VOCAL SYMPHONY for Mezzo-soprano solo, speaker, chorus & orch (1958)
φ   3(2picc)3(ca)2+E♭cl+bcl.3(cbsn/4331/
timp.perc.tamtam.xyl/cel.hp.pf/str   31'35"   Panton,1965   Misc 8147

SOMMERFELDT, Øistein (1919-

SINFONIA, op.12 (La Betulla)(1974)
φ   2+picc.222/4331/timp.perc.xyl/str   18'   Norsk,1976   Misc 9050
SUITE for chamber orch, op.7b (1958, rev 1973)(orig for pf)
  1. Liten marsj (Miniature march)   4. Liten jente (Lassie)
  2. Bånsull (Lullaby)   5. Stribukken (Hard-head)
  3. Vals (Waltz)
φ   1(picc)121/2110/1perc(timp.tamtam.xyl)/str   9'   Norsk,1975   Misc 9049

SOMMERFELT, Waldemar

NORWEGIAN RUSTIC WEDDING   PC   1111/2110/timp/str   AH & C   2648 B

SOMMERLATTE, Ulrich

DADDY-SUITE
  1. Hallo Daddy!   3. Der neue Hut
  2. Daddy träumt   4. Der Autokavalier
                    PC   2(picc)11+bcl.1/3330/perc(glock.xyl)/
                         cel.gtr.hp/str   Baváriaton,1957(H)   PL 533
TRAUMBALLETT (Dream ballet): suite
  1. Wandernde Schatten   3. Pan und Flöte
  2. Die schwarzen Schwäne   4. Tanz in den Morgen
                    φ   2121/2230/timp.perc/hp.pf/str   12'   Canzonetta,1960   Misc 6363

SONDHEIM, Stephen (1930-

A LITTLE NIGHT MUSIC: musical play
  Extracts
    Remember
      arr P.Knight for Soprano & Tenor soli & orch
          φPC 1+picc.1+ca.22/4100/timp.perc/hp.pf(cel)/
               str   (Arranger)   26716

SONG AND TUNE SHEETS, arr Herbert

No. 1   Love's old sweet song, by J.Molloy, in F   Drink to me only, attrib R.Mellish, in A♭
         The bonnie banks of Loch Lomond, in F
                    PC   112.sx.2/41.cnt.30/perc/str   Boosey   7241 Ap B
No. 2 Sea shanties
         Hullabaloo balay, by S.T.Harris, in A♭   Stormalong, in D♭
         A long time ago, in A♭   Fire down below, in F
         Roll the wood-pile down, in E♭
                    PC   1122/2230/perc/str   Boosey   7334 Ap
No. 3   John Brown's body, in B♭   Marching through Georgia, by H.C.Work, in A♭
         The tramp, tramp, tramp, by G.F.Root, in B♭   The farmer's boy, in B♭
                    PC   1132/23.3cnt.30/perc/str   Boosey   8079

SONG AND TUNE SHEETS (cont)

No. 4	Off to Philadelphia, adapted B.Haynes, in C	My ain folk, by L.Lemon, in Eb
	The road to the isles, adapted Kennedy-Fraser, in Ab	The drunken sailor, in C
	PC 1132/2330/perc/str	Boosey 7390 Bp C
No. 5	Good-night (Shine, shine moon, by Scott-Gatty, in Bb	Old folks at home, by Foster, in Db
	De ole banjo, by Scott-Gatty, in C	Missouri (Shenandoah), in Eb
	PC 1132/4330/perc/str	Boosey 7488 Aj
No. 6	On guard, by W.H.Squire, in G	Keep on hopin', by K.Heron-Maxwell,
	We won't stop singing, by S.Dickson, in Eb	in C
	PC 1132/23.cnt.30/perc/str	Boosey 8084
No. 7	Charlie is my darling, in C	Robin Adair, in Ab
	Annie Laurie, by Lady J.Scott, in C	Auld lang syne, in F
	Mary of Argyle, by S.Nelson, in F	
	P.C 113.2sx.2/4430.euph/perc/str	Boosey 8083 Ap
No. 8	John Peel, in Eb	Clementine, by P.Montrose, in Ab
	There is a tavern, in C	Buy a broom (Air 'Liber Augustin',
	Here's a health unto His Majesty, by J.Saville, in Gb	attrib A.Lee), in F
	PC 1132/2330/perc/str	Boosey 8082
No. 9	Sacred night, holy night, by F.Grüber, in Bb	When evening's twilight, by J.L.
	Farewell to the forest (Abschied), by Mendelssohn,	Hatton, in Ab
	in Db	Sweet and low, by J.Barnby, in C
	PC 1121/2230/perc/str	Boosey 1650 Ap
No.10	Land of my fathers, by J.James, in Eb	The ash grove, in Ab
	All through the night (trad), in F	Men of Harlech, in F
	PC 1(picc)13.2sx.2/4330/perc/str	Boosey 8081 Ap C
No.11	Carols	
	The first Nowell, in Eb	It came upon the midnight clear, in F
	O come all ye faithful, in Ab	While shepherds watched, in F
	Good King Wenceslas, in Ab	
	PC 113.2sx.2/4330.euph/perc/str	Boosey 8080 Dp
No.12	Oft in the stilly night, attrib S.Stevenson, in Bb	The minstrel boy, in Eb
	Come back to Erin, by Claribel, in C	Killarney, by W.M.Balfe, in F
	PC 1132/2231/str	Boosey 5299
No.13	Grace: 'For these and all thy mercies', in F	Lead kindly light, by J.B.Dykes, in F
	Vesper hymn, in Eb	Abide with me, by W.H.Monk, in Eb
	Allelulia (An Easter Hymn), in Eb	
	PC 1132/2430/perc/str	Boosey 8085 Ap
No.15	The march of the Cameron men, in C	Scotch reel, in C
	The hundred pipers, in Eb	The flowers of the forest: lament,
	Bonnie Dundee, attrib C.Sainton-Dolby, in Eb	in Ab
	PC 113.2sx.2/2230/perc/str	Boosey 10698 Ap
No.16	Set of toasts	
	God save the Queen (The Queen), in F	God bless the Prince of Wales, in Ab
	The British grenadiers (The army), in Bb	The red, white and blue (The navy),
		in Bb
	The girl I left behind me (The army), in Eb	Hearts of oak (The navy), in Bb
	PC 1121/4230/perc/str	Boosey 12807
No.17	Set of toasts	
	Rule Britannia (England), in F	Wearing of the green (Ireland), in Eb
	Scots wae hae (Scotland), in Bb	Land of my fathers (Wales), in Eb
	Blue bells of Scotland (Scotland), in Eb	Men of Harlech (Wales), in Bb
	St. Patrick's day (Ireland), in Bb	
	PC 1121/2230/perc/str	Boosey 9249 Ap Cs
No.18	Set of toasts	
	The roast beef of old England (For dinner), in Bb	Here's to the maiden, in Bb
	For he's a jolly good fellow (The host), in F	See the conquering hero, in Bb
	Fine old English gentleman (Private gentleman), in Eb	Home sweet home (Return home), in F
	Here's a health to all good lasses (The ladies), in F	Auld lang syne (At parting), in F
	PC 1121/2230/perc/str	Boosey 9248 Bp Cp

SONG AND TUNE SHEETS (cont)

No.19 Set of toasts
    A life on the ocean wave (Navy, etc.), in A♭   John Peel (Hunting song), in E♭
    Let Erin remember (Ireland), in E♭   Speed the plough: country dance, in B♭
    The last rose of summer (Ireland), in E♭   Glorious Apollo (for harmony), in E♭
    Will ye no come back (Scotland), in F   The mistletoe bough (Christmas), in B♭
        PC 112.2sx.1/4230/perc/str
                                                              Boosey   9222 Ap B

No.20 They all love Jack, by S.Adams, in E♭   The sailor's hornpipe, in F
    Away for Rio Grande: sea shanty, in E♭
        PC 1122/22.cnt.30/perc/str
                                                              Boosey   9221 Bp C

No.21 Come lasses and lads: country dance, in E♭   The Irish washerwoman: jig, in E♭
    Sir Roger de Coverley: country dance, in F   The college hornpipe, in C
    Tullochgorum: highland fling, in F
        PC 112.2sx.1/2230/str
                                                              Boosey   386 Bp

No.23 Glorious Devon, by E.German, in D♭   Widdicombe fair, in A♭
        PC 1121/2230.euph/perc/str
                                                              Boosey   552 Ap

SONIN, Ray

The ONE THAT GOT AWAY: song
  in E♭, arr B.Thompson   ø 1110/0000/hp.pf/str   (Evans & Lowry,1947)   LM G 8881

SONNINEN, Ahti (1914-

El AMOR PASA: 4 poems for flute, Soprano & chamber orch, op.40
  1. Los sospiros   3. Hoy como ayer
  2. Hoyla tierra   4. Los invisibles
           ø 0.picc.110/2000/perc/str   11'   Composer,1953   21160

SONNTAG, Eugen

MAIENTÄNZE   ø 1121/2210/perc.glock/hp/str   Afa-Verlag   Misc 34

SONNTAG, G.

NIBELUNGEN MARSCH
  arr Hoffmann   PC 2+picc.222/4331/perc/str   Schott   4800

SONTINI, R.

MIRAMAR: waltz
  arr A.Lotter   PC 1+picc.222/4230/perc/str   Hawkes   120

SONTONGA, Enoch

MUNGU IBARKI AFRICA: National Anthem of Tanzania (formerly of Tanganyika: retained on union with
  Zanzibar, 1964)
  in F, arr G.French   ø 2222/2230/timp.perc/str   Arranger/Blandford   25520
  in G, arr N.Fulton   ø 2222/4230/timp/str   (Lovedale Press,S.Africa)   23456 +

SONZOGNO, Giulio Cesare (1906-1976)

BOULE DE SUITE: opera
  Complete   ø 2222+cbsn/4331/timp.perc.xyl/hp.pf/str
                  Offstage: 0000/1000
                                                       Curci,1970   Misc 8290
QUADRI RUSTICI
  1. Adillio Montano   2. Battibecchi
           ø 12(ca)11/2210/perc/hp/str   Suivini Zerboni   14350

SOPRONI, Joszef (1930-

EKLYPSIS (1969)   ⌀   322+bcl.2/3441/timp.perc.bells.mba/
                                   cel.hp.pf/str   8'   Ed Musica,1971   Misc 7613

SORABJI, Kaikhosru Shapurji (1892-

CONCERTO for piano & orch, no.2 (1920)
                              ⌀   2+picc+bfl.2+ca.2+bcl.2+cbsn/4431/
                                   timp.perc.tamtam.xyl/cel.hp/str   Curwen   Misc 848 B

SORESINA, Alberto (1911-

SONATA for small orch   ⌀   1111/2100/timp/str   Curci,1962   Misc 8244

SORO, Enrique (1884-1954)

RECUERDO
    arr A.Schmid   PC   1121/2210/timp.perc/str   G.Schirmer   2637

SOUKKARI, Dia

SACT EL ZIND (1967)   ⌀   1110/0000/perc/pf/str   (Composer)   Misc 7556

SOUSA, John Philip (1854-1932)

ANCHOR AND STAR: march
    arr M.L.Lake   PC   112.2sx.1/2210/perc/str   C.Fischer   10091 Ap
The BLACK HORSE TROOP: march PC   112.3sx.1/2210/perc/str   Sam Fox   11859 Ap
BULLETS AND BOYONETS: march PC   1(picc)222/2210/perc/str   G.Schirmer   9706 Ap
Les CADETS: High School Cadets march
    arr F.Salabert   ⌀   112.3sx.1/2230.euph/perc/str   Salabert   13727 Bp
    arr F.Salabert   ⌀   1121/2210/perc/str (additional parts by A.Franzel)   Salabert   12658
CAMERA STUDIES: suite
    1. The flashing eyes of Andalusia   3. The children's ball
    2. Drifting to loveland
                              PC   1121/2210/timp.perc/str   10'30"   Sam Fox   5159
El CAPITAN: march   ⌀   3(picc)222/4231/timp.perc/str   J.Church   47 Cni Dp E
A CENTURY OF PROGRESS: High School Cadets march
    arr F.Salabert   PC   1121/4230/perc/str   Presser   10086 Ap
The CHANTYMAN'S MARCH
    arr M.L.Lake   PC   112.sx.1/2210/perc/str   C.Fischer   10090 Ap
COMRADES OF THE LEGION: march PC 1121/1210/perc/str   Sam Fox   4735 Ap
The CRUSADER MARCH   ⌀   1(picc)221/2211/perc/str   Coleman   16864
The DIPLOMAT MARCH   PC   1222/2210/perc/str   Salabert   13726 Ap
DWELLERS IN THE WESTERN WORLD: suite
    1. The red man   2. The white man   3. The black man (3'30")
        arr Merz   ⌀   2+picc.222/4231/perc/str   J.Church   14645
        arr Merz   PC   2+picc.222/4231/perc/str   J.Church   515
The FAIREST OF THE FAIR: march PC 1(picc)121/2231/perc/str   J.Church   7543
The GALLANT SEVENTH: march   PC   112.2sx.1/2210/perc/str   Sam Fox   4739 Ap B
The GLADIATOR: march
    arr A.Winter   ⌀   222.2sx.2/4231/perc/str   2'45"   Boosey & H   2310 Bp C
The GLORY OF THE YANKEE NAVY: march
                              ⌀   3222/4231/timp.perc/hp/str   3'15"   J.Church   2337
The GRIDIRON CLUB MARCH   PC   122.3sx.1/2210/perc/str   Sam Fox   11858 As B
HANDS ACROSS THE SEA: march ⌀   3222/4231/timp.perc/str   J.Church   1913 Bp

SOUSA, John Philip (cont)

IMPERIAL EDWARD: march	∅	2+picc.222/4231/perc/str	2'30"	Salabert	5596
The INVINCIBLE EAGLE: march	PC	1121/1210/timp/str		J.Church	2069
KING COTTON: march	PC	222.2sx.2/2210/perc/str		J.Church	1414 Bp C
	∅	2222/2231/timp.perc/hp/str		J.Church	1302
The LIBERTY BELL: march					
arr A.Winter	∅	2+picc.2+ca.2+bcl.2/4331.euph/perc/str		Hawkes	860 Dp
LOYAL LEGION: march	∅	3222/4231/timp.perc/hp/str	2'30"	Hawkes	3387
MANHATTAN BEACH: march	PC	222.2sx.2/2230/perc/str		Hawkes	852
NATIONAL FENCIBLES: march	PC	2(picc)121/2211/perc/str		C.Fischer	1422
The NATIONAL GAME: march	PC	112.3sx.1/2210/perc/str		Sam Fox	11857
NEW YORK HIPPODROME: march	∅	2222/4231/perc/str	2'40"	FD & H	16863
NOBLES OF THE MYSTIC SHRINE: march					
	PC	112.2sx.1/2210/perc/str		Sam Fox	4740
The NORTHERN PINES	∅	3(picc)22.2sx.2/4231/timp.perc/hp/str	3'	G.Schirmer	12640
ON THE CAMPUS: march	PC	112.2sx.1/2210/perc/str		Sam Fox	4737
POWHATAN'S DAUGHTER: march	PC	2222/4231/perc/str		J.Church	16865
PRESIDENTIAL POLONAISE	∅	1(picc)221/2211/perc/str		Coleman	16864

3 QUOTATIONS: suite

1. The King of France   3. In darkest Africa
2. I, too, was born in Arcadia

	PC	1(picc)2+ca.22/2210/timp.perc/str		J.Church	2853 B
SABRE AND SPURS: march of the American Cavalry (2 versions)					
'A' version, arr S.Robinson		2+picc.222/40.2cnt.31/timp.perc/hp/str		Sam Fox	4736
'B' orig printed version	PC	1121/20.2cnt.1[=2]0/perc/str		Sam Fox	4736
SEMPER FIDELIS: march	PC	2(picc)121/2211/perc/str	3'	C.Fischer	1422 Ap
arr A.Winter	∅	2(picc)22.2sx.2/4231/perc/str		Boosey & H	3254 C
SESQUI CENTENNIAL EXPOSITION MARCH					
	PC	112.3sx.1/2210/perc/str		Sam Fox	11856 B
SOLID MEN TO THE FRONT: march	PC	1121/2210/perc/str		G.Schirmer	7477

SOUSA MARCH FOLIO

1. Stars and Stripes forever   8. Hail to the Spirit of Liberty
2. Powhatan's daughter   9. Man behind the gun
3. Free lance (On to victory)   10. Hands across the sea
4. The diplomat   11. The charlatan
5. Jack Tar   12. The bride-elect
6. Imperial Edward   13. Yorktown centennial march
7. Invincible eagle   14. The white plume

	PC	212.2sx.2/2230/perc/str		J. Church	6858 B
STARS AND STRIPES FOREVER: march					
	∅	2(picc)222/423[1]/timp.perc/hp/str		J.Church	2023 Ap Cm Dwe E
The THUNDERER: march					
arr Seredy	PC	2+picc.222/4231/timp.perc/hp/str	2'30"	C.Fischer	5932
The WASHINGTON POST: march	∅	1121/2220/perc/str		Hawkes	862
WEDDING MARCH	PC	1121/2210/perc/str		Sam Fox	4753
The WHITE PLUME: march	PC	1222/2210/perc/str		J.Church	1912

SOUSTER, Tim (1943-

SONATA for cello, piano, 7 wind instruments & percussion (1978-9)(BBC Commission)

∅	1(picc,afl)1(ca)0.Ebcl.bcl.1/0101/perc.3Japanese bell. 2crot.Chinese cym.8Moroccan pottery dm.hihat.mbn. metal plate.2tamtam.2timb.2tomtom.vib/pf/vlc		Composer,1979	26676
SONG OF AN AVERAGE CITY (1973/4) ∅	1(picc)+picc.1+ca.1(bcl)+Ebcl.2+cbsn/1111/elec/str		(Composer,1974)	25722

TRIPLE MUSIC II for 3 orchestras (1969-70)

∅	orch I str			
	orch II vib/cel.bgtr.2hp.org.Horg.2pf/2sound mixers			
	orch III: 4(2picc,afl)2+ca.4(bcl)+Ebcl.4sx.2+2cbsn/ 6431	28'35"	(Composer,1970)	25066 +

SOWANDE, Fela

AFRICAN SUITE
   1. Joyful day (6'45")   4. Onipe (2'45")
   2. Nostalgia (3'45")   5. Akinla (3'30")
   3. Lullaby   (6'15")
                      ø hp/str   23'   Chappell,1955   21596
A FOLK SYMPHONY: a symphony of Nigerian folk-melodies (1960)
                  ø   21+ca.22/4231/timp.perc.cbell/hp/str   (Composer)   Misc 8782

SOWERBY, Leo (1895-1968)

COMES AUTUMN TIME: programme overture
                  ø 2+picc.22+bcl.2/4331/timp.perc.bells/
                      cel.hp/str   5'35"   Boston Music Co Misc 782
CONCERT OVERTURE (1941)   ø 2+picc.222/4331/timp.perc.bells/hp/str   Music Press,1941 Misc 2387
FROM THE NORTHLAND: impressions of Lake Superior country
   1. Forest voices   3. Burnt rock pool
   2. Cascades   4. The shining big sea water
                  ø 222+Ebcl+bcl.2+cbsn/4331/timp.perc/cel.hp/str   Schirmer   18778
The IRISH WASHERWOMAN: country dance tune, arr
                  ø 2+picc.2+ca.22/433[1]/perc/hp.pf/str   Boston Music Co 8052 B
MONEY MUSK: country dance tune, arr
                  ø 3(2picc)22+bcl.2/433[1]/perc/hp/str   Birchard   7682

SPAIN-DUNK, Susan

The FARMER'S BOY: overture   1000/0000/str   6'   Cranz   13316 B
2 SCOTTISH PIECES
   1. By St. Mary's loch   2. Kerrera
                  ø 1(picc)121/2210/timp.perc/str   Stainer & B   14832
SERENADE DE CAPRI
   arr Adlington   PC 1121/2230/timp.perc/str   4'45"   Hawkes   10157 B
SPANISH DANCES: suite, arr
   1. El Ole (3')   3. Aragonaise (2')
   2. El Jaleo (3')   4. Pepita   (2')
                  PC 1121/2210/timp.perc/str   10'   Universal   13873
WEALD OF KENT: fantasie   112.3sx.1/2210/timp.perc/str   4' Screen Mus Pub Co 15771

SPARROW, Fred W.

The LITTLE PLACE FOR YOU: song
   in D   org.pf/str   Chappell,1918   18203

SPAWFORTH, J.

ENTR'ACTE in D   2222/4230/timp.perc/hp/str   Boosey   17624 B

SPEAKS, Oley (1874-1948)

MORNING: song
   in C min, B min & Bb min, arr G.Stacey
                      pf/str   (Chappell)   LM G 3467
   orch B.Thompson   ø hp.pf/str   BBC   MS 20283
ON THE ROAD TO MANDALAY: song
   in C & Bb, arr G.Stacey   pf/str   (Boosey)   LM G 3695
   in C, arr S.Torch   ø 2(picc)1+ca.22/4330/timp.perc/hp.pf(cel)/str   (Boosey)   23973 +
   in C, arr J.Turner   ø 1110/1000/hp/str   (Boosey)   LM G 9280

SPEAKS, Oley (cont)

The PRAYER PERFECT: song
   in F, arr L.Woodgate   ø   1122/2000/hp/str   BBC   MS 8317
SYLVIA: song
   in E♭, arr A.Franzel   ø   1110/0000/acdn.hp.pf/str   (Boosey)   LM G 3434
   in G, arr A.Franzel   pf/str   (Boosey)   LM G 3434
   orch O.Langey   PC 112.3sx.1/2210/timp/str   Boosey & H   10734
   orch Phillips   PC 112.3sx.1/2210/timp.perc/hp/str   Boosey   10979

SPEER, William Henry (1863-1937)

FESTIVAL OVERTURE, op.9   ø   2222/2230/timp/str   Novello   Misc 3532

SPELMAN, Timothy Mather (1891-1970)

BARBARESQUES: suite   ø   2(picc)2(ca)22/2120/timp.perc.glock/hp/str   Chester   Misc 2964 B
JAMBOREE: a rustic carnival ø   113.4sx.1/1331/perc/2hp.pf/str   (C.Connelly) 18669

SPENCE, Lee

The MERRY MIDDY
   arr Dulay   PC [1][1][1]0/0000/str   Ashdown   5806

SPENDYAROV, Aleksandr Afanasyevich (1871-1928)

ESQUISSES DE LA CRIMÉE, op.9
   1. Air de danse   3. Chanson à boire
   2. Chanson élégiaque   4. Air de danse 'Khaîtarma'
                     ø   2+picc.2+ca.22/4231/timp.perc/hp/str   Bessel   3315
2 MORCEAUX, op.3
   1. Menuet   2. Berceuse
                     ø   2222/2000/hp/str   Bessel   6709 B
OUVERTURE DE CONCERT, op.4, in D
                     ø   2+picc.222/4231/timp/str   Bessel   14599
PRÉLUDE FUNÈBRE, op.20   ø   2022/4000/perc/hp/str   Belaieff   Misc 1772
Les TROIS PALMIERS: symphonic poem, op.10
                     ø   2+picc.2+ca.3(bcl)2+cbsn/4231/timp.perc/
                       2hp/str   19'   Belaieff   6067
VALSE DE CONCERT, op.18   ø   3(picc)2(ca)22/4231/timp.perc/hp/str   Jurgenson 2859

SPERGER, Johann Matthias (1750-1812)

CASSATIONS
   in D
     ed R.Malarić   ø   1000/2000/str   Doblinger,1980 26965 *
   in G
     ed R.Malarić   ø   0000/2000/str   Doblinger,1980 26966 *

SPIALEK, Hans

BEAU GESTE: film see BRADFORD, James: BEAU GESTE: film - music by J.Bradford & H.Spialek
The TALL CITY: suite
   1. General view   4. Moon over the city
   2. The avenue   5. Holiday
   3. A shanty between two sky-scrapers
                     ø   3(3picc)2+ca.3+bcl.[3sx].2+cbsn/4431/
                       timp.perc.bells.vib.xyl/cel.hp.pf/str 20' Chappell   Misc 889
WOLGA-GIPSIES: overture, op.39 PC 1110/0110/timp.perc/str   Bote & B   11914

SPIEGL, Fritz

Z CARS: signature tune   see   FRY, Bridget: Z CARS: signature tune by B.Fry & F.Spiegl

SPIER, Larry

MEMORY LANE: song by Spier & Conrad
    in F, arr C.Grant   1121/2210/timp.perc/str   Chappell,1924   18301
    in G, arr G.Stacey   1010/0000/perc/pf/str   (Chappell)   LM A 111

SPIES, Ernst

COMIC OVERTURE for 4 wind instruments, op.61, in A
                   ø   1011/1000   Oertel   8804

SPINDLER, Fritz (1817-1905)

HUSARENRITT, op.140, no.3   ø   1+picc.121/221[1]/perc/str   2'15"   Kistner & S   5435

SPINKS, Charles

CONCERT TOCCATA for organ & brass, op.9
                   ø   0000/4331   (Lengnick,1957)   Misc 4793
FARM FARE: signature tune & links based on the folk song 'Mrs Bond', arr C.Spinks & F.Wade
                   ø   1100/1000/cel/str   (Lengnick)   MS 30720
SUITE for flute & string orchestra, op.14
                        str   Lengnick,1958   22735

SPINNER, Leopold (1906-1980)

CANTATA ON GERMAN FOLKSONG TEXTS, for Mezzo-soprano solo, chorus & orch, op.20
                   ø   11+ca.1+bcl.0/110.btbn.0/perc/cel.hp/
                        vln.vla.vlc.cb   Boosey & H,1978   Misc 9765
CONCERTO for piano & chamber orch, op.4
                   ø   111+bcl.0/1110/cym.tamtam.xyl/hp/str 4-tet   Boosey & H,1968   Misc 6703
PRELUDE AND VARIATIONS, op.18 ø 11+ca.1+bcl.0/1111/timp.perc.glock.tamtam.vib/
                        cel.hp/str   12'   Boosey & H   Misc 6039

SPISAK, Michael (1914-1965)

CONCERTO GIOCOSO for chamber orch
                   ø   2222/2211/timp.xyl/hp.pf/str   Leduc,1960   Misc 5547
SUITE for strings   ø   str   16'   Polish SM   Misc 2740 B
SYMPHONIE CONCERTANTE no.2 (1956)
                   ø   1111/0000/2vln.vla.vlc-soli.str   Polish SM,1959   Misc 6269

SPITZMÜLLER, Alexander (1894-1962)

CONCERT DANS L'ESPRIT LATIN, op.37
    1. Sinfonia   3. Permutazioni
    2. Serenata del Corso   4. Commedia
                   ø   1011/0100/perc/pf/str   19'   Hawkes,1952   Misc 3857
3 HYMNES À LA PAIX, op.27
    Magnificat   Prière   Frénésie
                   ø   2(picc)2+ca.22+cbsn/4331/timp.perc/2hp/str   Universal   Misc 3064
40e MAI (18/5/42): suite for chamber orch, op.25
    Très vif   2. Angélique   3. Allègre
                   ø   1(picc)111/2200/timp.perc.xyl/cel/str   Universal   Misc 3063

SPIVAKOVSK, Michael

MEMOIR	pf/str		3'	Schott	19739
TANGO OF VIOLINS					
arr R.Hanmer	PC 1121/2320/timp.perc/gtr/str			F.Benson,1955	21716

SPOHR, Louis (1784-1859)

Der ALCHYMIST: opera					
Overture	2+picc.222/4230/timp/str			Schlesinger	23914
ALRUNA, DIE EULEN-KÖNIGIN: opera					
Overture	∅	2222/2220/str		André [1814]	21153 +
Der BERGGEIST: opera, op.73					
Overture		2222/4230/timp/str		Peters	23916
CONCERT OVERTURE 'Im ernsten Styl', op.126					
	∅	2222/4230/timp/str		Kistner & S	6472
CONCERTANTE					
2 violins & orch					
No. 1, op.48, in A min	∅	1222/2000/str		Peters,1850	21393
No. 2, op.88, in B		2022/2000/str		Simrock,1834	21402
CONCERTI					
Clarinet & orch					
No. 1, op.26, in C min	∅	2202/2200/timp/str	23'	(Peters)	23426 +
ed F.Leinert	∅	2202/2200/timp/str		Bärenreiter,1957	Misc 5039 B
No. 2, op.57, in E♭	∅	2202/4200/timp/str		(GB:Lam)	Misc 9921
No. 4, in E min (1828/9)					
ed H.Genser	∅	2222/22[=2clarini]10/timp/str		Spohr Gesellschaft,1976.CW 5	MRL
ed G.E.Rischka	∅	2222/4230/timp/str		(D.D.Rundfunk)	Misc 5787
String quartet & orch, op.131					
	∅	2222/2230/timp/str		Breitkopf,1846	21148 + & mf 177
ed K.Weelink	∅	2222/2230/timp/str		K.W.Verlag,1963	24000
Violin & orch					
No. 1, op. 1, in A					
ed F.Göthel	∅	1222/2010/timp/str		Bärenreiter,1955	Misc 4427
No. 3, op. 7, in C min		2222/2200/str		Peters,1806	21149 +
No. 6, op.28, in G min	∅	2222/3000/str		Haslinger,1835	21396 +
No. 7, op.38, in E min		2222/2200/timp/str	27'	Breitkopf	23296
ed F.Göthel	∅	2222/2200/timp/str		Spohr Gesellschaft,1963.CW 1	Misc 8988 & MRL
No. 8, op.47, in A min ('in Form einer Gesangscene')					
	∅	1021/2000/str	20'	Breitkopf	6902 +
No. 9, op.55, in D min	∅	2222/2230/timp/str		Richault,1823	21397
Rondo: finale only	∅	2222/2230/timp/str		BBC	Misc 3207
No.12, op.79, in A	∅	2222/2200/timp/str		Schlesinger,1828	21398
Violin, harp & orch	∅	2222/2000/timp/str		(R.C.M)	24993 * & mf 320
FAUST: opera, op.60					
Overture	∅	2222/4230/timp/str	5'	Breitkopf	13409
Extracts					
Folg' dem Freunde (Dearest let thy footsteps): duet					
in F (orig)		2022/2000/str		(Siddell)	17868
Liebe ist die zarte Blüthe (Clad in brightest beauty): aria					
Der Hölle selbst: recit					
in F (orig), orch L.Wurmser					
	∅	2(picc)222/4030/timp/str		BBC	22576 +
Der FRÜHLING (Festgesang): cantata for SSA soli, chorus & orch					
	∅	2022/2000/str		BBC	Misc 3328
GOTT, DU BIST GROSS (God, thou art great): cantata for SATB soli, chorus & orch, op.98					
	∅	2222/2230/timp/str		Novello	10794
	∅	2222/2230/timp/str		Simrock	Misc 3418

SPOHR, Louis (cont)

IRDISCHES UND GÖTTLICHES IM MENSCHENLEBEN   see   SYMPNONIES, no.7, op.21
JESSONDA: opera, op.63
   Complete
     ed Kogel   φ 2(picc)222/4230/timp.perc/str   Peters   Misc 1638
   Overture   φ 2(2picc)222/4230/4230/timp/str   8'   Breitkopf   4243 B
     ed A.de Almeida φ 2(2picc)222/4230/timp/str   Heugel,1962 Misc 23661
     arr Audibert   PC 2(picc)222/2230.euph/timp.perc/str 8'   Lafleur   3327
     arr Kogel   φ 2(2picc)222/4230/timp/str   Peters   Misc 3390
   Extracts
     Die iht Fühlended betrübet: aria
     Als in Mitternächt 'ger (Yes, when all around): recit
        in G min (orig)   φ 2222/2000/str   (Siddell)   17862
     Schönes Mädchen (Fairest maiden): duet
        in Ab (orig)   2022/2200/timp/str   (Siddell)   17861
Die LETZTEN DINGE (The Last Judgement): oratorio for SATB soli, chorus & orch
   Complete   φ 2222/2230/timp/str   Novello   14697
   Overture   φ 2222/2230/timp/str   Novello   5233
   Introduction, part 2   , 2222/2230/timp/str   Novello   2366
MACBETH: overture & incidental music, op.75
   Overture   φ 2222/4000/str   Peters,1827 21154 +
NOTTURNO for wind instruments, op.34   Peters   18686 Б
                   φ 0.2picc.222/2210/timp.perc
PIETRO VON ALBANO: opera, op.76
   Overture   2222/4000/str   Schlesinger,1828 21155
POLONAISE for violin & orch, op.40
                   2021/2000/timp/str   Peters   24134 *
SYMPHONIES
   No.1, op.20, in Eb   φ 2222/2230/timp/str   (GB-LVp)   Misc 7536
     Slow mvt only   φ 1222/2000/timp/str   BBC   19791
   No.3, op.78, in C min φ 2222/4230/timp/str   Schlesinger Misc 756
     ed H.Heussner   φ 2222/4230/timp/str   Bärenreiter,1957 Misc 5700
   No.4, op.86, in F (Die Weihe der Töne)
                   φ 2(picc)222/4230/timp.perc/str   40'-46' Haslinger   8319
   No.5, op.102, in C min φ 2222/4230/timp/str   Haslinger   22153
   No.6, op.116, in G ('Historical symphony')
                   φ 2(picc)222/4230/timp.perc/str   Pietro Mechetti 11810 B
   No.7, op.121, in C for 2 orchs (Irdisches und Göttliches im Menschenleben)
     1. Kinderwelt   2. Zeit der Leidenschaften   3. Endlicher Sieg des Göttliches
                   φ orch I : 1111/2000/str
                      orch II : 2121/2230/timp/str   Schuberth   16888
     ed J.Berrett   φ orch I : 1111/2000/str
                      orch II : 2121/2230/timp/str Schuberth,1843/Garland,1980 Misc 10284
   No.8, op.137, in G min φ 2222/4230/timp/str   Peters,1854 21156
   No.9, op.143 ('The Seasons')
                   φ 2222/4231/timp/str   Schuberth,1853 21147
TU M'ABBANDONI INGRATO: song, op.71
   in A   2022/2000/str   Peters   17863
ZEMIRE UND AZOR: opera
   Extracts
     Rose wie bist du (Rose softly blooming)
        in G   1022/0000/str   (Siddell)   17540
        in A   φ 1022/0000/str   (Siddell)   17539
     in A & Bb, arr G.Stacey
                 pf/str   (Cramer)   LM G 4789

SPOLIANSKY, Mischa

DEDICATION from film 'Idol of Paris'
    arr G.Zalva   PC   2121/2230/perc/hp/str   6'   Chappell   19074 D
FREDERIC HOLLAENDER MELODIES, arr
                            gtr/str   Arranger MS:BBC   MS 30665
The HAPPIEST DAYS GALOP
    arr A.Birkby   2121/2230/perc/hp/str   Chappell   19905 Cp
L'HEURE BLEUE: nocturne
    arr Irwin   PC   112.3sx.1/2210/perc/2bjo/str   Chappell   8732 B
IMPERIAL CANTATA for Benito Mussolini's birthday: radio production
                         ϕ   2140/2330/timp.perc/gtr.hp.pf/str   Composer MS:BBC MS 30475
LAPPENKRANK, arr   ϕ   110.sx.1/1000/gtr.hp   Arranger MS:BBC MS 30106
LIED FUR DIE DEUTSCHEN FRONTSOLDATEN
    in Bb   ϕ   1110/0230/timp.perc/gtr.pf/str   Composer MS:BBC MS 8483
LOVE IS NOTHING NEW: song
    in F, arr C.Mackerras   ϕ   2222/4230/timp.perc/hp.pf/str   (K.Prowse)   21876 +
MARZIA NATIONALE, arr   ϕ   1110/0230/timp.perc/gtr/str   Arranger MS:BBC MS 8481
MISTER MERRYMAN AND HERR SCHON: song
    in F   gtr.pf/str   Arranger MS:BBC MS 30122
MY SONG FOR YOU: song
   Extracts
      My song for you: song
        in C, arr P.Cardew   ϕ   2222/4230/timp.perc/hp/str   (Cinephonic,1957) 22206 +
        in C, arr P.Hope (Refrain only, used in programme 'Friday night is Music Night')
                      ϕ   2222/4230/timp.perc/hp/str   Cinephonic   23284
PAINTING THE WHOLE TOWN RED: song
    in Eb, arr M.Mackie   ϕ   2222/4230/timp.perc/hp.pf/str   Composer,1956   21835 +
The RED FLAG (Air: Tannenbaum), arr
                      ϕ   1+picc.222/4230/cym/str   Arranger MS:BBC MS 8343 ϕ only
SANDERS OF THE RIVER: film
   Extracts
      Canoe song
        in F, arr J.Byfield for Baritone solo, mv-chorus & orch
                      ϕ   2(picc)221/4230/timp.perc/hp/str   (C.Connelly,1957) 22236 +
SCHERZO   gtr.pf/str   Composer MS:BBC MS 30659
SERENADE OUT OF THE NIGHT
    arr Baynes   PC   212.3sx.1/2230/timp/gtr/str   P.Maurice   11381 B
SONG OF CAPRI
    arr Zalva   PC   2121/2230/timp.perc/hp/str   Chappell   19476 Bp
STACHELDRAHT, arr   ϕ   0.picc.010/0100/perc/pf/str   Arranger MS:BBC MS 30107
SUMMERTIME: lullaby
    in B min   gtr.pf/str   Composer MS:BBC MS 30660
TELL ME TONIGHT: film
   Extracts
      Tell me tonight: song
        in C, arr H.Carruthers ϕ   1111/0000/perc/acdn.hp.pf/str   (Chappell)   LM G 5709
        in Db, arr K.Warner   ϕ   0010/0000/pf/str   (Chappell)   LM G 5103
        in D, arr F.Cramer   pf/str   (Chappell)   LM G 5195
        in D, arr M.Mackie   1122/0220/timp/pf/str   (Chappell)   22141
      arr Reber: serenade-intermezzo
                     PC   111.3sx.1/2210/timp/str   Chappell   10605
TICO-TICO: samba   ϕ   gtr/str   Composer MS:BBC MS 20140
VERBOTEN: potpourri   gtr/str   Composer MS:BBC MS 30666
VIENNA
    Introduction & nos. 1-6   ϕ   2(picc)222/4230/timp.perc/cel.gtr.hp.pf/
                             str   Composer MS:BBC MS 8357 ϕ only

SPOLIANSKY, Mischa (cont)

WALTZ: song
  in F   perc/gtr.hp.pf/str   Composer MS:BBC MS 30663
WIR WANDERN: marching song, arr
        φ 111.4sx.1/0330/perc/gtr.hp.pf/str   Arranger MS:BBC MS 8358 φ only

SPONTINI, Gasparo (Luigi Pacifico)(1774-1851)

see BOUVET, Charles: Spontini. Paris: Riedner, 1930   BRL

AGNES VON HOHENSTEIN: opera
 Extracts
   O Re dei cieli (Nein König droben): aria (Act II)
    in Ab   φ 2222/2000/str   Otos-Florence 24068
FERNANDO CORTEZ, ou La conquête du Mexique: opera   (Misc 3646-7 &
  Complete   φ 2(picc)+picc.222/4230/timp.perc/str   Erard [1817] (mf 59-60
  Act 3 (complete) φ 2+picc.222/4230/timp.perc/str   Composer 19766
  Extracts
   C'en est donc fait: aria (Act I, scene 6)
        φ 0222/2300/timp/str   (Erard,1809) Misc 6185 C
   Les Espagnoles: aria (Act I, scene 7)
        φ 0222/2300/timp/str   (Erard,1809) Misc 6185 C
   Hélas, elle n'est plus: air
    in Ab (orig) φ 0222/2000/str   5'   (Erard)   20591
   O mon roi, o mon roi: quartet & chorus, with finale 'Quels cris' (Act 1, scene 7)
        φ 0222/2230/str   (Erard,1809) Misc 6185 C
   Quittons, quittons ces bords: chorus (Mutiny scene)
    in Eb (orig) φ 0222/2230/timp/str   (Erard)   20592
JULIE, or Le pot de fleurs: opera (1805)
 Overture
   rev L.Tozzi φ 0.2picc.222/2000/timp/str   4'30"Boccaccini & S,1978 Misc 10031
MILTON: opera
  Complete   φ 2222/2000/str   Erard [1804] Misc 5070
OLIMPIE (OLYMPIA): opera (1st perf 1819; rev 1821 as Olympia, rev 1826)
 2nd version (1821)
  Complete   φ 2+picc.2+ca.23/4330/timp.perc.tamtam/hp/str
        On stage: 0000/2410.oph/perc
        Off stage: 0000/4230/bell   Delahante,c.1826/Garland,1980 Misc 10318
 3rd version (1826)
   Overture   φ 2+picc.2+ca.24/4230/timp/str   9'15"-10' Schlesinger 11629
  Act 1, scenes 6 & 7 (pages 198-154 in Erard score)
   A la voix de ses dieux: aria, in D (orig)
   Ah, voici le moment: marche religieuse (with chorus), in Bb (orig)
   Dieux, auteurs de mon être: trio & double chorus, in Db (orig)
   De fraiches guirlandes: soli & chorus, in Bb (orig)
        φ 22+ca.23/4230/timp/hp/str   (Erard)   20594
  Extracts
   Dance at the marriage of Olympie and Cassandra
        φ 2222/2000/str   6'30"   (Erard)   20593
   O triomphe: part of Act 3 Scene 6 (pages 198-255 in Erard score)
        φ 2+picc.222/4230/timp.perc/hp/str
        On stage: 0000/4410.oph/perc   ([Erard]) Misc 3978 & mf 57
OLIMPIE: tragic finale for Soprano solo, chorus & orch
        φ 2222/4230/timp/2hp/str   10' Boccaccini & S,1979 Misc 10454
OLYMPIA see OLIMPIE (OLYMPIA): opera
La VESTALE: opera
  Complete   φ 2+picc.222/4230/timp.perc/2hp/str   Ricordi   Misc 1253
        φ 2(picc)+picc.222/4230/timp.perc.tamtam/2hp/
        str   Erard,c.1808/Garland,1979 Misc 9936

SPONTINI, Gasparo (cont)

La VESTALE: opera (cont)

Overture	∅	2+picc.222/4230/timp/str		8'15"-10'	Ricordi	Misc 3967 B
	PC	1121/2210/timp/str or 1010/0000/str			Cranz	5799

Extracts

Adieu mes tendres soeurs: duet						
in C min (orig)	∅	0112/0000/str			(Ricordi)	20590
Les dieux prendront pitié: aria						
in A♭ (orig)	∅	2222/4230/timp/str		3'30"	(Ricordi)	20587
Fille du Ciel: hymne du matin (Chorus of priestesses)						
in E♭ (orig)	∅PS	2222/2000/str			Leuckart	Misc 2667
in E♭	∅	2222/2000/str			(Ricordi)	20586 +
Impitoyables dieux: aria						
Julia! je l'entends: recit						
in C min (orig)	∅	2222/4230/timp/str		4'45"	(Ricordi)	20587
Non, non, je vis encore: aria						
Qu'ai-je vu: recit						
in G min (orig)	∅	2222/2230/timp/str		3'30"	(Ricordi)	20589
O crime! ô désespoir, and Finale Act II						
	∅	2222/2230/timp/str		8'30"	(Ricordi)	20588
Quel trouble! quels transports!: duet						
in B♭ (orig)	∅	2222/4230/timp/str		2'45"	(Ricordi)	20587

SPORCK, Georges (1870-1943)

PAYSAGES NORMANDS: suite
  1. À Villerville   4. Élégie
  2. Au marche   5. À travers champs
  3. Au Calvaire   6. Marche normande

	∅	1121/2230/timp.perc/str		Édn moderne des classiques	9903

SPURGIN, Anthony (1907-

CHINSTRAP	∅	0.picc.021/0210.euph/timp.perc/pf/str		Composer MS:BBC	MS 30711 ∅ only

READY THE BAND: songs & marches of the British Army (1957)
  Bruces's address   Love Farewell
  Ça Ira   The Sodger's Return
  Garryowen   Johnnie Cope
  Savourna Deelish   The Owl

	∅	1(picc)000/1100/perc/hp/str		Arranger MS:BBC	MS 31191

SQUIRE, William Henry (1871-1963)

The CORPORAL'S DITTY: song						
in E♭, arr R.Chignell	∅	1121/2110/timp.perc/str			(Boosey)	MS 4894
IF I MIGHT COME TO YOU: song						
in C, arr G.Stacey		1010/0000/perc/acdn.pf/str			(Boosey)	LM A 18
in C, arr J.Turner	∅	1110/1000/hp/str			(Boosey & H)	LM G 8541
in A♭, arr Dyck		1121/2230/perc/str			Boosey	3645
IN AN OLD FASHIONED TOWN: song						
in E♭		1(picc)221/2020/timp.perc/str		2'15"	Boosey	3643 Bp C
in E♭, arr Hartley	PC	1010/0000/str			Boosey	16875
in E♭ & F, arr H.Carr	∅	2121/2230/perc/hp/str			(Boosey)	TO 893
in F, arr H.Carruthers		hp.pf/str			(Boosey)	LM G 5430
in F, arr B.Thompson	∅	1110/1000/hp/str/solo voice.chorus			(Boosey)	LM G 7521
in F		2(picc)121/2130/perc/str			Boosey	15672
in G, arr J.Turner		112.2sx.1/2220/perc/hp.pf/str			Arranger MS:BBC	MS 20419

SQUIRE, William Henry (cont)

The JOLLY SAILOR
   March, arr G.Byng   PC 1(picc)121/2230.euph/timp/str   Chappell   2289
LAZY-LANE: waltz
   arr C.Woodhouse   PC 1+picc.222/2230.euph/perc/str   AH & C   6461
LIGHTERMAN TOM see COLLINSON, F: LIGHTERMAN TOM, arr
MEDITATION in C
   arr Baynes   PC 2122/2230/timp/str   Boosey   3443
The MERRY NIGGER   PC 2222/2230/perc/str   Bosworth 1016
The MOONLIT ROAD: song by W.H.Squire & P.J. O'Reilly
   in G, arr S.Baynes   2122/2230/timp/hp/str   Boosey,1923 17078
MOUNTAIN LOVERS: song
   in C   2222/2220/timp/str   4'   (Siddell) 17983
   in E♭   1(picc)121/2200/timp/str   Boosey   5058 Bp
   in E♭   2+picc.222/2320/timp/str   (Siddell) 17982
   in E♭, arr H.Carr & Groves   φ 2121/2230/perc/hp/str   (Boosey) TO 52
   in E♭, arr G.Stacey   1110/0000/perc/acdn.pf/str   (Boosey) LM A 31
   arr Hartley (non-vocal)   PC [1]0[1]0/0000/str   Boosey   14963
MY PRAYER: song
   in E♭, arr S.Baynes   PC 2122/2230/timp.perc/str   Boosey   3646 B
   in E♭, arr J.Turner   φ 1110/1000/hp/str   (Boosey) LM G 9056
   in D, arr F.Cramer   pf/str   (Boosey) LM G 5820
   in D, arr G.Stacey   [1]0[1]0/0000/pf/str   (Boosey) LM G 3684
ON GUARD: song
   in G, arr S.Herbert for solo cornet & orch
                  PC 1132/2330/perc/str   Boosey   8084
SERENADE, op.15   PC 1010/0000/str   Augener   6204 B
SERGEANT OF THE LINE: song
   in F, arr G.Stacey   pf/str   (Boosey) LM G 3259
The SINGING LESSON: duet
   in F, arr A.Franzel   φ 1110/0000/perc/hp.pf/str   (Boosey) LM A 629
SQUIRE'S SONGS: selection, arr S.Baynes
                  PC 2(picc)122/2230/timp.perc/str   Boosey   308 D
SUMMER DREAMS: entr'acte   PC 2+picc.222/4230/perc/hp/str   Boosey   3461 C
SWEET BRIAR   φ 2+picc.222/2230/perc/str   Bosworth 4657
SYLVANIA: idyll   φ 2222/2230/timp.perc/str   7'-9'   W.H.Squire 3979
THREE FOR JACK: song
   in F, arr F.Cramer   pf/str   (Chappell) LM G 7490
   in A♭, arr R.Chignell   φ 1111/0000/timp/str   (Chappell) MS 5536
WHEN YOU COME HOME: song
   in E♭   PC 1222/2120/timp.perc/str   4'30"   Boosey   4975 C
   in E♭, F & G, arr H.Carr   φ 2121/2230/perc/hp/str/[chorus] (Boosey) TO 95
   in G   1221/2220/perc/str   (Boosey) LM G 3963
   in G, arr G.Stacey   pf/str   (Boosey) LM G 3349
The YEOMANRY PATROL: march PC 2+picc.222/4230/timp.perc/str Boosey   2268 B

STACEY, Gilbert

BARBARA ALLEN: trad song, arr
   in D   pf/str   (W.Rogers) LM G 3861
BELLISSIMA   PC str   Liber   14117
EN PASSANT PAR LA LORRAINE, arr   1110/0000/acdn.hp.pf/str   (Heugel) 3553
HEART OF OAK: trad song, arr   φ 2222/4230/timp.perc   Arranger MS:BBC MS 20392 φ only
HO RO MY NUT BROWN MAIDEN: trad song, arr
   in A   pf/str   Arranger   LM G 5415
The LARK IN THE CLEAR AIR: trad song, arr
   in A & A♭   pf/str   Arranger   LM G 5167

STACEY, Gilbert (cont)

SKYE BOAT SONG: trad song, arr
    in Bb
                              1110/0000/perc/acdn.pf/str   (Cramer)   LM A 122
WHEN EVENING SHADOWS FALL: song
    in Ab
                              1111/2210/timp/str   Osborne,1918   17109

STACHOWSKI, Marek (1936-

CHOREIA (1980)   φ 3+picc.33+bcl.3/6430/timp.perc.gong.tamtam.tomtom/
                              str (control copy only)   (Composer)   Misc 10481

STADLMAIR, Hans

CONCERTO for trumpet & strings, in D
                           φ str   Peters/Litolff,1972   Misc 7893

STADTFELDT, Alexander (1826-1853)

HAMLET: opera
    Overture
      arr Atzler   PC 1+picc.121/2210/timp.perc/str   Cranz   580C

STAFFORD-SMITH, J.

CANTATE DOMINO: chant setting   1121/20.2cnt.30/perc/str   Boosey & H   20417

STAGGINS, Nicholas (d.1700)

CALISTO, or The Chaste Nymphe: masque (1674)
    Extracts
      Minutte for the flageoletts
        ed P.Holman   φ 0.2rec.000/0000/str/cont   Editor   Misc 10169
      Scotch Tune
        ed P.Holman   φ 0200/0000/str/cont   Editor   Misc 10169

STAHL, F.

DOBRA-DOBRA   see   SKALKA, M: DOBRA-DOBRA

STAHLBERG, Heinz

NAGAIKA   PC 2(picc)222/3330/perc.gong/org/str   Monte-Ferro,1981   26934
REMEMBER OF TALES (Märchen-Erinnerungen)
                           PC 2(picc)222/3330/timp.perc.bells/org/str Monte-Ferro,1975   25832
WINDSPIEL   PC 2(picc)222/3330/perc.bells/org/str   Monte-Ferro,1972   25833

STAINER, John (1840-1901)

LOVE DIVINE ALL LOVES EXCELLING: hymn
                           PC 1121/0000/timp.perc/org/str   Hawkes   4970
THERE'S A FRIEND FOR LITTLE CHILDREN: hymn
                           PC 1121/0000/timp.perc/org/str   Hawkes   4970

STAMITZ, Anton (1750-ca.1809)

see   European Broadcasting Union; Catalogue no.8: Johann, Carl and Anton Stamitz. Brussels:
      B.R.T.B., 1973   BRL

CONCERTI
    Flute & orch, in D
      ed W.Lebermann   φ 0200/2000/str   Breitkopf,1964.EDM 1:51   MRL

STAMITZ, Anton (cont)

CONCERTI (cont)
   Viola & strings, no.4, in D
      ed W.Lebermann   φ   str   Breitkopf,1973   Misc 8455

STAMITZ, Carl (1745-1801)

see   European Broadcasting Union; Catalogue no.8; Johann, Carl and Anton Stamitz. Brussels:
       B.R.T.B.,1973

ANDANTINETTA
   arr Q.Maganini   φ   str   Edn Musica   16598
CONCERTI
   Bassoon & orch
      in F
         ed R.Meylan   φ   0200/2000/str   Ars Viva/[BBC]   26674 +
   Cello & orch
      in C
         ed W.Upmeyer   φ   0200/2000/str   Bärenreiter   21159
      in G
         ed W.Upmeyer   φ   2000/2000/str   Bärenreiter,1953   21000
      in A
         ed W.Upmeyer   φ   2000/2000/str   Bärenreiter,1951   20512
   Clarinet & orch
      in E♭
         ed J.Wojciechowski φ 0200/2000/str   13'   Sikorski,1953   21075
      in F
         ed G.Balassa   φ   0200/2000/str   Edn Musica/Boosey & H,1970   Misc 7552
      in B♭ [no.3]
         ed J.Wojciechowski φ 0200/2000/str   Peters,1957   Misc 5081
      in B♭ [no.10]
         ed & arr J.Michaels φ 0200/2000/str   Sikorski,1958   23409
   2 clarinets (or clarinet & violin), in B♭
         ed W.Lebermann   φ   0[2]00/[2]000/str   Litolff,1968/Peters   24982
   Flute & orch
      in D
         ed W.Leberman   φ   str   Breitkopf,1964.EDM 1:51   MRL
      in D (also attrib J.Stamitz, not the same as previous work)
         ed & arr D.Sonntag φ 0000/2000/str   Sikorski,1958   23408
      in G (op.29)
         ed W.Lebermann   φ   0[2]00/[2]000/str   15'-17'   Schott   25807
   Flute, oboe & orch
      in G   φ   2[=2ob]000/2000/str   [BBC]   25846 +
   Oboe & orch
      in B♭
         ed J.Wojciechowski φ 0000/2000/str   Simrock,1963   Misc 7047
   Viola & orch
      op.1, in D   φ   0200/2000/str   22'25"   Peters   21426
   Violin & orch
      in G
         ed M.Hochkofler φ 2000/2000/str   Eulenberg,1957   22430
      in B♭
         ed D.Hellmann   φ   2000/2000/str   Breitkopf,1973   Misc 8029
QUARTETS for orchestra
   in C [no.1]   φ   str
      ed H.Mönkemeyer φ str   Schott,1959   24439
   in F
      arr Geiringer   φ   str   13'10"   Universal   19169

STAMITZ, Carl

SINFONIE CONCERTANTE
    Flute, oboe, clarinet, 2 horns, violin & cello soli & orch
        in F   φ   timp/str   16'   Universal   Misc 570 B
    Violin, viola & orch
        in D
            ed F.Kneusslin   φ   0000/2000/str   Kneusslin,1953   26174 B
    2 violins & orch
        in C
            ed F.Kneusslin   φ   2[=2ob]000/2000/str   Hug,1947   19919
SYMPHONIES
    op. 8, no.5, in B♭
        ed H.Riemann   φ   0000/2000/str/cont   (Broude)   26979 +
    op.13, no.1, in E♭   02[=2fl]00/2000/str   Preston,1781   21593
        ed G.Lenzewski   φ   2000/2000/str   11'15"   Vieweg   10251 +
        ed H.Riemann   φPS 02[=2fl]00/2000/str   Breitkopf,1906.DDTB 7/2   MRL & 26836
        ed H.Riemann   φ   02[=2fl]00/0000/str   Broude   Misc 6296
        Andante (2nd mvt) only
            ed H.Riemann   φ   str   (Breitkopf.DDTB 14) 19682
        Presto (3rd mvt) only
            ed H.Riemann   φ   2000/2000/str   Breitkopf,1906.DDTB 7/2/(Preston)   26726 Ani
    op.13, no.2, in B♭   02[=2fl]00/2000/str   Preston [1781]   21593
    op.13, no.3, in D   02[=2fl]00/2000/str   Preston [1781]   21593
    op.13, no.4, in G   02[=2fl]00/2000/str   Preston [1781]   21593
        ed H.Riemann   φ   2000/2000/str   Broude   (Misc 6296 &
                                                                                                         (25837 + Ani
    op.13, no.5, in C
                                          02[=2fl]00/2000/str   Preston [1781]   21593
                                          02[=2fl]00/2000/str   Preston [1781]   21593
    op.13, no.6, in F
    in E min   (Editor)   26375
        ed A.E.F.Dickinson   φ   2000/2000/str

STAMITZ, Johann (c.1717-c.1757)

see   European Broadcasting Union; Catalogue no.8: Johann, Carl and Anton Stamitz.   Brussels:
      B.R.T.B., 1973   BRL

CONCERTI
    Clarinet & orch
        in B♭
            ed R.Fiske   φ   str   Editor/[Thurn & Taxissche]   21331 & mf 40
            ed W.Lebermann   φ   0000/[2]000/str   Schott,1967   25714
    Flute & orch
        in D
            ed W.Lebermann   φ   str   Eulenburg,1961   23654
        in G
            ed W.Lebermann   φ   str   Breitkopf,1964.EDM 1:51   MRL
    Oboe & orch
        in C
            ed & arr H.Töttcher & H.F.Hartig
                                     φ   str/cont   Sikorski,1957   23410
    Violin & orch
        in C (Dresden Concerto)
            ed W.Lebermann   φ   str   Heinrichshofen/Pegasus,1965   25126
        in B♭   φ   str   17'40"   (D-brd DO)   Misc 4667 B +

STAMITZ, Johann (cont)

ORCHESTRAL TRIOS
   op.1, no.1, in C

ed H.Riemann	φ	str/cont		Breitkopf	25544
ed H.Riemann	φ	str/cont		Breitkopf,1902.DDTB 3/1	MRL
ed H.Riemann	φ	str/cont		Broude	Misc 6256

   op.1, no.2, in A

ed H.Riemann	φ	str/cont		Breitkopf	25545

SYMPHONIES
   op. 3, no.1, in G (The Periodical Overture)

ed H.Riemann	φ	02[=2fl]00/2000/str/cont		Breitkopf,1902.DDTB 3/1	MRL
ed H.Riemann	φ	02[=2fl]00/2000/str		Broude	Misc 6256

   op. 3, no.2, in D (Sinfonia a 11 (8))

ed H.Riemann	φ	02[=2fl]00/2200/timp/str/cont		Breitkopf,1902.DDTB 3/1	MRL & 20388 +
ed H.Riemann	φ	02[=2fl]00/2200/timp/str	11'20'	Broude	Misc 6256

   op. 3, no.3, in G

arr A.Carse	φ	0000/[2]00/str	7'30"-12'	Augener	15532

   op. 4, no.2, in D (Symphonie pastorale)

ed W.Upmeyer	φ	02[=2fl]00/2000/str/cont	13'45"	Vieweg	10252

   op. 4, no.6, in Eb

ed H.Riemann	φPS	0200/2000/str		Breitkopf,1906.DDTB 7/2	MRL & mf 39
ed H.Riemann	φ	0200/2000/str		Broude	Misc 6256

   op. 5, no.2, in D

ed H.Riemann	φ	2202/2000/str/cont		Breitkopf,1906.DDTB 7/2	21737 +
ed H.Riemann	φ	2202/2000/str/cont		Broude	Misc 6256

   op. 8, no.5, in Bb

ed H.Riemann	φ	0000/2000/str/cont		Breitkopf,1902.DDTB 3/1	MRL
ed H.Riemann	φ	0000/2000/str/cont		Broude	Misc 6256

   op.11, no.1, in D (La Melodia Germanica no.1)

ed H.Riemann	φ	0220/2000/str		Breitkopf,1902.DDTB 3/1	MRL
ed H.Riemann	φ	0220/2000/str		Broude	Misc 6256

   in D (Reitersinfonie)

ed Sondheimer	φ	2000/2000/str		Bernoulli	Misc 1377

   in Eb (La Melodia Germanica no.3)

ed Lenzewski	φ	02[=2fl]00/2000/str	12'	Vieweg	10249
ed H.Riemann	φ	0201/2000/str/cont		Breitkopf,1906.DDTB 7/2	19664 & MRL &)
					mf 39)
ed H.Riemann	φ	02[=2fl=2cl]00/2000/str/cont		Broude	Misc 6256

   in A (Frühlingssinfonie)

	φ	2000/2000/str	15'30"	Bernoulli	Misc 1376

   in Bb (1740)

	φ	pf/str		Bernoulli,1937	Misc 2559

STAMPER, Dave (1883-

ZIG ZAG: revue

Selection, arr Jones	PC	2(picc)121/2230/timp.perc/str	FD & H	3743 B

   Extracts
     Beware of Chu Chin Chow: song

in G min, arr J.Beaver	φ	2121/2230/perc/hp/str	(FD & H)	TO 327

     Hello! my dearie: song

in Eb, arr J.Beaver	φ	2121/2230/perc/hp/str	(FD & H)	TO 328

STANDEN, Richard

THREE HIGHLAND PICTURES	φ	2(picc)120/2230/perc(tplbl.glock.cel)/hp/str	Metro	MLO 418

STANDFORD, Patric (1939-

ANTITHESIS for 15 strings, op.37 (1971)
        φ   str   Novello/CML.,1973   Misc 8291
CELESTIAL FIRE: ballet suite (1969)
  1. Prologue   5. Doll's dance
  2. Pas de deux   6. Valse
  3. March   7. Round dance
  4. Intermezzo
        φ   2222[=1+tbn]/2200/timp.perc.glock.xyl/str   19'30"   (Composer)(H)   PL 527
        φ   2222/2200/timp.perc.glock.xyl/str   Redcliffe,1976   Misc 9364
A CHRISTMAS CAROL SYMPHONY (1977-8)
        φ   2+picc.222/2100/timp.perc.bells.glock.tamtam/
           hp/str   Redcliffe,1978   Misc 9868
CONCERTI
  Cello & orch, op.32   φ   22(ca)2+bcl.2(cbsn)/2111/timp.perc(tamtam.vib.xyl)/
           hp.pf/str   Redcliffe,1976   Misc 9366
  Piano & orch, op.44   φ   2(picc)1+ca.22/2000/perc.glock/str   17'   Redcliffe,1979   Misc 10009
  Violin & orch, op.34   φ   22+ca.2+bcl.2+cbsn/2100/timp.perc/hp/str   Redcliffe,1976   Misc 9365
3 PASTORAL DANCES   φ   2(picc)1+ca.21/2000/perc(glock)/str   9'   (Composer)(H)   PL 538
SUITE for small orch (1966)   φ   2121/2000/str   Novello   Misc 9402
SYMPHONY no.1 (1971/2)   φ   2+picc.2+ca.2+Ebcl+bcl.asx.2+cbsn/4331/
           timp.perc.bells.glock.xyl/cel.hp/str   (Composer)   Misc 8640

STANFORD, Charles Villiers (1852-1924)

AWAY TO THE WARS: song, arr
  in Ab, orch H.Carr   φ   2121/2230/perc/hp/str   BBC   TO 142
BECKET: incidental music, op.48 (1892)
  Funeral March (The Martyrdom)
   Original version for small orch
        φ   1122/2210/hp/str   Stainer & B   Misc 9124
   Version for large orch   φ   2222[+cbsn]/2230/timp.perc/hp/str   Stainer & B   Misc 9124
BOLD UNBIDDABLE CHILD: song
  in F   φ   1121/2210/perc/str   (Stainer & B)   MS 3590
The CANTERBURY PILGRIMS: opera (1884)
  Overture   φ   2222/4330/timp/str   (Composer)   26262 +
CONCERT VARIATIONS on the theme 'Down among the dead men', for piano & orch, op.71
        φ   2222[+cbsn]/4230/timp/str   20'   Bosworth   27016
CONCERTI
  Clarinet & orch, op.80, in A min
        φ   2202/4200/timp/str   21'30"-23'   (Stainer & B)   19131 * str only
        φ   2202/4200/timp/str   Stainer & B   Misc 9524
        φ   2202/4200/timp/str(12.12.8.8.8)   Cramer,1977   26788
  Piano & orch, no.2, op.126, in C min
        φ   2222/4230/timp/str   30'   Stainer & B   9888
The FAIRY LOUGH: song, op.77, no.2 (from An Irish Idyll' - orig voice & pf)
  in D   φ   2022/4000/hp/str   3'45"   (Boosey)   19914
FATHER O'FLYNN: song, arr
  in Bb   φ   1121/2110/timp/str   2'30"   (Siddell)   18077
  in Bb & Ab, arr S.Robinson, orch H.Carr
        φ   21+ca.2+bcl.2/4230/timp/str   (Boosey)   TO 1704
The FISHERMAN OF LOUGH NEAGH   see   IRISH RHAPSODIES, no.4
GREAT BRITAIN: NATIONAL ANTHEM, arr for chorus & orch
        φ   2222+cbsn/4231/timp.perc/hp.org/str/[Soprano solo]   Boosey & H   14280
The IRISH REEL
  in Bb, orch V.Tausky   φ   1111/4000/str   Boosey   Ni 39

STANFORD, Charles Villiers (cont)

IRISH RHAPSODIES
    No.1, op.78, in D min   ø   2(picc)2(ca)2(bcl)2+cbsn/4331/timp.perc/
                                           hp/str   12'30"-13'45" Stainer & B   4244 Cwa Ds E
    No.4, op.141, in A min ('The fisherman of Lough Neagh and what he saw')
                           ø   2+picc.2+ca.22/4331/timp.perc/hp/str   20'30"   Stainer & B   Misc 759 C
    No.5, op.147, in G min   ø   2222/4231/timp.perc/hp/str   (Stainer & B) 27140 + &)
JOHN KELLY: song   mf 201)
    in D, arr C.Helliwell   ø   1121/2210/hp/str   (Stainer & B) MS 3591
LAST POST: song for chorus & orch, op.75
                           ø   2222+cbsn/43.bugle.31/timp.perc/hp/str   8'30"   Boosey   8284 B
LITTLE SNOWDROP (Spring): song (from Songs from 'The Elfin Pedlar' - orig voice & pf)
    orch L.Wurmser   ø   2+picc.222/2000/timp.perc/hp/str   0'35"   (Stainer & B) 20163
MY LOVE'S AN ARBUTUS: song, arr
    in F & Eb   ø   1122/0000/str   Boosey   MLO 628
OEDIPUS REX: prelude, op.29   ø   22(ca)22/2230/timp/hp/str   10'   Stainer & B   8513
PHAUDRIG CROHOORE: ballad for chorus & orch, op.62
                           ø   2222/4230/timp/str   20'-24'   Boosey   9906
The PIPER OF SPRING: song (from Songs from 'The Elfin Pedlar' - orig voice & pf)
    in Eb, arr H.Carr   ø   2222/4000/hp/str   2'   (Stainer & B) 18417
QUICK WE HAVE BUT A SECOND: song
    in Bb, arr C.Helliwell   ø   1121/2210/str   0'35"   (Boosey)   MS 3086 ø only
REQUIEM, for SATB soli, chorus & orch
                           ø   22+ca.22+cbsn/4331/timp/hp/str   60'-79'   Boosey   Misc 1335
The REVENGE (A ballad of the fleet), for chorus & orch, op.24
                           ø   2+picc.222/4231/timp.perc/str   Novello   13812
SHAMUS O'BRIEN: opera, op.61
    Overture   ø   2122/2230/timp/hp/str   5'-5'40"   Boosey   14533
                                 1122/2220/timp/hp/str   Boosey   1396
SONGS OF THE FLEET, for Baritone solo, chorus & orch, op.117
    1. Sailing at dawn   4. The little admiral
    2. The song of the sou' wester   5. Farewell
    3. The middle watch
    Complete   VS   2222/4231/timp/hp/str   23'   Stainer & B,1910 Misc 1668
    No.4 only
      in C, arr G.Stacey   pf/str   (Stainer & B) LM G 3185
SONGS OF THE SEA, for Baritone solo, mv-chorus & orch, op.91
    1. Devon, O Devon, in G min   4. Drake's drum, in D min
    2. Outward bound, in Ab   5. Homeward bound, in Db
    3. The Old Superb, in Bb
    Complete   ø   2+picc.22+bcl.2/4231/timp.perc/str   Boosey   5013 C +
    No.1 only
      in Bb, arr G.Stacey   pf/str   (Boosey)   LM G 3627
    No.3 only
      in Bb (orig), arr S.Robinson
                           ø   2(picc)121/2230/timp.perc/str   3'   (Boosey)   TO 58
      in Bb, arr G.Stacey   pf/str   (Boosey)   LM G 3466
      in Ab   ø   2+picc.222/4230/timp.perc/str   (Boosey)   23563 +
    No.4 only
      in D min (orig), arr G.Stacey
                              pf/str   (Boosey)   LM G 3049
      in C min   2222/4231/timp.perc/str   3'   (Boosey)   3990
    Suite, arr T.Dunhill for small orch
      1. Drake's drum   3. Homeward bound
      2. Devon, O Devon   4. The Old Superb
                       PC   1+picc.121/2220/timp.perc/str   Boosey   675 B

STANFORD, Charles Villiers (cont)

SUITE for violin & orch, op.32   φ   2222/4200/timp/str   Novello   4683
SUITE OF ANCIENT DANCES, op.58 (arr from 'Ten Dances', op.58 - orig for pf solo)
   1. Morris dance   4. Minuet
   2. Saraband   5. Passepied
   3. Branle
                    φ   2222/2200/timp.perc/str   Boosey   7 B

SYMPHONIES
  op.28, in F min ('Irish Symphony')
                    φ   2222/4330/timp/hp/str   39'   Novello   2155 Bwe C
  op.31, in F (No.4)   φ   2222+cbsn/4230/timp/hp/str   Novello   2168
  op.56, in D ('L'Allegro ed il Pensieroso')(No.5)
                    φ   2222/4230/timp/[org]/str   39'   Stainer & B   2812
  op.124, in D min (No.7) φ   2222/4230/timp/str   Stainer & B   16321
TE DEUM LAUDAMUS in B♭ (from Communion service, op.20)
                   2222/4230/timp/str   Novello   5044 B

The TRAVELLING COMPANION: opera
        φ   2+picc.2+ca.2+bcl.2+cbsn/4331/timp.perc.glock/
           hp/str
           On stage: 0000/0200/tmc.wmc   Stainer & B,1923   Misc 89 B

TROTTIN' TO THE FAIR: song
  in D   1121/0220/pf/str   (Boosey)   LM G 5427
  in F, E♭ & C   2022/2000/str   (Boosey)   TO 89
  arr C.Woods as signature tune for programme 'Golden Treasury'
           1000/0000/pf/str/mv-chorus (TTBB)   Boosey   LM lib

The VEILED PROPHET OF KHORASSAN: opera
  Extracts
    There's a bower of roses: song
      in B♭ min   2222/2000/perc/str   (Siddell)   17883

STANGE, Max

DAMON: song
  in E, arr S.Robinson   φ   3222/4000/str   4'   (Bosworth)   TO 1487

STANHOPE, Erroll

I WOULD! I WOULD!: song by E.Stanhope & G.Arthurs
  in C   PC   1111/1110/perc/str   (FD & H)   MS 89

STANLEY, Cecil

ROMANTIC SUITE
  1. Courtship   2. The wedding morn   3. Festivities
          PC   1+picc.121/2220/timp.perc/str   Hawkes   2646 C

STANLEY, John (1713-1786)

6 CANTATAS for voice & instruments, op.3
  1. Who'll buy a heart   4. By heav'n I'll stoop no more
  2. By the moon's soft-beaming light   Cymon, a rough unpolish'd swain: recit
    Aloft, and near her highest noon: recit 5. Alas, my Julia
  3. Cease Eugenio thus to gaze   6. No sooner had my infant face
    Complete   φ   1200/0000/str/cont   J.Stanley [1742]   Misc 3015
    No. 5 only
      in G (orig)   φ   str   9'15"   J.Stanley [1742]   22465 +

STANLEY, John (cont)

CONCERTI
  6 Concerti for 2 violins & orch

No.1, in D		str/cont		I.Walsh [1745]	26163
ed G.Finzi	∅	[pf]/str	10'-11'	Boosey & H	20788
No.2, in B min		str/cont		I.Walsh [1745]	26163
ed G.Finzi	∅	pf/str	14'	Boosey & H	20789
No.3, in G		str/cont		I.Walsh [1745]	26163
ed G.Finzi	∅	pf/str	8'-9'	Boosey & H	19857 C
No.4, in D min		str/cont		I.Walsh [1745]	26163
ed G.Finzi	∅	[pf]/str	9'	Boosey & H	21385
No.5, in A		str/cont		I.Walsh [1745]	26163
ed G.Finzi	∅	[pf]/str		Boosey & H	21382
No.6, in B♭		str/cont		I.Walsh [1745]	26163
ed G.Finzi	∅	[pf]/str	8'	Boosey & H	21927

  6 Concerti for organ (or harpsichord or piano), with 2 violins & bass, Op.10

No.4, in C min				
ed & arr C.L.Cudworth	∅	str (no vla)	Arranger/[Harrison,c.1775]	20947

PAN AND SYRINX (composed J.Stanley, formerly attrib W.Boyce)
  Overture

arr C.Lambert	∅	0201/0000/str	3'	OUP	14577 B

The POWER OF MUSIC (composed J.Stanley, formerly attrib W.Boyce)
  Overture

arr C.Lambert	∅	0201/0000/str	3'	OUP	14578 C

TERAMINTA: opera (also attrib J.C.Smith)

	∅	0200/0200/timp/str/cont	(GB-Lbm)	21354 + & mf 67

TRUMPET TUNE, arr Coleman (from suite for organ)

		0000/0100/str	3'45"	OUP	18793

STANSBURY, G.F. (1800-1845)

SHE SMILED AND I COULD NOT BUT LOVE: song

in G	∅	0000/2000/str	Composer	MS 30878

STANTON, Geoffrey

The SONG OF THE ROAD

in D, arr G.Stacey	∅	2121/0220/perc/pf/str	(Cramer)	MS 20490 ∅ only

STANTON, Michael

SALE TIME

orch H.Dexter	PC	1121/2230/timp.perc/hp/str	FD & H,1955	22008

STANTON, Noel

FLANAGAN'S MARE

arr A.Fones	PC	2121/2330/perc/hp/str	N.Gay,1951	20470

STANTON, Walter Kendall (1891-

ALL POOR MEN AND HUMBLE: Welsh traditional carol

arr W.K.Stanton & C.Roberts	∅	str	OUP	2852

The CRADLE: carol

arr W.K.Stanton & M.Shaw	∅	str	OUP	18981

The FIRST NOWELL: carol

arr W.Stanton & M.Shaw	∅	str	OUP	16688

STANTON, Walter Kendall (cont)

The GARDEN OF JESUS: carol
   arr W.K.Stanton & G.Shaw   ø   str   OUP   18985
The HOLLY AND THE IVY: carol
   arr W.K.Stanton, C.Sharp & M.Shaw
                           ø   str   OUP   18984
IN DULCI JUBILO: carol
   arr W.K.Stanton   ø   str   OUP   15545
JOSEPH DEAREST, JOSEPH MINE: carol
   arr W.K.Stanton & R.V.Williams
                           ø   str   OUP   13587
REJOICE AND BE MERRY: carol
   arr W.K.Stanton & M.Shaw   ø   str   OUP   16457
ROCKING: carol
   arr W.K.Stanton & M.Shaw   ø   str   OUP   18986

STARKE, Hermann

WITH SWORD AND LANCE: march   ø   2+picc.222/4231/timp.perc/hp/str   2'30"   Hawkes   18847
                                PC   2222/4230.euph/perc/str   Hawkes   863 Bp

STAROKADOMSKI, Mikhail (1901-

CONCERTO for orchestra, op.14
   ed Sheldon   ø   2+picc.2+ca.2+E♭cl.2+cbsn/4331/timp.perc/str   Leeds Music Corp   Misc 2622

STARR, Hattie

LITTLE ALABAMA COON: song
   in D♭, arr R.Bernell   ø   2121/2200/perc/str   (Darewski)   TO 299

STARZER, Josef (1727-1787)

DIVERTIMENTI
   in C
      ed Horwitz & Riedel   ø   str   Artaria,1908.DTÖ 31   MRL
   in A min
      ed Horwitz & Riedel   ø   str   Artaria,1908.DTÖ 31   MRL

STATKOWSKI, Roman (1859-1925)

KRAKOWIAK: Polish dance
   arr O.Langey   PC   1121/2210/perc/str   G.Schirmer   11754

STECK, Arnold
                                                                                         (no hire
IMPORTANT OCCASION   PC   2(picc)121/2230/timp.perc/hp/str   (Chappell)(H)   PL 391 (fees
MORNING CANTER
   orch C.Milner   PC   2121/2230/perc/hp/str   2'40"   Chappell,1953   21095 Ap C

STECK, P.A.

COQUETTERIE (Flirtation): valse intermezzo
                              ø   str   Decourcelle   8911
   arr A.Schmid   PC   1121/2000/str   Hawkes   2905

STEER, Michael

CORIOLANUS: incidental music for radio productioon (1979)
                        1(picc)1(ca).shm.00/0121/timp.perc.
                        anv.2gong.sistrum/org   Composer,1979   MS 31798
CRY GOD FOR HARRY: incidental music for radio production (1977)
                        0.pipe & tabor.0.ob-d'a.shm.0.ssx.0/
                        0302.skbt(2askbt)/perc(timp)/hurdy-gurdy   Composer   MS 31763
The FILE ON LEO KAPLAN: music for radio production (1980)
                    ∅   perc.gro.rhythm-kit.tomtom/gtr.bgtr/
                        pf.syn/2vln.vla   Composer   MS 31793
A LIFE: music for radio production (1978)
                    ∅   1(picc,afl)1(ca)1(bcl)1(cbsn)/1100/timp.perc.glock/
                        hp.mand/2vln.2vlc.cb   (Composer,1978)   MS 31803
VANITY FAIR: music for radio series
    Material consists of original opening and closing music, plus Steer's adaptations of other
    material, including:
        HOOK: Hornpipe   MAURER: March
        HUMMEL: Octet   SPERGER: Rondo
        KROMMER: Octet-Partita, op.79
                        2(picc)111/2000/perc.glock/hp/str   (Composer,1978)   MS 31785 pts only

STEFANI, Jan (1746-1829)

CRACOVIANS AND HIGHLANDERS, or The supposed miracle (Krakowiacy i górale): opera
    Overture
        arr G.Fitelberg   ∅   2(picc)222/2110/timp/str   4'30"   Polish SM,1951   Misc 4894
    3 dances, arr G.Fitelberg
        1. Polonez   2. Krakowiak   3. Oberek
                          ∅   2(picc)22+Ebcl.2/4331/timp.perc/str   Polish SM,1953   Misc 4395

STEFFAN, Joseph Anton   see   ŠTĚPÁN, Josef Antonin

STEFFAN, Wolfgang   see   STEFFEN, Wolfgang

STEFFANI, Agostino (1654-1728)

ALARICO IL BALTHA: opera (1687)
    Complete
        ed H.Riemann   ∅   2201/0300/timp/pvln.str/cont(hpsd)   Breitkopf,1912.DDTB 11/2   MRL
    Extracts
        Già comincio a farmi piangere: aria
            in D min (orig)   hpsd/str   (DDTB)   MS 30123
AMOR VIEN DAL DESTINO (Il Turno): opera (1709)
    Overture & extracts for solo voices & orch
        ed H.Riemann   ∅   0100/0000/str/cont(pf)   Breitkopf,1912.DDTB 12/2   MRL
BRISEĪDE: opera (1696)
    Overture & extracts for solo voices & orch,
        ed H.Riemann   ∅   1100/0000/str/cont(pf)   Breitkopf,1912.DDTB 12/2   MRL
HENRICO LEONE: opera (1689)
    Overture & extracts for solo voices & orch
        ed H.Riemann   ∅   str/cont(pf)   Breitkopf,1912.DDTB 12/2   MRL
    Overture
        arr Werner   ∅   str   Nagel   19487
La LIBERTA CONTENTA (Alcibiade): opera (1693)
    Overture & extracts for solo voices & orch
        ed H.Riemann   ∅   2101/0000/str/cont(pf.hpsd)   Breitkopf,1912.DDTB 12/2   MRL

STEFFANIN, Agostino (cont)

La LOTTE D'HERCOLE CON ACHELOO: opera (1689)
  Overture & extracts for solo voices & orch
    ed H.Riemann   ø str/cont(pf)   Breitkopf,1912.DDTB 12/2   MRL
MARCO AURELIO: opera (1681)
  Overture & vocal extracts
    ed H.Riemann   ø str/cont(pf)   Breitkopf,1912.DDTB 12/2   MRL
NIOBE: opera (1688)
  Overture & extracts for solo voices & orch
    ed H.Riemann   ø 2000/0000/str/cont(hpsd)   Breitkopf,1912.DDTB 12/2   MRL
  Extracts
    Come padre e come Dio: aria (Act 1, Sc.21a)
      in C min (orig), ed H.Riemann
                  ø str/cont   (Breitkopf,1912.DDTB 12/2) 19420
    Sfere amiche: aria (Act 1, Sc.13) Del alma stanca: recit
      in F, ed H.Riemann   ø str/cont   (DDTB 12/2)   19517
ORLANDO GENEROSO: opera (1691)
  Overture & extracts for solo voices & orch
    ed H.Riemann   ø 0201/0000/str   Breitkopf,1912.DDTB 12/2   MRL
  Overture
    ed H.Riemann   ø 0201/0000/str/cont   (DDTB 12/2)   19594
La RIVALI CONCORDI (Atalanta): opera (1692)
  Complete: facsimile of autograph (GB-Lbm)
                  ø 0.2rec.201/0000/str/cont   Garland,1977   MRL facs
  Overture & extracts for solo voices & orch
    ed H.Riemann   ø str/cont   Breitkopf,1912.DDTB 12/2   MRL
La SUPERBIA D'ALLESSANDRO (Il Zelo di Leonato): opera (1691)
  Overture & extracts for solo voice & orch
    ed H.Riemann   ø str/cont   Breitkopf,1912.DDTB 12/2   MRL
SERVIO TULLIO: opera (1685)
  Overture
    ed H.Riemann   ø str/cont   Breitkopf,1912.DDTB 12/2   MRL
TASSILONE: opera (1709)
  Overture
    ed G.Croli   ø 0201/0000/str/cont(hpsd)   Schwann,1958.Denk Rhein 8 MRL
  Overture & extracts for solo voices & orch
    ed H.Riemann   ø 0100/0100/str/cont(pf)   Breitkopf,1912.DDTB 12/2   MRL
TRIONFI DEL FATO (La Gloire d'Eneau): opera
  Overture & extracts for solo voices & orch
    ed H.Riemann   ø str/cont   Breitkopf,1912.DDTB 12/2   MRL

STEFFE, W.

JOHN BROWN'S BODY: song, arr
  in B♭, arr R.Barsotti   PC 1+picc.12.4sx.2/4230/perc/str   Boosey & H   21039 B
  in B♭, arr S.Herbert   PC 1132/23.cnt-solo.30/perc/str   Boosey   8079 D
  in B♭, arr M.L.Lake   PC 1+picc.12.2sx.1/2210/perc/str   C.Fischer   19720

STEFFEN, Wolfgang (1923-

POLYCHROMIE for piano & 10 instruments, op.38 (1970)
                  ø 1(picc)111/1000/perc(bamboo rattle.timp.xba)/
                     str-4tet   11'   Bote & B,1976   Misc 9581

STEFFENS, Walter (1934-

GUERNICA: elegy for viola & orch, op.32 (1976-8)
          ø 3(picc)3(ca)3(bcl)3(cbsn)/4331/timp.perc.sirens.wmc/
            cel.hp/str(12-14.10-12.8-10.6-8.4-5)   15'-18'   Hansen,1979   M9sc 10065

STEIGER, Hans

MOUNTAIN MARCH
    arr L.Young   PC   2121/0320/perc/str   FD & H,1958   22860 Ap

STEIN, Egon (1903-

SINFONIETTA for strings   ∅   str   Eulenburg,1959   Misc 6351

STEINBACHER, Johann Michael (c.1700-c.1750)

CONCERTI
    Harpsichord & strings
        in F
            ed G.M.Schmeiser   ∅   str   Akademische Druck,1975   Misc 8748 B
        in A min
            ed G.M.Schmeiser   ∅   str   Akademische Druck,1975   Misc 8748 B

STEINBERG, Maximilian Osseyevich (1883-1946)

FANTAISIE DRAMATIQUE, op.9 (1910)
                              ∅   3(picc)2+ca.2+bcl.2+cbsn/4331/timp.perc(tamtam)/
                                   cel.hp/str   Belaieff,1912   Misc 9417
6 FOLKSONGS, op.19
    1. Prisoner of the Tartars   4. Turkish love song
    2. Abdurachmans plaint   5. Altai
    3. Dudeck (Tartar song)   6. 'Ça ira'
                                   2(picc)2(ca)22/2200/perc/cel.hp/str   Universal   16993
        No.4 only
            in B♭ min   11+ca.11/1000/tamb/cel/str   (Anglo-Soviet)   TO 1745
6 FOLKSONGS, op.22
    1. Tartar cradle song   4. Hungarian emigrants' song
    2. Dagestan   5. Dyginn
    3. Shepherds' song   6. Cossack song
                                   1(picc)122/2200/perc.xyl/str   Universal   12086
        No.6 only
            in A   1122/2200/tamb/str   (Anglo-Soviet)   TO 1730
METAMORPHOSES: ballet, op.10
    Suite
        1. Introduction   4. Apollo; Dance of the muses
        2. Crowning of Jupiter's statue   5. Transformation of Adonis
        3. Pan
                              ∅   3(picc,bfl)+picc.2+ca.3(E♭cl)+bcl.2+cbsn/42.2cnt.31/
                                   timp.perc.bells.tamtam.xyl/cel.2hp.[pf]/str   Belaieff   Misc 2357
SYMPHONIC PRELUDE, op.7   ∅   3(picc)2+ca.32+cbsn/6331/timp.perc.bells.tamtam/
                                   2hp.pf/str   Belaieff   Misc 1532
SYMPHONIES
    No.2, op. 8   ∅   3(picc)2+ca.32+cbsn/6332/timp.perc.tamtam/
                                   [pf]/str   Belaieff   Misc 1805
    No.3, op.18   ∅   3(picc)2+ca.2+bcl(Dcl)2+cbsn/4331/
                                   timp.perc.bells.tamtam/cel.hp/str   Russian SM   Misc 1677
    No.4, op.24 ('Turksib')   ∅   3(picc)2+ca.32+cbsn/4331/timp.perc/2hp/str 37'-40' Russian SM 14335

STEINBRECHER, Alexander

ICH KENN EIN KLEINES WEGERL: song
    in F, arr H.Carruthers   ∅   1021/0210/perc/acdn.gtr.mand.pf/str   Arranger   MS 30042

STEINER, Max (1888-1971)

GONE WITH THE WIND: film
  Extracts
    My own true love: song
       in Eb, arr K.Pakeman ∅ 2222/4230/timp.perc.glock/hp/str   (Feldman)   23285 +
A STAR IS BORN: song
    in Eb, arr B.Berlin   ∅ 2121/2000/perc/hp/str   (Stirling)   TO 79

STEININGER, F.

MARCHING ALONG TOGETHER: song by F.Steininger & E.Pola
  in G, arr G.Vinter for chorus & orch
                 ∅ 1+picc.222/4230/timp.perc/hp/str   (P.Maurice,1957) 22192 +

STEKEL, Eric P.

GRENOBLE: overture, op.29   ∅ 2222/4330/timp.perc/hp/str   7'   Paterson,1955   Misc 4339

STENHAMMAR, Wilhelm Eugen (1871-1927)

CONCERTO for piano & orch, no.2, op.23, in D min
                 ∅ 2222/4231/timp/str   Nordiska,1971   Misc 10336
FLOREZ OCH BLANZEFLOR for Baritone solo & orch, op.3
                 ∅ 2222/2200/timp/str   Nordisk   Misc 1818
MIDVINTER, op.24   ∅ 2+picc.223/4331/timp/str/chorus   12'   Hansen   13400
SERENADE, op.31
   1. Overtura   4. Notturno
   2. Canzonetta   5. Finale
   3. Scherzo
                 ∅ 2222/4230/timp.perc/str   22'   Edn.Suecia   15086
SYMPHONY no.2, in G min, op.34 ∅ 2222/4230/timp/str   40'-45' Hirschs Förlag   Misc 766

ŠTĔPÁN, Josef Antonín (STEFFAN, Joseph Anton)(1726-97)

CONCERTI
  Piano & orch
    in D
      ed H.Picton   ∅ 0000/2000/vln-solo.str   30'   OUP,1976   Misc 9001
    in Bb
      ed H.Picton   ∅ 0000/2000/str   A-R Edns,1980   Misc 10275

STEPHEN, David (1869-1946)

LOCH LOMOND, arr, in A   str   (Paterson)   TO 304
SCOTTISH FANTASIA   PC 2(picc)121/2230/timp.perc/str   Hawkes   2224 C
SCOTTISH SERENADE   PC 1121/2230.euph/timp.perc/str   Hawkes   3018 B
WILLY'S RARE AND WILLY'S FAIR: Scottish folk song, arr
  orch D.Darlow   ∅ 1122/2000/hp/str   (Paterson)   20324

STEPT, S.H.

FUNNY SIDE UP: musical play by S.H.Stept, L.Brown & C.Tobias
  Extracts
    Comes love: duet
      in G min, arr P.Cardew ∅ 2222/4230/timp.perc/hp/str   (Chappell)   22684
    It's me again: song
      in C, arr R.Hanmer   ∅ 2222/4230/timp.perc/pf/str   (Chappell)   20895

STERNBERG, Erich-Walter (1898-1974)

MY BROTHER JONATHAN, for SATB soloists (or chorus) & orch (1969)
                              φ   str   Israeli Music,1973   Misc 8661 B

The STORY OF JOSEPH: suite
  1. The Shepherd Joseph   7. Joseph and Potiphar's wife
  2. His brethren deride him   8. Joseph's advancement
  3. Joseph's dreams (Theme and variations)   9. The Brethren come before Joseph
  4. And they cast him into a pit   10. Joseph makes himself known to his brethren
  5. Joseph is sold into bondage   11. Reconciliation and gladness
  6. Jacob's grief
                              φ   str   35'   Novello   16918

STERNDALE-BENNETT, William   see   BENNETT, William Sterndale

STERNE, Ashley

SNAPDRAGON
  Extracts
    If I hold your hand: song
      in E♭, arr H.Carr   φ   2121/2230/perc/hp/str   [Arranger]   TO 505

STERNE, Marcel

DIVERTISSEMENT for small orch   φ   111.sx.1/1110/timp.perc.tamtam.xyl/pf/str   Eschig   Misc 2990

STEUERMANN, Edward (1892-1964)

AUF DER GALERIE, for soli, chorus & orch (1964)
                              φ   2(picc:bfl)2(ca)2+bcl.2(cbsn)/2220/timp.perc.
                                  glock.mba.vib.xyl/gtr.hp.pf/str   (Composer,1964)   Misc 6970
MUSIC FOR INSTRUMENTS (1959-1960)
                              φ   2+picc.2+ca.2+bcl.2+cbsn/2231/timp.perc.mba.xyl/
                                  hp.pf/str   [Composer]   Misc 6091

STEVENS, Bernard (1916-

CHORIAMB, op.41	φ	2222/4231/timp.perc/str	12'	Novello,1973	Misc 8632
CONCERTO for piano & orch, op.26					
	φ	2222/4231/timp.perc/str	27'	(Composer)	Misc 10134
ECLOGUE, op.8	φ	1111/2000/timp/str	7'	Lengnick	19759
INTRODUCTION, VARIATIONS & FUGUE on a theme of Giles Farnaby, op.47					
	φ	2222/2200/timp/str	13'	(Lengnick)	Misc 10276
RICERCAR, op.6	φ	str	12'	Lengnick	19050
SINFONIETTA, op.10	φ	str	14'-16'	Lengnick	19760

STEVENS, James

ECHO AND NARCISSUS: radio production
                            φ   1010/0000/perc/acdn.cel.hp.pf/str   Composer MS:BBC   MS 31277 φ only
GHOST STORY: radio production (1960)
                            φ   1010/1110/timp.perc.glock.vib/cel.hp/str/voices   Composer MS:BBC   MS 31333 +
The SALVATION OF FAUST: radio production (1960)
                            φ   1(picc)01(bcl)0/0100/perc/hp.pf/str   Composer MS:BBC   MS 31323 + φ only

STEVENS, Richard John (1757-1837)

SIGH NO MORE, LADIES: song
    in A, arr S.Robinson   str   (Novello)   MS 5671

STEVENSON, John (1761-1833)

FALLEN IS THY THRONE O ISRAEL
    in F   0011/0000/str   (Siddell)   17877
OFT IN THE STILLY NIGHT, attrib
    arr R.Barsotti   PC 1+picc.12.4sx.2/4230/perc/str   Boosey & H   21039 B
    arr M.L.Lake   PC 1+picc.12.2sx.1/2210/perc/str   C.Fischer   19720

STEVENSON, Ronald (1928-

CONCERTO for piano & orch, no.2 ('The Continents')(1972)
                            ∅   2(picc)222/4231/timp.perc.xyl/cel.2hp/str   OUP,1972   Misc 7756 C

STEWART, James E.

ONLY TO SEE HER FACE AGAIN: song
    in E♭   1020/0110/str   Bosworth,1906   18206

STEWART, W.

TRUMPET TUNE in the 17th century style
    arr Wright   PC 212.3sx.1/2230/timp/str   Paxton   18606

STICH, Jan Václav (Johann Wenzel)   see   PUNTO, Giovanni

STILL, Robert (1910-1971)

CONCERTI
    Piano & orch   ∅   2222/4330/timp/str   Lengnick   Misc 7600
    Violin & orch   ∅   2222/4330/timp.perc/str   Lengnick   Misc 7601

STILL, William Grant (1895-1978)

AFRO-AMERICAN SYMPHONY   ∅   32+ca.3+bcl.2/4331/timp.perc.vib/cel.hp/str 23'45"-26'27"
                                                                        J.Fischer,1935 Misc 1704
    Scherzo only   PC 112.3sx.1/2210/timp/bjo/str   J.Fischer   16193
IN MEMORIAM (The Colored soldiers who died for democracy)
                            ∅   3(picc)0.ca.2+bcl.2/4331/timp.perc/hp/str   Delkas Mus,1943   Misc 6025
The LITTLE SONG THAT WANTED TO BE A SYMPHONY, for narrator, SSA soli & orch
                            ∅   2[-3](picc)2+[ca].2+[bcl]2/3[-4]32[-3]1/
                                timp.perc.bells.glock.xyl/cel.hp/
                                str [solo str can substitute for SSA soli]   Eastman School,1974   Misc 8570

STILLMANN-KELLEY, E.   see   KELLEY, Edgar Stillman

STIMMER, Karl

ET IN ARCADIA EGO   ∅   2+picc.22.2sx.2+cbsn/4330.cbtuba/hp/str K.Stimmer   Misc 1502
KONZERTSATZ for piano & orch, op.10
                            ∅   2+picc.22.asx.tsx.2+cbsn/3221/str   K.Stimmer   Misc 1503

STIX, Carl

FLITTERWOCHEN: waltz caprice, op.147
         ø str   André 8254
HABANERA, op.139   ø 2000/0000/perc/hp/str   André 8258

STOCK, Frederick (1872-1942)

SYMPHONIC VARIATIONS on an original theme, op.7
         ø 3(2picc)2+ca.2+bcl.2+cbsn/43[=4]31/timp.perc/
          hp.[org]/str   Rahter,1910 Misc 788
SYMPHONY no.1, op.18, in C min ø 3(picc)+picc.2+ca.3(bcl)3+cbsn/4432/timp.perc/
          hp/str   Breitkopf Misc 1699

STOCKHAUSEN, Karlheinz (1928-

see MACONIE, Robin: The works of Karlheinz Stockhausen. London: OUP, 1976
   WÖRNER, K.H: Stockhausen: Life and work. London: Faber & Faber, 1973

The numbers after each title are the composer's own numbering system and serve as opus numbers

CARRÉ, for 4 orchs & choruses, no.1 (1959/60)
         ø 2+afl.2+ca.3+bcl.3sx.3/63+Dtpt+btpt.41/
          4perc.vib/cimb.pf/str(no cb) 30' Universal,1971 Misc 8009
FORMEL, no.^{1}/6 (1951) ø 0333/3000/1perc(glock.vib)/amphp.cel.pf/
          str(6.0.0.3.3)   Universal,1974 Misc 8620
FRESCO, for 4 orchestral groups, no.29 (1969)
     Group 1 ø Conductor(ob)   2222/3221/perc(mba.vib)
     Group 2 ø Conductor(harm) str(6.5.4.3.2)
     Group 3 ø Conductor(pf)   1111/2110/str(2.2.2.2.2)
     Group 4 ø Conductor(acdn.hca) str(7.4.3.3.2) Universal,1969 Misc 9539
GRUPPEN, for 3 orchs, no.6
       ø orch 1: 1(picc)+afl.1+ca.11/221.bvtbn.1/
            4(perc.5cbell,3cym.2African slotted dm.sdm.
            glock.mbn.3tamb.tamtam)/1kglock[=cel].hp/
            str(10.-.2.4.2)
        orch 2: 2(picc)10.E♭cl.asx(cl).barsx.1/321+btbn.0/
            4(perc.14bell.4cbell.3cym.2African slotted dm.
            4dm.sdm.ratchet.tamb.tamtam.2tri)/egtr.pf/
            str(8.-.4.2.2)
        orch 3: 1(picc)1+ca.1+bcl.1/320.2bvtbn+cbtbn[=tuba].0/
            4(perc.4cbell.3cym.2African slotted dm.4dm.sdm.
            tamb.tamtam.xba)/cel.hp/str(8.-.4.2.2)
               23'30"-25' Universal,1963 Misc 5831 C
HYMNEN: a score for reading (transcribed from the electronic tape), no.22 (1966/67)
         ø OS.tape   113' Universal,1968 Misc 6796
KONTRA-PUNKTE, no.1 (1952) ø 101+bcl.1/0110/hp.pf/vln.vlc 10'-12' Universal,1952 52774
         ø 101+bcl.1/0110/hp.pf/vln.vlc   Universal,1953 Misc 4750 B
MIXTUR for orch, sine-wave generators, ring modulators & loudspeakers
  no.16 (1964)
    recommended average instrumentation
         ø 3(3picc)33(E♭cl;bcl)3(cbsn)/5331/perc/1[=2]hp/
          str   16'-27' Universal,1966 Misc 6391
  no.16^1/$_2$ (version for chamber orch, sine-wave generators & ring modulators (1967)
         ø 1(picc)11(E♭cl,bcl)1(cbsn)/2110/str Universal,1968 Misc 6795
PUNKTE, no.^{1}/$_2$ (1952/62) ø 3(3picc;bfl)3(ob-d'a;ca)1+E♭cl+bcl.3(cbsn)/3321/
          timp.perc.bells.glock.mbn.vib.xyl/2hp.2pf(cel)/
          str   Universal,1963 Misc 5848
   1964 revision   ø 3(3picc;afl)3(ob-d'a;ca)1+E♭cl+bcl.3(cbsn)/3321/
          timp.perc.bells.glock.mba.vib/2hp.2pf(cel)/
          str   Universal,1964 Misc 6509

STOCKHAUSEN, Karlheinz (cont)

SPIEL, no.$^1/_4$ (1952, rev 1973)   φ   0333+cbsn/3000/9perc(ptimp.bell.Indian bell.
cinelli.crot.sizzle cym.glock.hihat.ratchet.
African pod rattle.2tamtam.tomtoms.vib.Japanese wdblk)/
cel(eorg).pf/str(12.-.-.6.6)
(str & ww players may take some perc parts; score
gives details & illustrations of perc instrs.)   Universal,1975   Misc 9855

STOP, for orch
  no.18 (1965)   φ   OS 6 characteristic groups of mixed instruments   Universal,1972   Misc 7757
  no.18$^1/_2$ (Paris version, 1969)
                           φ   Group 1: 0100/0001/pf
                               Group 2: 0000/0100/elektronium/vlc
                               Group 3: 000.bcl.0/0000/vib/vlc
                               Group 4: 000.bsthn.1/0000/vla
                               Group 5: 001(E♭cl;acl)0/0000/vln
                               Group 6: 1+afl.000/0000/hp/vla   Universal,1972   Misc 7757

STERNKLANG (Starsound): Parbmusic (Parb music), no.34 (1971)
                           φ   OS for 1 perc(bell.cbell.tamtam).electronics.
                               5 torchbearers & 5 groups of 4(unspecified)
                               singers & players   Stockhausen,1977   Misc 9488

TRANS, for orch, no.35 (1971)   φ   444+bcl.1+cbsn/0411/4perc(bells.cinelli.cbell.cym.
                               bdm.infantry dm.gongs.Indian bell.wreath.tamtams.
                               tomtoms.vib)/ampcel.eorg/str(22.-.8.6.4)/
                               tape.elec   Stockhausen,1978   Misc 9580

YLEM, for 19 or more players or singers, no.37 (1972)
                           φ   4 electronic instrs.5non-portable instrs.10 or more
                               portable instrs   19'-23' Stockhausen,1977   Misc 9489

STODDON, R.S.

COMMUNITYLAND: selections
  No.1   PC   111.3sx.1/2210/timp.perc/str   8'   Feldman   7414 Bp Cin Dtv
  No.2   PC   1+picc.11.3sx.1/2210/timp.perc/2bjo/str   8'   Feldman   6816 Atv Bp
DIXIELAND: selection of jazz classics
                           PC   1+picc.11.3sx.1/2210/perc/bjo/str   Feldman   10289
MELODYLAND: selection   PC   1+picc.020/0210/perc/str   Feldman   16600
OLD TIMES: selection no.1 PC   111.3sx.1/2210/perc/bjo/str   Darewski   14307 Ap B
SHAMROCKLAND: selection   PC   2(picc)11.3sx.1/2210/perc/bjo/str   Feldman   13281
WALTZLAND: selection of popular old time waltz songs
                           PC   1(picc)11.3sx.1/2210/perc/bjo/str   Feldman   10997

STOESSEL, Albert (1894-1943)

CONCERTO GROSSO   φ   pf/str   22'30" C.Fischer   13934
DUTCH PATROL on 2 Netherland airs
  arr O.Langey   PC   1121/2210/timp.perc/str   Boston Music 1757
HISPANA: suite
  1. Seguidilla   3. In old Castile: minuet
  2. La Media noche: serenade 4. Jota
                           φ   2+picc.22.2sx.2/4331/timp.perc/hp/str   C.Fischer   6645
SOUTHERN IDYL   PC   1121/2210/timp/str   Boston Music 506
SUITE ANTIQUE for 2 violins & chamber orch
  1. Bourée   3. Rigaudon   5. Gigue
  2. Sarabande   4. Ana
                           φ   1111/1000/str   G.Schirmer   7998

STOKER, Richard (1938-

CHORALE for strings (1967)	φ	str	4'30"	Fennette,1974	25770 *
LITTLE SYMPHONY	φ	OS orchestration unspecified	8'	Boosey & H,1973	Misc 8603 B
PERMUTATIONS, op.25	φ	orchestration variable: composer suggests 2222[=3333]/4230/str, with various optional instruments		Fenette,1973/CML,1973	Misc 8604

STOJOWSKI, Sigismond (1869-1916)

CHANT D'AMOUR, op.26, no.3					
arr Hupperts	PC	2121/2110/timp.perc/str	3'	Peters	3937
CONCERTI					
Piano & orch					
No.1, op.3, in F#	φ	2(picc)2+ca.22/4230/timp.perc/str		Lucas	Misc 785 B
Violin & orch					
op.22, in G	φ	2222/4230/timp/hp/str		Schmidt	Misc 727
Le PRINTEMPS: cantata for chorus & orch					
	φ	2+picc.222/4231/timp.perc/hp/str		Lucas	Misc 2454
SUITE, op.9, in E♭					
1. Thème varié 3. Rêverie et Cracovienne					
2. Intermède polonais					
	φ	3(picc)2+ca.22/4431/timp.perc/hp/str		Stanley	10308
SYMPHONY, op.21, in D min	φ	3(picc)2+ca.2+bcl.2/4231/timp.perc/hp/str		Peters	2810

STOKES, John

TO YOU: song					
in C, arr R.Binge	φ	1111/1220/perc/pf/str		(Boosey)	LM G 4790
arr P.Cardew (used in programme 'Friday night is music night')					
	φ	2222/4330/timp.perc/hp.pf/str		Boosey	23059 +

STOKOWSKI, Leopold (1882-1978)

TRADITIONAL SLAVIC CHRISTMAS MUSIC for brass & strings			4'		
	φ	0000/2331/str		Tetra Music/(Broude,1969)	Misc 7117

STOLLBERG, Sascha von

KASTILIANA: serenade	PC	2222/4231/timp.perc/hp/str	4'30"	Helbling	20354

STOLOFF, Morris

SONG WITHOUT END (Based on 'Un Sospiro' by Liszt), by M.Stoloff & G.W.Duning					
arr A.F.Fones	PC	2121/2230/perc/hp/str	2'45"	Chappell,1960	23355 Ap

STOLTE, Siegfried (1925-

CONCERTINO for descant recorder & strings (1974)					
	φ	str		DVfM,1979	Misc 10077

STOLZ, Robert (1880-1975)

AFRICAN MOON	PC	1121/2100/perc/gtr.hp/str	2'55"	Chappell,1959	22922 Cs Dp
The BELLS OF ST. STEPHEN'S					
arr B.Fahey	PC	2121/2230/timp.perc/hp/str	3'	Chappell,1960	23120 Cs Dp
The BLUE TRAIN: musical comedy					
Selection, arr H.Carr	PC	2(picc)222/2230/timp.perc/hp.org/str		Metzler	1900 B
Extracts					
When a girl is in love with a man (The blue train waltz): waltz					
arr S.Baynes	PC	111.3sx.1/2210/timp.perc/2bjo/str		Metzler	5603

STOLZ, Robert (cont)

DON'T ASK ME WHY: song for Tenor solo & orch
   arr J.Fox ϕ 21+ca.22/4030/2perc.glock.vib/cel.hp/str   (Campbell Connelly)   26263
EASTER PARADE IN VIENNA: waltz, op.837
   arr V.Charrosin   PC 112.3sx.1/2230/timp.perc.acdn.org/str   Bosworth   19535
Ein EINZIGE NACHT: operetta
  Selections
    Fantasy selection, arr Malkine
                 PC 1121/2210/timp.perc/str   Eschig   12015
    Selection, arr Ralph   PC 112.2sx.1/2220/timp.perc/bjo/str   Drei-Masken Verlag   9279 B
FRÜHLING IN WIEN: song, op.300 PC 2(picc)222/4230/perc/hp/str   Bruder Mändl   16177
FÜNF-UHR-TEE BEI R.STOLZ: selection, arr Dostal from the music of R.Stolz
           PC 2(picc)22.3sx.2/4231/ timp.perc/bjo.hp/str   Alrobi   11648 B
GOD BLESS MY HOMELAND: song
   arr D.Caryll   PC 112.3sx.1/2230/timp/str   Dix   16639
L'HEURE BLEUE: serenade, op.716
   arr G.Zalva   PC 112.3sx.1/2230/timp.perc/str   Boosey & H   16513 B
ICH WILL NICHT WISSEN: film
  Extracts
    So eine Nacht wie heute müsste es sein: Italian tango-serenade, op.568
                 PC 111.3sx.0/0210/perc/bjo/str   Alrobi   11778
IM PRATER BLÜHN: song
   in D min, arr P.Cardew ϕ 2222/4330/timp.perc/cel.hp.pf/str   (Brull)   18419
LILAC IN VIENNA
   arr L.Williams   PC 2121/2220/perc/hp/str (or pf/str)   3'40"Fanfare Mus Co,1960   23190
The MAGIC OF ROBERT STOLZ: selection, arr R.Docker form the music of R.Stolz
  Waltzing in the clouds   Goodbye
  Don't say goodbye   Two hearts in waltz time
  You, just you
           ϕ 2(picc)2(ca)22/4231/timp.perc.glock.vib/hp/
                 str   7'45"-8'   (Arranger)   26775
MEIN HERZ RUFT NACH DIR: film
  Extracts
    Der verhexte Speisesaal: novelty foxtrot
                 PC 222.3sx.1/4230/perc/bjo.hp/str   Wiener Boheme   3572
MEMORIES OF ROBERT STOLZ, arr J.Fox from the music of R.Stolz for Soprano & Tenor soli, chorus &
   orch (1976)
   1. My song of love   5. You, just you
   2. Don't ask me why   6. Waltzing in the clouds
   3. Two hearts in waltz time   7. Don't say goodbye (reprise)
   4. Don't say goodbye
           ϕ 22(ca)22/4331/timp.perc(glock.vib.xyl)/hp.pf(cel)/
                 str   [Arranger]   26171
PERSIAN NOCTURNE
   arr Mordish   PC 112.4sx.1/2220/perc/gtr/str   Liber-Southern   19373
RAINBOW SQUARE: musical play
  Extracts
    What a day: song
      in G, arr R.Green ϕ 1110/0000/hp.pf/str   (C.Connelly,1951)   LM G 8894
      in G, arr R.Tilsley ϕ 2222/4230/timp.perc/hp/str   (C.Connelly)   22392 +
REMINISCING WITH ROBERT STOLZ: selection, arr H.Jacques from the music of R.Stolz
           PC 112.3sx.1/2220/timp.perc/str   Dix   12754
ROBERT STOLZ MELODIES: selection arr F.Rapley from the music of R.Stolz
           PC 212.3sx.1/2230/timp.perc/hp/str   Chappell,1931   23157 Ap Ds
SERVUS DU: song, op.102
   in C   PC 2122/2230/timp.perc/hp/str   Robitschek   19322

STOLZ, Robert (cont)

SPRING PARADE: film
   Extracts
      Waltzing in the clouds: song
         in Eb, arr K.Pakeman   φ 102.asx.tsx.0/0220/timp.perc.glock/pf/str   Feldman   MLO 1644
         in F, arr R.Tilsley   φ 2140/2330/perc/hp.pf/str   (Feldman)   LM G 7869
         arr R.Docker (non-vocal)
                        φ 2222/4300/timp.perc/hp.pf/str   (Feldman)   23182 +
      When April sings: song
         in G, arr P.Hope   φ 2122/3000/timp.perc/hp/str   (Feldman)   22600 +
         in Ab   2121/2230/perc/str   (Feldman)   TO 662

TWO HEARTS IN WALTZ TIME: duet for Soprano & Baritone soli & orch
   in Bb (includes version in C)   2'45"
                 φ 21+ca.22/4331/timp.perc.glock.vib/hp.pf/str   (Chappell & Connelly) 26113

VIENNA BY NIGHT (Lovely Vienna mine): waltz
               PC 1120/0210/timp.perc/str   Dix   6705

WHIRLED INTO HAPPINESS: musical play
   Selection, arr M.Morgan   PC 1121/2230/timp.perc/str   AH & C   633 Bp
   Extracts
      Robinson Crusoe's isle: song
         in A min, arr R.Hanmer φ 2222/4230/timp.perc/str   (AH & C)   18439
      The World's a stage: song
         in D, arr J.Brown   φ 2232/4230/timp.perc/hp.pf/str   (AH & C)   18438

The WHITE HORSE INN, by R.Stolz & R.Benatzky
   Selection
      arr P.Cardew   2222/4230/timp.perc/hp.pf/str   (Chappell)   21848
      arr R.Docker for Soprano & Bass soli, chorus & orch
                        hp.pf(cel)/str   (Chappell)   24771 +
      arr R.Hanmer (vocal medley)
                   φ 2222/4330/timp.perc/hp/str   (Chappell)   18463
      arr Jones   PC 2122/2230/perc/str   7'   Chappell   9630 D
   Extracts
      Goodbye: song
         in Eb (orig)   1110/0210/pf/str   (Chappell)   LM G 3893
         in Eb, for mv-chorus & orch
                   φ 2121/2230/perc/str   (Chappell)   MS 6369
         in F, arr R.Binge   φ 1111/2210/perc/str   (Chappell)   LM G 4738
         in F, arr F.Cramer   pf/str   (Chappell)   LM G 4431
      It would be wonderful: song (Benatzky)
         in Ab (orig), orch H.Carr
                   φ 2121/2230/perc/hp/str   (Chappell)   TO 1221
      My song of love: song (Stolz)
         arr Dostal   PC 112.3sx.1/2210/timp.perc/2bjo/str   Chappell   10271
      You too: duet (Stolz)
         in G, arr M.Mackie φ 2222/4230/timp.perc/hp/str   (Chappell)   22584 +

WILD VIOLETS: operetta (English version of Wenn die kleinen Veilchen bluhmen)
   Selection
      arr Dostal (from orig version 'Wenn die kleinen Veilchen bluhmen')
                 PC 2(picc)22.3sx.2/4231/perc/bjo/str   Drei-Masken Verlag 10946
      arr Jones   PC 212.sx.1/2230/timp.perc/str   8'   Chappell   10556 Dp
      arr L.Wurmser   φ 32+ca.22/4231/timp.perc/cel.hp/str   (Chappell)   TO 1611

STÖLZEL, Gottfried Heinrich (1690-1749)

CONCERTO for oboe & strings, in D
   ed H.Töttcher   φ str   Sikorski,1953   21174
CONCERTO GROSSO A QUATTRO CHORI, in D
   ed A.Schering   φ 1301/0600/2timp/2hpsd/str   (Breitkopf & H.DDT 29/30) 24307

STONE, Gregory

HORA IMPROMPTU: Roumanian gypsy caprice
   arr T.Seidel   ∅   str   Marks   16584

STORACE, Stephen (1763-1796)

La CAMERIERA ASTUTA: opera
   Extracts
      Beaux yeux: air
         in G min   ∅   1202/2000/str   (GB-Lbm)   22571 + & mf 101
      È di matti questo mondo: air
         in F   ∅   2000/2000/str/cont(hpsd)   (GB-Lbm)   22572 + & mf 101
      Jeunes coeurs soyez fidelles: gavotte in G
                                 ∅   1202/2000/str   (GB-Lbm)   22571 + & mf 101
The CHEROKEE: opera
   Overture (without Largo intro. used as overture to 'Gli Sposi Malcontenti')
      ed R.Fiske   ∅   2202/2200/timp/str   Editor   22568 + & mf 80
Gli EQUIVOCI: opera (1786)
   Complete   ∅   2.piffera.222/2200/timp.perc/str   (D-ddr DI) Misc 8336 & mf 81
LULLABY, for voice & orch
   arr G.Langford   ∅   hp/str   Arranger   24575 +
NO SONG, NO SUPPER: ballad opera [1790]
   Complete   ∅   2222/2000/glock/str   (GB-Lbm)   21408 + & mf 71
   Overture
      arr Dailey   ∅   2222/2000/str   Augener   15023
   Extracts
      With lowly suit and plaintive ditty: song
         in Bb, arr D.Arundell   ∅   0020/2000/str   BBC   24567 +
The PRETTY CREATURE: song, attrib
   in A, arr L.Wilson, orch H.Carr
                                 ∅   2222/2000/hp/str   (Boosey & H) TO 1421
PRIGIONIERA ABBANDONATA: aria   see INSANGUINE, Giacomo: PRIGIONIERA ABBANDONATA: aria
The SIEGE OF BELGRADE: opera (including material from MARTÍN'S 'Una Cosa Rara')
   Extracts
      The Rose and the lily: song
         in F   ∅   2121/2200/timp/hpsd/str   (GB-Lbm)   MS 27
Gli SPOSI MALCONTENTI
   Overture   see The CHEROKEE: opera - Overture

The STORY OF THE BALLET: radio production.

   Selection of extracts from various ballets, [arr M.Seiber]
                                 ∅   2(picc)222/4200/timp.perc.glock/cel.hp/str/
                                     chorus   BBC   MS 8242

STOTHART, Herbert

CUBAN LOVE SONG: film music by H.Stothart, J.McHugh & D.Fields
   Extracts
      Cuban love song: song
         in Eb, arr R.Tilsley (refrain only)
                                 ∅   2222/4030/perc/hp/str   (K.Prowse) 22207
ROSE MARIE   see   FRIML, Rudolph: ROSE MARIE
The WILDFLOWER   see   YOUMANS, Vincent: The WILDFLOWER

STOTT, Wally

ANGEL CAKE: arranged as Signature Tune of 'Soundstage'
                                  φ   2(picc)222/433[1]/timp.perc.bells.glock.vib/
                                      [gtr].hp.pf(cel)/str   BBC   25493
MISS UNIVERSE   φ   2(picc)12+bcl.1/1100/timp.perc.glock.vib/   (no hire
                                      gtr.hp/str   (Chappell)(H)   PL 399   (fee

STRACHEY, Jack (1894-1972)

ASCOT PARADE
   arr R.Hanmer   PC 112.3sx.1/2231/timp.perc/str   Paxton   19576
BELINDA FAIR: musical play
   Selection, arr L.Stevens PC 1+picc.12.4sx.1/2230/timp.perc/hp/str   Chappell   19335 B
A BOY, A GIRL AND THE MOON: song
   in C, arr J.Beaver   φ   2121/2230/timp/hp/str   (Boosey)   TO 977
CAESAR HAVING DEPARTED: song
   in B♭ min, arr B.Berlin φ   2121/2220/perc/hp/str   Arranger   TO 832
DEAR LITTLE BILLIE: musical play by J.Strachey & H.B.Hedley   see   HEDLEY, H.D: DEAR LITTLE BILLIE
EROS IN PICCADILLY
   arr D.Bowden   PC 212.4sx.1/2330/perc/str   Boosey & H   19245
GIVE THEM A WALTZ TUNE: song
   in C, arr M.Lubbock   φ   2121/2230/perc/hp/str   Arranger   TO 659
IN PARTY MOOD   PC 112.3sx.1/2230/perc/str   Bosworth   13337 Bp
KNIGHTS OF MALTA: march   incomplete parts only (no score)   (FD & H)   TO 1128
LADY LUCK: musical play by J.Strachey & H.D.Hedley   see   HEDLEY, H.D: LADY LUCK
MAYFAIR PARADE
   arr A.Franzel   PC 1+picc.12.3sx.1/2230/perc/acdn/str   3'15"   Bosworth   18992
NEW FACES: revue
   Extracts
     If you were Ginger Rogers: song
       in D, arr E.Griffiths φ   2222/4230/timp.perc/hp.pf/str   (P.Maurice)   18407
     Thank you for the party, Mr. Pollinger: song
       in D♭, arr B.Berlin   φ   2121/0220/perc/str   (P.Maurice)   TO 833
OVERTURE AND BEGINNERS: march
   arr R.Hanmer   PC 213.3sx.1/2220/perc/str   P.Maurice   18695 Ap
PINK CHAMPAGNE: waltz
   arr A.Franzel   PC 1+picc.12.3sx.1/2230/timp.perc/hp/str   Bosworth   19250
SHAFTESBURY AVENUE: march
   arr A.Franzel   PC 112.3sx.1/2230/timp.perc/str   Bosworth,1948   20907
SONG OF THE MAY TREE
   in D, arr J.Beaver   φ   2121/2230/perc/hp/str   BBC   TO 868
STARLIGHT CRUISE: beguine
   arr K.Warner   PC 2+picc.121/2230/timp.perc/acdn.gtr.hp/str 3'   Boosey & H,1955 21604 B
THEATRELAND: march
   arr D.Bowden   PC 112.4sx.1/2330/timp/str   4'   Boosey & H   16822 C
THESE FOOLISH THINGS: song (from 'Spread it Abroad')
   in C, D & E♭, arr J.Brown   φ   21+ca.2+bcl.2/4230/timp.perc/cel.hp/str   (Boosey)   18378
   in D♭, arr P.Cardew   PC 112.4sx.1/2330/perc/gtr/str   Boosey & H   13594 Bp C
   in D♭, arr F.Hartley   PC 1010/0000/gtr/str   Boosey & H   7479
   in D, E♭ & A♭, arr B.Campbell φ   0010/0100/cel.gtr.hp.pf/str   (Boosey)   LM G 8921
TRAMWAY QUEEN: song
   in C, arr B.Berlin   φ   2121/2230/perc/hp/str   BBC   TO 869
UP WITH THE CURTAIN
   arr D.Bowden   PC 2+picc.12.3sx.1/2330/timp.perc/str   4'40"   Hawkes,1954   21236

STRADELLA, Alessandro (1642-1682)

ARIA DI CHIESA (Air d'église): Pietà Signore [authenticity doubtful]
   in C min   0202/2000/str   (Siddell)   17338
   in D min   ϕ   2222/2000/str   BBC   20898
   in A min   0202/2000/str   (Siddell)   17339
   in B♭ min   ϕ   0022/2000/str   6'40"   BBC   TO 2017
   orch, arr & transcr G.Cristiani for cello & orch
                  ϕ   2hp.org/str   Carisch,1948   Misc 2756

Il BARCHEGGIO: serenata
  Part 1
    Sinfonia
      ed R.P.Block   ϕ   0000/0100/2vln/cont   Musica Rara,1973 25726
  Part 2
    Sinfonia
      ed R.P.Block   ϕ   0000/0200/2vln/cont(inc tbn)   Musica Rara,1971 25533 B

CANTATA À 6 CON I STROMENTI PER IL SS. NATALE, for SSS.Mz.A.Bar soli, SSATB chorus & orch
   ed R.Giazotto   ϕ   hp.hpsd.lute.org/str   Curci,1962   Misc 8238

ECHO CONCERTO for concert band
   adapted A.Antonini, arr J.Cacavas
                  ϕ   1+picc.23+E♭ac]+[E♭cl]+bcl±[cbcl].4sx.1/
                     41.3cnt.21+bar/timp.perc/[org]/cb   Chappell,1971   MB 4505

QUAL PRODIGIO E GH'IO MIR?! serenata
  Sinfonia, in D
    ed F.Chrysander   ϕ   2vln.vlc-soli.str/cont   Breitkopf & H,1889.Handel CW supp 3   25449 + & MRL
  Extracts
    Amor, Amor: aria for Soprano solo & orch (no.9)
      in F, ed F.Chrysander ϕ 2vln.vlc-soli.str/cont   Breitkopf & H,1889.Handel CW supp 3   25404 + & MRL
    Io pur seguirò: aria for Soprano solo & orch (no.13)
      in C, ed F.Chrysander ϕ 2vln.vlc=soli.str/cont   Breitkopf & H,1889.Handel CW supp 3   25451 +
    Seguir non voglio più: aria for Bass solo & orch (no.14)
      in A, ed F.Chrysander ϕ 2vln.vlc-soli.str/cont   Breitkopf & H,1889.Handel CW supp 3   25450 +
    Sinfonia Concertata, in B♭ (no.10)
      ed F.Chrysander   ϕ   2vln.vlc-soli.str/cont   Breitkopf & H,1889.Handel CW supp 3   25401 +

SAN GIOVANNI BATTISTA: oratorio for SSSATB soli, SSATB chorus & orch
  ed J.Crowther from I MOe MS.MUS.F 1136-7
                  ϕ   str/cont   (Editor)   26787

SE NEL BEN SEMPRE INCOSTANTE: aria
   in G   ϕ   0001/0000/str   (Siddell)   17879

SERENATA for strings
   transcr G.F.Malipiero ϕ   str   7'   Ricordi,1930   Misc 3159

SINFONIA in G, arr from the Sinfonia for violin
   arr A.Gentili   ϕ   str   Carisch,1948   21646

SONATA for trumpet & strings
   ed O.Jander   ϕ   str/cont   7'15" R.King Mus Co,1960 23835

STRANO, Alfredo

SULLA VIA MAESTRA: opera
  Complete   ϕ   2+picc.2+ca.2+bcl.2/4340/timp.perc/hp/str   Curci,1968   Misc 8304

STRAESSER, Joep (1940-

CHORAIN (Fields)(1966)   ϕ   perc.tamtam.vib/hp/str   12'   Donemus,1967   Misc 6628
EN RADE, for SSAB chorus & orch (1963)
                  ϕ   3221/0110/perc.glock.xyl/gtr.pf/str   10'   Donemus,1967   Misc 6629

STRANKS, Allan

WHEN NIGHT IS THRO': song by A.Stranks & P.Patterson
    in A   000.sx.0/0000/str   (P.Maurice)   19423

STRASSER, Alfred

BLUES SINFONIQUE, op.58   PC 111.3sx.0/0210/perc/bjo/pf/str   Heinrichshofen   12320

STRASSER, Ewald (1867-?)

SYMPHONY, op.22, in G   ø   2+picc.2(ca)22+cbsn/4231/ptimp.perc/str   Tischer & J,1910   Misc 9244

STRATICO, Michele (c.1721-c.1782)

CONCERTO for violin & orch, in D
    ed M.Roeder   ø   str/cont(hpsd - real R.Chapman)   Presser,1976   Misc 9039

STRAUS, Christophorus (1580-1631)

MISSA PRO DEFUNCTIS: Requiem for SSTT & TBBBBB choruses, strings & continuo
    ed G.Adler   ø   str/cont(org)   Universal,1923.DTÖ 59   MRL

STRAUS, Oscar (1870-1954)

ABRAKADABRA-HEXEREI, or Das Zaubermittel: polka-française on motives from 'Zur indischen Witwe'
                            PC 2(picc)222/4230/timp.perc/str   Bosworth   11980
ALT-WIENER-REIGEN, op.45   ø   str   Schott   8145
                            PC 2(picc)222/4230/timp/str   Schott   16557
The CHOCOLATE SOLDIER: operetta
    Complete   1121/2220/timp.perc/hp/str   (Doblinger,1908)   21843
    Selections
        Selection, arr Lampe PC 1(picc)121/2210/perc/hp/str   Remick   1680 D
        Vocal selection, arr D.Edge, orch R.Burston
                        ø   2222/4231/perc/hp/str   (Feldman)   TO 911
        Waltz selection, arr Danmark
                      PC 1121/2210/timp.perc/str   6'15"-8' Feldman   102
    Extracts
        Bulgarian march   ø   0.2picc.222/4230/perc/str   Doblinger   9528
        Come, come, I love you only (My hero): song
          in C   2222/4230/perc/hp.pf/str   (Feldman)   LM G 4450
          in Db   1121/00.2cnt-solo.10/perc/str   (Feldman)   LM G 4627
          in D   PC 2222/4130/tlmp/hp/str   3'45"   Doblinger   5467
          in D, arr Smith   1121/20.2cnt.10/2timp.perc/pf/str   Remick   3948
          in Eb   2121/2130/perc/hp.pf/str   (Feldman)   LM G 5452
          in Eb, arr G.Stacey   1010/0000/perc/acdn.pf/str   (Feldman)   LM A 117
          in Eb, arr K.Warner ø   0010/0000/gtr.pf/str   (Feldman)   LM G 5102
        Entr'acte and Letter song: intermezzo
                      PC 2222/4230/timp.perc/str   3'   Doblinger   9526
      In the evening when you are good: song
        non-vocal arrangement PC 2222/4230/perc/hp/str   Doblinger   9529
      Soldier's march   PC 1+picc.222/4230/timp.perc/str   Doblinger   9527
CLEOPATRA: operetta by O.Straus & A.Wood
    Selection, arr Wood   PC 2(picc)121/2230/timp.perc/str   AH & C   3312 C
DIDI: waltz on motives from operetta 'Didi'
                      PC 2(picc)121/2230.euph/timp.perc/str   Chappell   3963
DREI WALZER: operetta (part 1 based on the music of J.Strauss (i), part 2 based on the music
    of J.Strauss (ii), part 3 by O.Strauss)
    Overture   ø   2(picc)222/4230/timp.perc.glock.vib/   str
                            cel.hp.2pf/str   BBC   TO 1774 ** only

STRAUS, Oscar (cont)

LAND WITHOUT MUSIC: film
   Extracts
      Heaven in a song
        in D, arr B.Berlin   ø   2121/2000/perc/hp/str   (Chappell)   TO 185

The LAST WALTZ: operetta
   Selection, arr H.Jaxon   PC 1121/2230/timp.perc/str   10'30"   AH & C   636
   Excerpts
      Introduction
      Love the minstrel: aria, in A (orig)
      When life and love are calling: duet, in Ab (orig)
      If this must be the last waltz: song, in Ab (orig G)
      Scene and Waltz (no.6), with additional finale
               ø 3(picc)22+bcl.2/4231/timp.perc/hp/str   (AH & C) TO 1469
   Extracts
      Laggard lover: song
        in F (orig)   incomplete parts only   (AH & C) TO 782
        arr P.Hope for chorus & orch
               ø 2(picc)222/4230/timp.perc(glock)/str/chorus   AH & C   26485 +
      The Magic valse
        arr H.Jaxon   PC 112.sx.1/2230/timp.perc/str   AH & C   606
      When life and love are calling: duet
        in Ab (orig), arr R.Chignell
               ø 2212/2120/timp/cel.hp/str   (AH & C) MS 5563

LOVE AND LAUGHTER: operetta
   Selection   PC 2(picc)222/2230/timp.perc/str   Metzler   7139

LOVE'S ROUNDABOUT see   La RONDE DE L'AMOUR

MARIETTA: operetta
   Selection   ø   1(picc)121/2210/timp.perc/str   15'30"   Salabert   12302
                    PC 2121/2220/timp.perc/hp/str   Karczag   12071

MOTHER OF PEARL: operetta
   Selection   PC 212.sx.1/2230/perc/str   6'   Chappell   10933 B
   Extracts
      Ev'ry woman thinks she wants to wander: song
        in Eb, arr B.Ebbinghouse
               ø 221+bcl.2/4230/timp.kit/hp.pf(cel)/str   (Chappell) 26875
        in Bb   ø   1121/2220/timp.perc/hp/str   (Chappell) 18498

MY SON JOHN: operette by O.Straus, V.Ellis & B.Thompson
   Selection, arr Hornsey   PC 1121/2210/timp.perc/str   AH & C   6977 B

The PASSING REGIMENT: march
   arr Paul   PC 112.3sx.1/2210/perc/2bjo/str   Chappell   8500

Die PRINZESSIN VON TRAGANT: operetta
   Extracts
      Die Schlossparade: Marsch excentrique
        arr Schott   PC 2(picc)222/4230/timp.perc/str   Doblinger 9162
      Soldatenliebe: polka
        arr Schott   PC 2(picc)222/4230/timp.perc/str   Doblinger 9160 B
      Tragant Walzer
        arr Schott   PC 2(picc)222/4230/perc/str   Doblinger 9161 B

La RONDE DE L'AMOUR: valse song (from film 'La Ronde')
   in F, arr A.Sandford   ø 2121/2220/timp.perc/hp.pf/str   (Cinephonic) 21782 +
   in F#   ø 21+ca.22/4000/perc/cel.hp/str   (Cinephonic) 23869 +
   in G, arr J.Brown   ø 21+ca.32/4230/timp.perc/cel.hp/str (Cinephonic) 18447
   arr M.Farren (non-vocal) ø 2(picc)222/4230/timp.perc/hp/str   (Cinephonic) 22491 +
   arr R.Green   ø 211+bcl.0/2220/perc.glock/gtr.pf/str Cinephonic MLO 17

RUND UM DIE LIEBE: operetta
   Overture   ø 2(picc)222/4231/timp.perc/hp/str   Doblinger 12085

STRAUS, Oscar (cont)

SERENADE, op.35, in G min	ø	str		Schott	5554
Das TAL DER LIEBE: opera					
Overture	ø	2(picc)222/4230/timp.perc/hp/str	4'	Doblinger	12298 +
TANZENDE WIENERINNEN (The dancing Viennese): waltz					
arr Fraliers	PC	1+picc.121/2230/perc/str		Schott	16760
TIRALALA: waltz on motives from 'The Chocolate Soldier'					
	PC	1+picc.222/4230/timp.perc/hp/str		Doblinger	9530

A WALTZ DREAM: operetta

Complete	ø	2(picc)222/4230/timp.perc/hp/str/solo & chorus parts			
		Stageband: 1000/0200/timp.perc/hmn.pf/			
		vln-solo.2vln.vlc.cb		Doblinger(H)	PL 267
Version for radio, arr M.Lubbock					
		0121/2000/perc/hp/str		(Chappell)	TO 783
Overture	ø	2(picc)222/4230/timp.perc/hp/str		Doblinger	13143
	ø	2(picc)211/20.2cnt.10/timp.perc/str	6'45"-7'30"	(Chappell)	MS 195 ø only
arr M.Schönherr	PC	2(picc)222/4230/timp.perc/hmn[=acdn].hp/			
		str		Doblinger,1959	23217
Selections					
	PC	1121/2210/perc/str		Ascher	1844 B
arr C.Godfrey, jnr	PC	2(picc)222/4230.euph/timp.perc/hp/str		Hawkes	2642 Ewe
Waltz on melodies from the operetta					
	PC	2(picc)222/4230/timp.perc/hp/str	11'45"-14'	Hawkes	3174 B
arr M.Lubbock for military band					
	ø	2(picc)121/2220/timp.perc		Arranger MS:BBC	MS 30091
Extracts					
I walked in the blossoming garden: waltz duet for Soprano & Baritone soli & orch (no.7)					
in G (orig)	ø	2222/4230/perc/hp/str	6'30"	(Chappell)	TO 783
Leh'n deine Wangen (Violin & piccolo): duet for Soprano & Baritone soli & orch					
in E	PC	2(Picc)221/2200/perc/hp/str		(Doblinger)	26444
arr as Piccolo! Piccolo! (non-vocal)					
	PC	1+picc.222/3230/perc/str		Hawkes	16087)
WALTZ-SCHERZO, op.43, no.2					
arr L.Artok	PC	2222/2210/timp.perc/str		Schott	9927
arr O.Langey	PC	1121/2210/timp.perc/str		G.Schirmer	10916
WHILE HEARTS ARE SINGING: song (from film 'The smiling lieutenant')					
Waltz, arr Mason	PC	112.3sx.1/2210/perc/2bjo/str		Chappell	11384

STRAUSS, Art

BLUE MIST				
arr Berry	PC	112.4sx.1/2320/timp.perc/hp/str	Cosmo Music Co	9093

STRAUSS, C.

DR. PICCOLO: galop, op.35 (on motives from Lecocq's operetta)				
	PC	1+picc.222/4231/perc/str	André	11346

STRAUSS, Eduard (1835-1916)

AUS DEM RECHTSLEBEN: waltz, op.126				
	PC	1+picc.222/4231/timp.perc/hp/str	Schreiber	3536
AUS DER STUDIENZEIT: waltz, op.141				
	PC	1+picc.222/4230/timp.perc/hp/str	Schreiber	16123
BAHN FREI! (The train galop): Polka schnell, op.45				
arr Atzler	PC	1121/2210/timp.perc/hp/str	Cranz	20824 +
arr W.Goehr	ø	2222/2230/timp.perc/hp/str	(Cranz)	TO 828

STRAUSS, Eduard (cont)

BALL-CHRONIK: waltz, op.167	PC	1+picc.222/4230/timp.perc/hp/str		Cranz	16125
BALL-ERINNERUNGEN: waltz, op.299 (op.300)					
		2(picc)122/4230/timp.perc/hp/str		Zimmermann	7402
arr Roth	PC	1222/2210/timp.perc/str		C.Fischer	1951
BALL-PROMESSEN: waltz, op.82	PC	1+picc.222/4230/timp.perc/hp/str		Cranz	16126
BLAUÄUGLEIN: polka française, op.254					
arr G.Walter	∅	2222/2230/timp.perc/hp/str	2'30"	(Cranz)	TO 829
BLÜTHENKRANZ: selection of waltzes of J.Strauss (ii), arr, op.292					
		2(picc)222/4230/timp.perc/hp.pf/str		Cranz	8239 B
CARNEVALSSTUDIEN: waltz, op.213					
	PC	1+picc.222/4230/timp.perc/hp/str		Cranz	16136
COLOMBINE: polka-mazurka, op.89					
		1+picc.222/4230/timp.perc/hp/str		Schreiber	3370
DEUTSCHE HERZEN: waltz, op.65	PC	1+picc.222/4231/timp.perc/hp/str		Cranz	16129
DOCTRINEN: waltz, op.79	PC	2222/2230.euph/timp.perc/str		Hammond	335 Bp
	∅	2222/4230.euph/timp.perc/str	8'	Hawkes	14368 B
EXPOSITIONEN: waltz, op.103	PC	2(picc)122/4230/timp.perc/hp/str		Schreiber	8435

FANTASIE ÜBER NEUERE DEUTSCHE LIEDER, arr, op.133

1. Der Trompeter (W.Speier)
2. Mein Liebster ist im Dorf der Schmied (G.Hölzel)
3. Es hat nicht sollen sein (F.Abt)
4. Schlaf wohl, du süsser Engel du (F.Abt)

5. Wie mirs im Herzen (F.Gumbert)
6. Fliege du Vöglein (F.Abt)
7. Von dir (F.Gumbert)
8. Gute Nacht du mein herziges Kind (F.Abt)

	∅	2(picc)122/4231/timp.perc/hp/str		Andre	3027
FESCHE GEISTER: waltz, op.75	PC	1+picc.222/4230/timp.perc/hp/str		Cranz	8374 B
	PC	2222/2230/timp.perc/str	6'15"	Hawkes	6414
FLEUR ROUMAINE: polka française, op.192					
		1+picc.122/4230/timp.perc/hp/str		Cranz	3915
FREIE LIEDER: waltz, op.188		1+picc.222/4230/timp.perc/hp/str		Cranz	5059
FREUDENSALVEN: waltz, op.249	PC	1+picc.222/4230/timp.perc/hp/str		Cranz	16122
GEFLÜGELTE WORTE: waltz, op.158	PC	1+picc.222/4230/timp.perc/hp/str		Cranz	16137
GLOCKENSIGNALE: waltz, op.198	PC	1+picc.222/4230/timp.perc/hp/str		Cranz	16118
GREETING: waltz on English airs					
	PC	2(picc)212/4230.euph/timp.perc/hp/str		Chappell	3721
HECTOGRAF: polka, op.186		1+picc.222/4230/timp.perc/str		Cranz	5448
HULDIGUNGEN: waltz, op.88	PC	1+picc.222/4231/timp.perc/hp/str		Spina	13394
INTERPRETATIONEN: waltz, op.97	∅	1+picc.222/4230/timp.perc/hp/str		Cranz	16127
KAISER FRANZ-JOSEF-JUBILÄUMS-MARSCH, op.109					
	PS	2+picc.21+E♭cl.2/4231/perc/hp/str		Cranz	25444 +
LEBENDE BLUMEN: waltz, op.205	PC	1+picc.122/4230/timp.perc/hp/str		Cranz	16135
LEUCHTKÄFERL'N: waltz, op.161	PC	1+picc.222/4230/timp.perc/hp/str		Cranz	16124
LUSTFAHRTEN: waltz, op.177	PC	1+picc.222/4230/timp.perc/hp/str		Cranz	16139
LUSTIG IM KREISE: polka, op.93		1+picc.122/4230/perc/hp/str		Schreiber	8877
MANUSCRIPTE: waltz, op.90	∅	1+picc.222/4230/timp.perc/hp/str	7'30"	Spina	12533
MÄRCHEN AUS DER HEIMATH: waltz, op.155					
	PC	1+picc.222/4230/timp.perc/str		Spina	2342
MEIN LIEBLINGSBLÜMCHEN: polka-mazurka, op.230					
		1+picc.122/4230/timp.perc/hp/str		Cranz	20666
MIT DAMPF: polka schnell, op.70					
	∅	1+picc.121/2220/perc/str	2'-2'45"	Cranz	10669
arr R.Hanmer	PC	1+picc.222/4231/timp.perc/hp/str		Dix	19491
MIT EXTRAPOST: polka, op.259		1+picc.122/4230/timp.perc/str		Cranz	25256
MIT FROHEM MUTH UND HEITER'M SINN: waltz, op.153					
		1+picc.122/4231/timp.perc/hp/str		Spina	3206
MOOSRÖSCHEN: polka-mazurka, op.169					
		1+picc.122/4230/timp.perc/hp/str		Spina	6367

STRAUSS, Eduard (cont)

MYRTHENSTRÄUSSCHEN: waltz, op.87
              ø 2(picc)222/4230/timp.perc/hp/str   Cranz   16128
Eine NEUE WELT!: Polka schnell, op.86
            1+picc.222/4230/timp.perc/str   Schreiber   7672
OHNE AUFENTHALT: polka, op.112   1+picc.222/4230/timp.perc/str   Schreiber   9849
ORIGINALBERICHT: polka française, op.189
            1+picc.122/4230/timp.perc/str   Cranz   10097
SCHLEIER UND KRONE: waltz, op.200
            1121/2210/perc/str   Cranz   7381
SCHMEICHELKÄTZCHEN: polka-mazurka, op.226
  arr G.Walter   ø   2222/2230/perc/hp/str   3'   (Cranz)   TO 830
SCHNEESTERNCHEN: polka française, op.157
          ø 2(picc)121/2230/timp.perc/str   2'30"-3'15"   Cranz   11108
SCHÜTZEN-QUADRILLE see STRAUSS, Johann (i): SCHÜTZEN-QUADRILLE
SEEKADET-QUADRILLE, op.151 (on motives from Genée's opera)
           1+picc.222/4230/timp.perc/str   Spina   10045
STILL UND BEWEGT: polka, op.187   1+picc.122/4230/timp.perc/hp/str   Cranz   2344
STIMMEN AUS DEM PUBLIKUM: waltz, op.104
           1+picc.222/4230/timp.perc/str   Schreiber   7366
The TRAIN GALOP see BAHN FREI
TRAUMGEBILDE: waltz, op.170   PC 1+picc.222/4230/timp.perc/hp/str   Cranz   16138
VERDICTE: waltz, op.137   PC 1+picc.222/4230/timp.perc/hp/str   Schreiber   5966
WIDMUNGSBLÄTTER: waltz, op.242 PC 1+picc.222/4230/timp.perc/str   Cranz   16121
WIENER DIALECT: waltz, op.237 ø 1+picc.2+ca.22/4231/timp.perc/str 6'15" Cranz   16115

STRAUSS, Johann (i)(1804-1849)

see SCHÖNHERR-REINÖHL: Das Jahrhundert des Walzers. Band 1 - J.Strauss (Vater). Vienna:
    Universal, 1954

Die ADEPTEN: waltz, op.216   1+picc.121/2210/timp.perc/str   Haslinger [1847] 22177
  ed H.Gal   ø 2(picc)11+Ebcl.1/2210/timp/str   Universal,1928.DTÖ 68 Misc 3252 & MRL
ALICE-POLKA, op.238
  arr R.Hanmer   PC 2121/2320/perc/gtr/str   2'50"   Dix,1953   21053
DEUTSCHE LUST, or Donaulieder ohne Worte (Joy and delight): waltz, op.127
  arr A.Winter   ø 2(picc)22.3sx.2/4230/timp.perc/hp/str   Boosey & H   9541
  arr A.Winter   PC 212.3sx.1/4230/timp.perc/str   6'45"   Boosey & H   20167
DREI WALZER see STRAUS, Oscar: DREI WALZER
ELISABETHEN-WALZER, op.71
  ed H.Gal   ø 1(picc)121/2410/timp/str   Universal,1928.DTÖ 68 Misc 3252 & MRL
  ed H.Gal: vla & vlc parts added V.Tausky   (26297 + ø see
          1(picc)+picc.121/2410/timp/str   (Universal,1928.DTÖ 68)   (Misc 3252
EXETER-POLKA, op.249
  orch B.Fry   ø 1+picc.222/2200/perc/str   BBC   22631 +
Die FRIEDENSBOTEN (The messengers of peace): waltz, op.241
         ø 1+picc.222/4230/timp/str   BBC   21482 +
HULDIGUNG DER KÖNIGEN VICTORIA (Hommage to Queen Victoria): waltz, op.103
         ø 1(picc)141/2210/timp.perc/str   Haslinger   18705
KATINKA-POLKA, op.210
  arr M.Lubbock   ø 2221/2230/timp.perc/hp.pf/str   Arranger   20192
LONDONER-SAISON: waltz, op.112 PC 1121/2210/perc/str   (Breitkopf)   22625 +
LORELEY-RHEIN-KLÄNGE: waltz, op.154
  with additions by S.Robinson & L.Wurmser   8'30"
         PC 1121/2220/perc/str   Cranz   3817 +
  arr S.Robinson   ø 2+picc.222/4331/timp.perc/hp/str   Arranger MS:BBC   24027 +
  arr M.Schönherr   PC 2222/4430/timp.perc/acdn/str   Krenn,1959   23044
  arr A.Winter   PC 212.2sx.1/2230/perc/str   Boosey & H   11232

STRAUSS, Johann (i)(cont)

MARSCH DER STUDENTENLEGION, op.223
| | φ | 1+picc.03+2E♭cl.0/46.cnt.4flg.30.bomb.euph/perc | | (Misc 4972 & |
| | | perc/cb | (Wiener Stadtbibliothek) | (mf 158 |

MASKENLIEDER: waltz, op.170
ed H.Gal	φ	1+picc.121/2410/timp.perc/str	Universal,1928.DTÖ 68	Misc 3252 & MRL
MYRTHEN: waltz, op.118		1+picc.121/2210/timp/str	(Breitkopf)	22624 +
ed H.Gal	φ	1(picc)121/0410/timp.perc/str	Universal,1928.DTÖ 68	Misc 3252 & MRL

Die NACHTWANDLER (Les somnambules): waltz, op.88
	PC	2222/2230.euph/perc/str	Hawkes	15819
arr S.Robinson	φ	3222/4231/timp.perc/hp/str	Arranger	TO 1624
OLD CHINA: polka	PC	1020/2230.euph/perc/str	Hawkes	1330

PHILOMELEN-WALZER, op.82
ed H.Gal	φ	1(picc)121/2410/timp/str	Universal,1928.DTÖ 68	Misc 3252 & MRL
RADETZKY-MARSCH, op.228	φ	1+picc.222/4230/timp.perc/str	2'45" Cranz	3569 + Bp Cm
	PC	1(picc)121/2230.euph/perc/str	Hawkes	19508

arr A.Franzel (wind & perc for use with Cranz edition)
| | φ | 1011/2220/perc | Arranger MS:BBC | MS 20136 ** |
| arr A.Hohenstein | PC | 2(picc)222/423[1]/perc/str | Benjamin | 16363 |

arr G.Jacob: E♭cl & bcl parts added P.Ryan)
	φ	1+picc.222/4331/timp.perc/hp/str	(Arranger)	25908 +
arr G. de Mauny	φ	2222/2220/perc/str	Arranger MS:BBC	MS 8295
arr M.Schönherr	PC	1+picc.22.3sx.2/4230/perc/str	Bosworth (Krenn)	22819

Die SORGENBRECHER: waltz, op.230
ed H.Gal	φ	1+picc.121/2410/timp/str	8' Universal,1928.DTÖ 68	Misc 3252 & MRL
ed H.Gal	φ	1+picc.122/2310/timp.perc/str	(Universal,1928.DTÖ 68)	21168 +
arr Grosz	φ	1+picc.122/2210/timp.perc/str	Universal	Misc 1386

SPERL-GALOPP, op.42
| arr M.Schönherr | PC | 1+picc.222/4230/timp.perc/str | Krenn | 25739 |

TÄUBERLN: waltz, op.1
| ed H.Gal | φ | 1020/2300/timp/str | Universal,1928.DTÖ 68 | Misc 3252 & MRL |

WALTZES FROM VIENNA: musical play   <u>see</u>   STRAUSS, Johann (ii): WALTZES FROM VIENNA

WIENER KARNEVAL: waltz, op.3
| ed H.Gal | φ | 1+picc.01+E♭cl.0/2300/timp.perc/str | Universal,1928.DTÖ 68 | Misc 3252 & MRL |
| ed H.Gal | φ | 1+picc.020/2300/str | (Universal,1928.DTÖ 68) | 21169 + |

STRAUSS, Johann (ii)(1825-1899)

COMPLETE WORKS

Johann Strauss (Sohn) Gesamtausgabe, ed F.Racek.   Vienna: Doblinger/Universal,1967-   MRL

| ABSCHIEDS-WALZER, op.post | φ | 2222/4230/timp.perc/str | Seeman,1900 | 9977 |

ACCELERATIONEN: waltz, op.234
arr M.Schönherr	PC	2(picc)22.3sx.2/4231/timp.perc/acdn.hp/str	Bosworth (Krenn,1960)	23441
arr A.Winter	PC	2(picc)22.3sx.2/2230/timp.perc/hp/str	Boosey & H	7279 + C
ADELEN-WALZER, op.424	PC	1121/2210/timp.perc/str	C.Fischer	1982

Die AFRIKANERIN-QUADRILLE, op.299, on themes from Meyerbeer's opera 'L'Africaine'[c.1865]
| ed F.Racek | φ | 1+picc.222/4231/timp.perc/str | Doblinger/Universal,1968.CW 1/18 | 26343 * & MRL |
| AMAZONEN: polka, op.9 | φ | 1+picc.121/2210/timp.perc/str | Cranz | 8376 |

AN DER SCHÖNEN, BLAUEN DONAU (The Blue Danube): waltz, op.314
| | φ | 2(picc)222/4211/timp.perc/hp/str | Breitkopf | 6860 + Bmv Cs |
| | φ | 2(picc)222/421[1]/timp.perc/hp/str | Cranz | 4301 B |

ed H.Gal for optional mv-chorus & orch
| | φ | 2(picc)222/4211/timp.perc/hp/str | Universal,1925.DTÖ 63 | Misc 3251 & MRL |
| ed F.Racek | φ | 2(picc)222/4211/timp.perc/hp/str | Doblinger/Universal,1967.CW 1/19 | Misc 6455 & MRL |

STRAUSS, Johann (ii)(cont)

AN DER SCHÖNEN, BLAUEN DONAU (The Blue Danube)(cont)
  arr F.Th.Cursch-Bühren for chorus & orch
                              PC 2(picc)222/4210/timp.perc/hp/str   Cranz   23607
      arr G.Davies   PC 111.2sx.1/2210/timp.perc/bjo/str   K.Prowse   14998
      arr F.Hartley   PC 1110/0000/timp.perc/gtr/str   4'   F.Hartley   15863
      arr I.Markevitch (concert transcription)
                              ∅ 32+ca.2+bcl.2+cbsn/4331/timp.perc/2hp/str   Zerboni   Misc 2666 C
      arr S.Robinson as 'Danube of Dreams': romantic paraphrase for orchestra of The Blue Danube, made
          from the original vocal version (1968)
                              2121/2230/timp.perc/cel.hp/str   (Elkin)   TO 1672
      arr M.Schönherr   PC 2222/4230/perc/hp/str   Bosworth   LM G 11490
      arr A.Wilkinson   ∅ 3(3picc)1+ca.22/4230/timp.perc/hp/str   (AH. & C,1954) 24246
      arr A.Winter   PC 212.2sx.2/2230/timp.perc/str   Hawkes   4539 Bp D
ANNEN-POLKA, op.117
      arr M.Schönherr   PC 1+picc.22.3sx.2/4230/timp.perc/str   Krenn/Bosworth,1964 24404
      arr G.Walter   PC 2(picc)222/4230/timp.perc/hp/str   Boosey & H   6622 B
      arr A.Wood   PC 112.3sx.1/2220/perc/str   Paxton   6898
      arr Grosz, orch H.Carr: vocal arrangement, in D
                              ∅ 2121/0000/str   (Boosey)   TO 1316
ARTIST'S LIFE   see   KÜNSTLERLEBEN: waltz, op.316
ARTIST'S QUADRILLE see KÜNSTLER-QUADRILLE, op.201
ASCHENBRÖDEL (Cinderella): ballet
  Overture
      arr M.Schönherr   ∅ 1+picc.222/4231/perc/hp/str   Bosworth,1957 22424
  Introduction to Act 3   PC 2121/2210/timp.perc/str   Weinberger 2818
AUF DER JAGD: polka, op.373, on motives from the operetta "Cagliostro in Wien"
                              ∅ 1+picc.222/4230/timp.perc/str   Schreiber   9201 +
      arr M.Schönherr (Hunting Polka)
                              PC 1+picc.22.3sx.2/4230/timp.perc/str   Bosworth,1957 22675
AUS DEN BERGERN: waltz, op.292
  ed F.Racek   ∅ 1+picc.21+Ebcl.2/4211/timp.perc/str Doblinger/Universal,1968.CW 1/18   MRL
BAL CHAMPÊTRE: quadrille, op.303
                              ∅ 1+picc.222/4321/timp.perc/str   Doblinger/Universal,1968.CW 1/18   MRL
Un BALLO IN MASCHERA: quadrille, op.272, on motives from Verdi's opera
                              1+picc.222/4230/timp.perc/str   Cranz   19873 +
BALLSTRÄUSSCHEN: polka, op.380 ∅ 1+picc.222/4230/timp.perc/hp/str   Cranz   5072
BANDITEN-GALOPP: polka schnell, op.378, on motives from the operetta "Prinz Methusalem"
                              ∅ 1+picc.222/4230/timp.perc/str   Cranz   25486 +
The BAT   see   Die FLEDERMAUS
BAUERN-POLKA, op.276   PC 1+picc.222/4210/timp.perc/str (∅ 'A' set)   Haslinger   12713 B
BEAUTIFUL BLUE DANUBE see AN DER SCHÖNEN, BLAUEN DONAU: waltz, op.314
BITTE SCHÖN!: polka française, op.372, on motives from the operetta "Cagliostro in Wien"
                              ∅ 1+picc.222/4230/timp.perc/str   3'   Cranz   16181 B +
      arr I.Geiger   PC 122.3sx.1/2230/timp.perc/acdn/str   Bosworth,1953 21998
BLINDEKUH: operetta
  Overture   ∅ 1+picc.222/4230/timp.perc/str   8'   Cranz   12373
The BLUE DANUBE   see   AN DER SCHÖNEN, BLAUEN DONAU: waltz, op.314
BLÜTHENKRANZ: selection of waltzes see STRAUSS, Eduard: BLÜTHENKRANZ
BÜRGERSINN: waltz, op.295   ∅ 1+picc.222/4211/timp.perc/str   Doblinger/Universal,1968.CW 1/18   MRL
                              1+picc.222/4211/timp.perc/str   Spina   8631
BÜRGERWEISEN: waltz, op.306 PC 1(picc)121/2210/timp.perc/hp/str   Cranz   6323
                              PC 1+picc.222/4211/timp.perc/hp/str   Cranz   16245
      ed F.Racek   ∅ 1+picc.222/4211/timp.perc(glock)/hp/str
                                                      Doblinger/Universal,1967.CW 1/19   MRL

STRAUSS, Johann (ii)(cont)

CAGLIOSTRO IN WIEN: operetta
   Overture   φ   2(picc)221/2230/timp.perc/str   Cranz   11628
     see also BITTE SCHÖN!: polka-française, op.372   LICHT UND SCHATTEN: polka-mazurka, op.379
CAGLIOSTRO-WALZER, op.370, on motives from the operetta
   arr Dumont   PC 1021/2210/timp.perc/str   C.Fischer   1965
Der CARNEVAL IN ROM (Carnival in Rome): operetta
   Overture
      arr Atzler   φ   1121/22.cnt.10/timp.perc/str   6'   Cranz   6311
      arr M.Schönherr   PC 2(picc)222/4230/timp.perc/acdn.hp/str   Krenn,1961 25443 +
     Ballet music, arr A.Waldenmaier
                   φ   2(picc)222/4330/timp.perc(glock)/hp/str   Mozart Ed,1976(H) PL 536
CASANOVA   see BENATZKY, R: CASANOVA
CHAMPAGNER-POLKA, op.211
   arr M.Schönherr   PC 1+picc.222/4230/timp.perc/hca/str   Krenn,1960 23393
CINDERELLA see ASCHENBRÖDEL (Cinderella): ballet
CONTROVERSEN: waltz, op.191   PS 1+picc.122/4211/perc/str   Haslinger   25287
COTILLON on various motives
   arr M.Schönherr   PC 1+picc.222/4230/timp.perc/hmn.hp/str   4'   Krenn   22764
CUCKOO POLKA see IM KRAPFENWALD'L: polka française, op.336
CZECHEN-POLKA, op.13   φ 1+picc.121/2210/timp.perc/str   Cranz   8392
   arr Lambert   PC 2+picc.121/2220/timp.perc/str   Boosey & H   19479
DAMENSPENDE: polka, op.305
   ed F.Racek   φ 1+picc.22+Ebcl.2/4210/timp.perc/str Doblinger/Universal,1967.CW 1/19 26627 & MRL
The DANCING PARTNER: music for radio feature arr D.Darlow from the music of Strauss (1962)
                 φ pf/str   Arranger MS:BBC MS 31390 +
DANUBE OF DREAMS see AN DER SCHONEN, BLAUEN DONAU: waltz, op.314, arr S.Robinson
DEMOLIRER-POLKA, op.269   PC 1+picc.222/4210/timp.perc/str   (Haslinger) 25859 +
DEUTSCHMEISTER-JUBILÄUMS-MARSCH: march, op.470
                 φ 2222/4230/perc/str   Cranz   10822 B
DONAUWEIBCHEN: waltz, op.427, on motives from the operetta "Simplicius"
               PC 2(picc)222/4230/timp.perc/hp/str   6'-7'   Cranz   16252
   arr A.Winter   φ 2(picc)22.2sx.2/4231/timp.perc/hp/str   Hawkes   7253 B
DREI WALZER see STRAUSS, Oscar: DREI WALZER
DU UND DU: waltz, op.367, on motives from the operetta "Die Fledermaus"
               φ 2(picc)222/4230/timp.perc/str   7'-8'15"   Breitkopf 3720 + Bs
               φ 2(picc)222/421[1]/timp.perc/hp/str   Cranz   4301 B
             PC 1121/2210/timp.perc/str   Cranz   4529 B
   arr A.Winter   PC 2(picc)22.2sx.2/2230/timp.perc/str   Hawkes   5323
EGYPTISCHER MARSCH: march, op.335
   with optional chorus   1+picc.222/4230/perc/str   3'30"   Cranz   9172 +
   arr Atzler   PC 2(picc)121/2230/perc/str   Cranz   2977 B
   arr M.Schönherr   PC 1+picc.222/4230/timp.perc/str   Bosworth   22698 +
ELEKTROPHOR: polka schnell, op.297
   ed F.Racek   φ 1+picc.222/4211/timp.perc/str Doblinger/Universal,1968.CW 1/18 26628 & MRL
ELJEN A MAGYAR: polka, op.332 φ 1+picc.222/4330/timp.perc/str   Cranz   6894
EMPEROR WALTZ see KAISER-WALZER, op.437
L'ENFANTILLAGE: polka, op.202 φ 1+picc.222/4231/timp.perc/str   2'15"   Haslinger   12183
EPISODE: polka française, op.296
   ed F.Racek   φ 1+picc.21+Dcl.2/4211/timp.perc/str Doblinger/Universal,1968.CW 1/18 MRL
ERINNERUNG AN COVENT GARDEN: waltz on English folk songs, op.329
               PC 1+picc.222/4231/timp.perc/str   Cranz   16210
   ed F.Racek   φ 1+picc.222/4231/timp.perc/str Doblinger/Universal,1971.CW 1/20 26342 * & MRL
ES GIBT NUR A KAISERSTADT see 'S GIBT NUR A KAISERSTADT: polka, op.291
ES WAR SO WUNDERSCHON: march, op.467, on motives from the operetta "Waldmeister"
                φ 1+picc.222/4230/timp.perc/hp/str   Bote & B   11150
EXCURSION TRAIN POLKA see VERGNÜGUNGSZUG (Excursion train): polka schnell, op.281

STRAUSS, Johann (ii)(cont)

EXPLOSIONS-POLKA, op.43	PC	1+picc.222/4230/timp.perc/hmn/str	Krenn/Bosworth,1958	25190
EXPRESS-POLKA: polka schnell, op.311				
ed F.Racek	∅	1+picc.222/4210/timp.perc/str	Doblinger/Universal,1967.CW 1/19	26424 * & MRL
FANNY ELSSLER THE DANCER see Die TÄNZERIN FANNY ELSSLER: operetta				
FATA MORGANA: polka mazurka, op.330				
ed F.Racek	∅	1+picc.222/4330/timp.perc/hp/str	Doblinger/Universal,1979.CW 1/21	26810 & MRL
arr M.Schönherr	PC	1+picc.222/4330/timp.perc/acdn.hp/str	Krenn,1959	23043
FEENMÄRCHEN: waltz, op.312		2(picc)222/4210/timp.perc/hp/str	Spina	8886
ed F.Racek	∅	2(picc)222/4210/timp.perc/str	Doblinger/Universal,1967.CW 1/19	MRL
FEST-MARSCH, op.452	PC	1+picc.222/4230/perc/hp/str	G.Lewy	11338
FEST-POLONAISE, op.352	PC	1121/2230.euph/timp.perc/str	Hawkes	2145
FEUILLETON: waltz, op.293	PC	1+picc.222/4211/timp.perc/str	Cranz	16221
ed F.Racek	∅	1+picc.222/4211/timp.perc/str	Doblinger/Universal,1968.CW 1/18	MRL
FIGARO-POLKA, op.320				
ed F.Racek	∅	1+picc.222/4210/timp.perc/str	Doblinger/Universal,1971.CW 1/20	MRL

Die FLEDERMAUS: operetta in 3 acts
  Complete

	∅	2(picc)222/4230/timp.perc(glock)/hp/str	Kalmus (Cranz)	22170
		2(picc)222/4230/timp.perc(glock)/hp/str	Cranz(H)	PL 264
ed F.Racek	∅	2(picc)222/4230/timp.perc(glock)/hp/str		
			Doblinger/Universal,1974.CW 2/ 3	PL 264

    ed & rev H.Swarowski (Added English text - C.Hassall)

	∅	2(picc)222/4230/timp.perc.bells.glock/		
		hp/str	Eulenburg,1968/J.Weinberger,1959	Misc 6918 B

  Radio version (without overture & ballet music)

	∅	2222/3230/timp.perc/hp/str	[Cranz]	TO 763
Overture	∅	2(picc)222/4230/timp.perc/str	8'-10'	Breitkopf	6252 Cs Dwa
	∅	2(picc)222/4230/timp.perc/str		Cranz	8811 + Bn C
	PC	2(picc)222/2230/timp.perc/hp/str		Heugel	5719
	PC	1121/2210/timp.perc/str		Cranz	3754
arr L.Artok	PC	2(picc)222/2230/timp.perc/str		Schott	9992
arr R.Jungnickel	PC	2(picc)222/4230/timp.perc/str		Jungnickel	1160
arr M.Schönherr	PC	2222/4230/timp.perc/acdn/str	8'	Krenn,1959	23042
arr A.Winter	PC	112.3sx.1/2230/timp.perc/str		Boosey & H	14440 Bm

  Selections

arr L.Artok	PC	2(picc)222/2230/timp.perc/str	16'	Schott	9996
arr A.Fones for Glamourous Nights, April 1980				
		2(picc)222/4230/timp.perc.bell/str (∅ of overture only)	(Breitkopf)	25743
arr G.Goldschmidt	PC	2(picc)222/4231/timp.perc/str		Cranz	7433
arr Kaps	PC	2222/4230/timp.perc/str	13'15"	Metzler	9475
arr Moses-Tobani & Seredy	PC	1121/2230/perc/org/str		C.Fischer	1996
arr Rhode	PC	2(picc)222/4231/timp.perc/str	15'	Benjamin	12167
arr S.Robinson (Gay Rosalinda)				
	∅	2+picc.222/3230/timp.perc/hp/str	Weinberger (Cranz)	19788 B +
arr Tavan	PC	2(picc)222/2231/timp.perc/str	Heugel	10238
arr A.Wood	PC	1+picc.12.3sx.1/2230/perc/str	Paxton	18889

  Extracts
    Dieser Anstand (Her behaviour): watch duet (Act 2, no.9)

in F	∅	2222/4230/timp.perc/str	[Cranz]	(Misc 5845 B + (pts - 22170 A

    Klänge der Heimat (Songs of my homeland): czardas

in D (orig)	PC	2121/2210/timp.perc/str	Cranz	7059
in D, arr G.Stacey		pf/str	[Cranz]	LM G 3404

    Laughing song   see   Mein Herr Marquis

STRAUSS, Johann (ii)(cont)

Die FLEDERMAUS (cont)
   Extracts (cont)
     Mein Herr Marquis (My dear Marquis): laughing song
       in G (orig)   φ   1121/2210/perc/str   Cranz   9685 B +
       in G   φ   2222/4230/timp/str   [Cranz]   21924
       in G, arr G.Stacey   1010/0000/perc/acdn.pf/str   or   pf/str   [Cranz]   LM G 3186
       in G♭, arr G.Stacey   1121/2210/perc/pf/str   [Cranz]   LM G 4741
FLEDERMAUS-POLKA, op.362, on motives from the operetta
                  PC   1(picc)121/2210/perc/str   Cranz   11555
                  PC   1+picc.222/4230/timp.perc/str   Cranz   11550
FLEDERMAUS-QUADRILLE, op.363, on motives from the operetta
   arr M.Schönherr   PC   1+picc.222/4230/timp.perc/hmn/str   Bosworth (Krenn)   24513
FLUGSCHRIFTEN: waltz, op.300   1+picc.222/4210/timp.perc/hp/str   Spina   8687
   ed F.Racek   φ   1+picc.222/4210/timp.perc/hp/str   Doblinger/Universal,1968.CW 1/18   MRL
FREIKUGELN: polka schnell, op.326
                  φ   1+picc.21+E♭cl.2/4331/timp.perc/str   (Cranz)   25524 +
                  φ   1+picc.222/4331/timp.perc/str   Doblinger/Universal,1971.CW 1/20   26338 & MRL
FREUT EUCH DES LEBENS (Eat, drink and be merry): waltz, op.340
                  φ   1+picc.222/4231/timp.perc/hp/str   (Krenn)   25644
                  PC   1122/2210/timp.perc/str   C.Fischer   1952
   arr A.Winter   PC   2+picc.22.2sx.2/4231/timp.perc/hp/str   Boosey & H   10525
FRISCH HERAN: polka, op.386   1+picc.222/4230/timp.perc/str   Cranz   9697
FRISCH INS FELD!: march, op.398 on motives from the operetta "Der lustige Krieg"
                  0.picc.121/2210/perc/str   Cranz   10821 B
FROHSINNSSPENDEN: waltz, op.73 PC   1+picc.222/4210/timp.perc/str   Cranz   8375
FRUHLINGSSTIMMEN (Voices of Spring): waltz, op.410
                  φ   1+picc.222/4230/timp.perc/hp/str   6'   Breitkopf   3763 B +
                  PC   1(picc)121/2210/perc/str   Cranz   8068
                  PC   1+picc.222/4230/timp.perc/hp/str   Cranz   8086
   arr Dumont   PC   1121/2210/perc/str   Fischer   1961
   arr A.Winter   PC   1+picc.22.2sx.2/2230/timp.perc/hp/str   Hawkes   9238 Ap Cn Dwe Em
   Vocal versions
     in B♭, arr Atzler φ   1(picc)121/2210/timp.perc/hp/str   Cranz   12400 B
     in B♭, arr Atzler (cuts and additional parts arr S.Torch)
                1+picc.242/4330/perc/hp.pf/str   S.Torch   LM G 7670
     in A, arr Elkin   φ   1101/2021/perc/hp/str   [Elkin]   TO 1528 **
GAY ROSALINDA see Die FLEDERMAUS: operetta - Selections; arr S.Robinson
Die GEMÜTLICHEN: waltz, op.70 φ   2+picc.222/4231/timp.perc/hp/str   Cranz   8391
GESCHICHTEN AUS DEM WIENERWALD (Tales from the Vienna Woods): waltz, op.325
                  φ   2(picc)222/4331/timp.perc/hp.zither/str   12'-13'   Breitkopf   1949 + Ds
                  PC   1+picc.222/4331/timp.perc/hp.zither/str   Cranz   4315
   ed F.Racek   φ   2(picc)222/4331/timp.perc/hp.zither/str
                              Doblinger/Universal,1971.CW 1/20   MRL
   arr M.Schönherr   PC   2222/4230/perc/str   Bosworth   LM G 11489
   arr A.Winter
   Vocal versions
     in E♭, arr W.Goehr φ   2121/2230/timp/hp/str   3'30"   (Chappell)   TO 764
     in E, arr E.Korngold & G.Stacey
                PC   str   (Schott)   LM G 3448
     in A♭, arr Mansfield & Carr for fv-chorus & orch
                φ   2222/4230/timp.perc/hp/str   (Bayley & F) 20916
     in A♭, arr G.Stacey   1000/0000/hp.pf/str   (Cranz)   LM G 3132
     in E♭, arr D.Tiomkin & A.Franzel
                φ   1110/0000/hp.pf/str   (Chappell)   LM A 664
     in A♭, arr Ulbricht φ   1121/2210/perc/str   Cranz   8926 B
The GIPSY BARON see Der ZIGEUNERBARON

STRAUSS, Johann (ii)(cont)

GRADUATION BALL: ballet in 1 act
   arr A.Dorati   φ 2222/4230/timp.perc/hp/str   26'40" Mills Music,1948 Misc 7471
The GREAT WALTZ: film music adapted by Dimitri Tiomkin from the music of J.Strauss
   Selection, arr G.Zalva   PC 112.3sx.1/2220/timp.perc/str   9'   Chappell 15552 Eni
   Extracts
      I'm in love with Vienna: song
         in F, arr P.Cardew   φ 2222/4230/timp.perc/hp/str   (Chappell) 23249 +
      One day when we were young: song
         in C, arr G.Stacey   PC str   (Chappell) LM G 3073
         in Db, arr P.Hope as duet
                        φ 2222/4330/timp.perc/hp/str   (Chappell) 23569 +
         in Db, arr G.Stacey   1010/0000/perc/acdn.pf/str   (Chappell) LM A 96
         in D   gtr/str   (BBC) MS 20152
         in D, arr G.Zalva   1121/2220/perc/pf/str   (Chappell) LM G 4471
         in Eb, arr G.Stacey PC [acdn=org].hp/str   (Chappell) LM G 3073
GROSS-WIEN (Merry old Vienna): waltz, op.440
                     PC 1121/2210/timp.perc/str   7'   Simrock 16368
G'SCHICHTEN AUS DEM WIENERWALD see GESCHICHTEN AUS DEM WIENERWALD: waltz, op.325
GUT BÜRGERLICH: polka, op.282   1+picc.222/4210/timp.perc/str   3'   Cranz 5170
HERMANN: polka, op.91   1+picc.122/4210/timp.perc/str 2'15"   Cranz 8380
HERRJEMINEH: polka française, op.464, on motives from the operetta "Waldermeister"
                     φ 1+picc.222/4230/timp.perc/hp/str   Bote & B 9581
Ein HERZ, EIN SINN: polka mazurka, op.323
                     PC 1+picc.222/4331/timp.perc/str   Cranz 7266
   ed F.Racek   φ 1+picc.222/4231/timp.perc/hp/str Doblinger/Universal,1971.CW 1/20 MRL
HERZENSKÖNIGIN: polka-mazurka, op.445
                     PC 1+picc.222/4230/timp.perc/hp/str   (Simrock,1893) 25634 +
HOCHZEITSREIGEN: waltz, op.453 ^
   arr M.Tobani   PC 1121/2210/timp.perc/str   C.Fischer 1964
HOFBALLTÄNZE (At the court ball): waltz, op.298
                     φ 2+picc.22.2sx.2/2231/timp.perc/str 9' Boosey & H 10524
                        1+picc.222/4211/timp.perc/hp/str   Spina 11828
   ed F.Racek   φ 1+picc.21+Ebcl.2/4211/timp.perc/hp/str
                               Doblinger/Universal,1968.CW 1/18 MRL
HOMMAGE AU PUBLIC RUSSE: potpourri
                     φ 2(picc)222/2210/timp.perc/str (Konsertföreningen,Stockholm) 22821 +
HUNTING POLKA see AUF DER JAGD: polka, op.373
HUSAREN-POLKA, op.42, on motives from the operetta "Der Zigeunerbaron"
                     PC 1+picc.222/4230/timp.perc/str   Cranz 5171
ILLUSTRATIONEN: waltz, op.331 PC 1+picc.222/4230/timp.perc/str   Cranz 16254
   ed F.Racek   φ 1+picc.21+Ebcl.2/4230/timp.perc/str Doblinger/Universal,1979.CW 1/21 26812 & MRL
IM KRAPFENWALD'L: polka française (Cuckoo polka), op.336
   arr M.Schönherr   PC 1+picc.22.3sx.2/4231/timp.perc/str   Bosworth 22699
   arr G.Vinter   PC 1+picc.12.4sx.1/2230/timp.perc/cel.gtr/str Liber-Southern 19215
INDIGO UND DIE VIERZIG RÄUBER: operetta
   Overture   φ 2(picc)222/4230/timp.perc/hp/str   7'   Cranz 13188
      arr M.Schönherr   PC 2(picc)222/4230/timp.perc(glock)/
                          acdn.hp/str   Krenn,1963 25070 +
   Bacchanale (no.16)
      in Eb (orig), orch K.Pakeman
                     φ 2222/4230/timp.perc/hp/str   (Cranz) 20694
     see also TAUSEND UND EINE NACHT: operetta
INDIGO-MARSCH, op.349   PC 1+picc.222/4231/perc/str   Cranz 10876
IN'S CENTRUM!: waltz, op.387 φ 1+picc.222/4230/timp.perc/hp/str   Cranz 20667

STRAUSS, Johann (ii) (cont)

ITALIENISCHER-WALTZER, op.407, on motives from the operetta "Der lustige Krieg"
                              PC 1+picc.222/4230/timp.perc/str   Cranz   7387
I-TIPFERL-POLKA, op.377, on motives from the operetta "Prinz Methusalem"
                                  1+picc.222/4230/timp/str   Spina   9554+
JOHANNIS-KÄFERLN: waltz, op.82 ø 2+picc.222/4231/timp.perc/hp/str   6'30"   Cranz   8353
JOURNALISTEN: waltz see Die LEITARTIKEL: waltz, op.273
JUBEL-MARSCH, op.126   PS 1+picc.121/4230/perc/str   (Austrian Radio) 26358
Die JUNGEN WIENER: waltz, op.7 ø 2(picc)121/2210/timp.perc/str   9'   Cranz
JURISTENBALLTÄNZE: waltz, op.177
                              ø   3222/4231/timp.perc/hp/str   8'30"   Hawkes   12170
JUX-POLKA, op.17   PC 1+picc.121/2210/timp.perc/str   Cranz   8390
KAISER-WALZER (Emperor Waltz), op.437
                              ø   2222/4230/timp.perc/hp/str   9'45"-12'   Breitkopf 5489 B
      rev S.Robinson   ø   3(picc)222/4331/timp.perc/str   8'45"   (Arranger) 22528 +
      arr A.Winter   PC 222.2sx.2/2230/timp.perc/hp/str   Hawkes   4542 D
KAMMERBALL-POLKA, op.230   ø   1+picc.222/4210/timp.perc/str   Haslinger Misc 1273
KARNEVALS-BOTSCHAFTER: waltz, op.270
      arr Atzler   PC 1+picc.121/2210/timp.perc/str   Cranz   16083
KENNST DU MICH?: waltz, op.381, on motives from the operetta "Blindekuh"
                                  2(picc)222/4230/timp.perc/hp/str   Spina   9605
KINDERSPIELE: polka, op.304 ø   1+picc.222/4211/timp.perc/str   Doblinger/Universal,1967.CW 1/19 MRL
                              ø   1+picc.222/4211/timp.perc/str   Spina   8718
KLIPP-KLAPP: galup, op.466, on motives from the operetta "Waldmeister"
                              ø   1+picc.222/4230/timp.perc/hp/str   Bote & B   11150
KÖNIGSLIEDER: waltz, op.334   1+picc.222/4230/timp.perc/str   Spina   18704
KREUZFIDEL: polka française, op.301
      ed F.Racek   ø   1+picc.222/4210/timp.perc/str   Doblinger/Universal,1968.CW 1/18 MRL
KRIEGERS LIEBCHEN: polka-mazurka, op.379, on motives from the operetta "Prinz Methusalem"
                                  1122/4230/perc/str   Spina   9561
KRIEGS-ABENTEUER: galop, op.419, on motives from the operetta "Der Zigeunerbaron"
                              ø   1+picc.222/4230/timp.perc/str   Cranz   4836
KÜNSTLERLEBE (Artist's Life): waltz, op.316
                              ø   1+picc.222/4230/timp.perc/str   (BBC)   2904
      ed F.Racek   ø   1+picc.222/4210/timp.perc/str   Doblinger/Universal,1967.CW 1/19 26629 B & MRL
      rev Keldorfer   ø   1+picc.222/4210/timp.perc/str   Eulenburg Misc 98
      arr M.Schönherr   PC 1+picc.22.2sx.2/4230/timp.perc/hmn/str   Bosworth   25200
      arr A.Winter   ø   212.2sx.2/2230/timp.perc/str   Hawkes,1928 1967 B
         'A' set contains alternate orchestration
                              ø   322.2sx.2/4231/timp.perc/str   (Hawkes,1928) 1967 A
      arr A.Winter   PC 212.2sx.2/2230/timp.perc/str   Boosey & H 16714 Bs
KÜNSTLER-QUADRILLE (Artist's Quadrille), op.201
                              PC 1+picc.222/4211/timp.perc/hp/str   (Haslinger) 25905
KUSS-WALZER, op.400, on motives from the operetta "Der lustige Krieg"
                                  1121/2210/perc/str   Cranz   20360
LAGUNEN-WALZER, op.411, on motives from the operetta "Eine Nacht in Venedig"
                              ø   3(picc)222/4231/timp.perc/hp/str   7'   Cranz   7432
      orch J.Tunbridge (vocal arrangement)
                              ø   1121/0220/timp/str   (Cranz)   Misc 4368
LEICHTES BLUT (With ease): polka schnell, op.319
                                  1+picc.222/4210/timp.perc/str   Spina   8356
      ed F.Racek   ø   1+picc.222/4210/timp.perc/str   Doblinger/Universal,1971.CW 1/20 26339 * & MRL
      arr B.Hartmann   PC 1121/2210/timp/str   Cranz   23547
LEITARTIKEL (Journalisten): waltz, op.273
                              PC 1111/0110.euph/timp.perc/str   Hawkes   15915
LICHT UND SCHATTEN: polka-mazurka, op.374, on motives from the operetta "Cagliostro in Wien"
                                  1+picc.222/4230/timp.perc/str   Schreiber 9278
LIEBE UND EHE: polka-mazurka, op.465, on motives from the operetta "Waldmeister"
                              ø   1+picc.222/4230/timp.perc/hp/str   Bote & B   9581

STRAUSS, Johann (ii)(cont)

LOB DER FRAUEN: polka, op.315   1+picc.222/4210/timp.perc/str   Spina   8887
    ed F.Racek   ⌀ 1+picc.222/4210/timp.perc/str   Doblinger/Universal,1967.CW 1/19   26425 * & MRL
Der LUSTIGE KRIEG (The Merry War): operetta
    Overture   ⌀ 2(picc)222/4230/timp.perc/hp/str   6'30"   Cranz   5549
        arr L.Weninger   PC 2(picc)222/4230/timp.perc/hp/str   Benjamin   13669
    Extracts
        Nur für Natur (no.11)   2121/4230/hp/str   Cranz   25016 +
            see also ITALIENISCHER-WALZER, op.407
Der LUSTIGE KRIEG: march, op.397, on motives from the operetta
                                 PC 1+picc.222/4230/perc/str   Cranz   10877
MÄRCHEN AUS DEM ORIENT: waltz, op.444
                                 PC 2(picc)222/4230/timp.perc/hp/str   8'   Simrock   2963 B
        arr A.Winter   ⌀ 2+picc.22.2sx.2/4230/timp.perc/hp/str   Boosey & H   11094
MEMORIES OF COVENT GARDEN   see   ERINNERUNG AN COVENT GARDEN
MEMORIES OF OLD VIENNA: selection of Johann Strauss (ii) melodies, arr W.Grosz
                                 PC 111.3sx.1/2230/perc/hp/str   P.Maurice   12245 B
MEPHISTOS HÖLLENRUFE WALZER, op.101
                                 ⌀ 1+picc.222/4230/timp.perc/str   6'30"   (Vienna Phil)   Misc 7966
METHUSALEM-QUADRILLE, op.376, on motives from the operetta "Prinz Methusalem"
                                 ⌀ 1+picc.222/4230/timp.perc/str   Spina (Cranz)   19872
MORGENBLÄTTER (Morning papers): waltz, op.279
                                 ⌀ 1+picc.22.2sx.2/2230/timp.perc/str   7'-8'   Hawkes   1954 B
                                 ⌀ 1+picc.222/4211/timp.perc/str   Cranz   13906
                                     1+picc.222/4211/timp.perc/str   (BBC)   MS 2631
                                 PC 1+picc.222/4211/timp.perc/str/[chorus]   Cranz   9808 B
        ed H.Gal   ⌀ 1+picc.222/4211/timp.perc/str   Universal,1925.DTÖ 63   Misc 3251 & M
        arr M.Schönherr   PC 1+picc.22.3sx.2/4331/timp.perc/str   Bosworth   22885
MUTIG VORAN!: polka schnell, op.432, from "Simplicus"
                                 PC 1121/2210/perc/str   Cranz   5226
MYRTENBLÜTEN: waltz, op.395   PC 2(picc)222/4230/timp.perc/str   Cranz   5166 B
Eine NACHT IN VENEDIG (A Night in Venice): operetta in 3 acts
    Complete   ⌀ 2(picc)222/4230/timp.perc(bells)/hp/str   (Wöllner)   24710
        ed F.Racek   ⌀ 2(picc)222/4230/timp.perc(glock.tamb.xyl)/
                                     gtr.hp.2zither/str   Doblinger/Universal,1970.CW2/ 9   Misc 9937 & M
    Overture
        arr L.Artok   PC 2(picc)121/2220/timp.perc/str   Schott   10004 B
        arr Korngold   ⌀ 2(picc)121/3230/timp.perc/hp/str   Cranz   11286
    Selections   PC 1121/2210/perc/str   Cranz   6407
        arr T.Moses-Tobani   PC 1121/2210/perc/str   C.Fischer   1973
        arr L.Weninger   PC 2222/4230/timp.perc/hp/str   15'   Rahter (Benjamin)   15938
    Extracts
        Gondellied
            arr Oelschlegel   PC 1121/2210/perc/str   Cranz   3455
        Lagunen-Walzer
            in E♭ (orig F)   ⌀ 2222/4230/timp.perc/str   (Cranz)   4875
        Mir ist auf einmal (Schwips Lied/Tipsy song)
            arr A.Paulik   VS 1+picc.222/0000/str   (Weinberger)   26686
        Sei mir gegrust, du holder Venetia: song
            in A♭ (orig), arr Korngold
                                 PC 1121/2210/hp/str   Cranz   5396
        Treu sein, das liegt mir nicht: song
            in D (orig)   PC 1121/2210/timp.perc/hp/str   Cranz   12855
                see also   SO ÄNGSTLICH SIND WIR NICHT: galop, op.413
NAPOLEON-MARSCH, op.156   ⌀ 1+picc.121/4230/perc/str   (Austrian Radio) 16358 +
NEU-WIEN: waltz, op.342   ⌀ 2+picc.222/4231/timp.perc/str   Cranz   6046
    ed H.Gal   ⌀ 2(picc)21+E♭cl.2/4231/timp.perc/str   Universal,1925.DTÖ 63   Misc 3251 & M

STRAUSS, Johann (ii)(cont)

NEUE PIZZICATO-POLKA, op.449, from "Fürstin Ninetta"
    arr M.Schönherr   PC glock/str   Bosworth   20462 B
NEWA-POLKA, op.288   PC 1+picc.222/4210/timp.perc/str   Cranz   10894
NINETTA: galop, op.450, on motives from the operetta "Fürstin Ninetta"
                      PC 1121/2210/perc/str   Cranz   10671
NITCHEVO (Nothing): polka   ø 1+picc.020/2210/timp.perc.glock/str   [Russian SM]   26822 +
NORDSEEBILDER: waltz, op.390 ø 1+picc.222/4230/timp.perc/str   7'40"   Cranz   5167
                          2(picc)222/4230/timp.perc/hp/str   Cranz   9797
O SCHÖNER MAI: waltz, op.375, on motives from the operetta "Prinz Methusalem"
                      PC 1+picc.222/4230/timp.perc/str   Cranz   11386
                            1+picc.222/4230/timp.perc/str   Spina   27
                      PC 1121/2210/perc/str   C.Fischer   1955
The OLD CAMPAIGNER: galop; on motives from the operetta "Der Zigeunerbaron"
    arr I.Geiger   PC 1+picc.22.3sx.1/2230/timp.perc/str   Bosworth,1953 21036
ONE THOUSAND AND ONE NIGHTS see TAUSEND UND EINE NACHT: waltz, op.346
ORAKELSPRÜCHE-WALZER, op.90   1+picc.222/4211/timp.perc/str   Cranz   8377
PAPACODA: polka, op.412, on motives from the operetta "Eine Nacht in Venedig"
                        2(picc)222/4230/timp.perc/str   Cranz   5172
PAR FORCE: polka, op.308   1+picc.222/4210/timp.perc/str   Spina   8533
    ed F.Racek   ø 1+picc.222/4211/timp.perc/str   Doblinger/Universal,1967.CW 1/19   26340 * & MRL
PAROXYSMEN: waltz, op.189   ø 1+picc.222/4210/timp.perc/hp/str   Haslinger   25288
PATRIOTEN-MARSCH, op.8   PC 1+picc.021/2200/str   Cranz   8352
PERPETUUM MOBILE, op.257   ø 3(picc)222/4210/timp.perc/hp/str   2'30"-4'   Haslinger   4653 + Cs
    arr H.Weber   PC 1(picc)121/2210/timp.perc/str   Cranz   11220
    arr A.Winter   PC 2(picc)22.3sx.2/4230/timp.perc/hp/str   Boosey & H 14167 Ap Cs
PERSISCHER-MARSCH, op.289   ø 1+picc.121/2210/perc/str   1'45"-2'30"   Cranz   5847 +
                      PC 1+picc.222/4230.oph/perc/str   Heugel   4584
                          1+picc.222/4230/perc/str   Spina   8623
    arr I.Geiger   PC 1+picc.12.3sx.1/2230/perc/str   Bosworth,1955 21967
PIZZICATO-POLKA by Johann Strauss (ii) and Josef Strauss
                      ø 1+picc.222/4230/perc/str   2'30"-3'   Heugel   4796 Amv B
                      PC 1121/2230/perc/str   Hawkes   2397 B
    arr M.Schönherr   PC glock/str   Bosworth   22702
    arr A.Winter   PC 1+picc.12.3sx.1/2230/timp.perc/str   Boosey & H 14434 Bwe
    arr A.Wood   PC 1(picc)12.3sx.1/2220/timp.perc/str   Paxton   6898
        see also NEUE PIZZICATO-POLKA
POSTILLON D'AMOUR: polka française, op.317
                      1+picc.222/4210/timp.perc/str   Spina   8356 +
    ed F.Racek   ø 1+picc.222/4210/timp.perc/str   Doblinger/Universal,1971.CW 1/20   MRL
Le PREMIER JOUR DE BONHEUR: quadrille, op.327
    ed F.Racek   ø 1+picc.222/4231/timp.perc/str   Doblinger/Universal,1971.CW 1/20   MRL
PRINZ METHUSALEM: operetta
    Overture   ø 1121/2210/perc/str   6'-6'30"   Cranz   16420
                      PC 2(picc)222/4230/timp.perc/str   Cranz   3008
      arr M.Schönherr   PC 1+picc.222/4230/timp.perc/hmn/str   6'   Krenn,1959   23041
      arr L.Weninger   PC 2(picc)222/4230/timp.perc/pf/str   Benjamin   13872
    Waltz from melodies of the opera, arr R.Hanmer
                      PC 2121/2230/perc/acdn/str   3'30"   Weinberger,1952 20507
        see also BANDITEN-GALOPP: polka schnell, op.378   O SCHÖNER MAI: waltz, op.375
                KRIEGS-ABENTEUER: galop, op.419
PROMOTIONEN: waltz, op.221   PC 1+picc.222/2210/timp.perc/hp/str   8'30"   C.Fischer   1958
    arr S.Robinson   ø 2222/4231/timp.perc/hp/str   (Cranz)   TO 1058
    arr A.Winter   PC 2(picc)22.2sx.2/2230/timp.perc/hp/str   Hawkes   3961
PROZESS-POLKA: polka, op.294
    ed F.Racek   ø 1 + picc.222/4211/timp.perc(glock)/str
                                                Doblinger/Universal,1968.CW 1/18   26630 & MRL

STRAUSS, Johann (ii)(cont)

Die PUBLIZISTEN: waltz, op.321   1+picc.222/4231/timp.perc/str   Spina   20348
    ed F.Racek   φ   1+picc.222/4231/timp.perc(glock)/str Doblinger/Universal,1971.CW 1/20   MRL
QUADRILLE SUR DES AIRS FRANÇAISES, op.290
                                    φ   1+picc.222/4230/timp.perc/str   Spina   8899
REITERMARSCH, op.428, from "Simplicius"
                                    PC 1121/2210/perc/str or 0020/0000/str   Cranz   10771
RHADAMANTUS-KLÄNGE: waltz, op.94
                                    PC 1+picc.222/4211/timp.perc/str   Cranz   8378
RITTER PÀSMÁN: comic opera, op.441
    Selection, arr Schlar   φ   1+picc.222/4230/timp.perc/hp/str   Simrock   5562
    Ballet music
        1. Polka (2'30")   2. Valse (5'45")   3. Czardas (8'30")
            arr Leopold   φ   2(picc)+picc.222/4230/timp.perc/hp/str   Simrock   5546
            arr Leopold   PC 2(picc)+picc.222/4230/timp.perc/hp/str   Simrock   11678 B
        No.3 only   2+picc.222/4230/hp/str   Simrock [1892]   26291 *
ROMANZEN
    No.1 for cello & orch, op.243, in D min
        arr M.Schönherr   2222/4210/perc/hp/str   Krenn,1956   22425
    No.2 for cello & orch, op.posth, in G min (Dolci Pianti)
        arr M.Schönherr   1002/3000/hp/str   Krenn,1956   22426
ROSALINDA: ballet arr J.Lanchbery from the operetta "Die Fledermaus"
    Nos 21 & 22   φ   2+picc[=2(picc)]222/4331/timp.perc.glock.vib[=glock].xyl/
                                        hp/str   (Cranz)   26701
ROSEN AUS DEM SÜDEN (Roses from the South): waltz, op.388, on motives from the operetta "Das
    Spitzentuch der Königin)
                                    φ   1+picc.222/4230/timp.perc/hp/str   9'   Breitkopf   7227 B +
                                    PC 1+picc.222/4230/timp.perc/hp/str   Cranz   7942 A Ap
    arr D.Gomm as signature tune for programme 'Grand Hotel'
                                        cel.org.pf/str   Arranger   MS LM Lib
        arr M.Schönherr   PC 1+picc.22.2sx.2/4230/timp.perc/str   Bosworth,1953 21314
        arr L.Weninger   PC 1+picc.222/4230/timp.perc/hp/str   Rahter   1701
        arr A.Winter   PC 1+picc.22.2sx.2/2230/timp.perc/hp/str 4'   Hawkes   9236 Ap C
RUSSISCHER MARSCH, op.426   PC 1121/2210/perc/str   3'   Cranz   3567 B
'S GIBT NUR A KAISERSTADT: polka, op.291
                                        1+picc.222/4210/timp.perc/str   Spina   8623
    arr C.Groves & S.Robinson   φ   2222/4230/timp.perc/str   (Cranz)   TU 1007
SÄNGERSLUST: polka française, op.328
                                    PC 1(picc)121/2210/timp.perc/str   Cranz   7280
    ed F.Racek   φ   1+picc.222/4331/timp.perc/str   Doblinger/Universal,1971.CW 1/20   26631 & MRL
    arr M.Schönherr   PC 1+picc.22.3sx.2/4331/timp.perc/str   Bosworth   22700
SCHATZ-WALZER, op.418, on motives from the operetta "Der Zigeunerbaron"
                                    PC 2121/2220/timp.perc/str   7'30"   C.Fischer   2015
    arr M.Schönherr   PC 222.3sx.2/4230/timp.perc/hp/str   Krenn,1958   22815
    arr A.Winter   φ   2(picc)22(sx)2/2230/timp.perc/str   Hawkes   9252
    in C, arr D.Edge & H.Carr (vocal arrangement- Treasure Waltz)
                                    φ   hp.pf/str   (Paxton)   TO 1265
SCHÜTZEN-QUADRILLE by Johann Strauss (ii), Josef Strauss & Eduard Strauss
                                    PC 1+picc.222/4430/timp.perc/str   (Cranz)   25415 +
SEID UMSCHLUNGEN MILLIONEN! (Be embraced, ye countless millions): waltz, op.443
    arr Atzler   PC 1121/2210/timp.perc/hp/str   10'-11'   Cranz   20310 +
    arr A.Franzel   φ   3(2picc)22+bcl.2/4231/timp.perc/hp/str   Simrock   24042 φ MS
    arr Leopold   φ   1121/2230/timp.perc/str   Simrock   12672
SERAILTÄNZE: waltz, op.5   PC 1+picc.121/2210/timp.perc/str   Cranz   8399
SINNEN UND MINNEN: waltz, op.435
                                    PC 2(picc)222/4230/timp.perc/str   Cranz   16220

STRAUSS, Johann (ii)(cont)

SINNGEDICHTE: waltz, op.1 (Poème d'amour)
                                   PC 1121/2210/timp.perc/str   Cranz   8388
SO ÄNGSTLICH SIND WIR NICHT!: galop, op.413, on motives from "Eine Nacht in Venedig"
                                   PC 1121/2210/perc/str   Fischer   1449
SPANISCHER MARSCH, op.433   ∅ 1+picc.222/4230/timp.perc/hp/str   4'30"   Cranz   11075
Das SPITZENTUCH DER KONIGEN: operetta
   Overture   PC 1(picc)121/2210/timp.perc/str   Cranz   11332
   Selection, arr Pausperth & Atzler
                      PC 1(picc)121/2210/timp.perc/hp/str   16'15"   Cranz   10961
   Extracts
     Ballet music (no.7)   ∅ 2222/4230/timp.perc.glock/cel.hp/str   (BBC)   TO 1466
     Du Märchenstadt im Donautal (Vienna stands in Danube's vale): song (no.10)
       in C (orig)   ∅ 2121/3230/timp.perc/hp/str   (BBC)   TO 1466
     Freunde, Ihr seid doch so reizend (When all the singers)(part of no.6)
       in Db   ∅ 2121/3220/timp.perc/hp/str   (BBC)   TO 1466
     Mit dem Kopfe (Love is not as poets sing): trio (no.14)
       in F (orig)   ∅ 2 222/4230/timp.perc/hp/str   (BBC)   TO 1466
     Rote Rose (Red rose): duet (no.4)
       in Db (orig)   ∅ 2222/3230/timp.perc.glock/cel/hp/str   (BBC)   TO 1466
     Rote Rose (Red rose) (part of no.6)
       in Db (orig)   ∅ 2222/2220/timp.perc.glock/cel.hp/str   (BBC)   TO 1466
     Sei mir gegrüst (Sleep on in love): waltz song (from no.3)
       in Bb (orig)   ∅ 1121/2220/timp/hp/str   (BBC)   TO 1466
     Wein und Musik: waltz duet (from no.13)
       in Bb (orig)   ∅ 2122/4230/timp.perc/hp/str   (BBC)   TO 1466
     see also ROSEN AUS DEM SÜDEN: waltz, op.388
              STÜRMISCH IN LIEB' UND TANZ: schnell-polka, op.393
SPRING IN MY HEART: song
   in C, arr H.Salter, orch G.Stacey
                      pf/str   (FD & H)   LM G 3074
   in C, arr G.Vinter   ∅ 2(picc)222/4230/timp.perc/hp/str   (FD & H)   23365 +
   arr H.Salter, orch P.Hope as vocal signature tune for 'Friday Night is Music Night'
                 ∅ 2222/4330/timp.perc/hp/str   (FD & H)   23366 +
STADT UND LAND (Town and country): polka-mazurka, op.322
                 ∅ 1+picc.222/4331/timp.perc/str   (Cranz)   25610 +
   ed F.Racek   ∅ 1+picc.222/4230/timp.perc/str   Doblinger/Universal,1971.CW 1/20   MRL
STRAUSS SELECTIONS
   BEIM WALZERKÖNIG STRAUSS   see   WEBER, Henry: WITH STRAUSS, J (ii)
   SELECTION OF OPERAS   see   SCHLOGEL, Ludwig: SELECTION FROM OPERAS BY JOHANN STRAUSS (ii)
   STRAUSS-FANTASIE   see   GOMM, Dennis: STRAUSS-FANTASIE
   STRAUSSIANA   see   BORSCHEL, Erich: STRAUSSIANA
   STRAUSSIANA   see   KORNGOLD, Erich Wolfgang: STRAUSSIANA
   TALES OF STRAUSS   see   KORNGOLD, Erich Wolfgang: TALES OF STRAUSS
STUDENTENLUST: waltz, op.285   1+picc.222/4211/timp.perc/str   Spina   7924
STÜRMISCH IN LIEB' UND TANZ: schnell-polka, op.393, on motives from "Das Spitzentuch der Königin"
SYLPHEN-POLKA, op.309   1+picc.222/4211/timp.perc/str   Spina   9533
   ed F.Racek   ∅ 1+picc.222/4211/timp.perc/str   Doblinger/Universal,1967.CW 1/19   26632 & MRL
TALES FROM THE VIENNA WOODS see GESCHICHTEN AUS DEM WIENERWALD: waltz, op.325
TALES OF STRAUSS see KORNGOLD, E: TALES OF STRAUSS
TÄNDELEI: polka-mazurka, op.310 PC 1+picc.222/4210/timp.perc/str   Spina   12175
   ed F.Racek   ∅ 1+picc.222/4210/timp.perc/str   Doblinger/Universal,1967.CW 1/19   MRL
Die TÄNZERIN FANNY ELSSLER (Fanny Elssler, the dancer): operetta
   Overture
     arr Stalla   ∅ 2(picc)222/4230/timp.perc/hp/str   7'30"   Weinberger   13355

STRAUSS, Johann (ii)(cont)

Die TÄNZERIN FANNY ELSSLER (cont)
   Extracts
      Draussen in Sievering: 'Es dämmert schon' (Act II, no.9)
        in F   φ 2222/4210/timp.perc/hp/str   (BBC)   24829 +
      Einmal im Traum (Once in a dream): song
        in Db (orig), arr L.Salter
                   φ 2122/2131/timp/hp/str   (Cranz)   TO 152
      Fanny-Elssler-Walzer, arr O.Stalla & H.Weber
             PC incomplete set of parts (full orchestration not known)
TARANTELLE VENEZIANA, on motives from the operet   Weinberger,1935   26137 **
TARANTELLE VENEZIANA, on motives from the operetta "Eine Nacht in Venedig"
   arr M.Schönherr   PC 2(picc)222/4230/perc/hp/str   Bosworth,1963   23995
Die TAUBEN VON SAN MARCO: polka, op.414, on motives from the operetta "Eine Nacht in Venedig"
              PC 2(picc)222/4230/timp.perc/str   Cranz   1763
TAUBENPOST: polka-française, op.237
              φ 1+picc.122/4210/timp.perc/hp/str   Haslinger   Misc 1271
TAUSEND UND EINE NACHT: operetta, arr Reiterer from "Indigo"
   Intermezzo
     arr Schmid   PC 112.2sx.1/2210/timp.perc/hp/str   G.Schirmer   9289
TAUSEND UND EINE NACHT: waltz, op.346, on motives from the operetta "Indigo"
   arr S.Robinson   φ 3222/4231/timp.perc/hp/str   7'30"-10'45" (Arranger) TO 1080 +
   arr A.Winter   φ 222.2sx.2/4230/timp.perc/str   Hawkes   1963 Bp Cs
TELEGRAMME WALTZ, op.318   2(picc)222/4210/timp.perc/str   Spina   9130
              PC 2221/2230.euph/timp.perc/str   Riviere & H 4664
   ed F.Racek   φ 2(picc)222/4210/timp.perc/str   9'
                             Doblinger/Universal,1971.CW 1/20   26426 * & MRL
   arr A.Winter   PC 2(picc)22.2sx.2/2230/timp.perc/str   Hawkes   4834 B
THUNDER AND LIGHTNING POLKA see UNTER DONNER UND BLITZ: polka, op.324
TIK-TAK: polka schnell, op.365, on motives from "Die Fledermaus"
              PC 1+picc.222/4230/timp.perc/str   3'   Cranz   8343 Am
   arr R.Hanmer   PC 2222/4230/timp.perc/hp/str   Dix   19202
   arr M.Schönherr   PC 1+picc.12.3sx.2/4230/timp.perc/str   Krenn,1956   22063
TRAU-SCHAU-WEM!: waltz, op.463, on motives from the operetta "Waldmeister"
              PC 1+picc.222/4230/timp.perc/hp/str   Bote & B   11505
TRAUMBILDER   φ 2222/4230/timp/hp/str   10'30"   Weinberger   10165
TREASURE WALTZ see SCHATZ-WALZER, op.418
TRITSCH-TRATSCH-POLKA, op.214
   arr P.Hope   φ 2(picc)120/2220/perc.glock.xyl/gtr.hp/str   (Arranger) MLO 358
   arr Schimak   φ 2+picc.222/4231/timp.perc/str   Haslinger   12182 B +
   arr M.Schönherr   PC 1+picc.22.3sx.2/4230/timp.perc/acdn.gtr/
                   vln-solo.str   Bosworth (Krenn,1964)   24636
   arr L.Weninger   PC 2(picc)22.2sx.2/4230/timp.perc/str   Schott   14298 Bni C
   arr A.Wilkinson   φ 2(picc)+picc.122/2220/timp.perc/hp/str   Arranger,1954 24268
   arr A.Winter   PC 2(picc)22.4sx.2/4230/timp.perc/str   Hawkes   3524 As Bm C
   arr A.Wood   PC 1(picc)12.2sx.1/2220/perc/str   Paxton   12500
   vocal version (Song of the Tritsch Tratsch) see LEONARD, Conrad: SONG OF THE TRITSCH TRATSCH
UNTER DONNER UND BLITZ (Thunder and Lightning Polka): polka, op.324
   ed F.Racek   φ 1+picc.222/4331/perc/str   Doblinger/Universal,1971.CW 1/20   26341 * & MRL
   arr R.Hanmer   PC 1+picc.222/4231/timp.perc/hp/str   Dix   19210 B
   arr H.Perry   φ 1+picc.222/4230/timp.perc/str   Boosey & H   19342 B
   arr M.Schönherr   φ 1+picc.22.2sx.2/4331/timp.perc/str   Bosworth   22701 +
VERBRÜDERUNGS-MARSCH, op.287   PC 1+picc.122/4230.bombardon/perc/str   Cranz   10894
VERGNÜNGUNGZUG (Excursion train): polka schnell, op.281
   arr M.Schönherr   PC 1+picc.22.2sx.2/4230/perc/str   Krenn (Bosworth) 23906
   arr D.Shostakovich φ 1+picc.222/4230/timp.perc.xyl/str   [Russian SM]   26823

STRAUSS, Johann (ii)(cont)

VIBRATIONEN: waltz, op.204	PC	2(picc)222/4221/timp.perc/hp/str		Haslinger	14842
arr S.Robinson	∅	2222/4231/timp.perc/hp/str	8'30"	(Arranger)	TO 1081

VOICES OF SPRING see FRÜHLINGSSTIMMEN: waltz, op.410

VON DER BÖRSE: polka française, op.337					
ed F.Racek	∅	1+picc.222/4230/timp.perc/hp/str		Doblinger/Universal,1979.CW 1/21	26811 & MRL
WAHLSTIMMEN WALZER, op.250	PC	1+picc.222/4210/timp.perc/hp/str		Haslinger [1861]	22176
WALDINE: polka-mazurka, op.385	PC	1+picc.222/4230/timp.perc/str		Cranz	9764
WALDMEISTER: operetta					
Overture	∅	2222/4230/timp.perc/hp/str	8'30"	Bote & B	8037 +
arr Atzler	PC	1121/2210/timp.perc/hp/str		Cranz	8698 +
arr M.Schönherr	PC	2222/4230/timp.perc/acdn.hp/str		Krenn	26385

       see also HERRJEMINEH: polka française, op.464

WALTZ TIME: operetta (adaptation of "Die Fledermaus")

  Extracts

    Come out, Vienna: song

in Db, arr B.Berlin	∅	2121/2000/perc/str		(Chappell)	TO 184

WALTZES FROM VIENNA: musical play, adapted by Korngold, Bittner, Clutsam & Griffiths from the

  music of Johann Strauss (i and ii)

Complete		2121/2230/timp.perc/str		(London Coliseum)	22116
Selection, arr Clutsam	PC	2(picc)121/2230/timp.perc/str		Chappell	6476 C
Extracts					
Today: song					
in Ab, arr F.Bye	∅	1121/2210/perc/str		(Chappell)	MLO 378
Waltz					
arr M.Irwin	PC	1121/2210/timp.perc/str		Chappell,1930	10869
WEIN, WEIB UND GESANG (Wine, women and song): waltz, op.333					
	∅	2(picc)222/4230/timp.perc/hp/str	7'15"-10'15"	Breitkopf	3678 C +
	∅	2(picc)222/4230/timp.perc/hp/str		Cranz	4301 B
arr Borch		1222/2210/timp.perc/str		Fischer	1959
arr Cursch-Buhren. Vocal arrangement, in C					
	PC	2(picc)222/4230/timp.perc/hp/str		Cranz	3384 B
arr G.Walter	∅	3222/4231/perc/hp/str		BBC	TO 121
arr A.Winter	PC	2(picc)22.2sx.2/2230/timp.perc/str		Hawkes	8097 Bp C

WHERE LEMON TREES BLOSSOM see WO DIE CITRONEN BLÜH'N: waltz, op.364

WIENER BLUT (Vienna Life): operetta

  Overture (on motives from the operetta)

arr M.Schönherr	∅	2+picc.222/4230/timp.perc/hp/str	7'	Krenn,1954	21557
Extracts					
Das Eine kann ich nicht verzeih'n (One thing I never can forgive): duet					
in C (orig)	∅	2222/4230/timp.perc/str		(Cranz)	TO 2032
WIENER BLUT: waltz, op.354	∅	2(picc)222/4230/timp.perc/str	7'-8'	Breitkopf	5114 + Amv C
arr L.Artok	PC	2222/2230/timp.perc/str		Schott	9991
arr L.Feigel	PC	2(picc)22.2sx.2/4230/timp.perc/hmn/str		Krenn	24239
arr A.Winter	PC	1+picc.22.2sx.2/2230/timp.perc/str		Hawkes	5979 Ap Dm F
arr L.Wright	PC	1121/2210/timp.perc/str		C.Fischer	1966
WIENER BONBONS: waltz, op.307	∅	1+picc.222/4211/timp.perc/str	9'	Spina	8719
ed F.Racek	∅	1+picc.222/4210/timp.perc/str		Doblinger/Universal,1967.CW 1/19	MRL+ 26625 *
arr Laurendeau	PC	1121/2210/perc/str		C.Fischer	1962
arr M.Schönherr	PC	1+picc.22.3sx.2/4230/timp.perc/str		Bosworth	22159 +
arr L.Weninger	∅	2+picc.222/4231/timp.perc/hp/str		Rahter	5939
WIENER FRAUEN: waltz, op.423	PC	2(picc)222/4230/timp.perc/str		Cranz	410
	PC	2(picc)22.2sx.2/2230/timp.perc/str		Boosey & H	10526
WILDFEUER: polka française, op.313					
	∅	1+picc.222/4210/timp.perc/str		Spina	7548
ed F.Racek	∅	1+picc.222/4210/timp.perc/str		Doblinger/Universal,1967.CW 1/19	26625 * & MRL

STRAUSS, Johann (ii)(cont)

WINDSOR-KLÄNGE: waltz, op.104	PC	2222/2230/perc/str		Hawkes	4833
arr B.Fry	PC	1(picc)222/2230.euph/perc/str		(GB-Lbm)	22632
WO DIE CITRONEN BLÜH'N: waltz, op.364					
	∅	2+picc.222/4230/timp/hp/str		Schreiber	7173
arr L.Artok	PC	2(picc)122/2230/perc/str		Schott	10001
arr Roth	PC	1222/4230/timp.perc/str		C.Fischer	1960
arr M.Schönherr	PC	2(picc)22.3sx.2/4230/timp.perc/hp/str		Krenn,1963/Bosworth	24924 +
arr A.Winter	∅	2(picc)222/2230/timp.perc/str		Boosey & H	10554
arr A.Winter	∅	2(picc)22.2sx.2/2230/timp.perc/str		Boosey & H	16545 Amv B
Die ZEITLOSE: polka française, op.302					
ed F.Racek	∅	1+picc.21+Ebcl.2/4210/timp.perc/str	Doblinger/Universal,1968.CW 1/18		MRL
Der ZIGEUNERBARON (The Gipsy Baron): operetta					
Complete		2(picc)222/4230/timp.perc/hp/str		Cranz(H)	PL 260
without overture & nos.14 & 15)					
	∅	2222/4230/timp.perc/hp/str		(Cranz)	TO 1361
Overture	∅	2(picc)222/4230/timp.perc/hp/str	8'	Cranz	8823 B +
	PC	1121/2210/timp.perc/str		Cranz	6320
arr L.Artok	PC	2(picc)222/2230/timp.perc/str		Schott	9990
arr M.Schönherr	PC	2222/4230/timp.perc/hmn.hp/str	6'	Krenn	22772
Selections					
arr L.Artók	PC	2222/2230/timp.perc/str	16'	Schott	10002
arr Atzler	PC	1121/2210/perc/str		Cranz	6925
arr R.Hanmer	PC	2121/2230/timp.perc/hp/str	8'	Weinberger,1955	21793

Extracts

Als flotter Geist (Barinkay's song)(Zigeunerbaron Waltz)					
in C min	∅	1+picc.222/4230/timp/str		Cranz	26041
in C, arr G.Stacey as 'Love, where ever I roam': song					
		pf/str		(Cranz)	LM G 3516
in C, arr C.Watters as 'Open road, open sky': song					
	PC	2222/4230/perc/hp.pf/str		[Schirmer]	LM G 10194
Einzugsmarsch	∅	2222/4230/perc/str		Cranz	26041
arr M.Schönherr	PC	222.3sx.2/4230/timp.perc/str	2'45"	Cranz	5240
Her die Hand, es muss ja sein (Werberlied)(no.12a)					
in F min (orig G min)		2(picc)222/4230/timp.perc.spurs		(Cranz)	27073 +
O habet Acht: Zigeunerlied (no.6)					
in D min (orig)		1+picc.222/4230/timp.perc/hp/str		(Cranz)	26685
in D min, arr Frost	PC	1121/2210/timp.perc/hp/str		Cranz	14721
Wer uns getraut (Who trusts us): song					
in Eb (orig)	PC	1121/2210/timp/str	4'	Cranz	5883
in Eb		2122/4010/timp.perc/hp/str		(Cranz)	26684
arr L.Artok for trumpet & orch					
	PC	1121/2110/perc/str	3'	Schott	10012
see also HUSAREN-POLKA, op.42 The OLD CAMPAIGNER: galop					

STRAUSS, Johann (iii)(1866-1939)

BUDAPESTER-POLKA, op.26	PC	1(picc)121/2210/timp.perc/str		Cranz	14742
DICHTERLIEBE: waltz, op.38	PC	2(picc)222/4230/timp.perc/str		Cranz	8549
IM GALOPP, op.34		1121/2220/perc/str	2'	Cranz	5815 B
vocal version in E & Eb, arr W.Goehr					
	∅	2(picc)222/4231/perc/str		(Cranz)	TO 125
KRÖNUNGS-WALZER, op.40	PC	1+picc.222/4230/timp.perc/hp/str		Cranz	8548
UNTER DEN LINDEN: waltz, op.30	∅	2(picc)222/2220/timp.perc/str		Cranz	9784
WIENER WEISEN: waltz, op.32	PC	2222/4230/timp.perc/hp/str		Cranz	7659

STRAUSS, Josef (1827-1870)

ACTIONEN: waltz, op.174	PC	1+picc.222/4210/timp.perc/hp/str		Cranz	16308 B
ALLERLEI: polka, op.219	∅	1+picc.222/4210/timp.perc/str		Spina	3555
AQUARELLEN: waltz, op.258	∅	2(picc)222/4430/timp.perc/hp/str	6'	[Cranz]	13120 +
ARM IN ARM: polka-mazurka, op.215					
	PC	1222/4210/timp.perc/hp/str		Cranz	25403
AUF FERIENREISEN: polka, op.133					
arr M.Schönherr	PC	1+picc.22.3sx.2/4230/timp.perc/str		Bosworth	22694
AUS DER FERNE: polka-mazurka, op.270					
		1+picc.222/4431/timp.perc/pf/str		Cranz	15964 +
		1+picc.222/4431/timp.perc/hp/str		Spina	6900
BUCHSTABEN: polka, op.252					
CHATTER-BOX: polka see PLAPPERMÄULCHEN: polka, op.245				Spina	1640
CONSORTIEN: waltz, op.260	PC	2(picc)222/4431/timp.perc/hp/str		Cranz	14402 +
DELIRIEN: waltz, op.212	∅	1+picc.222/4230/timp.perc/hp/str	9'	Bosworth	LM G 11488
arr M.Schönherr	PC	2222/4230/perc/hp/str		Spina	12250
DEUTSCHE GRÜSSE: waltz, op.191		1+picc.222/4211/timp.perc/hp/str		Hawkes	7726
DISPUTATIONEN: waltz, op.243	PC	2122/2230/perc/str		Spina	16176
		1+picc.222/4431/timp.perc/hp/str			
DORFSCHWALBEN AUS ÖSTERREICH (The Village Swallows): waltz, op.164			6'-8'15"		
	∅	2+picc.222/4210/timp.perc/hp/str		Universal,1931.DTÖ 74	20712 + & MRL
		2(picc)222/4210/timp.perc/hp/str		BBC	MS 2633
	PC	1(picc)121/2210/timp.perc/str		Cranz	6443
ed Botstiber	∅	1+picc.21+E♭cl.2/4210/timp.perc/hp/str		Universal,1931.DTÖ 74	Misc 3253 & MRL
arr H.Daeblitz	PC	2(picc)222/4230/timp.perc.birdwhistle/hp/str		Bosworth	26252
arr A.Winter	∅	2(picc)22.2sx.2/2230/timp.perc/hp/str		Boosey & H	7198
DYNAMIDEN (Geheime Anziehungskräfte): waltz, op.173					
	PC	1+picc.222/4210/timp.perc/hp/str		Spina	8900
EINGESENDET: polka, op.240		1+picc.222/4431/timp.perc/str		Spina	6989
EISLAUF: polka, op.261		1+picc.222/4431/timp.perc/str		Spina	7412
Die EMANCIPIRTE: polka-mazurka, op.282					
	∅	1+picc.222/4331/timp.perc/hp/str		(Cranz)	25876 +
ERNST UND HUMOR: waltz, op.254		2(picc)222/4431/timp.perc/hp/str		Spina	12817
EXPENSNOTEN: waltz, op.194		1+picc.222/4211/timp.perc/hp/str		Spina	7418
EXTEMPORE: polka, op.241		1+picc.222/4431/perc/str		Spina	6989
FASHION-POLKA, op.165		1+picc.222/4210/timp.perc/str		Cranz	2851 +
FEUERFEST: polka, op.269	PC	1(picc)121/2210/timp.perc/str	2'50"	Cranz	7353
	PC	1+picc.222/4431/timp.perc/str		Cranz	15964 +
arr M.Schönherr	PC	2(picc)22.3sx.2/4231/timp.perc/str		Krenn (Bosworth)	23107
FLATTERGEISTER: waltz, op.62					
arr Zeitlberger	PC	1110/0110/timp.perc/str		Bosworth	16723
FRAUENHERZ: polka-mazurka, op.166					
	PC	1121/2210/timp.perc/str	2'30"	Cranz	9916
	∅	1+picc.222/4210/perc/hp/str		Cranz	2851 +
ed Botstiber	∅	1+picc.21+E♭cl.2/4210/perc/hp/str		Universal,1931.DTÖ 74	Misc 3253 & MRL
arr M.Schönherr	PC	1+picc.22.3sx.2/4230/timp.perc/str		Bosworth	22695
FRAUENWÜRDE: waltz, op.277		1+picc.222/4331/timp.perc/hp/str		Spina	11868
FREUDENGRÜSSE: waltz, op.128	∅	1+picc.222/4230/timp.perc/hp/str		Cranz	5165
FRIEDENSPALMEN: waltz, op.207		1+picc.222/4210/timp.perc/hp/str		Spina	11988
FROHES LEBEN: waltz, op.272		1+picc.222/4431/timp.perc/hp/str		Spina	3499
FROHSINN: polka, op.264		1+picc.222/4431/timp.perc/str		Spina	7412
Die GALANTE: polka-mazurka, op.251					
		1+picc.222/4431/timp.perc/hp/str		Spina	6900
GALLOPIN: polka, op.237		1+picc.222/4431/timp.perc/str		Spina	3589
GEDENKBLÄTTER: waltz, op.178		1+picc.222/4211/timp.perc/hp/str		Spina	2819
GEHEIME ANZIEHUNGSKRÄFTE see DYNAMIDEN: waltz, op.173					

STRAUSS, Josef (cont)

HELENEN-WALZER, op.197		1+picc.222/4210/timp.perc/hp/str		Spina	12305
HERBSTROSEN: waltz, op.232		1+picc.222/4211/timp.perc/hp/str		Spina	4939
arr A.Winter	PC	1+picc.22.2sx.2/2231/timp.perc/hp/str		Boosey & H	6562 +
HERZTÖNE: waltz, op.172		1+picc.222/4211/timp.perc/str		Spina	8639
HESPERUS-BAHNEN: waltz, op.279		1+picc.222/4331/timp.perc/hp/str		Spina	11871
HOCHZEITZKLÄNGE: waltz, op.242		1+picc.222/4431/timp.perc/hp/str		Spina	3360
JOKEY-POLKA, op.278					
arr H.Carr	⌀	2222/2230/timp.perc/hp/str		(Cranz)	TO 821 +
arr M.Schönherr	PC	1+picc.222/4331/timp.perc/str		Krenn,1960/Bosworth	24780
KRÖNUNGSLIEDER: waltz, op.226		1+picc.222/4431/timp.perc/hp/str		Spina	4750
Die LIBELLE (Dragon-fly): polka-mazurka, op.204					
	PC	1+picc.222/4210/timp.perc/hp/str		Cranz	6045 +
arr Roth	PC	1222/2210/timp.perc/str		C.Fischer	6592
LUSTSCHWÄRMER: waltz, op.91		1+picc.222/4210/timp.perc/hp/str		Haslinger	20668
MARIEN-KLÄNGE: waltz, op.214	⌀	1+picc.222/4210/timp.perc/hp/str		Spina	6000
MEIN LEBENSLAUF IST LIEB' UND LUST:	waltz, op.263				
	PC	1(picc)121/2210/timp.perc/str	7'30"	Cranz	14733 +
ed H.Botstiber	⌀	1+picc.222/4431/timp.perc/hp/str	Universal,1931.DTÖ 74		Misc 3253 & M
arr H.Carr	⌀	2122/2230/perc/hp/str		(Cranz)	TO 813
arr M.Schönherr	PC	1+picc.22.3sx.2/4431/timp.perc/hp/str		Bosworth	22696
MOULINET: polka, op.57					
arr M.Schönherr	PC	1+picc.222/4231/timp.perc/hp/str	3'05"	Krenn,1961	24937
MUSIC OF THE SPHERES see SPHÄRENKLÄNGE: waltz, op.235					
NACHTSCHATTEN: polka-mazurka, op.229					
		1+picc.222/4431/timp.perc/hp/str		Spina	4940
OHNE SORGEN: polka, op.271	PC	1+picc.222/4331/perc/acdn/vln-obblig.str	1'40"	Krenn,1962	24656 +
PIZZICATO POLKA, by Johann Strauss (ii) and Josef Strauss					
	⌀	1+picc.222/4230/perc/str	2'30"-3'	Heugel	4796 Amv B
	PC	1121/2230/perc/str		Hawkes	2397 B
arr M.Schönherr	PC	glock/str		Bosworth	22702
arr A.Winter	PC	1+picc.12.3sx.1/2230/perc/str		Boosey & H	14434
arr A.Wood	PC	1(picc)12.3sx.1/2220/timp.perc/str		Paxton	6898
PLAPPERMÄULCHEN (Chatter-box): polka, op.245					
arr M.Schönherr	PC	1+picc.222/4331/timp.perc/hmn/str	3'	Krenn	22766
POLKA POTPOURRI, arr S.Robinson	⌀	2+picc.222/4231/timp.perc/str		BBC	4904
RUDOLFSKLÄNGE: waltz, op.283	⌀	1+picc.222/4331/timp.perc/hp/str	6'-7'	Cranz	1688
SCHÜTZEN-QUADRILLE see STRAUSS, Johann (i): SCHUTZEN-QUADRILLE					
Die SCHWÄTZERIN: polka-mazurka, op.144					
arr M.Schönherr	PC	1+picc.222/4210/timp.perc/str		Krenn,1964	25738
SCHWERT UND LEIER: waltz, op.71					
arr Schimak	PC	1121/2210/perc/str		Wrede	11003
SPHÄRENKLÄNGE (Music of the Spheres): waltz, op.235					
	⌀	2(picc)222/4431/timp.perc/hp/str	6'-9'	Cranz	12492 Cm +
ed H.Botstiber	⌀	2(picc)222/4431/timp.perc/hp/str	Universal,1931.DTÖ 74		Misc 3253 & MR
arr B.Hartmann	PC	2(picc)222/4231/timp.perc.vib/hp/str	7'	Cranz,1960	25798
arr M.Mackie	⌀	cel/str		Arranger MS:BBC	MS 30651
arr S.Robinson (excerpt)	⌀	2(picc)222/4230/timp.perc/hp/str		(Boosey)	20168 B
rev S.Robinson	⌀	3222/2230/timp.perc/hp/str		(Cranz)	TO 814
arr Seredy	PC	1121/2210/timp/str		C.Fischer	10176
arr G.Walter	PC	2(picc)222/4230/timp.perc/str		Boosey & H	16574 Amv Dwa
SPRINGINSFELD: polka, op.181	PC	1(picc)121/2210/timp.perc/str		Cranz	10670
STUDENTENTRÄUME: waltz, op.222		1+picc.222/4210/timp.perc/hp/str		Spina	13610
TANZADRESSEN: waltz, op.234		1+picc.222/4431/timp.perc/hp/str		Spina	3061
TANZPRIORITÄTEN: waltz, op.280	PC	1+picc.222/4331/timp.perc/hp/str		Cranz	16309
TANZREGULATOR: polka, op.238		1+picc.222/4431/timp.perc/str		Spina	6989

STRAUSS, Josef (cont)

THEATER-QUADRILLE, op.213		1+picc.222/4210/timp.perc/str		Spina	3294
TRANSACTIONEN: waltz, op.184	∅	2(picc)222/4230/timp.perc/hp/str	7'	Cranz	12755
UNGARISCHER KRÖNUNGSMARSCH, op.225					
	∅	2+picc.222/4431/perc/str		Spina	3555
VEREINSLIEDER: waltz, op.198	PC	1+picc.222/4211/timp.perc/hp/str		Spina	6824
VICTORIA: polka, op.228		1+picc.222/4210/timp.perc/str		Spina	4940

VILLAGE SWALLOWS see DORFSCHWALDEN AUS ÖSTERREICH: waltz, op.164
WALZERKRIEG: waltz potpourri on themes of Josef Strauss & J.Lanner, from the film see
        GROTHE, F: WALZENKRIEG

WIENER FRESKEN: waltz, op.249	PC	1+picc.222/4431/timp.perc/hp/str		Cranz	16200 B
	PC	1121/2210/timp.perc/str		Cranz	14310
WIENER KINDER: waltz, op.61	PC	1+picc.222/4211/timp.perc/str		Schlesinger	11136
WIENER STIMMEN: waltz, op.239		2(picc)222/4431/timp.perc/hp/str		Spina	5210
arr Atzler	PC	1(picc)121/2210/timp.perc/str		Cranz	12751
Die WINDSBRAUT: polka, op.221		1+picc.222/4210/timp.perc/str		Spina	10970

STRAUSS, Joseph (de Paris)

QUADRILLE (for Offenbach's 'Orphée aux Enfers')

	PC	1222/42.2cnt.31/timp.perc/str	Heugel	23826

STRAUSS FAMILY see also the following works based on the music of the STRAUSS family

CASANOVA	see	BENATZKY, R: CASANOVA
GEMS OF STRAUSS	see	WINTER, A: GEMS OF STRAUSS
LANNERS ZEITGENOSSEN	see	ABSENGER, A: LANNERS ZEITGENOSSEN
SOUVENIRS DES TROIS STRAUSS	see	SALABERT, F: SOUVENIRS DES TROIS STRAUSS
A STRAUSS GARLAND	see	WINTER, A: A STRAUSS GARLAND
A STRAUSS SALAD	see	HAYWOOD, J: A STRAUSS SALAD

STRAUSS, Richard (1864-1949)

see MUELLER von ASOW, E.H.: Richard Strauss Thematisches Verzeichnis. Vienna: Doblinger,1955

Die ÄGYPTISCHE HELENA: opera, op.75
    Selection, arr Singer & Rudolf

	PC	2222/2230/timp.perc/str		Fürstner	8652

ALLERSEELEN (All Soul's Day), op.10, no 8 see LIEDER, op.18, no.8
Eine ALPENSINFONIE, op.64   ∅   4(2picc)3(ca).heck.3(bcl)+Ebcl.4(cbsn)/8(4ttuba)442/
                                   2timp.3perc(bdm.cbells.cym.glock.sdm.tamtam.tri.
                                   tmc.wmc)/cel.2hp.org/str(18.16.12.10.8)
                    Offstage: 12hn.2tpt.2tbn   Leuckart,1915   Misc 813 E +

ALSO SPRACH ZARATHUSTRA: symphonic poem, op.30
                        ∅   3(picc)+picc.3+ca.2+Ebcl+bcl.3+cbsn/6432/
                             timp.perc.bell.glock/2hp.org/
                             str(16.16.12.12.8)   29'30"-33'   Aibl   10615 + Amv
                        ∅   3(2picc)+picc.3+ca.2+Ebcl+bcl.3+cbsn/6432/
                             timp.perc.bell.glock/2hp.org/
                             str(16.16.12.12.8)   Peters (Aibl,1896)(H)   PL 664 Amv

ANDANTE MA NON TROPPO (from sonata for cello, op.6)
    arr Bauer   PC   1121/2210/timp/str   6'   Universal   11121
ARABELLA: opera, op.79
    Complete   ∅   3(picc)2+ca.3+bcl.3(cbsn)/4331/timp/hp/str Boosey & H/F.Strauss,1960 5186
    Prelude, Act 3   ∅   3(picc)2+ca.3+bcl.3/4330/timp/hp/str   5'   Fürstner,1933/34   Misc 30
    Selections
        Phantasy on themes from the opera, arr L.Weninger
                    PC   2(picc)222/4231/timp/hp/str   Fürstner   11742

STRAUSS, Richard (cont)

ARIADNE AUF NAXOS: opera, op.60
  Complete (2nd version 1915-16)

	∅	2(picc)222/2110/timp.perc(glock)/cel.hmn.2hp.pf/			
		str	100'	Fürstner	Misc 2352 B
Prelude and dance scene	∅	2222/2000/str	9'-10'	Boosey & H	Misc 3577 B
Selection, arr E.Tavan	PC	2222/2231/timp.perc/str		Fürstner	6114
Extracts					

    Sein wir wieder gut: excerpt from prelude

orig keys	∅	2222/2110/timp.perc/cel.hp.pf/str	3'	Boosey	20206 ∅ Misc

AUS ITALIEN: symphonic fantasy, op.16

	∅	2+picc.2(ca)22+cbsn/4230/timp.perc/hp/str	47'	Aibl	9897

AUSTRIA, for mv-chorus & orch, op.78

	∅	22+ca.2+bcl.2/4431/timp.perc/2hp/str	10'	Bote & B	Misc 824

BEFREIT, op.39, no.4 see LIEDER, op.39, no.4
BEIM SCHLAFENGEHEN   see   4 LETZTE LIEDER
Le BOURGEOIS GENTILHOMME: suite
  Overture Act 1 (Jourdain-der Bürger)(3'45")
  Minuet (1'30")
  The Fencing Master (Der Fechtmeister)(1'30")
  Entrance and dance of the tailors (Auftritt und Tanz der Schneider)(5')
  The Minuet of Lully (2')
  Courante (3')
  Entrance of Cléonte (4'30")
  Prelude, Act 2.   Intermezzo (Dorantes und Dorimene - Graf und Marquise)(3')
  The dinner (Tafel musik und Tanz des Küchenjungen)(10')

Suite	∅	2(2picc)2(ca)22(cbsn)/2110/timp.perc/hp.pf/			
		str		Fürstner,1923	Misc 809 B
	∅	2(2picc)2(ca)22(cbsn)/2110/timp.perc(glock)/			
		hp.pf/str		Russian SM,1968	Misc 6765
Selection, arr E.Tavan	PC	2222/2231/timp.perc/str		Fürstner	6174 B

BURLESKE for piano & orch, in D min

	∅	2+picc.222/4200/timp/str	16'15"-21'	Steingraber	7699 Amv B

CÄCILIE, op.27, no.2 see LIEDER, op.27, no.2
CAPRICCIO: opera, op.85

Complete	∅	3(picc)2+ca.3+bcl.bthn.3(cbsn)/4230/timp.perc/			
		2hp.hpsd/str		Boosey & H,1942	Misc 5907

CONCERTI
  Horn & orch

No.1, op.11, in E♭	∅	2222/2200/timp/str	16'-18'	Aibl	10118 +
	∅	2222/2200/timp/str		Universal,1973	Misc 8305
No.2, in E♭ (1942)	∅	2222/2200/timp/str	18'10"-25'	Boosey & H,1950	Misc 3268
	∅	2222/2200/timp/str		Boosey & H(H)	PL 564
Oboe & orch	∅	20.ca.22/2000/str	22'-23'	Boosey & H	Misc 2718 C &
Violin & orch					PL 672 An
op.8, in D min	∅	2222/4200/timp/str	28'30"	Universal,1897	Misc 24

DAPHNE: opera, op.82

Complete	∅	3(picc)2+ca.3+bcl.bthn.3+cbsn/4331/timp.perc(tamtam)/			
		2hp/str			
		Offstage: 2 alphn/org		Boosey & H,1938	Misc 5935 B

Des DICHTERS ABENDGANG, op.47, no.2 see LIEDER, op.47, no.2
DIVERTIMENTO for small orch on harpsichord pieces by Couperin

	∅	22+ca.22/2110/timp.perc/cel.hpsd.hp.org(hmn)/			
		str(3-6.3-6.2-4.2-4.2)		Oertel,1942	Misc 3351

DON JUAN: symphonic poem, op.20

	∅	3(picc)2+ca.22+cbsn/4331/timp.perc/hp/str	15'45"-17'15"	Universal	9291 + Bmv Cr
	∅	3(picc)2+ca.22+cbsn/4331/timp.perc/hp/str		Peters(H)	PL 431 An Bmv

STRAUSS, Richard (cont)

DON QUIXOTE: symphonic poem for cello & orch, op.35
         ø   2+picc.2+ca.2(E♭cl)+bcl.3+cbsn/6332+ttuba/
           timp.perc/hp/str   Aibl   9895 + Amv B
         ø   2+picc.2+ca.2+E♭cl)+bcl.3+cbsn/6331+ttuba/
           timp.perc.wmc/hp/str(16.16.12.10.8)   Peters(H)   PL 665 Amv
DU MEINES HERZENS KRÖNLEIN, op.21, no.2   see   LIEDER, op.21, no.2
DUET CONCERTINO for clarinet, bassoon & orch
         ø   hp/str   18'-20'   Boosey & H,1949   Misc 3020 C
ELEKTRA: opera, op.58
  Complete   ø   3(picc)+picc.3(ca).heck.4+E♭cl+bcl.2bthn.3+cbsn/
           8(4tuba)6+btpt.3+cbtbn.0.cbtuba/timp.perc(glock.tamtam)/
           [cel].2hp/str   Boosey & H   Misc 2439 B +
         ø   3(picc)+picc.3+ca.heck.4+E♭cl+bcl.2bthn.3+cbsn/
           8(4tuba)6+btpt.3+cbtbn.0.cbtuba/2timp.3-4perc(glock.
           switch.tamtam)/[cel].2hp/str(vln:8.8.8.vla:6[=6vln]
           6.6.vlc.6.6.cb.8)   Fürstner,1908   Misc 1613
   Selection, arr E.Tavan   PC   2222/2231/timp.perc/str   Fürstner   6115
FANFARE (for the opening ceremony of Vienna Music Week, Sept.1924)
           0000/8662/2timp   Boosey & H,1960   23737
FEIERLICHER EINZUG DER RITTER DES JOHANNITERORDENS
         ø   0000/4.15.42/timp/str   Schlesinger,1909   Misc 839
FEST MARSCH, op.1, in E♭   ø   2+picc.222/4231/timp/str   7'30"   Breitkopf   6357 +
FESTLICHES PRAELUDIUM for organ & orch, op.61
         ø   4+picc.4+ca.4+E♭cl.4+cbsn/8441/timp.perc/
           org/str   12'
           offstage: 6[=12]tpt   Fürstner,1913   Misc 814 B
FESTMUSIK DER STADT WIEN   see   MILITARY BAND CATALOGUE
FEUERSNOT: opera, op.50
  Selection, arr Regnis & Doebber
         PC   2(picc)2(2ca)22/4230/timp.perc/hp/str   Fürstner   6409
  Extracts
   Liebesszene   ø   3(picc)3(ca)3(E♭cl,bcl)3(cbsn)/4331/
           timp.perc/3hp/str   7'   Fürstner   10847
Die FRAU OHNE SCHATTEN: opera, op.65
  Complete   ø   4(2picc)3(ca)5(E♭cl,bcl,bthn)4(cbsn)/8(4ttuba)440.btuba)/
           timp.perc(bdm.cast.5Chinese gongs.glass hca.glock.sbells.
           tamb.tamtam.tdm.tri.xyl)/2cel.2hp/str(vln.16.16.vla.6.6.
           vlc.6.6.cb.8)
           on stage: 2121/1660/perc(4tamtam.tmc.wmc)/org   Fürstner   Misc 3372
FREUNDLICHE VISION, op.48, no.1   see   LIEDER, op.48, no.1
FRÜHLING   see   4 LETZTE LIEDER
GESANG DER APOLLOPRIESTERIN, op.33, no.2   see   LIEDER, op.33, no.2
GUNTRAM: opera, op.25
  Overture   ø   3(picc)2+ca.2+bcl.3+cbsn/43+btpt.31/timp.perc/
           str   Aibl   Misc 1746
  Overture, Act 2   ø   2+picc.333+cbsn/43+btpt.31/timp.perc/str   Aibl   7426
  Extracts
   Ich schaue ein glanzvoll prunkendes Fest (Guntram's Friedenserzählung/Guntram's peace narration)
    orig keys   ø   32+ca.33+cbsn/43+btpt.31/timp/hp/str   Aibl   2386
Die HEILIGEN DREI KÖNIGE, op.56, no.6   see   LIEDER, op.56, no.6
Ein HELDENLEBEN: symphonic poem, op.40
         ø   3+picc.4(ca)2+E♭cl+bcl.3+cbsn/8532/
           timp.perc/2hp/str   40'-45'30"   Leuckart   10315 + Amv
HYMNE AN DIE LIEBE, op.71, no.1   see   Drei HYMNE

STRAUSS, Richard (cont)

Drei HYMNEN, for voice & orch, op.71
  No.1: Hymne and die Liebe, op.71, no.1
    in F   ∅   32+ca.3+bcl.3/4331/timp/2hp/str   Fürstner,1921   20861
  No.3: Die Liebe, op.71, no.3
    in E   ∅   32+ca.3+bcl.3+cbsn/4231/2hp/str   Fürstner,1921   20862
HYMNUS, op.33, no.3 see LIEDER, op.33, no.3
ICH LIEBE DICH, op.37, no.2 see LIEDER, op.37, no.2
IM ABENDROT see 4 LETZTE LIEDER
INTERLUDIO   ∅   2222/4230/str   Heinrichshofen(H)   PL 426
INTERMEZZO, op.9, no.3 (from "Stimmungsbilder" for piano)
  arr A.Schmid   PC   1121/2210/timp.perc/str   G.Schirmer   10914
INTERMEZZO: opera, op.72
  4 symphonic entr'actes
    1. Reisefieber und Walzerszene (8'45")   3. Am Spieltisch   (3'15")
    2. Träumerei am Kamin   (5'30")   4. Fröhlicher Beschluss (2'15")
                           ∅   22(ca)22/3220/timp.perc/hp.pf/str   21'   Fürstner   9612
JAPANISCHE FESTMUSIK, op.48 (Festmusik for the 2600th anniversary of the Japanese Empire)
                           ∅   3(picc)2+ca.4+bcl.3+cbsn/8441/timp.5perc.glock.
                               gong.tamtam/2hp.org[=2hn.3tpt.4tbn.tuba in addition
                               to those already listed]/str   Fürstner   Misc 3350
JOSEPHS LEGENDE: ballet, op.63
                           ∅   4+picc.3(ca).heck.2+Dcl+bcl.4(cbsn)/6442/timp.perc(glock.
                               wmc.xyl)/4hp/str   60'   Fürstner,1914   Misc 1612
KAMPF UND SIED (Battle & Victory)
                           ∅   2+picc.222/4331/timp.perc/str   5'15"Heinrichshofen,1930 Misc 833 B
5 KLEINE LIEDER on poems by Arnim & Heine, op.69 (orig voice & pf)
  No.5 Schlechtes Wetter
    in F,arr Rudolf   PC   2222/2230/timp/str   Fürstner   16201
KÖNIGSMARSCH   ∅   2[=4]+2picc.2[=4].2[=4]+Ebcl.2[=4]+cbsn/8441/
                               timp.perc/2hp/str(12.12.8.8.6)
                               offstage: 8tpt.12dms   Fürstner   1617
4 LAST SONGS see 4 LETZTE LIEDER
4 LETZTE LIEDER (4 Last songs) for Soprano solo & orch
  No.1: Frühling (Spring)
    in A min   ∅   22+ca.2+bcl.3/4000/hp/str   4'
  No.2: September
    in D   ∅   32+ca.2+bcl.2/4200/hp/str   4'30"
  No.3: Beim Schlafengehen (On going to sleep)
    in Db   ∅   2+ca.2+bcl.2/4231/cel/str   2'50"
  No.4: Im Abendrot (At dusk)
    in Eb   ∅   2(picc)2+ca.2+bcl.2+cbsn/4331/timp.perc/str 6'   (Misc 6082,
    Complete   ∅   3(picc)2+ca.2+bcl.3(cbsn)/4331/timp.perc/   (Misc 3095-8
                               cel.hp/str   18'20"-23'Boosey & H,1950   (PL 553
Die LIEBE, op.71, no.3 for voice & orch see Drei HYMNE
Die LIEBE DER DANAE: symphonic fragment from the opera, op.83
                           ∅   3(picc)0.ca.3+bcl.bthn.3+cbsn/6331/timp.perc(glock)/
                               cel.2hp/str   9'   Boosey & H,1954   Misc 4211 B
LIEBESHYMNUS, op.32, no.3 see LIEDER, op.32, no.2
LIEDER
  op.10: 8 LIEDER (orig voice & pf)
    No.1: Zueignung
      in C, ed F.Trenner   ∅   2223/4300/timp/2hp/str   Fürstner/Boosey & H,1965.CW 4   MRL
      in G, arr Catalinet ∅   202+bcl.2/4210/timp/hp/str   2'   (Boosey)   TO 1808
    No.8: Allerseelen (All Soul's Day)
      in Db, arr Heger   222+bcl.2/4210/timp/hp/str   Arranger MS:BBC MS 3494 **

STRAUSS, Richard (cont)

LIEDER (cont)
  op.17: 6 LIEDER (orig voice & pf)
    No.2: Ständchen
      in D, arr H.Carr   ø 3222/4231/timp/hp/str   (Lengnick)   18738
      in E, arr H.Carr from F.Mottl arrangement, with revised ending
                      ø 3222/4130/timp/2hp/str   (Lengnick)   20086
      in E, arr F.Mottl   3222/4130/timp/2hp/str   (Rahter)   MS 3492
      in F, arr F.Mottl   ø 3222/4130/timp/2hp/str   Rahter   13992
      in Gb, arr F.Mottl   ø 3222/4130/timp/2hp/str   (Rahter)   20087
  op.21: 5 LIEDER (orig voice & pf)
    No.2: Du meines Herzens Krönelein (Pride of my heart)
      in E, arr Wilke   PC 1121/2210/timp/str   Universal   12766
  op.27: 4 LIEDER (orig voice & pf)
    No.1: Ruhe meinen Seele!
      in C, ed F.Trenner   ø 2+picc.2+ca.2+bcl.2/4231/timp/cel.hp/
                          str   Fürstner/Boosey & H,1965.CW 4   MRL
    No.2: Cäcilie
      in Eb   ø 2222/4231/timp/hp/str   2'30"   Universal   9845
      in Eb   ø 2222/4231/timp/hp/str   Universal,1911 Misc 808 C
      in Eb, arr F.Trenner   ø 2222/4231/timp.perc/hp/str(10.10.6.6.4)Fürstner/Boosey & H,1965.CW 4   MRL
    No.4: Morgen!
      in G   ø 0000/3000/hp/vln-solo.str   Universal,1911 Misc 808 C
      in G   ø 0000/3000/hp/vln-solo.str   Universal   6642
      in G, ed F.Trenner   ø 0000/3000/hp/str(10+vln-solo.10.6.6.4) Fürstner/Boosey & H,1965.CW 4   MRL
      in G, arr Wilke   PC 1121/2100/timp/str   Universal   9074
  op.29: 3 LIEDER (orig voice & pf)
    No.1: Traum durch die Dämmerung
      in E, arr Catalinet ø 202+bcl.2/4010/hp/str   2'   (Universal)   TO 1809
      in E, arr R.Heger   2032/4010/hp/str   (Universal)   MS 3493
  op.32: 5 LIEDER (orig voice & pf)
    No.3: Liebeshymnus (Love's pleading)   (25144 &
      in B   ø 3222/2100/str(8+4vln-soli.8.6.4.4.)   Universal,1911 (Misc 808 C
      in B, ed F.Trenner   ø 3222/4100/str(8+4vln-soli.8.6.4.4.) Fürstner/Boosey & H,1965.CW 4   MRL
  op.33: 4 LIEDER for voice & orch
    No.1: Verführung
      in E   ø 32+ca.2+bcl.3+cbsn/4231/timp/hp/str   Bote & B   11464
      in E   ø 32+ca.2+bcl.3+cbsn/4231/timp/1[=2]hp/
                          str(12.12.8.8.6)   Aibl   Misc 1746
      in E, ed F.Trenner   ø 322+bcl.3/4000/timp/hp/str(12.12.8.8.6)Fürstner/Boosey & H,1965.CW 4   MRL
    No.2: Gesang der Apollopriesterin
      in C   ø 3333+cbsn/4340/timp.perc/str   Bote & B   14745
      in C   ø 3333+cbsn/4340/timp.perc/str(12.12.8.8.6)   Aibl   Misc 1746
      in C, ed F.Trenner   ø 3233/4340/timp.cym/str(12.12.8.8.6) Fürstner/Boosey & H,1965.CW 4   MRL
    No.3: Hymnus
      in Db   ø 222+bcl.2/4230/timp.perc/hp/str   Bote & B   14741
      in Db, ed F.Trenner   ø 322+bcl.2/4230/timp.perc/vln- vla- vlc-soli.
                          str   Fürstner/Boosey & H,1965.CW 4   MRL
    No.4: Pilgers Morgenlied
      in Eb   ø 2+picc.22+Ebcl.3/4231/timp/str   4'30"   Bote & B   9418
      in Eb, ed F.Trenner   ø 2+picc.22+Ebcl.3/4231/timp/str Fürstner/Boosey & H,1965.CW 4   MRL
  op.36: 4 LIEDER (orig voice & pf)
    No.1: Das Rosenband
      in A   ø 2+picc.22+bcl.2/2000/str   3'   Universal,1911 Misc 554
      in A   ø 2+picc.22+bcl.2/2000/str   Universal   Misc 808 C
      in A, ed F.Trenner   ø 2+picc.22+bcl.2/2000/str(10.10.6.6.4) Fürstner/Boosey & H,1965.CW 4   MRL

STRAUSS, Richard (cont)

LIEDER (cont)
  op.37: 6 LIEDER (orig voice & pf)
    No.2: Ich liebe dich

in E♭, ed F.Trenner	∅	2222/4230/timp/str		Fürstner/Boosey & H,1965.CW 4	MRL

    No.3: Meinem Kinde

in G♭	∅	2002/0000/hp/str(1.1.1.1.1.)		Universal,1911	Misc 808 C
in G♭ & F	∅	2002/0000/hp/str		(Universal)	21741
in G♭, ed F.Trenner	∅	2002/0000/hp/str(1.1.1.1.1.)		Fürstner/Boosey & H,1965.CW 4	MRL

    No.4: Mein Auge

in F, ed F.Trenner	∅	2222/2200/hp/str		Fürstner/Boosey & H,1965.CW 4	MRL

  op.39: 5 LIEDER (orig voice & pf)
    No.4: Befreit

in E min, ed F.Trenner	∅	22+ca.2+bcl.2+cbsn/4231/timp/hmn.hp/ str		Fürstner/Boosey & H,1965.CW 4	24737 + & MRL

  op.41: 5 LIEDER (orig voice & pf)
    No.1: Wiegenlied

in D	∅	22+ca.22/2000/2hp/str	3'45"	Leuckart	10956 B +
in D, ed F.Trenner	∅	22+ca.22/2000/1[=2]hp/str(8+3vln-soli.8.6. 4+2vlc-soli.1)		Fürstner/Boosey & H,1965.CW 4	MRL

  op.43: 3 LIEDER (orig voice & pf)
    No.2: Muttertändelei

in F, ed F.Trenner	∅	22+ca.22/2000/cym.tri/str(8.8.6.6.0)		Fürstner/Boosey & H,1965.CW 4	MRL

  op.44: Zwei Grösse Gesange for voice & orch
    No.1: Notturno

in A	∅	2+picc.2+ca.2+bcl.2+cbsn/0030/str(12+vln-solo. 12.8.7.6.)		Forberg	Misc 838
in A, ed F.Trenner	∅	2+picc.2+ca.2+bcl.2+cbsn/0030/str		Fürstner/Boosey & H,1965.CW 4	MRL

    No.2: Nächtlicher Gang

in C min, ed F.Trenner	∅	4+2picc.2+ca.2+E♭cl+bcl.2+cbsn/6431/ timp.perc(cast.tamtam.xyl)/hp/ str(12.12.8.8.8)		Fürstner/Boosey & H,1965.CW 4	MRL

  op.47: 5 LIEDER (orig voice & pf)
    No.2: Des Dichters Abendgang

in D♭	∅	32+ca.2+bcl.2/4331/timp/2hp/str	10'	Fürstner	Misc 1902
in D♭, ed F.Trenner	∅	32+ca.2+bcl.2/4331/timp/2hp/str		Fürstner/Boosey & H,1965.CW 4	MRL

  op.48: 5 LIEDER (orig voice & pf)
    No.1: Freundliche Vision

in D	∅	2002/4220/str	4'	Fürstner	Misc 1901
in D, ed F.Trenner	∅	2002/4220/str		Fürstner/Boosey & H,1965.CW 4	MRL

    No.4: Winterweihe

in E♭	∅	0122/3000/str	4'	Fürstner	Misc 1900

    No.5: Winterliebe

in E	∅	2+picc.222/4230/timp.perc/str	3'	Fürstner	Misc 1899

  op.49: 8 LIEDER (orig voice & pf)
    No.1: Waldseligkeit

in G♭	∅	202+bcl.2/2000/hmn.hp/str	5'	Fürstner	Misc 1898

  op.56: 6 LIEDER (orig voice & pf)
    No.6: Die Heiligen drei Könige

in C	∅	32+ca.22/3231/timp.perc/cel.2hp/ vln- vla- vlc-soli.str		Bote & B	14740 +

4 LETZTE LIEDER <u>see</u> 4 LETZTE LIEDER

MACBETH: symphonic poem, op.23	∅	3(picc)2+ca.2+bcl.2+cbsn/4431/timp.perc/str	17'30"-19'	Aibl	9907 +
	∅	3(picc)2+ca.2+bcl.2+cbsn/43+btpt.31/ timp.perc(tamtam)/str		Eulenburg	5377 B

MEIN AUGE, op.37, no.4 <u>see</u> LIEDER, op.37, no.4
MEINEM KINDE, op.37, no.3 <u>see</u> LIEDER, op.37, no.3

STRAUSS, Richard (cont)

METAMORPHOSEN: study for 23 solo strings
                        φ   str(10.-.5.5.3)   23'30"-28'30" Boosey & H   Misc2312 C

2 MILITARY MARCHES, op.57
  No.1: Militärmarsch   φ 2+picc.232/4230/timp.perc/str   2'40"-3'   Peters   6503
  No.2: Kriegsmarsch   φ 4+2picc.242/6431/timp.perc/str   Peters   6503

MORGEN, op.27, no.4 <u>see</u> LIEDER, op.27, no.4

MÜNCHEN: ein Gedächtniswaltzer (2nd version)
                        φ 3(picc)2+ca.2+E♭cl+bcl.2+cbsn/4331/timp.perc/
                           hp/str   9'-9'30" Boosey & H,1951 Misc 3457 B

MUTTER TÄNDELEI, op.43, no.2 <u>see</u> LIEDER, op.43, no.2

NÄCHTLICHER GANG, op.44, no.2 <u>see</u> LIEDER, op.44, no.2

NOTTURNO, op.44, no.1 <u>see</u> LIEDER, op.44, no.1

PARERGON ZUR SYMPHONIA DOMESTICA, for piano (left hand) & orch (fantasy on themes from 'Symphonia
    Domestica'), op.73
                        φ 22+ca.2+bcl.2+cbsn/4231/timp/hp/str   18'   Boosey & H,1964 Misc 5915

PILGERS MORGENLIED, op.33, no.4 <u>see</u> LIEDER, op.33, no.4

Das ROSENBAND, op.36, no.1 <u>see</u> LIEDER, op.36, no.1

Der ROSENKAVALIER: opera, op.59
  Complete   φ 3(picc)3(ca)3(Dcl,E♭cl)+bcl(bthn)3(cbsn)/4331/
                         timp.perc(glock)/cel.2hp/str
                         Stageband: 2122/2100/sdm/hmn.pf/str(1.1.1.1.1.)   Fürstner   Misc 1610
    rev C.Krauss   φ 3(picc)3(ca)3(Dcl,E♭cl)+bcl(bthn)3(cbsn)/4331/
                         timp.perc(glock.bells.cast)/cel.2hp/
                         str(16.16.12.10.8)
                         Stageband: 212+E♭cl.2/2100/perc/hmn/pf/
                               str(1.1.1.1.1)   Boosey & H   Misc 2438 B
  Suite
    Revised version (1945) φ 3(picc)3(ca)2+E♭cl+bcl.3+cbsn/4331/cel.2[=1]hp/
                       str   20'-22'15"Boosey & H,1945 Misc 1329 C
                  φ 3(picc)2(ca)2+E♭cl+bcl.3(cbsn)/4331/timp.perc(glock)/
                       cel.2[=1]hp/str
                       (alt MS pts for clarinets in lieu of E♭cl)   Boosey & H(H) PL 246
  Suite, arr Hambert   φ 2222/4230.euph/timp.perc/cel.hp/str   Fürstner   3151 B
  Film music, arr O.Singer & K.Alwin
                  PC no full score exists - for orch material
                      apply Strauss Archiv, Garmisch   Fürstner,1926 Misc 5562 +
  Selection, arr H.M.Higgs PC 2(picc)222/2230/timp.perc/hp/str   Chappell   1789 Bwa
  Extracts
    Act 1
      Concert ending only, arr S.Robinson
                  φ 0222/4000/timp/str   (Boosey)   TO 1569
      Da geht er hin: Monolog der Marschallin (Act 1)
        in F (orig) φ 2222/0000/timp/str   6'   (Boosey)   TO 1569 φ only
    Waltz (Act 2)
      arr Doebber   PC 2222/4231.euph/timp.perc/hp/str   8'30"-9'30"Fürstner,1911 1824
      arr R.Douglas PC 2222/3230/timp.perc/hp/str   Boosey & H   10959 B
    Waltz sequence, no.1 (Acts 1 & 2)
                  φ 232+E♭cl.bthn.3/4331/timp.perc/2hp/str 12'30"   Boosey & H   Misc 2354
      arr M.J.Isacc   φPC str   Boosey & H,1946 LM G 10522
      arr S.Robinson φ 33+ca.4+bcl.3+cbsn/4331/timp.perc/hp.pf/str   (Chappell)   TO 1151
      arr Singer, orch Doebber
                  φ 2(picc)222/4230/timp.perc/hp/str   Fürstner,1911 7662 B
      abridged version, adapted for the Radio Orchesta from the version arr Singer & Doebber
                PC 2(picc)121/4441/timp.perc.glock/gtr.hp.pf/str   Boosey & H,1943 24665 Ap

RUHE, MEINE SEELE, op.27, no.1 <u>see</u> LIEDER, op.27, no.2

STRAUSS, Richard (cont)

SALOME: opera, op.54
    Complete   ∅ 3+picc.2+ca.heck.4+E♭cl+bcl.3+cbsn/6441/timp.perc.
                                   glock.tamtam.xyl/cel.2hp/str
                                   Offstage: hmn.org   Fürstner   Misc 1611
                      ∅ 3+picc.2+ca.heck.4+E♭cl+bcl.3+cbsn/6441/timp.perc.
                                   cast.glock.tamtam.tri.xyl/hmn.org/
                                   str(16.16.10-12.10.8.)   Boosey & H   Misc 2437
    Selection, arr Doebber   PC 1010/0110/timp.perc/str   Fürstner   5254
    Extracts
        Dance of the Seven Veils ∅ 3+picc.2+ca.heck.4+E♭cl+bcl.3+cbsn/6441/
                                   timp.perc(glock.tamtam)/cel.2hp/str   Fürstner,1905 Misc 826 B
                      ∅ 3+picc.2+ca.heck.4+E♭cl+bcl.3+cbsn/6441/
                                   timp.perc(glock.tamtam.xyl)/cel.2hp/str Russian SM,1968 Misc 6912
          arr J.Hartley & W.Hill ∅ 2221/2230/timp.perc/cel.hp.pf/str   (BBC)   TV 1388 A
          arr for wind band   ∅ 2+picc.2+[ca]4+2E♭cl+A♭cl+acl+bcl.ssx.asx.tsx.barsx.2+cbsn/
                                   40.4E♭tpt.[E♭cntto].E♭cnt.B♭cnt.2thn.42.bar[=euph]/
                                   timp.perc.cast.[glock].tamb.tamtam.xyl/
                                   [cel]/[cb]   Fürstner   Misc 1605
        Final scene (solo scene) ∅ 3+picc.2+ca.heck.4+E♭cl+bcl.3+cbsn/6441/timp.perc.
                                   glock.tamtam/cel.2hp.org/str   12'   Boosey & H   Misc 2327
          Reduced version   ∅ 3(picc)2+ca.2+bcl.3(cbsn)/4331/timp.perc/
                                   cel.hp/str   Boosey & H,1943 Misc 2327

SCHERZO, op.3, no.2 (orig pf)
    arr Wilks   PC 2221/2220/timp.perc/str   Universal   11120

SCHLAGOBERS, op.70
    1. In der Konditorküche Marsch   5. Marschtemps: Tanz der Prinzessin: Walzer
    2. Tanz der Teeblüte   6. Tanz der kleinen Pralinees: Springtanz, Galopp
    3. Tanz des Kaffees: Träumerei   7. Menuett: Pas de deux
    4. Schlagobers-Walzer   8. Finale: Allgemeiner Tanz
                      ∅ 3+picc.2+ca.2+bcl.3+cbsn/4331/timp.perc/cel.2hp/
                         str   Fürstner   10319

SCHLECHTES WETTER: song, op.69, no.5 see   5 KLEINE LIEDER, op.69
SEPTEMBER see   4 LETZTE LIEDER
SERENADE for 13 wind instruments, op.7
                      ∅ 2222+cbsn[=btuba]/4000   9'-11'   Aibl   51467
       arr Bauer for orch   PC 1121/2210/timp/hmn/str   Universal   9574
       arr Borch for orch   PC 1121/2210/timp/org[=hmn]/str   Schirmer   7940
SONATINES
    No.1, in F for 16 wind instruments
                      ∅ 223+bcl.bthn.2+cbsn/4000   28'   Boosey,1964   Misc 5982 B
    No.2, in E♭ see SYMPHONIE FÜR BLÄSER
STÄNDCHEN, op.17, no.2 see LIEDER, op.17, no.2
SUITE for 13 wind instruments, op.4, in B♭
                      ∅ 2222+cbsn[=tuba]/4000   25'   Leuckart,1911 25504
SYMPHONIA DOMESTICA, op.53   ∅ 3+picc.2+ca+ob-d'a.3+Dcl+bcl.4sx.4+cbsn/8431/
                         timp.perc(glock)/2hp/str   Universal   Misc 830 E +
SYMPHONIE FÜR BLÄSER "Fröhliche Werkstatt" (formally 'Sonatine no.2 für Bläserinstrumente, in E♭),
    op. posth.
                      ∅ 223+bcl.bthn.2+cbsn/4000   36'   Hawkes,1952   Misc 3798 B
SYMPHONY, op.12, in F min   ∅ 2222/4231/timp/str   41'-45'   Aibl   10460 +
TANZSUITE (Dance suite)(arr from harpsichord pieces by F.Couperin)
    1. Einzug und feierlicher Reigen: pavane (Entry & Ceremonious Round Dance)
    2. Courante
    3. Carillon
    4. Sarabande
    5. Gavotte
    6. Wirbeltanz (Whirling dance)
    7. Allemande
    8. Marsch
                      ∅ 22(ca)22/2110/perc/cel.hpsd.hp/str   Fürstner   10571

STRAUSS, Richard (cont)

Das THAL, op.51, no.1, for voice & orch
   in Bb   ø   322+bcl.bthn.2+cbsn/4200/str   8'15"   Fürstner,1903   Misc 840 B
TILL EULENSPIEGELS LUSTIGE STREICHE: symphonic poem, op.28
                     ø   3+picc.3+ca.2+Dcl+bcl.3+cbsn/8[=4]6[=3]31/
                         timp.perc.rattle/str   14'   Peters(H)   PL 666 Amv
                     ø   3+picc.3+ca.2+Dcl+bcl.3+cbsn/8631/timp.perc/
                         str
                         ('C' set reduced for triple woodwind)   Universal   7384 + Amv Cn
TOD UND VERKLÄRUNG (Death and Transfiguration): symphonic poem, op.24
                     ø   32+ca.2+bcl.2+cbsn/4331/timp.perc/2hp/str   21'30"-24'   Aibl   9896 + Amv C
                     ø   32+ca.2+bcl.2+cbsn/4331/timp.tamtam/2hp/str   Novello   Misc 8693
                     ø   32+ca.2+bcl.2+cbsn/4331/timp.perc/2hp/str   Universal   Misc 2610
    Facsimile of composer's MS   ø   3(picc)2+ca.2+bcl.2+cbsn/4331/timp.tamtam/
                         2hp/str   Aibl,1890/Peters,1932   MRL facs
TRAUM DURCH DIE DÄMMERUNG, op.29, no.1 see LIEDER, op.29, no.1
VERFÜHRUNG, op.33, no.1 see LIEDER, op.33, no.1
WALDSELIGKEIT, op.49, no.1 see LIEDER, op.49, no.1
WANDERERS STURMLIED, op.14, for chorus & orch
                     ø   2+picc.222+cbsn/4230/timp/str   16'   Aibl   Misc 819 E
WIEGENLIED, op.41, no.1   see LIEDER, op.41, no.1
WINTERLIEBE, op.48, no.5   see LIEDER, op.48, no.5
WINTERWEIHE, op.48, no.4   see LIEDER, op.48, no.4
ZUEIGNUNG, op.10, no.1   see LIEDER, op.10, no.1

STRAUSS, Wolfgang

SUITE for chamber orch (1977)
   1. Fantasie   3. Notturno
   2. Scherzo   4. Saltarito
                     ø   [gong[=tamtam]]/str(6.5.4.3.1.)   13'   Neue Musik,1979   Misc 10378
SYMPHONY no.1 for orchestra, op.49 (1967)
                       ø   2+2picc.2+ca.2+bcl.2+cbsn/4331/timp.4perc(glock.
                         gongs.mba.tomtoms.vib)/cel.hp/str   20'   DVfM,1971   Misc 9614

STRAVINSKY, Igor Feodorovitch (1882-1971)

see WHITE, Eric Walter: Stravinsky: The Composer and his works. London; Faber & Faber, 1966;
     2nd edition, 1979

AGON: ballet (1954-57)   ø   3(picc)2+ca.2+bcl.2+cbsn/4430/timp.perc.   (Misc 4811 D &
                         3tomtom.xyl/hp.mand.pf/str   20'-24'   Boosey & H,1957   (PL 696 Amv
APOLLON MUSAGÈTE: ballet (1928, rev 1947)
   rev version, 1947   ø   str   28'30"-30'30"   Ed Russe   Misc 2850 D
BABEL: cantata for mv-chorus, narrator & orch (1944)
                     ø   3(picc)22+bcl.2+cbsn/4330/timp/hp/str   6'30"-7'   Schott,1953   Misc 3981
Le BAISER DE LA FÉE see The FAIRY'S KISS
BASLE CONCERTO see CONCERTI: Strings
BLUE BIRD PAS DE DUEX from The Sleeping Beauty by P.I.Tchaikovsky see TCHAIKOVSKY, P.I: The
     SLEEPING BEAUTY
La BONNE CHANSON see 2 SONGS on poems by Verlaine
CANON (on a Russian popular tune) for concert introduction or encore (1965)
                     ø   2+picc.2+ca.2+bcl.2+cbsn/4331/timp.bdm/
                       hp.pf/str   Boosey & H,1973   Misc 9531
CANTATA ON OLD ENGLISH TEXTS for Soprano and Tenor soli, fv-chorus & orch (1952)
                     ø   22(ca)00/0000/vlc   27'50"   Boosey & H   Misc 3858 C

STRAVINSKY, Igor Feodorovich (cont)

CANTICUM SACRUM ad honorem Sancti Marci nominis, for Tenor & Baritone soli, chorus & orch
ø   12+ca.02+cbsn/03.Btpt.3+cbtbn.0/hp.org/
vlas.cbs   Boosey & H,1956   Misc 4732
CAPRICCIO for piano & orch (1929)
rev ed, 1949   ø   2+picc.2+ca.2+bcl.2/4231/timp/str   18'30"   Boosey & H   Misc 3851 C
The CARD PARTY: ballet (1936) ø   2(picc)2(ca)22/4231/timp.perc/str   21'30"-22'30"   Schott   Misc 411 C
Le CHANT DU ROSSIGNOL: symphonic poem (1917)
ø   2(picc)22(E♭cl)2/4331/timp.perc/
cel.2hp.pf/str   18'15"-21'   Ed Russe   Misc 801 C
CHORAL VARIATIONEN über das Weihnachtslied 'Von Himmel hoch da komm' ich her', by J.S.Bach (1956)
ø   22+ca.02+cbsn/0330/hp/vla.vlc   12'15'   Boosey & H,1956   Misc 4731 B
CIRCUS POLKA for a young elephant (1942)
ø   2+picc.222/4231/timp.perc/str   5'   AMP   Misc 2275 B
CONCERTI
Chamber orch   (Misc 2006 &
in E♭ 'Dumbarton Oaks'   ø   1011/2000/str   12'-14'   Schott   (PL 574 Amv
Jazz band see EBONY CONCERTO
Piano & wind instruments (1924)
rev version, 1950   ø   2+picc.2+ca.22(cbsn)/4331/timp/cb   20'   Boosey & H,1968   Misc 6686 B
Strings
in D 'Basle concerto' (1946)
orig version   ø   str   11'30"-14'35" Boosey & H   18925
rev version, 1947   ø   str   Boosey & H,1947   Misc 6976
Violin & orch
in D (1931)   ø   2+picc.2+ca.3(E♭cl)3(cbsn)/4331/timp.perc/
str   19'-22'   Schott   Misc 803 C
DANSES CONCERTANTES for chamber orch (1942)
1. Marche: introduction   4. Pas de deux
2. Pas d'action   5. Marche: conclusion
3. Thème variée
ø   1111/2100/timp/str(6.-.4.3.2.)   20'   AMP   Misc 2276
DIVERTIMENTO: symphonic suite from the ballet 'Le baiser de la fée' (1934)
rev version, 1949   ø   2+picc.2+ca.2+bcl.2/4331/timp.perc/hp/str   20'-23'   Boosey & H   Misc 3460 Cwe
DUMBARTON OAKS see CONCERTI: Chamber orch, in E♭
EBONY CONCERTO for jazz band (1945)
ø   001+bcl.2E♭asx.2B♭tsx.E♭barsx.0/1530/perc/
gtr.hp.pf/cb   8'20"-9'20"
Charling Music   Misc 2776 B
4 ÉTUDES for orch (1914-1929)
1. Danse   2. Excentrique   3. Cantique   4. Madrid
rev version, 1952   ø   3(picc)3(ca)2+E♭cl+bcl.2/4231/timp.perc/   (Misc 7554 &
hp.pf/str   Boosey & H,1971   (PL 599 Amv
The FAIRY'S KISS (Le Baiser de la fée): ballet (1928)(see also DIVERTIMENTO)
rev version, 1950   ø   3(picc)2+ca.3(bcl)2/4331/timp.perc/hp/str 45'   Boosey & H   Misc 3859 B
The FAUN AND THE SHEPHERDESS (Le Faune et la Bergère): song suite for Mezzo-soprano & orch, op.2
1. The Shepherdess   2. The Faun   3. Torrent
ø   2+picc.222/4231/timp.perc/str   Belaieff   18942 B
The FIREBIRD (Oiseau de feu): ballet (1910)
ø   2+2picc.3+ca.3(Dcl)+bcl.3(cbsn)+cbsn/4331/
timp.perc.bells.tamtam.xyl/cel.3hp.pf/str
Offstage: 0000/0302+2ttuba   Jurgenson,1910   Misc 1517
ø   2+2picc.3+ca.3(Dcl)+bcl.3(cbsn)+cbsn/4331/
timp.perc.bells.tamtam.xyl/cel.3hp.pf/str
Offstage: 0000/0302+2ttuba   Russian SM,1964   Misc 6113 C

STRAVINSKY, Igor Feodorovich (cont)

The FIREBIRD (cont)
  Suites
    No.1 (1911)
      1. Introduction   4. The Princesses' Khorovod (Rondo)
      2. Supplication of the firebird   5. Infernal dance of Kastcheis' subjects
      3. The Princesses' game with the golden apples
                  ø 3(picc)+picc.3+ca.3(E♭cl)+bcl.3(cbsn)+cbsn/4331/
                      timp.perc/cel.3hp.pf/str   Jurgenson,1912   10502 Bmv
    No.2 (1919)
      1. Introduction (3'15")   5. Infernal dance of King Kastchei (4'30")
      2. The firebird and its dance)   6. Lullaby (3')
                         (1'30")
      3. Variation of the firebird)   7. Finale (3')
      4. The Princesses' Khorovod (Rondo)(4'30")
                  ø 2(picc)2(ca)22/4231/timp.perc/hp.pf/str   26'   Chester,1920   4245 Amv
    No.3 (1945)
      1. Introduction   7. Scherzo - Dance of the Princesses
      2. Prelude & dance of the firebird   8. Pantomime 3
      3. Variations - firebird   9. Khorovod (Rondo)
      4. Pantomime 1   10. Infernal dance
      5. Pas de deux - firebird & Ivan Tsarevitch 11. Lullaby
      6. Pantomime 2   12. Final hymn
                  ø 2(picc)222/4231/timp.perc/hp.pf/str   Leeds,1947/Schott   Misc 5681 B
  Lullaby
    arr Q.Maganini   ø   str   Ed Musicus   16594 B
FIREWORKS: fantasy, op.4 (1908)
                  ø 2+picc.2+ca.3(bcl)2/6331/timp.perc.bells/
                      cel.2hp/str   3'45"-5'   Schott,1910   Misc 821 F
The FLOOD: musical play for TBB soli, SAT chorus, narrator and speaking voices & orch
                  ø 3(picc)+afl.2+ca.2+bcl+cbcl.2+cbsn/4330.cbtuba/
                      timp.perc/cel.hp.pf/str   Boosey & H,1963   Misc 5804
The FOX (Reynard): burlesque story for TTBB soli & orch
                  ø 11(ca)1(E♭cl)1/2100/timp.perc/cimb/str   15'27"-20' Chester,1917   Misc 1512 C +
GREETING PRELUDE for the 80th birthday of Pierre Monteux (1955)
                  ø 2+picc.222+cbsn/4231/timp.perc/hp/str   0'45"   Boosey & H,1956   Misc 4598
L'HISTOIRE DU SOLDAT (The Soldier's Tale): a story to be told, acted and danced (1918)
                  ø 0011/00.cnt.10/perc/vln.cb   35'   Chester,1924   Misc 1718 C
8 INSTRUMENTAL MINIATURES   ø 2222/1000/2vln.2vla.2vlc   6'   Chester,1963   24048
3 JAPANESE LYRICS for Soprano & orch (orig Soprano & pf)(1913)
  1. Akahito   2. Mazatsumi   3. Tsaraiuki
                  ø 2(picc)02(bcl)0/0000/str   Boosey & H,1956   Misc 4321 D
                  ø 2(picc)02(bcl)0/0000/str   Ed Russe   Misc 1046 B
JEU DE CARTES   see   The CARD PARTY
MASS for chorus & wind ensemble (1944-48)
                  ø 02+ca.02/0230   18'15"-20'45" Boosey & H   Misc 2782
MAVRA: opera in one act (1922)
                  ø 2+picc.2+ca.2+E♭cl.2/4431/timp/str   25'   Boosey & H,1969   Misc 7006
MONUMENTUM PRO GESUALDO DI VENOSA AD CD ANNUM: three madrigals by Gesualdo recomposed for
    instruments (1960)   ø 0202/4230/str(no cb)   6'45"-7' Boosey & H,1960   Misc 3212
MOVEMENTS for piano & orch (1959)
                  ø 2(picc)1+ca.1+bcl.1/0230/cel.hp/str   7'49"-10'Boosey & H,1960   Misc 5294 B
The NIGHTINGALE (Le Rossignol): opera
  Complete
    rev version   ø 2+picc.2+ca.3+bcl.3(cbsn)/4431/timp.perc.
                      bells.tamtam/cel.[gtr].2hp.[mand].pf/str   Boosey & H,1962   Misc 5697 B
The NIGHTINGALE'S SONG   see   Le CHANT DU ROSSIGNOL

STRAVINSKY, Igor Feodorovich (cont)

Les NOCES see The WEDDING
4 NORWEGIAN MOODS (1942)
   1. Intrada   2. Song   3. Wedding dance   4. Cortège
              ɸ 2(picc)2(ca)22/4221/timp/str   8'30"   AMP   Misc 1758
ODE: elegiacal chant in three parts (1943)
   1. Eulogy   2. Eclogue   3. Epitaph
              ɸ 3(picc)222/4200/timp/str   8'   Schott   Misc 2365 C
                                                                    (Misc 2872 C
OEDIPUS REX: opera-oratorio (1927, revised 1948)
   rev version, 1948   ɸ 32+ca.2+E♭cl.2+cbsn/4431/timp.perc/str   51'   Ed Russe   (PL 562 Amv
L'OISEAU DE FEU see The FIREBIRD
ORPHEUS: ballet (1947)   ɸ 2+picc.2(ca)22/4220/timp.perc/hp.pf/str 29'45"-33'20" Boosey & H Misc 2720 C
PERSÉPHONE: melodrama for Tenor solo, chorus, narrator & orch (1934, revised 1949)
   rev version, 1949   ɸ 3333/4331/timp.perc/2hp.pf/str   45'-56' Boosey & H,1949 Misc 3621 B
PETRUSHKA: ballet (1911, rev 1947)
   Complete
      orig version   ɸ 4(2picc)4(ca)4(bcl)4(cbsn)/42(Dtpt).2cnt.31/
                      timp.perc/cel.2hp.pf/str   Ed Russe   10016 Amv
         ed C.Ham with crit. analysis
                   ɸ 4(picc)4(ca)4(bcl)4(cbsn)/42(Dtpt).2cnt.31/
                      timp.perc.glock.xyl/cel.2hp.pf/str   W.W.Norton,1967 Misc 6696
   rev version, 1947   ɸ 3(picc)2+ca.3+bcl.2+cbsn/4331/timp.perc.tamtam.xyl/   (Misc 260? D
                      cel.pf/str   29'   Boosey & H   (PL 330 An B
   Extracts
     Danse des cochers et Danse russe
        arr H.Carr   2222/4230 (wind parts only)   (Jurgenson)   TO 1087 **
     Danse russe
        arr F.Guenther, ed J.E.Maddy
               ɸ 2(picc)22.3sx[=2hn].2/233[1]/timp.perc/pf/str E.B.Marks   3679 B
2 POEMS OF BALMONT for high voice & chamber orch (orig voice & pf, 1911, orch 1954)
   1. The flower   2. The dove
               ɸ 2020/0000/pf/str(2vln.vla.vlc)   2'30" Boosey & H,1955 Misc 4321 D
PRAELUDIUM for jazz ensemble (1937, vew arrangement 1953)   2'
               ɸ 000.4sx.0/0320/timp.perc/cel.gtr/3vln.vla.vlc.cb Boosey & H,1968 54331
PRIBAOUTKI: song games for Baritone & orch (1914)
   1. Kornillo   2. Natashka   3. The Colonel   4. The old man and the hare
               ɸ 11(ca)11/0000/str-5tet   Chester,1971   52381
PULCINELLA: ballet for STB soli & orch, based on music by G.B.Pergolesi (1920)
   rev ed   ɸ 2(picc)202/2110/2vln- vla- vlc- cb-soli.str 35' Boosey & H,1966 Misc 6460
   Suite
     1. Sinfonia (2')   5. Toccata (1')
     2. Serenata (3')   6. Gavotte (2')
     3. Scherzino (2')   7. Duetto (1'30")
     4. Tarantella (1')   8. Minuetto (2') & Finale (2')
      orig version, 1922
        ed Spalding   ɸ 2(picc)202/2110/2vln- vla- vlc- cb-soli.str   Ed Russe   Misc 796
      rev version, 1949   (Misc 2883 &
        ed Spalding   ɸ 2(picc)202/2110/2vln- vla- vlc- cb-soli.str   Boosey & H (325 Amv Bn
RAGTIME for 11 instruments (1918)
               ɸ 1010/10.cnt.10/perc.cimb/str   4'   Chester,1920   Misc 1162 B
The RAKE'S PROGRESS: opera (1947-51)
   Complete   ɸ 2(picc)2(ca)22/2200/timp/hpsd[=pf]/str   Boosey & H,1951 Misc 5698
REQUIEM CANTICLES for Contralto & Bass soli, chorus & orch (1965-6)
               ɸ 3(picc)+afl.002/4230/2timp.2perc(bells.vib.xyl)/   (Misc 6518 C
                     cel.hp.pf/str   15'   Boosey & H,1967 (PL 653 Amv
REYNARD see The FOX

STRAVINSKY, Igor Feodorovich (cont)

The RITE OF SPRING (Le Sacre du printemps): ballet
  orig version   ø   3(picc)+picc+afl.4(ca)3(bcl)+bcl.4(cbsn)+cbsn/
                                 8(2ttuba)4(btpt)+Dtpt.32/timp.perc.tamtam/str   Ed Russe,1921   Misc 6386
  rev version, 1947
    ed F.H.Schneider   ø   3(picc)+picc+afl.4(ca)+ca.3(bcl)+bcl+Dcl(Ebcl)4(cbsn)+cbsn/
                                 8(2ttuba)4(btpt)+Dtpt.32/timp.perc.tamtam/str
                                        Ed Russe,1921/Boosey & H,1947 Misc 795
    ed F.H.Schneider   ø   3(picc)+picc+afl.4(ca)+ca.3(bcl)+bcl+Dcl(Ebcl)4(cbsn)+cbsn/
                                 8(2ttuba)4(btpt)+Dtpt.32/timp.perc.tamtam/str
                                        Ed Russe,1921/Boosey & H,1967 Misc 795
  rev version, 1947, with corrections, 1965
    ed F.H.Schneider   ø   3(picc)+picc+afl.4(ca)+ca.3(bcl)+bcl+Dcl(Ebcl)4(cbsn)+cbsn/
                                 8(2ttuba)4(btpt)+Dtpt.32/timp.perc.tamtam/str
                                     Boosey & H,1947/Russian SM,1965 Misc 7393
  rev version, 1947, re-engraved 1967
                      ø   3(2picc)+picc+afl.4(2ca)+ca.3(bcl)+Ebcl(Dcl)+bcl.4(cbsn)+cbsn/
                                 8(2ttuba)4(btpt)+Dtpt.32/2timp.perc.crot.gro.tamtam/   (Misc 10024 &
                                 str   33'   Boosey & H,1967   (PL 410 B
  reduced version with barring simplified by R.Rudolf
                      ø   3(picc,afl)2+ca.3(bcl)3(cbsn)/4331/timp.2(perc.
                               crot[=glock])/str   33'   Belwin Mills,1974 Misc 8791
  facsimile of sketches (1911-13)   Boosey & H,1969 Misc 7075
Le ROI DES ÉTOILES: cantata for TTBB chorus & orch (1912)
                      ø   3+picc.4(ca)3+Ebcl.3+cbsn/8331/timp.perc/
                                 cel.2hp/str   6'Forberg/Jurgenson,1971 Misc 7571 B
Le SACRE DU PRINTEMPS see The RITE OF SPRING
SAGESSE see 2 SONGS on poems by Verlaine
SCÈNES DE BALLET (1944)   ø 2(picc)221/2331/timp/pf/str   15'30"-18' Chappell,1965 Misc 4126
SCHERZO À LA RUSSE (1944)
  Symphonic version (1944) ø 2+picc.222/4231/timp.perc.xyl/hp.pf/str 3'45"   Schott Misc 3854 C
SCHERZO FANTASTIQUE, op.3 (1909) ø 3(picc,bfl)+picc.2+ca.3(Dcl)+bcl.2+cbsn/42+Btpt.00/
                             cel.3hp/str   12'-16'   Jurgenson   3087
A SERMON, A NARRATIVE AND A PRAYER: cantata for Contralto & Tenor soli, narrator, chorus & orch   (Misc 5567 B &
                      ø   221+bcl.2/4331/3tamtam/hp.pf/str   16'   Boosey & H,1961 (PL 600 Amv
The SOLDIER'S TALE see L'HISTOIRE DU SOLDAT
The SONG OF THE NIGHTINGALE see Le CHANT DU ROSSIGNOL
SONG OF THE VOLGA BOATMEN, arr for wind & percussion
                      ø   1+picc.223/4331/timp.perc   2'   Chester   10757
2 SONGS on poems by Verlaine
  1. La bonne chanson   2. Sagesse
                      ø   2020/2000/str   4'   Boosey & H,1953 Misc 3934 B
The STARFACE ONE see le ROI DES ÉTOILES
SUITES for small orch
  No.1
    1. Andante   (1'30")   3. Española (1'15")
    2. Napolitana (1'15")   4. Balalaika (1')   (Misc 856 &
                      ø   2(picc)222/1111/perc/str   4'30"-5' Chester,1926 (PL 588 Ani
                      ø   2(picc)222/1111/perc/str   Russian SM,1967 Misc 6567
  No.2
    1. Marche   (1'15")   3. Polka (1')
    2. Valse   (2'15")   4. Galop (2')
                      ø   2(picc)122/1211/perc/pf/str   6'30"   Chester,1925 Misc 857 B
                      ø   2(picc)122/1211/timp.perc/pf/str   Russian SM,1967 Misc 6567
SYMPHONY in 3 movements (1945) ø 2+picc.22+bcl.2+cbsn/4331/timp.perc/hp.pf/
                                  str   20'30"-25'   AMP   Misc 2356 E

STRAVINSKY, Igor Feodorovich (cont)

SYMPHONY OF PSALMS (1930, revised 1948)
   orig version   ∅   5(picc)4+ca.03+cbsn/44+Dtpt.31/timp.perc/
                        hp.2pf/vlc.cb   22'30"   Ed Russe,1931   Misc 6567
                        ∅   5(picc)4+ca.03+cbsn/44+Dtpt.31/timp.perc/
                        hp.2pf/vlc.cb   Russian SM,1969   Misc 7437
   rev version,1948   ∅   5(picc)4+ca.03+cbsn/44+Dtpt.31/timp.perc/
                        hp.2pf/vlc.cb   20'15"-22'30"   Boosey & H   Misc 2735 E

SYMPHONIES OF WIND INSTRUMENTS (1920)
   rev ed, 1947   ∅   32+ca.33(cbsn)/4331   10'-12'
                                  Ed Russe,1926/Boosey & H,1952   Misc 3850 E

SYMPHONIES
   in C (1938-40)   ∅   2+picc.222/4231/timp/str   27'30"-29'30"   Schott   Misc 2951 C
   in E♭ (1905-7)   ∅   3(picc)232/4331/timp.perc/str   28'-30'   Jurgenson   4246 Amv
TANGO (orig pf solo,1940)
   orch F.Guenther   ∅   322+bcl.3sx.2/2331/perc/gtr.pf/str   Mercury Mus   Misc 2316 B
THRENI (Id est Lamentationes Jeramiae Prophetae) for SATTBBp soli, chorus & orch (1957)
                        ∅   22+ca.2+acl+bcl.0.sarr/40.flg.31/timp.tamtam/
                        cel.hp.pf/str   35'   Boosey & H,1958   Misc 5018
VARIATIONS (ALDOUS HUXLEY IN MEMORIAM)(1964)
                        ∅   2+afl.2+ca.2+bcl.2/4331/hp.pf/str   4'45"-5'30"Boosey & H,1965   Misc 6257 B
VON HIMMEL HOCH DA KOMM' ICH HER: variations <u>see</u> CHORAL VARIATIONS
The WEDDING (Les Noces): choreographic scenes (1917)
                      ∅   timp.perc.bell.2crot.dms.xyl/4pf   26'45"   Chester   Misc 799 F
ZVEZDOLIKI <u>see</u> Le ROI DES ÉTOILES

STREABBOG, L.

VIVE LA CANADIENNE
   arr M.L.Lake   PC   1+picc.12.2sx.1/2210/perc/str   C.Fischer   19720

STREET, Georges

SCARAMOUCHE by G.Street & A.Messager   <u>see</u>   MESSAGER, André: SCARAMOUCHE

STRELEZKI, Anton (1859-1907)

DREAMS: song
   in D, arr A.Schmid   PC   1121/2210/timp/str   G.Schirmer   7813

STREICHER, Theodore (1874-1940)

MIGNON'S EXEQUIEN (Mignon's Requiem from Goethe's "Wilhelm Meister") for cv-chorus, chorus & orch (1907)
                      ∅   33(ca)3(bcl)3/6331/timp/hp/str   Breitkopf,1907   Misc 9245

STRICKLAND, Lily Teresa (1887-1958

MAH LINDY LOU: song
   in C, arr A.Collins   ∅   1020/0000/str   (Chappell)   MS 6326
   in C, arr G.Stacey   ∅   pf/str   (Chappell)   LM G 5414
   in E♭, arr Clark   PC   1121/2210/timp.perc/str   G.Schirmer   7813
   in G & C   1010/0000/str   (Chappell)   MLO 327 **

STRINGFIELD, Lamar (1897-1959)

CHIPMUNKS   PC   1011/2110/timp/pf/str   Ed Musicus   9807
SOUTHERN MOUNTAINS: suite, op.41
   Mountain song (5'30")   At evening   Cripple Creek (3')
                      ∅   1+picc.12.3sx.2/4230/timp.perc/str   C.Fischer   13071

STRONG, George Templeton (1856-1948)

ELEGIE for cello & orch (1916)   φ   22+ca.2+bcl.2/4231/timp/hp/str   Henn,1922   25575
Die NACHT: four little symphonic poems (1913)
   1. Beim Sonnenuntergang (At Sunset)
   2. Kriegsmarsch der Bauern (Peasants' battle-march)
   3. Im tiefen Wald (In an old forest)
   4. Das Erwachen der Waldgeister (The awakening of the forest-spirits)
                          φ   3(picc)2+ca.2+bcl.3/4330.cbtuba/timp.perc/str   Jost,1914   25647
Le ROI ARTHUR: symphonic poem (1916)
                          φ   3(picc)2+ca.3+bcl.2+cbsn/43.2cnt.31/timp.perc/
                              str   Henn,1922   25721 ** str only
SUITE for cello & orch (1923)
   1. Sarabande   3. Danse   5. Impromptu
   2. Mélodie   4. Adagio
                          φ   21+ca.2+bcl.2/2200/str   Henn,1928   25720
SYMPHONY no.2, in G min (Sintram)(1888)
                          φ   3(picc)2+ca.2+bcl.3/4330.cbtuba/timp.perc/str   Jost   25645

STRONG, Michael

The VILLAGES OF ENGLAND: song
   in Eb, arr G.Stacey   1010/0000/pf/str   (AH & C)   LM G 3656

STROUSE, Charles (1928-

I AND ALBERT: musical play
   Extracts
      This gentle land: song
         in G, arr G.Langford for chorus & orch, vocal parts arr N.Brooks
                          φ   2222/4231/timp.perc.glock.vib/hp/str   2'30"   (Edwin Morris) 25584 +

STUART, Graeme

ECCENTRIC COURTIER: polka   PC 212.3sx.1/2230/timp.perc/cel.hp/str   4'   Bosworth   18990
THAMES CASTLES: suite
   1. The Tower Beefeaters: processional   3. Windsor Castle
   2. Hampton Court: minuet
                                PC 212.3sx.1/2230/timp.perc/cel/str   Bosworth   18989

STUART, Leslie (pseud of Thomas A.Barrett)(1864-1928)

The BANDOLERO: song
   in Ab   φ   1121/2220/timp.perc/str   (Siddell)   17978
   in Ab   φ   2(picc)222/2230/perc/str   (Chappell)   Misc 4599
   in Ab, arr G.Stacey φ   pf/str   (Chappell)   LM G 5192
   in Bb, arr Buerger   2121/2230/timp.perc/str   (Chappell)   MS 4329
   in Bb, arr Moore   PC 1+picc.222/2230/perc/str   Chappell   3999 C
   in Bb, arr J.Turner φ   1110/1000/hp/str   (Chappell)   LM G 9067
   in Bb, arr G.Williams for Baritone & orch
                       φ   1121/2210/timp.perc/str   Chappell   MLO 222
BELLE OF MAYFAIR: musical comedy
   Selection, arr C.Kiefert PC 1(picc)222/4230.euph/perc/str   FD & H   11499
   Extracts
      I am a military man: song
         in C (orig)   PC 2121/2220/timp.perc/pf/str   FD & H   11524
      Why do they call me a Gibson Girl: song
         in G (orig)   str   (FD & H)   TC 355

STUART, Leslie (cont)

FLORODORA: musical comedy
   Selection, arr C.Kiefert   PC 2(picc)222/4230.euph/perc/str   Hawkes   1633
   Extracts
      He loves me, he loves me not: song
        in Eb (orig), arr S.Robinson
                ø 2121/2220/timp.perc/str   (FD & H)   MS 7 ø only
      I want to be a military man: song
        in Bb (orig)   ø 2121/2220/timp.perc/str   (FD & H)   MS 4 ø only
      I want to marry a man: song
        in F (orig)   ø 2121/2220/str   (FD & H)   MS 6 ø only
      The Millionaire: song
        in C (orig)   ø 2121/2220/timp.perc/str   (FD & H)   MS 3 ø only
        in C, arr P.Cardew ø 1121/2230/timp.perc/pf/str   (FD & H)   18343
      Phrenology: song
        in Ab (orig)   ø 2121/2220/perc/str   (FD & H)   MS 2 ø only
      Queen of the Phillipine Islands: song
        in G (orig)   ø 2121/2220/perc/str   (FD & H)   MS 5 ø only
      The Shade of the palm: song
        in Ab, arr R.Chignell ø 2122/4231/timp/cel.hp/str   (FD & H)   MS 5169
      Silver star of love: song
        in Ab (orig)   ø 2121/2220/timp.perc/str   (FD & H)   MS 9 ø only
      Tact: song
        in D (orig)   ø 2121/2220/timp.perc/str   (FD & H)   MS 1 ø only
        in D, arr P.Cardew ø 1121/2230/timp.perc/pf/str   BBC   18342
      Tell me, pretty maiden: song
        in Eb, arr S.Torch for Soprano & Baritone soli, & orch
                ø 22(ca)2(bcl)2/4330/timp.perc.glock.xyl/cel.hp.pf/
                   str   (FD & H)   24556 +
HAVANA: musical play
   Selection, arr C.Kiefert   PC 2(picc)222/2230.euph/timp.perc/str   Chappell   3317 B
LILY OF LAGUNA: song
   in Ab   PC 111.3sx.1/2210/timp.perc/str   FD & H   8468 Ap C
   in Ab   PC 111.3sx.1/2210/timp.perc/bjo/str   FD & H   MLO 2471
   in Ab, arr S.Robinson ø 0010/0000/str   (FD & H)   TO 628
   in G, arr P.Cardew   ø 1121/2230/timp.perc/pf/str   (FD & H)   18344
LITTLE DOLLY DAY DREAM: song
   refrain only, arr R.Douglas (non-vocal)
                ø 2222/2230/timp.perc/str   (FD & H)   MS 30092
LOUISIANA LOU: song
   in F   ø 1111/0120/perc/str   (FD & H)   MS 6954
   in F, arr P.Cardew   ø 1121/2210/timp.perc/pf/str   (FD & H)   18345
MEMORIES OF LESLIE STUART: selection for Soprano & Baritone soli, mv-chorus & orch, arr Young
                ø 2(picc)222/4331/timp.perc(glock.kit.vib)/
                   gtr.hp.pf/str   (FD & H)   26367
MY LITTLE OCTAROON: song
   in Ab, arr H.Carr   ø 2121/2230/perc/hp/str   (FD & H)   TO 1181
PEGGY: musical comedy
   Selection, arr C.Kiefert   PC 2(picc)222/2230.euph/perc/str   Chappell   5374 B
   Extracts
      Dance fascination   PC 1+picc.121/2230.euph/timp.perc/str Chappell   7509
The SCHOOL GIRL: musical comedy
   Extracts
      The Honeymoon girl: song
        in Bb (orig), arr H.Carr
                ø 2121/2230/timp.perc/hp/str   (FD & H)   TO 285
      My little canoe: song
        in Eb (orig), arr R.Hanmer
                ø 2222/4230/timp.perc/str   (FD & H)   20913

STUART, Leslie (cont)

SELECTIONS OF LESLIE STUART'S SONGS
    arr Allan   PC 1(picc)121/0210.euph/str   FD & H   2514 B
    arr Baynes   PC 000.3sx.0/0220/timp.perc/bjo/str   FD & H   11658 B
The SHADE OF THE PALM
    orch R.Chignell   ϕ 2222/4231/timp/cel.hp/str   BBC   MS 5169
The SILVER SLIPPER: musical play
    Selection, arr Allan & C.Kiefert
                        PC 2222/4230.euph/timp.perc/str   FD & H   3793
SILVER STAR OF LOVE: song
    in Ab, arr P.Cardew   ϕ 1121/2230/timp.perc/pf/str   (FD & H)   18341
The SOLDIERS OF THE QUEEN: song
    in D, arr L.Wurmser & Clements
                        ϕ 3222/4231/perc/str   (FD & H)   TO 1471
    in Eb, arr P.Cardew   ϕ 1121/2230/timp.perc/pf/str   (FD & H)   18336
    arr Barsotti   PC 1+picc.12.4sx.2/4230/perc/str   Boosey & H 21039 B
    arr J.Greebe   ϕ 2222/2230/perc/str   (FD & H)   MS 6958
    arr M.Lubbock   2121/2220/timp.perc/pf/str   BBC   MS 30091
    see also   DOCKER, R: SALUTE TO THE QUEEN
SWEETHEART MAY: song
    in F, arr J.Greebe   1111/1120/perc/str   (FD & H)   MS 6959
    in G, arr P.Cardew   ϕ 1121/2230/timp.perc/pf/str   (FD & H)   18349
    in Ab, arr J.Greebe   2222/2220/perc/str   (FD & H)   MS 63

STUART, R.P.

HOLY FATHER, IN THY MERCY: hymn
    arr D.Godfrey   PC 2222/4230/timp.perc/str   Chappell   2867

STUNTZ, H.

Le RHIN SUISSE: Swiss air
    arr Scassola   ʳ   1221/2230/timp.perc/str   Foetisch   6425

STURDY, L.

OLD KENSINGTON: suite
    1. In old Victorian days   3. Boats on the pond
    2. Peter Pan   4. A morning's walk
      arr Owen   PC 1121/2210/perc/str   Bosworth   956

STUTELY, Gordon

SALT O' THE SEA: suite   ϕ str   OUP   2574

STYNE, Jule (1905-

BELLS ARE RINGING: musical play
    Selections
      arr R.Docker for Soprano & Baritone soli & orch
                        ϕ 22(ca)22/4330/timp.perc.glock.xyl/
                           gtr.hp.pf(cel)/str   10'   (Chappell) 25147 +
      arr F.Rapley   PC 212.3sx.1/2230/timp.perc/hp/str   8'   Chappell,1957 22400 Cp
    Extracts
      The party's over: song
        in Bb & C, arr B.Richards
                        ϕ 2121/2230/perc/hp.pf/str   (Chappell) LM G 10396

STYNE, Jule (cont)

DO-RE-MI: musical comedy
  Selection, arr F.Rapley   PC 2(picc)12.3sx.1/2230/timp.perc/hp/str   7'   Chappell,1961   23463 Ap
  Extracts
    Cry like the wind, in E min φ 2131/0020/perc/pf/str   Chappell   LMG 10302
FUNNY GIRL: musical show
  Overture
    arr R.Russell Bennett   PC 2(picc)12.3sx.1/2230/timp.perc/xyl/hp/str 6' Chappell,1963-4 24451 Cp
  Extracts
    Don't rain on my parade: song
      arr P.Knight for orch with rhythm section
          φ 2(picc)1+ca.22/4331/rhythm-cab.kit.tgl.bgtr.gtr.pf/
             timp.glock.vib.xyl/hp/str   (E.H.Morris)   26751
    The Greatest star: song for Soprano & orch
      in C, arr R.Docker   φ 2222/4331/perc.glock.vib./gtr.hp.pf(cel)/str 4' (Chappell)   26095 +
    People: song
      in A,Ab,C & B, arr A.Fones
          φ 2222/4330/timp.perc.glock.vib/hp.pf/str   (Chappell)   24459 +
GYPSY: musical play
  Selection, arr P.Hope for Soprano & Tenor soli, chorus & orch
          φ 2(picc)2(ca)22/4331/timp.perc.glock.vib.xyl/
             gtr.hp.pf(cel)/str   8'   (Chappell)   25661
  Extracts
    Everything's coming up roses: song
      arr P.Knight for orch with rhythm section
          φ 2(picc)222/4331/rhythm-kit.bgtr.gtr.pf/
             timp.perc.glocl.vib.xyl/hp/str   (Chappell)   26756
HIGH BUTTON SHOES: musical play
  Selection, arr G.Zalva   PC 1+picc.12.3sx.1/2230/timp.perc/hp/str   E.H.Morris   19217 B
  Extracts
    Papa, won't you dance: song
      in Eb, arr M.Mackie φ 2131/2230/timp.perc/hp.pf/str   (E.H.Morris) 18573
I SAID NO!: song
  in Bb   φ 2121/2230/perc/str   (Chappell)   TO 993
IT'S MAGIC
  Selection, arr R.Hanmer   PC 212.4sx.1/2330/timp.perc/hp/str   C.Connelly   20330

SUBOTNICK, Morton (1933-

PARALLEL LINES for piccolo, electronics & instruments
          φ 01(ca)1(bcl)0/0110/2perc(timp.bells.crot.glock.   (Misc 10542
             mba.tamtam.vib.xyl)/hp/vla.vlc   Presser,1979   (& picc

SUBRT, Miroslav

RHAPSODY (St John 8, 1-11: He that is without sin...[Kdo z vás je bez hřichn...])
          φ 2(picc)222+cbsn/3231/timp.perc/str   (Composer)   Misc 7684
STALINGRAD 1943: overture   φ 2+picc.222.2-4bsn-soli/3331/timp.perc/str (Composer)   Misc 7912

SUCHOŃ, Eugen (1908-

METAMORFÓZY: suite (1954)   φ 3(picc)33(bcl)2+cbsn/4331/timp.perc.bells.xyl/
             hp.pf/str   30'   Czech SM,1955   Misc 4794 B
6 PIECES (Šesť Skladieb)(1955/63) φ str   27'   Panton,1967   Misc 7535

SUDESSI, P.

MYTHOLOGIA: scènes de ballet
  1. Les centaures: cortège   3. Ode à l'amour: duetto appassionata
  2. Le pas des muses: valse de ballet   4. Les bacchantes: finale
          PC 2(picc)222/2230/timp.perc/str   Marchetti   10275

SUESSE, Dana (1911-

AND ON WE GO: revue
  Extracts
    The night is young: song
      in Eb, arr J.Beaver   1122/1220/timp.perc/cel.hp.pf/str   (Chappell)   22235 +

SUK, Joseph (1874-1935)

ASRAEL, op.27 see SYMPHONIES, op.27, in C min
CHANSON D'AMOUR, op.7, no.1
  arr H.Geehl   φ 112.2sx.1/2210/timp.perc/str   7'   K.Prowse   15534
  arr H.Geehl   PC 112.2sx.1/2210/timp.perc/str   K.Prowse   1786 C
ÉLÉGIE, op.7, no.5
  arr Eber   PC 1(picc)121/2210/timp.perc/str   Universal   14888
EPILOGUE, op.37, for SBarB soli, chorus & orch (1920-32)
          φ 3+picc.3+ca.3+bcl.3+cbsn/6331/timp.perc/hp/
             str   39' Hudebni Matice,1939 Misc 4786 B
FAIRY-TALE SUITE (Pohádka), op.16
  1. Liebe und Leid der Königskinder (10'45")   3. Intermezzo: Trauermusic   (7'30")
  2. Intermezzo: Volkstanz   (3')   4. Königin Runa's Fluch;Sieg der Liebe (7'45")
          φ 2+picc.2+ca.2+bcl.2/4231/timp.perc/hp/str 30'   Simrock   7584
    Nos 1 & 2 only
        arr Becce   PC 1121/2210/timp.perc/str   Simrock   13921
LEGEND OF DEAD VICTORS (Legenda o mrtvých vítezích), op.35b
          φ 2+picc.2+ca.2+bcl.2+cbsn/6331/timp.perc.tamtam/
             hp/str   Hudebni Matice   Misc 12 C
MEDITATION ON AN OLD BOHEMIAN CHORALE, op.35a
          φ str   7'-8'   Urbanek   6722 Cwe +
MINUET
  arr O.Langey   PC 1121/2210/timp.perc/str   Schirmer   7082
Un POCO TRISTE, op.17, no.3
  arr Becce   PC 1121/2220/timp.perc/str   4'   Simrock   10538 B
PRAGUE: symphonic poem, op.26 φ 3(picc)2+ca.2+bcl.2+cbsn/4331/timp.perc/
             hp.org/str   Czech SM,1953   Misc 4456
SCHERZO FANTASTIQUE, op.25   φ 2+picc.2+ca.2+bcl.2/4231/timp.perc/hp/str 13'15"-15' Breitkopf   9656 B +
SERENADE, op.6, in Eb   φ str   25'   Simrock   2756 Bwe
A SUMMER TALE (Pohádka léta): symphonic poem, op.29
          φ 2+picc.2(ca)+ca.2+bcl.2+cbsn/6331/timp.perc/
             cel.2hp.org.[pf]/str   55'   Universal   Misc 2251
SYMPHONIES
  op.14, in E   φ 2(picc)222/4231/timp/str   36'   Simrock,1900   Misc 3772 B
  op.27, in C min (Asrael) φ 2+picc.2+ca.2+bcl.2+cbsn/4331/timp.perc/
             hp/str   60'-66' (Breitkopf)   20991 +
TOWARDS A NEW LIFE (V nový život): march (with optional chorus), op.35c
          φ 2+picc.222/4331/timp/str   Hudebni Matice   Misc 3994
  arr B.Leopold (without chorus)
          φ 2+picc.232/4331/timp.perc/str   Hudebni Matice   13101
         PC 2+picc.232/4331/timp.perc/str   Hudebni Matice   6857
A WINTER'S TALE: overture after Shakespeare's play, op.9
          φ 2+picc.2+ca.2+bcl.2+cbsn/4231/timp.perc/str   Czech SM,1950   Misc 5234
ZRÁNÍ (Harvest-tide, or Ripening): symphonic poem, op.34
          φ 3(2picc)3(ca)3(bcl)3(cbsn)/6331/timp.perc.bells/
             cel.2hp.pf/str   40'   Hudebni Matice   Misc 825 D

SUK, Vāsa (1861-1933)

The FOREST KING (Lesnoy Tzar): opera
   Polka   φ 2222/4230/timp.perc/[hp]/str   2'30"   Zimmermann   10173

ŠULEK, Stjepan (1914-

CONCERTO for cello & orch   φ 3(picc)22(bcl)2/4331/timp.perc/str   26'   (BBC)   Misc 5525 B
SYMPHONY no.1, in A min   φ 2+picc.2+ca.2+bcl.2+cbsn/4331/timp.perc.tamtam/
                           str   Hrvatsk,1950   Misc 3198

SULLIVAN, Arthur (1842-1900)

The BEAUTY STONE: operetta   {PL 185 & TO
   Complete   2122/2230/perc/str   (Chappell)(H) (382 str on]
   Selection
      arr Godfrey & Moore   PC 1122/2230.euph/timp.perc/str   Chappell   4544 C
   Extracts
      I am Loyse from St. Denis: waltz song (from no.8, Act 1)
        in B (orig)   φ 2122/2220/timp.perc/str   (Chappell)   TO 382 φ on]
      When the rose-leaf lies: song (from no.9, finale act 1)
        in C (orig)   φ 2122/2220/timp.perc/str   (Chappell)   TO 382 φ on]
BUNTHORNE'S BRIDE see PATIENCE
CASTLE ADAMANT see PRINCESS IDA
The CAVES OF CARRIG-CLEENA see The EMERALD ISLE
The CHIEFTAIN: operetta (new version of 'Contrabandista')
   Selection   PC 2(picc)222/2230/timp.perc/str   Boosey   3788 C
   Extracts
      Ah! oui j'étais une pensionaire: duet(Act 2, no.4)
        in Eb (orig)   φ 2121/2000/perc/str   (Boosey & H)   TO 382 φ on]
      From rock to rock: song (Act 1, no.8)
        in Eb   φ 1+picc.122/20.2cnt.30/str   [BBC]   TO 382 str o
      Let us lead a life of pleasure (from finale act 1)
        in Bb (orig)   φ 2122/2220/perc/str   2'55"   (Boosey & H)   TO 382 φ on]
The CHORISTER: song
   in F, arr H.M.Higgs   1121/2230.euph/timp/hp/str   Metzler   17954
COX AND BOX, or The Long Lost Brothers: operetta
   Complete (without overture) φ 2121/2220/perc/str   55'   [BBC]   TO 1161
   Overture
      arr N.Richardson   φ 2(picc)121/2220/timp.perc/str   2'10"-2'50"
                                                        Boosey & H,1966 24496
   Extracts
      The Buttercup dwells on the lonely mead: duet for Tenor & Baritone (no.7)
        in Bb (orig)   1121/2000/str   (Chappell)   23926 φ TO
        in Bb   1121/2000/str   (Boosey & H) TO 382 φ on]
      Finale - complete (not shortened for show)
                      1121/2220/perc/str   [BBC]   TO 1161 +
      Hush'd is the bacon on the grid: lullaby for Tenor & orch (no.4)
        in F (orig)   0021/2000/str   (Boosey & H) TO 382 φ on]
        in F#   0021/2000/str   (Chappell)   TO 1161
DAY DREAMS (from Piano suite, op.14)
   arr H.Finck   φ 2(picc)121/2230/timp.perc/str 5'30"-8' Boosey & H   13616
   arr H.Finck   PC 2(picc)121/2230/timp.perc/str   Boosey & H   12168 B
DI BALLO: overture   φ 2(picc)222/4231/timp.perc/str   9'30"   Novello   2154 Cmv Dni
DOMINE SALVAM FAC REGINAM see TE DEUM LAUDAMUS and DOMINE FAC SALVAM FAC REGINAM
The EMERALD ISLE, or The Caves of Carrig-Cleena: operetta (unfinished; completed Edward German)
   Complete   φ 2122/2230/perc/str   Chappell(H)   PL 201
      concert version   2122/2230/perc/str   Chappell(H)   PL 269

SULLIVAN, Arthur (cont)

The EMERALD ISLE (cont)
   Selections   PC 1(picc)122/2230.euph/timp.perc/str   Chappell   2392 Cwe

Selections	PC	1(picc)122/2230.euph/timp.perc/str		Chappell	2392 Cwe
arr C.Godfrey	φ	2(picc)122/2230.euph/timp.perc/str		Chappell	16443

   Excerpts
      Chorus & dance of Peasants, in F (orig)
      Come away, sighs the fairy voice, in G (orig)(2'50")
      Goodbye my native town, in Ab (orig)(2'30")
      Jig
      Now this is the song of the Devonshire men, in D (orig)(2'45")
      Oh setting sun: song, in E (orig)
      On the heights of Glantaun: trio, in G (orig)(2'30")
                         φ   2122/2000/perc/str   (Chappell)   TO 1803
   Extracts
      Oh setting sun: song (No.10, act 1)
         in F   2022/2000/str   (Chappell)   18198

The FLOWERS OF PROGRESS   see   UTOPIA LIMITED

The GOLDEN LEGEND: cantata   φ   2+picc.2+ca.2+bcl.2+cbsn/42.2cnt.31/timp.bells/
                                   str   105'   Novello   Misc 792 B

The GONDOLIERS, or The King of Barataria: operetta

Complete	PS	2(picc)222/4230/timp.perc/str	126'	(Chappell)(H)	PL 287 B
Overture		2122/20.2cnt.30/str		(Chappell)	25869
	φ	2122/2230/timp.perc/str		[BBC]	8889 B
Selections	φ	2(picc)222/2220/timp.perc/str/chorus		[BBC]	TO 738 φ only
arr A.Cruikshank	PC	2+picc.12.3sx.1/2230/timp.perc/hp/str	9'20"	Chappell,1950	19836 Cp
arr Godfrey	PC	2(picc)222/2230.euph/timp.perc/str	13'30"	Chappell	87 Cni D
arr R.Hanmer	PC	212.4sx.1/2230/timp.perc/acdn.hp/str	7'30"	Paxton,1950	23006 Bs
arr V.Hely-Hutchinson	φ	2222/2230/timp.perc/str	14'30"	[BBC]	14968 B

   Extracts
      Dance a Cachucha: chorus & dance (Act 2, no.5)
                       φ   2(picc)222/4331/timp.perc/str   [BBC]   TO 738
      Fanfare from finale Act 2 PC 0000/0230/perc   [BBC]   TO 738
      For the merriest fellows are we, for Baritone solo, chorus & orch (from act 1, no.1)
         in G (orig)   1+picc.122/20.2cnt30/perc/str   (Chappell)   25870 (φ TO 738)
      From the sunny Spanish shore: quartet for SATBar soli & orch (Act 1, no.2)
         in C (orig)   φ   2122/20.2cnt.00/perc/str   (Chappell)   25871
      Gavotte   see   I am a courtier
      I am a courtier, for SAT.2Bar soli & orch (Act 2, no.11)
         in D (orig)   φ   2122/2200/str   [BBC]   TO 738
         arr Czibulka (op.36)   PC 2(picc)122/2230/timp.perc/str   2'18"   Bosworth   8647
      In a contemplative fashion: quartet for SSTBar soli & orch (Act 2, no.7)
         in Eb (orig)   φ   0022/0000/str   (Chappell)   25872
      In enterprise of martial kind: song for Baritone solo & orch (Act 1, no.3)
         in C (orig)   φ   2122/2000/perc/str   (Chappell,1965)   24332 (φ TO 738)
      I stole the Prince: song (Act 1, no.6)
         in Eb (orig)   φ   1+picc.122/2000/str   Chappell   25939
      Kind sir, you cannot have the heart: song for Soprano solo & orch (from finale act 1)
         in Bb (orig)   2122/2000/str   (Chappell)   23687 +
         in Bb   2122/20.2cnt.30/perc/str   (Chappell)   25873
      List and learn, for chorus & orch (from act 1, no.1)
         in D (orig)   φ   2122/2230/timp.perc/str   [BBC]   26524
      O rapture, when alone together: duet for Soprano & Tenor soli & orch (Act 1, no.4)
                       φ   2122/2240/timp/str   [BBC]   26516
      On the day when I was wedded: song for Contralto solo & orch (Act 2, no.9)
         in F   φVS 2(picc)122/20.2cnt.30/timp/str   (Chappell)   24008 +

SULLIVAN, Arthur (cont)

The GONDOLIERS (cont)
   Extracts (cont)
      Once more gondolieri: chorus (from finale act 2)
        in F (orig)   PC 2122/2230/timp.perc/str   (Chappell)   26101
      Regular Royal Queen see Then one of us will be a queen
      See, see, at last they come to make their choice: link between 'For the merriest fellows are
          we' & 'We're called Gondolieri' (from act 1, no.1)
                        2122/2230/perc/str   (Chappell)   26601 **
      Small titles and orders: duet for Contralto & Baritone soli & orch (Act 2, no.10)
        in Ab (orig)   φ 2122/2000/str   (Chappell)   26335
      Thank you gallant gondolieri (from finale act 1)
        in D (orig)   2(picc)122/2230/timp.perc/str   (Chappell)   26611 B
      Then one of us will be a queen: quartet for SMzTBar soli & orch (from finale act 1)
        in F (orig)   2122/20.2cnt.30/perc/str   (Chappell)   25873
      There lived a King: song for T.2Bar soli & orch (Act 2, no.6)
        in C (orig)   φ 2122/2000/str   (Chappell)   23942 +
      There was a time: duet for Soprano & Tenor soli & orch (Act 1, no.5)
        in F# (orig)   φ 2122/2000/str   (Chappell)   25938
                              φ 2122/2400/str   [BBC]   26516
      We're called Gondolieri: duet for Tenor & Baritone soli & orch (from act 1, no.1)
        in F (orig)   2122/2230/perc/str   (Chappell)   23941 +
      When a merry maiden marries: song for Mezzo-soprano solo, chorus & orch (Act 1, no.9)
        in F (orig)   2(picc)122/2000/str   (Chappell)   24007 +
      When alone together see O Rapture, when alone together
      With ducal pomp, for chorus & orch (Act 2, no.8)
        in Bb (orig)   2122/20.2cnt.30/perc/str   (Chappell)   26737
The GRAND DUKE, or The Statutory Duel: operetta
   Complete
      ed S.Robinson (nos.21 & 28a orch S.Robinson), with additional parts for the overture
                    φ 2122/20.2cnt.30/timp.perc.bells/str   97'   (Chappell)   24593 +
   Selections
      arr C.Godfrey   PC 2(picc)122/2230.euph/timp.perc/str   Chappell   9782
   Extracts
      Take my advice: song for Tenor solo, chorus & orch (no.27, act 3)
        in E (orig Db), orch S.Robinson
                    φ 2(picc)122/2230/timp.perc.glock/str   (Chappell)   25494
HADDON HALL: operetta
   Selections
      arr C.Godfrey   PC 2(picc)222/2230.euph/timp.perc/str   Chappell   444 B
   Extracts
      Red of the rosebud: song (Act 1, no.8a)
      Why weep and wail: recit
                    φ 2121/2000/str   [BBC]   TO 382 **
      Today it is a festal time: chorus (Act 1, no.1)
        in F (orig)   φ 2122/2000/str   [BBC]   TO 382 **
      When the budding bloom: madrigal (Act 1, no.1b)
        in G (orig)   φ 2122/2000/str   [BBC]   TO 382 **
      Ye stately homes of England: chorus (from introduction)
        in G (orig)   φ 2122/2000/str   [BBC]   TO 382 **
HENRY VIII (Youth will needs have Dalliance): incidental music
   Suite for solo, chorus & orch
      1. March   3. Graceful dance
      2. King Henry's song   4. Water Music
                    φ 2(picc)222/4231/timp.perc/str   18'   Metzler   2609 Bs Fn

SULLIVAN, Arthur (cont)

HENRY VIII (cont)
   Extracts

Graceful dance	φ	2(picc)222/4200/perc/str	4'-45"	Metzler	10273 B
King Henry's song					
in Eb		2021/0000/str/mv-chorus (arr C.Groves)		(Metzler)	MS 7436
Orpheus with his lute: song					
in Bb & Ab	φ	1022/2000/str	3'15"-4'	(Siddell)	17471
in Bb, arr R.Chignell	φ	1121/2220/timp/hp/str		[BBC]	MS 5418

H.M.S.PINAFORE, or The Lass that loved a Sailor: operetta

Complete	PS	2(picc)222/4230/timp.perc/str	52'-70'	(Chappell)(H)	PL 290
ed J.Bauser	φ	2(picc)121/20.2cnt.20/timp.perc/str		Kalmus,1978	Misc 9887
ed S.Robinson, without overture					
	φ	2121/2220/timp.perc/str		(Chappell)	Misc 10106
Overture					
orig version	φ	2(picc)121/20.2cnt.20/timp.perc/str	4'30"	Musicprint,1981	Misc 10514
Selections	PC	1121/2230/timp/str	7'45"	Metzler	23
arr Cruikshank	PC	2+picc.12.3sx.1/2230/timp.perc/hp/str		Chappell,1950	19984
arr R.Hanmer	PC	2(picc)12.4sx.1/2230/timp.perc/acdn.hp/str		Paxton,1951	23903 As
arr V.Hely-Hutchinson	φ	2(picc)121/2220/timp.perc/str	9'30"	(Chappell)	11313 & mf 161
arr Jacobi	PC	2222/4230.euph/perc/str	8'30"	Hawkes	805
arr S.Robinson (vocal medley)					
	φ	2(picc)222/4330/timp.perc/str		[BBC]	TO 622 +
arr Urich	PC	1+picc.222/2230.euph/timp.perc/str		Lafleur	359

   see also   COOTE, C: LANCERS: selection

Extracts

A maiden fair to see: aria for Tenor solo, mv-chorus & orch, in C (No.3, act 1)
The nightingale: scena for Contralto & Tenor soli, mv-chorus & orch, in Ab

	2121/2000/str	(Chappell)	26024

A simple sailor see The hours creep on apace
Carefully on tiptoe stealing: chorus

in G		2222/4230/timp.perc/str	(Chappell)	23845 +

Fair moon, to thee I sing: song for Baritone solo & orch (No.13, act 2)

in D (orig)		2122/2000/str	(Chappell)	26734 +
in C		2122/2000/str	(Chappell)	26733

Farewell my own: octet & chorus (No.19, act 2)

	2121/20.2cnt.20/timp.perc/str	Chappell	26023

The Hours creep on apace: aria for Soprano solo & orch (No.15, act 2)

in G min (orig)		2122/2000/str	(Chappell)	26736
		2121/2000/timp/str	(Chappell)	24949

I am the captain of the Pinafore, for Baritone solo, mv chorus & orch (No.4, act 1)
My gallant crew good morning: recit

in A (orig)	φ	2122/20.2cnt.20/timp/str	Chappell	25944

I'm called little Buttercup: song for Contralto solo & orch (No.2, act 1)
Hail, men-o-wars men: recit

in C (orig)	2122/2000/str	Chappell	25945

Let's give three cheers for the sailor's bride (from finale act 1)

in Eb (orig)	φ	1+picc.122/20.2cnt.20/perc/str	Chappell	25943

My gallant crew, good morning see I am the captain of the Pinafore
Never mind the why and wherefore: trio for Soprano & Baritone soli & orch (No.16, act 1)

in E (orig)	φ	2121/2000/perc/str	(Chappell)	25370 +

The Nightingale see A maiden fair to see
Refrain, audacious Tar: duet for Soprano & Tenor soli & orch (No.11, act 1)

in F min (orig)	2121/2000/str	(Chappell)	23693 +

Things are seldom what they seem: duet for Contralto & Baritone soli & orch (No.14, act 1)

in D (orig)	2122/2000/perc/str	(Chappell)	26735

SULLIVAN, Arthur (cont)

H.M.S.PINAFORE (cont)
  Extracts (cont)
    We sail the ocean blue: chorus (No.1, act 1)
      in C   2122/20.2cnt.20/timp/str   (Chappell)   25946
    When I was a lad: song for Baritone solo, chorus & orch (No.9, act 1)
      in Bb (orig)   2121/2220/perc/str   (Chappell)   23785

I WOULD I WERE A KING: song
  in D, arr R.Chignell   ø 1111/0110/timp/str   (Boosey)   MS 5104
  in D, arr F.Cramer   pf/str   (Boosey)   LM G 4835

IF DOUGHTY DEEDS MY LADY PLEASE: song
  in Eb, arr H.Carr   ø 2122/2230/perc/hp/str   2'   (Chappell)   TO 741

L'ÎLE ENCHANTÉE: ballet
  Complete   2222/4231/timp.perc/hp/str   7'   (Covent Gdn) 19939

IMPERIAL MARCH   ø 2+picc.22+bcl.2/4432/timp.perc/hp/str 3'40"-6'25" Chappell   8888

IN MEMORIAM: overture, in C ø 2222/4230.oph/timp.perc/org/str 10'-12'   Novello   2153 E

IOLANTHE, or The Peer and the Peri: operetta
  Complete   PS 2(picc)222/4230/timp.perc/str   118'   (Chappell)(H) PL 280
    arr S.Robinson, without overture
                    ø 2121/2220/timp.perc/str   (Chappell)   Misc 10107
  Overture
    arr Cruikshank   PC 2121/2220/timp.perc/str   7'-10'   Chappell   20072 Cni Dwa
    additional wind parts, arr S.Robinson
                    ø 2(picc)121/4321/timp.perc/str   [BBC]   8800 C +
  Selections   PC 1(picc)222/2230/timp.perc/str   Chappell   149 Dwa
    arr Cruikshank   PC 2+picc.12.3sx.1/2230/timp.perc/hp/str 8'45" Chappell,1950 19834 Cn
    arr V.Hely-Hutchinson (from act 1)
                    ø 2121/2220/timp.perc/str   12'30"   [BBC]   5913 B
    arr V.Hely-Hutchinson (from act 2), for piccolo, flute & trombone soli & orch
                  PC 1+picc.121/2220/timp.perc/hp/str 12'   [BBC]   7199 B
    arr Rivière   1121/0210/perc/pf/str   [BBC]   TO 761-2 +
  Extracts
    Entrance & march of the Peers see Loudly let the trumpets bray
    Good-morrow, good mother: song (Act 1, no.3)
      in D   ø 2120/0000/str   (Chappell)   23966 +
    If we're weak enough to tarry: duet for Soprano & Tenor soli & orch (Act 2, no.9)
                    ø 2121/20.2cnt.20/perc/str   [BBC]   26522
    In Good Queen Bess's glorious day see When Britain really ruled the waves
    Loudly let the trumpets bray (Entrance & march of the Peers): chorus (Act 1, no.6)
                  PC 2(picc)121/20.2cnt.20/perc/str   (Chappell)   26333 B
                  ø 2+picc.222/4331/timp/str   [BBC]   TO 761
    Love unrequited robs me of my rest see When you're lying awake
    Nightmare song see When you're lying awake
    None shall part us from each other: duet for Soprano & Tenor soli & orch (Act 1, no.5)
      in G (orig)   ø 2121/2000/str   [BBC]   26520
                      2121/2000/str   (Chappell)   25368 +
    O foolish Fay: song for Contralto solo, fv-chorus & orch
      in Db (orig)   PC 2121/2220/timp.perc/str   [BBC]   TO 761 **
    Soon as we may (finale act 2)
                  ø 2121/2220/timp.perc/str   [BBC]   26521
    Song of the Sentry see When all night long
    Spurn not the nobly born (Blue blood): song for Tenor solo, mv-chorus & orch (Act 1, no.10)
      in Eb (orig)   2122/20.2cnt.20/str   (Chappell)   26739
    When all night long a chap remains: song for Bass solo & orch
      in Bb (orig)   øPC 2121/2220/timp/str   [BBC]   TO 761 **

SULLIVAN, Arthur (cont)

IOLANTHE (cont)
   Extracts
      When Britain really ruled the waves: song for Baritone solo, chorus & orch (Act 2, no.3)

in A (orig)		2121/20.2cnt.20/timp/str		[BBC]	26452
in G	φ	2121/2220/timp/str		[BBC]	TO 761 +
in G		2121/2220/timp/str		(Chappell)	26334

      When you're lying awake (Nightmare song), for Baritone solo & orch (Act 2, no.7)
      Love unrequired robs me of my rest: recit

φ	2(picc)121/2000/timp/str	[BBC]	26515

IVANHOE: opera
   Complete   φ 2+picc.2+ca.2+bcl.2/4231/timp.perc/hp/str   Chappell   Misc 789-791
      with cuts & marking by P.Pitt
             φ 2+picc.22+bcl.2/4231/timp/hp/str   Chappell   Misc 938

   Selections
      arr D.Godfrey   PC 2+picc.22+bcl.2/42.2cnt.31.euph/timp.perc/hp/
                   str   Chappell   398 B

   Extracts
      Drink, drink ye all

in A min (orig)	φ	2(picc)122/2230/str		[BBC]	TO 382 ** ww

      Her southern splendour: aria
      Woo thou thy snowflake: recit

in Gb (orig)	φ	21+ca.22/4231/timp/hp/str	(Siddell)	Misc 3597
in Gb, arr F.Cramer		pf/str	(Chappell)	LM G 4262

      Ho, jolly Jenkins: song

in F (orig) & D	2222/4031/timp/str	2'45"	(Chappell)	TO 287
in F & D, arr G.Stacey	pf/str		(Chappell)	LM G 3757

      Lord of our chosen race (Rebecca's prayer): song for Soprano solo & orch

in Ab (orig)	φ	20.ca.22/4000/hp/str	4'40"	(Siddell)	26191 +
in F		1110/0000/timp/str		(Siddell)	18321

The KING OF BARATARIA   see   The GONDOLIERS
The LASS THAT LOVED A SAILOR   see   H.M.S.PINAFORE
LET ME DREAM AGAIN: song
   in Eb   φ 1222/4000/str   (Siddell)   17875
A LIFE THAT LIVES FOR YOU: song
   in D   2222/2230/str   (Siddell)   17873
The LIGHT OF THE WORLD: oratorio
   Extracts
      Elegy
         arr Hickling   PC 1022/2210/timp/org/str   Cramer   4693
      Refrain thy voice from weeping: air
         in Ab (orig)   2122/4000/str   (Siddell)   17870
The LONG LOST BROTHERS   see   COX AND BOX
The LOST CHORD: song

in F & Eb	φ	2222/4130.oph/str	(Siddell)	17010
in F, arr H.Carr	φ	3222/4231/perc/hp.org/str/chorus	[BBC]	TO 1716
in F, arr Marriott	PC	2222/2230.euph/timp/str	Boosey	10707
in F, arr Marriott	PC	2222/2230.euph/timp/str	Boosey	3644 C
in F, G & Ab, arr S.Robinson	φ	2122/2230/timp/hp/str	(Boosey)	TO 698 +
in F, Eb & Bb, arr G.Stacey		pf/str	(Boosey)	LM G 3486

   in Ab, arr J.Turner for chorus & orch

φ	1110/1000/hp/str	(Boosey)	LM G 9442

   arr F.Mahl for cornet solo & orch

PC	1121/2210/str	Boosey	1981

SULLIVAN, Arthur (cont)

LOVE LAID HIS SLEEPLESS HEAD: song
    in G, arr R.Chignell   φ 1121/2220/timp/str   (Boosey)   MS 5126
MACBETH: incidental music
    Complete   φ 2(2picc)222/4231/timp.perc/hp/str   (Chappell)(H)   PL 403
    Overture   φ 2222/4231/timp.perc/hp/str   6'15"-8'15"   Chappell   Misc 762 D (
The MARTYR OF ANTIOCH: sacred music drama   copy in PL
    Extracts
        Come, Margarita, come: aria
           in Bb (orig)   2222/2000/str   (Siddell)   17871
MEMORIES OF SIR ARTHUR SULLIVAN, arr C.W.Bennet see   BENNET, C.W: MEMORIES OF SIR ARTHUR SULLIVAN
The MERCHANT OF VENICE: incidental music
    1. Introduction   5. Valse (4'30")
    2. Barcarolle (Serenade)   6. Melodrama
    3. Introduction & bourée   7. Finale
    4. Danse grotesque

                        φ 2(picc)222/4230/timp.perc/str   Bosworth   3850 Dwa Es G
        arr V.Nemeti   PC 1(picc)110/0110/timp.perc/str   12'   Bosworth   969 B
The MERRY MAN AND HIS MAID see   The YEOMAN OF THE GUARD
The MIKADO, or The Town of Titipu: operetta
    Complete   PS 2(picc)222/4230/timp.perc/str   90'-130'   (Chappell)(H)   PL 281
                        φ 2(picc)121/20.2cnt.20/timp.perc/str   [Chappell]/Kalmus 26714
                        φ 2(picc)121/20.2cnt.20/timp.perc/str   [BBC]   Misc 73
       Facsimile of autograph in R.A.M.London
                        φ 2(picc)121/20.2cnt.20/timp.perc/str   Gregg,1968   MRL facs
    Overture
        arr Cruikshank   PC 2121/2220/timp.perc/str   7'-10'   Chappell,1950 19880 Cp Dwa
        arr S.Robinson   φ 2121/2220/timp.perc/str   [BBC]   8799
    Selections
        arr Cruikshank   PC 2+picc.21.3sx.1/2230/timp.perc/str   9'30"   Chappell,1950 19835 Cp
        arr V.Hely-Hutchinson (from act 1) for flute & trombone soli & orch
                        φ 1+picc.121/2220/timp.perc/str   26'15"   [BBC]   10709 B
        arr V.Hely-Hutchinson (from act 2) for flute & trombone soli & orch
                        φ 2+picc.2+ca.22/2220/timp.perc/str   [BBC]   1059 B
        arr G.Williams   PC 1+picc.222/2230.euph/timp.perc/str   Chappell   4495 Dni
        arr Winterbottom   PC 2(picc)222/4230.euph/perc/str 14'45"-15'30"   Chappell   89 C
    Extracts
        Alone and yet alive: recit & scena for Contralto solo & orch (Act 2, no.10)
          in Db   2121/2220/str   (Chappell)   25893
        And I have journeyed for a month: recit for Tenor & Baritone soli & orch (Act 1, no.4a)
                        2121/20.2cnt.20/str   Chappell   25942
        As someday it may happen: song for Tenor solo, chorus & orch (Act 1, no.5a)
          in Eb   2121/2000/str   Chappell   25941
        Behold the Lord High Executioner, for Tenor solo, chorus & orch (Act 1, no.5)
          in Eb (orig)   φ 2121/20.2cnt.20/perc/str   2'30"   (Chappell)   25263 +
        Brightly dawns our wedding day: madrigal for SATBar soli & orch (Act 2, no.3)
          in F (orig)   0121/0000/str   (Chappell)   25177 +
        The Criminal cried: trio for Soprano & 2 Baritone soli & orch
          in E (orig)   2121/2220/perc/str   (Chappell)   26122 +
        Entrance of the Mikado see Mi-ya-sa-ma
        The flowers that bloom in the Spring: duet for 2 Tenors with SABar soli as chorus (Act 2, no.9)
          in A   2021/2220/perc/str   (Chappell)   25895
        For he's gone and married Yum-Yum: finale to act 2
          in Eb (orig)   2121/2220/perc/str   (Chappell)   25896
        Here's a how-de-do!: trio for STT soli & orch (Act 2, no.4)
          in E (orig)   2121/2000/str   (Chappell)   25367 +

SULLIVAN, Arthur (cont)

The MIKADO (cont)
  Extracts (cont)
    I am so proud: trio for Tenor & 2 Baritone soli & orch (Act 1, no.10)
       in B (orig)   2121/2220/timp/str   (Chappell)   26121 +
    If you want to know who we are: chorus for mv-chorus & orch (Act 1, no.1)
       in C (orig)   1+picc.121/2220/timp/str   (Chappell)   23808 +
    Mikado's song see A More humane Mikado never did in Japan exist
    Mi-ya-sa-ma, mi-ya-sa-ma: duet for Contralto & Bass soli, chorus & orch (Act 2, no.5)
       in C (orig)   2121/2000/perc/str   Chappell   25940 +
    A More humane Mikado never did in Japan exist (Mikado's song) for Bass solo, chorus &
       orch (Act 2, no.6)
       in A (orig)   2121/2220/perc/str   (Chappell)   23901 +
    On a tree by a river: song for Tenor solo & orch (Act 2, no.11)
       in Ab (orig)   ∅   1+picc.121/2000/str   (Kalmus)   23578 +
    See how the Fates their gifts alot: glee for SA2BarB soli & orch (Act 2, no.8)
       in F (orig)   str   (Chappell)   25894
    So please you sir, we much regret: quartet for SMzABar soli, fv-chorus & orch (Act 1, no.8)
       in G (orig)   2121/2000/perc/str   (Chappell)   26120 +
    The Sun whose rays are all ablaze: song for Soprano solo & orch (Act 2, no.2)
       in G (orig)   1110/0000/str   (Chappell)   23656 B +
    There is beauty in the bellow of the blast: duet for Contralto & Tenor soli & orch (Act 2, no.12)
          (also includes fanfare, no.21a)
       in Eb   2121/2220/perc/str   (Chappell)   26123 +
    Tit Willow see On a tree by a river
    Three little maids from school are we: trio for SMzA soli, fv-chorus & orch (Act 1, no.7)
       in C (orig)   2121/20.2cnt.00/perc/str   (Chappell)   25264 +
    A Wand'ring minstrel I: aria for Tenor solo, mv-chorus & orch (Act 1, no.2)
       in F (orig)   ∅   2121/20.2cnt.20/timp/str   (Chappell)   23695 Bs +
    Were you not to Koko plighted: duet for Soprano & Tenor soli & orch (Act 1, no.9)
       in F (orig)   2121/2000/str   (Chappell)   23686 +
    Your revels cease!: extracts from finale act 1, for Contralto solo, chorus & orch (commences
          bar 167)
                                2121/2220/timp.perc/str   (Chappell)   26124 +
MY DEAREST HEART: song
    in Bb   ∅   2222/4000/str   3'30"   (Siddell)   17071 B
    in G, arr D.Darlow   ∅   3222/3230/hp/str   (Boosey)   19715
ON SHORE AND SEA: cantata   2(picc)222/4231/timp.perc/str   Boosey   10421
ONCE AGAIN: song
    in F#   2222/4330/timp/hp/str   (Siddell)   17874
    in F   ∅   1121/2210/perc/str   (Boosey)   MS 5413
ONWARD CHRISTIAN SOLDIERS: hymn (St. Gertrude)
    arr D.Godfrey   PC   2222/4230/timp.perc/str   Chappell   2867
    arr M.L.Lake   PC   1+picc.12.2sx.1/2210/perc/str   C.Fischer   19720
    arr H.Perry   PC   1121/0000/timp.perc/org/str   Hawkes   4970
ORPHEUS WITH HIS LUTE see HENRY VIII
OVERTURE in C see IN MEMORIAM
PATIENCE, or Bunthorne's Bride: operetta
    Complete   PS   2121/2220/timp/str   76'-125' (Chappell)(H) PL 282
      arr S.Robinson, without overture
                           ∅   2121/2220/timp/str   (Chappell)   Misc 10108
    Overture   ∅   2(picc)121/2220/timp.perc/str   4'40"-5'55" [BBC]   8802 B
    Selections
      arr R.Binding   PC   1(picc)222/2230.euph/timp.perc/str 17'30" Hawkes   441 Ap Cni
      arr Cruikshank   PC   212.3sx.1/2230/timp.perc/hp/str   8'30"   Chappell   19807 Cp
      arr V.Hely-Hutchinson ∅   2122/2220/timp.perc/str   13'30"   [BBC]   6909 + & mf 161

<u>SULLIVAN, Arthur</u> (cont)

PATIENCE (cont)
   Extracts

     After much debate: song & chorus (Act 2, no.11 - finale)
       in Eb   2(picc)121/2220/timp.perc/str   (Chappell)   25848
     I cannot tell what this love may be: aria for Soprano solo & orch (Act 1, no.2)
     Still brooding: recit
       in Eb   2121/2000/str   (Chappell)   24038 +
     If Saphir I choose: quintet (Act 2, no.8)
       in Eb   2(picc)121/2000/perc/str   (Chappell)   25850
     If you're anxious for to shine: song for Baritone solo & orch, in D
     Am I alone: recit in G min (Act, no.6)
                         2(picc)121/2220/timp/str   (Chappell)   25947
     It's clear that mediaeval art: trio for TBarB soli & orch (Act 2, no.7)
       in C   0021/0000/str   (Chappell)   25849 +
     Love is a plaintive song: song for Soprano solo & orch (Act 2, no.5)
       in A   2121/2000/str   (Chappell)   23685 +
     The Magnet and the churn <u>see</u> A Magnet hung in a hardware shop
     A Magnet hung in a hardware shop: song for Baritone solo, fv-chorus & orch (Act 2, no.4)
       in Ab   2121/2220/perc/str   (Chappell)   26336
     Prithee, pretty maiden: duet for Soprano & Baritone soli & orch (Act 1, no.8)
       in A   2020/0000/str   (Chappell)   23692
     Silvered is the raven hair: aria for Contralto solo & orch (Act 2, no.2)
     Sad is the woman's lot: recit
       in Eb   2121/2000/str   (Chappell)   24038 +
     When I go out of doors: duet for 2 Baritones & orch (Act 2, no.9)
       in G   str   1'20"   (Chappell)   23937 +

The PEER AND THE PERI <u>see</u> IOLANTHE

PINEAPPLE POLL: ballet suite, arr form the music of Sullivan by C.Mackerras
   Suite
     1. Opening number (3'35")   5. Jasper's dance (2'25")
     2. Poll's dance (1'15")   6. Belaye's hornpipe (1'30")
     3. Captain Belaye's dance (1'50")   7. Reconciliation of Poll and Jaspar (1'35")
     4. Pas de troi (1'40")   8. Finale (2'35")

                 ϕ 2+picc.2+ca.22/4231/timp.perc/hp/str   16'10"-22'35"
                                                      Chappell,1951   20791
               PC 2+picc.2+ca.22/4231/timp.perc/hp/str   Chappell   20390 Cp D
               ϕ 3(2picc)2+ca.2+bcl.2+cbsn/4331/timp.perc.glock.
                   tamtam.xyl/cel.hp/str   (Chappell)   24160 + & mf
      Montage, arr C.Mackerras for 'The Gilbert & Sullivan Story'
                    2+picc.222/4231/timp.perc/hp/str   (BBC,1955)   21993 +

The PIRATES OF PENZANCE, or The Slave of Duty: operetta
   Complete   PS 2121/2220/timp.perc/str   89'40"   (Chappell)(H)   PL 279
     arr S.Robinson, without overture (incomplete score)
               ϕ 2121/2220/timp.perc/str   (Chappell)   Misc 10109
   Overture
     orig version   ϕ 2(picc)121/20.2cnt.20/timp.perc/str   8'   Musicprint,1981 Misc 10515
                  ϕ 2(picc)121/2220/timp.perc/str   [BBC]   8803 B +
   Selection
     arr Cruikshank   PC 212.3sx.1/2230/timp.perc/hp/str   9'   Chappell   19806
     arr V.Hely-Hutchinson ϕ 2(picc)121/2220/timp.perc/str   10'-12'15" (Chappell)   11053 B +
     arr Hiller   PC 1+picc.121/2210/timp.perc/str   Chappell   151 Cni D
   Extracts
     Ah leave me not to live alone <u>see</u> Stay, Frederic, Stay
     Climbing over rocky mountains, for fv-chorus & orch (Act 1, no.5)
       in Bb (orig)   2121/20.2cnt.20/perc/str   (Chappell)   25178 +

SULLIVAN, Arthur (cont)

PIRATES OF PENZANCE (cont)
  Extracts
    I am the very model of a modern Major General: song for Baritone solo, chorus & orch (Act 1, no.13)
      in Eb (orig)   ø 2121/2220/timp/str   (Chappell)   TO 890
    O here is love   see   Stay, Frederic, Stay!
    Oh is there not one maiden: song for Tenor solo, fv-chorus & orch (Act 1, no.7)
        (for recit see Stop, Ladies, pray)
      in Db (orig)   2121/2000/str   (Chappell)   25948
    The Policeman's song   see   When a felon's not engaged
    Poor wand'ring one: aria for Soprano solo, fv-chorus & orch (Act 1, no.8)
      in Ab (orig)   ø 1+picc.121/2210/timp.perc/str   3'   (Siddell)   17953
                     2(picc)121/20.2cnt.20/perc/str   Chappell   25949
      reprise (finale act 2)   2(picc)121/22.cnt.20/perc/str   (Chappell)   23988 +
    Pour, oh pour the pirate sherry, for Baritone solo, mv-chorus & orch (Act 1, no.1)
      in Eb (orig)   2121/2000/timp.perc/str   Chappell   25947
    A Rollicking band of pirates we: aria for Bass solo, mv-chorus & orch (Act 2, no.11)
                     2121/20.2cnt.20/timp.perc/str   (Chappell)   24586 +
    Sighing softly to the river: song for Baritone solo, mv-chorus & orch (Act 2, no.14)
    Hush, hush. Not a word: recit (Act 2, no.13)
                     2(picc)121/2000/str   (Chappell)   26602
    Stay, Frederic, Stay!: duet for Soprano & Tenor soli & orch (Act 2, no.8
        (includes 'Ah leave me not alone' and 'O here is love')
      in Bb (orig)   2121/2000/str   (Chappell)   23688 +
    Stop, ladies, pray: recit for Tenor solo, fv-chorus & orch (Act 1, no.6)
        (for aria   see   Oh is there not one maiden)
                     1+picc.121/2000/str   (Chappell)   26610
    When a felon's not engaged in his employment: song for Bass solo, mv-chorus & orch (Act 2, no.10)
      in F (orig)   ø str   (Chappell)   TO 890
    When the foeman bares his steel: song for Soprano & Bass soli, chorus & orch (Act 2, no.3)
      in C (orig)   2121/20.2cnt.20/perc/str   Chappell   25969
    With cat-like tread: aria for Baritone solo, mv-chorus & orch (Act 2, no.11)
      in D (orig)   2121/20.2cnt.20/timp.perc/str   (Chappell)   24586 +
PRINCESS IDA, or Castle Adamant: operetta
  Complete   PS 2121/2220/timp.perc/str   80'20"   (Chappell)   PL 283
    arr S.Robinson, without overture
                    ø 2121/2220/timp.perc/str   (Chappell)   Misc 10110
  Overture   PC 2121/2220/timp.perc/str   (Chappell)   25900 +
  Selections
    arr V.Hely-Hutchinson (no.1)
                    ø 2121/2220/perc/str   10'   (BBC)   10716 + & mf 161
    arr V.Hely-Hutchinson (no.2)
                    ø 2121/2220/perc/str   (BBC)   18639 & mf 161
    arr Riviere   PC 2222/2230.euph/timp.perc/str   18'30"   Hawkes   3158
  Extracts
    And thus to Empyrean height, for chorus & orch (No.10, act 2)
      in Bb   VS 2121/2220/timp/str   (Chappell)   25897 +
    Gently, gently: trio for TTBar soli & orch (No.12, act 2)
                   VS 2(picc)121/2220/timp.perc/str   (Chappell)   25742
    I am a maiden: trio for TTBar soli & orch (No.13, act 2)
                   VS 2(picc)121/2220/timp.perc/str   (Chappell)   25742
    Ida was a twelve month old: song for Tenor solo & orch (No.3, act 1)
    Today we meet: recit
                     2121/2000/str   (Chappell)   23690 B +
                   VS 2121/2000/str   (Chappell)   25898 +
    Mighty maiden with a mission, for chorus & orch (No.9, act 2)
                   VS 2121/2220/timp/str   (Chappell)   25897 +

SULLIVAN, Arthur (cont)

PRINCESS IDA (cont)
  Extracts (cont)
    O Goddess wise: aria for Soprano solo & orch (No.10, act 2)
    Minerva: recit

	VS	2121/2220/timp/str	2'45"	(Chappell)	25897 +

    Oh joy! Our chief is saved: ensemble (finale act 2)

in Eb	VS	2121/2220/timp.perc/str		(Chappell)	25901 +

    If you give me your attention: song (No.6, act 1)

in Eb	VS	2121/2000/str	2'15"	(Chappell)	25899 +

    A Lady fair: song (No.15, act 2)

	VS	2121/2220/perc/str	2'45"	(Chappell)	25902 +

    This helmet, I suppose: trio for soli, chorus & orch

	VS	2(picc)121/2220/timp.perc/str		(Chappell)	25742

    Today we meet **see** Ida was a twelve month old
    Would you know the kind of maid: song for Tenor solo & orch (No.19, act 1)

in F	2121/2000/str		(Chappell)	23691 +

    The Women of wisest wit: quintet (No.16, act 2)

in Db	2121/2220/perc/str		(Chappell)	26026

    The World is but a broken toy: quartet (No.14, act 2)

in B	2021/2000/str		(Chappell)	26025

The PRODIGAL SON: oratorio
  Love not the world

in Eb	2020/2000/str		(Siddell)	17869

The ROSE OF PERSIA, or The Story-teller and the Slave: operetta
  Selection, arr D.Godfrey, jnr

	PC	2122/2230.euph/timp.perc/str	11'	Chappell	7871 B

  Extracts
    Drinking song **see** I care not if the cup
    From morning prayer the Sultan: chorus & march (No.3, act 2)

	∅	2122/2230/str	BBC	TO 382

    Hassan thy pity I entreat: song
    With Martial gait: chorus

	∅	2122/2000/str	[BBC]	TO 382 ∅ only

    I care not if the cup (Drinking song) for solo, chorus & orch (No.9, act 1)

in Bb (orig)	∅	2122/2230/timp.perc/str	[BBC]	TO 382 +
arr G.Stacey		pf/str	(Chappell)	LM G 3973

    Oh life has put into my hand: song (No.3, act 1)

in D	∅	2122/2030/str	[BBC]	TO 382

    Our tale is told: song (No.23, act 2)

in G (orig)	∅	2122/2000/str	[BBC]	TO 382
Sultan's march	PC	1+picc.222/4230/timp.perc/str	Bosworth	8640

RUDDIGORE, or the Witch's Curse: operetta

Complete	PS	2121/2220/timp.perc/str	88'	(Chappell)(H)	PL 286

    arr S.Robinson, without overture

	∅	2121/2220/timp.perc/hp/str	(Chappell)	Misc 10111

  Overture

orig version	∅	2(picc)222/4230/timp.perc/str	(Chappell)	24532 + & mf
arr Cruikshank	PC	2+picc.121/2220/timp.perc/str	Chappell,1950	19945 Cp Dwa
ed & arr S.Robinson		2(picc)121/2220/timp.perc/str	(Chappell)	24532 + & mf
arr G.Toye	∅	2(picc)121/2220/timp/str	[BBC]	8801 B

  Selections

arr V.Hely-Hutchinson	∅	2121/2220/timp.perc/str		[BBC]	13678
arr H.Rapley	PC	2+picc.12.3sx.1/2230/timp.perc/hp/str	8'15"	Chappell,1950	19837
arr Winterbottom	PC	2(picc)222/4230.euph/timp.perc/str	13'-14'30"	Chappell	7867 Cp

SULLIVAN, Arthur (cont)

RUDDIGORE (cont)
  Extracts
    The battle's roar is over: duet (Act 1, no.8)
      in Ab   2121/2000/str   (Chappell)   26337
    From the briny sea: chorus (Act 1, no.5)
                    2(picc)121/2220/timp.perc/str   (Chappell)   25324
    The ghosts' high noon see When the night wind howls
    Happily coupled are we: duet & chorus (Act 2, no.2)
      in Eb (orig)   2121/2220/timp.perc/str   (Chappell)   25323
    Henceforth all the crimes: song (Act 2, no.7)
    Away, remorse: recit, in F
      arr S.Robinson   φ   1021/2000/str   (Chappell)   24826 +
    I shipp'd d'ye see: song for Tenor solo & orch (Act 1, no.6)
                    2(picc)121/2220/timp.perc/str   (Chappell)   25324
    If somebody there chanced to be: song for Soprano solo & orch (Act 1, no.3)
      in A min   2121/2000/str   (Chappell)   23689 +
    In sailing o'er life's ocean: trio (Act 1, no.10)
      in Ab (orig)   2121/2000/str   (Chappell)   25369 +
    Painted emblems of a race (Chorus of Ancestors): chorus (Act 2, no.4)
                φ   2(picc)121/2220/timp/str/TTBB chorus   [BBC]   26491
    Sir Rupert Murgatroyd: song for Contralto solo, chorus & orch (Act 1, no.2)
                φ   2121/2200/str   [BBC]   26450
    When a man has been a naughty baronet, for soli & chorus (finale act 2)
      in Eb (orig), arr S.Robinson
                φ   2(picc)221/2220/timp.perc/str   (Chappell)   24825 + & mf 322
    When the night wind howls: song for Bass solo, chorus & orch (Act 2, no.5)
      in D min   2(picc)121/2220/perc/hp/str   (Chappell)   23891 +
The SAILOR'S GRAVE: song
  in F   2222/2230/timp/str   (Siddell)   17881
  in F   φ   2222/2210/str   (Novello)   TO 696
  in F, arr R.Chignell   φ   1120/2210/timp/str   (Ashdown)   MS 5527
  in F, arr A.Morelli for cornet solo & orch
               PC 1222/2130.euph/timp/str   Lafleur   17880
SAVOY REMINISCENCES: selection, arr Moore, W see MOORE, W: SAVOY REMINISCENCES
SHE IS NOT FAIR TO OUTWARD VIEW: song
  in Ab, arr R.Chignell   φ   1121/2210/timp/str   [BBC]   MS 5517
The SLAVE OF DUTY see The PIRATES OF PENZANCE
The SONG OF THE WRENS see The WINDOW
The SORCERER: operetta
  Complete
    (with slips ed S.Robinson)
               PS 2121/2220/timp.perc/str   78'25"   (Chappell)(H)   PL 285 & TO 1024
    arr S.Robinson, without overture
               φ   2121/2220/timp.perc/str   (Chappell)   Misc 10112
  Selections
    arr Urich   PC 2222/2230/timp.perc/str   Lafleur   3823
  Extracts
    The air is charged see Time was when love and I were well acquainted
    Dear friends, take pity on my lot: ensemble for Soprano & Bass soli, chorus & orch (No.16, act 2)
      arr S.Robinson   2222/4000/str   [BBC]   TO 1024
    For love alone see Love feeds on many kinds of things
    I rejoice that it's decided: quintet for SAT2Bar soli & orch (No.18, act 2)
      in Gb   VS 2021/2000/str   (Chappell)   25857 +
    Incantation see Sprites of earth and air
    It is not love see Thou hast the power

SULLIVAN, Arthur (cont)

The SORCERER (cont)
  Extracts (cont)
      My name is John Wellington Wells: song for Baritone solo & orch (No.12, act 1)
          in Eb   VS 2021/2000/perc/str   2'20"   (Chappell)   25856 +

      Oh, happy young heart: aria for Soprano solo & orch (No.6, act 1)
      My kindly friends: recit
          in G (orig)   VS 2(picc)121/20.2cnt.20/perc/str   2'25"   (Chappell)   25853 +
      Ring forth ye bells: chorus (No.1, act 1)
          in D   VS 2(picc)121/20.2cnt.20/perc/str   (Chappell)   25852 +
      Sprites of earth and air: incantation for STBar soli, chorus & orch (No.13, act 1)
          in Gb (orig)   VS 1+picc.121/20.2cnt.20/timp/str   (Chappell)   25858 +
      Time was when love and I were well acquainted: ballad for Baritone solo & orch (No.3a, act 1)
      The air is charged: recit
          in D (orig), arr S.Robinson
                                       21+ca.22/2000/str   [BBC]   TO 1024 +
      Thou hast the power: ballad for Tenor solo & orch (No.17, act 2)
          arr S.Robinson   2222/4000/str   [BBC]   TO 1024
      Welcome joy! adieu to sadness: duet for Contralto & Baritone soli & orch (No.9, act 1)
          in Eb   VS 2121/2000/str   2'55"   (Chappell)   25854 +
The STATUTORY DUEL   see   The GRAND DUKE
The STORY TELLER AND THE SLAVE   see   The ROSE OF PERSIA
SULLIVAN'S POPULAR SONGS, arr W.Henky (op.40)
                                   PC 2(picc)222/2230.euph/perc/str   14'30"   Boosey   2061 Cni
SYMPHONY in E (Irish Symphony)   ø   2222/4230/timp/str   35'-41'05" Novello   2150
TE DEUM LAUDAMUS (A song of thanksgiving for victory, 1900), for chorus & orch
                                   ø   0000/42.4cnt.2flg.40.2euph/timp/org/str   Novello   7824
TE DEUM LAUDANMUS and DOMINE SALVAM FAC REGINAM (for the Prince of Wales' recovery, 1872), for
      Soprano solo, chorus & orch
                                   ø   2(picc)222+cbsn/4230.oph/timp/org/str   Novello   8288
The TEMPEST: incidental music, op.1
  Complete   ø   2+picc.222/2230/timp.perc/str   26'   Novello   2152 C
  Extracts
      3 dances
        Masque   Banquet   Dance of nymphs and reapers
                                   ø   2222/2230/timp.perc/str   12'   Novello   2151 B
      Where the bee sucks: song
          in Db   2222/4200/timp/str   1'40"   (Siddell)   17872
THOU'RT PASSING HENCE: song
  in Ab (orig)   ø   2222/2230/timp/str   Chappell   7757
  in Ab   2222/4330.euph/timp/str   (Siddell)   17461
  in G, arr H.Carr   ø   10.ca.2+bcl.2/2230/perc/hp/str   (Chappell)   TO 742
The TOWN OF TITIPU   see   The MIKADO
TRIAL BY JURY
  Complete   ø   2121/2220/timp.perc/str   32'-34'   (Chappell)(H)   PL 284
  arr S.Robinson   ø   2121/2220/timp.perc/str   (Chappell)   Misc 10113
UTOPIA LIMITED, or The Flowers of Progress: operetta
  Complete
      arr S.Robinson   ø   2(picc)222/4331/timp.perc/str   101'   (Chappell)   Misc 10114
  Selections
      arr C.Godfrey jnr   PC 2(picc)122/2230.euph/timp.perc/str   10'   Chappell   2098 C
      Selections of extracts for Prom, 1969
                                       incomplete parts   (Chappell)   26846 **
  Extracts
      Drawing Room Music   2(picc)122/2230/perc/str   (Chappell)   26846
      Eagle high: chorus (No.17, act 2)
                                       2112/2230/timp.perc/str   (Chappell)   26846

SULLIVAN, Arthur (cont)

UTOPIA LIMITED (cont)
   Extracts (cont)
     O Zara, my beloved   see   A Tenor all singers above
     Tarantella (No.24b, act 2)

arr S.Robinson		2+picc.222/4231/timp.perc/str		(Chappell)	26846

     A Tenor all singers above: song for Tenor solo & orch (No.12, act 2)
     O Zara, my beloved: recit

in F min (orig)	ø	2122/2030/str	3'35"	Chappell	23701 +

VICTORIA AND MERRIE ENGLAND: ballet
   Suite no.1
     1. Introduction   4. Mistletoe dance
     2. Berceuse   5. May day festivities
     3. Druids' march

	PC	2(picc)122/4230/timp.perc/hp/str	9'35"-13'10"	Metzler	6575 B

WALTZING WITH SULLIVAN: potpourri of waltzes, arr G.Vinter

ø	2222/4230/timp.perc/hp/str		[BBC]	22497 +

The WILLOW SONG

in E		2222/2000/hp/str	(Siddell)	17876
in A, arr R.Douglas	ø	2222/2000/timp.perc/hp/str	[BBC]	20244

The WINDOW, or The Song of the Wrens: song-cycle (orig voice & pf)

arr V.Hely-Hutchinson	ø	2(picc)222/2200/timp/str	(J.Williams)	6222

The WITCH'S CURSE   see   RUDDIGORE
The YEOMAN OF THE GUARD, or The Merry man and his Maid: operetta

Complete	PS	2122/2230/timp.perc/str	89'	(Chappell)(H)	PL 278 B

   arr S.Robinson, without overture

	ø	2122/2230/timp.perc/str		(Chappell)	Misc 10115
Overture	ø	2(picc)122/2230/timp/str	4'30"-5'30"	[BBC]	8891 B +
arr F.Rapley	PC	2+picc.121/2230/timp.perc/str		Chappell,1950	19946 Cp Dwa G

   Selections

arr C.Godfrey jnr	PC	2(picc)222/2230.euph/timp.perc/str		Chappell	88 Cp Eni
arr V.Hely-Hutchinson	ø	1+picc.121/2231/timp.perc/str		(Chappell)	10793
arr F.Rapley	PC	2+picc.12.3sx.1/2230/timp.perc/hp/str	8'30"	Chappell,1950	19838 Cp

   Extracts
     Comes the pretty young bride (finale act 2)

in D	2122/2230/timp/str		(Chappell)	25867 +

     Free from his fetters grim: song for Tenor solo & orch (Act 2, no.4)

in Eb	2022/2000/str		(Chappell)	25868 +

     Here upon we're both agreed: duet for 2 Baritones & orch (Act 2, no.3)

in G	1+picc.122/2000/str		(Chappell)	23940 +

     Here's a tale of cock and bull   see   Here upon we're both agreed
     I have a song to sing, O!: duet for Soprano & Baritone soli & orch (Act 1, no.7)

VS	2(picc)122/20.2cnt.30/str		(Chappell)	23940 +

     Is life a boon: song for Tenor solo & orch (Act 1, no.5)

in Db (orig)	2202/0000/str		(Chappell)	23684 +

     A man who would woo: trio for SAT soli & orch (Act 2, no.7)

in D (orig)	2122/2000/str		(Chappell)	23846 +

     Night has spread her pall once more: chorus (Act 2, no.1)

in Bb	2122/2000/str		(Chappell)	25866 +

     Oh! a private buffoon: song for Baritone solo & orch (Act 2, no.2)

in Eb	2122/2000/str		(Chappell)	25865 +

     Strange adventure: quartet for SATB soli & orch (Act 1, no.5)

in G	0100/0000/str		(Chappell)	24031 +

     This is the autumn of our life: song for Baritone solo & orch (Act 1, no.2)

in Ab	2122/20.2cnt.30/perc/str		(Chappell)	25322 +

SULLIVAN, Arthur (cont)

The YEOMAN OF THE GUARD (cont)
    Extracts
        Though tear and long drawn sigh: song for Soprano solo & (Act 1, no.10)
        Tis done, I am a bride: recit
                                φ   2122/2200/str   (Chappell)   TO 1741 +
        Tower warders under orders, for double chorus (Act 1, no.2)
            in C   2122/20.2cnt.30/perc/str   (Chappell)   25322
        Were I thy bride: song for Contralto solo & orch (Act 1, no.11)
                                2022/2000/str   (Chappell)   23847 +
        When a wooer goes a-wooing: quartet for SATBar soli & orch (Act 2, no.8)
            in Db   2122/2000/str   (Chappell)   26738
        When our gallant Norman foes: song for Contralto solo, chorus & orch (Act 1, no.3)
            in Eb   2121/20.2cnt.30/perc/str   (Chappell)   25952
            in G, arr S.Robinson   2222/2230/perc/str   (Chappell)   TO 1741
YOUTH WILL NEEDS HAVE DALLIANCE   see   HENRY VIII: incidental music

SULLIVAN, Henry (1893-

BOW BELLS
    Selections
        arr Jones   PC   212.sx.1/2230/perc/str   Chappell   10178 B
    Extracts
        Mona Lisa: song
            in C min, arr J.Beaver φ   21+ca.21/2230/timp.perc/hp/str   (Chappell)   TO 403
HOME AND BEAUTY: revue by H.Sullivan & N.Brodsky   see   BRODSKY, N: HOME AND BEAUTY

SUMMERS, T.

MAKER OF EARTH AND SEA: Australian song
                        PC   2(picc)222/4220/str   Benjamin   16364

SUMSION, Herbert (1899-

A MOUNTAIN TUNE: intermezzo   str   6'   OUP   18792

SUPPÉ, Franz von   (1819-1895)

Die AFRIKAREISE: operetta
    Selections
        Titania waltz: waltz based on themes from the operetta
                        2000/0000/str   Cranz   11634
BANDITENSTREICHE (Jolly Robbers): operetta
    Overture   φ   1+picc.222/4230/timp.perc/gtr/str   6'50"   Kistner & S   5736
                        PC   1+picc.222/4230.euph/timp.perc/str   Hawkes   2705 C
The BEAUTIFUL GALATHEA: operetta   see   Die SCHONE GALATHEA
BOCCACCIO (Giovanni Boccaccio): operetta
    Complete
        microfilm only of MS full score
                        φ   1+picc.110/2220/timp/cel/str   Danish Radio mf 123
        ed L.Wurmser (Radio version 'cuts')(English translation - J.Barker)
                        φ   2(picc)222/4230/timp.perc/str   (Weinberger) Misc 6220
    Overture   φ   1121/2210/perc/str   Cranz   3491
        arr R.Jungnickel   PC   1+picc.222/4231/timp.perc/str   Jungnickel   3612
    Selections
        Boccaccio march, arr A.Winter
                        PC   222(2sx)2/2230/perc/str   3'   Hawkes   2133 +
        Boccaccio waltz, arr Eduard Strauss on motives from Suppés operetta   see   STRAUSS, Eduard

SUPPÉ, Franz von (cont)

BOCCACCIO (cont)
  Extracts
    Hab' ich nur Deine Liebe: song (Act 1, sc.6)   (24803 + ∅ use
      in A♭   2222/4230/timp.perc/str   (Weinberger)   (VS
    Mia bella Fiðrentina: duet (Act 3, no.18)
      in D   2222/4230/timp/str   (Weinberger)   25543 +
CARNIVAL: overture
  arr A.Lotter   PC 2(picc)222/4230/timp.perc/str   6'30"-7'30"   Hawkes   8600
COLETTA WALTZ   see   Das MODELL
DAME VALENTIN: operetta
  Overture   PC 1+picc.222/2230/timp.perc/str   8'15"-9'15"   Boosey   8921 B
DICHTER UND BAUER (Poet and Peasant): operetta
  Overture   ∅   1+picc.222/4230.oph/timp.perc/hp/str   9'-11'   Aibl   9119 +
    arr Godfrey & Winter PC 2222/4230.euph/timp.perc/hp/str   Hawkes   3150
DONNA JUANITA: comic opera
  Overture   PC 1121/2210/timp.perc/str   Junne   12063
FATINITZA: comic opera
  Overture   ∅   2(picc)222/4230/timp.perc/str   6'15"   Cranz   12756
  Selections
    arr Meyder   PC 1+picc.121/1230.euph/timp.perc/str   Hawkes   3165
    arr Paepke   PC 2(picc)222/4230/timp.perc/hp/str   Bote & B   8287
    Fatinitza march on motives from the opera, arr Genée
                          ∅   1+picc.121/4230/perc/str   Cranz   8219
FLOTTE BÜRSCHE: operetta
  Overture
    arr Atzler   PC 1(picc)121/2210/timp.perc/pf/str   6'   Cranz   11999
FORTUNE'S LABYRINTH: overture   see   Die IRRFAHRT UMS GLÜCK
FRANZ SCHUBERT: operetta
  Overture   ∅   2222/4230/timp.perc/str   6'   Kistner & S   5744
    arr Gruenwald   PC 1121/2210/timp.perc/str   Cundy-Bettoney 9690
Die FRAU MEISTERIN (The Mistress): operetta
  Overture   ∅   1+picc.222/4230/timp.perc/str   8'   Kistner & S   5741
                        PC 1+picc.222/4230.euph/timp.perc/pf/str   Hawkes   2894
Der GASCOGNER: comic opera
  Overture   PC 1+picc.222/4230/timp.perc/str   Cranz   8878
  Extracts
    March   1+picc.122/4230/perc/str   Cranz   20665
GLÜCKSWALZER   PC 2+picc.222/4230/timp.perc/str   Cranz   8628
Die IRRFAHRT UMS GLÜCK: overture (Fortune's Labyrinth)
                            ∅   2(picc)222/4231/timp.perc/str   7'30"   Kistner & S   5739
  arr A.Evans   PC 1+picc.122/4230.euph/timp.perc/str   Hawkes   980 Bwa
ISABELLA: overture   ∅   2(picc)222/4230/timp.perc/str   7'45"   Aibl   9587
JOLLY ROBBERS: operetta   see   BANDITENSTREICHE
Der KRÄMER UND SEIN COMMIS: burlesque
  Overture   ∅   1+picc.222/4210/timp.perc/str   BBC   Misc 1180
LEICHTE CAVALLERIE (Light Cavalry): operetta
  Overture   ∅   1+picc.222/4230/perc/str   7'-8'   Kistner & S   5735 Bs Dwa
    arr C.Godfrey, jnr   PC 2222/2230.euph/perc/str   Hawkes   3505 Ap Cwa
    arr A.Winter   PC 2222/2230.euph/perc/str   Boosey   16774 Cwe
The MISTRESS: operetta   see   Die FRAU MEISTERIN
Das MODELL: operetta
  Overture   PC 2(picc)222/4230/timp.perc/str   5'45"   Weinberger   8880
    arr A.Waldenmaier   ∅   3(picc)222/4331/timp.perc/hp/str   Mozart Ed,1976(H) PL 535
  Selection: waltz
    Coletta waltz, on motives from the operetta
                          PC 2222/4230/timp.perc/str   Weinberger   8856

SUPPÉ, Franz von (cont)

Ein MORGEN, EIN MITTAG, EIN ABEND IN WIEN (Morning, Noon and Night in Vienna): overture
	ø	2(picc)222/4230/timp.perc/str	9'	Kistner	5743 B
arr C.Godfrey	PC	1+picc.222/4230.euph/timp.perc/str		Hawkes	3504 Am Cwe

MOZART (An Artist's Life): musical play arr L.Wolmuth from music of Mozart and Suppé
	ø	2222/4220.oph/timp.perc/str	BBC	Misc 1344

PARAGRAPH III: operetta
Overture
	ø	2(picc)222/4230/timp.perc/str	9'	Aibl	5856
	PC	1010/0110/timp.perc/str		Aibl	11698
arr A.Winter	PC	2(picc)222/4230/timp.perc/str		Boosey & H	13590

Die PARISERIN (Parisian Woman): operetta
Gavotte
arr A.Waldenmaier	ø	2(picc)222/4330/timp.perc(glock)/hp/str		Mozart Ed(H)	PL 545

Das PENSIONAT: comic opera
Selection, arr Paepke
	PC	2(picc)222/4230/timp.perc/hp/str	Bote & B	8253

Extracts
Prelude, chorale and dance
	PC	1(picc)121/2210/timp.perc/str	R.Fischer	6756 B

PIQUE DAME: operetta
Overture
	ø	2(picc)222/4230.oph/timp.perc/str	6'30"-8'	Kistner & S	5742
arr A.Evans	PC	2(picc)222/4230.euph/timp.perc/str		Hawkes	3326 Cwa Dwa
arr A.Winter	PC	2(picc)222/4230.euph/timp.perc/str		Boosey & H	16718

POET AND PEASANT: operetta see DICHTER UND BAUER

PRINZ EUGEN, DER EDLE RITTER: operetta
Complete
	ø	2(picc)222/4210/timp.perc/str	(Non autograph MS ca 1884)		Misc 5963

Die SCHÖNE GALATHEA: operetta
Complete
	ø	1+picc.222/2210/timp.perc/str	Cranz	21893

Overture
arr L.Artok	PC	1121/2210/timp.perc/str	6'45"-7'30"	Schott	13855
arr R.Jungnickel	ø	1+picc.222/4231/timp.perc/str		Schirmer	7870 C +

SUMMERNIGHT'S DREAM: overture
arr Margis-Berger	PC	1222/2210/timp.perc/str	C.Fischer	9778

SUPPÉ SELECTIONS
SIGNALS FROM SUPPÉ	see	URBACH, E: SELECTIONS from the works of various composers - SUPPÉ
SUPPÉ ILLUSIONEN	see	MICHAELOFF, M: SUPPÉ ILLUSIONEN
SUPPÉ ON PARADE	see	PALMER, (Cedric) King: SUPPÉ ON PARADE
Ein WIENER SOUPER	see	HRUBY, V: Ein WIENER SOUPER

TANTALUSQUALEN: operetta
Overture
	ø	1+picc.222/4230/timp.perc/str	5'30"-6'30"	Kistner & S	5740
arr A.Evans	PC	1+picc.222/4230.euph/timp.perc/str		Hawkes	2708

TEN MAIDENS AND NO MAN: operetta see ZEHN MÄDCHEN UND KEIN MANN

TEUFEL AUF ERDEN: operetta
Extracts
Teufelsmarsch
	PC	1+picc.222/4230/perc/str (== 1+picc.121/2210/perc/str)	Cranz	5142

TITANIA WALTZ see Die AFRIKAREISE

TRICOCHE UND CACOLET: burlesque
Overture
	PC	2(picc)222/4230.oph/timp.perc/str	Kistner & S	5738

TRIUMPH-OUVERTÜRE
	PC	1+picc.121/2210/timp.perc/str	Cranz	3490

Des WANDERERS ZIEL (The Wanderer's Goal): overture
	ø	2(picc)222/4230.oph/timp.perc/hp/str	9'	Kistner & S	5737
arr A.Evans	PC	1+picc.222/4230.euph/timp.perc/hp/str		Hawkes	2683

WIENER JUBEL: overture (Vienna Jubilee)
	øPC	1121/2210/perc/str	6'30"	Cranz	8822
arr Moses-Tobani	PC	1121/2210/perc/str		C.Fischer	10977 B

ZEHN MÄDCHEN UND KEIN MANN (Ten maidens and no man): operetta
Overture
arr Kretschmer	PC	1222/2210/timp/str	7'30"	C.Fischer	5880
Selection	PC	1121/2210/timp.perc/str		Cranz	8338

SUPRON, Lionel

MEXICAN CARNIVAL
   arr R.Jones   ø   212+bcl.0/2220/timp.latin/gtr.pf/str   D.Toff   MLO 852

SURINACH, Carlos (1915-

ACROBATS OF GOD: ballet
  Symphonic version

1. Fanfare	6. Interlude
2. Interlude	7. Minuet
3. Antique Dance	8. Interlude
4. Interlude	9. Spanish Gallop
5. Bolero	

                  ø   3(2picc)3(ca)3(bcl)2+cbsn/4331/timp.perc(tamtam.xyl)/
                      hp.3mand/str   AMP,1972   Misc 8248

CONCERTI
  Piano & orch   ø   3(picc)3(ca)3(bcl)2+cbsn/4331/timp.3perc(glock.
                      tamtam.xyl)/str   23'   AMP,1976   Misc 9237
    Strings (Composer's transcription of his String Quartet)
                  ø   str   25'   AMP,1978   Misc 9846
DOPPIO CONCERTINO for violin, piano & chamber orch
                  ø   1(picc)1(ca)11/1100/timp.perc.glock.xyl/cb 15   Rongwen Music,1956   Misc 4956
DRAMA JONDO: overture for orchestra
                  ø   3(1picc)3(ca)3(bcl)2/4331/timp.perc(xyl)/
                      hp/str   8'   AMP,1967   Misc 7836
MADRID, 1890: suite for chamber orch

1. Waltz	3. Tango	5. Schottische
2. Polka	4. Mazurka	

                  ø   1(picc)1(ca)11/1100/timp.perc.glock.xyl/
                      pf/str   12'-13'   AMP,1955   Misc 4375
The MISSIONS OF SAN ANTONIO: a symphonic Canticle in 5 parts
                  ø   3(2picc)3(ca)3(bcl)2+cbsn/4331/timp.perc(bells.
                      crot.glock.xyl)/cel.hp.pf/str   22'   AMP,1970   Misc 8248
Les TROMPETAS DE LOS SERAFINES: overture (1973)
                  ø   3(2picc)3(ca)3(bcl)2+cbsn/4331/timp.3perc(bells.
                      glock.xyl)/hp/str   8'30"   AMP,1975   Misc 8610

SUSATO, Tielman (Tylman)(ca.1500-1564)

SUSATO SUITE (from 'Danserye', [1551])

1. La Mourisque	4. Basse Danse Bergeret
2. Bransle Quatre Branles	5. Ronde - Mon Amy
3. Ronde	6. Pavane Bataille

    ed & arr J.Iveson   ø   0000/1(tambour)4[=3+hn]4[=3+hn]1   Chester,1975   26061

SÜSSMAYER, Franz Xaver (1766-1803)

12 MINUETS (1795)
    ed W.Jerger   ø   2(2picc)222/2200/timp/str(no vlas)   Doblinger,1974   25756

SUTER, Robert (1919-

3 NOCTURNES for viola & orch (1968-9)
                  ø   1122/4000/timp.3perc(Siamese gongs.tamtam.xmbn)/
                      cel.cim.gtr.hp/str   30'   Bärenreiter   Misc 7405
SONATA for orchestra (1967) ø   3(picc)2(ca)3(bcl,Ebcl)2(cbsn)/4331/timp.4perc(bgos.
                      claves.tamtam.tomtoms.tplbl.xmbn)/cel.hp/
                      str(12.10.8.6.4)   18'30" Bärenreiter,1967   Misc 9586

SUTERMEISTER, Heinrich (1910-

DIVERTIMENTO no.1 for strings
   revised edn   ø   str   20'   Schott,1960   Misc 5425
LIEDER UND TÄNZE for string orch
                             ø   str   W.Muller,1962   Misc 6859
MARCHE FANTASQUE   ø   3(2picc)2+ca.2+bcl.2+cbsn/4331/timp.perc.xyl/
                                 2pf/str   15'   Schott   Misc 3982
MISSA DA REQIUEM, for Soprano & Baritone (or Bass) soli, chorus & orch
                             ø   3(picc)2+ca.2+bcl.3(cbsn)/4331/timp/hp.pf/
                                 str   47'   Schott,1960   Misc 5326
ROMEO AND JULIA: opera
   Symphonic suite   ø   3+picc.2+ca.2+bcl.2+cbsn/4331/timp.perc.glock.xyl/
                                 cel.hp.pf/str   18'   Schott   11256

SUTHERLAND, Gavin

SAILING
   arr J.McCarthy for chorus & orch
                           ø   2(picc)222/4331/timp.perc.kit/gtr.hp.pf/str   (Island)   26661 +

SUTHERLAND, Iain

COPENHAGEN CARNIVAL (Danish folk-song), arr
                           ø   2(picc)222/4331/timp.perc.kit.glock.ratchet/
                                 hp.pf(cel)/str   Arranger,1979   26641 +
DARLING CHARLIE (Charlie is my darling): traditional song, arr for orch with rhythm section
                           ø   2(picc)22(bcl)2/4331/rhythm-kit.egtr.bgtr.pf/
                                 timp.perc.finger-cyms.xyl/hp/str   Arranger   26873
FANFARE for 'A Salute to St.Andrew' (Friday Night is Music Night, Nov 1981)
                           ø   2(picc)222/4331/timp.perc.gong/hp.pf/str   Composer,1981   27118
OVERTURE TO FIFTY YEARS OF BRITISH MUSICALS for orch with rhythm section
                          SS   3(picc)2+ca.3(bcl)2/4331/rhythm-gtr.kit.pf(cel)/
                                 timp.perc.glock.xyl/hp/str   (Composer)   26694 +
SCOTTISH MUSIC-HALL MEDLEY for Tenor solo & orch
   Here's to the Gordons (Stewart, Garden & Wilson; pub.J.S.Kerr)
   Campbelltown Loch (A.Stewart; pub.Lochside)
   I belong to Glasgow (W.Fyffe; pub FD & H)
   I love a lassied (H.Lauder; pub FD & H)
   Stop your ticklin', Jock (H.Lauder; pub FD & H)
   The laddies who fought and won (H.Lauder; pub FD & H)
                           ø   2(picc)22(bcl)2/4331/timp.perc.bells.glock.kit.rattle.
                                 whistle.xyl/[egtr].hp.pf(cel)/str   Arranger,1981   27119
THREE CASTLES SUITE
   1. Edinburgh Castle (Prince's Street)
                           ø   2(picc)[=1(picc)]121/2[=1]3[=2]3[=2, or 2tbn.tuba]0/
                                 hp.pf/str   4'05"   Senlac   25802
     version for military band & orch
                         ø   22[=1]22[=1]/4[=2]3[=2]3[1]/timp.perc.glock/
                                 [hp]/str
                               Military band: 0.picc.13+Ebcl.asx.tsx.0/20.2cnt.31.euph/
                                              bdm (parts included in set)   Senlac   26959
WEE WILLIE WINKIE (traditional), arr for Soprano solo & strings (or str-4tet)
                         ø   str   (Argyll)   26693 +

SVEINBJÖRNSSON,Svenibjorn (1847-1927)

O GUD VORS LANDS: National Anthem of Iceland

		2222/4230/timp/str	[BBC]	Misc 510
	PC	2(picc)222/4230/timp.perc/str	Breitkopf	14305
arr A.Franzel	∅	2222/42.2cnt.31/timp.perc/str	Arranger	19518
arr G.French	∅	2222/2230/timp.perc/str	Arranger/Blandford	25512 +

SVENDSEN, Johann Severin (1840-1911)

ANDANTE FUNÈBRE	∅	2222/4231/timp/str	6'	Hansen	4349
CARNIVAL IN PARIS: episode, op 9					
	∅	2+picc.222/4231/timp.perc/str	10'30"-11'30"	Kistner & S	3089 An C
arr L.Weninger	PC	1(picc)121/2210/timp.perc/str		Kistner & S	14315
CONCERTI					
Cello & orch, op.7, in D	∅	2222/2200/timp/str		Siegel	4703
Violin & orch, op.6, in A	∅	2222/2200/timp/str		(E.W.Fritzsch)	19737
CORONATION MARCH for Oscar II, op.13					
	∅	2222/4331/timp.perc/str		Kistner & S	5704 B
	PC	2222/4331/timp.perc/str		Kistner & S	1517

FANTASIA on compositions of Johan Svendsen, arr Reesen, E   see   REESEN, E: FANTASIA on compositions
    of Johan Svendsen

I FJOL GJAETTE GJEITINN: Norwegian folk melody					
	∅	str		Kistner & S	7983
2 ICELANDIC MELODIES					
1. Maestoso 2. Moderato					
	∅	str	7'	Kistner & S	7168
NORWEGIAN ARTISTS' CARNIVAL, op.14					
	∅	2+picc.222/4331/timp.perc/str	6'	Peters	2767 Bs C
2 OLD SWEDISH FOLK SONGS					
1. Allt under himmelens fäste 2. Du gamla, du friska, du fjellhöga Nord					
	∅	str	7'	Hansen	4247 Bwa
PERSIAN DANCE	PC	1010/0110/perc/pf/str		Hansen	7564
POLONAISE, op.12	∅	2+picc.222/4331/timp.perc/str	8'	Hansen	4348
arr Hansen	PC	1(picc)010/0110/timp.perc/pf/str		Hansen	4602
PRELUDE					
arr Hansen	PC	1010/0110/timp/pf/str		Hansen	4634
RHAPSODIES NORVÉGIENNES					
No.1, op.17, in B	∅	2222/4230/timp/str	10'-11'30"	Hansen	4325
arr A.Schmid	PC	2222/4230/timp/str		Hawkes	164 B
No.2, op.19, in A	∅	2(picc)222/4230/timp/str	8'45"	Hansen	4326
No.3, op.21, in C	∅	2(picc)222/4230/timp/str	12'	Hansen	4327
arr Roberts	PC	1(picc)121/2210/timp/org/str		Hansen	1276
No.4, op.22, in D	∅	2(picc)222/4230/timp/str	11'-12'	Hansen	4328
ROMANCE for violin & orch, op.26, in G					
	PC	1122/2000/timp/str	8'	Hansen	4860 B
ROMEO AND JULIET: fantasy overture, op.18					
	∅	2222/4231/timp/str	12'	Breitkopf	4248
SIGURD SLEMBE: overture, op.8	∅	2222/4231/timp/str	7'-9'15"	Kistner & S	6519
SYMPHONIES					
No.1, op. 4, in D	∅	2222/4230/timp/str	29'	Fritzsch	13969
No.2, op.15, in B♭	∅	2222/4230/timp/str	29'-35'	Fritzsch	4476 Bs
ZORAHAYDA: legend, op.11	∅	2222/4230/timp/str	11'-14'30"	Hansen	4307
	PC	1010/0110/timp/pf/str		Hansen	4632
	∅	2222/4230/timp/str		Warmuth	Misc 1408

SVENSSON, Bernh.

BERCEUSE
   arr Rybrandt   PC   1121/2210/perc/str   Nordiska   19017

SVIRIDOV, Georgi Vasilevich (1915-

KURSK SONGS: cantata for chorus & orch
                           φ   2(picc)+picc.2+ca.3(E♭cl:bcl)2+cbsn/4331/timp.perc.glock/
                              cel.2hp.pf/str   Russian SM,1975   Misc 8807
MINIATURE TRIPTYCH (1964)   φ   3(2picc)3(ca)2+bcl.3(cbsn)/4331/timp.bells/
                              cel.2hp.pf/str   Russian SM,1972   Misc 7892
MUSIC FOR CHAMBER ORCHESTRA (1964)
                           φ   0000/1000/pf/str   Russian SM,1971   Misc 7646
ORATORIO PATHÉTIQUE, for Soprano & Baritone soli, chorus & orch (1959)
   (English version - H.Marshall)
                           φ   2+2picc.33+bcl.2+cbsn/8661/timp.perc.bells.tamtam/
                              cel.2hp.org.2pf/str   Russian SM,1964   Misc 6040
RUSSIA THE WOODEN: cantata for Tenor solo, TB chorus & orch
                           φ   3(picc)22+bcl.2+cbsn/2331/perc.bell.glock/
                              cel.2hp.pf/str   Russian SM,1975   Misc 8807
SNOW IS FALLING: cantata for boys' chorus, fv-chorus & orch
                           φ   2(picc,afl)020.cbsn/0000/perc.bells/cel.2hp/
                              str(10.8.6.4.2.)   Russian SM,1975   Misc 8807
The SNOWSTORM: musical illustrations to Pushkin's tale
                           φ   2+picc.2+ca.2(E♭cl)2+cbsn/4331/timp.perc.bells.glock/
                              cel.2hp.pf/str   Russian SM,1978   Misc 9751
SPRINGTIME CANTATA, for chorus & orch
                           φ   2(2picc)+afl.3(ca)32+cbsn/4021/perc.bells.glock.vib/
                              2hp/str   Russian SM,1974   Misc 8807

SWAN, Timothy (1758-1842)

LEGHORN)
LONDON   ) see GOLDMAN, R.F: LANDMARKS OF EARLY AMERICAN MUSIC, collected & arr by R.F.Goldman & R.Smith

SWANN, Donald (1923-

EMILY BUTTER (1954)
   arr M.Saunders   φ   1+picc.121/0010/timp.perc/hpsd.pf/str   Arranger MS:BBC   MS 30786
The HIPPOPOTAMUS SONG
   in A♭, arr P.Hope for chorus & orch
                      φ   2222/4230/timp.perc/str   (Chappell)   22297 +
O MY LOVE'S LIKE A RED, RED ROSE: song
   in E♭, arr J.Byfield   pf/str   (Morgan)   LM G 4368
The WARTHOG SONG
   in B♭, arr P.Pattison   φ   1110/0000/hp.pf/str   (Chappell)   LM G 6979

SWANSON, Howard (1909-1978)

NIGHT MUSIC for woodwind, horn & strings
                    φ   1111/1000/str   9'   Weintraub,1951   Misc 4082
SHORT SYMPHONY   φ   2222/2210/timp/str   11'   Weintraub,1951   Misc 4083

SWANSON, O.E.

MODER SVEA: selection of Swedish songs and dacnes, arr
   arr Borch   PC   1121/2210/timp.perc/str   C.Fischer   10105

SWANSTROM, A.

SONS O' GUNS: musical play by A.Swanstrom, B.Davis & J.F.Coots
  Selection, arr Jones   PC 212.sx.2/2230/perc/str   Chappell   9367 B
  Extracts
    Why: song
      in E♭   ø 112.3sx.1/2220/perc/str   (Chappell)   TO 393
      in E♭, arr G.Vinter (refrain only)
                  ø 1+picc.222/4230/timp.perc/str   (Chappell)   22644 +

SWEELINCK, Jan Pieterszoon (1562-1621)

PRAELUDIUM
  arr M.Flothuis   ø 4303+cbsn/1440/str   5'20"   Donemus,1958   Misc 5270

SWIETEN, Gottfried van (1733-1803)

SYMPHONY in E♭ (also attrib J.Haydn (H.I: Es 1))
                  ø 0200/2000/str   7'   Kistner & S   611

SWINSTEAD, Felix (1880-

SCARLATTI SUITE, arr from the harpsichord sonatas of D.Scarlatti
                  ø pf/str   Novello   11363 Bwa

SWOLKIEN, Henryk

SERCE GENERAVA: march by H.Swolkien & A.Wisnieski
                  ø 103+E♭cl.0/4.thn.4.2cnt.32.bar/perc   Polish SM,1948 MB 4559 ø only

SYLVA, B.G.de librettist, for works by de Sylva see relevant composer, e.g. HENDERSON, Ray

SYLVA, Johann Elias de

SYMPHONY in D
  ed W.Senn   ø 0000/00.2clni.00/str/cont   Universal.DTÖ 86 MRL

SYLVESTER, P.W.

LOM PALANKA: march   1+picc.222/2230.euph/timp.perc/str   Boosey   17258

SZABADI, F.J.

TOROK MAGYAR: Hungarian march
  arr A.Winter   PC 222.2sx.2/2230/timp.perc/str   4'   Boosey & H   11960

SZABELSKI, Bolesław (1896-1979)

MARSZ ZOLNIERSKI, for chorus & brass instruments (or piano)
                  ø 0000/4231   Polish SM   Misc 2991
PRELUDE FOR CHAMBER ORCHESTRA (1963)
                  ø 1+picc.110/2210/perc/pf/str   6'40"   Polish SM,1964 Misc 6479
SONETY (Sonnets)(1958)   ø 2+picc.222/4230/timp.perc.xyl/pf/str 17'   Polish SM,1961 Misc 7348
SYMPHONY no.3 (1951)   ø 2(picc)222/4331/timp.perc.tamtam/str 45'   Polish SM,1954 Misc 4166
TOCCATA, op.10   ø 2(picc)222/4231/timp.perc/hp.pf/str 5'   Polish SM,1950 Misc 3841 C

SZALONEK, Witold (1927-

GESTÄNDNISSE for speaker, chorus & chamber orch (1959)
          ø   101+bcl.0.cbsn/1110/perc.vib.xyl/hpsd/str   Moeck,1960   Misc 7347

SZAŁOWSKI, Antoni (1907-1973)

CONCERTINO for strings	ø	str		(Composer) 19069
OVERTURE	ø	2+picc.222/4331/timp.perc.tamtam/str	6'45"-8'	Polish SM,1939 Misc 3761
	ø	2+picc.222/4331/timp.perc/str		(Composer) 18709

SZARZYŃSKI, Stanisłav Sylwester (late 17th cent)

COMPLETORIUM for chorus & orch ø 0000/0200/2vln/cont(org)   Polish SM,1980   Misc 10330

SZÉKELY, Endre (1912-

FANTASMA (1969)	ø	3(picc)2+ca.2+Ebcl+bcl.2+cbsn/4331/timp.perc.bells.		
		vib.xba/cel.hp.pf/str	10'	Ed Musica,1971 Misc 7614
MUSICA NOTTURNA (1967)	ø	1111/1000/pf/str(1.1.1.1.1.)	8'	Ed Musica,1968 Misc 8880

SZELIGOWSKI, Tadeusz (1896-1963)

EPITAPH (in memoriam Karol Szymanowski) for strings
          ø   str   13'30"   Polish SM,1948   Misc 4198

SZENTIRMAY, E.

THERE'S ON EARTH BUT ONE PRECIOUS PEARL: song
  in B min, arr Korbay, orch B.Orr
          ø   str   (Schott)   LM G 9893

SZERVÁNSZKY, Endre (1911-

CONCERTO for clarinet & orch (1965)
          ø   20.ca.0.bcl.1/3220/timp.3perc/cel.hp/str 14'-15' Ed Musica,1970 Misc 7864

SERENADES				
Clarinet & orch	ø	2212/4200/timp/str	17'	Hungarian SM,1952 Misc 4154 C
Strings	ø	str		Hungarian SM,1949 Misc 3294 B

SZOKOLAY, Sándor (1931-

BALLATA SINFONICA   ø   3(picc)3(ca)3(bcl)2+cbsn/4331/timp.perc.glock.
                  vib.xyl/cel.hp.pf/str   Ed Musica/Peters/Litolff,1970 Misc 9184

SZÖLLÖSKY, András (1921-

CONCERTI				
No.3 (1968)	ø	16 str(9.3.3.1)(cb player also plays bell) 13'		Ed Musica,1970 Misc 8363 B
No.4 (1970)	ø	2222/0220/str(18.6.5.4)		Ed Musica,1971 Misc 8403
SONORITA (1974)	ø	404+bcl.0/4000/str(8.8+8.8.6.4.)[=10.10+10.10.8.6]		
			13'	Ed Musica,1977 Misc 9159

SZÖNYI, Erzsébet (1924-

CONCERTO for organ & orch (1958)	ø	0122/2200/timp.perc/hp/str	18'	Ed Musica,1966 Misc 9183
DIVERTIMENTO, no.2 (1951)	ø	2(picc)121/2200/timp.perc/hp.pf/str	12'	Hungarian SM,1952 Misc 4153

SZULC, Józef (1875-1956)

FLOSSIE: operetta
   Selection, arr F.Salabert   PC 1121/2230/perc/str   Salabert   9497
ZOU! operetta
   Selection, arr F.Salabert   PC 1121/2230/perc/str   Salabert   4671

SZYMANOWSKI, Karol (1882-1937)

see   MICHAŁOWSKI, Kornel: Karol Szymanowski 1882-1937. Thematic catalogue of works and bibliography.
      Kraków: Polish SM,1967   BRL

COMPLETE WORKS

Karol Szymanowski: Complete edition, general editor T.Chylińska. Polish SM/Universal/Eschig,1973-

AGAWE, for Contralto solo, fv-chorus & orch, op.38
   facsimile edition   ɸ   3(picc)3(ca)3+Ebcl+bcl.2+cbsn/6231/timp.perc/
                               cel.hp/str   Polish SM,1975.CW 9   MRL
CONCERTI
   Violin & orch
      No.1, op.35   ɸ   3(picc)3(ca)3(Ebcl)+bcl.3(cbsn)/4331/timp.perc.bells/
                               cel.2hp.pf/str   20'-25'30"   Universal   Misc 1230 B
         ed B.Konarska   ɸ   3(picc)3(ca)3(Ebcl)+bcl.3(cbsn)/4331/timp.perc.bells/
                               cel.2hp.pf/str(12.12.8.8.6)   Polish SM,1976.CW 3   MRL
      No.2, op.61   ɸ   2(picc)2(ca)2(Ebcl)2(cbsn)/4231/timp.perc/
                               pf/str   Eschig,1934   Misc 3348 B
         ed A.Neuer   ɸ   2(picc)2(ca)2(Ebcl)2(cbsn)/4231/timp.perc/
                               pf/str   Polish SM,1976.CW 3   MRL
                     ɸ   2(picc)2(ca)2(bcl)2(cbsn)/4231/timp.perc/
                               pf/str   Russian SM,1971   Misc 7645
CONCERT-OVERTURE, op.12   ɸ   3(picc)3(ca)3(Ebcl)+bcl.2+cbsn/6331/timp.perc/
                               hp/str   Universal   Misc 1913
DEMETER for Contralto solo, fv-chorus & orch, op.37b (1917, re orch 1924)
   ed Z.Helman   ɸ   2+picc.1+ca.2+bcl.2/4020/timp.perc/cel.2hp.pf/
                               str(12.12.8.8.6.)   Polish SM,1975.CW 9   MRL
KING ROGER: opera, op.46
   ed T. Chylińska   ɸ   3(picc)3(ca)3(Ebcl)+bcl.3(cbsn)/4731/timp.perc.
                               bells.tamtam.xyl/cel.2hp.org.pf/str   Polish SM,1973.CW 14   MRL
LITANY TO THE VIRGIN MARY: 2 fragments for Soprano solo, fv-chorus & orch, op.59
                     ɸ   21+ca.22/4200/timp.perc/hp/str   Polish SM,1951   Misc 4200
   ed Z.Helman   ɸ   21+ca.22/4200/timp.perc.tamtam/hp/str   Polish SM,1975.CW 8   MRL
LOVE SONGS OF HAFIZ, for voice & orch, op.26
   ed T.Chylińska   ɸ   2+picc.2(ca)2+Ebcl+bcl.2/4200/timp.perc.glock/
                               cel.2hp.pf/str   Polish SM,1978.CW 5   MRL
PENTHESILEA for Soprano & orch, op.18
   ed T.Chylińska   ɸ   22+ca.2+bcl.2+cbsn/4231/timp.perc/hp/str   Polish SM,1978.CW 5   MRL
5 SONGS for voice & orch, op.46 bis
   ed T.Chylińska   ɸ   1111/1000/pf/2vln.2vla.vlc.cb   Polish SM,1978.CW 5   MRL
SONGS OF THE FAIRY PRINCESS for voice & orch, op.31
   ed T.Chylińska   ɸ   1+picc.12(Ebcl)1/2200/perc.glock/pf/str   Polish SM,1978.CW 5   MRL
SONGS OF THE INFATUATED MUEZZIN for high voice & orch, op.42
   ed T.Chylińsak   ɸ   2(picc)2(ca)21/2200/timp.perc/pf/
                               str(12.12.8.8.4.)   Polish SM,1978.CW 5   MRL
SYMPHONIE CONCERTANTE   see   SYMPHONIES, no.4
SYMPHONIES
   No.2, op.19, in Bb
      ed G.Fitelberg   ɸ   3(picc)2+ca.2+bcl(Ebcl)2+cbsn/4331/timp.perc/
                               hp/str   35'   Polish SM,1954   Misc 4201

SZYMANOWSKI, Karol (cont)

SYMPHONIES (cont)

No.3, op.27 'Das Lied von der Nacht' (The song of the night)
                                  ϕ   3+picc.3+ca.3+E♭cl+bcl.3+cbsn/6441/timp.perc.
                                        bells.tamtam/cel.2hp.org.pf/str(16.14.12.10.8)/
                                        Tenor solo.chorus   Universal,1925   Misc 1486
      ed T.Chylińska   ϕ   3+picc.3+ca.3+E♭cl+bcl.3+cbsn/6441/timp.perc.
                                          bells.tamtam/cel.2hp.org/pf/str(16.14.12.10.8)/
                                        Tenor solo.chorus   Polish SM,1973.CW 2   MRL

No.4, op.60 'Symphonie concertante' for piano & orch
      ed T.Chylińska   ϕ   2(picc)2(ca)2(E♭cl)2(cbsn)/4331/timp.perc.tamtam/
                                          hp/str   Polish SM,1973.CW 4   Misc 8618 &

VENI CREATOR, for Soprano Solo, chorus & orch, op.57
      ed Z.Helman   ϕ   3(picc)3(ca)32+cbsn/4331/timp.perc.bells.hbells.tamtam/
                                          hp.org/str   Polish SM,1975.CW 8   MRL

TABACHINK, Michael (1942-

MOVIMENTI	φ	1(afl)+picc.1(ca)+ob-d'a.1(bcl)+E♭cl.2(cbsn)/ 2221/4perc(bells.crot glock.2mba.vib/str (8.6.6.4.4.)		Ricordi,1973	Misc 9392 B
SILLAGES for 32 strings (1972)	φ	str [16.6.6.4]	17'	Ricordi,1973	Misc 8438
SUPERNOVAE (1967)	φ	1(afl)010/0110/timp.4perc(bells.crot. 2glock.mba.2mbn.vib)/cel.2hp.amphsd. 2pf/vla.vlc.cb.		Fairfield,1969	Misc 8602 B

TABRAR, Joseph

DADDY WOULDN'T BUY ME A BOW-WOW: song					
in D	φ	1020/0110/timp/str		(F D & H)	MS 763
in D arr R.Chignell	φ	1121/0210/pf/str		(F D & H)	MS 3346
in D arr F.M.Collinson	φ	2222/2220/timp/hp.pf/str		Arranger	MS 30850 φ only

TAEYE, Alex de

PAYSAGES FLAMANDS: suite arr Delsaux
   Part I
      1. Chanson du ruisseau
      2. Noces villageoises et carillon

	PC	1122/2220/timp.perc/hp/str		Choudens	6138

   Part 2
      3. Sous le grand orme (D'après un noël flamand du 16e siècle)
      4. Kermesse flamande (sur des airs populaires)

	PC	2(picc)022/2230/timp.perc/str		Choudens	6136

TAGELL, Rogelio   see   HUGUET Y TAGELL, Rogelio

TAGORE, Rabindranath

JANĂ GÁNĂ MANĂ = national anthem of India (adopted 1950)

arr G.French	φ	2222/2230/timp.perc/str		Arranger/Blandford	25226 +
arr H.Murrill	φ	2.2+ca.2+bcl.2+cbsn/4231/timp.perc/ str		Arranger	19805
arr S.Sharan		2222/4230/timp.perc/hp[=pf]/str		Music Board,Calcutta	Misc 3224

TAGLIAFERRI, E.

CITY OF SONG (Nun me sieta): song					
in E	φ	2020/0220/timp/hp/str		(Ricordi)	MS 2064

TAILLEFERRE, Germaine (1892-

CONCERTO FOR 2 PIANOS, CHORUS & ORCHESTRA					
		SATB chorus parts only	14'30"	(Heugel)	MS 2199
SARABANDE on a theme from the opera 'Camille' by A.Campra					
	φ	2222/2200/timp/str		Salabert	Misc 4163

TAKÁCS, Jenö (1902 -

CONCERTO for piano & orch, no.2, op.60					
	φ	perc/str	32'	Sidem,1948	Misc 3295

TAKÁCS, Jenő (cont)

LÄNDLICHES BAROCK: suite for orch, op.48
                      φ 2(picc)222/2210/timp.perc/hp[=pf]/str   8'   Universal,1953   Misc 4356
PASSACAGLIA for strings, op.73   φ str   13'   Doblinger,1961   Misc 6548

TAKEMITSU, Tōru (1930-

CORAL ISLAND for Soprano solo & orch (1962)
   Accumulation I
   Poem I
   Accumulation II with "corona" for strings
   Poem II
   Accumulation II
                      φ 3(picc:afl).03(bcl)0/2220/5perc(crot.
                         2glock.mba.tamtam.vib.xyl)/cel.hp.pf/str
                         (12.10.8.6.6)   Salabert,1970   Misc 9108
EUCALYPTS   φ 1100/0000/hp/str(8.6.4.4.2.)   Salabert,1970   Misc 9109
GARDEN RAIN for 2 brass groups (1974)
                        Group I   0000/1211
                        Group II   0000/0230   Salabert,1974   Misc 8828
REQUIEM for string orch (1957)   φ str   Salabert,1962   Misc 8483

TAL, Joseph (formerly GRUENTHAL) (1910 -

EXODUS: choreographic poem for Baritone & orch
                      φ 2+picc.2+ca.2+bcl.2+cbsn/4331/timp.perc.
                         tamtam.xyl/[cel]hp.str(score also contains
                         pf redn.of Baritone solo   Hargail Press   Misc 3086
SYMPHONY No.3 (1978)   φ 2+picc.2+ca.2+bcl(Ebcl)2+cbsn/4331/5perc(timp.
                         bells.3bgo.Turkish scym.gro.mba.tamtam.4tplbl.
                         vib.xyl)/hp/str   15' Israel Mus.Inst,1979 Misc 9915

TALBOT, Howard (1865-1928)

The ARCADIANS: musical play by H.Talbot & L.Monckton
   Complete   φ 3222/4231/perc/str   Chappell   12620 B
   Overture, arr A.Wood   PC 1+picc.222/2230/timp.perc/str   Chappell   313 Cs Dm
   Selection   φPC 2(picc)121/2230.euph/timp.perc/str   Chappell   324 E
      see also: MONCKTON, L.
AUTUMN MANOEUVRES: musical play   see KÁLMÁN, E
The BELLE OF BRITTANY: musical play
   Selection arr I.A.de Orellana   PC 2(picc)122/2220/timp.perc/str   K.Prowse   1928 Bp
The BLUE MOON: musical play by H.Talbot & P.Rubens
   Selection arr A.W.Ketèlbey   PC 1+picc.122/2230.euph/timp.perc/str   Chappell   7140 Bp
      see also ROUBENS, P.
The BOY: musical play by H.Talbot & L.Monckton
   Selection arr H.M.Higgs   PC 2(picc)122/2230.euph/timp.perc/cel.hp/str   Chappell   1595 C
      see also MONCKTON, L.
The CARNIVAL: march   PC 2(picc)122/2230.euph/perc/str   Chappell   2954
A CHINESE HONEYMOON: musical play
   Selection arr Godfrey   PC 2(picc)121/2230.euph/timp.perc/str   12'30"   Hawkes   1638 C
The GIRL BEHIND THE COUNTER: musical play
   Selection arr Ketèlbey & Moore   1(picc)122/2230.euph/timp.perc/pf/str   Chappell   2264 Ap
HIGH JINKS: musical play by H.Talbot & R.Freemann
   Selection arr   PC 1(picc)121/2230.euph/timp.perc.glock/str   Lafleur   10528

TALBOT, Howard (cont)

HIGH JINKS: musical play by H.Talbot & R.Friml (cont)
  Extracts
    Jim: song
      in C (orig D) arr H.Carr   φ 2121/2230/timp.perc/hp/str   (Chappell)   TO 561
        see also FRIML, R.
KITTY GREY: musical play by H.Talbot, L.Monckton & A.Barratt
  Selection   PC 1(picc)122/2220.euph/perc/str   Boosey   1334
MADEMOISELLE PIROUETTE: song
  in Eb arr H.Carr   φ 2121/2230/timp.perc/cel.hp/str   (Ascherberg) TO 180
The MOUSMÉ: musical play by H.Talbot & L.Monckton
  Complete   1121/2210/perc/str   Chappell(H) PL 214
  Selection arr H.M Higgs & Wood PC 2(picc)222/2230.euph/timp.perc/str   Chappell   548 D
  Selection of excerpts
    Opening chorus, Act 1 (Monckton)(No.1)
    Introduction to 'I know nothing of life'
    My Samisen: in D min (No.12)
    Opening of Act 2
    Introduction & opening chorus to Act 3: in G (No.17)(3'45")
    The temple bell: in Bb (No.18)(3')
                 φ 3(picc)2+ca.3(bcl)2/4231/timp.perc.vib/hp/str (Chappell) TO 1476
  Extracts
    I know nothing of life (Monckton): song
      in Ab   φ 212+bcl.1/3230/timp.perc/hp/str (Chappell) MS 5287
    Waltz
      arr C.Kiefert   PC 1(picc)121/2230.euph/perc/str   (Chappell) 3708
MR. MANHATTEN: musical play
  Selection, arr Cortenay & Carr PC 2121/2230/timp/str   A H & C   2211 B
  Extracts
    I shall flirt with anyone: song
      in C (orig), arr E.Griffiths
               φ 2222/4230/timp.perc/hp.pf/str   (A H & C) 18356
MY LADY FRAYLE: musical play by H.Talbot & H.Finck
  Selections   PC 2(picc)222/2230/timp.perc/hp/str Hawkes   1634 C
  Extracts
    Day by day: song
      in C (orig)   2222/2230/str   (A H & C) MS 42
    Song of the bowl: song (H.Finck)
      in Bb   φ 1111/2210/str   (A H & C) MS 2822
MY NIECES: musical play
  Selection, arr H.Finck   PC 1+picc.122/2230/timp.perc/str A H & C   2720 B
The PEARL GIRL: musical play by H.Talbot & H.Felix
  Selection, arr H.M Higgs   PC 2(picc)122/2230.euph/perc/str Chappell   1594
  Extracts
    Waltz, arr H.M.Higg & Wood PC 1(picc)121/2230.euph/perc/str Chappell   3670
The WHITE CHRYSANTHEMUM: musical play
  Selection, arr Ketèlby & Godfrey PC 2(picc)122/2230.euph/timp.perc/str Chappell 3960
  Extracts
    The Butterfly and the flower: song
      in G (orig D)   1010/2000/timp/str   (Chappell) MS 221
    O wandering breeze:
      in C (orig)   2121/2230/timp.perc/str   (Chappell) TO 388
WHO'S HOOPER?: musical play by H.Talbot & I.Novello
  Selection, arr H.Jaxon   PC 2(picc)121/2230/timp.perc/hp/str A H & C 2106 B
  Extracts
    If you were the king of Babylon: song (I.Novello)
      in Ab, orch H.Carr   φ 2121/2230/ti p.perc/hp/str   (A H & C) TO 523
    Pierrot dance   PC 2(2picc)121/2220/timp.perc.xyl/hp.pf/str A H & C 6830
        see also NOVELLO, I.

TALLEDO, Eduardo Marquez

GREY CLOUD (Nube Gris)   PC 2121/2220/timp.perc/acdn.gtr/str   2'15"   Weinberger,1950   23138

TALLIS, Thomas (ca 1505-1585)

SANCTUS, arr for orchestra   1121/20.2cnt.30/perc/str   Boosey & H   20417
VENITE, EXULTATE DOMINO: (Psalm 95): chant setting, arr for orchestra
                                         1121/20.2cnt.30/perc/str   Boosey & H   20417

TAMBERG, Eino (1930-

CONCERTO GROSSO   Concertino: 1(picc)01.asx.1/0100/pf
                                   Ripieno: timp.perc.xyl/cel.hp/str   Russian SM,1968   Misc 8660

TANEYEV, Aleksandr Sergeyevich (1850-1918)

FESTIVE MARCH, op.12   PC 2+picc.222/4331/timp.perc/hp/str   5'   Zimmerman   5516 B
HAMLET: overture   φ   3(picc)2+ca.2+bcl.2/4331/timp.perc/hp/str 14'-19' Zimmerman   5192
2 MAZURKAS, op.15
   No.1   PC 2+picc.222/4231/timp.perc/str   6'   Zimmerman   5515
   No.2   PC 32(ca)22/4231/timp.perc/str   6'   Zimmerman   5514
SUITES
   op.9
      1. Introduction   3. Berceuse   5. Rêverie
      2. Sérénade   4. Valse   6. Finale
                                   φ   3(picc)21+ca.2+bcl.2/4231/timp.perc/hp/str   (Rahter)   12006
   op.14, in F
      1. Tema con variazioni   3. Andantino
      2. Menuette   4. Finale
                                   φ   3(picc)2(ca)22/4231/timp.perc/hp/str   Zimmerman   13056
SYMPHONY no.2 op.21, in B♭ min   φ   3(picc)2(ca)22/4231/timp.perc.glock/hp/str 36'   Zimmerman   5525

TANEYEV, Sergei Ivanovich (1856-1915)

ADAGIO
   ed P.Lamm   φ   2222/2200/timp/str   Russian SM,1950   Misc 3949
CANTATAS
   op.1, for chorus & orch (from Tolstoy's 'John of Damascus')
                                   φ   2222/4231/timp/str   Jurgenson   Misc 2133
   op.36, no.2 (Upon reading a psalm)(1914), for SATB soli, double chorus & orch
      ed I.Iordan & G.Kirkor   φ   3(picc)3(2ca)3(bcl)3+cbsn/4331/timp.perc/hp/str Russian SM,1960 Misc 5616
CONCERTO for piano & orch (1876)   φ   2222/4231/timp/str   Russian SM,1957   Misc 5927
ORCHESTEIA (L'Orestie): opera op.6
   Overture   φ   3(picc)222/4231/timp.perc.glock/hp/str   19'   Belaieff   8595
   Entr'acte   φ   3222/4231/timp/2hp/str
                                       Offstage: perc   Belaieff,1901   25546
OVERTURE ON RUSSIAN THEMES
   ed P.Lamm   φ   2+picc.222/4231/timp.bells/str   Russian SM,1948   Misc 4084
SUITE DE CONCERT for violin & orch, op.28
   1. Prelude   4. Theme with variations
   2. Gavotte   5. Tarantella
   3. Fairy-tale
                                   φ   2(picc)2(ca)22/2200/timp.perc/hp/str   Russian SM,1971   Misc 6683

TANEYEV, Sergei Ivanovich (cont)

SYMPHONIES
    [no.1], in E min
      ed P.Lamm   φ   2222/4230/timp/str   32'   Russian SM   Misc 3951
    [no.3], in D min
      ed B.Yavorsky   φ   2+picc.222/2230/timp/str   Russian SM,1947   Misc 3950
    [no.4], in C min, op.12 (orig published as No.1 by Belaieff)
                            φ   3(picc)232+cbsn/4331/timp.perc/str   Belaieff/Russian SM,1963   15470 B
VALSE MÉLANCOLIQUE from quartet no.2, op.28
                            φ   2122/2000/str   7'   Zimmerman   1182

TANSMAN, Alexandre (1897-

CONCERTI
    for Orchestra (1954)   φ   2222/4331/timp.perc.glock.xyl/cel.pf/str 20'   Eschig,1956   Misc 4748 B
    for Piano & orch, no.2, in E φ   2+picc.2+ca.2+bcl.2/4331/timp.perc/str   Eschig,1930   Misc 2516
CONCERTINO for Piano & orch   φ   2+picc.2(ca)2(bcl)2/4300/timp.perc/cel/
                                 str   18'-19'30"   Eschig,1936   Misc 3112 B
4 DANSES POLONAISES
    1. Polka   2. Kujawiak   3. Dumka   4. Oberek
                              φ   2+picc.2+ca.22/4331/timp.perc.glock.xyl/cel.pf/
                                 str   Eschig,1932   Misc 1192 C
6 ÉTUDES   φ   2+picc.222/4330/timp.perc.bells.glock.
                                 vib.xyl/cel.pf/str   25'
                                                Ed.Françaises de Musique,1963   Misc 6179
HOMMAGE À ERASME DE ROTTERDAM   φ   2220/4331/perc.glock.xyl/cel.pf/str   15'   Eschig,1971   Misc 8462
LIED & TOCCATA for orch (1944) φ   2+picc.2+ca.22+cbsn/4331/timp.xyl/pf/str   Universal,1952   Misc 3830
6 MOVEMENTS for strings (1962-3)
    1. Introduction & allegro giocoso   4. Intermezzo
    2. Dirge   5. Scherzino
    3. Perpetuum mobile   6. Fuga
                            φ   str   Ed.Françaises de Musique,1963   Misc 6178
PSALMES 118, 119, 120 for Tenor solo, chorus & orch (1960-61)
                            φ   2+picc.222/4331/timp.perc.glock.gong.
                               vib. xyl/cel(pf)/str   Eschig,1964   Misc 10124
RICERCARI (1949)   φ   2+picc.222/4331/timp.perc.bells.xyl/
                               cel.hp.pf/str   14'40"   Leeds,1953   Misc 4775
SHORT SUITE for instrumental groups & orch
                            φ   2222/3331/perc.xyl/pf/str   Delkas,1944   Misc 3021
SINFONIETTA for chamber orch φ   1111/1120/timp.perc/cel.pf/str   16'   Universal,1926 Misc 1601
SINFONIETTA no.2 (1979)   φ   1(picc)110/1000/timp.perc.vib.xyl/str 15'30" Eschig,1981   Misc 10482
SONATINE TRANSATLANTIQUE in 3 parts
    1. Fox-trot   2. Spiritual and blues   3. Charleston
                            φ   2+picc.2(ca)2+bcl.sx.2/timp.perc.xyl/
                             cel.pf/str   Leduc,1930   Misc 812
SUITE BAROQUE
    1. Entrée   2. Sarabande   3. Divertissement   4. Aria   5. Rigaudon
                                2(picc)222/2000/timp.perc/pf(cel)/str 10'
                                                Universal,1958   Misc 5148 B
                                                              PL 632 Ani
SYMPHONY in A min   φ   2+picc.2+ca.2+bcl.2+cbsn/6441/timp.perc.
                               glock.tamtam/cel.2[=1]hp.pf/str 26'   Eschig,1931   Misc 261
TOCCATA   φ   2+picc.2+ca.2+bcl.2+cbsn/4431/timp.perc.
                               glock.xyl/cel.hp.pf/str   8'   Eschig,1932   Misc 734
TOMBEAU DE CHOPIN
    1. Nocturne   2. Mazurka   3. Postlude
                              str   Leeds Music Corp   51931

TANSMAN, Alexandre (cont)

TRIPTYQUE	φ	str			18'	Eschig,1931	Misc 1285

VARIATIONS ON A THEME BY GIROLAMO FRESCOBALDI

φ   str   Ass.Mus.Pub.NY   Misc 1727

TAPKOV, Dimitre

CANTATE POUR LA PAIX (Peace Cantata) for Mezzo soprano solo, children's chorus & strings
   1. Passacaglia (Retrospection)
   2. In mode di sonate (Compte á rebours: Backwards counting)
   3. Rondo (Chant d'hiver pour la colombe: Winter song about the dove)
                            φ   str   Bulgarian SM   Misc 9154

TAPP, Frank

BEACHYHEAD: overture   PC 212.3sx.1/4230/timp.perc.glock/cel.hp/str 5'30"-7' Chappell   15462 B
ENGLISH LANDMARKS: suite
   1. Ascot: Waltz   (3')
   2. Tintern Abbey   (3')
   3. Whitehall: march   (3')
                            PC 1121/2220/timp.perc.glock/cel.hp/str   9'   P.Maurice   11820 B
LAND OF FANCY: suite, arr J.Engleman
   1. A swing song at morn   (3'15")
   2. Sprites lullaby   (3')
   3. The pixies parade   (5'30")
                            PC 1121/2230/timp.perc/str   11'45"   Bosworth   9036
A WAYSIDE MELODY: entr'acte   PC 1121/2220/timp/cel.hp/str   3'30"-4' P.Maurice   11662
WOODLAND ECHOES, arr A.W.Leggett PC 112.sx.1/2230/timp.perc/str   8'   Bosworth   6706

TĂRANU, Cornel

DIALOGUES II (Intercalations) for piano & orch
                            φ   2(picc)222/2110/perc.vib/hp.pf/str 10'-11' Rumanian SM,1972 Misc 7923

TARDOS, Béla (1910-

CONCERTO for violin & orch (1962) φ 2(picc)2(ca)2(bcl)2(cbsn)/4330/timp.
                                      perc.vib.xyl/cel.hp/str   Ed.Musica,1970   Misc 8300

TARENGHI, Mario

SCENA ORIENTALE op.17   φ   2+picc.222/4231/timp.perc/hp/str   Fantuzzi   10277

TARP, Svend Erik (1908 -

CONCERTINO for flute & orch, op.30 φ 0202/2000/perc/str   Ed.Dania,1939   Misc 933
COMEDY OVERTURE (Lustspiel Ouverture) op.36
                            φ   2222/4330/timp.perc.xyl/str   Ed.Dania,1943   Misc 3510
MOSAIK: suite op.35
   1. Harmonica   5. Bagpipe
   2. Shalm   6. Tempo di valse
   3. The old violin   7. Callopade
   4. Choral
                            φ   2[=1]2[=1]22[=1]/4[=2]3[=2]10/
                                timp.perc/cel/str   8'30"   Hansen,1942   Misc 3356 B

TARP, Svend Erik (cont)

SUITE ON OLD DANISH FOLK SONGS (1933)
    1. Ravnen, han flyver om Aften   3. Liden Kirstens Dans
    2. Skaemtevise   4. Hr. Ramund
                                    ∅   22(ca)22/2200/timp/str   12'   Hansen,1936   Misc 2363
SYMPHONY, op.50, in E♭   ∅   2+picc.222/2200/timp.perc.xyl/str   Dania,1949   Misc 5511

TARTINI, Giuseppe (1692-1770)

see   CAPRI, A. Giuseppe Tartini.   Garzanti, 1945
      DOUNIAS, M. Die Violinkonzerte Giuseppe Tartinis.   Berlin: Kalmeyer, 1935.   The numbers prefixed
      'D' refer to entries in this book.

COMPLETE WORKS

Le Opere di Giuseppe Tartini, 1st series, ed E.Farina & C.Scimone.   Milan: Carish, 1971   CAT IN MAIN LIB

ANDANTE
    arr H.Elkan   ∅   [pf]/str   Elkan   11715
ANDANTE & PRESTO for violin & orch
                                    ∅   2+picc.202/2000/timp/str   (Schott)   19923
ANDANTE CANTABILE for flute (or violin & oboe) & strings
    transcr N.Ticciati, ed R.Jacques
                                    ∅   str   OUP,1961   23395
CONCERTINO for clarinet & orch, selected & arr by G.Jacob from sonatas of Tartini
                                    ∅   str   Boosey & H   19897 B
CONCERTI
    Cello & orch
      in D
        ed Delune   ∅   0000/2000/str   12'-16'   Breitkopf   16920
        ed Hindemith   PC 0000/2000/hpsd/str   Schott   6834
      in A
        ed O.Ravanello   str   12'   Zanibon   15414
    Flute & orch
      in G
        ed Brinckmann & Mohr   ∅   str/cont   11'   Sikorski,1954   21449
    2 oboes, 2 horns & strings
      in F (No.58)
        ed Bonelli   ∅   str   12'   Zanibon,1948   22174 B
    Violin & orch
      D.12, in D
        ed C.Scimone (includes alternative first mvt)
                                    ∅   str/cont   Carisch,1975   Misc 8743
      D.15, op.1, no.4, in D
        ed M.Abbade   ∅   str/cont   22'   Ricordi,1971   Misc 7710
      D.21, in D
        ed C.Scimone   ∅   0000/[2]000/str/cont   Carisch,1976   Misc 9854
      D.24, in D
        ed E.Farina   ∅   str/cont   Carisch,1971   Misc 8742
      D.28, in D
        ed Bonelli   ∅   0000/2200/timp/str   20'-22'   Zanibon,1953   21259
      D.45, in D min
        ed R.Baumgartner   ∅   str   Hug,1958   Misc 5211
        ed Pente   str   Benjamin   7588
      D.56, in E min
        ed C.Scimone   ∅   str/cont   Carisch,1975   Misc 8741
      D.67, in F
        ed E.Farina   ∅   str/cont   Carisch,1971   Misc 8740
        ed Ross   ∅   str/cont   Smith College,1972   Misc 3811
      D.78, in G
        ed C.Scimone   ∅   str/cont   Carisch,1972   Misc 8739
      D.83, in G
        ed E.Farina   ∅   str/cont   Carisch,1975   Misc 8738

TARTINI, Giuseppe (cont)

CONCERTI (cont)
  Violin & orch (cont)
    D.85, in G min
      ed G.Guglielmo   ∅   str/cont   14'30"   Zanibon,1972   25659
    D.86, in G min
      ed Rostel   str/cont   20'   Novello,1952   Misc 3716
    D.92, in A
      ed Schroeder   ∅   str/cont(hpsd)   Eulenburg,1959 23256 B
    D.96, in A
      ed E.Farina   ∅   str/cont   Carisch,1971   Misc 8737
    D.105, in A, ed Brosa   str   20'   BBC   19670
    D.115, in A min
      ed Ross with cadenzas   str/cont   Simith College,1947 Misc 3811
    D.117, in B♭
      ed C.Scimone   ∅   str/cont   Carisch,1975   Misc 9002 B
    D.125, in B min
      ed E.Farina   ∅   str/cont   Carisch,1971   Misc 8736
The DEVIL'S TRILL: sonata
    ed R.Becker   ∅   0222/2000/timp/str   20'   Breitkopf   18690
SYMPHONIES
    in D, ed H. Erdmann   ∅   str   Schott,1956   24325 +
    in D 'Sinfonia Pastorale' ed A.Schering
                             ∅   str   Kahnt,1926   25653
    in A, ed H.Erdmann   ∅   str   Bärenreiter   20214

TATE, Arthur F.

ETERNAL DAY: song, in A♭   2222/2220/timp/str   (Siddell)   18322
LOVE'S DEVOTION: song
    in D♭ arr S.Baynes   2122/2230/timp/str   Larway   18009
    in E♭ arr S.Baynes   2122/2230/timp/str   Larway   18008 B
    in F arr S.Baynes   2122/2230/timp/str   Larway   18007
SLEEP AND THE ROSES: song
    in G arr E.Austin   1111/2210/timp.perc/str   Larway,1915   17249
SOMEWHERE A VOICE IS CALLING: song
    in D arr C.Windeatt   PC   1021/2230/timp.perc/str   Larway   51 Ap C
    in E♭ arr C.Windeatt   1121/2230/timp/str   Larway   17307
    in F arr C.Windeatt   PC   1121/2230/timp.perc/str   Larway   16572 B
    in F arr B.Thompson   ∅   cel.hp/str   (Ashdown)   LMG 4394
    in F arr G.Stacey   pf/str   (Larway)   LMG 3233
    in G arr J.O.Turner   ∅   1110/1000/hp/str/solo voice & SATB chorus (Larway) LMG 7527
    in G arr C.Windeatt   PC   1120/2230/timp.perc/str   Larway   11864
WHEN LOVE SHALL CALL: song
    in E♭   PC   1121/2220/perc/str   (Larway)   16357
WHEN YOU COME BACK: song, in G   1111/2210/timp.perc/str   (Siddell)   18323
YOUR HEART WILL CALL ME HOME: song
    in E♭   1121/2230/timp.perc/str   Larway,1912   17253
    in F   1121/2230/timp.perc/str   Larway,1912   17254

TATE, James W.

The BEAUTY SPOT
  I have to make the old man do: song
    in A♭, arr A.Sandford   ∅   1121/2220/timp.perc/hp/str   (F D & H)   18432

TATE, James W. (cont)

A BROKEN DOLL: song
    in A♭ & B♭ arr Chappelle   1131/0220/perc/pf/str   (F D & H)   LMG 4730
COME OVER THE GARDEN WALL: song
    in D arr E.Griffiths   φ   2+picc.121/0220/perc/pf/str   (Feldman)   LMG 8323
EV'RY LITTLE WHILE: song
    in E♭ arr H.Carr   φ   2121/2230/timp.perc/hp/str   (F D & H)   TO 336
    in B♭ arr J.Beaver   φ   2121/2230/timp.perc/hp/str   (F D & H)   TO 938
I WAS A GOOD LITTLE GIRL: song
    in F   PC 2121/2220/perc/str   (F D & H)   MS 157
    in F   1132/0220/perc/pf/str   (F D & H)   LMG 4404
IF I SHOULD PLANT A TINY SEED OF LOVE: song
    in E♭ arr H.A Carruthers   φ   2121/0220/timp/pf/str   (Feldman)   MS 20178
    in B♭ arr H.A.Carruthers   2121/0220/perc/pf/str   (Feldman)   LMG 4820
MAID OF THE MOUNTAINS: musical play by H.Fraser-Simson & J.W.Tate   see   FRASER-SIMSON, Harold: THE
    MAID OF THE MOUNTAINS
The PEEP SHOW
    Selection   PC 1(picc)121/2230/perc/str   F D & H   12594
ROUND IN FIFTY: musical play
    Extracts
        Shovel on a few more coals: song
           in F arr R.Hanmer   φ   1+picc.222/4230/timp.perc/str   (F D & H)   18362
ROW ME OVER THE RIVER, ROMEO: song
    in A arr H.A.Carruthers   φ   2121/0220/perc/pf/str   (F D & H)   MS 30114

TATE, Phyllis (1911-

The LADY OF SHALOTT: cantata for Tenor solo & small orch
    1. Prologue
    2. Moto perpetuo
    3. All marcia
    4. Barcarolle & Epilogue
                    φ   perc/cel.2pf/vla   (OUP)   Misc 6610
The LODGER: opera
    Concert suite: for Soprano & Bass soli, chorus & orch
        1. Prelude and Cockney chorus
        2. Duet and polka
        3. Interlude and song
        4. Valse
        5. Finale
                    φ   2(picc)2(ca)2(bcl)2/4230/timp.perc.bells.xyl/
                        cel.pf/str   BBC,1965   24324 +
LONDON FIELDS: suite (1958)
    1. Springtime at Kew
    2. Hampton Court - the maze
    3. St James' Park
    4. Hampstead Heath: rondo for roundabouts
    Complete   φ   2(picc)2(ca)22/4230/timp.perc/cel.hp/
                       str   12'-13'
                                          Composer,1958   22901 +
    No.4 only, arr D.Stone   φ   2121/2230/timp.perc/[pf duet]/str
                       (minimum orch: pf.duet/str(no cb))   OUP,1964   24632
NOCTURNE FOR 4 VOICES   φ   cel/str/cont/Mz.T.Bar.B.soli   OUP   Misc 2962 H

TATTENHALL, Barry

| HEYDAY: novelty | PC | 112.3sx.1/2220/perc/acdn(org)/str | 2'40" | Bosworth | 833 |
| VIE DE PLAISIRS (revised) | ∅ | 2121/2330/perc.vib/gtr.hp[pf]/str | 2' | Bosworth | 25232 |

TAUBE, Evert

PIERINA: song
  in E♭ arr G.Vinter   ∅   2222/4230/timp.perc/hp/str   (Gehrman)   22645 +

TAUBER, Richard (1892 - 1948)

HEART'S DESIRE by R.Tauber & G.H.Clustsam
    Selection arr A.Wood   PC   2(picc)12.3sx.1/2230/timp.perc/str   K.Prowse   13209
OLD CHELSEA: musical play by R.Tauber & B.Grun
    Selection arr H.Geehl   PC   212.3sx.1/2230/timp.perc/hp/str   L.Wright   18634 Bp
    Selection arr C.Young for Soprano & Tenor soli, chorus & orch
        1. There are angels outside Heaven
        2. Your love could be everything to me
        3. Why did I have to awake from my dreams?
        4. My heart and I
                               ∅   2(picc)2(ca)22/43[=2]3[1]/timp.perc(glock.
                                   kit.vib)/str/[chorus]   (L.Wright)   26357

    My heart and I: song
        in D (orig)   1110/0000/hp.pf/str   (L. Wright)   LMG 3751
        in D & C arr H.Carr   ∅   2121/2230/timp.perc/hp/str   (L.Wright)   TO 1272
        in D arr V.Harker   1131/2230/perc/hp/str   L.Wright   LMG 4267
        in D & E♭ arr Stacey   pf/str   L.Wright   LMG 3262
        in D♭ arr P.Cardew   ∅   222.4sx.2/4440/timp.perc/hp.pf/str   (L.Wright)   18466 +
        in D♭ arr R.Binge   ∅   1111/1210/perc/str   MS(L.Wright) LMG 4725
        in C arr V.Harker   111.3sx.1/1220/perc/str   L.Wright   18624 Ap
WHY DID I HAVE TO AWAKE?: song
    in A arr Stacey   pf/str   (L.Wright)   LMG 5144

TAUBERT, Ernst Eduard

SUITE IN D op.67
    1. Praeludium
    2. Allegretto grazioso
    3. Larghetto
    4. Gavotte
    5. Finale
                               ∅   str   Kahnt   11624 B

TAUBERT, Wilhelm (1811-1891)

GEBURSTAGS-MARSCH op.146   ∅   2+picc.222/2230/timp.perc/str   Bote & B   Misc 2305
TAUSEND UND EINE NACHT
    Overture op.139   ∅   2222/4000/timp/str   Kistner   Misc 1823

TAUSCH, Franz (1762-1817)

CONCERTO for clarinet & orch in E♭
    ed G.Balassa   ∅   0200/2000/str   Ed Musica,1978 Misc 9749

TAUSCH, Julius (1827-1895)

CONCERTO (SLOW MARCH AND POLONAISE) for 6 timpani & orch
                             ∅   2022/2200/str   (GB-Lcm)   23768 *

TAUSKY, Vilem (1910 -

BUTTERMILK LONEY: Irish reel	φ	2222/4230/timp.perc/cel/str		Arranger	22649 +
COVENTRY: meditation	φ	str		Chester(H)	PL 608
The CZECHS ARE MARCHING	PC	222.3sx.2/4230/timp.perc/str		Dix	10033
GREENSLEEVES for violin & orch	φ	str	4'	Chandos,1967	24688 An B Cgg
MEN OF TOMORROW: festival march	φ	2222/4331/timp.perc/str		(Bensin)	22372 C +
The PRETTY BROWN GIRL: Irish set tune					
	φ	2(picc)121/0000/car/cel.hp.pf/str		Arranger	22680 +
SOHO: scherzo for orch	φ	2(picc)2(ca)22/4230/timp.perc/cel.hp/str	5'30"	Mozart Ed (H)	PL 469
UNDER CZECH SKIES: fantasy on Czech folk songs					
	PC	2(picc)222/4230/timp.perc/hp/str		Dix	8918
WALTZING THROUGH CZECHOSLOVAKIA: based on Czech folk tunes			7'	Dix 1942	21806
WHITTINGHAM FAIR: trad ballad in C min arr					
	φ	1121/2000/timp.perc/hp/str		Arranger	23609 +

TAVAN, Emile

L'ALGÉRIENNE	PC	2222/2230/timp.perc/str	Marguaritat	1142
BEETHOVEN: mosaïque on Beethoven's works				
	PC	2222/2230/timp/str	Margueritat	1122
La CANADIENNE: characteristic piece	PC	2(picc)222/2231/timp.perc/str	Margueritat	5851
La FÉE AUX PERLES: overture	PC	2(picc)222/2231/timp.perc/str	Enoch	12090
La FÊTE DE SÉVILLE: suite by Tavan & Marchetti				
1. Bolero				
2. Sierra Morena				
3. Jota				
4. Sevillanas				
5. Marche des Troubadours				
arr R.Jungnickel	φ	2(picc)222/4231/timp.perc/str	Jungnickel	7873
GAVOTTE LOUIS XV	PC	2222/2000/timp/str	Margueritat	3594
GOUNOD: mosaïque on Gounod's works	PC	2222/2231/timp.perc/str	Leduc	1132
HAYDN: mosaïque on Haydn's works	PC	2222/2230/timp/str	Margueritat	1097
MENDELSSOHN: mosaïque on Mendelssohn's works				
	PC	2222/2231/timp.perc/str	Margueritat	1111
MENUET HENRY IV	PC	1121/1000/timp/str	Margueritat	3521
MOZART: mosaïque on Mozart's works	PC	2222/2230/timp.perc/str	Margueritat	1112
RONDE DES GARDES LORRAINES	PC	1121/2210/timp/str	Ricordi	560
ROSSINI: mosaïque on Rossini's works				
	PC	2222/2231/timp/str	Margueritat	7804
WEBER: mosaïque on Weber's work				
	PC	2222/2[2]31/timp.perc/str	Margueritat	1098

TAVENER, John (1944-

CAIN AND ABEL: a dramatic cantata	φ	2(picc)222(cbsn)/3330/timp.perc.bell/hp/str	22'	Chester,1967	Misc 6718
CELTIC REQUIEM for Soprano, children's choir chorus & orch (1969)					
	φ	0010/01(ptpt)10[Aeolian bagpipes]/timp.perc. xyl/pf.org/egtr(bgtr)/str	22'-23'	Chester,1972	Misc 7746 F
A GENTLE SPIRIT: opera	φ	1(picc)01(bcl)0/1110/timp.perc.hbells.claves. 3gong.tamtam.5tomtom.whip/pf/2vln.vla. vlc.cb	45'	Chester,1978	Misc 9829
IN ALIUM for Soprano & orch	φ	perc/pf.org.Horg(4 hands)/tape/str	15'	Chester,1968	Misc 6760 B
KYKLIKE KINÉSIS for Soprano solo, chorus, cello & orch (1977)					
	φ	0101/1110/3perc(timp.bells.bgos.clv.gongs. tomtoms)/pf/str	45'	Chester,1980	Misc 10133

TAVENER, John (cont)

The WHALE: Biblical fantasy for speaker, Mezzo-soprano & Baritone soli, chorus, pre-recorded tape,
   6 male performers with loud hailers & orch (1965-6)

            ⌀ 2(picc.bfl)22(bcl)2(cbsn)/4331/timp.perc.
               glock.mba.3gongs.tamtam.bells.Sanctus.
               bells.hand-bells.football rattle.2 metronomes
               glass sheet.xyl/cel.hp.org.Horg.pf/str(no vlns)   Chester,1969   Misc 7020

TAVARES, Hekel arr

PAPA CORUMIASCU: Brazilian folksong
   orch J.Serrallonga   ⌀ 1+picc.0.ca.22/2000/hp/str   1'05"   (Sampaio Araujo)   20200

TAXIN, Ira

SABA (1974)   ⌀ 2+picc.2+ca.2+E♭cl.2+cbsn/4331/
               timp.perc(tamtam)/hp.pf/str   Presser   Misc 9267

TAYLOR, Avril COLERIDGE-   see   COLERIDGE-TAYLOR, Avril

TAYLOR, COLERIDGE   see   COLERIDGE-TAYLOR, Samuel

TAYLOR, Colin

PRELUDE AND SARABANDE   ⌀ str   3'   OUP   2308

TAYLOR, Deems (1885-1966)

CAPTAIN STRATTON'S FANCY: song
   in F arr F.Cramer   pf/str   (Boosey)   LMG 4645
CIRCUS DAY, op.18: 8 pictures from memory
   1. Street parade
   2. The big top
   3. Bareback riders
   4a. The lion cage   b. The dog & monkey circus   c. The waltzing elephants
   5. Tight-rope walker
   6. Jugglers
   7. Clowns
   8. Finale
           ⌀ 3(picc)2+ca.2+E♭cl.3sx.2/4331/timp.perc.
               xyl.glock/str   21'   J.Fischer,1934   Misc 1076
FANFARE FOR RUSSIA
   arr J.Turner   ⌀ 0000/4331/timp.perc   Boosey & H,1944 Misc 2974
The PORTRAIT OF A LADY op.14   ⌀ 1111/1000/pf/str   12'   J.Fischer,1932   Misc 1354
THROUGH THE LOOKING GLASS op.12 ⌀ 3(picc)2+ca.2+bcl.2+cbsn/4331/timp.
               perc.glock.xyl/pf/str   J.Fischer   7268

TAYLOR, H.J.

MEMORIES   ⌀ str   Stainer & B   Misc 3619 B

TAYLOR, Iris

DREAMY AFTERNOON arr F.Hartley   PC 111.4sx.0/0210/perc/gtr/str   P.Maurice   18833
JAPANESE GOWN arr F.Hartley   PC 1110/0210/perc.xyl/gtr/str   3'30" Hartley,1940   20416
STARRY NIGHT arr R.Hanmer   PC 1(picc)12.3sx.1/2220/timp.perc/hp/str   P.Maurice   6810

TAYLOR, W.H.

SO DEAR TO ME: song
   in Eb arr R.G.Brown   pf/str   Cross,1919   18214

TCHAIKOVSKY, André

CONCERTO for piano & orch (1966-71)
                     ø   2(picc)22(Ebcl)2/4201/timp.perc.tamtam.xyl/
                        str(16-24.0.12.8.6-2cbs must be 5-stringed)   Weinberger,1975   Misc 10480

TCHAIKOVSKY, Boris Aleksandr (1925 -

CHAMBER SYMPHONY (1967)   0200/2000/hpsd/str   Russian SM,1971   Misc 7640
CONCERTO for cello & orch   ø 3000/0330/timp.perc.glock.vib.xyl/hp/str   Russian SM,1970   Misc 6570
CONCERTO for violin & orch ø 0000/4431/timp/str   Russian SM,1978   Misc 9795
SYMPHONY no.2 (1967)   ø 4(2picc)44(bcl)4/4440/timp.perc.bells.mba.vib/
                        cel.hp/str   Russian SM,1970   Misc 7539
THEME & 8 VARIATIONS   ø 4444/6441/timp.perc.bells.glock/cel.hp/str 19' Russian SM,1978   Misc 9815

TCHAIKOVSKY, Pyotr Ilyich (1840-1893)

see   SYSTEMATISCHES VERZEICHNIS DER WERKE VON PJOTR ILIJITSCH TSCHAIKOVSKY. Hamburg: Hans Sikorski,1973

COMPLETE WORKS

P.I.Tchaikovsky: complete edition of compositions. Moscow & Leningrad. Russian SM, 1940-71. MRL

AGAIN, AS BEFORE, ALONE see   LYRIC SUITE
AGITATO, in E minor (1863-64)   ø 2222/0000/str   Russian,1967 CW 58   MRL
AH, WEEP NO MORE op.6 no.4 (orig voice & pf)
   in Eb, arr Siddell   ø 1121/2000/str   (Siddell)   18109
   in Eb, arr G.Stacey   pf/str   BBC   LMG 3622
   in F [arr]   2121/2000/pf/str   BBC   LMG 3850
   orch arr Arends (Trembling tears)
                     ø 2122/2100/str   Jurgenson   9187
ALBUM FOR THE YOUNG op.39 (see also 'INTERNATIONALE': suite)(orig pf)
   Suite no.1 (orig.numbers in brackets)
      1. Playing hobby-horses (No.3)
      2. Mama (No.4)
      3. March of the wooden soldiers (No.5)
                PC 1(picc)121/2230/timp.perc/str   Salabert   94
   Suite no.2
      1. Song of the lark (No.22)
      2. Sweet reverie (No.21)
      3. In church (No.24)
      4. The witch (No.20)
                PC 1(picc)121/2230/timp.perc/str   Salabert   53
   No.8 Valse   pf/str   1'20"   Hawkes   6184
     arr H.Germer   ø str   Bosworth   8417
   No.19 Polka, arr Rowley ø 1111/2110/timp/str   J.Williams   19751
   No.21 Sweet reverie   pf/str   1'45"-2'15" Hawkes   6184
     arr H.Germer   ø str   Bosworth   8417
   No.24 In church, arr Pribik ø 2022/2000/tamtam/str   Jurgenson   Misc 831
ALLEGRO MA NON TANTO in G (1863-64)
                    ø str   Russian SM,1967 CW 58   MRL
ALLEGRO VIVO in C min (1863-64) ø 2222/2200/str   Russian SM,1967 CW 58   MRL
ANDANTE (from string quartet in E minor op.30)
   arr A.Glazunov   ø str   Jurgenson   9867 AmvB
   arr Q.Maganini   ø pf[str]   Ed.Musicus 16597

TCHAIKOVSKY, Pyotr Ilyich (cont)

ANDANTE from Suite no.3, op.55   see   BALLET SUITE
ANDANTE AND FINALE for pinao & orch, op.79
   orch Taneyev from sketches   ∅   2+picc.222/4231/timp.perc/str   18'30"   Belaieff   10384
ANDANTE CANTABILE (arr from string quartet in D, op.11)
                                 ∅   vlc-solo.str   Russian SM.CW 30b   MRL
   arr S.Hughes   ∅   str   8'   BBC   9988
   arr Schmid   str   Hawkes   2306 Amv Dwe
ANDANTE MA NON TROPPO and ALLEGRO MODERATO in A (1863-64)
                                ∅   2222/4000/str   Russian SM,1967.CW 58   MRL
AT THE TCHAIKOVSKY SPRING: selection of Tchaikovsky's works   see   URBACH, E: AT THE TCHAIKOVSKY SPRING
AURORA'S WEDDING   see   The SLEEPING BEAUTY
AUTUMN (Herbst)(No.14 of Children's songs, op.54)
   orch Taneyev   ∅   2022/3000/str   Jurgenson   Misc 2224
BALLET SUITE, arr Becce
   1. Polacca, op.72, no.7   3. Andante (from SUITE no.3, op.55)
   2. Valse ('Christmas' from The SEASONS) 4. Fughetta a danza (from SUITE no.3, op.55)
                             PC   2121/2210/timp/str   Bote & B   1672
BERCEUSE TRISTE, op.16, no.1 (arr of 'Cradle song')
   arr Torke   PC   1111/2110/str   Kuhl   3262
BLUEBIRD VARIATION, arr Stravinsky   see   The SLEEPING BEAUTY
CANTATA (Hymn) for the Jubilee of the singer Osip Afanasyevich Petrov, for Tenor solo, chorus & orch (1875)
                                ∅   2+picc.222/4230/timp/str   Russian SM.CW 27   MRL
CANTATA in honour of the 200th anniversary of the birth of Pyotr Veliski for Tenor solo, chorus & orch(1872)
                                    2+picc.222/4231/timp.perc/str   Russian SM.CW 27   MRL
Les CAPRICES D'OSANE   see   OXANA'S CAPRICES
CAPRICCIO ITALIEN   see   ITALIAN CAPRICE
CASSE NOISETTE   see   The NUTCRACKER
CATHARINE: musical play based on Tchaikovsky's music
   Selection, arr Morgan   PC   1121/2230/timp.perc/str   AH & C   2270 C
CATHERINE: waltz   see   CHANT SANS PAROLES
CHANSON TRISTE (from 12 pieces), op.40, no.2
                             PC   1121/2210.euph/timp/str   2'30"   Lafleur   368
   arr R.Douglas   ∅   21+ca.22/4030/timp/hp/str   BBC   TO 1765
   arr Pribik   ∅   1121/2000/str   Jurgenson   10170 B
   see also   2 PIECES, arr W.Stewart
CHANT ÉLÉGIAQUE (from 18 pieces), op.72, no.14
   orch A.Schmid   PC   2(picc)1+ca.22/4230/timp.perc/hp/str 6'15"-7'15"   Hawkes   724
   see also LYRIC SUITE no.3
CHANT SANS PAROLES, op.2, no.3 (from SOUVENIR DE HAPSAL)
   arr Erdmannsdörger   ∅   2222/2000/timp/hp/str   3'   Jurgenson   10169 Bs
   arr Kretschmer   PC   1121/2210/timp/str   C.Fischer   1301
   arr A.Winter   ∅PC   2222/2000/timp/hp/str   Hawkes   3247 B
   waltz, arr (as Catherine)   PC   112.2sx.1/2210/perc/str   Weinberger   8650
CHARACTERISTIC DANCE (from 18 pieces for pf), op.72, no.4
   arr F.Salabert   PC   1010/0010/timp.perc/str   Salabert   11751
CONCERT FANTASY for piano & orch, op.56
                                 ∅   3222/4230/timp.perc.glock/str   27'45"-31'   Rahter   10301 B
                                ∅   3222/4230/timp.perc.glock/str   Russian SM.CW 29   MRL
CONCERT SUITE OF TCHAIKOVSKY'S WORKS   see   NEMETI, J: CONCERT-SUITE
CONCERTI
   Piano & orch   Fn   )
     No.1, op.23, in B♭   ∅   2222/4230/timp/str   34'   Rahter   4595 + Amv Es)
                          ∅   2222/4230/timp/str   Russian SM.CW 29   MRL
       'Concerto Pastiche',arr from themes of op.23 by C.King Palmer
                        PC   112.3sx.1/2230/timp/str   4'   Paxton   19563
       'Intermezzo pomposo': fragments of op.23, arr L.Artok
                        PC   2(picc)222/2230/timp.perc/str   5'   Schott   10350

TCHAIKOVSKY, Pyotr Ilyich (cont)

CONCERTI (cont)
  Piano & orch (cont)
    No.2, op.44, in G
      orig version   ϕ   2222/4200/timp/str   Russian SM.CW 28   MRL
      ed A.Siloti   ϕ   2222/4200/timp/str   28'30"-32'30"   Rahter   6029 B
    No.3, op.75, in E♭   ϕ   3(picc)222/4231/timp/str   15'30"   Jurgenson   1113
                             ϕ   3(picc)222/4231/timp/str   Russian SM.CW 29   MRL

  Violin & orch
    op.35, in D   ϕ   2222/4200/timp/str   30'-33'30"   Rahter   4695 Amv C
                             ϕ   2222/4200/timp/str   (alt.reduction -
                                 2121/2210/timp/str)   Breitkopf   23930 As

      Canzonetta only
        arr M.Baron   PC 1121/2210/timp.perc/str   G.Schirmer   3044 B
        arr E.Haensch   PC 1121/2000/str   Benjamin   7573 B
CONSOLATION   see   AH, WEEP NO MORE
CORONATION CANTATA   see   MOSCOW
CORONATION MARCH for the coronation of Alexander III, 1883
                             ϕ   2+picc.2+ca.22/42.2cnt.31/timp.perc/str   Jurgenson   4383
                             ϕ   2+picc.2+ca.22/42.2cnt.31/timp.perc/str   Russian SM.CW 25   MRL
The CROWN OF ROSES   see   A LEGEND
DANSE RUSSE, oo.40, no.10   see   2 PIECES, arr A.Schmid
DAWN: duet for Soprano & Mezzo soprano soli & orch, op.46, no.6
                             ϕ   2222/4000/str   Russian SM.CW 27   MRL
DMITRI THE PRETENDER: incidental music to play
  Introduction to Act 1, and Mazurka
                             ϕ   1122/2110/timp.perc/str   Russian SM,1962.CW 14   MRL
DO NOT LEAVE ME (O go not from me)(No.3 of 6 songs, op.27)
                             ϕ   0122/2000/str   Jurgenson   Misc 2116 B
DON JUAN'S SERENADE (No.1 of 6 songs, op.38)
    in B min   ϕ   1121/2210/timp/str   2'55"   (Siddell)   17538
    in B min   ϕ   2(picc)222/4231/timp.tri/hp/str   BBC   TO 488 **
    in B min, arr Torke for voice (or pf) & orch
                             PC 1111/2110/timp/str   Kuhl   3390
    in B♭ min   ϕ   2222/4230/timp.perc/hp/str   (Siddell)   17537
    in B min, A min & G min, arr F.Cramer
                                 pf/str   (J.Williams)   LM G 4263
DREAMING AND WAKING   see   WHY?, op.28, no.3
1812, Festival overture (Overture solonelle), op.49
                             ϕ   2+picc.2+ca.22/42.2cnt.31/timp.perc/   Es)
                                 org/str   15'30"-18'   Rahter   2446 Amv Dn +)
                             ϕ   2+picc.2+ca.22/42.2cnt.31/timp.perc/
                                 org/str   Russian SM.CW 25   MRL
    arr G.Borch   PC 2(picc)121/2210/timp.perc/str   C.Fischer   1863
    arr A.Schmid   PC 2(picc)222/4231/timp.perc/str   Hawkes   776 B
ELEGIE no.2, in G (to the memory of J.Samarine)
                             ϕ   str   7'   Rahter   8912
                             ϕ   str   Russian SM.CW 26   MRL
    arr L.Weninger   PC 1110/0110/timp/str   Benjamin   498
      [N.B. also used as entr'acte in Hamlet]
The ENCHANTRESS (The Sorceress): opera
                             ϕ   3(picc)2+ca.22/42.2cnt.31/timp.perc.tamtam/hp/str
                                 Onstage: 4hn   Russian SM.CW 8a-b   MRL
L'ESPIÈGLE (from 18 pieces, op.72 no.12)(used by composer as an interpolation in "Swan Lake" ballet)
    arr Drigo   ϕ   1222/2000/bells/hp/str   Jurgenson   8055
    arr Schmid   PC 1121/2210/timp.perc/str   G.Schirmer   7348 B

TCHAIKOVSKY, Pyotr Ilyich (cont)

ÉTUDES EN FORME DE VARIATIONS (12 Études Symphoniques) for piano, by R.Schumann
    Variations 11 & 12 Adagio & Allegro, transcr for orch

		∅	2+picc.222/4231/timp/str	Russian SM,1967.CW 58	MRL
EUGENE ONEGIN: opera, op.24					
Complete		∅	2+picc.222/4230/timp.perc/hp/str	Jurgenson	6022 +
		∅	2+picc.222/4230/timp/hp/str	Russian SM.CW 4	MRL
		∅	2+picc.222/4230/timp/hp/str	Russian SM,1965	Misc 6240
Overture		∅	2222/4000/str	(Jurgenson)	9610 B
Selection, arr C.Godfrey jnr		PC	2(picc)222/4230.euph/timp/str	Hawkes	1379 Cwe
Extracts					

All men surrender to love's power: aria (Prince Gremin)(No.20a, act 3)

		∅	2222/4000/str	[Jurgenson]/E.F.Kalmus	26830

Could I pursue (If in this world)(Se dell' imen la dolce): aria (Onegin)(No.12, act 1)

in B♭ (orig)		∅	2122/3000/str	(Russian SM)	Misc 6180
2 Écossaises, arr Kleinecke		∅	1+picc.222/4230/timp/str	Jurgenson	9158 B
Excerpts (links and codas)			slips only	BBC	TO 484

For dull despair: aria (Olga's scene & aria)

in E♭ (orig)		∅	2222/4000/str	Jurgenson	Misc 4424

How far ye seem: aria (Introduction scene & Lenski's aria)(No.17, act 2)

in E min (orig)		∅	2222/4230/timp/str	5'-6'45"	Russian SM	10210
arr & orch L.Weninger			1121/2210/timp/str	7'	Benjamin	5295
Polonaise		∅	2222/4230/timp/str	4'-5'	Rahter	422 Amv Bs D +
		PC	2(picc)222/4231/timp.perc/str		Benjamin	1058
arr O.Langey		PC	1121/2210/timp.perc/str		G.Schirmer	3889

Tho' I should die for it: aria (Tatyana's letter song)(No.9, act 1)

		∅	2222/4230/timp/hp/str	10'	Russian SM	10211 Amv B +
		∅	2222/4230/timp/hp/str		(Siddell)	18001
Waltz		∅	3(picc)222/4230/timp/str	6'	Jurgenson	4251 Amv C +
arr A.Lotter		PC	2(picc)222/4231/timp/str		Hawkes	3324 Cm D
arr Roberts		PC	1121/2210/perc/str		C.Fischer	1850 Ap

EVENING: song op.46 (No.1 of 6 duets for Soprano & Contralto)

in A♭			2+picc.222/4000/str	(Siddell)	18030
FATE: symphonic poem, op.77		∅	2+picc.2+ca.22/4331/timp.perc/hp/str	10'	Belaieff	5783 +
		∅	2+picc.2+ca.22/4331/timp.perc/hp/str	Russian SM.CW 22	MRL

FIFINELLA (Pimpinella): song, op.38 (No.6 of 6 songs, op.38)

in G, arr H.Carr		∅	3222/4000/tri/hp/str	BBC	TO 2019

FRANCESCA DA RIMINI: fantasy after Dante, op.32   En

		∅	3(picc)2+ca.22/42.2cnt.31/timp.perc/hp/str	18'-25'	Bote & B	6344 + Amv Cs
		∅	3(picc)2+ca.22/42.2cnt.31/timp.perc.tamtam/hp/str	Russian SM,1946	Misc 6638
		∅	3(picc)2+ca.22/42.2cnt.31/timp.perc.tamtam/hp/str	Russian SM.CW 24	MRL

FUGHETTA A DANZA from suite no.3, op.55   see   BALLET SUITE

HAMLET: fantasy overture, op.67a	∅	3(picc)2+ca.22/42.2cnt.31/timp.perc/str	17'30"-20'45"	Rahter	2447 Amv B +
		∅	3(picc)2+ca.22/42.2cnt.31/timp.perc/str	Russian SM.CW 29	MRL
HAMLET: incidental music, op.67b	∅	2222/2210/timp.perc.glock/str			
			Stage band: 0222/2210/tamb	Jurgenson	9619
		∅	2222/2210/timp.perc.glock/str			
			Stage band: 0222/2210/tamb	Russian SM.CW 14	MRL
Overture					
arr O.Haensch		PC	2222/2210/timp.perc/str	Benjamin	5161
Funeral march		∅	2222/2210/timp.perc/str	Jurgenson	9623

HUMORESQUE, op.10, no.2

transcr S.Dodgson		∅	2221/[2]100/[perc]/str	Novello,1964	24674

    see also 2 PIECS, arr W.Stewart

ICHABOD see WHY ARE THE ROSES SO PALE

IN THE VILLAGE (No.7 of 12 pieces for piano, op.40)

		PC	1121/2210/timp.perc/str	Ascher	8010
arr J.Németi		PC	1121/2230/timp/str	Kistner & S	9951 B

- 1878 -

TCHAIKOVSY, Pyotr Ilyich (cont)

INTERMEZZO POMPOSO   see   CONCERTI, Piano & orch, no.1, op.23
INTERNATIONALE: suite (extracts from 'Album for the young', op.39), arr J.Gilbert
  1. Mazurka: Polish dance (No.10)   5. Kamarinskaya: Russian dance (No.13)
  2. Old French air (No.16)   6. Tyrolean dance (No.17)
  3. Polka: Bohemian dance (No.14)   7. March of the wooden soldiers: Hungarian march (No.5)
  4. Italian air (No.15)   8. Neapolitan air (No.18)

		PC	1122/2210/perc/str	Benjamin	5227 B
IOLANTHE (Yolande): opera, op.69					
Complete		φ	3(picc)2+ca.22/4231/timp/2hp/str	Jurgenson	3955
		φ	3(picc)2+ca.22/4231/timp/2hp/str	Russian SM.CW 10	MRL
Overture		φ	32+ca.22/4000/(no strings)	Jurgenson	10418
Selection, arr L.Weninger		PC	2(picc)222/4231/timp.perc/hp/str	10'45"-12'	Benjamin 6845 B
Extracts					
Matilda: aria (No.6)					
in E (orig)		φ	2121/2230/perc/hp/str	BBC	TO 891
The Minstrel's canzonet (orch arr of Act 1, sc.1)					
arr Q.Maganini		φ	hp[=pf]/str	Ed Musicus	16539 B
ITALIAN CAPRICCIO, op.45		φ	3(picc)2+ca.22/42.2cnt.31/timp.perc/hp/str 14'15"	Rahter	4250 Amv Bgg)
					Cs En)
		φ	3(picc)2+ca.22/42.2cnt.31/timp.perc/hp/str	Russian SM.CW 25	MRL
arr A.Schmid		PC	22+[ca]22/4231/timp.perc/hp/str	Hawkes	847 Agg B
arr L.Weninger		PC	1(picc)121/2210/timp.perc/str	Benjamin	14098
JOAN OF ARC: opera					
Complete		φ	32+ca.22/42.2cnt.31/timp.perc.bells/hp.org/str	Jurgenson	Misc 572
		φ	3(picc)2+ca.22/42.2cnt.31/timp.perc.bell/hp.org/		
			str		
			Stage band: 0000/0440/sdm	Russian SM,1964.CW 5a-b	MRL
Prelude to Act 1		φ	32+ca.22/4431/timp.perc/hp/str	6'40"	(Jurgenson) 20632 +
Extracts					
Adieux forêts: aria (Act 1)					
in D min (orig)		φ	32+ca.22/4231/timp/str	6'30"-8'15"	Jurgenson 11763 Amv B
in D min		φ	32+ca.22/4231/timp/str	(Siddell)	17548 B
in B min		φ	32+ca.22/4231/timp/str	(Siddell)	17549
in B min		φ	32+ca.22/4231/timp/str	(Siddell)	17550
in B min, arr M.Saunders		φ	cel.org.pf/str	(BBC)	LM G 10782
Most gracious King (Ehr' würd'ger Herr!)(Joan's narration)(Act 2)					
in A♭ (orig)(translated A.Jacobs)					
		φ	32+ca.22/42.2cnt.31/timp/hp/str	(Jurgenson)	24054
Le LAC DES CYGNES see SWAN LAKE					
LARGO and ALLEGRO, in D (1863-64)	φ	2000/0000/str		Russian SM,1967.CW 58	MRL

A LEGEND (Christ in His garden): song for Tenor solo & orch (No.5 of Children's songs, op.54)

	φ	0222/2000/str	Jurgenson	Misc 2117
	φ	0222/2000/str	Russian SM.CW 27	MRL
arr G.Stacey		pf/str	(Boosey & H)	LM G 3512
in E min, arr Stanton as The Crown of roses				
	φ	str	OUP	18982
in E min & F min, arr M.Saunders				
	φ	str	Arranger	22792 +

LYRIC SUITE, arr G.Becce from the works of Tchaikovsky
  1. Mid sombre days, op.73, no.5 (Canto appasionato)(1'30")
  2. Again, as before, alone, op.73, no.6 (Canto lirico)(2')
  3. Elegiac song, op.72, no.14 (Canto elegiaco)(3'30")
  4. Oh, if you knew, op.60, no.3 (Canto d'amore)(1'30")
  5. Andante cantabile from 'Francesca da Rimini', op.32 (6')

	PC	2121/2210/timp/str	Bote & B 1674

The MAID OF ORLEANS   see   JOAN OF ARC

TCHAIKOVSKY, Pyotr Ilyich (cont)

MANDRAGORE: opera (unfinished)
Extant parts   φ   2222/4000/timp/hp/str   Russian SM.CW 2   MRL
Extracts
   Chorus of flowers & insects
    orch A.Glazunov   φ   2222/4000/timp/hp/str   Jurgenson   15754
MANFRED SYMPHONY, op.58   φ   32+ca.2+bcl.3/42.2cnt.31/timp.perc.glock/
             2hp/str   53'-61'   Jurgenson   9292 + Amv Cn
MARCHE SLAVE, op.31   φ   2+picc.222/42.2cnt.31/timp.perc/str   9'-11'   Rahter   4253 Amv C
  arr Haensch   PC   2(picc)222/4231/timp.perc/str   Benjamin   13620
  arr Roberts   PC   2+2picc.222/4431/timp.perc/str   C.Fischer   1878 B
  arr F.Salabert   PC   2(2picc)121/2230/timp.perc/str   Salabert   13778
MARCHE SOLENNELLE (op.posth)   φ   2+picc.2+ca.22/4231/timp.perc/2hp/str   Jurgenson   2166 Amv C
  arr L.Weninger   PC   1(picc)121/2210/timp.perc/hp/str   Benjamin   5062
MAZEPPA: opera
Complete   φ   3(picc)2+ca.22/42.2cnt.31/timp.perc/hp/str
      Offstage: banda   Russian SM,1969.CW 6a-b   MRL
Overture   φ   3(picc)2+ca.22/42.2cnt.31/timp.perc/str   7'30"   Jurgenson   9107 Amv
Extracts
   The Battle of Poltava (No.15, act 3)
     φ   2+picc.2+ca.22/42.2cnt.31/timp.perc/str
     Stage band: banda   7'   Rahter   4249 Amv B
   Cossack dance   φ   2+picc.2+ca.22/42.2cnt.31/timp.perc/str   4'   Rahter   6071 Amv B
    arr L.Weninger   PC   2+picc.2+ca.22/4431/timp.perc/str   Rahter   8809 Amv B
   O manà, manà: arioso des Mazeppa (No.10, act 2)
    in Gb   φ   32+ca.22/4231/hp/str   (Simrock/Rahter)   23628 +
MAZURKA DE SALON, op.9, no.3 <u>see</u> PETITE SUITE (Valse Creole)
MÉDITATION (No.5 of 18 pieces, op.72)
  arr O.Langey   PC   1121/2210/timp.perc/str   G.Schirmer   7075
MID SOMBRE DAYS <u>see</u> LYRIC SUITE
MOSCOW (Coronation cantata) for Soprano & Baritone soli, chorus & orch
     φ   3222/4231/timp/hp/str   Jurgenson   Misc 140
     φ   3222/4231/timp/hp/str   Russian SM.CW 27   MRL
MOZARTIANA <u>see</u> SUITES, no.4
MUSICAL GEMS OF TCHAIKOVSKY: selection, arr O.Langey
     PC   1121/2210/timp.perc/str   G.Schirmer   2527
NATA VALSE (No.4 of 6 pieces for piano, op.51)
  arr L.Weninger   PC   1121/2210/timp.perc/hp/str   3'30"   Benjamin   11290 B
NATURE AND LOVE for SSA soli, chorus & orch, op.posth.   (Misc 5598 B &
  orch H.Wood   φ   32+ca.2+bcl.2/4331/timp/hp/str   (GB-Lam)   (mf 170
NOCTURNE, op.10, no.1 <u>see</u> PETITE SUITE
NOCTURNE for cello solo & orch (No.4 of 6 pieces for piano, op.19)
     φ   2222/2000/str   Russian SM.CW 30b   MRL
  arr L.Weninger   PC   1121/2210/timp/hp/str   Benjamin   11391
   see also 2 PIECES, arr A.Schmid
NONE BUT THE WEARY HEART (No.6 of 6 pieces for voice & pf)
  in C   1121/2230/perc/str   BBC   LM G 4421
  in C, Db & D, arr G.Stacey   pf/str   (Schott)   LM G 3202
  in Db, arr B.Thompson   φ   hp.pf/str   BBC   MS 20390
  in Db, Eb & F, arr S.Robinson   φ   3(bfl)222/4231/timp/str   2'30"-3'55"   BBC   TO 487
  in D   1110/2000/timp/pf/str   (Siddell)   18020
  in Eb, arr A.Sandford   str   BBC   LM G 4589
  arr Pribik (non-vocal)   φ   2121/3200/str   Jurgenson   9188
  arr Roberts   PC   1121/2210/timp/str   C.Fischer   1266
  arr Schmid   PC   2222/22.cnt-solo.30/timp/str   Hawkes   889 B

TCHAIKOVSKY, Pyotr Ilyich (cont)

The NUTCRACKER (Casse-Noisette): ballet, op.71
  Complete   ϕ 3+picc.2+ca.2+bcl.2/4230/timp.perc/
                                 cel.2hp/str
                                 Stage band of toy instrs (vocal parts to
                                 Act 1)   Tchaikovsky Foundation NY   22082 +
                     ϕ 3(2picc)2+ca.2+bcl.2/4231/timp.perc.glock/
                                 cel.2hp/str
                                 Stage band of toy instrs   Russian SM,1955.CW 13a-b   23309 + & MRL
  Shortened version as broadcast at Birmingham, April 1952

Act 1	Act 2
1. Excerpt from scene 1	10. Scene
3. Children's galop and parents' entrance	12a. Chocolate
4. Dancing scene	14. Pas de deux
5. Grandfather's scene and dance	15. Dance of the sugar-plum fairy
6. Scene 'twelve chimes'	
8. Scene	
9. Waltz of the snowflakes	

                     ϕ 2+picc.2+ca.2+bcl.2/4231/timp.perc/cel.2hp/
                        str   (Rahter)   20550
  Final waltz and Apotheosis
    (str & hp parts arr J.Blore)
                     ϕ 2+picc.2+ca.2+bcl.2/4231/timp.perc/cel.hp/str   BBC   19088
  Golden waltz
    arr J.O.Turner   PC 2222/2230/timp/str   Boosey & H   19049 B
  Pas de deux (no.14)   ϕ   2+picc.2+ca.2+bcl.2/4231/timp.perc/hp/str   Tchaikovsky Foundation NY   26244 (ϕ 22082)
                     ϕ 3(picc)2+ca.2+bcl.2/4231/timp.perc/cel.2hp/
                        str   (Russian SM)   23910 +
  Waltz of the snow-flakes   ϕ   2+picc.2+ca.2+bcl.2/4231/timp.perc.glock/
                        2hp/str/24 female voices or children's voices   Jurgenson   25681

The NUTCRACKER: suite [No.1], op.71a
  1. Miniature overture (3'-4')
  2. Characteristic dances

a. March	(2'30")	d. Arab dance	(3'30")	
b. Dance of the sugar-plum fairy	(1'30")	e. Chinese dance	(1')	
c. Russian dance 'Trepak'	(1'15")	f. Dance of the reed-pipes	(2'15")	

  3. Waltz of the flowers (6'-7')
    Complete   ϕ   3+picc.2+ca.2+bcl.2+cbsn/4231/timp.perc/   (2485 + Amv
                      cel.hp/str   22'   Rahter   (Bgg Cs Dn E
                    ϕ   3(picc)2+ca.2+bcl.2/4231/timp.perc.bells/
                      cel.hp.[pf]/str   Russian SM   Misc 1876
      arr Roberts   PC 1121/2210/timp.perc/str   C.Fischer   1857
      arr L.Weninger PC 1(picc)121/2110/timp.perc/str   Benjamin   483 B
    No.1 only   ϕ   2+picc.222/2000/perc/str(no vlc or cb)   4'   Jurgenson   12209 B
    Nos.1, 2b, 2c & 2d only   (1520 Bp Ewa
      arr Schmid   PC 2222/4230/timp.perc/cel/str   Hawkes   (Gwa Jtv
    Nos.2a, 2f & 3 only
      arr Schmid   PC 2(picc)222/4231/timp.perc/hp/str   Hawkes   1533 Ewa Htv
    No.3 only   ϕ   2+picc.222/4231/timp.tri/hp/str   Jurgneson   1860 B
      arr Frolow   ϕ   2(picc)121/2210/timp.perc/str   Jurgenson   9127
      arr Griffiths   pf/str   (Schirmer)   LM G 5674
      arr Schmid   PC 2(picc)222/4230/timp.perc/hp/str   Boosey & H   16716 Bwe
OH! IF YOU KNEW   see   LYRIC SUITE
ONDINE: opera (1869)
  Excerpts   ϕ   2+picc.222/4231/timp.perc/hp.pf/str   Russian SM.CW 2   MRL
ONLY FOR THEE (Ob heller Tag)(No.6 of 7 romances, op.47)
  in C, arr R.Chignell ϕ 2222/4220/timp/str   (Arranger)   MS 5422

TCHAIKOVSKY, Pyotr Ilyich (cont)

ONLY ONE WORD: song (No.6 of 6 songs, op.28)(orig voice & pf)
   in F# min, orch Taneyev   ø 0122/2000/str   Jurgenson   Misc 2225
The OPRICHNIK: opera
   Complete   ø 2+picc.222/4231/timp.perc/hp/str   Russian SM.CW 3a-b   MRL
   Overture   ø 2+picc.222/4231/timp.perc/str   5'   Bessel   10887
   Dance   ø 2+picc.222/4231/timp.perc/str   Bessel   10010
OVERTURE ON THE DANISH NATIONAL HYMN, op.15
                          ø 2+picc.222/4231/perc/str   15'   Jurgenson   7956 B
                          ø 2+picc.222/4231/perc/str   Russian SM.CW 22   MRL
OVERTURE SOLONELLE (1812)   see   1812
OVERTURES
   in F (2 versions, 1865 & 6)   ø 2222/4230/timp/str   Russian SM.CW 21   MRL
   in C min (1866)   ø 2+picc.222/4231/timp.perc/str   Russian SM.CW 21   MRL
OXANA'S CAPRICES (Tcherevichky)(The little shoes): opera, op.14 (Revised version of Vakula the Smith)
   Complete   ø 2+picc.222/4231/timp.perc/hp/str
                             Stage band: banda   Russian SM.CW 7   MRL
   Overture   ø 2+picc.222/4231/timp.perc/str   Jurgenson   7955 + Amv
   Suite
      1. Introduction, exorcism and snow-storm   4. Russian dance
      2. Menuet   5. Cossack dance
      3. Introduction to act 3   6. Finale
                          ø 2+picc.222/4231/timp.perc/hp/str   Jurgenson   10050 Amv B
   Extracts
      Fair Oxana you are here at last, for soli & chorus (Act 2, no.14)
         in A   ø 2+picc.222/4231/timp/str   Russian SM.CW 7a   23979 + & MRL
      Fairer than the rose, for soli & 3 choruses (Act 2, no.13)
         in A   ø 2+picc.222/4231/timp/str   Russian SM.CW 7a   23979 + & MRL
      Polonaise (Act 3, no.19)
         orch L.Salter   ' 0.picc.01+Ebcl.0/20.2cnt.21/timp (stage band only)   BBC   25165 **
      Scene (Act 3, no.23)
         orch L.Salter   101+Ebcl.0/20.cnt.01/timp (stage band only)   BBC   25164 **
PETITE SUITE
   1. In the Troika, op.37b, no.11   3. Valse Creole, op.9, no.3 (Mazurka de salon)
   2. Nocturne, op.10, no.1
                         PC 2222/42.2cnt.30/timp.perc/str   11'30"   Boosey   1370 B
PETITE VALSE, op.40, no.8   see   2 PIECES, arr A.Schmid
PEZZO CAPRICCIOSO for cello & orch, op.62
                          ø 2222/4000/timp/str   9'   Jurgenson   8131 +
                          ø 2222/4000/timp/str   Russian SM.CW 30b   Misc 6706 & MR
2 PIECES, arr W.Stewart
   1. Chanson triste, op.40, no.2   2. Humoreske, op.10, no.2
                          PC 2111/2100/str   Hawkes   907 C
2 PIECES, arr A.Schmid
   1. Rêverie interrompue, op.40, no.12   2. Danse russe, op.40, no.10
                          ø 2+picc.222/4231/perc/hp/str   Hawkes   10706
                          PC 2(picc)222/4230/timp.perc/hp/str   Hawkes   201 B
2 PIECES, arr A.Schmid
   1. Nocturne, op.19   2. Valse, op.40, no.8
                          PC 2(picc)222/4230/timp.perc/hp/str   Hawkes   4624 B
PILGRIM'S SONG   see   TO THE FOREST
PIMPINELLA   see   FIFINELLA
PIQUE DAME   see   QUEEN OF SPADES
Un POCO DI CHOPIN (No.15 of 18 pieces for piano, op.72)(used by composer as an interpolation in "Swan
    Lake" ballet
   arr Drigo   ø 2222/4030/timp/str   Jurgenson   8057
POLACCA, op.72, no.7   see   BALLET SUITE

TCHAIKOVSKY, Pyotr Ilyich (cont)

The QUEEN OF SPADES: opera, op.68
    Complete   ∅ 2+picc.2+ca.2+bcl.2/4231/timp.perc.toy instrs/hp/
                                   str
                                                                    Jurgenson   3898 B +
                                ∅ 2+picc.2+ca.2+bcl.2/4231/timp.perc.toy instrs/hp/
                                   str
                                                                    Jurgenson   Misc 347-9
                                ∅ 2+picc.2+ca.2+bcl.2/4231/timp.perc.toy instrs/hp/
                                   str   Russian SM.CW 9a   MRL
    Selection, arr L.Weninger   PC 2(picc)222/4230/timp.perc/str   Benjamin   5157
    Extracts
        The faithful Shepherdess: interlude (no.14)
            1. Chorus of Shepherds & Shepherdesses   3. Daphnis & Chloë
            2. Sarabande   4. Finale
              orch L.Weninger   PC 1121/2210/timp/str   Benjamin   292 B
        Suite, arr W.Hofmann
            1. Sarabande   3. Menuet
            2. Daphnis & Chloë   4. Shepherd's chorus
                                PC 2222/4230/timp/str   Rahter   8540 B
    A queer old creature: aria (no.5)(Tomski's scene & ballet)
        in E min (orig)   ∅ 1+picc.222/4200/str   BBC   TO 623
    'Twill soon be midnight now: aria (no.20)(Lisa's scene & aria)
        in E min (orig) with 54 bars of no.21
                                ∅ 322+bcl.2/4231/timp/str   (Jurgenson)   14667 +
RÊVERIE INTERROMPUE, op.40, no.12 see 2 PIECES, arr A.Schmid
ROMANCE IN F MINOR, op.5 (1868)
    arr Frolow   ∅ 2+picc.121/2210/timp/str   5'15" (Jurgenson)   9856
    arr Lavotta   PC 1121/1000/timp/str   Noel   8054
    arr A.Wood, transposed to F# min
                                PC 2121/2230/timp.perc/str   AH & C   646 B
ROMANCE IN F, op.51, no.5 (orig pf)(1882)
    arr Gillet   PC 1121/2210/str   G.Schirmer   7182
ROMEO AND JULIET: fantasie-overture
    1869 version   ∅ 2+picc.2+ca.22/4231/timp.perc/hp/str Russian SM.CW 23   MRL
    1870 version
        fragments only   ∅ 2+picc.2+ca.22/4231/timp.perc/hp/str Russian SM.CW 23   MRL
    1880 version   ∅ 2+picc.2+ca.22/4231/timp.perc/hp/str Bote & B   5366 Amv Cs Dn
                                ∅ 2+picc.2+ca.22/4231/timp.perc/hp/str Russian SM,1963   24504
                                ∅ 2+picc.2+ca.22/4231/timp.perc/hp/str Russian SM.CW 23   MRL
    arr Bauman   PC 2+picc.2+ca.22/4231/timp.perc/hp/str Bote & B   6757
    arr J.Hollingsworth for radio production (1958)
                                ∅ 22(ca)22/4231/timp.perc/hp/str   Arranger   MS 31254
    arr F.Salabert   PC 2(picc)1(ca)21/2230/timp.perc/hp/str Salabert   13672
ROMEO AND JULIET ('Ah! no my love the morning has not come')('N'entends-tu pas le rossignol?'): duet for
    Soprano & Tenor soli, completed & orch by Tanayev
                                ∅ 22+ca.22/4200/timp/hp/str   Jurgenson   22433 + B
                                ∅ 22+ca.22/4200/timp/hp/str   Russian SM.CW 62   MRL
The SEASONS, op.37b (orig pf)
    1. January 'By the hearth'   7. July 'Reaper's song'
    2. February 'Carnival time'   8. August 'Harvest'
    3. March 'Song of the lark'   9. September 'The Hunt'
    4. April 'Snowdrop'   10. October 'Autumn song' (4'15")
    5. May 'Bright nights'   11. November 'In the Troika' (3')
    6. June 'Barcarolle' (6')   12. December 'Christmas' (5')
    Complete
        arr F.Salabert   PC 1121/2230/timp.perc/hp/str   Salabert   5470 Ap B

TCHAIKOVSKY, Pyotr Ilyich (cont)

The SEASONS (cont)

No.6 only				
arr A.Lotter	PC	2222/3000/str	Hawkes	10750
arr Novacek	PC	2222/3000/str	Jurgenson	Misc 2226
No.10 only				
arr A.Lotter	PC	hmn.pf/str(no vla)	Hawkes	2626
No.11 only				
arr L.Weninger	PC	2(2picc)222/4231/timp.perc/hp/str	Benjamin	5203
No.12 only				
arr F.Salabert	PC	1121/2230/timp.perc/str	Salabert	13268
arr A.Seidel		1+picc.222/4230/timp.bells/str	Oertel	27051

see also BALLET SUITE

SERENADE for strings, op.48
1. Pezzo in forma di sonatina (8'50")   3. Elegie (7')
2. Waltz (4')   4. Finale (Russian theme)(7'30")   (4285 Amv D

	∅	str	Rahter	(Ewa
	∅	str	Breitkopf	24123
	∅	str	Russian SM.CW 20	MRL
No.2 only				
arr L.Weninger	PC	1121/2210/timp/str	Benjamin	10708
No.3 only	∅	str	Rahter	8608

SERENADE for small orch (1872)		1020/1100/str	Russian SM.CW 24	MRL
SÉRÉNADE MÉLANCOLIQUE, for violin & orch, op.26				
	∅	2222/4000/str	9'30"-10' Jurgenson	8036

SLEEP ON, OH HEART'S DELIGHT (No.4 of 7 romances for voice & pf, op.47)

	PC	1020/0210/timp/str	Rattig	16910

The SLEEPING BEAUTY (The Sleeping Princess)(La belle Dormante)(Dornröschen): ballet, op.66   (20806 B +

Complete	∅	2+picc.2+ca.22/42.2cnt.31/timp.perc/hp.pf/str	(GB-Lam)	(mf 229
	∅	2+picc.2+ca.22/42.2cnt.31/timp.perc/2hp.pf/str	Eulenburg	Misc 7439
	∅	2+picc.2+ca.22/42.2cnt.31/timp.perc/hp.pf/str	Russian SM.CW 12a	MRL
Selection, arr F.Rapley	PC	2(picc)12.3sx.1/2230/timp.perc/hp/str	W.Disney,1959	23017 Cs

Suite no.1, arr Douglas
  Introduction   3. Rose adagio (3'30")
  1. The lilac fairy (2'10")   4. The three Ivans (1'15")
  2. The silver fairy (1')   5. Polonaise (4'45")

	PC	2+picc.2+ca.22/4231/timp.perc/cel.hp/str	Boosey & H	19561 Bm Ct

Suite no.2, arr Douglas
  6a. Allegro (0'10")   7c. Valse (1')
  6b. Panorama (2'50")   7d. Allegro vivace (2'35")
  7a. Allegro vivo (0'25")   8. Waltz (4'30")
  7b. Moderato con moto (1')

	PC	2+picc.2+ca.22/4231/timp.perc/hp/str	Boosey & H	19734 C

Extracts

No. 6 Waltz	∅	2+picc.2+ca.22/42.2cnt.31/timp.perc/str	Jurgenson	6002 B
arr A.Schmid	PC	2(picc)222/4230/timp.perc/str	Hawkes	180 Agg Cp D
No. 8c Aurora variation	∅	2+picc.2+ca.22/42.2cnt.31/timp/hp/str	(Rahter)	19569
No.22 Polacca		2+picc.2+ca.22/42.2cnt.31/timp/str	(GB-Lam)	20809 +
No.23 Pas de quatre, polka	∅	2+picc.1+ca.22/4000/glock/str	Jurgenson	14984
	∅	2+picc.1+ca.22/4000/glock/str	Jurgenson	16842

No.25 Pas de quatre - adagio
  Var.1 'Cinderella and the prince'
  Var.2 'Bluebird'
  Coda

	∅	3+picc.222/2220/timp/str	BBC	TV BL 24
	∅	2+picc.222/2220/timp.perc/str	BBC	22414
arr S.Robinson	∅	3222/42.2cnt.31/timp/str	Arranger	TO 1009

TCHAIKOVSKY, Pyotr Ilyich (cont)

The SLEEPING BEAUTY: ballet (cont)
  Extracts (cont)
    No.25 (cont)   (GB-Lam)   Misc 2714
      Pas de quatre only   ∅   2+picc.112/2230/str
      Var 2 only, orch Stravinsky∅   1121/1220/timp/pf/str   5'15"   Schott,1953   Misc 4019 B
    No.30 Finale   ∅   2+picc.2+ca.22/42.2cnt.31/timp.perc/str (GB-Lam)   Misc 2715
The SLEEPING BEAUTY (The Sleeping Princess)(La Belle Dormante)(Dornröschen): suite, op.66a
  1. Introduction 'The lilac fairy' (La Fée des Lilas)(4'30")   4. Panorama (3'30")
  2. Adagio 'Pas d'action' (6')   5. Waltz (4'30")
  3. Characteristic dance (2')
                                  ∅   2+picc.2+ca.22/42.2cnt.31/timp.perc/hp/str   Eulenburg,1965   Misc 6157 C
                                  ∅   2+picc.2+ca.22/42.31/timp.perc/hp/str   Jurgenson   4256 + Bmv Cs)
                                                                                                           Dn E)
        arr L.Weninger   PC 1(picc)1(ca)21/2210/timp.perc/hp/str   Benjamin   5156 Cni
The SLIPPERS   see   OXANA'S CAPRICES
The SNOWMAIDEN: incidental music, op.12
  Complete   ∅   2+picc.2+ca.22/4231/timp.perc/str/Mz.TT soli.chorus   Jurgenson   Misc 2015
                                  ∅   2+picc.2+ca.22/4231/timp.perc/str/Mz.TT soli.chorus
                                                                              Russian SM.CW 14   MRL
    Extracts
      Narrentana (Dance of the clowns)
                                  ∅   2+picc.222/4231/timp.perc/str   (Jurgenson)   25115 +
SONATA for piano, no.2, op.39, in Ab (J.199) by C.M.von Weber
  Menuetto capriccioso only, transcr for orch
                                  ∅   2222/4000/str   Russian SM,1967.CW 58   MRL
SONATA for violin & piano, op.47, in A by L.van Beethoven (The Kreutzer), arr
  Exposition from 1st mvt only, transcr for orch
                                  ∅   2222/4230/timp/str   Russian SM,1967.CW 58   MRL
SOUVENIR DE FLORENCE: sextet for strings, op.70 (see also   CHAMBER CATALOGUE)
                                  ∅   vln 1 & 2.vla 1 & 2.vlc 1 & 2.added cb pt 35'   Jurgenson   10302 +
SOUVENIR D'UN CHATEAU (from 'Souvenir de Hapsal', op.2)
  arr Vladimirov   ∅   3(picc)2+ca.22/4431/timp.perc/hp/str   Jurgenson   4254 B
SOUVENIR D'UN LIEU CHER for violin & orch, op.42, orch A.Glazunov (orig vln & pf)
  1. Meditation   2. Scherzo   3. Melody
                                  ∅   2222/2000/hp/str   Jurgenson   4771 +
The STORM: overture to Ostrovsky's play, op.76
                                  ∅   2+picc.2+ca.22/4231/timp.perc/hp/str 10'-14'   Belaieff   5782
                                  ∅   2+picc.2+ca.22/4231/timp.perc/hp/str   Russian SM.CW 21   MRL
STRING QUARTET IN D   see   ANDANTE CANTABILE
STRING QUARTET IN F MINOR   see   ANDANTE
SUITES
  No.1, op.43, in D
    1. Introduction and fugue (10')   3b. Miniature march (2')
    2. Divertimento   4. Scherzo
    3a. Intermezzo   5. Gavotte (5')
      Complete   ∅   3+picc.21+Ebcl.2/4200/timp.perc.glock/str 46'   Jurgenson   8075 Amv B
                                  ∅   3+picc.21+Ebcl.2/4200/timp.perc.glock/str   Russian SM.CW 19a   MRL
        arr F.Salabert   PC 2+picc.121/2230/timp.perc/hp/str   Salabert   13683
      No.2 only
        arr L.Weninger   PC 1121/2210/str   Benjamin   7554
      No.3b only   ∅   2+picc.220/0000/glock.tri/str   (Rahter)   873
  No.2, op.53, in C
    1. Jeu des sons   4. A child's dream
    2. Waltz   5. Baroque dance (in the style of Dargomijsky)
    3. Humerous scherzo (4acdn ad lib)
      Complete   ∅   32+ca.22/4231/timp.perc/hp/str   Jurgenson   8073 +
                                  ∅   32+ca.22/4231/timp.perc/hp/str   33'-38' Russian SM.CW 19b   MRL

TCHAIKOVSKY, Pyotr Ilyich (cont)

SUITES (cont)

No.3, op.55, in G
1. Elegy   3.   3. Scherzo
2. Melancholic waltz   4. Theme and variations   (4255 Amv Cn
   Complete   φ   3(picc)2+ca.22/4231/timp.perc/hp/str   Bote & B   (Dwe
                       φ   3(picc)2+ca.22/4231/timp.perc/hp/str   Eulenburg,1978   Misc 9721
                       φ   3(picc)2+ca.22/4231/timp.perc/hp/str   Russian SM.CW 20   MRL
                       φ   3(picc)2+ca.22/4231/timp.perc/hp/str   Russian SM,1960   Misc 5510 C
     arr F.Salabert   PC 2(picc)121/2230/timp.perc/hp/str   20'20"   Salabert   9512
   Final polacca and elegy only
     arr Roberts   PC 3(picc)222/4231/timp.perc/hp/str   C.Fischer   1867
          see also   BALLET SUITE

No.4, 'Mozartiana', op.61 (based on works by W.A.Morzart)
1. Gigue (K.574)   3. Ave verum corpus (Preghiera)(K.618 as transcr by F.Liszt)(5'30")
2. Menuet (K.355)   4. Theme and variations on a theme by L.Gluck (K.455)(14'30")
   Complete   φ   2222/4200/timp.perc.glock/hp/str   Rahter   4467 Amv Cs D
                       φ   2222/4200/timp.perc.glock/hp/str   Russian SM.CW 20   MRL
     arr Roberts   φ   2222/4210/timp/hp/str   C.Fischer   1039
   No.2 only
     arr V.Németi   PC 1121/2230/timp/str   Kistner & S   9951 B

SWAN LAKE (Le lac des Cygnes): ballet in 4 acts, op.20
   Complete   φ   2+picc.222/42.2cnt.31/timp.perc.bells.tamtam/
                           hp/str   Jurgenson   14185 B
                       φ   2+picc.222/42.2cnt.31/timp.perc.bells.tamtam/
                           hp/str   Russian SM.CW 11   MRL
   ed I.Iordan & G.Kirker φ 2+picc.222/42.2cnt.31/timp.perc.bells.tamtam/
                           hp/str   Russian SM,1966   Misc 6698-9
Selections
     arr Fr.G.Charrosin PC 2(picc)12.2sx.1/2230/timp.perc/hp.org/str   Bosworth   9793
     arr K.Palmer   PC 112.3sx.1/2230/timp.perc/str   Paxton   18903
Suite
1. Scene (3'10")   4. Scene (3')
2. Valse (5')   5. Hungarian dance (2'45")
3. Dance of the little swans (1'30")   6. Scene
                       φ   2+picc.222/42.2cnt.31/timp.perc/hp/str   Eulenburg   Misc 7161 Bni
                       φ   2+picc.222/42.2cnt.31/timp.perc/hp/str   Jurgenson   4252 + Amv B
     arr A.Winter   PC 2+picc.222/42.2cnt.31/timp.perc/hp/str   Boosey & H   13900 + Cwe D
Suite, arr Roberts
1. Scene (3'30")   2. Dance of the little swans (1'15")   3. Hungarian dance (2'15")
                       PC 1121/2210/timp.perc/str   7'30"   C.Fischer   1273 B
Extracts
   3 Interpolated pieces added by the composer (orig from 18 pieces for piano, op.72)
     1. Espiègle (op.72, no.12)   3. Un poco di Chopin (op.72, no.15)
     2. Valse-bluette (op.72, no.11)
          see individual titles
   Scene & Introduction
     arr J.Németi   PC 1121/2230/timp/str   Kistner & S   9951 B
   Scene (Act 1, no.1) φ 2+picc.222/42.2cnt.31/timp.perc/str   (Jurgenson)   26868
   Scene 4
     arr J.Németi   PC 1121/2230/timp/str   Kistner & S   9951 B
   Scene 10 (Act 2), used as signature tune to 'Music from the ballet'
                       φ   0100/0000/hp/str   (Jurgenson)   23061
   Waltz selection, arr G.Vinter
                       φ   2(picc)12[=1]2[=1]/4[=2]230/timp.perc/hp/str   Arranger   25597

TCHAIKOVSKY, Pyotr Ilyich (cont)

SYMPHONIES

No.1, op.13, in G min (Winter day-dreams)

	φ	2+picc.222/4231/timp.perc/str	44'-46'	Jurgenson	6294 + Amv Cwa
	φ	2+picc.222/4231/timp.perc/str		Russian SM.CW 15a	MRL
	φ	2+picc.222/4231/timp.perc/str		Russian SM,1961	24503

No.2, op.17, in C min (Little Russian)

	φ	2+picc.222/4231/timp.perc/str	31'-35'	Bessel	7112 As Bn C +
	φ	2+picc.222/4231/timp.perc.tamtam/str		Bruckner	Misc 2842 B
	φ	2+picc.222/4231/timp.perc/str		Russian SM,1963	23992 Bmv Cwe
	φ	2+picc.222/4231/timp.perc/str		Russian SM.CW 15b	MRL
Presto only	φ	2+picc.222/4331/timp.perc.tamtam/str		BBC,1965	24244 + An

No.3, op.29, in D (Polish)

	φ	2+picc.222/4231/timp/str	43'-47'	Jurgenson	4257+Amv Bn D
	φ	2+picc.222/4231/timp/str		Breitkopf	Misc 5670
	φ	2+picc.222/4231/timp/str		Bruckner	Misc 3000 B
	φ	2+picc.222/4231/timp/str		Russian SM,1963	24172 Bwe
	φ	2+picc.222/4231/timp/str		Russian SM.CW 16a	MRL

No.4, op.36, in F min

	φ	2+picc.222/4231/timp.perc/str	38'-43'	Breitkopf	24953 Awe
	φ	2+picc.222/4231/timp.perc/str		Boosey & H	Misc 2475
	φ	2+picc.222/4231/timp.perc/str		Rahter	2444 + Amv Bgg) Ds En)
	φ	2+picc.222/4231/timp.perc/str		Russian SM,1946	Misc 19
	φ	2+picc.222/4231/timp.perc/str		Russian SM.CW 16b	MRL

Andantino in modo di canzona (2nd mvt)

arr Godfrey	PC	2222/4230/timp.perc/str	10'	Hawkes	7541
arr Roberts	PC	1121/2210/timp/org/str		C.Fischer	1877

Scherzo 'Pizzicato ostinato' (3rd mvt)

arr Godfrey	PC	2+picc.222/4230/timp/str	4'30"	Hawkes	7542
arr Roberts	PC	1222/4231/timp/org/str		C.Fischer	1998

Finale

arr Roberts	PC	1121/2210/timp/org/str	10'	C.Fischer	2000

No.5, op.64, in E min

	φ	3222/4231/timp/str	45'-48'30"	Rahter	2445 + Amv Bgg) Cs Dn)
	φ	3222/4231/timp/str		Breitkopf	12163 Awe
	φ	3222/4231/timp/str		Boosey & H	Misc 2475
	φ	3(picc)222/4231/timp/str		Russian SM	24502
	φ	3222/4231/timp/str		Russian SM.CW 17a	MRL

Andante cantabile (2nd mvt)

arr Godfrey	PC	3(picc)222/4231/timp/str	11'	Hawkes	7538
arr Roberts	PC	1(picc)121/2210/timp/org/str		C.Fischer	2013

Valse (3rd mvt)

arr Godfrey	PC	3(picc)222/4230/timp/str		Hawkes	7539
arr Roberts	PC	1121/2210/timp/str		C.Fischer	1974

No.6, op.74, in B min (Pathétique)

	φ	3(picc)222/4231/timp.perc/str	42'-45'	Boosey & H	Misc 2475
	φ	3(picc)222/4231/timp.perc/str		Forberg	4294 Amv Bgg +) Es Fn)
	φ	3(picc)222/4231/timp.perc/str		Russian SM.CW 17b	MRL
	φ	3(picc)222/4231/timp.perc/str		Russian SM	14983 Awe

Facsimile of autograph including a few sketches

	φ	3+picc.222/4231/timp.perc/str		Russian SM,1970	MRL facs
ed R.Eller	φ	3(picc)222/4231/timp.perc/str		Bruckner	Misc 2843
arr Schmeling	φ	3(picc)222/4231/timp.perc.tamtam/str		Breitkopf	27050 **
alternative version	φ	2121/2210/timp.perc/str		Breitkopf	27050 **

1st & 2nd mvts only

arr A.Schmid	PC	2(picc)222/4231/timp.perc/str		Hawkes	850 Bwa

3rd & 4th mvts only

arr A.Schmid	PC	2(picc)222/4230/timp.perc/str		Hawkes	849 Bwa

No.7, in E♭ (1892)

(reconstructed and edited by S.Bogatryryev from sketches)

	φ	3(picc)222/4231/timp.perc/hp/str		Russian SM,1961	23679 B +

TCHAIKOVSKY, Pyotr Ilyich (cont)

TCHAIKOVSKIANA: selection   see   PALMER, (Cedric) King: TCHAIKOWSKIANA
TCHAIKOVSKY IN THE BALLROOM   see   BOWDEN, D: TCHAIKOVSKI IN THE BALLROOM
TCHAIKOVSKY WALTZ MEMORIES   see   WINTER, A: TCHAIKOVSKY WALTZ MEMORIES
TCHEREVICHKY: opera   see   OXANA'S CAPRICES
The TEMPEST (after Shakespeare): fantasie

	φ	2+picc.222/4231/timp.perc/str	23'	Jurgenson	8058 Amv B +
	φ	2+picc.222/4231/timp.perc/str		Russian SM.CW 24	MRL

TO JOY: cantata for 4 solo voices, chorus & orch

	φ	2+picc.222/4231/timp.perc/str	Russian SM.CW 27	MRL

TO SLEEP, for chorus & orch   φ   2222/2200/timp/str   Russian SM.CW 27   MRL
TO THE FOREST (Pilgrims' song), op.47, no.5

in D	φ	1122/2131/str	4'	(Siddell)	17489 B
in E♭	φ	1122/2031/str		(Siddell)	17490
in E♭ & F, arr G.Stacey		pf/str		(Boosey)	LM G 3535
in E	φ	1122/2031/str		(Siddell)	17491
in E, arr G.Stacey		pf/str		(Ashdown)	LM G 3741
in E 'I bless you forests'	φPC	2122/4221/timp/str		Ashdown	6355
in F	φ	1122/2031/str		(Siddell)	17488
in G	φ	2+picc.122/2031/str		(Siddell)	17492

'TWAS APRIL: song, op.38, no.2

in D♭, arr H.Carr	φ	2121/2230/hp/str	(Boosey)	TC 632

UNDINE: opera

Complete	φ	2+2picc.222/4231/timp.perc/hp/str	Russian SM.CW 2	MRL

VAKULA THE SMITH   see   OXANA'S CAPRICES
VALSE, op.40, no.8   see   2 PIECES, arr A.Schmid
VALSE BLUETTE (No.11 of 18 pieces, op.72)(used by composer as an interpolation in "Swan Lake" ballet

arr Drigo	φ	2222/4000/tri/hp/str	Jurgenson	8056

VALSE CREOLE   see   PETITE SUITE
VALSE-SCHERZO for violin & orch, op.34

	φ	2222/2000/str		Jurgenson	23074 +
	φ	2222/2000/str		Russian SM.CW 30a	MRL
arr F.Salabert	φ	2222/2230/timp/str	8'	Salabert	9503

VARIATIONS ON A ROCOCO THEME for cello & orch, op.33 (1876)

original version	φ	2222/2000/str		Russian SM,1973	Misc 8201
revised version	φ	2222/2000/str	15'-19'30"	Rahter	4850 Amv Cn

VARIATIONS ON A THEME BY TCHAIKOVSKY   see   ARENSKI, A.S: VARIATIONS ON A THEME BY TCHAIKOVSKY
The VOYEVODE: opera, op.3 (1867-68)

Complete	φ	2+picc.2+ca.22/4230/timp.perc/hp/str		Russian SM.CW 1a-c	MRL
Overture	φ	2+picc.2+ca.22/4231/timp.perc/str	12'	Jurgenson	8975 +
Suite					
Entr'acte Airs de ballet					
	φ	2+picc.222/4231/timp.perc/hp/str		Jurgenson	6371 Amv
arr F.Salabert	PC	2(picc)121/2230/timp.perc/str		Salabert	13670
Intermezzo	φ	2111/0000/hp/str		(BBC)	19773

The VOYEVODE: incidental music to play by Ostrovsky (1886)
   Melodrama for the 'Domovoy' scene

	φ	2111/0000/hp/str	Russian SM.CW 14	MRL

The VOYEVODE: symphonic ballad, op.78 (1890-91)

	φ	32+ca.2+bcl.2/4231/timp.perc/cel.hp/str	10'	Belaieff	4365 B
	φ	32+ca.2+bcl.2/4231/timp.perc/cel.hp/str		Russian SM.CW 27	MRL

WAS I NOT A LITTLE BLADE OF GRASS?: song for Soprano solo & orch, op.47, no.7

	φ	2222/4000/str	Russian SM.CW 27	MRL

WHY? (Dreaming and waking), op.28, no.3 (orig voice & pf)

arr Torke	PC	1111/2110/timp/str	Kuhl	10104

WHY ARE THE ROSES SO PALE?: song, op.6, no.5 (orig voice & pf)

in D, arr F.Cramer		pf/str	(Enoch)	LM G 4592
arr Torke	PC	1111/2110/timp/str	Kuhl	10103

WHEN I SING: song
   in B♭, arr F.Cramer from waltz from 'Sleeping Beauty' used in film 'It started with Eve'

	pf/str	(FD & H)	LM G 5235

TCHAIKOVSKY, Pyotr Ilyich

YEVGENI ONEGIN   see   EUGENE ONEGIN
YOLANDE   see   IOLANTHE

TCHAKOPP, Ivan

DANCE SUITE
  1. Sambo's holiday: Danse afrique   3. Pekoe dance: polka elegante
  2. Cossack revels: Danse grotesque   4. Valse russe
    arr Roberts   PC   1121/2210/perc/str   C.Fischer   6996

TCHÉRÉPNIN, Aleksandr Nikolayevich (1899-1977)

CONCERTINO for violin, cello, piano & strings, op.47
                 φ   str   15'   Universal,1931   Misc 3535
CONCERTI
  Piano & orch
    No.2, op.26   φ   2222/4231/timp.perc/str   18'   Heugel,1969   Misc 7486
    No.3, op.48, in B♭   φ   2222/4231/timp.perc/str   17'   Universal,1932   Misc 3535
    No.5, op.95   φ   3(picc)2+ca.2+bcl.2+cbsn/4331/timp.perc.
                     bell.tamtam.xyl/hp/str   21'   Belaieff,1968   Misc 7004
    No.6, op.99   φ   2+picc.222/4231/timp.perc.bells.glock.xyl/
                     hp/str   24'   Belaieff,1970   Misc 8384
CONCERTO DA CAMERA for flute, violin & small orch, op.33
                 φ   0000/20.2cnt.00/timp/str   Schott   Misc 1060
DIVERTIMENTO, op.90   φ   2+picc.2+ca.3+bcl.2+cbsn/4431/timp.perc.bells/
                   str   23'   Boosey & H   Misc 6329 B
GEORGIANA: suite, op.92
  1. Ceremonial   4. Kartsuli
  2. Veils and Daggers   5. Apotheosis
  3. Chota and Thamar
                 φ   2(picc)222/4231/timp.perc.bells/str   Eulenburg,1959   Misc 6352
Die HOCHZEIT DER SOBEIDE: opera
  Festmusik: suite, op.45b   φ   2(picc)222/4231/timp.perc.tamtam/hp/str   Universal   Misc 1179
IVAN THE FOOL: incidental music for SATB soli, SSAATTBB chorus & orch (1968)
                 φ   1(picc)1(ca)1(E♭cl)1/1221/timp.perc.
                     bells.vib.xyl/hp/str
                     (with tape recorded electronic music by
                     Serge Tchérépnin)   35'   Composer   MS 31535 +
The LOST FLUTE for narrator & orch, op.89 (1954)
                 φ   2(picc)222/2210/timp.perc.bells.Chinese temple-bells.
                     Chinese small dm[=sdm].glock.3Chinese gong.tamtam.
                     Chinese scissors[=tri].xyl/Chinese str-instrs.str   Templeton,1954   Misc 10504
MAGNA MATER, op.41   φ   2222/4231/timp.perc.tamtam/str   Universal   Misc 890
ROMANTIC OVERTURE, op.67   φ   2+picc.2(ca)22/4231/timp.perc.bells.glock.xyl/hp.pf/
                   str   8'30"   G.Schirmer,1955 Misc 4455
RUSSIAN DANCES: suite   φ   2(picc)2(ca)2(E♭cl)2/4231/timp.perc.xyl/hp/
                   str   Ed Pro Musica   13621
SONATINE, op.61   φ   2(picc)2(ca)12/1210/timp.xyl   Belaieff,1967   CM 54978
SYMPHONIC MARCH, op.80   φ   3(picc)222/4331/timp.perc.xyl/cel.hp.pf/str   Leeds,1956   Misc 4776
SYMPHONIES
  No.1, op.42, in E   φ   2(picc)222/4331/timp.perc/str   20'   Durand   Misc 888
  No.2, op.77 (1945-51)   φ   3(picc)2+ca.2+bcl.2+cbsn/4331/timp.perc(bells.xyl)/
                   cel.hp.pf/str   25'   Russian SM,1971 Misc 7641
  No.3, op.83   φ   2+picc.2+ca.2+bcl.2+cbsn/4331/timp.perc.bells.xyl/
                   cel.hp.pf/str   28'   Templeton,1955   Misc 8715

TCHÉRÉPNIN, Aleksandr Nikolayevich (cont)

SYMPHONIES (cont)
No.4, op.91   ∮   2+picc.2+ca.2+E♭cl+bcl.2+cbsn/4331/timp/
                                    hp/str   24'   Hawkes,1959   Misc 5235 B

TCHÉRÉPNIN, Nikolai Nikolayevich (1873-1945)

CHANT DE SAPHO, for Soprano solo, fv-chorus & orch, op.5
                               ∮   2222/2000/hp/str   Belaieff,1899   Misc 3103
FANTAISIE DRAMATIQUE, op.17   ∮   32+ca.32/5331/timp.perc/hp/str   15'   Belaieff   5787
GAVOTTE   ∮   2222/4200/str   2'   Jurgenson   8102
MACBETH   see   The WITCHES SCENE IN SHAKESPEARE'S MACHBETH
NARCISSE ET ECHO: mythological poem
                               ∮   4+picc.2+ca.32+cbsn/6331/timp.perc.glock.xyl/
                                    cel.2hp/str   Jurgenson   15020
Le PAVILLON D'ARMIDE: ballet
   Complete
      ed J.Turner   ∮   2121/2220/timp.perc/cel.hp/str   BBC   TV 708
   Suite, op.29
      1. Introduction & 1st scene (6'25")
      2. Courantes - danses des heures (1'55")
      3. La scène d'animation du gobalin (3'30")
      4. Grand valse noble (4'25")
      5. La plainte d'Armide (2'45")
      6. Danse des gamins (1'55")
      7. Bacchus et les Bacchantes (2'30")
      8. Entrée des magiciens et danse des ombres (2'20")
      9. Danse des bouffons (2'45")
                               ∮   3(picc)2+ca.32+cbsn/4331/timp.perc.xyl/
                                    cel.2hp/str   28'   Belaieff   4357 C
         No.5 only   pf/str   Belaieff   3434
   Grande valse   ∮   3(picc)232/4331/timp.perc.glock/hp/str   Belaieff   4258
   Intermezzo
      arr A.Rudd   PC   1121/2210/timp.perc/str   Enoch   10930
   Valse lente
      arr A.Rudd   PC   1121/2210/timp.perc/str   Enoch   11978
La PRINCESSE LOINTAINE: overture, op.4
                               ∮   2+picc.222/4231/timp/hp/str   8'   Belaieff   4369
The ROMANCE OF A MUMMY: ballet
   Suite, arr A.Goossens
      1. Entrance of the grand priestess and Lot's dance   3. Dance of the little slaves
      2. Sacred dance   4. Love duet
                               PC   1+picc.121/4230/perc.glock/cel.hp/str   Chester   3875 B
Le ROYAUME ENCHANTÉ: symphonic poem, op.24
                               ∮   42+ca.32/4331/timp.perc.glock.xyl/cel.2hp.pf/
                                    str   Jurgenson   9726 C
SIX MUSICAL ILLUSTRATIONS   ∮   3(picc)2+ca.2+acl.2+cbsn/4331/timp.perc(glock.
                                    tamtam.xyl)/cel.2hp.pf/str   Russian SM,1969   Misc 6998
The WITCHES SCENE IN SHAKESPEARE'S MACBETH for orch, op.12
                               ∮   3(picc)22+bcl.2+cbsn/4331/timp.perc/str 20' Belaieff   5788

TEDESCO, Mario Castelnuovo   see   CASTELNUOVO-TEDESCO, Mario

TEIKE, C.

ALTE KAMERADEN (Old comrades): march
   arr C.Woodhouse   ∮PC 1+picc.222/4231.euph/timp.perc/hp/str 2'30"-4' Hawkes   229 Bp C
   arr P.Hope for military band & orch
                               ∮   2(picc)222/433[1]/3perc(timp.glock)/hp/str (Boosey)   26207 + ∮ &
                                                                                                      mil band

TEIKE, C (cont)

GRAF ZEPPELIN: march   PC 2(picc)211/4230/perc.glock/str   Bellmann & Tüner   12584
IN TREUE FEST (Steadfast and true): march
                                PC 1+picc.222/4230.euph/perc/str   Hawkes   2875 B
OLD COMRADES   see   ALTE KAMERADEN

TELEMANN, Georg Philipp (1681-1767)

see: HOFFMANN, A. - "Die Orchestersuiten Georg Philipp Telemann TWV 55"
                        (With thematic index) Zürich: Möseler Verlag, 1969
      KROSS, S.   - "Das Instrumentalkonzert bei G.Ph. Telemann"
                        (With thematic index) Tutzing: Schneider,1969
      BACH, J.S.   - Cantatas 141, 146 & 160

COMPLETE WORKS

George Philipp Telemann: Musikalische Werke. Kassel & Basel: Bärenreiter, 1950.

ALLEIN GOTT IN DER HÖH SEI EHR: Christmas cantata for Bass (or Baritone) solo, chorus & orch
    ed K.Hofmann   ø   000[1]/0[1]00/str/cont(org)   Hänssler,1977   26949 *
ALLES REDET JETZT UND SINGET: cantata for Soprano & Bass soli & orch
    ed W.Menke   ø   2201/0000/str(vln.vla)/cont   Bärenreiter,1955   Misc 4738 B
Das BEFREITE ISRAEL: for SATBB soli, chorus & orch
    ed W.Hobohm   ø   22+ob-d'am[=ob].01/10+3clno.00/timp/
                                cont(org[=hpsd].vlc.bass.bsn)   Bärenreiter,1971.CW 22   MRL
La BOURSE: Suite (1720)   see   OVERTURES in Bb, no.11
CHACONNE in F min   see   SUITE in F min
La CHANGEANTE: suite for strings (TWV 55:g2)   see   OVERTURES in G min, no.2
CONCERTI(for one or more similar instruments)
    Numbering and definition of solo instruments from KROSS, Siegfried: Das Instrumentalkonzert bei
    Georg Philipp Telemann. Tutzing: Schneider, 1969
    Cello   see   OVERTURES in D no.6
    2 Chalumeaux (Clarinets)
       in D min
          ed H.Dechant   ø   str/cont   Musica Rara,1973   25675
    Chalumeaux
       in D min
          ed C.Lowson   ø   str/cont   (Editor)   26936
    Flute
       in D, No.1, Concerto à 5, ed & arr Brinckmann & Mohr
                              ø   str/cont(hpsd)   Sikorski,1959   23264
       in D, No.4
          ed F.Schroeder   ø   str/cont   Eulenburg,1968   26010 **
       in E min
          ed F.Schroeder   ø   str/cont(hpsd)   Eulenburg   23951
       in G, no.2
          ed W.Upmeyer   ø   str(no vla)/cont   Bärenreiter,1955   52833
    2 flutes (or recorders)
       in A min, ed F.Stein   ø   str/cont   10'   Nagel,1953   21226
       in Bb
          ed W.Birke   ø   str/cont   Vieweg,1938   Misc 4250
          ed A.Hoffmann   ø   str/cont   Möseler,1949   Misc 6102
    Horn (corno da caccia)
       in D, ed E.Leloir, cont   ø   0100/0000/str/cont(hpsd: real H.Majewski)   Heinrichshofen,1964   24681

TELEMANN, Georg Philipp (cont)

CONCERTI (cont)

2 horns
   in Eb (Musique de Table III, 1733)

ed W.Bergmann	φ	str/cont	10'	Eulenburg,1935	Misc 10121
ed W.Bergmann	φ	str/cont		(Eulenburg,1935)	51804
ed W.Bergmann	φ	str/cont		Eulenburg,1935	52686
ed J.P.Hinnenthal	φ	str/cont		Bärenreiter,1963 CW 14	MRL
ed M.Seiffert, rev.H.J.Moser					
	φ	str/cont		Breitkopf,1959 DDT 61/2	MRL

3 horns
   in D, ed E.Leloir, cont. real. K.Weelink

	φ	0[2]00/0000/solo vln.str/cont(hpsd)	Ka We,1966	Misc 6412 B

Oboe

in C min, ed R.Lauschmann	φ	str/cont	5'	Sikorski,1977	Misc 9302
in D min, ed H.Töttcher	φ	str/cont		Sikorski,1953	21116
in E minor, ed H.Töttcher	φ	str/cont(hpsd)		Sikorski,1954	23030
in F minor					
ed F.Schroeder	φ	str/cont(hpsd)	10'	Eulenburg,1957	22609
ed F.Stein	φ	str/cont		Hinrichsen,1932	21353

Oboe d'Amore

in E min, ed J.P. Hinnenthal	φ	str/cont	Hinnenthal	Misc 3777
in G, ed & arr H. Töttcher	φ	str/cont	Sikorski,1963	23964
in A, ed F.Schroeder	φ	str/cont	Eulenburg	23650

Orchestra

in D, ed G.Fleishhsauer	φ	0[2]0[1]/0300/str/cont	Peters,1968	25011
in D, ed H.Köbel, cont.real. E. Meyerolbersleben				
	φ	2001/0000/str(2vln.vla[vlc])	Heinrichshofen,1971	25307
in D, ed K.M.Komma	φ	0200/0300/timp/str/cont	Breitkopf Erbe Reichs II	MRL
ed K.M.Komma	φ	0200/0300/timp/str/cont	(Erbe Reichs II)	19604 +
ed R.P.Block	φ	020[1]/03[=3cln]00/timp/str/cont	Musica Rara,1975	26107 *
in Bb, ed K.M.Komma	φ	2200/0000/str(no vla)/cont	Erbe Reichs II	MRL

Recorder
   in C: treble recorder & orch

ed I.Hechler	φ	str/cont(hpsd)	Hoeck,1960	Misc 9907
in A min see OVERTURES in A min, no.2				
in F, ed M.Ruetz	φ	str/cont	Bärenreiter,1955	52659

2 recorders
   in Bb for 2 recorders   see   CONCERTO in Bb for 2 FLUTES

Strings
   in D "Eine Kleine Tanzsuite"
     1. Allemande   2. Ballo   3. Giga

arr W.Upmeyer	φ	str/cont(hpsd)	Bärenrenreiter,1950	20204
in G "Concerto Polonois"				
ed F.Schroeder	φ	str/cont	Schott,1977	Misc 9461
in Bb "Polish Concerto"				
cont real K.Sikorsky	φ	str/cont(hpsd)	Polish State,1964	Misc 6104

Trumpet

in D see SONATA (concerto) in C for trumpet & orch				
in D, ed K.Grebe	φ	str(no vla)/cont(hpsd)	Sikorski,1959	23031
ed R.P.Block	φ	0001/0000/str(no vla)/cont	Musica Rara,1976	26132 *
in D, ed H.Töttcher & K.Grebe (not same concerto as above)				
	φ	0200/0000/str/cont	Simrock,1961	23959
ed & real R.P.Block	φ	0201/0000/str/cont(hpsd)	Musica Rara,1976	26128

     see also CONCERTO for 2 oboes & trumpet
          OVERTURE in D, no.8, for trumpet, strings & continuo
          SONATA in D for trumpet, strings & continuo

TELEMANN, Georg Philipp (cont)

CONCERTI (cont)
  3 trumpets
    in D, no.1
      ed K.M.Komma   ø 020[1]/0000/timp/str/cont   Breitkopf,1938. EDM.I,II   19604 & MRL
      ed R.P.Block   ø 120[1]/0000/timp/str/cont   Musica Rara,1975   26107
    in D, no.2
      ed G.Fleischhauer   ø [0201]/0000/timp/str/cont(hpsd)   Peters,1968   25011
  Viola
    in G, ed H.C.Wolff   ø str   Bärenreiter   19986 + B
    in A, ed J.P.Hinnenthal ø str(no vla)/cont   Hinnenthal,1955   22359
  Viola da gamba see OVERTURES in D no.6
  2 violas (violetti)
    in G, ed W.Lebermann   ø str/cont   Schott,1970   25252
      ed K.Flattschacher, cont real G.Frotscher
                         ø str/cont   Müller,1966   25615
  Violin
    in C, no.1, ed S.Kross ø 0201/0000/str/cont(hpsd)   Bärenreiter,1973.CW 23(no.1) MRL
    in C, no.2 see Der NEUMODISCHE LIEBHABER DAMON
    in D [no.1] (D-brd.DS.Mus Ms 1033/71)
      ed S.Kross   ø str/cont(hpsd)   Bärenreiter,1973.CW 23(no.2) MRL &
                                                                    Misc 8984
    in D, no.2, ed S.Kross ø str/cont(hpsd)   Bärenreiter,1973.CW 23(no.3) MRL
    in D, ed H.Töttcher & K.Grebe
                         ø 0000/0100/str(vln.I.II.III.,vla.I.II.,
                              vlc.obl)/cont   Sikorski,1965   Misc 6264
    in E, ed S.Kross   ø str/cont(hpsd)   Bärenreiter,1973.CW 23(no.4) MRL
    in E min, ed S.Kross   ø str/cont   Bärenreiter,1973.CW 23(no.5) MRL
    in F, ed S.Kross   ø str(vln.I.II.[=violettas].vla.vlc)/cont(hpsd)
                                              Bärenreiter,1973.CW 23(no.6) MRL
    in F (Concerto-suite)
      ed A.Schering   ø 220[1]/0200/timp/str/cont   Breitkopf,1905.DDT.29-30 19625 + & MRL
      ed A.Schering, rev A.Möser ø 220[1]/0200/timp/str/cont   Breitopf,1958   MRL
    in G, no.1, ed S.Kross ø 0201/0000/str/cont(hpsd)   Bärenreiter,1973.CW 23(no.7) MRL
      Ed F.Schroeder   ø str/cont   Eulenburg   23950
    in G. no.4, ed S.Kross ø str(vln.I.II[=violettas].vla.vlc)/
                              cont(hpsd)   Bärenreiter,1973.CW 23(no.8) MRL
    in G min, ed S.Kross   ø str/cont(bsn.hpsd)   Bärenreiter,1973.CW 23(no.9) MRL
    in A min, no.1, ed S.Kross ø str/cont   Bärenreiter,1973.CW 23(no.10) MRL
    in A min, no.2, arr H.C.Wolff ø str/cont   Bärenreiter,1950   20140
    in Bb, no.1, ed S.Kross ø str/cont(hpsd)   Bärenreiter,1973.CW 23(no.11) MRL
    in Bb (Concerto grosso per il Signor Pisendel)
      ed W.Hobohm   ø str/cont(real.W.H.Bernstein)   Peters,1964   27085
    in B min, ed S.Kross   ø str/cont(hpsd)   Bärenreiter,1973.CW 23(no.12) MRL
  2 violins
    in G min, ed F.Schroeder ø str/cont(hpsd)   Peters,1977   Misc 9576
  3 violins
    in F (Musiene de Table II, 1733)
      ed J.P.Hinnenthal   ø str/cont   15'05" Bärenreiter,1962   MRL
      ed M.Seiffert, rev.H.J.Moser
                       ø str/cont   Breitkopf,1959.DDT.61/2 51799 & MRL

TELEMANN, Georg Philipp (cont)

CONCERTI for 2 or more different instruments & orch
  in C min, for oboe & violin
    ed K.Beckmann   φ 000[1]/0000/str/cont   8'   Breitkopf,1981   Misc 10441
  in D, for 2 flutes & calchedon[=bassoon]
    ed H.Kölbel   φ str/cont(real E.Meyerolbersleben)   Heinrichshofen,1971   25307
  in D, for 2 oboes & trumpet
    ed R.P.Block   φ str/cont   Musica Rara,1976   26128
      (called 'Concerto no.3' in this edition)
    ed H.Töttcher & K.Grebe   φ str/cont   Simrock,1961   23959
  in D, for violin & cello
    (classified thus by Kross, but virtually a solo violin concerto)
    ed H.Töttcher & K.Grebe   φ 0000/0100/str/cont   Misc 1965   Misc 6264
  in E, for flute, oboe d'amore, viola d'amore [=vln con sord] & orch
    ed F.Stein   φ str/cont   Litolff,1938   Misc 9509
                                                             20495 +
  in E min, for flute & recorder
    ed H.Kölbel   φ str/cont   Bärenreiter,1954   52467
                      φ str/cont   (D-brd DS MS 1033/84) m/f 408
  in E min, for 2 flutes & violin
    ed F.Schroeder   φ str/cont   Eulenburg,1959   23255
  in F, for flute & bassoon
    ed G.Angerhöfer   φ str/cont (hpsd real W.H.Bernstein)   Breitkopf [1966] 24592
  in F, for oboe & violin
    ed A.Wiklund   φ str/cont   Musica Rara,1978   26644 *
  in F, for recorder & bassoon
    ed I.Hechler   φ str/cont   Heinrichshofen,1964   53666
  in F, for recorder & bassoon
    ed G.Angerhöfer   φ str/hpsd   Breitkopf,1965   24592
  in A, for flute & violin (Musique de Table I, 1733)
    ed J.P.Hinnenthal   φ str/cont   35'
                                  Bärenreiter,1959 (Mus Werke 12) 25800 & MRL
    ed M.Seiffert, rev H.J.Moser φ str/cont   Breitkopf,1959 (DDT 61/2) 51794 & MRL
  in B♭ for 2 flutes & 2 oboes
    ed K.M.Komma   φ str/cont   Breitkopf 1938 EDM Reichs 1/2 MRL
CONCERTI for orchestra, without solo instruments
  in D (Eine kleine Tanzsuite)
    ed W.Upmeyer   φ str/cont(hpsd)   Bärenreiter,1950   20204
  in D see CONCERTI, 3 trumpets
  in G 'Concerto polonois'
    ed F.Schroeder   φ str/cont(hpsd)   Schott,1977   Misc 9461
  in B♭ 'Concerto polonois'
    ed T.Ochlewski   φ str/cont(hpsd real K.Sikorsky)   PWM,1964   Misc 6104
CONCERT SUITE in A, for violin & orch see OVERTURES in A, no.8
CONCLUSIONS
  in D (Musique de Table II, 1733)
    ed J.P.Hinnenthal   φ 0100/0100/str/cont   Bärenreiter,1962 CW 13   MRL
    ed M.Seiffert, rev H.J.Moser φ 0101/0100/str/cont   Breitkopf,1959,DDT 61/2 MRL
  in E min (Musique de Table I, 1733)
    ed J.P.Hinnenthal   φ 2000/0000/str/cont   Bärenreiter,1959CW 12   MRL
    ed M.Seiffert, rev H.J.Moser φ 2000/0000/str/cont   Breitkopf,1959,DDT 61/2 MRL
  in B♭ (Musique de Table III, 1733)
    ed W.Bergmann   φ 0200/0000/str/cont   Eulenburg,1935   Misc 10121
    ed J.P.Hinnenthal   φ 0200/0000/str/cont   Bärenreiter,1963 (Mus Werke 14) MRL
    ed M.Seiffert, rev H.J.Moser φ 0200/0000/str/cont   Breitkopf,1959 (DDT 61/2) MRL

TELEMANN, Georg Philipp (cont)

DA, JESU, DEINEN RUHM ZU MEHREN: cantata for Soprano (or Tenor) solo & instruments
   ed K.Hofmann   φ 0.rec[=vln].1[=vln].00/0000/cont
                          or 0.[rec].[1]/0000/str/cont/[chorus]   12'   Hänssler,1981   26950 *
DAMON see Der NEUMODISCHE LIEBHABER DAMON
DAS IST JE GEWISSLICH WAHR: cantata for ATB soli, SATB chorus & orch
   [formerly attrib J.S.Bach]   φ 0200/0000/str/cont   Breitkopf.BG 30   MRL
DER FÜR DIE SÜNDE DER WELT GEMARTERTE UND STERBENDE JESUS: Passion Oratoria
                   φ 2+2rec.201/2200/vla-d'a.str/cont(hpsd) (D-brd DS MUS 1283) Misc 6267

DIVERTIMENTI
   in A, ed F.Oberdörffer   φ str/cont   Vieweg,1936   20150
   in Bb, ed F.Oberdörffer   φ str/cont   Vieweg,1937   20151
DON QUICHOTTE: opera
   Ein wahrer Held eilt schon im Feld: aria (Don Quichotte)
      ed C.Ottzer   φ str   Ebering,1902   Misc 3349
DON QUICHOTTE: suite see OVERTURES, in G, no.10
Die DONNERRODE: 'Wie ist dein Name so gross': music for the 17th Sunday after Trinity, 1756
   for SATBB soli, chorus & orch
      ed W.Hobohm   φ 22+ob-d'a.02/02+3clno.00/timp/
                          cont(hpsd.vlc.cb.bsn)   Bärenreiter,1971 CW 22 MRL
EHRE SEI GOTT IN DER HÖHE (Weihnachtskantate) for SATB soli, chorus & orch
   ed G.Fock   φ 0000/0300/timp/str/cont(org)   Bärenreiter,1969   Misc 10084
EMMA UND EGINHARD: opera (1728)
   Overture see CONCERTI, violin, in A min no.1
   Sinfonia
      ed C.Ottzenn
                    φ str/cont   Ebering,1902   Misc 3349
FESTLICHE SUITE in A see OVERTURES in A, no.5
FUNERAL MUSIC see HAMBURGISCHE TRAUERMUSIK
Der GEDULDIGE SOCRATES: opera
   Complete
      ed B.Baselt   φ 0.2rec.201/0300/timp/str/cont(hpsd) Bärenreiter,1967.CW 20 MRL
   Overture (NB. this is the same as Overture in G, no.4 'Ouverture des Nations Anciens et Modernes')
      ed C.Ottzer   φ str   Ebering,1902   Misc 3349
   Extracts
     Ach Adon, Adon ist hin: chorus
       ed C.Ottzer   φ 0200/00+3clno.00/str   Ebering,1902   Misc 3349
     Io nò non cedero, non cedero : duet (Xantippe & Amitta)
       ed C.Ottzer   φ str   Ebering,1902   Misc 3349
GOTT DER HOFFNUNG ERFÜLLE EUCH: cantata for SAT soli, SATB chorus & orch [formerly attrib J.S.Bach, BWV 218]
                   φ 0000/2000/str/cont   Breitkopf BG 41   MRL
GOTT SEI MIR GNÄDIG: cantata for SAB soli, chorus & orch
   ed T.Fedtke   φ str/org[=hpsd]   Hänssler,1963   25233
GRILLEN-SYMPHONIE: concerto
   ed P.Thalheimer   φ 1[=picc=1+picc]11[=chalumeau]0/0000/
                       2cb[=2vlc]=soli.str   11'   Hänssler,1978   26941 *
HAMBURGISCHE TRAUERMUSIK: 5 instrumental pieces from the Trauermusik for Gerhard Schröder (1723) and
   for Daniel Stockfleth (1739)
      ed K.Hofmann   φ 0200/0300/timp/str/cont(hpsd[=org])   Hänssler,1976   26951 *
HERZLICH TUT MICH VERLANGEN: cantata for Tenor & Bass soli, chorus & orch
   ed K.Hofmann   φ str/cont(org)   18'   Hänssler,1981   26947 *
ICH DANKE DEM HERRN (Psalm 111) for SATB soli, chorus & orch
   ed K.Hofmann   φ 0.[2rec].201/0100/str/cont   25'   Hänssler,1977   26944 *

TELEMANN, Georg Philipp (cont)

IN DULCE JUBILO: Christmas cantata for ATB soli, chorus & orch
    ed F.Stein   φ   0000/2000/str/cont(org)   Merseburger,1957   25241
INO: cantata for Soprano solo & orch
                      φ   2000/2000/str/cont   (D-ddr Bds Mus Ms 21781)   Misc 10471
                                                                   m/f 410
    ed M.Schneider   φ   200[1]/2000/str/cont(hpsd)   (DDT 28)   Misc 10208
    ed M.Schneider   φ   200[1]/2000/str/cont(hpsd)   Breitkopf.DDT 28   26931 & MRL
JAUCHZET DEM HERRN (Psalm 100): cantata for bass solo & orch
    ed K.Hofmann   φ   0001/0100/str/cont(org)   Hänssler,1974   26942 *
    ed F.Schroeder   φ   0000/ 1[=ob]00/str/cont   Leuckart,1975   Misc 8865
Ein KINDELEIN SO LÖBELICH: cantata for SATB soli, chorus & orch
    ed K.Schultz-Mauser   φ   str/cont(org)   Vieweg,1963   Misc 5960
Eine KLEINE TANZSUITE: see   CONCERTI: Orchestral concerti, in D
KLEINE SUITE in D
    1. Overture   4. Menuet 1
    2. Rondeau   5. Menuet 2
    3. Loure   6. Rigaudon
      ed H.Höckner   φ   str/cont (real F.W.Lethar)   Bärenreiter,1963   21002
LAUDATE PUERI DOMINUM (Psalm 112) for Soprano (or Tenor) solo & instruments
    ed K.Hofmann & F.Schroeder   φ   0[2]00/0000/2vln/cont(hpsd)   Hänssler,1981   26948 *
LOBET DEN HERRN, ALLE HEIDEN (Psalm 117)(from Cantata 11, 1744) for SS soli, SS[=A][B] chorus & instruments
    ed & real K.Hofmann   φ   0000/0[3]00/[timp]/str(2vln[2vla])/cont   Hänssler,1974   Misc 8685
LOBT GOTT, IHR CHRISTEN ALLZUGLEICH: Christmas cantata for STB soli, chorus & orch
    ed A.Adrio   φ   0000/05[=5 ob]00/timp/str/cont(org)   Merseburger,1947   20615
LUSTIGE SUITE in C
    1. Overture   5. Menuett 2
    2. Loure   6. Entrée
    3. Rigaudon   7. Pastourell
    4. Menuett 1
      arr A.Hoffmann   φ   pf/str   Kallmeyer,1944   19911 B
La LYRA   see   SUITE in E♭
MACHET DIE TORE WEIT: Cantata for the first Sunday of Advent for STB soli, chorus & orch
    ed T.Fedtke   φ   0201/0000/org[=hpsd]/str   Hänssler,1963   25234
    ed T.Fedtke & K.Hofmann, for soli, chorus & orch
                       φ   020[1]/0000/str/cont   Hänssler,1975   26919
MAGNIFICAT (Kleines Magnificat) for Soprano & instruments, in A min (formerly attrib J.S.Bach, BWV Anh 21)
    ed H.Hellman   φ   1000/2vln.vltta[vlc]/cont(org) with complete
                          facsimile   Hänssler,1961   25578
    ed H.Schouman   φ   1000/0000/2vln.vltta[=vla]/cont(org.vlc) Brockmans & Poppel,1978   26654
    ed E.Pascanella (with facsimile)
                       φ   1000/0000/str/cont(org)   Santis,1958   Misc 4883
MAGNIFICAT in G for SATB soli, chorus & orch
    ed K.Hofmann   φ   0.2tblrec.201/0000/str/cont(org)   Hänssler,1980   26940
MEINE SEELE ERHEBT DEN HERRN   see   MAGNIFICAT
Der MESSIAS: oratorio for SATB soli & orch (1759)
                      φ   22(ob-da)02/0000/str/cont   (D-ddr Bds Telemann 25)   Misc 10223 &
                                                                mf 405
MIRINAYS: opera
    Die Dankbarkeit mir dich verpflichten: aria (Zemir)
      in E, ed C.Ottzenn   φ   str   Ebering 1902   Misc 3349
MUSIQUE DE TABLE (1733)
    Complete
      ed J.P.Hinnenthal   φ   1000/2000/str/cont   Bärenreiter,1959-63(Mus Werke 12-14)   MRL
      ed M.Seiffert, rev H.J.Moser φ   1000/2000/str/cont   Breitkopf,1959.DDT 61/2   MRL

TELEMANN, Georg Philipp (cont)

MUSIQUE DE TABLE (cont)
   3ème Production
     ed W.Bergmann   φ 0000/2000/str/cont   Eulenburg,1935   Misc 10121
       [For the Overtures, Concertos and Conclusions listed below, see under their individual titles;
         other works are included in the Chamber catalogue]
   1ère Production Overture in E min, no.1
                Concerto in A for flute, violin, strings & cont
                Conclusion in E min
   2ème Production Overture in D, no.1
                Concerto for 3 violins, strings & cont in F
                Conclusion in D
   3ème Production Overture in B♭, no.1
                Concerto for 2 horns, strings & continuo in E♭
                Conclusion in B♭
Der NEUMODISCHE LIEBHABER DAMON (Die Satyrn on Arcadien): Comic opera (1724)
   Complete
     ed B.Baselt   φ 0.2rec.202/2200/str/cont   Bärenreiter,1969.CW 21   MRL
   Extracts
     Concerto in C, for violin & orch
       ed A.Hoffmann   φ (1)[=rec].200/0000/str/cont   Möseler,1971   Misc 8301
       ed C.Ottzenn   φ 0200/0000/str   Ebering,1902   Misc 3349
         (No.7 of "Telemann als Opernkomponist")
     "Still, still, hört, hört": recit (Mirtilla)
       ed C.Ottzer   φ str   Ebering,1902   Misc 3349
     Sarabande, Gigue & Gavotte
       ed C.Ottzer   φ str   Ebering,1902   Misc 3349
         (Nos.8, 9a,9b,9c, of "Telemann als Opernkomponist")
O JESU CHRIST DEIN KRIPPLEIN IST: Cantata for chorus & orch
   ed G.Braun   φ str/cont(org=hpsd)   Hänssler,1966   Misc 6521
OUVERTURE BURLESQUE: see OVERTURES in B♭ no.8
OUVERTURE DES NATIONS ANCIENS ET MODERNES: see OVERTURE in G no.4
OVERTURES (SUITES) Numbering from HOFFMANN, Adolf. Die Orchestersuiten Georg Philipp Telemanns, TWV 55.
   Zürich: Möseler,1969
OVERTURES
   in C, no.1
     1. Ouverture   4. Menuet I & II
     2. La complaisance   5. Loure
     3. L'indignation   6. Très viste
       ed H.Mönkemeyer   φ 3vln.vlc   Heinrichshofen,1964   Misc 5985
   in C, no.3 "Wasser-Ouverture" (1723)
     1. Ouverture
     2. Sarabande: Die schlaffende Thetis
     3. Bourrée: Die erwachende Thetis
     4. Loure: Der verliebte Neptunes
     5. Gavotte: Die spielenden Naiaden
     6. Harlequinade: Der schertzende Tritonus
     7. Der stürmende Aeolus
     8. Menuet: Der angenehme Zephyr
     9. Gigue: Ebbe und Fluth
    10. Canerie: Die lustigen Bots-Leut
       ed F.Noack   φ 2(picc.2rec)201/0000/str/cont(hpsd)   Bärenreiter,1955 CW 10   25715 & MRL
   in D, no.1 (Musique de Table II,1733)
     1. Ouverture
     2. -5 Airs I-IV
       ed J.P.Hinnenthal   φ 0100/0100/str/cont   26'30"
                                                    Bärenreiter,1962 CW 13   MRL
      ed M.Seiffert,rev.H.J.Moser
                     φ 0100/0100/str/cont   Breitkopf,1959 DDT 61/2   51797 & MRL

TELEMANN, Georg Philipp (cont)

OVERTURES (cont)

  in D, no.6
    1. Ouverture   5. Bourrée
    2. La trompette 6. Courante & double
    3. Sarabande   7. Gigue
    4. Rondeau
      ed W.Schulz   ø   vlc[=vla-dg]solo.str/cont(hpsd)   Peters   20688

  in D, no.8 ["Suite 1" in this edition]
    1. Ouverture   6. Sarabande
    2. Marche   7. Gigue
    3. Menuet I & II 8. Passepied I & II
    4. Aria   9. Rondeau
    5. La Réjouissance
      ed R.P.Block   ø   tpt/str/cont   Musica Rara.1978   26639 *

  in D, no.12 "Perpetuum mobile"
    1. Ouverture   5. Menuet I & II
    2. Perpetuum mobile 6. Tourbillon
    3. Sarabande   7. Gigue
    4. Bourrée
      ed F.Schroeder   ø   str/cont   Doblinger,1975   26064 *

  in D, no.21 (for Landgrave Ludwig VIII of Hessen-Darmstadt, 1765)
    1. Ouverture   5. Tintamare
    2. Plainte   6. Loure
    3. Réjouissance   7. Menuet I & II
    4. Carillon
      ed F.Noack   ø   0201/2000/str/cont(hpsd)   Bärenreiter,1955 CW 10   25242 & MRL

  in D (combined with a tragi-comic Suite)(H.D.22)
    Ouverture
    Le podagre (Der Gichtgeplagte)
    Remède expérimenté: La poste et la danse (Erprobtes Heilmittel: Postfahrt und Tanz)
    L'hypocondre (Der eingebildete Kranke)
    Remède: Souffrance héroïque (Heilmittel: Heldenhaftes Ertragen)
    Le petit-maître (Der Geck)
    Remède: Petite-maison (Heilmittel: Das Freudenhaus)
      ed W.Hobohm   ø   000[1]/0300/timp/str/cont   Breitkopf,1981   Misc 10440

  in D min "Ouverture à la Polonoise" [orig. for hpsd: Der getreue Musikmeister, p.72]
    arr R.Rikorski & T.Ochlewski ø   str   Polish SM,1973   Misc 9466

  in E flat, no.3 "La Lyra"
    1.   Ouverture
    2.(4) Menuet I & II
    3.(5) La vielle
    4.(6) Sicilienne avec cadenze
    5.(7) Rondeau
    6.(2) Bourrée I & II
    7.(3) Gigue
      [Mvt nos from Eulenburg ed; alternatives from Hoffmann catalogue]
      ed W.Bergmann   ø   str/cont (hpsd)   Eulenburg,1962   23952

  in E flat, no.4
    7. Polonaise
      ed A.Hoffmann   ø   str/cont   Möseler,1951   20539

  in E min, no.1 (Musique de Table I, 1733)
    1. Ouverture   5. Passepied
    2. Réjouissance   6. Air
    3. Rondeau   7. Gigue
    4. Loure
      ed J.P.Hinnenthal   ø   2000/0000/str/cont   22'15"
                                                   Bärenreiter,1959 CW 12 MRL
    ed M.Seiffert, rev.H.J.Moser
                      ø   2000/0000/str/cont   Breitkpf,1959 DDT 61/2 51792 & MRL

TELEMANN, Georg Philipp (cont)

OVERTURES (cont)

in F, no.4
1. Ouverture
2. Pastorelle en rondeau
3. Sarabande
4. Menuet
5. Bourrée
    ed H.Böttner   ø   0000/2000/str(no vla)/cont(hpsd)   Eulenburg,1939   20852

in F, no.7 "Ouverture à la Pastorelle"
1. Ouverture   5. Gigue
2. Viste   6. Caprice
3. Menuet   7. Carillon
4. Air
    ed F.Schroeder   ø   str/cont   Doblinger,1974   26019

in F, no.11 "Alster-Ouverture"
1. Ouverture   6. Der Alsterschäfer Dorfmusik
2. Die kanonierende Pallas   7. Die konzertierenden Frösche und Krähen
3. Das Alster-Echo   8. Der ruhende Pan
4. Die Hamburgischen Glockenspiele   9. Der Schäfer und Nymphen eilfertiger Abzug
5. Der Schwanen Gesang
    ed J.Braun   ø   0201/4000/str/cont   Eulenburg,1967   Misc 6658

in F min, no.1
Chaconne
    ed F.Brüggen   ø   0.2tbl.rec.000/0000/str   Schott,1971   25455
    ed H.Hoffmann   ø   0.2tbl.rec.000/0000/str   Hänssler,1977   26946 *

in F# min
1. Ouverture   5. Loure
2. Les Plaisirs   6. Menuet I & II
3. Angloise   7. Courante
4. La Badinerie italienne   8. Le Batelage
    ed F.Noack   ø   str/cont(hpsd)   Bärenreiter,1955 CW10   25624 & MRL

in G, no.4 "Ouverture des nations anciens et modernes"
1. Ouverture (Overture to "Der gedultige Socrates")
2. Menuet I & II
3. Les Allemands anciens
4. Les Allemands modernes
5. Les Suédois anciens
6. Les Suédois modernes
7. Les Danois anciens
8. Les Danois modernes
9. Les vielles femmes
    ed F.Noack   ø   str/cont(hpsd)   Bärenreiter,1955 CW10   24331 & MRL
    ed G.Lenzewski   ø   str/cont(hpsd)   Vieweg,1928   10138

in G, no.10 "Burlesque de Quixotte"
1. Ouverture   5'12"
2. Le reveil de Quixotte   1'30"
3. Son attaque des moulins à vent   1'45"
4. Ses soupirs amoureux après la Princesse Dulcinée 1'30"
5. Sanche Panse berné   1'35"
6. Le galop de Rosinante   )2'48"
7. Celui d'ane de Sanche Panse   )
8. Le couché de Quixotte   1'10"
    ed G.Lenzewski   ø   str/cont   Vieweg,[1927]   10029
    ed F.Schroeder   ø   str/cont   Vieweg, 1963   Misc 10470

TELEMANN, Georg Philipp (cont)

OVERTURES (cont)

  in G, appendix no.1 ("La Putain")

1. Ouverture	7. Marche
2. Masquerade: Die Schneckenpost	8. Gasconnade: In der Laussherberg
3. Loure: Die Bauren Kirchweyh	9. Menuet & Trio
4. Menuet	10. Bourrée: Die Baass Lissabeth
5. Rondeau: Der Hexen-Tantz	11. Hornpipe: Der Vetter Michel Ziehbart
6. Sarabande	

      ed F.Noack ϕ str/cont(hpsd)   Bärenreiter,1955 CW 10   24331 & MRL

      ed F.Noak ϕ str/cont   Bärenreiter   26792

  in G min, no.2 ("La Changeante")

1. Ouverture	5. La plaisanterie
2. Loure	6. Hornpipe
3. Les scaramouches	7. Avec douseur
4. Menuet I & II	8. Canerie

      ed A.Hoffmann ϕ str/cont   Möseler,1971   Misc 8256

  in G min, no.4

1. Ouverture	5. Loure
2. Rondeau	6. Gasconnade
3. Les irresoluts	7. Menuet I & II
4. Les capricieux	

      ed F.Noack ϕ 0301/0000/str/cont(hpsd)   Bärenreiter,1955 CW 10   Misc 4372 &

  in A, no.2

    7. Polonaise

      ed A.Hoffmann ϕ str/cont   Möseler,1951   20539

  in A, no.5 (Festliche Suite)

1. Ouverture	4. Gavotte I & II
2. Marche	5. Passepied & double
3. Plainte	6. Gigue

      ed A.Hoffmann ϕ str[no vla]/cont   Kallmeyer,1938   19912

  in A, no.8 (Concert suite)

1. Ouverture	5. Menuet I & II
2. Passepied I & II	6. Fanfare (Fantaisie)
3. Aria I & II	7. Air
4. Rondeau	8. Gigue

      ed B.Martens ϕ vln solo str/cont(hpsd)   Breitkopf,1967   Misc 6769

  in A min, no.1

1. Ouverture	5. Rigaddon
2. Rondeau	6. Forlane
3. Gavotte	7. Menuet I & II
4. Courante	

      ed A. Schering ϕ str/cont(hpsd)   Kahnt [1906]   25621

  in A min, no.2

1. Ouverture	5. Réjouissance
2. Les plaisirs I & II	6. Passepied I & II
3. Air à l'italien	7. Polonaise
4. Menuet I & II	

      ed H.Büttner ϕ tblrec/str/cont(hpsd)   Eulenburg,1936   19163

  in B♭, no.1 (Musique de Table III,1733)

1. Ouverture	5. Flatterie
2. Bergerie	6. Badinage
3. Allégresse	7. Menuet
4. Postillons	

      ed W.Bergmann ϕ 0200/0000/str/cont   19'30"   Eulenburg,1935   Misc 10121

      ed J.P.Hinnenthal ϕ 0200/0000/str/cont   Bärenreiter,1963 CW 14   MRL

      ed M.Seiffert ϕ 0200/0000/str/cont   Breitkopf,1928   51802

      ed M.Seiffert,rev H.J.Moser

                      ϕ 0200/0000/str/cont   Breitkopf,1959 DDT 61/2   MRL

TELEMANN, Georg Philipp (cont)

OVERTURES (cont)
   in B♭, no.8 "Ouverture burlesque"
     1. Ouverture   5. Pierrot
     2. Scaramouches   6. Menuet I & II
     3. Harlequinade   7. Mezzetin en Turc
     4. Colombine
      ed A.Hoffmann   ϕ   str/cont   Möseler,1975   Misc 8750
   in B♭, no.11 "La Bourse" (1720)
     1. Ouverture   4. Les vainqueurs vaincus
     2. Le repos interrompu   5. La solitude associée
     3. La guerre en la paix   6. L'éspérance de Mississippi
      ed A.Hoffmann   ϕ   0201/0000/str/cont   Möseler,1968   25577 Ani
OVERTURE POLONOISE see OVERTURE in D min
OVERTURE A LA PASTORELLE see OVERTURE in F
PASSIONS
   St.Luke (1728) for soli, chorus & orch (1728)
     ed H.Hörner & M.Ruhnke   ϕ   0.rec.101/0000/str/cont   Bärenreiter,1964 CW 15   MRL
   St.Luke (1744) for soli, chorus & orch (1744)
     ed F.Schroeder   ϕ   11(ob-d'a)01/0000/str/cont   Hänssler,1966   26952 *
        see also DER FÜR DIE SÜNDE DER WELT GEMARTERTE UND STERBENDE JESUS
PERPETUUM MOBILE see OVERTURE (Suite) in D
PIMPINONE (Die Ungleiche Heirat): Zwischenspiel
   Complete
     ed T.W.Werner   ϕ   str/cont   Erbe Reichs 6   MRL
   Extracts
     Chi mi vuol son cameniera: aria (vespetta)
      ed C.Ottzer   ϕ   str(vln I.II.cb)   Ebering,1902   Misc 3349
     Höflich reden Lieblich singen: aria
      ed T.W.Werner   ϕ   str/cont   (Erbe Reichs 6)   19446
     Schweig hinkünftig (duet vespetta, tipione)
      ed C.Ottzer   ϕ   str   Ebering,1902   Misc 3349
POLONAISES
   in A see OVERTURES, in A no.2
   in E♭ see OVERTURES, in E♭, no.4
PSALM 96 see SINGET DEM HERRN
PSALM 100 see JAUCHZET DEM HERRN
PSALM 112 see LAUDATE PUERI DOMINUM
La PUTAIN (Die Dirne) see OVERTURES, in G, appendix no.1
Die SATYRN IN ARCADIEN see Der NEUMODISCHE LIEBHABER DAMON
SELIGES ERWÄGEN: Oratorio (1719)
   Sinfonia in F, ed A.Hoffmann   ϕ   [2]201/0000/str/cont   Möseler,1971   Misc 8301
SIE, ES HAT ÜBERWUNDEN DER LÖWE: cantata for SAB soli, chorus & orch
   [formerly attrib J.S.Bach, BWV 219]
                        ϕ   0000/0200/str/cont   Breitkopf BG 41   MRL
SIEG DER SCHÖNHEIT: opera (1722)
   Overture, in D
     ed A.Hoffmann   ϕ   [2=2ob]00[1]/0000/str/cont   Möseler,1971   Misc 8301
   Extracts
     Placidia, mein schönstes Kind: aria: (Olybrius)
      ed C.Ottzenn   ϕ   100+chal.1/0000/str/cont   Ebering,1902   Misc 3349
     Schönheit ist nur Fantasie: duet: (Melite & Trasimundus)
      ed C.Ottzenn   ϕ   2vln/cont   Ebering,1902   Misc 3349

TELEMANN, Georg Philipp (cont)

SINFONIA MELODIA in C (for the Landgrave of Darmstadt)
   ed F.Oberdörffer   φ 0200/0000/str   Vieweg,1936   20152
SINGET DEM HERRN EIN NEUES LIED (Psalm 96) for SATB soli, chorus & orch
                      φ str/cont   20'   Hänssler,1978   26943 *
SO DU MIT DEINEM MUNDE: cantata movement for sopran & contralto soli, chorus & orch
   [published with Bach: Cantata 145]
                      φ 0[2]00/0100/str/cont   Breitkopf BG 30   MRL
                      φ 0[2]00/0100/str/cont   Bärenreiter NBA 1/10   MRL
SOCRATES   see Der GEDULDIGE SOCRATES
SONATA (Concerto) for trumpet & orch, in D
   ed & arr H.Winschermann   φ str/cont   Sikorski,1964   24923
SONATA in F min
   ed K.Hofmann   φ 2vln.2vla.vlc.[cb]/cont   Bärenreiter,1971   CM 55065
Der STERBENDE JESUS: Passion (Brockes
                      φ 2+3rec.201/2200/str/cont(hpsd)   Photo Hessische Landes und
                                       Hochschul-bibliotek,Darmstadt(Mus.1283)   Misc 6267
SUITES   see OVERTURES
SYMPHONIE ZUR SERENATE (1765)
    Die alte Welt
    Die mittlere Welt
    Die jüngere Welt
      ed & arr W.Brückner-Rüggeberg
                      φ 1101/0000/str/cont   Simrock,1972   Misc 9826
Der TAG DER GERICHTS (The day of judgement)
   ed M.Schneider   φ 0202/3200/timp/str   Breitkopf DDT 28   MRL & 21176
TELEMANN ALS OPERNKOMPONIST: operatic extracts from Der NEUMODISCHE LIEBHABER DAMON,
   DON QUICHOTTE, SIEG DER SCHONHEIT, EMMA UND EGINHARD, MIRINAYS, PIMPINONE, and
   Der GEDULDIGE SOCRATES :
     For details see individual operas   Ebering,1902   Misc 3349
Der TOD JESU for SMzTB soli, chorus & orch (1755)
   ed P.Czornyj   φ 2201/0000/str/cont   (Editor)   26915
TRAUERMUSIK see HAMBURGISCHE TRAUERMUSIK
UNS IST EIN KIND GEBOREN: cantata for Christmas, for [SS]ATB soli, [S]ATB chorus & orch
   ed H.Jaedtke   φ 2200/0000/str/cont   Möseler,1963   Misc 6529
WEIHNACHTSKANTATE see LOBT GOTT, IHR CHRISTEN ALLZUGLEICH
WIDER DIE FALSCHEN PROPHETEN (Beware of false prophets): cantata for Soprano solo,
   SAB chorus & orch
     (No. 50 of Musicalisches Lob Gottes in der Gemaine des Herrn (1744))
                      φ str/cont   Eulenburg,1967   Misc 6578
WIE IST DEIN NAME SO GROSS   see Die DONNERODE

TELLAM, H.

En SOURDINE: petite serenade   PC 1010/1000/str   Boosey & H   12441

TELLIER, A.

HERZEN UND BLUMEN (Hearts and flowers): waltz, arr Tellier from melody by Czibulka
                      PC 2(picc)222/42.cnt.30/
                          timp.perc/str   Bosworth   7724
JAPANESE BRIDAL PROCESSION   PC 1121/2210/perc/str   Bosworth   4656
PARFUM DE ROSE   PC 2222/4230/timp.perc/[hp]/str   Bosworth   13

TEMPLE, Gordon

IN SWEET KILLARNEY: song
   in Eb, arr W.Williams   1121/2200.euph/timp/str   Larway   17311

TEMPLE, Gordon (cont)

The MOTHERLAND'S A-CALLING: song
    in G arr H.E.Geehl   1121/2210/timp.perc/str   Larway,1909   18285
The OLD GREEN ISLE: song
    in E♭ arr W.Williams   1121/2200.euph/timp/str   Larway   17305
SWEET VALE OF AVOCA: song
    in E♭ arr P.Graener   1121/2110/timp/str   Larway   17250
    in G arr W.Williams   1121/2210/timp/str   Larway   17251

TEMPLE, Hope

IN SWEET SEPTEMBER: song
    in F arr R.Hanmer   ϕ   2222/4230/timp.perc/hp/str   (Boosey & H)   18401
An OLD GARDEN: song
    in G arr G.Stacey   pf/str   (Boosey)   LMG 3538
    in A♭ arr L.Wurmser   ϕ   21‡ca.1+bcl.2/4000/perc/hp/str   3'40"   (Boosey)   TO 1431

TEMPLETON, Alec (1910-1963)

BACH GOES TO TOWN
    arr used as signature tune for programme 'Edward Rubach Quintet'
                           perc/gtr.org.pf/cb   F D & H   Property of
                                                                           E.Rubach

SPRINGTIME IN THE VILLAGE: rustic dance
    arr H.Hutchinson   PC 1(picc)121/2210/timp.perc/str   UMP   11665

TEMPLETON STRONG   see   STRONG, Templeton

TEN BRINK, Jules   see   BRINK, Jules ten

TENNENT, H.M.

ONE LITTLE MOMENT
    arr Wilkinson   ϕ   111.5sx.1/2430/timp.perc/gtr.hp.pf/str   (Chappell)   20209

TERRADELLAS, Domenico (1713-1751)

La MEROPE: opera
    Excerpts, transc & rev R.Gerhard ϕ   2202/2200/hpsd/str   (Bib Cent Barcelona,1951)   21122 +
In VASTO MARE INFIDO: motet for Soprano, violins & cont
    ed Davison & Apel   ϕ   str/cont   (OUP,1950)   S.31365

TERRASSE, Claude (1867-1923)

AU TEMPS DES CROISADES: operetta
    Valse des pêches: duet in G   ϕ   1111/2200/perc/str   (Schott)   Misc 3354

TERRY, Ray

HARRY WOOD'S HITS: selection   PC 111.3sx.1/2220/perc.gtr/str   Cinephonic   495

TERRY, Richard (1865-1938)

BLOW THE MAN DOWN: song, arr
    in E♭ orch A.Evans   ϕ   1031/0210/perc/pf/str   (Curwen)   MS 9133

TERRY, Richard (cont)

BOUND FOR THE RIO GRANDE: song, arr
   in Eb, orch H.Carr   φ 2121/2230/perc/hp/str   (Curwen)   TO 990
The DRUMMER AND THE COOK (Capstan shanty)
   in G, orch S.Robinson   φ 3+picc.222/4231/timp/str   1'55"   (Curwen)   20351
FIRE DOWN BELOW: song
   in F orch H.Carr   φ 2121/2230/perc/hp/str   (Curwen)   TO 991
HAUL AWAY JOE: song
   in D arr R.Chignell   φ 2222/2200/str   (Curwen)   MS 5000
SEA SHANTIES
   Potpourri   orch J.Buerger
      Male voices and orch   φ 2(picc)121/2230/timp.perc.glock.xyl/hp/str   MS   MS 7000
SHENANDOAH (Windlass and capstan shanty)
   in Eb, orch C.Groves   φ 1111/2000/timp/hp/str   (Curwen)   TO 988
   in D & Eb arr F.Bye   11+ca.21/0000/hp/str   (Curwen)   MLO 769
WHISKY JOHNNY
   in Ab orch H.Carr   φ 2121/2230/perc/hp/str   (Curwen)   TO 989

TER-TATEYOSYAN, Dzhon Gurgenovich (1926-

SYMPHONY   φ 3(picc)2+ca.2(bcl)+Ebcl.2/4331/timp.perc(tamtam.xyl)/
                         hp.pf/str   Russian SM,1959   Misc 8053

TERTRE, Estienne du [16th cent]

SUITE OF FRENCH DANCES by Claude Gervaise & Estienne du Tertre, arr Paul Hindemith
                φ 1+picc.1+ca.01/0100/lute/str   Schott,1958   Misc 5042

TERZIAN, Alicia

CARMEN CRIATURALIS (1971)   φ 0000/1000/cym.vib/str   Ricordi,1971   Misc 9913

TESCHNER, Melchior (1584-1635)

ALL GLORY LAUD AND HONOUR: hymn (Tune St.Theodulph)
   arr H.Perry   PC 1121/0000/timp.perc/org/str   Hawkes   4970

TESTI, Flavio (1923-

CORI DI SANTIAGO for SABar-soli, 3choruses & orch, op.32
                φ 3333/4440/timp.perc.vib.xmba/cel.gtr.hp/
                     str   Ricordi,1975   Misc 9411
MUSICA DA CONCERTO no.6, for viola & chamber orch (1970)
                φ 1111/2000/str   17'   Ricordi,1971   Misc 7588
OPUS 21 for orch   φ 2222/2200/str   13'   Ricordi,1972   Misc 7784
OPUS 23 for 2 pianos, 3 trumpets, 3 trombones, timpani (con una caldaia piccola) & 2 chamber orchs
                φ Orch I: 1111/2000/str (6.6.4.4.2)
                   Orch II: 1111/2000/str (6.6.4.4.2)   Ricordi,1973   Misc 8318

TEUSCHER, Hans (1907-

CONCERTINO for piano & strings   φ str   21'   Grahl,1952   Misc 8883

TEXIDOR, Jaime

AMPARITO ROCA: Spanish march
   arr A.Winter   PC 1+picc.12.2sx.2/2231/perc/str   2'15"-3'   Boosey & H   11652 Cv

TEXIDOR, Jaime (cont)

BONDS OF FRIENDSHIP (Lozos de Amistand): Spanish march
    arr A.Winter   PC 2(picc)22.2sx.2/2230/perc/str   2'40"-3'   Boosey & H   13407 Bp
CARRASCOSA: Spanish march
    arr A.Winter   PC 2(picc)22.2sx.2/2230/perc.glock/str   3'   Boosey & H   13406

TEYBER, Anton (1756-1822)

CONCERTO for horn & orch, in E♭
    ed F.Gabler   φ   0202/2000/str   Doblinger,1976   26144 *

THAL, Dennis van

CHARLOT'S CHAR-A-BANG: fox-trot medley
    arr J.Lally   PC 111.3sx.1/2210/perc/bjo.gtr/str   K.Prowse   13298 Ap
FRENCH FILMS: song
    in E♭ arr B.Berlin   φ   2121/2000/perc/hp/str   K.Prowse   TO 551
The SHEPHERDESS
    in G, male chorus arr J Beaver   φ   2121/2230/perc/hp.pf(cel)/str   K.Prowse   TO 1068
TOO OLD AT TEN: song
    in C & E♭, arr H.Carr   φ   2121/2000/hp/str   K.Prowse   TO 552

THALBERG, S. (1812-1871)

HEXAMÉRON   see under   LISZT, Franz
TARANTELLA op.65
    arr A.Winter   PC 2(picc)22.3sx.2/4230/timp.perc/str   7'   Boosey & H   14862

THÄRICHEN, Werner

CONCERTO for timpani & orch, op.34 φ 2222/4331/perc.glock.tamtam.xyl/str   Bote & B,1956   Misc 6153
    revised version   φ 2222/4331/perc.glock.tamtam.xyl/str   Bote & B,1966   Misc 7109

THAYER, Pat

COME ON FEET, LET'S GO: song
    in D arr B.Berlin   φ   2121/2220/perc/str   (F D & H)   TO 808
FOR LOVE ALONE: song
    in A & C arr F.Cramer   pf/str   (A H & C)   LMG 5232
I TRAVEL THE ROAD, WHO CARES   see   P's & Q's
The OLD ARGEE: song in F   φ   1110/0000/hp/pf/str   Box & Cox   LMG 8889
P's & Q's: musical play
    I travel the road, who cares: song
        in D   PC 1111/2210/timp/str   2'30"   K.Prowse   19013
        in D arr G.Stacey   1110/0000/hp[acdn]/str   (K.Prowse)   LMA 116
        in D arr G.Stacey   pf/str   (K.Prowse)   LMG 3053
        in E♭   PC 1120/0210/timp/str   (K.Prowse)   MS 2511
SNOWBIRD: song
    in E♭ arr F.Cramer   pf/str   (A H & C)   LMG 5306
    in E♭ arr M.Mackie   φ   3222/4231/timp.perc/hp/str   A H & C   TO 1717
A WAYSIDE INN: song in G   2121/0000/timp/str   Composer   MS 2555 φ only

THEILE, Johann (1646-1724)

PASSION according to St Matthew, for SSATB chorus & orch (1673)
    ed F.Zelle   φ str/viols)/cont   Breitkopf DDT 17   MRL

THEIMER, J.Lindsay   see   LINDSAY-THEIMER, J

THEODORAKIS, Michael (1925-

SERPICO (film): Theme
    arr I.Sutherland   φ   2(picc)1+ca.22/4331/timp.perc.mba.vib/gtr.hp.pf/
                                        str   (Chappell)   25762

THIELE, Richard

DEUTSCHES FLAGGENLIED: German national song
                         PC   2(picc)222/4231/timp.perc/str   Benjamin   16363 +
    arr M.L.Lake   PC   112.2sx.1/2210/perc/str   C.Fischer   19720

THIELE, Siegfried (1934-

MUSIC FOR ORCHESTRA (1968)   φ   3(picc)3(ca)3(E♭cl:Bcl)3(cbsn)/4331/
                                         timp.2perc(tamtam.tomtom.xyl)/hp.pf/
                                         str   17'   DVfM,1971   Misc 9616
SONATINE for youth string orchestra φ   str   Peters,1971   Misc 7700

THIERE, Charles le   see   Le THIERE, Charles

THIERIOT, Ferdinand

SERENADE for strings, op.44   φ   str   Rieter Biedermann   Misc 884

THIMAN, Eric (1900-1975)

DANCE FOR A CHILDREN'S PARTY   PC   2(picc)222/4230/timp.perc/hp/str   2'15"-2'30"   Boosey & H   13588
An EASTER PRAYER: in B min
    orch S.Robinson   φ   2222/4230/timp.perc/hp/str   2'20"   (Cramer)   18422
ELEGIAC MELODY   φ   org/str   4'30"   J.Williams   8211
FITTLEWORTH FAIR: suite founded on English trad tunes
    1. Morris   3. Air
    2. Pastoral   4. Jig
                               PC   2(picc)222/2220/timp.perc/hp/str   Goodwin & Tabb   16207 B
HIGHLAND SCENES   φPC 1+picc.222/4230/timp.perc/hp/str   7'   Bosworth   18765 B
2 IRISH MELODIES
    1. Moll Roone   2. The Coulin
                               φ   str   Boosey & H,1960   22545
2 IRISH PIECES
    1. My love's an Arbutus
    2. Sligo dance tune
                               φ   pf/str   4'30"   Hinrichsen   19568 Bni
2 PIECES, freely arr
    1. Shenandoah
    2. Billy boy: Northumbrian song
                                   pf/str   Boosey & H   12813
2 SEVENTEENTH CENTURY TUNES, arr
    1. Barbara Allen
    2. Green meadows
                                   pf/str   Goodwin & Tabb   13926 B
The SILVER SWAN
    in C min arr D.Darlow   φ   2222/4030/timp/hp/str   2'   (Novello)   TO 1547
STIRLING CASTLE: march   PC   2(picc)22.3sx.2/4230/timp.perc/str   Bosworth   18677 B
VARIATIONS ON A THEME OF ELGAR φ   str   12'   Novello   16514 B

THOBRITHER, Joseph

The COPENHAGEN POLKA   arr A.Fones   PC 2121/2330/timp.perc/hp/str   Chappell   21285 C

THOMAS, Afan

DAWNS Y GWANWYN (I Seindorf Linnynol)
                                     ∅ pf/str   OUP   10128 B

THOMAS Ambroise (1811-1896)

Le CAID: operetta in 2 acts
    Overture   ∅ 1+picc.222/4230/timp.perc/str   4'30"   Heugel   15535 Awa
        arr A.Evans   PC 2(picc)222/2230.euph/timp.perc/str   Hawkes   779
    Selection arr E.Tavan   PC 2222/2231/timp.perc/str   Heugel   5397
Le CARNAVAL DE VENISE: opera
    Overture   ∅ 2(picc)222/4230/timp.perc/str   8'   (Lemoine)   14191
        arr G.Auvray   ∅ 1+picc.1121/2230/timp.perc/str   Lemoine   9034
        arr R.Jungnickel   1+picc.222/4231/timp.perc/hp/str   Jungnickel   3119
La DOUBLE ECHELLE: opera
    Overture   ∅ 2(picc)222/4230/timp.perc/str   6'45"-7'   Lemoine   9005
FRANÇOISE DE RIMINI: opera
    Ballet music
        Barcarolle
        Pantomime & recit
        Valse, dance & chant
            Airs de ballet
                1. Adagio   2. Scherzo   3. Capriccio   4. Pas de six   5. Habanera   6. Saltarelle & Sevillana
                                     ∅ 2(picc)22.sx.2/42.2cnt.sxhn.30/
                                        timp.perc/2hp.hca/str   20'   Heugel   5789

GILLE ET GILLOTIN: opera
    Complete   ∅ 2(picc)222/4230/timp.perc/str   Colombier,c.1874 Misc 5526
    Selection   PC 2222/2231/timp.perc/str   Margueritat 5201
HAMLET: opera
    Selection   PC 2222/2231/timp.perc/str   Heugel   1456
    Suite
        1. Divertissement (danse villageoise)   5'15"
        2. Pas des chasseurs   2'30"
        3. Pantomime   1'30"-2'00"
        4. Valse Mazurka   3'30"
        5. Scène du bouquet   0'55"
        6. La Freya   2'15"
        7. Strette finale   6'55"
                                     ∅ 2+picc.22.2sx.2/42.2cnt.31/timp.perc/str 23'   Heugel   6866
            arr H.Mouton   PC 1121/2210/timp.perc/str   Heugel   1361 B
        arr A.Winter, with introduction, & omitting No.5
                                     ∅PC 2+picc.22.2sx.2/4231/timp.perc/str   Boosey   15720 B
    Partagez-vous mes fleurs: aria in Bb (Mad Scene)
    À vos yeux: recit   ∅ 22+ca.12/4230/perc/str   (Siddeli)   17033 B
LUSTSPIEL OVERTURE on themes by Ambroise Thomas
    arr Artok & Homann-Webau   PC 1111/1110/perc/str   Schott   11724
MIGNON: opera
    Complete   2222/4230/timp.perc/hp/str   Kalmus NY   22499
    Broadcast version   ∅ 2222/4230/timp.perc/hp/str   (UMP)   TO 1592
    Overture   PC 1+picc.222/4230/timp.perc/hp/str   8'   Lafleur   350 Cwa
                                     ∅ 2(picc)222/4230/timp.perc/hp/str   Heugel   5785 Bs C
        arr Roberts   PC 1(picc)222/4230/timp.perc/hp/str   C.Fischer   1871

THOMAS, Ambroise (cont)

MIGNON (cont)
  Selections
    arr Audibert & C.Godfrey Jnr PC 1+picc.222/2230.euph/timp.perc/str   Lafleur   1376 B
    arr Finck '5 minuet operatic selection'
                    PC 1010/0210/timp.perc/str   A H & C   12204
    arr Seredy   PC 1121/2220/timp.perc/str   C.Fischer   1875 B
    arr Tavan   PC 2(picc)222/2231/timp.perc/str   Heugel   60
  Extracts
    Adieu Mignon: aria
      in G (orig)(Farewell)   φ   2122/2000/str   (Siddell)   18250
      in Gb   2222/2000/str   (Heugel)   TO 165
    Connais-tu le pays? (Knowest thou the land?): aria
      Tomorrow: recit
        in Db (orig)   φPC 2(picc)222/2000/str   5'   Bote & B   418
        in Db   φ   1020/2000/str   (Siddell)   17990
        in Db & Eb arr Stacey   pf/str   (Schott)   LMG 3487
        in Eb   1020/2000/str   (Siddell)   17992
        in F   1020/2000/str   (Siddell)   17991
        in D   1020/2000/str   (Siddell)   17989
    Elle ne croyait pas (In her simplicity): aria
      in C (orig)   φ   2+picc.122/2000/str   (Siddell)   18127
      in Db   2+picc.122/2000/str   (Siddell)   18128
    Entr'acte gavotte   φ   2222/4230/timp/str   Heugel   6922 Bgg
                    PC 1+picc.222/2230.euph/timp.perc/str   La Fleur   364 Bni Cwa
      arr H.Mouton   PC 1121/2200/str   Heugel   13344
    La Forlane   PC 1121/2230/timp.perc/str   2'15"   Heugel   9568
    Here, in beauty's home am I: Gavotte song (from English version)
      in Eb (orig): in F   φ   2222/2000/str   2'30"   (Siddell)   17580
      in Eb, arr F.Cramer   hp.pf/str   (Schott)   LMG 4277
    Je connais un pauvre enfant (Once a maiden sad and wan): aria
      in D (orig)   φ   1+picc.222/2200/perc/str   (Siddell)   Misc 4101
    Je suis Titania: polonaise
      in Bb (orig)   φ   2+picc.222/4230/timp.perc/str   5'   (Siddell)   17032
      in Bb arr F.Cramer   cel.pf/str   (Schott)   LMG 4617
      in Bb   φ   2222/4230/timp.perc/str   Bote & B   9066
      orch arr L.Artok   PC 1121/2210/timp.tri/str   Schott   12106
        see also URBACH, Ernst: THOMAS: "Mignon Erinnerungen"

Le PANIER FLEURI: opera
  Overture   φ   2(picc)222/4230/timp.perc/str   5'30"   Heugel   3863
RAYMOND: opera
  Overture   φ   2(picc)222/4230/timp.perc/str   8'   Heugel   2619 Ac Bn
    arr A.Evans   PC 2(picc)222/2230.euph/timp.perc/str   Hawkes   3322 CweDwa
    arr A.Winter   PC 2(picc)222/2230.euph/timp.perc/str   Boosey & H   16743 B
Le ROMAN D'ELVIRE: opera
  Overture   φ   2(picc)222/2230.euph/timp.perc/str   7'15"   Joubert   11100
  Selection, arr Gauwin   PC 2(picc)222/2230/timp.perc/str   Joubert   9438
Le SONGE D'UNE NUIT D'ÉTÉ: opera
  Overture   φ   2(picc)222/4230   Lafleur   14642
                    PC 2(picc)222/4230.euph/perc/str   7'30"   Lafleur   16937
    arr H.Mouton   PC 1121/2210/timp.perc/str   Heugel   772
La TONELLI: opera
  Overture   φ   1+picc.222/4230/timp/str   Heugel   3251

THOMAS, Arthur Goring (1850-1892)

AMOURS VILLAGEOISES: song
    in Gb   ∅   2222/4200/timp.tri/hp/str   BBC   3416
The BLACKSMITH: song
    in F   ∅   2222/2210/timp.perc/str   BBC   11513
ESMERALDA: opera
    Extracts
        Ballet music   ∅   2(picc)222/4040/timp.perc/str   16'   BBC   22668 +
        O vision entrancing: aria
            in Gb (orig)   ∅   2222/4000/hp/str   (Siddell) 17418 B
            in Gb arr Stacey   pf/str   (Boosey)   LMG 3609
            in F   ∅   2222/4000/hp/str   (Siddell) 17419
        Polacca: in Eb   ∅   2222/4231/timp.perc/hp/str   BBC   12946
L'EXTASE: song in Eb   ∅   2222/4231/timp.perc/hp/str   BBC   5332
NADESHDA: opera
    Complete   ∅   2+picc.222/4241/timp.perc/str   (Carl Rosa) Misc 5807
                                 ∅   2+picc.222/4240/timp.perc/hp/str   Erben   Misc 2210
    Prelude   ∅   2222/4230/timp.perc/str   BBC   8249
    Selection, arr S.Baynes   PC 1+picc.122/2230/timp.perc/str   Boosey   5310 B
    Extracts
        As when the snow drift: aria
            in Ab (orig)   ∅   2222/4231/timp.perc/str   (Siddell) 17416
        Dear love of mine: duet
            in F (orig.Bb)   ∅   2121/2230/timp/hp/str   3'30"   (Boosey)   MS 7853
            in F arr H.Carr   ∅   2121/2000/hp/str   (Boosey)   19104
        O, my heart is weary: aria in Ab: What means Ivan: recit
                                 ∅   2222/4031/timp/hp/str   (Siddell) 17458 B
Une RÊVE D'AMOUR: romance   PC 1121/2230/str   J.Williams 4873
SION: scène religieuse: in G   ∅   2222/4020/timp/str   BBC   11405
A SUMMER NIGHT: song
    in Db arr J.Turner   ∅   1110/1000/hp/str   4'   (Cramer)   LMG 9278
    in C   1121/2000/str   (Siddell) 18251
    in C, D & Db arr Stacey   pf/str   (Cramer)   LMG 3465
    in D & Db orch. J.Buerger   ∅   2121/2030/hp/str   (Cramer)   MS 3770
    in D arr A.Franzel   ∅   1110/0000/perc/acdn.hp.pf/str   (Boosey)   LMA 607
The WILLOW: song
    in A arr Stacey   1010/0000/perc/pf/str   (Cramer)   LMA 51
    in F arr F.Cramer   pf/str   (Cramer)   LMG 4561

THOMAS, Huw Llewellyn

NEMESIS for orch   ∅   2(picc)222/4230/timp.perc.glock.vib.xyl/hp.pf/
                                     str   (Composer,1974) 25705

THOMAS, J.R. (1829-1896)

EILEEN ALANNAH: song
    in Ab arr G.Williams   1121/2210/str   Swan   9551
    in Bb arr J.O.Turner   ∅   1110/1000/hp/str.solo voice/chorus   (Arranger) LMG 7548
    in Db, arr G.Williams for tenor, chorus & orch
                                 ∅   1121/2210/hp/str   (Swan)   MLO 259

THOMAS, Lloyd

COUNTRY CAPERS, arr J.Engleman   PC 112.3sx.1/2230/perc/str   Cinephonic   15120 B
SCARLET AND GOLD: march arr Vinter PC 2(picc)222/2230/perc/str   Leonard, Gould & Bottler   16754 C

THOMAS, Mansel (1909-

DANCE OF THE FOUR CLOGS   ∅   2222/4230/perc/hp/str   1'45"   Composer   Welsh 13
DANCE OF THE RED CLOAK   ∅   2222/2230/perc/hp/str   1'30"   Composer   Welsh 12
GOING WITH DEIO TO TOWYN?   ∅   2222/2230/perc/hp/str   1'40"   Composer   Welsh 14

THOMAS, Vincent

2 ENTR'ACTES
   1. Pastorale   3'30"
   2. Torch dance
                                    PC 2222/4230/timp.perc/hp/str   Hawkes   1901 Bwa
2 PIECES
   1. Lady Margaret's minuet
   2. Lady Mary's gigue
                                    ∅   hp[=pf]/str   Elkin,1937   Misc 7340
TALES BY MOONLIGHT: suite
   1. Told on the promenade
   2. Told at the garden gate
   3. Told at the carnival
                                    PC 2222/2200/hmn/str   Hawkes   1380 Bwa

THOMÉ, François (1850-1909)

ANDANTE RELIGIOSO op.70   PC 2222/4210.euph/timp/str   Hawkes   899 B
   arr L.Wurmser   ∅   222+bcl.2/4231/perc.hp/str   BBC   TO 1678
ANGELUS from 'Scènes champêtres'   bells/str   Hamelle   3123
AU PRINTEMPS (Primavera): waltz
   arr Hall   PC 1+picc.222/2230.euph/perc/str   Chappell   7935
AUBADE op.102   ∅PC 2010/2210/perc/hp/str   Lemoine   9819
BADINAGE: scherzo   ∅   2222/2200/timp.tri/str   Heugel   6483 B
Un BAL À LA COUR: suite in ancient dance style
   1. Passacaille   3. Madrigal
   2. Menuet   4. Gaillarde
      arr Domergue   ∅PC 2(picc)222/0200/str   Lemoine   6064
CARNAVALESQUE: suite
   1. Fête au village   3. Polichinelle
   2. Pierrot; air de ballet 4. Gigue
      arr Domergue   ∅   2(picc)222/2231/timp.perc/str   Lemoine   4814
CLAIR DE LUNE: romance sans paroles
   arr Tobani & Seredy   PC 1121/2210/bells/str   C.Fischer   1872
ENTR'ACTE - PIZZICATO op.39   ∅PC 2222/2000/perc/str   Lemoine   3899 B
L'EXTASE   ∅PC 2222/2230.euph/timp.perc/hp/str   4'30"   Hawkes   14789
                                   PC 2222/2230.euph/timp.perc/hp/str   Hawkes   972 B
GUITARE: morceau de genre
   arr Gauwin   PC 1121/2200/timp.perc/str   Deiss & Crepin   10360
LÉGENDE for harp & orch op.122   ∅PC 2(picc)2(ca)22/2200/timp.perc/str   Hamelle   5873
LÉGENDE DE L'UKRAINE op.28
   arr Turin   PC 1+picc.121/2210/timp.perc/str   Durand   4321
MADRID: caprice espagnol
   arr Gauwin   PC 2(picc)222/2231/timp.perc/str   Deiss & Crepin   10358
Le MENUET DE LA MARIÉE op.89   PC 2222/2220/timp.tri/str   Lemoine   9820
                                       str   Schott   16231

THOMÉ, François (cont)

MINUETTO op.68		str	Schott	16231

Les NOCES D'ARLEQUIN: suite op.73

1. Préambule	3'30"	4. Cassandre	4'	
2. Sérénade	6'	5. Cortège	2'	
3. Duo d'amour	3'15"			

	∅	2(picc)2(ca)22/4230.oph/timp.perc/hp/str	17'-19'15"	Lemoine	8528
SCARAMOUCHE: air de ballet op.26					
arr Turin	PC	1+picc.121/2210/timp.tri/str		Durand	4320
SIMPLE AVEU for cello & orch op.25	∅PC	1011/1000/str	3'30"	Hawkes	886 C
	∅	1011/1000/str		Hawkes	14989
	PC	1010/1000/str		Durand	16712
SOURIRE DU MATIN op.160	PC	1122/2230/timp.perc/str		Hamelle	5887
TRICOTETS: morceau dans le style ancien					
arr Gauwin	PC	2122/2231/timp/str		Hachette	10359
VIEIL AIR, JEUNE CHANSON					
arr H.Mouton	PC	1121/2210/timp.perc/str		Ed de la Sirene	3456 B

THOMMESSENS, Reider

SOLREGN (Norwegian text)				
in C, arr R.Levin	PC	0100/0100/acdn.gtr/str	Iversen (Oslo)	19341

THOMPSON, Bert (1856-1945)

ADMIRAL BENBOW: song, arr for solo voice, TTBB chorus & orch				
	∅	1(picc)120/1000/hp/str	(Arranger)	LMG 10935
The AGINCOURT SONG: song, arr for TTBB chorus & orch				
	∅	1120/1000/hp/str	(Arranger)	LMG 10922
The BARLEY MOW: song, arr				
in F-G	∅	1120/1000/hp/str	(Arranger)	LMG 10981
BEAUTIFUL CITY OF SLIGO: song, arr				
in G	∅	1120/1000/hp/str	(Arranger)	LMG 10935
BELIEVE ME IF ALL THOSE ENDEARING YOUNG CHARMS: song, arr				
in F	∅	1120/1000/hp/str	(Arranger)	LMG 10922
BEN BACKSTAY: song, arr				
in F-G	∅	1120/1000/hp/str	Arranger :BBC	LMG 10981
BLAYDON RACES: song, arr for chorus & orch				
in G	∅	1120/1000/hp/str	(Arranger)	LMG 10894
BLOW THE MAN DOWN: song, arr				
in Db-E	∅	1120/1000/hp/str	(Arranger)	LMG 10981
The BOAR'S HEAD CAROL: carol, arr				
in C	∅	1120/1000/vib/hp/str	(Arranger)	LMG 10982
The BONNY EARL O'MORAY: song, arr				
in Bb	∅	1120/1000/hp/str	(Arranger)	LMG 10922
BROCKLESBY FAIR: song, arr for solo voice, chorus & orch				
in F	∅	1120/1000/hp/str	(Arranger)	LMG 10935
A CAPITAL SHIP: song, for solo voice, TTBB voices & orch				
in C	∅	1(picc)12(bcl)0/1000/hp/str	(Arranger)	LMG 10935
The CARTER: song, arr				
in F min	∅	1120/1000/hp/str	(Arranger)	LMG 10935
COASTS OF BARBARY: song, arr for solo voice, TTBB, chorus & orch				
in G min	∅	1120/1000/hp/str	(Arranger)	LMG 10922

THOMPSON, Bert (cont)

COME, TAKE YOUR LUTE: song, arr				
in A	φ	cel.hp/str	Arranger MS:BBC	MS 20364 φ
COMIN' THRO' THE RYE: song, arr				
in G	φ	1110/1000/hp/str	(Composer)	LMG 7510
CORN RIGS ARE BONNIE: song, arr				
in A	φ	1120/1000/hp/str	(Arranger)	LMG 10981
DARBY KELLY: song, arr for TTBB voices & orch				
in A	φ	1120/1000/hp/str	(Arranger)	LMG 10894
The DEAR LITTLE SHAMROCK: song, arr for solo voice, chorus & orch				
in G	φ	1120/1000/hp/str	(Arranger)	LMG 10922
DECK THE HALL: song, arr	φ	1120/1000/bells/hp/str	(Arranger)	LMG 10982
DUNCAN GRAY: song, arr				
in Ab	φ	1120/1000/hp/str	(Arranger)	LMG 10935
FIRE DOWN BELOW: song, arr				
in F	φ	1120/1000/hp/str	(Arranger)	LMG 10982
GREENSLEEVES: song, arr				
in G min	φ	1111/2000/perc/hp.pf/str	(Ashdown)	MS 30048
The GREY MARE: song, arr	φ	1120/1000/hp/str	(Arranger)	LMG 10981
HERE AWA' THERE AWA': Scottish song, arr				
in F	φ	1120/1000/hp/str	(Arranger)	LMG 10935
HERE'S TO THE MAIDEN: song, arr for solo voice, TTBB chorus & orch				
in D	φ	1120/1000/hp/str	(Arranger)	LMG 10935
The HIGHLAND LAD: song, arr				
in C	φ	1120/1000/hp/str	(Arranger)	LMG 10922
HOT CODLINGS: song, arr	φ	1120/1000/hp/str	(Arranger)	LMG 10981
HOW DEAR TO ME THE HOUR: Irish song, arr				
in G	φ	1120/1000/hp/str	(Arranger)	LMG 10922
I AM A BRISK AND SPRIGHTLY LAD: song, arr				
in D-Eb	φ	1120/1000/hp/str	(Arranger)	LMG 10981
I'M SEVENTEEN COME SUNDAY: song, arr				
in D min	φ	1120/1000/hp/str	(Arranger)	LMG 10895
I MARRIED A WIFE: song, arr for solo voice, TTBB chorus & orch				
in Ab	φ	1120/1000/hp/str	(Arranger)	LMG 10935
I'LL BID MY HEART BE STILL: song, arr				
in A min	φ	1120/1000/hp/str	(Arranger)	LMG 10935
JOCK O'HAZLEDEN: song, arr				
in Eb	φ	1120/1000/hp/str	(Arranger)	LMG 10895
JOE THE CARRIER LAD: song, arr for solo voice, TTBB chorus & orch				
in Ab	φ	1120/1000/hp/str	(Arranger)	LMG 10922
JOHNNY TODD: song, arr				
in F	φ	1120/1000/hp/str	(Arranger)	LMG 10935
KITTY OF COLERAINE: song, arr				
in A	φ	1120/1000/hp/str	(Arranger)	LMG 10981
The LAMBTON WORM: song, arr for solo voice, TTBB chorus & orch				
in G	φ	1120/1000/hp/str	(Arranger)	LMG 10922
LAND OF MY FATHERS: song, arr for solo voice, chorus & orch				
in Eb	φ	1120/1000/hp/str	(Arranger)	LMG 10935
The LAND O' THE LEAL: Scottish song, arr				
in Gb	φ	1120/1000/hp/str	(Arranger)	LMG 10935
The LAST ROSE OF SUMMER: song				
in F	φ	1110/1000/hp/str	(Arranger)	LMG 7525
in F, arr J.Stevenson orch Stacey		1010/0000/pf/str	(Paxton)	LMG 3680
LOVE IS THE SWEETEST THING: song				
	φ	111.4sx.1/2430/timp.perc/hp/str	F D & H	MS 20197

THOMPSON, Bert (cont)

LOVE WILL FIND OUT THE WAY: 17th century song, arr
   in G   φ 1120/1000/hp/str   (Arranger)   LMG 10935
MARY MORISON: song, arr
   in F min   φ 1120/1000/hp/str   (Arranger)   LMG 10894
NEAR WOODSTOCK TOWN: song, arr
   in D♭   φ 1120/1000/hp/str   (Arranger)   LMG 10935
The NORTH COUNTRY LASS: song, arr
   in G   φ 1120/1000/hp/str   (Arranger)   LMG 10935
AN OLD MAN HE COURTED ME: song, arr for solo voice, chorus & orch
   in F   φ 1120/1000/hp/str   (Arranger)   LMG 10935
OLD ROSIN THE BEAU: song, arr
   in F   φ 1120/1000/hp/str   (Arranger)   LMG 10922
ON CHRISTMAS NIGHT: song, arr
   in A♭   φ 1120/1000/cel.hp/str   (Arranger)   LMG 10982
The ONLY ONE FOR ME: Irish song, arr
   in G   φ 1120/1000/hp/str   (Arranger)   LMG 10922
O SALLY MY DEAR: song, arr
   in D min   φ 1120/1000/hp/str   (Arranger)   I.MG 10981
The OXFORD SPORTING BLADE: song, arr
   in F   φ 1120/1000/hp/str   (Arranger)   LMG 10935
The PIGEON: song, arr
   in G   φ 1120/1000/hp/str   (Arranger)   LMG 10894
The PRESS GAME: song, arr
   in F min   φ 1(picc)120/1000/hp/str   (Arranger)   LMG 10935
RICH AND RARE: song, arr
   in D   φ 1120/1000/hp/str   (Arranger)   LMG 10895
The ROAD TO THE ISLES: song, arr (1946)
                        φ hp.pf/str   (Boosey & H)   MS 20335
                                                                               (φ only)

The ROAST BEEF OF OLD ENGLAND: song, arr
   in B♭   φ 1120/1000/hp/str   (Arranger)   LMG 10935
The SAILOR LIKES HIS BOTTLE-O: song, arr
   in F-G   φ 1120/1000/hp/str   (Arranger)   LMG 10981
SEARCHING FOR LAMBS: song, arr
   in A min   φ 1120/1000/hp/str   (Arranger)   LMG 10894
SERENADE TO A LONELY STAR, arr B.Thompson, orch G.Melachrino (1946)
                        φ 1110/0000/timp/gtr.hp.pf/str   3'   A H & C   MS 20233
SHE MUST BE MINE: song, arr
   in G   φ 1120/1000/hp/str   (Arranger)   LMG 10935
SHOW ME THE WAY: song   φ hp.pf/str   Arranger MS:BBC   MS 20403
                                                                                (φ only)

SIGN OF THE BONNIE BLUEBELL: song, arr
   in E min   φ 1120/1000/hp/str   (Arranger)   LMG 10922
SIR EGLAMORE: song, arr
   in G   φ 1120/1000/hp/str   (Arranger)   LMG 10981
The SKATERS: song, arr
                        φ gtr.hp.pf/str   3'25"   A H & C   MS 20404
                                                                                (φ only)

SMILE AGAIN MY BONNIE LASSIE: song, arr
   in E♭   φ 1120/1000/hp/str   (Arranger)   LMG 10894
SMUGGLER'S LULLABY: Manx folksong, arr
   in E   φ 1120/1000/hp/str   (Arranger)   LMG 10922
SONG IN LONELINESS: song in G   φ cel.hp.pf/str   (Boosey)   MS 20367
A SONG IN THE NIGHT: song, arr
                        φ hp.pf/str   Arranger MS:BBC   MS 20407
                                                                                (φ only)

THOMPSON, Bert (cont)

The STAR: song				
in Db	φ	hp.pf/str	(Chappell)	MS 20327
STEAL AWAY TO JESUS: spiritual				
in Eb	φ	hp.pf/str	(Ricordi)	MS 20338
SWEET YESTERDAY: song				
in C	φ	hp.pf/str	(K.Prowse)	MS 20304
The SWEETEST FLOWER THAT BLOWS: song				
in E	φ	cel.hp/str	(Boosey)	MS 20303
THERE'S MY LOVE: song, arr				
in E min	φ	1120/1000/hp/str	(Arranger)	LMG 10894
The THORN: song, arr				
in Bb	φ	1120/1000/hp/str	(Arranger)	LMG 10935
The TIME I'VE LOST IN WOOING: song, arr				
in G	φ	1120/1000/hp/str	(Arranger)	LMG 10935
TI, TUM, TI: song, arr				
in G	φ	1120/1000/hp/str	(Arranger)	LMG 10894
TO LADIES EYES: song, arr for solo voice, TTBB chorus & orch				
in G	φ	1120/1000/hp/str	(Arranger)	LMG 10935
TURMUT HOEING: song, arr for solo voice, TTBB chorus & orch				
in F	φ	1120/1000/hp/str	(Arranger)	LMG 10922
TWANKYDILLO: song, arr for solo voice, TTBB chorus & orch				
in F-F#-G	φ	1120/1000/hp/str	(Arranger)	LMG 10935
The VERY THOUGHT OF YOU: song, arr B.Thomson, orch G.Melachrino				
	φ	212.3sx.1/2430/kit.glock/gtr.hp.pf/		
		str	(Campbell Connelly & Co.Ltd)	MS 20192
VILLIKINS AND HIS DINAH: song, arr				
in C-Db	φ	1120/1000/hp/str	(Arranger)	LMG 10935
The WAY YOU LOOK TONIGHT: song, arr B.Thompson, orch G.Melachrino				
	φ	111.5sx.1/2430/kit/hp.pf/str	(Chappell)	MS 20195(φ
The WASSAIL SONG: song, arr				
in E min	φ	1120/1000/cel.hp/str	(Arranger)	LMG 10982
WE MAY ROAM THRO' THIS WORLD: song, arr				
in Db	φ	1120/1000/hp/str	(Arranger)	LMG 10895
A WELL THERE IS: Cornish air				
in Db	φ	1120/1000/hp/str	(Arranger)	LMG 10895
WE'RE ALL BOUND TO GO: song, arr				
in Bb-C	φ	1+picc.120/1000/hp/str	(Arranger)	LMG 10981
WHEN THE KYE COME HAME: song, arr				
in Bb	φ	1120/1000/hp/str	(Arranger)	LMG 10894
WHA WADNA FECHT FOR CHARLIE: Scottish song, arr for solo voice, TTBB chorus & orch				
in D	φ	1120/1000/hp/str	(Arranger)	LMG 10935
WI' A HUNDRED PIPERS AN' A': song, arr for solo voice, chorus & orch				
in E	φ	1(picc)120/1000/hp/str	(Arranger)	LMG 10935
WIDDICOMBE FAIR: song, arr for solo voice, chorus & orch				
in F:G:Ab	φ	1120/1000/hp/str	(Arranger)	LMG 10935
WITHIN A MILE OF EDINBURGH TOWN: song, arr				
in G	φ	1120/1000/hp/str	(Arranger)	LMG 10935
YOUNG ROGER THE PLOUGHBOY: song, arr				
in A	φ	1120/1000/hp/str	(Arranger)	LMG 10981

THOMPSON, Billy

MY SON JOHN   see   STRAUS, Oscar: MY SON JOHN

THOMPSON, Jack

COME SING TO ME: song
in Eb, arr F.Cramer		pf/str	(Enoch)	LMG 4940
in Eb, arr G.Stacey		pf/str	(Enoch)	LMG 5818
in F	PC	org.pf/str(no vla)	Enoch	3316 B
in D		1121/2210/timp.perc/hp/str	(Siddell)	17314

I'LL SING TO YOU: song
in F	PC	2121/2230/timp/str		Enoch,1916	18299

THOMPSON, Randall (1899-

SYMPHONIES
No.1	∅	3(picc)2+ca.2+bcl.2+cbsn/4231/timp.perc/			
		hp.org/str	24'		
			Eastman School of Mus,1931		Misc 4185
No.2	∅	3(picc)3(ca)33/4331/timp.perc/str	31'45"	Birchard	Misc 1980
No.3 in A min	∅	3+picc.02+ca.32+cbsn/4331/timp.perc/str		C.Fischer	19895

THOMSON, Virgil (1896-

FANFARE FOR FRANCE ed E.Goossens	∅	0000/4330/perc		Boosey & H	Misc 2974
THE FEAST OF LOVE: for Baritone solo & small orch (1964)					
	∅	112(bcl)1/0000/cym.glock/hp/str	8'	G.Schirmer,1977	Misc 9149
A JOYFUL FUGUE	∅	3(picc)3(ca)3(bcl)3/4331/timp.perc/str		G.Schirmer 1949/65	Misc 7838
LOUISIANA STORY: film music					
Suite for orch	∅	2(picc)2(ca)2(bcl)2(cbsn)/4231/timp.2perc(cym.			
		mildm.sdm.glock.xyl)/hp/str	18'	G.Schirmer	Misc 3014
Acadian songs & dances	∅	2(picc)2(ca)22/2220/perc.xyl(glock/acdn.hp/str		G.Schirmer,1951	23323
Boy fights alligator (fugue)	∅	2222/4231/timp.perc/str	4'	Schirmer,1972	25874
METROPOLITAN MUSEUM FANFARE	∅	0000/42.3cnt.31/timp.perc.glock.mba.xyl		Schirmer,1972	25732
ODE TO THE WONDERS OF NATURE for brass & percussion					
	∅	0000/2330/timp.perc		Schirmer/Chappell,1968	24995
PILGRIMS AND PIONEERS	∅	11(ca)2(bcl)1/4200/perc/str	10'	Schirmer,1971	Misc 8234
The PLOW THAT BROKE THE PLAINS: suite (from U.S.A. Govt documentary film)(1936)					

1. Prelude   4. Blues (Speculation)
2. Pastorale (Grass)   5. Drought
3. Cattle   6. Devastation

	∅	11+[ca]2([asx])+bcl[=tsx=bxn2].1/2220/timp.perc.		
		(cbell.cym.dms.horses hooves.tamb.tomtom.tri.		
		wdbl)/bjo.gtr[=hp.pf]/str(N.B. For complete list		
		of alternative combinations of woodwind see score)	Mercury Mus	25217
The RIVER: suite		1(picc)2(ca)2(bcl)1/2220/timp.perc/bjo/str	25'	Southern,1958	Misc 5058
SEA PIECE WITH BIRDS: orch	∅	3(picc)333/4330/perc/str	5'	G.Schirmer,1954	Misc 4247
The SEINE AT NIGHT	∅	3(picc)3(ca)3(bcl)3(cbsn)/4331/perc.tamtam/			
		cel.2hp/str		G.Schirmer,1949	Misc 2530
A SOLEMN MUSIC (1961)	∅	2+picc.3(ca)3(bcl)3/4331/timp.perc/str		G.Schirmer 1949/65	Misc 7838
SYMPHONY ON A HYMN TUNE	∅	2(picc)222/4231/timp.perc/str	19'	Southern NY,1954	Misc 4137
SYMPHONY No.2 in C	∅	3(picc)2+ca.3(bcl)3(cbsn)/4231/timp.perc/str		Leeds,1954	Misc 4777
WHEAT FIELD AT NOON: orch	∅	3(picc)3(ca)3(bcl)3(cbsn)/4330/perc.xyl.tamtam/			
		str	6'	G.Schirmer	Misc 4248

THORMAN, F.

GAVOTTE-LIEBESGLÜCK: voice or solo cornet & orch
in G	2222/2230.[euph]./timp/str		Boosey	17054

THORNE, Donald

LIGHTS O' LONDON: suite by D.Thorne & T.Lowry
 1. Dawn (In Kew Gardens)   3'00"
 2. Noon (Oxford Street & Hyde Park) 3'00"
 3. Dusk (Limehouse)   2'00"
 4. Midnight (Piccadilly)   5'00"
           PC 1+picc.12.3sx.1/2220/timp.perc/str   13'   Boosey 8988 B

THORNE, Francis (1922-

ELEGY   φ 2(picc)2(ca)2(bcl)2/4231/timp.2perc(gong)/
            hp/str   13' Marks,1963/80 Misc 10443

THORNTON, R.S.

LEGIONS OF THE AIR: quick march
 arr B.Tattenhall   PC 112.2sx.1/2230/perc/str   Bosworth 16762

THORPE DAVIE, Cedric (1913-

AULD LANG SYNE, arr for Soprano solo, chorus & orch
        φ 2+picc.33.2+cbsn/4331/timp.perc.xyl/
          hp/str   (Composer,1979) 26637
DIVERSIONS ON A TUNE BY DR.ARNE (1954)
        φ 2+picc.222/4331/timp.perc.bell.glock.gong.xyl/
          hp/str   15' (Stainer & B) Misc 9933
ORPHEUS & EURIDICE: radio play φ 22(ca)22+cbsn/4231/timp.perc/hp/str/
         chorus/speaking voices   BBC MS 30294
ROYAL NILE: march (1953) φ 2+picc.222+cbsn/4231/timp.perc/str   (BBC) 26692
The TRUMPETER OF FYVIE: radio play φ 2+picc.2+ca.22/4231/timp.perc/cel/str 9' BBC 18854

THUILLIER, Ch.(Jnr)

CENTRAL 81 - 37: galop PC 112.2sx.1/2230/perc/str   Salabert 10616

THURBAN, Thomas W.

AFRICANA: suite
 1. Serenade to Owani
 2. Moonlight on the Orange River
 3. Prayer and war dance of the Basutos
        PC 1121/2230/perc/str   Paxton 2669 C
AMERICANA: suite
 1. The tiger's tail: march   3'
 2. When Malindy sings: serenade 4'30"
 3. The watermelon fête: sketch
        PC 2(picc)222/2230.euph/perc/str   Hawkes 185 Bwa Cp
BROOKLYN CAKE WALK arr G.Walter φ 3222/4231/perc/pf/str   1'50" (F D & H) TO 124
        PC 1+picc.222/4230/perc/str   Benjamin 9134
DIXIANA: suite
 1. Dixieland revels
 2. Dixieland serenade
 3. Dixieland rhythm
        PC 111(sx)2sx.1/2230/timp.perc.banjo/str Paxton 12290 Awa
INCIDENTAL & DRAMATIC MUSIC (Collection No.1)
        PC 2222/2231/timp.perc/str   Haekes 18850

THURBAN, Thomas W. (cont)

ITALIANA: suite
  1. In sunny San Marino   2'
  2. A Venetial love song   3'
  3. Chimes of St. Peter   4'

	PC	1121/2230/perc.bells/str	9'	Boosey	8708 Awa
MUMBLIN' MOSE: American march	PC	1121/2210.euph/perc/str		C.Sheard	16777

PARISIANA: Parisian suite
  1. The gaiety of the Champs Élysées
  2. The dream of an Apace
  3. Air to the memory of Joan of Arc

	PC	1121/2230/timp.perc/str	British & Dominions Mus Co	12011
TWILIGHT DREAMS: a reverie	PC	1121/2210/perc/str	Boosey	3480

VOICE OF THE BELLS: an Alpine fantasy

	PC	1(picc)122/2230/timp.perc/str	K.Prowse	5188

YANKIANA: suite
  1. March 'Mighty America'
  2. Serenade 'Song of the bells'
  3. Sketch 'Arrival of the Coontown cadets'

	PC	1+picc.121/2230.euph/timp.perc/str	Boosey	1398

YASHMAK-LAND: suite
  1. On the Bosphorus
  2. The mosque of St. Sophia
  3. In a Stamboul bazaar

	PC	1(picc)122/2230/timp.perc/str	Paxton	4824 Awa

TIERNEY, Harry (1890-1965)

IRENE: musical play
  Selection
    (1943 edition, now out of print)

	PC	1111/2210/timp.perc/str	Darewski	4538 D
New arr D.Caryll	PC	112.3sx.1/2330/timp.perc/str	F D & H	14359 +

  Selection, arr J.Fox for SBar soli, optional chorus & orch

	φ	2(picc)2(ca)22/4331/timp.perc.glock.xyl/		
		hp.pf(cel)/str	[Arranger]	26181

  Alice blue gown: song
    in Eb, arr R.Burston

	φ	2121/2230/perc.cel/hp/str	(F D & H)	TO 377
in C	PC	2021/1230/perc/hp/str	Darewski	11538 Ap

    in C, arr D.Edge orch B.Berlin (SATB)

	φ	2121/2230/timp.perc/hp/str	(F D & H)	TO 1056 +
in D, arr B.Berlin	φ	2121/2230/timp.perc/hp/str	(F D & H)	TO 1056 +
in D:Db, arr S.Torch	φ	cel.hp/str	(F D & H)	24740 +

  Once the King of Normandy: song
    in F: SATB arr C.Groves

	φ	2121/2230/perc/str	(Darewski)	TO 467

RIO RITA: musical play & fil
  Selection, arr Pether

	PC	111.3sx.1/2210/timp.perc.bjo/str	F D & H	239

  Extracts
    The rangers' song: male chorus
      in G, arr R.Hanmer

	φ	2222/4330/perc/pf/str	(F D & H)	18446

    Rio Rita: song: SATB chorus & orch

in G, arr R.Tilsley	φPC	2222/4230/perc/hp/str/chorus pts	(F D & H)	22104 +
in Eb, arr P.Cardew	φ	2222/4330/timp.perc/hp.pf/str	(F D & H)	22744

TIERSOT (Jean Baptiste Élisée) Julien (1857-1936)(coll)

EN PASSANT PAR LA LORRAINE (Les TROIS CAPITAINES): French national song
    arr for solo voice, chorus & orch

	∅ 1+picc.221/2330/timp.perc/hp/str		Arranger	TO 1286
arr Stacey	1110/0000/timp/acdn.hp/str		Arr/Heugel	3553

TIESSEN, Heinz (1887-1971)

KONZERTANTE VARIATIONEN for piano and orch, op.60

∅ 2(picc)222/4200/timp.perc/glock.xyl/			
str	23'	Ries & E,1962	Misc 6089

TOTENTANZ-SUITE: 3 pieces for violin & small orch, op.29

∅ 2(picc)22(Ebcl)2/2100/timp.perc(tamtam)/str		Ries & E,1928	Misc 9421

TILSLEY, Henry

CLASSICA: selection of standard favourites, arr H.Tilsley & M.Ewing   see EWING, Montague: CLASSICA
CAPSTAN AND WINDLASS: sea shanties   see REEVES, Ernest

TILSLEY, Reginald

INTO THE HIGH HILLS: medley of trad Scottish tunes arr

	∅ 1+picc.1+ca.22/4330/timp.perc/hp/str		Arranger	22635 +
LITTLE DONKEY	∅ 2222/4230/timp.perc/hp/str		Composer	22738
MARINE PARADE	∅ 2(picc)222/4230/timp.perc/hp.pf/str	4'20"	Composer,1958	22891 +
La MATTCHICHE: French trad dance, arr				
	∅ 1+picc.2(ca)22/4330/timp.perc/hp/str		Composer	22746
OVERTURE TO A HORSE OPERA	∅ 22(ca)22/4330/timp.perc/hp/str		(Benson)	22688 +
PARIS SOIR (Evening in Paris)	PC 2121/2330/perc/str	2'30"	L.Wright 1961	23411 Bp
The TORTOISE AND THE HARE: fable for orch & narrator				
	∅ 2222/4330/timp.perc/hp/str		Composer	22777 +

A WELSH FANTASY arr from national songs
    1. Suo gan
    2. David of the white rock
    3. All through the night
    4. Men of Harlech

        ∅ 2222/4230/timp.perc/hp/str/chorus

TILZER, Albert von (1878-1956)

HELLO AMERICA
  Give me the moonlight: song

in Bb orch J.Beaver	∅ 2121/2230/perc/hp/str	(F D & H)	TO 241

I'LL BE WITH YOU IN APPLE BLOSSOM TIME: song

in C arr G.Stacey	1010/0000/perc.pf/str	(F D & H)	LMA 109

TEASING: song for female chorus

in G	∅ 2121/2230/perc/cel/str	(F D & H)	TO 171

TILZER, Harry von (1872-1946)

DOWN AT THE OLD BULL AND BUSH: song

in C	∅ 1121/2220/perc/str	(Feldman)	MS 585
in C & Eb	1121/2220/perc/str	(Feldman)	LMG 5289

TIMBERG, Sammy

GULLIVER'S TRAVELS, by S.Timberg, L.Robin, R.Rainger & W.Sharples
    Selection, arr G.L.Zalva   PC   1(picc)12.3sx.1/2220/timp.perc/str   10'   Victoria MP   16235 B

TINEL, Edgar (1854-1912)

FRANCISCUS: oratorio op.36   ∅   2+picc.22/4331/timp.perc.tamtam/2hp.org/str   Breitkopf   Misc 1658

TIOMKIN, Dimitri

The GREAT WALTZ: film music adapted from the music of Johann Strauss (ii) see STRAUSS, Johann
The GREEN LEAVES OF SUMMER
    arr A.Roper   ∅   21(ca)22/2220/perc.kit/gtr.pf/str   Robbins   MLO 262

TIPPETT, Michael (1905-

A CHILD OF OUR TIME: oratorio for SATB soli, chorus & orch
                                 ∅   22+ca.22+cbsn/4330/timp.perc/str   61'-68'35"   Schott,1944   Misc 6361 B

CONCERTI
    Double string orch   ∅   str   22'30"   Schott   Misc 2125 E
    Orchestra   ∅   21+ca.1+bcl.1+cbsn/3221/timp.perc
                                     tamtam.xyl/hp.pf/str   31'   Schott,1964   Misc 5945 B
    Piano & orch   ∅   2(picc)222/4230/timp/cel/str   32'-33'35"   Schott,1957   Misc 7150 B
DIVERTIMENTO for chamber orch 'Sellinger's round'
                                 ∅   1111/1100/str   16'   Schott,1954   Misc 4243 B
FANFARE FOR BRASS   ∅   0000/4330   Schott,1971   26071
FANTASIA CONCERTANTE on a theme of Corelli for 2 violin soli, cello solo & strings   (PL 516 Amv
                                 ∅   str   16'   Schott   (Misc 3968 B
LITTLE MUSIC   ∅   str   8'30"-10'   Schott,1949   25212
The MIDSUMMER MARRIAGE: opera
    Complete   ∅   2(picc)222/4231/timp.perc/cel.hp/str   Schott,1954   Misc 8701
    Ritual dances   ∅   2(picc)222/4230/timp.perc/str/[chorus] 16'-17'   Schott   19496+
MUSIC: unison song for voices, strings & piano in D
                                 ∅   pf/str   Schott,1960   23246
PRAELUDIUM for brass, bells & perc ∅ 0000/6332/perc.bells   6'   Schott,1962   Misc 5755
                                                                                                            Misc 8283 B

SEVERN BRIDGE: variations on a Welsh folk song "Braint" by Malcolm Arnold & others (1966)
    Variation 6 "Braint"   ∅   3232/2210/timp.perc.bells.glock.xyl/
                                     cel.hp/str   BBC,1966   24805
SONGS FOR DOV, for tenor & orch ∅   2(2picc)1+ca.1+bcl.1+cbsn/3110/timp.
                                     perc.bells.xyl.vib/egtr.hp.pf/str   25'   Schott,1972   Misc 7796
SUITE in D (Birthday suite)(1948)
    1. Intrada   4. Carol
    2. Berceuse   5. Finale
    3. Procession & dance
                                 ∅   2222/4231/timp.perc/hp/str   14'30"-17'25"   Schott,1950   PL 531 Amv &
                                                                                                            Misc 8188

SYMPHONIES
    No.1 (1945)   ∅   3(3picc)222+cbsn/4331/timp/str   32'-35'45"   Schott,1948   Misc 2591 D &
                                                                                                            PL 674 Amv

    No.2   ∅   2(2picc)222/4231/timp.perc/cel.hp.pf/str 32'   Schott,1958   Misc 4952 C
    No.3   ∅   3(2picc) 2+ca.2+[Ebcl]+bcl.2+cbsn/
                                     42(flg)31/timp.perc.bells.crot.glock.vib.xyl/
                                     cel.hp.pf/str/soprano solo   Schott,1974   Misc 8227

TIPPETT, Michael (cont)

SYMPHONIES (cont)
No.4 (1977)   φ 2(2picc)2+ca.2+bcl.2+cbsn/6332/timp.4perc
          (glock.mba.vib.wmc.xyl)/hp.pf/str   Schott,1977 Misc 9457

TRIPLE CONCERTO for violin, viola, cello & orch
     φ 1(picc,afl)1+ca bob)2+2bcl[=2(bcl)+bcl].1+cbsn/
       4220/timp.perc.clv.glock.mba.vib.bells/
       str(min.8.8.6.4.4)   32' Schott,1981 Misc 10529

The VISION OF ST. AUGUSTINE, for Baritone solo, chorus & orch
     φ 2(2picc)1+ca.1+bcl.1+cbsn/42(Dtpt)31/timp.perc.
       glock.mba.tamtam.xyl)/cel.hp.pf/str 31'30"-35' Schott,1966 Misc 6205

TIRCUIT, Heuwell

CONCERTO for solo percussionist & orch
     φ 2+picc.2+ca.22/4331/timp.3perc.bells.
       kijoshige.tamtam.xyl/hp/str
       solo perc: timp.bell-chain.crot.gongs.
            prayer-bell.taiko.wind-chimes   AMP,1975 Misc 9238

MANGA (1959, rev 1966) φ 2+picc.222+cbsn/4231/timp.perc.bells.
       chime-bar.xyl/hp/str   6' AMP,1975 Misc 8844

GDORU KATACHI (Dance Patterns) for solo percussion & orch (1962)
     φ 1(picc)111/1110/timp/hp/str
       solo perc incl: Atare-gane[=tri].prayer-bells.
           sbells.gong.tamtam.xyl 14' AMP,1978 Misc 9869

TISHCHENKO, Boris (1939-

CONCERTO for cello, 17 wind instruments, percussion & harmonium, op.23
     φ 02+ca.2+Ebcl.2+cbsn/2321/timp.perc.xyl/
       harm[=org]   Russian SM,1968 Misc 6733

TITL, A. Emil

OVERTURE ON SLAVONIC AIRS
 arr A.Roth   PC 2222/2210/perc/str   .Fischer 14035

SERENADE in F
 Flute, horn & orch, arr L.Weninger
       PC 1122/2210/timp.perc/str 3'15"-4'20" Benjamin 10789 **

 Flute, cello & orch, arr Zoeller
       PC 0121/2230/timp/str   Lafleur 1886

TOBANI, Moses see MOSES TOBANI, Theodore

TOBIAS, Henry

FUNNY SIDE UP: musical play
 Extracts
  Comes love: duet
   in G min, arr P.Cardew φ 2222/4230/timp.perc/hp/str   (Chappell) 22684
  It's me again: song
   in C, arr R.Hanmer φ 2222/4230/timp.perc/pf/str   (Chappell) 20895

SWEET & LOVELY: song by H.Tobias, G.Arnheim & J.Lemare
 in Bb, arr R.Tilsley (1957) φ 2222/4030/perc/hp/str   K.Prowse 22197

The WEDDING OF THE BIRDS, by H.Tobias & C.Kisco
 arr A.Wilkinson PC 212.3sx.1/2320/perc/acdn.hp/str K.Prowse,1930 22427

TOCCHI, Gian Luca (1901-

CANTI DI STRAPAESE
    Suite 1: voice & 11 instruments φ 1110/1100/pf/str   Ricordi,1938   Misc 4414
    Suite 2: voices & 11 instruments φ 1110/1100/pf/str   25'45"   Ricordi,1938   Misc 4415
LUNA PARK: suite for a ballet   φ 1+picc.11.sx.1/2221/perc.bells.xyl/cel.pf/
                               str   25'   Universal   Misc 2682 B

TOCH, Ernst (1887-1964)

BIG BEN variations on the Westminster chimes, op.62
                       φ 2+picc.2+ca.2+E♭cl.2/4431/timp.perc.glock.xyl/
                         cel.hp/str   AMP   Misc 980
BUNTE SUITE op.48
    1. Marschtempo   4. Marionetten - Tanz
    2. Intermezzo   5. Galante passacaglia
    3. Adagio espressivo   6. Karussel
                       φ 2(picc)1+ca.22/2210/timp.perc.glock.xyl/
                         pf/str   12'   Schott   Misc 1368
Die CHINESISCHE FLUTE: chamber symphony for 14 solo instruments, Soprano solo & orch, op.29
                       φ 2(picc)01(E♭cl)+bcl.01/0000/timp.perc.xyl/
                         cel/str   20'   Schott   Misc 2003
CIRCUS: overture   φ 2+picc.222/3330/timp.perc/pf/str   Aff Mus Inc,1954   22307
CONCERTO for cello & chamber orch, op.35
                       φ 1111/1000/timp.perc/str   25'   Schott   Misc 1058
EPILOGUE   φ 2+picc.222/2220/timp.perc.bells.xyl/str 2'55" Mills Music,1962   Misc 6172
FANAL for organ & orch, op.45   φ 2+picc.1+ca.2+E♭cl+bcl.2+cbsn/4431/timp.
                         perc.tamtam/org/str   5'   Schott   Misc 854
HYPERION: dramatic prelude op.71 φ 2+picc.2+ca.2+bcl.2+cbsn/3331/timp.perc.xyl/
                         hp/str   12'   Leeds,1950   Misc 4778
INTERMEZZO   φ 2222/2200/timp.perc.vib/hp[=pf]/str 4'25" Mills Music,1962   Misc 6169
KLEINE THEATER-SUITE op.54   φ 2+picc.22+E♭cl.2/2231/timp.perc.glock.xyl/
                         hp/str   16'   Schott   Misc 3266
MUSIK FÜR ORCHESTER UND EINE BARITONSTIMME op.60
                       φ 222+E♭cl.2/2220/timp.perc/str   Schott,1932   Misc 3340
NOTTURNO, op.77 (1953)   φ 2222/2230/xyl/hp/str   14'   Mills,1957   Misc 9499
PETER PAN: a fairy tale for orch, op.76
                       φ 2(2picc)1+E♭cl.11/4120/timp.perc/hp/str 17'   Schott,1958   Misc 4896
PINOCCHIO: overture   φ 2+picc.222/2230/timp.perc.xyl/str   6'   AMP,1937   Misc 3721 B
POEMS TO MARTHA for medium voice & strings, op.66
                       φ str   Delhas,1943   51780
Die PRINZESSIN AUF DER ERBSE: opera
    Vorspiel   φ 2(picc)111/1101/timp.perc/str   Schott   Misc 91
PRELUDE & FUGUE (transcription of J.S.Bach solo violin sonata no.3, BWV 1005)
                       φ str   Mills Music   Misc 4530
SYMPHONIES
    No.1 op.72   φ 3(picc)3(ca)3(bcl)2/3331/timp.perc.vib.xyl/
                       str   39'   Schott,1951   Misc 3558
    No.2 op.73   φ 3(picc)3(ca)3(E♭cl/bcl)2/3331/timp/hp.pf
                       (4 hands)org/str   30'   AMP,1953   Misc 3969
    No.3 op.75   φ 2+picc.2+ca.2+E♭cl.2+cbsn/4330/timp.perc/
                       org/str   Mills Mus Inc,1957
    No.6 op.93   φ 2(picc)222/3330/timp.perc.bells.glock.vib.
                       xyl/str   23'   Mills Music,1966   Misc 6365
TANZ-SUITE op.30   φ 1(picc)010/0000/perc/vln.vla.cb   Schott   Misc 2992
UNSER DUMMER POBEL MEINT: variations for piano & orch by W.A.Mozart, K.455, transcribed E.Toch
    see under MOZART, W.A.

TOESCHI, Carlo Giuseppe ([1731]-1788)

CONCERTO for flute & orch, in F
  ed W.Lebermann   ø 0000/2000/str   Erbe Reichs 51   MRL
SYMPHONIES
  op.3,no.3 (Sinfonia à 8)
    ed H.Riemann   ø 0200/2000/str   Broude   Misc 6296
    ed H.Riemann   ø 0200/2000/str   Breitkopf & H   DTB8/2
    in D, arr Carse   ø 02[=2fl].000/2000/str   11'15"   Augener   13878

TOGNI, Camillo

HELIAN DI TRAKL, op.39   ø 1+picc.110/1111/timp.bells.xyl/cel.gtr.pf/str   (BBC)   Misc 5183
                                                                                                AP'S only

TOLAR, Jan Křtitel (Jan Baptist)(17th cent)

3 BALLETTI, ed J.Polanka
  No.1, in G   ø hpsd/str   Artia 1959.MAB XL   Misc 5225
  No.2, in F   ø hpsd/str   Artia 1959.MAB XL   Misc 5225
  No.3, in D min   ø hpsd/str   Artia 1959.MAB XL   Misc 5225
SONATAS, ed J.Polanka
  à 10   ø 0001/0130/org/str   Artia 1959.MAB XL   Misc 5225
  à 13   ø 0001/02.2cntto.40/org/str   Artia 1959.MAB XL   Misc 5225
MISERERE MEI DEUS: for SATB soli, chorus & orch
  ed J.Höfler   ø str/cont   Akad.Druck.1974   Misc 8294
MISSA SOPRA LA BERGAMASCA for SSATB voices & orch
                  ø 0000/0240/org/str   (Narodni Mus,Prague)   Misc 6595

TOLDRÁ, Edouardo (1895-1962)

CANÇO DE L'OBLIT: canción espagnole
  in F# min   1011/0110/pf/str   (Composer)   19729
CANÇO DE PASSAR CANTANT: canción espagnole
  in A   1011/0110/pf/str   (Composer)   19727
La JARIGOLA: in F   1011/0110/pf/str   (Composer)   19728
MENTA I JARIGOLA:
  in Bb   1011/0110/pf/str   (Composer)   19727
ROMANZA SENSE PARAULES:
  in Bb   1011/0110/pf/str   (Composer)   19727
VORETTA LA MAR:
  in F   1011/0110/pf/str   (Composer)   19728

TOLENTINO, Arturo

OJOS DE JUVENTUD (Eyes of youth): Mexican waltz
  arr Lazarano   ø 2222/2230/timp.perc/str   5'35"   (Composer)   13121

TOLHURST, Henry

GENTLE MAIDEN: Irish folk song, arr
                    PC org/str   Paxton   18627

TOLLETT, Thomas (d. 1696)

LOVERS LUCK: incidental music
  ed L.Leonard (from GB-Lbm Add 24889)
                    ø str   [Editor]   22394

TOMA, Frantisĕk Ignáz Antonín (1704-1774)

PARTITAS
  in C min rev & ed J.Racek & V.Belsky
                φ org[=hpsd]/solo-vln.str(no vlas)   Artia,1965:MAB 67   Misc 6542
  in D min rev & ed J.Racek & V.Belsky
                φ org[=hpsd]/solo-vln.str(no vla)   Artia,1965:MAB 67   Misc 6542

SONATAS
  in E min (1741) rev & ed J.Racek & V.Belsky
                φ org/str   Artia,1965:MAB 67   Misc 6542
  in E min rev & ed J.Racek & V.Belsky
                φ 0001/0020/org/str(no vla)   Artia,1965:MAB 67   Misc 6542
  in A min rev & ed J.Racek & V.Belsky
                φ 0001/0000/org/str   Artia,1954:MAB 67   Misc 6542
  in A min ed J.Racek & V.Belsky φ 0001/0000/org/2vln-soli.str(no vla) Artia,1965:MAB 67   Misc 6542
  in A ed J.Racek & V.Belsky   φ 0001/0000/org/2vln-soli.str(no vla) Artia,1965:MAB 67   Misc 6542

SYMPHONIES
  in G rev & ed J.Racek & V.Belsky φ str/cont(hpsd)   Artia,1965:MAB 67   Misc 6542
  in A, rev & ed J.Racek & V.Belsky
                φ str/cont(hpsd)   Artia,1965:MAB 67   Misc 6542
  in B♭, rev & ed J.Racek & V.Belsky
                φ str/cont(hpsd)   Artia,1965   Misc 6542

TOMASI, Henri (1901-1971)

COLOMBA: symphonic tableaux
  1. Moderato   2. Agitato   3. Andante
                  φ 2(picc)2(ca)22(cbsn)/4231/timp.perc.tamtam/
                    str   13'   Eschig,1938   Misc 1290

CONCERTO for trumpet & orch   φ 3(picc)2+ca.22/4031/timp.perc.xyl/cel.hp/
                    str   Leduc,1966   Misc 10213

5 DANSES PROFANES ET SACRÉES
  1. Danse agreste   4. Danse nuptiale
  2. Danse profane   5. Danse guerrière
  3. Danse sacrée
                  φ 0111/1001/timp.perc.mba.vib.xyl/
                    cel[=glock].pf/str   Leduc,1962   Misc 6300

DIVERTIMENTO CORSICA
  1. Paghiella   3. Danse-sérénade
  2. Cimetière Marin   4. La foire du Niolo
                  φ 0111/0000/hp[=pf]/str   Leduc,1962   20755

DON JUAN DE MAÑARA: suite
  1. Le jardin de Girolama   3'30"
  2. La dernière sérénade de Don Juan   3'30"
  3. Procession   4'00"
  4. Dimanche de Pâques à Seville   2'00"
                PC 22+ca.22/2210/timp.perc/cel.hp/str   Leduc,1952   19710

FANFARES LITURGIQUES
  1. Annonciation   3. Apocalypse (Scherzo)
  2. Evangrile   4. Procession du Vendredi-Saint
                  φ 0000/4341/timp.perc   Leduc,1952   21049

HIGHLANDS BALLAD (Ballade Écossaise) for harp solo, woodwind trio & strings   Leduc,1967   Misc 6965
                  φ 0111/0000/str   12'

JEUX DE GEISHAS: Japanese suite
  1. Danse des parasols   4. Prière Bouddhique
  2. Les guerriers   5. Le Samourai et le Geisha
  3. Danse des papillons
                  φ 1(picc)1(ca)11/1000/perc.xyl/hp[=pf]/str   Eschig   Misc 3113

TOMASI, Henri (cont)

3 LETTRES DE MON MOULIN
  1. Les trois messes basses
  2. Le secret de Maître Cornille
  3. L'elixir du R.P.Gaucher

	φ	3(picc)2(ca)22/433[1]/timp.perc.xyl.vib/ cel.hp/str		Leduc,1958	Misc 5219

Les NOCES DE CENDRES: symphonic suite

	φ	2+picc.2+ca.2+bcl.2+cbsn/4331/timp.perc. xyl.glock.ondes martenot/str	40'	Leduc,1955	Misc 4428

NUITS DE PROVENCE: Évocations

	φ	2(picc)2(ca)22/4231/timp.perc.glock.xyl. tamtam/hp/str		Leduc,1954	Misc 4289

PIÈCES BRÈVES: suite
  1. Et s'il revenait un jour   4. Air à danser
  2. Menuet   5. Espiègleries
  3. Le Lied que chante mon coeur

	φ	1(picc)121/2110/timp.perc/hp[pf]/str	Lemoine	9805

Le ROSIÈRE DU VILLAGE: ballet
  Suite d'orchestre

	φ	2+picc.222/4231/timp.perc.xyl/cel.hp/str	13'	Leduc,1950	Misc 3624

SINFONIETTA PROVENÇALE (Le Tombeau de Mireille)

	φ	1(picc)101/1000/hpsd[=pf]/perc.vib.xyl/ cel/str	Leduc,1960	Misc 5311

TOMASINI, Luigi (1741-1807)

CONCERTO for violin & orch, in A
  ed E.Schenk

	φ	0000/2000/str	Universal.DTÖ 124	MRL

TOMBELLE, F. de la   see   LA TOMBELLE, F.de

TOMLINS, Greta

VARIATIONS ON A THEME OF PAISIELLO: φ str   Weeke,1949   Misc 3472

TOMLINSON, Ernest (1924-

CANTILENA	φ	2(picc)1(ca)21/223[:2]0/perc/hp/str	3'15"	Mozart	25387
CANZONET	PC	2121/2110/perc.glock/str	3'15"	Arcadia,1957	22344 B

CINDERELLA
  pantomime for radio by E.Tomlinson & E.Coates

	φ	2222/4230/timp.perc/hp/str	3'45"	Composer MS:BBC	MS 31099

  Waltz: adaptation (used as signature tune for programme 'All for your delight')

				22390 C 8
	φ	2(picc)222/4230/timp.perc/hp/str	Benson	23644

A COMEDY OVERTURE	φ	3[=2](picc)2[=1]22[=1/44[=2]3[1/ timp.perc.glock/hp/str	3'45	F D & H (H)	PL 382
CONCERT JIG	PC	2+picc.121/2230/timp.perc/hp/str	3'30"	Metro Music,1952	21559 B
	φ	2(picc)22[bcl]2/22[=3]30/timp.perc.cel/ hp/str		Metro Music,1952	24662

CUMBERLAND SQUARE: based on tradional tunes

	PC	2(picc)222/4330/timp.perc/hp/str	Arcadia,1960	23341 B
	PC	2(picc)222/4330/timp.perc/hp/str	Arcadia,1960	MLO 238

DO YOU REMEMBER: signature tune	φ	2222/4230/timp.perc/hp/str	Composer	22846 +

ENGLISH PAGEANT: suite
  1. March: Men-At-Arms   3. My Lady's Pavane
  2. The Jester   4. The Fiddler at the Fair

	φ	2[=3](2picc)1[=2]21[=2]/2[=4]2[=3]3[1]/ timp.perc.glock.xyl/hp/str	16'	Belwin-Mills 1961 CML 1974	Misc 858

TOMLINSON, Ernest (cont)

FAIRY COACH	PC	2222/4330/timp.perc/cel.hp/str		Benson,1958	22893

FESTIVAL SUITE
    1. Festive overture   2. Saraband   3. Carnival dance

	∅	3(picc)2(ca)22/4331/timp.perc/cel.hp/str		(Inter-art)	Misc 6348

3 GAELIC SKETCHES

1. The Fairy cobbler	PC	2121/2210/perc/glock[=cel]hp/str	2'40"	F.Benson,1958	24334
2. Gaelic lullaby	PC	1110/1000/glock/hp/str	2'35"	F.Benson,1958	24335
3. Legend of the sea	PC	21+ca.22/2230/timp.perc/cel.hp/str		F.Benson,1958	23081
	PC	11+ca.21/2230/timp.perc/cel.hp/str		F.Benson,1958	24336
A GEORGIAN MINIATURE	PC	2121/0000/str		Boosey	LM G 11207

GEORGIAN SUITE [Suite in F], arr from the works of T.Arne

	∅	2222/2200/perc/hp/str	18'30"	(Arranger)	PL 596

The KING AND THE MERMAID (An Irish Fantasy)(1956)

	∅	22+ca.2+bcl.2/4330/timp.perc.glock/cel.hp/str		BBC	MS 31189
LITTLE SERENADE	PC	2121/4000/perc/hp/str	3'	Benson,1956	21844 Bwa

LYRICAL SUITE

Nocturne	PC	2121/1230/timp.perc/hp/str	2'15"	Inter-art,1957	22928
MARIONETTE	PC	2121/3210/timp.perc/acdn.hp/str	2'50"	Hawkes,1957	22221 B

A MEDITERRANEAN SUITE
    1. A Cafe on the Croisette   (2'15")
    2. Mediterranean Daydream   (3'40")
    3. American in St. Tropez   (2'35")
    4. Monte Carlo Regatta

	PC	2(picc)121/2230/timp.perc.glock.xyl/bjo.gtr/ str		Weinberger,1969(H)	PL 451 Aca Bs Cm Dni

2 MINIATURE DANCES
    1. Gavotte   (2'10")   2. Rigadoon   (2')

	∅	2121/2220/timp.perc/hp/str		Metro Music	Misc 6561

NAUTICAL INTERLUDE arr from 'A-roving' and 'Billy Boy'

	PC	2222/4330/timp.perc/hp/str	2'50"	Arcadia,1956	22032
PASSEPIED	PC	1121/2110/perc/str	3'	Arcadia,1952	21467 B

3 PASTORAL DANCES
    1. Bourrée   2. Minuet   3. Hornpipe

No.3 only	∅	2222/2230/timp.perc/hp/str	2'30"	Boosey & H,1953	21732
SHENANDOAH	∅PC	2121/2230/timp/hp/str	3'15"	(Arcadia,1965)	24319 +
	∅	hp/str		(Arcadia)	LM G 11116
SOLILOQUY	PC	1110/1000/glock/hp/str	3'	Benson,1956	22987
SPANISH FESTIVAL DANCE	∅	2121/2230/perc/hp/str		Mozart Ed	LM G 10824

SUITE OF ENGLISH FOLK DANCES taken from various editions of John Playford's 'The English dancing master'
    1. Jenny pluck pears   4. Nonesuch
    2. Ten pound lass   5. Hunt the squirrel
    3. Dick's maggot   6. Woodicock

	∅	2(picc)222/4230/timp.perc/hp/str	13'	Novello	22138 Cni D

SYMPHONY '65: symphony orch & jazz band

	∅	3(2picc)3(ca)3(bcl)3(cbsn)/4331/timp.perc. glock.vib.xyl/hp/str Jazz band: 1(picc)05(bcl).5sx.0/0440/perc/ egtr.pf(cel)		(Composer,1965)	24276 An +

TOMLINSON, Frederick

A-BEGGING WE WILL GO: song arr
    in B♭

	∅	111+bcl.0/1000/hp/str		(Arranger)	LM G 10981

TOMLINSON, Frederick (cont)

AIKEN DRUM: song for solo voice, chorus & orch
   in G   φ   1120/1000/hp/str   (Arranger)   LM G 10935

The ANGLER'S SONG: arr for solo voice, TTBB chorus & orch, arr
   in E♭   φ   1120/1000/hp/str   (Arranger)   LM G 10895

ARISE, ARISE: song, arr
   in G   φ   1120/1000/hp/str   (Arranger)   LM G 10981

AS I WALKED THROUGH THE MEADOWS: song, arr
   in B♭   φ   1120/1000/hp/str   (Arranger)   LM G 10922

AWAY IN A MANGER: carol, arr
   in F   φ   1120/1000/cel.hp/str   (Arranger)   LM G 10982

BILLY BOY: song arr for solo voice, chorus & orch
   in C   φ   1120/1000/hp/str   (Arranger)   LM G 10895

The BOLD FISHERMAN: song, arr
   in G   φ   111+bcl.0/1000/hp/str   (Arranger)   LM G 10981

CA' HAWKIE THROUGH THE WATER: song for solo voice, SSAA chorus & orch
   in E min   φ   1120/1000/hp/str   (Arranger)   LM G 10935

CALLINO CUSTUREME: song, arr for solo voice, chorus & orch
   in B♭   φ   1120/1000/hp/str   (Arranger)   LM G 10894

The CARMAN'S WHISTLE: song, arr
   in F   φ   0+picc.01+bcl.0/1000/hp/str   (Arranger)   LM G 10981

CAWSAND BAY: song, arr for solo voice, chorus & orch
   in D   φ   1(picc)120/1000/hp/str   (Arranger)   LM G 10922

CHEVY CHASE: song, arr for solo voice, TTBB chorus & orch
   in D   φ   1120/1000/hp/str   (Arranger)   LM G 10895

CHRISTMAS IS COMING: song, arr
   in D-E♭   φ   1120/1000/perc/cel.hp/str   (Arranger)   LM G 10982

COME LASSIES AND LADS: song, arr for chorus & orch
   in C   φ   1120/1000/hp/str   (Arranger)   LM G 10935

The DERBY RAM: song, arr
   in C   φ   1120/1000/hp/str   (Arranger)   LM G 10981

EAGLE'S LULLABY: song, arr for solo voice, SSAA chorus & orch
   in F   φ   1120/1000/hp/str   (Arranger)   LM G 10935

FAIRY LULLABY: song, arr
   in A♭   φ   1120/1000/hp/str   (Arranger)   LM G 10981

FLOWERS IN THE VALLEY: song, arr
   in A   φ   1120/1000/hp/str   (Arranger)   LM G 10981

FOR I LIVE NOT WHERE I LOVE: song, arr
   in E♭   φ   1120/1000/hp/str   (Arranger)   LM G 10981

The FOX JUMPED OVER THE PARSON'S GATE: song, arr for solo voice, TTBB chorus & orch
   in B♭   φ   1120/1000/hp/str   (Arranger)   LM G 10935

GATHERING PEASCODS: song, arr for SSAA chorus & orch
   in G   φ   1120/1000/hp/str   (Arranger)   LM G 10895

GOOD MORROW GOSSIP JOAN: SATB & orch, arr
   in C   φ   1120/1000/hp/str   (Arranger)   LM G 10935

GREEN GROW THE RUSHES O: song, arr for solo voice, chorus & orch
   in C   φ   1120/1000/hp/str   (Arranger)   LM G 10935

HAVE YOU SEEN BUT A WHYTE LILLIE GROW: song, arr
   in F   φ   1120/1000/hp/str   (Arranger)   LM G 10895

HE THAT WILL NOT MERRY MERRY BE: song, arr for solo voice, TTBB chorus & orch
   in A min   φ   1120/1000/hp/str   (Arranger)   LM G 10935

HOB Y DERRY DANDO: song, arr
   in G♭   φ   112(bcl)0/1000/hp/str   (Arranger)   LM G 10935

HUSHABYE DARLING: song, arr
   in A♭   φ   111+bcl.0/1000/hp/str   (Arranger)   LM G 10981

HUSH YE MY BAIRNIE: song, arr
   in E♭   φ   111+bcl.0/1000/hp/str   (Arranger)   LM G 10981

TOMLINSON, Frederick (cont)

I AM A LUSTY LIVELY LAD: song, arr
   in D   φ   1120/1000/hp/str   (Arranger)   LM G 10935
I RODE MY LITTLE HORSE: song, arr
   in G   φ   1120/1000/hp/str   (Arranger)   LM G 10981
I WISH I WERE WHERE HELEN LIES: song, arr
   in A   φ   111+bcl.0/1000/hp/str   (Arranger)   LM G 10981
JOAN'S ALE IS NEW: song, arr for solo voice, TTBB chorus & orch
   in D   φ   1120/1000/hp/str   (Arranger)   LM G 10935
The KEEPER: song, arr for chorus & orch
   in D   φ   1120/1000/hp/str   (Arranger)   LM G 10922
LITTLE RED BIRD: song, arr for solo voice, chorus & orch
   in G min   φ   112(bcl)0/1000/str   (Arranger)   LM G 10935
LOVELY JOAN: song, arr for medium voice & orch
                                 φ   1120/1000/hp/str   (Arranger)   LM G 10935
LOWLANDS AWAY: song, arr
   in C min   φ   1120/1000/hp/str   (Arranger)   LM G 10895
The MERRY MILKMAIDS: song, arr for solo voice, SSAA chorus & orch
   in F   φ   1120/1000/hpEstr   (Arranger)   LM G 10922
MISTER STORMALONG: song, arr for solo voice, chorus & orch
                                 φ   112(bcl)0/1000/hp/str   (Arranger)   LM G 10935
MY JOHNNIE WAS A SHOEMAKER: song, arr
   in Eb   φ   111.bcl.0/1000/hp/str   (Arranger)   LM G 10981
O GOOD ALE: song, arr for solo voice, TTBB chorus & orch
   in E min   φ   112(bcl)0/1000/hp/str   (Arranger)   LM G 10935
OLD JOHN BRADDLEUM: song, arr
   in F   φ   1120/1000/hp/str   (Arranger)   LM G 10981
ONE MORE DAY: song, arr for solo voice, chorus & orch
   in G   φ   1120/1000/hp/str   (Arranger)   LM G 10922
ORANGES AND LEMONS: song, arr for solo voice, chorus & orch
   in F   φ   1120/1000/hp/str   (Arranger)   LM G 10922
OVER THE HILLS AND FAR AWAY: song, arr for solo voice, TTBB chorus & orch
   in Ab   φ   1120/1000/hp/str   (Arranger)   LM G 10895
OVER THE STONE: song, arr
   in G min   φ   1120/1000/hp/str   (Arranger)   LM G 10981
PACE-EGGING SONG: song, arr for solo voice, TTBB chorus & orch
   in Ab   φ   1120/1000/hp/str   (Arranger)   LM G 10894
PAST THREE O'CLOCK: song, arr
   in Ab   φ   1120/1000/vib/cel.hp/str   (Arranger)   LM G 10982
PORTSMOUTH-YOUTH'S THE SEASON: song, arr
   in G & C   φ   1120/1000/hp/str   (Arranger)   LM G 10935
PRETTY CAROLINE: song, arr for solo voice, chorus & orch
   in Eb   φ   1120/1000/hp/str   (Arranger)   LM G 10894
PRETTY LITTLE POLLY PERKINS: song, arr for solo voice, chorus & orch
   in Bb   φ   112/bc10/1000/hp/str   (Arranger)   LM G 10894
SELLENGER'S ROUND: song, arr for solo voice, SSAA chorus & orch
   in Bb   φ   1120/1000/hp/str   (Arranger)   LM G 10894
SHALLOW BROWN: song, arr for solo voice, chorus & orch
   in Bb   φ   1120/1000/hp/str   (Arranger)   LM G 10894
SLUMBER SONG: song, arr for solo voice, chorus & orch
   in A min   φ   1120/1000/hp/str   (Arranger)   LM G 10895
The SPRING IS COMING: song, arr
   in Eb   φ   1120/1000/hp/str   (Arranger)   LM G 10981

TOMLINSON, Frederick (cont)

THERE WAS A GIRL WENT TO THE MILL: song, arr 　　in Ab　　　　φ　1120/1000/hp/str		(Arranger)	LM G 1098
THERE WAS A SIMPLE MAIDEN: song, arr for chorus & orch 　　in G　　　　φ　1120/1000/hp/str		(Arranger)	LM G 1093
TOBACCO'S BUT AN INDIAN WEED: song, arr for solo voice, TTBB chorus & orch 　　in C min　　φ　112(bcl)0/1000/hp/str		(Arranger)	LM G 1093
TO THE MAYPOLE AWAY: song, arr 　　in G　　　　φ　1120/1000/hp/str		(Arranger)	LM G 1089
TO THE MAYPOLE HASTE AWAY: song, arr for solo voice, chorus & orch 　　in D min　　φ　1120/1000/hp/str		(Arranger)	LM G 1089
'TWAS ONE OF THOSE DREAMS: song, arr 　　in F　　　　φ　1120/1000/hp/str		(Arranger)	LM G 1089
The TWELVE DAYS OF CHRISTMAS: carol, arr 　　in F　　　　φ　111+bcl.0/1000/cel.hp/str		(Arranger)	LM G 1098
WESTERN LULLABY: song, arr for solo voice, SSAA chorus & orch 　　in Bb　　　φ　1120/1000/hp/str		(Arranger)	LM G 1093
WHISKY JOHNNY: song arr 　　in Ab　　　φ　111+bcl.0/1000/hp/str		(Arranger)	LM G 1098
WITH JOCKEY TO THE FAIR: song, arr for solo voice, chorus & orch 　　in F　　　　φ　112(bcl)0/1000/hp/str		(Arranger)	LM G 1093
YOUNG RICHARD OF TAUNTON DENE: song, arr 　　in F　　　　φ　1120/1000/hp/str		(Arranger)	LM G 1093

TOMMASI, A

SALVE REGINA: chorus & orch　　φ　2222/4000/hp/str		Ed Trebbi,Bologna	Misc 154

TOMMASINI, Vincenzo (1878-1950)

Il BEATO REGNO: poem　　φ　2+picc.2+ca.2+bcl.2/4231/timp.perc.bells.tamtam/ 　　　　cel.hp.pf/str			Ricordi,1925	Misc 882
Il CARNEVALE DI VENEZIA: variations after Paganini 　　φ　3(2picc)2+ca.Ebcl.2+bcl.2+cbsn/4331/timp.perc. 　　　　bells.xyl/hp/str	12'		Ricordi,1929	Misc 805
CHIARI DI LUNE 　　1. Chiese e ruine　　2. Serenata 　　φ　2+picc.2+ca.2+bcl.2/40+2cnt.31/timp.perc. 　　　　tamtam/cel.hp/str	14'		Ricordi,1921	Misc 800
CONCERTO for strings　　φ　str	30'		Zerboni,1942	Misc 320
The GOOD-HUMOURED LADIES　see　SCARLATTI, Domenico. The GOOD-HUMOURED LADIES				
2 MELODIES for voice & orch 　　1. Lungi, lungi ...　　2. Disperata 　　φ　2+picc.22+bcl.2/4231/timp.perc.tamtam/ 　　　　cel.hp/str	8'30"		Ricordi,1933	Misc 222
NÁPULE (Napoli): fantasia for orch　φ　3(picc)2+ca.2+Ebcl±bcl.2+cbsn/63+Dtpt. 　　　　31/timp.perc.bells/hp/str	20'		Adler	14601
PAESAGGI TOSCANI: rhapsody on a popular theme 　　φ　2+picc.2+ca.22/4231/timp.perc.bells/str			Ricordi,1926	Misc 879
4 PEZZI (Pieces) 　　1. Sinfonia　　3. Valzer lento 　　2. Notturno　　4. Rondo scherzoso 　　φ　3(picc)2+ca.2+Dcl+bcl.2+cbsn/4231/timp. 　　　　perc/cel.hp/str	24'30"		Ricordi,1937	Misc 19
PRELUDIO, FANFARA E FUGA　φ　2+picc.2+ca.2+bcl.2+cbsn/4331/timp.perc. 　　　　bells/cel.hp/str	13'15"		Ricordi,1928	Misc 80

TOMMASINI, Vincenzo (cont)

SCHERZO for cello & orch
  transcr L.Silva   ø   2(picc)201/2100/hp/str   Zanibon,1938   Misc 8677 B
                                                                          (ø + vlc part)

TONI, Alceo (1884-1969)

Il CAVALIER ROMANTICO: overture   ø   2+picc.222/4231/timp.perc/str   Carisch,1931   Misc 1382

TOOTELL, George

MANX SCENES: suite
   1. Crag and sea: fantasy-prelude
   2. At the trysting place: romance
   3. A Manx wedding: finale
                        PC   2122/2220/timp.perc/org/str   Paxton   6129

TORCH, Sidney

ALL STRINGS AND FANCY FREE   PC   2(picc)120/000/[hp]/str   Chappell   18842
AMORE MIO: Neapolitan serenade, arr

                      PC   2120/2230/timp.perc/acdn.hp/str   3'   Chappell,1952   22481 D
   arr   ø   2120/2330/cym.glock.vib/hp.mand.pf/str 3'   (Chappell)   24733
BARBECUE   PC   2121/2230/timp.perc/hp/str   2'55" Chappell,1952   20765 B
CATARI! CATARI! (Core ingrato)(S.Cardillo), for Tenor & orch, arr
                      ø   21+ca.22/4331/timp.perc.glock.vib/
                          hp[pf]/str   3'   (Ricordi)   25292 +
COLISEUM CAVALCADE, for chorus & orch
                      ø   21+ca.22/4331/timp.perc.bells.cbells.
                          glock.vib.xyl/cel.hp.org/str   (Arranger)   25033 +
COMIC CUTS   ø   2(picc)12+[bcl]1/2230/timp.perc/hp/str   (Chappell)   24742
The DREAM OF OLWEN for piano & orch (C.Williams)
                      ø   21+ca.22/4331/timp.perc/hp/str   (L.Wright)   24882 +
DUEL FOR DRUMMERS: suite   ø   2(picc)2(ca)22/4331/timp.perc/hp/str   Arranger,1960   23207 +
EDWARDIAN ECHOES: selection for soli & chorus
                      ø   2(picc)222/4330/timp.perc/hp/str   (Chappell/Glocken.Verlag)   24219 +
The ENCHANTMENT OF VICTOR HERBERT   see   HERBERT, Victor: The ENCHANTMENT OF VICTOR HERBERT
FANDANGO   PC   2121/2230/perc/hp/str   Chappell   19237 Ani B
FRIDAY NIGHT IS MUSIC NIGHT: medley, arr (12.10.1962)
   1. Spanish Gipsy dance, for orch (P.Marquina)(Schauer & M)
   2. Valencia, for chorus & orch, in F (J.Padilla)(Feldman)
                      ø   2(2picc)222/4330/timp.perc/hp.pf/str   (Arranger)   23716 +
  Medley (for Barry) of choruses (15.5.1970)
     1. Who were you with last night (Godfrey & Sheridan)(Feldman)
     2. If you were the only girl (Ayer) (Feldman)
     3. I wouldn't leave my little wooden hut (Mellor & Collins)(F D & H)
     4. We'll keep a welcome (Joshua, Harper & Jones)(E.Cox)

                                                        (Arranger)   25057 +
The GLAMOUR OF TODAY for Soprano, Soubrette, Tenor & Baritone soli & orch
                      ø   2(picc)2(ca)22/4331/timp.perc.bells.glock.xyl/
                          gtr.hp.org.pf/str   15'   (Arranger,1976) 24486 +
GOING FOR A RIDE   PC   2121/2230/timp.perc/hp/str   Chappell   19530 Cp
HIGHLIGHTS OF AMERICAN MUSICAL COMEDY: selection for Soprano, Baritone & orch
                      ø   2(picc)2(ca)22/4331/timp.perc/hp.org/str
                                        (Williamson,Chappell & Frank)   23403 +

TORCH, Sidney (cont)

INTRODUCTION TO "A TRIBUTE TO RICHARD RODGERS": arrangement of introduction to "The Sound of Music"
     φ 20.ca.22/0000/hp/str   00'45" (Williamson) 25476 +

ITALIAN CARNIVAL: medley for soloists, solo piano, chorus & orch, arr
     φ 2(picc)222/4331/timp.perc/acdn.hp.pf/str   (Ricordi) 23622 +

ITALIAN INTERLUDE: medley for chorus & orch (chorus arr J.McCarthy)
     φ 2(picc)222/4331/timp.perc.glock.vib.xyl/
       hp.2mand.pf(cel)/str   (Arranger) 25075

LATIN-AMERICAN FIESTA: medley for Soprano, Baritone & Bass-baritone soli, chorus & orch, arr
     φ 2222/4331/timp.perc/gtr.hp.pf/str   (Arranger) 23890 +

LONDON MUSICAL TRANSPORT: suite
 1. The Hansom cab
 2. Rosie, the red omnibus
 3. The 5.52 from Victorloo
     φ 2(picc)222/4231/timp.perc/hp/str   6'30" (Composer) 22373 +
 No.1 only   PC 2(picc)121/2230/timp/hp/str   2'10" Chappell,1958 22503 Cp

MEANDERING   PC 2+picc.121/2230/timp.perc/str 2'10" Chappell,1952 20779 B

MEDITATION (from "Thaïs" by J.Massenet) for optional chorus & orch
     φ 21+ca.22/4030/timp/cel(pf)hp/str   (Arranger,1969) 24914 +

MEMORIES OF NOËL COWARD: selection, arr
     φ 2(picc)222/4230/timp.perc/hp/str   (Chappell) 23359 +

METROPOLITAN MUSIC: signature tune for programme
     φ 2140/2330/timp.perc/hp.pf/str   Composer MS LM Lib

MOON MEDLEY for Soprano, Mezzo-soprano & Baritone soli & orch
     φ 2222/4330/perc/hp.pf/str   (Arranger) 24443 +

MUSIC FOR SWEETHEARTS, for Soprano & Baritone soli & orch
     φ 21+ca.22/4331/timp.perc/glock.vib/
       cel.pf/str   (Arranger,1969) 24971 +

MUSIC WE LOVE: signature tune to radio programme (based on Cavatina by J.Raff)
 Opening & closing music φ 22(ca)22/4230/timp.perc/hp/str   (Arranger) 23643 +

MUSICAL COMEDY MEMORIES: selection arr
     φ 22(ca)3+bcl.2/4330/timp.perc/hp/str 10' (Chappell) 22651 +

MUSICAL FLY (Marches of the R.A.F.): medley for military band & orch
     φ 2(picc)222/4330/timp.perc/hp/str 3'30" (Arranger,1965) 24329 +

MY WALTZ FOR YOU   PC 2121/2230/timp.perc/hp/str 3'15" Chappell,1948 20909

NO, NO, NANETTE: selection, arr see YOUMANS, Vincent: No, No, NANNETTE - Selection, arr

ON A SPRING NOTE   PC 2+picc.121/2230/perc/hp/str 2'35" Chappell,1952 20480 Cp
     PC 2+picc.121/2330/perc/hp/str   Chappell,1952 20480'A's

OO-LA-LA   φ 2(picc)121/2330/timp.perc.glock.xyl/hp/str (Chappell)(H) PL 390 (N
                           hire fe

OUR WALTZING YEARS: medley of British waltz tunes, arr
     φ 2(picc)1+ca.22/4331/timp.perc.glock.vib/
       hp.pf(cel)/str   17'20" (Arranger) 24807 +

Les PETITES VALSES PARISIENNES φ 2(picc)2(ca)22/4331/timp.perc.glock.xyl/
       hp.[pf]/str   (Arranger) 25247

Un PREMIER BOUQUET (Time remembered): waltz, op.201 (E.Waldteufel)
     φ 212[=4]2/2330/perc/hp.pf/str   (A H & C) 24856

RAINBOW RIDE   φ 2(picc)1(ca)21/2330/perc/hp/str   Composer 24444 Ani

El RANCHO GRANDE: Latin-American song fantasy for Soprano, Baritone & chorus, and orch.
     φ 2(picc)2(ca)2(bcl)2/4330/timp.perc/hp.pf/str (Arranger) 23726 +

RENDEZVOUS IN VIENNA: medley for Soprano & Tenor soli & orch (1969)
     φ 2(picc)2(ca)22/4331/timp.perc.glock.vib/
       cel.hp.hpsd.pf.zither/str   (Arranger) 25014 +

The ROMANCE OF IVOR NOVELLO: medley for Soprano & Tenor soli & orch
     φ 2(picc)222/4331/timp.perc/hp.pf/str   (Chappell) 23893 +

TORCH, Sidney (cont)

ROMANCE WITH ROMBERG   see   ROMBERG,Sigmund ROMANCE WITH ROMBERG
ROMANY RHAPSODY: medley for violin, Mezzo-soprano & Tenor soli, chorus & orch
                          φ   2(picc)2(ca)22/4331/timp.perc.sbells.glock.
                               xyl/hp/str
                                                                (Arranger)   24487 +
SALUTE THE SOLDIER: song medley for soli, chorus, military band & orch
                          φ   2(picc)2(ca)22/4330/timp.perc/hp/str   15'
                                              (Boosey/L.Wright/Harmony/Prowse)   24037 +
SAMBA SUD   PC   2+picc.121/2230/perc/hp/str   3'   Chappell   18944 B
SHOOTING STAR   PC   2121/2230/timp.perc/hp/str   Chappell   19239 C
SHORTCAKE-WALK   PC   1+picc.121/2230/perc/hp/str   2'15"   Chappell 1952 20481
SHOW MUSIC OF THE SIXTIES: medley for Soprano & Baritone soli & orch
                          φ   2(picc)222/4331/timp.perc/hp.pf/str
                                                                (Chappell)   23621 +
SIXTY YEARS OF SHOWS: vocal selection for chorus and orch
                          φ   2222/4331/timp.perc/hp/str   Composer MS:BBC,1960   23242
A SLAVONIC RHAPSODY, for 2 pianos & orch
                          φ   2(picc)2(ca)22/4331/timp.perc.xyl/hp/str   9'
                                                                (Arranger)   25203 +
SONG OF NORWAY: operetta based on the music of Grieg, arr Wright & Forrest
     Strange music: song
       in A (duet version) for Soprano & Baritone
                          φ   21+ca.22/4331/timp.perc/hp/str
                                                                (E.Morris)   24957 +
SONGS OF THE SEA: medley for Soprano & Baritone soli, male-voice chorus & orch
                          φ   2222/4331/timp.perc/hp.pf/str
                                                                Arranger   23877 + D
The SOUND OF RICHARD ROGERS: medley for Soprano & Baritone soli, chorus & orch
                          φ   2222/4331/timp.perc/gtr.hp.org.pf/str
                                                                (Williamson)   23889 +
The STUDENT PRINCE (S.Romberg): Selection for Soprano & Baritone soli, TB chorus & orch
                          φ   22(ca)22/4331/timp.perc/[cel].hp.pf/str
                                                                (Chappell)   24878 +
THOROUGHLY MODERN MILLY: medley of songs by various composers for soloists, chorus & orch
                          φ   2(picc)1+ca.22/4331/timp.perc.glock.xyl/
                               hp.pf/str   5'   (Arranger)   24686 +
The TRAPEZE WALTZ   PC   112[=1]1/02[=1]20/[acdn].gtr/str   2'45 Chappell,1963 23813 Ani
TRIBUTE TO COWARD   see   COWARD, N. TRIBUTE TO COWARD
TUESDAY TUNE TIME: radio programme opening & closing music to "Tuesday Tune Time"
                          φ   2222/4230/timp.perc.glock/hp/str   Arranger   23315
     Showboat: opening music   φ 21.ca.22/4330/timp.perc/cel.hp/str   Arranger   23316
THEATRE ROYAL MELODIES: vocal selection for Soprano, chorus & orch
                          φ   2(picc)2(ca)22/4331/timp.perc/hp.pf/str
                                                                (Chappell)   22943 +
VICTOR HERBERT MELODIES: selection arr
                          φ   2(picc)2(ca)2(bcl)2/4230/timp.perc/hp/str
                                                                Feldman   23376 +
VICTORIAN VANITIES: medley of 21 Victorian songs, for 4 soli, mv-chorus & orch (1967)
                          φ   2(picc)2(ca)22/4331/timp.perc.bells.glock.xyl/
                               hp.pf/str
                                                                (Arranger)   24599 +
WALTZING WITH LOVE   φ   2(picc)2(ca)22/4331/timp.perc.bells.glock.xyl/
                               hp.pf(cel)/str   7'45" (Arranger,1972) 25398 +
WALTZING WITH THE LADIES!   φ 2(picc)1+ca.22/4331/timp.perc.bells.glock/
                               hp.pf(cel)/str
                                                                (Arranger,1969)   24956 +
WAY OUT WEST, for Soprano & Baritone soli, chorus & orch
                          φ   222(bcl)2/4330/timp.perc/str   15'   (Arranger,1965) 24203 +

TORÉ, John

GOLDEN CITY
     Selection, arr Zalva   PC 212.3sx.1/2230/timp.perc/hp/str   9'   Chappell,1950 19927 Cp
MOONLIGHT ON THE RIVER: song
     in B, arr C.Watters   φ   1121/0210/perc/hp.pf/str   (Chappell)   LM G 4463

TORELLI, Giuseppe (1658-1709)

see   GIEGLING, Franz. Giuseppe Torelli Thematisches Verzeichnis. Kassel, Bärenreiter, 1949.
      Numbers prefixed by the letter 'G' refer to entries in this work.   BRL

CONCERTI
    for strings (Concerto à 4), op.5 no.2,G.118, in D min
        ed W.Kolneder   ∅   str/cont   Doblinger,1979   26671 *
    trumpet & orch, G.2-3, in D (made up of G2 & G3)
        rev & cont real J.F. Paillard ∅ str/cont   Costallat,1962   23838
            in D, ed E.H.Tarr (Not in Giegling)
                                 ∅   str/cont   Musica Rara,1968   24892
    2 trumpets & strings, G.18, in D
        rev & cont real P.Santi ∅   str/cont   8'   Ricordi,1971   25586
CONCERTI GROSSI, Op.8
    no.1, G.153, in C
        ed W.Kolneder   ∅   2vln-soli.str/cont(hpsd=org)   Doblinger,1980   26967 *
        rev P.Santi   ∅   2vln-soli.str/cont   Zerboni,1959   Misc 5636
        ed.D.Stevens   ∅   2vln-soli.str/cont(lute)   Editor/(Siluani,1709) 21126 mf
    no.2, G.154, in A min
        ed D.Stevens   ∅   2vln-soli.str/cont(lute)   Editor/(Siluani 1709) 21126 + m
        ed Paumgartner   ∅   2vln-soli.str/cont   Schott,1956   23594 B
    no.3, G.155, in E
        rev P.Santi   ∅   str/cont   Zerboni,1959   Misc 5637
        ed D.Stevens   ∅   2vln-soli.str/cont(lute)   Editor/(Siluani,1709) 21126 + m
    no.4, G.156, in B♭
        ed D.Stevens   ∅   2vln-soli.str/cont(lute)   Editor/(Siluani,1709) 21126 + m
    no.5, G.157, in G
        ed A.Casella   ∅   2vln-soli.str/cont   8'-8'55" Zerboni,1960   Misc 5568
        ed M.Sidwell   ∅   2vln-soli.str/cont(hpsd)   Editor/(Siluani,1709) 24774
        ed D.Stevens   ∅   2vln-soli.str/cont(lute)   Editor/(Siluani,1709) 21126 + m
    no.6, G.158, in G min
        ed A.Schering   ∅   2vln-soli.str/cont   Kahnt,1928   20427
        ed D.Stevens   ∅   2vln-soli.str/cont   Heinrichsen,1957   Misc 4878
        ed D.Stevens   ∅   2vln-soli.str/cont   Editor/(Siluani,1709) 21127 + m
    no.7, G.159, in D min
        ed & rev P.Santi   ∅   vln-solo.str/cont   Zerboni,1959   Misc 5635
        ed D.Stevens   ∅   vln-solo.str/cont   Editor/(Siluani,1709) 21127 + mf
    no.8, G.160, in C min
        ed E.Praetorius   ∅   vln-solo.str/cont   Eulenburg   19613
        ed D.Stevens   ∅   vln-solo.str/cont(lute)   Editor/(Siluani,1709) 21127 + mf
    no.9, G.161, in E min
        ed B.Paumgartner   ∅   vln-solo.str/cont   Hug,1950   20280
        ed & rev P.Santi   ∅   vln-solo.str/cont   Zerboni,1959   Misc 5638
        ed D.Stevens   ∅   vln-solo.str/cont(lute)   Editor/(Siluani,1709) 21127 + mf
    no.10, G.162, in A min
        ed D.Stevens   ∅   vln-solo.str/cont(lute)   Editor/(Siluani,1709) 21127 + mf
    no.11, G.163, in F
        ed D.Stevens   ∅   vln-solo.str/cont(lute)   Editor/(Siluani,1709) 21127 + mf
    no.12, G.164, in D
        ed D.Stevens   ∅   vln-solo.str/cont(lute)   Editor/(Siluani,1709) 21127 + mf
SONATAS
    trumpet, strings & continuo, G.1, in D (1690)
        ed E.H.Tarr   ∅   str/cont   Musica Rara,1973   25725 B
    trumpet, strings & continuo, G.3, in D à 5
        ed F.Schroeder   ∅   str/cont   Doblinger,1975   26065
    trumpet, strings & continuo, G.5, in D (c.1690)
        ed E.H.Tarr   ∅   str/cont   Musica Rara   25864 B
    trumpet, strings & continuo, G.6, in D
        ed E.H.Tarr   ∅   str/cont   Musica Rara,1975   25964 *

TORELLI, Giuseppe (cont)

SONATAS (cont)
   trumpet, strings & continuo, G.7, in D

ed R.P.Block & E.H.Tarr	ø	cello solo-str/cont		Musica Rara,1976	26146 *

SYMPHONIES
   G.2, in D

ed E.H.Tarr	ø	0000/0100/str/cont		Musica Rara,1974	25780 *

   G.3, in D

ed E.H.Tarr	ø	0000/0100/str/cont		Musica Rara,1974	25794 B

   G.4, in D (1693)

ed E.H.Tarr	ø	0000/0100/str/cont		Musica Rara,1974	25863 B

   G.8, in D

ed R.P.Block & E.H.Tarr	ø	0000/0100/str/cont		Musica Rara,1976	26145
ed F.Schroeder	ø	0000/0100/str/cont		Doblinger,1975	26066 *

   G.14, in D

ed E.H.Tarr	ø	0000/0100/str/cont		Musica Rara,1975	25963 *

   G.26, in D

rev & cont real P.Santi	ø	0200/0200/str/cont	8'	Ricordi,1971	Misc 7534

   G.29, in D (1707)

ed F.Schroeder	ø	0201/0210/str/cont		Doblinger,1971	25273

   G.33, in C

ed E.H.Tarr	ø	0402/0410/timp/str/cont		Musica Rara,1974	25801 B*

   G.117 (op.5, no.1) in A min

ed W.Kolneder	ø	str(no vlas)/cont		Doblinger,1979	26672 *

   G.119 (op.5,no.3) in C

ed W.Kolneder	ø	str/no vlas)/cont		Doblinger,1979	26673 *

TORRALBA, R.

HIMNO REPUBLICANO ESPAÑOL (REPUBLICAN HYMN): Spanish patriotic song

PC	111.2sx.1/2210/perc/str	Garzon	12762

TORRANDELL, A.

LAS VENTAS DE MADRID	PC	1+picc.111/2230/timp/str	2'30-3' Deiss & Crepin	12220

TORRI, Pietro (c1650-1737)

ADELAIDE: opera

Excerpts	ø	0000/02.cor-dc.2clno./perc/str/cont	Breitkoph,1920.DDTB 19-20	MRL

EDIPPO: opera

Excerpts	ø	str/cont	Breitkopf,1920.DDTB 19-20	MRL

ENONE: opera

Excerpts	ø	str/cont	Breitkoph,1920.DDTB 19-20	MRL

L'EPAMINONDA: opera

Excerpts	ø	str/cont	Breitkopf,1920.DDTB 19-20	MRL

GRISELDA: opera

Excerpts	ø	str/cont	Breitkopf,1920.DDTB 19-20	MRL

IPPOLITO: opera

Excerpts	ø	0000/0.cor-dc.000/str/cont	Breitkopf,1902.DDTB 19-20	MRL

ISMENE: opera

Excerpts		0.flag.000/0000/str/cont	Breitkopf.1920.DDTB 19-20	MRL

La MEROPE: opera

Act 3 only	ø	str/cont	Breitkopf.1920.DDTB 19-20	MRL

ORESTE: opera

Excerpts	ø	str/cont	Breitkopf.1920.DDTB 19-20	MRL

TORMÉ, Mel

CHRISTMAS SONG: song by M.Tormé & R.Wells
   in Ab, arr J.Spence   ø   2121/2030/timp/gtr.hp.pf/str   (Edwin Morris)   LMG 9421

TORROBA, Federico Moreno

MADRILENAS: suite (orig gtr solo)
   1. Bolero   2. Cupla   3. Tirana
                PC   2121/2230/timp.perc/hp/str   Musica del Sur,1956   23748

TOSATTI, Vieri (1920 -

DIONISO: musical drama
   Two fragments
      1. Preludio a Dioniso
      2. Le nozze d'Arianna
              ø   2+picc.2+ca.2+bcl.2+cbsn/4331/timp.perc.bells.tamtam/
                  cel.hp/str   Ricordi,1954   Misc 4416
DIVERTIMENTO for chamber orch (1950)
              ø   1011/2000/str   15'   Ricordi,1955   Misc 5481

TOSELLI, Enrico (1883-1926)

SERENATA No.1, op.6 'Come back'
   in F   PC   1121/2230/perc/str   3'10"   (Walsh Holmes)   10910 Ap
   in E arr E.Griffiths   pf.str(vln.obbl. arr Byfield)   (Freeman)   LMG 5481
   orch arr Gervasio   ø   hp/str   Walsh Holmes   11248
   orch arr E.Reeves   PC   1121/2[=2cnt]000/perc/str   Walsh Holmes   9200 Bp C
   orch arr Gervasio   hp/str   Walsh Holmes   376 B
SERENATA No.2 'Notte nostalgica'
   orch arr H.Geehl   PC   2122/2210/timp.perc.bells/str   3'15"   K.Prowse   1748

TOSTI, Francesco Paolo (1846-1916)

A VUCCHELLA: song
   in Eb & F, arr R.Chignell   ø   2121/2220/timp.perc/hp/str   2'-3'   (Ricordi)   MS 4788 +
APRIL
   arr E.Tavan   PC   1110/0000/str   Ricordi   1719
FOR EVER AND FOR EVER (Per sempre e ancor' per sempre)
   in F   PC   1020/2110/str   Ricordi   1767
GOODBYE: song
   in Ab, arr G.Stacey   pf.hp/str   (Ricordi)   LMG 5509
   in Ab, arr L.Wurmser   ø   31+ca.22/4231/timp.perc/hp/str   (Ricordi)   TO 1526
   in F, arr H.Finck   PC   2122/2210/timp/str   Ricordi   268
IDEALE 'My love for you'
   in A & Bb, arr L.Wurmser ø   21+ca.1+bcl.2/4230/timp/cel.hp/str   (Ricordi)   TO 1423
   in F   ø   21+ca.2+bcl.2/4230/timp/cel.hp/str   (Ricordi)   TO 1804
IVANO-SERENADE arr E.Tavan   PC   1110/0000/str   Ricordi   432
MARECHIARE: Neapolitan song
   in C min, arr E.Tavan   ø   1110/0000/pf/str   2'45"-3'40" (Ricordi)   LM G 4264
   in D min, arr P.Hope for chorus & orch
              ø   3(picc)2+ca.2+bcl.2/4331/timp.perc/hp/
                 str   (Ricordi)   23868 +
   in D min, arr P.Hope for solo voice, chorus & orch
              ø   2222/4330/timp.perc.glock.xyl/hp.pf/str   (Ricordi)   26921(voca
                                               i

TOSTI, Francesco Paolo (cont)

MARECHIARE: (cont)
   in D min & E min, arr S.Robinson

	∅	2222/2230/hp/str	2'45"-3'40"	(Ricordi)	TO 1912 +
in D min & B min, arr E.Tavan		pf/str		(Ricordi)	LM G 3632
orch & arr E.Tavan (non-vocal)	PC	1110/0000/str		Ricordi	1152

MATTINATA: song

in F	PC	1111/2110/perc/str		(Ricordi)	MS 4412
in G, arr Billi	PC	1111/2110/perc/str		Ricordi	3488

MY DREAMS: song

in D♭, arr Moore	PC	2222/2230.euph/timp/str		Chappell	3654 CpDEp
in E♭, arr H.Carr	∅	2222/4230/perc/hp/str		(Chappell)	TO 53
in E♭, arr B.Thompson		pf.hp/str		(Chappell)	MS 20328
in E♭ & B♭, arr Stacey		pf/str		(Chappell)	LM G 3080
in E♭, arr J.Turner	∅	1110/1000/hp/str		(Chappell)	LM G 8559

MY LOVE FOR YOU see IDEALE

PARTED: song

in G & B♭ (2 settings)		1101/0000/str	4'30"	(Siddell)	18171
in G	∅PC	1121/2210/timp/str		Ricordi	894 BpC
in B♭, arr H.Carr		hp[=pf]/str		(Ricordi)	LM G 5487
in B♭, arr G.Williams, for tenor & chorus					
	∅	1121/2210/glock.hp/str		(Ricordi)	MLO 108

Il PESCATORE CANTA! arr E.Tavan	PC	2222/2220/str	2'15"	Ricordi	11356

RAPSODIE NAPOLETANE: selection of Tosti's popular songs

arr Culotta	∅	1010/1210/perc/str		Ricordi	12140
arr Culotta	PC	1010/1210/perc/str		Ricordi	10861

La SERENADE

in F, arr G.Stacey		pf/str		(Ricordi)	LM G 3405
arr E.Tavan	PC	1110/0000/str		Ricordi	719

TOSTI'S SONGS: selection

arr C.Godfrey jnr	PC	2(picc)221/2230.euph/timp.perc/str		Chappell	2400 B

L'ULTIMA CANZONE arr Billi

in B♭ min, arr Catelinet	∅	1111/2110/perc/str	3'-5'	(Ricordi)	TO 1805

VENETIAN SONG: duet

in D		1222/2000/perc/str		(Chappell)	20971
in D♭, arr L.Salter	∅	1022/1000/str		(Chappell)	TO 1579
in F, orch J.Buerger	∅	2121/2000/tri/hp/str		(Chappell)	MS 3765

TOURNIER, Marcel-Lucien (1879-1951)

FÉERIE: Prelude & dance for harp & strings

	∅	str	L.Roulier,1920 & Leduc	23564

TOURS, Frank, E.

The DAIRYMAIDS: musical play by F.E.Tours & P.A.Rubens see under RUBENS, P.A.
The DASHING LITTLE DUKE: musical play

Selection, arr C.Godfrey jnr	PC	2212/2230.euph/timp.perc/str	A H & C	2436 B
Rose of the world: song in F	∅	1121/2220/timp.perc/str	(A H & C)	MS 4911

MOTHER O'MINE: song

in B♭, arr J.Turner	∅	1110/1000/hp/str	(Chappell)	LM G 9445

SEE-SEE: comic opera by F.Tours & S.Jones

Selection	PC	2(picc)222/4230.euph/timp.perc/str	Hawkes	2896 B
SWEET NELL: waltz arr M.Irwin	PC	112.3sx.1/2210/perc.2bjo/str	Chappell	6248

TOVEY, Donald Francis (1875-1940)

CONCERTO for piano & orch, op.15, in A
                φ   2222/4200/timp/str   30'   Schott,1906   Misc 1137
CONCERTO for cello & orch, op.60, in C, bowed and fingered by P.Casals
                φ   2(picc)222/4230/timp/str   55'-62'   OUP   Misc 1909
The SULTANS HYMN: former national anthem of Zanzibar
   arr M.L.Lake   PC 112.2sx.1/2210/perc/str   C.Fischer   19720

TOWERS, Leon

WHEN YOU LOVE: song
   in F min, arr F.Barber   φ   2222/4330/timp.perc/hp.pf/str   (Southern)   18491

TOYE, Francis (1883-1964)

The INN (tarantella): song
   in Eb, orch L.Wurmser   φ 31+ca.2+bcl.2/4231/timp.perc/cel.pf/str 4'05"   Composer   TO 1594

TOYE, Geoffrey (1889-1942)

The HAUNTED BALLROOM: ballet
   Waltz arr L.Lucas   φ hp/str   4'45"-6'   (P.Maurice)   8740
     arr Tapp   3222/4231/timp.perc/cel.hp/str   P.Maurice   12872 CpD
     arr G.Vinter   φ 2222/4230/timp.perc/hp/str   (P.Maurice)   22450 +
HENDRICKJE'S DEATH (from Rembrandt) for chorus & orch
                φ 2222/4331/timp.bells/hp/str   6'10"   Composer   TO 1111
The KEEPER   φ 0000/2231/chorus   2'30"   (Boosey)   TO 766
The RED PEN: radio opera (1927)   2122/2220/timp.perc/str   Composer MS:BBC   MS 3859

TRAETTA, Tommaso (1727-1779)(Michele Francesco Saverio)

ANTIGONE: opera (1772)
   rev A.Rocchi   φ 2222/3200/str/cont   Maggio Musicale Florentino,1962   Misc 5786
   Excerpts for solo voices, chorus & orch
     ed H.Goldschmidt   φ 0200/0000/str/cont(hpsd)   Breitkopf 1916 DTB 14/1   MRL
CARI SPOSI AMOR COSTANTE: aria
   in C   φ 0001/0000/str/cont(hpsd)   BBC   21209
Il FARNACE: opera
   Excerpts for solo voices & orch
     ed H.Goldschmidt   φ 0001/2000/str/cont(pf)   Breitkopf 1916 DTB 14/1   MRL
Le FESTE D'IMENEO: opera
   Excerpts for solo voices, chorus & orch
     ed H.Goldschmidt   φ 0200/2000/str/cont(hpsd)   Breitkopf 1916 DTB 14/1   MRL
IFIGENIA IN TAURIDE: opera (1763)
   Complete. Facsimile of contemporary MS I(Fc MS)
                φ 22(ca)02/2000/str/cont   Garland,1978   MRL facs
   Excerpts for solo voices, chorus & orch
     ed H.Goldschmidt   φ 2200/0000/str/cont(hpsd)   Breitkopf 1916 DTB 14/1   MRL
   Extracts
     Crude larve! for solo & chorus (Act II sc.4)
       in Eb ed L.Wurmser   φ 0200/2000/str/cont   [Editor]   19704
     Dormi Oreste; chorus in Eb (Act II sc.4)
       ed L.Wurmser   0200/2000/str/cont   [Editor]   19704 +
     Gli strali tremendi; soli & chorus in C min (Act II Sc.8)
       ed L.Wurmser   0200/0000/str/cont   3'15"   [Editor]   23433
     Nere figlie dell' Erebo; chorus in D (Act II sc.4)
       ed L.Wurmser   φ 0200/2000/str/cont   [Editor]   19704 +
     Oh, come presto a sera; soli & chorus (Act I sc.6)
       in A min ed L.Wurmser   φ 2200/0000/str   [Editor]   19703 & mf

TRAETTA, Tommaso (cont)

OMBRA CARA: in E min   ∮   str   (Ricordi)   20868
La SOFONISBA: opera
   Excerpts for solo voices & orch
      ed H.Goldschmidt   ∮   0202/2000/str/cont(hpsd)   Breitkopf 1916.DTB 14/1   MRL
   Extracts
      Mà, chimèi la mano, perchè mi trema?: aria
      Sofonisba, che aspetti?: recit (Act III sc.10)
         in A min, ed L.Wurmser   ∮   0202/2000/str/cont   4'10"   [Editor]   19704 mf 42
      Nume adorabile: chorus & orch, in C (Act II sc.4)
         ed L.Wurmser   ∮   0200/2000/str/cont   [Editor]   23435 +
      Sposa infelice a te farò ritorno: recit & aria in F (Act I sc.10)
         ed L.Wurmser   ∮   2202/2000/str/cont   10'40"   [Editor]   23435 +
STABAT MATER, for Soprano & contralto soli, chorus & strings
   ed R.A.Rocchi   ∮   str   35'   Ricordi,1965   Misc 6573
I TANTARIDI (1760): opera
   Excerpts for solo voices & orch
      ed H.Goldschmidt   ∮   0000/2000/str/cont(pf)   Breitkopf 1916.DTB 14/1   MRL
   Extracts
      Dove mi guide: Ombra cara: recit & cavatina in G min (Act II sc.3)
         ed L.Wurmser   ∮   0000/2000/str/cont   9'   [Editor]   23432 +

TRAJKOVIĆ, Vlastimir

DAY (Dan/Le Jour): 4 hymns   ∮   3(2picc)3(ca)3(bcl)2+cbsn/6341/timp.
                                          6perc(bells.mba.rattle.tamtam.vib.whip.xyl)/
                                          pf(cel.epf)/str(14.12.10.10.8)
                                          (4 cbs must be 5-stringed)   Yugoslav SM,1977   Misc 10207
DUO, for piano & orch, op.4   ∮   2+picc.2+ca.2+bcl.2+cbsn/4331/
                                          timp.perc.bells.glock.xyl/hp/str   Yugoslav SM,1973   Misc 8467

TRAMA, J.

COSSACK RIDE
   arr A.Roper   ∮   2(picc)120/2220/timp.perc.gong/
                                          pf/str   Toff   MLO 127

TRANCHELL, Peter (1922-

ZULEIKA: musical play
   Selection arr F.Rapley orch C.Mackerras
                                     PC   2(picc)12.3sx.1/2230/timp.perc/
                                          hp/str   5'30"   Chappell,1957   22303 B

TRANSLATEUR, S.

Ein BALLNACHTSTRAUM (A ball-night vision): waltz intermezzo
                                     PC   2222/3230/timp.perc/str   Musikverlag Lyra   15875
DREAM FLOWERS: waltz - intermezzo   PC   2121/2230/perc/str   Hawkes   9239
HOCHZEITSZUG, IN LILIPUT op.165   PC   2(picc)211/2230/timp.perc/str   Musikverlag Lyra   6660

TRAPP, Max (1887-1971)

CONCERTO for orchestra, op.32
                                     ∮   3222/4331/timp/str   30'   Leuckart   Misc 1632
DIVERTIMENTO op.27   ∮   1111/1111/timp/str   17'-20'   Eulenburg   Misc 939 B

TRAPP, Max (cont)

SYMPHONIES
No.4, op.24, in B♭ min	∅	3(2picc)2+ca.2+bcl.2+cbsn/4331/timp.perc/ str	29'	Eulenburg	Misc 978 B
No.5, op.33, in F	∅	322[E♭cl]2/4331/timp.perc/str		Leuckart	Misc 1001

TRAVERS, Alison

The COMPASS SUITE, arr Baynes
   1. North - the arctic zone
   2. South - the south Pacific
   3. East - the Chinese bazaar
   4. West - the prairie

MAY DAY SUITE, arr Baynes	PC	2(picc)122/2230/timp.perc/str	Boosey	4680

   1. A May morning
   2. Noon reverie
   3. Around the maypole

	PC	2(picc)122/2230/timp.perc/str	Boosey	4662

TRAVIS, Roy
CONCERTO for piano & orch (1969)	∅	2(picc)222(cbsn)/2210/ptimp/str	19'	OUP,1976	Misc 9922

TREDICI, David Del   see   DEL TREDICI, David

TREFORD, Michael
AGGIE THE DRESSER: song in C, arr J.Beaver	∅	2121/2220/perc/str	Composer	TO 461
TILL THE SEASON CLOSES: song in E♭, arr B.Berlin	∅	2121/2000/perc/hp/str	Composer	TO 555

TREHARNE, Bryceson
OLWEN: song in G, arr J.Burger	∅	1111/1000/timp/hp/str	(Snell & Sons)	MS 6937

TREIBMANN, Karl Ottomar
SYMPHONY for strings	∅	str(min.5.4.3.2.1)	15'	DVfM,1980	Misc 10442

TRELAWNY, Jack
IN GOD'S GOOD TIME: song in C, arr Austin	1111/2210/timp/str	Larway,1915	18272
WOMEN WHO STAY AT HOME: song in F, arr E.Austin	1111/2210/perc/str	Larway,1914	18277

TREMAIN, Ronald (1923-
ALLEGRO FOR STRINGS (1958)	∅	str	Wai-te-ata Press,1969	Misc 7215

TREMBLAY, A.L.
AIRMAIL: galop arr Baron	PC	0.picc.010/0210/perc/str	I.Berlin	10843

TRÉMISOT, Edouard

La DANSE DE PAMINA, op.47	PC	22(ca)22/4230/timp.perc/2hp/str		Enoch	17052
ICARE: symphonic poem	PC	2(picc)222/4231/hp/str		Salabert	10611
La MER: symphonic poem	PC	2122/4230/timp/hp.org/str		Salabert	10595
PYRAMÉ ET THISBÉ: overture	∅	3(picc)2+ca.2+bcl.2/4431/perc/2hp/str		Grus	12025

TRENET, Charles

BATEAU D'AMOUR: song					
in B min, arr B.Berlin	∅	1121/2000/perc/str		(Roaul)	TO 1164
BOUM: song					
in Eb, arr B.Berlin	∅	2121/2000/timp.perc/str		(K.Prowse)	TO 1118
PIGEON VOLE: song					
in Eb, arr B.Berlin	∅	2121/2220/timp.perc/hp/str		(Roaul)	TO 1163
POLKA DU ROI: song					
in Eb, arr B.Berlin	∅	2121/2000/perc/str		(K.Prowse)	TO 1188
in D, arr G.Stacey		1010/0000/perc/pf/str		(Breton)	LM A 92
Le SOLEIL ET LA LUNE: song					
in Eb, arr B.Berlin	∅			Arranger	TO 1223
THERE WAS A TIME: song					
in Bb, arr R.Frank	∅	0010/0000/gtr.pf/str		Leeds	LM G 8053

TRÉPARD, Émile

| L'ANGÉLUS: symphonic poem | ∅ | 3(picc)2.ca.23/4231/timp/2hp/str | | Grus | 8452 |

TREVALSA, Joan

| MY TREASURE: song | | | | | |
| in G, arr B.Thompson | ∅ | 1110/1000/hp/str | | (Boosey & H) | LMG 7530 |

TREW, Arthur

| BROTHER JAMES' AIR, arr | | [pf]/str/unison voices | | OUP | Misc 471 |
| The RANTERS HYMN (c.1649), arr | | [pf]/str | | OUP | 16668 |

TREW, C.A.

| CORNISH CARNIVAL | | | | | |
| arr R.Farnon | PC | 1+picc.121/2230/timp.perc.glock/hp/str | 2'05" | (K.Prowse) | 26149 + |

TRIENES, Hermann

| OTHELLO | | | | | |
| Overture | ∅ | 2222/4230/timp/str | | Oertel | Misc 887 |

TRIFUNOVIĆ, Vitomir (1916-

ANTINOMIA	∅	2020/0100/timp.perc.gong.3tomtom.vib.xyl/			
		str(8-16.8-16.6-12.6-12.4-8)		Yugoslav SM,1972	Misc 10209
ASOCIJACIJE	∅	3(picc)332/4330/timp.perc.bells.vib.xyl/			
		str[16.14.12.12.10])		Jugoslav SM	Misc 8908
IMPULSE I for double bass & orch	∅	2222/2220/timp.perc.gong.5tomtom.vib/str			
		(10-12.10-12.8-10.6-8.4-6)		Yugoslav SM,1975	Misc 10210
INTEGRALS (1976-7)	∅	str(6-12.6-12.4-10.2-10.2-10.2-8)		Yugoslav SM,1977	Misc 10211

TRIMBLE, Joan (1915-

MAQUIRE'S MARCH, arr   φ   1+picc.11/3130/timp.perc/str   Arranger   14266

TRINDALE, Ferrer

SONG OF THE SEA, arr A.Fones   PC   2121/2230/perc/gtr.hp/str   Chappell,1954   21419

TRINKHAUS, George, J.

FOUR WINDS: suite
    1. Erirus - An eastern dance
    2. Zephyr - A western episode
    3. Boreas - A northern idylle
    4. Sirocco - Southern serenade   1(picc)121/2210/perc/pf/str   Witmark   8121
ROMANCE OF THE ROSE   PC   112(2sx)1/2210/timp.perc/str   Witmark   667

TROIANI, Gaetano

2 PEZZI, for strings, transc B.Bandini
                               φ   str   5'   Ricordi,1938   Misc 2

TROJAN, Václav (1907-

HUMOROUS VARIATIONS (Rozmarné variace) on Mendelssohn's 'Spring Song' (1936, rev.1971)
                               φ   1+picc.12.sx.tsx.2/4231/timp.perc.bells.
                                   glock.gong.2tamtam/bjo.cel.1[=2]hp.pf/str/
                                   S-solo   34'   Czech SM,1977   Misc 9

TROST, Gustav

CASCADES, arr H.Mielenz   PC   2121/2230/timp.perc/acdn/str   L.Southern,1953 21662

TROTÈRE, Henry (1855-1912)(pseud of Henry Trotter)

ASTHORE: song
    in G min, arr J.Turner   φ   1110/1000/hp/str   (Cramer)   LM G 9
The DEATHLESS ARMY: song
    in A, arr E.Griffiths   pf/str   4'35"   (Boosey)   LM G 5
    in Bb   φPC 2222/2230.euph/perc/str   Boosey   5433 C
    in Bb   1+picc.222/2230.euph/perc/str   Boosey   10707
GO TO SEA: song
    in F, arr H.A.Carruthers   φ   2121/0220/perc/pf/str   (Boosey)   MS 204
I DID NOT KNOW: song
    in C   1111/2230/timp/str   (Leonard)   18502
    in Ab   1121/2230/timp/str   Leonard,1910   18300
    in Bb, arr G.Stacey   pf/str   (L G & B)   LM G 3
    in Bb, arr J.Turner   φ   1110/1000/hp/str   (L G & B)   LM G 9
IN OLD MADRID: song
    in C & Ab, orch.Bürger   φ   1111/1120/timp.perc/str   (Cramer)   MS 267
    in Ab, arr J.O.Turner   φ   1110/1000/hp/str   (Cramer)   LM G 7
    in Bb, arr Bürger   φ   2111/1120/timp/str   (Cramer)   MS 480
    arr Ascher (non-vocal)   1121/2210/timp/pf/str   Ascher   8014 A
IN YOUR DEAR EYES: duet for soprano & tenor
    in F arr J.Cockerill   φ   1110/0000/perc/hp.pf/str   (Cramer)   LM A 6

TROTÈRE, Henry (cont)

MY OLD SHAKO: song
   in C   PC 1+picc.122/2230/timp.perc/str   Boosey   5996 Bp
   in C & B♭, arr G.Stacey   pf/str   (Boosey)   LM G 3181
   in B♭   1122/2230/perc/str   (Boosey)   LM G 4515
   in B♭ orch Bürger   1111/1120/timp.perc/str   Boosey   MS 2672
RUM-TUM-TUM: polka   PC 1121/2230.euph/str   Chappell   6487
SONGS BY H.TROTÈRE arr J.Engleman PC 1121/2230/timp.perc/hp/str   11'30"   Cramer   14732

TRUNK, Richard (1879-1968)

Eine KLEINE SERENADE, op.55   ∅   str   15'   Leuckart   10943

TSIMBALIST, E.   see   ZIMBALIST, Efrem

TUBIN, Edvard (1905-

SYMPHONY no.5, in B min   ∅   32+ca.2+bcl.2+cbsn/4331/timp/str   Körlings Förlag   Misc 3041 B

TUCCI, Terig

EDELMA, orch W.Hill Bowen   PC 212.3sx.1/2230/perc/gtr.hp/str   Bosworth,1955   21456
LITTLE SERENADE: song in C   ∅   3121/1330/perc/gtr.hp.pf/str   (Macmelodies)   LM G 8348

TUCKER, William (d.1679)

EASTER ANTHEM: chant setting
   anonymous, orch   1121/20.2cnt.30/perc/str   Boosey & H   20417

TUCKEY, William (1708-1781)

'ERECT YOUR HEADS': psalm 24
   arr Goldman & Smith   VS 1121/2230/perc/str   Mercury Music   19040

TULL, Fisher (1934-

CONCERTINO for oboe & str (1970)   ∅   str   8'30"   Boosey& H,1979   Misc 9985

TUNBRIDGE, J. & WALLER, J.   see   WALLER, J.

TUNDER, Franz (1614-1667)

ACH HERR, LASS DEINE LIEBEN ENGELEIN: aria
   in C min arr G.Göhler   ∅   str/cont(hpsd.org)   Breitkopf   20453
DA MIHI DOMINE: for Bass solo & instruments
   ed M.Seiffert   ∅   str/cont   Breitkopf.1900 DDT3   MRL
DOMINUS ILLUMINATIO MEA for SSATB chorus & instruments
   ed M.Seiffert   ∅   2vln/cont(org)   Breitkopf & H.1900 DDT3   MRL
Eine FESTE BURG IST UNSER GOTT for SSTB voices & orch
   ed M.Seiffert   ∅   str/cont(org)   Breitkopf.1900 DDT3   MRL
   ed & arr N.Stone   ∅   str/cont(org)   Editor   20329
HELFT MIR GOTT'S GUTTE PREISEN for SSATB voices & orch
   ed M.Seiffert   ∅   str/cont(org)   Breitkopf.1900 DDT3   MRL
HERR, NUN LÄSSEST DU DEINEN DIENER for 2 Bass soli & instruments
                             ∅   str/cont(org)   Breitkopf.1900 DDT3   MRL

TUNDER, Franz (cont)

HOSIANNA DEM SOHNE DAVIDS: cantata for SSATB soli, chorus & orch
   ed W.Hinnenthal   ø   str/cont(org)   Bärenreiter   Misc 3226
   ed M.Seiffert for [=S][=S]ATB soli, chorus & orch
                       ø   000[1]/0000/str/cont(org)   Breitkopf.1900.DDT3   MRL
Ein KLEINES KINDELEIN: aria for Soprano solo & orch
   ed M.Seiffert   ø   str/cont(org)   Breitkopf.1900.DDT3   MRL
                       ø   str/cont(org)   Kistner & S   Misc 1602
NISI DOMINUS for SSBsoli & orch
   ed M.Seiffert   ø   str/cont(org)   Breitkopf.1900.DDT3   MRL
   ed M.Seiffert, for SSATBsoli, chorus & orch
                       ø   str/cont(org)   Breitkopf.1900.DDT3   MRL
O JESUS DULCISSIME for Bass solo & instruments
   ed M.Seiffert   ø   2vln/cont(org.vlne)   Breitkopf.1900.DDT3   MRL
SALVE MI JESU for Contralto solo & instruments
                       ø   str/cont(org)   Breitkopf.1900.DDT3   MRL
STREUET MIT PALMEN: aria for SSATB voices & orch
   ed M.Seiffert   ø   str/cont(org)   Breitkopf.1900.DDT3   MRL
WEND' AB DEINEN ZORN for SSATTB voices & orch
   ed M.Seiffert   ø   str/cont(org)   Breitkopf.1900.DDT3   MRL

TURCHI, Guido (1916-

Il BUNO SOLDATO SUEJK: opera
   Excerpts: music de geste see MUSIQUE DE GESTE
CINQUE COMMENTI ALLE 'BACCANTI DI EURIPIDE'
                       ø   2(picc)2+ca.2+bcl.2/4221/timp.perc/
                          vla.vlc.cb   20'   Boosey & H   Misc 3576
CONCERTO for orchestra (piccolo concerto notturno)
                       ø   2(picc)1+ca.1+bcl.2/2210/timp.perc.tamtam.
                          xyl/cel.hp/str   14'   Ricordi   Misc.4023
CONCERTO for strings   ø   str   22'30" De Santis,1950 Misc 3383
DEDALO: ballet
   1. Preambolo   4. Recitativo (Monologo)
   2. Variazioni   4a.Variazioni riepilogo (Danse pour Minosse)
   3. Labirinto (Dedalo II)   5. Epilogo (lied)
                       ø   2+picc.2+ca.2+bcl.2+cbsn/4331/timp.perc.
                          bells.glock/cel.hp.pf/str   Ricordi,1971   Misc 8407
MUSIQUE DE GESTE: rhapsody in 3 metamorphoses for orchestra (From the opera 'Il Buno soldato svejk')
                       ø   3(picc)2+ca.2+Ebcl+bcl.2+cbsn/4331/timp.perc.
                          bell.glock.tamtam.xyl/cel.hp/str   Ricordi,1970   Misc 8166

TURINA, Joaquin (1882-1949)

À LA MÉMOIRE D'UN BÉBÉ op.21, no.7 (from Ninerias: orig pf)
   arr S.Chapelier   PC 1+picc.121/2200/timp.perc/str   Rt Lerolle   9849 B
3 ARIAS, op.26 (orig voice & pf)
   1. Romance   2. El pescador   3. Rima
     arr F.Salabert   PC 1121/2230/timp.perc/hp/str   UMFE   9608
Les BUVEURS DE MANZANILLA op.47 no.4 (from Contes d'Espagna, 2nd series)
   arr S.Chapelier   ø   1121/2210/perc/str   2'   Rt Lerolle   1682
CHANSON MAURESQUE op.47 no.3 (from Contes d'Espagne, 2nd series (orig pf)
   arr S.Chapelier   PC 1111/1110/perc/str   1'45"   Rt Lerolle   2495
Le CHEMIN DE LA ALHAMBRA op.20 (from Contes d'Espagne, 1st series (orig pf)
   arr S.Chapelier   PC 1+picc.121/2230/timp.perc/str   Rt Lerolle   6881

TURINA, Joaquin (cont)

COINS DE SÉVILLE op.5
  1. Rondes d'enfants
  2. Soir d'été sur la terrasse
  3. Danse de 'Seises' dans la cathédrale
  4. À los toros
      arr S.Chapelier   PC 1+picc.121/2230/timp.perc/str   Eschig   11843

CORDOUE EN FÊTE op.47 no.1 (Contes d'Espagne, 2nd series, orig pf)
      arr S.Chapelier   PC 1121/2210/timp.perc/str   2'15"   Rt.Lerolle   7183

CUENTOS DE ESPAGNA (orig pf)   see   Les BUVEURS DE MANZANILLA
                                          CHANSON MAURESQUE
                                          CORDOUE EN FÊTE
                                          MIRAMAR

DANSE CASTILLANE 'Baile Castizo'(from Verbena Madrilena, orig pf)
      arr S.Chapelier   φ 1121/2230/timp.perc/str   4'   Rt Lerolle   20172

DANSE DES POUPÉES op.21 no.5 (from Ninerias: series 1, orig pf)
      arr S.Chapelier   φPC 1+picc.121/2230/timp.perc/str   4'   Rt.Lerolle   5687 B

DANS LES JARDINS DE MURCIA op.20 (from Contes d'Espagne, 1st series, orig pf)
      arr S.Chapelier   PC 1+picc.121/2200/timp.perc/str   Rt.Lerolle   3883 B

DANZAS FANTASTICAS, op.22
  1. Exaltacion   2. Ensueno   3. Orgia
                        φ   3(picc)2+ca.2+bcl.2+cbsn/4331/timp.perc.
                            hp/str   13'   UMFE   5268
      arr F.Salabert   φ   2(picc)1(ca)21/2230/timp.perc/hp/str   UMFE   13580

DÉFILE DES SOLDATS DE PLOMB
      arr S.Chapelier   PC 2(picc)121/2230/timp.perc/str   Rt Lerolle   5690

FARRUCA: in D   φ   2222/2200/timp.perc/str   BBC   19731
                              0120/0000/str   BBC   19731

HABANERA, arr S.Chapelier   PC 1121/2200/timp.perc/str   3'   Rt Lerolle   13456

JEUX op.21 no.8 (from Ninerias, series 1)
      arr S.Chapelier   PC 1+picc.121/2230/timp.perc/str   Rt.Lerolle   5688 B

MIRAMAR, op.20 (from contes d'Espagne, series 1)
      arr S.Chapelier   PC 2(picc)121/2230/timp.perc/str   Rt.Lerolle   6262 B

NINERIAS: suite for piano   see   À LA MEMOIRE D'UN BÉBÉ: DANSE DES POUPÉES

NUIT SUR LA BAIE DE PALMA op.44 no.2 (from Mallorca: suite)
      arr S.Chapelier   PC 1111/1110/timp.perc/str   3'   Rt.Lerolle   14713
      arr S.Chapelier   φ   1111/1110/timp.perc/str   Rt.Lerolle   20171

El PESCADOR: aria   see   3 ARIAS

La PROCESSION DU ROCIO: suite op.9
  1. Friana en fête
  2. La procession
                        φ   2+picc.2+ca.2+bcl.2+cbsn/4331/timp.perc/
                        hp/str   Rt Lerolle   7767 B

RAPSODIA SINFONICA for piano & orch
                        φ   str   8'15"-9'   (UME)   11297 B

RIMA: aria   see   3 ARIAS
ROMANCE: aria   see   3 ARIAS

SEVILLA: suite pittoresque (orig pf)
  1. Sous les orangers
  2. Le Jeudi Saint à minuit
  3. La Feria
      arr S.Chapelier   1+picc.121/2230/timp.perc/str   Eschig   11840

SINFONIA SEVILLANA op.23   φ   3(picc)2+ca.2+bcl.2+cbsn/4331/timp.perc.glock/
                              cel.hp/str   UME   7395 Bwa

SUR LA GIRALDA arr S.Chapelier   PC 1121/2200/timp.perc/str   Rt Lerolle   14707

TURLET, A. arr

Le REGIMENT DE SAMBRE ET MEUSE: march (on Planquette's song)
ϕ   2+picc.222/4231/perc/hp/str   4'   Joubert   2961 C

TURNER, G.

FANFARE, CHORALE & FINALE: brass inst
ϕ   0000/4331   9'   Arrow Music,1946   Misc 2
GREGORIAN OVERTURE: double str orch
ϕ   str   (American Music Centre)   Misc 2

TURNER, James, O.(1905-

THE AULD HOUSE: song, arr
    in G♭   ϕ   1120/1000/hp/str   (Arranger)   LM G 1
THE BEE PROFFERS HONEY: song, arr
    in A   ϕ   1120/1000/hp/str   (Arranger)   LM G 1
BLACKBIRDS AND THRUSHES: song, arr
    in G   ϕ   1120/1000/hp/str   (Arranger)   LM G 1
A BRISK YOUNG SAILOR: song
    in A♭   ϕ   112(bcl)0/1000/hp/str   (Arranger)   LM G 1
THE BRISK YOUNG WIDOW: song, arr J.O.Turner & C.J.Sharp
    in C   ϕ   1120/1000/hp/str   (Arrangers)   LM G 1
COLD BLOWS THE WIND, for solo, SSAA chorus & orch, arr
    in F min   ϕ   112(bcl)0/1000/hp/str   (Arranger)   LM G 1
COME MY OWN: song
    in A   ϕ   1120/1000/hp/str   (Arranger)   LM G 1
COUNTRYWISE   ϕPC 2121/1000/perc/hp/str   (Mozart Ed)   LM G 1
THE COVENTRY CAROL, arr
    in G min   ϕ   1120/1000/cel.hp/str   (Arranger)   LM G 1
THE CRYSTAL SPRING: song, arr
    in E   ϕ   1120/1000/hp/str   (Arranger)   LM G 1
DABBLING IN THE DEW: song, arr
    in E min   ϕ   1120/1000/hp/str   (Arranger)   LM G 1
THE ENGLISH WAY: song
    in E♭, arr G.Daines ϕ   1110/0000/hp.pf/str   (Unit)   LM G
THE FAIRY SWEETHEART: song, arr
    in F   ϕ   1120/1000/hp/str   (Arranger)   LM G
FALSE LOVE: song
    in G   ϕ   112(bcl)0/1000/hp/str   (Arranger)   LM G
THE FOGGY FOGGY DEW: song, arr
    in G
                 ϕ   1120/1000/hp/str   (Arranger)   LM G
HOW SWEET I ROAMED: song in F ϕ   1110/1000/hp/str   Boosey   LM G
JOHN ANDERSON, MY JO: song, arr
    in F min   ϕ   112(bcl)0/1000/hp/str   (Arranger)   LM G
THE KEYS OF HEAVEN: Cheshire folksong, arr
    in A   ϕ   1110/1000/hp/str   (Cramer)   LM G
THE LITTLE TURTLE DOVE: song
    in A min   ϕ   112(bcl)0/1000/hp/str   (Arranger)   LM G
MELODIES AND MEMORIES: SATB
    in D   ϕ   1110/1000/hp/str   BBC   21535
    in D (introduction only) ϕ   1110/1000/hp/str   BBC   22027
MILKING SONG: Hebridean song, arr from M.Kennedy Frazer
    in F   ϕ   112(bcl)0/1000/hp/str   (Boosey)   LM G
MOLLY BAWN: song, arr
    in D   ϕ   1120/1000/hp/str   (Arranger)   LM G

TURNER, James, O. (cont)

SANDGATE LASS'S LAMENT: song, arr				
in D	φ	1(picc)120/1000/hp/str	(Arranger)	LM G 10935
THE SEEDS OF LOVE: song, arr				
in F	φ	1120/1000/hp/str	(Arranger)	LM G 10935
SERENADE FOR SUSAN		[1][1][1]0/0000/hp[=pf]/str	S & Bell	9484
THE SILENT MUSIC				
arr Cardew (used in programme 'Friday night is music night'				
	φ	2222/4330/timp.perc/hp.pf/str	Boosey & H	23195
THE SPRING OF THYME: song, arr				
in G	φ	112(bcl)0/1000/hp/str	(Arranger)	LM G 10935
TARRY TROUSERS: song				
in E min	φ	1120/1000/hp/str	(Arranger)	LM G 10981
THE TREES THEY DO GROW HIGH: song, arr				
in G min	φ	112(bcl)0/1000/hp/str	(Arranger)	LM G 10935
WON'T YOU BUY MY PRETTY FLOWERS for SSAA soli and orch				
in G	φ	1120/1000/hp/str	(Arranger)	LM G 10935

TURNER, Olive

ARUNDEL SUITE
1. The old town   3'00"
2. Where the Arun flows   3'15"
3. The castle   3'00"
  orch H.J.Stafford   PC   1(picc)12.3sx.1/2320/timp.perc/str   L.Southern   16403

TURNER, Robert

OPENING NIGHT: theatre overture   φ   2+picc.222/4331/timp.perc/str   9'   BMI,Canada,1960   Misc 5433 B

TURNER, William (1651-1740)

I WILL ALWAYS GIVE THANKS (The Club Anthem by John Blow, Pelham Humfrey & William Turner) for ATB soli,
  SATB chorus   φ   str   Stainer & B,1972: Mus Brit 34   25633 & MRL
PRESERVE ME, O GOD: verse anthem for AATBB soli, chorus & orch
  ed B.Wood   φ   str/cont(org)   (Editor,1978)   26647

TURNER, William [18th C]

BEAUTY MORE POWERFUL THAN WAR: song
  in Ab, arr F.Collinson   φ   1121/2220/timp.perc/hp/str   Arranger   MS 30917
EPISTLE DEDICATORY (To the subscribers)
  in G# min arr F.Collinson   φ   0022/2200/perc/str   Arranger   MS 30924

TURSKI, Zbigniew (1908-

CONCERTO for violin & orch (1951)   φ   2(2picc)2(ca)22/2220/timp.perc.bells.xyl/
                        cel.hp/str   31'   Polish SM 1958   Misc 7346
PETITE OVERTURE (Mała uwertura)(1955)
                φ   2+picc.2+ca.22+cbsn/4331/timp.perc/str   4'10"   Polish SM,1959   Misc 7345

TWINN, Sydney

GOSSIP JOAN   φ   str   Mills,1955   23159

TYRWHITT-WILSON, Gerald   see   BERNERS, Lord

UCCELLINI, Marco (ca 1603-1680)

GRAN BATTAGLIA, La (Sinfonia)   2vlns & vlc   BBC   MS 30125

UGOLINI, Giovanni

CONCERTO PER ARCHI (1957)   ∅   str   13'   Curci,1961   Misc 8284

UHL, Alfred (1909-

4 CAPRICEN
    1. Musikanten   3. Gaukler
    2. Fahrende Sänger   4. Komödianten
                           ∅   2(picc)2(ca)2(E♭sx)bcl.2/4331/timp.perc
                               glock.xyl/hp.[org]/str   28'   Universal   Misc 3067
INTRODUCTION AND VARIATIONS on a 16th century melody "Es geht eine dunkle Wolk' herein"
                           ∅   str   15'   Universal   Misc 3066
SINFONIA CONCERTANTE for clarinet & orch (1943)
                           ∅   2(2picc)2(ca)2(bcl)2/4321/timp/str   Universal,1971 Misc 10000

UHL, Martin

MUTED STRINGS   PC 1120/2000/str   Dix   11
ÖSTERREICHISCHE MARSCHPERLEN   see   BERNHAUER, Anton

ULDALL, Hans

MUSIC FOR BRASS AND PERCUSSION
    1. Hanseatische Turmmusik
    2. Tanzstück
    3. Kriegsmarsch   ∅   0000/22.2flg.2thn.21/perc   14'   Leuckart   Misc 1672

ULIERTE, Enrique de

SUITE ESPAGNOLA
    1. Fandango (1'45")   3. Malaguena (2'30")
    2. Granadina (1'45")   4. Zapateado (2')
       orch C.Watters   PC 2121/2230/timp.perc/hp/str   Hawkes 1953   21086 B

ULNER, Georges

PIGALLE for voice, chorus & orch
    in E♭, arr R.Green   ∅   2122/2330/timp.perc/hp.pf(cel)/str   (C.Connelly) 24797

UMLAUF, Ignaz (1746-1796)

Die BERGKNAPPEN: Singspiel
    ed R.Haas   ∅   0202/2000/str   Artaria,1911,DTO 36 MRL

ÜNGER, Joseph B.

WE WILL LIVE AGAIN: song
    in F, arr S.Robinson for chorus & orch
                           ∅   3222/4231/timp.perc/hp/str   1'30"   BBC   TO 1601

ÜNGÖR, Osman Zeki

KORKMA,SÖNMEZ BU SAFAK Istiklâl Mars (The March of Independence): National anthem of Turkey (adopted 1921)

	PC	2(picc)222/4230/timp.perc/str	Breitkopf	14305
arr G.French	φ	2222/2230/timp.perc/str	Arranger/Blandford	25209 +

URAY, Ernst Ludwig (1906-

CONCERTO GROSSO (1968)   φ   str   17'   Doblinger,1969   Misc 7219
SLAWISCHE IMPRESSIONEN: symphonic sketches
  1. Festlicher Tanz (1'30") 5. Bohmische Volksweise (1'20")
  2. Am grossen Strom (3')   6. Kosakentanz (2')
  3. Furiant (1'40")   7. Legende (3')
  4. Hochzeitsreigen (2')   8. Trepak (1'30")
    arr M.Schönherr   φ 2(picc)222/4330/timp.perc/hp/str   J.Kliment   15260

URBACH, Ernst

SELECTIONS from the works of various composers:

ADAM: "In Adams Paradies"	PC	1+picc.222/4230/perc/str		Wrede	13257
AUBER: "Aubers Marionetten"	PC	2(picc)222/4230/perc/str		Wrede	12498
BACH, J.S.: "Der fromme Bach"	PC	2222/4230/timp.perc/str		Wrede	9398
BELLINI: "Opernball bei Bellini"	PC	2(picc)222/4230/timp.perc/str		Wrede	5992
BIZET: "Bizets Wünderklänge"	PC	2(picc)222/4230/timp.perc/str	15'30"-17'	Wrede	7101
DELIBES: "Ein Plauderstündchen mit Delibes"					
	PC	2(picc)222/4230/timp.perc/str	13'	Wrede	12258
DONIZETTI: "Donizettis Triumphzug"					
	PC	2(picc)222/4230/timp.perc/str		Wrede	9018
GLINKA: "Glinka Juwelen"	PC	2(picc)222/4230/timp.perc/str		Wrede	9452
GODARD, B.: "Ein Godard Zyklus"	PC	2(picc)222/4230/timp.perc/str	16'	Wrede	9519
GOUNOD: "Im Sonnenwagen Gounods"					
	PC	2(picc)222/4230/timp.perc/str		Wrede	9409 B
HALÉVY: "Durch Halévys Operngucker"					
	PC	2222/4230/timp.perc/str		Wrede	13261
HANDEL: "Handels Reichtum"	PC	2222/4230/timp/str		Wrede	9864
HAYDN: "Haydns Himmelsgrusse"	PC	2222/2210/perc/str		Wrede	4613
LISZT: "Ein Soiree bei Liszt"					
	PC	2222/4230/timp.perc/str	15'	Wrede	6835
LORTZING: "Lortzings Lieblingskinder					
	PC	2(picc)222/4230/perc/str		Wrede	13271
MARSCHNER: "Aus Marschners Truhe"					
	PC	2222/4230/perc/str		Wrede	9839
Ein MELODIENTRAUM	PC	2222/4230/str		Wrede	7340
MENDELSSOHN: "Im Rosengarten Mendelssohns"					
	PC	2(picc)222/4230/timp/str		Wrede	9489
MEYERBEER: "Also sprach Meyerbeer"					
	PC	2(picc)222/4230/perc/str		Wrede	13260
MOZART: "In Mozarts Reich"	PC	2222/2210/perc/str	17'	Wrede	6233 B
MUSIKALISCHE SEIFENBLÄSEN		2(picc)222/4220/str		Wrede	12187
NOTENREGEN	PC	1(picc)222/4000/str		Wrede	13270 **
OFFENBACH: "Aus Offenbachs Musterkoffer"					
	PC	2222/2000/perc/str		Wrede	12533
PER ASPERA AD ASTRA: march					
arr Salabert	PC	2222/4230/perc/str		Salabert	5638
ROSSINI: "Am Hofe Rossinis"	PC	2222/4230/timp.perc/str	7'45"-10'	Wrede	7497
RUBINSTEIN: "Rubinstein Poesie"					
	PC	1222/4230/timp.perc/str		Wrede	9549

URBACH, Ernst (cont)

SELECTIONS (cont)
  SCHUBERT: "Aus Schuberts Skizzenbuch"

	PC	2222/4230/timp.perc/str		Wrede	9342

  SCHUMANN: "Frühlingstau auf Schumanns Grab"

	PC	2(picc)222/4230/perc/str		Wrede	9470
SMETANA: "Smetanas Vermachtnis"	PC	2222/4230/timp.perc/str		Wrede	9425
SUPPÉ: "Im Zeichen Suppés"	PC	2(picc)222/4230/timp.perc/str		Wrede	2029
THOMAS: "Mignon Erinnerungen"	PC	2(picc)222/4230/timp.perc/str		Wrede	9648 B

  WAGNER: "Der Nibelungen Flammenzeichen"

	PC	2(2picc)222/4220/perc/str		Wrede	13272
WAGNER: "Wagners Heldenbuch"	PC	2222/4230/timp.perc/str	20'	Wrede	7100
WEBER: "Durch Webers Zauberwald"	PC	2222/4230/timp.perc/str	17'15"	Wrede	9412

URBANCIC, Victor (1903-

OUVERTURE ZU EINE KOMODIE (1952)	∅	3(picc)222/3301/timp.perc/str		Doblinger,1971	Misc 7549

URBANNER, Erich (1936-

CONCERTINO for flute (1958)	∅	0000/2000/timp.perc.bells/cel.hp.pf/str	12'	Doblinger,1971	Misc 7696

CONCERTI

Double-bass & orch (1973)	∅	2(picc)11+bcl.1/1011+ct.tuba/timp.3perc(bells. glock.mbn.vib)/6vln	22'	Doblinger,1975	Misc 8675
Oboe & chamber orch (1966)	∅	010+bcl.1+cbsn/1110/timp.perc.glock.vib.xyl/ cel.cemb/hp/str(no vlas)	12'	Doblinger,1970	Misc 7223
Violin & orch (1971)	∅	3(picc)2+ca.2+bcl.3/3000/2vla.2vlc.2cb	20'	Doblinger,1976	Misc 8928

  'Wolfgang Amadeus' for 3 trombones, celeste & double orch (1972)

	∅	orch I: 1202/2200/2[=3timp]/str(6.5.4.3.2)			
	∅	orch II:102.2bthn.1/2000/str(6.5.4.3.2)		Doblinger,1974	Misc 8352 B

RETROSPEKTIVEN 1974/75: 4 pieces (rev.1979)

	∅	4(picc.afl)4(ca.ob-d'a)3+bcl.3+cbsn/43+Cbtpt.31/ timp.4perc(bells.3bgo.glock.mba.tamtam.3tomtom. vib.xba)/cel.hp.2pf/str	18'	Doblinger,1979	Misc 10005
RONDEAU (1967)	∅	3(picc)2+ca.2+bcl.2+cbsn/4331/timp.perc.bells glock.mba.xyl/cel.hp.pf/str		Doblinger,1970	Misc 7224

URIO, Francesco Antonio (17th-18th cent)

TE DEUM (c.1700)
  Complete

ed F.Chrysander	∅	0200/2000/org/str		Denkmäler(Weissenborn)	Misc 2781

  Laudamus, laudamus (1st chorus)only for SSATB voices & orch

	∅	0200/0200/str/cont		GHS	25447 +

USHER, Julia

The BRIDGE	∅	2(picc)222/4311/timp.perc.bells.crot.glock. tamtam.vib.xyl/str		Primavera,1980	Misc 10180

DE REVOLUTIONIBUS (1975)
  1. Geocentric   2. Chaos   3. Heliocentric

	∅	2(picc)22(E♭cl[])2/3210/timp.perc.bells[crot].glock. gong.mtl.xyl/lute/str		Primavera,1980	Misc 10232
GORDALE SCAR	∅	3(picc)232/2221/timp.perc.glock.vib/str		Primavera,1980	Misc 10233

2 IMAGES
  1. Peace-offering   2. An Ocean of light

	∅	[hp]/str		Primavera,1980	Misc 10179

USIGLIO, Emilio (1841-1910)

Le DONNE CURIOSE: opera (after Goldoni)
  Overture   PC   1121/2110/timp.perc/str   Sonzogno   12062

VACCAI, Nicola (1790-1848)

GIULETTA E ROMEO: opera
   Ah, se tu dormi (Ah, if thou sleepest): aria
      È questo il loco:recit
         in Eb   2022/2000/hp/str   (Siddell)   17904
     Se Romeo: aria
         in G   1021/2200/timp/str   (Siddell)   17905

VACEK, Karel

CAFÉ IN VIENNA: tango   PC 112.3sx.1/2210/perc/2acdn.bjo/str   Feldman   7958

VAČKÁŘ, Dalibor (1906-

PRÉLUDE ET MÉTAMORPHOSES   ø 3(picc)2+ca.2+bcl.2+cbsn/4331/timp.perc.
                             glock.tamtam/cel.hp/str   Czech SM,1958   Misc 8186
SYMFONIETTA (1947)   ø 0000/1000/timp/pf/str   Czech SM,1961   Misc 8187

VÁGVÖLGYI, Béla

LILIAN: musical play
   Ballet music   ø 1+picc.222/4230/timp.perc.bells/cel.hp/str   Pressler   Misc 1201
   Sousi march   ø 2222/3230/timp.perc/str   Pressler   Misc 1200

VALCARCEL, Teodoro (1900-1942)

SURAY SURITA: Peruvian suite
   1. Los Balseros
   2. El cortejo nupcial
   3. La puna Nevada
   4. Danza del combate
     arr & orch L.Holzmann   ø 2+picc.2+ca.22/4331/timp.perc/cel.hp/str   Arranger   19475

VALDEZ, Charles Robert

SÉRÉNADE DE TSIGANE   PC 1121/2210/timp.perc/str   C.Fischer   11076

VÁLEK, Jiří (1923-

SYMPHONY No.7 (Frescoes of Pompeii)(1968-70)
                         ø 2+picc.222/2200/timp.ptimp.perc.clv.glock.8gong.
                            mrc.2tomtom.vib.xyl/cel.pf(hpsd)/str(12.8.6.4.4)
                                         17'   Czech SM,1973   Misc 10389
SYMPHONY No.9 (Revolutionary)(1974)
                         ø 1(picc)111/3331/6perc(timp.bells.glock.
                           gong.rattle.vib.xyl)/cel/str(14.12.12.8.6)
                         Solo group 1: vln.vla.pf
                         Solo group 2: 1111/1000   20'   Czech SM,1975   Misc 10388

VALEN, Fartein (1887-1952)

CANTICO DI RINGRAZIAMENTO, for orch, op,17. no.2
                         ø 2222/2210/perc/str   7'   Lyche,1959   Misc 6893
Le CIMETIÈRE MARIN, op.20   ø 2222/2230/timp/str   8'30"-10'   Lyche,1951   Misc 4025 C
CONCERTI
   Piano & orch, op.44   ø 1111/1000/str   12'   Lyche,1953   Misc 6892
     Violin & orch, op.37
       ed. Fjeldstad   ø 1122/2100/timp/str   12'   Lyche,1948   Misc 4566

VALEN, Fartein (cont)

La ISLA DE LAS CALMAS, op.21	φ	2222/1000/str	5'30"	Lyche	Misc 990 B
PASTORALE, op.11	φ	2222/1000/timp/str	3'	Norsk	Misc 379 C
SONETTO DI MICHELANGELO, op.17 no.1					
	φ	2222/1000/str	5'	Norsk	18877
SYMPHONY no.3, op.41	φ	2222/3110/timp/str	20'	Lyche,1949	Misc 4290
TO HOPE, op.18 no.2	φ	2222/1100/hp/str		Norsk	18876

VALENTE, Nicola

TORNA A SORRENTO: film
  Torna: song

in Db, orch F.Rapley	φ	2222/4230/timp.perc/hp/str	(Bixio,1955)	21623 +
in B,arr R.Tilsley	φ	1110/1000/perc/gtr.hp.pf/str	(Boosey)	LM G 6874

VALENTIN, A.

The COCKNEY BAND	PC 1+picc.222/2230.euph/perc/str	Hawkes	3660

VALENTINI, Giuseppe (1681-1740)

CONCERTO for oboe, violin, strings & continuo

rev R.Fasano	φ	str/cont(hpsd)	10'	Ricordi,1959	Misc 5132

SYMPHONIES
  Christmas Symphony (Per il Santissimo Natale/Weihnachts-Symphonie),op.1, no.12

ed F.Schroeder	φ	str/cont	15'	Vieweg,1961	23522

VALÉRE, Paul

QUAND JE M'ENFUIS EN RÊVE (Had I the moon)

arr M.Saunders	φ	str		Ricordi	2693

VALLINI, Mario

ECHI TOSCANI RAPSODIA SU TEMI POPULARI: selection, arr (op.45)   8'-9'15"

φ 2+picc.121/2210/timp.perc/cel/str		Ricordi	11807
PC 0.picc.121/2210/timp.perc/str		Ricordi	4337
FIOR D'APRILE (Serenata) op.56 φ 1111/2100/timp/tri/str	3'45"	Ricordi	13472

SUITE ITALIANA
  1. Venezia (Gondoliera)   2. Firenze (la Festa del Grillo): scherzo

φ 1121/2210/timp.perc/cel/str		Ricordi	16334 φ to no.1 only

VALLS, Francisco (1665-1747)

MASS "Scala Aretina", for 3 choruses & orch (1702)
  Kyrie only

transcr & real J.Lopez-Calo φ 0200/0300/hp.org/str (no vla)	Tesoro Sacro musical 4-1971	BRL

VALLS, Josep (1904-

CONCERTO for solo string quartet and orchestra

φ 2222/2210/timp/str	22'15"	Senart	Misc 1935

VALVERDE, Joaquín (1846-1910)

CADIZ: operetta by J.Balverde & F.Chueca
  Selections,arr Serrallonga   φ 21+ca.22/4231/timp.perc/cel.hp/str

	(Chester)	TO 1261

VALVERDE, Joaquín (cont)

Las GOLONDRINAS (The Swallows) by J.Valverde & F.Chueca
	PC	1+picc.222/2230/timp.perc/str	9'	Lafleur	9647

La GRAN VIA: operetta by J.Valverde & F.Chueca
Selection, arr H.Finck	φ	2(picc)222/4230.euph/timp.perc/str	9'	Hawkes	171

Extracts
Cadiz march	PC	1(picc)222/2230/timp.perc/str		Hawkes	2871

The LAND OF JOY
Selection, arr Min t	PC	1121/2210/perc/str		G.Schirmer	5833

TOLEDANA: danse espagnole
arr Billaut	PC	1221/2230/perc/str		G.Lorette	7919

VAN DELDEN, Lex   see   DELDEN, Lex van

VANE, Lee

GOOD LUCK LANE: song
in E♭	1121/2230/timp/str		(Siddell)	18302

VANGARDE, Daniel

DANCING IN THE SUN (Un raye de sol)
arr P.Hope	φ	2121/2330/perc[glock]/cel[=pf].gtr.hp/str	Ardmore & Beechwood	26607

VAŇHAL, Jan Křtitel (Johann Baptist) (1739-1813)

CONCERTI
  Double bass & orch
    in E♭ (orig D)
ed R.Malaric	φ	0200/2000/str/cont		Doblinger,1971	26416

  Organ & Orch
    in F
ed F.Haselbock	φ	str		Doblinger,1973	CM 55199

  Viola & orch
    in F
ed A.Weinmann	φ	0000/2000/str/cont		Doblinger,1978	26470

DIVERTIMENTO for strings (originally Divertimento for orch, arr V.Tausky)
arr V.Tausky	φ	str	14'	OUP,1960	24978

SYMPHONIES
in C	φ	2000/2000/str		Bernoulli	Misc 1378
in D		0202/2000/str		(D-brd DO)	22874 + negs only
in D min		0200/2000/str		(D-brd DO)	22875 + negs only
ed C.Bennett	φ	2200/4000/str		(D-brd DO/A-R Edns)	26945 +
in E min		0200/2000/str		(D-brd DO)	22873 + negs only
in F (c.1771)					
ed P.Bryan	φ	220[1]/2000/str		Doblinger,1978	26519
in G min	φ	0200/4000/str		(A-KR)	21781 + mf 69
ed W.Hofmann	φ	0200/2000/str		Litolff/Peters,1966	25660
ed H.C.Robbins Landon	φ	0201/4000/str		Doblinger,1965	24562
in A min					
ed F.Kneusslin	φ	2[=2ob]000/0000/str		Hug,1947	25568 Awe
in A♭		0200/2000/str		(D-brd DO)	22876 + negs only
in B♭ (Periodical Overture: Symphony à B)					
	φ	0200/2000/str/cont		(US-NYp,1934)	27023 +

in B♭ attrib F.J.Haydn   see   HAYDN, F.J.   SYMPHONIES - Spurious & doubtful, in B♭ Hl:Bll

TE DEUM LAUDAMUS for SATB voices & orch
ed M.P.Eckhardt	φ	0000/2000/str/cont(org)	Doblinger/Ed Musica,1970	25468

VANIS, Charles

NELSON'S CALL: march   PC   2+picc.222/4231/timp.perc/str   Hawkes   2135 B

VARÈSE, Edgar (1885-1965)

AMÉRIQUES (1921)
  rev & ed C.Wen-Chung   ∅   2+2picc+afl.3+ca.heck.3+Ebcl+bcl.3+2cbsn/
                                         864+cbtbn.1.cbtuba/2timp.9perc(bells.sbells.cym.
                                         scym.2bdm.sdm.cast.glock.gong.lion's roar.rattle.
                                         siren.tamb.whip.xyl)/2hp/str   23'   Colfranc,1973   Misc 8164
ARCANA   ∅   2+3picc.3+ca.heck.2+2Ebcl+cbcl.3+2cbsn/
                                         853+cbtbn.1+cbtuba/timp.perc.bells.glock.
                                         tamtam.xyl/str   16'   Franco Colombo,1964 Misc 6531 C
DÉSERTS   ∅   2(picc)02(Ebcl,bcl)0/2231+cbtuba/timp.perc/
                                         pf/2 magnetic tapes   23'30-26'30"   Ricordi,1959   Misc 5133 C
ECUATORIAL   ∅   0000/0440/timp.perc.tamtam/2om.org.pf   Ricordi,1961   Misc 5848 E
HYPERPRISM for wind instruments and percussion
                                    ∅   1(picc)010/3230/perc.tamtam.siren   F.Colomba,1961/Ricordi Misc 941 B
INTÉGRALES for small orchestra and percussion
                                    ∅   0.2picc.11+Ebcl.0/122+cbtbn.0/perc.tamtam 9'50"-11'   Ricordi   Misc 1228 + E
IONISATION for two groups of percussion instruments
                                         percussion ensemble for 13 players   New Music Orch Series(Ricordi) Misc 1667 C
NOCTURNAL for solo soprano, mv chorus (basses) & orch (1961)
  ed & completed C.Wen-Chung   ∅   1(picc)+picc.11+Ebcl.1/11+Dtpt.2+cbtbn[=btbn]0/
                                         6 perc(timp.sbells.bgos.cym.scym.sdms.tdm.bdm.
                                         cencerros.claves.flex.gro.gongs.mrc.metal sheet.
                                         ratchets.tplbl)/pf/str   Colfranc,1973   Misc 8020
OFFRANDES (Offerings) for Soprano and chamber orchestra
    1. Chanson de là-haut   4'
    2. La croix du sud   4'
                                    ∅   1+picc.111/1110/perc/hp/str   7'50"   Ricordi,1960   Misc 5332 B

VARLAMOV, Aleksandr Igorevich (1801-1848)

The RED SARAFAN: ballad
  arr J.Fitz-Gerald   PC   2222/2230/timp.perc/str   Hawkes   1839

VARNEY, Louis (1844-1908)

La FÉE AUX CHÈVRES: operetta
  Suite, arr Gauwin
      1. Farandole de la vendange
      2. Ronde de nuit
      3. L'orage
      4. Le rêve d'Yvette: valse
                                    PC   2(picc)122/2230/timp/str   Joubert   627
Les MOUSQUETAIRES AU COUVENT: operetta
  Selection, arr E.Tavan   PC   1121/2230/perc/str   Margueritat 16277

VARNEY, Pierre (1811-1879)

MOURIR POUR LA PATRIE: Choeur des Girondins: French national song
  arr M.L.Lake   PC   112.2sx.1/2210/perc/str   C.Fischer   19720
                                   PC   2(picc)222/4231/timp.perc/str   Benjamin   16363 +

VAŠATA, Rudolf Leo

ANNABELLA: serenata
  arr B.Leopold   PC 112.2sx.1/2210/timp.perc/hp/str   Bosworth   18680

VASILENKO, Sergei Nikiforovich (1872-1956)

Les BOHÉMIENS   see   The GYPSIES
CHINESE SUITE, no.1, op.60
   1. Procession to the temple of Ancestors
   2. A spring evening
   3. Funeral
   4. Merry dance
   5. Lament of the Princess
   6. Echo and the golden lakes; Chinese market
                             ∅ 3(picc)2+ca.22/4331/timp.perc/cel.hp.pf/str   Universal   15208
EPIC POEM, op.4   ∅ 3(picc)232+cbsn/4331/timp.perc/hp/str   15'   Jurgenson   9633
The GARDEN OF DEATH: symphonic poem op.12
                             ∅ 3(picc)2(ca)2+bcl.2+cbsn/4331/timp.perc/
                                tamtam[glock]/[cel].[hp].[org]/str   Jurgenson   Misc 749
The GYPSIES (Les Bohémiens): ballet, op.90
   Suite   ∅ 2+picc.2+ca.22/4331/timp.perc.bells.xyl/
                                cel.hp/str   Russian SM,1947   Misc 4089
HINDU SUITE, op.42b
   1. Introduction   6. Najas dance
   2. Dithyramb   7. Dance of the young men
   3. Dance of the maidens   8. Duet on the theme "Ghusal"
   4. People's festival; Wedding procession 9. Rolling dance
   5. Hindu dance   10. Before sunrise; Legend; Finale
                             ∅ 3(picc)2+ca.3+Ebcl+bcl.2+cbsn/43.2cnt.31/
                                timp.perc/2hp.org/str/[chorus]   42'   Universal   16994
MIRANDOLINA: ballet
   Suite   ∅ 3(picc)2+ca.2+bcl.sx.2/4331/timp.perc.bells.
                                vib.xyl/cel.2hp.mand/str   Russian SM,1949   Misc 4088
SYMPHONY No.4, op.82 (Symphonie Arctique)
                             ∅ 2(picc)2(ca)3(bcl)2+cbsn/4631/timp.perc.
                                windmachine/2hp/str
                                ad lib: 0001/0300/windmachine/2[=1]hp   Russian SM   Misc 1888
TURKMENIAN PICTURES, op.68
   1. The Steppe blooms   3. In the night
   2. The Nomads   4. March
                             ∅ 3(picc)2+ca.2+bcl.2/4331/timp.perc.bells/
                                hp/str   Russian SM   Misc 1827
VALSE FANTASTIQUE, op.18   ∅ 3(picc)2+ca.22/4000/tri/hp/str   5'   Jurgenson   9108

VASZY, Viktor

LUSTSPIEL OVERTURE (Vígjáték nyitány)
                             ∅ 2222/4230/timp.perc/str   Universal   Misc 1880

VAUGHAN, Lynn

SAILING: march arr of song by G.Marks
                             PC 2(picc)12.2sx.1/2230/perc/str   K.Prowse   12040 Ap B

VAUGHAN WILLIAMS, Ralph (1872-1958)

see   KENNEDY, Michael: The Works of R.Vaughan Williams: London. OUP. 1964

A DESTE FIDELES (O come all ye faithful), attrib John Reading, arr for chorus & orch
   in A   ∅ bells/str   OUP   MS 20495

VAUGHAN WILLIAMS, Ralph (cont)

ALL PEOPLE THAT ON EARTH DO DWELL (Old 100th) for chorus, congregation & orch
  Rescored R.Douglas   ϕ   0000/0300/[timp]/org   OUP,1969   25128
AS I WALKED OUT: Essex folksong, arr
  in E min   ϕ   1111/1000/str   (Novello)   MS 7572
BENEDICITE, for Soprano solo, chorus & orch (1929)
                     ϕ   2(picc)2[=1]22[=1]/4[=2]2[=1]3[=1]0)/
                       timp/[cel].pf/str   15'   OUP,1969   Misc 7173
CA' THE YOWES: Scottish folksong, arr
  orch S.Robinson   ϕ   211+bcl.1/2230/timp/hp/str   (Curwen)   TO 1277
CHARTERHOUSE SUITE (orig pf)
  1. Prelude   (2')   4. Slow air   (3'30")
  2. Slow dance (1'30")   5. Rondo   (2')
  3. Quick dance (2'15")   6. Pezzo ostinato (2'15")
    arr J.Brown   ϕ str   15'30"   Stainer & B 5220 Bs Cni
COASTAL COMMAND: film music (1942)
  See the vacant sea: suite   ϕ 21(ca)12/2230/perc/hp/str   Composer MS:BBC MS 1525
CONCERTO GROSSO for three string groups (1950)
  1. Intrada   4. Scherzo
  2. Burlesca ostinata   5. March and reprise
  3 Sarabande
                  ϕ str   17'   OUP,1950   20022 B
CONCERTI
  Oboe & strings, in A min (1944)ϕ str   17'-18'52"   OUP, 1967 Misc 6504 B
  Piano (or 2 pianos) & orch, in C (1926-31)
                  ϕ   This edition includes both the original solo part
                     and the version for 2 pianos made by J.Cooper in
                     collaboration with the composer
                     2(picc)222/4231/timp.perc.tamtam/[org]/str 25' OUP,1972 Misc 7945
  Tuba & orch, in F min (1954) ϕ 2(picc)121/2220/timp.2[=1]perc/str   20'   OUP,1979 Misc 9926 &
                                                             PL 688 Amv
  Violin & strings, in D min 'Concerto accademico' (1924-5)
                  ϕ str   14'30"-15'30"   OUP   Misc 936 B
COVENTRY CAROL, arr
  in G min   ϕ bells/str   (OUP)   MS 20495
DEATH OF TINTAGILES: radio production
                  ϕ   0110/1000/str   (Composer) MS 31719
DIVES AND LAZARUS   see   5 VARIANTS OF 'DIVES AND LAZARUS'
DONA NOBIS PACEM: cantata for Soprano & Baritone soli, chorus & orch (1936)
                  ϕ   3(picc)222+cbsn/44[=2]5[=3]1/timp.perc.bells.
                     glock/hp.[org]/str   35'15"-40'   OUP,1971 Misc 7508
ENGLAND, MY ENGLAND: song
  in D, arr G.Williams for Soprano & Tenor soli, SAT chorus & orch
                  ϕ   1121/2210/timp.perc/pf/str   OUP   MLO 77
The ENGLAND OF ELIZABETH: film music (1955)
  3 Portraits, arr H.Mathieson
    1. Explorer   2. Poet   3. Queen
                  ϕ   2(picc)1+ca.21/2230/timp.perc.bells.glock.[vib]/
                     [cel].hp/str   16'30"   OUP,1964 Misc 5933
ENGLISH FOLKSONG SUITE (orig military band, 1923)
  1. Seventeen come Sunday (3'15")
  2. My bonny boy (3'15")
  3. Folksongs from Somerset (3'30")
    arr G.Jacob   ϕPC 2(picc)121/2220/timp.perc/str   10'30" Boosey & H,1924 13551
    arr G.Jacob   ϕPC 2(picc)121/2220/timp.perc/str   Boosey,1924   3074
FANTASIA (quasi variazione) on 'The Old 104th' Psalm tune, for piano, chorus & orch (1949)
                  ϕ   2(picc)222/4231/timp.perc.glock/org/str
                     or org/str   12'   OUP,1973 Misc 7963

VAUGHAN WILLIAMS, Ralph (cont)

FANTASIA ON A THEME BY TALLIS for double string orch (1910, rev 1919)

| | ϕ | str | 14'-18'30" | Curwen | 3083 Amv |
| | | | | | Cs Es Fwa |

FANTASIA ON CHRISTMAS CAROLS for Baritone solo chorus & orch

| | ϕ | 2222/4231/timp.tri[bells]/org/str | 12'-13' | Stainer & B | 11392 B |

FANTASIA ON GREENSLEEVES (orch R.Greaves from the music to 'Sir John in Love')

	ϕ	[2]000/0000/hp[=pf]/str	4'30"	OUP	11911 Bmv Cp
					Ds En Fwa
					Gwe H

FLOS CAMPI: suite for viola, chorus & small orch (1925)

| | ϕ | 1(picc)111/1100/perc/cel.hp/str | 19'-22'30" | OUP,1928 | Misc 945 B |

FOLK SONGS OF THE FOUR SEASONS: cantata for SSAA voices & orch (1949)

Suite for small orch, arr R.Douglas

1. To the ploughboy & May song   (3'30")
2. The green meadow & An Acre of land   (2')
3. The sprig of thyme & The Lark in the morning (3'15")
4. The cuckoo   (1'30")
5. Wassail song & Children's Christmas song   (3'15")

| | PC | 2(picc)2(ca)22/2230/timp.perc/hp/str | 13'30" | OUP | 22094 B |

FORTY NINTH PARALLEL: film (1940-41)

Prelude

arr R.Douglas	PC	21(ca)22/4231/timp.cym/hp/str			
		(orig orchestration with cues for			
		reduced orch)		OUP,1960	23199

arr R.Douglas for string orch

| | ϕ | str | | OUP | LM G 9720 |

GOLDEN CAROL 'Now is Christemas y-come'

in C, for Soprano & Tenor soli, & unison chorus

| | ϕ | bells/str | | (OUP) | MS 20495 |

GREENSLEEVES   see   FANTASIA ON GREENSLEEVES

HEART'S HAVEN   see   The HOUSE OF LIFE, no.4

HODIE (This Day): Christmas cantata for STBar soli, TrSATBchorus & orch (1953-4)

| | ϕ | 3[=2](picc)2[=1]+ca.22+[cbsn]/4[=2]3[=2]31/ | | | |
| | | timp.perc.bells.glock/cel.[hp].[org].pf/str | | OUP,1967 | Misc 7807 |

THE HOUSE OF LIFE: song cycle (orig voice & pf)

No.1 Love Sight: song

| in A, arr M.Johnstone | ϕ | hp[=pf]/str | 5'30" | (Ashdown,1968) | Misc 7366 |

No.2 Silent noon; song

in Db & Eb, arr F.Cramer		pf/str		(Ashdown)	LM G 7735
in D, arr M.Johnstone	ϕ	hp[=pf]/str	4'35"	(Ashdown,1968)	Misc 7366
in Eb, arr H.Geehl	ϕ	2222/2000/timp.perc/hp/str		(Ashdown)	Misc 4754

No.4 Heart's Haven: song

| in E, arr M.Johnstone | ϕ | hp[=pf]/str | 3'30" | (Ashdown,1968) | Misc 7366 |

HOUSEHOLD MUSIC: three preludes on Welsh hymn tunes (1940-41)

1. Crug-y-Bar: fantasia
2. St.Denio: scherzo
3. Aberystwyth: variations

| | ϕ | str 4-tet, or alternative instrs | 15' | OUP | 19122 |

HUGH THE DROVER: opera (1910-14, rev 1956)

Introduction

| arr S.Robinson (4 bars) | ϕ | 2222/4230/timp.perc/str/chorus | | Composer MS:BBC | MS 6998 |

Bright is the ring of words: song

| in D, arr G.Stacey | | pf/str | | (Boosey) | LM G 3793 |

Horse hoofs, horse hoofs, thunder down the road (Hugh's song of the road)

| in Ab, arr G.Stacey | | pf/str | | (Curwen) | LM G 3696 |
| in Ab, arr G.Williams | ϕ | 2121/2230/perc/hp str | | (Curwen) | TO 1256 + |

VAUGHAN WILLIAMS, Ralph (cont)

HUGH THE DROVER (cont)
  Sweet little linnet (Song of the linnet)
    in G, arr G.Williams   ϕ   1121/2000/str   (Curwen)   TO 1256 +
HYMN TUNE PRELUDE ON 'SONG 13' by Orlando Gibbons (orig pf.solo.1928)
    arr H.Glatz   ϕ   str   OUP,1953   20904
2 HYMN TUNE PRELUDES for small orch (1936)
    1. Eventide (Monk)
    2. Dominus regit me (Dykes)
                                  ϕ   1111/1000/str   6'   OUP,1960   23319
IN THE FEN COUNTRY: symphonic impression (rev 1935)
                                  ϕ   32+ca.2+bcl.2/4231/timp/str   14'   OUP,1969
JOB: a masque for dancing   ϕ   3[=2](picc)+bfl.2[2[=3]+bcl.[E♭sx].
                                       2+[cbsn]/43[=2]31/timp.[perc].[glock].   PL 76 Amv &
                                       [tamtam].[xyl]./2[=1]hp.[org]/str   40'-47'   OUP   Misc 1521 F
JOSEPH BEING AN OLD MAN: carol
    in A min, arr for unison chorusϕ   bells/str   OUP   MS 20495
JOSEPH DEAREST, JOSEPH MINE: 14th century German carol, arr
                                  ϕ   str   OUP
The LARK ASCENDING for violin & orch
                                  ϕ   2122/2000/tri/str
                                       or 1111/1000/tri/str   11'30"-13'35"   OUP   5886 Amv B
LINDEN LEA: Dorset song for voice & strings, arr
                                  ϕ   str   (Boosey & H)   MS 6288
    in F   ϕ   str   (Boosey)   MLO 252
    in F & A, arr H.Carr   ϕ   2121/2230/timp/hp/str   (Boosey)   TO 223 +
    in F & A, arr G.Stacey   ϕ   str   (Boosey)   LM G 5168
    in F & A, arr G.Stacey   1110/0000/pf/str   (Boosey & H)   LM A 123
    in G   ϕ   str   (Boosey)   MLO 252
    in A   ϕ   str   (Boosey)   MLO 252
    arr H.Perry   PC   1121/2210/timp/str   Boosey & H   20107
LORD, THOU HAST BEEN OUR REFUGE (Psalm 90): motet for chorus & semi-chorus (1921)
                                  ϕ   2222/4331/timp/str   (Curwen)   20049
LOVE SIGHT   see   The HOUSE OF LIFE, no.1
NORFOLK RHAPSODY, no.1, in E min (1955-6)
                                  ϕ   2(picc)2+ca.2([E♭cl])2/4231/timp.perc/
                                       hp/str   9'-11'45"   OUP   6770 Amv +
NOTHING IS HERE FOR TEARS: song
    in C   0000/0230/timp/org/str   Composer MS:BBC MS 2549
NOW IS CHRISTEMAS Y-COME: see   GOLDEN CAROL
O COME ALL YE FAITHFUL: see   ADESTE FIDELES
O LITTLE TOWN OF BETHLEHEM: carol (trad), arr
    arr R.Jaques for chorus & orch ϕ   [2222]/[2200]/str   OUP,1971   26752
OLD KING COLE: a ballet for orchestra (1923)
                                  ϕ   3[=2]+picc.2[=1].22/4=2]23[=2][1]/
                                       timp.perc/[cel].hp/str/[chorus]   Curwen,1925   6223
ON CHRISTMAS NIGHT (Sussex carol), arr
    in G, arr F.Bye   ϕ   2222+cbsn/4030/perc/hp/str   OUP   MLO 2744
ON WENLOCK EDGE: song cycle for Tenor & orch (1923)
    1. On Wenlock edge, in G min   4. Oh, when I was in love with you, in D min
    2. From far, from eve and morning, in E 5. Bredon Hill
    3. Is my team ploughing?, in D min   6. Clun, in A
                                       pf/str   Boosey,1911   18106
PARTITA for double string orch (from Double Trio, 1938) (1946-8)
                                  ϕ   str   19'25"-20'   OUP,1951   Misc 3572

VAUGHAN WILLIAMS, Ralph (cont)

The PILGRIM'S PROGRESS: opera (1949, rev 1951-2)
    Prelude   ϕ 2+picc.2+ca.22/4331/timp.perc(bells.xyl)/
                           hp/str   (Composer)   mf 371
    Parts 1 & 2   ϕ 2+picc.2+ca.22/4331/timp.perc.bells.xyl/hp/str   (Composer)   MS 20235
The POISONED KISS: opera
    Overture, arr S. Robinson   ϕ 0101/2030   6'50"   (OUP)   TO 1097
    Extracts
      It's really time: duet
        in Db   0021/2000/hp/str/(for use with hire material)   (OUP)   TO 853
PRELUDE founded on the Welsh tune 'Rhosymedre' or 'Lovely' (orig org solo)
    orch A.Foster   ϕ 2122/2100/str (or str orch)   3'30"   Stainer & B   14985 Dwa
PRELUDE founded on the Welsh hymn tune ·'Hyfrydol'(R.H.Prichard)(orig org solo)
    orch A.Foster   ϕ 2222/2200/timp/str   4'   Stainer & B   20581
RICHARD II: incidental music to radio production
                        ϕ 2+picc.222/4330/timp.perc/hp/str   (Composer MS:BBC)   MS 1594
RIDERS TO THE SEA: opera in 1 act ϕ 21+ca.0.bcl[=cl+bsn2].1/2100/timp.
                           perc.sea machine/str(max.6.6.4.4.2)   OUP,1972   Misc 7888
The ROADSIDE FIRE see SONGS OF TRAVEL
The RUNNING SET (1933)   ϕ 1+picc.222/2200/perc/pf/str   5'   OUP,1952   20634
SANCTA CIVITAS (The Holy City): oratorio for Tenor & Baritone soli, 3 chorus & orch (1923-25)
                        ϕ 3(picc)2+ca.22+cbsn/4331/timp.perc/hp.pf/str
                            or 2(picc)1+ca.22/2330/timp.perc/hp[=pf]/str   (Curwen)   (Misc 6000 &
                                                                                (mf 219
SEA SONGS: march   ϕPC 2(picc)2[=1]22[=1]/4[=2]23[1]/timp.perc/str 3'45"   Hawkes   11492 Am·B
SEA SYMPHONY see SYMPHONIES, no.1
SERENADE TO MUSIC for 16 solo voices or SATB soli & chorus or chorus & orch
                        ϕ 21+ca.22/4231/timp.perc/hp/str   9'30"-11'40" OUP,1961   Misc 5324
SHEPHERDS OF THE DELECTABLE MOUNTAINS: a pastoral episode for 2SA2T2Bar.Bsoli & orch (1921)
                        ϕ 21+ca.00/0000/str(min 2.2.2.1;
                            max 6.6.4.4.2)
                          off stage: 0000/0200/bells/hp   20'15"   OUP,1925   25809

SILENT NOON see The HOUSE OF LIFE, no 2
SINFONIA ANTARCTICA see SYMPHONIES
SONGS OF TRAVEL: song cycle (orig voice & pf)
    The Roadside fire
      in C & F   ϕ 2222/4200/timp/hp/str   2'15"   (BBC)   TO 2028
      in Db & F, arr G Stacey   pf/str   (Boosey)   LM G 3794
      in Db, arr G.Stacey   ϕ 1110/0000/perc/hp/str   (Boosey)   LM A 676
    The Vagabond
      in C min, arr G.Stacey   ϕ 1110/0000/perc/hp/str   (Boosey)   LM G 11683
      in C min & B min, arr G.Stacey pf/str   (Boosey)   LM G 3444
      in D min   VS 2222/4200/timp.perc/str   Boosey & H(H) PL 684 +
SUITE for viola & small orch (1934)
    Group 1: Prelude, Carol, Christmas dance
    Group 2: Ballad, Moto Perpetuo
    Group 3: Musette, Polka Melancolique: Galop
                        ϕ 2(picc)122/2200/timp.perc/cel.hp/str   23'   OUP,1966   Misc 6259
SYMPHONIES
    No.1 'Sea Symphony' (1903-9) ϕ 3[=2](picc)2[=1]+ca.2+Ebcl+[bcl].2+[cbsn]/
                                4331/timp.perc/2[=1]hp.[org]/str/Soprano &
                                Baritone soli, chorus   57'-68' Stainer & B,1918 13923
    No.2 'London Symphony' 1912-13
      Revised versión 1920   ϕ 3[=2](picc)2[=1]+ca.2+[bcl].2+[cbsn]/
                                42.[2cnt].31/timp.perc.glock/hp/str   41'-46'   Stainer & B   2813 Am.v Bs

VAUGHAN WILLIAMS, Ralph (cont)

SYMPHONIES (cont)

No.3 'Pastoral Symphony'(1921) ∅   3[=2](picc)2[=1]+ca.3[=2]+[bcl]2/
                                   43[=2]31/timp.perc/cel.hp/str[Soprano
                                   & Tenor solo]   34'-39'   Curwen   3080 Amv Bs

   rev R.Douglas   ∅   3[=2](picc)2[=1]+ca.3[=2](bcl)2/43[=2]31/
                                   timp.perc/cel.hp/str[Soprano & Tenor solo] 33'-34'

                                                          Boosey & H/Curwen[1977]   Misc 9391

No.4, in F min (1931-4)   ∅   3[=2](picc)3[=2]+ca.2+[bcl]2+[cbsn]/4231/
                                   timp.2perc/str   32'   OUP   Misc 1660 &
                                                                                                   PL 101 Amv

No.5, in D (1938-43)   ∅   2(picc)1+ca.22/2230/timp/str   36'-41'   OUP,1946   Misc 2335 D
                                                                                                   PL 85 Amv

No.6, in E min (1944-47)   ∅   3(picc)2+ca.2+bcl.tsx.2+cbsn/4331/
   rev version (1948)   timp.perc/1[=2]hp/str   31'35'   OUP,1948   Misc 2719 C
                                                                                                   PL 153 Amv

   rev version, new impression (1950)
                              ∅   3(picc)2+ca.2+bcl(tsx).2+cbsn/44[=3]31/
                                   timp.perc.xyl/hp/str   OUP,1950   Misc 4864 B
No.7 'Sinfonia antartica   ∅   3(picc)2+ca.2+bcl.2+cbsn/4331/timp.perc.
                                   glock.vib.wmc.xyl/cel.hp.org.pf/str/
                                   SSA chorus   42'   OUP, 1953   Misc 3972 C &
                                                                                                   PL 255 Amv

No.8, in D min (1953-55)   ∅   2(picc)223[=2]/2230/timp.perc.bells.glock.
                                   vib.xyl/cel.2[=1]hp/str   26'30"-30'   OUP,1956   Misc 4649 B &
                                                                                                   PL 256 Amv

   2nd mvt only 'Scherzo alla marcia'
                              ∅   2(picc)223/2230   3'45"   OUP   22615
   3rd mvt only 'Cavatina'   ∅   str   7'45"   OUP   22614
No.9, in E min (1956-7, rev 1958)
                              ∅   3(picc)2+ca.2+bcl.3sx.2+cbsn/42.flg.31/
                                   timp.perc.glock.tamtam.xyl/cel.2hp/str 30'-33'45" OUP,1958   Misc 4982 C
THANKSGIVING FOR VICTORY   ∅   226+bcl.2+cbsn/4631/timp.perc/2hp.org/str   BBC   13029
THIS DAY   see   HODIE
TOWARD THE UNKNOWN REGION for chorus & orch
                              ∅   32+ca.2+bcl.2/4331/timp/2hp[org]/str 12'40"-14'   Stainer & B   20166
5 TUDOR PORTRAITS: choral suite for Contralto (or mezzo), Baritone solo, chorus & orch (1936)
   1. The Tunning of Elinor Rumming: ballad
   2. Pretty Bess: intermezzo
   3. Epitaph on John Jayberd of Diss: burlesca
   4. Jane Scroop: romanza
   5. Jolly Rutterkin: scherzo

                              ∅   3(picc)2(ca)22+cbsn/4231/timp/perc.glock/
                                   hp/str   45'   OUP,1971   Misc 7528
5 VARIANTS OF 'DIVES AND LAZARUS' ∅ 1[=2]hp/str   12'-12'30"   OUP   16671 Amv B
The WASPS OF ARISTOPHANES: incidental music for Tenor & Baritone soli, mv chorus & orch
   (English translation J.Edwards) ∅ 2[=1](picc)122[=1]/2100/timp.perc/hp/str   (GB-Cfm)   Misc 6726 &
                                                                                                   mf 297
   Overture   ∅   2(picc)2[=1]22[=1]/2[4]2[=1][3]0/timp.perc/
                                   hp/str   Curwen   23971
Suite (1909)
   1. Overture (9')
   2. Entr'acte (2'30")
   3. March past of the kitchen utensils (3'15")
   4. Entr'acte (3'30")
   5. Ballet & final tableau (6'15")
                              ∅   2(picc)2[=1]22[=1]/4[=2]2[=1][3]0/timp.perc/
                                   hp/str
                                                                                     Curwen   2815 + Amv Bn
                                                                                                   Cs Dni G

VAUGHAN WILLIAMS, Ralph (cont)

The WASPS OF ARISTOPHANES (cont)
  March past of Kitchen utensils ⌀   1+picc.2[=1]22[=1]/2100/timp.perc
                                     str   Curwen,1964   Misc 5924
The WATER MILL: song
  in C   ⌀   21+ca.2+bcl.2/4000/hp/str   3'35"   (BBC)   19606
WHILE SHEPHERDS WATCHED: carol
  in F, arr for chorus & orch   ⌀   bells/str   (OUP)   MS 20495

VECSEY, Armand

BALLET SUITE
  1. Carnival   (2')   4. Oriental   (2'30")
  2. Love scene   (2 30")   5. Finale   (2')
  3. Pierrot and Pierrette (2')
     arr O.Langey   PC   2(picc)222/4331/timp.perc/hp/str   11'15"   G.Schirmer   2560 B
HUNGARIAN FANTASIA
     arr O.Langey   PC   2(picc)222/4231/timp/str   G.Schirmer   3047

VEERHOFF, Carlos H. (1926-

3 CANTOS DE TÖDÄ, for solo voices & orch
                         ⌀   1(picc)111/0210/perc.glock.vib.xyl/cel.hp.pf/
                             str   (Autograph)(H)   PL 454
SINFONIA 'PANTA RHEI' (1953)   ⌀   3(picc)2+ca.3(bcl)3(cbsn)/4431/timp.perc.xyl/
                             hp.pf/str   (Autograph)(H)   PL 452
TEXTUR for strings   ⌀   str   12' Peters/Litolff,1972   Misc 7894

VEJVANOVSKÝ (Weywanowský), Pavel Joseph (c.1640-1693)

(Numbers in brackets refer to the Kroměříž Archives)

INTRADA (B.XIV:124)(1683)
  ed C.Mackerras   ⌀   02+ca.01/0200/timp/str/cont   Editor/Artia MAB 49   23550 + # & MRL
SERENADE (B.XIV:45)(1679)
  ed C.Mackerras   ⌀   02+ca.01/0320/timp/2vla-dg.str/cont   5'30" Editor/Artia MAB 49   23549 + # & MRL
SERENADE (B.XIV: 91)(1670)
  ed J.Pohanka & J.Racek ⌀   0000/0200/str/cont   Artia,1958 MAB 36   Misc 5544 & MRL
SONATA à 4 (1666)
  ed J.Pohanka   ⌀   0000/02[1]0/str/cont(org)   Artia,1958 MAB 36   Misc 5544 & MRL
SONATA à 5 (1666)
  ed J.Pohanka   ⌀   0000/02[1]0/str/cont(org)   Artia MAB 47   MRL
SONATA à 6 (1666)
  ed J.Pohanka   ⌀   str/cont(org)   Artia MAB 47   MRL
SONATA à 7 (1666)
  ed J.Pohanka   ⌀   0000/020[3]/str/cont   Artia MAB 47   MRL
SONATA à 8 (IV:10)
  ed C.Mackerras   ⌀   0001/0130/str/cont   5'10" Artia MAB 49   23551 + & MRL
SONATA à 10 (1666)
  ed J.Pohanka   ⌀   0001[=tbn]/0220/str/cont   Artia MAB 47   MRL
SONATA à 10 (1665)
  ed J.Pohanka   ⌀   0000/0200/str/cont(org)   Artia MAB 47   MRL
SONATA à 10 (IV: 147)(1665)   ⌀   0001/0200/2vla-dg.str/cont   3'25" Artia MAB 49   MRL
  ed C.Mackerras   ⌀   0001/0200/2vla-dg.str/cont   Editor   23572 +
SONATA LAETITIAE (1666)
  ed J Pohanka   ⌀   str/cont   Artia MAB 47   MRL

VEJVANOVSKÝ (Weywanowský), Pavel Joseph (cont)

SONATA PASCHALIS (1666)
   ed J.Pohanka   φ   str/cont   Artia MAB 47   MRL
SONATA PRIMA à 5 (1666)
   ed J.Pohanka   φ   str/cont   Artia MAB 47   MRL
SONATA SANCTI SPIRITUS (1666)
   ed J.Pohanka   φ   str/cont(org)   Artia MAB 47   MRL
SONATA SECUNDA à 6
   ed J.Pohanka   φ   str/cont   Artia MAB 47   MRL
SONATA VENATORIA (B.IV:199](1684)
   ed J.Pohanka & J Racek   φ   0000/0200/str/cont   Artia MAB 36   Misc 5544 &
SONATA VESPERTINA à 8 (1665)
   ed J.Pohanka   φ   0000/02[3]0/str/cont(org)   Artia MAB 47   MRL

VEJVODA, Timm

ROLL OUT THE BARREL: song by T.Vejvoda & L.Brown
   in C arr G.Williams   φ   2131/2231/timp.perc/pf/str   (K.Prowse)   MS 20076
   arr   D.Darlow   φ   3222/4231/timp.perc/hp/str   (K.Prowse)   TO 1599

VELÁZQUEZ, Consuelo

KISS ME (Besame mucho): song
   in F min arr E.Griffiths   φ   1121/2230/perc/hp.pf/str   (Southern)   LM G 4473

VELÁZQUEZ, Leonardo

ADAGIO & SCHERZO for strings 1971 φ   str   (Composer)   Misc 9983

VELEBIL, Hans

NOCHE DE FIESTE: Episodio español φ   2222/4330/timp.perc.xyl/hp/str   Adler   24661

VENTO, Mattia(1735-1776)

SOFONISBA: pasticcio by M.Vento, A.Sacchini & G.F. di Maio
  The favourite songs
    Overture   Se m'accendo ad altra face: in Bb (Vento)
    Invan celar pretende: in F (Maio)   Mio sposo, mia vita: in Bb (Vento)
    Crudo fato aversa: in A (Sacchini)   Che bramate o giusti Dei: in A (Vento)
           φ   2222/20.2clno.00/str/cont   Bremner,1770   Misc 550

VEPRIK, Aleksandr (1899-1958)

5 KLEINE ORCHESTERSTÜCKE, op.17   φ   11+ca.1+bcl.1/2220/timp.perc.tamtam/str   12'   Russian SM   Misc 1711

VERACINI, Francesco Maria (1690-1768)

ARIA SCHIAVONA
   arr F.Margola   φ   str   Zanibon,1953   Misc 4195
CONCERTO GRANDE DA CHIESA (O della incoronazione) for violin & orch
   transcr Damerini   φ   0200/0200/timp/str/cont(org=cel)   12'   Zanibon,1958   Misc 5274
CONCERTO for violin & orch in D
   ed B.Paumgartner   φ   str/cont   Bärenreiter,1959   23188
LAMENT
   arr L.Bridgewater   pf/str   Universal   16383
PASSACAGLIA for strings
   ed & arr R.Lupi   φ   str   Carisch,1965   Misc 6041

VERACINI, Francesco Maria (cont)

4 PEZZI, transcr. E.Bonelli from Sonate Accademiche, op.2
   1. Largo   (5')   3. Giga (4')
   2. Allegro assai (4'30")   4. Aria rustica (2'30")
                                ø   str   Zanibon,1964   26004 B
TOCCATA E CAPRICCIO from op.2 no.1
   transcr F.Previtali   ø   str/cont   10'   Ricordi,1934   Misc 1906

VERDI, Giuseppe (1813-1901)

see   HOPKINSON, Cecil. A Bibliography of Giuseppe Verdi.   New York: Broude Bros., 1973   MRL

AIDA: opera
   Complete   ø   3(picc)2+ca.2+bcl.2/4230.cimbasso/timp.
                                 perc.tamtam/2hp/str
                                 Onstage: 6 Egyptian tpt.banda.2hp
                                 Offstage: 0000/0440/bdm   E.F.Kalmus   Misc 6487
                            ø   3(picc)2+ca.2+bcl.2/4230.cimbasso/timp.
                                 perc.tamtam/2hp/str
                                 Onstage: 6 Egyptian tpt.banda.2hp
                                 Offstage: 0000/0440/bdm   Ricordi,1913   Misc 870
      New edition with correctionsø 3(picc)2+ca.2+bcl.2/4230.cimbasso/timp.
                                 perc.tamtam/2hp/str
                                 Onstage: 6 Egyptian tpt.banda.2hp
                                 Offstage: 0000/0440/bdm   Ricordi,1976   Misc 870
   Prelude   ø   2+picc.222/4231/timp/str   3'45"   Leduc   Misc 1438
   Prelude (1872)
      ed P.Spada   ø   2+picc.222/4231/timp.perc/str   Boccaccini & S   Misc 10029
   Selections
      arr E.Tavan   PC   2(picc)222/0231/perc/str   15'   Leduc   2396 Cni
      arr E.Tavan(new selection) PC 2(picc)222/2231/timp.perc/str   Ricordi   85
   Suite arr S.Robinson   ø   3(2picc)222/4231/timp.perc/hp/str   Ricordi   16347
   Extracts
      Ballet music
         arr G.Hinrichs
            1. Andante con moto   2. Allegro giusto   3. Marziale
                            PC   3(picc)222/4231/timp.perc/hp/str   G.Schirmer   16199
      Celeste Aida (Heavenly Aida): aria
         Se quel guerrier (If only I were chosen):recit
            in Bb (orig)   ø   2222/4230/str   (Siddell)   17899
            in Bb, arr F Cramer pf/str   Ricordi   LM G 4788
      Triumphal march (Grand march)(Marche des trompettes)(Finale, Act 2)
         arr L.Artok   PC   2(picc)222/4231/timp.perc/str   Schott   12267 Amv B
         arr H.Carr   ø   2+picc.222/4431/timp.perc/str   (Ricordi)   TO 1236 **
         arr H.Mielenz   PC   2(picc)222/4230/timp.perc/str   Schott,1940   24916 +
         arr H.Mouton   PC   1121/2230/timp.perc/str   Leduc   9958
         arr Stefani   PC   1+picc.020/2110/timp.perc/str   Ricordi   1690 Bn +
         arr D.Stone   ø   1121/2210/timp.perc/pf/str   Boosey & H,1964 Misc 6051
         arr M.Tobani (op.328) rev Seredy
                            PC   1+picc.22.2sx.2/4231/perc/str   C.Fischer   16348
AIR DU KHEDIVE (Song of the Khedive: former national anthem of Egypt (attrib Verdi; authenticity doubtful)
                            PC   2(picc)222/4230/timp.perc/str   Breitkopf   14305
                            PC   2(picc)222/4220/str   Benjamim   16364
      arr F.Salabert   PC   1(picc)221/223[1]/timp.perc/str   Salabert   3816
      arr M.L.Lake   PC   112.2sx.1/2210/perc/str   C.Fischer   19720

VERDI, Giuseppe (cont)

ATTILA: opera
  Opening scene
    Facsimile (instruments not specified after first page)
                  φ 1+picc.222/4420.cimbasso/timp/str   (F-Pn)   Misc 7632 &
                                                                                                          mf 347

  Te sol quest anima: trio
    in C (orig Db)   1012/2000/str   (Siddell)   17899

Un BALLO IN MASCHERA (Masked Ball): opera
  Complete   φ 1+picc.222/4230/timp.perc/hp/str
                            Offstage: banda.bell   Ricordi,1914 Misc 871 C
    revised edition 1959   φ 2(picc)2(ca)22/4230.cimbasso/timp.perc/
                            hp/str
                            Offstage: banda.bell   Ricordi,1914 Misc 5082
  Selections
    arr H.Finck   PC 1010/0210/perc/str   A H & C   12233
    arr E.Tavan   PC 2222/2231/timp.perc/str   Heugel   19437 Ani
    arr E.Tavan   PC 2222/2231/timp.perc/str   Ricordi   76 E
    arr M.T.Tobani (op.387) rev Seredy
                  PC 1121/2210/timp.perc/org/str   C.Fischer   16944
  Extracts
    E scherzo (But food for mirth): quintet
      in Bb (orig)   1222/4200.oph/str   (Siddell)   17895
    Eri tu (And would'st thou): aria
      Alzatil là tuo figlio (Get thee up): recit
        in D min (orig)   φ 2222/4220.euph/timp/hp/str   (Siddell)   17165 B +
        in D min, arr R.Chignell
                   φ 1121/2210/timp/hp/str   (Ricordi)   MS 5545
        in D min, arr F.Cramer   pf/str   (Ricordi)   LM G 4271
        in D min, arr G.Stacey   pf/str   (A H & C)   LM G 3597
        in C# min   φ 2222/4220.oph/timp/hp/str   (Siddell)   17166
        in C min   φ 2222/4220.oph/timp/hp/str   (Siddell)   17167
    Ma dall'arido (When at last): aria
      Ecco l'orrido campo (Lo! the spot): recit
        in Ab (orig)   φ 1+picc.2+ca.22/4231/timp.perc/str   (Siddell)   18133
    Ma se m'è forza perditi (But though for aye): aria
      Forse la soglia (Haply the step): recit
        in C min (orig)   1222/2000/str   (Siddell)   18254
    Saper vorreste (You'd fain be hearing): canzone
      in G (orig)   φ 1+picc.222/2000/str   2'   (Siddell)   17351
      in F   φ 1222/2130/timp/str   (Siddell)   17350
    Volta la terrea (Reading the stars)
      in B (orig)   φ 1+picc.222/4231/timp/str   2'   (Ricordi)   17896
      in Bb, arr R.Chignell   1121/2110/timp/str   (Ricordi)   MS 5546

La BATTAGLIA DE LEGNANO: opera
  Overture arr Mattioli   PC 1020/2210/timp.perc/str   8'   Ricordi   1783

DON CARLOS: opera (1867)
  Original Paris version, ed A.Porter [completing the hire material from Ricordi and Chelsea Opera Group]
    Act 1 Scene 1   φ 2+picc.224/42.2cnt.30.oph/timp.perc/str
                          Offstage: 0000/4000.euph[=2hn] φ & offstage band pts only
    Act 2 Part 1 (Scenes 1, 2 & 3)
                       φ 2+picc.224/42.2cnt.31/timp.bells/str
    Act 2 Part 2 (No.7)·   φ 2+picc.224/42.2cnt.31/timp/str
    Act 3 (Opening)   φ 2+picc.224/42.2cnt.31/timp.perc/str
    Act 4 (No.12)   φ 2+picc.224/42.2cnt.31/timp/str
    Act 4 (No.13)   φ 2+picc.224/42.2cnt.31/timp/hp/str
    Act 4 (Finale)   φ 2+picc.224/42.2cnt.31/timp.perc/str
    Act 5 (Duet & Finale)   2224/42.2cnt.31/timp.perc.tamtam/hp/str   (Editor)   25664 +

VERDI, Giuseppe (cont)

DON CARLOS (cont)
  Paris version
    Act 2 only   φ 2+picc.224/42.2cnt.30.oph/timp.perc/str   (I-Nc:MS 41-5-15a)   Misc 8322
    Prelude to Act 2   φ 2+picc.221/2000/timp/str   2'30"   Sadlers Wells   20828
  Extracts
    Ella giammai m'amo: aria
      in D min (orig)   φ 1222/4000/str   8'   (Ricordi)   20430
    Nel giardin del bello (Canzone del velo) for soli, SSA chorus & orch (Act 1, no.8)
                       φ 2+picc.224/40.2cnt.00/timp.perc/str   Ricordi(H)   PL 611
    O don fatale: aria
      in F   φ 2+picc.223/42.2cnt.30.euph/timp/str   (Siddell)   17217
      In F, arr H.Carr   φ 2121/2230/timp   (Ricordi)   TO 1171 **
      in F,arr F.Cramer   pf/str   (Ricordi)   LM G 4459
  German stage version
    ed J.Kapp & K.Soldan (Unsuitable for use with any other version)
      Complete   φ 3(picc)2(ca)24(cbsn)/42.2cnt.31/timp.perc/
                          hp/str
                          Onstage (no.17) 0020/42.3flg.32.bomb.
                          Offstage (no.1) 0000/22.4cnt.4.0.bar/bells.
                          cast.tamb/hp   Peters,1947   Misc 4202
    Extracts
      Erbarmt euch meiner: scene & aria (AB-3 no.21)
        in G min, ed K.Soldan
                φ 2+picc.224/42.2cnt.31/timp/str   Peters,1947   Misc 6754,mf 299
      In dem stillen Haine: aria for chorus & orch (Act 1, no.8)
        in A, ed K Soldan φ 2+picc.224/40.2cnt.00/timp.perc/str   Peters,1947   Misc 6753,mf 299
      Wie so lieblich ist's: chorus & scene (Act I, no.7)
        in B, ed K.Soldan φ 2+picc.224/42.2cnt.31/timp.perc/str   Peters,1947   Misc 6753,mf 299
EGYPT: national anthem   see AIR DU KHEDIVE
ERNANI: opera
  Selections
    arr M.L.Lake   PC 1121/2210/perc/str   C.Fischer   5490
    arr M.T.Tobani   PC 1121/2210/timp.perc/str   C.Fischer   1372
  Extracts
    Ernani! involami (Ernani, o come fly with me): aria
      Sorta è le notte ('Tis near the dawning): recit
        in Bb (orig)   φ 1+picc.222/4230.oph/timp/str   (Siddell)   17129
    Infelice! (How I trusted): aria
      Che mai vegg': recit
        in Ab(orig)   φ 2222/4230.oph/str   (Siddell)   17176
    Oh de' verd' anni miai (O bright and fleeting shadows): aria
      Gran Dio! (Great Heaven): recit
        in Ab (orig)   2222/4230.oph/timp/str   (Siddell)   17894
FALSTAFF: opera
  Complete   φ 3(picc)2+ca.2+bthn.2/4340/timp.perc.bell/
                          gtr.hp/str
                          Offstage: horn   Ricordi/Kalmus   24207 + *
  Complete (facsimile of orig.MS)φ 3(picc)2+ca.2+bthn.2/4340/timp.perc.bell/
                          gtr.hp/str
                                              Ricordi   Misc 3620
  Selection, arr E.Tavan PC 2222/2231/timp.perc/str   Ricordi   84
  Extracts
    Minuet (Act III)
      arr Mazzone   PC 1020/2000/str   Ricordi   5621 B
      arr S.Robinson   φ 2121/2000/str   2'15"   (Ricordi)   TO 19

VERDI, Giuseppe (cont)

La FORZA DEL DESTINO: opera

Complete (1862 version)	∅	1+picc.22(bcl)2/4231/timp.perc/2hp.org/str		(Composer/Peters)	Misc 10078
(1862 version)	∅	1+picc.22(bcl)2/4231/timp.perc/2hp/str		(BBC)	27002
(1869 version)	∅	1+picc.22(bcl)2/4230.cimbasso/timp.perc/2hp/str			
		Offstage: 0000/0600/perc/org		(F-Pn MS ResF 1659)	Misc 8321 m
rev G.Göhler	∅	1+picc.22(bcl)2/4231/timp.perc/2hp.org/str		Peters,1960	Misc 5528
Overture	∅	1+picc.222/4231/timp.perc/2hp.org/str	7'-8'30"	Eulenburg	Misc 4395
	∅	1+picc.222/4231/timp.perc/2hp/str		Ricordi(H)	PL 372 Agg
	∅	1+picc.222/4231/timp.perc/2hp/str		[Ricordi]/E.F.Kalmus	26783 Amv
arr Fumagalli	PC	1020/2210/timp.perc/str		Ricordi	1784
arr R.Jungnickel	PC	1+picc.222/4231/timp.perc/2hp/str		Jungnickel	3118 Awe B

Selections

arr Mattioli	PC	1020/2210/perc/str		Ricordi	13428
arr M.T.Tobani(op.416)	PC	1121/2210/perc/str		C.Fischer	3773

Extracts

Oh tu che in seno (I think of thee in heaven above): aria

La vita inferno ('Tis hell on earth): recit

in Ab (orig)	∅	1122/2000/str		(Siddell)	17376

Pace, pace, mio Dio (Father of heaven): aria

in Bb (orig)	∅	2222/4231/timp/hp/str	5'	(Siddell)	18093

Tarantella

arr S.Robinson	∅	2121/2230/perc/str	2'15"	(Ricordi)	TO 321 **

GIOVANNA D'ARCO: opera

Overture	∅	1+picc.222/4231/timp.perc/str		Choudens	8336 *
arr Ludovic	PC	1020/2100/perc/str	8'	Ricordi	1788
arr Roberts	PC	1121/2210/timp.perc/org/str		C.Fischer	6624

Extracts

Triumphas march	∅	2+picc.222/4230.oph/timp.perc/str		Choudens	4447

IO LA VIDI E A QUAL'ASPETTO: aria (c.1835)(facsimile)

in Eb	∅	2222/2230/str		(Pierpont Morgan Lib)	Misc 7631

The LADY AND THE FOOL: suite from the ballet arr C.Mackerras from music of Verdi

1. Tarantella (3'15")   4. Romantic pas de deux (4'30")
2. Pas seul (1'30")   5. Divertissement (3')
3. Pas de trois: galop (1'20") 6. Finale (3'30")

	∅	3+picc.2+ca.22/4331/timp.perc/cel.hp/str		Ricordi,1955	21405 B
No.6 only (Grand Adage)		2(picc)222/4331/timp.perc.glock.tamtam/cel.hp/str		(ROH)(H)	PL 592

I LOMBARDI ALLA PRIMA CROCIATA: opera

Selection, arr Baynes	PC	2(picc)122/2230.euph/timp.perc/hp/str		Boosey	1934

Extracts

La mia letizia

in A (orig)	∅	2222/4030/str		(Siddell)	17900

O signore: Coro di crociati e pellegrini

in E (orig C) arr L.Wurmser

	∅	2111/1110/timp/str		(Ricordi)	MS 8389

Scena e terzetto (orch version) arr Culotta

	PC	2222/2230/timp.perc/str		Ricordi	16264

LUISA MILLER: opera (1849)

Overture	∅	2+picc.222/4230.cimbasso/timp.perc/str		Ricordi,1954	Misc 8546 B
arr I.Culotta	PC	2221/2230/timp.perc/str	8'30"	Ricordi	9334

Extracts

Quando le sere al placido: aria

Oh! fede negar potessi: recit

in G (orig Ab)		1112/4000/str		(Siddell)	17901

VERDI, Giuseppe (cont)

MACBETH: opera
  Orig version (1847)   φ   1+picc.2(ca)2(bcl)2/4231[=btbn]/timp.perc
                             tamtam/hp/str
                             Onstage: 0.picc.26+Ebcl.2+cbsn/42+Ebtpt.flg.31/
                                      dm.2sdm
                             (Extra drums & trumpets needed for Battle
                             scene in Act 4)   (BBC)   26658

Complete					
revised version	φ	1+picc.2(ca)2(bcl)2/4231[=btbn]/timp.perc. tamtam/hp/str			
		Onstage:1262+cbsn/2210/sdm		(Kalmus)	24299 *
Prelude	φ	1+picc.222/4240/timp/hp/str		(Ricordi)	21458
arr Culotta	PC	1+picc.121/2230/timp.perc/str	3'30"	Ricordi	13208
Extracts					
Ballabile	PC	1+picc.222/2230/timp.perc/str	10'	Ricordi	11027 B
Come dal ciel: aria (Banquo)					
Studia il passo: recit					
in E min (orig)	φ	1+picc.222/4231/timp/str		(Ricordi)	20555
Una maccia è qui tutt' ora: aria (Sleepwalking scene)					
in Db (orig)	φ	1+picc.2+ca.22/4231/timp.perc/str		(Ricordi)	21327 +
Vieni! t'affretta: aria					
Ambizioso spirito: recit					
in Db (orig)	φ	1+picc.2+ca.22/4231/timp.perc/str		(Ricordi)	21327 +

MARCH formerly used as national anthem of Egypt <u>see</u> AIR DU KHEDIVE

NABUCCO (Nabucodonosor): Opera in 4 Acts

Complete	φ	1+picc.222/4230.cimbasso(spt)/timp.perc/hp/str			
		Stageband: banda		(Ricordi)	Misc 7475
Overture	φ	2222/4210.euph/timp.perc/str	8'	Hawkes	316
Extracts					
D'Egitto la sui lidi:cavatina					
Sperato o figli: recit					
in C (orig)		1+picc.222/4230.oph/timp/str		(Siddell)	17903
Oh dischiuso è il firmamento: Romanza for Soprano solo & orch					
	φ	1+picc.222/4200/hp/str		Donizetti-Press[1977]	Misc 9234
Va, pensiero, sull'ali dorate (Chorus of Hebrew slaves)					
in F#	φ	1+picc.222/4230.cimbasso/timp/str	5'	Ricordi (H)	PL 485

O DOLORE ED IO VIVA: romance, in Db

	φ	1222/4000/hp/str		(Museo Teatrale alla Scala 1113)	Misc 7910

OBERTO, CONTE DI SAN BONIFACIO: opera

Extracts					
Ah, Riccardo amia Vagio: duet					
Basta, basta O fedeli: recit					(Misc 7972 &
Facsimile	φ	1+picc.122/4230/str		(I-Nc)	(mf 357
Un amplesso ricevi: cabaletta (duet)					(Misc 7971 &
Facsimile	φ	1+picc.122/4230/str		(I-Nc)	(mf 357
Dove corri, osciagurata: duet (as performed, Genoa 1841)					(Misc 7970 &
Facsimile	φ	1+picc.222/4231/perc/str		(I-Nc)	(mf 357

OTELLO: opera

Complete	φ	3(picc)224/42.2cnt.40/timp.perc/hp.org/str			
		Offstage: 01.bagpipes[=2ob]11/0000/gtr[=hpsd]mand[=hp]/vln			
				Ricordi	Misc 872 C
Selections					
arr C.Godfrey	PC	2(picc)2(ca)22/4230.euph/timp.perc/str		Hawkes	8473
arr E.Tavan	PC	2222/2231/timp.perc/str		Ricordi	80
Extracts					
A terra (Act 3 ensemble)					
Revised version for Paris production, 1894					
	φ	2+picc.224/4440/timp.perc/str		(Ricordi,1894)	Misc 10064

VERDI, Giuseppe (cont)

RIGOLETTO (cont)
  Extracts (cont)
    Quartet <u>see</u> Un di se ben

Questa o quella (Yes the one is as fair): aria			2'		
in A♭ (orig)	φ	2222/2000/str		(Siddell)	17159 B
in A♭ arr R.Chignell	φ	1121/2100/str		(Ricordi)	MS 5489
in A♭ arr E.Griffiths		pf/str		(Ricordi)	LM G 6556
in A♭ arr Stacey		1010/0000/pf/str		(Ricordi)	LM A 39
in G		1+picc.222/4000/str		(Siddell)	17160
Pari siamo (recits etc. to precede aria "Figlia")(no.7)					
in F (orig) arr R.Chignell					
	φ	1121/2100/str		(A H & C)	MS 5491
Signor ne principe (Riches and dignity): scena and duet					
in G (orig)		1+picc.222/4231/str	6'30"	(Siddell)	18161
Tutte le feste al tempio (While at the altar praying): duet			3'		
in E min (orig) arr R.Chignell					
	φ	1111/1000/str		(BBC)	MS 5487
Un di se ben (One day if I remember well): quartet					
in E (orig)		1+picc.222/4231/str		(Siddell)	17898
arr Missa (orch version)	PC	1121/2210/timp.perc/str		Grus	6553

SICILIAN VESPERS <u>see</u> I VESPRI SICILIANI

SIMON BOCCANEGRA: opera
  Original version 1857

Complete	φ	1+picc.222/4230.cimbasso[=oph]/timp.perc/ str		(I-Mc)	Misc 8122 & mf 361
ed A.Boustead	φ	1+picc.222/4230/cimbasso[=oph]/timp.perc/str Stageband: 0000/0330/perc		(Editor)	25975 + ** Awa (φ & inserts only)

  Prelude to 1857 version

ed P.Spada	φ	1+picc.222/4231/timp/str		Boccaccini & S,1978	Misc 1028

  Extract
    Il lacerato spirito: Fiesco's romance
      A te l'estremo addio: recit

in F# (orig)	φ	1112/4231/timp/str	4'30"	Ricordi	5572
in F#	φ	2222/4230.oph/timp/str		(Siddell)	17504 B

STABAT MATER for chorus & orch	φ	3222/4340/timp.perc/hp/str	14'-16'15"	Ricordi	Misc 1198
ed K.Soldan	φ	3224/4340/timp.bdm/hp/str	12'-16'15"	Peters	23368

STIFFELIO: opera
  Complete

ed L.Gardelli	φ	2+picc.222/4230.cimbasso/timp.perc/str		Editor,1979	Misc 9976
TE DEUM for double chorus & orch	φ	32+ca.2+bcl.4/4340/timp.perc/str	16'	Ricordi	Misc 1908 B

La TRAVIATA: opera

Complete	φ	2(picc)222/4231/timp.perc/str Offstage: banda.hp	111'	Ricordi/Kalmus,1914	Misc 866 F
	φ	2(picc)222/4230.cimbasso/timp.perc/str Offstage: banda.hp		E.F.Kalmus	Misc 6489
Prelude Act 1	φ	1112/4000/str		(Ricordi)	23227 +
arr L.Artok	PC	2122/2110/timp/str	4'	Schott	12402
arr Mattioli	PC	1020/2110/timp/str		Ricordi	7510
Introduction Act 1 (no.2) for stage band					
	φ	0.picc.040/23+flg.20/sdm/2cb		(Ricordi,c.1870)	Misc 7625
Prelude Act 3	φ	1122/1000/str		(Ricordi)	23228 Bn +
Selections					
arr C.Godfrey	PC	2(picc)222/2230.euph/timp.perc/str		Hawkes	2163 B
arr E.Tavan (old selection)	PC	2(picc)222/2231/timp.perc/str		Margueritat	5046 Cni
arr E.Tavan (new selection)	PC	2222/2231/timp.perc/str		Ricordi	82
arr L.Weninger	PC	2(picc)222/4231/timp.perc/str	14'	Benjamin	12659

VERDI, Giuseppe (cont)

La TRAVIATA (cont)
    Extracts
        Addio, del passato (Forever I must leave thee): aria
          È tardi! attendo (It is late): recit
            in A min (orig) arr F.Cramer

		pf/str		(Ricordi)	LM G 7794

        Ah, fors' è lui (Ah, was it him): aria in F min (orig) — 6'50"
          È strano (How wond'rous): recit
          Follie! (What folly): recit
          Sempre libera (I'll fulful the round): aria in A♭ (orig)

orig. keys	∅	1+picc.222/4231/hp/str	4'	(Siddell)	17029
orig keys arr R.Chignell					
	∅	1121/2110/hp/str		BBC	MS 5130
orig keys arr F.Cramer		cel.pf/str		Schirmer	LM G 5264
in E♭ min (aria only)		1+picc.202/2000/str		BBC	MS 30030

        Di Madrido noi siam mattadori: chorus of matadors, for solo voices, STB chorus &
          orch (Act 2: No.7 - extract)

in G (orig)	1+picc.222/4231/timp.perc/str		(Siddell)	27044

        Di miei bollenti spiriti (Fevered and wild): aria
          Lunge da lei (When we are parted): recit — 2'

in E♭ (orig)	1+picc.222/4230.oph/timp/str		(Siddell)	17893

        Di provenza il mar (Hath they love): aria
          Mio figlio (Despair not): recit

in D♭ (orig)	∅	2022/2000/str	(Siddell)	17495 B
in D♭ (without recit) arr E.Griffiths				
		pf/str	(Ricordi)	LM G 5682
in C		2022/2000/str	(Siddell)	17496

        Largo al quadrupede (Lo, where the pride): baccanale
          in D (orig) arr S.Robinson

	φ	2222/4230/bdm/str	(Ricordi)	TO 550

        Libiamo (Where beauty & truth)(Drinking song): aria

in B♭ (orig)	∅	2+2picc.222/4230.cimbasso/timp.perc/str	3'	Ricordi(H)	PL 483
in B♭					
arr F.Cramer		pf/str		(Ricordi)	LM G 5201

        Non gradireste (Shall we with dancing): waltz
          Un di felice (Oh day for ever remembered): duet
            in E♭

arr S.Robinson	φ	2+picc.232/4231/timp.perc/hp/str	(Ricordi)	TO 550

        Parigi, o cara (Far from the busy throng): duet

in A♭ (orig)		0222/2000/str	(Siddell)	17892
in A♭	φ	1+picc.222/4240/timp/str	Ricordi(H)	PL 482

        Sempre libera: aria   <u>see</u>   Ah, for' è lui

Il TROVATORE: opera

Complete	φ	1+picc.222/4230.cimbasso/timp.perc.bell/hp/str	Ricordi	Misc 869E
	φ	2(picc)222/4230.cimbasso/timp.perc.bells/org.hp/str		
		Offstage: 0000/1000/perc.bell/hp	E.F.Kalmus	Misc 6490

    Selections

arr H.Finck and Baynes	PC	1010/0210/perc/str	A H & C	12282
arr C.Godfrey	PC	2(picc)222/2230.euph/timp.perc/str	Hawkes	1483 Dwa
arr E.Tavan (old selection)	PC	2(picc)122/2230.oph/timp.perc/str	Margueritat	5893
arr E.Tavan (new selection)	PC	2(picc)222/2231/timp.perc/str	Ricordi	83

    Extracts
        Ah si ben mio (Ah yes thou'rt mine): aria

in F min (orig)	0.picc.222/4230.oph/timp/str		(Siddell)	18019
in F min, arr F.Cramer	pf/str		(Ricordi)	LM G 4261

VERDI, Giuseppe (cont)

II TROVATORE (cont)
  Extracts (cont)
    II balen (Ah could I behold): aria   3'
      Tutte è deserto (All have departed): recit
        in Ab   ∅   1112/4000/str   (Siddell)   17532
        in A   1112/4000/str   (Siddell)   17531
      in Bb (orig)(without recit)
                               1222/2000/str   (Siddell)   17530
    Condotta ell' era in ceppi (In galling fetters): aria
      in A min (orig)   1+picc.222/4231/timp.perc/str   4'30"   (Siddell)   18114
    D'amor sull' ali rosee (Breeze of the night): aria
      in F min (orig)   ∅   1+picc.122/4230.oph/timp.perc/hp/str   (Ricordi)(H)   PL 195
      in F min   1122/4230.oph/timp.perc/hp/str   (Siddell)   17891
      aria only, in F min ∅ 1122/1000/str   (Siddell)   17918
    Di quella pira (Strike down that dread pyre): aria
      in Bb (orig C)   2222/4231/timp.perc/str   2'   (Ricordi)   TO 1810
    Home to our mountains   see   Si la stanchezza
    Miserere scene and aria   see   D'amor sull'ali rosee
    Si la stanchezza (Yes, I am weary): duet (including 'Home to our mountains')
      in G (orig)   1222/2000/str   (Siddell)   17890
      in G arr Glover, orch F.Cramer
                               pf/str   (F.Harris)   LM G 4874
      in G arr J.Turner   1110/1000/str   (BBC)   LM G 8570
    Stride la vampa (Fierce flames are raging)
      in E min (orig)   ∅   0222/0000/str   (Siddell)   18010
    Tacea la notte ('Twas night): aria (including 'Di tale amor' (To tell of love))
      in Ab (orig)   ∅   2222/4230.oph/timp/str   5'   (Siddell)   17136
      in Ab arr J.Byfield ∅ acdn.pf/str   (Ricordi)   LM G 7864
      in Ab arr R.Chignell ∅ 1121/2110/timp/str   (Arranger)   MS 5085
    Vedi! le fosche notturne: cori di Zingari, for STB chorus & orch (Anvil Chorus)(Act 2: No.4)
      in E min (orig)   1+picc.222/4231/timp.perc.anv/str   (Siddell)   27043

VERDI SELECTIONS
  Verdi's opera memories, arr I.Geiger   see   GEIGER, Isy: VERDI'S OPERA MEMORIES
  Verdi reminiscences, arr F.Godfrey & Millars   see   GODFREY, Fred: VERDI REMINISCENCES
  Verdi Variationen, arr R.Heger   see   HEGER, Richard: VERDI-VARIATIONEN
  Verdi memories, arr H.Worch   see   WORCH, Herman: VERDI MEMORIES

I VESPRI SICILIANI (Les vêpres siciliennes): opera
  Complete (orig French text - E.Scribe & C.Duveyrier)
                       ∅   2(picc)222/42.2cnt.31/timp.perc.bells/hp/str   (Ricordi)   Misc 6885
  Overture   ∅   1+picc.222/42.2cnt.30.cimbasso/timp.perc/str   Ricordi   Misc 9731
    arr R.Jungnickel   ∅   2+picc.222/4431/timp.perc/str   Jungnickel   5279 Awe
    arr F.Salabert   PC 1121/2230/timp.perc/str   9'   Salabert   9492
  Selection
    arr Godfrey   PC 2(picc)222/4231/timp.perc/hp/str   Hawkes   831 Cwe Dwa
  Extracts
    Barcarolle
      arr Luporini   PC 1020/2100/tri/str   (Ricordi)   1791
    Del vostro amico dona: siciliana
      in A min (orig)   2222/4230.oph/timp.perc/str   (Siddell)   17897
      in A min arr Franzel (Merce dilette amiche)
                         ∅   3222/4231/timp.perc/hp/str   (Siddell)   TO 1754
    O tu, Palermo: aria (Act 2)
      O patria: recit
        in Gb (orig)   ∅   2222/4230.oph/timp/str   (Siddell)   17170 B
        in Gb   ∅   2+picc.222/4231/timp/str   (Ricordi)   20435 +

VERDI, Giuseppe (cont)

I VESPRI SICILIANI (cont)
  Extracts (cont)
    O tu, Palermo: aria (Act 2) (cont)
      O patria: recit (cont)

in G♭ arr J.Byfield		pf/str.orch		(A H & C)	LM G 7740
in G♭ (orig), arr S.Robinson					
	∅	1+picc.222/42.2cnt.40/str		(Ricordi)	24121 +
Tarantella					
arr Luporini	∅	2121/2220/perc/str	3'30"	Ricordi	1791

VERDIER (17th cent)

ALLEMANDE				
ed Écorcheville	OS	Instruments unspecified	M.Fontin,1906	Misc 3027 B
COURANTE				
ed Écorcheville	OS	Instruments unspecified	M.Fortin,1906	Misc 3027 B

VERESS, Sándor (1907-

CONCERTO for piano & orch	∅	timp.perc.tamtam.xyl/str	27'	Zerboni,1956	Misc 4838
The MAGIC FLUTE (Csodafurulya): ballet					
	∅	3(picc)3(ca)3(bcl)3(cbsn)/4331/timp.perc.xyl/			
		hp/str	17'	Universal	Misc 2769 D
SONATA PER ORCHESTRA	∅	1(picc)121/2100/timp.perc/str	10'	Zerboni,1953	Misc 4763
4 TRANSYLVANIAN DANCES	∅	str	12'	Zerboni,1950	Misc 3278

VARIATIONS ON A THEME OF ZOLTÁN KODÁLY see KODÁLY, Zoltán: VARIATIONS ON A THEME OF ZOLTÁN KODÁLY

VERETTI, Antonio (1900-

I SETTE PECCATI: Mystery in music and dance
  Frammenti sinfonici (Two suites can be made from these fragments: see introductory note)

	∅	3(picc)3(ca).2+E♭cl+bcl.asx.tsx.3(cbsn)/			
		4331/timp.perc.bullroarer.cast.scym.glock.			
		rattle.tamb.tamtam.xyl/cel.2hp.pf/str	24'	Ricordi,1956	Misc 9726
SINFONIA ITALIANA (The people and the prophet)					
	∅	3(picc)2+ca.2+bcl.2+cbsn/4431/timp.perc.tamtam/			
		2hp.pf/str		Ricordi	Misc 2599 B
SINFONIA SACRA for men's voices and orch (1946)					
	∅	0000/4.Dtpt.331/timp.perc.bells.tamtam.vib.xyl/			
		2hp.2pf/str		Zerboni	Misc 2777

SUITE in C (1934)
  1. Preludio   4. Minuetto-pastorale
  2. Ninna-Nanna   5. Finale
  3. Scherzo

	∅	2(picc)1+ca.22/4221/timp.perc.bells.xyl/hp/pf			
		str	15'	Ricordi,1935	Misc 2600

VERMEULEN, Matthijs (1888-1967)

SYMPHONY No.1 (1942)	∅	3(2picc)3(3ca)2+2E♭cl+bcl.3/4331/timp.		
		perc.tamtam/2hp/str	Donemus,1953	Misc 10575

VERNON, Joseph (1738-1782)

STRAWBERRY HILL: song
   in G, arr F.Collinson   ø   1121/2200/perc/hp.pf/str   Arranger   MS 30978
WHO IS SYLVIA: song
   in Eb, arr F.Collinson   ø   1121/2200/str   Arranger   MS 30982

VEROLI, M.di   see   DI VEROLI, M.

VERROUST

La CHASTE SUZANNE for trombone and orch
   arr A.Evans   PC 2(picc)222/2220/perc/str   Boosey & H   11231
VESPER HYMN: trad air
   in B   ø   1110/2000/perc/hp.org/str   Composer   4840

VICTORY, Gerard (1921-

GAELIC GALOP   PC 2121/2230/perc/str   2'50"   Bosworth,1960   23272 B
The ISLAND PEOPLE: radio production (1968)
                    ø   2(picc/221/2220/timp.perc.glock.vib.xyl/
                        cel.hp/str   Composer MS:BBC   MS 31630
The PENNINE WAY (Music Workshop stage 2): (1971)
                    ø   11(ca)10/1210/timp.perc/hp/voices   Composer MS:BBC   MS 31669

VIDAL, Paul (1863-1931)

La MALADETTA: BALLET
   Suite pyrénéenne
      arr Wittmann   ø   2(picc)2(ca)22/4230.oph/timp.perc/hp/str   Choudens   9801
PETITE SUITE ESPAGNOLE
   1. Introduction et danse de cour   4. Rêverie
   2. Sarabande   5. Pastorale
   3. Danse moresque
                    PC 2222/2000/timp.perc/hp/str   Heugel   8492
VARIATIONS JAPONAISES   PC 3333+cbsn/42.2.cnt.31/timp/cel.hp/str   3'30"   Heugel   8624
ZINO ZINA: ballet
   Scènes galantes
      1. Marche des cadeaux   4. Tambourin
      2. Ballabile: ballet des cadeaux   5. Volte
      3. Musette
   Danses anciennes
      6. Menuet   8. Courante à la française
      7. Sarabande   9. Gavotte
   Danse tanagréenes
     10. Danse des ménades   12. Danse des crotales
     11. Danse d'Aphrodite
       Complete   ø   2(picc)2(ca)22/41.2cnt.31/timp.perc/hp/str   Heugel   7557-9
       Scènes galantes ø   2(picc)2(ca)22/41.2cnt.31/timp.perc/hp/str   Heugel   15116

VIDERIQUE, A

ROSES AND THORNS: Mexican dance
   arr H.Balfour   PC 2222/2230.euph/timp.perc/str   Hawkes   4663

VIERLING, Georg

AN DEN WASSERN ZU BABEL (PSALM 137) for T-solo, chorus & orch, op.22
ø   2222/4230/timp/str   Leuckart   Misc 9242

VIEUXTEMPS, Henri (1820-1881)

BALLADE ET POLONAISE DE CONCERT for violin and orch, op.38
ø   1222/2200/timp/str   10'   J.Schuberth   6310
CONCERTI
   Cello & orch, op.46, in A min-maj
ø   2222/2200/timp/str   (Brandus)   27116
     Violin & orchestra
       No.3, op.25, in A   PC   2(picc)222/4230/timp.perc/str   25'   Joubert   11822
       No.4, op.31, in D min   ø   2222/4230/timp/hp/str   André   14190 C
       No.5, op.37, in A min   ø   1222/2200/timp/str   17'   Eulenburg   6300 +
       No.6, op.47, in G   PC   str   20'   Brandus   11823
       No.7, op.49. in A min   PC   2222/2230/timp/hp/str   Brandus   11824
FANTASIA APPASSIONATA: Concertstück for violin and orch, op.35
ø   1222/2200/timp/str   16'   J.Schuberth   9844
RÊVERIE op.22 no.3
   arr R.Jungnickel   PC   2222/4231/timp/str   Jungnickel   7860
   orch E.Sauret   ø   2222/2000/timp/str   Bote & B [c.1870] 26292
SALTARELLE op.54a
   arr B.Godard   ø   2+picc.222/2231/timp.perc./str   Joubert   10321 B

VILBAC, Alphonse Charles Renaud de (1829-1884)

MARCHE SERBE   ø   1+picc.222/4231/timp.perc/str   Enoch   6965

VILLA-LOBOS, Heitor (1887-1959)

AMAZONAS: ballet for orchestra   ø   2+picc.2+ca.2+E♭cl+bcl.2+cbsn.sarr/
42.2cnt.31/timp.perc/cel.hp.pf/violinophone.
vla-d'a.str   11'   Eschig   16142
BACHIANAS BRASILEIRAS
   No.1 for 8 solo cellos
      1. Introduction (Embolada)
      2. Preludio (Modinha)
      3. Fugue (Conversa)
ø   8vlc (or vlc, 2vlas)   18'   AMP,1948   25050 +
   No.2 for orchestra
      1. Preludio (O Canto do Capadocio)
      2. Aria (O Canto da Nossa Terra)
      3. Dansa (Lembranca do Sertão)
      4. Tocata (O Tremzinho do Caipíra)(The little train)
ø   1(picc)11.sx.1+cbsn/2010/timp.perc.tamtam/
cel.pf/str   Ricordi,1953   Misc 4094 B
   No.3 for piano and orchestra
      1. Preludio (Ponteio)
      2. Fantasia (Deraneio)
      3. Aria (Modinha)
      4. Tocata (Picapao)
ø   2+picc.2+ca.2+bcl.2+cbsn/4241/timp.xyl.pf/str   Ricordi,1953   Misc 4095 B

VILLA-LOBOS, Heitor (cont)

BACHIANAS BRASILEIRAS (cont)
    No.4 for orchestra
        1. Preludio (Introdução)
        2. Coral (Canto do Sertão)
        3. Aria (Cantiga)
        4. Dansa (Modinha)

	⌀	2+picc.2+ca.22+cbsn/4331/timp.perc.xyl/ cel/str		Ricordi,1953	Misc 4095 B
No.5 for soprano and orchestra of cellos					
	⌀	vlcs	11'	AMP,1947	Misc 3722 C
arr J.Krance for full orch	⌀	2(picc)1+ca.2(bcl)2/2220/timp.perc.bells/ cel.gtr.hp/str	6'40"	AMP,1971	Misc 8235
arr J.Krance for string orch	⌀	[gtr]/str		AMP,1971	Misc 8236
No.6 for flute and bassoon	⌀	fl.bsn		AMP	V 1810
No.8 for orch	⌀	2+picc.2+ca.2+bcl.2+cbsn/4231/timp.perc. xyl/cel/str	25'	Eschig,1969	Misc 7245
No.9 for string orch	⌀	str	15'	Eschig,1969	Misc 7246

CAIXINHA DE BOAS FESTAS, or Vitrine Encantada (The Magic Window): children's ballet (symphonic poem)

	⌀	2+picc.2+ca.2+bcl.2+cbsn/4321/timp.perc.tamtam. xyl/cel.hp.pf/str	30'	Ricordi,1952	Misc 4086 B

CANTO DO CYSNE NEGRO (The black swan): song

in A min arr W.Goehr	⌀	2(picc)0.ca.21/2230/perc/cel.hp/str		Arranger	TO 1079

CHÔROS (nos.2,3,4,7   see   CHAMBER CATALOGUE)

No.8 for orchestra	⌀	2+picc.2+ca.2[=4]+bcl.sx.2+cbsn/4341/ timp.perc.tamtam.xyl/cel.2hp.2pf/str	18'	Eschig	Misc 880
No.10 'Rasga o Coraçaó': for SAT.Bar.B chorus & orch					
	⌀	2+picc.22.sx.2+cbsn/3220/timp.perc/hp.pf/ str	10'30"	Eschig	Misc 881
	⌀	2+picc.22.sx.2+cbsn/3220/timp.perc/hp.pf/ str		Russian SM,1970	Misc 7250

CIRANDA DAS SETE NOTAS, for bassoon and strings

	⌀	str		(Southern NY,1961)	24244

CONCERTO

Guitar & orch (1951)	⌀	1111/1010/str	20'	Eschig,1971	Misc 8120

DANSES AFRICAINES (Danses des Indiens Métis de Brésil)

	⌀	2+2picc.2+ca.22+cbsn/4431/timp.perc.tamtam. xyl/cel.2hp.pf/str	20'	Eschig	Misc 878

EROSÃO (Erosion): Légende indienne No.1 (Les Origines de l'Amazone): symphonic poem   Eschig,1955   Misc 4504

	⌀	2+picc.2+ca.2+bcl.2+cbsn/4341/timp.perc.xyl/cel.hp.pf/ str	15'	Eschig,1955	Misc 4504

FANTASIA for saxophone, 3F horns & strings (1948)

	⌀	str		Southern NY,1963	Misc 6875

FANTASY IN THREE MOVEMENTS in the form of a 'chôros', for wind orchestra

	⌀	6+2picc.6+2ca.6+Ebcl+acl+bcl+cbcl.6+2cbsn/ 63.flg.2Ctpt.61/timp.perc.vib.xyl/ cel.hp.[pf]/2cb		Peters,1959	Misc 5304

NONETTO

	⌀	111.sx.1/0000/perc/cel.hp.pf	18	Eschig,1954	Misc 4187 B

L'ODYSÉE D'UNE RACE: symphonic poem

	⌀	2222/cbsn/4231/timp.perc/xyl/cel.2hp.pf/ str str		Israeli Mus Pub,1954	Misc 3507

OUVERTURE DE L'HOMME TEL from 'Suite Sugestiva' for orchestra

		1(picc)111/1110/timp.perc/cel.pf/str		Eschig,1954	Misc 4186

Le POLICHINELLE from 'Prole do Bêbê': suite for piano

arr F.Guenther	PC	2+picc.22.3sx.2/2321/perc/hp/str		E.B.Marks	3680 B

VILLA-LOBOS, Heitor (cont)

SINFONIETTAS for small orchestra
No.1	φ	2222/2220/timp/str	20'	Southern NY,1955	Misc 4452
No.2	φ	1(picc)1(ca)1(bcl).sx.1/3221/timp.perc.xyl/			
		cel.hp/str	20'	Southern NY,1960	Misc 5279
UIRAPURÛ: ballet for orchestra	φ	2+picc.2+ca.2+bcl.2+cbsn/4331/timp.perc.			
		glock.xyl/cel.2hp.pf/violinophone.str	18'	AMP,1948	Misc 3695

VILLE, P.B.de   see   DE VILLE, P.B.

VILLIERS, M.L.de

Die STEM VAN SUIT-AFRIKA: national anthem of South Africa
	PC	2(picc)222/4230/timp.perc/str	Breitkopf	14305
arr Franzel	φ	2+picc.22.2+cbsn/4231/timp.perc/str	Arranger	19651
arr G.Jacob	φ	2+picc.222/4331/timp.perc/str	Arranger	20734

VINCENT, George F.

The FLAG THAT FLEW AT TRAFALGAR: song
in C	2222/2220/timp.perc/str	Schirmer 1914	18291

VINCENTI, Benedetto

BOLIVIANOS, EL HADO PROPICIO: national anthem of Bolivia (adopted 1842)
	PC	2(picc)222/4220/str	Benjamin	16364
arr M.L.Lake	PC	112.2sx.1/2210/perc/str	C.Fischer	19720
	PC	2(picc)222/4230/timp.perc/str	Breitkopf	14305
arr G.French	φ	2222/2230/timp.perc/str	Blandford	25228 +

VINCI, Leonardo (1690-1730)

ALESSANDRO NELL' INDIE
Symphony, in D	φ	0200/2200/str	Bernoulli,1954	21207

CATONE IN UTICA: opera (1728)
  Extracts
    Con si bel nome: aria for Soprano & orch
in D	φ	0100/0000/str/cont	Arno Volk,1976 Analecta Mus 16	BRL φ only

DIDONE ABBANDONATA: opera (1726)
  Complete with intro, by H.M.Brown
  Facsimile of contemporary MS score
	φ	020[1]/2200/str/cont	Garland,1977	MRL Facs

  Extracts
    Ardi per me fedele: aria for Soprano solo & orch
in D (orig), ed R.Strohm	φ	0000/2000/str/cont	Arno Volk,1976 Analecta Mus 16	BRL φ only

La FESTA DE BACCO: opera (1722)
  Extracts
    Si mbe so'nzemprecella: aria for Soprano solo & orch
in A (orig), ed R.Strohm	φ	str/cont	Arno Volk,1976 Analecta Mus 16	BRL φ only

LIONEL AND CLARISSA: opera
  Extracts
    Come then, pining, peevish lover: song
in Eb arr G.Williams	φ	1000/0000/hpsd/str	Arranger	9555

PER L'AFRICANE ARENE: aria for Contralto solo & orch (Inserted in Handel's 'Poro')
ed F.Chrysander	φ	0000/2000/str/cont	Breitkopf.Handel CW,1880/Kalmus	Misc 8995

La ROSMIRA FELELE: opera (1727)
  Extracts
    Al mio tesoro: aria for Tenor solo & orch
in C (orig) ed R.Strohm	φ	020[1]/0000/str/cont	Arno Volk,1976.Analecta Mus 16	BRL φ only

VINCI, Leonardo (cont)

SEMIRAMIDE RICONOSCIUTA: opera (1729)
    Extracts
        Tradita, sprezzata: aria for Soprano & orch
           in C min (orig), ed R.Strohm
                φ str/cont   Arno Volk,1976.Analecta Mus 16   BRL φ only

SIROE: opera (1726)
    Extracts
        Gelido in ogni vena: aria for Tenor & orch
           in B♭ (orig), ed R.Strohm
                φ str   Arno Volk,1976.Analecta Mus 16   BRL φ only

VINCZE, Imre (1926-1969)

RAPSODIA CONCERTANTE for piano & orch (1966)
               φ 2+picc.222/4231/timp.,erc.bells.glock/str   Ed Musica,1972   Misc 8299 B

VINTER, Gilbert (1909-1969)

ALLA POLKA	PC	1+picc.12.4sx.1/2230/timp.perc/cel.hp/str		Liber-Southern	19204
AUBADE	φ	str		Polyphonic Rep	LM G 10893
AU PRÈS DE MA BLONDE: Canadian trad song, arr					
	φ	2(picc)222/4230/perc/hp/str		Arranger	23371 +
A CELTIC LILT	PC	212.4sx.1/2230/timp.perc/str	4'	Bosworth	18812
The CHANTRYMAN (A Seascape for orchestra)					
	PC	2(picc)222/2230/timp.perc/str	5'30"	Boosey & H	14923 B
CHIHUAHUA: fantasy on Mexican airs & dances					
	PC	1+picc.12.4sx.1/2230/timp.perc/acdn.hp/str		Boosey & H	19478 B
CHIN CHIN JOSS		2121/2220/perc/hp/str		Composer	TO 1363
A CHRISTMAS FANTASY		22+ca.22/2230/timp.perc/cel.hp/str	12'	Composer	21696 B +
CHRISTMAS SINFONIETTA	φ	2(picc)12(bcl)1/2230/perc.glock.vib/ cel.hp/str	10'	Universal/Kalmus,1956	Misc 4686
An ENGLISH RHAPSODY	φ	22(ca)22/4230/timp.perc.glock.xyl/hp/str		Polyphonic Rep,1966	24539
ESCENA INDIA	φ	2+picc.2+ca.22/4231/timp.perc/hp/str	7'	Composer,1956	21787 +
FÊTE BASQUE	φ	2222/4230/timp.perc/hp/str	4'	(Composer)	24457 + Am
FOLK TUNE SELECTIONS, arr					
Austria	φ	2121/2230/timp.perc/hp/str		Arranger MS:BBC	MS 20342 Am
Britain	φ	2(picc)1(ca)2(bcl)1/2230/timp.perc/hp/str		Arranger MS:BBC	MS 20277 Am
Bulgaria	φ	2(picc)1(ca)21/2230/perc/hp/str		Arranger MS:BBC	MS 20341 Am
Denmark	φ	2(picc)121/2230/timp.perc/hp/str		Arranger MS:BBC	MS 20321 Am
Finland	φ	2(picc)121/2230/perc/hp/str		Arranger MS:BBC	MS 20346 Am
France	φ	2(picc)121/2230/timp.perc/hp/str		Arranger MS:BBC	MS 20320 Am
France (2nd selection)		2(picc)12(bcl)1/2230/perc/hp/str		Arranger MS:BBC	MS 20348 Am
Greece	φ	2(picc)1(ca)2(bcl)1/2230/timp.perc/hp/str		Arranger MS:BBC	MS 20323 Am
Holland	φ	2(picc)121/2230/timp.perc/hp/str		Arranger MS:BBC	MS 20278 Am
Hungary	φ	2(picc)121/2230/timp.perc/hp/str		Arranger MS:BBC	MS 20319 Am
Iceland	φ	2(picc)1(ca)2(bcl)1/2230/timp.perc/hp/str		Arranger MS:BBC	MS 20428 Am
Norway	φ	2(picc)12(bcl)1/2230/timp.perc/hp/str		Arranger MS:BBC	MS 20279 Am
Poland	φ	2(picc)1(ca)21/2230/timp.perc/hp/str		Arranger MS:BBC	MS 20350 Am
Portugal	φ	2(picc)1(ca)21/2230/perc/hp/str		Arranger MS:BBC	MS 20322 Am
Rumania	φ	2(picc)1(ca)21/2230/timp.perc/hp/str		Arranger MS:BBC	MS 20351 Am
Russia	φ	2(picc)1(ca)2(bcl)1/2230/perc/hp/str		Arranger MS:BBC	MS 20349 Am
Spain	φ	2(picc)121/2230/perc/hp/str		Arranger MS:BBC	MS 20347 Am
Switzerland	φ	2(picc)12(bcl)1/2230/perc/hp/str		Arranger MS:BBC	MS 20343 Am

FRIDAY NIGHT IS MUSIC NIGHT: medley of choruses (1957)
    1. The King's horses (N.Gay)   (L.Wright)
    2. Oh, oh, Antonio (Murphy & Lipton)   (F ♩ & H)
    3. The Roses of Picardy (H.Wood)   (Chappell)
    4. The Soldiers in the park (L.Monckton)   (Chappell)
                   φ 1+picc.222/4230/timp.perc/str   Arranger MS:BBC   22157 +

VINTER, Gilbert (cont)

FRIDAY STREET for oboe & orch	φ	cel[=hp]/str		5'	Polyphonic Rep,1961	23580
Las GOLONDRINAS: Mexican song, arr						
in A	φ	2222/4230/timp.perc/hp/str			Arranger MS:BBC	21934
HEY, NONNY NO, for chorus & orch	φ	2(picc)222/4230/timp.perc.glock.xyl/hp/str			(Polyphonic Rep)	24519
HIGH PLAIN AND PAMPAS: suite	PC	2(picc)222/4230/timp.perc.tamb/hp/str			Mills,1959	26604 A B**
HUNTERS MOON for horn and orchestra						
	φ	2121/0000/perc/hp/str		5'30"	Boosey,1966	24497
IRISH JOURNEY	PC	21.ca.21/2230/timp.perc/hp/str		3'30"	A H & C,1955	21447 B
JEUNE FILLE	PC	212+bcl.1/2000/timp.perc/hp/str		4'	Inter-Art 1956	22071
LATIN-AMERICA: suite						

1. Alla cueca   2. Lamento   3. Alla rumba

	PC	2+picc.1+ca.2.3sx.1/2230/timp.perc/				
		acdn.org/str		13'	Bosworth	19297
The LITTLE ISLAND RHAPSODY	φ	1000/0000/hp/str			Universal London,1959	22778 B
MARCH MEDLEY (World War I) for military band & orch						

1. Colonel Bogey (K.J.Alford)   (Boosey & H)
2. On the quarter deck (K.J.Alford)   (Boosey & H)
3. El Abanico (A.Javaloyes)   (Boosey & H)
4. National Emblem (E.E.Bagley)   (Wood Ms Co)
5. Le Regiment de Sambre et Meuse (A.Turlet)   (Lafleur)
6. Blaze away (A.Holzmann)   (Feldman)
7. The Great little army (K.J.Alford)   (Boosey & H)

	φ	2(2picc)222/4230/timp.perc/hp/str				24079 +
MEN OF HARLECH: Welsh song, arr for male voices and orch						
in Bb, arr H.Evans	φ	2222/4230/timp.perc/str			(Ed Pub Co Wrexham)	22384 +
MEXICAN FANTASIA arr	φ	2(picc)+picc.1(ca)21/2230/timp.perc/hp/str			BBC	4743
MR KNOW-ALL: overture	φ	2(picc)222/4331/timp.perc/hp/str		3'30"	Composer,1960	23173 +
MUSIC OF THE PEOPLE: signature tune for radio programme						
	φ	hp/str			BBC	MS 20476 +
OVERTURE TO A NEW VENTURE (1965)	φ	2(picc)2(ca)22/4230/timp.perc/hp/str		7'30"	Composer,1965	24192 +
PEEP SHOW: a humoureske for woodwind						
	φ	2(picc)121[=bcl]		2'20"	C.Connelly	LM G 7307
PRAISE TO THE LORD: hymn (No.536. The English Hymnal) arr						
in G, arr for solo voice, chorus & orch						
		org/str			(OUP)	23313 +
REVERIE: a signature tune, arr	φ	2222/4230/timp.perc/hp/str			(OUP)	21917 +
RHAPSODY ECUADOR	φ	2222/4230/timp.perc/hp/str			(orig)	22982 +
SCREWBALL for violin (or xylophone) solo and orch						
	PC	222.3sx.2/2230/perc/str			Hawkes	20565
SONG-DANCE: suite						

1. Song-Dance   2. Fado   3. Kolo

	φ	2(picc)1+ca.21/2230/timp/cel.hp/str			Mozart Ed	24863
SONG MEDLEY (refrains only), arr						

All the nice girls (B.Scott)   My bonnie (trad)
You made me love you (J.Monaco)   Avalon (Jolson & Rose)

	φ	2(picc)222/4230/timp.perc/pf/str			(Feldman,1957)	22241 +
SONG SELECTIONS						
Africa ('Music of Africa')	φ	222(bcl)2/4220/timp.perc/hp/str			Composer MS:BBC	MS 31123 Am
The Afrikaans	φ	2(picc)222/4230/perc/hp/str			Composer MS:BBC	MS 31127 Am
The American Negro	φ	2(picc)1(ca)21/2230/perc/cel.hp/str			Composer MS:BBC	MS 31124 Am
Argentina	φ	2(picc)1(ca)21/2220/perc/hp/str			Composer MS:BBC	MS 31126 Am
Australia	φ	2(picc)22(bcl)2/2230/perc/hp/str			Composer MS:BBC	MC 31125 Am
The Balearic islands	φ	2(picc)2(ca)22/4230/perc/hp/str			Composer MS:BBC	MS 31130 Am
The Basque	φ	2(picc)2(ca)2(bcl)2/4230/timp.perc/hp/str			Composer MS:BBC	MS 31132 Am
Brazil	φ	2(picc)2(ca)2(sx)2/4230/perc/hp/str			Composer MS:BBC	MS 31133 Am
The British	φ	2(picc)222/2230/timp.perc/hp/str			Composer MS:BBC	MS 20241 Am
The British dominions	φ	2(picc)121/2230/timp.perc/hp/str			Composer MS:BBC	MS 20478 Am

VINTER, Gilbert (cont)

SONG SELECTIONS (cont)

The British grenadiers	φ	2222/4230/perc/cel/str	Composer MS:BBC	MS 31128 Am
British Guiana	φ	222.sx.2/4230/perc/hp.pf/str	Composer MS:BBC	MS 31129 Am
British Isles	φ	0.2picc.222/4231/timp.perc/hp/str	Composer MS:BBC	MS 31131 Am
Canada	φ	2(picc)2(ca)22/4230/timp.perc/hp/str	Composer MS:BBC	MS 31134 Am
Children's songs	φ	2(picc)2(ca)22/4230/timp.perc/cel.hp/str	Composer MS:BBC	MS 31135 Am
Chile	φ	2(picc)1(ca)21/2230/perc/hp/str	Composer MS:BBC	MS 31136 Am
China	φ	2(picc)2(ca)22/4230/perc/cel.hp/str	Composer MS:BBC	MS 31137 Am
The Commonwealth	φ	2(picc)2(ca)22/4230/timp.perc/hp/str	Composer MS:BBC	MS 31140 Am
Cuba	φ	2(picc)12(bcl)sx.1/2220/timp.perc/hp.pf/str	Composer MS:BBC	MS 31138 Am
Czechoslovakia	φ	2(picc)1(ca)21/2230/timp.perc/hp/str	Composer MS:BBC	MS 31139 Am
The English	φ	2(picc)222/2230/timp.perc/hp/str	Composer MS:BBC	MS 20163 Am
The English (sel.No.2)	φ	2(picc)2(ca)22/4230/perc/hp/str	Composer MS:BBC	MS 31143 Am
Germany	φ	2121/2230/timp.perc/hp/str	Composer MS:BBC	MS 31141 Am
The Greek Islands	φ	21.ca.1.2sx.2/4230/timp.perc/pf/str	Composer MS:BBC	MS 31142 Am
The Irish	φ	2(picc)222/2230/timp.perc/hp/str	Composer MS:BBC	MS 20239 Am
Israel	φ	21.ca.22/4230/perc/str	Composer MS:BBC	MS 31144 Am
Italy	φ	2(picc)121/2230/perc/hp/str	Composer MS:BBC	MS 31145 Am
Japan	φ	2(picc)2(ca)22/4220/perc/hp/str	Composer MS:BBC	MS 31146 Am
Latin-America	φ	2(picc)1(ca)2(bcl)1/2230/timp.perc/hp/str	Composer MS:BBC	MS 20477 Am
Luxembourg	φ	2(picc)121/2230/timp.perc/str	Composer MS:BBC	MS 20429 Am
The Manxman	φ	222(bcl)2/4230/timp.perc/hp/str	Composer MS:BBC	MS 31148 Am
The Maori	φ	21(ca)21/2230/perc/hp/str	Composer MS:BBC	MS 31147 Am
Old London	φ	2(picc)222/4330/perc/hp/str	Composer MS:BBC	MS 31149 Am
Peru	φ	2(picc)1ca.22/4230/timp.perc/hp/str	Composer MS:BBC	MS 31150 Am
The Scottish	φ	2(picc)222/2230/timp.perc/hp/str	Composer MS:BBC	MS 20216 Am
The Sea (Sea chanties)	φ	2(picc)1(ca)21/2230/timp.perc/hp/str	Composer MS:BBC	MS 31152 Am
Sweden	φ	2(picc)121/2230/perc/cel.hp/str	Composer MS:BBC	MS 31151 Am
The U.S.A.	φ	2(picc)1(ca)2(bcl)1/2230/timp.perc/hp/str	Composer MS:BBC	MS 20466 Am
The Welsh	φ	2(picc)222/2230/timp.perc/hp/str	Composer MS:BBC	MS 20194 Am
Yugoslavia	φ	2(picc)1(ca)2(bcl)1/2230/timp.perc/hp/str	Composer MS:BBC	MS 20427 Am

SONGS OF FRANCE: (No.3 pf 'A heritage of melody') arr
                   PC   2121/2230/timp.perc/hp/str   Planetary-Kahl,1959   23071

SONGS OF THE BRITISH ISLES: fantasia for Soprano solo, chorus, string trio, concert (military)band & orch
  Men of Harlech; Last rose of summer; Road to the isles; Heart of Oak
                   φ   2222/4230/perc/hp/str   Composer MS:BBC   22658 +

THEATRE ROYAL MELODIES: vocal selection arr G.Vinter, R.Docker & S.Torch, for Soprano, chorus & orch
  Excerpts from various musical plays, arr
                   φ   2(picc)2(ca)22/4331/timp.perc/hp.pf/str   (Chappell)   22943 +

WALTZING WITH SULLIVAN: potpourri of waltzes, arr
                   φ   2222/4230/timp.perc/hp/str   Arranger MS:BBC   22497 +

El YUMBO (on an Aboriginal Ecuadorian melody)]
                   φ   1+picc.0.ca.2+bcl.1/2230/timp.perc/hp/str   Arranger MS:BBC   21915

VIOLA, Anselmo (1738-1798)

CONCERTO for bassoon and orchestra, in F   Montestier de Montserrat.1936.
  ed D.Pujol   φ   0200/0200/str/cont   Mestres de L'Escolania Vol.2   MRL

VIOTTI, Giovanni Battista (1755-1824)

CONCERTI
  Cello & orch
    in C, ed I.Gomez   φ   0200/2000/str   A.Bruzzichelli,1968   Misc 6806
  Piano & orch
    in G min, rev R.Giazotto   φ   2222/2200/timp/str   41'   Ricordi,1960   Misc 5391

VIOTTI, Giovanni Battista (cont)

CONCERTI (cont)

No.7, in Bb						
ed C.White	φ	0200/2000/str			A-R Edns,1976	Misc 9040
No.13, in A						
ed C.White	φ	0200/2000/str			A-R Edns,1976	Misc 9040
No.17, in D min						
ed D.Da Deppe: cadenzas by C.Rossi						
	φ	str			Otos,1977	Misc 9487
No.18, in E min						
ed C.White	φ	0200/2000/str			A-R Edns,1976	Misc 9041
No.19, in G min						
rev & cadenza by R.Giazotto						
	φ	2220/2000/str		33'	Ricordi,1964	24470
No.22, in A min	φ	1222/2200/timp/str		27'	Breitkopf	20960 +
ed A.Einstein	φ	1222/2200/timp/str			Eulenburg,1929	Misc 4087 (
No.27, in C						
ed C.White	φ	1202/2000/str			A-R Edns,1976	Misc 9041

SINFONIE CONCERTANTI

No.1,for two violins, 2 oboes, 2 horns & strings					
arr F.Quaranta	φ	str		Carisch,1960	Misc 5987
No.2, for 2 violins & orchestra					
arr F.Quaranta	φ	2222/2000/str		Carisch,1946	21640

VIRGO, Edwin

PLAISIRS INCONNUE: waltz					
arr H.Carruthers	PC	2121/2230/timp.perc/hp/str	4'45"	Hawkes,1953	22013

VISKI, János (1906-1961)

CONCERTO for violin & orch	φ	3(picc)2(ca)22/4331/timp.perc.xyl/cel.hp/			
		str	31'	Ed Musica,1958	Misc 5088

VITALI, Giovanni Battista (1644-1692)

CAPRICCIO for strings				
arr G.Lenzewski	φ	str	Vieweg	Misc 992

VITALI, Tommaso Antonio (1663-1745)

CIACCONA					
orch O.Respighi for violin, organ & strings					
	φ	str	10'	G.Schmidl,1911	Misc 1457

VĪTOLINS, Jānis

LATVIAN RHAPSODY No.1	φ	2(picc)222/4231/timp.perc.vib/cel.hp/str	14'45"	Universal	Misc 1933

VITTADINI, Franco (1884-1948)

ANIMA ALLEGRA: fantasia	PC	2(picc)222/2230/timp.perc/str		Ricordi	11353
SCHERZO	φ	2+picc.2+ca.2+bcl.2+cbsn/4300/timp.perc/			
		cel.2hp.pf/str		Ricordi 1931	Misc 8817

VIVALDI, Antonio (1675-1741)

    see   RYOM, Peter. Verzeichnis der Werke Antonio Vivaldis. Leipzig: DVfM, 1974. Vivaldi's works are numbered in accordance with this index, prefix RV. Conversion tables are to be found at the end of the sequence. Only the 18th century opus numbers are quoted (op.1-op.14)

COMPLETE WORKS

    Le opere di Antonio Vivaldi. Ricordi, 1947 (Instituto Antonio Vivaldi. Direzione artistica di Gian Francesco Malipiero)

AL SANTO SEPOLCRO see SONATA for strings, RV 130, in E♭, and CONCERTI for strings, RV 169, in B min

ALLA MADRIGALESCA see CONCERTI for strings, RV 129, in D min

ALLA RUSTICA see CONCERTI for strings, RV 151, in G

ANDANTE	str	[BBC/M.Pincherle]	19389 pts only

(ϕ with   )
M.Pincherle)

ARMIDA AL CAMPO D'EGITTO

    Sinfonia, RV 699 (see also RV 710)

ed J.Szabolczi	ϕ	str	Hungarian SM,1961	Misc 5647

BEATUS VIR (Psalm 111/112)

    RV 597, in C, for soli, double chorus & orch

        ed B.Maderna for SST soli, double chorus & orch

                ϕ   orch 1: 0200/0000/str/cont

                    orch 2: str/cont   Ricordi,1967   25199

        ed R.Fasano for SSAATBB soli, double chorus & orch

                ϕ   orch 1: 0200/0000/str/cont

                    orch 2: str/cont   Philharmonia,1972   Misc 7931

        ed R.Fasano with additional editing & realisation

                ϕ   orch 1: 0200/0000/str/cont(org=hpsd)

                    orch 2: str/cont(org=hpsd)   Universal,1972   Misc 7931 B

    RV 598, in B♭, for SSA soli, chorus & orch

ed A.Corghi	ϕ	str/cont	Ricordi,1970	Misc 7248
ed K.H.Füssl	ϕ	str/cont	Philharmonia,1967	25197
ed K.H.Füssl	ϕ	str/cont(org=hpsd)	Universal,1969	25197

La CACCIA see CONCERTI: violin, RV 362, in B♭ (3rd mvt of 'The Seasons' has the same title)

CANTO IN PRATO: motet for Soprano (or Tenor) & orch, RV 623, in A

ed R.Blanchard	ϕ	str/cont	Heugel,1968	Misc 9060

CESSATE OMAI CESSATE: cantata for Contralto & orch, RV 684

ed B.Martinotti	ϕ	str/cont	Zerboni,1972	Misc 7871

La CETRA: 11 concerti for violin, strings & cont, 1 concerto for 2 violins, strings & continuo, op.9

    1. RV 181(a), in C   7. RV 359, in B♭

    2. RV 345, in A   8. RV 238, in D min

    3. RV 334, in G min   9. RV 530 (for 2 violins), in B♭

    4. RV 263, in F   10. RV 300, in G

    5. RV 358, in A min   11. RV 198, in C min

    6. RV 348, in A   12. RV 391, in B min

        Complete, ed D.Stevens   ϕ str/cont   (BBC/Le Cene [1727])   20641-2+& mf 144

        see also separate entries under individual concerti

Il CIMENTO DELL'ARMONIA E DELL'INVENZIONE: 12 concerti for violin, strings and continuo, op.8

    (Nos 1-4 are 'The Seasons')

    1. RV 269, in E   7. RV 242, in D min 'Per Pisendel'

    2. RV 315, in G min   8. RV 332, in G min

    3. RV 293, in F   9. RV 236 & 454, in D min (for vln or ob)

    4. RV 279, in F min   10. RV 362, in B♭

    5. RV 253, in E♭ 'La Tempesta   11. RV 210, in D

       di Mare'   12. RV 178 & 449, in C (for vln or ob)

    6. RV 180, in C, 'Il Piacere'

       see also entries under individual concerti and 'The SEASONS' for nos. 1-4

VIVALDI, Antonio (cont)

CONCERTI FOR 1 (OR MORE THAN 1 SIMILAR) SOLO INSTRUMENT
  Bassoon

RV 466, in C						
ed G.F.Malipiero	φ	str/cont(hpsd)		10'	Ricordi,1957.CW 274	Misc 4922
RV 467, in C						
ed G.F.Malipiero	φ	str/cont(hpsd)		10'30"	Ricordi,1956.CW 239	Misc 4707
RV 469, in C						
ed G.F.Malipiero	φ	str/cont(hpsd)		11'30"	Ricordi,1956.CW 237	Misc 4708
RV 470, in C						
ed G.F.Malipiero	φ	str/cont(hpsd)		10'	Ricordi,1958.CW 281	Misc 5089
RV 471, in C						
ed G.F.Malipiero	φ	str/cont(hpsd)			Ricordi,1958.CW 282	Misc 5091
see also version for oboe, RV 450, in C						
RV 472, in C						
ed G.F.Malipiero	φ	str/cont(hpsd)		8'30"	Ricordi,1956.CW 238	Misc 4706
RV 473, in C						
ed G.F.Malipiero	φ	str/cont(hpsd)			Ricordi,1951.CW 118	Misc 3672
RV 474, in C						
ed V.Amendola	φ	str/cont(hpsd)			Ricordi,1949.CW 47	26551 & MRL
RV 475, in C						
ed G.F.Malipiero	φ	str/cont(hpsd)		9'	Ricordi,1957.CW 267	Misc 4924 &
RV 476, in C						
ed G.F.Malipiero	φ	str/cont(hpsd)		7'30"	Ricordi,1958.CW 277	Misc 5092 &
RV 477, in C						
ed G.F.Malipiero	φ	str/cont(hpsd)		11'	Ricordi,1955.CW 224	Misc 4580 &
RV 478, in C						
ed A.Ephrikian	φ	str/cont(hpsd)			Ricordi.1949.CW 34	Misc 2937 &
RV 479, in C						
ed G.F.Malipiero	φ	str/cont(hpsd)		9'30"	Ricordi,1957.CW 272	Misc 4923 &
RV 480, in C min						
ed G.F.Malipiero	φ	str/cont(hpsd)		9'	Ricordi,1955.CW 225	Misc 4581 &
RV 481, in D min						
ed G.F.Malipiero	φ	str/cont(hpsd)		9'	Ricordi,1949.CW 67	Misc 3136 &
see also version for cello, RV 406, in D min						
RV 483, in E♭						
ed G.F.Malipiero	φ	str/cont(hpsd)		9'	Ricordi,1957.CW 273	26504 + & M
RV 484, in E min						
ed G.F.Malipiero	φ	str/cont(hpsd)		10'-12'	Ricordi,1949.CW 71	Misc 3137 &
RV 485, in F (see also version for oboe, RV 457, in F)						
ed G.F.Malipiero	φ	str/cont(hpsd)		10'	Ricordi,1951.CW 109	Misc 3679 &
RV 486, in F						
ed G.F.Malipiero	φ	str/cont(hpsd)			Ricordi,1957.CW 268	Misc 4934 &
RV 487, in F						
ed G.F.Malipiero	φ	str/cont(hpsd)		8'30"	Ricordi,1956.CW 236	Misc 4718 &
RV 488, in F						
ed G.F.Malipiero	φ	str/cont(hpsd)		11'30"	Ricordi,1956.CW 240	Misc 4719 &
RV 489, in F						
ed G.F.Malipiero	φ	str/cont(hpsd)		10'	Ricordi,1957.CW 266	Misc 4933 &
RV 490, in F						
ed G.F.Malipiero	φ	str/cont(hpsd)		10'	Ricordi,1958.CW 278	Misc 5099 &
RV 491, in F						
ed G.F.Malipiero	φ	str/cont(hpsd)		8'30"	Ricordi,1957.CW 271	Misc 4931 &
RV 492, in G						
ed G.F.Malipiero	φ	str/cont(hpsd)			Ricordi,1957.CW 275	Misc 4937 &

VIVALDI, Antonio (cont)

CONCERTI (cont)

Bassoon (cont)

RV 493, in G
ed G.F.Malipiero	φ	str/cont(hpsd)	7'	Ricordi,1958.CW 276	Misc 5105 & MRL

RV 494, in G
ed G.F.Malipiero	φ	str/cont(hpsd)	10'	Ricordi,1958.CW 300	Misc 5104 & MRL

RV 495, in G min
ed G.F.Malipiero	φ	str/cont(hpsd)	11'	Ricordi,1957.CW 269	Misc 4940 & MRL

RV 496, in G min
ed G.F.Malipiero	φ	str/cont(hpsd)	11'30"	Ricordi,1955.CW 214	Misc 4590 & MRL

RV 497, in A min
ed L.Hara & O.Nagy	φ	str/cont(hpsd)		Ed Musica,1970	Misc 7551
ed G.F.Malipiero	φ	str/cont(hpsd)	10'	Ricordi,1949.CW 72	Misc 3138 & MRL

RV 498, in A min
ed A.Ephrikian	φ	str/cont(hpsd)		Ricordi,1949.CW 28	21481 & MRL

RV 499, in A min
ed G.F.Malipiero	φ	str/cont(hpsd)	9'	Ricordi,1955.CW 233	Misc 4571 & MRL

RV 500, in A min
ed G.F.Malipiero	φ	str/cont(hpsd)	10'	Ricordi,1951.CW 119	Misc 3661 & MRL

    see also version for oboe, RV 463, in A min

RV 501, in Bb 'La Notte'
ed A.Ephrikian	φ	str/cont(hpsd)	10'	Ricordi,1947.CW 12	Misc 2572 & MRL
ed F.Schroeder	φ	str	10'	Eulenburg,1964	25976

RV 502, in Bb
ed G.F.Malipiero	φ	str/cont(hpsd)	12'	Ricordi,1957.CW 270	Misc 4943 & MRL

RV 503, in Bb
ed G.F.Malipiero	φ	str/cont(hpsd)	9'	Ricordi,1958.CW 298	Misc 5112 & MRL

RV 504, in Bb
ed G.F.Malipiero	φ	str/cont(hpsd)	11'	Ricordi,1958.CW 299	Misc 5111 & MRL

Cello

RV 398, in C
ed G.F.Malipiero	φ	str/cont(hpsd)	8'30"	Ricordi,1955.CW 218	Misc 4575 & MRL

RV 399, in C
ed G.F.Malipiero	φ	str/cont(hpsd)	7'30"	Ricordi,1955.CW 211	Misc 4576 & MRL

RV 400, in C
ed G.F.Malipiero	φ	str/cont(hpsd)	11'30"	Ricordi,1955.CW 204	Misc 4574 & MRL

RV 401, in C min
ed G.F.Malipiero	φ	str/cont(hpsd)	11'	Ricordi,1947.CW 19	Misc 2579 & MRL

RV 402, in C min
ed F.Zobeley	φ	str/cont(hpsd)	10'	Ricordi,1972	Misc 8000
ed G.F.Malipiero	φ	str/cont(hpsd)		Ricordi,1952.CW 527	MRL

RV 403, in D
ed G.F.Malipiero	φ	str/cont(hpsd)	8'	Ricordi,1956.CW 235	Misc 4710 & MRL

RV 404, in D
ed G.F.Malipiero	φ	str/cont(hpsd)		Ricordi,1970.CW 500	Misc 7273 & MRL
ed E.Rapp	φ	str/cont(hpsd)		Schott,1951	21631

RV 405, in D min
	φ				
ed F.Zobeley	φ	str/cont(hpsd)	10'	Ricordi,1972	Misc 7994
ed F.Zobeley	φ	str/cont(hpsd)		Ricordi,1967.CW 524	MRL

RV 406, in D min
ed G.F.Malipiero	φ	str/cont(hpsd)		Ricordi,1955.CW 212	26570 & MRL
ed F.Schroeder	φ	str/cont(hpsd)		Eulenburg	24044

RV 407, in D min
ed F.Zobeley	φ	str/cont(hpsd)	11'	Ricordi,1972.CW 523	Misc 7993 & MRL

VIVALDI, Antonio (cont)

CONCERTI (cont)

  Cello (cont)

    RV 408, in E♭

      ed G.F.Malipiero   ϕ   str/cont(hpsd)   10'   Ricordi,1955.CW 206   Misc 4586 &

    RV 409, in E min

      ed G.F.Malipiero   ϕ   0001/0000/str/cont(hpsd)   10'   Ricordi,1952.CW 137   Misc 3884 &

    RV 410, in F

      ed G.F.Malipiero   ϕ   str/cont(hpsd)   10'30" Ricordi,1956.CW 243   Misc 4715 &

    RV 411, in F

      ed G.F.Malipiero   ϕ   str/cont(hpsd)   6'30" Ricordi,1956.CW 233   Misc 4714 &

    RV 412, in F

      ed G.F.Malipiero   ϕ   str/cont(hpsd)   7'   Ricordi,1955.CW 221   Misc 4588 &

    RV 413, in G

      ed G.F.Malipiero   ϕ   str/cont(hpsd)   10'   Ricordi,1956.CW 231   26586 & MRL

    RV 414, in G

      ed G.F.Malipiero   ϕ   str/cont(hpsd)   11'   Ricordi,1960.CW 317   Misc 5355 &
        (see also version for flute, RV 438, in G)

    RV 415, in G

      ed F.Zobeley   ϕ   str/cont(hpsd)   9'   Ricordi,1972.CW 523   Misc 7992 &
                      ϕ   str/cont(hpsd)   Ricordi.CW 522   MRL

    RV 416, in G min

      ed F.Zobeley   ϕ   str/cont(hpsd)   Ricordi,1972.CW 526   Misc 7999 &

    RV 417, in G min

      ed G.F.Malipiero   ϕ   str/cont(hpsd)   9'30" Ricordi,1926.CW 234   Misc 4723 &

    RV 418, in A min

      ed G.F.Malipiero   ϕ   str/cont(hpsd)   10'   Ricordi,1956.CW 244   Misc 4729 &

    RV 419, in A min

      ed G.F.Malipiero   ϕ   str/cont(hpsd)   7'   Ricordi,1955.CW 220   Misc 4568 &

    RV 420, in A min

      ed F.Zobeley   ϕ   str/cont(hpsd)   Ricordi,1972.CW 521   Misc 7991 &

    RV 421, in A min

      ed G.F.Malipiero   ϕ   str/cont(hpsd)   7'   Ricordi,1956.CW 232   Misc 4728 &

    RV 422, in A min

      ed G.F.Malipiero   ϕ   str/cont(hpsd)   10'   Ricordi,1955.CW 205   Misc 4567 &
      ed W.Upmeyer   ϕ   str/cont(hpsd)   Nagel,1952   21297

    RV 423, in B♭

      ed F.Zobeley   ϕ   str/cont(hpsd)   Ricordi,1972.CW 525   Misc 7995 &

    RV 424, in B min

      ed G.F.Malipiero   ϕ   str/cont(hpsd)   10'   Ricordi,1955.CW 219   26584 & MRL

  2 Cellos

    RV 531 in G min

      ed G.F.Malipiero   ϕ   str/cont(hpsd)   10'   Ricordi,1949.CW 61   26555 & MRL

Flute

  (see also CONCERTI: Recorder)

    RV 427, in D

      ed G.F.Malipiero   ϕ   str/cont(hpsd)   12'   Ricordi,1951.CW 102   Misc 3675 & M

    RV 428, in D (op.10,no.3)(see also version for flute, oboe, bassoon, violin & cont, RV 90, in D)
                         Chamber Catalogue)

      ed A.Einstein   ϕ   str/cont(hpsd) 'Il Gardellino'   Eulenburg,1930   22051
                      ϕ   str/cont(hpsd)   Broude   20657
      ed F.G.Malipiero   ϕ   str/cont(hpsd)   Ricordi,1953.CW 456   Misc 6833 &
      1st mvt only, ed Lenzewski

                      ϕ   str/cont(hpsd)   Vieweg   19623

    RV 429, in D

      ed G.F.Malipiero   ϕ   str/cont(hpsd)   10'   Ricordi,1953.CW 153   Misc 4044 & M

VIVALDI, Antonio (cont)

CONCERTI (cont)
  Flute (cont)
    RV 433, in F (op.10, no.1) 'La Tempesta di Mare' (see also version for flute, oboe, bassoon
                                                    & orch, RV 570, in F)

      ed G.F.Malipiero   ∅   str/cont(hpsd=org)   Ricordi,1968.CW 454   26574 & MRL
      arr W.Fortner for str & cont
                              ∅   str/cont(hpsd)   8'   Schott,1938   21251
    RV 434, in F (op.10, no.5)(see also version for recorder & orch, RV 442, in F)
      ed A.Ephrikian   ∅   str/cont(hpsd)   10'   Ricordi,1949.CW 46   26550 & MRL
      ed W.Fortner   ∅   str/cont(hpsd)   Schott   13958
    RV 435, in G (op.10, no.4)
      ed W.Fortner   ∅   str/cont(hpsd)   8'   Schott   13959
      ed G.F.Malipiero   ∅   str/cont(hpsd)   Ricordi,1968.CW 457   Misc 6834 & MRL
    RV 436, in G
      ed G.F.Malipiero   ∅   str/cont(hpsd)   9'30"   Ricordi,1953.CW 151   Misc 4052 & MRL
    RV 437, in G (op.10,no.6)
      ed G.F.Malipiero   ∅   str/cont(hpsd)   10'   Ricordi,1968.CW 458   Misc 6835 & MRL
        (see also version for flute, oboe, bassoon & continuo, RV 101, in G, Chamber Catalogue)
    RV 438, in G
      ed G.F.Malipiero   ∅   str/cont(hpsd)   10'30" Ricordi,1952.CW 138   Misc 3888 & MRL
        (see also version for cello & orch, in G, RV414)
    RV 439, in G min 'La Notte' (op.10,no.2)
      ed G.F.Malipiero   ∅   str/cont(hpsd)   10'   Ricordi,1968.CW 455   Misc 6832 & MRL
      ed A.Ephrikian   ∅   0001/0000/2vln/cont(hpsd)   Ricordi,1949.CW 33   23374 +
    RV 440, in A min
      ed G.F.Malipiero   ∅   str/cont(hpsd)   9'   Ricordi,1952.CW 148   26565 & MRL
    RV 441, in C min   see   CONCERTI: recorder, RV 441, in C min
  2 Flutes
    RV 533, in C
      ed G.F.Malipiero   ∅   str/cont(hpsd)   8'   Ricordi,1951.CW 101   Misc 3669 & MRL
      ed F.Schroeder   ∅   0001/0000/str/cont(hpsd)   Eulenburg,1963   24045
    RV 585, in F, for 2 flutes & double string orchestra
                              ∅   str/2cont(org)   5'   Acc Mus Chigiana,1949   Misc 4509,MRLfacs

  2 Horns
    RV 538, in F
      ed G.F.Malipiero   ∅   str/cont(hpsd)   6'-7'   Ricordi,1950.CW 91   21522 & MRL
    RV 539, in F
      ed G.F.Malipiero   ∅   str/cont(hpsd)   9'   Ricordi,1951.CW 121   Misc 3680 & MRL
                              ∅   str/cont   Eulenburg,1966   25977 B

  Mandolin
    RV 425, in C
      ed G.F.Malipiero   ∅   str/cont(hpsd)   7'   Ricordi,1950.CW 98   Misc 3482 B & MRL
  2 Mandolins
    RV 532, in G
      ed G.F.Malipiero   ∅   str/cont(org)   12'   Ricordi,1951.CW 104   Misc 3683 & MRL
  Oboe
    RV 447, in C (see also version for bassoon, RV 470, in C)
      ed G.F.Malipiero   ∅   str/cont(hpsd)   14'30" Ricordi,1955.CW 216   Misc 4578 & MRL
    RV 448, in C
      ed G.F.Malipiero   ∅   str/cont(hpsd)   10'   Ricordi,1955.CW 217   Misc 4577 & MRL
    RV 449, in C (for oboe or violin)
      ed G.F.Malipiero   ∅   str/cont(hpsd)   Ricordi,1950.CW 85   Misc 3478 & MRL
    RV 450, in C
      ed G.F.Malipiero   ∅   str/cont(hpsd)   10'   Ricordi,1958.CW 283   23327 & MRL
        (see also version for bassoon, RV 471, in C)

VIVALDI, Antonio (cont)

CONCERTI (cont)
  Oboe (cont)
    RV 451, in C
      ed G.F.Malipiero   φ   str/cont(hpsd)   9'30"   Ricordi,1955.CW 222   26585 & MR|
    RV 452, in C
      ed G.F.Malipiero   φ   str/cont(hpsd)   Ricordi,1951.CW 520   Misc 7673
    RV 453, in D
      ed G.F.Malipiero   φ   str/cont(hpsd)   9'   Ricordi,1958.CW 279   Misc 5093
    RV 454, in D min (op.8 no.9) (for oboe or violin) (see also version for violin, RV 236, in D min)
      ed R.P.Block   φ   str/cont   7'30"   Musica Rara,1978   26689 *
      ed A.Ephrikian   φ   str/cont(hpsd)   Ricordi,1947.CW   2   21503+B & |
    RV 455, in F .
      ed R.P.Block   φ   str/cont   10'   Musica Rara,1979   26698 *
      ed A.Ephrikian   φ   str/cont(hpsd)   Ricordi,1947.CW   14   Misc 26546
    RV 456, in F
      ed G.F.Malipiero   φ   str/cont(org=hpsd)   9'   Ricordi,1970.CW 488   Misc 7263 &
    RV 457, in F (see also version for bassoon, RV 485)
      ed G.F.Malipiero   φ   str/cont(hpsd)   9'   Ricordi,1960.CW 315   Misc 5354 &
    RV 461, in A min
      ed R.P.Block   φ   str/cont   Musica Rara,1979   27133 *
      ed G.F.Malipiero   φ   str/cont(hpsd)   9'   Ricordi,1955.CW 215   26572
    RV 463, in A min (see also version for bassoon, RV 500)
      ed R.P.Block   φ   str/cont   Musica Rara,1979   27132 *
      ed G.F.Malipiero   φ   str/cont(hpsd)   Ricordi,1960.CW 316   Misc 5361 &
    RV 464, in B♭ (op.7, no.7)
      ed G.F.Malipiero   φ   str/cont(org=hpsd)   7'   Ricordi,1966.CW 448   Misc 6483 &
    RV 465, in B♭ (op.7, no.1)
      ed G.F.Malipiero   φ   str/cont(org=hpsd)   6'   Ricordi,1967.CW 442   Misc 6477 &
  2 Oboes
    RV 534, in C
      ed G.F.Malipiero   φ   str/cont(hpsd)   10'30" Ricordi,1952.CW 139   Misc 3876 &
    RV 535, in D min
      ed D.Lasocki   φ   str/cont(hpsd)   Musica Rara   25728
      ed G.F.Malipiero   φ   str/cont(hpsd)   9'   Ricordi,1957.CW 264   26582 & MRL
    RV 536, in A min
      ed G.F.Malipiero   φ   str/cont(hpsd)   8'   Ricordi,1957.CW 263   Misc 4941 &
Piccolo   see   Recorder: Sopranino Recorder
Recorder
  Sopranino Recorder (or piccolo)
    RV 443, in C
      ed G.F.Malipiero   φ   str/cont(hpsd)   11'   Ricordi,1951.CW 105   Misc 3670 &
      ed F.Schroeder   φ   str/cont(hpsd)   Eulenburg,1963   24043
    RV 444, in C
      ed D.Lasocki   φ   str/cont(hpsd: real R.P.Block)   Musica Rara,1972   25433
      ed G.F.Malipiero   φ   str/cont(hpsd)   10'   Ricordi,1951.CW 110   Misc 3671 &
    RV 445, in A min
      ed G.F.Malipiero   φ   str/cont(hpsd)   10'   Ricordi,1953.CW 152   26564 & MRL
  Treble Recorder (or flute)
    RV 441, in C min
      ed G.F.Malipiero   φ   str/cont(hpsd)   13'   Ricordi,1953.CW 159   Misc 4041 &
      ed F.Schroeder   φ   str/cont(hpsd)   Eulenburg,1969   Misc 7163 B
    RV 442, in F
      ed A.Ephrikian   φ   str/cont(hpsd)   Ricordi,1949.CW   46   26550 & MRL
      arr W.Fortner   φ   str/cont(hpsd)   Schott   13958

VIVALDI, Antonio (cont)

CONCERTI (cont)

   Strings (for concerti with various string inst <u>see</u> concerti for relevant solo instrument)

RV 109, in C					
ed G.F.Malipiero	φ	str/cont(hpsd)	6'30"	Ricordi,1954.CW 185	Misc 4262 & MRL
RV 110, in C					
ed G.F.Malipiero	φ	str/cont(hpsd)	4'30"	Ricordi,1954.CW 200	Misc 4258 & MRL
RV 111, in C (Il Giustino)					
transcr & ed M.Bruin	φ	str/cont(hpsd)	6'	Carisch,1959	23730
RV 112, in C (sinfonia)					
ed G.F.Malipiero	φ	str/cont(hpsd)	6'	Ricordi,1971.CW 507	Misc 7661 & MRL
RV 113, in C					
ed G.F.Malipiero	φ	str/cont(hpsd)		Ricordi,1971.CW 509	Misc 7663 & MRL
RV 114, in C					
ed G.F.Malipiero	φ	str/cont(hpsd)		Ricordi,1970.CW 493	Misc 7266 & MRL
RV 115, in C					
ed G.F.Malipiero	φ	str/cont(hpsd)	4'	Ricordi,1960.CM 309	Misc 5340 & MRL
RV 116, in C					
ed G.F.Malipiero	φ	str/cont(hpsd)	8'	Ricordi,1951.CW 506	Misc 7665 & MRL
RV 117, in C					
ed G.F.Malipiero	φ	str/cont(hpsd)	7'	Ricordi,1960.CW 308	Misc 5341 & MRL
RV 118, in C min					
ed B.Maderna	φ	str/cont(hpsd)		Ricordi,1949.CW 32	26600 & MRL
RV 119, in C min					
ed G.F.Malipiero	φ	str/cont(hpsd)	6'	Ricordi,1954.CW 177	Misc 4263 & MRL
RV 120, in C min					
ed B.Maderna	φ	str/cont(hpsd)		Ricordi,1949.CW 30	26548 & MRL
RV 121, in D					
ed G.F.Malipiero	φ	str/cont(hpsd)	6'30"	Ricordi,1956.CW 246	Misc 4711 & MRL
RV 122, in D					
ed G.F.Malipiero [with inauthentic wind parts]					
	φ	0[1]0[1]/0000/str/cont(hpsd)	5'	Ricordi,1962.CW 362	Misc 5737 & MRL
RV 123, in D					
ed G.F.Malipiero	φ	str/cont(hpsd)	6'	Ricordi,1951.CW 114	Misc 3677 & MRL
RV 124, in D					
ed A.Ephrikian	φ	str/cont(org or hpsd)		Ricordi,1968.CW 464	Misc 6841 & MRL
RV 126, in D					
ed G.F.Malipiero	φ	str/cont(hpsd)	6'	Ricordi,1951.CW 113	Misc 3676 & MRL
RV 127, in D min					
ed G.F.Malipiero	φ	str/cont(hpsd)	5'	Ricordi,1954.CW 176	Misc 4268 & MRL
RV 128, in D min					
ed H.Landshoff	φ	str/cont(hpsd=pf)		Music Press	19151
ed G.F.Malipiero	φ	str/cont(hpsd)	6'	Ricordi,1957.CW 251	Misc 4927 & MRL
RV 129, in D min 'Concerto Madrigalesco'					
ed A.Ephrikian	φ	str/cont(hpsd)		Ricordi,1949.CW 36	Misc 2941 & MRL
RV 130, in E♭ 'Al Santo Sepulchro'					
ed A.Ephrikian	φ	str/cont(hpsd)		Ricordi,1947.CW 21	19386 & MRL
RV 131, in E					
ed G.F.Malipiero	φ	str/cont(hpsd)	5'	Ricordi,1953.CW 161	Misc 4046 & MRL
RV 132, in E					
ed G.F.Malipiero	φ	str/cont(hpsd)		Ricordi,1971.CW 515	Misc 7669 & MRL
RV 133, in E min					
ed G.F.Malipiero	φ	str/cont(hpsd)		Ricordi,1970.CW 492	Misc 7265 & MRL
RV 134, in E min					
ed G.F.Malipiero	φ	str/cont(hpsd)	12'	Ricordi,1949.CW 56	Misc 3141 & MRL

VIVALDI, Antonio (cont)

CONCERTI (cont)
  Strings (cont)
    RV 135, in F
      ed G.F.Malipiero [with inauthentic wind parts]
                            ϕ   000[1]/[2]000/str/cont(hpsd)   6'   Ricordi,1962.CW 363   Misc 5738 & MRL
    RV 136, in F
      ed G.F.Malipiero   ϕ   str/cont(hpsd)   5'   Ricordi,1949.CW 59   Misc 3140 & MRL
    RV 137, in F
      ed G.F.Malipiero   ϕ   str/cont(hpsd)   7'   Ricordi,1971.CW 516   Misc 7670 & MRL
    RV 138, in F
      ed G.F.Malipiero   ϕ   str/cont(hpsd)   8'   Ricordi,1958.CW 288   Misc 5100 & MRL
    RV 140, in F
      ed G.F.Malipiero   ϕ   str/cont(hpsd)   6'30" Ricordi,1956.CW 242   Misc 4716 & MRL
    RV 141, in F
      ed G.F.Malipiero   ϕ   str/cont(hpsd)   7'   Ricordi,1956.CW 241   Misc 4717 & MRL
    RV 142, in F
      ed A.Ephrikian   φ   str/cont(hpsd)   8'   Ricordi,1947.CW   6   Misc 2566 & MRL
    RV 143, in F min
      ed G.F.Malipiero   ϕ   str/cont(hpsd)   6'   Ricordi,1958.CW 289   Misc 5101 & MRL
    RV 144, in G
      ed G.F.Malipiero   ϕ   str/cont(hpsd)   10'   Ricordi,1971.CW 512   Misc 7667 & MRL
    RV 145, in G
      ed G.F.Malipiero   ϕ   str/cont(hpsd)   4'   Ricordi,1957.CW 252   Misc 4935 & MRL
    RV 146, in G
      ed H.Landshoff   ϕ   str/cont(hpsd)   Peters,1935   15071
      ed F.Schroeder   ϕ   str/cont(hpsd)   Eulenburg,1965   Misc 6156 B
      ed G.F.Malipiero   ϕ   str/cont(hpsd)   6'   Ricordi,1962.CW 361   Misc 5724 & MRL
    RV 148, in G
      ed G.F.Malipiero   φ   [1]000/0000/str/cont   Ricordi,1962   Misc 5736
    RV 149, in G
      ed H.Landshoff   ϕ   str/cont   6'   Peters   13027
      ed G.F.Malipiero   ϕ   str/cont(hpsd)   Ricordi,1960.CW 321   MRL
    RV 150, in G
      ed G.F.Malipiero   ϕ   str/cont(hpsd)   5'   Ricordi,1958.CW 290   25697 & MRL
    RV 151, in G 'Alla Rustica'
      rev A.Casella   ϕ   str/cont(hpsd)   Carisch,1960   23782
      ed G.F.Malipiero   ϕ   str/cont(hpsd)   Ricordi,1949.CW 49   26552 & MRL
      ed F.Schroeder   ϕ   str/cont   Eulenburg,1965   25990 *
    RV 152, in G min
      ed G.F.Malipiero   ϕ   str/cont(hpsd)   6'   Ricordi,1956.CW 226   Misc 4724 & MRL
      Finale only
        ed G.F.Malipiero   str   (Editor)   19388
    RV 153, in G min
      ed G.F.Malipiero   ϕ   str/cont(hpsd)   7'   Ricordi,1958.CW 287   Misc 5107 & MRL
    RV 154, in G min
      ed G.F.Malipiero   ϕ   str/cont(hpsd)   6'30" Ricordi,1960.CW 310   Misc 5357 & MRL
    RV 155, in G min
      ed G.F.Malipiero   ϕ   str/cont(hpsd)   12'   Ricordi,1947.CW 11   Misc 2571 & MRL
    RV 156, in G min
      ed G.F.Malipiero   ϕ   str/cont(hpsd)   6'   Ricordi,1951.CW 115   Misc 3684 & MRL
    RV 157, in G min
      ed G.F.Malipiero   ϕ   str/cont(hpsd)   7'   Ricordi,1954.CW 182   Misc 4275 & MRL
    RV 158, in A
      ed A.Ephrikian   ϕ   str/cont(hpsd)   10'   Ricordi,1947.CW   8   26544 & MRL

VIVALDI, Antonio (cont)

CONCERTI (cont)
  Strings (cont)
    RV 159, in A
      ed A.Ephrikian   ∅   str/cont(hpsd)   6'   Ricordi,1947.CW   5   26543 & MRL
    RV 160, in A
      ed G.F.Malipiero   ∅   str/cont(hpsd)   5'30"   Ricordi,1954.CW 184   Misc 4253 & MRL
    RV 161, in A min
      ed G.F.Malipiero   ∅   str/cont(hpsd)   4'30"   Ricordi,1955.CW 201   Misc 4569 & MRL
    RV 162, in B♭
      ed G.F.Malipiero   ∅   [2201]/0000/str/cont(hpsd)   4'   Ricordi,1962.CW 359   Misc 5735 & MRL
    RV 163, in B♭
      ed A.Ephrikian   ∅   str/cont(hpsd)   5'   Ricordi,1947.CW   9   Misc 2569 & MRL
    RV 164, in B♭
      ed G.F.Malipiero   ∅   str/cont(hpsd)   Ricordi,1949.CW 20   Misc 2943 & MRL
    RV 165, in B♭
      ed G.F.Malipiero   ∅   str/cont(hpsd)   5'   Ricordi,1953.CW 172   Misc 4034 & MRL
    RV 166, in B♭
      ed G.F.Malipiero   ∅   str/cont(hpsd)   7'   Ricordi,1947.CW   7   Misc 2567 & MRL
    RV 167, in B♭
      ed G.F.Malipiero   ∅   str/cont(hpsd)   5'   Ricordi,1954.CW 190   Misc 4256 & MRL
    RV 168, in B min
      ed G.F.Malipiero   ∅   str/cont(hpsd)   Ricordi,1971.CW 518   Misc 7671 & MRL
    RV 169, in B min 'Sinfonia al Santo Sepolcro'
      ed A.Fanna   ∅   str/cont   Ricordi,1947.CW 23   19387 & MRL
  2 Trumpets
    RV 537, in C   ∅   str/cont(bsn.hpsd.vlne)   Eulenburg,1965   25992
      ed G.F.Malipiero   ∅   str/cont(hpsd)   7'   Ricordi,1950.CW 97   25360 & MRL
  Viola d'amore
    RV 392, in D
      ed G.F.Malipiero   ∅   str/cont(hpsd)   10'   Ricordi,1960.CW 337   26580 & MRL
    RV 393, in D min
      ed G.F.Malipiero   ∅   str/cont(hpsd)   10'30" Ricordi,1954.CW 198   Misc 4267 & MRL
    RV 394, in D min
      ed G.F.Malipiero   ∅   str/cont(hpsd)   8'   Ricordi,1954.CW 196   Misc 4266 & MRL
    RV 395(a), in D min
      ed G.F.Malipiero   ∅   str/cont(hpsd)   9'   Ricordi,1954.CW 197   Misc 4265 & MRL
    RV 396, in A
      ed G.F.Malipiero   ∅   str/cont(hpsd)   10'   Ricordi,1954.CW 189   26567 & MRL
    RV 397, in A min
      ed G.F.Malipiero   ∅   str/cont(hpsd)   9'   Ricordi,1961.CW 431   26579 + MRL
  Violin
    RV 170, in C
      ed G.Prato   ∅   str/cont(hpsd)   11'   Ricordi,1963.CW 379   Misc 5862 & MRL
    RV 171, in C
      ed G.F.Malipiero   ∅   str/cont(hpsd)   10'   Ricordi,1954.CW 194   Misc 4259 & MRL
    RV 172, in C
      ed G.F.Malipiero   ∅   str/cont(hpsd)   11'   Ricordi,1960.CW 322   Misc 5338 & MRL
    RV 173 (op.12, no.4), in C
      ed A.Ephrikian   ∅   str/cont(org=hpsd)   8'   Ricordi,1968.CW 465   Misc 6842 & MRL
    RV 175, in C
      ed G.F.Malipiero   ∅   str/cont(hpsd)   Ricordi,1971.CW 580   Misc 7660 & MRL
    RV 176, in C
      ed G.F.Malipiero   ∅   str/cont(hpsd)   Ricordi,1970.CW 495   Misc 7268 & MRL
    RV 177, in C
      ed G.F.Malipiero   ∅   str/cont(hpsd)   12'   Ricordi,1953.CW 160   Misc 4037 & MRL

VIVALDI, Antonio (cont)

CONCERTI (cont)
  Violin (cont)
    RV 178 (op.8,no.12), in C
      ed G.F.Malipiero   φ   str/cont(org=hpsd)   9'   Ricordi,1950.CW 85   Misc 3478 & MRL
      (see also concerti: Oboe, RV 449, in C)
    RV 179, in C 'Per la S.S.Assunzione di Maria Vergine' for double orch
      ed B.Maderna   φ   str/cont(2hpsd)   12'-14'Ricordi,1949.CW 55   26554 & MRL
    RV 180 (op.8,no.6), in C 'Il Piacere'
      ed G.F.Malipiero   φ   str/cont(hpsd/org)   8'   Ricordi,1950.CW 81   25320 B & MRL
    RV 181, in C (op.9, no.1) from 'La Cetra'
      ed G.F.Malipiero   φ   str/cont(hpsd=org)   10'   Ricordi,1951.CW 122   Misc 3668 & MRL
      ed D.Stevens   φ   str/cont(hpsd=org)   (Le Cene,[1727])   20641 + & mf 144
    RV 182, in C
      ed G.F.Malipiero   φ   str/cont(hpsd)   13'   Ricordi,1954.CW 195   Misc 4260 & MRL
    RV 183, in C
      ed G.F.Malipiero   φ   str/cont(hpsd)   9'   Ricordi,1957.CW 256   Misc 4920 & MRL
    RV 184, in C
      ed G.F.Malipiero   φ   str/cont(hpsd)   11'   Ricordi,1961.CW 328   Misc 5575 & MRL
    RV 185 (op.4,no.7), in C from 'La Stravaganza'
      ed A.Ephrikian   φ   str/cont/(hpsd.org)   9'   Ricordi,1965.CW 424   Misc 6288 & MRL
    RV 186, in C
      ed B.Maderna   φ   str/cont(hpsd)   10'   Ricordi,1947.CW 13   Misc 2573 & MRL
    RV 187, in C
      ed G.F.Malipiero   φ   str/cont(hpsd)   12'   Ricordi,1960.CW 311   Misc 5339 & MRL
    RV 188 (op.7,no.9), in C
      ed G.F.Malipiero   φ   str/cont(hpsd)   9'   Ricordi,1966.CW 443   Misc 6478 & MRL
    RV 189, in C
      ed G.Prato   φ   str/cont(hpsd)   12'   Ricordi,1963.CW 376   Misc 5859 & MRL
    RV 190, in C
      ed G.F.Malipiero   φ   str/cont(hpsd)   13'   Ricordi,1951.CW 120   Misc 3667 & MRL
    RV 191, in C
      ed G.F.Malipiero   φ   str/cont(hpsd)   12'30" Ricordi,1957.CW 259   Misc 4921 & MRL
    RV 192, in C
      ed G.F.Malipiero   φ   str/cont(hpsd)   8'   Ricordi,1953.CW 162   Misc 4036 & MRL
    RV 194, in C
      ed G.F.Malipiero   φ   str/cont(hpsd)   8'30" Ricordi,1953.CW 167   Misc 4038 & MRL
    RV 195, in C
      ed G.F.Malipiero   φ   str/cont(hpsd)   Ricordi,1970.CW 481   MRL
    RV 196, in C
      ed A.Ephrikian   φ   str/cont(hpsd=org)   Ricordi,1966.CW 427   Misc 6468 & MRL
      (see also KREISLER, F. CONCERTO IN THE STYLE OF VIVALDI)
    RV 197, in C min
      ed G.F.Malipiero   φ   str/cont(hpsd)   10'   Ricordi,1953.CW 173   Misc 4040 & MRL
    RV 198a (op.9,no.11), in C min, from 'La Cetra'
      ed A.Casella   φ   str/cont(org)   15'   Universal,1937   Misc 1955
      ed G.F.Malipiero   φ   str/cont(org=hpsd)   10'   Ricordi,1952.CW 133   Misc 3879 & MRL
      ed D.Stevens   φ   str/cont(org=hpsd)   10'   (Le Cene,[1727])   20642 & mf 144
    RV 199, in C min 'Il Sospetto'
      ed A.Ephrikian   φ   str/cont(hpsd)   12'   Ricordi,1947.CW 4   Misc 2564 & MRL
      ed F.Schroeder   φ   str/cont(hpsd)   Eulenburg   23799
    RV 201, in C min
      ed G.F.Malipiero   φ   str/cont(hpsd)   12'   Ricordi,1956.CW 230   Misc 4709 & MRL
    RV 202, in C min (op.11,no.5)
                       φ   str/cont   (GB Lbm-g.33/e(1)) 22020 +
      ed G.F.Malipiero   φ   str/cont(org=hpsd)   14'   Ricordi,1968.CW 461   Misc 6838 & MRL

VIVALDI, Antonio (cont)

CONCERTI (cont)
  Violin (cont)
    RV 204 (op.4,no.11), in D
    . ed A.Ephrikian   ∅   str/cont(hpsd=org)   8'   Ricordi,1966.CW 428   Misc 6470 & MRL
    RV 205, in D 'Fatto per il M.Pisendel'
       ed G.F.Malipiero   ∅   str/cont(hpsd)   8'   Ricordi,1961.CW 331   Misc 5578 & MRL
    RV 206, in D
       ed G.F.Malipiero   ∅   str/cont(hpsd)   Ricordi,1970.CW 497   Misc 7270 & MRL
    RV 207, in D
       ed G.F.Malipiero   ∅   str/cont(hpsd)   11'   Ricordi,1954.CW 188   Misc 4264 & MRL
    RV 208, in D
       ed G.F.Malipiero   ∅   str/cont(hpsd)   13'   Ricordi,1960.CW 314   Misc 5342 & MRL
       ed F.Schroeder   ∅   str/cont(hpsd)   13'   Eulenburg,1961   23659
    RV 208(a)(op.7,no.11), in D
       ed G.F.Malipiero   ∅   str/cont(org=hpsd)   Ricordi,1968.CW 452   Misc 6829 & MRL
    RV 209, in D
       ed G.F.Malipiero   ∅   str/cont(hpsd)   7'   Ricordi,1958.CW 286   Misc 5095 & MRL
    RV 210 (op.8,no.11), in D
       ed G.F.Malipiero   ∅   str/cont(org=hpsd)   13'   Ricordi,1950.CW 84   26558 & MRL
    RV 211, in D
       ed G.F.Malipiero   ∅   str/cont(hpsd)   13'   Ricordi,1957.CW 261   Misc 4925 & MRL
    RV 212, in D 'Concerto fatto per la Solennità della S.Antonio - 1712'
       ed N.Jenkins   ∅   str/cont(hpsd)   Eulenburg,1958   22886
       ed G.F.Malipiero   ∅   str/cont(hpsd)   13'   Ricordi,1960.CW 312   Misc 5343 & MRL
    RV 213, in D
       ed G.F.Malipiero   ∅   str/cont(hpsd)   12'   Ricordi,1961.CW 347   Misc 5594 & MRL
    RV 214 (op.7,no.12), in D
       ed G.F.Malipiero   ∅. str/cont(org=hpsd)   Ricordi,1968.CW 453   Misc 6830 & MRL
       ed F.Schroeder   ∅   str/cont(hpsd)   Eulenburg,1959   23254
    RV 215, in D
       ed G.F.Malipiero   ∅   str/cont(hpsd)   7'30" Ricordi,1960.CW 305   Misc 5345 & MRL
    RV 216 (op.6,no.4), in D
       ed G.F.Malipiero   ∅   str/cont(hpsd=org)   6'   Ricordi,1966.CW 439   Misc 6474 & MRL
    RV 217, in D
       ed G.F.Malipiero   ∅   str/cont(hpsd)   11'   Ricordi,1949.CW 69   Misc 3131 & MRL
    RV 218, in D
       ed G.F.Malipiero   ∅   str/cont(hpsd)   10'   Ricordi,1960.CW 307   Misc 5347 & MRL
    RV 219, in D
       ed G.F.Malipiero   ∅   str/cont(hpsd)   12'   Ricordi,1960.CW 335   Misc 5582 & MRL
    RV 220, in D
       ed G.F.Malipiero   ∅   str/cont(hpsd)   Ricordi,1970.CW 482   Misc 7257 & MRL
    RV 221, in D
       ed G.F.Malipiero   ∅   str/cont(hpsd)   6'   Ricordi,1955.CW 203   Misc 4582 & MRL
    RV 222, in D
       ed G.F.Malipiero   ∅   str/cont(hpsd)   14'   Ricordi,1958.CW 294   Misc 5094 & MRL
    RV 223, in D
       ed G.F.Malipiero   ∅   str/cont(hpsd)   Ricordi,1970.CW 494   Misc 7267 & MRL
    RV 224, in D
       ed G.F.Malipiero   ∅   str/cont(hpsd   11'   Ricordi,1961.CW 343   Misc 5590 & MRL
       facsimile   ∅   str   11'   Acc.Mus.Chigiana 1949   Misc 4509
    RV 225, in D
       ed G.F.Malipiero   ∅   str/cont(hpsd)   13'   Ricordi,1953.CW 174   Misc 4042 & MRL
    RV 226, in D
       ed G.F.Malipiero   ∅   str/cont(hpsd)   10'   Ricordi,1968.CW 302   Misc 5344 & MRL

VIVALDI, Antonio (cont)

CONCERTI (cont)
  Violin (cont)
    RV 227, in D
      ed G.F.Malipiero   ∅   str/cont(hpsd)   Ricordi,1971.CW 513   Misc 7668 & MRL
    RV 228, in D
      éd G.F.Malipiero   ∅   str/cont(hpsd)   7'30" Ricordi,1961.CW 345   Misc 5592 & MRL
    RV 229, in D
      ed G.F.Malipiero   ∅   str/cont(hpsd)   11'   Ricordi,1951.CW 117   Misc 3674 & MRL
    RV 230, in D (op.3,no.9), from 'L'Estro Armonico'
      [op.3,no.7 in this ed.]   ∅   str/cont   I.Walsh,1722   19843+
      ed R.Eller   ∅   str/cont   Eulenburg,1966   25978
      ed G.F.Malipiero   ∅   str/cont(hpsd)   7'   Ricordi,1965.CW 414   Misc 6278 & MRL
      arr G.Dandelot   ∅   str   Eschig,1928   22353
    RV 231, in D
      ed B.Maderna   ∅   str/cont(hpsd)   Ricordi,1949.CW 31   Misc 2930 & MRL
    RV 232, in D
      ed G.F.Malipiero   ∅   str/cont(hpsd)   13'   Ricordi,1949.CW 68   Misc 3130 & MRL
    RV 233, in D
      ed G.F.Malipiero   ∅   str/cont(hpsd)   10'   Ricordi,1960.CW 306   Misc 5346 & MRL
    RV 234, in D 'L'Inquietudine'
      ed A.Ephrikian   ∅   str/cont(hpsd)   Ricordi,1949.CW 37   Misc 2932 & MRL
    RV 582, in D 'Per la S.S.Assunzione di Maria Vergine'
      ed G.F. Malipiero   ∅   double str orch/2 cont(hpsd) 14' Ricordi,1952.CW 141   26562 & MRL
      ed F.Schroeder   ∅   double str orch/2 cont(hpsd)   Eulenburg,1960   23647
    RV 235, in D min
      ed G.F.Malipiero   ∅   str/cont(hpsd)   11'   Ricordi,1957.CW 258   Misc 4926 & MRL
    RV 236, (op.8,no.9) in D min, (for violin or oboe)
      see version for oboe, RV 454, in D min
    RV 237, in D min
      ed G.F.Malipiero   ∅   str/cont(hpsd)   10'   Ricordi,1960.CW 325   Misc 5350 & MRL
    RV 238 (op.9, no.8) in D min, from 'La Cetra'
      ed G.F.Malipiero   ∅   str/cont(org=hpsd)   Ricordi,1952.CW 131   Misc 3883
      ed D.Stevens   ∅   str/cont(org=hpsd)   (Le Cene, [1727])   20641-2+ mf 144
    RV 239 (op.6,no.6) in D min
      ed G.F.Malipiero   ∅   str/cont(hpsd=org)   9'   Ricordi,1966.CW 441   24945 & MRL
    RV 240, in D min
      ed G.F.Malipiero   ∅   str/cont(hpsd)   12'   Ricordi,1960.CW 324   Misc 5349 & MRL
      facsimile   ∅   str/cont   Acc.Mus.Chigiana 1949   Misc 4509 MRL facs
    RV 241, in D min
      ed G.F.Malipiero   ∅   str/cont(hpsd)   9'30" Ricordi,1961.CW 336   Misc 5583 & MRL
    RV 242 (op.8,no.7) in D min, 'Per M.Pisendel'
      ed G.F.Malipiero   ∅   str/cont(org=hpsd)   6'30" Ricordi,1950.CW 82   Misc 3483 & MRL
    RV 243, in D min, 'Senza Cantin'
      ed G.F.Malipiero   ∅   str/cont(hpsd)   Ricordi,1949.CW 45   Misc 2946 & MRL
    RV 244 (op.12,no.2) in D min
      ed A.Ephrikian   ∅   str/cont(org=hpsd)   9'30" Ricordi,1968.CW 463   Misc 6840 & MRL
      ed T.Nachez   ∅   str/cont   Schott   14276
    RV 245, in D min
      ed G.F.Malipiero   ∅   str/cont(hpsd)   8'   Ricordi,1961.CW 333   Misc 5580 & MRL
    RV 246, in D min
      ed G.F.Malipiero   ∅   str/cont(hpsd)   8'30" Ricordi,1958.CW 285   Misc 5096 & MRL
    RV 247, in D min
      ed G.F.Malipiero   ∅   str/cont(hpsd)   7'   Ricordi,1958.CW 296   Misc 5097 & MRL
    RV 248, in D min
      ed G.F.Malipiero   ∅   str/cont(hpsd)   12'30" Ricordi,1949.CW 74   Misc 3133 & MRL

VIVALDI, Antonio (cont)

CONCERTI (cont)
  Violin (cont)
    RV 249 (op.4,no.8) in D min, from 'La Stravaganza'

ed A.Ephrikian	⌀	str/cont(hpsd)	8'	Ricordi,1965.CW 425	Misc 6289 & MRL

    RV 250, in Eb

ed G.F.Malipiero	⌀	str/cont(hpsd)	8'	Ricordi,1956.CW 227	Misc 4712 & MRL

    RV 251, in Eb

ed G.F.Malipiero	⌀	str/cont(hpsd)	10'30"	Ricordi,1957.CW 254	Misc 4929 & MRL

    RV 252, in Eb

ed G.F.Malipiero	⌀	str/cont(hpsd)	10'	Ricordi,1961.CW 349	Misc 5596 & MRL

    RV 253 (op.8,no.5) in Eb, 'La Tempesta di Mare'

ed G.F.Malipiero	⌀	str/cont(hpsd=org)	8'	Ricordi,1950.CW 80	25361 & MRL

    RV 254, in Eb

ed A.Ephrikian	⌀	str/cont(hpsd)	12'	Ricordi,1949.CW 38	Misc 2931 & MRL

    RV 256, in Eb, 'Il Ritiro'

ed G.F.Malipiero	⌀	str/cont(hpsd)		Ricordi,1961.CW 502	Misc 7664 & MRL

    RV 257, in Eb

ed G.F.Malipiero	⌀	str/cont(hpsd)	10'	Ricordi,1954.CW 193	Misc 4269 & MRL

    RV 258, in Eb

ed G.F.Malipiero	⌀	str/cont(hpsd)	12'	Ricordi,1953.CW 169	Misc 4045 & MRL

    RV 259, in Eb

ed G.F.Malipiero	⌀	str/cont(hpsd=org)	10'	Ricordi,1966.CW 437	Misc 6467 & MRL

    RV 260, in Eb

ed G.F.Malipiero	⌀	str/cont(hpsd)	11'	Ricordi,1962.CW 352	Misc 5731 & MRL
facsimile	⌀	str/cont(hpsd)		Acc.Mus.Chigiana,1949	Misc 4509

    RV 261, in Eb

ed G.F.Malipiero	⌀	str/cont(hpsd)	10'	Ricordi,1960.CW 304	Misc 5351 & MRL

    RV 262, in Eb

ed G.F.Malipiero	⌀	str/cont(hpsd)	10'	Ricordi,1961.CW 340	Misc 5587 & MRL

    RV 263a (op.9,no.4) in E, from 'La Cetra'

ed G.F.Malipiero	⌀	str/cont(org=hpsd)	11'	Ricordi,1951.CW 123	Misc 3678 & MRL
	⌀	str/cont(hpsd=org)		(Le Cene, [1727])	20641 + mf 144

    RV 264 in E

ed G.F.Malipiero	⌀	str/cont(hpsd)	10'	Ricordi,1953.CW 166	Misc 4047 & MRL

    RV 265 (op.3,no.12) in E

	⌀	str/cont(hpsd)		Walsh,1722	19843 +
ed H.Husmann	⌀	str/cont(hpsd)		Eulenburg	20095
ed G.F.Malipiero	⌀	str/cont(hpsd)		Ricordi,1965.CW 417	26575

    RV 266, in E

ed G.F.Malipiero	⌀	str/cont(hpsd)	12'	Ricordi,1954.CW 180	Misc 4270 & MRL

    RV 267, in E

ed G.F.Malipiero	⌀	str/cont(hpsd)	6'30"	Ricordi,1961.CW 327	Misc 5574 & MRL

    RV 268, in E

ed A.Ephrikian	⌀	str/cont(hpsd)		(Editor)	19624
ed A.Ephrikian	⌀	str/cont(hpsd)		Ricordi,1949.CW 29	19624 & MRL

    RV 269 (op.8,no.1) in E, 'La Primavera' from 'The Seasons'

ed N.Jenkins	⌀	str/cont(hpsd)		Eulenburg,1959	23174
ed G.F.Malipiero	⌀	str/cont(hpsd=org)	10'-11'15"		
				Ricordi,1950.CW 76	22290 Misc 9427 & MRL
ed A.Toni	⌀	str/cont(hpsd=org)		Carisch,1924	25986
transcr B.Molinari	⌀	str/cont(hpsd=org)		Ricordi,1927	Misc 1813

    RV 270, in E, 'Il Riposo'

ed A.Fanna	⌀	str		Ricordi,1947.CW 15	Misc 2575 & MRL

VIVALDI, Antonio (cont)

CONCERTI (cont)

  Violin (cont)

    RV 271, in E, 'L'Amoroso'

ed G.F.Malipiero	⌀	str/cont(hpsd)		8'	Ricordi,1958.CW 297	Misc 5098 & MRL

    RV 273, in E min

ed G.F.Malipiero	⌀	str/cont(hpsd)		12'	Ricordi,1953.CW 164	Misc 4048 & MRL

    RV 275, in E min

ed G.F.Malipiero	⌀	str/cont(hpsd)			Ricordi,1970.CW 484	MRL

    RV 276, in E min

ed G.F.Malipiero	⌀	str/cont(hpsd)			Ricordi,1970.CW 480	Misc 7255 & MRL

    RV 277 (op.11,no.2) in E min, 'Il Favorito'

ed G.F.Malipiero	⌀	str/cont(org=hpsd)		14'	Ricordi,1968.CW 459	26573 & MRL
ed G.F.Malipiero	⌀	str/cont			GB LO-BL(BM.g.33/ e(3)	22169 +

    RV 278, in E min

ed G.F.Malipiero	⌀	str/cont(hpsd)		11'	Ricordi,1950.CW 93	Misc 3489 & MRL

    RV 279 (op.4,no.2), in E min, from 'La Stravaganza'

ed A.Ephrikian	⌀	str/cont(hpsd)		10'	Ricordi,1965.CW 419	Misc 6283 & MRL
arr Mistowski	⌀	str			OUP	5422
arr W.Upmeyer	⌀	str/cont(hpsd)			Bärenreiter	20054

    RV 280 (op.6,no.5), in E min

ed G.F.Malipiero	⌀	str/cont(org=hpsd)		9'	Ricordi,1966.CW 440	Misc 6475 & MRL

    RV 281, in E min

ed G.F.Malipiero	⌀	str/cont(hpsd)		12'	Ricordi,1953.CW 168	Misc 4049 & MRL

    RV 282, in F

ed G.F.Malipiero	⌀	str/cont(hpsd)		9'	Ricordi,1950.CW 87	Misc 3492 & MRL

    RV 283, in F

ed G.F.Malipiero	⌀	str/cont(hpsd)		13'	Ricordi,1960.CW 301	Misc 5352 & MRL

    RV 284 (op.4,no.9), in F

ed A.Ephrikian	⌀	str/cont(hpsd)		8'	Ricordi,1066.CW 426	Misc 6466 & MRL

    RV 285, in F

ed G.F.Malipiero	⌀	str/cont(hpsd)		9'	Ricordi,1061.CW 346	Misc 5593 & MRL

    RV 285a (op.7,no.5), in F

ed G.F.Malipiero	⌀	str/cont(hpsd=org)		10'	Ricordi,1966.CW 446	Misc 6482 & MRL

    RV 286, in F, 'Per la Solennità di San Lorenzo'

ed G.F.Malipiero	⌀	str/cont(hpsd)		16'	Ricordi,1949.CW. 70	Misc 3132 & MRL

    RV 287, in F

ed G.F.Malipiero	⌀	str/cont(hpsd)		10'30"	Ricordi,1954.CW 187	Misc 4271 & MRL

    RV 288, in F

ed G.F.Malipiero	⌀	str/cont(hpsd)		8'30"	Ricordi,1949.CW 66	Misc 3129 & MRL

    RV 289, in F

ed G.F.Malipiero	⌀	str/cont(hpsd)		10'30"	Ricordi,1955.CW 165	Misc 4051 & MRL

    RV 291, in F

ed G.F.Malipiero	⌀	str/cont(hpsd)		10'	Ricordi,1970.CW 479	Misc 7254 & MRL

    RV 292, in F

ed G.F.Malipiero	⌀	str/cont(hpsd)		10'	Ricordi,1962.CW 357	Misc 5733 & MRL

    RV 293 (op.8,no.3), in F, 'L'Autunno' from 'The Seasons' (3rd mvt is 'La Caccia')

ed N.Jenkins	⌀	str/cont(hpsd)			Eulenburg,1959	23176
ed G.F.Malipiero	⌀	str/cont(hpsd=org)		10'	Ricordi,1950.CW 78	22292 Misc 9427 & MRL
ed A.Toni	⌀	str/cont(org)			Sonzogna,1924/Carisch,1942	25988
transcr Molinari	⌀	str/cont(hpsd=org)			Ricordi,1927	Misc 1815
rev F.Oubradous	⌀	str/cont(hpsd=org)			Ed.Mus.Trans.1959	Misc 5251

    RV 294, in F

ed G.F.Malipiero	⌀	str/cont(org=hpsd)			Ricordi,1968.CW 451	Misc 6828 & MRL

VIVALDI, Antonio (cont)

CONCERTI (cont)
  Violin (cont)
    RV 295, in F
      ed G.F.Malipiero   φ   str/cont(hpsd)   9'30" Ricordi,1960.CW 303   Misc 5353 & MRL
    RV 296, in F
      ed G.F.Malipiero   φ   str/cont(hpsd)   13'   Ricordi,1953.CW 158   Misc 4050 & MRL
    RV 297 (op.8,no.4), in F min 'L'Inverno' from 'The Seasons
      ed N.Jenkins   φ   str/cont(hpsd)   Eulenburg,1959   23177
      ed G.F.Malipiero   φ   str/cont(org=hpsd)   Ricordi,1950.CW 79   22293 Misc 9427
                                                                                                        & MRL
      ed A.Toni   φ   str/cont(org)   Carisch,1924   25989
      transcr Molinari   φ   str/cont(hpsd)   Ricordi,1927   Misc 1816
      rev F.Oubradous   φ   str/cont(hpsd)   Ed.Mus.Trans.1959   Misc 5246
    RV 298 (op.4,no.12) in G
      ed A.Ephrikian   φ   str/cont(hpsd)   Ricordi,1966.CW 429   Misc 6471 & MRL
      ed T.Nachez   φ   str/cont   Schott,1921   26289
    RV 299 (op.7,no.8), in G
      ed G.F.Malipiero   φ   str/cont(hpsd=org)   7'   Ricordi,1966.CW 449   Misc 6484 & MRL
      ed F.Sondheimer   φ   str/org   Bernoulli,1933   Misc 1375
        2nd mvt, Largo Cantabile, only
          ed F.Sondheimer   φ   str/cont   Bernoulli,1957   22167
    RV 300 (op.9,no.10) in G, from 'La Cetra'
      ed G.F.Malipiero   φ   str/cont(hpsd=org)   10'   Ricordi,1951.CW 124   Misc 3682 & MRL
      ed F.Schroeder   φ   str/cont(hpsd)   Eulenburg   23804
      ed D.Stevens   φ   str/cont(hpsd=org)   (Le Cene, [1727])   20642 +
    RV 301 (op.4,no.3) in G, from 'La Stravaganza'
      ed A.Ephrikian   φ   str/cont(hpsd=org)   12'   Ricordi,1965.CW 420   Misc 6284 & MRL
      ed W.Upmeyer   φ   str/cont(org)   Bärenreiter   20055
    RV 302, in G
      ed G.F.Malipiero   φ   str/cont(hpsd)   11'   Ricordi,1962.CW 358   Misc 5734 & MRL
    RV 303, in G
      ed G.F.Malipiero   φ   str/cont(hpsd)   13'30" Ricordi,1956.CW 228   Misc 4721 & MRL
    RV 306, in G
      ed G.F.Malipiero   φ   str/cont(hpsd)   7'   Ricordi,1954.CW 186   Misc 4272 & MRL
    RV 307, in G
      ed G.F.Malipiero   φ   str/cont(hpsd)   10'   Ricordi,1957.CW 255   Misc 4936 & MRL
    RV 308, in G
      ed G.F.Malipiero   φ   str/cont(hpsd)   13'   Ricordi,1968.CW 460   Misc 6837 & MRL
    RV 310 (op.3,no.3) in G, from 'L'Estro Armonico'
                              φ   str/cont   Walsh,1722   19843
      ed Heller   φ   str/cont   Peters,1973   Misc 8368
      ed Kücher & Herrmann   φ   str/cont   Hug,1957   Misc 4762
      ed G.F.Malipiero   φ   str/cont(hpsd)   8'   Ricordi,1965.CW 408   Misc 6272 & MRL
      arr A.Egigi for violin, piano, and strings (original slow mvt replaced by Adagio from oboe concerto
      by Marcello) in F   φ   str/cont(pf)   Vieweg,1926   Misc 991
      arr for mandolin & orch of plucked instr
                              φ   mands.gtr/cbs   E.Kalmus   26414
    RV 311, in G
      ed G.F.Malipiero   φ   str/cont(hpsd)   5'30" Ricordi,1955.CW 202   Misc 4591 & MRL
    RV 312, in G
      ed G.F.Malipiero   φ   str/cont(hpsd)   9'   Ricordi,1956.CW 247   Misc 4722 & MRL
    RV 313, in G
      ed G.F.Malipiero   φ   str/cont(hpsd)   8'   Ricordi,1953.CW 156   Misc 4053 & MRL
    RV 314, in G 'Per Pisendel'
      ed G.F.Malipiero   φ   str/cont(hpsd)   13'   Ricordi,1954.CW 192   Misc 4273 & MRL

VIVALDI, Antonio (cont)

CONCERTI (cont)
  Violin (cont)
    RV 315 (op.8,no.2) in G min, 'L'Estate' from 'The Seasons'
      ed N.Jenkins   ∅   str/cont(hpsd)   Eulenburg,1959   23175
      ed G.F.Malipiero   ∅   str/cont(org=hpsd)   10'   Ricordi,1950.CW 77   22291.Misc 9427
                                                                                                        & MRL

      ed A.Toni   ∅   str/cont(org)   Carisch,1924   25987
      transcr Molinari   ∅   str/cont(hpsd=org)   Ricordi,1927   Misc 1814
    RV 316a (op.4,no.6) in G min, from 'La Stravaganza'
      ed A.Ephrikian   ∅   str/cont(hpsd=org)   10'   Ricordi,1965.CW 423   Misc 6287 & MRL
      arr Franko   ∅   str/cont(pf)   Ries & Erler   10889
      arr Mistowski   ∅   str/cont(pf)   12'30"-14'30"   OUP   8931 B
    RV 317 (op.12,no.1), in G min
      ed A.Ephrikian   ∅   str/cont(hpsd)   13'   Ricordi,1968.CW 462   Misc 6839 & MRL
      ed T.Nachez   ∅   str/cont(org)   Schott   7743
    RV 318 (op.6,no.3) in G min
      ed G.F.Malipiero   ∅   str/cont(org=hpsd)   9'   Ricordi,1966.CW 438   Misc 6473 & MRL
    RV 319, in G min
      ed R.Eller   ∅   0201/0000/str/cont(hpsd)   Breitkopf   Misc 5773
      ed G.F.Malipiero   ∅   str/cont(hpsd)   10'   Ricordi,1962.CW 351   Misc 5730 & MRL
    RV 321, in G min
      ed G.F.Malipiero   ∅   str/cont(hpsd)   10'   Ricordi,1958.CW 292   Misc 5108 & MRL
    RV 323, in G min
      ed G.F.Malipiero   ∅   str/cont(hpsd)   7'30"   Ricordi,1961.CW 329   Misc 5576 & MRL
    RV 324 (op.6,no.1), in G min
      ed A.Einstein   ∅   str/cont(org)   Eulenburg   19765
      arr Gerheuser   ∅   str/cont(pf)   Nagel   14166
      ed G.F.Malipiero   ∅   str/cont(org=hpsd)   10'   Ricordi,1966.CW 436   Misc 6472 & MRL
    RV 325, in G min
      ed G.F.Malipiero   ∅   str/cont(hpsd)   9'   Ricordi,1957.CW 253   Misc 4938 & MRL
    RV 326 (op.7,no.3), in G min
      ed G.F.Malipiero   ∅   str/cont(hpsd=org)   7'   Ricordi,1966.CW 444   Misc 6488 & MRL
    RV 327, in G min
      ed G.F.Malipiero   ∅   str/cont(hpsd)   11'30"   Ricordi,1957.CW 257   Misc 4939 & MRL
    RV 328, in G min
      ed G.F.Malipiero   ∅   str/cont(hpsd)   9'   Ricordi,1954.CW 178   26566 & MRL
    RV 329, in G min
      ed G.F.Malipiero   ∅   str/cont(hpsd)   11'   Ricordi,1961.CW 334   Misc 5581 & MRL
    RV 330, in G min
      ed G.F.Malipiero   ∅   str/cont(hpsd)   9'   Ricordi,1950.CW 92   Misc 3498 & MRL
    RV 331, in G min
      ed G.F.Malipiero   ∅   str/cont(hpsd)   14'   Ricordi,1958.CW 295   Misc 5106 & MRL
    RV 332 (op.8,no.8), in G min
      ed G.F.Malipiero   ∅   str/cont(hpsd)   8'30"   Ricordi,1949.CW 65   26556 & MRL
    RV 333, in G min
      ed G.F.Malipiero   ∅   str/cont(hpsd)   13'   Ricordi,1953.CW 175   Misc 4054 & MRL
    RV 334 (op.9,no.3), in G min from 'La Cetra'
      ed G.F.Malipiero   ∅   str/cont(hpsd=org)   10'   Ricordi,1952.CW 127   Misc 3889 & MRL
      ed D.Stevens   ∅   str/cont(org)   (Le Cene, [1727])   20641+ mf 144
    RV 335, in A (Il Cucu)
      ed G.F.Malipiero   ∅   str/cont(hpsd)   Ricordi,1970.CW 487   Misc 7262 & MRL
    RV 336, in A
      ed G.F.Malipiero   ∅   str/cont(hpsd)   12'   Ricordi,1954.CW 191   Misc 4251 & MRL
    RV 338, in A
      ed G.F.Malipiero   ∅   str/cont(org=hpsd)   Ricordi,1970.CW 485   Misc 7260 & MRL

VIVALDI, Antonio (cont)

CONCERTI (cont)
  Violin (cont)
    RV 339, in A
      ed G.F.Malipiero   ∅   str/cont(hpsd)   12'   Ricordi,1970.CW 496   Misc 7269 & MRL
    RV 340, in A 'Per Pisendel'
      ed H.Landshoff   ∅   str/cont(hpsd)   Peters   15070
      ed G.F.Malipiero   ∅   str/cont(hpsd)   10'   Ricordi,1960.CW 323   Misc 5359 & MRL
    RV 341, in A
      ed G.F.Malipiero   ∅   str/cont(hpsd)   9'30" Ricordi,1961.CW 330   Misc 5577 & MRL
    RV 342, in A
      ed Guarnieri   ∅   str/cont(hpsd)   Ricordi,1918   5358
      ed G.F.Malipiero   ∅   str/cont(hpsd)   11'   Ricordi,1970.CW 489   Misc 7264 & MRL
    RV 343, in A
      ed G.F.Malipiero   ∅   str/cont(hpsd)   11'   Ricordi,1950.CW 100   Misc 3474 & MRL
    RV 344, in A
      ed G.F.Malipiero   ∅   str/cont(hpsd)   12'   Ricordi,1961.CW 339   Misc 5586 & MRL
    RV 345 (op.9,no.2) in A, from 'La Cetra'
      ed G.F.Malipiero   ∅   str/cont(hpsd=org)   9'   Ricordi,1952.CW 126   Misc 3865 & MRL
      ed D.Stevens   ∅   str/cont(hpsd=org)   (Le Cene, [1727])   20641 + mf 144
    RV 346, in A
      ed G.F.Malipiero   ∅   str/cont(hpsd)   11'   Ricordi,1956.CW 229   Misc 4727 & MRL
    RV 347 (op.4,no.5) in A, from 'La Stravaganza'
      ed A.Ephrikian   ∅   str/cont(hpsd)   10'   Ricordi,1965.CW 422   Misc 6286 B & MRL
    RV 348 (op.9,no.6) in A, from 'La Cetra'
      ed G.F.Malipiero   ∅   str/cont(hpsd)   Ricordi,1952.CW 129   Misc 3866 & MRL
      ed D.Stevens   ∅   str/cont(hpsd=org)   12'   (Le Cene, [1727])   20641 +
    RV 349, in A
      ed G.F.Malipiero   ∅   str/cont(hpsd)   11'30" Ricordi,1958.CW 293   Misc 5109 & MRL
    RV 350 (op.9,no.15), in A from 'La Cetra'
      ed G.F.Malipiero   ∅   str/cont(hpsd)   11'   Ricordi,1956.CW 245   Misc 4726 & MRL
    RV 352, in A
      ed B.Maderna   ∅   str/cont(hpsd)   7'   Ricordi,1947.CW 16   Misc 2576 & MRL
    RV 353, in A
      ed G.F.Malipiero   ∅   str/cont(hpsd)   9'   Ricordi,1960.CW 313   Misc 5360 & MRL
    RV 354 (op.7,no.4) in A min
      ed G.F.Malipiero   ∅   str/cont(hpsd=org)   Ricordi,1966.CW 445   24942 & MRL
    RV 355, in A
      ed G.F.Malipiero   ∅   str/cont(hpsd)   Ricordi,1971.CW 519   Misc 7672 & MRL
    RV 536 (op.3,no.6), in A min, from 'L'Estro Armonico'
      [op.3,no.8 in this ed] ∅   str/cont   Walsh[1722]   19843 +
      ed A.Einstein   ∅   str   Eulenburg,1952   20773
      G.F.Malipiero   ∅   str/cont(hpsd)   5'   Ricordi,1965.CW 411   Misc 6275 & MRL
      ed T.Nachez   ∅   str/org   Schott   7745
    RV 357 (op.4,no.4) in A min, from 'La Stravaganza'
      ed A.Ephrikian   ∅   str/cont   10'   Ricordi,1965.CW 421   Misc 6285 & MRL
    RV 358 (op.9,no.5) in A min, from 'La Cetra'
      ed G.F.Malipiero   ∅   str/cont(org=hpsd)   Ricordi,1952.CW 128   26560 & MRL
      ed D.Stevens   ∅   str/cont(hpsd=org)   (Le Cene, [1727])   20641 +
    RV 359 (op.9,no.7) in Bb, from 'La Cetra'
                             ∅   str/cont(hpsd=org)   (GB-Lbm.g.33/e(1)) 20642 +
      ed G.F.Malipiero   ∅   str/cont(hpsd=org)   Ricordi,1952.CW 130   Misc 3875 & MRL
    RV 361 (op.12,no.6) in Bb
      ed A.Ephrikian   ∅   str/cont(org=hpsd)   14'   Ricordi,1968.CW 466   Misc 6843 & MRL
    RV 362 (op.8,no.10), in Bb, 'La Caccia'
      ed G.F.Malipiero   ∅   str/cont(org=hpsd)   7'30" Ricordi,1950.CW 83   26557 & MRL

VIVALDI, Antonio (cont)

CONCERTI (cont)
  Violin (cont)
    RV 363, in B♭ 'Il corneto da posta'
      ed G.F.Malipiero   φ   str/cont(hpsd)   9'   Ricordi,1961.CW 348   Misc 5595 & MRL
    RV 364, in B♭
      ed G.F.Malipiero   φ   str/cont(org=hpsd)   Ricordi,1970.CW 483   Misc 7258 & MRL
    RV 365, in B♭
      ed G.F.Malipiero   φ   str/cont(hpsd)   12'   Ricordi,1953.CW 163   Misc 4032 & MRL
    RV 366, in B♭
      ed G.F.Malipiero   φ   str/cont(hpsd)   10'   Ricordi,1961.CW 332   Misc 5579 & MRL
    RV 367, in B♭
      ed A.Ephrikian   φ   str/cont(hpsd)   13'   Ricordi,1947.CW   1   Misc 2561 & MRL
    RV 368, in B♭
      ed G.F.Malipiero   φ   str/cont(hpsd)   9'   Ricordi,1958.CW 291   Misc 5113 & MRL
    RV 369, in B♭
      ed G.F.Malipiero   φ   str/cont(hpsd)   10'   Ricordi,1953.CW 157   Misc 4031 & MRL
    RV 370, in B♭
      ed G.F.Malipiero   φ   str/cont(hpsd)   12'   Ricordi,1954.CW 199   Misc 4255 & MRL
    RV 371, in B♭
      ed G.F.Malipiero   φ   str/cont(hpsd)   12'   Ricordi,1957.CW 262   Misc 4942 & MRL
    RV 372, in B♭
      ed G.F.Malipiero   φ   str/cont(hpsd)   Ricordi,1958.CW 284   Misc 5110 & MRL
    RV 373 (op.7,no.9) in B♭
      ed G.F.Malipiero   φ   str/cont(hpsd=org)   12'   Ricordi,1966.CW 450   Misc 6485 & MRL
    RV 374 (op.7,no.6) in B♭
      ed G.F.Malipiero   φ   str/cont(hpsd=org)   8'   Ricordi,1966.CW 447   Misc 6481 & MRL
    RV 375, in B♭
      ed G.F.Malipiero   φ   str/cont(hpsd)   10'   Ricordi,1950.CW 86   Misc 3476 & MRL
    RV 376, in B♭
      ed G.F.Malipiero   φ   str/cont(hpsd)   10'   Ricordi,1953.CW 170   Misc 4033 & MRL
    RV 377, in B♭
      ed G.F.Malipiero   φ   str/cont(hpsd)   Ricordi,1970.CW 499   Misc 7272 & MRL
    RV 379, in B♭
      ed G.F.Malipiero   φ   str/cont(hpsd)   12'30"   Ricordi,1954.CW 183   Misc 4254 & MRL
      ed T.Nachez   φ   str/cont(org)   Schott   7736
    RV 380, in B♭
      ed G.F.Malipiero   φ   str/cont(hpsd)   12'   Ricordi,1949.CW 64   Misc 3127 & MRL
    RV 381, in B♭
      ed Frenkel   φ   str/cont   Ries & Erler,1933   Misc 1400
      ed G.F.Malipiero   φ   str/cont(hpsd)   Ricordi,1971.CW 514   Misc 7674 & MRL
      arr W.Upmeyer   φ   str/cont   Bärenreiter   20053
    RV 382, in B♭
      ed G.F.Malipiero   φ   str/cont(hpsd)   Ricordi,1961.CW 511   Misc 7666 & MRL
    RV 383, in B♭
      ed G.Prato   φ   str/cont(hpsd)   8'   Ricordi,1963.CW 377   Misc 5860 & MRL
    RV 383a (op.4,no.1) in B♭, from 'La Stravaganza'
      ed A.Ephrikian   φ   str/cont(hpsd & org)   12'   Ricordi,1965.CW 418   Misc 6282 & MRL
    RV 583, in B♭
      ed G.F.Malipiero   φ   double str orch/2cont(hpsd)   14'   Ricordi,1952.CW 136   25085* & MRL
    RV 384, in B min
      ed G.F.Malipiero   φ   str/cont(hpsd)   9'   Ricordi,1961.CW 326   Misc 5573 & MRL
    RV 385, in B min
      ed G.F.Malipiero   φ   str/cont(hpsd)   12'   Ricordi,1970.CW 498   Misc 7271 & MRL
    RV 386, in B min
      ed G.F.Malipiero   φ   str/cont(hpsd)   12'   Ricordi,1957.CW 260   Misc 4944 & MRL

VIVALDI, Antonio (cont)

CONCERTI (cont)
  Violin (cont)
    RV 387, in B min
      ed G.F.Malipiero   ∅   str/cont(hpsd)   13'   Ricordi,1954.CW 179   Misc 4257 & MRL
    RV 388, in B min
      ed G.F.Malipiero   ∅   str/cont(hpsd)   9'   Ricordi,1963.CW 378   Misc 5861 & MRL
    RV 389, in B min
      ed G.F.Malipiero   ∅   str/cont(hpsd)   11'   Ricordi,1950.CW 96   Misc 3477 & MRL
    RV 390, in B min
      ed G.F.Malipiero   ∅   str/cont(hpsd)   12'30" Ricordi,1953.CW 171   Misc 4035 & MRL
    RV 391 (op.9,no.12) in B min, from 'La Cetra'
      ed G.F.Malipiero   ∅   str/cont(hpsd=org)   12'   Ricordi,1957.CW 125   Misc 3664 & MRL
      ed D.Stevens   ∅   str/cont(hpsd=org)   (Le Cene, [1727])   20642 +
  2 Violins
    RV 505, in C,
      ed G.F.Malipiero   ∅   str/cont(hpsd)   9'30" Ricordi,1954.CW 181   Misc 4261 & MRL
    RV 506, in C
      ed G.F.Malipiero   ∅   str/cont(hpsd)   Ricordi,1961.CW 342   Misc 5589 B & MRL
    RV 507, in C
      ed G.F.Malipiero   ∅   str/cont(hpsd)   11'   Ricordi,1951.CW 112   26559 & MRL
    RV 508, in C
      ed G.F.Malipiero   ∅   str/cont(hpsd)   11'   Ricordi,1951.CW 116   Misc 3666 & MRL
    RV 509, in C min
      ed R.Olivieri   ∅   str/cont(hpsd)   Ricordi,1949.CW 48   Misc 2933 & MRL
    RV 510, in C min
      ed G.F.Malipiero   ∅   str/cont(hpsd)   7'   Ricordi,1949.CW 60   Misc 3126 & MRL
    RV 511, in D
      ed G.F.Malipiero   ∅   str/cont(hpsd)   10'   Ricordi,1950.CW 89   Misc 3486 & MRL
    RV 512, in D
      ed G.F.Malipiero   ∅   str/cont(hpsd)   10'   Ricordi,1951.CW 108   Misc 3673 & MRL
    RV 513, in D
      ed G.F.Malipiero   ∅   str/cont(org=hpsd)   Ricordi,1970.CW 486   Misc 7261 & MRL
    RV 514, in D min
      ed G.F.Malipiero   ∅   str/cont(hpsd)   10'   Ricordi,1955.CW 209   26569 & MRL
    RV 515, in E♭
      ed G.F.Malipiero   ∅   str/cont(hpsd)   12'30" Ricordi,1955.CW 210   Misc 4587 & MRL
    RV 516, in G
      ed A.Ephrikian   ∅   str/cont(hpsd)   Ricordi,1949.CW 27   26512 B & MRL
    RV 517, in G min
      ed G.F.Malipiero   ∅   str/cont(hpsd)   9'   Ricordi,1955.CW 207   26568+ & MRL
    RV 519 (op.3,no.5) in A, from 'L'Estro Armonico'
                              ∅   str/cont   Walsh [1722]   19843 +
      ed G.F.Malipiero   ∅   str/cont(hpsd)   7'   Ricordi,1965.CW 410   26576 & MRL
    RV 521, in A
                              ∅   str/cont   Eulenburg,1966   25970
      ed G.F.Malipiero   ∅   str/cont(hpsd)   10'   Ricordi,1961.CW 344   Misc 5591 & MRL
    RV 522 (op.3,no.8), in A min, from 'L'Estro Armonico'
      [op.3,no.6 in this ed] ∅   str/cont   12'30" Walsh [1722]   19843 +
      ed A.Einstein   ∅   str/cont(hpsd)   (Eulenburg)   19585+
      ed Franko   ∅   str/cont(hpsd)   G.Schirmer   9184
      ed G.F.Malipiero   ∅   str/cont(hpsd)   10'   Ricordi,1965.CW 413   Misc 6277 & MRL
      ed T.Nachez   ∅   str/cont(org)   Schott   13869
    RV 523, in A min
      ed G.F.Malipiero   ∅   str/cont(hpsd)   10'   Ricordi,1952.CW 140   Misc 3869 & MRL

VIVALDI, Antonio (cont)

CONCERTI (cont)

2 Violins (cont)

RV 524, in B♭
   ed G.F.Malipiero   φ   str/cont(hpsd)   11'   Ricordi,1959.CW 107   Misc 3662 & MRL

RV 525, in B♭
   ed G.F.Malipiero   φ   str/cont(hpsd)   10'   Ricordi,1952.CW 145   26563 & MRL

RV 527, in B♭
   ed G.F.Malipiero   φ   str/cont(hpsd)   10'   Ricordi,1955.CW 208   Misc 4572 & MRL

RV 529, in B♭
   ed G.F.Malipiero   φ   str/cont(hpsd)   11'   Ricordi,1951.CW 111   Misc 3663 & MRL

RV 530 (op.9,no.9) in B♭, from 'La Cetra'
   ed G.F.Malipiero   φ   str/cont(org=hpsd)   10'   Ricordi,1952.CW 132   Misc 3874 & MRL
   ed D.Stevens   φ   str/cont   (Le Cene, [1727]) 20641-2+ mf 144

3 Violins

RV 551, in F
   ed G.F.Malipiero   φ   str/cont(hpsd)   9'   Ricordi,1950.CW 88   Misc 3494 & MRL
   ed G.Schumann   φ   str/cont(hpsd)   9'   Wernthal   10575

4 Violins

RV 549 (op.3,no.1) in D, from 'L'Estro Armonico'
                   φ   str/cont   Walsh,1722   19843+
                   φ   str/cont   Eulenburg,1966   25979
   ed Heller   φ   str/cont(hpsd)   Peters,1973   Misc 8367
   ed G.F.Malipiero   φ   str/cont(hpsd)   10'   Ricordi,1965.CW 412   Misc 6270 & MRL

RV 550 (op.3,no.4) in E min, from 'L'Estro Armonico'
                   φ   str/cont   Walsh,1722   19843 +
   ed Heller   φ   str/cont(hpsd)   Peters   Misc 8371
   ed G.F.Malipiero   φ   str/cont(hpsd)   8'   Ricordi,1965.CW 409   26420 & MRL

RV 552, in A
   ed G.F.Malipiero   φ   str/cont(hpsd)   Ricordi,1960.CW 319   Misc 5358 & MRL
   ed K.Straube   φ   str/cont(hpsd)   Breitkopf,1930   Misc 3821

RV 553, in B♭
   ed G.F.Malipiero   φ   str/cont(hpsd)   Ricordi,1952.CW 134   26561

CONCERTI FOR 2 DIFFERENT SOLO INSTRUMENTS

CONCERTI RV 1 - 108 <u>see</u> CHAMBER CATALOGUE

RV 409, in E min, for bassoon, cello, strings & continuo <u>see</u>   CONCERTI : cello, RV 409

RV 540, in D min, for viola d'amore, lute, strings & continuo
   ed G.F.Malipiero   φ   str/cont(hpsd)   9'   Ricordi,1960.CW 320   26702 +# & MRL

RV 541, in D min, for violin, organ, strings & continuo
   ed G.F.Malipiero   φ   str/cont(hpsd)   8'   Ricordi,1951.CW 95   Misc 3484

RV 542, in F, for violin, organ, strings & continuo
   ed G.F.Malipiero   φ   str/cont(org)   9'   Ricordi,1962.CW 353   26578 & MRL
   ed F.Schroeder   φ   0001/0000/str/cont   Eulenburg,1968/9   24966

RV 543, in F, for oboe, violin, strings & continuo
   ed G.F.Malipiero   φ   str/cont(hpsd)   Ricordi,1957.CW 265   Misc 4932 & MRL

RV 544, in F, for violin, cello, strings & continuo 'Il Proteo: ∂ sia, il Mondo al Rovescio'
   ed G.F.Malipiero   φ   str/cont(hpsd)   11'   Ricordi,1952.CW 125   Misc 3885 & MRL

RV 545, in G, for oboe, bassoon, strings & continuo
   ed D.Lasocki   φ   str/cont(real R.P.Block)   Musica Rara,1974   25748
   ed G.F.Malipiero   φ   str/cont(hpsd)   11'   Ricordi,1958.CW 280   26581

RV 546, in A, for violin, cello, strings & continuo
   ed G.F.Malipiero   φ   str/cont(hpsd)   10'   Ricordi,1952.CW 146   Misc 3867

RV 547, in B♭, for violin, cello, strings & continuo
   ed A.Ephrikian   φ   str/cont(hpsd)   Ricordi,1949.CW 35   26549 & MRL

RV 548, in B♭, for oboe, violin, strings & continuo
   ed G.F.Malipiero   φ   str/cont(hpsd)   8'30"-9'30"
                                              Ricordi,1949.CW 73   24578 B+ & MRL

VIVALDI, Antonio (cont)

CONCERTI (cont)
  2 different solo instruments (cont)
    RV Anh 17, for oboe, violin, strings & continuo
      _ ed D.Lasocki   φ   str/cont(real R.P.Block)   Musica Rara,1973   25729
CONCERTI FOR 3 (OR MORE) DIFFERENT SOLO INSTRUMENTS
    RV 549, in D, for 4 violins with cello solo in 1st mvt   see   CONCERTI, 4 violins, RV 549, in D
    RV 554, in C, for flute, oboe or cello, 2 violins (or violin & organ), strings & continuo
      ed G.F.Malipiero   φ   str/cont(hpsd)   12'   Ricordi,1956.CW 250   Misc 4705 & MRL
    RV 555, in C, for 2 recorders, oboe, salmoé, 2 trumpets, violin, 2 viole all'Inglese, strings &
        continuo
      ed G.F.Malipiero   φ   21+ca.00/0000/vln.2vla.str/cont(hpsd)   10'   Ricordi.1952.CW 142   Misc 3877 & MRL
    RV 556, in C, for 2 recorders, 2 oboes, 2 clarinets, bassoon, 2 violins, strings &
        continuo 'Per las Solennità di S.Lorenzo'
      ed E.Ephrikian   φ   str/cont(hpsd)   14'-15'Ricordi,1949.CW 54   26553 & MRL
    RV 557, in C, for 2 recorders, 2 oboes, bassoon, 2 violins, strings & continuo
      ed G.F.Malipiero   φ   str/cont(hpsd)   8'   Ricordi,1950.CW 90   Misc 3481 & MRL
    RV 558, in C, for 2 recorders, 2 salmoé, 2 trumpets, 2 mandolines, 2 theorbos, 2 violins,
        cello, strings & continuo
      rev A.Casella   φ   str/cont(hpsd)   Carisch,1943   23781
      rev P.Giorgi with bassoon replacing salmoés (from Dresden Mss 2389/0/4)
                                 φ   str/cont(hpsd)   Del Turco Editore.CIDM. Vol 2   MRL (pts hire)
      ed G.F.Malipiero   φ   str/cont(hpsd)   10'   Ricordi,1960.CW 318   Misc 5337 & MRL
    RV 559, in C, for 2 oboes, 2 clarinets, strings & continuo
      ed A.Ephrikian   φ   str/cont(hpsd)   15'   Ricordi,1947.CW 10   26545 & MRL
      2nd mvt ed A.Ephrikian   φ   str/cont(hpsd)   Ricordi,1947   21323
    RV 562, in D, for 2 oboes, 2 horns, violin, strings & continuo
      ed G.Prato   φ   str/cont (2 org)   16'   Ricordi,1963.CW 380   Misc 5863 & MRL
    RV 563, in D, for 2 oboes, violin, strings & continuo
      ed G.F.Malipiero   φ   str/cont   8'   Ricordi,1971.CW 510   Misc 7662 & MRL
    RV 564, in D, for 2 violins, 2 cellos, strings & continuo
      ed G.F.Malipiero   φ   str/cont(hpsd)   11'   Ricordi,1950.CW 99   Misc 3487 & MRL
    RV 565, (op.3,no.11) for 2 violins, strings & continuo, from 'L'Estro Armonico'
                                 φ   str/cont(hpsd)   9'45"-13'15"   Walsh,1722   19843+
      ed A.Einstein   φ   str/cont   Eulenburg,1952   20602
      ed G.F.Malipiero   φ   str/cont(hpsd)   9'   Ricordi,1965.CW 416   Misc 6280 & MRL
      arr Raphael   φ   str   Breitkopf   9404 B
      arr F.Schroeder   φ   str/cont   Tonger   9307
      orch D'Antalffy from J.S.Bach's transcription (BWV 595)
                                 φ   3(picc)2+ca.2+bcl.2+cbsn/4331/timp.bells/
                                     hp.org.pf/str   Boosey & H,1940   Misc 2406
    RV 566, in D min, for 2 recorders, 2 oboes, bassoon, 2 violins, strings & continuo
      ed G.F.Malipiero   φ   str/cont(hpsd)   10'   Ricordi,1955.CW 213   26571 & MRL
    RV 567 (op.3,no.7) in F, for 4 violins, cello, strings & continuo, from 'L'Estro Armonico'
      [op.3,no.9 in this edn] φ   str/cont   Walsh,1722   19843+
      ed R.Eller   φ   str/cont   Eulenburg,1969   Misc 7164 B
      ed Heller   φ   str/cont   Peters,1973   Misc 8370
      ed G.F.Malipiero   φ   str/cont(hpsd)   18'   Ricordi,1965.CW 412   Misc 6276 & MRL
      arr W.Upmeyer   φ   str/cont   Bärenreiter,1954   21446
    RV 568, in F, for 2 oboes, bassoon, 2 horns, violin, strings & continuo
      rev P.Giorgi from Dresden MSS 2389/0/47
                                 φ   str/cont(hpsd)   Del Turco Editore.CIDM vol 2   MRL
      ed G.F.Malipiero   φ   str/cont(hpsd)   10'30" Ricordi,1961.CW 338   Misc 5585 & MRL
    RV 569, in F, for 2 oboes, bassoon, 2 horns, violin, strings & continuo
      ed A.Ephrikian   φ   str/cont(hpsd)   Ricordi,1949.CW 43   Misc 2945 & MRL
      ed Straube   φ   str/cont(hpsd)   Breitkopf   19175

VIVALDI, Antonio (cont)

CONCERTI (cont)
  3 (or more) different solo instruments (cont)
    RV 570, in F, for flute, oboe, bassoon, strings & continuo, 'La Tempesta di Mare'
      (see also Concerto for flute, in B, RV 433)

ed G.F.Malipiero	ϕ	str/cont(hpsd)		Ricordi,1952.CW 150	Misc 3886 & MRL
ed G.F.Schroeder	ϕ	str/cont(hpsd)		Eulenburg,1965	25991*

    RV 571, in F, for 2 oboes, bassoon, 2 horns, violin, strings & continuo

ed G.F.Malipiero	ϕ	str/cont(org)	10'	Ricordi,1961.CW 350	Misc 5597 & MRL

    RV 574, (op.46,no.3) in F, for 2 oboes, bassoon, violin, strings & continuo

ed G.F.Malipiero	ϕ	str/cont(hpsd)	11'	Ricordi,1950.CW 94	Misc 3495 & MRL

    RV 575, in G, for 2 cellos, 2 violins, strings & continuo

ed A.Ephrikian	ϕ	str/cont(hpsd)		Ricordi,1949.CW 26	Misc 2934

    RV 576, in G min, for 2 flutes, 3 oboes, bassoon, violin, strings & continuo

ed G.F.Malipiero	ϕ	str/cont(hpsd)	11'	Ricordi,1956.CW 249	26583 & MRL
arr Torrefranca	ϕ	2202/0000/str/cont		Carisch	14695

    RV 577, in G min, for violin, 2 flutes, 2 oboes, 2 bassoons, strings & continuo 'Per
      L'Orchestra di Dresda' (Dresden Concerto)

	ϕ	str/cont(hpsd)	10'	Swift	Misc 4847
ed A.Ephrikian	ϕ	str/cont	10'	Ricordi,1947.CW 25	26547 & MRL
rev F.Oubradous	ϕ	str/cont(hpsd)	10'	Ed.Mus.Trans,1959	Misc 5245

    RV 578 (op.3,no.2) in G min, for 2 violins, cello, strings & continuo, from L'Estro Armonico'

	ϕ	str/cont		Walsh [1722]	
arr Baud-Bovy	ϕ	str/cont		Eulenburg	19162
ed G.F.Malipiero	ϕ	str/cont(hpsd)	10'	Ricordi,1965.CW 407	19843 +

    RV 579, in Bb, for oboe, salmoé, violin, 3 viola all'Inglese. (Concerto funèbre)

ed A.Ephrikian	ϕ	01+ca.00/0000/2vla,vlc-soli.str/			
		cont(hpsd)	12'	Ricordi,1949.CW 51	Misc 3142

    RV 580 (op.3,no.10), in B min, for 4 violins, cello, strings & continuo from 'L'Estro Armonico'

	ϕ	str/cont		Walsh [1722]	19843
ed A.Einstein	ϕ	str/cont		Eulenburg	19240 B
ed G.F.Malipiero	ϕ	str/cont	11'	Ricordi,1956.CW 415	25769 We & MRL
ed W.Wohel	ϕ	str/cont		Hinrichsen,1937	24490
arr Bouvet	ϕ	str/cont		Eschig	12660
arr M.Esposito	ϕ	str/cont		OUP	11692
arr W.Upmeyer	ϕ	str/cont		Bärenreiter,1954	Misc 4246
transcr J.S.Bach for 4 kbd instr & str:		see		BACH,J.S. CONCERTI for 4 kbd instr & str (BWV 1065)	

    RV 585, in A, for 4 recorders, 4 violins, 2 cellos, organ, theorbo (or organ) & double string orch

ed R.Meylan	ϕ	str/cont(2hpsd)	14'	Universal	Misc 5247
ed G.Prato	ϕ	str/cont(2org)		Ricordi,1963.CW 381	Misc 5864 & MRL

CONCERTO FUNEBRE   see   CONCERTI for 3 or more different instruments, RV 579 in Bb

CREDO for SATB chorus & orch, RV 591, in E min

rev & ed R.Fasano	ϕ	str/cont	Universal/Philharmonica,1961	25205
ed G.F.Malipiero	ϕ	str/cont(org)	Ricordi,1970	Misc 9695

DANZA PASTORALE   see   The SEASONS, 3rd movement of 'Spring'

DIXIT DOMINUS (Psalm 109) for SSATB soli, 2 choruses & 2 orchs, RV 594, in D

ed G.F.Malipiero	ϕ	0200/0200/org/str/cont)		
		str/cont)	35'	Ricordi,1970	Misc 7472

DRESDEN CONCERTO   see   CONCERTO FOR 3 (OR MORE) DIFFERENT SOLO INSTRUMENTS, RV 577, in G min

ERCOLE SUL TERMODONTE: opera, RV 710
  Extracts
    4 Arias
      1. Da due venti   2. Onde chiare   3. Ama, risponde il Pio   4. Con aspetto lusinghieri

	ϕ	str	[BBC]	19390

      No.1 only
        in G, rev A.Casella

	ϕ	str/cont	Carisch,1940	23790

      No.2 only
        in D, rev A.Casella

	ϕ	str/cont	Carisch,1940	23790

L'ESTATE see CONCERTI, Violin, RV 315

VIVALDI, Antonio (cont)

L'ESTRO ARMONICO op 3: 12 Concerti for various instruments [NB. modern editions may have different order]

1.	RV 549, in D for 4 vln	7.	RV 567 in F for 4 vln, vlc
2.	RV 578 in G min for 2 vln, vlc	8.	RV 522, in A min for 2 vln
3.	RV 310, in G for vln	9.	RV 230, in D for vln
4.	RV 550, in E min for 4 vln	10.	RV 580, in B min for 4 vln, vlc
5.	RV 519 in A for 2 vln	11.	RV 565, in D min for 2 vln, vlc
6.	RV 356 in A min for vln	12.	RV 265, in E for vln

                                                                                            (19843+, &
    Complete   ⌀   str/cont   Walsh,[1722]   (26163 & mf 55-6
    see also separate entries under CONCERTI

FANTASMI   see   CONCERTO for violin in G min, RV 317 ('La Notte', 2nd Mvt)

La FIDA NINFA: opera, RV 714
    ed R.Monteresso   ⌀   0.4rec.000/2000/perc/hpsd/str   Antheanum Cremonense,1964.CW 1/3   MRL

FIUME CHE TORBIDO: aria for Bass solo & strings (not in Ryom)
                              ⌀   str   L.S.Olschki,1978   Misc 10593

FUNEBRE   see   CONCERTO FOR 3 (OR MORE) DIFFERENT SOLO INSTRUMENTS, RV 577, in G min

II GARDELLINO   see CONCERTO for flute, RV 428, in D (The Goldfinch) and CONCERTO for fl.ob.bsn.vln & cont
                    RV 90 in CHAMBER CATALOGUE

GLORIA for SSA soli, chorus and orchestra, RV 589, in D
    ed G.F.Malipiero   ⌀   0100/0100/str/cont(org)   Ricordi,1970   Misc 7228
    ed G.Westerman   ⌀   0100/0100/str/cont(org)   E.F.Kalmus   24697

L'INCORONAZIONE DI DARIO: opera, RV 719

    Sinfonia, in C
      ed H.La shoff   ⌀   str/cont(hpsd)   Peters   15071

IN FURORE: motet for soprano (or tenor) solo and orchestra, RV 626, in C min
    ed N.Fechner   ⌀   str/cont   DVfM,1977   Misc 9512

L'INQUIETUDINE   see   CONCERTO for violin, RV 234, in D
L'INVERNO   see   The SEASONS

INVICTAI BELLATE: motet for soprano & orch, RV 628, in G
    ed R.Blanchard   ⌀   str/cont   Heugel,1968   Misc 9060 B

JUDITHA TRIUMPHANS: oratorio for S Ms AAA soli, chorus & orch, RV 644
    ed A.Zedda   ⌀   22.2salmoé.00/02.2clarino.00/timp/mand.4theorbos/
                                  hpsd.org/vla d'a str   120' Ricordi,1971   Misc 7680
    facsimile   ⌀   2200/0200/timp/str/cont   Acc.Mus.Chigiana Misc 2393 B facs
    miscellaneous parts only   vla-d'a.mand.hpsd/cont(vlc)   BBC   20625

    Veni, veni: aria
      ed A.Zedda   ⌀   00.salmoé.00/0000/str/cont   Ricordi,1971   26937 *

KYRIE for double chorus & double orch, RV 587
    ed J.Braun with SSAA soli ⌀ str/2cont(org/hpsd)   Eulenburg,1969   25018
    ed F.Degrada   ⌀   str/2cont(org)   Universal,1969   25206

LAUDA JERUSALEM (Psalm 147) for SS soli, chorus & double string orch, RV 609, in E min
    ed J.Braun   ⌀   str/cont(org)   Eulenburg,1969   25097
    ed F.Degrade   ⌀   str/cont(org)   Ricordi,1973   Misc 8185

LAUDATE PUERI DOMINUM (Psalm 112) for soprano & orch, RV 600, in C min
    transcr & real G.Spinelli ⌀ str/cont(org)   26'   Carisch,1970   Misc 7512

LAUDATE PUERI DOMINUM (Psalm 112) for soprano & orch, RV 601, in G
    ed A.Ephrikian   ⌀   1200/0000/str/cont   26'   Ricordi,1970   26525 B

LONGE MALA UMBRAE TERRORES: motet for soprano solo & orch, RV 629, in G min
    ed R.Blanchard   ⌀   str/cont   Heugel,1968   Misc 9060 B

MAGNIFICAT
    RV 610   Original version for SSAT soli, chorus & orch, in G min
      ed H.C.Robbins Landon   ⌀   [0201]0.cntto.1301/str/cont   Universal,1961   Misc 9380
      ed G.F.Malipiero   ⌀   0200/0000/str/1[2=]cont   14'   Ricordi,1959   23369
    RV 610a, Revised version for SSAT soli, double chorus & double orch, in G min
      ed G.F.Malipiero (Includes version with substitute solo mvts for SSSAA[=SA] soli, chorus & orch)
                              ⌀   020[1]/0000/str/cont   Ricordi,1970   Misc 9387

VIVALDI, Antonio (cont)

MIO COR POVERO COR   see   SERENATA A TRE
NISI DOMINUS (Psalm 126) for contralto solo & orch, RV 608
   ed F.Degrada   φ   str/cont   24'   Ricordi,1971   Misc 7792
   transcr & rev M.Bruni

                       φ   str/org   24'   Carisch,1959   23729
La NOTTE   see   CONCERTI, flute, RV 439 in G min; bassoon, RV 501 in E♭
NULLA IN MUNDO PAX SINCERA: motet for soprano (or tenor) & orch in F, RV 630
   ed R.Blanchard   φ   str/cont(hpsd)   Heugel,1968   Misc 9060 B
O QUI COELI: motet for soprano (or tenor) & orch, RV 631, in E♭
   ed R.Blanchard   φ   str/cont(hpsd)   Heugel,1968   Misc 9060 B
OLIMPIADE: opera, RV 725
   Overture,arr Mortari   φ   str   Carisch   16426
ORRIBILE LO SCEMPIO: aria for Bass solo & strings (not in Ryom)
                       φ   str   L.S.Olschki,1978   Misc 10593
La PASTORELLA   see   CHAMBER CATALOGUE
PER LA SS ASSUNZIONE DI MARIA VERGINE   see   1. CONCERTO for violin, RV 179, in C
                                           2. CONCERTO for violin, RV 389, in D
PER LA SOLENNITÀ DI SAN LORENZO   see   1. CONCERTO for violin, RV 286, in F
                                           2. CONCERTO for 3 (or more) different instruments
                                                 RV 556, in C
PER L'ORCHESTRA DI DRESDA   see   CONCERTO for 3 (or more(different instruments,
                                                 RV 577, in G min
Il PIACERE   see   CONCERTO for violin, RV 180 (op.8,no.6) in C
PISENDEL, concerti for J.G.Pisendel   see   1. CONCERTO for violin, RV 242, in D min
                                           2. CONCERTO for violin, RV 314, in G
                                           3. CONCERTO for violin, RV 340, in A
                                           4. CONCERTO for violin, RV 205, in D

La PRIMAVERA   see   The SEASONS
Il PROTEO: O SIA, IL MONDO AL ROVESCIO   see   CONCERTO FOR 3 (OR MORE) DIFFERENT INSTRUMENTS, RV 544, in F
PSALM 109   see   DIXIT DOMINUS
PSALM 112   see   LAUDATE PUERI
PSALM 126   see   NISI DOMINUS
PSALM 147   see   LAUDA JERUSALEM
Il RIPOSO   see   CONCERTO for violin, RV 270, in E
SALVE REGINA for contralto & double orch, RV 616
   ed A.Ephrikian   φ   2000/0000/str/2cont(org   Ricordi,1970   26541
SCORRE IL FIUME MORMORANDO: aria for bass solo & strings (not in Ryom)
   ed F.Piva   φ   str   L.S.Olschki,1978   Misc 10592
The SEASONS: concerti for violin & strings & continuo, op.8,nos.1-4
   No.1, RV 269, in E, Spring (La Primavera)
   No.2, RV 315, in G min, Summer (L'Estate)
   No.3, RV 293, in F, Autumn (L'Autonno)
   No.4, RV 297, in F min, Winter (L'Inverno)
     Complete
       ed N.Jenkins   φ   str/cont   Eulenburg   Misc 9025 &
                                                                               23174-7
       ed G.F.Malipiero   φ   str/cont   Ricordi,1950   Misc 9427 &
                                                                               22290-3
       ed B.Molinari   φ   str/cont   Ricordi,1927   Misc 1813-6 C
       ed A.Toni   φ   str/cont   Carisch,1924   25986
   No.3 only
       ed F.Oubradous   φ   str/cont   Ed.Mus.Transc.,1959   Misc 5251
   No.4 only
       ed F.Oubradous   φ   str/cont   Ed.Mus.Transc.,1959   Misc 5246

VIVALDI, Antonio (cont)

SENZA CANTIN   see   CONCERTO for violin, RV 243, in D min
SERENATA A TRE: aria for 2 sopranos, tenor & orch, RV 690
     ed L.Sgrizzi   ⌀ 0201/2000/str/cont(hpsd   (Editor)   Misc 9575
SINFONIAS
     RV 112, in C   see   CONCERTI for strings & continuo, RV 112, in C
     RV 116, in C   see   CONCERTI for strings & continuo, RV 116, in C
     RV 192, in C   see   CONCERTI for violin, RV 192, in C
     RV 669 & 710, in C see   ARMIDA AL CAMPO D'EGITTO
     RV 719, in C   see   L'INCORONAZIONE DI DARIO
     RV 122, in D   see   CONCERTI for strings & continuo, RV 122, in C
     RV 131, in E   see   CONCERTI for strings & continuo, RV 131, in E
     RV 132, in E   see   CONCERTI for strings & continuo, RV 132, in E
     RV 134, in E min see   CONCERTI for strings & continuo, RV 134, in E min
     RV 135, in F   see   CONCERTI for strings & continuo, RV 135, in F
     RV 137, in F   see   CONCERTI for strings & continuo, RV 137, in F
     RV 140, in F   see   CONCERTI for strings & continuo, RV 140, in F
     RV 146, in G   see   CONCERTI for strings & continuo, RV 146, in G
     RV 148, in G   see   CONCERTI for strings & continuo, RV 148, in G
     RV 149, in G   see   CONCERTI for strings & continuo, RV 149, in G
     RV 16 , in B♭   see   CONCERTI for strings, RV 162, in G
     RV 168, in B min see   CONCERTI for strings & continuo, RV 168, in B min
SIROE: opera (1727)
    Extracts
        Gelido in ogni vena: aria for tenor & orch
           in F min, (orig)
               ed R.Strohm   ⌀   str/cont   Arno Volk,1976.Analetica Mus 16   BRL ⌀ only
SONATAS
    for strings, RV 130, in E♭ 'AL SANTO SEPULCRO'
                              ⌀   str/cont(hpsd)   (Ricordi)   19386
    see also CHAMBER CATALOGUE
SONATAS DA CAMERA (orig chamber ensemble)
    RV 40, in E min
       arr H.Bazelaire for cello & orch
                              ⌀   str   21'10"   Leduc,1942   21261
    RV 67, in G
       arr J.Brown for piano & strings
                              ⌀   str   Stainer & Bell   1694
Il SONNO   see   CONCERTO for flute, RV 439, in G min, (4th mvt)
Il SOSPETTO   see   CONCERTO for violin, RV 199, in C min
STABAT MATER for contralto, str & cont, RV 621, in F min
    rev A Casella   ⌀   str/cont(org)   Carisch,1949   23789
    rev R.Fasano   ⌀   str/cont(hpsd or org)   20'   Universal,1969   25198
    ed G.F.Malipiero   ⌀   str/cont(org)   27'   Ricordi,1970   26542
La STRAVAGANZA: 12 CONCERTI for violin, str & cont, (op.4)
    1. RV 381 & 383, in B♭   7. RV 185, in C
    2. RV 279, in E min   8. RV 249, in D min
    3. RV 301, in G   9. RV 284, in F
    4. RV 357, in A min   10. RV 196, in C min
    5. RV 347, in A   11. RV 204, in D
    6. RV 316, in G min   12. RV 298, in G
      see separate entries under CONCERTI
La TEMPESTA DI MARE   see   1. CONCERTI, violin, RV 253, in E♭
                            2. CONCERTI, flute, RV 433 & CONCERTI for 3 (or more) different instruments,
                                            RV 570, in F
The TRIAL OF HARMONY AND INVENTION   see   Il CIMENTO DELL'ARMONIA E DELL'INVENZIONE

VIVALDI, Antonio (cont)

CONCORDANCE TABLES FOR VIVALDI'S ORCHESTRAL WORKS (Further tables may be found in the Ryom Thematic
Catalogue)

OPUS NUMBERS (original opus nos. not Rinaldi)
op.3 L'ESTRO ARMONICO [1711]
NB. The Roger edition and the Walsh edition do not have the pieces in the same order.

Roger:

1. RV 549	4. RV 550	7. RV 567	10. RV 580
2. RV 578	5. RV 519	8. RV 522	11. RV 565
3. RV 310	6. RV 356	9. RV 230	12. RV 265

Walsh:

1. RV 549	4. RV 550	7. RV 230	10. RV 580
2. RV 578	5. RV 519	8. RV 356	11. RV 565
3. RV 310	6. RV 522	9. RV 567	12. RV 265

op.4 LA STRAVAGANZA: 12 Concerti for violin & orch [1714]
NB. The Roger & Walsh editions do not have the pieces in the same order.

Roger:

1. RV 383a	4. RV 357	7. RV 185	10. RV 196
2. RV 279	5. RV 347	8. RV 249	11. RV 204
3. RV 301	6. RV 316a	9. RV 284	12. RV 298

Walsh:

1. RV 383a	4. RV 284	7. -	10. -
2. RV 279	5. RV 204	8. -	11. -
3. RV 357	6. RV 291	9. -	12. -

op.6, 6 Concerti, for violin & orch [1716-1721]

1. RV 324	4. RV 216
2. RV 259	5. RV 280
3. RV 318	6. RV 239

op.7, 2 Concerti for oboe, 10 Concerti for violin & orch [1716-1721]

1. RV 465(ob)	4. RV 354	7. RV 464(ob)	10. RV 294a
2. RV 188	5. RV 285a	8. RV 332	11. RV 208a
3. RV 326	6. RV 374	9. RV 373	12. RV 214

op.8, IL CIMENTO DELL'ARMONIA & DELL'INVENZIONE: 12 Concerti, for violin & orch (nos.9 & 12 also
for oboe) [1725]

1. RV 269	4. RV 297	7. RV 242	10. RV 362
2. RV 315	5. RV 253	8. RV 332	11. RV 210
3. RV 293	6. RV 180	9. RV 236	12. RV 178
		& 454(ob)	& 449(ob)

op.9, LA CETRA: 11 Concerti, for violin & orch; 1 Concerto, for 2 violins & orch [1727]

1. RV 181a	4. RV 263a	7. RV 359	10. RV 300
2. RV 345	5. RV 358	8. RV 238	11. RV 198a
3. RV 334	6. RV 348	9. RV 530	12. RV 391

op.10, 6 Concerti, for flute & orch [c1728]

1. RV 433	4. RV 435
2. RV 439	5. RV 434
3. RV 428	6. RV 437

VIVALDI, Antonio (cont)

CONCORDANCE TABLES (cont)
  OPUS NUMBERS (cont)
    op.11, 5 Concerti, for violin & orch; 1 Concerto, for oboe & orch [1729]
            1. RV 207   4. RV 308
            2. RV 277   5. RV 202
            3. RV 336   6. RV 460(ob)

    op.12, 5 Concerti, for violin & orch; 1 Concerto, for str & cont
            1. RV 317   4. RV 173
            2. RV 244   5. RV 379
            3. RV 124   6. RV 361

PINCHERLE TO RYOM
  Sinfonias (Concerti)

#	RV	#	RV	#	RV	#	RV
1. Anh.	4	14. RV	179	53. RV	536	94. RV	113
2. RV	116	15. RV	526	54. RV	557	95. RV	111
3. RV	149	16. RV	558	55. RV	468	96. RV	310
4. RV	140	17. RV	508	56. RV	475	97. RV	550
5. RV	135	18. RV	506	57. RV	476	98. RV	279
6. RV	147	19. RV	172	58. RV	561	99. RV	301
7. RV	122	20. RV	170	59. RV	190	100. RV	298
8. RV	146	21. RV	177	60. RV	161	101. RV	280
9. RV	719	22. RV	184	61. RV	110	102. RV	299
10. RV	700)	23. RV	507	62. RV	187	103. RV	300
10. RV	736)	24. RV	422	63. RV	115	104. RV	435
11. RV	162	25. RV	741	64. RV	117	105. RV	437
12. RV	148	26. RV	176	65. RV	505	106. RV	277
13. RV	132	27. RV	114	66. RV	171	107. RV	308
14. RV	125	28. RV	523	67. RV	109	108. RV	276
15. RV	111a	29. RV	189	68. RV	182	109. RV	275
16. RV	739	30. RV	400	69. RV	474	110. RV	272
17. RV	137	31. RV	398	70. RV	498	111. RV	314
18. RV	699)	32. RV	419	71. RV	478	112. RV	302
18. RV	710)	33. RV	399	72. RV	497	113. RV	133
19. RV	131	34. RV	421	73. RV	560	114. RV	150
20. RV	192	35. RV	418	74. RV	559	115. Anh.	12
21. RV	169	36. RV	554(a)	75. RV	537	116. Anh.	11
22. RV	168	37. RV	397	76. RV	533	117. RV	311
23. RV	112	38. RV	183	77. RV	108	118. RV	414)
		39. RV	191	78. RV	444	118. RV	438)
Concerti		40. RV	194	79. RV	443	119. RV	409
1. RV	356	41. RV	447	80. RV	440	120. RV	413
2. RV	522	42. RV	461	81. RV	87	121. RV	303
3. RV	357	43. RV	448)	82. RV	88	122. RV	312
4. RV	185	43. RV	470)	83. RV	445	123. RV	145
5. RV	188	44. RV	451	84. RV	556	124. RV	307
6. RV	354	45. RV	472	85. RV	534	125. RV	273
7. RV	180	46. RV	477	86. RV	129	126. RV	281
8. RV	178)	47. RV	499	87. RV	555	127. RV	134
8. RV	449)	48. RV	467	88. RV	186	128. RV	492
9. RV	181a	49. RV	469	89. RV	500	129. RV	545
10. RV	358	50. RV	450)	90. RV	473	130. RV	494
11. RV	173	50. RV	471)	91. RV	452	131. RV	493
12. RV	195	51. RV	466	92. RV	355	132. RV	516
13. Anh.	15	52. RV	479	93. RV	175	133. RV	532

VIVALDI, Antonio (cont)

CONCORDANCE NUMBERS (cont)
  PINCHERLE TO RYOM (cont)
    Concerti (cont)

134.	RV	425	184.	RV	389	236.	RV	352	286.	RV	97
135.	RV	575	185.	RV	390	237.	RV	346	287.	RV	395
136.	RV	306	186.	RV	225	238.	RV	546	288.	RV	394
137.	RV	484	187.	RV	453	239.	RV	353	289.	RV	393
138.	RV	313	188.	RV	564	240.	RV	265	290.	RV	286
139.	RV	431	189.	RV	512	241.	RV	269	291.	RV	141
140.	RV	436	190.	RV	511	242.	RV	263	292.	RV	142
141.	RV	438	191.	RV	123	243.	RV	267	293.	RV	235
142.	RV	432	192.	RV	222	244.	RV	268	294.	RV	128
143.	RV	151	193.	RV	209	245.	RV	264	295.	RV	296
144.	RV	278	194.	RV	215	246.	RV	271	296.	RV	289
145.	RV	144	195.	RV	233	247.	RV	266	297.	RV	566
146.	RV	549	196.	RV	218	248.	RV	270	298.	RV	487
147.	RV	230	197.	RV	126	249.	RV	567	299.	RV	488
148.	RV	580	198.	RV	92	250.	RV	565	300.	RV	491
149.	RV	204	199.	RV	231	251.	RV	284	301.	RV	543
150.	RV	216	200.	RV	232	252.	RV	291	302.	RV	535
151.	RV	208	201.	RV	217	253.	RV	249	303.	RV	482
152.	RV	214	202.	RV	387	254.	RV	239	304.	RV	486
153.	RV	210	203.	RV	427	255.	RV	258a	305.	RV	489
154.	RV	391	204.	RV	95	256.	RV	294	306.	RV	455
155.	RV	90)	205.	RV	429	257.	RV	293	307.	RV	490
	RV	428)	206.	RV	91	258.	RV	242	308.	RV	544
156.	RV	207	207.	RV	94	259.	RV	236)	309.	RV	584
157.	RV	124	208.	RV	234		RV	454)	310.	RV	243
158.	RV	220	209.	RV	93	260.	RV	238	311.	RV	541
159.	RV	513	210.	RV	563	261.	RV	433	312.	RV	247
160.	RV	203	211.	RV	227	262.	RV	434	313.	RV	138
161.	RV.	224	212.	RV	519	263.	RV	244	314.	RV	283
162.	RV	228	213.	RV	347	264.	RV	456	315.	RV	295
163.	RV	213	214.	RV	345	265.	RV	573	316.	RV	248
164.	RV	582	215.	RV	348	266.	RV	540	317.	RV	287
165.	RV	212	216.	RV	336	267.	RV	568	318.	RV	485
166.	RV	392	217.	RV	338	268.	RV	571	319.	RV	574
167.	RV	219	218.	RV	Anh.14	269.	RV	240	320.	RV	538
168.	RV	384	219.	RV	335	270.	RV	241	321.	RV	539
(169.			220.	RV	520	271.	RV	292	322.	RV	100
(444.	RV	562	221.	RV	342	272.	RV	246	323.	RV	99
170.	RV	226	222.	RV	552	273.	RV	569	324.	RV	288
171.	RV	229	223.	RV	344	274.	RV	542	325.	RV	282
172.	RV	388	224.	RV	521	275.	RV	285	326.	RV	578
173.	RV	205	225.	RV	349	276.	RV	245	327.	RV	383)
174.	RV	223	226.	RV	585	277.	RV	237		RV	381)
175.	RV	121	227.	RV	341	278.	RV	551	328.	RV	316
176.	RV	404	228.	RV	340	279.	RV	136	329.	RV	324
177.	RV	206	229.	RV	343	280.	RV	127	330.	RV	318
178.	RV	385	230.	RV	160	281.	RV	514	331.	RV	564
179.	RV	221	231.	RV	159	282.	RV	406)	332.	RV	326
180.	RV	424	232.	RV	339		RV	481)	333.	RV	374
181.	RV	403	233.	RV	396	283.	RV	412	334.	RV	465
182.	RV	211	234.	RV	350	284.	RV	411	335.	RV	373
183.	RV	386	235.	RV	158	285.	RV	410	336.	RV	315

VIVALDI, Antonio (cont)

CONCORDANCE NUMBERS (cont)
   PINCHERLE TO RYOM (cont)
      Concerti (cont)

337.	RV	332
338.	RV	362
339.	RV	334
340.	RV	359
341.	RV	530
342.	RV	439
343.	RV	317
344.	RV	379
345.	RV	361
346.	RV	364a
347.	RV	360
348.	RV	322
349.	RV	370
350.	RV	363
351.	RV	319
352.	RV	323
353.	RV	383
354.	RV	329
335.	=	
414.	RV	259
356.	RV	369
357.	RV	328
358.	RV	366
359.	RV	576

RICORDI TOMO TO RYOM
(Ricordi tomo numbers refer
to the volumes of the
collected works)

1.	RV	367
2.	RV	454
3.	RV	560
4.	RV	199
5.	RV	159
6.	RV	142
7.	RV	166
8.	RV	158
9.	RV	163
10.	RV	559
11.	RV	155
12.	RV	501
13.	RV	186
14.	RV	455
15.	RV	270
16.	RV	352
17.	RV	71
18.	RV	86
19.	RV	401
20.	RV	83
21.	RV	130
22.	RV	169
23.	RV	103
24.	RV	77
25.	RV	577
26.	RV	575
27.	RV	516
28.	RV	498
29.	RV	268
30.	RV	120
31.	RV	231
32.	RV	118
33.	RV	104
34.	RV	478
35.	RV	547
36.	RV	129
37.	RV	234
38.	RV	254
39.	RV	92
40.	RV	107
41.	RV	106
42.	RV	90
43.	RV	569
44.	RV	108
45.	RV	243
46.	RV	442
47.	RV	474
48.	RV	509
49.	RV	151
50.	RV	164
51.	RV	579
52.	RV	101
53.	RV	561
54.	RV	556
55.	RV	581
56.	RV	134
57.	RV	68
58.	RV	70
59.	RV	136
60.	RV	510
61.	RV	531
62.	RV	93
63.	RV	82
64.	RV	380
65.	RV	332
66.	RV	288
67.	RV	481
68.	RV	232
69.	RV	217
70.	RV	286
71.	RV	484
72.	RV	497
73.	RV	548
74.	RV	248
75.	RV	85
76.	RV	269
77.	RV	315
78.	RV	293
79.	RV	297
80.	RV	253
81.	RV	180
82.	RV	242
83.	RV	362
84.	RV	210
85.	RV	178
86.	RV	375
87.	RV	282
88.	RV	551
89.	RV	511
90.	RV	557
91.	RV	538
92.	RV	330
93.	RV	278
94.	RV	574
95.	RV	541
96.	RV	389
97.	RV	537
98.	RV	425
99.	RV	564
100.	RV	343
101.	RV	533
102.	RV	427
103.	RV	105
104.	RV	532
105.	RV	443
106.	RV	100
107.	RV	524
108.	RV	512
109.	RV	485
110.	RV	444
111.	RV	529
112.	RV	507
113.	RV	126
114.	RV	123
115.	RV	156
116.	RV	508
117.	(RV	229)
118.	RV	473
119.	RV	500
120.	RV	190
121.	RV	539
122.	RV	181a
123.	RV	263a
124.	RV	300
125.	RV	391
126.	RV	345
127.	RV	334
128.	RV	358
129.	RV	348
130.	RV	359
131.	RV	238
132.	RV	530
133.	RV	198a
134.	RV	553
135.	RV	544
136.	RV	583
137.	RV	409
138.	RV	438
139.	RV	534
140.	RV	523
141.	RV	582
142.	RV	555
143.	RV	88
144.	RV	94
145.	RV	525
146.	RV	546
147.	RV	99
148.	RV	440
149.	RV	91
150.	RV	570
151.	RV	436
152.	RV	445
153.	RV	429
154.	RV	95
155.	RV	87
156.	RV	313
157.	RV	369
158.	RV	296
159.	RV	441
160.	RV	177
161.	RV	131
162.	RV	192
163.	RV	365
164.	RV	273
165.	RV	289
166.	RV	264
167.	RV	194
168.	RV	281
169.	RV	258
170.	RV	376
171.	RV	390
172.	RV	165
173.	RV	197
174.	RV	225
175.	RV	333
176.	RV	127
177.	RV	119
178.	RV	328
179.	RV	387
180.	RV	266
181.	RV	505
182.	RV	157
183.	RV	379
184.	RV	160
185.	RV	109
186.	RV	306
187.	RV	287
188.	RV	207
189.	RV	396

VIVALDI, Antonio (cont)

CONCORDANCE NUMBERS (cont)
  RICORDI TOMO TO RYOM (cont)

190.	RV	167								
191.	RV	336	224.	RV	418	297.	RV	271	350.	RV	571
192.	RV	314	245.	RV	350	298.	RV	503	351.	RV	319
193.	RV	257	246.	RV	121	299.	RV	504	352.	RV	260
194.	RV	171	247.	RV	312	300.	RV	494	353.	RV	542
195.	RV	182	248.	RV	98	301.	RV	283	354.	RV	96
196.	RV	394	249.	RV	576	302.	RV	226	355.	RV	84
197.	RV	770	250.	RV	554	303.	RV	295	356.	RV	28
198.	(RV | 393)	251.	RV	128	304.	RV	261	357.	RV	292
199.	RV	370	252.	RV	145	305.	RV	215	358.	RV	302
200.	RV	110	253.	RV	325	306.	RV	233	359.	(RV | 162)
201.	RV	161	254.	RV	251	307.	RV	218	360.	(Anh. | 68)
202.	RV	311	255.	RV	307	308.	RV	117	361.	RV	146
203.	RV	221	256.	RV	183	309.	RV	115	362.	(RV | 122)
204.	RV	400	257.	RV	327	310.	RV	154	363.	RV	135
205.	RV	422	258.	RV	235	311.	RV	187	364.	RV	10
206.	RV	408	259.	RV	191	312.	RV	212a	365.	RV	12
207.	RV	517	260.	RV	386	313.	RV	353	366.	RV	3
208.	RV	527	261.	RV	211	314.	RV	208	367.	RV	15
209.	RV	514	262.	RV	371	315.	RV	457	368.	RV	5
210.	RV	515	263.	RV	536	316.	RV	463	369.	(RV | 2)
211.	RV	399	264.	RV	535	317.	RV	414	370.	RV	29
212.	RV	406	265.	RV	543	318.	RV	558	371.	(RV | 25)
213.	RV	566	266.	RV	489	319.	RV	552	372.	RV	6
214.	RV	496	267.	RV	475	320.	RV	540	373.	RV	26
215.	RV	461	268.	RV	486	321.	RV	149	374.	RV	34
216.	RV	447	269.	RV	495	322.	RV	172	375.	RV	53
217.	RV	448	270.	RV	502	323.	RV	340	376.	RV	189
218.	RV	398	271.	RV	491	324.	RV	240	377.	RV	383
219.	RV	424	272.	RV	479	325.	RV	237	378.	RV	388
220.	RV	419	273.	RV	483	326.	RV	384	379.	RV	170
221.	RV	412	274.	RV	466	327.	RV	267	380.	RV	562
222.	RV	451	275.	RV	492	328.	RV	184	381.	RV	585
223.	RV	499	276.	RV	493	329.	RV	323	382.	RV	73
224.	RV	477	277.	RV	476	330.	RV	341	383.	RV	67
225.	RV	480	278.	RV	490	331.	RV	205	384.	RV	61
226.	RV	152	279.	RV	453	332.	RV	366	385.	RV	66
227.	RV	250	280.	RV	545	333.	RV	245	386.	RV	69
228.	RV	303	281.	RV	470	334.	RV	329	387.	RV	62
229.	RV	346	282.	RV	471	335.	RV	219	388.	RV	65
230.	RV	201	283.	RV	450	336.	RV	241	389.	RV	64
231.	RV	413	284.	RV	372	337.	RV	392	390.	RV	75
232.	RV	421	285.	RV	246	338.	RV	568	391.	RV	78
233.	RV	411	286.	RV	209	339.	RV	344	392.	RV	79
234.	RV	417	287.	(RV | 153)	340.	RV	262	393.	RV	63
235.	RV	403	288.	RV	138	341.	RV	397	394.	RV	27
236.	RV	487	289.	RV	143	342.	RV	506	395.	RV	31
237.	RV	469	290.	RV	150	343.	RV	224	396.	RV	14
238.	RV	472	291.	RV	368	344.	RV	521	397.	RV	20
239.	RV	467	292.	RV	321	345.	RV	228	398.	RV	36
240.	RV	488	293.	RV	349	346.	RV	285	399.	RV	1
241.	RV	141	294.	RV	222	347.	RV	213	400.	RV	8
242.	RV	140	295.	RV	331	348.	RV	363	401.	RV	23
243.	RV	410	296.	RV	247	349.	RV	252	402.	RV	16

VIVALDI, Antonio (cont)

CONCORDANCE NUMBERS (cont)
  RICORDI TOMO TO RYOM (cont)

403.	RV	21	435.	RV	72	467.	RV	54	499.	RV	377
404.	RV	9	436.	RV	324	468.	RV	56	500.	RV	404
405.	RV	32	437.	RV	259	469.	RV	57	501.	RV	52
406.	RV	549	438.	RV	318	470.	RV	59	502.	RV	256
407.	RV	578	439.	RV	216	471.	RV	55	503.	RV	44
408.	RV	310	440.	RV	280	472.	RV	58	504.	RV	39
409.	RV	550	441.	RV	239	473.	RV	47	505.	Anh.	4
410.	RV	519	442.	RV	465	474.	RV	41	506.	RV	116
411.	RV	356	443.	RV	188	475.	RV	43	507.	RV	112
412.	RV	567	444.	RV	326	476.	RV	45	508.	RV	175
413.	RV	522	445.	RV	354	477.	RV	·40	509.	RV	113
414.	RV	230	446.	RV	285a	478.	RV	46	510.	RV	563
415.	RV	580	447.	RV	374	479.	RV	291	511.	RV	382
416.	RV	565	448.	RV	464	480.	RV	276	512.	Anh.	70
417.	RV	265	449.	RV	299	481.	RV	195	513.	RV	227
418.	RV	383a	450.	RV	373	482.	RV	220	514.	RV	381
419.	RV	279	451.	RV	294a	483.	RV	364	515.	RV	132
420.	RV	301	452.	RV	208a	484.	RV	275	516.	RV	137
421.	RV	357	453.	RV	214	485.	Anh.	65	517.	RV	49
422.	RV	347	454.	RV	433	486.	RV	513	518.	RV	168
423.	RV	316a	455.	RV	439	487.	(RV | 335)	519.	RV	355
424.	RV	185	456.	RV	428	488.	RV	456	520.	RV	452
425.	RV	249	457.	RV	435	489.	RV	342	521.	RV	420
426.	RV	284	458.	RV	437	490.	RV	48	522.	RV	415
427.	RV	196	459.	RV	277	491.	RV	19	523.	RV	407
428.	RV	204	460.	RV	308	492.	RV	133	524.	RV	405
429.	RV	298	461.	RV	202	493.	RV	114	525.	RV	423
430.	RV	18	462.	RV	317	494.	(RV | 762)	526.	RV	416
431.	RV	30	463.	RV	244	495.	RV	176	527.	RV	402
432.	RV	33	464.	RV	124	496.	RV	339	528.	RV	60
433.	RV	35	465.	RV	173	497.	RV	206	529.	RV	24
434.	RV	76	466.	RV	361	498.	RV	385	530.	RV	42

VLAD, Roman (1919-

CADENZE MICHELANGIOLESCHE for soprano (or tenor) solo & orch (1966)
  φ   33(ca)3(bcl)3(cbsn)/4331/timp.perc.vib/
      2hp.pf/str(12.12.12.6.6)   15'   Ricordi,1966   Misc 8911
DIVERTIMENTO for 11 instruments φ 1111/0000/hpsd/str   Hawkes,1954   Misc 4281

VLADIGEROV, Panchu (1899-

VARDAR: Bulgarian rhapsody op.16
  φ   2+picc.2+ca.22/4331/timp.perc.glock/
      hp/str   8'   Universal   Misc 1455 B

VLIJMEN, Jan van (1935-

GRUPPI (1962)   φ   4 groups= 1. 1001/0100
                                      2. xyl.vib/hp/6vln
                                      3. 0110/000.btbn.0/perc.bells/cb
                                      4. 0000/1001/4vla   9'   Donemus,1962   Misc 8863
SERENATA 1, for 13 players (1944,rev 1967)
                        φ   2222/2100/perc.xba   Donemus,1962   Misc 9228

VOGEL, Ernst

MOIRA: Musik für Streichen (1926)
| | φ | str(4.4.3.3.1) | 18' | Doblinger,1977 | Misc 9327 |
PROGRAMME for orchestra (1974 | φ | 2+picc.2+ca.2+bcl.2+cbsn/4231/ | | | |
| | | timp.perc(tamtam)/str | 15' | Doblinger,1978 | Misc 9644 |

VOGEL, Johann Christoph (1756-1788)

SINFONIA CONCERTANTE for oboe, bassoon and small orchestra, in C
| | φ | 02[=2cl]00/2000/str | 21' | Leuckart | Misc 3453 |

VOGEL, Vladimir (1896-

CONCERTI cello & orch	φ	2(picc)2(ca)2+bcl.2/0220/			
		timp.perc/str	24'10"	Zanibon,1957	Misc 5571
violin & orch (1937)	φ	2(2picc)222/2[=4]220/timp.perc/			
		hp[=pf]/str	35'	Vogel	Misc 5866 B
DEVISE (1934)	φ	0000/0231/perc.tamtam/str		Composer	27045

2 ETÜDEN
  1. Ritmica funebre
  2. Ritmica scherzosa | φ | 2(picc)+picc.2+cà.2+Ebcl+bcl.2+cbsn/
		4331/timp.perc.tamtam.vib/str	11'30"-14'30"	Bote & Bock	Misc 946
RITMICA OSTINATA	φ	2(picc)+picc.2+ca.2+Ebcl+bcl.2+cbsn/			
		4331/timp.perc/str (with composer's corrections)			
THYL CLAES: epic oratorio			6'30"	Universal	Misc 1215
Part 1.					
6 fragments for reciter, voice & orch					
	φ	2(picc)02+Ebcl.2sx.2/4220/perc/pf/str	43'	Ricordi,1950	Misc 4647
3 suites (1958)	φ	2(picc)03.2sx.2/0220/timp.perc/pf/str	25'20"	Ricordi,1959	Misc 5450
TRIPARTITA	φ	1+picc)+picc.22+bcl.2+cbsn/4231/			
		timp.perc/str	14'	Ars Viva	Misc 1108

VOGLER, Georg Joseph (Abbé Vogler) (1749-1814)

VARIATIONS SUE L'AIR DE MARLBOROUGH: for piano and small orchestra
  arr F.Schröder | φ | 2002/[2]000/str | 28' | Schott,1951 | Misc 3473 |

VOGT, J

ARMONS-NOUS: Swiss air
  arr Scassola | φ | 1221/2230/timp.perc/str | | Foetisch | 6425 |

VOIGT, G.B.

HEIMATHS-SEHNEN: romance for oboe & str
| | φ | str | | Kahnt | 5867 |

VOLKMANN, Robert (1815-1883)
| CONCERT-OUVERTURE, in C | φ | 2222/2200/timp/str | 5' | Breitkopf | 8000 |
RICHARD III: incidental music
  Overture op.68
    arr Grohmann | PC | 1(picc.)121/2210/perc/str | 14'15" | Cranz | 3489 |
| SERENADE No.2, op.63 in F | φ | str | | Schott | 133 |

VOLLSTEDT, Robert

BLUMEN DER LIEBE: waltz, op.11	PC	1+picc.222/4230/timp.perc/zither/str		H.Thiemer	5600
IM ORIENTALISCHEN CAFE, op.390	PC	1+picc.222/4230/timp.perc/str		Benjamin	4915
JAPANISCHE WACHTPARADE: march, op.92					
	PC	1121/2210/perc/str		Cranz	5807
LUSTIGE BRÜDER: waltz	PC	2222/2230/perc/str	7'	Hawkes	457
arr Douglas	ø	1+picc.222/4230/timp.perc/hp/str		(Boosey)	MSS 30092
arr H.Noble	PC	112.2sx.1/2230/timp.perc/str		Boosey & Hawkes	18619
arr M.Lubbock (Albert Whelan signature tune)					
	ø	1021/2230/str		BBC	TO 1217
MONDNACHT AM RHEIN, op.53	PC	222/2230.euph/perc/str		Hawkes	925
OLD LOVE IS NEVER FORGOTTEN	PC	1222/2230/perc/str		Hawkes	3389
ORIENTALISCHER BAUCHTANZ, op.188	PC	1222/2210/timp.perc/str	3'	Benjamin	4552
SPANISCHES LIEBESLEBEN: grand valse espagnol, op.50					
	PC	1+picc.220/0000/str		Doss & Heidegger	15176 **

VOLPATTI, F. jnr

Los BANDERILLEROS: marche espagnole					
	PC	1+picc.221/2231/perc/str		Gaudet	8834
BIFOLCO PARADE: characteristic piece					
	PC	2(picc)222/2231/perc/str		Salabert	5605
The BLUE MEDITERRANEAN (Souvenir de Nice)					
	PC	1121/2210/bells/str		C.Fischer	9777
CANTO DI SIRENA see 2 ITALIAN SONGS					
CHANTONS L'AVRIL see 2 ITALIAN SONGS					
ENVOLÉE: caprice	PC	2210/0231/str		Salabert	5634 **
ITALIA: march	PC	1+picc.222/4231/perc/str		Joubert	7095
2 ITALIAN SONGS: Canto di Sirena; Chantons l'avril					
	PC	2222/2231/timp.perc/str		Liber	12097 B
MARCHE MAURESQUE	PC	1+picc.222/42.2cnt.31/timp.perc/str		Joubert	7096
MINUETTO		str		Gaudet	12118
NAPOLE MIO	PC	2(picc)110/0000/str		Decourcelle	5113 **
RAPSODIE SLAVE	PC	1+picc.222/4231/timp.perc/hp/str	5'30"	Salabert	3925
ROMANESQUE: overture by F.Volpatti, jnr, & J.Delaforêt					
	PC	1+picc.222/2231/timp.perc/hp/str		Gaudet	12505
SÉRÉNADE NIÇOISE	PC	2020/2000/bells/str		Decourcelle	5108

VOLTI, Carl

The COTTAR'S SATURDAY NIGHT: overture				
	PC	1+p cc.020/0210.euph/perc/str	A.H.& C.	6945
JACOBITE AIRS: selection	PC	1+picc.020/0210.euph/perc/str	A.H.& C.	6949
PRINCE CHARLIE OR THE '45: overture on Jacobite airs				
	PC	1+picc.020/0010.euph/perc/str	Kerr	7218
SEA SONGS				
1st Selection	PC	1222/2230euph./perc/str	A.H.& C.	6945
2nd Selection	PC	1+picc.020/0210.euph/perc/str	A.H.& C.	6948

VOORMOLEN, Alexander Nicholas (1895-

ARETHUSA: symphonic myth	ø	2+picc.2+ca.2+bcl.2+cbsn/4431		
		timp.perc.bells.tamtam/cel.2hp.org/str	Donemus,1948	Misc 1341
The THREE KNIGHTS (De drie Ruitertjes): variations on a Dutch folksong				
	ø	3(picc.)2+ca.2+bcl.2+cbsn/4331/		
		timp.perc.tamtam/cel.2hp/str	Alsbach	Misc 1154 C

VOORN, Joop

SONG OF ENITHARMON for chorus & orch (1979-80)
       φ 3(picc)3(ca)33/4331/timp.perc.tamtam/
        str   20'   Donemus,1980 Misc 10152

VOŘÍSEK (Worzischek), Jan Hugo (Jan Udclav) (1791-1825)

SYMPHONY, in D   φ 2222/2200/timp/str   23'40"-27' Artia,1957 25747
          2222/2200/timp/str   MAB 34 MRL

VOSS, Friedrich (1930-

CONCERTO for violin & orch
 2nd version, 1962 φ 2222/4231/timp/str   21'   Breitkopf,1966 Misc 7344

VOTISHENKO, Sasha

EASTER CHIMES IN LITTLE RUSSIA PC 2(picc)222/4231/timp.perc/hp/str 9'   C.Fischer 6509 B

VOYE, de la see DE LA VOYE

VRANICKÝ, Pavel (1756-1808)

SYMPHONY (Quodlibet) in D φ 2222/2200/timp/hpsd/vln-solo/str   (A:Wn SM 11086) Misc 10102

VREULS, Victor (1876-1944)

CORTÈGE HÉROIQUE (1894) φ 2+picc.2+ca.2+bcl.2/4231/timp.perc/hp/str   Breitkopf Misc 9420
Un SONGE D'UNE NUIT D'ETE: opera
 Le lever du soleil: interlude, Act 3
        φ 2+picc.2+ca.2+bcl.2+cbsn/4431/timp.perc/
         hp.pf/str   Cranz   16968

VRIES, Klaas de

REFRAINS for 2 pianos & orch φ 111+bcl.2/1221/2perc(vib.2xba)/str   Donemus,1973 Misc 9227

VUATAZ, Roger (1898-

PETIT CONCERT, op.39   φ 1(picc)111/2110/timp.perc/cel.hp/str 14'-17'45 Hawkes,1955 Misc 4320

VUILLEMIN, Louis

4 DANCES, suite of old French dances, op.16
 1. Bourée 2. Gigue 3. Pavane 4. Passepied
        φ 3(picc)2(ca)23(cbsn)/4331/timp.perc/
         hp.pf/str   10'   Durand   7289
EN KERNO: suite
 1. Notre-Dame de Kerineo
 2. Le pêcher en goguettes
 3. Sous les hêtres
  arr Branga   PC 1121/2200/perc/str   Durand   12105 B

VULPIUS, Melchior (1560-1616)

MY SOUL THERE IS A COUNTRY (Christus der ist mein Leben)
 arr H.Perry   PC 1121/0000/timp.perc/org/str   Hawkes   4970

VYCPÁLEK, Ladislav (1882-1969)

CONCERNING THE LAST THINGS OF MAN (O poslednich věcech člověka): cantata, op.16
         ϕ   3(picc)2+ca.2+bcl.2/4230/
            timp.perc.tamtam.xyl/str   H.Matice   Misc 2764

The VAGRANTS (Tuláci): cantata for male chorus with woodwind, op.10
         ϕ   11.ca.22/0000/str   H.Matice,1924   Misc 2860

WACHS, Paul Étienne Victor (1851-1915)

La BERRICHONNE
    arr Allier   PC   1+picc.121/2230/perc/str   Leduc   5324
CHANSON BASQUE   PC   1100/0000/str   Enoch   9471
MADRILENA: fantaisie espangnole
    arr Schneklud   PC   2121/2231/timp.perc/str   Leduc   11205
NADIA   PC   1121/2210/perc/str   G.Schirmer   923

WADE, Frank

FARM FARE: signature tune and links based on the folk song 'Mrs Bond', arr F.Wade & C.S.Rinks
                                 ø   1100/1000/cel/str   (Lengnick)   MS 30720

WADDELL, J.M.

The FAIR MAID OF PERTH: overture
    arr Hartmann   PC   1122/2230.euph/perc/str   Hawkes   2222 B

WADHAM, Walter

BY THE RIVER: song
    in D   2020/0110.euph/timp/str   Reid   18101
COME TO ME: song
    in E   2020/0110.euph/timp/str   Reid   18101
The VOICE I LOVED: song
    in F   2020/0110.euph/timp/str   Reid   18101

WAGEMANS, Peter-Jan (1952-

MUSIC I for wind & percussion, op.7 (1974)
                                 ø   2+2picc+afl.4(ca)2+2Ebcl+bcl+cbcl.1+cbsn/
                                     4+2wtuba.441+cbtuba/4perc(timp.plate-bell)   Donemus,1975 Misc 10339

WAGENAAR, Bernard (1894-1971)

FANFARE FOR AIRMEN
    ed Goossens   ø   0000/4331/timp.perc   Boosey & H   Misc 2974
SINFONIETTA for small orchestra ø   1111/1111/timp.perc.xyl/hp.pf/str   25'   Cos Cob Press Misc 392

WAGENAAR, Diderik

TAM TAM (1978-9)   ø   0.2pan-pipes.00.2asx.0/0000/2conga.mba/
                                     2bgtr.4pf(2fender-pf)   25'-30'   Donemus,1980 Misc 10157

WAGENAAR, Johan (1862-1941)

CYRANO DE BERGERAC: overture, op.23
                                 ø   3(picc)222/4331/timp.perc/str   12'   Leuckart   4387
SAUL UND DAVID: symphonic poem, op.24
                                 ø   3(picc)2+ca.2+bcl.2/4331/timp.perc.glock/
                                     2hp/str   Leuckart   Misc 1120
Der WIDERSPENSTIGEN ZÄHMUNG (The Taming of the Shrew): overture
                                 ø   3(picc)222/4331/timp.perc/hp/str   6'   Leuckart   Misc 1119
WIENER DREIVIERTELTAKT (Rhythme de la vie viennoise), op.38
                                 ø   3(picc)2+ca.2+bcl.2+cbsn/4330/timp.perc/
                                     cel.hp/str   Wagenaar   6448

WAGENSEIL, Georg Christoph (1715-1777)

see SCHOLZ-MICHELITZCH, Helga: Das Orchester- und Kammermusikwerke von Georg Christoph Wagenseil,
     thematischer Katalogue. Vienna: Böhlaus, 1972. (Vol 6 of Tabulae Musicae Austriace): The
     numbers prefixed 'WagsWV' refer to entries in this book.

CONCERTI
  Cello & orch
    WagsWV 341, in C (1763)
      ed F.Racek   ⌀ 0200/2200/str/[cont]   Doblinger,1963   23957
    WagsWV 348, in A (1752)
      ed Mainardi & F.Racek ⌀ str/cont(hpsd)   Doblinger,1960   23180
  Harpsichord & orch
    WagsWV 290, in E♭
      ed A.Copland   ⌀ 2200/2000/str   17'   Universal,1979   Misc 10118
    WagsWV 294, in F
      ed G.M.Schmeiser   ⌀ str(no vla)   Akad Druck   Misc 8747
    WagsWV 298, in D
      ed G.M.Schirmer   ⌀ str(no vla)   Breitkopf & H   24088
    WagsWV 335, in B♭
      ed G.M.Schmeiser   ⌀ str(no vla)   Akad Druck   Misc 8747 B
  Trombone & orch
    WagsWV 346, in E♭
      ed P.Bryan   ⌀ 2000/2000/str/cont   13'   Universal,1979   Misc 10122
SYMPHONIES
  WagsWV 361, in C
    ed B.Paumgartner   ⌀ 0200/2000/str   Doblinger,1979   26817 *
  WagsWV 368, in D
    ed K.Horwitz & K.Riedel
                           ⌀ 0200/2000/timp/str   Artaria,1908/Akad Druck,1959.DTÖ 31   MRL
    1st mvt only
    ed K.Horwitz & K.Riedel
                           ⌀ 0201/2000/timp/str   (DTÖ 31)   19665 #
  WagsWV 374, in D
    ed B.Paumgartner   2000/2000/str   Doblinger,1978   26518
    ed R.Sondheimer   ⌀ 2000/2000/str   8'30"   Bernouilli   14970
  WagsWV 376, in D
    ed K.Horwitz & K.Riedel
                           ⌀ str(no vla)/cont   Artaria,1908/Akad Druck,1959.DTÖ 31   MRL
  WagsWV 393, in E
    ed B.Paumgartner   ⌀ 0200/0000/str   Doblinger,1975   26133 *
  WagsWV 398, in F
    ed B.Paumgartner   ⌀ 0000/2000/str/cont   Doblinger,1975   26067 *
  WagsWV 418, in G min
    ed A.Copland   ⌀ 0200/0000/str   15'   Universal,1972   Misc 2167
  WagsWV 421, in A
    ed B.Paumgartner   ⌀ 0200/2000/str   Doblinger,1979   26818 *

WAGNER, Alfred

CONCERTO PICCOLO for violins   ⌀ vlns (4 groups)   Neue Musik,1977   26938 *

WAGNER, Joseph F.

UNDER THE DOUBLE EAGLE: march, op.159
                   PC 1222/4230.euph/perc/str   4'30"   Hawkes   3401 B

WAGNER, Larry

OH MY LOVE - OH MY HEART: song by L.Wagner, L.Singer & J.Eaton
  in G, arr B.Sharpe   ⌀ 1110/0000/hp.pf/str   (Feldman)   LM G 8876

WAGNER, Max

VON DER SCHAUENBURG: symphonic poem, op.18
                        ∅   2+picc.222/4230/timp.perc/str   Scheithauer   Misc 924

WAGNER, Richard (1813-1883)

COMPLETE WORKS

Richard Wagners Musikalische Werke, ed M.Balling.   Leipzig: Breitkopf & H, 1912-22. 10 vols   MRL
Richard Wagner sämtliche Werke, ed C.Dahlhaus.   Mainz: Schott, 1970-   MRL

ALBUM SONATA (orig pf solo)
    orch K.Müller-Berghaus   ∅   3(picc)2+ca.2+bcl.2/4231/timp/hp/str   Schott   5555
ALBUMBLATT, in C (orig pf)(Romanze)(1861)
    arr Mulder, in A   PC pf/str   Boosey   10756 B
    arr Reicheilt, in C   ∅   1122/2200/timp/str   4'30"   Kistner & S 5720
    arr Popper for cello & orch, in E
                              ∅   2022/2000/perc/str   Siegel   6814
    arr Weninger for violin & orch, in D
                              PC 1121/2210/timp/str   Benjamin   11670
    arr Wilhlmj for violin & orch, in A
                              ∅   1022/2000/str   Siegel   6988
                              PC 1022/2000/str   Siegel   10482
ALBUMBLATT, in E♭ (orig vln & pf)(1875)
    arr Singer for violin & orch ∅ 2222/2000/timp/str   Schott   11609
    arr Tourbie   PC 1010/0100/timp.perc/str   Schott   4672
ALLEGRO TO AUBRY'S ARIA (Doch jetzt wohin ich blicke)(Interpolated in Marschner's 'Der Vampyr')
                              ∅   2222/2200/timp/str   (Breitkopf)   23791 +
CHRISTOPHER COLUMBUS: overture
    arr F.Mottl   ∅   2+picc.222/4631/timp/str   8'   Breitkopf   2981
CONCERT OVERTURE, in D min   ∅   2222/4200/timp/str   Breitkopf,1926 Misc 900
DESCENTE DE LA COURTILLE, for chorus & orch (1840)
    ed M.Balling   ∅   1+picc.222/21.cnt.30/timp.perc/str   Breitkopf & H,1913.CW 16 Misc 8306 & MRL
EINLAGE ZU V.BELLINIS OPER NORMA, for Baritone solo, TB chorus & orch [1837]
    ed M.Balling   ∅   2+picc.222/4230.spt/timp.perc/str   Breitkopf & H,1914.CW 1   S.32718 #
EINLAGE ZU MARIE, MAX UND MICHEL (Singspiel), for Baritone solo & orch (1837)
    ed M.Balling   ∅   1+picc.122/4200/timp.perc/str   Breitkopf & H,1914.CW 1   S.32718
Der ENGEL   see   WESENDONCK LIEDER
ENREACTE TRAGIQUE, no.1
    Fragment only, ed E.Voss ∅   2202/2210/timp/str   Schott,1973.CW 18/1   MRL
3 FANFARES   ∅   0000/00.4signal tpt.00/timp   M.Hieber   11044
Eine FAUST-OUVERTÜRE   ∅   2+picc.223/4231/timp/str   11'30"-13'30" Breitkopf 6404
    arr Roberts   PC 2(picc)222/4231/timp/str   C.Fischer   9311
Die FEEN (The Fairies): opera
    Complete
        ed M.Balling   ∅   2+picc.222/4230/timp/hp/str
                                 Onstage: 2020/0240   Breitkopf & H,1912.CW 13   MRL
    Act 3 only   ∅   2222/4240/timp/hp/str   Breitkopf   Misc 9561
    Overture   ∅   2222/4230/timp/str   12'   Breitkopf   4710 Amv
        ed A.de Almeida   ∅   2222/4230/timp/str   Heugel,1964 24227
    Excerpts from Acts 1 & 2 ∅   2+picc.222/4230/timp/str   (Breitkopf)   23805 +
Der FLIEGENDE HOLLÄNER (The Flying Dutchman): opera
    Complete   ∅   3(picc)2(ca)22/4231/timp.perc/hp/str
                                 Offstage: 0.picc.000/6000/wmc   Fürstner   Misc 965 C
                             ∅   2+picc.2+ca.22/4231/timp.perc/hp/str
                                 Offstage: 0.3picc.000/7000/perc   Meser (Fürstner) Misc 3225
        ed P.Pitt   ∅   3(picc)2(ca)22/4231/timp.perc/hp/str
                                 Offstage: 0.picc.000/6000/wmc   Durand   Misc 1644
    Overture   ∅   2+picc.2(ca)22/4231/timp/hp/str 9'45"-10'30" Fürstner 12589 Amv Bn C
        arr Hoffmann   ∅   3(picc)2(ca)22/4231/timp/hp/str   Breitkopf   4260
        arr L.Weninger   PC 1110/0111/timp/str   Benjamin   7761

WAGNER, Richard (cont)

Der FLIEGENDE HOLLÄNDER (cont)
   Selections
      arr C.Godfrey, jnr   PC 2(picc)222/2230.euph/timp/str   Hawkes   6678
      arr E.Tavan   PC 2(picc)2(ca)22/22.2cnt.31/timp.perc/str   Margueritat 1669
   Extracts
      Jo-ho-hoe! Traft ihr das Schiff (Saw ye the ship)(Senta's ballad): aria for Soprano solo & orch
        in G min (orig)   ϕ 2+picc.222/4231/timp/str   7'15"-11'   Fürstner   5019 C
        in G min (publ with Spinning chorus)
                            ϕ 2+picc.222/4231/timp/str   [Breitkopf & H]/E.F.Kalmus   26708
        in G min, arr R.Chignell
                            ϕ 2+picc.222/4230/timp/str   Arranger   MS 4940
           see also   Summ und brumm
      Mit Gewitter und Sturm (On the wings of the storm)(Steersman's song): aria for Tenor solo & orch
        in B♭ (orig)   ϕ 2+picc.222/4231/timp.perc/str   Fürstner   9223 B
        in B♭, arr R.Chignell   ϕ 2+picc.222/4231/timp.perc/str   Arranger   MS 4941 ϕ only
        arr F.Haensch with sailor's chorus (non-vocal)
                            ϕ 2(picc)222/4231/timp/str   Benjamin   5610
      Senta's ballad   see   Jo-ho-hoe
      Steersman's song   see   Mit Gewitter und Sturm
      Summ und brumm' (Spinning chorus): chorus for fv-chorus & orch
        in A (publ with Senta's ballad)
                          ϕ 2+picc.222/4221/timp/str   [Breitkopf & H]/E.F.Kalmus   26708
        Non-vocal versions
           arr Kasanli   PC 2121/2210/str   Zimmeramnn 6886
           arr A.Winter   PC 2222/4000/str   Boosey & H   14860
      Wie oft in Meeres tiefsten Schlund (How oft in ocean's seething deep): aria
      Die Frist ist um: recit
        in C min (orig)   ϕ 2+picc.222/4231/timp/str   9'   Fürstner   6791 B
        in C min, arr R.Chignell
                            ϕ 2(picc)222/2230/timp/str   Arranger   MS 4947

GESANG ZUR ENTHÜLLUNG DES DENKMALS SR. MAJESTÄT DES HOCHSELIGEN KÖNIGS FRIEDRICH AUGUST DES GERECHTEN,
   for TTBB chorus & brass (1843)
                         ϕ 0000/4331   Breitkopf & H,1913.CW 16   Misc 8309 & MRL

GÖTTERDÄMMERUNG   see   Der RING DES NIBELUNGEN

GROSSER FEST MARSCH: American centennial march
                         ϕ 3+picc.333+cbsn/43+btpt.31/timp.perc/str 12'   Schott   4302 C

Die HOCHZEIT: unfinished opera
   Fragments for Tenor & Bass soli, SSATTBB chorus & orch
      Introduction
      Vereint, vereint, ertönet: chorus
      Sie sind vermählt: recit
      Willkommen sei mir: septet
      Vereint, vereint: chorus
        ed M.Balling   ϕ 2222/4200/timp/str   Breitkopf & H,1913.CW 12   Misc 2203 & MRL
        ed M.Balling   ϕ 2222/4200/timp/str   (Breitkopf & H,1913.CW 12)   Misc 8307
      Introduction, chorus, recit & chorus only
        ed M.Balling   ϕ 2222/4200/timp/str   (Breitkopf)   23792 +

HULDIGUNGSMARSCH   ϕ 2+picc.22+bcl.2/4331/timp.perc/str 5'   Schott   7344

KAISER-MARSCH (Marche imperiale)
                         ϕ 2+picc.333/4331/timp.perc/str/[chorus] 9'   Peters   5340 B

KINDER-KATECHISMUS, for children's voices & small orch (1873)
   Score includes facsimile of autograph
                       ϕPS 1121/2000/str   Schott,1937   Misc 4471

KÖNIG ENZIO: overture
      arr F.Mottl   ϕ 2222/4200/timp/str   10'30"   Breitkopf   2980
      arr E.Voss   ϕ 2222/4210/timp/str   Schott,1973.CW 18/1   MRL

WAGNER, Richard (cont)

Das LIEBESMAHL DER APOSTEL, for men's chorus & orch

	∅	2+picc.224+cbsn/4431/timp/str	32'30"	Breitkopf	11660 B +
ed M.Balling	∅	2+picc.224.spt/4331/timp/str	Breitkopf & H,1913.CW 16		Misc 8309 & MRL
arr R.Hofmann (non-vocal)	∅	2222/4331/timp/str		Breitkopf,1905	Misc 3604
Selection, arr Baumgartel	PC	1110/0110/timp.perc/str		Wrede	6853

Das LIEBESVERBOT, oder Die Novize von Palermo: opera

Complete

∅	2+picc.222/4430.oph/timp.perc/str			(Misc 5794 B &
	Onstage: military band	(Breitkopf & H.CW 14)		(mf 182

Overture ∅ 2+picc.222/4430.oph/timp.perc/str Breitkopf 8790 +

Selection of excerpts from Acts 1 & 2

∅	2+picc.222/4230.oph/timp.perc.bells/str		
	Stage band: 0.2picc.054/4630.oph/timp.perc.bells	Breitkopf	23806 +

LOHENGRIN: opera

Complete

∅	3(picc)3(ca)3(bcl)3/4431/timp.perc/hp.org/str		
	Offstage: 3222/4.10.00/perc/hp	Breitkopf,1906	Misc 963 D
∅	3(picc)3(ca)3(bcl)3/4431/timp.perc/hp.org/str		
	Offstage: 3222/4.10.00/perc/hp	Peters,1917	Misc 954

(English & French texts; with intro by D.Cooke)

∅	3(picc)3(ca)3(bcl)3/4431/timp.perc/hp.org/str		
	Offstage: 3222/4.10.00/perc/hp	Eulenburg	Misc 963

ed M.Balling

∅	3(picc)3(ca)3(bcl)3/4431/timp.perc/hp.org/str		
	Offstage: 3222/4.10.00/perc/hp	Breitkopf & H.CW 4	MRL

ed P.Pitt

∅	3(picc)3(ca)3(bcl)3/4431/timp.perc/hp.org/str		
	Offstage: 3222/4.10.00/perc/hp	Breitkopf	1645-7

Prelude ∅ 32+ca.2+bcl.3/4331/timp.perc/str Breitkopf 4262 Amv Cwe Dn

Prelude (Introduction) to Act 3

∅	3333/4231/timp.perc/str	Breitkopf & H	4263 Cs Dn

with ending by A.Toscanini

∅	3333/4231/timp.perc/str	Breitkopf & H	4263 Amv B

arr H.Carr

reduced wind parts only for use with strings in previous sets

∅	2222/4230/perc	BBC	TO 519

| arr A.Evans | PC | 3333/43.3cnt.31/timp.perc/str | Hawkes | 3790 B Cwe |
| arr Hoffmann | PC | 2222/4231/timp.perc/str | Breitkopf & H | 6321 |

Coda only, compiled D.Bowden

∅	3333/4331/timp.perc/str	(Arranger)	Misc 4538 B +

Selections

arr Fletcher for chorus & orch (Choral fantasia)

	1121/2210/timp.perc/str	Curwen	5032
arr Luigini	∅	2222/4331/timp.perc/hp/str	Durand	1771
arr H.Mouton	PC	1121/2210/timp.perc/str	Durand	9905
arr W.H.Myddleton	PC	2(picc)222/4230.euph/timp.perc/hp/str	Hawkes	1383
arr V.Nemeti	PC	1121/2210/str	Bosworth	6558

arr E.Tavan (1st fantasia)

PC	2(picc)222/22.2cnt.31/perc/str	Margueritat	380

arr E.Tavan (2nd fantasia)

PC	2(picc)222/22.2cnt.31/perc/str	Margueritat	381

Extracts

Bridal chorus see Treulich geführt

Einsam in trüben Tagen (Lonely amid my sorrow)(Elsa's dream): aria for Soprano (Act 1, Sc.2)

∅	32+ca.2+bcl.3/2300/timp/hp/str	6'	Breitkopf	5022
∅	32+ca.2+bcl.3/2300/timp/hp/str		Durand	19716
∅	32+ca.2+bcl.3/2300/timp/hp/str		(Siddell)	17354 B

Elsa's dream see Einsam in trüben Tagen

Entrance of the guests see Gesegnet soll sie schrieten

WAGNER, Richard (cont)

LOHENGRIN (cont)
   Extracts (cont)
      Euch lüften, die mein klagen (Ye breezes): aria for Soprano (Elsa)(Act 2, Sc.2)
        in Bb (orig)   32+ca.2+bcl.3/2000   5'   BBC   18105
      Finale Act 1 (from Sc.2 'Wer hier in Gotteskampf', with cuts to end of Act 1)
        orch version arr Hoffmann

           φ   3(picc)2(ca)2(bcl)2/4331/perc/hp/str   Breitkopf   7361
      Gesegnet soll sie schrieten (May blessings shower..): chorus (Act 2, Sc.4)
        in E (orig)   φ   32+ca.2+bcl.3/4331/timp/str   9'30"   Breitkopf   4561 B
                  φ   32+ca.2+bcl.3/4331/timp/str   Durand   9840
      In fernem Land (In distant land)(Lohengrin's narration): aria for Tenor (Act 3, Sc.3)
        in A (orig)   φ   3223/4331/timp/str   6'   Breitkopf   5043 Amv B
        in A   φ   3+picc.333/4331/perc/str   Durand   19718
        in A, arr R.Chignell   φ   2222/2230/timp/str   Arranger   MS 5135 **
        in Ab   φ   3333/4331/timp.perc/str   (Siddell)   17204
      Lohengrin's narration see In fernem Land
      Mein Herr und Gott (O heaven in prayer)(King's prayer)(from Act 1, Sc.3)
        in Eb (orig)   φ   33+ca.3+bcl.3/4331/timp/str   Breitkopf   3731
        in Eb   φ   22+ca.2+bcl.3/4331/timp/str   (Siddell)   17355
        arr Hoffmann (non-vocal)
           PC 2222/4231/timp/hp/str   Breitkopf   6332
      Mein lieber Schwan (Beloved swan)(Lohengrin's farewell)(from Act 3, Sc.3)
        in A (orig)   φ   22+ca.23/4231/timp/str   6'   Breitkopf   7810 C
        in A   φ   22+ca.23/4231/timp/str   Durand   19717
        in A   φ   22+ca.23/4231/timp/str   (Siddell)   17206
      Nun sei bedankt (My thanks be thine)(Lohengrin's arrival): aria for Tenor (Act 1, Sc.3)
        in A (orig)   φ   32+ca.22/0000/str   Breitkopf   25816
      Das Süsse Lied verhallt (The song has died away)(love duet): duet for Soprano & Tenor (Act 3, Sc.2)
        in E (orig)   φ   33+ca.3+bcl.3/4331/timp/str   25'   Breitkopf   19942
        in E, arr H.Carr   φ   22+ca.2+bcl.2/4231/timp/str   Arranter   TO 788
      Treulich geführt (Guided by us): bridal chorus (Act 3, Sc.1)
        in Bb (orig)   φ   3323/4231/perc/hp/str
                  Offstage: 3222/4200/perc/hp   Breitkopf   Misc 1242
        in Bb, arr H.Carr φ   2222/4230/tri/hp/str   BBC   TO 486 +
        arr A.Winter, with march (non-vocal)
           PC 2223/4230/hp/str   Hawkes   2093
LOVE FEAST OF THE APOSTLES see LIEBESMAHL DER APOSTEL
Die MEISTERSINGER VON NÜRNBERG: opera
   Complete   φ   2+picc.222/4331/timp.perc.glock/hp.lute/str
                  Offstage: 0000/0100/sdm/org   246'   Schott   Misc 956-7
           φ   2+picc.222/4331/timp.perc.glock/hp.lute/str
                  Offstage: 0000/0100/sdm/org   Eulenburg Misc 966-7 B
           φ   2+picc.222/4331/timp.perc.glock/hp.lute/str
                  Offstage: 0000/0100/sdm/org   Peters   Misc 950-1
      ed P.Pitt   φ   2+picc.222/4331/timp.perc.glock/hp.lute/str
                  Offstage: 0000/0100/sdm/org   Schott   Misc 1648-9
   Act 1 with prelude
      ed E.Voss   φ   3+picc.222/3331/timp.perc.glock/hp/lute
                  Offstage: 0000/0100/org   Schott,1979.CW 9/1   MRL
   Prelude (Overture)   φ   2+picc.222/4331/timp.perc/hp/str   8'45"-10'   Schott   3093 + Amv Bs Dn
      arr Gorter   PC 1121/2110/timp.perc/str   Schott   12628
      arr Hoffmann   φ   2+picc.222/4331/timp.perc/hp/str   Breitkopf   7843 B
      arr H.Mouton   PC 1121/2230/timp.perc/str   Heugel   1081
   Prelude to Act 3   φ   2122/4231/str   6'15"   Eulenburg Misc 1404 B
               φ   2122/4231/str   Schott   14805

WAGNER, Richard (cont)

Die MEISTERSINGER VON NÜRNBERG (cont)
   Suite
      Prelude Act 3   Entry of the Mastersingers
      Dance of the Apprentices   Hamage to Sachs

	⌀	2+picc.222/43.stage tpt.31/timp.perc/hp/str 12'-13'45"		Schott	8152 Amv Bs C
arr Hutschenruyter	⌀	2+picc.222/4331/timp.perc/hp/str		Breitkopf	4468 Amv Ds En
arr F.Salabert	PC	1121/2230/timp.perc/hp/str		Salabert	9960

   Selections

arr H.Finck	PC	1010/0210/timp.perc/str		AH & C	12238
arr C.Godfrey, jnr	PC	2(picc)222/4231.euph/timp.perc/hp/str		Hawkes	1508

   Extracts
      Am stillen Herd (By silent hearth)(Act 1, Sc.3)

in D (orig)	⌀	2222/4200/hp/str	4'15"	Schott	1608 C

      Apotheosis of Hans Sachs   see   Wach auf!
      Dance of the Apprentices
         arr A.Schmid (reduced orch version)

PC	2(picc)222/4230/timp.perc/str		Hawkes	994 B

      Fanget an! so rief der Lenz in den Wald (Now begin, so cried the Spring)(Trial song): aria for
         Tenor (Act 1, Sc.3)

in F (orig)		2+picc.222/4231/timp/hp/str	3'30"	Schott	10848 B

      Morgenlich leuchtend (Bathed in the sunlight)(Prize song): aria for Tenor (Act 3, Sc.5)

in C (orig)	⌀	2222/4230/timp/hp/str	4'45"	Schott	5023 Amv D
in B		2222/4231/timp/hp/str		(Siddell)	17211

         arr Scmid (reduced orch version)

PC	2222/4230/timp/hp/str		Hawkes	16967

         arr Wilhelmj, paraphrase for violin & orch

⌀	2222/4000/hp/str		Schott	2716 B

         arr Jungnickel (from Wilhelmj's paraphrase)

⌀	2222/4230/timp/hp/str		Jungnickel	7934

      Nun hört und versteht (Now hear, and understand)(Pogner's address): aria for Tenor (Act 1, Sc.3)

in F (orig)	⌀	3222/4331/timp/str	Schott	17449

      Pogner's address   see   Nun hört und versteht
      Prize song   see   Morgenlich leuchtend
      Sachs mein Freund (Sachs, my friend)(Act 3, Sc.5)

in G (orig)		2222/4100/str	(Siddell)	18125

      Sachs' first monologue   see   Was duftet doch der Flieder
      Sachs' second monologue   see   Wahn! Überall Wahn!
      Selig, wie die Sonne: quintet for SSTTB soli (Act 3, Sc 4)
         Non-vocal versions

arr Sandré	⌀	str	Schott	13236
arr Windsperger	PC	1010/0110/timp.perc/str	Schott	6713

      Trial song   see   Fanget an! so rief der Lenz in den Wald
      Verachtet mir die Meister nicht (Disdain our masters not): aria for Bass (Act 3, Sc.5)

in C (orig)	⌀	2+picc.222/4331/timp.perc/str	Schott	18110

      Wach auf (Awake)(Apotheosis of Hans Sachs): chorus (Act 3, Sc.5)
         in G (orig), arr Kistler

⌀	2+picc.222/4431/timp.perc/str		Schott	6890

      Wahn! Überall Wahn (Madness, madness)(Sachs' second monologue): aria for Bass (Act 3, Sc.1)

in D	⌀	2+picc.222/4331/timp/hp/str	Schott	7407 B

      Was duftet doch der Flieder (The elder's scent)(Sachs' first monologue): aria for Bass (Act 2, Sc.3)

⌀	2+picc.222/4000/timp/hp/str	6'	Schott	8883 B

MIGNONNE (Die Rose): song

in E, arr F.Mottl	⌀	1110/1000/str	Fürstner	4748

MINUET from piano sonata in B♭

arr Baselt	⌀	2222/3200/str	Breitkopf	8246

WAGNER, Richard (cont)

NEUJAHRS-KANTATE for chorus & orch (1834)
    ed M.Balling   ∅   2+picc.222+cbsn/4230/timp.perc/str
                                Offstage: 2222/2000   Breitkopf & H,1913.CW 16   Misc 8306 # & MR▌
Der NIBELUNGEN FLAMMENZEICHEN: selection, arr E.Urbach see URBACH, Ernst: Der NIBELUNGEN FLAMMENZEICHEN
NICOLAI: Volk-Hymne for Soprano (or Tenor) solo, chorus & orch (1837)
    ed M.Balling   ∅   2+picc.222+cbsn/4330.oph/timp.perc/str Breitkopf & H,1913.CW 16   Misc 8306 & MRL
OVERTURES
    in C (Konzert-overture, no.2)(1830)
                            ∅   2222/4230/timp/str   9'30"   Breitkopf   13253
       ed E.Voss   ∅   2222/4230/timp/str   Schott,1973.CW 18/1   MRL
    in D (Konzert-overture, no.1)
       Orig version
          ed E.Voss   ∅   2222/4200/timp/str   Schott,1973.CW 18/1   MRL
       Rev version   ∅   2222/4200/timp/str   Breitkopf,1926   Misc 900
          ed E.Voss   ∅   2222/4200/timp/str   Schott,1973.CW 18/1   MRL
PARSIFAL: opera
    Complete   ∅   33+ca.3+bcl.3+cbsn/4331/timp.perc/2hp/str
                                Offstage: 0000/0660/bells.sdm   Ricordi   Misc 974
                            ∅   33+ca.3+bcl.3+cbsn/4331/timp.perc/2hp/str
                                Offstage: 0000/0660/bells.sdm   Schott   Misc 898 B
                            ∅   33+ca.3+bcl.3+csbn/4331/timp.perc/2hp/str
                                Offstage: 0000/0660/bells.sdm   Eulenburg   Misc 962 B
                            ∅   33+ca.3+bcl.3+cbsn/4331/timp.perc/2hp/str
                                Offstage: 0000/0660/bells.sdm   Peters   Misc 953 B
    Act 1
       ed E.Voss & M.Geck   ∅   3(picc)3+ca.3+bcl.3+cbsn/4331/timp/str
                                Offstage: 0000/0660/bells.dm.tmc   Schott,1971.CW 14/1   MRL
    Act 2
       ed E.Voss   ∅   3(picc)3+ca.3+bcl.3+cbsn/4331/timp/2hp/str
                                Offstage: 0000/0660/bells.dm.tmc   Schott,1971.CW 14/2   MRL
    Act 3
       ed E.Voss with critical notes
                            ∅   3(picc)3+ca.3+bcl.3+cbsn/4331/timp/2hp/str
                                Offstage: 0000/0660/bells.dm.tmc   Schott,1973.CW 14/3   MRL
    Prelude
       arr Hutschenruyter   ∅   33+ca.33+cbsn/4331/timp/str   16'30"   Breitkopf   7259 Amv Bs
       arr Schmid   PC 22(ca)22/4231/timp/str   Hawkes   992
    Prelude and closing scene ∅ 33+ca.3+bcl.3+cbsn/4331/timp/2hp/str   Schott   4266 Amv C
    Selections
       arr O.Langey   PC 2222/4231/timp/hp/str   G.Schirmer   10263
       arr Wilhelmj, paraphrase for violin & orch
                            ∅   2222/4230/timp/hp/str   Schott   2294
    Extracts
       Amfortas' prayer   see   Nein, lasst ihn unernthüllt
       Chorus of flower maidens, and Klingsor's magic garden
          Orchestral versions
             arr Hoffmann (reduced orch)
                            PC 22(ca)22/4230/timp/hp/str   Schott   6769
                arr Steinbach ∅ 32+ca.32/4231/timp/hp/str   13'   Schott   3097 Amv Bs
             Chorus of flower maidens only
                arr Schmid   PC 2222/4231/timp/hp/str   Hawkes   995 B
       Closing scene, Act 1 see Transformation music and closing scene from Act 1
       Dies alles (Full surely): duet for Soprano & Tenor (Act 2)
          orig keys   ∅   02+ca.3+bcl.3/4031/str   (Siddell)   18050

WAGNER, Richard (cont)

PARSIFAL (cont)
    Extracts (cont)
        Du könntest murden (Thou coulds't do murder)(Gurnemanz' reproach): aria for Bass (Act 1)
            orig keys   ⌀   33+ca.3+bcl.3/4000/hp/str   (Siddell)   17467
        Good Friday music   ⌀   33+ca.3+bcl.3+cbsn/4331/timp/str   10'-16'   Schott   4267 Amv Cs
                                     ⌀   33+ca.3+bcl.3+cbsn/4331/timp/str   Breitkopf   2384
                                     PC 22+ca.2+bcl.2+cbsn/4231/timp/hp/str   Benjamin   1042
        Gurnemanz' reproach   see   Du könntest murden
        Ja! Wehe Weh' über mich (Aye, woe is me): aria for Baritone (Act 3)
                                     ⌀   13+ca.33+cbsn/4331/timp.perc/str   (Siddell)   17413
        Klingsor's magic garden   see   Chorus of flower maidens
        Nein, lasst ihn unenthüllt (Amfortas' prayer): aria for Baritone (Act 1)
            orig keys   ⌀   33+ca.3+bcl.3+cbsn/4231/timp/str   8'   Schott   12131 Amv
            orig keys   ⌀   23+ca.3+bcl.3/4231/timp/str   (Siddell)   18135
        Procession of the Grail (reduced orch)
            arr Kistler   ⌀   3222+cbsn/4331/timp.perc/str   Schott   4721
            arr Schmid   PC 2222/4231/timp.perc/str   Hawkes   1000 B
        Titurel, der fromme Held (Titurel, the hero pure): aria for Bass (Act 1)
            orig keys   ⌀   33+ca.3+bcl.3+cbsn/4331/timp.perc/str   (Siddell)   17466
        Transformation music and closing scene from Act 1 (from 'Vom Bade kehrt' to end of Act): concert
            version for AT.Bar.BB soli, mv-chorus, boys' chorus & orch
            in orig keys   ⌀   33+ca.3+bcl.3+cbsn/4331/timp.perc/str
                                         Onstage: 0000/0660/bells.dm   Schott   10145 Amv C
            reduced version (non-vocal)
                                     ⌀   2222/4231/timp.perc/str   Schott   3098 Amv
POLONAISE (orig pf)
    arr Hoffmann   PC 2(picc)2(ca)22/4231/timp.perc/hp/str   Breitkopf   6164
POLONIA: overture
    arr F.Mottl   ⌀   2+2picc.222/4431/timp.perc/str   11'   Breitkopf   2982
Das RHEINGOLD   see   Der RING DES NIBELUNGEN
RIENZI, DER LETZTE DER TRIBUNEN: opera
    Complete   ⌀   2+picc.223(spt)/4430.oph/timp.perc/hp/str
                                         On stage: 0000/0.12.60.4oph/perc.bells.tamtam/
                                                  org   Fürstner   Misc 972 D
        ed E.Downes & E.Warburton   ⌀   2232.spt/4430.oph/timp.perc/hp/str
                                         On stage: 0000/0.12.60.4oph/perc.bells.tamtam/
                                                  org   (Fürstner)   25878 + & mf 373
    Act 1
        ed R.Strohm & E.Voss   ⌀   3(picc)223+cbsn.spt/2+2nathn.2+2nattpt.30.oph[=tuba]/
                                         timp.perc/str
                                         Offstage: tpt   Schott,1974.CW 3/1   MRL
    Act 2
        ed R.Strohm & E.Voss   ⌀   3(picc)233+cbsn.spt/2+2natth.2+2nattpt.30.oph[=tuba]/
                                         timp.perc.tamtam/str   Schott,1975.CW 3/2   MRL
    Act 3
        ed R.Strohm & E.Voss   ⌀   3(Picc)233+cbsn.spt/2+2nathn.2+2nattpt.30.oph[=tuba]/
                                         timp.perc/str
                                         Offstage mil band: 0000/04+4nattpt.60.4oph/bdm   Schott,1976.CW 3/3   MRL
    Overture   ⌀   2+picc.222.spt/4431/timp.perc/str   Fürstner   14687 An Bs
                                     PC 2(picc)222/2230.euph/timp.perc/str   Lafleur   3822
        arr C.Godfrey   PC 2+picc.223/4431/timp.perc/str   Hawkes   2583
        arr Hoffmann   ⌀   3(picc)223.spt/4431/timp.perc/str   12'   Breitkopf   4259 Amv Cn
    Selections
        arr Ritter & C.Godfrey, jnr
                                     PC 2(picc)222/2230.euph/timp.perc/str   Hawkes   1511
        arr E.Tavan   PC 2(picc)222/22.2cnt.31/perc/str   Margueritat 1666

WAGNER, Richard (cont)

RIENZI, DER LETZTE DER TRIBUNEN (cont)
  Extracts
    Allmächt'ger Vater, blick' herab (Almighty father, strong to save), for Tenor (introduction to
        Act 5, and prayer)(no.13)
      in Bb (orig)   ∅   2222+cbsn/4230/timp/hp/str   Fürstner   17158 C
    Ballet music   .
      1. Introduction   4. Auftritt der Jungfrauen
      2. Waffentanz   5. Festlicher Tanz
      3. Gladiatoren-Kampf
                          ∅   2+picc.222.spt/4331/timp.perc/str   Fürstner   4980
          arr Haensch   PC 2(2picc)222/4220/timp.perc/str   Benjamin   5150
    Ihr Römer, hort die Kunde (We hail with joyful ditties): introduction to Act 2 and chorus of
        the messengers of peace
                          ∅   2222/4230/timp/str   Fürstner   15802
    In seiner Blüte bleichen (Nipped in the bud): aria (no.9)
    Gerechter Gott (Ye powers above): recit
      in G (orig)   ∅   2+picc.222+cbsn/4231/timp.perc/str   7'30"   Fürstner   Misc 923
      in G   2222.spt/4231/timp.perc/str   (Siddell)   18053
      in Eb   ∅   2222.spt/4231/timp.perc/str   (Siddell)   18055
      in F   2222/0031/timp.perc/str   (Siddell)   18054 **
    Peace march from finale to Act 4
                          ∅   2+picc.222.spt/4330/timp/str   6'   Fürstner   6790
    Santo Spirito Cavaliere: battle hymn see War march and Battle hymn
    War march & Battle hymn (Santo Spirito Cavaliere)(finale Act 3)
                          ∅   2+picc.222.spt/4432/timp.perc/str
                              On stage: 0000/0.12.60.oph/6mildm.2dm 6'   Fürstner   6794
        Miscellaneous 'inserts' incorporating stage band within orchestral parts
          arr L.Wurmser   see bag for details   (Fürstner)   23977
Der RING DES NIBELUNGEN
  1. Das RHEINGOLD
    Complete   ∅   3(picc)+picc.4(ca)3+bcl.3(cbsn)/
                              8(4wtuba)3+btpt+cbtpt.3(cbtbn)0.cbtuba/
                              timp.perc.glock/6hp/str
                              Offstage: hp   154'   Eulenburg   Misc 961 An C
                          ∅   3(picc)+picc.4(ca)3+bcl.3(cbsn)/
                              8(4wtuba)3+btpt+cbtpt.3(cbtbn)0.cbtuba/
                              timp.perc.glock/6hp/str   Schott   Misc 1003 B
                          ∅   3(picc)+picc.4(ca)3+bcl.3(cbsn)/
                              8(4wtuba)3+btpt+cbtpt.3(cbtbn)0.cbtuba/
                              timp.perc.glock/6hp/str   Schott   Misc 1425-6
      Selection (Tonbilder aus Rehingold), arr Stansy
                          ∅   2(picc)222/4231/timp.perc/hp/str   Schott   11526
    Extracts
      Entry of the gods into Valhalla
        Orchestral versions
          ed Zumpe   ∅   2222/4331/timp.perc/hp/str   8'   Schott   4764 Amv Ds
          arr Hutschenruyter
                          ∅   2+picc.2+ca.2+bcl.2/4431/timp.perc/2hp/str   Breitkopf   9855
          arr Langey   PC 2(picc)222/4230/timp/hp/str   Hawkes   997 B
      Erda's warning see Weiche, Wotan! weiche
      Immer ist Undank Loge's Lohn (Thankless was ever Loge's toil): aria for Tenor & orch (Sc.2)
        orig keys   ∅   22+ca.3+bcl.3/4100/timp/str   Schott   17453
      Weich, Wotan! weiche (Yield it, Wotan)(Erda's warning)(Sc.4)
        orig keys   ∅   33+ca.3+bcl.3/4045/timp.perc/str   Schott   5033
        arr S.Robinson (with optional concert ending)
                          ∅   3[=2]2[=1]+ca.2+[bcl]3[=2]/403[1]/timp.tamtam/str BBC,1961   23338 +

WAGNER, Richard (cont)

Der RING DES NIBELUNGEN (cont)
   2. Die WALKÜRE

Complete	∅	3(picc)+picc.4(ca)3+bcl.3(cbsn)/ 8(4wtuba)3+btpt.4(cbtbn)0.cbtuba/timp.perc.glock/ 6hp/str	Eulenburg	Misc 960 An B
	∅	3(picc)+picc.4(ca)3+bcl.3(cbsn)/ 8(4wtuba)3+btpt.4(cbtbn)0.cbtuba/timp.perc.glock/ 6hp/str	Peters	Misc 955 B
	∅	3(picc)+picc.4(ca)3+bcl.3(cbsn)/ 8(4wtuba)3+btpt.4(cbtbn)0.cbtuba/timp.perc.glock/ 6hp/str	Schott	Misc 1097 C
	∅	3(picc)+picc.4(ca)3+bcl.3(cbsn)/ 8(4wtuba)3+btpt.4(cbtbn)0.cbtuba/timp.perc.glock/ 6hp/str	Schott	Misc 1413-5 B
ed P.Pitt	∅	3(picc)+picc.4(ca)3+bcl.3(cbsn)/ 8(4wtuba)3+btpt.4(cbtbn)0.cbtuba/timp.perc.glock/ 6hp/str	Schott	1635

    Selections

arr V.Nemeti	PC	1(picc)121/2210/timp/hp/str	Bosworth	707
arr E.Tavan	PC	2(picc)222/2231/timp.perc/str	Margueritat	1099

    Extracts

      Brünnhilde's battle cry <u>see</u> Ho-jo-toho

      Ho-jo-toho (Brünnhilde's battle cry), for Soprano & orch (Act 3, Sc.1)(<u>see also</u> Ride of
          the Valkyries)

	∅	33+ca.3+bcl.3/4331/timp.perc/str	(Siddell)	17560

      Lebewohl du kühnes herrliches Kind (Farewell then valliant, glorious child)(Wotan's
          farewell and Fire music)

orig keys	∅	2(picc)222/4231/timp.perc/hp/str ('B' set with MS amendments. For details, see score)	Schott	5025 Amv D
Orchestral versions	∅	2(picc)222/4231/timp.perc/hp/str	Schott	5959 Cs
ed W.Hutschenruyter	∅	3(picc)3+ca.2+bcl.3/4331/timp.perc/hp/str	Breitkopf	9113 Bn +
arr A.Hohenstein (reduced orch)	PC	2(picc)222/4231/timp.perc/str	Benjamin	9175

      Ride of the Valkyries
        Orchestral versions

	∅	2+2picc.3+ca.3+bcl.3/8341/timp.perc/str	5'	Schott	3095 Amv Bs C
arr W.Hutschenruyter	∅	2+picc.2+ca.3+bcl.3/6331/timp.perc/str		Breitkopf	7952 Amv C
arr O.Langey (reduced orch)	PC	2(picc)222/4231/timp.perc/str		Hawkes	996 B

      Siegmund, sieh auf mich (Siegmund, look on me): duet for Soprano & Tenor (Act 2, Sc.4)

orig keys	∅	33+ca.3+bcl.3/4441/timp.perc/hp/str	Schott	16059

      Winterstürme wichen dem Wonnemond (Winter storms have waned): aria for Tenor

in B♭ (orig)	∅	33+ca.3+bcl.3/4000/hp/str	3'-4'	Schott	7811 Amv E
Orchestral versions	∅	2222/4120/hp/str		Schott	1238
	PC	2222/4230/timp/hp/str		Hawkes	993 B

      Wotan's farewell and Fire music <u>see</u> Lebewohl du kühnes herrliches Kind

Der RING DES NIBELUNGEN (cont)
   3. SIEGFRIED

Complete	∅	3(picc)+picc.4(ca)3+bcl.3(cbsn)/ 8(4wtuba)3+btpt.4(cbtbn)0.cbtuba/timp.perc.glock/ 6hp/str	Eulenburg	Misc 964 An B

WAGNER, Richard (cont)

Der RING DES NIBELUNGEN (cont)
    3. SIEGFRIED (cont)
        Complete (cont)   ∮ 3(picc)+picc.4(ca)3+bcl.3(cbsn)/
                                8(4wtuba)3+btpt.4(cbtbn)0.cbtuba/timp.perc.glock/
                                6hp/str   Schott   Misc 1006 B
                             ∮ 3(picc)+picc.4(ca)3+bcl.3(cbsn)/
                                8(4wtuba)3+btpt.4(cbtbn)0.cbtuba/timp.perc.glock/
                                6hp/str   Schott   Misc 1416-8 B
        Extracts
            Forest murmers
                Orchestral versions
                    ed Zumpe   ∮ 2(picc)222/4230/timp.perc/str   9'   Schott   3096 Amv B
                    arr W.Hutschenruyter
                                ∮ 3(picc)2+ca.33/4330/timp.perc/str   Breitkopf   8913 Amv B
            Forging song no.1 see   Nothung! Nothung!
            Forging song no.2 see   Hoho! hoho! Schmeide mein Hammer
            Hoho! hoho! Schmeide mein Hammer (Shape me my hammer)(Forging song no.2)
                orig keys   ∮ 2+picc.3+ca.33/8(4wtuba)3+btpt.00/timp.anvil/
                                  str   5'30"   Schott   10849
            Nothung! Nothung! (Forging song no.1): aria for Tenor
                orig keys   ∮ 3+picc.3+ca.3+bcl.3/8(4wtuba)3+btpt.00.cbtuba/
                                  timp/6hp/str   Schott   10850 B
            Siegfried's ordeal by fire (finale Act 3, Sc.2)
                reduced orch version, arr P.Pitt
                        PC 2(picc)222/4231/timp.perc/hp/str   Hawkes   5187
            Wache, Wala! Wala! Erwach! (Waken, Wala): duet for Contralto & Bass (Act 3, Sc.1)
                orig keys   ∮ 3+picc.3+ca.3+bcl.3/8(4wtuba)400/timp.perc/hp/str Schott   18051
Der RING DES NIBELUNGEN (cont)
    4. GÖTTERDÄMMERUNG
        Complete   ∮ 3(picc)+picc.4(ca)3+bcl.3(cbsn)/
                                8(4wtuba)3+btpt.4(cbtbn)0/timp.perc.glock/
                                6hp/str   Eulenburg   Misc 970-1 An B
                             ∮ 3(picc)+picc.4(ca)3+bcl.3(cbsn)/
                                8(4wtuba)3+btpt.4(cbtbn)0/timp.perc.glock/
                                6hp/str   Schott   Misc 981 B
            ed P.Pitt   ∮ 3(picc)+picc.4(ca)3+bcl.3(cbsn)/
                                8(4wtuba)3+btpt.4(cbtbn)0/timp.perc.glock/
                                6hp/str   Schott   Misc 1637-9
        Act 1, with prelude
            ed H.Fladt   ∮ 3(picc)+picc.3+ca.3+bcl.3/8(4wtuba)3+btpt.3+cbtbn.2/
                                timp.perc/6hp/str
                                Offstage: 0000/1100/4hp   Schott,1981.CW 13/1   MRL
        Act 2
            ed H.Fladt   ∮ 3(picc)+picc.3+ca.3+bcl.3/8(4wtuba)3+btbn.3+cbtbn.2/
                                timp.perc/2hp/str   Schott,1980.CW 13/2   MRL
        Extracts
            Altgewohntes Geräusch (Sounds familiar of old): duet for Soprano & Mezzo soprano (Act 1, Sc.3)
                orig keys (long intro in parts only)
                             ∮ 3+picc.3+ca.3+bcl.3/8(4wtuba)400/timp.perc/hp/str   Schott   17558
            Brünnhilde's apotheosis and Closing scene see   Starke Scheite schichtet mir dort
            Frau Sonne sendet lichte Strahlen (Fair sunlight sendeth rays): song of the Rhine-maidens
                (Act 3, Sc.1)
                Concert version for three voices, omitting Siegfried's solos
                    orig keys, arr Volbach
                             ∮ 2222/4231/timp/hp/str   10'   Schott   18045
                Orchestral concert version
                    ed Zumpe   ∮ 2222/4230/timp.perc/hp/str   Schott   5327
                    arr H.Mouton PC 1121/2230/timp.perc/str   Heugel   6051

WAGNER, Richard (cont)

Der RING DES NIBELUNGEN (cont)
   4. GÖTTERDÄMMERUNG (cont)
      Extracts (cont)
        Funeral music (Act 3)

	∅	3+picc.3+ca.3+bcl.3/8(4wtuba)4+btpt.40.cbtuba/			
		timp.perc/6hp/str	8'	Schott	6812 Amv
arr W.Hutschenruyter					
	∅	2+picc.3+ca.2+bcl.3/8(4wtuba)3+btpt.30.cbtuba/			
		timp.perc/hp/str		Breitkopf	19935
arr W.Hutschenruyter (with additional MS intro 'Death of Siegfried)					
	∅	2+picc.32+bcl.3/8(4wtuba)3+btpt.30.cbtuba/			
		timp.perc/hp/str		Breitkopf	4872
arr Stasny (reduced orch)					
	∅	2(picc)222/4231/timp.perc/hp/str		Schott	6750
arr L.Weninger	PC	1112/4111/perc/str		Benjamin	1033

Hagen assembles the vassals   <u>see</u>   Ho! ho! Ihr Gibich's Männen
Hagen's watch   <u>see</u>   Hier sitz' ich zur Wacht
Hier sitz' ich zur Wacht (Here sit I on guard)(Act 1, Sc.2)

orig keys	∅	22+ca.22/4231/timp/str		(Siddell)	17403

Ho! ho! Ihr Gibich's Männen (Ye Gibich vassals): aria for Bass & mv-chorus (Act 2, Sc.3)
   solo version, omitting choral sections, orig keys

	∅	3+picc.333/84.cowhorn.51/timp/str		(Siddell)	17404

Mime heiss ein mürrischer (Mime, know ye then, was a dwarf)(Siegfried's narration)
    (Act 3, Sc.2)
   orig keys (Mime heiss, to end of funeral music)

	∅	3+picc.3+ca.3+bcl.3/8441/timp.perc/hp/str		Schott	18052 +

Siegfried's journey to the Rhine (Act 1 prelude)
   Orchestral concert versions

	∅	2+picc.22+bcl.2/4331/timp.perc/hp/str	10'	Schott	4497 Amv C
arr M.Johnstone (Bowden)					
	∅	3(picc)2+ca.2+bcl.3/4331/timp.perc/hp/str		Lengnick(H)	PL 375 An

Siegfried's narration   <u>see</u>   Mime heiss ein mürrischer Zwerg
Song of the Rhine-maidens   <u>see</u>   Frau Sonne sendet lichte Strahlen
Starke Scheite schichtet mir dort (Mighty logs I bid you now pile)(Brünnhilde's apotheosis
    and closing scene, to end of Act): aria for Soprano

orig keys	∅	3+picc.3+ca.3+bcl.3/8(4wtuba)3+btpt.40.cbtuba/			
		6hp/str	17'15"-20'	Schott	9606 B

ROMANCE in E   <u>see</u>   ALBUMBLATT in C
Die ROSE   <u>see</u>   MIGNONNE
RULE BRITANNIA: overture

arr F.Mottl	∅	2+2picc.22+Fcl.2+cbsn/4430.oph/timp.perc/			
		str	10'	Breitkopf	2983

SCHMERZEN   <u>see</u>   WESENDONCK LIEDER
SIEGFRIED   <u>see</u>   Der RING DES NIBELUNGEN   (4268 Amv Ds

SIEGFRIED IDYLL	∅	1121/2100/str	16'30"-18'30"	Schott	(Ewe Fn
	∅	1121/2100/str		Breitkopf	13326 B +
Facsimile of autograph	∅	1121/2100/str		Drei Masken,1923	Misc 4005
arr A.Schmid	PC	1121/2100/str		Hawkes	729
arr R.Jungnickel (from paraphrase arr Wilhelmj)					
	∅	2222/2230/timp/hp/str		Jungnickel	16561

STEHE STILL   <u>see</u>   WESENDONCK LIEDER

SYMPHONY in C	∅	2222+cbsn/4230/timp/str	33'30"	Brockhaus	10420
ed E.Voss	∅	2222/4210/timp/str		Schott,1973.CW 18/1	MRL

Der TAG ERSCHEINT   <u>see</u>   GESANG ZUR ENTHÜLLUNG

WAGNER, Richard (cont)

TANNHÄUSER: opera
  Complete
    Orig version (1842-5)   φ   3(picc)22+bcl.2/4331/timp.perc/hp/str
                                      Stageband: 4+2picc.4+ca.66/12.12.40/perc   Fürstner   Misc 1419-21
      with new Venusberg music in supplement
                                 φ   3(picc)22+bcl.2/4331/timp.perc/hp/str
                                      Stageband: 4+2picc.4+ca.66/12.12.40/perc   Müller   Misc 897
      with Paris version in supplement
                                 φ   3(picc)22+bcl.2/4331/timp.perc/hp/str
                                      Stageband: 4+2picc.4+ca.64/12.12.40/
                                         timp.perc/hp
                                      Additions to stageband for Paris
                                      version: hp/timp.cast   Eulenburg [1929] Misc 3208 Bn
      with Paris version inserts in sequence
                                 φ   3(picc)22+bcl.2/4331/timp.perc/str
                                      Stageband: 4+2picc.4+ca.66/12.12.40/perc
                                      Additions to stageband for Paris
                                      version: hp/timp/str   Peters,1972   Misc 7846 B
      with Paris version in supplement
                                 φ   3(picc)22(bcl)2/4331/timp.perc/hp/str
                                      Stageband: 4+2picc.4+ca.66/12.12.40/perc
                                      Additions to stageband for Paris
                                      version: hp/timp.cast   Peters   Misc 949
      with variants up to 1860
        Act 1, with overture
                                 φ   3(picc)22+bcl.2/4331/timp.perc/hp/str
                                      Stageband: 4+picc.4+ca.64/12.000   Schott,1980.CW 5/1   MRL
      Paris version (1860-61)
        ed P.Pitt   φ   3(picc)22+bcl.2/4331/timp.perc/hp/str
                                      Stageband: 4+picc.4+ca.64/12.12.40/perc/hp   Durand   Misc 901
  Overture   φ   2+picc.222/4331/timp.perc/str   12'-14'30"   Fürstner   12673 Amv B
                                 φ   2+picc.222/4331/timp.perc/str   Hawkes   796 B
    arr Hoffmann   φ   3(2picc)222/4331/timp.perc/str   Breitkopf   4261 Amv Bs En
  Overture and Venusberg music (Paris version)
                                 φ   3(picc)222/4331/timp.perc/hp/str   23'   Fürstner   4935 + Amv
  Selections
    arr C.Godfrey, jnr   PC   2222/2230.euph/timp/str   Hawkes   1509
    arr Luigini   PC   3(picc)22(bcl)2/4231/timp/hp/str   Durand   3320
    arr W.H.Myddleton   PC   2(picc)222/4230.euph/timp.perc/hp/str   Hawkes   1383
    arr S.Robinson   φ   3222/4331/timp.perc/hp/str   Arranger   TO 729
  Extracts
    Allmächt'ge Jungfrau (All holy Virgin)(Elizabeth's prayer)
      in Gb (orig)   φ   322+bcl.2/4030/[str]   (Siddell)   18013
      in Gb, arr R.Chignell   φ   221+bcl.2/2230/[str]   Arranger   MS 5531
        see also Beglückt darf nun dich
    As du in kühnem (As for the palm in song): aria (Cavatina) for Baritone (Act 1, Sc.4)
      in B min   φ   2222/0000/str   (Fürstner)   Misc 1155 B
    Beglückt darf nun dich (In joy once more): pilgrims' chorus (Act 3, Sc.1)
      orig keys, including Elizabeth's prayer
                                 φ   322+bcl.2/4031/timp/str   Fürstner   10591
      arr H.Schmid with Shepherd's song (Act 1, Sc.3)(non-vocal)
                                 PC   22(ca)22/4230/timp/str   Hawkes   7516
    Blick' ich umher (Gazing around): aria for Baritone (finale Act 2)
      in Eb (orig)   φ   1[=2]hp/vlas.vlcs   4'30"-5'30"   Fürstner   6802
      in Eb   φ   1[=2]hp/vlas.vlcs   (Siddell)   17352

WAGNER, Richard (cont)

TANNHÄUSER (cont)
  Extracts (cont)
    Dich, teure Halle (O hall of song)(Elizabeth's greeting)
      in G (orig)   φ 2222/4000/timp/str   3'15"-5'   Fürstner   5020 C
      in G (short intro)   φ 2222/4000/timp/str   (Siddell)   17218
      in G, arr R.Chignell (short intro)
                          φ 2222/2220/str   (Fürstner) MS 5529
      in G, arr G.Stacey (short intro)
                          pf/str   Arranger   LM G 3626
    Elizabeth's greeting see Dich, teure Halle
    Elizabeth's prayer see Allmächt'ge Jungfrau
    Entry of the guests at Wartburg see Freudig begrüssen
    Frau Holda kam aus dem Berg (Shepherd's song)
      arr Schmid (non-vocal) PC 22(ca)22/4230/timp/str   Hawkes   7516
    Freudig begrussen (Joyous we greet thee)(Entry of the guests at Wartburg)
      orig keys   φ 2(picc)222/4331/perc/str (12 stage tpts)   Fürstner   14723
      orig keys   PC 2+picc.222/4330.oph/timp.perc/str 3 stage tpts)   Durand   8592
      Orchestral versions   φ 2(picc)222/4331/timp.perc/str   Fürstner   11902
        arr Hoffmann   φ 3222/4331/timp.perc/str   Breitkopf   5764
        arr A.Winter   PC 2222/4330.euph/timp.perc/str   6'30"   Hawkes   2607
    Inbrunst im Herzen (Contrite in spirit)(Tannhäuser's return): aria
    Hör' an Wolfram (Hear all, Wolfram): recit
      orig keys   φ 3+picc.222/4231/timp.perc/str   (Siddell)   17501
    Introduction Act 3 see Tannhäuser's pilgrimage
    O du mein lieber Abendstern (O star of eve): aria
    Wie Todesahnung (As death's foreboding): recit
      in G (orig)   φ 2212/0031/hp/str   5'30"   Fürstner   5021
      in G   φ 2212/0031/hp/str   (Siddell)   17917 D
      in G, arr E.Griffiths (without recit)
                          pf/str   Arranger   LM G 6772
      in G, arr G.Stacey   pf/str   Arranger   LM G 3572
      in F   φ 2212/0031/hp/str   (Siddell)   17916
      in B   φ 2222/0030.oph/hp/str   (Siddell)   17915
      arr Atzler for trombone & orch
                         PC 1121/2100/hp/str   Cranz   3306
    O Fürstin (O princess): duet for Soprano & Tenor (Act 2, Sc.2)
      in A♭ (orig)   φ 2222/4230/timp/hp/str   BBC   17502
    O Himmel! Lass! dich jetzt erflehen (Oh Heaven, hear me): aria for Baritone (Act 2, Sc.4)
      in E♭ (orig)   φ 0022/2030/timp/hp/str   Fürstner   10764
    Pilgrims' chorus see Beglückt darf nun dich
    Tannhäuser's pilgrimage (Introduction Act 3)
      Orig version, as performed in early productions, 1845 et seq
                        φ 3(picc)222/4331/timp/str   Novello   8243
      Rev, shortened version φ 3(picc)222/4331/timp/str   Fürstner   9159
                        φ 3(picc)222/4331/timp/str   Durand   4954
        arr W.Hutschenruyter
                        φ 3(picc)222/4331/timp/str   Breitkopf   5906
    Tannhäuser's return see Inbrunst im Herzen
    Venusberg music (Bacchanale)(Act 1)
      Orig version
        arr A.Schmid (parts of orig version with parts of overture, arr without chorus)
                      PC 2(picc)222/4230/timp.perc/hp/str   6'   Hawkes   7705
      Paris version
        with chorus   φ 3(picc)222/4331/timp.perc/hp/str   Durand   12130
        without chorus   φ 2+picc.222/4331/timp.perc/hp/str   12'-13'   Fürstner   9155
          rev M.Hochkofler (1936)
                      φ 3(picc)222/42+Dtpt.31/timp.perc/hp/str   Eulenburg Misc 6954

WAGNER, Richard (cont)

TRAUERSINFONIE for wind instruments (written for the funeral of Weber, based on melodies from Euryanthe)
φ   5.7.20.10/14.6.4.1/perc
(actual parts - 1242/4231/perc)   Breitkopf,1926   Misc 902

TRÄUME   see   WESENDONCK LIEDER
TRISTAN UND ISOLDE: opera
  Complete   φ   3(picc)2+ca.2+bcl.3/4331/timp.perc/hp/str
                            Stageband: 00.ca.00/6330   226'   Breitkopf & H   Misc 969 C
                            φ   3(picc)2+ca.2+bcl.3/4331/timp.perc/hp/str
                            Stageband: 00.ca.00/6330   Peters   Misc 952 B
    ed P.Pitt   φ   3(picc)2+ca.2+bcl.3/4331/timp.perc/hp/str
                            Stageband: 00.ca.00/6330   Breitkopf & H   Misc 1636
  Prelude
    Wagner's concert ending   φ   32+ca.2+bcl.3/4231/timp/hp/str   9'30"-11'   Breitkopf   5871
  Prelude and Liebestod (Prelude to Act 1 and finale to Act 3 from 'Mild und leise')
    Concert versions
      Vocal version for Soprano
        orig keys   φ   3(picc)2+ca.2+bcl.3/4331/timp/hp/str   16'-18'45"   Breitkopf   9570
    Concert versions (non-vocal)
                  φ   3(picc)2+ca.2+bcl.3/4331/timp/hp/str   Breitkopf & H   4265 Amv Cb +
      arr A.Schmid   PC 2222/4230/timp/hp/str   Hawkes   991
           see also Mild und leise (Liebestod)
  Selections
    arr Hoffmann 'Tonbilder aus Tristan'
                  φ   2(picc)2(ca)2+bcl.2/4231/timp/hp/str   15'   Breitkopf   1723 C
    arr E.Tavan   PC 2(picc)2(ca)22/2230/timp.perc/str   Margueritat   2096
  Extracts
    Act 2, Sc.1   condensed horn and stage horn part only, arr
                        S.Robinson   Composer   TO 2001
    Bist du nun todt (Art thou then dead)(Tristan's vision) for Tenor (Act 3, Sc.1)
      arr A.Seidel (non-vocal)
                  φ   22+ca.2+bcl.2/4231/timp/hp/str   Breitkopf   1781
    Introduction Act 3
      arr A.Seidel   φ   01+ca.22/4000/timp/str   8'-9'30"   Breitkopf   4264 Bs
    Isolde's Liebestod   see   Mild und Leise
    Isolde's narration   see   Wie lachend sie mir liedern singen
    Mild und leise (Mild and softly)(Liebestod): finale to Act 3 for Soprano
      orig keys   φ   2+picc.2+ca.2+bcl.3/4331/timp/hp/str   Breitkopf & H   9243 B
        see also   Prelude and Liebestod
    Tristan's vision   see   Bist du nun todt
    Wie lachend sie mir liedern singen (How scoffingly they sing): aria for Soprano (Act 1, Sc.3)
      orig keys   φ   3(picc)2+ca.2+bcl.3/4331/timp.cym.tri/str   8'45"-10'   (Siddell)   17442

VAMPYR ARIE: Allegro zur Arie des Aubry in H.Marschners Vampyr, for voice & orch (1833)
                  φ   2222/2200/timp/str   Breitkopf,1914.CW 1   S.32718

WAGNER SELECTIONS
  GRAND CHRONOLOGICAL SELECTION OF WAGNERS OPERAS   see   KRAUS, H: RICHARD WAGNER
  WAGNER'S HELDENBUCH   see   URBACH, Ernst: WAGNER
  WAGNERIANA   see   HAND, Hermann: WAGNERIANA
Die WALKÜRE   see   Der RING DES NIBELUNGEN
WESENDONCK LIEDER
  1. Der Engel, in G   φ   2222/2000/str
  2. Stehe still   φ   2222/4100/timp/str
  3. Im Treibhaus (Studie zu Tristan und Isolde), in D min
                  φ   2222/4000/str
  4. Schmerzen, in C min   φ   2222/4100/str
  5. Träume, in A♭   φ   0022/2000/str
  Complete   φ   2222/4100/timp/str   Schott   9065 B +
    orch F.Mottl; foreword by L.Salter - orig piano version printed beneath full score
      (Also includes Wagner's own orchestration of No.5)
                  φ   2222/4100/timp/vla-solo(no.5 only).str   Eulenburg,1979   Misc 9986

WAGNER, Richard (cont)

WESENDONCK LIEDER (cont)

No.1 only						
in G, orch F.Mottl	∮	2222/2000/str		3'15"	Schott	17510
No.2 only						
in C min, orch F.Mottl	∮	2222/4100/timp/str		3'30"	Schott	17511
No.3 only						
in D min, orch F.Mottl	∮	2222/3000/str		6'45"	Schott	17512
No.4 only						
in C min, orch F.Mottl	∮	2222/4100/str		2'40"	Schott	17513
in A min	∮	2222/2131/str			(Siddell)	17514
No.5 only						
in A♭, orch F.Mottl for voice or solo instrument						
	∮	0022/2000/str		5'20"	Schott	4690
in A♭, orch F.Mottl for voice or solo instrument						
		0022/2000/str			(Siddell)	17515
in A♭, orch A.Schmid	PC	2222/4230/timp/hp/str			Hawkes	481 Cp
in F, orch F.Mottl	∮	0022/2000/str			(Siddell)	17516
in F, orch G.Stacey		pf/str			Schott	LM G 3558
Non-vocal versions						
orch Mulder	PC	2222/4210/timp/hp/str			Boosey	11301
orch Svendsen	PC	2222/2000/timp/str			Schott	3101
orch Wagner for solo violin & orch			in Complete edition,			
	∮	0022/2000/str	with foreward L.Salter.Eulenburg,1979			Misc 9986
orch A.Winter for violin & orch						
	PC	2222/4000/timp/hp/str			Boosey & H	14965

WAGNER, Robert

MEDLEY OF FRENCH FOLKSONGS, for chorus & orch, arr

1. Frère Jacques		3. Sur le Pont d'Avignon			
2. Au Clair de la lune		4. En passant par la Lorraine			
	∮	2222/4231/timp.perc/cel.hp/str		BBC	23852 +

WAGNER, Rudolf

FRÜHLINGSJUBEL: overture, op.96	∮	2(picc)222/4230/timp.perc/str		Kistner & S	5711

WAGNER-RÉGENY, Rudolf (1903-1969)

5 GESÄNGE DES ABSCHIEDS (Hermann-Hesse-Gesänge), for Baritone & orch (1968/69)
1. Wie sind die Tage (Wie sind die Tage schwer!)
2. Abendgespräch (Was blickst du träumend ins verwölkte Land?)
3. Gang bei Nacht (Busch und Wiese, Feld un Baum)
4. Nach dem Fest (Von der Tafel rinnt der Wein)
5. Der Künstler (Was ich schuf in heisser Jahre Glut)

	∮	0222/2200/perc/pf/str	Peters,1971	Misc 7777

3 ORCHESTERSÄTZE (1952)
1. Langsam   2. Andante rubato   3. Lebhaft

	∮	3(picc)2+ca.3(bcl)3(cbsn)/4331/timp.perc/str	Bote & B,1956	Misc 5220

WAGNER, Siegfried (1869-1930)

Der BÄRENHÄUTER: opera

Overture	∮	2+picc.222/4231/timp.perc/str	Brockhaus	18688

WAHLBERG, Rune (1910-

NOCTURNE for orchestra	∮	2222/2220/timp.perc/hp/str	5'	Gehrmans,1941	Misc 2662

WAINWRIGHT, Derek

IDLING   PC   1121/2230/timp.perc/str   Weinberger,1951   20322

WAINWRIGHT, John (1723-1768)

CHRISTIANS AWAKE: hymn
   in D, arr G.Williams   ∅   1111/0000/perc/hp/str/chorus   Arranger   MS 20312
   arr H.Perry   PC   1121/0000/timp.perc/org/str   Hawkes   4970 B

WAITE, E.W.

Les DIABOLTINS for piccolo & orch
                                PC   1121/2230.euph/timp.perc/str   Lafleur   6690

WAL-BERG

DANSE DES ÉTOILES   PC   2121/2230/timp.perc/hp/str   Brull,1951   20577
DANSE DES POIGNARDS   ∅PC 2232/2330/timp.perc/gtr.hp.pf/str   5'-5'30"   Méridien,1952   Misc 8668
La FOLLE RONDE
   arr R.Binge   PC   2222/2230/timp.perc/hp/str   Brull,1951   20574
MARIONETTES
   arr P.Bonneau   ∅   2(picc)2(ca)2(bcl).asx.2/3330/timp.perc.glock.
                                     kit.vib.whip.xyl/cel.gtr.hp.[om].pf/str   Chappell(H)   PL 640
MONTMARTRE: waltz   ∅   2(picc)2(ca)2+bcl.[3sx].2/2230/timp.perc.glock.
                                     vib.xyl/cel.[gtr].hp/str   4'20"   Mills,1953   24603
PAYSAGES MÉDITERRANÉES: suite
   1. La Macédoine   2. L'Arabie   3. L'Andalousie
                                ∅   2(picc)2(ca)22/4331/timp.2perc.mba.xyl/
                                     cel.hp/str   11'   Marbot,1961   Misc 8669
WELTSTADTRHAPSODIE (Musique sur la ville)(Music on the town)
                                ∅   2(picc)2(ca)2+bcl.2/433[1]/timp.perc.glock.vib.xyl/
                                     [gtr].hp/str   Crescendo,1961   Misc 7576

WALCH, Joh. Heinrich (1776-1855)

FUNERAL MARCH (Trauermarsch)(attrib to Beethoven)
                                PC   2222/2231/perc/str   Benjamin   1060

WALDIMIR, Sune

SWEDISH FOLK MELODIES: selection, arr
                                PC   1020/0210/timp.perc/gtr/str   Gehrman,1938   22220

WALDENMAIER, August Peter

SERENADE, op.9, in A   ∅   str   Mozart Edn   LM G 11208

WALDSTEIN, Ferdinand (Ernst Gabriel), Count (1762-1823)

SYMPHONY, in D
   ed L.Schiedermair   ∅   2200/2200/timp/str   L.Schwann,1951.Denk Rhein vol 1   MRL

WALDTEUFEL, Berthe

AIMÉE: waltz   PC   1121/2231/timp.perc/str   Zook   1129

WALDTEUFEL, Émile (1837-1915)

À TOI: waltz, op.150   PC   1+picc.222/4231/timp.perc/str   AH & C   6668
   arr Seredy   PC   1122/2210/timp.perc/str   C.Fischer   19628
ABANDON: waltz, op.213   PC   1121/2210/timp.perc/str   C.Fischer   1421

WALDTEUFEL, Émile (cont)

ACCLAMATIONS: waltz, op.223	PC	2+picc.222/4230.euph/timp.perc/str		AH & C	11307
arr M.Tobani	PC	1222/2210/perc/str	5'30"	C.Fischer	1420
AMITIÉ: waltz	PC	2+picc.222/2230.euph/timp.perc/str		AH & C	10922
AMOUR ET PRINTEMPS: waltz	PC	1+picc.222/4231/timp.perc/str		Schott	7468
	PC	1121/2210/perc/str	6'	C.Fischer	1426
ANGE D'AMOUR: waltz, op.241	PC	1122/2210/perc/str	7'-8'15"	C.Fischer	1419
	PC	1121/22.cnt.10/perc/str		Cranz	15874
ARC EN CIEL: waltz, op.237					
arr G.Borch	PC	1121/2210/timp.perc/str		C.Fischer	1428
AU REVOIR: waltz, op.149	PC	1121/2210/perc/str		C.Fischer	10219
AUS SCHÖNER ZEIT (Autrefois): waltz, op.167					
	PC	1+picc.222/4230.oph/timp.perc/str		Litolff	25830
Les BAISERS PARLENT	∅	2+picc.222/4231/timp.perc/str	4'30"	(Heugel)	MS 5637
La BARCAROLLE: waltz, op.178	PC	1+picc.222/4231/timp.perc/str		AH & C	12136 C
arr G.Borch	PC	1121/2210/timp.perc/str	7'30"	C.Fischer	1427
BELLA: polka-mazurka, op.113					
arr R.Jungnickel	PC	2222/4230/timp.perc/str		Jungnickel	3124
BÉOBILE: pizzicato for strings	∅	str		BBC	MS 7134
La BERCEUSE: waltz, op.161	PC	1+picc.222/4230.euph/timp.perc/str		AH & C	2865
arr Seredy	PC	1122/2210/timp.perc/str		C.Fischer	19628
BIEN AIMÉS: waltz, op.143	∅	2(picc)+picc.222/4231/perc/str		AH & C	3236
arr M.L.Lake	PC	1122/2210/timp.perc/str		C.Fischer	19628
BLUEBELLS: waltz	PC	1+picc.121/2230.euph/timp.perc/str		AH & C	497
BLEUETS ET COQUELICOTS: waltz, op.259					
	PC	1+picc.222/4230.euph/timp.perc/str	7'	Metzler	6467
Les BOHÉMIENS: polka, op.216	PC	1+picc.222/2230.euph/timp.perc/str		AH & C	12494
BONNE BOUCHE: polka, op.163	PC	1+picc.222/4230.euph/timp.perc/str		AH & C	11424 B
BRUNE OU BLONDE: waltz, op.162					
arr Roth & Seredy	PC	1222/4230/perc/str		C.Fischer	10225
arr Seredy	PC	1122/2210/timp.perc/str		C.Fischer	19628
CHANSON D'AUTREFOIS: gavotte					
orch J.Buerger		2121/2230/timp.perc.glock/str		(Fonotipia)	MS 7135
CHANT D'OISEAUX: waltz, op.251	PC	1+picc.121/2210/timp.perc/str		Cranz	5811
CHANTILLY: waltz, op.171	∅	1+picc.222/4230.euph/timp.perc/str		AH & C	3298
arr G.Borch	PC	1122/2210/timp.perc/str		C.Fischer	19628
CHÂTEAUX EN ESPAGNE: waltz, op.225					
	PC	1+picc.222/2230.euph/timp.perc/str		AH & C	12493
CHRISTMAS ROSES see ROSES DE NOËL					
COEUR BRISÉ: waltz	PC	1+picc.221/4230/timp.perc/str		Apollo Verlag	12443
CONFIDENCES: waltz, op.214	PC	1121/2210/timp.perc/str		C.Fischer	1448
COQUETTERIE: waltz, op.218					
arr Seredy	PC	1121/2210/timp.perc/str		C.Fischer	1447
COÛTE QUE COÛTE: waltz, op.261	PC	1+picc.222/4230.euph/timp.perc/str		Metzler	12565
DANS LES NUAGES: waltz, op.208					
arr White	PC	1222/2210/timp.perc/str		C.Fischer	1435
DANS TES YEUX: waltz, op.227	PC	1222/2210/timp.perc/str		C.Fischer	1436
DOLORES: waltz, op.170	∅	1+picc.222/4230.euph/timp.perc/str		AH & C	3939
	PC	1222/2210/perc/str		C.Fischer	1429
concert edn, 1944	PC	2(picc)222/2230/perc/str		AH & C	7316 Bm
ed S.Robinson	∅	3(picc)222/4231/timp.perc/hp/str		AH & C	6490
DOUCES PAROLES: waltz, op.210	PC	1+picc.222/2230.euph/timp.perc/str		AH & C	9543
Un DOUX POÈME: waltz, op.249	PC	1+picc.222/4231/timp.perc/str		Cranz	8229
	PC	1222/2210/timp.perc/str		Cranz	5848
	PC	1+picc.222/2210/timp.perc/str		C.Fischer	1451
ENTRE-NOUS: waltz, op.144	PC	2+picc.222/4230/timp.perc/str		Litolff	25831

WALDTEUFEL, Émile (cont)

L'ESPACE: waltz, op.268		1222/4230/timp.perc/str		Heugel	11303
ESPAÑA: waltz on Chabrier's Rhapsody, op.236					(740 Agg Bs Cp
	PC	1+picc.221/2231/timp.perc/str	7'	Enoch	(Dni Ewa Fm G
arr S.Torch (used as signature tune for 'Torchlight on Music')					
	ø	1+picc.222/4330/perc.glock/cel.hp.pf/str		Arranger	25195
arr A.Wilkinson	ø	3(3picc)1+ca.22/4230/timp.perc/hp/str		BBC	24254
L'ESPRIT FRANÇAIS: waltz, op.182					
	PC	1+picc.222/4230.euph/timp.perc/str		AH & C	12372 B
	PC	1222/2210/perc/str		C.Fischer	1449
L'ESTUDIANTINA: waltz, op.191	PC	1+picc.121/4231/timp.perc/hp/str	6'		
		(ø 'A' set)	6'	AH & C	258 + Am Bp C
	PC	1+picc.121/4231/timp.perc/str		Enoch	7225
	PC	1111/2231/timp.perc/str		Litolff	6597 **
ETINCELLES: waltz, op.229	PC	1+picc.222/2230.euph/perc/str		AH & C	5817
ÉTOILE POLAIRE: waltz, op.238	PC	1222/2210/timp.perc/str		C.Fischer	1452
La FIANCÉE: waltz, op.245					
arr M.Tobani	PC	1222/2210/perc/str		C.Fischer	10214
FIN DE SIÈCLE: waltz, op.250	PC	1121/2210/perc/str		Cranz	5812
FIVE MINUTES WITH WALDTEUFEL'S WALTZES: selection from the works of Waldteufel, arr F.Hartley					
	PC	1110/0000/perc/str		AH & C	2309
Les FLEURS: waltz, op.190	PC	2(picc)121/2231/timp.perc/str		Durand	14650
FLEURS ET BAISERS: waltz	PC	2+picc.222/4230/timp.perc/str		Apollo Verlag	12444
FLOTS DE JOIE: waltz, op.145	PC	2+picc.222/4230/timp.perc/str		AH & C	3356
		2+picc.222/4230/timp.perc/str		Litolff	20669
Les FOLIES: polka, op.157					
arr for cornet solo & orch	PC	1+picc.222/2230.euph/perc/str		AH & C	12371
FONTAINE LUMINEUSE: waltz, op.247					
	ø	1(picc)121/2210/timp.perc/str		Cranz	5813
FORGET-ME-NOT: waltz, op.101					
arr Seredy	PC	1121/2210/perc/str		C.Fischer	1453 B
FRANCINE: waltz	PS	2222/20.2cnt.30.euph/timp.perc/str		Cramer	25351
GAIETÉ: waltz, op.164	PC	1+picc.121/4231/timp.perc/str		Litolff	20503
arr Roth	PC	1222/4230/timp.perc/str		C.Fischer	10102
GOUTTES DE ROSÉE: waltz, op.222					
	PC	1+picc.222/2230.euph/timp.perc/str		AH & C	3943
GRANDE VITESSE: galop, op.146	ø	1+picc.222/4232/timp.perc/str	2'	Durand	14649
The GRENADIERS: waltz, op.207	ø	1+picc.222/2230.euph/timp.perc/str	5'	AH & C	13870
	PC	1+picc.222/2230/timp.perc/str		AH & C	1329 Bp Fs G
arr S.Robinson		3222/4331/timp.perc/str		(AH & C)	TO 1245
HABANERA: waltz	PC	1+picc.222/4230.euph/timp.perc/str		Metzler	6474
HEBE: waltz, op.228	PC	1+picc.222/2230/timp.perc/str		AH & C	2662
HOMMAGE AUX DAMES: waltz, op.153					
	PC	1+picc.222/2221/perc/str		AH & C	9542 B
IDYLLE: waltz, op.209		1+picc.222/20.2cnt.30.euph/perc/str		AH & C	25825
ILLUSION: waltz, op.204	PC	1+picc.222/4230/timp.perc/str		AH & C	12277
INVITATION À LA GAVOTTE, op.246	ø	2222/2230.oph/timp.perc/hp/str	5'45"	Cranz	8232
JE T'AIME: waltz, op.177	PC	1+picc.222/4230.euph/timp.perc/str		Chappell	13439 Am
arr S.K.Wright	PC	1122/2210/timp.perc/str		C.Fischer	19628
JEU D'ESPRIT: polka, op.196	PC	1+picc.212/2200/timp.perc/str		AH & C	12543
		1+picc.222/4230.oph/timp.perc/str		Litolff	25826
JEUNESSE DORÉE: waltz	PC	2(picc)222/4231/timp.perc/str		AH & C	3932 Am B
JOIE ENVOLÉE: waltz, op.198	PC	1+picc.222/2230.euph/timp.perc/str		AH & C	15919
Un JOUR À SEVILLE: waltz, op.252					
	PC	1+picc.222/4231/timp.perc/str (also contains arrangement for small orch)		Cranz	5810

WALDTEUFEL, Émile (cont)

JOYEUX PARIS: polka	PC	1+picc.221/2230.euph/timp.perc/str		AH & C	12496
KAMERADEN-POLKA, op.197		2(picc)122/4230.oph/timp.perc/str		Litolff	25826
LONGCHAMPS FLEURI: waltz, op.254					
arr Atzler	PC	1121/2210/timp.perc/str		Cranz	5808
LUNE DE MIEL: waltz, op.205	∅	1+picc.122/2230.euph/timp.perc/str		AH & C	12375
MA CHARMANTE: waltz, op.166	PC	1+picc.222/4231/timp.perc/str		Hawkes	453
MA VOISINE: polka, op.206	PC	1+picc.121/2230.euph/timp.perc/str		AH & C	16676
MADELEINE: waltz, op.126	PC	1121/2230.euph/perc/str		Lafleur	1124
La MANOLA: waltz, op.140	PC	1+picc.12.3sx.1/2230/perc/str		Boosey & H	1007
MARIANA: waltz, op.185	∅	1+picc.222/4230.euph/timp.perc/str	7'30"	AH & C	2921 Am
MELLO: waltz, op.123	PC	1121/2230.euph/perc/str	6'	Hawkes	1009
MINUET: polka, op.168	PC	1+picc.222/2230.euph/timp.perc/str		AH & C	16216
MODESTIE: waltz, op.220	PC	1+picc.222/2230.euph/timp.perc/str		AH & C	2919
MON RÊVE: waltz, op.151	∅	1+picc.222/4231/timp.perc/str	6'-10'	AH & C	13908 Am
	PC	1+picc.222/4231/timp.perc/str		AH & C	135 Bp
arr G.Borch	PC	1122/2210/timp.perc/str		C.Fischer	19628
NAPLES: waltz, op.179	PC	2(picc)222/4231/timp.perc/str	5'30"	AH & C	2288
NID D'AMOUR: waltz, op.195	∅	1+picc.221/4230.euph/timp.perc/str	6'30"	AH & C	9518
NUIT ETOILEE: waltz, op.231	PC	1122/2210/perc/str		C.Fischer	1430 Ap
PAPILLONS BLEUS: waltz, op.224	PC	1+picc.222/2230.euph/perc/str		AH & C	1481
PAR-CI, PAR-LÀ: polka, op.239	PC	1+picc.121/2230.euph/timp.perc/str		AH & C	12544
Les PATINEURS (The Skaters' Waltz): waltz, op.183					
	PC	1+picc.222/4230.euph/perc/str		AH & C	(12374 Ap Bm Cs
					(Fwe Gwa
	∅	1+picc.222/4230/timp.perc/str		AH & C	14673
arr A.Colville, orch F.Cramer: waltz-song, in F					
		pf/str		(AH & C)	LM G 4884
arr B.Thompson: waltz-song, in F					
	∅	gtr.hp.pf/str		(AH & C)	MS 20404
arr G.Walter	∅	3222/4231/perc/hp/str		(AH & C)	TO 129
arr A.Wilkinson	∅	3(3picc)1(ca)22/2230/timp.perc/hp/str		(AH & C,1954)	24249
arr A.Wilkinson	∅	3(3picc)1(ca)22/2230/timp.perc/hp/str		(Chappell,1954)	24253
arr Wright	PC	1122/2210/perc/str		C.Fischer	1437 Ap
PLUIE D'OR: waltz, op.160	PC	1+picc.222/4230.euph/timp.perc/str		AH & C	3936
arr Seredy	PC	1122/2210/timp.perc/str		C.Fischer	19628
La PLUS BELLE: waltz, op.158	PC	1+picc.222/4230.euph/timp.perc/str		AH & C	13562
POLKA POTPOURRIS					
No.1, arr S.Robinson	∅	1+picc.222/4231/timp.perc/str		Arranger MS:BBC	MS 5573
No.2, arr S.Robinson	∅	1+picc.121/2230/timp.perc.glock/str		Arranger MS:BBC	MS 7136
POMONE: waltz, op.155	∅	2+picc.222/4231/timp.perc/hp/str	8'	AH & C	2275 B
see also TALES OF AUTUMN					
Un PREMIER BOUQUET (Time remembered): waltz, op.201					
	PC	1+picc.121/2230.euph/timp.perc/str		AH & C	16042 B
arr S.Torch	∅	212[=4]2/2330/perc/hp.pf/str		(AH & C)	24856
PRESTISSIMO, op.152	∅	1+picc.222/2230.euph/timp.perc/str		AH & C	14778
PRINCESS MAY: waltz	PC	1+picc.222/4230.euph/timp.perc/str		Chappell	1676
REINE DES COEURS: waltz, op.192					
	PC	1+picc.221/2230.euph/timp.perc/str		AH & C	3203
RETOUR DES CHAMPS: polka, op.203					
	PC	1+picc.121/2230.euph/timp.perc/str		AH & C	12545
RETOUR DU PRINTEMPS: waltz, op.244					
	PC	1121/2210/perc/str		Cranz	9787
	PC	1222/2210/perc/str		C.Fischer	1417
RÊVE DIVIN					
in G, arr J.Bürger as 'O vision deceiving'					
	∅	2322/2230/timp.perc/hp/str	5'15"	(Arranger)	MS 5636

WALDTEUFEL, Émile (cont)

RÊVERIE: waltz, op.202	⌀	2+picc.222/4230.euph/timp.perc/hp/str		AH & C	11780
arr S.K.Wright	PC	1122/2210/timp.perc/str		C.Fischer	19628
RÊVES DE BOIS: waltz, op.105					
arr R.Jungnickel	PC	2222/4231/timp.perc/str		Jungnickel	3029
ROSÉE: waltz					
arr Raimon		1(picc)221/2230/timp.perc/str		AH & C	12504
ROSES DE NOËL (Christmas Roses): waltz, op.230					
	⌀	1+picc.222/2230.euph/timp.perc/str	7'	AH & C	3296
concert edn, 1948	PC	1+picc.222/2230/timp.perc/str		AH & C	19224
Les SIRÈNES: waltz, op.154	PC	1+picc.222/4231/timp.perc/str	7'30"	AH & C	3942 B
arr G.Borch	PC	1122/2210/timp.perc/str		C.Fischer	19628
The SKATERS' WALTZ see Les PATINEURS					
SKATING SCENE, arr J.Bürger from 'Les Patineurs' and other waltz themes by Waldteufel					
	⌀	2(picc)122/2230/perc/str		(Arranger)	MS 2297
SOIR D'AMOUR: waltz	PC	1+picc.222/4231/timp.perc/str		AH & C	10907
SOIRÉE D'ÉTÉ: waltz, op.188	PC	1222/2210/perc/str		C.Fischer	10218
arr G.Borch	PC	1122/2210/timp.perc/str		C.Fischer	19628
SOLEIL LEVANT					
in B♭, arr H.Carr	PC	1010/2000/hp/str		(AH & C)	TO 2005
SOLITUDE: waltz, op.174	PC	2+picc.222/4231/timp.perc/str		AH & C	3237 B
La SOURCE: waltz, op.180	PC	2(picc)222/4231/timp.perc/str		AH & C	3938
Les SOURIRES: waltz, op.187	PC	1+picc.222/2230.euph/perc/str		AH & C	2929
SOUS LA VOÛTE ETOILÉE: waltz, op.253					
	PC	1222/2210/timp.perc/str		Cranz	5809
SOUVENIR D'ESPAGNE: waltz	PC	1+picc.222/2230.euph/timp.perc/str		Metzler	16227
SOUVERAINE: mazurka, op.255	PC	1+picc.222/4231/timp.perc/str		Cranz	8228
SOUVIENS-TOI: waltz, op.173	PC	1+picc.222/4231/timp.perc/str		AH & C	12251
arr Seredy	PC	1122/2210/timp.perc/str		C.Fischer	19628
SUR LA PLAGE: waltz, op.234	⌀	1+picc.222/4230.oph/timp.perc/str	8'	AH & C	15473 Bm
	PC	1+picc.222/4231/timp.perc/str		AH & C	2927
TALES OF AUTUMN: abridged version of waltz 'Pomone', arr S.Baynes					
	PC	112.3sx.1/2230/timp.perc/gtr/str		AH & C	5948
TENDRES BAISERS: waltz, op.211	PC	1+picc.222/2230.euph/timp.perc/str		AH & C	15588
TERESA: waltz, op.133	PC	1121/2210/perc/str		C.Fischer	10220
TOUJOURS AIMÉE: waltz	⌀	2+picc.222/4230.oph/timp.perc/str		(AH & C)	Misc 3765
arr S.Robinson	PC	2+picc.222/4231/timp.perc/hp/str (⌀ 'A' set)		AH & C,1953	20979 B
TOUJOURS FIDÈLE: waltz, op.169	⌀	2+picc.222/4230.euph/timp.perc/hp/str		AH & C	3941 B
arr M.L.Lake	PC	1122/2210/timp.perc/str		C.Fischer	19628
TOUJOURS OU JAMAIS: waltz, op.156					
	PC	2+picc.222/4231/timp.perc/str (⌀ 'A' set)		AH & C	3933
arr G.Borch	PC	1122/2210/timp.perc/str		C.Fischer	19628
TOUT À VOUS: waltz		2(picc)222/40.2cnt.30.euph/timp.perc/str		AH & C	25835
TOUT EN ROSE: waltz, op.200	PC	1+picc.222/2230.euph/timp.perc/str		AH & C	12403
TOUT OU RIEN: polka, op.219	PC	2+picc.222/2230.euph/timp.perc/str		AH & C	12495
TOUT-PARIS: waltz, op.240	⌀	2+picc.222/4230.oph/timp.perc/str		Cranz	11476
	PC	1121/2210/perc/str	7'15"	Cranz	11452
TRÈS JOLIE: waltz, op.159	⌀	1+picc.222/4230.oph/timp.perc/str	7'	Hawkes	14534
	PC	1+picc.222/4231/timp.perc/str		Hawkes	7346 Ap Cm Dwe
arr S.K.Wright	PC	1122/2210/timp.perc/str		C.Fischer	19628
TRÉSOR D'AMOUR: waltz, op.199	⌀	3(picc)222/4230.euph/timp.perc/hp/str		AH & C	3202
	PC	2(picc)121/2210/perc/str	7'	C.Fischer	1450
VÉNITIENNE: waltz	PC	1222/2210/perc/str		C.Fischer	1423
Les VIOLETTES: waltz, op.148	PC	1222/4230/timp.perc/str		AH & C	243 Ap
		1+picc.222/4230/timp.perc/str		Litolff	20670
VISION: waltz, op.235	PC	1+picc.222/2230.euph/timp.perc/str		AH & C	10581

WALDTEUFEL, Émile

WALDTEUFEL MEMORIES: selection from the music of Waldteufel, arr H.Finck
                         PC   2(picc)121/2230/timp.perc/str   AH & C   8601 Cni
WALDTEUFELEIEN: selection from the music of Waldteufel, arr Kling
                         PC   1+picc.222/4230/timp.perc/str   13'15"   Oertel   9053
WALTZ WITH WALDTEUFEL: selection from the music of Waldteufel, arr A.Wilkinson
                         PC   2222/2320/timp.perc/hp/str   5'15"   AH & C,1956   22445
WALTZING WITH WALDTEUFEL: selection from the music of Waldteufel, arr R.Docker
                         ∅   2(picc)2(ca)22/4331/timp.perc/hp/str   6'50"   (AH & C)   23657 +
    rev version   ∅   2(2picc)2(ca)22/4331/timp.perc.2glock.vib.xyl/
                              hp/str   5'40"   (Arranger,1972) 25474 +
ZIGZAG: polka, op.248   PC   1+picc.222/42.cnt.31/timp.perc/str   Cranz   4847

WALFORD DAVIES   see   DAVIES, H.Walford

WALKER, Ernest (1870-1949)

CORINNA'S GOING A-MAYING: song
   in G, arr F.Collinson   ∅   1121/2220/timp.perc/hp/str   Arranger   MS 30920

WALKER, Geo. Oastlere (18th-19th cent)

RIGHT O' THE LINE: march   PC   2+picc.222/4230.euph/perc/str   2'30"   Hawkes   861

WALKER, James (1929-

ENCORE FOR WINDS: scherzo   ∅   2222/2200   2'30"   Schirmer,1975 26038

WALKER, William

BALLYHOO: revue
   Extracts
      The world is so small: song
         in E♭, arr B.Berlin   ∅   2121/2000/perc/hp/str   Arranger/(K.Prowse) TO 946
BEARDS: song
   in D, arr B.Berlin   ∅   1121/2000/str   Arranger   TO 159
The CHARGE OF THE LATE BRIGADE: song
   in D, arr B.Berlin   ∅   2121/2220/timp.perc/str   Arranger   TO 156
FADE AWAY OLD FAITHFUL: song
   in E♭, arr J.Beaver   ∅   2121/2230/perc/hp/str   (S.French)   TO 339
LIBERTY HALL: song
   in C, arr B.Berlin   ∅   1121/2000/perc/str   Arranger   TO 157
SPREAD IT ABROAD: revue
   Overture and finale, in D♭ ∅   2121/2230/perc/hp/str   (K.Prowse)   TO 341

WALL, Alfred M.

RECREATIONS: suite
   1. Overture   3. Idyll
   2. Siciliano   4. Minuet and Rigaudon
                         ∅   str   OUP   4984 Bwa

WALLACE, Oliver

DUMBO: film by O.Wallace & F.Churchill
   Selection, arr G.Zalva   PC   112.3sx.1/2220/timp.perc/str   Chappell   16728 C

WALLACE, Raymond

WEAR A TOP-O'-THE-MORNING SMILE: song
  in B♭, arr B.Berlin   ø 2121/2220/perc/str   (Southern)   TO 569

WALLACE, (William) Vincent (1812-1865)

The AMBER WITCH: opera
  Extracts
    My long hair is braided: rondo
      in A♭ (orig A), arr Reynolds
                  ø 2121/2000/perc/hp/str   [BBC]   TO 1337
    The Tyrant shall wake: soldiers' song & chorus
      in E, arr A.Reynolds & J.Clements
                  ø 2121/2230/perc/hp/str   [BBC]   TO 1336
    When the elves at dawn do pass: ballad
      in A♭ (orig)   2222/4000/str   (Siddell)   17927
The BELLRINGER: song
  in E♭   1021/0100/str   4'30"   (Siddell)   17926
The DESERT FLOWER: opera
  Extracts
    Through the pathless forest: song
      in B min, arr A.Reynolds
                  ø 2121/2230/perc/str   Arranger   TO 1335
LURLINE: opera
  Overture   PC 2222/2230.euph/timp.perc/str   Lafleur   1374
  Selection, arr Urich   PC 2222/2230.euph/perc/str   Lafleur   7493
  Extracts
    Ave Maria 'Peace to the mem'ry of the brave'
      in E (orig)   ø 2222/2200/timp/str   (Goodwin & T)   TO 1334
    Gentle troubadour: ballad
      in F (orig)   1011/0000/str   (Siddell)   17923
    My home, my heart's first home: song
    Home of my heart: recit
      in E (orig)   1012/2000/str   (Siddell)   17925
    Our barque in moonlight: romance
      in D min (orig)   ø 2222/4000/perc/str   (Goodwin & T)   TO 1333
    Peace to the mem'ry of the brave   <u>see</u> Ave Maria
    Sweet Spirit hear my prayer (Oh thou, to whom this heart)
      in A♭ (orig)   1222/2000/str   (Siddell)   17924
      arr (does not agree with vocal score)
        in B♭   ø 2222/2000/str   (Goodwin & T)   TO 82
MARITANA: opera
  Overture
    arr A.Evans   PC 2222/4230.euph/timp.perc/str   10'-12'   Hawkes   586 B
    arr Hoffmann   ø 2(picc)222/4231/timp.perc/hp/str   Breitkopf   10262
  Selection, arr Ritter   PC 2(picc)222/4230.euph/timp.perc/str   Hawkes   987 Cp
  Extracts
    Ah confusion: song
      in C (orig), arr R.Chignell
                  ø 2(picc)222/4230/timp/str   Arrnager   MS 5213
    Alas, those chimes: song
      in A (orig)   2222/2000/str   (Siddell)   17921
      in G, arr S.Robinson   2121/2000/str   (Novello)   MS 6381
    Angels, that around us hover (Angelus): song
      in E♭ (orig)   ø 2222/4200/hp/str   (Goodwin & T)   TO 1331

WALLACE, (William) Vincent (cont)

MARITANA (cont)
  Extracts (cont)
    The Harp in the air: romance
      in Eb (orig), arr S.Robinson

	ϕ	1021/2010/hp/str	(Novello)	MS 6380

    Hear me gentle Maritana (The mariner in his barque): cavatina
      in D (orig)   1222/2000/str   (Siddell)   17922
    In happy moments
      in F (orig)   ϕ   1122/2110/str   (Siddell)   17465
    O Maritana: duet
      in Ab (orig)   1222/2200/hp/str   (Siddell)   17919
    Of fairy wand had I the power: duet
      in C (orig)   ϕ   2221/4000/str   (Goodwin & T)   TO 1331
    Remorse and dishonour: song
      in G (orig), arr R.Chignell

                    2122/4231/timp/str   Arranger   MS 5220
    Scenes that are brightest: song
      in F (orig)   ϕ   1122/2000/hp/str   (Siddell)   17015 B
      in F   ϕ   1112/0000/hp/str   (Goodwin & T)   TO 1331
      in F, arr R.Chignell   ϕ   1122/2000/hp/str   Arranger   MS 5216
      in F, arr E.Griffiths   pf/str   (Novello)   LM G 7006
      in F, arr M.Mackie   ϕ   cel/str   Arranger   MS 30651
    There is a flower that bloometh: song
      in Db (orig)   1122/2210/str   (Siddell)   17920
      in Db   ϕ   1122/2000/str   Boosey   26405
      in Db, arr J.Turner   ϕ   1110/1000/hp/str   (BBC)   LM G 9449
    To my courage: song
      in E   ϕ   2222/4230/timp/str   (Siddell)   Misc 4102
    Yes, let me like a soldier fall: song
      in C (orig)   1222/4130/timp.perc/str   (Siddell)   17914
      in C   ϕ   1212/4220/timp.perc/str   (Goodwin & T)   TO 1331

MERRILY WE ROLL ALONG: song by W.V.Wallace & H.Carr
  in Eb   ϕ   1+picc.122/2230/perc/hp/str/chorus   (P.Maurice)   TO 261
OUR HANDS HAVE MET BUT NOT OUR HEARTS: song
  in Eb, arr J.Turner   ϕ   1110/1000/hp/str   (BBC)   LM G 9271
SWEET AND LOW: cradle song
  in A   1012/2000/hp/str   (Siddell)   17928

WALLACE, William (1860-1940)

FREEBOOTER SONGS
  No.3 Son of mine   PC   2122/2000/str   Cramer   6984
                   PC   2122/2200/timp/str   Cramer   5946 B
The PASSING OF BEATRICE: symphonic poem no.1 on the 31st canto of Dante's 'Paradiso'
                 ϕ   2222/4230/timp/hp/str   13'-16'   Schott,1911   Misc 922
VILLON: symphonic poem no.6   ϕ   3(picc)2+ca.2+bcl.2/4331/timp.perc/hp/str   16'30"   Schott   5563

WALLBANGER, Harvey (1857-1923)

IN BLAUER LAUNE: suite   ϕ   2(picc)2+ca.2+bcl.2/4230/timp.perc.bouteillophone.
                       glass hca/2hp/str   Weinberger,1920   Misc 905

WALLER, Jack

DEAR LOVE: musical play by J.Waller, J.Tunbridge & H.Wood
  Selection   PC   212.sx.2/2230/perc/str   Chappell   703

WALLER, Jack (cont)

HE WANTED ADVENTURE: musical play by J.Waller & J.Tunbridge
   Selection, arr Somers   PC 1(picc)11.3sx.1/2230/timp.perc/str   Chappell   11011 B
PLEASE TEACHER: musical play by J.Wallace & J.Tunbridge
   Extracts
      Song of the cello (adapted from Beethoven)
         in Eb, arr M.Lubbock   φ   212.3sx.1/2000/str   (Chappell)   TO 394
PRINCESS CHARMING: musical play by J.Waller, R.Bennett, H.Ruby & A.Sirmay
   Selection, arr H.M.Higgs   PC 2122/2230/timp.perc/cel.hp/str   Chappell   6884 C
   Extracts
      A palace of dreams: song
         in F, arr L.Salter   φ   2220/2000/perc/hp/str   (Chappell)   TO 1505
         arr Irwin (non-vocal) PC 112.3sx.1/2210/perc/str   Chappell   8500
      Swords and Sabres: song (R.Bennett), for Tenor & Bass soli, chorus & orch
         in G min, arr P.Cardew φ 2(picc)121/2230/timp.perc/hp.pf/str (Chappell)   22937
SILVER WINGS: musical play by J.Wallace & J.Tunbridge
   Selection, arr Jones   PC 2122/2230/perc/str   Chappell   8184 C
   Extracts
      Asleep in my heart: song
         in F, arr M.Mackie   φ   2131/2230/timp.perc/hp.pf/str   (Chappell)   18532 +
TELL HER THE TRUTH: musical play by J.Wallace & J.Tunbridge
   Selection, arr Jones   PC 1121/2230/perc/str   Chappell   10324 B
   Extracts
      Hoch, Caroline: song
         in Db, arr P.Cardew   φ   2222/4330/timp.perc/hp.pf/str   (Chappell)   18429
      Sing brothers: song
         in D, arr G.Vinter (refrain only)
                    φ   1+picc.222/4230/timp.perc/str   (Chappell)   22182 +
VIRGINIA: musical comedy by J.Waller & J.Tunbridge
   Selection, arr H.M.Higgs   PC 212.sx.2/2230/timp.perc/cel.hp/str   Chappell   8433 Ap C
   Extracts
      Roll away clouds, for chorus & orch
         in F, arr A.Masters   φ   2222/4330/perc/hp.pf/str   (Chappell)   23723 +
WALLER AND TUNBRIDGE MELODIES: selection of melodies by J.Wallace & J.Tunbridge, arr S.Robinson
                    φ   322+bcl.sx.2/4231/perc/cel.hp/str   (Chappell)   TO 420
YES, MADAM?: musical play by J.Wallace & J.Tunbridge
   Extracts
      The Girl the soldiers always leave behind: song
         in D, arr J.Beaver   φ   2121/2230/perc/hp/str   (Feldman)   TO 398

WALLERSTEIN (Wallerston), Anton (1813-1892)

La FÊTE CHAMPÊTRE: polka
   arr M.Lubbock   φ   1+picc.021/0100/str   (Arranger)   MS 30785
The GREAT EXHIBITION POLKA OF 1851
   arr M.Lubbock   φ   1+picc.121/2200/perc/hp.pf/str   (Arranger)   20191
JENNY LIND'S FAVOURITE POLKA, op.28, no.4
   arr D.Berry   PC 101.4sx.0/0320/perc/gtr/str   Paxton   8317
   arr M.Lubbock   φ   2+picc.121/2200/perc/hp.pf/str   (Arranger)   20191

WALLOND, Wally

MEDLEY, arr for solo voices, chorus & orch
   Roses (L.Monckton)   Where the rainbow ends (H.Finck)
   A hundred years ago (L.Monckton)
                    φ   1121/2220/perc/str   Arranger   MS 787 φ only

WALLOND, Wally (cont)

OLD AND NEW COON SONGS (Kentucky Minstrels): medley arr for solo voices, chorus & orch
 Coon drum major (L.Stuart)   (FD & H)
 Whistling coon (Raeburn)   (FD & H)
 Doan ye cry my honey (A.W.Noll)   (FD & H)
 Lazy bones (Mercer & Carmichael)   (L.Wright)
 Dixie Lee (A.Hill)   (P.Maurice)
 Great day (V.Youmans)   (C.Connelly)
        φ 111.3sx.1/2220/timp.perc/pf/str   Arranger MS 333 φ only
PLANTATION MEDLEY (Kentucky Minstrels), arr for mv-chorus & orch
        φ 221.4sx.1/1430/perc/str   Arranger MS 75 φ only
SCOTTISH MEDLEY: medley of Scottish folksongs for radio programme 'Monday at Seven', arr for Baritone
   solo, chorus & orch
        φ 1130/0210/timp/gtr.pf/str   Arranger MS:BBC MS 5447 φ only

WALPURGIS, Maria Antonia (1724-1780)

PRENDI L'ULTIMO ADDIO: aria for Soprano solo & strings [c.1750]
 in G (orig), ed H.Schouwmann φ str/cont   Broekmans 1977 26453 *

WALSWORTH, Ivor

The INN OF THE BIRDS   string parts only, for use with material on hire
                from the composer   Composer   19308

WALTER, Georg (pseud of Walter GOEHR)

CAVALCADE OF STRAUSS WALTZES, arr
       PC 112.3sx.1/3230/timp.perc/hp/str   K.Prowse   14845 B
DELIBES IN VIENNA: waltz fantasy, arr
       PC 2(picc)1(ca)21/2230/timp.perc/hp/str   Liber-Southern 18711
The FLEMISH LION: Flemish air, arr
 in B♭   φ 1010/2220/perc/str   Arranger MS:BBC MS 20095
GOUNOD IN VIENNA: fantasy in waltz time, arr
       PC 1(picc)121/2230/timp.perc/hp/str   Liber-Southern 1116 B
GROENINGE: Flemish air, arr φ 1010/2220/perc/str   Arranger MS:BBC MS 20096
MARCHING ON
 arr Wright   PC 2(picc)121/4230/timp.perc/str   AH & C   16954 C
RHWYM WRTH DY WRECYS (Forth to the battle)(Captain Morgan's march): Welsh song, arr
 in G   φ 2121/2230/timp.perc/hp/str   Arranger MS:BBC MS 7841
SELECTION OF BRAHMS' WALTZES from op.39
       PC 1121/2230/timp.perc/hp/str   Liber-Southern 19123 B
SPELLBOUND: film
 Excerpts, arr G.Zalva φ 1111/2120/perc/hp.pf/str   (Chappell)   TO 812
 Extracts
  Spellbound: valse intermezzo
   arr G.Zalva   PC 102.3sx.0/0220/perc/str   (Chappell)   TO 812
The STORY OF THE WALTZ: a radio potpourri of waltz music
        φ 2(picc)121/3231/timp.perc.gong.xyl/acdn.cel.gtr.
         hp.hpsd.mustel-org.2pf/str/S.Bar soli.chours.mv-chorus BBC   MS 6214-9

WALTERS, Gareth (1928-

DIVERTIMENTO FOR STRINGS φ str   Composer,1960 23056 +
ELEGY for strings   φ str   Ricordi   Misc 7380 B
A GWENT SUITE   φ 2222/4230/timp.perc/str   Mozart Edn(H) PL 621 Ani

WALTERS, Gareth (cont)

PRIMAVERA: overture	∅	2(picc)222/4230/timp.perc/hp/str		(Ricordi)	Misc 5898
SINFONIA BREVE	∅	str	17'	Anglo-Cont.,1964	Misc 10453

WALTERS, Owen

POODLE POLKA				
arr C.Watters	PC	1121/2230/timp.perc/hp/str	FD & H,1952	21639

WALTHEW, Richard Henry (1872-1951)

CONVERSATION GALANTE				
arr Taylor	∅	1121/2000/timp/str	Augener	7130
GLEANERS' SLUMBER SONG				
in E♭, orch Bürger	∅	212(bcl)2/2000/hp/str	(Boosey)	MS 2789
INTERMEZZO (Aladdin's Cave)	∅	1021/2000/tri/str	Stainer & B	2747
IT WAS A LOVER AND HIS LASS: duet				
in D, arr H.Carr	∅	2121/2230/timp/hp/str	Arranger	19132
in D, arr F.Cramer		pf/str	(Boosey)	LM G 4913
in D, arr A.Franzel	∅	1110/0000/perc/hp.pf/str	(Boosey)	LM A 623
in A, arr B.Thompson	∅	1110/1000/hp/str	(Boosey)	LM G 7523
MINUET (Intermezzo)	∅	str	Stainer & B	859
TABLE MUSIC: suite				
arr J.Brown	∅	str	Stainer & B	16311

WALTON, Albert E.

CALL OF THE ANGELUS: intermezzo				
	PC	1111/2230/timp/str	Lafleur	19449

WALTON, William (1902-

see CRAGGS, Stewart R.: William Walton: a thematic catalogue. London, OUP,1977   BRL

ANNIVERSARY FANFARE (may be used as introduction to 'Orb & Sceptre')					
	∅	0000/09[=6]4[=2].3[=2]btbn/timp.perc	1'	OUP,1975	Misc 8958 B
The BEAR: extravaganza in one act					
	∅	1111/1110/2perc(timp.bells.crot[=glock].vib.xyl)/			
		hp.pf/2vln.vla.vlc	40'	OUP,1977	Misc 9398
BELSHAZZAR'S FEAST for Baritone solo, chorus, 2 brass ensembles & orch					
	∅	2+picc.23(E♭cl;bcl)asx[=ca]2+cbsn/4331/			
		timp.3[=4]perc(anvil.bdm.gong.glock.wdbl.xyl)/			
		2hp.org.[pf]/str			
		2 brass ensembles: 0000/0662	33'30"	OUP,1957	Misc 4749 B
CAPRICCIO BURLESCO	∅	2+picc.2+ca.2+E♭cl+bcl.3(cbsn)/4331/timp.perc.xyl/			
		hp/str	7'	OUP,1969	Misc 7103
CHRISTOPHER COLUMBUS: musical drama for SATBB soli, chorus, 4 speakers & orch					
	∅	2+picc.2+ca.2+bcl.2+cbsn/4331/timp.perc.rumba sticks.xyl/			
		gtr.hp/str		Composer MS:BBC	MS 8429
CONCERTI					
Cello & orch (1956)	∅	2(picc)2(ca)2(bcl)2(cbsn)/4231/timp.perc/cel.hp/			
		str	27'-28'30"	OUP,1957	Misc 4832 D
Viola & orch (1929, rev 1962)					
orig version	∅	3(picc)2+ca.2+bcl.2+cbsn/4331/timp/str	24'	OUP,1930	Misc 1696 D
rev version	∅	2(picc)2(ca)2(bcl)2/4230/timp/hp/str	23'	OUP,1964	Misc 6081
Violin & orch (1938/39)	∅	2(picc)2(ca)22/4230/timp.perc.xyl/hp/str	29'45"-33'	OUP,1945	Misc 308 C

WALTON, William (cont)

CROWN IMPERIAL: Coronation march (1937, rev 1963)
    orig version
        arr Greenbaum   PC   112.2sx.1/2210/timp.perc/str   8'30"   OUP   14631 Cs Dp
        arr D.Stone   ∅   2221/2230/timp.perc.bell.tamtam/pf-duet/
                                  str   7'   OUP,1969   Misc 8088
    rev version   ∅   3(picc)2+ca.2+bcl.2+cbsn/4331/timp.2perc/hp.[org]/
                                  str   OUP,1967   Misc 8277
        reduced version by V.Tausky
                             ∅   2(picc)1+ca.22/4331/timp.perc.bell.glock.gong/
                                  hp.[org]/str   OUP,1967(H) PL 607
    excerpts (signature tune for programme 'An invitation to music')
                                  2(picc)1+ca.22/4230/timp.perc/hp/str   OUP(H)   PL 273
FAÇADE: an entertainment for reciter and chamber orch (1926)
    Complete
        orig version   ∅   1(picc)01(bcl).sx.0/0100/perc/vlc   38'40"   OUP,1951   CM 57383
    Orchestral versions
    Suite no.1
        1. Polka   (1'10")   4. Tango-Pasodoble   (1'45")
        2. Valse   (3')   5. Tarantella sevillana (2'15")
        3. Swiss yodelling song (2'50")
                             ∅   2(picc)2(ca)22/4[=2]11/timp.perc/str   11'   OUP   Misc 1807
                             ∅   2(picc)2(ca)22/4[=2]11/timp.perc.glock.xyl/   (Misc 6884 Cn &
                                  str   OUP,1968   (PL 307 Amv Bn Dni
    Suite no.2
        1. Fanfare   4. Noche espagnole
        2. Scotch rhapsody   5. Popular song   (4')
        3. Country dance   6. Old Sir Faulk   (1'45")   (Misc 1248 E &
                             ∅   2(picc)2+ca.2.sx.2/2210/perc/str   8'-10'30"   OUP,1938   (PL 308 Amv Bn Dni
    Special suite (1968)
        1. Polka   5. Popular song
        2. Valse   6. Old Sir Faulk
        3. Swiss yodelling song   7. Tarantella sevillana
        4. Tango-Pasodoble
                             ∅   2(picc)2+ca.2.sx.2/4[=2]210/timp.perc.glock.xyl/
                                  str   OUP,1968(H) PL 427 Amv
    Four dances, arr W.Goehr
        1. Polka (1'15")   3. Popular song: tap dance (2'15")
        2. Tango (1'50")   4. Tarantelle   (2'15")
                             PC   2(picc)121/2230/timp.perc/hp/str   OUP   16299 Dp Ewa Fs
    Tarantella sevillana
        arr S.Robinson   ∅   2222/0211/str   (OUP)   TO 1416
FAÇADE 2 for reciter & instruments (1917)
        1. Came the great popinjay   5. The Octogenarian
        2. Aubade   6. Gardener Janus catches a niad
        3. March   7. Water party
        4. Madam mouse toots   8. Said King Pompey
                             ∅   1(picc)01.asx.0/0100/perc/vlc   12'   OUP,1979   CM 56989 ∅ only
FANFARE: memorial for Sir Henry Wood
                             ∅   6+3picc.999/12.10.9.3/2timp.perc/3hp.org/str 2'30"   (Composer,1945) 25418 ∅ only
The FIRST OF THE FEW: film see SPITFIRE PRELUDE AND FUGUE
GOD SAVE THE QUEEN: National Anthem of Great Britain, arr
    in G   ∅   2+picc.32+bcl.2+cbsn/4331/timp.perc/2hp/str   Composer,1965 24162 + C
    Introduction to the National Anthem
                             ∅   0000/0330/mildm   OUP,1980   CM 57131
GLORIA for ATB soli, SSAATTBB chorus & orch (1961)
                             ∅   2+picc.2+ca.2+bcl.2+cbsn/4331/timp.perc(bells.xyl)
                                  hp.[org]/str   18'35"   OUP,1961   Misc 9220

WALTON, William (cont)

HAMLET: film music (1947)
   Extracts
     Fanfare in F
       arr M.Sargent   φ 0000/4331/timp.perc   OUP,1965   24304
     Funeral March
       arr M.Mathieson   φ 1+picc.222/423[1]/timp.perc/hp/str   OUP,1963   Misc 5841
     Hamlet and Ophelia: a poem for orchestra
       Concert version, arr M.Mathieson
                     φ 2(picc)2(ca)22/4231/timp.perc.glock/cel.hp/
                       str   13'-14'   OUP,1968   Misc 6674
HENRY V: film music
   Suite for chorus & orch
     1. Overture - The Globe Playhouse   3. Touch her soft lips and part
     2. Passacaglia: Death of Falstaff   4. Agincourt song
                     φ 3(2picc)2+ca.32/4331/timp.perc/hp.hpsd/str   (OUP)   15057 +
   Suite for chorus & orch, arr M.Mathieson
     1. Overture - The Globe Playhouse   3. Charge and Battle   5. Agincourt song
     2. Passacaglia - Death of Falstaff   4. Touch her soft lips and part   (Misc 5895 D &
       ed M.Sargent   φ 2(2picc)3(ca)33/4331/timp.perc/hp/str   OUP,1964   (PL 478 Amv
   Two pieces for strings
     1. Passacaglia: Death of Falstaff (2'45")   2. Touch her soft lips and part (1'45")
                     φ str   OUP,1947   21982 Bwe Ds
IMPROVISATIONS on an impromptu of Benjamin Britten
                     φ 3(picc)3(ca)3(bcl)3(cbsn)/4331/timp.perc.bells.glock.xyl/
                       hp/str   14'-15'   OUP,1970   Misc 7236
JOHANNESBURG FESTIVAL OVERTURE (1956)
                     φ 3(picc)2+ca.33(cbsn)/4431/timp.perc/hp/str 7'   OUP,1958   Misc 4867
   reduced version - V.Tausky   φ 2(picc)2(ca)22/4231/perc/hp/str   OUP(H)   PL 302 Agg
MUSIC FOR CHILDREN (1940)   φ 2(picc)2(ca)22/4231/timp.perc.glock.xyl/   (Misc 2083 B &
                       hp/str   12'   OUP,1941   (PL 602 Ani
NATIONAL ANTHEM   see   GOD SAVE THE QUEEN
ORB AND SCEPTRE: coronation march (1953)
   in E (orig), arr R.Douglas   PC 2+picc.222/4231/timp.perc/str   8'30"   OUP   21059
   in F, arr R.Douglas   φ 2(picc)222/4231/timp.perc/hp/str   OUP,1953   26328 +
     see also   ANNIVERSARY FANFARE
PARTITA for orchestra (1957)
   1. Toccata   2. Pastorale siciliana   3. Giga burlesca
                     φ 3(picc)2+ca.3(bcl)3(cbsn)/4331/timp.perc/
                       hp/str   OUP(H)   PL 376 As
PORTSMOUTH POINT: overture (1925)
                     φ 2(picc)+picc.2+ca.2+bcl.2+cbsn/4331/   (Misc 926 D &
                       timp.perc.tamtam.xyl/str   5'30"   OUP,1928   (PL 295 Amv Bn
A QUEEN'S FANFARE (for NATO Parliamentarians' Conference, London, June 1959)
                     φ 0000/0840   0'40"   OUP,1972   Misc 7780
The QUEST: ballet
   Suite
     1. Introduction (Storm) & The Magician and the transformation
     2. Siciliana (The Spell)
     3. The Challenge
     4. The Reunion (Passacaglia)
                     φ 2(picc)2(ca)22/4230/timp.perc.kglock/cel.hp/str   OUP,1962   Misc 5659 B
RICHARD III: film music (1955)
   Prelude
       arr M.Mathieson   φ 22(ca)2(bcl)2/423[1]/timp.perc/hp/str   7'30"   OUP,1964   Misc 5894 C
   A Shakespeare suite, arr M.Mathieson
     1. Fanfare   4. With drum and Colours
     2. Music plays   5. I would I knew thy heart
     3. The Princes in the Tower   6. Trumpets sound
                     φ 22[=1]22[=1]/4[=2]23[=2]0/[hp]/str   OUP,1964   24020

WALTON, William (cont)

SCAPINO: comedy overture (1940)   (Misc 3291 B &
    1950 rev edn   φ   3(picc)2+ca.3(bcl)2/4331/timp.perc.glock.xyl/   (mf 64
                 hp/str   8'-9'40"   OUP,1950

A SHAKESPEARE SUITE   see   RICHARD III
SIESTA for small orch (1926)   φ   1(picc)121/2000/str   4'-5'30"   OUP   14317 + Amv C
SINFONIA CONCERTANTE for piano & orch (1926-7, rev 1943)
   orig edn   φ   2+picc.2+ca.2+bcl.2+cbsn/4331/timp.perc/str 17'40"-19'   OUP,1928   Misc 930 C
   rev edn with reduced orch   φ   2+picc.2+ca.22/4231/timp.perc.glock.xyl/
                 pf/str   OUP,1953   Misc 3922 C

SONATA FOR STRING ORCHESTRA (adapted from String Quartet in A min)
                φ   str   25'   OUP,1973   25974

SPITFIRE PRELUDE AND FUGUE (from film 'The First of the Few')
                φ   2(picc)121/423[1]/timp.perc/hp/str   (Misc 5495 &
                  (with 2nd ob & 2nd bsn added by V.Tausky)   7'30"   OUP,1961   (PL 305 Agg

The STAR-SPANGLED BANNER (attrib J.S.Smith): National Anthem of the United States of America, arr
                φ   2+picc.32+bcl.2+cbsn/4331/timp.perc/2hp/str   Arranger,1965 24161 C +

SYMPHONIES   (Misc 1721 D &
   No.1, in Bb min (1935, corrected 1968)   (PL 272 Amv Bn
     orig edn   φ   2+picc.222/4331/timp.perc/str   39'-45'30"   OUP,1936
     corrected edn   φ   2(picc)222/4331/timp.perc/str   OUP,1968   Misc 7431
   No.2   φ   3(picc)3(ca)3(bcl)3(cbsn)/4331/timp.perc.glock.   (Misc 5419 &
                 vib.xyl/cel.2hp.pf/str   27'-28'30"   OUP,1960   (PL 270 Amv Bn

UNDER THE GREENWOOD TREE: song (from film 'As you like it')
   in G min, orch R.Douglas   φ   21+ca.22/2000/hp/str   (OUP)   20048
VARIATIONS ON A THEME BY HINDEMITH (1963)
                φ   3(picc)2+ca.2+bcl.2+cbsn/4331/timp.perc.bells.glock/
                 hp/str   21'-23'   OUP,1963   Misc 1440 C

VARII CAPRICCI (free transcriptions of 5 Bagatelles for guitar)
                φ   3(picc)2+ca.3(bcl)2/4331/timp.3perc(cel.glock.xyl)/
                 hp/str   14'   OUP   Misc 9443

The WISE VIRGINS: ballet suite arr from the works of J.S.Bach
   1. What God hath done is rightly done (2'30")   4. Ah! how ephemeral   (1'45")
   2. Lord, hear. my longing   (2'20")   5. Sheep may safely graze (6'45")
   3. See what His love can do   (3'55")   6. Praise be to God   (1'35")
     Complete   φ   2(picc)2(ca)22/4230/timp/hp/str   16'-19'30"   OUP   Misc 2154 D
     No.5 only   φ   21+ca.22/4000/hp/str   OUP   11816 B
       see also BACH, J.S. CANTATA no.208

WANGENHEIM, Volker (1928-
SINFONIA NOTTURNA   φ   2222/4231/timp/str   33'   Boosey & H,1965 Misc 6058

WANHAL, J.K.   see   VANHAL, J.K.

WANSKI, Jan (1762-c.1800)

SYMPHONIES
   in D (based on themes from the opera "Pasterz nad Wisla")
                φ   2000/1000/str   Polish SM,1962 Misc 6311
   in G (based on themes from the opera "Kmiotek")
                φ   2000/1000/str   Polish SM,1962 Misc 6311

WARD, David

CONCERTO for cello & orch (1978) φ   2(picc)1+ca.1+bcl+cbcl.1(cbsn)/31+Dtpt.flg.31/
                     timp.perc.crot.glock.kit.mrc.vib/hp/
                     str(12[=16].-.10[=12].8[=10].6[=8]) 35'   (Composer,1978) 26656 +

WARD, David (cont)

The DEATH OF FERDIA: chamber opera for male speaker, female dancer, S.Mz.TB soli & ensemble (1973)
     ϕ 1(picc;afl)0.ob-d'a.1+bcl.0/00[1]+btbn.0/
      dm-kit.dbm.mba.tamtam/hp/vla.vlc.cb   Composer 26062 +
A FULL MOON IN MARCH: chamber opera (1962/8)
     ϕ 1(picc)1(ca)1(bcl)0/0010/ptimp.perc.crot.glock.xyl/
      hp.2mand[1 player]/2vln.vla.vlc.cb   (Composer,1968) Misc 9931

WARD, Francis

INCANTATION: orchestral fantasy (1966)
     ϕ 2(picc)222/4230/timp.1perc(glock.tamtam.xyl)/
      hp.pf/str   8'30"   (Composer) Misc 9305

WARD, Lionel

L'HEURE GALANTE: baroque suite after Domenico Scarlatti
     PC 2222/2110/str   10'   Boosey & H 16360 B

WARD, Robert (1917-

INVOCATION AND TOCCATA ϕ 3+picc.2+ca.2+bcl.2/4331/timp.perc/str 9' Highgate Press,1975 Misc 8653
SYMPHONY no.1   ϕ 3(picc)2+ca.2+bcl.2+cbsn/4331/timp/str 15'
                  American Music Center Inc Misc 2183

WARE, Peter (1951-

TSANKAWI (1978)   ϕ 2(picc)222([cbsn])/3231/timp.perc.crot.glock.gong.
      3tomtom.vib/str   6'30" Alpheus,1978 Misc 10335

WARING, H.W.

GENTLEMAN JOHN: song
 in F, arr F.Collinson ϕ 1121/2220/perc/hp/str   Arranger MS 30965

WARLOCK, Peter (pseud of Philip Heseltine)(1894-1930)

CAPRIOL SUITE (1926, arr for orch 1928)
 1. Basse-danse   4. Bransles (2')
 2. Pavane (2')   5. Pieds en l'air (2'20")
 3. Tordion   6. Mattachins
  orig version   ϕ str   10'   Curwen 555 Bni Cs En Fwa
  orchestral version ϕ 2(picc)222/2231/perc/str   Curwen 8797 Cp Dn E
CAPTAIN STRATTON'S FANCY: song (orig voice & pf)
 in D, arr F.Cramer   pf/str   (Augener) LM G 4519
 in F, arr P.Hope   ϕ 2222/4230/timp.perc/hp/str   (Augener) 24682 +
The COUNTRYMAN: song (orig voice & pf)
 arr G.Williams for Tenor & orch
         ϕ 1121/2210/perc/str   Boosey & H MLO 299
The CURLEW: song cycle for Tenor & orch (1920-22)
         ϕ 10.ca.00/0000/str   Stainer & B CM 51423 B
6 ENGLISH TUNES, transcr & ed
 1. The Witch   4. Tickle my toe
 2. Daphne   5. Sweet youth
 3. Strawberry leaves 6. A Toy
         ϕ str   OUP 7209

WARLOCK, Peter (cont)

6 ITALIAN DANCE TUNES, transcr & ed
    1. Zorzi   4. La Manfrolina
    2. La Gamba   5. Le Forze d'Hercole
    3. Paduana del re   6. El Salterello

		φ str	8'15"	OUP	7210 Cwa
MR. BELLOC'S FANCY: song for voice & orch					
in E, arr F.Bye	φ	1121/0220/hp/str		Augener	MLO 760
in G, arr J.Brayfield	φ	pf/str		(Augener)	LM G 7910
An OLD SONG	φ	1110/1000/str	5'45"	Chester	4545 C
SERENADE for strings (1921-2)	φ	str	6'-7'30"	OUP	4688 Cwa
SORROW'S LULLABY for Soprano & Baritone soli & orch					
	φ	str-4tet or strings		OUP,127	3450 B
A VIRGIN UNSPOTTED: traditional song, arr					
in F		2222/4230/timp/hp/str/chorus		(Novello)	MLO 987
YARMOUTH FAIR: Norfolk folk song (orig voice & pf), arr					
in D, arr K.Regan		2(picc)222/4231/timp.perc/hp/str		(OUP)	22434 +
in E & G	VS	str		(OUP)	MLO 779

WARNER, H.Waldo (1874-1945)

The BROAD HIGHWAY (Sketches from a tramp's diary): suite, op.47
    1. Morning mist   5. The Church in the valley
    2. Blue hills   6. The Broad highway
    3. The Brook   7. Sundown
    4. Siesta

	φ	1(picc)111/2210/timp.perc/pf/str		J.Fischer	13932

3 ELFIN DANCES, op.10
    1. Elves   2. Nymphs   3. Gnomes

	PC	3(picc)222/4231/timp.perc/hp/str	10'	Chappell	3762 C

WARNER, Ken

ALWAYS ON THE FIDDLE	PC	112.3sx.1/0220/perc/gtr/str		P.Maurice	12294
FIDDLE FOR A LIVING	PC	112.3sx.0/0210/perc/gtr/str		P.Maurice	5139 B
FIDDLER'S DELIGHT	PC	112.3sx.1/0220/perc/gtr/str		P.Maurice	16582
HURRIED INTERLUDE		str		Paxton	19557 B
MINUET FOR AN IDLE MOMENT	PC	1111/0000/hp/str	4'	Hawkes,1954	21237 B
PIZZICATO PIECE	PC	str	2'30"	Paxton,1949	19832
SCRUB, BROTHER, SCRUB	PC	2(picc)22.3sx.1/0220/perc/gtr/str		P.Maurice	4927 Bp C
SHOPPING DAY	PC	2121/2230/timp.perc/acdn.hp/str	2'15"	Hawkes,1954	21388
TO AN IRISH LAKE					
arr F.Hartley	PC	1121/2220/perc/hp/str		P.Maurice	18834

WARR, Eric (1905-

The SONGS ERIN SINGS: traditional air, arr

in E♭	φ	str	Arranger MS:BBC	MS 20254

WARREN, Cyril

SO LITTLE TIME: song

in D, arr J.Turner	φ	1110/1000/hp/str	(Boosey)	LM G 9447
in D, arr C.Watters	φ	1110/1000/perc/cel.gtr.hp.pf/str	(Boosey)	LM G 6869

WARREN, Elinor Remick (1906-

SONNETS for Soprano solo & string orch
    1. Night is my sister
    2. Not in a silver casket
    3. Clearly my ruined garden
    4. If in a widened silence

	∅	str [=str-4tet]		Fischer,1974	Misc 8745

WARREN, Harry (1893-1981)

DAMES: film
  I only have eyes for you: song
    in C, arr P.Cardew   ∅ 2222/4330/timp.perc/hp.pf/str   (Feldman)   23699
The GLENN MILLER STORY: film
  I know why
    arr R.Green   ∅ 2222/4230/timp.perc/hp/str   2'45"   (Feist)   18433
The GOLD DIGGERS OF 1933: film
  Shadow waltz: song
    arr A.Sandford (non-vocal) ∅ 2222/4230/timp.perc/hp/str   (Feldman)   22196 +
SEPTEMBER IN THE RAIN: song
  in E♭, arr K.Warner (refrain only)
          ∅ 2222/4230/timp.perc/hp/str   (Feldman)   22248 +
  in G, arr R.Docker for chorus & orch
          ∅ 2120/0330/perc/gtr.hp.pf(cel)/str   3'   (Feldman)   25103 +
SONG OF THE MARINES ("We're shovin' right off again"): march
  arr Mason & Petersen   PC 111.4sx.1/2320/perc/gtr.mand/str   Feldman   15022
SUN VALLEY SERENADE: film
  Selection, arr D.Edge, orch B.Berlin
          ∅ 2121/2230/perc/hp/str/chorus   (FD & H)   TO 912
WEEK-END IN HAVANA: film
  Selection, arr D.Edge, orch B.Berlin
          ∅ 2121/2230/timp.perc/hp/str/chorus   (Boosey)   TO 985
WOULD YOU LIKE TO TAKE A WALK: song
  in E♭, arr J.Beaver   2121/2230/perc/hp/str   (FD & H)   TO 266

WARREN, Norman

MEMORIES COME GENTLY: music for TV production 'The Secret War', by N.Warren, A.Richards & L.Osborne
  arr I.Sutherland (1977)   ∅ 2100/4000/timp.perc(kit.vib)/gtr.pf/str   Arranger   MS 31782

WARREN, Raymond (1928-

MUSIC FOR HARLEQUIN: serenade for woodwind, brass & percussion
    1. Fanfare
    2. Pierrot
    3. Muted fanfare
    4. Harlequin and Columbine
    5. Pantaloon

          ∅ 1[=2]1[=2]3[=2][2]/2[=4]3[=2]2[1][=btbn=ttbn]/
            timp.perc   Novello,1966   24921

WASHBURN, Robert

PROLOGUE AND DANCE   ∅ 2(picc)222/4331/timp.2perc.bells.xyl/
             str   7'   OUP,1974   Misc 8568

WASSENAER, Unico Wilhelm, Graaf van (1692-1766)

see   DUNNING, Albert: Count Unico Wilhelm van Wassenaer. Buren: F.Knuf, 1980. Contains facsimile
      of MS of the 6 Concerti plus an essay on their authorship

6 CONCERTI ARMONICI (Concertini), 1st publ. C.Ricciotti, The Hague, 1740. (Walsh edn, 1755, attrib
      Ricciotti, later edns attrib Pergolesi)
      No.1, in G   No.2, in G   No.3, in A   No.4, in F min   No.5, in Eb   No.6, in Bb
      Complete 1-6, as attrib Pergolesi
                                    str   Gli Amici della Musica da Camera,1940   16981
      Complete facsimile of MS ∅ in copyist's hand, with annotations in composer's hand
                                    str/cont   F.Knuf,1980   BRL
      No.1, in G
            ed F.Caffarelli   str/cont   Gli Amici,1940   26981
            ed F.Caffarelli   ∅   str/cont   Gli Amici,1940   26982
            ed R.Fasano   ∅   str/cont   Ricordi,1961   25459
      No.2, in G
            ed F.Caffarelli   ∅   str/cont   Gli Amici,1940   26981
            ed F.Caffarelli   ∅   str/cont   Gli Amici,1940   26983
            ed T.Harvey   str   (Gli Amici,1940)   20264
            ed J.P.Hinnenthal   ∅   str/cont   Bärenreiter   26985
      No.3, in A   ∅   str/cont(org)   Henn   Misc 2501
            ed F.Caffarelli   str/cont   Gli Amici,1940   26981
            ed F.Caffarelli   str/cont   Gli Amici,1940   26984
            ed F.Caffarelli   str/cont   (Gli Amici,1940)   20378
      No.4, in F min
            ed F.Caffarelli   str/cont   Gli Amici,1940   21705 +
            ed F.Caffarelli   str/cont   Gli Amici,1940   26981
            ed J.P.Hinnenthal   ∅   str/cont   Bärenreiter   25677
      No.5, in Eb
            ed F.Caffarelli   ∅   str/cont   Gli Amici,1940   21381
            ed F.Caffarelli   str/cont   Gli Amici,1940   26981
            ed R.Fasano   ∅   str/cont   Ricordi,1961   25459
      No.6, in Bb
            ed F.Caffarelli   ∅   str/cont   Gli Amici,1940   20770 +
            ed F.Caffarelli   str/cont   Gli Amici,1940   26981

WASSIL, Bruno

GRAN VALZER (Intermezzo)   PC   2222/2210/timp.perc/str   Edn Cora   18950
MEDITAZIONE   PC   1111/2210/pf/str   Ricordi   19033
PRELUDIO   PC   1111/2210/str   Ricordi   19032

WATERS, Charles F.

IDYLL   ∅   str   Stainer & B,1938   25357

WATKINS, Michael Blake   see   BLAKE-WATKINS, Michael

WATSON, J.

JOHN ANDERSON MY JO
      arr M.L.Lake   PC   1+picc.12.2sx.1/2210/perc/str   C.Fischer   19720

WATSON, Michael

ANCHORED: song
      in G   1020/2210/perc/str   (AH & C)   LM G 4457
      in G, arr G.Stacey   [hp].org/str   (Blockley)   LM G 5499
HUSH YO' GENTLY, HONEY: song
      in Db, arr H.Carr   ∅   10.ca.2+bcl.1/2230/perc/hp/str   (Darewski)   TO 624

WATSON, Michael (cont)

I WISH TO TUNE MY QUIVERING LYRE
    in D, arr R.Burston as duet   φ   2121/2230/perc/hp/str   (AH & C)   TO 36
The POWDER-MONKEY: song
    in F, arr H.Carr   φ   112+bcl.1/2230/perc/hp/str   (Ashdown)   TO 707
The PRESS-GANG: song
    in G, arr A.Collins   φ   1+picc.121/2230/timp.perc/str   (Ashdown)   MS 7791

WATSON, Rosabel

The ROSE WITHOUT A THORN: incidental music
    Act 1 To open   Act 3 To open; after Sc.1; end of Sc.2; mummer's dance
    Act 2 To open; masque
                        pf.spinet/str   S.French   14253

WATTERS, Cyril

BARGAIN BASEMENT   PC 1121/2230/perc/hp/str   Boosey & H   19293
PICCADILLY SPREE   PC 2121/2230/timp.perc/acdn.gtr.hp/str   2'40"   Hawkes,1954   21387 C
The WILLOW WALTZ   φ   22(ca)22/4000/perc/hp/str   (Boosey & H,1958)   22949

WATTS, Wintter (1884-1962)

JOY: song
    in G, arr H.Carr   φ   31+ca.22/4231/timp.perc/hp/str   (Chappell)   TO 1789
The LITTLE SHEPHERD'S SONG
    in C, arr G.Stacey   pf/str   (Ricordi)   LM G 4282

WAYNE, Bernie

PORT-AU-PRINCE
    arr N.Riddle   φ   2121[=bcl]/2330/timp.perc.glock/str   2'20"   (Bosworth)   24791

WAYNE, Mabel (1904-

RAMONA: song
    in F   1121/2220/perc/pf/str   (FD & H)   LM G 4383

WEATHERLY, Fred

DANNY BOY: song
    in C, orch Redman   VS 1110/0210/perc/str   (Boosey)   LM G 4981

WEBB, Evelyn

SING ALOUD UNTO GOD OUR STRENGTH, **for SSAATTBB chorus & instruments**
                     φ   0000/0330/timp   Schott,1973   Misc 8050

WEBBE, Samuel (1740-1816)

COME YE DISCONSOLATE
    arr M.L.Lake   PC 1+picc.12.2sx.1/2210/perc/str   C.Fischer   19720
The MANSION OF PEACE **for voice & instruments**
                     φ   1000/2000/str/cont   I.Bland [c.1790]   CM 56847 φ on]

WEBBER, Andrew Lloyd (1948-

EVITA: musical
  Extracts
    Don't cry for me, Argentina
      arr P.Hope   ∅   2(picc)2(ca)22/4331/timp/hp.pf(cel)/str   Evita Music   26529
      arr J.McCarthy   ∅   2(picc)222/4331/timp.perc(kit.tamb.vib)/
                               gtr.hp.pf/str/[chorus]   (Arranger)   26493 +

WEBBER, W.L.Lloyd

LENTO in E   ∅   str   Hinrichsen   19419
3 SPRING MINIATURES
  1. Gossamer: a little waltz   3. Tree tops: a toccatina
  2. Willow song: a lament
                          PC   1111/0000/str   Elkin,1954   22329
WALTZ, in F min   ∅   str   Hinrichsen   19418

WEBER, Alain (1930-

ALPHA: 5 easy pieces
  Nos 1-3 only   ∅   1000/0000/str(no vla or cb)(fl in no.2 only)   EMT,1978   Misc 9969

WEBER, Carl Maria von (1786-1826)

see   JÃHNS, F.W.: Chronologisch-thematisches Verzeichniss.   Berlin: Schlesinger, 1871.
      The numbers prefixed 'J' refer to entries in this book

COMPLETE WORKS

C.M. von Weber: Musikalische Werke: erste kritische Gesemtausgabe, ed H.J.Moser, W.Kaehter &
L.K.Mayer. Ausburg: Filser, 1926

ABU HASSAN: opera, J.106
  Complete (corrected to agree with Boosey's hired material)
    arr W.W.Göttig   ∅   2(picc)222/2210/timp.perc/gtr/str   44'30"
                                                           Werner Dohany (Offenbach am Main,c.1925)   Misc 4011 B
      English translation by D.Harris
                          ∅   2222/2210/timp.perc/2gtr/str   (Schlesinger)   21273 +
    Overture   ∅   1+picc.222/2210/timp.perc/str   3'35"-4'   Schlesinger   4826 + Amv BsCn D
                          PC   1+picc.222/4231/timp.perc/str   Benjamin   1064
      arr A.Winter   PC   1+picc.222/2230/timp.perc/str   Boosey & H   12820 B +
  Extracts
    Wass nun zu machen (What shall I do?): aria (no.2)
      in E (orig D).   English by D.Harris
                          2202/2200/timp/2gtr/str   (Schlesinger)   21274
        O Fatima: aria (part of no.2)
          in Eb (orig F)   1022/2000/str   (Siddell)   17913
ADAGIO AND RONDO for harmonichord (or harmonium) & orch, J.115
                          ∅   2202/2200/timp/str   Peters   Misc 2113
ANDANTE AND RONDO UNGARESE for viola & orch, J.79
  ed G.Schünemann   ∅   2202/2200/timp/str   9'   Schott,1938   22488
  adapted for bassoon & orch, op.35, J.158
                          PC   2202/2200/timp/str   R.Lienau   24689
                          ∅   2202/2200/str   (Schlesinger)   Misc 4188 +
ANDANTE CON VARIAZIONE, op.10, no.3, J.83, in G (orig pf duet)
  orch & arr Schreiner   ∅   str   Geissel   8795

WEBER, Carl Maria von (cont)

AUFFÖRDERUNG ZUM TANZ (Invitation to the dance), J.260 (orig pf duet)

arr H.Berlioz	∅	1+picc.224/42.2cnt.30/timp/2hp/str	8'30"-10'30"	Joubert	16742
arr H.Berlioz	∅	1+picc.224/42.2cnt.30/timp/2hp/str		Breitkopf	4271 + Amv Bs C
arr H.Berlioz with ending by A.Toscanini					
	∅	1+picc.224/42.2cnt.30/timp/2hp/str		Breitkopf	4271 + Amv only
arr B.Berlin for voices & orch, in C					
	∅	2121/2220/timp.perc/hp/str/voices		BBC	TO 222
arr M.Johnstone	∅	2+picc.222/4230/timp.perc.glock/hp/str	9'	Lengnick(H)	PL 301 An
arr M.Johnstone (signature tune for programme 'Invitation to the dance')					
		2122/4000/hp/str		Lengnick	23747 + (∅ PL 3(
arr Lind & Gibilaro for voices & orch, in B♭					
		pf/str		(Boosey)	LM G 3295
arr G.Stacey for voices & orch, in C					
		00[1]0/0000/[acdn].pf/str		(FD & H)	LM G 3063
arr F.Weingartner	∅	2+picc.32+E♭cl.3/4330/timp.perc.glock/hp/str		Fürstner	6132 Amv B
arr L.Weninger	PC	1+picc.222/4230/timp/hp/str		Benjamin	464 C
arr A.Winter	∅PC	1121/1210.euph/perc/str		Boosey & H	14238
arr C.Woodhouse	PC	2222/2230.euph/perc/str		Lafleur	906
arr C.Woodhouse & F.Weingartner for voices & orch, in D					
	PC	1121/2221/timp.perc/hp/str		Hawkes	9048 Bgg D
arr C.Woodhouse & F.Weingartner					
	∅	2(picc)222/4231/timp.perc.glock/hp/str		Boosey & H	16440

Finale only (last 13 bars)

arr A.Toscanini	∅	1+picc.220/4020/str		(Arranger)	Misc 4537

BEHERRSCHER DER GEISTER: overture, op.27, J.122 (probably a revision of an earlier overture to
'Rubezahl')

	∅	1+picc.222/4230/timp/str	5'15"-7'	Breitkopf	8437 + Amv Cn
arr Schreiner	PC	1+picc.222/4230/timp.perc/str		Benjamin	1037

BLÜTHENKRANZ (Musical blossoms): selection of famous melodies by Weber, arr Schreiner & L.Weninger for
oboe & trumpet soli & orch

	PC	2(picc)222/4230/perc/str		Benjamin	474

CONCERTI (see also CONCERTINI)

Bassoon & orch

op.75, J.127, in F	∅	2202/2200/timp/str	18'	Schlesinger	3459 B +

Clarinet & orch

No.1, op.73, J.114, in F min

	∅PC	2202/3200/timp/str	19'	Breitkopf	6420 +

No.2, op.74, J.118, in E♭

	∅	2202/2200/timp/str	22'	Breitkopf	8579 B +

Piano & orch

No.1, op.11, J.98, in C	∅	2202/2200/timp/str	18'	J.André	22273 +
rev Schönzeler	∅	2202/2200/timp/str		Eulenburg	Misc 5379 B
No.2, op.32, J.155	∅	2022/2200/timp/str	22'	Schlesinger	20893 +
rev Schönzeler	∅	2022/2200/timp/str		Eulenburg	Misc 5380 B

CONCERTINI

Clarinet & orch, op.26

op.26, J.109, in E♭	∅	1202/2200/timp/str	10'	Breitkopf	7826
	∅	1022/2200/timp/str		Eulenburg,1954	Misc 9185
rev R.Fiske	∅	1022/2200/timp/str		Eulenburg,1954/1971	Misc 9185 B only

Horn & orch

op.45, J.188, in E min	∅	1022/2200/timp/str		Schlesinger	10268 +

Oboe & wind

in C

ed H.Dechant	∅	1042/2110/cb		Musica Rara,1981	27068

CONCERTSTÜCK for piano & orch, op.79, J.282, in F min

	∅	2222/2210/timp/str	16'20"	Breitkopf	6177 Amv B
	∅	2222/2210/timp/str		Simrock	14156

<u>WEBER, Carl Maria von</u> (cont)

Die DREI PINTOS: unfinished comic opera, J.Anh 1, no.5
   Completed by G.Mahler   φ 2222/4331/timp.perc/str   Kahnt   Misc 3210
   Extracts
       Höchste Lust ist treues Lieben: arietta (no.9)
         in D   φ 2222/2000/perc/str   (Kahnt)   Misc 5629 +
DURCH WEBERS ZAUBERWALD (In the magic wood of Weber): selection on works of Weber, arr E.Urbach
                PC 2222/4230/timp.perc/str   17'15"   Wrede   9412
6 ÉCOSSAISES, J.29-34 (orig pf), arr de Kresz
               φ str   5'   Chester   916
ERNTE-CANTATA: overture, J.Anh IV, no.107 (authenticity doubtful)
                  2222/2210/timp/str   Peters,1854 22101
Der ERSTE TON: music for reciter, chorus & orch, J.58 (1808, rev 1810)
   English translation by B.Asheore
               φ 2222/2230/timp/str   BBC   24638 + & mf 256
EURYANTHE: opera, J.291
   Complete   φ 2222/4230/timp/str
                   On stage: 0.2picc.222/4330/timp   152'Schlesinger/Gregg,1969 Misc 6958
      ed F.Stiedry   φ 2222/4230/timp/str
                   On stage: 0.2picc.222/4330/timp   Novello   21629 +
   Overture   φ 2222/4230/timp/str   7'45"-8'30" Breitkopf 4269 +AmvBs En Fwa
      ed E.Elgar   φ 2222/4230/timp/str   Peters   R Misc 3839
      arr A.Winter   φ 2222/4230/timp/str   Hawkes   6091 C
   Extracts
       Glöcklein in Thale (Euryanthe's cavatine): aria (Act 1, no.5)
         in C (orig)(Bells in the valley)
                 PC 2222/2000/str   4'   Bote & B   406
         in C (Morn now is breaking)
               φ 2222/2000/str   (Siddell) 17906
       Unter blüh'nden Mandelbäumen (Adolar's romance): aria (Act 1, no.2)
         in Bb (orig)(When the orb of day)
                 2022/2000/str   (Siddell) 17907
       Wehen mir Lüfte Ruh': aria (Act 2, no.12)
         in Ab (orig)(Waft me, ye Zephyrs)
                 PC 2022/0000/str   Bote & B   1057
         in Ab   2022/0000/str   (Siddell) 17908
       Wo berg' ich mich: scene & aria (Act 2, no.10)
         in C min (orig)(I fain would hide)
                 2222/4200/timp/str   Breitkopf 10260 B
Der FREISCHÜTZ: opera, J.277
   Complete   φ 2+2picc.222/4231/timp/str
                   On stage: 0020/2100/2vln.vlc   Peters   Misc 7602
               φ 2+2picc.222/4231/timp/str
                   On stage: 0020/2100/2vln.vlc   Schlesinger 21189 + B
      ed H.Albert, rev S. de Haan
               φ 2+2picc.222/4230/timp/str
                   On stage: 0010/2100/2vln.vlc   Eulenburg,1976 Misc 9186
      ed K.Soldan   φ 2+2picc.222/4230/timp/str
                   On stage: 0010/2100/2vln.vlc   Peters,1926 Misc 6306 B
   Overture   φ 2222/4230/timp/str   9'-10'20" Breitkopf 4270 Amv Cs Dn Fwa G
      ed E.Elgar   φ 2222/4230/timp/str   Peters   R Misc 3839
      ed Pringsheim & Artok φ 1121/2210/timp/str   Schott   12662
      arr L.Weninger PC 2222/4230/timp/str   Benjamin 786 Cwe
      arr A.Winter   φ 2222/4230/timp/str   Hawkes   11552 Cwe
   Selections
      arr Fétras   PC 2(picc)222/4230/timp.perc/str   13'   Benjamin 12396
      arr Jullien, orch C.Mackerras
               φ 2222/4230/timp.perc/str   (GB-Lbm) 22919 + & mf 109

WEBER, Carl Maria von (cont)

Der FREISCHÜTZ (cont)
   Selections (cont)
      arr O.Langey   PC   2222/2230.euph/perc/str   Hawkes   3164
      arr Moses   PC   1121/2210/timp.perc/str   C.Fischer   16946
   Extracts
      Durch die Wälder (Through the forests): aria (Act 1, no.3)
      Nein, länger trag' ich nicht die Qualen: recit
         in Eb (orig)   2222/4000/timp/str   7'   Breitkopf   17157 B
         in Eb   ø   2222/4230/timp/str   BBC   TO 500
         in Eb   ø   2222/4000/timp/str   Bote & B   9265
      Einst träumte meiner sel'gen Base (My aunt, poor soul): aria (Act 3, no.13)
         in G min (orig)   2022/2000/str   (Siddell)   18249
      Entr'acte to Act 2   ø   2222/4210/timp/str   BBC   19401
      Hier im ird'schen Jammerthal (Drinking song): rondo (Act 1, no.4)
         in B min (orig)(Life is darkened)
                         2202/0000/str   (Siddell)   18012
      Kommt ein schlanker Bursch gegangen (Comes a gallant youth): aria (Act 2, no.7)
         in C (orig)   ø   2202/2000/str   3'30"   (Siddell)   18075
      Leise, leise (Softly sighs): aria (Act 2, no.8)
      Wie nahte mir (Before my eyes): recit
         in E (orig)   ø   2222/4000/str   8'-8'25"   Bote & B   20423
         in E   ø   2222/4000/str   Breitkopf   6178 Amv C
         in E   ø   2222/4000/timp/str   Bote & B   9266
      Schelm! Halt fest (Come, be gay): duet (Act 2, no.6)
         in A (orig)   2022/2000/str   (Siddell)   18243
      Schweig', schweig' (Haste, haste): Caspar's aria (Act 1, no.5)
         in D min (orig)   2+picc.222/4230/timp/str   3'   (Siddell)   18011
         in E min   ø   2+2picc.222/4230/timp/str   BBC   TO 439
      Und ob die Wolke sie verhülle (Though clouds): aria (Act 3, no.12)
         in Ab (orig)   ø   0202/2000/str   4'-5'30"   (Siddell)   18017
         in A   0202/2000/str   (Siddell)   18016
FROM CHINDARA'S WARBLING FOUNT I COME: aria for Soprano, J.308 (from Thomas Moore's 'Lalla Rookh')
   in C, orch T.Müller-Reuter   ø   2222/2000/str   (BBC)   21755
GRAND POLONAISE, op.21, J.59
   arr Schmidt-Kothen   PC   2121/3220/timp.perc/str   8'   Oertel   7775
GRAND OUVERTURE À PLUSIEURS INSTRUMENTS   see   PETER SCHMOLL: overture
HOLD IST DER CYANENKRANZ: song for the festival 'Weinberg an der Elbe', for SATB soli, chorus & orch,
   J.260   ø   2222/2200/timp/str   Peters   18675
IN SEINER ORDNUNG SCHAFFT DER HERR: hymn for SATB soli, chorus & orch, op.36, J.154
                ø   2222/2210/timp/str   Schlesinger   Misc 2663 C
INVITATION TO THE DANCE   see   AUFFÖRDERUNG ZUM TANZ
JUBEL-CANTATA, for SATB soli, chorus & orch, op.58,J.244
                ø   2222/4230/timp/str   Schlesinger   Misc 2544
JUBEL-OVERTURE: concert overture, op.54, J.243
                ø   2+picc.222/4230/timp.perc/str   9'   Breitkopf   431
   ed E.Elgar   ø   2+2picc.222/4230/timp.perc/str   Peters   R Misc 3839
   arr A.Winter (with alternative ending, omitting 'God save the King')
                PC   2222/4230/timp.perc/str   Hawkes   1415
KAMPF UND SIEG: cantata for soli, chorus & orch, op.44, J.190
                ø   2(picc)222/4230/timp.perc/str   Schlesinger   5679 +
MARCH for wind ensemble, J.307, in C (1826)(rev of pf duet, J.13)
   ed G.Meerwein   ø   1222/2210   DVfM,1975   26140
   ed G.Meerwein   ø   1222/2210   Musica Rara [1976]   26140 B only
MASSES
   No.1, op.75, J.224, in Eb, for SATB soli, chorus & orch
                ø   2222/2200/timp/org/str   Richault   22000

WEBER, Carl Maria von (cont)

MASSES (cont)
    No.2, op.76, J.251, in G, for SATB soli, chorus & orch
                                ∅   2222/2200/str   Haslinger   Misc 2415 B
                                ∅   2222/4201/timp/str   Novello   25349
        Offertorium only, J.250 ∅   2222/2200/timp/str   (D-ddr Bds)   26104 & mf 285
MOMENTO CAPRICCIOSO for piano & orch, op.12, J.56
    arr F.Salabert   PC   1110/0110/timp.tri/str   Salabert   10829 B
OBERON: opera, J.306
    Complete   ∅   2+2picc.222/4230/timp.perc/str   Schlesinger   21506 + ∅ & negs
    Overture   ∅   2222/4230/timp.perc/str   8'45"-9'45" Breitkopf   4272 Amv Bwe Cs)
                                                                                                   Fn Gwa)
                                PC   2222/4230.euph/timp.perc/str   Hawkes   767 B
        ed E.Elgar   ∅   2222/4230/timp.perc/str   Peters   R Misc 3839
        arr J.Burger   PC   1111/1110/timp.perc/str   Schott   12627
    Selections
        arr Hubans   PC   2(picc)122/2230/timp.perc/str   Margueritat   1360
        arr E.Tavan   PC   2222/2231/timp.perc/str   Margueritat   4506
    Extracts
        From boyhood trained: aria
            in Db   2222/4210/timp/str   Arranger   19399
        I revel in hope: aria (Act 3, no.20)
            in Eb   2222/2000/str   (Schlesinger)   25611
        Lonely Arab maid: arietta
            in E min (orig)   ∅   2022/0000/str   (Siddell)   17912
        March   ∅   1+picc.222/4440/timp.perc/str   Arranger   19398
        O Araby, dear Araby: Fatima's romance
            in G min (orig)   2022/0000/str   (Siddell)   17910
        Ocean, thou mighty monster (Ozean, du Ungeheuer): scene & aria
            in Eb (orig)   ∅PC 2222/4230/timp/str   9'30"   Breitkopf   5027 Amv B
            in Eb   ∅   2222/4230/timp/str   Bote & B   4863
        Oh 'tis a glorious sight: aria (Interpolation, not in original score), J.306/23
        Yes, even love: recit
            in D (orig)   1222/4230/timp/str   (Siddell)   17909
            in Db   1122/4221/timp/str   Arranger   19400
        Over the dark blue waters: quartet
            in D (orig)   1222/2200/str   (Siddell)   17911
PERPETUUM MOBILE (Rondo 'L'Infatigable' from sonata for piano no.1, op.24), J.138.
    arr G.Szell   ∅   2+picc.222/4231/timp.perc/[cel]/str Boosey & H   Misc 2082 C
    in C, arr Flotsam (i.e.J.P.Hilliard), for chorus & orch
                                ∅   2121/2230/timp/hp str   BBC   TO 61
PETER SCHMOLL UND SEINE NACHBARN: opera, J.8
    Complete   ∅   2(picc)222/2210/timp/str   Filser,1926.CW 2/1 MRL
    Overture, J.54 (not the original overture, but a revised version of 1807, also published with the
            title 'Grande Ouverture à plusieurs instruments')
                                ∅   2222/2210/timp/str   Schlesinger   11390 Bp
        arr A.Evans   PC   2222/2230.euph/timp/str   Hawkes   231 B
6 PIECES FOR PIANO, op.3   see   SERENADE
POLONAISE BRILLANTE for piano & orch, op.72, J.268 (orig pf solo)
    orch F.Liszt [S.367]   ∅   2222/2230/timp.perc/str   8'   Schlesinger   16899
    arr Schmidt-Kothen (Polacca brillante)
                                PC   2121/3220/timp.perc/str   Oertel   7775
PRECIOSA: opera, J.279
    Complete   ∅   2222/2200/timp.perc/str   Schlesinger   Misc 2280
        ed L.K.Mayer   ∅   2(2picc)222/4220/timp.perc/str
                                On stage: 0.2picc(fl)022/4000/perc   Filser,1939.CW 2/3 MRL

WEBER, Carl Maria von (cont)

PRECIOSA (cont)
   Overture   ø   2222/2200/timp.perc/str   7'-8'   Breitkopf   4273

Overture	ø	2222/2200/timp.perc/str	7'-8'	Breitkopf	4273
arr Evans	PC	2222/2230.euph/timp.perc/str		Hawkes	2895 Awa Bwa
ROMANZE APPASSIONATA for cello & orch					
	PC	2222/2210/timp.perc/str		Oertel	7777
RUBEZAHL: opera, J.44-6					
Fragments only	ø	2222/2300/timp/str		Filser,1928.CW 2/2	MRL
see also BEHERRSCHER VON DER GEISTER: overture					
SCHERZO, op.39, J.199 (orig pf)					
orch A.Schmid	PC	1121/1210/timp.perc/str		G.Schirmer	4934
SERENADE (from 6 pieces for pf, op.3)					
arr H.Freudenthal	ø	str		Gehrmans,1944	22146
SILVANA: opera, J.87					
Complete	ø	2(picc)222/2210/timp/str		Filser.CW 2/2	MRL
Overture	ø	2202/2210/timp/str	6'30"	Schlesinger	6395
arr Schimak	PC	1110/0110/timp/str (no vlas)		Wrede	10623
arr A.Winter	PC	2222/4230/timp/str		Boosey & H	12044
Extracts					
Wie war ich so heiter: aria					
Er geht! er hört mich nicht: recit					
in C (orig)	ø	2202/2000/str		([Filser.CW 2/2])	21315
Das STUMME WALDMÄDCHEN: opera, J.Anh.1					
Fragments only					
ed A.Lorenz	ø	2200/2200/timp/str		Filser.CW 2/1	MRL
SYMPHONIES					
No.1, op.19, J.50, in C	ø	1202/2200/timp/str	21'45"-23'	André	6172 Amv +
ed F.Oeser	ø	1202/2200/timp/str		Bruckner-verlag	21252
No.2, J.51, in C	ø	1202/2200/timp/str	21'	Schlesinger	13440
TURANDOT: incidental music, op.37, J.75					
Overture					
arr Gorgel	PC	1+picc.222/2210/timp.perc/str	6'	Benjamin	7880
Overture & March	ø	1+picc.222/2210/timp.perc/str	3'20"	Breitkopf	4807
Das WALDMÄDCHEN see Das STUMME WALDMÄDCHEN					

WEBER, Henry

Die TONI VON OBERAMMERGAU: Ländler & waltzes on original Bavarian melodies				
	PC	112.3sx.1/2231/perc.glock/str	Cranz (Odeon)	12138
WITH STRAUSS, J. (ii): selection from waltzes by Johann Strauss (ii)				
	PC	1(picc)12.3sx.1/2220/timp.perc/str	Cranz	10962

WEBER, Ludwig (1899-1947)

STREICHERMUSIK	ø	str	Kallmeyer,1927	Misc 3847

WEBERN, Anton von (1883-1945)

Das AUGENLICHT (The light of the eye), for chorus & orch, op.26				
	ø	111.sx.0/1110/timp.glock.xyl/cel.hp.mand/str(no cb)	5'20"-7'09"	Universal,1956	Misc 4756
CANTATAS				
No.1, op.29, for Soprano solo, chorus & orch (1944)				
	ø	111+bcl.0/1110/timp.perc/cel.hp.mand/str	7'15"-8'47"	Universal,1957	Misc 4812
No.2, op.31, for Soprano & Bass soli, chorus & orch (1944)				
	ø	1+picc.1+ca.1+bcl.sx.1/1111/bells.glock/cel.hp/str	12'50"-16'	Universal,1956	Misc 6294

WEBERN, Anton von

IM SOMMERWIND: idyll (1904)   ∅   32+ca.4+bcl.2/6200/timp.perc/2hp/str   12'08"   C.Fischer,1966   Misc 6293

LIEDER <u>see</u> SONGS

5 MOVEMENTS for strings, freely transcribed from quintet, op.5 (1929)
                       ∅   str   Universal,1961   Misc 5643

PASSACAGLIA, op.10   ∅   2+picc.2+ca.2+bcl.2+cbsn/4331/timp.perc.tamtam/
                            hp/str   9'10"-11'15"   (Misc 904 D &
                                                   Universal,1922/50   (PL 556 Amv

5 PIECES for small orch, op.10   ∅   1(picc)11+Ebcl+bcl.0/1110/perc.glock.xyl/
                               cel.hmn.hp.mand/str-5tet   Universal,1923/51   Misc 1505 E

5 PIECES (1913)
    ed F.Cerha (Nos.2 & 4 are incomplete)
                          ∅   2+picc.2+ca.2+Ebcl+bcl.2+cbsn/43+Ebbtpt.31/
                               timp.perc.bells.glock.tamtam/cel.gtr.hmn.hp/
                               vln.vla.vlc.cb   Fischer,1971   Misc 9788

6 PIECES, op.6
    orig version for large orch   ∅   4(2picc;afl)2+2ca.3(Ebcl)+bcl.2(cbsn)/6641
                                     3timp.perc.bells.glock.tamtam.whip/cel.2hp/
                                     str   9'59"-12'   (Misc 1142 C &
                                               Universal,1961/Philharmonia   (PL 585
    reduced orchestration   ∅   2(picc)22+bcl.2(cbsn)/4441/timp.perc.bells.glock.tamtam/
                                     cel.hp/str   10'45"-12'20"
                                                 Universal,1956   Misc 5551 B
    arr for chamber ensemble   ∅   111(Ebcl)0/0000/perc.bells.tamtam/hmn.pf/
                                     2vln.vla.vlc   (Composer)   Misc 8160

SKETCHES (1926-1945).   Facsimile reproductions from the composer's autograph sketchbooks in the
      Moldenhauer Archive - [the works contained are all unpublished]
    commentary by E.Krenek, with a foreward by H.Moldenhaur   C.Fischer,1967   Misc 6896 MRL fac s

3 SONGS for Soprano & small orch
    1. Leise Düfte (Gentle fragrance)   3. O sanftes Glühn der Berge (Oh gentle maintain radience)
    2. Knufttag III (Advent III)
      ed P.Westergaard, with completion of no.2
                        ∅   0.picc.1+ca.1+bcl.0/1120/timp.perc.bells.glock/
                               cel.gtr.hmn.hp.mand/vln.vla.vlc.2cb-soli   Boosey & H,1968   Misc 7378

4 SONGS for Soprano & small orch (1917-18)
    1. Wiese im Park (Lawn in the park)(2'30")   3. In der Fremde (In a strange land) (1')
    2. Die Einsame (Lonely girl)(1'30")   4. Ein Winterabend (A winter evening)(2')
    English words E.Smith   ∅   1(picc)01+bcl.0/1110/glock/cel.hp/str   Universal,1954   Misc 6042

SYMPHONY for small orch, op.21   ∅   001+bcl.0/2000/hp/str   8'40"-10'10"   Universal   (Misc 903 C &
                                                                       (PL 677 Amv

VARIATIONS for orch, op.30   ∅   111+bcl.0/1111/timp/cel.hp/str   5'50"-6'15"   (Misc 4511 &
                                                       Universal,1956   (PL 676 Amv

WEBSTER, J.B.

' IN THE SWEET BY AND BY: song
    in G, arr M.L.Lake   PC   1+picc.12.2sx.1/2210/perc/str   C.Fischer   19720

WEBSTER, P.F.

LOVE IS A MANY SPENDOURED THING: song by P.F.Webster & S.Fain
    in C, arr P.Hope   ∅   0010/0000/gtr.pf/str   Robbins   LM G 8142
    in E, arr S.Torch for Soprano & Baritone soli
                      ∅   21+ca.22/4331/timp.perc.glock.vib/pf/str   (Robbins)   24788 +

WECKER, Georg Kaspar (1632-1695)

ALLEIN GOTT IN DER HÖHE SEI EHR: Geistliches Konzert for SSATTB voices & orch
    ed A.Sondberger   ∅   0001/02.2cnt.00/org/str(2vln.2vla.vlne)/
                               cont   Breitkopf & H,1901.DDTB 6/1   MRL

WECKER, Georg Kaspar (cont)

HERR JESU, ZEUCH MICH DIR NACH: Geistliches Konzert am h.Himmelfahrts-Fest, for SS[=T]AB voices & orch
   ed A.Sondberger   ø 2vln[=2ob].vla/org[=vlne]/cont   Breitkopf & H,1901.DDTB 6/1   MRL
ICH WEISS, DASS MEIN ERLÖSER LEBET: Geistliches Konzert for SS[=T]AB voices & orch (1695)
   ed A.Sondberger   ø org[=vlne]/str/cont   Breitkopf & H,1901.DDTB 6/1   MRL

WECKERLIN, Jean Baptiste (1821-1910)

La FORÊT: symphony, in F	ø	2(picc)222/4230/timp.perc/org/str		Brandus	Misc 618
JEUNES FILLETTES: 18th cent. bergerette					
in A min, orch S.Robinson	ø	str		(Heugel)	21859 +
MAMAN, DITES-MOI: 18th cent. bergerette					
in D, orch S.Robinson	ø	str	2'35"	(Heugel)	21860 +
NON, JE N'IRAI PLUS AU BOIS: 18th cent. bergerette					
in A min, orch S.Robinson	ø	2222/1000/hp/str		(Heugel)	21861
La ROMANESCA	ø	2222/2000/perc/hp/str		Richault [c.1866]	Misc 861
RUY BLAS					
Stars of night: serenade, arr H.Balfour					
	PC	1222/2230.euph/str		Hawkes	2898 B

WECKMANN, Matthias (1619-1674)

ES ERHUB SICH EIN STREIT, for SSSAATTBB chorus & orch				
ed M.Seiffert	ø	0000/0300/str	Breitkopf & H,1901.DDT 6	MRL
KOMMET HER ZU MIR ALLE		str/cont(hpsd)		BBC MS 30126
WEINE NICHT: motet for ATB voices & instruments				
ed M.Seiffert	ø	str(vln.1.2.3.vla-d'g.1.2.3)	Breitkopf & H,1901.DDT 6	MRL
WENN DER HERR DIE GEFANGENEN ZU ZION, for SATB voices & orch				
ed M.Seiffert	ø	org/str	Breitkopf & H,1901.DDT 6	MRL & Misc 2045

WEERSMA, Melie

PENNY SERENADE: song			
in F, arr K.Warner	ø	2222/1230/timp.perc/hp/str	(World Wide) 22237 +

WEHRLI, J.U.

SEMPACH: Swiss air			
arr A.Scassola	VS	1221/2230/timp.perc/str	Foetisch 6425

WÉI, Jūe

The WHITE-HAIRED GIRL
    1. Towering, irrepressible anger   4. Deep hatred
    2. The North wind blows   5. Fleeing the tiger-lair
    3. A Thread of red wool   6. Celebrating liberation
           ø 2+picc.222/4231/timp.perc.glock.tamtam/hp/
               str (also various Chinese instruments: see
               score for details)   [Chinese SM]   Misc 9843

WEIGL, Karl (1881-1949)

RHAPSODY in D min, op.30	ø	str	30'	Universal Misc 2832

WEILL, Kurt (1900-1950)

AUFSTIEG UND FALL DER STADT MAHAGONNY: opera
   Suite   ø 2(2picc)11.asx.tsx(ssx)2/223[1]/timp.perc/
                   bgtr.bjo.pf/str   25'   Universal,1968   Misc 7875

<u>WEILL, Kurt</u> (cont)

Das BERLINER REQUIEM for TBar soli, mv chorus [=TBarB soli] & orch (1928, rev 1931)
    ed D.Drew   ∅   002.2asx(tsx)2/222[1]/timp.perc/bjo.gtr.org[=hmn]   Universal,1967   Misc 9372

CONCERTO for violin & wind instruments, op.12
                       ∅   2(picc)122/2100/timp.perc.xyl/cb   Universal,1965   Misc 6100

Die DREIGROSCHENOPER (The Beggar's Opera): opera in 3 acts
    Complete   ∅   1(picc)02(4sx;bcl)1/0210/timp.perc.bells/
                                bandoneon(mand).bjo(Hawaian gtr).gtr.hmn(cel).pf/   (Misc 7872 &
                                vlc.cb   Universal,1956   (26603 **

    Extracts
        Die Moritat von Mackie Messer
            arr R.Hanmer   PC   212.4sx.1/2330/timp.perc/acdn.gtr/str   Acardia,1956   21909 B
          <u>see also</u>   KLEINE DREIGROSCHENMUSIK

HAPPY END: opera
    ed A.Boustead (score only)   ∅   1(cl,asx)01(tsx,bsx)00/0210/1perc(bells.tamtam.
                                 tomtoms)/bjo(bandoneon[=acdn],bgtr,Hawaian gtr[=mand],
                                 pf(hmn)   Universal,1980   CM 57374

    Extracts
        Surabaya Johnny
            arr G.Langford for Contralto solo & orch with rhythm section
                         ∅   1221/0210/rhythm-[gtr].kit.pf/str   (Universal)   26691

KLEINE DREIGROSCHENMUSIK (Little Threepenny Music): suite for **wind** ensemble
    1. Ouverture (Overture)(2'30")
    2. Die Morität von Mackie Messer (The Moritat of Mack the Knife)(1'30"-2'30")
    3. Anstatt dass (The Instead-of-Song)(1'30"-2')
    4. Die Ballade von angenehmen Leben (The Ballad of the easy life)(3')
    5. Pollys Lied (Polly's Song)(2'30"-3')
    5a.Tang-Ballade (Tango-Ballad)(2'30"-3')
    6. Kanonen-song (Cannon Song)(2'30"-3')
    7. Dreigroschen-finale (Threepenny finale)(3'30"-4'30")
                       ∅   2(picc)02.asx.tsx(ssx)2/0211/timp.perc/bells/
                              [acdn].bjo.[gtr].[hp].pf   Universal,1929/56   26018

Der LINDBERGHFLUG: cantata for Tenor & Baritone soli, chorus & orch (1929)
                       ∅   2022/0220/timp.perc/pf/str   40'   Universal   Misc 1622

QUODLIBET (Suite from Zaubernacht), op.9 (1923)
                       ∅   2222/2220/timp.perc.glock/str   20'   Universal,1926   Misc 4423

SEPTEMBER SONG: song
    arr R.Docker for chorus & orch
                       ∅   21+ca.20/3030/perc/gtr.hp.pf(cel)/str   3'   (Chappell)   25105 +

SYMPHONIES
    No.1, in one movement (1921)
        ed D.Drew   ∅   2(picc)12(bcl)2/2[=4]110/timp.perc.bells/
                              str   24'30"   Schott,1968   Misc 6932
    No.2 (1933)   ∅   2(picc)222/2220/timp/str   28'   Schott,1966   Misc 6413 B

The THREEPENNY OPERA <u>see</u> DREIGROSCHENOPER

Der ZAR LÄSST SICH PHOTOGRAPIEREN: opera buffa (1927)
    Extracts
        Tango Angèle, transcr M.Coe
                       ∅   000+Ebcl.ssx.asx.0/0210/2perc(bells.glock.xyl)/
                               bjo.hmn.pf/2vln.vlc.cb
                               (For use with hired set for complete opera
                               only)   (Universal)   26899

ZAUBERNACHT: ballet with song
    Suite   see   QUODLIBET

WEINBERG, Jacob (1883-1956)

GETTYSBURG ADDRESS: symphonic ode for Baritone solo, chorus & orch
         φ 3(picc)2+ca.2+bcl.2+cbsn/4431/timp.perc/
           2hp.org.pf.[theremin]/str   Witmark   Misc 2080

WEINBERGER, Jaromir

The BIRD'S OPERA
  1. Overture   3. Junior reception
  2. Nuptial ceremonies   4. Fugue of many subjects
         φ 2+picc.22.sx.2/4331/timp.perc.glock.xyl/
           cel.2pf/str   30'   Southern NY,1940 Misc 4138

BOHEMIAN SONGS & DANCES					
Nos 1-6	φ	2222/4230/timp.perc/cel.hp/str	24'	Universal	Misc 919 B
No.1	φ	2222/4230/perc/cel.hp/str	5'	Universal	Misc 2678
No.2	φ	2222/4230/timp.perc/cel.hp/str		Universal,1930	Misc 4090
No.6	φ	2222/4230/perc/cel.hp/str		Universal,1930	Misc 4091

BOSNIAN RHAPSODY for Soprano solo, chorus & orch
        φ 3(picc)1+ca.22/4330/cel.2hp.mand/str   Universal   Misc 1186

CZECH RHAPSODY   φ 2+picc.22.[3sx]2/4231/timp.perc/hp/str   K.Prowse   2313

HEBRAIC SONG for chorus & orch φ 3(picc)2+ca.2+bcl.2+cbsn/4331/timp.perc.tamtam/
           hp/str   Storch-Marien   Misc 2258

OVERTURE TO A KNIGHTLY PLAY   φ 1111/2210/perc/hmn.pf/str   8'30"-10' Universal   Misc 1267

OVERTURE TO A MARIONETTE PLAY see PUPPETSHOW OVERTURE

PRELUDE & FUGUE ON 'DIXIE' φ 3(picc)222/4331/timp.perc/hp.[org]/str
           Stage band: 0000/2220/perc   Boosey & H   Misc 2239 B

PRÉLUDES RÉLIGIEUX ET PROFANES
  Vol.1
    1. To the chief musician upon Neginah (5')   3. Mon cher, tes violons sont partis (5')
    2. Les illusions perdues (4')
        φ 3(picc)222/4330/timp.perc.bell.tamtam/hp/
           str   38'30"   Boosey & H   Misc 4158 B
  Vol.2
    4. Anthem to St. Wenceslas (5')   6. Of yester-year (4'30")
    5. A folk ballad (6')
        φ 3(picc)222/4330/timp.perc.bell.tamtam/hp/
           str   Boosey & H   Misc 4149 B
  Vol.3
    7. Narrante (2'30")   8. Adoration of St. Cecilia (6'30")
        φ 3(picc)222/4330/timp.perc.bell/str   Boosey & H,1954 Misc 4160 B

PUPPETSHOW OVERTURE   φ 2(picc)222/4330/timp.xyl/cel.hp/str 6'30"-10' Universal   Misc 1144 B
  arr V.Nemeti   PC 1(picc)121/2230/timp.perc/cel.hp/str   Universal   13793

SCHWANDA THE BAGPIPER (Švanda Dudak): opera
  Overture   φ 3(picc)2(ca)2(bcl)2(cbsn)/43.4nattpt.31/timp.perc/
           cel.2hp.org/str   Universal   Misc 913
  Act 1 from bar 1255 to end, orig keys
          vlc & cb pts only   BBC   19503
  Selections
    arr Bauer   PC 2(picc)121/2220/timp.perc/st   14'40" Universal   14344 B
    arr Bauer   φ 2(picc)121/2220/timp.perc.glock/hp/str
          hp/str   (Universal)   15781
  Suite
    1. Polka   3. Furiant   5. Fugue
    2. Bohemian song & dance 4. Odzemek
        φ 3(picc)222/4331/timp.perc/cel.hp.[org]/str   Universal   10196

WEINBERGER, Jaromir (cont)

SCHWANDA THE BAGPIPER (cont)
  Extracts
    Bohemian polka

arr Bauer	PC	1110/2210/perc/str	2'	Universal	13795
Furiant					
arr Bauer	PC	1121/2210/perc/str	3'	Universal	13794
Intermezzo from Act 1	∅	2222/4[=2]230/timp.perc/hp/str			
Polka	PC	2(picc)221/4231/timp.perc.glock/hp/str	2'30"-3'	Boosey & H	16542 Cp

    Wie kann ich dann vergessen? (How can I then forget?)
      in F# (orig), arr H.Carr

	∅	20.ca.21/2230/perc/cel/str		(Universal)	TO 492
SONG OF THE HIGH SEAS	∅	3(picc)2[=1]+ca.2+[bcl].2+cbsn/4331/timp.perc.tamtam/			
		hp.[org]/str	9'30"	Boosey & H	Misc 2070

UNDER THE SPREADING CHESTNUT TREE: variations & fugue on an old English theme

	∅	3(2picc)222/4330/timp.perc/hp.[org].pf/str	14'30"-18'	Boosey & H	Misc 4 B
rev version	∅	3(2picc)222/4331/timp.perc.glock/hp.pf/str	20'	AMP,1941	Misc 6503

WEIHNACHTEN (Váncoe), for organ & orch

	∅	3(picc)2+ca.2+bcl.2+cbsn/4331/timp.perc.bells/			
		cel.2hp.org.pf/str		Universal	Misc 934

WEINER, Leó (1885-1960)

BALLATA for clarinet & orch, op.28					
	∅	2222/4230/timp/hp/str	10'	Hungarian SM	Misc 4249
CONCERTINO for piano & orch, op.15					
	∅	2(picc)222/2200/timp/str	19'30"	Universal	Misc 112 B

CSONGOR ÉS TÜNDE: incidental music, op.10
  Suite (op.10b)

1. Night	3. Fairy dance	5. Witches cauldron
2. Callo	4. The grieving Tünde	6. Golden apple-tree

	∅	2(picc)222/4230/timp.perc/hp/str	24'	Hungarian SM	Misc 3977
Introduction & scherzo	∅	2(picc)222/4230/timp/hp/str		Hansen	Misc 2806

DIVERTIMENTI
  No.1, op.20 (on old Hungarian dances)

			9'30"		
	∅	str		Rózsavölgyi,1934	20548

  No.2, op.24, in A min

1. Lakodalmas	3. Panaszos ének
2. Tréfálkozás	4. Kanas - nóta

	∅	str	13'	Rózsavölgyi	Misc 2059

  No.3, op.25, in A (Impressioni Ungheresi)

	∅	2(picc)222/4230/timp.perc.glock/hp/str	14'	Rózsavölgyi,1950	Misc 5766
PASSACAGLIA, op.44	∅	2(picc)222/4231/timp/hp/str		Hungarian SM	Misc 6007

PASTORALE, PHANTAISIE ET FUGUE, for string orch, op.23

	∅	str	14'	Rózsavölgyi,1941	Misc 5767

PRELUDIO, NOTTURNO E SCHERZO DIABOLICO, op.31

	∅	2(picc)222/4230/timp/hp/str		Hungarian SM	Misc 6328

WEINER, Stanley

SYMPHONY no.1, op.18 (1967)	∅	3(picc)333+cbsn/4331/timp.perc/str	31'15"	MCA Music,1971	Misc 7599

WEINGARTNER, Felix (1863-1942)

La BURLA: suite, op.78

1. Marcia	3. Notturno (Duettino)	5. Introduzione e valzer
2. Mazurka	4. Symphonie à la minute	6. Scherzetto

	∅	2(picc)2(ca)22/4200/timp.perc.glock/hp/str		Birnbach	10915

WEINGARTNER, Felix (cont)

DAME KOBOLD: opera
   Overture   ø   2222/3200/timp/hp/str   8'   Universal   Misc 1760
   Extracts
     Waltz   ø   2222/4230/timp.perc/hp/str   10'   Universal   Misc 1759
FRÜHLING: symphonic poem in form of variations, op.80
                ø   3(picc)2+ca.2+bcl.3(cbsn)/4331/timp.perc.tamtam/
                   hp/str   16'-17'30"   Challier   Misc 1026
Das GEFILDE DER SELIGEN (The fields of heaven): symphonic poem, op.21
                ø   3(picc) +bfl .2+ca.2+bcl.3+cbsn./43+btpt.31/
                   timp.perc.glock/2hp/str   17'   Breitkopf   Misc 1641
GENESIUS: opera   ø   3(picc)3(ca)2+bcl.3(cbsn)/43+btpt.31/
                   timp.perc.glock.tamtam/2hp/str
                   Offstage: 0000/0610   Bote & B   Misc 1642
KING LEAR: symphonic poem, op.20
                ø   3(picc)+picc.333+cbsn/43+btpt.31/timp.perc.tamtam/
                   str   20'   Breitkopf   Misc 1468
LÜSTIGE OUVERTURE, op.53   ø   2+picc.222+cbsn/4231/timp.perc/hp/str   Breitkopf   6167

PLAUDERWÄSCHE (Tell-tale laundry song), for Mezzo-soprano (or Tenor) solo & orch, op.27, no.1, in G♭
                ø   2222/2000/str   Breitkopf   26488
SERENADE, op.7
   1. Andante quasi allegretto   3. Andante sostenuto
   2. Intermezzo, allegro ma non troppo   4. Molto vivace
                ø   str   11'   Ries & E   8898
SYMPHONIES
   No.1, op.23, in G   ø   3(picc)2(ca)22/4200/timp/hp/str   Breitkopf   Misc 767
   No.3, op.49, in E   ø   4(picc)2+aob+heck.2+Dcl+bcl.3+cbsn/
                   63+btpt.31/timp.perc/cel.2hp.[org]/str   Breitkopf   Misc 1241

WEINZWEIG, John (1913-

DIVERTIMENTI
   No.1 for flute & strings   ø   str   10'30"   Boosey & H,1951   Misc 3455 C
   No.2 for oboe & strings   ø   str   3'30"   Boosey & H,1951   Misc 3456 B
INTERLUDE IN AN ARTIST'S LIFE for strings
                ø   str   7'   Leeds Music,1961   Misc 5762
SYMPHONIC ODE for orchestra   ø   2+picc.2+ca.2+bcl.2/4331/timp.perc.xyl/str 9' Leeds Music,1962   Misc 5760

WEIR

MAY-BLOSSOM TROOP
   arr R.Barsotti   PC   1+picc.12.4sx.2/4230/perc/str   Boosey & H   21039 B

WEISS, Carl Flemming (1898-

INTRODUCTION GRAVE   pf/str   6'-7'   Hansen   Misc 2645
MUSICAL OVERTURE   ø   str   5'
                                   Skandinavisk Musikforlag,1955   21663

WEISGALL, Hugo David (1912-

AMERICAN COMEDY 1943   ø   2+picc.2+ca.2+bcl.2/4331/timp.perc/pf/str 12' (Composer)   6502
An ENGLISHMAN LOOKS AT AMERICA   ø   1120/2210/pf/str   Composer MS:BBC   MS 8480

WEISMANN, Julius (1879-1950)

CONCERTINO for horn & orch, op.118
       φ 2222/1000/timp.perc/str   15'   Birnbach Misc 2848
CONCERTO for orch, op.106 φ 1011/0110/timp/str   Tischer & J Misc 8 B
SERENADE for flute, oboe, clarinet, bassoon, horn, violin & strings, op.113
       φ str   Birnbach Misc 2847
SINFONIA BREVIS, op.116 φ 2222/4221/timp/str   Birnbach Misc 2846
TANZ-FANTASIE, op.35a φ 2(picc)222/4230/timp.perc/str   Tischer & J Misc 2862

WEISS, Willoughby Hunter (1820-1867)

The SLAVE DREAM: song
  in A   φ 2121/2230/hp/str   Composer MS:BBC MS 4616
The VILLAGE BLACKSMITH: song
  in C & B♭   φ 1011/0110/str   (Siddell) 17929
  in F, orch J.Bürger φ 1111/1110/timp.perc/hp/str   (Curwen) MS 2127

WEISSBERG, Julia

DANSE DES MATELOTS
  La petite fée des eaux φ 2+picc.222/4231/timp.perc/str   Russian SM Misc 999 B

WEISSENBURG, Heinz see ALBICASTRO, Enrico

WEISSHAUS, Imre see ARMA, Paul

WEITZ, G.

Le JOLI TAMBOUR
  arr G.Stacey   1110/0000/timp/acdn.hp/str   Arranger/Chester 3553

WEITZENDORF, Heinz

AURORA: symphonic prologue (1977)
       φ 3(picc)220/4330/timp.5perc(tamtam.4tomtom)/
         pf/str   8'   Neue Musik,1978 Misc 10338

WEJWANOWSKÝ, P.J. see VEJVANOVSKÝ, P.J.

WEKERLIN, J.B. see WECKERLIN, J.B.

WELDON, John (1676-1736)

The JUDGEMENT OF PARIS: masque for solo voices, chorus & orch   φ only)
       φ 2201/0100/timp/str   (Folger Shakespeare Lib.[c.1735]) Ch Lib 13753)
The TEMPEST, or The Enchanted Island: opera (attrib) see PURCELL, H: The TEMPEST
The WAKEFUL NIGHTINGALE: song
  in G min, arr F.Collinson φ 1121/1000/str   (Boosey) MS 30945

WELLEJUS, Hennig

FRÈRE JACQUES GOES WRONG: galop, op.23
       φ 2222/2210/timp.perc/str   Warnys,1959 23123
The MAIL COACH IS ROLLING (Postvognen ruller): overture, op.16
       φ 2222/2210/timp.perc/str   Warnys,1959 23004

WELLESZ, Egon (1885-1974)

CANTICUM SAPIENTIAE for Baritone solo, chorus & orch, op.104 (1968)

     φ   3(picc)3(ca)2+Ebcl+bcl.2+cbsn/4331/timp.perc.xyl/
       cel.hp/str   Doblinger   Misc 8641

CONCERTO for violin & orch, op.84 (1961)

     φ   2+picc.2+ca.2+bcl.2/2231/timp.perc/hp/str   31'20"Heinrichshofen,1961   Misc 7506

DIVERTIMENTO, op.107 (1969)   φ   1(picc)11+bcl.1/1100/timp.perc/cel.hp/str   12'   Doblinger,1971   Misc 7701

DUISNER ELEGIE (Rainer Maria Rilke) for Soprano solo, chorus & orch, op.90

     φ   21+ca.1+bcl.2/2220/timp.perc.tamtam/cel.hp/
       str   20'42"-23' Doblinger,1965   Misc 6254 B

MIRABILE MYSTERIUM for speaker, SSBar soli, chorus & orch, op.101

   1. Die Prophezeiung   5. Die Anbetung der Engel
   2. Et tu Bethlehem   6. Das Wunder
   3. Klage Josephs   7. Hymne der Glaubigen
   4. Hymne

     φ   2(picc)2(ca)2+bcl.2/2331/timp.perc.glock/
       cel.hmn.hp.pf/str   Doblinger,1967   Misc 8598

MUSIC FOR STRINGS in one movement, op.91

     φ   str   12'   Doblinger,1965   Misc 6253

ODE AN DIE MUSIK (Ode to music), for Contralto (or Baritone) & chamber orchestra, op.92

     φ   1111/1100/hp/str   5'   Doblinger,1966   Misc 6336 B

PROSPEROS BESCHWÖRUNGEN (Prospero's incantation)(Prospero's spell): 5 symphonic pieces

   1. Prosperos Beschwörungen   4. Caliban
   2. Ariel und der Stern   5. Ferdinand und Miranda
   3. Ariels Gesang

     φ   3(picc)2+ca.2+bcl.2+cbsn/4331/timp.perc/hp/str   Doblinger,1964   Misc 6030 D

4 SONGS OF RETURN, for Soprano solo & instruments, op.85 (1961)

   1. Where suddenly the wanderer comes (4')   3. The stubble was pale (5')
   2. Separate the shrivell'd moon (4')   4. Befriend us fortune (6')

     φ   1010/0000/hp.pf/str-4tet   19'   Heinrichshofen,1962   Ch Lib

SYMPHONIC EPILOGUE, op.108   φ   2+picc.2+ca.2+bcl.2+cbsn/4331/timp.perc.xyl/
       hp/str   12'   Doblinger,1974   Misc 8211 C

SYMPHONIES

No.1, op.62, in C	φ	3332/4331/timp.perc/str	42'	Schott	Misc 2973 B
No.5, op.75	φ	2+picc.2+ca.2+bcl.2/4331/timp.perc/str	35'	Sikorski,1957	Misc 5222 C
No.6, op.95 (1965)	φ	3(picc)2+ca.2+bcl.2+cbsn/4331/timp.perc/ cel.hp/str	25'-26'05"	Doblinger,1966	Misc 6317 B
No.7, op.102	φ	3(picc)3(ca)2+bcl.2+cbsn/4331/timp.perc.xyl/ cel.hp/str	24'	Doblinger,1968	Misc 6851 B
No.8, op.110 (1970)	φ	3(picc)3(ca)2+bcl.2+cbsn/4331/timp.perc.xyl/ hp/str	21'30"	Doblinger,1972	Misc 7723
No.9, op.111 (1971)	φ	3(picc)3(ca)2+bcl.2+cbsn/4331/timp.perc.tamtam.xyl/ cel.hp/str	27'	Doblinger,1973	Misc 8006 C

VORFRÜHLING (Spring's awakening): symphonic poem, op.12

     φ   32+ca.33/4330/timp.perc.tamtam/cel.hp/str   Universal   Misc 2858

WELLINGS, M.

HUSH-A-BYE: song
  in A, arr S.Robinson   str   Arranger   MS 5678

WENDT, T.

GLORIANA: a ballad to Queen Elizabeth
  in Eb   φ   1+picc.222/4230/timp.perc/hp/str   (Composer)   TO 1626   φ only

WENINGER, Leopold

AUF WIEDERHOVEN! (Knick-knacks): selection of famous melodies, arr
                      PC   2(picc)222/4231/timp.perc/hp/str   Benjamin   7941

BLÜTHENKRANZ (Musical blossoms): selection on famous melodies by C.M.Weber, arr L.Weninger &
    A.Schreiner for oboe, trumpet & orch
                      PC   2(picc)222/4230/perc/str   Benjamin   474

BRITELODIA: selection of British melodies, arr L.Weninger & F.Humphries
                      PC   2(picc)22.sx.2/4231/timp/hp/str   13'   Rahter   7671

HALALI (Happy hunting songs): march potpourri, arr
                      PC   2(picc)222/4230/timp.perc.bells/str   Rahter   12205

JUNG-DEUTSCHLAND (Young Germany): selection of marching songs, arr
                      PC   2(picc)222/4230/timp.perc.bells/str   Benjamin   9881

ÖSTERREICHISCHE BAUERNMUSI: suite
  1. Auf der Alm (5'30")   3. Beim Heurigen (5'30")
  2. Dorfhochzeit (6')   4. Am Kirta (4'30")
                      PC   2(picc)222/4230/timp.perc/hp/str   22'   Hofmeister   15148

SCHENKT WAN SICH ROSEN   see   ZELLER, C.F: Der VOGELHÄNDLER
ZION: selection of Hebrew melodies, arr L.Weninger & M.Philippson
                      PC   2222/4231/perc/hp/str   Benjamin   4535

WENRICH, Percy (1880-

PERSIAN LAMB RAG: a pepperette PC   1121/2210/perc/str   B.F.Wood   4997

WENTZELI (WENTZELY), Nicolaus Franz Xaverius (Nicolaus Francisco Xaverio)(ca.1643-1722)

FLORES VERNI (5 Masses)
  Mass no.2: Non confunder in aeternum, for SATB voices & orch
                   ø   0000/0030/org/str   (CS Pnm)   Misc 6597

WENZEL, Leopold

VINELAND: selection from the ballet
  arr A.Schmid   PC   2(picc)222/4230/timp.perc.bells/str   Boosey   3462

WERDER, Felix

ACTOMOS (Acdumos): choral prelude (elegy), for strings, op.10
                   ø   str   BBC,1954   Misc 6140 +

WERNER, Gregor Joseph (c.1695-1776)

CONCERTI
  Flute & orch
    ed R.Moder   ø   2vln/cont.   Doblinger,1971   25384
  Organ & orch
    ed R.Moder   ø   000.2chal.0/0000/str(no vla)   Doblinger,1975   26053 *
SYMPHONIAE SEX SENAEQUE SONATAE nos.1-6   see   CHAMBER CATALOGUE
WIENERISCHER TANDLMARKT, for TTBB soli, mv-ch
  ed R.Moder   ø   str/cont   Doblinger,1961   23434

WERNER, Sven Erik (1937-

COMBINATIONS (1967-1969)   ø   2(picc)222/2220/timp.perc.xyl   10'   Hansen,1969   Misc 7568 C

WERNER-KERSTEN, M.

LAZY PETE (Bummel-Petrus)   PC 1121/2210/perc/str   Liber   6786

WERNICK, Richard (1934-

VISIONS OF TERROR AND WONDER for Mezzo-soprano solo & orch
                                   ∅   4(2picc,2afl)4(ca)4(2E♭cl,bcl)4(cbsn)/4331/
                                       2timp.5perc(bells.2large bells.bell tree.
                                       crot.flox.glock.mba.3tamtam.vib.xyl)/cel.hp/
                                       str   28'   Presser,1978   Misc 9746

WESLEY, Charles (1757-1834)

CONCERTO for harpsichord (or organ) & orch, no.4, op.2, in C
    ed & arr G.Finzi   ∅   0[2]00/0000/str   17'   Hinrichsen,1956   23482
SOLDIERS OF CHRIST, ARISE (St. Ethelwald)
                                   ∅   str   BBC   MS 20035

WESLEY, Samuel (1766-1837)

BEGIN,BEGIN THE NOBLE SONG: ode to St. Cecilia for SABar soli, SSATB chorus & orch (1799)
    ed F.Routh   ∅   0202/2200/timp/str/cont(org)   65'   Redcliffe,1977   Misc 9437
ODE TO ST. CECILIA   see   BEGIN, BEGIN THE NOBLE SONG
OVERTURE in D (1778)
    ed M.Channon (rough pencil copy only)
                                   ∅   0200/2000/str   Editor   Misc 10503
SYMPHONIES
    in D (1784)
        ed R.Platt   ∅   0000/2000/str   15'   OUP,1976   Misc 9053
    in A (c.1790)
        ed R.Platt   ∅   0000/2000/str/[cont]   15'   OUP,1974   Misc 8574 B

WESLEY, Samuel Sebastian (1810-1876)

ASCRIBE UNTO THE LORD: anthem for SSSATTB soli, chorus & orch (c.1852)
                                   ∅   2222/4230/timp/org/str   (RCM)   26091 +
The CHURCH'S ONE FOUNDATION (Aurelia)
    arr Perry   PC 1121/0000/timp.perc/org/str   Hawkes   4970
I HAVE BEEN YOUNG: sacred song for Baritone solo & orch (c.1832)
    ed H.Keyte   ∅   2222/2000/str   Editor/(GB-Lcm)   26080 + Ap's st
SYMPHONY (or Overture) in C (c.1827)
    ed H.Keyte   ∅   2222/2230/timp/str   Editor/(GB-Lcm)   26082
The WILDERNESS, for SSAATB soli, SSATTB chorus & orch
                                   ∅   2222/4430.oph.spt/timp/str   (Composer)   26052

WESLY, Emile

NEERLANDIA
    Overture   PC 2+picc.222/4231/timp.perc/hp/str   Gaudet   12624

WESSLANDER, E.

NORDISCHER SUITE
    1. Die Sennerin   3. Gebirgsklänge
    2. Auf der Wanderung   4. Schwedischer Bauerntanz
                                 PC 1121/2210/timp.perc/str   Hoffman-Wesslander   13484
SCHWEDISCHER SUITE no.1
    1. Im Dorfe (Pastorale)   3. Hochzeitszug
    2. Auf der Wiese   4. Ländlicher Tanz
                                 PC 1121/0210/timp/str   Edn International (A.E.Wappler)   1652

WESSLANDER, E. (cont)

SCHWEDISCHE SUITE no.2
  1. Auf der Senne   3. In den Schären
  2. Die Hochzeit auf Solsta 4. Tanz in der Scheune
                  PC 1121/2210/timp.perc/str   Hoffman-Wesslander   13159

WEST, Alfred H.

MAFEKING NIGHT (refrain)
  in Bb & D (2 settings), arr R.Chignell
                ø 1121/2220/timp.perc/str   (Reynolds)   MS 5363

OUR COURT BALL: song
  in D, arr Tapp   ø 1121/2220/perc/pf/str   (Reynolds)   MS 795 ø only
PROMENADE MILITARIE   PC 2222/2230/timp.perc/str   AH & C   2846

WEST, John Ebenezer (1863-1929)

MAYPOLE DANCE   PC 1+picc.222/2231/timp.perc/str   Novello   2832 E

WESTBERG, Eric (1892-1944)

GASK (Kneipe): symphonic poem in rondo form
                ø 2(picc)12(bcl).2sx.1(cbsn)/2210/timp.perc.2glock/
                    bjo.cel.hp/str   Edn Suecia   10570
LUSTSPIEL OUVERTURE   ø 2(picc)222/223[1]/timp.perc/str   Edn Suecia   10564 B

WESTERHOUT, Nicola (Niccoló) van (1857-1898)

RONDE D'AMOUR
  arr M.Tobani   PC 1121/2210/timp.perc/str   C.Fischer   9192

WESTON, Harris

STOP, GO: revue
  Extracts
    Olga Pullofski: song
      in D, arr H.Carr   ø 2122/2230/perc/hp/str   (FD & H)   TO 702
      in Bb, arr R.Green ø 1120/0320/perc/gtr.pf/str   FD & H   LM G 10991

WESTON, R.P.

AMERICA ANSWERS THE CALL: song by R.P.Weston & others
  in F, arr H.Carr   ø 2121/2230/perc/hp/str/chorus   FD & H   TO 899
ANY DIRTY WORK TO-DAY? (Rogues rejoicing), by R.P.Weston & B.Lee
  in D min, arr H.Carr ø 2121/2230/perc/hp/str   (FD & H)   TO 433
The CO-OPTIMISTS by R.P.Weston & B.Lee
  Give three cheers for the dustman: song
    in D, arr R.Hanmer ø 2222/4230/timp.perc/hp.pf/str   (FD & H)   20856
FAN FAIR
  I wonder why poor Nelly never writes: song
    in Eb, arr H.Carr   ø 2121/2230/perc/hp/str   (FD & H)   TO 703
The GIPSY WARNED ME: song by R.P.Weston & B.Lee
  in F, arr M.H.Lubbock ø 2121/2230/glock/str   (Feldman)   TO 23
  in G & Bb, arr R.Chignell ø 2121/2220/perc/hp/str   (FD & H)   MS 7337
WHAT A MOUTH!
  arr J.McCarthy for chorus & orch
             ø 1+picc.222/4230/perc(xyl)/hp/str   FD & H   24576
WHILE THE RICH MAN RIDES BY IN HIS CARRIAGE AND PAIR: song by R.P.Weston & B.Lee
  in C, arr H.Carr   ø 2121/2230/perc/hp/str   (FD & H)   TO 978

WETHERELL, Eric (1925-

BEAU NASH: overture	∅	2222/4230/timp.perc/hp/str	Anglo-Continental(H)	PL 635 Ani

WELSH DRESSER: suite
    1. The Dove   4. New Year's Eve
    2. The Holly Tree   5. Girl from Pendryn
    3. Love Dance

∅ 2(picc)122/2230/timp.perc/hp/str (10.8.6.6.4)		Mozart Edn(H)	PL 578 Ani B

WETZEL, Peppi

GNOMEN-PARADE	PC 1+picc.222/4231/timp.perc/str			Benjamin	2688 B
KOMODIANTEN (The comedian): overture					
arr Meissner	PC 223.4sx.2/4330/perc/hp/str	11'		Symphonic Music	15425 B
STRAHLENDER SUDEN (Sunny south): waltz					
	PC 222.3sx.2/4230/perc/bjo/str	7'		Symphonic Verlag	13887

WETZLER, Hermann Hans (1870-1943)

Die BASKISCHE VENUS: opera, op.14
    Extracts
        Symphonic dances
            1. Fandango   3. Moderato misterloso   5. Arin-arin
            2. Zortziko   4. Ézpatadantza

∅ 3(2picc)2+ca.3(E♭cl)+bcl.3(cbsn)/4331/ timp.perc.glock.tamtam/cel.2[=1]hp/str/mv-chorus		Brockhaus	Misc 925

VISIONEN, op.12
    1. Introduzione
    2. Cantico d'annl e di pechati pieno (Michelangelo sonnet)
    3. Scherzo demoniaco
    4. Intermezzo ironico
    5. Fugato
    6. Risonanza estrema

∅ 3(3picc)2+ca.2+bcl.3/4331/timp.perc/cel.2hp/ str	40'	Brockhaus	14681 B

WIE ES EUCH GEFÄLLT (As you like it): incidental music, op.7
    1. Page's duet   4. The hunter's bugle call
    2. Love scene   5. Rosalinde's farewell
    3. Dance of the shepherds, no.1   6. Dance of the shepherds, no.2

PC 1121/2210/timp/str	Benjamin	6600

WEYRAUTH (WEYRAUCH), August Heinrich von (1788-?)

ADIEU: song (formerly attrib F.Schubert)

in E♭, orch C.Clarke as duet	1121/2200/pf/str/[ST soli.mv-chorus]	BBC	TV MS 130
in E♭, arr M.Tobani	PC 2222/2210/str	C.Fischer	11060
arr for cornet & orch	PC 1122/2200/str	Hawkes	6481

WEYSE, E.F. (1774-1842)

SONG OF DENMARK 'Der er et Land': Danish National song

PC 2(picc)222/4231/perc/str	Benjamin	16363

WEYSENBERGH, Heinrich   see   ALBICASTRO, Enrico

WEYWANOWSKÝ, P.J.   see   VEJVANOVSKÝ, P.J.

WHEELER, Clarence E.

The LITTLE CLOCK ON THE MANTEL   PC   1121/2210/perc/str   G.Schirmer   3102 B

WHELEN, Christopher (1927-

The ACHARNIANS: radio production (1955)
                        φ   2202/2200/timp.perc/hp/str   Composer MS:BBC   MS 31057 +
The ATHEIST: radio 3 drama production for The Soldier's fortune (1980)
                        φ   1(picc)100/1001/timp.perc.anv.4bjo.4gong.
                            tamtam.xyl/pf(hmn.hpsd)/voices   Composer MS:BBC   MS 31796
The BACCHAE: radio production (1964)
                        φ   1(picc)100/1221/timp.perc/2hp/solo voices.chorus Composer MS:BBC   MS 31485 +
The BEGGAR'S OPERA: radio production, arr (1961)
                        φ   perc.vib/cel(hpsd).cimb.2gtr(egtr).hp.mand/
                            str   Arranger MS:BBC   MS 31349 +
The BULL FROM THE SEA: radio production (1965)
                        φ   2(picc)000/0101/timp.perc/hp(cel)/str/voice   Composer MS:BBC   MS 31546 +
The CANCELLING DARK: radio opera, op.2 (1965)
                        φ   2(picc)2(ca)2(bcl)2(cbsn)/3221/timp.perc/
                            hp.pf(cel)/str/SAT.2Bar.B soli.spk voice   Composer MS:BBC   (MS 31513 + &
                                                                                                (mf 225
The CHANGELING: radio production (1960)
                        φ   0000/2220/timp.perc/gtr.org/str   Composer MS:BBC   MS 31313 φ only
A CHASTE MAID IN CHEAPSIDE: radio play (1979)
                        φ   0101(cbsn)/1000/perc.ptimp.bjo.glock/
                            hp.hpsd.pf(cel)/voices   Composer MS:BBC   MS 31788
CUMULUS: a fable for radio in words and music (Commisioned by radio 3)(1978)
                        φ   01(ca)1(Ebcl,bcl)0/3321/3perc.anv.5bgo.claves.
                            crot.scym.2tdm.glock.4gong.rattle.tamtam.2tblbl.
                            vib.xyl/pf(cel)/2vln.vla.2vlc.cb   Composer MS:BBC   MS 31784
The DEMON KING: radio feature (1962)
                        φ   001(bcl)0/0010/timp.perc/cel/vln-solo.str/
                            voices   Composer MS:BBC   MS 31394 +
The DOUBLE GALLANT: radio feature (1962)
                        φ   1(picc)101/2000/timp.perc/hp.hpsd/str/Bar solo   Composer MS:BBC   MS 31385 +
EASTWARD HO: radio production (1961)
                        φ   1(picc)101/1100/perc/lute.hp.hpsd/str-5tet   Composer MS:BBC   MS 31337 φ only
The FINDINGS: radio opera (1970-71)
                        φ   3110/3321/timp.perc.glock.vib.xyl/hp.pf(cel)/
                            vlc.cb   Composer MS:BBC   25191 +
The FROGS: radio production (1956)
                        φ   0.picc.200/2400/timp.perc/hp/cb   Composer MS:BBC   MS 31165 φ only
INCIDENT AT OWL CREEK: radio opera in 1 act (1968)
                        φ   2(picc)22+Ebcl.2/4231/timp.perc.bells.glock.
                            vib.xyl/hp.mand.pf[=org=cel]/str   Composer MS:BBC   24883 + & mf 303
KING LEAR: radio production (1974)
                        φ   000.bcl.1/2211/1perc(timp.bells.tamtam)/
                            hp.pf(cel,hmn)/male singer   Composer MS:BBC   MS 31765
The LINCOLN PASSION: radio feature (1963)
                        φ   2(picc)1(ca)01/1111/timp.perc/cel.hp/
                            vlas.vlc.cb/solo voice.chorus.cv-chorus   Composer MS:BBC   MS 31416 +
LYSISTRATA: radio production (1957)
                        φ   0200/3100/perc/cel.hp.hpsd/cb   Composer MS:BBC   MS 31210 Ap's φ
MEDEA: radio production (1962) φ   1(picc)1(ca)01/2211/timp.perc/hp/2cb/fv-chorus Composer MS:BBC MS 31378 + φ only
OEDIPUS IN QUAD: radio production (1973)
                        φ   0000/1111/timp.perc.bells.gong/cel.2hp/
                            spoken voices   Composer MS:BBC   MS 31713 + φ only

WHELEN, Christopher (cont)

The PEACE (Aristophanes): radio production (1957)
             ø 1(picc)000/2000/timp.perc/cel.hp.hpsd/str   Composer MS:BBC   MS 31199 ø only

PHILOCTETES: radio feature (1963)
             ø 2(2picc)000/2201/2hp/vla.vlc/Bar solo.TB chorus   Composer MS:BBC   MS 31408 +

POLLY (Pepusch/Gay): radio production (1961)
             ø 1(picc)100/2100/timp.perc.glock.bells/hp.hpsd(cel).gtr/
                 str   Composer MS:BBC   MS 31363 +

The RESTORER: incidental music for radio production (1976)
             ø 0.rec.000/4000/3perc(timp.bells.2anvil.5bgos.crot.
                 glock.4gongs.3mexican cbells.3tamtam.tplbl.vib.xyl)/
                 hpsd(pf,cel).org/str-4tet   Composer MS:BBC   MS 31738

TAMBURLAINE: radio production (1963)
             ø 2(picc)1(ca)00/2221/timp.perc/hp.mand.pf[=cel]   Composer MS:BBC   MS 31430 +

The TEMPEST: radio production (1964)
             ø 1(picc)000/0101/timp.perc/cel.hp.hpsd/vlc/
                 voices   Composer MS:BBC   MS 31480 +

TIMON OF ATHENS: radio production (1974)
             ø 0300/2200/1perc(ptimp.bells.crot)/hp.org/
                 str(0.0.2.5.1)   Composer MS:BBC   MS 31762 ø only

TO THE OFFICE AND BACK: radio opera (notes toward a portrait of Wallace Stevens)(1978)
             ø 0000/4000/perc(bells.bgos.crots.cym.glock.gongs.sdm.
                 rattle.tamtam.vib.xyl)/cel(pf)   Composer MS:BBC   MS 31778

TWELFTH NIGHT: radio production (1956)
                 0201/2100/perc/hp/str   Composer MS:BBC   MS 31093

VALENTINIAN: radio production (1959)
             ø 1100/2200/timp.perc/hp.mand/str   Composer MS:BBC   MS 31281 ø only

VENICE PRESERVED: radio production (1960)
             ø 1[=picc]100/2210/perc/cel.hp.hpsd.mand/str   Composer MS:BBC   MS 31324 + ø only

WHETTAM, Graham (1927-

CONCERTINO for oboe & strings, op.12, no.2
             ø str   9'   De Wolfe,1952   Misc 3898

CONCERTO for cello & orch (1962)
             ø 3(picc)222/4230/timp.2perc(glock.vib.xyl)/cel.hp/
                 str   22'   Meriden   Misc 9248

CONCERTO SCHERZOSO for harmonica (or flute) & orch, op.9
             ø 0121/2000/timp/str   De Wolfe   Misc 3899

The DEMON HUNTER OF THE MOOR: concert overture, op.13
             ø 2(picc)2+ca.22/4230/timp.perc/str   De Wolfe   Misc 3900

HYMNOS (1978)   ø str   7'   Meriden,1978   Misc 10039

SINFONIA DRAMMATICA (1976-8) ø 3(picc)2+ca.3(Ebcl,bcl)3(cbsn)/4331/timp.5perc(large scym.
                 Tibetan cym.glock.tamtam.2xyl/hp.pf/str   30'   Meriden,1978   Misc 9961

SINFONIA INTREPIDA (1976)   ø 4(2picc,afl)4(2ca)4(Ebcl,bcl)3+cbsn/6432(cbtuba)/
                 2timp.6perc(bells.cast.crot.glock.tamb.tamtam.xyl)/
                 2hp/str   45'-50' Meriden Mus,1976 Misc 9535

SINFONIETTA for strings   ø str   De Wolfe   Misc 3901

VARIATIONS on an original theme, for oboe, bassoon & strings (1961)
             ø str   11'   (Composer)   Misc 10164

WHITAKER, John (?1776-1847)

OH, SAY NOT WOMAN'S HEART IS BOUGHT: song
  in F   ø 1022/2000/str   (Siddell)   17930

SLEEP MY BABE: song
  in D   1010/2000/str   (Siddell)   17931

WHITE, Clarence Cameron (1880-1960)

BANDANNA SKETCHES: suite of Negro spirituals, op.12
    1. Chant (Nobody knows de trouble I've seen)
    2. Lament (I'm troubled in mind)
    3. Slave song (Many thousand gone)
    4. Negro dance (Sometimes I feel like a motherless child)
                  PC · 1121/2210/timp.perc/str   C.Fischer   6526

WHITE, Cool

BUFFALO GALS: Minstrel song (also ascribed to D.D.Emmett)
    in F, arr H.Carr   ø   1+2picc.222/4231/timp.perc/hp/str   (J.M.Chapple)   TO 2012

WHITE, Edward

CABANA	PC	1+picc.121/2230/perc/hp/str		Boosey & H	18904
CAPRICE FOR STRINGS	PC	1120/0220/timp/glock/gtr/str		Cosmo	1795
The CLOCKWORK CLOWN	PC	2121/2230/timp.perc/hp/str		Boosey & H	20291 B
FAIRY ON THE FIDDLES	PC	1121/2220/perc/cel/str	3'30"	Boosey & H	18724 B
IDLE JACK	PC	1+picc.121/2220/timp.perc.glock.xyl/str	3'40"	Hawkes,1953	22014
PARIS INTERLUDE	PC	2121/2230/timp.perc/str	3'05"	Lafleur	19565
arr composer	PC	str		Lafleur	19735
PUFFIN' BILLY	PC	2+picc.121/2230/timp.perc/hp/str	3'35"	Chappell,1954	21165 Cp
ROUNDABOUT	PC	1+picc.121/2220/timp.perc/hp.org/str		Boosey & H	19236
RUNAWAY ROCKING HORSE	PC	1(picc)12.4sx.1/2220/timp.perc.glock.xyl/ hp/str	4'30"	Boosey & H	12133 D
WHITE WEDDING	PC	2(picc)121/2230/timp.perc.glock/acdn.gtr.hp/ str	2'55"	Boosey & H,1954/7	22438 B
YODELLING STRINGS	PC	2+picc.121/2220/timp.perc/gtr.hp/str	3'	Boosey & H,1954	21648

WHITE, Felix (1884-1945)

ARIETTA	ø	str	2'45"	Curwen	6210
La CHARMANTE for piano & orch		1111/2210/timp.tri/str		Liber	16528 B
MY LITTLE PRETTY SWEETING	PC	1121/2000/hp/str		Liber	16529
'TO MIRANDA': serenade					
arr J.Brown	ø	str		Stainer & B	14684

WHITE, Joseph

La BELLA CUBANA	PC	2121/0030/perc/str	3'05"	Chappell,1960	23232 Ap

WHITE, Maude Valerie (1855-1937)

ABSENT YET PRESENT: song					
in A♭	ø	2222/2230/timp/hp/str		(Lengnick)	MS 4791
The DEVOUT LOVER: song					
in E♭, arr S.Andrews	ø	hp.pf/str		Arranger MS:BBC	MS 20377
in E♭, D & F, arr F.Cramer		pf/str		(Ricordi)	LM G 3889
in F		str	4'25"	Ricordi	1738
KING CHARLES	ø	2(picc)222/2230/timp.perc/str	2'25"	(Boosey)	6081 Ap
in F	ø	1111/2210/timp/str		(Boosey)	TO 1393 ø & str)
					only)
MARCHING ALONG: song					
in F, arr G.Williams for Baritone solo, mv-chorus & orch					
	ø	1121/2320/timp.perc/str		Chappell	MLO 717

WHITE, Maude Valerie (cont)

SO WE'LL GO NO MORE A ROVING: song
     in C, arr H.Carr   φ   2222/2000/perc/hp/str   4'50"   (Chappell)   TO 1396
     in E, orch J.Bürger   2121/2000/perc/hp/str   (Chappell)   MS 2129
     in E & E♭, arr S.Robinson   φ   1111/1110/perc/str   (Chappell)   MS 5701
     in E, arr G.Stacey   1010/0000/pf/str   (Chappell)   LM G 3681
     in E & D♭, arr G.Stacey   pf/str   (Chappell)   LM G 4253
WHEN THE SWALLOWS HOMEWARD FLY: song
     in A   φ   2121/2230/timp.perc/hp/str   (Chappell)   MS 4617 φ only

WHITE, Paul Taylor (1895-

5 MINIATURES
     1. By the lake   3. Waltz for Teenie's doll   5. Mosquito dance
     2. Caravan song   4. Hippo dance
                             φ   0.picc.0.ca.01/2230/perc.bells.xyl/cel/str   Elkan-Vogel   Misc 2478

WHITE, Teddy

HOLIDAY IN HARLEM   PC   000.sx.0/0320/timp.perc/gtr/str   Cosmo   7306

WHITELEY, Norman

DUSKY ARISTOCRAT: an impression
     arr R.Hanmer   PC   1121/2230/timp.perc/str   Cramer,1954   22009
GRANNY'S SPINNING WHEEL
     arr H.Evans   PC   2221/2220/timp.perc/hp/str   Leonard Gould & B 19571
KATHLEEN MARY   PC   1121/2220/timp/hp/str   Cramer   19474

WHITEMAN

PINS AND NEEDLES: musical play by Whiteman, Pitts, Egan & Marsh
     Extracts
         I never knew: song
            in F, arr M.Mackie   φ   2131/2230/timp.perc/hp.pf/str   (FD & H)   18556

WHITHORNE, Emerson (1884-1958)

The DREAM PEDLAR: symphonic poem, op.50
                            φ   3+picc.3+ca.3+bcl.3+cbsn/4331/timp.perc.bells/
                                cel.hp/str   16'   Cos Cob Press   Misc 1092
FATA MORGANA: symphonic poem, op.44
                            φ   3(picc)2+ca.2+bcl.2+cbsn/4331/timp.perc.bells.tamtam/
                                cel.hp/str   24'   Cos Cob Press   Misc 818
PELL STREET (Chinatown), op.40, no.3
     arr Roberts   PC   2222/4231/timp.perc.xyl/str   C.Fischer   1047
SATURDAY'S CHILD: an episode in colour for voices & chamber orch, op.42
                            φ   1(picc,bfl)111/1000/timp.perc.xyl/pf/str   20'   Birchard   Misc 462
SYMPHONY no.2, op.56   φ   3(picc)2+ca.2+bcl.2+cbsn/4331/timp.perc.bells.
                                tamtam.xyl/cel.hp/str   33'   C.Fischer,1940 Misc 2797

WHITING, Arthur (1861-1936)

The GOLDEN CAGE: dance pagenant for small orch
                            φ   1000/0000/str   G.Schirmer   Misc 456

<u>WHITING, Richard A.</u> (1891-1938)

INNOCENTS OF PARIS: film
   Louise: song
     in F, arr H.Carr   φ 2122/2000/perc/hp/str   (Connelly)   TO 748
MONTE CARLO: film by R.A.Whiting & W.F.Harling
   Beyond the blue horizon: song
     in Bb, arr R.Tilsley for solo voice & chorus (refrain only)
                  φ 2222/4230/timp.perc/hp/str   (Chappell)   22123
ROCK AND ROLL: song
   in C, arr J.Beaver for SATB voices & orch
                  φ 2121/2230/timp.perc/hp/str   (Sterling)   TO 357
WHERE THE BLACK-EYED SUSANS GROW: song
   in F & G (2 settings), arr B.Berlin
                  φ 2121/2220/perc/str   (Feldman)   TO 577
The WHIRLIGIG
   The Japanese sandman: song
     in Db, arr M.H.Lubbock   φ 2121/2230/perc/hp/str   (Feldman)   TO 38

<u>WHITING, W.</u>

ETERNAL FATHER STRING TO SAVE (For those in peril on the sea)
   arr R.Barsotti   PC 1+picc.12.4sx.2/4230/perc/str   Boosey & H   21309 B
   arr D.Godfrey   PC 2222/4230/timp.perc/str   Chappell   2867

<u>WHITNEY, Joan</u>

MY SISTER AND I: song by J.Whitney, H.Zaret & A.Kramer
   in A, arr B.Berlin   φ 2121/2230/timp.perc/hp/str   (C.Connelly)   TO 902

<u>WHITTAKER, William Gillies</u> (1876-1944)

BILLY BOY: north country song, arr
   in Eb, orch F.Bye   φ 1121/2000/hp/str   (Curwen)   MLO 335
BLOW THE WIND SOUTHERLY: traditional, ed
   in F, arr M.Saunders   φ hp/str   (Curwen)   LM G 8589
BOBBY SHAFTOE: north country song, arr
   in Ab, orch F.Bye   φ 1121/2000/hp/str   (Curwen)   MLO 336
   in Bb, orch S.Robinson   str   (Stainer & B)   MS 5613
The KEEL ROW: traditional tune, arr
   in E, orch F.Bye   φ 1121/2000/str   Curwen   MLO 375
A LYKE-WAKE DIRGE for chorus & orch
                  φ 2(2picc)222+cbsn/4231/timp.perc/str
                or   timp/pf/str
                or   timp/2pf   Stainer & B   Misc 5275
MA BONNY LAD: traditional tune, arr
   in G, orch F.Bye   φ 2122/2000/hp/str   Curwen   MLO 486
The OAK AND THE ASH: traditional tune, arr
   in A min, orch G.Williams φ 2222/4230/str   Arranger   12819

<u>WHYTE, Ian</u> (1901-1960)

AIRS AND DANCES FROM THE SCOTTISH PAST, arr
   Part 1
     1. Money in both your pockets   3. Love me as I deserve   5. In ane inch, I warrant you
     2. Killiekrankie   4. The fit is come owre me
                φ str   15'   Universal   20058
   Part 2
     1. Put on your sark on Monenday (3'30")   4. The Ladye Louthian's lilte (2'30")
     2. La voici (3'30")   5. The carrier (3'30")
     3. My Lady Balcleuch's ayre (3')
                φ str   16'   Universal   3301

WHYTE, Ian (cont)

QUEEN AND COMMONWEALTH: ceremonial march
                              ø   3222/4331/timp.perc/str   BBC   20816 + As
SCOTTISH DANCES   ø   2+picc.2+ca.2+bcl.2+cbsn/4331/timp.perc/str   BBC   MS 3671
WILLIE'S GANE TO MELVILLE CASTLE: song, arr
   in Db, for SATB voices & orch ø   str   BBC   TO 98

WICHENHAUSSER, Richard

SUITE, op.24, in F
   1. Praeludium   3. Gavotte   5. Gigue
   2. Air   4. Saraband
                        ø   str   Kistner & S   9016

WIDOR, Charles Marie (1845-1937)

CHORAL ET VARIATIONS, op.74	ø	2(picc)222/4231/timp.perc/str	13'	Heugel	5230
CONCERTI					
Cello & orch, op.41	ø	2222/4230/timp.perc/str		Hamelle	Misc 3018
Piano & orch, op.39	ø	2222/4230/timp/str		Hamelle	Misc 1125
CONTE D'AVRIL: incidental music					
Complete	ø	2222/4230/timp.perc/str		Heugel	9198

Suite no.1, arr H.Mouton
   1. Romance   2. Sérénade Illyrienne   3. Marche nuptiale
                        PC 1121/2210/timp.perc/str   10'   Heugel   1092 B
Suite no.2, arr H.Mouton
   1. La rencontre des amants (strings only)   2. Guitare   3. Aubade
                        PC 1121/2000/timp.tri/str

				Heugel	1090
ESPAGNOLE: overture	ø	2(picc)222/42.2cnt.30/timp.perc/str	7'	Heugel	5710
FANTASIE for piano & orch, op.62					
	ø	2222/42.2cnt.31/timp.perc/str		Durand & Schoenewerk	Misc 1124

La KORRIGANE: ballet
  Suite
   1. Prélude: alla marcia   4. Scherzando
   2. Tempo di Mazurka   5. Valse lente
   3. Adagio   6. Finale
            ø   2(picc)222/42.2cnt.30.oph/timp.perc/hp/str 20'   Heugel   7727
MAÎTRE AMBROS: opera, op.56
  Suite
   1. Overture   4. Ronde de nuit
   2. Intermezzo   5. Kermesse
   3. Marine
            ø   2222/42.2cnt.31/timp.perc/str   Heugel   9295
NERTO: lyric drama
  Overture
            ø   3(picc)2+ca.2+bcl.2+cbsn/4431/timp.perc/str 6'   Heugel   13618
La NUIT DE WALPURGIS: symphonic poem
   1. Overture   2. Adagio   3. Bacchanale
            ø   2+picc.2+ca.22/4431/timp.perc/str   Heugel   10371 B
Les PÊCHEURS DE SAINT JEAN: opera
  Symphonic framgments
   1. Overture   3. Marche de noël (Prelude to Act 3)
   2. Le calme de la mer (Prelude to Act 2)
            ø   2(picc)+picc.222/42.2cnt.31/timp.perc/hp/str   Heugel,1904 Misc 4876
SALVUM FAC POPULUM TUUM, op.84 ø   0000/0330/timp/org   Heugel   20099 B
SÉRÉNADES
  in A
   arr L.Artok   PC 1111/2110/timp.perc/str   4'20"   Schott   2534 B
  in Bb, op.10   ø   2(picc)222/2200/timp/hp/str   6'15"   Hamelle 14472
   arr F.Salabert   PC 1121/2230/timp/str   Salabert 10497

WIDOR, Charles Marie (cont)

SINFONIA SACRA for organ & orch, op.81
       φ 0110/0130/timp/str   Hamelle   Misc 1694

SYMPHONIES
  No.1, op.16   φ 2222/3200/timp/str   Durand   Misc 2658
  No.2, op.54   φ 2+picc.222/42.2cnt.31/timp.perc/str   Durand   25101
  No.5, op.42, in F min
   Toccata only, for organ & orch
    arr S.Torch   φ 2+picc.2+ca.22+cbsn/4331/timp.perc.glock.tamtam/
           hp/str   (Hamelle/UMP)   24295 +

WIECHOWICZ, Stanislaw (1893-1963)

CHMIEL (The hop): symphonic scherzo
       φ 3(picc)2+ca.2+bcl.2+cbsn/4331/timp.perc/
         hp.pf/str   6'   Polish SM   Misc 2993 B

WIEDOEFT, Rudy

RUBENOLA for saxophone & orch, by R.Wiedoeft & H.Frey
  arr Frey   PC 101.3sx.0/0210/perc/bjo.pf/str   Robbins   12634

WIÉNER, Jean (1896-

CONCERTO for piano & strings, no.1 'Franco-Américain'
       φ str   15'   Eschig   Misc 36 B

WIENIAWSKI, Henry (1835-1880)

ADAGIO ÉLÉGIAQUE, op.5
  arr A.Schmid   PC 1121/2210/timp.perc/str   G.Schirmer   7083
CHANSON POLONAISE, op.12, no.2   PC 1021/2000/str   Cranz   7751
CONCERTI
  Violin & orch
   op.14 (no.1), in F# min
    [critical edition]   φ 2222/2230/timp/str   Polish SM,1962   Misc 5800
   op.22 (no.2), in D min   φ 2222/2230/timp/str   23'-24'50"   Schott   7357
    [critical edition]   φ 2222/2230/timp/str   Polish SM,1962   Misc 5801
   2nd mvt only (Romanze)
    arr Ralf   PC 1110/0000/str   Schaper   7165
DUDZIARZ: marzurka (Le Ménétrier), op.19, no.2
       PC 1121/2210/timp/str   Cranz   6924
FANTAISIE BRILLANTE on themes from Gounod's 'Faust', for violin & orch, op.20
       φ 2+[picc].222/2230/timp/str   [Composer]   26170
  ed A.Wilhelmj   PC 2222/2230/timp/str   Schott   8924
KUYAWIAK: polonaise   φ 1121/2000/str   3'   Jurgenson   14696
LÉGENDE, op.17   φ 2222/2000/timp/str   7'   Kistner   8820 B
  arr Roberts   PC 1121/2210/timp/str   C.Fischer   1283
  arr F.Salabert   PC 1110/0110/timp/str   Salabert   10828
OBERTASS: mazurka, op.19, no.1   PC 1121/2210/timp/str   3'   Cranz   6923
POLONAISES for violin & orch
  No.1, op.4, in D   φ 2222/2210/timp/str   5'15"   [BBC]   Misc 5625
  No.2, op.21, in A   2222/2230/timp/str   Schott   21400
       φPC 2222/2230/timp/str   Schott   13197
SCHERZO-TARANTELLE for violin & orch, op.16
  arr Gilson   φ 2222/2200/timp.perc/str   Kistner   23896 +

WIENIAWSKI, Józef (1837-1912)

CONCERTO for piano & orch, op.20 φ   2222/4230/timp/str   Cranz   7593
GUILLAUME LE TACITURNE: overture, op.43
                         φ   2222/4230.oph/timp.perc/str   Schott   8025
ROMANTIQUE: suite, op.41
  1. Evocation   3. Idylle
  2. Scherzo   4. Mazourka villageoise
                         φ   2+picc.222/4230.oph/timp.perc.glock/hp/str   Schott   8024

WIESLANDER, Ingvar (1917-1963)

LITTLE SUITE for chamber orchestra
  1. Marcia Giocosa   2. Andante   3. Scherzo
                         φ   1011/0000/str   7'30"   Ed Suecia 26403 *

WIHTOL, Joseph (1863-1948)

The FEAST OF LIGO: symphonic picture on Latvian folk tunes, op.4
                         φ   2+picc.222/4231/timp.perc/hp/str   16'   Belaieff   6126
7 LETTISH FOLK SONGS, op.29a   φ   3(picc)2+ca.22/4000/timp.perc/str 13'   Belaieff   6125
OUVERTURE DRAMATIQUE, op.21   φ   2+picc.222/4231/timp.perc/str   Belaieff   Misc 1456
SPRIDITIS: overture, op.37   φ   2+picc.2+ca.22/4231/timp.perc.glock/hp/str   Belaieff   6124 B
VARIATION no.2 for 'Variations on a Russian theme' by various composers
                         φ   2+picc.222/4231/timp.perc/hp/str   13'   Belaieff,1903 8973

WIKLUND, Adolf (1879-1950)

3 PIECES
   1. I Folkton: tranquillo   3. Molto ritmico: allegro
   2. Andante espressivo
                         φ   hp/str   Ed Suecia 18823

WILD, Eric (1910-

REPARTEE   φ   2+picc.222/4231/timp.perc.glock.xyl/[hp]/
                             str   2'30"   Berandol,1974 Misc 8482

WILDER, Alec

WHILE WE'RE YOUNG by A.Wilder & M.Palitz
   arr D.Bowden   PC   1121/2230/timp.perc/hp/str   2'30"   Cavendish 20714

WILDMAN, Charles

SWEDISH RHAPSODY for piano & orch
   arr R.Douglas   φ   21+ca.2+bcl.2+cbsn/4231/timp.perc/hp/str
                           or   2121/2220/timp/hp/str   K.Prowse,1942 Misc 6549
   Theme only
   arr R.Douglas   PC   101.3sx.0/0210/timp/str   K.Prowse   19371

WILDGANS, Friedrich (1913-1965)

CONCERTO for trumpet, strings & percussion
                         φ   str   16'   Doblinger,1971 Misc 7695

WILEY, L.

GOT THE SOUTH IN MY SOUL: song by L.Wiley & V.Young
   in F, arr W.Wallond for soli, chorus & orch
                         φ   111.3sx.1/2220/perc/bjo/str   (Victoria) MS 336

WILHELM VI, Landgraf von Hesse (1629-1663)

SARABANDE
  ed Écorcheville   OS   instrumentation unspecified   M.Fortin,1906   Misc 3027 B

WILHELM, Carl (1815-1873)

Die WACHT AM RHEIN (The watch on the Rhine)
                          PC   2(picc)222/4231/timp.perc/str   Benjamin   16363 +
  arr M.L.Lake   PC   112.2sx.1/2210/perc/str   C.Fischer   19720

WILHELMJ, August (1845-1908)

ALLA POLACCA for violin & orch   2222/4230/timp/str   Schlesinger [1885]   25305
ALL' UNGHERESE for violin & orch (after Liszt)
                          ϕ   2222/4210/timp.perc/str   Schlesinger   8072
                          ϕ   2+picc.222/4231/timp.perc/str   BBC   15800
BALLADES for violin & orch   ϕ   2222/4000/str   BBC   Misc 921 B
IN MEMORIAM for violin & orch   ϕ   2222/2010/timp/str   Schlesinger   9029
ROMANZE for violin & orch   ϕ   1122/2000/str   Schlesinger [1874]   26307

WILKINSON, Arthur (1919-1968)

The BEATLE CONCERTO for piano & orch (based on 'All my loving' by Lennon & McCartney, in the
       style of the finale of Beethoven's 5th Piano Concerto)
                          ϕ   2222/2200/timp/str   (Arranger)   26743
DANCE, LITTLE LADY: song by N.Coward, arr
                          ϕ   1(picc)11.5sx.1/2430/kit/gtr.hp.pf/str   Chappell   MS 20196 ϕ only
DANCE MEXICAINE   PC   2(picc)122/2330/timp.perc/hp/str   3'45"   Arcadia   22281
FANTASY ON THE HELSTON FURRY DANCE: Cornish caprice, arr
                              2121/2220/perc/pf/str   4'55"   BBC   WE 363
HOWARD KEEL MEDLEY, arr   ϕ   2(picc)222/2230/timp.perc/hp.pf/str   BBC   24274
MELODY HOUR: opening & closing themes for radio programme
                          ϕ   2222/4230/timp.perc/hp/str   Composer   23114 +
NOVELLO-ITIS
  arr B.Thompson   ϕ   1110/0000/hp.pf/str   (Chappell)   MS 20299
SONGS OF LONDON: selection, arr
                          ϕ   2222/2230/timp.perc/hp/str   BBC   24250
SONGS OF VIENNA: vocal selection for soli, chorus & orch, arr
                          ϕ   2222/4230/timp.perc/hp/str   Weinberger/Chappell,1960   23215

WILKINSON, Philip G. (1929-

SHAKESPEAREAN SUITE for small orch (1958)
   1. Fanfare-prelude   3. Scherzetto   5. Aubade
   2. Threnody   4. Country dance   6. Fanfare-prelude
                          ϕ   2(picc)222/2200/timp.perc/str   15'   Novello,1960   25043

WILKINSON, Stephen

VARIATIONS ON 'GO FROM MY WINDOW' (Anon), ed for string sextet or string orch
                          ϕ   str   6'45"   OUP,1958   CM 52936

WILLAN, Healey (1880-1968)

see   BRYANT, G: Healey Willan Catalogue.   Ottowa: National Library of Canada, 1972

AGINCOURT SONG, arr
  in C, orch C.Groves for mv-chorus & orch
                          ϕ   0000/2400/timp/str   Arranger   TO 969

WILLAN, Healey (cont)

CONCERTO for piano & orch, in C min (1944, rev 1949)
       ϕ 2222/4230/timp/str   25'   B.M.I.Canada,1960   Misc 5434
CORONATION MARCH   ϕ 2+picc.222+cbsn/4331/perc/cel.hp/str   (Composer)   4608
OVERTURE TO AN UNWRITTEN COMEDY (1951)
       ϕ 1111/2220/timp/hp/str   4'05"   Berandol,1974   Misc 8652
TRANSIT THROUGH FIRE   PS only   (Composer)   Misc 2998

WILLARD, James

MY HEART SINGS: song
  in F, arr G.French   ϕ 1110/0000/gtr.hp.pf/str   (Boosey)   LM G 4912
  in F, arr E.Griffiths ϕ org.pf(cel)/str   (Boosey)   LM G 7911

WILLCOCKS, David (1919-

3 CHRISTMAS CAROLS for chorus & orch from 'Carols for Choirs, Bk.1', orch R.Jacques & D.Willcocks
  1. See amid the winter's snow (orch Willcocks)   3. Good King Wenceslas (orch Jacques)
  2. O Little town of Bethlehem (orch Jacques)
       ϕ [2222]/[2200]/[timp.perc]/str   OUP,1971   27652 An Dwa
5 CHRISTMAS CAROLS for chorus & orch from 'Carols for Choirs, Bk.1'
  1. God rest you merry gentlemen   4. The First Nowell
  2. O Come, all ye faithful   5. Hark! The herald angels sing
  3. Unto us is born a Son
       ϕ 2(picc)222/2200/timp/org[=pf]/str   OUP,1967   26540 An Dwa

WILLEBY, Charles

CROSSING THE BAR: song
  in F min, arr G.Stacey   pf/str   (Boosey)   LM G 3432
The FORTUNE HUNTER: song
  in C, arr G.Stacey   1010/0000/pf/str   (Boosey)   LM G 3686
MOON MADRIGAL   PC 1+picc.121/2220/perc.glock/str   J.Church   3827

WILLIAMS, Albert

The GATHERING OF THE CLANS: Scottish patrol
  arr A.Winter   PC 1+picc.222/4230/timp.perc/str   4'30"   Hawkes   7632

WILLIAMS, Alberto (1862-1952)

ETERNO REPOSO: symphony no.7, op.103, in D
       ϕ 3+picc.3+ca.3+bcl.3+cbsn/4441+cbtuba/   La Quena Casa de Musica.
          timp.perc.tamtam.xyl/cel.hp/str   Buenos Aires   Misc 2187
OUVERTURE DE CONCERT no.2, op.18 ϕ 2+picc.222/4231/timp.perc/str   A.Williams   Misc 1945

WILLIAMS, Charles (1893-

The BELLS OF ST. CLEMENTS   2222/4230/timp.perc.bells.glock.vib/hp.org/
          str   4'40"   (C.Williams)   18469 +
BIG BEN   ϕ 1111/2110/perc/hp/str   Composer   MS 20028
BLUE DEVILS: march
  arr A.Lotter   PC 1+picc.222/4230/perc/str   3'45"   Hawkes,1929   8991
DEVIL'S GALOP   ϕ 1+picc.122/2220/timp.perc/pf/str   Chappell(H)   PL 668
The DREAM OF OLWEN   see   WHILE I LIVE
The FALCONS
  arr C.Milner   PC 2+picc.12.5sx.1/2230/timp.perc/hp/str   2'50"   L.Wright,1950   20024

WILLIAMS, Charles (cont)

FLESH AND BLOOD: film					
Throughout the years	PC	2121/2230/timp.perc/hp/str	3'-3'30"	Chappell,1951	20242 B
HEART O' LONDON					
arr C.Milner	PC	2121/2230/timp.perc/hp/str	2'45"	Chappell,1956	21725 Ap C
JEALOUS LOVER	PC	2121/2230/timp.perc/hp/str		L.Wright,1949	20795
MODEL RAILWAY					
arr C.Milner	PC	2121/2220/timp.perc/str		Lafleur,1951	20296
The MUSIC LESSON	PC	1111/1000/timp.perc/str	2'30"	Chappell,1955	21636 Cp
The NIGHT HAS EYES: film					
Theme from the film					
arr G.Zalva	PC	212.3sx.1/2230/timp.perc/str		Chappell,1942	14579 Cp
The NURSERY CLOCK	PC	1120/0210/perc.glock.xyl/str		Liber,1933	11046
The OLD CLOCKMAKER	PC	2121/2230/timp.perc/hp/str		Chappell,1949	19808 C
A QUIET STROLL	PC	2121/2000/perc/hp/str	3'05"	Chappell,1952	20729 B
RHYTHM ON RAILS	PC	2+picc.121/2230/timp.perc/hp/str	2'30"	Chappell,1956	21710 Ap C
SALLY TRIES THE BALLET					
arr C.Milner	PC	2121/2230/timp.perc/hp/str	3'	L.Wright,1951	20223
SHEILA AND JIMMY: serenade	PC	1121/2230/perc/str	3'	Liber,1933	11048
SIDEWALK	PC	212+bcl.2/2220/timp.perc/hp/str	2'50"	Chappell	21104
SLEEPY MARIONETTE					
arr C.Milner	PC	2121/2210/perc.vib.xyl/hp/str	3'05"	Lafleur,1950	20110
STARLINGS					
arr C.Milner	PC	2121/2000/timp.perc/hp/str	3'	Chappell,1956	21709 Ap C
THROUGHOUT THE YEARS see FLESH AND BLOOD					
WHILE I LIVE: film					
The Dream of Olwen					
arr H.Geehl	PC	2121/2230/perc/hp/str		L.Wright,1947	19457 Ap
arr S.Torch for piano & orch					
	∅	21+ca.22/4331/timp.perc/hp/str		(L.Wright)	24882 +

WILLIAMS, Francis

A CHRISTMAS MINIATURE	∅	pf/str	4'	Boosey & H	13131 Cwa

WILLIAMS, Gene (pseud of Lawrence Wright)(1888-1964)

WYOMING LULLABY					
arr R.Farnon	∅	22(ca)3[=2+cbsn]+bcl[=bsn].0/4231/perc(glock.vib)/ hp/str		Composer(H)	PL 542
arr G.Langford	∅	2222/43[=2]3[1]/3perc(timp.bells.glock.kit.vib)/ [cel].hp/str	3'40"	(L.Wright)	26432

WILLIAMS, Gerrard (John Gerrard)(1888-1947)

AS I WALKED OUT: Essex folksong, arr for Tenor & small orch					
	∅	1111/1000/str		Arranger MS:BBC	MS 7572 ∅ only
AS SALLY SAT A-WEEPING: Dorset folksong, arr (collected by H.E.D.Hammond)					
in D	∅	1010/1000/hp/str		Arranger MS:BBC	MS 8140

A BACH SUITE

1. Prelude (English suite no.3)   5. Minuet (French suite no.1)
2. Allemand (French suite no.2)   6. Bourrée no.1 (English suite no.2)
3. Sarabande (English suite no.4)   7. Bourrée no.2 (English suite no.2)
4. Gavotte (French suite no.5)   8. Gigue (French suite no.5)

	∅	1111/0100/timp/str or str	23'	OUP	6464

WILLIAMS, Gerrard (cont)

The BATTLE OF THE BOYNE, arr	∅	2+picc.2+ca.2+bcl.2+cbsn/4331/timp.perc/ hp/str		Arranger	13699
BEAUTIFUL NANCY: Gloucestershire folksong, arr					
in G min	∅	1111/1000/str		Arranger MS:BBC	MS 7689
The BEGGARS OPERA					
Selection of melodies, arr	∅	0200/2000/str		Arranger	18713-4
The BONNY BUNCH OF ROSES: Norfolk folksong, arr					
in Bb		1121/2200/perc/hp/str		Arranger MS:BBC	MS 30062
BRISK YOUNG WIDOW: Somerset folksong, arr					
in Bb	∅	1111/1000/timp.perc/str		Arranger MS:BBC	MS 7688
CANNY CUMMERLAN': folksong, arr					
in C	∅	0.picc.111/0000/str		Arranger MS:BBC	MS 6866
La CARMAGNOLE, arr for Baritone solo, chorus & orch					
in F	∅	2221/2230/timp.perc/hp/str		Arranger	TO 1286
CAROL OF SERVICE: old French tune, arr					
in D min	∅	2222/0000/hp/str		Arranger	23446

4 CAROLS, arr G.Williams & S.Wilson

1. The Boar's Head, in C	3. God rest ye merry gentlemen, in E min	
2. In the bleak midwinter, in F	4. Gloria in excelsis, in F	

		1000/0000/str		Arrangers MS:BBC	MS 20034
CHAPS OF COCAIGNY: Somerset folksong, arr					
in E min	∅	1111/0000/str		(Novello)	MS 8197
CHARMING CHLOE	∅	1111/1000/timp.perc/str/SATB soli.chorus		Composer MS:BBC	MS 30054 ∅ only
The CLAUDY BANKS 'As I roved out one evening all in the month of May': Hampshire folksong, arr					
in G min	∅	1111/0000/perc/str		Arranger MS:BBC	MS 8141
CORTÈGE ON A GROUND BASS		2222/4331/timp.perc.glock/hp/str		BBC	19190
The COTSWOLDS: incidental music					
	∅	2(2picc)222/2230/timp.perc/hp/str		Composer MS:BBC	MS 30223
COVENT GARDEN: Sussex folksong, arr (noted by R.Vaughan Williams)					
in F min	∅	1010/0000/str		Arranger MS:BBC	MS 8196

The CUCKOO: folksong, arr

Dorset version (collected by H.E.D.Hammond)					
in Eb	∅	1111/1000/perc/str	4'-5'	Arranger MS:BBC	MS 8195
Somerset version (collected by C.Sharp)					
in E min	∅	1111/2200/perc/str		(Novello)	MS 6865
Surrey version (collected by F.Keel)					
in E min	∅	1111/2000/timp/str		Arranger MS:BBC	MS 7350
CUPID THE PLOUGHBOY: Dorset folksong, arr (collected by H.E.D.Hammond)					
in E min	∅	1111/0000/str		Arranger MS:BBC	MS 8142
DÛ BRÂUCHS MER NEISCHTZE SCHWIÊREN: Luxembourg song, arr					
	∅	1010/0000/str		Arranger	1146
DUKE OF MARLBOROUGH: Somerset folksong, arr					
in C	∅	1111/2100/perc/str		Novello	MS 7072
EPISODE: theme song, arr & orch					
	∅	2121/2230/timp.perc/hp/str		Arranger MS:BBC	MS 3421 ∅ only
FACETS: aspects of an original theme					
	∅	2222/4231/timp.perc/str		BBC	19189
3 FANFARES: radio feature: Italian Surrender Programme					
		0000/3430/timp.perc		Composer MS:BBC	MS 30377
FAREWELL, NANCY: Somerset folksong, arr					
in G	∅	1111/2000/str		(Novello)	MS 6136
The FIRST NOWELL, arr					
in D	∅	1111/0000/glock/hp/str/chorus		Arranger MS:BBC	MS 20311

FOLK-TUNE MEDLEYS, arr

No. 1

1. The Glory of the West	3. Mundesse	
2. New, new nothing		

	∅	1111/2000/timp.perc/str	4'	Arranger MS:BBC	MS 6134

WILLIAMS, Gerrard (cont)

FOLK-TUNE MEDLEYS (cont)

No. 2
    1. Rose is red and rose is white   3. Mage on a Cree
    2. The Saraband
               ø 1111/2000/timp.perc/str   3'   Arranger MS:BBC   MS 6133

No. 3
    1. The milk mayd's Bobb   3. Lulle me beyond thee
    2. An old man is a bed full of bones
               ø 1111/2200/timp.perc/str   Arranger MS:BBC   MS 6132

No. 4
    1. Prince Rupert's march   3. Goddesses
    2. All a mode de France
               ø 1111/2000/timp.perc/str   Arranger MS:BBC   MS 6131

No. 5
    1. Lord of Carnarvon's jigg   3. The bonny bonny broome
    2. Irish trot
               ø 1(picc)111/2100/perc/str   Arranger MS:BBC   MS 6868

No. 6
    1. Down the groves (2 versions)   2. The Manchester 'Angel'
               ø 1(picc)111/2100/timp.perc/str   Arranger MS:BBC   MS 6867

No. 7
    1. Flowers of Edinburgh   3. Lads a bunchum
    2. Cuckoo's nest
               ø 1111/1110/timp.perc/str   (Novello)   MS 7073

No. 8
    1. Nonesuch   3. The Cherping of the larke
    2. Argeers
               ø 1121/2110/timp.perc/str   Arranger MS:BBC   MS 7074

No. 9
    1. Bacca pipes jig: morris dance (6 variants)
               ø 1111/2120/perc/str   (Novello)   MS 7352

No.10
    1. The fool's jig   3. Glorisheers
    2. Princess Royal
               ø 1(picc)121/2210/timp.perc/str   (Novello)   MS 7353

No.11
    1. Maid of the mill: morris dance (4 variants)
               ø 1111/2210/timp.tri/str   (Novello)   MS 7354

No.12
    1. Millison's jigge   3. Grimstock
    2. The Old mole
               ø 1111/2200/timp.perc/str   (Novello)   MS 7355

No.13
    1. The Beaux of London   3. Bobby and Joan
    2. Heel and toe
               ø 1111/2200/perc/str   Arranger MS:BBC   MS 7571

No.14
    1. Cockle shells   3. Mr. Lane's maggot
    2. Softly, Robin
                  1111/2100/timp.perc/str   Arranger MS:BBC   MS 7687

No.15
    1. Soldiers joy   2. Morpeth rant
          ø   str   Arranger MS:BBC   MS 30057
         ø 1111/2220/perc/str   Arranger MS:BBC   MS 8145

No.16
    1. Blew Cap   3. Wooddicock
    2. Greenwood
               ø 1111/2100/timp.perc/str   Arranger MS:BBC   MS 8146

WILLIAMS, Gerrard (cont)

FOLK-TUNE MEDLEYS (cont)

No.17
1. Fourpence-halfpenny-farthing   3. King of Poland
2. Mall Peatly

           ∅   1111/2000/perc/str   Arranger MS:BBC   MS 8193

No.18
1. The Merry milkmaids   3. Chelsea Reach
2. The Black nag

           ∅   1+picc.111/2200/timp.perc/str   Arranger MS:BBC   MS 8194

FOUR PRESENTS: folksong, arr
   in F   ∅   2222/4230/timp.perc/str   Arranger MS:BBC   MS 20331

GEORDIE: Somerset folksong, arr
   in A min   ∅   0111/1000/str   (Novello)   MS 6869

GOD SAVE THE QUEEN: National Anthem, arr
           ∅   1121/2220/perc/str   Arranger(H)   PL 36
           ∅   2+picc.2+ca.2+bcl.2+cbsn/4331/timp.perc/
              hp/str   Arranger   19643 B

GOOD KING WENCESLAS, arr
   in A   ∅   1111/0000/glock/hp/str   Arranger MS:BBC   MS 20310

HARK, SAYS THE FAIR MAID: Dorset folksong, arr (collected by H.E.D.Hammond)
   in E♭   ∅   1111/0000/tri/str   Arranger MS:BBC   MS 8198

The HIGH ROAD TO LYNN: folksong, arr
   in A   ∅   1111/2100/timp/str   Arranger MS:BBC   MS 7349
   arr as dance tune   str   Arranger MS:BBC   MS 20270

HOW COLD THE WINDS DO BLOW: folksong, arr
   in C   ∅   1111/2000/perc/str   Arranger MS:BBC   MS 8199

I LOVED A LASS, A FAIR ONE
   in G   str   BBC   19191

IN BRUTON TOWN: Somerset folksong, arr (collected by C.Sharp)
   in E min   ∅   1111/1100/perc/str   Arranger MS:BBC   MS 6871

IN POLAND THERE'S AN INN: song, arr
   in B♭   ∅   2222/4230/timp.glock/hp/str   BBC   23447

JACK THE JOLLY TAR: Somerset folksong, arr
   in D min   ∅   1111/1110/perc/str   3'   Arranger   TO 490
   in D min   ∅   1111/1110/timp/str   Arranger MS:BBC   MS 7070

The JOLLY MILLER: 17th century song, arr for Contralto & Tenor soli, chorus & orch
           ∅   2121/2230/timp/hp/str   Arranger   MLO 1257

KALYANI: a little fantasy on the Indian song
           ∅   1110/0000/str   BBC   MS 20274

KINGS' MUSIC: music by Henry VIII and other royal composers, arr
1. Fanfare   8. Pastime with good company (Henry VIII)
2. Fanfare   9. Fanfare
3. Fanfare   10. Fanfare
4. O my heart (Henry VIII)   11. Mark how the blushful morn
5. Alas what shall I do for love (Henry VIII)   12. I pass all my hours (words Charles II;
6. Green grows the holly (Henry VIII)   music Pelham Humfrey)
7. O death, rock me on sleep (words Anne Boleyn)   13. Standchen (Prince Albert)
           ∅   1111/2200/hp/str/STBar soli   Arranger MS:BBC   MS 4571 ∅ only

LEEZIE LINDSAY: traditional tune, arr
   in E♭ for Soprano & Baritone soli, chorus & orch
           ∅   1121/2210/perc/hp/str   Arranger   MLO 155

The LINCOLNSHIRE FARMER: folksong, arr (collected by R.Vaughan Williams)
   in B♭   ∅   1111/1000/timp/str   Arranger MS:BBC   MS 8143

The LITTLE CRAB FISH: folksong, arr (collected by C.Sharp)
   in E♭   ∅   1111/2000/perc/str   (Novello)   MS 8144

WILLIAMS, Gerrard (cont)

The LITTLE TURTLE DOVE: Somerset folksong, arr (collected by C.Sharp)
   in A min   ɸ 2121/2230/timp.perc/hp/str   (Novello)   MS 7690
LLANOVER WELSH REEL, arr   ɸ 1121/220.btbn.0/timp.perc/str   3'   Arranger MS:BBC   MS 31371
LONELY JOAN: Norfolk folk tune, arr (collected by R.Vaughan Williams)
   in G min   ɸ 1111/1000/timp/str   (Novello)   MS 7351
LONELY ON THE WATER: Norfolk folk tune, arr (tune noted by F.Kedson)
   in E min   ɸ 1111/1000/str   (Paterson)   MS 7071
LORD RENDAL: Somerset folksong, arr for Contralto & Baritone soli & orch
   in D   ɸ 1121/2210/perc/hp/str   Arranger   MLO 271
LOVELY JOAN: Norfolk folk tune, arr for small orch (tune noted by R.Vaughan Williams)
                      ɸ 1111/1000/str   Arranger MS:BBC   MS 7351 ɸ only
MAGUIRE'S MARCH: Irish tune, arr
                      ɸ 2(picc)121/2230/timp.perc/hp/str   3'   Arranger   TO 1417 ɸ only
MEN OF HARLECH: Welsh tune, arr
                      ɸ 2222/4231/timp.perc/str   Arranger   5293
The MERMAID: Dorset folk tune (noted by H.E.D.Hammond)
   in F   ɸ 1111/1000/str   (Novello)   MS 7573
The MERRY GREEN BROOM: Herefordshire folk tune (collected by R.Vaughan Williams)
                      ɸ 1111/1000/str   (Novello)   MS 7348
The MINSTREL BOY: traditional song, arr
   in E   ɸ 1121/2210/perc/hp/str   Arranger   MLO 587
MY DANCING DAY: folksong, arr
   in G   ɸ 0100/0000/str   Arranger MS:BBC   MS 20330
O CAN YE SEW CUSHIONS: traditional Scottish lullaby, arr
   in F   ɸ 1100/0000/perc/hp/str   BBC   23442
O COME, ALL YE FAITHFUL: Christmas carol, arr for chorus & orch
                      ɸ 1111/0000/timp.perc/hp/str   Arranger MS:BBC   MS 20308
O PONDER WELL (from the Beggar's opera)
   in F   ɸ str   1'28"   BBC   12379
OH EARLY EARLY ALL IN THE SPRING: Lincolnshire folksong, arr (noted by F.Kidson)
   in G   ɸ 1011/1000/timp/str   Arranger MS:BBC   MS 8200
OH! THE DAYS ARE GONE: Irish song 'Love's young dream', arr
   in Eb   ɸ 2222/2000/perc/hp/str   Arranger MS:BBC   MS 1681 ɸ only
OLD MOTHER OXFORD: morris dance tune, arr (collected by C.Sharp)
                      ɸ 2222/2200/perc/str   BBC   20490
ON ILKLA MOOR: traditional song, arr
   in C   ɸ 2222/4230/timp.perc/str   BBC   6113
ONE MAN SHALL MOW: folksong, arr
   in G   ɸ 2222/4230/perc/hp/str   BBC   23444
ONE MAY MORNING, arr
   in Bb   ɸ 1111/1000/perc/str   Arranger   TO 489
OVER THE HILLS AND FAR AWAY (from the Beggar's opera), arr
   in A (duet)   ɸ 1000/0000/hpsd/str   BBC   2529
OVER THE HILLS AND THE MOUNTAINS: Northumberland folk tune, arr (collected by R.Vaughan Williams)
   in A min   ɸ 1111/1000/str   Arranger MS:BBC   MS 7887
PRECESSION: radio production   ɸ 1(picc)100/1100/perc/hp/str   Composer MS:BBC   MS 20380
PRETTY POLLY OLIVER: traditional song, arr
   in G, arr for Jubilee Programme, 1935
                      ɸ 2222/4200/timp.perc/hp/str   Arranger MS:BBC   MS 1684 ɸ only
POT-POURRI: cycle of fragments for orch

1. Lavender (2'30")	5. Roses	(1')	Epilogue: potpourri
2. Thyme (2')	6. Musk	(1')	
3. Pinks (1')	7. Rosemary & rue	(1'30")	
4. Cassia (1')	8. Lilies of the valley	(2')	

                      ɸ 3(picc)2+ca.2+bcl.2+cbsn/4200/timp.perc.glock/cel.2hp/
                      str   Novello   Misc 295 B

WILLIAMS, Gerrard (cont)

The SAILOR'S TEST: Dorset folksong, arr (noted by H.E.D.Hammond)
    in D   ϕ 0011/1000/hp/str   (Novello)   MS 7575
SCOTTISH MEDLEY, based on the traditional tunes 'Come under my plaidie' and Wha'll be king but
    Charlie?'
                      ϕ 2+picc.222/4221/timp.perc/str   BBC   20489
The SHEPHERD AND HIS FIFE: Gloucestershire folksong, arr (noted by C.Sharp)
    in B min   ϕ 1111/0000/tri/str   (Novello)   MS 7576
The SKYE BOAT SONG: Jacobite song, arr (attrib A.C.MacLeod)
    in G   ϕ 1121/2210/perc/hp/str   Cramer   MLO 74
SOLDIER, SOLDIER: traditional song, arr
    in G   ϕ 1110/2000/perc/hp/str   Arranger   MLO 284
SPRIG OF THYME: Dorset folksong, arr (noted by H.E.D.Hammond)
    in C min   ϕ 1111/1000/str   Arranger MS:BBC   MS 8201
SWEET NIGHTINGLAE: folksong, arr
    in G, for Baritone solo & orch
                      ϕ 2222/4230/timp.perc/hp/str   BBC   19225
The THREE SONS: Somerset folksong, arr
    in D   ϕ 1111/2220/timp/str   (Novello)   MS 7691
The TURN OF THE SCREW: radio play
                      ϕ 2021/4220/timp.perc/str   Composer MS:BBC   MS 20442 ϕ only
TURNE YE TO ME, arr see LAWSON, Malcolm: TURN YE TO ME
TWANKYDILLO: Sussex folksong, arr for treble chorus
    in G   ϕ 2222/4230/xyl/hp/str   BBC   23445
The UNFORTUNATE LAD: Yorkshire folk tune, arr (noted by F.Kidson)
    in D min   ϕ 1111/1100/timp/str   (Paterson)   MS 7069
UPIDEE: song, arr for Baritone solo, chorus & orch
                      ϕ 1121/2210/perc/str   (Arranger)   MLO 272
VALENTINE O'HARA: Irish tune, arr (Joyce 1909)
                      ϕ 3(picc)222/4231/timp.perc.xyl/hp/str   BBC   Misc 2844
WAIT TILL THE WORK COMES ROUND, arr (tune noted by F.Kidson)
                      ϕ 2222/4220/timp.perc/str   BBC   9389
                      ϕ 1+picc.121/2230/timp.perc/str   BBC   13227
WHAT SHALL WE DO WITH THE DRUNKEN SAILOR?: traditional song, arr for **solo** voice, chorus & orch
    in G min   ϕ 1121/1000/timp.perc/str   Ricordi   MLO 213
WHEN JOHNNY COMES MARCHING HOME: traditional song, arr for Mezzo-soprano solo & orch
    in A min & G min   ϕ 1121/0320/sdm/pf/str   Arranger   MLO 721
WHILE SHEPHERDS WATCHED: Christmas carol, arr
                      ϕ 1111/0000/glock/hp/str/chorus   Arranger MS:BBC   MS 20313 ϕ only
WILLIAM TAYLOR: Somerset folkson, arr (colllected by C.Sharp)
    in G   ϕ 1111/2200/perc/str   Arranger MS:BBC   MS 6870
YANKEE DOODLE: traditional American song, arr
                      ϕ 1+picc.121/2230/timp.perc/str   BBC   13227

WILLIAMS, Grace (1906-1977)

AMERICAN FOLKSONGS from the Appalachian folksongs, arr (collected by C.Sharp)
    1. Some love coffee   4. The Wisconsin emigrant
    2. Birnoire   5. The Swapping song
    3. The Two sisters

                      ϕ 0100/0000/hp/vln.vlc   (OUP)   CM 52795 Awa
BALLADS FOR ORCHESTRA   ϕ 3(picc)2(ca)2(bcl)2/4231/timp.perc.bells.bgos.glock.
                         mrc.tamtam.whip.xyl/hp/str   [BBC]   Misc 9822
The END OF A WORLD: incidental music for radio play
                      ϕ 2121/2230/timp.perc/hp/str   (BBC)   19965 Awa
FANTASIA ON WELSH NURSERY TUNES
                      ϕ 2222/4230/timp.perc/hp/str   10'   OUP   22065

WILLIAMS, Grace (cont)

FOLK SONGS AND CAROLS used in Rhythm & melody series

Winter, 1946 'Six carols'
   1. Ding dong merrily
   2. Rocking carol
   3. Flemish carol
   4. Patapan
   5. Wassail song
   6. The Twelve days of Christmas
                   2222/4230/timp.perc/cel.hp/str   (OUP/Stainer & B)   19964 Awa

Winter, 1947 'Six carols'
   1. Susanni: German carol
   2. A Christmas song: Gascon carol
   3. Sledging: Russian folk tune
   4. O little one: German carol
   5. The Kingdom: Angevin carol
   6. Shepherds in the field abiding: French traditional tune
            ø 2121/2230/timp.perc/hp/str   (OUP)   19963 Awa

Easter, 1947 'Six folksongs'
   1. Mocking bird
   2. Annie the miller's daughter
   3. The Wood pigeon
   4. The Feng-Yang drum: Chinese tune
   5. The Musician: French tune
   6. My horses ain't hungry: Kentucky song
            ø 2222/4230/timp.perc/hp/str   BBC   19961 Awa

Winter, 1948 'Three carols'
   1. Wassail song
   2. While shepherds watched their flocks by night
   3. Down in yon forest
            ø 2121/2230/timp.perc/hp/str   BBC   19962 Awa

Easter, 1948
   1. The Keeper   (Novello)
   2. High Barbaree   (Curwen)
   3. Time for man to go home   (Boosey)
   4. Carol of service   (OUP)
   5. Git along, little dogies: American cowboy song
            ø 2121/2230/timp.perc/hp/str   BBC   19960 Awa

Easter, 1949 'Five folksongs'
   1. The Tailor and the mouse
   2. Come, mah little darlin'
   3. Newcastle: English folk dance
   4. Little red bird
   5. Spinning wheel
            ø 1121/2210/timp.perc/hp/str   (Curwen/Stainer & B)   19959 Awa

Summer, 1949 'Three folksongs'
   1. My bonny cuckoo: Irish song
   2. Sing, said the mother: Appalachian song
   3. Cradle song: Czech song
            ø 2121/2230/timp.perc/hp/str   BBC   19958 Awa

Easter, 1950 'Four folksongs'
   1. O rare Turpin, in F min
   2. The Shepherdess, in A
   3. Bonny at morn, in F min
   4. Song of the flax, in B♭
            ø 2+picc.121/2200/timp.perc/hp/str   BBC   19789 Awa

WILLIAMS, Grace (cont)

FOLK SONGS AND CAROLS (cont)
    Summer, 1950 'Three folksongs'
        1. Bill Bones' hornpipe
        2. Out in the garden   (Novello)
        3. The Derby ram   (OUP)
                                                                                (Cramer)
                φ   2+picc.1+ca.21/2230/timp.perc/hp.pf/str   BBC   19890 Awa
    Winter, 1950 'Four carols'
        1. King Herod and the cock: Worcestershire carol
        2. Today in Bethlehem: Lithuanian carol   (Novello)
        3. Jesus, Jesus rest your head: American carol   (Schirmer)
        4. A merry Christmas: English West Country carol   (Schirmer)
                φ   1000/0100/perc/hp/str   (Evans)
    Easter, 1951 'Five folksongs'   BBC   20042 Awa
        1. A fairy lullaby: Gaelic song
        2. What say you?: Finnish song   (Bayley & Ferguson)
        3. Andulko: Czech song   (OUP)
        4. Buriano: Bulgarian song   (Schirmer)
        5. Hark to the mill wheels: French song   (Schirmer)
                φ   1+picc.111/0100/str   BBC   20126 Awa
    Summer, 1951 'Two folksongs'
        1. The wonderful inn: children's song
        2. The Drummer boy: French folksong   (Novello)
                φ   2+picc.222/3230/timp.perc/hp/str   (Macmillan)
    Winter, 1951 'Folksong & three carols'   BBC   20226 Awa
        1. The Mallow fling: English folksong
        2. The Cradle: Austrian carol   (Nelson)
        3. Infant holy: Polish carol
        4. Come, ye lofty: Breton carol
                φ   1+picc.111/0000/perc/hp/str   BBC   21242 Awa
    Easter, 1952 'Four folksongs'
        1. Tik-tak: Serbian folksong
        2. Lullaby (English air by S.Storace, from 'The Pirates': opera, c.1792)   (G.Schirmer)
        3. The cuckoo: English air
        4. Holahi, holaho: German air   (Curwen)
                φ   2+picc.222/2230/timp.perc/hp/str   BBC   21243 Awa
    Summer, 1952 'Four folksongs'
        1. Per Spelmann: Norwegian folksong
        2. Robin-a-thrush: English folksong
        3. Dorabella (Tchaikovsky)   (Curwen)
        4. Git along, little dogies: American cowboy song   (Curwen)
                φ   2222/2230/timp/hp/str   (Arnold)
    Winter, 1952 'Folksong & carol'   BBC   20614 Awa
        2. Sally Anne: Appalachian folksong
        2. Bethlehem calls you: Hungarian carol   (OUP/G.Schirmer)
                φ   2222/2230/timp.perc/hp. /str   BBC   21244 Awa
    Easter, 1953 'Four folksongs'
        1. Donkey riding: Lancashire sea song (1'48")
        2. Hilo somebody: Northumbrian shanty (2'30")   (OUP)
        3. Gentle Mary: Irish air (2'25")   (Curwen)
        4. Charlie is my darling: Scottish air (1'46")
                φ   2+picc.222/2230/timp.perc/hp/str   BBC   20823 Awa
    Summer, 1953 'Four folksongs'
        1. The meeting of the waters: Irish song
        2. Honza: Czech folksong
        3. Come, mah little darling: Negro folksong   (Schirmer)
        4. Barley mow   (Curwen)

                φ   2222/2230/timp.perc/hp/str
                                                                    BBC   20932 Awa

WILLIAMS, Grace (cont)

FOLK SONGS AND CAROLS (cont)
  Winter, 1953 'Folksong & carol'
    1. Kukulienka: Slovakian folksong (2')
    2. Sleep my little son: German carol (2'50")
                          ⌀ 1121/0220/timp.perc/hp/str   BBC   21038 Awa
  Easter, 1954 'Four folksongs'
    1. Winter has gone: German folksong, in A   (Schofield & Sims)
    2. The Holly: Welsh folksong, in D   (University of Wales Press)
    3. Faithful Johnnie: Scottish song, in E♭
    4. Oh! 'twas in the broad Atlantic: song, in F   (Ashdown)
                          ⌀ 1+picc.121/0220/timp.perc/hp/str   BBC   21203 Awa
  Summer, 1954 'Three songs'
    1. Tooralo, tooraly, tooralo: Czech folksong, in E♭   (Harrap)
    2. Lullaby (attrib Mozart), in G
    3. Blow the man down: English sea shanty, in E♭   (Curwen)
                          ⌀ 2+picc.121/2230/timp.perc/hp/str   BBC   21246 Awa
  Winter, 1962 'Folksongs & Carols'
    1. The Handsome butcher: Hungarian folksong
    2. A Recipe for fish: French traditional tune
    3. Mr. Frogs wedding: American folksong
    4. The Raggle taggle gypsies: English folksong
    5. Aunt Hessie's white horse: South African folksong
    6. In nightly stillness: Polish carol
    7. What shall we give: Catalan carol
    8. Christmas day in the morning: carol by E.J.Moeran
                          ⌀ hp/str/chorus   Arranger MS:BBC MS 31400
  Summer, 1963 'Five folksongs'
    1. Blow away the morning dew
    2. O Waly, waly
    3. One more river
    4. River Wisla
    5. Yeo, yeo, sir
                          ⌀ perc/hp/str/voices   Arranger MS:BBC MS 31421 +
PENILLION for orchestra   ⌀ 2(picc)2(ca)22/4230/timp.perc/hp/str   13'35"   OUP,1962 Misc 4657
SEA SKETCHES: suite
  1. High wind   4. Breakers
  2. Sailing song   5. Calm sea in summer
  3. Channel sirens
                          ⌀ str   16'-17' OUP,1951 20211 Bwa
SEVERN BRIDGE: varitaions on a Welsh folk song ['Braint'], by Malcolm Arnold and others
  Variation 5   Chorale prelude
                          ⌀ 2+picc.2+ca.2+bcl.2+cbsn/4231/timp.perc/
                             hp/str   BBC,1966 24805
SQUIRRI, WIRRI, WIP: Norwegian folksong, arr
                          ⌀ 0020/0000/hp/str   Arranger MS:BBC MS 30132
VARIATIONS ON A SWEDISH TUNE 'The SHOEMAKER', for piano & orch (used in Rhythm & Melody series, 1950)
                          ⌀ 2121/2230/timp.perc/hp/str   BBC   19889 Awa
WELSH NURSERY SONGS, arr for Soprano & Baritone soli & orch
  Set 1   Set 2
    1. Jim Cor Crystyn   1. Prybach yn mynd
    2. Gee, geffyl bach   2. Deryn y Bwn
    3. Cadi ha   3. Migildi Magildi
    4. Ble'rwyt ti'n myned   4. Ble'r Eidi
    5. Lali lwli   5. Oes gafr eto
    6. Pwsi meri mew   6. Robin Ddiog
    7. Blc'vel di heno   7. Mae gen i gworwrdd
    8. Modryb Elin enwog   8. Si so jac y do
                          ⌀ 0010/0000/perc.glock/2pf   BBC   19966 Awa

WILLIAMS, Harry

IT'S A LONG, LONG WAY TO TIPPERARY, for chorus & orch by H.Williams & J.Judge
  arr S.Robinson   ø 2(picc)121/2230/perc/str   BBC   TO 104

WILLIAMS, J.Lloyd

WHEREVER HEARTS ARE TRUE: Welsh traditional song (Tra-db-dau), arr
  in A, orch H.Carr   ø 2121/2000/timp/hp/str   (Boosey & H)   TO 96

WILLIAMS, John (1941-

CLOSE ENCOUNTERS OF THE THIRD KIND: film music
  arr I.Sutherland (Excerpts from Symphonic Orchestral Suite)
                    ø 2222/4331/perc/hp.pf/str   (Screen Gems/EMI Music)   26468
SUPERMAN: film music
  Concert overture, based on themes from the film, by David Francis
              ø 2(picc)2(ca)2(bcl)2/4331/timp.perc.bell tree.kit.vib/
                  hp.pf(cel)/str   (Warner-Tamerlane)   26705
STAR WARS: film
  Main theme   ø 2+picc.22+bcl.2/4331/timp.perc.glock.tamtam.vib/
                  hp.pf(cel)/str   (Fox Fanfare,1977)   Misc 9968

WILLIAMS, John Gerrard   see   WILLIAMS, Gerrard

WILLIAMS, Ralph Vaughan   see   VAUGHAN WILLIAMS, Ralph

WILLIAMS, T.

The LARBOARD WATCH: song
  in G, arr J.Turner   ø 1110/1000/hp/str   BBC   LM G 9057

WILLIAMS, Warwick

ALL THE GIRLS: selection, arr   PC 1+picc.222/2230.euph/timp.perc/str   FD & H   6870 B
BEST OF THE BUNCH: selection, arr
                    PC 1+picc.222/2230.euph/timp.perc/str   FD & H   5432
CHEVALIER'S COSTER SONGS: selection no.2, arr W.Williams & C.Godfrey
                    PS 2(picc)222/0200.euph/timp.perc/str   Reynolds   2390
CONVIVIALIA: selection, arr   PC 1(picc)222/2230.euph/timp.perc/str   FD & H   10763
The FESTIVE SEASON: selection, arr
                    PC 1+picc.222/2230.euph/timp.perc/str   FD & H   5291
The GOLD MINE: selection, arr   1+picc.222/2030.euph/timp.perc.bells/str   FD & H   10797
HARRY LAUDER'S SONGS: selection, arr
                    PC 1(picc)121/2230.euph/perc/str   FD & H   6869 C

WILLIAMSON, Bill

The GIRL I LEFT BEHIND ME, arr   2121/2220/perc/pf/str   2'50"   BBC   WE 366

WILLIAMSON, Malcolm (1931-

The BRIDGE THAT VAN GOGH PAINTED ø str   3'30"   E.B.Marks,1976   Misc 8869
CONCERTI
  Organ & orch (1961)   ø 1(picc)01+bcl.1(cbsn)/4331/timp.perc.xyl/
                    2hp/str   BBC   23423 +

WILLIAMSON, Malcolm (cont)

CONCERTI (cont)
  Piano & orch
    No.2   ∅   str   16'   Chappell,1961   24125
    No.3 (1962)   ∅   2(picc)2(ca)2(bcl)2(cbsn)/3231/timp.perc/str   Weinberger   Misc 6882
    2 pianos & strings (1972/3) ∅   str   Weinberger,1973   Misc 8219
  Violin & orch
      version for violin & chamber orch
                                ∅   1(picc)111(cbsn)/1000/str   Weinberger,1965   Misc 6077
CONCERTO GROSSO for string quartet & orch (1965)
                                ∅   2+picc.2+ca.33/43+Dtpt.31/timp.perc.glock.vib.xyl/
                                    hp/str   10'
                                                                            Weinberger,1965/CML,1972   Misc 8044
EPITAPHS FOR EDITH SITWELL (1966)
                                ∅   str   7'   Weinberger,1972   Misc 8111
HAMMARSKJOLD PORTRAIT: song cycle for Soprano solo & strings (1974)
    1. Prayer of Acceptance   4. Nocturne
    2. Pastoral   5. Apotheosis
    3. The Path of Unself
                                ∅   str   (Composer)   Misc 8871
The HOUSE OF WINDSOR: incidental music to radio production
                                    perc.glock.bells.tamtam/str   Composer MS:BBC   MS 31753 +
The ICY MIRROR: cantata for Soprano, Mezzo Soprano & 2 Baritone soli, chorus & orch (Symphony no.3)(1962)
                                ∅   1+picc.1+ca.1+bcl.1+cbsn/4331/timp.perc.glock.xyl/
                                    hp.pf/str   Weinberger,1972/CML,1973   Misc 8289
JUBILEE HYMN for chorus & orch (1977)
                                ∅   2+picc.2+ca.2+bcl.2+cbsn/44+Dtpt+Ftpt.31/
                                    6perc(2 sets bells.glock.3gongs.vib.xyl)/hp/
                                    str   Weinberger,1977   Misc 9261
LENTO for strings   ∅   str   Chappell(H)   PL 401
MASS OF CHRIST THE KING for SSTBar soli, double chorus & orch (1978)
                                ∅   3(picc,afl)3(ca)2+bcl.3(cbsn)/44(Dtpt)31/
                                    timp.2perc(anv.bells.crot.glock.3gong.tamtam.vib.xyl)/
                                    hp/str   Weinberger,1978   Misc 10511-2
OUR MAN IN HAVANA: opera (1963)
    Suite for STB soli, chorus & orch
      1. Prelude and scene   4. Beatrice's aria
      2. Hasselbacher's Scena   5. Intermezzo
      3. Serenade   6. Threnody and finale
                                ∅   2(picc)222/4230/timp.perc.glock/cel.gtr.hp/
                                    str   Weinberger,1963   Misc 6905
    Suite for orch in 5 mvts   ∅   2(picc)2(ca)2(bcl)2(cbsn)/4330/timp.perc/hp/
                                    str   20'   Weinberger,1965/69   Misc 6973 B
2 PIECES for strings
    1. Timid pink flamingoes   2. Parade-Cockarde
                                ∅   str   1'50"   E.B.Marks,1976   26172
SANTIAGO DE ESPADA: overture (1956)
                                ∅   1+picc.222/3231/timp.perc/str   6'30"   Boosey & H,1969   Misc 7007 B
SINFONIA CONCERTANTE for piano, 3 trumpets & strings (1960-62)
                                ∅   str   Boosey & H,1965   Misc 5981 C
SINFONIETTA (1965)
    1. Toccata   2. Elegy   3. Tarantella
                                ∅   2(picc)222(cbsn)/4331/perc.glock.xyl/hp/str 18' Weinberger,1966   Misc 6366 B
      version with prelude as used in Frederick Ashton's ballet
                                ∅   2(picc)222(cbsn)/4331/perc.gong/hp/str   Weinberger,1966/75   Misc 10364
The STONE WALL: cassation for audience & orch
                                ∅   2(picc)22(bcl)2(cbsn)/4331/perc.bells.xyl/hp/
                                    str   Weinberger,1971   Misc 7538 C

WILLIAMSON, Malcolm (cont)

SYMPHONIC VARIATIONS (1965)
   Serenade and Aubade only   φ   1(picc)111/1000/hp/str4-tet.str   Weinberger,1965   Misc 6881
SYMPHONIES
   No.2 (1969)   φ   3(2picc)3(ca)3(E♭cl,bcl)3(cbsn)/43+Dtpt.31/
                         timp.perc.bells.glock.vib/cel.hp/str   Weinberger,1969   Misc 7597

   No.3 see The ICY MIRROR

WILLIAMSON, W.L.

BICYCLES: radio feature (Export Jigsaw no.6) .
                    φ   1110/2000/timp.perc/str   Composer MS:BBC   MS 30349
La CUCARACH: traditional song, arr
  in A♭ for solo voice, chorus & orch
                    φ   1121/2220/perc/hp.pf/str   (FD & H)   LM G 4542
ESCAPE OR DIE: radio series
   Title music   φ   1111/1220/timp.perc/hp/str   Composer MS:BBC   MS 30050 φ only
   No. 2: The Escape of Charles II
                    φ   1111/1220/timp.perc/hp/str   Composer MS:BBC   MS 20451 φ only
   No. 3: Horned pigeons   φ   1111/1220/perc/hp/str   Composer MS:BBC   MS 20452 φ only
   No. 4: The Blenden Hall φ   1111/2220/timp.perc/hp/str   Composer MS:BBC   MS 30036 φ only
   No. 5: Road to Endor   φ   2121/2220/perc.vib/hp/str   Composer MS:BBC   MS 20483 φ only
   No. 6: Lord Nithsdale in the Tower of London
                    φ   1111/2220/timp.perc/hp/str   Composer MS:BBC   MS 20497 φ only
   No. 7: No stars to guide φ   2(picc)221/2220/timp.perc.vib.xyl/hp/str Composer MS:BBC   MS 30015 φ only
   No. 8: Boomerang   φ   2121/2220/Chinese high block/hp/str   Composer MS:BBC   MS 30003 φ only
   No.11: Submarine K13   φ   212(bcl)1/1220/timp.perc/hp/str   Composer MS:BBC   MS 30035 φ only
GO DOWN MOSES: traditional song, arr
  in A min   φ   1121/2220/perc/hp/str   BBC   LM G 4576
LAURA: radio production (1949)
                    φ   1100/1000/hp/str   Composer MS:BBC   MS 30372
LEATHER: radio feature (Export Jigsaw no.4)
                    φ   1110/2000/timp.perc/str   Composer MS:BBC   MS 30343
De OLD ARK A-MOVERING: traditional song, arr
  in G for solo voice, chorus & orch
                    φ   1121/2220/perc/hp/str   BBC   LM G 4584
READY THE BAND (Songs and Marches of the British Army)(1957)
   Lilliburlero   Hot stuff
   Over the hills   Happy soldier
   Glass

                    φ   1011/1110/perc/str(no cb)
                       drum & fife band: 2B♭ fifes, Ffl.bass.sdm.tdm Arranger MS:BBC MS 31190
SWING THAT KILT: Scottish medley in swingtime
                     000.4sx.0/00.2cnt.10/perc/bjo.gtr/str   FD & H   15686 Ap

WILLING, C.E.

WE ARE BUT LITTLE CHILDREN WEAK : hymn
  arr H.Perry   PC 1121/0000/timp.perc/org/str   Hawkes   4970

WILLNER, Arthur (1881-1959)

BAGPIPES: concerto for piano & orch, op.78
                 [1]0[1]0/0000/[perc]/str   Hinrichsen   Misc 2029
Die INSTRUMENTE STELLEN SICH VOR (The instruments introduce themselves), op.75
   1. Violinen   5. Zwei Flöten   8. Fagott   11. Harfe
   2. Viola   6. Oboe   9. Vier Hörner   12. Posaunen und Tuba
   3. Violoncell   7. Klarinetten   10. Zwei Trompeten   13. Pizzicati
   4. Contrabass

                    φ   212+bcl.1/4231/timp/hp/str   Willner   12976

WILLSON, Meredith (1902-

The GREAT DICTATOR: film by M.Willson & C.Chaplin
    Selection, arr D.Edge, orch E.Irving
                          ⌀   21+ca.21/2331/timp.perc/hp/str   BBC   TO 573
I SEE THE MOON: song for solo voice, chorus & orch
    in G, arr K.Papworth   ⌀   2222/4220/timp.perc/hp.2pf/str   (Feldman)   18379
The MUSIC MAN: musical play
    Selection, arr F.Rapley   PC   2(picc)12.3sx.1/2230/timp.perc/hp/str   Frank Mus Co,1961 23361 Cs
    Extracts
        Seventy-six trombones
            arr P.Knight for orch, with rhythm section
                              2(2picc)222/4331/rhythm-kit.[bgtr].gtr.pf/
                              timp.perc.glock/hp/str   6'30"   (Frank Music)   26776
            arr A.Roper   ⌀   2120/2220/timp.perc/gtr.pf/str   (Frank Music)   MLO 428

WILM, Nicolai von (1834-1911)

CONCERTSTÜCK for harp & orch, op.122
                          PC   2222/4230/timp/str   Kistner   7406

WILMS, Jan (1772-1847)

WIEN NEERLANDS BLOED: alternative Netherlands National Anthem
                          PC   2(picc)222/4231/timp.perc/str   Benjamin   16363 +
    arr M.L.Lake   PC   1+picc.12.2sx.1/2210/perc/str   C.Fischer   19720

WILSON, Brett

HEY PRESTO!
    arr T.Duncan   PC   2+picc.121/2230/timp.perc/acdn.gtr.hp/str
                          or   str   Boosey & H   21129

WILSON, Dennis

La CUNA (The Cradle) by D.Wilson & I.Slaney
                          PC   2121/2220/cast/hp/str   2'15"   B.Wood,1958   22861 Ap
LAND'S END TO JOHN O'GROATS: suite
    1. Land's End   2. John O'Groats   3. Windermere
                          ⌀   2120/2220/timp.perc.glock/cel.gtr/str   B.Wood   MLO 779
The SWANEE WHISTLER, by D.Wilson & I.Slaney
                          PC   2121/2220/timp.perc/str   B.Wood,1959   22877 Cs
VISION OF A ROSE   PC   2121/0000/timp.perc/acdn/str   2'30"   B.Wood,1958   22837 Cs

WILSON, Henry Lane (1871-1915)

BEFORE YOU CAME: song
    in Eb   org.pf/str   Cramer,1912   18217
BEGGAR'S SONG: song
    in G, arr F.Cramer   pf/str   Boosey   LM G 4845
CARMENA: song
    in E, arr J.O.Turner & linked with 'I'll sing thee songs of Araby' by F.Clay (for London Trascription
        Service)   ⌀   1110/1000/perc/hp/str   (Chappell,1955)   21700
    in F, arr F.Cramer   str   3'   (Reed & Walsh)   LM G 7372
    orch Clark (non-vocal) PC   1121/2210/timp.perc.bells.xyl/str   G.Schirmer   10123
    orch H.Geehl (non-vocal) PC   1121/2210/perc/str   Reed & Walsh   18745 C
COME LET'S BE MERRY: traditional song, arr
    in Bb   pf/str   (Boosey)   LM G 3619

WILSON, Henry Lane (cont)

PHILLIS HAS SUCH CHARMING GRACES
    in Bb min, arr G.Stacey   pf/str   (Boosey & H)   LM G 3805
The PRETTY CREATURE: song, arr (attrib J.Storace)
    in A, orch H.Carr   ϕ 2222/2000/hp/str   (Boosey)   TO 1421
The SAILOR'S LIFE: song, arr for solo voice, chorus & orch
    in D, orch G.Vinter   ϕ 2(picc)222/4230/perc.siren/hp/str   (Boosey)   23329 +
The TWO BEGGARS: duet for Tenor & Bass soli & orch
    in D, arr H.Carr   ϕ 2121/2220/timp/hp/str   (Dix)   19000
WHEN DULL CARE: song
    in G, arr G.Stacey   pf/str   (Boosey)   LM G 3756

WILSON, Hugh (1766-1824)

O FOR A CLOSER WALK WITH GOD (Martyrdom): hymn
  arr H.Perry   PC 1121/0000/timp.perc/org/str   Hawkes   4970

WILSON, J. (1591-1674)

FROM THE FAIR, LAVINIAN SHORE
  in A, arr F.Collinson   ϕ 1121/2200/str   Arranger MS:BBC   MS 30925

WILSON, R.Barclay

TUDOR SUITE, transcr from compositions attrib King Henry VIII (1509-1547)
    1. Pavyn   2. Saraband   3. Galyard   4. Chaunt
                  ϕ 2[=2ob]020/001[=bsn]0/perc/str   Ashdown   16484 B
The WINTER'S TALE: incidental music and trumpet fanfares
                  ϕ 0000/0500/str   Composer MS:BBC   MS 3050

WILSON, Sandy (1924-

The BOY FRIEND: musical play
  Extracts
    I could be happy with you: duet
      in Eb, arr R.Docker   ϕ 2122/4000/2pf/str   (Chappell)   24713 +
      in Eb, arr E.Tomlinson ϕ 2222/3230/timp.perc/hp/str   (Chappell)   21959
    It's never too late: duet
      in Bb, arr R.Docker   ϕ 2122/4000/2pf/str   (Chappell)   24713 +
    A Room in Bloomsbury: song
      in C, arr P.Cardew   1122/1230/timp.perc/hp.pf/str   (Chappell)   22788 +
The BUCCANEER: musical play
  Selection, arr F.Rapley PC 212.3sx.1/2230/timp.perc/hp/str   5'   Chappell,1955   Cp
VALMOUTH: musical play
  Selection   PC 2121/2230/perc/hp/str   (N.Gay,1958)   22821

WILSON, Stanley

SKYE SYMPHONY, op.30   ϕ 2+picc.22+bcl.2+cbsn/4331/timp.perc.bells.glock/
                      hp/str   28'   Stainer & B   Misc 911

WILSON, Thomas (Brendan)(1927-

TOUCHSTONE: a portrait for orch, op.27
                  ϕ 2+picc.2+ca.2+bcl.2+cbsn/4331/timp.perc.glock[=xyl].
                  tamtam/cel.hp.pf/str   10'
                                  International/AH & C,1967   Misc 6664 B

WIMBERGER, Gerhard (1923-

MOMENTO VIVERE for Mezzo soprano & Baritone soli, 3 speakers, chorus & orch (1974)
ϕ   2(2picc)1+ca.1+bcl.1+cbsn/1120/timp. 3perc(byos.
glock.gongs.mbn.tamtams.tomtoms.timbales.vib.xyl)/
gtr(egtr).ebgtr.eorg.org/str(6.-.3.3.3)   50'   Bärenreiter,1977   Misc 9578

PLAYS (1975)
  1. Konfrontation   2. Ostinato   3. Nostalgia   4. Swing
ϕ   2221+cbsn/2221/timp.2perc(bells.glock.4gongs.
kit.mba.tamtam.tomtoms.vib)/bgtr/12vlc   20'   Bärenreiter,1975   Misc 9525

WINDEATT, Corelli A.

SERENADE ESPAGNOLE   PC 1121/2230/timp.perc/str   Hawkes   571

WINDEATT, George

MASQUE OF MONTHS
  May's song
    in E   ϕ   2222/3231/timp.perc/hp/str   2'   (Boosey)   TO 1590

WINDSOR, B.

The CHIMES: waltz
  arr A.Lotter   PC 1+picc.122/4230/perc.bells/str   Hawkes   939

WINDT, Herbert (1894-1965)

ANDANTE RELIGIOSO for Baritone solo & chamber orch, op.6 (1926)
ϕ   1(picc)1+ca.1+bthn+bcl.1+cbsn/1110.euph[=wtuba]/
timp.perc(glock.tamtam.xyl)/cel.2hp.pf/st
str(6.0.4.3.2 or 24.0.12.9.6)   Universal,1922   Misc 9240

WINKLER, Alexander Adolfovitch (1865-1935)

En BRETAGNE: overture-fantasy, op.13
ϕ   2+picc.222/4231/timp.perc/hp/str   Belaieff   6123

WINKLER, Gerhard (1906-

FESTTAGS-STÄNDCHEN
  arr R.Etlinger   PC 2222/4230/timp.perc/acdn.gtr/str   4'30" Edn Insel-Ton,1952   5874
Die GRATULANTEN KOMMEN: intermezzo
  arr R.Etlinger   PC 2222/4230/timp.perc/acdn.gtr/str   5'   Edn Insel-Ton,1952   5874
NEAPOLITAN SERENADE   PC 112.3sx.1/2230/perc/acdn/str   3'30"   Bosworth   18922

WINLAW, Maurice

IN A FAERY GARDEN: suite
  1. Dawn   3. Whispering woods
  2. The elfin dance   4. The faery garden
    arr Bradley   PC 1121/2230/timp.perc/str   Paxton   2667

WINNE, Jesse M.

BENEATH A BALCONY   PC 112.3sx.1/2210/perc/bjo/str   Ricordi   11032

WINNER, Septimus (1826-1902)

LISTEN TO THE MOCKING BIRD
   arr M.L.Lake   PC 1+picc.12.2sx.1/2210/perc/str   C.Fischer   19720

WINSTONE, Eric

OASIS
   arr D.Bowden   PC 112.4sx.0/0320/perc/gtr/str   Lafleur   16636 Cp

WINTER, Aubrey

ALPINE MEMORIES 'By the lake of the four cantons': fantasias on Swiss melodies, arr
                         PC 2(picc)22.2sx.2/2230/timp.perc/acdn/str   Boosey & H   11229 Atv
BRITISH GRENADIERS: march, arr
   in   PC 1222/2230/perc/str   Hawkes   6100
CHARM OF THE VALSE: medley of famous English & Continental valses, arr
                         PC 2(picc)22.4sx.2/2330/timp.perc/gtr/str   Hawkes   12313
FESTIVALIA: echoes of old-time dances, arr
                         PC 2(picc)22.2sx.2/2230/perc/str   9'-10'30"   Hawkes   11418 +
FINCK-A-LINCKE: lancers   PC 222.3sx.2/2230/timp.perc/str   Boosey & H   20358
GEMS OF GUNG'L: waltz   PC 2222/2230/perc/str   Hawkes   124
GEMS OF STRAUSS: waltz   PC 2222/2230.euph/perc/str   Hawkes   2126 B
GOLDEN OPERA: lancers   PC 1+picc.22.4sx.2/2230/perc/str   Boosey & H   19027
The GOLDEN VALSE: valse medley PC 2(picc)22.2sx.2/2230/perc.glock.vib/str   7'15"-11' Boosey & H   10011 Ap B
LOCH LOMOND: Scottish tune, arr
   in F   PC 1222/2230/perc/str   Hawkes   7977
The MARCHING LANCERS   PC 1+picc.22.2sx.2/2230.euph/perc/str   Boosey & H   19035
MARTIAL MOMENTS: march medley PC 2(picc)222/4230/perc.glock/str   8'15"   Hawkes   3792 Ap C
MEN OF HARLECH: Welsh tune, arr PC 1(picc)222/2230/timp.perc/str   Hawkes   8735
The MINSTREL BOY, arr
   in Eb   PC 1+picc.222/2230/timp.perc/str   Hawkes   8734
NAUTICAL MOMENTS: allegro marziale
                         PC 2(picc)22.2sx.2/4230/perc/str   6'15"-7'30" Boosey & H   9174 Ap B
O'DONNELL ABOO
   in C   PC 1+picc.222/2230/timp.perc/str   Hawkes   8734
The PASSING OF THE REGIMENTS: march potpourri
                         PC 1+picc.22.2sx.2/2230/perc/str   7'45"-8'   Hawkes   10015 B
REVIEW-PAGEANTRY: grand fantasia of British Regimental marches
                         PC 2(picc)22.3sx.2/2230/timp.perc/str   15'   Boosey & H   14148 Bs
ST. PATRICK'S DAY
   in G   PC 1+picc.222/2230/timp.perc/str   Hawkes   8734
STEPS OF GLORY: march potpourri
                         PC 2(picc)22.2sx.2/2230/perc/str   8'30"   Hawkes   13129 Atv
The STORY OF THE OVERTURES: selection, arr
                       PC 2(picc)22.2asx.2tsx.2/4330/timp.perc/hp/str   Boosey & H   13132 *
A STRAUSS GARLAND: fantasia on works of the Strauss family
                       PC 2(picc)22.2sx.2/2230/timp.perc.vib/cel/str 10'-12' Hawkes   683
TCHAIKOVSKY WALTZ MEMORIES: selection, arr
                       PC 2+picc.222/4231/timp.perc/str   Boosey & H   11992 C
YANKEE DOODLE: traditional American song, arr
                       PC 2222/2230/perc/str   Hawkes   6103 Ap

WINTER, Banks

WHITE WINGS: song
   in Bb, arr R.Chignell for solo voice, chorus & orch
                       φ 1121/2220/timp.perc/str   (Paxton)   MS 5568
   in Bb, arr B.Thompson for solo voice, chorus & orch
                       φ 1110/1000/hp/str   BBC   LM G 7544

WINTER, Peter von (1754-1825)

CONCERTANTE, op.20, in Bb   φ   soli: 0111/0000/vln.vla.vlc
                                   orch: 1222/2000/str   Breitkopf [c.1814]   21981
MASS, in D   φ   2200/2200/timp/org/2vln.vla   von Falter [c.1800]   20274

WINTERBOTTOM, Frederich

AMERICAN NATIONAL AIRS, arr   PC 2(picc)122/2230.euph/timp.perc/str   Hawkes   2411 B
CHARLIE IS MY DARLING: traditional air, arr for bassoon & orch
                                 PC 1+picc.122/2230.euph/timp.perc/str   Hawkes   4521

WINTERFIELD, Max   see   GILBERT, Jean

WIRÉN, Dag Ivar (1905-

BALLET SUITE, op.24a
   1. Overture (2'30")   4. Promenade (1'35")
   2. Characters (2'15")   5. Introduction & polka (4')
   3. Viennese waltz (4'20")
                              φ   2222/4230/timp.perc/hp/str   14'40"   Gehrmans,1953   Misc 4228 B
CONCERTO for piano & orch, op.26 φ 2(picc)222(cbsn)/4210/timp.perc/str 19'   Gehrmans,1951   Misc 4386
LITTLE SUITE, op.17   φ   2(picc)222/2210/timp.perc/str   11'   Gehrmans,1944   Misc 2854 C
ROMANTIC SUITE, op.22   φ   1111/1000/str   12'   Gehrmans,1955   Misc 4764 C
SCHERZO, op.7b   φ   2+picc.222/2210/timp/str   4'   Gehrmans,1941   19861 B
SERENADE, op.11
   1. Preludium   3. Scherzo
   2. Andante espressivo   4. Marcia
                              φ   str   14'30"-16'
                                                                      Edn Suecia/Gehrmans,1944 16755 Bni C
SINFONIETTA, op.7   φ   2222/2210/timp.perc/str   18'   Universal,1951   Misc 2853 B
SYMPHONIES
   No.3, op.20   φ   2222/4231/timp.perc/str   23'   Gehrmans   18804
   No.4, op.27   φ   2(picc)222/4231/timp.perc/str   17'30"   Gehrmans,1954   Misc 5073

WIRGES, W.F.

FASCINATIN'MANIKIN   PC 112.3sx.1/2210/perc/bjo/str   Luz NY   11058
MISSISSIPPI LAMENT: symphonic transcription
   arr Grofe   φ   112.3sx.1/2320/timp.gong.vib/bjo/str   C.Fischer   11244

WISCHNEGRADSKI, A.

La NONNE: symphonic poem   φ   2+picc.2+ca.32+cbsn/4331/perc.bells/
                                  cel.hps/str   Belaieff   365
SUITE
   1. Andante   2. Valse   3. Tarantelle
                              φ   3(picc)2+ca.32+cbsn/4331/timp.perc/hp/str   Zimmermann 4725
SYMPHONIES
   op. 7, in Bb min   φ   3(picc)1+ca.32+cbsn/4331/timp.perc/str   Bote & B   10888
   op.12, in C min (no.4)   φ   3(picc)2+ca.3(bcl)2+cbsn/4331/timp.perc.bells/
                                  cel.hp/str   Belaieff   Misc 2300

WISE, Samuel [fl.1770]

CONCERTI for organ (or harpsichord) & orch
   No.1, in G   No.3, in Bb   No.5, in G
   No.2, in D   No.4, in C   No.6, in Bb
                                  str/cont [lacks solo & vln 2]   Mrs Johnson [c.1770]   26163 *

WISHART, Peter Charles (1921-

CAROL POTPOURRI (1953
   1. Ding dong merrily on high   3. Good King Wenceslas
   2. Love came down at Christmas
                  ø   1010/0100/pf/str/chorus   OUP   MLO 988
CONCERTO PICCOLO, in B♭
   1. Allegro   2. Ballet en Rondeau   3. Rondo
                    1111/1000/timp.perc/str   13'   Hinrichsen,1961   Misc 5451 C
COVENTRY CAROL, arr for Soprano & Contralto soli & orch
                  ø   1000/0000/str   Arranger   MLO 1849
DING DONG MERRILY ON HIGH: carol, arr
   in B♭   ø   2222/4230/timp.perc.bells.glock/hp/str   Arranger MS:BBC   MS 2562
FANTASIA ON CHRISTMAS CAROLS, arr for voices & orch
    God rest ye merry gentlemen   Away in a manger   The first Nowell
                  ø   11[=cl]00/1[=tpt]000/str   Arranger   MLO 1852
HERE WE COME A WASSAILING: Christmas carol, arr for SSA voices & orch
   in G   ø   1010/0100/timp.perc/pf/str   OUP   MLO 2535
The HOLLY AND THE IVY: Christmas carol, arr for chorus & orch
   in G   ø   1+picc.222/4000/hp/str   (OUP)   MLO 2507
I SAW THREE SHIPS: Christmas carol, arr
   in G   ø   1100/1000/tri/str   Arranger   MLO 1850
JINGLE BELLS: Christmas carol, arr for chorus & orch
                  ø   1+picc.222/4230/timp.perc.sbells.glock/str   Arranger   MLO 991
O COME ALL YE FAITHFUL: Christmas carol, arr
                  ø   1100/0100/pf/str   Arranger   MLO 1848
SYMPHONY no.2, op.71 (1972)   ø   2+picc.2+ca.2+bcl.2+cbsn/4231/timp.perc.glock/
                       hp.pf/str   Stainer & B/CML,1973   Misc 8261

WISSMER, Pierre Alexandre (1915-

DIVERTIMENTO   ø   2(picc)2(ca)22/4230/timp.perc.xyl/hp.pf/str 14'   P.Noël   Misc 4978

WISZNIEWSKI, Zbigniew (1922-

AD HOMINEM: ballet (1963)   ø   222+bcl.2/4230/3perc(cel.gong.vib)/pf/
                       str/ABarB chorus   25'-27' Polish SM,1976   Misc 9115
TRE PEZZI DELLA TRADIZIONE, for chorus & orch (1964)
                  ø   11+ca.01/2220/perc.bells.vib.xyl/cel.hp.pf/
                     str   7'   Polish SM,1966   Misc 6407

WITHERS, Herbert (1880-

FÊTE GALANTE, based on the music of Rameau and Couperin
                  ø   str   Lengnick   19761

WITMARK, I.

SHANGHAI
   I'm in love: song
     in F, arr M.Mackie   ø   2131/2230/timp.perc/hp.pf/str   (Feldman)   18548

WITT, Friedrich (1771-1837)

JENA SYMPHONY (formerly attrib Beethoven)
   ed Stein   ø   1202/2200/timp/str   21'15"   Breitkopf   4021
SONATA à 7, in C   0001/0100/str/cont   BBC   MS 30141

WITT, L.O.de

12 ENGLISH SONGS, arr
    1. British Grenadiers (traditional)
    2. Sally in our Alley (H.Carey)
    3. The Anchor's weighed (J.Braham)
    4. My Pretty Jane, or When the bloom is on the rye (H.Bishop)
    5. Twickenham Ferry (T.Marzials)
    6. The Midshipmite (S.Adams)
    7. Black Eyed Susan (R.Leveridge)
    8. The Bay of Biscay (J.Davy)
    9. Vicar of Bray (traditional)
    10. Goodbye, sweetheart, goodbye (J.L.Hatton)
    11. Ever of thee (F.Hall)
    12. Roast beef of old England (R.Leveridge)
            PC 1(picc)121/22.cnt-solo.11/perc/str   C.Fischer   5924

12 IRISH SONGS, arr
    1. The Minstrel Boy (traditional)
    2. Savourneen Delish (traditional)
    3. Killarney (M.W.Balfe)
    4. Come back to Erin (Claribel)
    5. Believe me, if all those endearing young charms (traditional)
    6. The Meeting of the waters (traditional)
    7. The Last rose of summer (traditional)
    8. The Pretty girl milking her cow (traditional)
    9. Dear little shamrock (J.W.Cherry
    10. Wearing of the green (traditional)
    11. The Harp that once through Tara's Halls (traditional)
    12. The Cruiskeen Lawn (traditional)
            PC 1(picc)121/22.cnt-solo.11/perc/str   C.Fischer   5923

The KICK-UP-A-ROW BRIGADE: march medley
            PC 1(picc)121/2210/perc/str   C.Fischer   10217

12 SCOTTISH SONGS, arr
    1. Auld Robin Gray (traditional)
    2. Logie o'Buchan (traditional)
    3. Ye Banks and Braes (traditional)
    4. Afton Water (A.Hume)
    5. Robin Adair (traditional)
    6. I dreamed I lay (traditional)
    7. Comin' thro' the rye (traditional)
    8. Within a mile of Edinburgh town (J.Hook)
    9. Maid of Dundee (traditional)
    10. Annie Laurie (Lady John Scott)
    11. Scots wha ha'e wi' Wallace bled (traditional)
    12. Auld Lang Syne (traditional)
            PC 1121/22.cnt-solo.11/perc/str   C.Fischer   5922

WITTGENSTEIN, Friedrich Ernst, Count of Sayn-Wittgenstein-Berleburg (1837-1915)

ANTONIUS AND CLEOPATRA: opera
            φ   2+picc.2+ca.2+bcl.2/4231/timp/str
            Offstage: 0000/0400   Wittgenstein   Misc 1640

WITTINGER, Robert (1945-

CONCENTRAZIONE, op.6 (1965-66)   φ   2(picc)+picc.1(ca)4(2sx,bcl)1(cbsn)/4331/timp.perc.
            bells.cimb.mba.vib.xyl/cel.hp.pf(4 hands)/str   Breitkopf,1967 Misc 7480

WITTINGER, Robert (cont)

CONCERTO LIRICO for orchestra, op.32 (1977)
      φ 3(picc)33+bcl.3(cbsn)/4331/timp.perc(bells.mbn.
        tamtam.vib.whip)/2[=1]hp.pf(cel)/
        str(16.14.12.10.8)   12'30"   Moeck,1978   Misc 9653

DIVERGENTI for orch, op.13 (1969)
      φ 3(picc)3(ca)3+bcl.3/4331/timp.perc.cimb.
        2mba.vib/cel.hp.pf(hpsd)/str   Breitkopf,1969 Misc 7327

ESPRESSIONI (1964-66) φ 11(ca)3(sx)+bcl.0/2110/timp.perc.bells.mbn.
        vib.xyl/cel.hp.2pf/str   Breitkopf,1967 Misc 7479

IRREVERSIBILITAZIONE, for cello & orch, op.10 (1968)
      φ 3(picc)1+ca.2+bcl.1/3220/perc.bells.vib/
        cel.hp/str   15'   Breitkopf,1968 Misc 6930

OM per orchestra, op.12 (1968) φ 3(3picc)3(2ca)+ca.3(bcl)3(2cbsn)/6331/
        timp.perc.bells.2mba.vib/cel.hp.2pf(2pianinos)/
        str   12'-14' Breitkopf,1968 Misc 6992 B

SINFONIAS
 No.1, op. 1 (1961-3, rev 1976)
  rev version   φ 3(picc)3(ca)3(bcl)3(cbsn)/4[=6]331/timp.perc.bells.
        [cimb].glock.xyl/hp.pf(cel)/str(16.14.12.10.8)/
        [chorus]   Breitkopf,1976 Misc 9026
 No.2, op.35 (1978-80) φ 4(2picc)4(ca)4(Ebcl,bcl)4(cbsn)/6441/5perc(timp.
        bells.4bgo.mba.4tamtam.4tomtom.vib.2whip.xyl)/
        cel.2hp.[org].pf/str(32.-.12.10.8)(4cbs must be
        5-stringed)/fv-chorus   41'-42' Moeck,1980 Misc 10489

WLADIGEROFF, Pantscha see VLADIGEROV, Panshu

WÖBER, Ottokar

JAPANISCHE KRIEGSBILDER (Japanese war pictures): suite
 1. Shotai: drill-song   3. Kimi ga yo: National hymn
 2. Ubergang (Transition)   4. Miyasan 'Mein Prinz, Reiterlied' (My prince, rider's song)
      φ 2(picc)222/4331/perc/str   Breitkopf   7991

WOHLFAHRT, Franz (1833-1884)

KINDER-KONZERT, op.76   pf/toy instrs   Forberg   16813

WOLF, Hugo (1860-1903)

COMPLETE WORKS

Hugo Wolf: Nachgelassene Werke, ed R.Haas & H.Schultz.   Leipzig: MWV, 1937- (abbreviated NW)
Hugo Wolf: Sämtliche Werke, ed H.Jancik & others.   Vienna: MWV, 1960- (abbreviated WW)

AN DEN SCHLAF (Song to sleep)
 in Ab   φ 2000/4000/str   Peters   20237 +
ANAKREON'S GRAB: song (orch 1893)
 in D   φ 2022/2000/str   Peters   16879
 in D, ed G.Raphael φ 2022/2000/str   Breitkopf,1934 Misc 4420 B
CHRISTNACHT (Christmas Night), for SATB soli, chorus & orch
 rev M.Reger & F.Foll (1903) φ 3222/4331/timp/hp/str 20'   Lauterbach Misc 2121
Der CORREGIDOR: opera
 Suite, arr H.Gal
  1. Prelude   2. Fandango & March   3. Spanish intermezzo   4. Notturno & entr'acte
      φ 3(picc)2(ca)22/4231/timp.perc/str 16' Hawkes,1955 Misc 4417 B
 Extracts
  In dem Schatten: aria
   in Bb   φ 2222/4000/hp/str   (BBC)   25744

WOLF, Hugo (cont)

DEM VATERLAND, for male voices & orch
   in C   ∅   2+picc.222/4331/timp.perc/str   Heckel   21609 + & mf 47
DENK' ES, O SEELE! (O soul, consider!): song (orch 1891)
   in D min   ∅   0222/2230/timp/str   Peters   21738 + & mf 49
   in D min, ed G.Raphael   ∅   0222/2230/timp/str   Breitkopf,1934   Misc 4420 B
   in F min   ∅   0222/2230/timp/str   (Peters)   25983
ELFENLIED for Soprano solo, fv-chorus & orch
   in B min   ∅   2+picc.222/2000/hp/str   4'15"   Fürstner   10174
   in D min, orch G.Raphael   ∅   1+picc.110/1100/hp[=pf]/str   Breitkopf   Misc 4421 B
EPIPHANIAS: song
   in G, orch N.Del Mar (1948) ∅   2+picc.22+bcl.2/4230/timp.tri/hp/str   Arranger   Misc 9022 B
ER IST'S (Song to spring): song (orch 1890)
   in G   2222/0200/timp/hp/str   Peters   19547 +
   in G, ed G.Raphael   ∅   2222/2200/timp/hp[=pf]/str   Breitkopf,1934   Misc 4420 B
Das FEST AUF SOLHAUG: incidental music to Ibsen's play
                                ∅   22+ca.22/4231/timp.perc/hp/str   (GB-Lbm)   21630 +
Der FEUERREITER: song arr & orch for chorus & orch (orch 1892)
                                ∅   2+picc.223/4331/timp.gong/str   5'10"-6'   Peters   11457 + & mf 49
Der FREUND: song
   in E, orch G.Raphael   ∅   2222/2200/timp/str   Breitkopf,1934   Misc 4420 B
   in E, arr M.Reger   ∅   2222/2200/timp/str   Peters   20234
FUSSREISE: song
   in D, orch G.Raphael   ∅   0022/2000/str   Breitkopf,1934   Misc 4421 B
Der GÄRTNER: song
   in D, orch G.Raphael   ∅   1111/1000/str   Breitkopf,1934   Misc 4421 B
GEBET 'Herr! Schicke was du willt': song (orch 1890)
   in E   ∅   0022/4000/str   Peters   18979
   in E, ed G.Raphael   ∅   0022/4[=2]000/vln-solo.str   Breitkopf,1934   Misc 4420 B
HARFENSPIELER I 'Wer sich die Einsamkeit': song (orch 1890)
   in D   ∅   2222/2000/hp/str   Peters   21607 + & mf 46
HARFENSPIELER II 'An die Türen will ich schleichen': song (orch 1890)
   in C min   ∅   0212/0000/str   Peters   20239 +
HARFENSPIELER III 'Wer nie sein Brot': song (orch 1890)
   in F min   ∅   2222/4000/hp/str   Peters   20240 +
HEIMWEH (Nostalgie)(Longing for Home): song
   in Eb, orch G.Huppertz   PC 2121/2110/timp/str   2'   Peters,1930   25344
   in Eb, orch J.Marx   ∅   2222/4100/timp/str   Peters,1934   Misc 87
   in Eb, orch G.Raphael   ∅   2222/2200/hp[=pf]/str   Breitkopf,1934   Misc 4420 B
ICH HAB' IN PENNA EINEN LIEBSTEN WOHNEN: song
   in F, arr J.Marx   ∅   2122/3100/timp/str   Peters   20231
IN DEM SCHATTEN see Der CORREGIDOR
IN DER FRÜHE (In the early morning): song (orch 1890)
   in D min   ∅   02+ca.22/4030/str   Peters   20230 + & mf 48
   in D min, ed G.Raphael   ∅   02+ca.22/4030/str   Breitkopf,1934   Misc 4420 B
ITALIENISCHE SERENADE   ∅   2222/2000/vla-solo.str   6'30"   Bote & B   4300 + Amv Bs C
                                ∅   str   9'   Bote & B   8836 Amv
   ed H.Jancik   ∅   2222/2000/vla-solo.str   15'   MWV,1965.NW 17/2 Misc 9187 & MRL
   arr Junk   PC 2222/2000/str   Bote & B   6747
   arr S.Robinson   ∅   2222/2000/str   7'55"   (Bote & B)   20064
KARWOCHE (Holy week): song (orch 1889)
   in Ab   ∅   2+picc.2+ca.22/4000/perc/str   Peters   20235 +
KENNST DU DAS LAND (Know'st thou the land): Mignon's song (orch 1890, rev 1893)
   1st instrumentation (1890), in Gb
                                ∅   22+ca.23/4230/timp/hp/str   Peters   21608 + & mf 48
   2nd instrumentation (1893), in Gb
                                ∅   22+ca.22/4130/timp/hp/str   (Peters)   19257

WOLF, Hugo

MANUEL VENEGAS: unfinished opera
   Extracts
      Frühlings-Chor
        in A   φ   32+ca.23/4331/timp.perc/hp/str   Peters   21606 +
MIGNON'S SONG see KENNST DU DAS LAND
MORGENHYMNUS (orch version of Morgenstimmung; arr & orch 1897)
   in E, arr W.Kähler   φ   22+ca.23/4331/timp.perc/hp/str   5'   Peters,1910   20227 + & mf 49
NEUE LIEBE: song (orch 1890)
   in Bb   φ   2222/4230/timp/str   Peters   18655 + & mf 48
2 ORCHESTERLIEDER aus dem Spanischer Liederbuch see 1) WENN DU ZU DEN BLUMEN GEHST
                                                   2) WER SEIN HOLDES LIEB VERLOREN

PENTHESILEA: symphonic poem
   orig version (1883)
      ed R.Haas & H.Schultz   φ   2+picc.2+ca.23/4331/timp.perc/hp/str   MWV,1937.NW 3/2   21263 + & MRL
      ed H.Jancik, based on 1837 edn by R.Haas
                   φ   2+picc.2+ca.23/4331/timp.perc/hp/str   MWV,1971.WW 16   MRL
   rev & shortened version, arr Hellmesberger
                   φ   2+picc.2+ca.23/4331/timp.perc/hp/str   Bote & B,1903   Misc 1492
PROMETHEUS: song
   in D min, arr W.Kähler   φ   2+picc.2+ca.23/4331/timp/str   Heckel   20228 + & mf 49
Der RATTENFÄNGER: song
   in A min, arr W.Kähler   φ   2+picc.222/2200/perc/str   Heckel   20229 + & mf 49
SCHERZO UND FINALE
   ed H.Schultz   φ   2+picc.222/4331/timp.perc/str   16'   MWV,1940.WW 3/3   20540 & MRL
SCHLAFENDES JESUSKING (Sleeping Christchild): song (orch 1890)
   in F   φ   2222/0000/str   3'45"   Peters   10146
   in F, ed G.Raphael   φ   2222/0000/str   Breitkopf,1934   Misc 4420 B
SEUFZER (A sigh): song
   in E min   φ   02+ca.02/0000/str   Peters   20236 + & mf 48
Das STÄNDCHEN: song
   in C & D (2 settings), arr M.Reger
                   φ   1111/1000/timp/str   Peters,1915   20233
STERB ICH, SO HÜLLT IN BLUMEN MEINE GLIEDER: song
   in Ab, orch M.Reger   1122/2000/timp/str   Peters,1915   20336
Der TAMBOUR: song
   in E, orch G.Raphael   φ   0022/1110/perc/str   Breitkopf,1934   Misc 4421 B
ÜBER NACHT: song
   in C, arr Pohle   φ   2222/4230/timp/hp/str   2'30"   Bote & B   14739
UND WILLST DU DEINEN LIEBSTEN STERBEN SEHEN: song
   in Ab, orch M.Reger   φ   1122/2000/timp/str   Peters,1915   20335
VERBORGENHEIT: song
   in Eb, orch G.Raphael   φ   1111/1000/str   Breitkopf   Misc 4421 B
   in Eb, arr J.Marx   φ   2122/3000/timp/str   4'   Peters   20232 +
WENN DU ZU DEN BLUMEN GEHST (Down the garden when you go): song (orch 1897)
   in A, ed R.Haas   φ   11+ca.22/3000/str   MWV,1937.WW 2/1   21745 + B & MRL
WER SEIN HOLDES LIEB VERLOREN (Him whose love has learned to scorn him): song (orch 1897)
   in F# min, ed R.Haas   φ   2222/4000/hp/str   MWV,1937.WW 2/1   21745 + B & MRL
WO FIND' ICH TROST (Where shall I find comfort): song (orch 1890)
   in C min   φ   22+ca.22/4230/timp/str   6'   Peters   11383 + & mf 48
ZUM NEUEN JAHR: Kirchengesang: song
   in A, orch G.Raphael   φ   2022/2000/str   Breitkopf,1934   Misc 4421 B

WOLF, Otto

ROMANZEN
   Cello & orch, op.64   φ   1022/2000/timp/str   Kahnt,1905   Misc 418
   Violin & orch, op.34   φ   2222/2000/str   Kahnt,1905   Misc 433

WOLF-FERRARI, Ermanno (1876-1948)

Gli AMANTI SPOSI: opera
  Complete   ø   2+picc.2+ca.2+bcl.2/4331/timp.perc/cel.hp/
                              str   Weinberger,1924   Misc 4666

L'AMORE MEDICO (Dr. Cupid): opera
  Overture   ø   2+picc.2+ca.2+bcl.2/4331/timp.perc/hp/str   8'30"-10'   Weinberger   11463 Amv
  Extracts
    Intermezzo   ø   22+ca.2+bcl.2/4000/hp/str   3'15"-3'45"
                                                                  Weinberger,1913   Misc 4619
      arr R.Docker   PC   11(ca)21/2220/timp/hp/str   4'50"   Weinberger,1953   25122

Il CAMPIELLO: opera
  Extracts
    Fantasia (Act 1)
      arr Maglio   PC   1120/0210/timp.perc/str   Ricordi   13833
    Fantasia (Act 2)
      arr Maglio   PC   1120/0210/timp.perc/str   Ricordi   13834
    Intermezzo (Act 2)   ø   2+picc.222/4230/timp/str   3'   Ricordi   Misc 2596 B
    Ritornello (Act 3)   ø   2222/4100/hp/str   2'-2'50"   Ricordi   Misc 2596 B
      arr Maglio   ø   1110/0000/str   Ricordi   13501
      arr Maglio   1110/0000/str   Ricordi   14447 B

CHAMBER SYMPHONY for piano & chamber orch, op.8, in Bb
                     ø   1111/1000/pf/str   32'30"-33'45"   Rahter   10300

CONCERTO for violin & orch, op.26, in D
  arr G.Bustabo   ø   2222/4330/timp/hp/str   C.R.Baher   Misc 2470 B

DIVERTIMENTO, op.20, in D
  1. Variazioni su un tema capriccioso   3. Siciliana
  2. Canzone pastorale   4. Rondo - finale
                     ø   2(picc)222/4330/timp.perc/str   21'   Leuckart   14452

Le DONNE CURIOSE (The Inquisitive Women): opera
  Overture   ø   2(picc)222/2200/timp/hp/str   Weinberger,1903   Misc 7039
    ed C.Mackerras   ø   2(picc)222/2200/timp/hp/str   Weinberger,1959(H) PL 386 As Bn Cgg
  Selection, arr Riesenfeld PC   1121/2210/timp.perc/str   G.Schirmer   3103 B
  Extracts
    Minuet & Furlana
      arr H.Schneider   PC   2122/2210/hp/str   2'45"   Weinberger,1954   21685

I GIOIELLI DELLA MADONNA (The Jewels of the Madonna): opera
  Suite
    1. Festa popolare (Volksfest)   3. Serenade (Intermezzo no.2)(Act 3)
    2. Intermezzo no.1 (Act 2)   4. Dance of the Camorrists (Danza napolitana)(Act 3)
                     ø   2+picc.223/4331/timp.perc.glock.xyl/
                           2gtr.hp.2mand/str   Weinberger,1941(H) PL 384 As Bn Cgg
  Selection, arr O.Langey PC   2(picc)222/4231/timp.perc/hp/str   G.Schirmer   3111 C
  Extracts
    Dance of the Camorrists (Danza napolitana)(Act 3)
      arr O.Langey   PC   2(picc)2+ca.23+cbsn/4331/timp.perc/hp/str   3'30"   G.Schirmer   3109 B
    Intermezzo no.1 (Act 2 introduction)
                     ø   2223/4000/hp/str   5'20"   G.Schirmer   1902 D
                     ø   2+picc.2+ca.2+bcl.3+cbsn/4000/hp/str   Weinberger   4877 B
    Intermezzo no.2 (Act 3 introduction)(Serenade)
                     ø   2+picc.2+ca.2+bcl.3+cbsn/4331/hp/str   3'15"   G.Schirmer   2903 D
                     ø   2+picc.2+ca.2+bcl.3+cbsn/4331/hp/str   Weinberger   3527 Bm
                    PC   1121/2210/timp/str   2'40"   Weinberger   26165
    Meeting of the Camorrists (Act 3)
      arr O.Langey   PC   2+picc.2+ca.2+bcl.2/4331/timp.perc/hp/str   G.Schirmer   3114
    Prayer
      arr O.Langey   PC   1121/2210/timp/str   G.Schirmer   3110 Bwe

WOLF-FERRARI, Ermanno (cont)

IDILLIO: concertino for oboe & orch, op.15, in A
                ø   0000/2000/str   17'30"   Ricordi,1932   23471
The JEWELS OF THE MADONNA   see   I GIOIELLI DELLA MADONNA
I QUATTRO RUSTEGHI (School for fathers): opera
  Prelude   PC 21+ca.21/3210/acdn.hp/str   Weinberger   20403
                    ø   21+ca.22/4000/hp/str   Weinberger,1934/65(H)   PL 385 As Bn Cgg
  Extracts
    Intermezzo   øPC 2(picc)222/3000/hp/str   3'45"   Weinberger   11883 B
                    ø   2(picc)222/3000/hp/str   Weinberger,1934/65(H)   PL 385 As Bn Cgg
                    PC 21+ca.21/3210/acdn.hp/str   Weinberger   18874
II SEGRETO DI SUSANNA (Sussana's Secret): opera in 1 act
  Complete   ø   2(picc)+picc.222/4230/timp.perc/cel.hp/str Weinberger,1909/10   24308
  Overture   ø   2+picc.222/4230/timp/hp/str   2'50"   Weinberger   7901 Amv B Cs
                    ø   2+picc.222/4230/timp/hp/str   Weinberger(H)   PL 383 As Bn Cgg
    arr Riesenfeld   PC 2(picc)121/2230/timp/hp/str   G.Schirmer   3112 B
    arr H.Schneider   PC 1+picc.121/2230/timp/str   Weinberger   21478 B
  Extracts
    Intermezzo
      arr G.Winter   PC 1121/2220/str   2'50" Weinberger,1951   20334 B
SERENADE in Eb   ø   str   18'-19'45"   Steingraber   2799 B
SLY: opera
  Selection, arr Fiorda PC 1121/2210/timp.perc.bells/cel.mand/str   Sonzogno   9258 B
SUITE: concertino for bassoon, 2 horns & strings, op.16, in F
  1. Notturno   3. Canzone
  2. Strimpellata   4. Finale
                    ø   str   20'-23'30" Ricordi,1932   Misc 1296
TALITHA KUMI (The daughter of Jairus), for chorus & orch, op.3
                    ø   1122/2[3][2]0/org/str   Rahter   Misc 1029 B
TRIPTYCHON, op.19
  1. In excelsis   3. Pregheira
  2. Agli eroi caduti
                    ø   2+picc.222/4331/timp/hp/str   Leuckart   14396
La VITA NUOVA: cantata, op.9
  Complete   ø   32+2ca.22/4331/2timp.perc/2hp.org.pf/str   Rahter   Misc 1402
  Dance of the angels PC 2121/0000/str   British Standard Mus,1928   23400
    arr L.Weninger   PC timp/str   Benjamin   11669

WOLFE, Jacques (1896-

De GLORY ROAD: song
  in C & Bb, arr T.Fones   ø 1121/2210/perc/hp.pf/str   (Schirmer)   LM G 4274
  in F min   ø 1121/1210/perc/str   (Boosey)   LM G 10178
SAILORMEN: song
  in C min, arr P.Akister ø 2121/1230/perc/pf(cel)/str   (Schirmer)   LM G 10251
SHORT'NIN BREAD: song
  in D, arr G.Stacey   pf/str   (Boosey & H)   LM G 5252
  in Eb, arr W.L.Williamson ø 1121/2220/perc/hp.pf/str   (Boosey & H)   LM G 4581

WOLFURT, Kurt von (1880-1957)

CONCERTO GROSSO for small orch, op.20
                    ø   2(picc)111/1100/timp.perc/str(5.4.3.2.2) 22'   Bote & B,1931   Misc 9419
TRIPELFUGE, op.16   ø   2+picc.2(ca)22/4331/timp.3perc/hp/str   Eulenburg,1929   Misc 9592

WOLPE, Stefan (1902-

SYMPHONY no.1 (1955/6)   ∅   3(picc)3+ca.3+bcl.3+cbsn/5331.2B♭bar=2foghn]/
                                     timp.perc.glock.xyl/cel.hp.pf/str   (Composer)   Misc 8424

WOLSELEY, Charles   see   CHARLES, Wolseley

WOLSTENHOLME, William (1865-1931)

ALLEGRETTO in E♭   PC   2222/2000/str   Novello   2034 C
ALLEGRETTO for viola & orch   ∅   1121/2000/str   3'10"   (Novello)   MS 4789
The ANSWER (Die Antwort)
   in B♭, arr R.Chignell   ∅   2121/2240/timp/hp/str   4'30"   (Lengnick)   MS 349 ∅ only
The QUESTION (Die Frage)
   in F, arr R.Chignell   ∅   2121/2240/timp/hp/str   3'   (Lengnick)   MS 349 ∅ only

WOLTMANN, Frederick   PL 436 &)

POEM for flute & orch   ∅   02+ca.22/2000/timp/str   (Composer)   Misc 2396   )

WOOD, Arthur

ALL CLEAR   PC   222.3sx.2/2230/perc/str   Paxton   8992 B
BALLERINA SUITE
   1. Theatre lights   3. Curtain up
   2. Flowers from a forgotten lover
                               PC   2(picc)12.3sx.1/2230/timp.perc/cel/str   10'   FD & H   13849 Cp
BARNSLEY FAIR: a Yorkshire rhapsody
                               PC   1+picc.222/4230/timp/hp/str   7'05"-8'   P.Maurice   12944 Bp
CLEOPATRA: operetta by O.Strauss
   Selection   PC   2(picc)121/2230/timp.perc/str   AH & C   3312 C
COQUETTERIE   1121/2230/perc/str   AH & C   7293
COUNTRY DANCE   PC   1121/2230/perc/hp/str   AH & C   4930
3 DALE DANCES (On Yorkshire folk tunes)
   1. Allegro con brio   3. Allegro moderato
   2. Andante molto espressivo
                               PC   2(picc)2(ca)22/2230/timp.perc/hp/str   8'-11'   AH & C   641 B
                               ∅   2(picc)2(ca)22/4230/timp.perc/hp/str   AH & C   16428
DEWSBURY MOOR PIG: song
   in C   ∅   2121/2230/timp/str   Composer MS:BBC   MS 1351 ∅ only
FAIRY DREAMS   PC   1+picc.121/2230/timp/str   2'   Chappell   1339 B
FIDDLERS THREE   PC   2(2picc)222/4230/perc/str   3'30"   Paxton   16479 Ap B
LANCASHIRE CLOG DANCE   PC   2121/2220/timp.perc/str   3'30"   P.Maurice   14691
LULLA-BYE   PC   2121/2220/timp.perc/str   AH & C   7347
3 MASK DANCES   PC   2(picc)121/2210/timp.perc/str   9'30"   Chappell   7342 B
MERRIMENT for piccolo & orch   PC   1222/2220/perc/str   Chappell   7271
MOORLAND FIDDLERS   PC   222.3sx.2/2230/timp.perc/mustel-org/str   3'40"-5'   P.Maurice   12273 C
3 MORE DALE DANCES (Yorkshire moors)
   1. Nidderdale (1'30")   3. Warfedale (2'45")
   2. Airedale (4'45")
                               ∅PC   2(picc)222/2230/timp.perc/str   8'   AH & C   7769 B
MY NATIVE HEATH: suite
   1. Knaresbro' status or Hiring fair   3. Bolton Abbey: slow melody
   2. Ilkley Tarn or Dance of the sprites   4. Barwick Green: Maypole dance
                               PC   2(picc)222/4230/timp.perc/hp/str   12'   Boosey   2860 Bp Cp E
NEXT MARKET DAY: song
   in E   ∅   1111/1110/perc/str   Composer MS:BBC   MS 2074

WOOD, Arthur (cont)

3 OLD DANCES
   1. True hearts   3. Gaiety
   2. Forget-me-not

arr Körke	PC	2(picc)222/4230/timp.perc/str		Bosworth	266
ORIENTAL SCENE	PC	2121/2230/timp.perc/hp/str		AH & C	3787
PETTICOAT FAIR: selection	PC	1(picc)121/2230/timp.perc/str		AH & C	2718 B
ROMANCE	PC	2222/2230/timp/str		AH & C	3903
SHIPLEY GLEN: overture	PC	2222/4230/timp.perc.vib/cel.hp/str	6'30"-7'15"	P.Maurice	14038 B
SPANISH DANCE: tango	PC	1+picc.121/2230/timp.perc/str		AH & C	11000
TOO MANY GIRLS	PC	1121/2030/timp.perc/str		AH & C	4894

The WIDOW MALONE: suite
   1. The Widow Malone   3. Irish Merrymaking: jig
   2. A Song of Erin: lament

	PC	2(picc)12.3sx.2/2220/timp.perc.glock/cel.hp/str		Paxton, 1937	24618

WOOD, Charles (1866-1926)

CHRIST, WHO KNOWS ALL HIS SHEEP: hymn

in F, arr S.Robinson	φ	str		Composer MS:BBC	MS 5619

COME SIT DOWN BESIDE ME

in F, orch H.Nelson	φ	1111/2000/perc/cel/str		Boosey	Ni 82

ETHIOPIA SALUTING THE COLOURS: song

in A♭, arr F.Cramer		pf/str		(Boosey & H)	LM G 4642

WOOD, Daniel

GARDEN OF HAPPINESS: song

in F	PC	1111/2210/timp/str		Enoch	12827

WOOD, Harry

HARRY WODD'S HITS: selection, arr Terry

	PC	111.3sx.1/2220/perc/gtr/str		Cinephonic	495

MANX AIRS: National melodies, arr

	PC	2+picc.222/2230/timp.perc/str		Boosey	7023

WOOD, Haydn (1882-1959)

An AMERICAN RHAPSODY	PC	2+picc.2+ca.22/4230/timp/hp.org/str	9'	Boosey & H	18980
APOLLO	φPC	222.3sx.2/2230/timp.perc/str	7'-8'30"	Boosey & H	12734 C
An AUTUMN SONG: morceau de concert					
		1222/2220/timp/pf/str		Chappell	6486
A BELL FOR ADANO	PC	2222/4230/timp.perc/hp/str		K.Prowse	18666
BIRD OF LOVE DIVINE: song					
in A♭	PC	2122/2000/str	2'40"	Boosey	3639
in A♭		2112/2000/str		Boosey	17272
in G, arr G.Zalva	φ	1121/0210/timp.perc/str		(Boosey)	Misc 4967
arr as intermezzo (non-vocal)	PC	212.3sx.1/2220/timp/str		Boosey	10386 Ap B
A BIRD SANG IN THE RAIN: song					
in A♭	φ	1121/2000/str	3'45"-4'05"	(AH & C)	TO 1428**
in A♭, arr G.Stacey		pf/str		(AH & C)	LM G 3189
in A♭, arr J.Turner	φ	1110/1000/hp/str		(AH & C)	LM G 9080
in F	PC	1121/1210/pf/str		(AH & C)	LM G 3978
BLUE MIST	PC	2222/2230/timp/str		P.Maurice	16753

WOOD, Haydn (cont)

A BOUQUET OF HAPPY MEMORIES: potpourri of popular songs for chorus & orch
	∅	2222/2230/timp.perc/str		Arranger	TO 1463
The BRITISH EMPIRE: fantasia	PC	2(picc)22.3sx.2/4230/timp.perc/hp/str	11'	Universal	14267 Cp
A BRITISH RHAPSODY	PC	2+picc.122/2230/timp.perc/hp/str	10'	AH & C	19137 B

A BROWN BIRD SINGING: song intermezzo
in Ab	PC	1111/2220/timp/str	3'20"-5'	(Boosey)	MS 9487 Ap
in Ab, arr G.Stacey	∅	1100/1000/perc/gtr.hp.pf/str		(Chappell)	LM G 4465
in G, arr J.O.Turner	∅	1110/1000/hp/str		(Chappell)	LM G 7508
non-vocal arr	PC	112.2sx.1/2230/perc/str		Chappell	10628 Ap B
non-vocal arr	∅	212.3sx.1/2230/timp.perc.glock/str		Chappell	16380

CASEY THE FIDDLER: song
in E, arr H.Carr	∅	2121/2230/timp.perc/hp/str		(Chappell)	TO 670
in E, arr J.Turner	∅	1110/1000/hp/str		(Chappell)	LM G 9303

CASH ON DELIVERY: musical play
Selection 'Clovertown', arr H.M.Higgs
	PC	2(picc)1+ca.22/2230.euph/timp.perc/cel.hp/str	Chappell	2267 B

Extracts
In a corner of somewhere: song
in G		org.pf/str	Chappell	18216

CITIES OF ROMANCE: suite
1. Budapest (Hungary)(5')   3. Seville (Fiesta)(3')
2. Venice (Soft eyes from a lattice window)(3')
	PC	2(picc)222/4230/timp.perc/str	11'-12'30"	AH & C	14565 B

The CITY   see   LONDON CAMEOS

CONCERTO for violin & orch, in B min
2nd mvt (Adagio) only	∅	2222/2000/timp/pf/str	Composer	22941
CONSOLATION	PC	2222/2220/timp/str	Chappell	2938
DAY DREAMS: morceau de concert	PC	2222/2220/timp.perc/str	Hawkes	8092

A DAY IN FAIRYLAND: ballet suite
1. Invocation (Dawn)(4'30")   3. A Dream fairy (Sunset)(2'30")
2. Dance of a whimsical elf (Noon)(3')   4. Fairy revels (Night)(5')
	∅	2(picc)2(ca)22/2230/timp.perc.glock.xyl/		
		cel.hp/str	15'	Boosey & H	11622

No.2 only
arr H.Perry	PC	[cel]/str	Boosey & H,1949	23639

DEAR LOVE: musical play by H.Wood, J.Tunbridge & J.Waller   see   WALLER, J: DEAR LOVE
DREAMING	PC	222.2sx.2/2220/timp/str	Hawkes	1479

EAST OF SUEZ: suite
1. Aziza, the temple dancer (5'15")   3. Suzuki, the Geisha (6'30")
2. Moti Lal, the charmer of snakes (4'15")
	PC	2(picc)222/2230/timp.perc/hp/str	16'	AH & C	15674 B

EGYPTA: suite
1. Dawn in the valley of the kings (2'30")   3. The court of Pharoah (5'30")
2. Slave dance (2'15")
	PC	2(picc)222/2230/timp.perc/str	10'15"	Hawkes	8666
An EGYPTIAN LOVE SONG	PC	2121/2210/timp.perc/str		K.Prowse	1699
An EIGHTEENTH CENTURY SCHERZO	∅	str	6'15"	Schott	19179 C

ELIZABETH OF ENGLAND: grand march
	PC	2222/2230/timp.perc/str	5'	AH & C	20551
EROS: overture	∅PC	2222/4230/timp.perc.glock/hp/str		P.Maurice	9607 B
An EVENING SONG	PC	2222/2220/timp/str		Hawkes	1814

3 FAMOUS CINEMA STARS: suite
1. Ivor Novello: valse apache   3. Charles Chaplin: humoreske
2. Dolores del Rio: romance
	PC	222.3sx.2/2230/timp.perc/cel/str		K.Prowse	8829 C

WOOD, Haydn (cont)

3 FAMOUS PICTURES: suite
  1. The village wedding (painting by Luke Fildes)   3. The Laughing cavalier (painting by Franz
  2. The Doctor (painting by Luke Fildes)   Hals)

	PC	2(picc)222/2230/timp.perc/org/str	10'	Hawkes	2127 C
FANFARE no.3		0000/04+E♭stpt.30		Boosey & H	15389
FANTASY-CONCERTO	∅	str		Schott	19812 B

FESTIVAL MARCH (for Light Music Festival, 1949)

	∅	2222/4331/timp.perc/hp/str		(Composer)	19300
	PC	2222/2231/timp.perc/hp/str		Chappell	19336 Cp

FIRELIGHT FANCIES: suite
  1. Firelight: caprice (4'30")   3. Dance of the flames: waltz (5'15")
  2. Reflections: nocturne (5'30")

	PC	2+picc.222/4230/timp.perc/hp/str	12'-15'30"	Boosey	19755 B

FLEURETTE, I SHALL NVER FORGET, for cornet (or euphonium) & orch

	PC	2122/2220/timp.perc/str		Chappell	3657

FRESCOES: suite
  1. Vienna, 1913 (4'35")   3. The bandstand, Hyde Park (4'10")
  2. Sea shanties (6'20")

	∅PC	2(picc)222/4231/timp.perc/str	15'15"	Boosey	13776 Bp C
GIPSY SERENADE	PC	2222/2230/timp.perc/hp/str		Schott	19349 B
HARLEQUINADE	∅	2222/2230/perc/str	6'-8'	Schott	20098 B

HARVEST TIME: suite
  1. Harvester's dance (4')   3. Harvest home (2'45")
  2. Interlude (4'30")

	∅PC	2(picc)222/4230/timp.perc/str	11'45"	Boosey	1402 C

HAYDN WOOD'S SONGS: selection, arr H.M.Higgs

	PC	2122/2230.euph/timp.perc/cel/str	16'30"	Chappell	316
HEATHER BELLS: entr'acte no.2	PC	2222/2210/timp.glock/cel/str		Chappell	6943
HOMAGE: march	PC	2222/4231/timp.perc/str	5'	AH & C	12685

I HEAR YOU CALLING ME (orch version of song by Marshall)

	PC	112.3sx.1/2220/perc/str		Boosey & H	10785 B

I LOVE YOUR EYES OF GREY: chansonette

	PC	2222/0220/timp/str		Chappell	341
I SHALL BE THERE	SC	2131/2220/perc/str		AH & C	6144 Ap
in E, arr K.Warner	∅	1010/0000/pf/str		(AH & C)	LM G 3555
I THINK OF YOU MY SWEET	PC	2(picc)12.3sx.1/2210/timp.perc/str		Chappell	9675 B

I WANT YOUR HEART: song

in F, arr Wright	PC	112.3sx.1/2210/timp/str		Chappell	10078 B

IN AN OLD CATHEDRAL TOWN: suite
  1. The sleepy city wakes   3. The Close at noon
  2. Jack-in-the-green   4. Market day

	PC	2222/2230/timp.perc/hp/str	17'	AH & C	11888 C

IT IS ONLY A TINY GARDEN, for violin & orch

	PC	pf/str		Chappell	4976 B

  in D, arr J.Clements for chorus & orch

	∅	cel.hp/str	3'05"	(Chappell)	TO 1475
The 'JIMMY SALE' RAG	PC	1+picc.222/2230.euph/perc/str		Chappell	3673
KING ORRY: rhapsody	∅	2(picc)222/4230/timp.perc/hp.org/str	9'30"	Hawkes	15695
LIFE AND LOVE: overture	∅	2(picc)222/4230/timp.perc/hp/str	10'-11'	AH & C	15142 Bwa

2 LITTLE PIECES
  1. Slumber song (2'15")   2. Elfin dance (1'45")

	∅	2121/2210/glock/str	4'	Stainer & B	14536

LITTLE YVETTE: song

in G		org.pf/str		Chappell	18162

WOOD, Haydn (cont)

LONDON CAMEOS: suite
   1. The City: miniature overture (4'30")   18830 B
   2. St. James' Park in spring (3'30")   8995 C
   3. State ball at Buckingham Palace (5'30")   18610 B
                              PC 2222/4230/timp/hp/str   AH & C
LONDON LANDMARKS: suite
   1. Nelson's column, Trafalgar Square   3. The Horse Guards, Whitehall
   2. Tower Hill
                              ∅PC 2(picc)222/4230/timp.perc/hp/str   Chappell   18633 Bp
LONGING   PC 212.2sx.2/2210/timp/hp/str   Hawkes   221
A LOVE SONG: morceau de concert PC 2222/2220/timp.perc/str   2'30"   Chappell   6976
LOVE'S GARDEN OF ROSES: song
   in G   2020/0220/timp/str   4'15"   Chappell   17229
   in A♭, arr G.Stacey   pf/str   (Chappell)   LM G 5508
   in B♭   str   Chappell   17230
   in B♭, orch J.O.Turner   ∅ 1110/1000/hp/str   (Chappell)   21538
   in B♭ & A, arr H.Carr   ∅ 2121/2230/timp/str   (Chappell)   TO 669
   in B♭, arr Griffiths   pf/str   (Chappell)   LM G 5504
   in B♭, arr G.Stacey   ∅ 1110/0000/perc/hp/str   (Chappell)   LM A 686
   arr H.M.Higgs for cornet (or euphonium) & orch
                              PC 1121/2230/timp.perc/str   Chappell   3658 Bp
MANNIN VEEN: a Manx tone poem (Dear Isle of Man)
                              PC 2222/2230/timp.perc/str   10'   Boosey   11088 B
A MANX COUNTRY DANCE (based on folk song 'Hunt the Wren')   see   MANX COUNTRYSIDE SKETCHES
MANX COUNTRYSIDE SKETCHES: suite
   1. Manx pastoral scene   2. A Manx country dance
                              PC 2(picc)222/2230/timp.perc/hp/str   3'55"-5'30" P.Maurice   259 B
A MANX OVERTURE (Isle of mountains and glens)
                              PC 2(picc)22.3sx.2/4230/timp.perc/str 7'30"-8'30" Boosey   14271 Bp C
A MANX RHAPSODY   PC 2(picc)222/2230/timp.perc/str   11'   Chappell   9629 Cp Dn
MARCH OF THE PATRIOTS   PC 2(picc)222/2230/timp.perc/str   3'50"   P.Maurice   11671 C
                                  2222/2230/perc/str   (Composer) TO 1380
A MAY DAY: overture   ∅PC 2(picc)222/2230/timp.perc/hp/str   8'   Hawkes   235
MINERVA: overture   2222/4230/timp.perc/hp/str   12'30"   Composer   22940
MOODS: suite
   1. Preldue (Dignity)   4. Romance (Peniveness)
   2. Novelette (Allurement)   5. Spring song (Felicity)
   3. Caprice (Coquetry)   6. Concert waltz (Joyousness)
                              PC 2222/2230/timp.perc/hp/str   20'   Chappell   10692 B
MORENA: tango   PC 212.3sx.2/2230/perc/2bjo/str   Chappell   8466
MYLECHARANE: Manx folksong (not the same work as MYLECHARANE: Manx rhapsody)
   in A, for Baritone solo & orch
                              ∅ 2222/2220/timp/str   (Boosey)   22942
MYLECHARANE: Manx rhapsody   PC 2(picc)222/2230/timp.perc/hp/str   P.Maurice   18623 B
NOW THAT I HAVE YOU: song
   in F   PC 112.2sx.1/2210/timp.perc/str   Chappell   10078 B
O FLOWER DIVINE: song
   in F, arr H.M.Higgs   PC 1121/2230/timp.tri/str   Chappell   3658 Bp
   in A♭, arr J.Turner   ∅ 1110/1000/hp/str   (Chappell)   LM G 9063
ODE TO GENIUS, for chorus & orch
                              ∅ 2222/4231/timp/hp.[org]/str   Composer   Misc 5085
OMAHA: intermezzo   PC 212.3sx.1/2230/timp.perc/str   FD & H   9476 B
PARIS: suite
   1. Waltz (Apache life)(4')   3. March (Montmartre)(4')
   2. Meditation (In the Tuileries garden)(6')
                              ∅PC 2222/4231/timp.perc/hp/str   14'   AH & C   13267 Bp Dwe

WOOD, Haydn (cont)

A PLAINTIVE MELODY	PC	2222/2230/timp.vib/str		Chappell	16214 B
PLEADING	PC	2222/2000/str		Hawkes	3403 B
PRELUDE	PC	2222/2230/timp.perc/hp/str	5'	AH & C	11417 B
PRINCESS ELIZABETH OF ENGLAND:	song				
in G, arr G.Stacey	PC	1010/0000/str		(AH & C)	LM G 3688
ROMANY LIFE: symphony	PC	2(picc)222/4230/timp.perc/hp/str		P.Maurice	1818 B
A ROSE STILL BLOOMS IN PICARDY:	song				
in F	PC	2121/2220/timp/str		Chappell	16771 B
ROSES OF PICARDY: song					
in C, arr R.Docker	φ	0110/1000/hp/str	4'15"	(Chappell,1970)	25163 +
in in C, D & Bb, arr G.Stacey		pf/str		(Chappell)	LM G 3066
in D	φPC	1121/2220/timp.perc/str	4'-5'	Chappell	12825
in D, arr J.O.Turner	φ	1110/1000/hp/str		(Chappell)	LM G 7535
in Bb, arr H.Carruthers	φ	2121/0220/timp.perc/pf/str		Arranger MS:BBC	MS 20498
non-vocal version					
	PC	222.3sx.2/2230/perc/cel/str	.	Chappell	11062 Ap
	PC	str		Chappell	2221
arr as waltz		1(picc)12.2sx.1/2230/perc/pf/str		Chappell	4701 Ap B
ROVING FANCIES	PC	2222/2210/timp.glock/hp/str		Bosworth	6953
ROYAL CASTLES: suite					
1. Balmoral (March)(4')		3. Windsor Castle (Gala night)(5')			
2. Caernarvon (Memories)(4')					
	φPC	2222/2230/timp.perc/str	13'	Manor Mus	20811 B
A ROYAL NIGHT OF VARIETY May 8, 1934					
Prologue	φ	1(picc)121/2220/timp.perc/str		BBC	3710 φ only
SCHERZO FANTASTIQUE for orch	φ	2222/4230/timp.perc/hp/str	4'	Composer	Misc 5084
3 SEA SONGS					
No.2 only for voice or cornet & orch					
		1+picc.222/2230/timp.perc/str		Boosey	3640 C
The SEAFARER: nautical rhapsody	PC	2(picc)222/4230/timp.perc/hp/str	8'	Boosey	16759 C
SERENADE AT SUNSET	PC	2222/2230/timp.perc/hp/str		AH & C	16573 B
SERENADE TO YOUTH	PC	2121/0000/str	3'	Boosey	21044 Awe B
SILVER CLOUDS: entr'acte	PC	2222/2220/perc.glock/str		Chappell	2941 C
SKETCH OF A DANDY	PC	212.3sx.1/2230/timp.perc/acdn/str	3'	Bosworth,1952	20718
SNAPSHOTS OF LONDON: suite					
1. Sadlers Wells (At the ballet)(6')		3. Wellington Barracks (4')			
2. Queen Mary's garden, Regent's Park (4')					
	PC	2+picc.222/4230/timp.perc/str	14'	Chappell	19118 B
SOLILOQUY	PC	2222/2230/timp.perc/hp/str		Chappell	19282 B
A SONG OF QUIETNESS					
in D	PC	1000/0000/str	2'45"-3'08"	(Chappell)	LM G 3815
in Db, D & Eb, arr H.Carr	φ	2121/2230/perc/hp/str		(Chappell)	TO 74
SOUVENIR DE VALENTINO: morceau de concert					
	PC	2222/2210/timp/str		Chappell	11523 B
A STANFORD RHAPSODY 'Westward Ho'					
	φ	2+picc.222/4231/timp.perc/hp/str	12'	Boosey	18897 B
The STARS LOOKED DOWN: song					
in G, arr D.Darlow		pf/str		(AH & C)	LM G 3371
SUPPLICATION	PC	2222/2230/timp/str	5'45"	Chappell	8765 B
THIS IS MY DREAM: song					
in F, arr G.Stacey		0010/0000/pf/str		(AH & C)	LM G 3671
THISTLEDOWN: entr'acte no.1	PC	2222/2210/perc/str		Chappell	7449
A THOUSAND BEAUTIFUL THINGS: song					
in D, Eb & Bb, arr G.Stacey		pf/str		(AH & C)	LM G 3584
TINA: musical play by H.Wood & P.A.Rubens					
Selection, arr H.M.Higgs	PC	2(picc)122/2230.euph/timp.perc/str		Chappell	1240 C

WOOD, Haydn (cont)

TORCH OF FREEDOM: march	PC	2(picc)22.4sx.2/4331/timp.perc/str		Hawkes	16535 B
VALE OF HEART'S DESIRE: song					
in G, arr D.Darlow		pf/str		(AH & C)	LM G 3370
VARIATIONS ON A ONCE POPULAR HUMOROUS SONG					
	⌀	2(picc)222/4230/timp.perc/str	7'-9'	Chappell	7011 B
VARIATIONS ON AN ORIGINAL THEME (1903)					
	⌀	2222/2230/timp.perc/str		Composer	25346 **
VENETIAN BARCAROLLE	PC	2222/2220/timp/str	3'	Hawkes	9240
The VILLAGE THAT NOBODY KNOWS: song					
in A♭, arr A.Franzel	⌀	1110/0000/perc/acdn.hp.pf/str		(AH & C)	LM A 604
VIRGINIA: a southern rhapsody	PC	22(ca)22/4230/timp.perc/str	7'-10'	Chappell	6269 Ewe
WHEN THE DAWN BREAKS THROUGH	PC	2121/2220/timp/str		Chappell	9427 B
WHENE'ER YOU CALL: song					
in C, arrA.Franzel	PC	1010/0000/str		(AH & C)	LM G 3723
WHEN THE HOME-BELLS RING AGAIN: song					
in B♭	PC	2121/2220/timp.bells/str		AH & C	3685
WHEN YOU ARE LONELY: song					
in F		org.pf/str		Chappell,1917	18182
WONDERFUL WORLD OF ROMANCE: song					
in F		org.pf/str		Chappell,1918	18215

WOOD, Henry Joseph (1869-1944)

FANTASIA ON BRITISH SEA SONGS	⌀	3[=2]+picc.3[=2]+[ca].2[=3].2+[cbsn]/			
		4[=6]2[=4]31[=euph]/timp.perc.glock.1[=2]hp/			
		str		Chappell(H)	PL 503
arr G.Zalva	PC	2(picc)222/4231/timp.perc/cel.hp/str	17'	Chappell	14903 B
Sailors' hornpipe	⌀	1000/0000/sdm/str		(GB-Lam)	20102
GOD SAVE THE QUEEN: National Anthem, arr					
	PC	2+picc.2+ca.2+bcl.2+cbsn/4331/timp.perc/2hp.org/			
		str		Curwen	6630 Amv
	PC	3+picc.3+ca.3+bcl.3+cbsn/4431/timp.perc/2hp.org/			
		str		Curwen	6630 Amv

SAILORS' HORNPIPE: see FANTASIA ON BRITISH SEA SONGS

WOOD, Hugh (1932-

SONG CYCLE TO POEMS OF PABLO NERUDA for high voice and chamber orch, op.19 (1974)					
	⌀	3(picc,afl)1(ca)3(cbl)0/1110/3perc.acym.glock.xyl/			
		cel.hp.pf/str(1.1.1.1.1)	22'	(Composer)	Misc 8485 B

WOOD, J.H.

BADINERIE by J.H.Wood & F.Gervais					
	PC	str		FD & H	16550

WOOD, M.L.

MY MARY VEEN, or The Manx sailor's farewell, for cornet & orch					
		1121/0010/str		(Blakemore)	16373

WOOD, Thomas (1892-1950)

2 FANFARES					
1. General salute: suggested by 'The Grenadiers' 2. C in C's: salute					
		1+picc.00.E♭cl.0/0330/cym.sdm		Composer M:SBBC	MS 1561
GREENSLEEVES, arr					
orch G.Williams	⌀	str		(BBC)	Misc 3016

WOOD-SCOTT   see   SCOTT-WOOD

WOODCOCK (Woodcocke), Clement (fl.ca.1575)

HACKNEY
  arr Warlock & Mangeot   ∅   str   Curwen   6994

WOODCOCK, Robert (late 17th cent-ca.1734)

CONCERTI
  Oboe, strings & continuo
     No.10   ∅   str   [N.P]   Misc 7371
     No.11   ∅   str   [N.P]   Misc 7372
     No.12, in E♭   see   HANDEL, G.F: CONCERTI for oboe & orch, in E♭

WOODFORDE-FINDEN, Amy (1860-1919)

A DREAM OF EGYPT: suite
  1. Introduction   4. Pomegranate in your mouth
  2. Beside the lonely Nile   5. I envy every circlet
  3. Within the Sphinx's solemn shade   6. I wakened when the moon
     arr S.Baynes   PC 2(picc)122/2230/timp.perc/str   Boosey   3318 B
4 INDIAN LOVE LYRICS: suite
  1. Temple bells (2')   3. Kashmiri song 'Pale hands I loved' (4')
  2. Less than the dust (4')   4. Till I wake (2')
     No.1, in D min   No.2, in A min   No.3, in B♭   No.4, in E♭
        arr S.Baynes   PC 2122/2230/timp.perc.bells/hp/str   Boosey   10312 Bp
     No.1, in E min   No.2, in C min   No.3, in D   No.4, in F
        arr S.Baynes   PC 2122/2230/timp.perc.bells/hp/str   Boosey   4648 Bp
        arr Fletcher (non-vocal)
                            PC 2222/2230.euph/timp.perc.glock/str   Boosey   156 Ap B
     No.1 only
        in D min, arr H.Carr   ∅ 10.ca.2+bcl.1/2130/perc.bells/hp/str   (Boosey)   TO 1157
        in D min, arr G.Stacey   pf/str   (Boosey)   LM G 3871
        in E min, arr J.Turner ∅ 1110/1000/hp/str   (Boosey,1959) LM G 9282
     No.3 only
        in D & B♭, arr G.Stacey   pf/str   (Boosey)   LM G 3737
        in D, arr J.O.Turner   ∅ 1110/1000/hp/str   (Boosey)   LM G 7554
        in D & E (2 settings), arr L.Wurmser
                            ∅ 21+ca.2+bcl.2/4330/perc/cel.hp/str   (Boosey)   TO 1408
        in E   2122/2230/timp.perc/hp/str   (Boosey)   MS 6033
        arr F.Hartley (non-vocal)
                            PC 1010/0000/str   Boosey   16648 B
     No.4 only
        in C min, arr H.Carr   ∅ 10.ca.2+bcl.1/2230/timp.perc/hp/str   (Boosey)   TO 1158
LOVER IN DAMASCUS: suite
  1. Far across the desert sands   4. How many a lonely caravan
  2. Where the Abana flows   5. If in the great bazaars
  3. Beloved in your absence   6. Allah be with us
     arr Fletcher   PC 2(picc)222/2230.euph/timp.perc/str   Boosey   162 B
     Nos.1-4 only, arr Fletcher ∅ 2(picc)222/2230.euph/timp.perc/str   (Boosey)   TO 885 ∅ only
     No.5 only
        in E♭   1121/2220/perc/str   (Boosey)   TO 886
ON JHELUM RIVER: suite
  1. Introduction & boat song   4. Ashoo at her lattice
  2. Song of the bride   5. Only a rose
  3. Will the red sun never set   6. Kingfisher blue
     arr S.Baynes   PC 2(picc)122/2230/timp.perc/str   Boosey   160 Bni

WOODFORDE-FINDEN, Amy (cont)

The PAGODA OF FLOWERS: suite
   1. Introduction & passing of priests   4. Blue lotus dance
   2. Midst the petals   5. The Return of Oomala
   3. Star flower tree
      arr Fletcher   PC 2(picc)222/2230.euph/timp.perc/str   Boosey   161 Bni
PETALS FROM A LOTUS LILY: suite
   1. A request   3. Song of the lotus lily
   2. Florida love song
      arr J.Engleman   PC 1121/2230/timp.perc/hp/str   Leonard, Gould & B   13097
STARS OF THE DESERT: suite
   1. Stars of the desert   3. The Rice was under water
   2. You are all that is lovely   4. Fate
      arr S.Baynes   PC 2122/2230/timp.perc/str   Boosey   1403 Cni

WOODGATE, Leslie (1902-1961)

BATTLE HYMN OF THE REPUBLIC, arr for solo voice, chorus & orch
   in Bb   2222/2220/perc/hp/str   Arranger MS:BBC   MS 8327
CHRISTMAS CAROLS PROGRAMME
   The first Nowell   A Child this day is born
   I saw three ships   God rest you merry gentlemen
   Unto us a boy is born   The Birds
   Here we come a-wassailing   Patapan
   Good King Wenceslas   Rocking
   The Holly and the Ivy   Good Christian men rejoice
                   φ perc/hp/str   BBC   Ch Ref Lib 343
COCKLES AND MUSSELS, arr
   in A   φ 2222/2000/perc/hp/str   Arranger MS:BBC   MS 8311
COME BACK TO ERIN, arr
   in Db   2222/2220/timp/hp/str   Arranger MS:BBC   MS 8316
The CRUISKEEN LAWN: Irish folksong, arr
   in A min   2222/2000/timp/hp/str   Arranger MS:BBC   MS 8310
DEAR LITTLE SHAMROCK: song by J.W.Cherry, arr
   in A   2222/2000/perc/hp/str   Arranger MS:BBC   MS 8308
ELEGY for Baritone solo, chorus & orch
                   φ 2222/4231/timp.perc/hp/str   (BBC)   9544
ENGLISH DANCE SUITE, op.12
   1. Pastoral dance (3'15")   3. Hornpipe (2'30")
   2. Country dance (3')
                   φ str   9'15"   Goodwin & T   9105 Bwa C
FANTASIA ON ENGLISH MELODIES   1121/2220/timp.perc/str   (Banks)   MS 8153
The HARP THAT ONCE THRO' TARA'S HALLS: Irish melody, arr
   in E, for mv-chorus & orch   PC 2222/2220/timp/hp/str   Arranger MS:BBC   MS 8307
HERE'S TO THE MAIDEN, for solo voice, mv-chorus & orch, arr
   in E   φ 2222/2220/timp/hp/str   Arranger MS:BBC   MS 8306
HYMN TO THE VIRGIN, op.1, no.1, for Baritone solo, mv-chorus & orch
                   φ org.pf/str   Stainer & B   7090
3 MINSTREL SONGS, arr
   1. My old Kentucky home (S.C.Foster)   3. Hear dem bells (McCosh)
   2. O dem golden slippers (J.A.Bland)
                   φ 2222/2230/perc/bjo/str   (Arranger)   9515
PLANTATION SONGS, arr for solo voices, chorus & orch
   Click clack (Scott-Gatty)(Boosey)   Good night (Scott-Gatty)(Boosey)
   De old banjo (Scott-Gatty)(Boosey)   Poor old Joe (S.C.Foster)(Bayley & Ferguson)
                   φ 1121/2230/perc/str   Arranger MS:BBC   MS 449

WOODGATE, Leslie (cont)

ROLLING HOME, arr for Baritone solo, chorus & orch

	φ 2222/4230/timp.perc/str		Arranger	10635
ROMANCE	φ 2121/2220/perc/hp/str	3'30"	Arranger	TO 1196

SACRED HYMNS AND SOLO: selection, arr

PC 1121/2220/timp.perc/hp/str		AH & C	10617 Atv

SEA SHANTIES, arr for Baritone solo, chorus & orch

φ 2222/4230/timp.perc/str	Arranger	11037

The WHITE ISLAND, for Tenor solo, mv-chorus & orch, op.1, no.2

φ org.pf/str	Stainer & B	7090

A WOOING SONG OF A YEOMAN OF KENT'S SON: Kentish ballad, arr
  in G, orch F.Bye

φ 1121/2000/hp/str	Cramer	MLO 498

WOODHOUSE, Charles (1879-1939)

3 ENGLISH MELODIES, arr
  1. Drink to me only   3. Home sweet home
  2. Oh! dear, what can the matter be

PC 112(bcl).2sx.1/2210/perc/str	Boosey & H	18726
WAIT FOR THE WAGGON PC 1+picc.222/2230.euph/perc/str	Hawkes	4869

WOODMAN, Raymond Huntington (1861-1943)

A BIRTHDAY: song
  in Db

PC 1121/2210/timp/.str	1'30"	G.Schiremr	8713

WOODS, Cecil

CONCERT VALSE	φ 222+bcl.2/2330/timp.perc.glock/hp.pf/str	Composer	20303

OFF TO THE FAIR: selection of old English fair tunes, coll & arr

PC 1121/2220/perc/acdn.hp/str	Weinberger	21784
WENDY DANCES: a fairy fantasy 1121/0000/cel/str	Dix	19754

The WRAGGLE TAGGLE GYPSIES O!: traditional song, arr

PC 1+picc.121/2230/timp.perc/hp/str	Dix,1951	20957 B

WOODS, Francis Cunningham (1862-1929)

GRESSENHALL SUITE
  1. Preamble   3. Slow air
  2. Norfolk folk tune   4. Jig and finale

pf/str	Hawkes	2421

SUITE IN F
  1. Prelude   4. Menuette & trio
  2. Allemande   5. Scherzo & trio
  3. Slow air

φ 2222/2000/timp/str	Breitkopf	9634 B

WOODS, Harry

EVERGREEN: musical play
  Film version
        arr Connelly & King   PC 112.3sx.1/2210/timp.perc.bells.glock.vib/
                                    bjo[=gtr]/str

	C.Connelly	11910

    Over my shoulder: song
      in C, for solo, chorus & orch, arr P.Cardew

φ 102.3sx.0/1220/timp.perc/pf/str	Cinephonic	LM G 9664

WOODS, Harry (cont)

IT'S LOVE AGAIN by H.Woods & S.Coslow
    Selection, arr Terry   PC 111.3sx.1/2210/timp.perc/gtr/str   Cinephonic   13813
POOR PAPA: song
    in G, arr B.Berlin   ∅   2121/2220/perc/str   (FD & H)   TO 646

WOODS, John J. (1849-1934)

GOD DEFEND NEW ZEALAND: National song
    arr R.Chignell   ∅   2222/4231/timp.perc/str   (Arranger)   13751
    arr R.Chignell   ∅   1121/2210/perc/hp/str   (Arranger)   13763
    arr M.L.Lake   PC 112.2sx.1/2210/perc/str   C.Fischer   19720

WOODWARD, Rev H.H.

The RADIANT MORN: anthem
    in E, arr R.Chignell   ∅   1121/20.2cnt.11/timp/hp/str   Arranger MS:BBC   MS 5509
TE DEUM LAUDAMUS: chant setting

                                     1121/20.2cnt.30/perc/str   Boosey & H   20417

WOODWARD, Kerry Russel (1939-

4 TRADITIONAL CAROLS, arr for chorus & orch
    1. Masters in this hall   3. Tomorrow shall be my dancing day
    2. The Angel Gabriel   4. Patapan
                                 ∅   2(picc)2(ca)22/4231/timp.perc.glock/cel.hp/str   (Composer,1970)   25148 +

WOODWORTH, Samuel

The OLD OAKEN BUCKET
    arr M.L.Lake   PC 1+picc.12.2sx.1/2210/perc/str   C.Fischer   19720

WOOLDRIDGE, David Humphry Michael (1931-

4 ARMENIAN DANCES (1965)
    1. Antelias   3. Kassab
    2. Eriván   4. Ván and Tátvàn
                                 ∅   2(picc)12+bcl.1/2200/timp.perc/cel.gtr[=hp].pf/
                                     str   9'   (Composer)(H)   PL 433
FIVE ITALIAN SONGS for Soprano solo & large orchestra (1978)
    1. Fase (Cycle)   4. In memoria (In memoriam)
    2. Silenzion in Liguria (Silence in Liguria)   5. Giugno (June)
    3. Sereno (Clear Sky)
                                 ∅   3(2picc,afl)3(ca)3(bcl,E♭cl)3(cbsn)/4331/
                                     timp.4perc(chimes.glock.eoliphone.qanum[=zither].
                                     tamb.tamtam.vib.xyl)/cel.hp.pf/str   (Misc 9598 &
                                     Offstage: ssx.nai[=ssx].2S-soli.[small str section]   Composer   (PL 665 Amv
The LEGEND OF LILLANONAH for orch
    1. Weantinock   3. Lillanonah's dance
    2. The Falls of Metichawon   4. The Vision of Waramaug
                                 ∅   2(picc)12(bcl)1/2220/timp(perc.vib)/hp.pf(cel)/
                                     str   (Composer)(H)   PL Ni 558
NIGHT CANTICLE for Contralto solo & instruments (1980)
                                 ∅   1(picc,afl)1(ca)1(bcl).asx.0/0000/perc.crot.gong.
                                     tabor.vib/hp/2vln.vla.vlc.cb/[4-5 male voices]
                                     (more strings may be used)   15'   (Composer)   Misc 10138

WOOLDRIDGE, David (cont)

Les PARAPLUIES
    1. Preamble   3. Nocturne
    2. Valse Caprice   4. Galop
                        ⌀ 2+picc.222/4231/timp.perc(glock.xyl)/hp/str   Mills   Misc 9262
PARTITA for small orch ⌀ 2(picc)12(bcl)1/2110/timp.perc.glock.xyl/
                           hp.pf(cel)/str   (Composer)(H) PL 434 +

WORCH, Hermann

CHOPIN MEMORIES: selection, arr   2(picc)22.3sx.2/2230/timp.perc/str   Bosworth   12347
VERDI MEMORIES: selection, arr PC 1+picc.22.3sx.2/2230/timp.perc/str   13'-15'   Bosworth   10753

WORDEN, Wilfred

2 IMPRESSIONS, op.27
    1. The lost cantref (4')   2. March of Glyndwr (2')
                        ⌀ 1(picc)121/2210/timp.perc/cel.hp/str   6'   Bosworth   16398

WORDSWORTH, William (1908-

The PEASANTS' REVOLT: radio production (1957)
                        ⌀ 1110/2100/timp.perc/hp/str   Composer MS:BBC MS 31213 + ⌀ only
PYTHEAS   ⌀ 1111/1000/timp.perc/hp/str/STBar soli.chorus   Composer MS:BBC MS 30075
SYMPHONY no.3, op.48, in C ⌀ 22+ca.22/4230/timp.perc/str   28'   Lengnick   Misc 4132 B

WORK, Henry Clay (1832-1884)

KINGDOM COMING: plantation song
    in C, arr A.Collins for solo voice, chorus & orch
                        ⌀ 2121/2210/perc/str   (Bayley & Ferguson) MS 6324
    in C, arr S.Robinson for chorus & orch
                        PC 2121/2230/perc/str   Arranger   TO 480
    arr M.L.Lake (non-vocal) PC 112.2sx.1/2210/perc/str   C.Fischer   19720
MARCHING THROUGH GEORGIA: American marching song
    arr R.Barsotti   PC 112.4sx.2/4230/perc/str   Boosey & H   21039 B
    arr J.Fitz-Gerald   PC 1222/2230.euph/perc/str   Hawkes   1841
    arr S.Herbert for voice (or cornet) & orch, in Ab
                        PC 1132/2330/perc/str   Boosey   8079 D
    arr M.L.Lake   PC 1+picc.12.2sx.1/2210/perc/str   C.Fischer   19720
    arr P.Hope   ⌀ 2(picc)222/4330/timp.perc/hp/str   (FD & H)   22669 + B

WORMSER, André (1851-1926)

AU BORD DU DANUBE: andante - rêverie, op.8
                        PC 1121/2000/str   Salabert   5646
DANSE DE LA SULAMITE   ⌀ 1101/2000/perc/hp/str   4'   Marcel Lion 8590
L'ENFANT PRODIGUE: pantomime (wordless play)
    Selection   PC 2(picc)222/2231/timp.perc/hp/str   12'30"-14'   Hawkes   232 Bwa
    Suite
        1. Introduction (Motif des vieux parents (5')   4. Rêverie (Pierrot à la fenêtre (2'15")
        2. Andantino (La veillée)(5'15")   5. Finale (Marche militaire)(5')
        3. Intermezzo (Valse de Phrynette)(4')
                        ⌀ 2(picc)222/4231/timp.perc/hp/str   Biardot   6614 B
    Suite
        1. Overture   4. Désespoir des parents & rêverie de Pierrot
        2. La veillée   5. Marche militaire
        3. Valse
                        PC 2(picc)222/4231/timp.perc/str   Salabert   5609 B
    Valse
        arr Desormes   PC 1+picc.222/2230/perc/str   6'30"   Hawkes   1670 B

WORMSER, André (cont)

GIGUE, op.12, no.2   ∅PC 1+picc.222/2000/str   2'35"   Heugel   9072 B
IMPRESSIONS DE PLEIN AIR: suite
   1. Clair de lune   (3'45")   3. Paysage (3'30")
   2. Idylle matinale (3'15")   4. Au pays des neiges-danse des promis (3'45")
                                 ∅   1+picc.222/2230/timp.perc/str   14'45"   Lemoine   5312
Les LUPERCALES: symphonic poem, op.5 (Fêtes de Pan)
                                 ∅   2+picc.1+ca.24/42.2cnt.31/timp.perc/str   Hartmann   12254
Les VIOLONS DE M. DE CONTY: rigaudon
                                 ∅   str   Lemoine   9400

WORZISCHEK, J.H.   see   VOŘÍŠEK, Jan Hugo

WREFORD, Reynell

The LAST RHAPSODY
   Theme for chorus, 2 pianos & orch
      in C, arr B.Couzens   ∅   2222/4230/timp.perc/hp/str   (AH & C)   23668 +ONLY A
ONLY A ROSE, from Horti-Mania ∅   1121/2000/timp/cel/str   BBC   MS 4961 ∅ only
POEMS OF THE PAST
   1. My love in her attire   5. Think of dress in every light
   2. Beauty sat bathing   6. She I love
   3. Follow a shadow   7. Me Cupid made a happy slave
   4. He that loves a rosy cheek
                                 1000/0000/hpsd/str   Composer MS:BBC   WE 66

WRIGHT, Denis (1895-1967)

CASINO CARNIVAL: overture for brass band & orch
                                 ∅   2(picc)222/4231/timp.perc/str   6'   Composer   22608 +
CORNISH HOLIDAY: fantasy for brass band & orch
                                 ∅   2(picc)222/4231/timp.perc/str   7'45"   Composer   22319 +
COLUMBINE: caprice for cornet & orch
   arr R.Chignell   ∅PC 2121/2230/timp.perc/hp/str   Composer   MS 4905
DANCE SUITE (Miniature), op.17 PC 2(picc)222/4230/timp.perc/str   Boosey   2260 B
HOMEWARD BOUND: march
   arr A.Franzel   ∅   2+picc.222/4331/perc.glock/str   Composer   19744
SUITE FOR STRINGS in 18th century style
                                 str   Composer   13130

WRIGHT, Ellen

FIDELITY: song
   in A♭, arr H.Finck   2122/2210/timp/str   Ricordi,1904   17980
   in A♭ & G (2 settings), arr H.Finck
                                    2122/2100/timp/str   (Siddell)   17789
   arr Baron   1+picc.12.4sx.1/2210/timp.bells/str   Ricordi   18928

WRIGHT, Geoffrey

BIG TOP: musical play
   Extracts
      Free French: song
         in D, arr B.Berlin   ∅   2121/2220/timp.perc/str   Arranger   TO 1120

WRIGHT, Geoffrey

CONFOUND THEIR POLITICS: musical play
    Selection of excerpts
        1. Au revoir: song for chorus & orch, in G
        2. Britannia's pickanninnies: song for fv-chorus & orch, in G
        3. Charters: song for unison chorus, in E♭ min
        4. Churchillians: song for chorus & orch, in C
        5. Grannie don't go down the mine: song for chorus & orch, in E♭
        6. Land girls: song for fv-chorus, in E
        7. Red, white & blue: song for chorus & orch, in C
                        φ   2121/2230/perc/hp/str (φ for no.2 only)   Composer   TO 1371
The GATE REVUE
    Extracts
        Transatlantic lullaby: song
            in E & E♭ (2 settings), arr J.Beaver for SATB voices & orch
                        φ   2121/2230/perc/cel.hp/str   3'30"   (AH & C)   TO 141
                arr M.Mackie (non-vocal)φ 2222/4230/timp.perc/hp/str   (AH & C)   22003 +
The MOON AND YOU: song
    in C, arr M.Lubbock   φ   2121/2230/perc/cel.hp/str   Arranger   TO 412
MY HEART IS MARCHING: song
    in F, arr J.Beaver & C.Groves for chorus & orch
                        φ   2121/2230/perc/hp/str   Arranger   TO 344
NURSE DUGDALE HAS A CLUE: radio feature
                        φ   0010/0000/pf/str/voice   Composer MS:BBC MS 20362
PHRYNE: radio operetta φ   1111/1100/perc/hp/str   Composer MS:BBC MS 30190
TAKE ME BACK TO MY HOME TOWN: song
    in D♭, arr B.Berlin   φ   2121/2220/timp.perc/hp/str   Arranger   TO 553
WINGS OF MORNING: incidental music
                        001+bcl.0/0000/str   Composer MS:BBC MS 20221
WITH A SONG
    in E♭, arr J.Beaver for chorus & orch
                        φ   2121/2230/perc/hp.pf/str   Arranger   TO 346

WRIGHT, Kenneth Anthony (1899-

BOHEMIA: fantasy on Bohemian airs
    arr A.Wood   PC 2(picc)12.3sx.1/2220/timp.perc/hp/str   9'35"   Goodwin & T   14869
DADDY LONG-LEGS   PC 2121/2220/perc.xyl/str   3'-4'15"   P.Maurice   13680 Ap
DAINTY LADY: intermezzo PC 1121/2220/perc/cel.hp/str   3'   P.Maurice   12788 Ap B
DANCING WITH THE DAFFODILS PC 112.3sx.1/2230/perc/hp/str   3'15"-3'45" Universal   14215
PERKY PIZZICATO   φ str   Mills,1955   23161
PIERETTE IN THE MOON GARDEN: song
    in E, arr R.Chignell φ   1111/1120/timp.perc/hp/str   Arranger MS:BBC MS 5476
TOBACCO SUITE
    1. Military shag: march   4. Virginia: lullaby
    2. Old Havana: tango   5. Irish twist
    3. Snuff: scherzo
                        φ   2+picc.2+ca.22/4230/timp.perc/cel.hp.pf/str   (Swan)   19573
                        PC 2+picc.121/2220/timp.perc/cel.hp.pf/str   FD & H   21821

WRIGHT, Lawrence (1888-1964) (see also   NICHOLLS, Horatio, O'HAGAN, Betsy, and WILLIAMS, Gene)

2 SONGS, arr F.C.Beck
    1. Ev'ry time he kissed her, in D   2. Down in the dell, in D
                        1111/2210/perc/str   L.Wright,1920   18279

WRIGHT, Robert (1914-

KISMET: musical play by R.Wright & G.Forrest, based on the music of A.Borodin
    Selections
            arr F.Rapley   PC 2+picc.1+ca.2.3sx.1/2230/timp.perc/hp/str   8'45"   Chappell   21433 Cp
        Vocal selections
            arr S.Torch for Soprano & Baritone soli, chorus & orch.
                Night of my nights   Baubles, bangles and beads
                And this is my beloved   Stranger in Paradise
                The Olive tree
                        ⌀   22(ca)22/4330/timp.perc.glock.xyl/cel.hp.pf/
                            str   10'   (Frank Mus Corp)   24557 +
            arr S.Torch for Soprano & Baritone soli & orch
                Overture   Stranger in Paradise
                And this is my beloved   (for concert ending, use Polovtsian Dances
                                                              from bag 4042)
                        ⌀   2(picc)222/4331/timp.perc/hp/str   (Frank Mus Corp)   23620 +
        Extracts
            And this is my beloved: song
                in E♭, arr E.Griffiths   pf/str   (Frank Mus Corp)   LM G 7079
                in E♭, arr E.Griffiths   1121/2230/perc/hp.pf/str   (Frank Mus Corp)   LM G 7072
            Fate: song
                in C min, arr P.Akister ⌀ 2121/2230/perc/gtr.hp.pf(cel)/str (Frank Mus Corp)   LM G 10219
            The Olive Tree: song
                in F, arr R.Tilsley   ⌀ 2130/3010/timp.perc/cel.gtr.hp/str (Frank Mus Corp)   LM G 7837
            Stranger in Paradise: duet for Soprano & Baritone soli & orch
                in F, arr S.Torch   ⌀ 2(picc)222/4330/timp.perc/cel.hp/str (Frank Mus Corp)   23932 +
                in F. arr S.Torch   ⌀ 2(picc)222/4331/timp.perc/hp/str   (Frank Mus Corp)   23620 +
The LOVE DOCTOR: musical play by R.Wright & G.Forrest
    Selection
            arr F.Rapley   2(picc)12.3sx.1/2230/timp.perc/hp/str   7'30"
                                                      Frank Mus Corp/(Chappell,1959)   22984 Cs
SONG OF NORWAY: operetta based on the music of Edvard Grieg, arr & adapted by R.Wright & G.Forrest
    Selections   PC 2(picc)12.3sx.1/2230/timp.perc/str   Chappell   18715 Cp
    Extracts
        Strange music: duet for Soprano & Baritone soli & orch
            in D♭, arr R.Docker   ⌀ 0010/0000/gtr.pf/str   (Chappell)   LM G 9763
            in G   ⌀ 1121/2210/timp.perc/hp.pf/str   (Chappell)   22790 +
            in A, arr C.Mackerras ⌀ 21+ca.22/4230/timp.perc/cel.hp/str   (Chappell)   22034 +
            in A, arr S.Torch   ⌀ 21+ca.22/4331/timp.perc/hp/str   (E.Morris)   24957 +

WRIGHT, T.Waugh

3 SCOTTISH SYMPHONIC DANCES
    1. The Cobbler   3. The Devil's elbow
    2. Keltic ballade
            PC 2+picc.222/2230/timp.perc/str   Boosey   1399

WRUBEL, A. (1905-

AMERICAN IDIOM
    Extracts
        Lullaby in blue: song
            in E♭, orch R.Burston ⌀ 2121/2230/timp.perc/hp/str   (P.Maurice)   TO 801
The FIRST TIME I SAW YOU: song
    in F (refrain only), arr P.Cardew
            ⌀ 2222/4230/timp.perc/hp/str   (C.Connelly)   22253 +

WÜERST, Richard Ferdinand (1824-1881)

TANZ DER MUCKEN, FLIEGEN UND KÄFER, op.87
      ∅ 1+picc.2+ca.22/4000/timp.perc/str   Ries & E   16507
VARIATIONS SUR CHANSON NÈGRE DE KENTUCKY, op.56
      ∅ 2222/4230/timp/str   Schott   Misc 2436

WUNSCH, Hermann (1884-1954)

KAMMERKONZERT for piano & small orch, op.22
      ∅ 1111/2000/str   Schott,1925 Misc 1059
KLEINE LUSTSPIEL: suite, op.37
  1. Heldische Fabel   3. Intrigenspiel
  2. Führszene   4. Finale
      ∅ 2(picc)222/4230/timp.perc/str   10' Eulenburg,1930 Misc 1209 B

WUORINEN, Charles (1938-

CHAMBER CONCERTO for cello & 10 instruements (1963)
      ∅ 11(ca)1(bcl)1/0000/timp.perc.glock.gong.vib.xyl/
        pf/vln.vla.cb   16'30" Peters,1972 Misc 8062
RINGING CHANGES: percussion ensemble (1970)
      ∅ timp.perc.4tamtam.bells.2vib/pf   Peters,1972 Misc 8060

WURMSER, Leo Russell (1905-1967)

BALLADE for cor anglais & small orch (1959)
      ∅ 2022/2000/str   (Composer) Misc 6534
The DOVE: Welsh song, orch & arr after G.Bantock's edn
  in G   ∅ 31+ca.1+bcl.2/2000/hp/str   2'45" (Paxton) 20019
ELEGY   ∅ 32+ca.2+bcl.2/4230/timp/hp/str   7'20" Composer TO 1633
FANFARE as used for Queen Mary's programme, 30 June, 1947
      ∅ 3222/4231/timp.perc/hp/str   Composer TO 1709
HUNTING THE HARE: Welsh song, arr
  in D♭   ∅ 2+picc.222/4220/timp.perc/str   (Paxton) 20021
IMPROVISATIONS on a Polish folk song
      ∅ 1(picc)1(ca)2(bcl)1/2000/timp.glock.xyl/hp/str Composer 24646 + & mf 267
An OLD WOMAN OF THE ROADS: song
  in D min ∅ 222+bcl.2/4000/str   2'40" (Boosey) TO 1632
  in D min, arr G.Stacey PC 1010/0000/str   (Boosey) LM G 3653
ROMANTIC VARIATIONS (on a simple song)(1942)
      ∅ 2222/4230/timp/hp/str   Composer 24645
SANTA LUCIA: Italian song, arr
  in E♭   ∅ 3(picc)222/.4231/perc/cel.hp/str/chorus Arranger TO 1773
4 SONGS for voice & orch (1937)
  1. Bei der Rückkehr, in E♭   01+ca.2+bcl.2+cbsn/4000/hp/str
  2. In der Fremde, in C min   222+bcl.2+cbsn/4230/timp.perc/str
  3. Kampf, in D min   1222/2000/hp/str
  4. Warum?, in E   2222/4000/hp/str
   Complete   ∅ 22(ca)2+bcl.2+cbsn/4230/timp.perc/hp/str Composer Misc 6536
5 SONGS for voice & orch (1945-47)
  1. Down by the Salley Gardens, in F min
         2222/2000/hp/str
  2. The song of the old mother, in F# min
         2+picc.222/2000/str
  3. Never give all the heart, in D
         21+ca.2+bcl.2/4231/timp/hp/str
  4. He wishes for the cloths of Heaven, in F#
         21+ca.2+bcl.2/4231/timp.perc/cel.hp/str
  5. He reproves the curlew, in A min
         2+picc.222/4231/timp/str
   Complete   ∅ 2+picc.1(ca)2+bcl.2/4231/timp.perc/hp/str Composer Misc 6535

WURMSER, Leo (cont)

SUR LE PONT D'AVIGNON: French song for children, arr
   in G   ∅   3222/4231/timp.perc/str   Arranger   TO 2002
SWEET AND LOW: song arr for SA chorus & orch
                     ∅   21+ca.1+bcl.2/3000/str   Arranger   Misc 6537
SYMPHONY   ∅   3(picc)2+ca.3(E♭cl,bcl)3(cbsn)/4331/timp.perc/
                      str   BBC   24680 +
VICTORIAN MELODIES
   Excerpts   ∅   3222/4231/perc/cel.hp/str   Arranger   TO 1474

WYLE, G.

WHISTLE MY LOVE: song by G.Wyle & E.Pola
   in C, arr K.Warner   ∅   2121/2000/timp.perc/hp/str   (Disney)   22944

WYNNE, David (David Wynne Thomas)

OCTAD for orch (1977)   ∅   2(picc)222/4331/timp.3perc(bells.glock.gong.
                      vib.xyl)/hp.pf(cel)/str   26'   Composer   26441 + Awa

XANROF, Léon (pseud of Léon Fourneau)(1867-1953)

Le FIACRE: song
    in C,arr G.Vinter   ∅   211.3sx.0/2230/perc/hp.pf/str   (P.Maurice)   LM G 7426

XENAKIS, Iannis (1922-

AKRATA(1964-65)   ∅   0.picc.10.E♭cl+ bcl+cbcl.1+2cbsn/2321   12'   Boosey & H,1968   Misc 6811
ATRÉES ST/10-3, 06 09 62: Hommage à Blaise Pascal (1957/62)
                            ∅   101+bcl.0/1110/3perc(gong.vib)/vln.vlc   Salabert,1968   Misc 9138
EMPREINTES   ∅   2+picc.3(ca)2(bcl)+E♭cl.2+cbsn/4441/
                                str(16.14.12.10.8)   Salabert,1975   Misc 10430 C
EONTA, for piano & brass   see   CHAMBER CATALOGUE
METASTASEIS[B] (1953-54)   ∅   1+picc.20.bcl.0/3220/timp.perc.xyl/str   7'   Boosey & H,1967   Misc 7144
PITHOPRAKTA (1955-56)   ∅   0000/0020/wdbl.xyl/str   10'   Boosey & H,1967   Misc 6643
ST/10-1, 080262   001+bcl.0/2000/perc/hp/str-5tet   Boosey & H,1967   54517
ST/48-1, 240162, for 48 instruments
                            ∅   1+picc.21+bcl.1+cbsn/2220/timp.perc.mbn.vib/
                                str   11'   Boosey & H,1967   Misc 7143
SUPPLIANTES D'ESCHYLE (Hiketides)
                            ∅   0000/0220/str(6.6.0.8.4)   Salabert,1972   Misc 9137
SYRMOS I (1959)
    Facsimile edition   ∅   str   15'   Boosey & H,1968   Misc 6963
WINDUNGEN [Retours], for 12 cellos (1976)
                            ∅   12vlc   8'   Salabert,1976   Misc 9664

YAN-JUN, Hua

The REFLECTION OF THE MOON AT ERH CHUAN
    arr Wu Zu-qiang for strings   ∅   str   [Chinese State]   Misc 9849

YANNIDIS, Costas, arr

4 GREEK SONGS
    1. Amersouda (2')   3. Otrabarifas (2')
    2. Tou Ghiannou i Floghera (2'30")   4. Gheraking (1'45")
                    ∅   1121/2210/perc/hp/str   Arranger   WE 359

YATES, A. arr

FRIDAY NIGHT IS MUSIC NIGHT: medley of choruses

    9.10.53   1. Wonderful Copenhagen (F.Loesser)   (Morris)
              2. Swanee (G.Gershwin)   (F D & H)
              3. By the light of the silvery moon (G.Edwards)   (Feldman)
              4. Don't dilly, dally on the way (Collins and Leigh)   (Feldman)
                    ∅   2222/4330/timp.perc/hp.pf/str   Arranger   18590
    16.10.53 1. In the shade of the old apple tree (Alstyne)   (F D & H)
              2. Moonlight and roses (Lemare, Black and Moret) (F D & H)
              3. I'm forever blowing bubbles (Kellette)   (Feldman)
              4. Roll out the barrel (Brown, Timm and Vejvoda) (K.Prowse)
                    ∅   2222/4330/timp.perc/hp.pt/str   Arranger   18591
NIGHTS OF GLADNESS
    12.10.54 Frances Day medley of choruses
              1. It's d'lovely (C.Porter)
              2. In my wildest dreams (H.Jacobson)
              3. My love for you (H.Jacobson)
              4. I've got the urge (H.Jacobson)
                    ∅   1122/4230/perc/hp.pf/str   (Chappell)   21820
    12.10.54 medley of choruses
              1. Most gentlemen don't like love (C.Porter)
              2. My heart belongs to daddy (C.Porter)
              3. My kind of music (Leslie-Smith)
                    ∅   2222/4230/perc/hp.pf/str   (Chappell)   21822
              Flanagan and Allen medley of choruses
              1. Home town (Kennedy and Carr)   (P.Maurice)
              2. Run, rabbit, run (N.Gay)   (N.Gay)
              3. Umbrella man (H.Rome)   (Chappell)
              4. Music, maestro, please (A.Wrubel)   (Chappell)
              5. F.D.R.Jones (H.Rome)   (Chappell)
                    ∅   2222/4230/timp.perc/hp.pf/str   Arranger   22134

YAYA, Alfa

LIBERTÉ: national anthem of Guinea
    arr G.French   ∅   2222/2230/timp.perc/str   Arranger/Blandford   25507 +

YELLEN, J.

KING OF JAZZ: film music by J.Yellen & M.Ager
    Selection arr D.Somers   PC 111.3sx.1/2210/timp.perc/bjo/str   (L.Wright)   9963 C
SONG OF THE DAWN by J.Yellen & M.Ager
    in Ab, arr R.Tilsley   ∅   2222/4230/timp.perc/hp/str   (L.Wright)   22124 +

YON, Pietro (1886-1943)

GESU BAMBINO: song
   in G, arr L.Lucas   φ 0100/0000/hp/str   (Boosey)   21064

YORK, B. see BOWEN, York

YORK, YORK, FOR MY MONEY: traditional song

   in D min   φ 1121/2210/perc/str   BBC   MS 4581

YORKE, Peter (1903-1966)

CARAVAN ROMANCE	PC	2121/2220/timp.perc/hp/str	3'	Chappell	22729 Cs
CARMINETTA	PC	1121/2210/timp.perc/str		Liber	18667
DAWN FANTASY, arr R.Gill	PC	2121/2230/timp.perc/hp/str		F D & H	19796 B

EVERGREEN MEDLEY, arr
   1. Poor little rich girl (N.Coward) Chappell
   2. If   (T.Evans)   Bron
   3. Ma belle Marguerite (V.Ellis)   Chappell
   4. We'll gather lilacs (I.Novello) Chappell

	φ	2222/4230/timp.perc/gtr.hp/str		MS,1960	23225

FADED LILAC: waltz intermezzo

arr R.Binge	PC	2121/2330/timp.perc/hp/str	4'	A H & C	19582
FIREFLIES	PC	2121/2230/perc/hp/str		Chappell	19348
FLAPJACK	PC	2121/2230/timp.perc/hp/str	3'	Chappell	21103 Cvo
FLYAWAY FIDDLES	PC	2121/2230/timp.perc/gtr/str	2'40"	K.Prowse,1959	22933
GOLDEN MELODY	PC	2121/2000/timp.perc/cel.hp/str	2'45"	Chappell	21863 B
HIGHDAYS AND HOLIDAYS	PC	212.3sx.1/2230/perc/acdn.hp/str	2'50"	Bosworth	20465

IN MY GARDEN: suite
   1. Rain in the trees (2'30")
   2. The bird bath   (3')
   3. The swing   (4')

	PC	2(picc)222/2230/timp.perc/str	9'30"	Liber	14118
MELODY OF THE STARS	PC	2121/2230/timp.perc/hp/str	3'	Chappell	19776 Cvo
MIDNIGHT IN MEXICO	PC	2121/2220/timp.perc/hp/str	2'30"	B.Wood 1958	22502
MISS IN MINK	PC	1121/1000/perc/gtr.hp/str		Chappell,1957	22360 B
MONICA	φ	perc/gtr.hp/str		(Berry Mus Co,1960)	23224
PARADE OF THE MATADORS	PC	212.3sx.1/2230/timp.perc/gtr/str	2'30	Arcadia,1956	22209
ROYAL MILE, arr R.Gill	PC	2121/2230/timp.perc/hp/str		F D & H	22306

SALVADORA

arr R.Hanmer	PC	212.4sx.1/2320/timp.perc/gtr.hp/str		Liber	22110
TOMPION'S GRANDFATHER CLOCK	PC	2121/2230/timp.perc/hp/str	2'50"	A H & C,1951	20280

YORKSTON, J.

COCKLES AND MUSSELS: song

in A, arr L.Woodgate	φ	2222/2000/perc/hp/str	Arranger	MS 8311
in Gb, arr P.Hope	φ	2122/3000/hp/str	(Arranger,1966)	24440
in G	PC	1131/0220/perc/str	BBC	LMG 4438
arr P.Hope (non-vocal)	φ	2222/4230/timp.perc/hp/str	Arranger	22801 +
transcr R.Binge	φ	2222/4231/timp.perc/hp/str	(Transcriber,1956)	21751 +

YOSHITOMO, Zimmer Carl (1869-1935)

ALL ROUND THE WORLD: selection arr PC 2(picc)222/4230/timp.perc/str   Kawi-Verlag   6848 B
Der HEILIGE BERG (The sacred mountain)
    Overture   PC 2(picc)222/4230/timp.perc/glock.xyl/str   Huhn   12157
IM GLOCKENTEMPEL (In the pagoda of bells)
                                    PC 2(picc)222/4230/perc/glock/str   5'   Birnbach   10440
IM TEEHAUS ZU DEN HUNDERT STUFEN (In the tea house with the hundred steps): Japanese reminiscence
                                    PC 2(picc)222/4230/timp.perc/str   5'   Birnbach   12309
JAPANISCHE SUITE
    1. Im Teehaus (In the tea rooms)
    2. Sommernachtsfahrt auf dem Sumidafluss (Midsummer's night on the Sumida river)
    3. Geisha und Schmetterling (Geisha & butterfly)
    4. Fest in Tokio (Festival in Tokio)
                                    PC 2(picc)221/2230/timp.perc/str   Roehr   9874
LIED DER TAUSEND VOGEL (The song of the thousand birds): Japanese legend
                                    PC 2(2picc)222/2230/timp.perc/str   Bosworth   12143
ÖSTASIATISCHE SUITE (East Asiatic suite)
    1. Lampenfest in Lahor (Festival of lamps in Lahore)
    2. Haru no hana (Vernal flower - Japanese song)
    3. Strassenszenen in Honkong (Street life in Hongkong)
                                    PC 2(picc)222/2230/timp.perc/str   Birnbach   10991

YOUFEROV, Sergei

ANTHONY AND CLEOPATRA op.24a
    Suite
        1. Prologue
        2. Danses
            a. Introduction   d. Danse des papillons
            b. Danse indienne   e. Valses des fleurs
            c. Danse egyptienne de la guêpe   f. Bacchanale
        3. Entr'acte
        4. La mort d'Antoine
                                    ∅ 3(picc)1+ca.2+bcl.2/4331/timp.perc/2hp/str   Zimmermann Misc 1886
SUITE DE BALLET op.49
    1. Introduction
    2. Danse des villageois
    3. In modo vecchio
        a. Rondinetto   d. Poco sostenuto
        b. Adagio   e. Coda
        c. Allegretto
    4. Valse triste
    5. Danse kourde
    6. Intermezzo
    7. Cortège nuptial
                                    ∅ 2+picc.2+ca.2+bcl.2+cbsn/42.2cnt.31/timp.perc/
                                       2hp.pf/str   Schott   14200

YOUMANS, Vincent (1898-1946)

GREAT DAY: musical play
    Selection, arr H.J.Stafford   PC 111.3sx.1/2210/timp.perc/vib/str   C.Connelly 14929 Bp
    Great day: song
        in D, arr W.Williamson   ∅ 1121/2220/perc/hp.pf/str.chorus   (C.Connelly) LMG 4569
        in F, arr R.Binge   ∅ 1111/1210/perc/gtr/str   (C.Connelly) LMG 4724

YOUMANS, Vincent (cont)

HIT THE DECK: musical play
   Selections
      arr H.M.Higgs   PC 2(picc)122/2230/timp.perc/str   6'15"   Chappell   7741 D
      arr R.Docker   φ   2(picc)2(ca)22/4330/timp.perc.vib.xyl/hp.pf
                                  str   5'   (Chappell)   25180 +
   Hallelujah: song
      in Eb, arr S.Torch for SSBB soli (or chorus)
                    φ   1+picc.1+ca.22/4330/timp.perc.glock/
                                    hp.pf/str   (Chappell)   24458 +
      in F, arr T.Harrison   1141/2230/perc/pf/str   (Chappell)   LMG 4896
      in F, arr M.Mackie   φ   2222/4230/perc/hp/str.chorus   (Chappell)   LMG 6573
   I know that you know: song
      in C, arr R.Docker   φ   2222/4330/timp.perc/hp.pf/str   Chappell   23069 +
   Join the navy: song
      in C, arr J.Brown for SATB φ   2232/4230/timp.perc/hp.pf/str   (Chappell)   18406
      in B: in D (2 settings, refrain only) arr H.Carr
                    φ   2121/2230/perc/hp/str   (Chappell)   TO 594
      in D: in F: in Eb   φ   2010/0200/timp.perc/str   (Chappell)   TO 313 φ only
   Sometimes I'm happy: song
      in F   φ   2010/0200/timp.perc/str   5'05"   (Chappell)   TO 313 φ only
MERCENARY MARY: musical play
   I'm a little bit fonder: song
      in D   φ   2121/0210/perc/str   (Chappell)   TO 314 φ only
   Tie a string: song
      in Eb   φ   2122/0210/timp.perc/str   (Chappell)   TO 314 φ only
      in G   φ   1111/0210/str   (Chappell)   18402
NO, NO, NANETTE: musical play
   Selection, arr H.M.Higgs   PC 2122/2230/timp.perc/bells/str   8'30"   Chappell   3609 Eni
   Selection for Soprano & Baritone soli, 2 pianos & orch, arr S.Torch
                    φ   21+ca.22/4331/timp.perc.bells.glock.vib/hp/
                                    str   7'30"   (Chappell)   25282 +
   I want to be happy: song
      in C (orig)   φ   1111/1210/perc/str   (Chappell)   TO 956
   No,no,Nanette: song for Soprano solo, male voice chorus & orch
      in Eb, arr G.Vinter   φ   2222/4230/perc.glock/str   (Chappell)   23480 +
   Tea for Two: song
      arr D.Shostakovich (non-vocal)
                    φ   1+picc.211/4210/timp.perc.glock.xyl/cel.hp/
                                    str   (Chappell)   Misc 10126
   You can dance: song
      in C (orig D) arr M.Mackie φ   2131/2230/timp.perc/hp.pf/str   (Chappell)   18563 **
The ONE GIRL: song
   in Eb, arr R.Green   φ   2141/2330/timp.perc/hp.pf/str   (C.Connelly) LMG 7071
RISE AND SHINE: musical play
   Rise 'n shine: song
      in Bb arr P.Akester   φ   001.sx.0/0100/gtr/cb   (Chappell)   TO 214
THROUGH THE YEARS: musical play
   Selection arr H.J.Stafford PC 101.3sx.0/0210/timp.perc.bells.glock.vib/
                                str   C.Connelly   7615
VINCENT YOUMAN'S MELODIES: selection arr C.Connelly
                    PC 111.3sx.1/2210/perc/gtr/str   C.Connelly   13576
The WILDFLOWER: musical play by V.Youmans & H.Stothart
   Selection, arr H.M.Higgs PC 2122/2230/timp.perc/bells/str   Chappell   5999 Cp
   You never can blame a girl for dreaming (Youmans)
      in Ab (orig) arr R.Hanmer φ   2222/4220/timp.perc/hp.pf/str   (Chappell)   18370

YOUMANS, Vincent (cont)

WITHOUT A SONG: song
    in F, arr R.Binge   ⌀   1111/1210/perc/str   (C.Connelly)   LMG 4766
    in E♭, arr G.Stacey   pf/str   (C.Connelly)   LMG 3257
    in E♭, arr S.Andrews   hp.pf/str   (C.Connelly)   MS 20371
    in D♭, orch R.Burston   ⌀   2121/2230/perc/hp/str   (C.Connelly)   TO 801
    in E♭, arr P.Cardew   ⌀   2222/4330/timp.perc/hp.pf/str   (C.Connelly)   23112 +
    arr R.Tilsley as signature tune to Friday night is music night
                                ⌀   2222/4230/timp.perc/hp/str   C.Connelly   23060

YOUNG

I DON'T WANT NOBODY BUT YOU: song by Young, Baer & Lewis
    in C, arr M.Mackie   ⌀   2121/2230/timp.perc/hp.pf/str   (F D & H)   18518

YOUNG, Anthony (ca 1685-after 1720)

PHILLIS HAS SUCH CHARMING GRACES: song
    in B min, arr G.Williams for tenor & orch
                                ⌀   1121/2000/timp/hp/str   (Boosey & H)   MLO 238
    in D♭, arr L.Wilson, orch S.Robinson
                                ⌀   2222/4230/hp/str   3'   (Boosey)   20090

YOUNG, Arthur

PRIM AND PROPER: entr'acte
    arr R.King   PC 111(3sx)0/0000/hp/str   2'45"   P.Maurice   9804

YOUNG, Arthur

NICOLETTE: intermezzo for saxophone & orch by A.Young & V.Phillips
    arr V.Phillips   PC 1121/2210/perc/cel/str   4'   Boosey & H   11987

YOUNG, Francis

BEAU BRUMMEL: minuet arr M.L.Lake   PC 1121/2210/timp/str   C.Fischer   3374

YOUNG, J.H. arr

IN CELLAR COOL (Ludwig Fischer) for bassoon & orch
                                PC 1121/2230.euph/perc/str   Hawkes   9004

YOUNG, L.

LOTTIE DUNDASS: radio production (1949)
                                ⌀   112.2sx.1/0220/perc/pf/str   Composer MS:BBC MS 30436
MIDSUMMER FIRE: radio production, incidental music (1951)
                                ⌀   112.bsx.1/1230/perc/cel/str   Composer MS:BBC MS 30436

YOUNG, Percy M. (1912-

KING JAMES' PLEASURE: suite, arr
    1. The Pages' masque
    2. Sir Francis Bacons' masque
    3. The Noblemenes masque tune
    4. The Baboons' dance
                                ⌀   02[=2rec]00/0000/[pf]/str[cb]   Hinrichsen,1959 Misc 5226

YOUNG, Percy (cont)

A SEVENTEENTH CENTURY SUITE, arr
   1. A masque at Fryers   4. The birds'dance
   2. Cuperaree or Graysin   5. The hay-makers' masque
   3. Cuperaree or Graysin the second

             φ   02[=2rec]00/0000/str   Hinrichsen,1941   22930

YOUNG, Peter

HOPE AND PRAY: song
   in Eb: in F: arr G.Stacey   1010/0000/pf/str   (K.Prowse)   LMG 3624
I GIVE THANKS FOR YOU: song
   in Eb,arr K.Warner   φ   0010/0000/pf/str   (Boosey)   LMG 3529
   in D, arr G.Stacey   φ   1110/0000/hp.pf/str   (Boosey)   LMG 4878
O BLESSED DAY: song
   in C: in F: arr G.Stacey   pf/str   (Boosey)   LMG 3412
YOU WILL RETURN: song
   in Bb, arr G.Stacey   pf/str   (Boosey)   LMG 3475

YOUNG, Victor (1900-1956)

AROUND THE WORLD IN EIGHTY DAYS: song (from the film)
   orch A.Fones   PC 1121/2220/timp.perc/hp/str   Chappell,1956   22382
   arr R.Docker for piano, SATB chorus & orch
             φ   2220/4000/glock.vib/gtr.hp/str   2'30"   (Chappell)   25173 +
   Beguine version (non-vocal), arr A.Fones
             φ   213(3sx)bcl(sx)0/2330/timp.perc/hp.pf(cel)/
                str   (Chappell)   24808
   Waltz version (non-vocal), arr A.Fones
             φ   2(picc)122/2330/timp.perc/(cel)hp.pf/str   (Chappell)   24804 +
GOT THE SOUTH IN MY SOUL by V.Young & L.Wiley
             φ   111.2asx.tsx.1/2220/timp.perc/bjo/str   Composer MS:BBC   MS 336 φ only
STELLA BY STARLIGHT
   arr D.Darlow   φ   000.asx.0/0000/timp.perc.glock.kit/pf/str   Arranger   MLO 1826
SUMMER LOVE, from 'Moonlight Serenade', arr A.Fones
          PC 1121/0000/perc/gtr.hp/str   2'50"
                                                V.Young/Chappell,1956   22986

YOUNG, William (? - 1671)

SONATAS
   No.1, in D min
      arr W.G.Whittaker   φ   pf/str   OUP   10406
   No.2, in D min
      arr W.G.Whittaker   φ   pf/str   4'05"   OUP   10659
   No.4, in F
      arr W.G.Whittaker   φ   pf/str   4'50"   OUP   10592
   No.5, in C
      arr W.G.Whittaker   φ   pf/str   4'20"-4'45"   OUP   10424
SUITE No.1
   1. 1st Allemande (1'25")   5. Second corrente (0'55")
   2. First Ayre (3'35")   6. Second ayre (1'25")
   3. First Corrente   7. Second Allemand
   4. Sarabande (2')
      arr W.G.Whittaker   φ   pf/str   OUP   10514

YOUNG

WHERE DID ROBINSON CRUSOE GO WITH FRIDAY ON SATURDAY NIGHT?: song by Young, Meyer & Lewis
  in F, arr R.S.Stoddon   PC 1020/0210/perc/str   Feldman   13493

YRADIER, Sebastián (1809-1865)

AY CHIQUITA arr H.Mouton   PC 1010/0000/str   Heugel   7123
HAVANAISE by S.Yradier & Shalmer
  orch Henders   PC 1121/2210/timp.perc/str   3'15"   Liber   16619
La PALOMA (The dove): Spanish serenade
                                  PC 222.2sx.2/2230/perc/str   4'   Lafleur   369 AvoB
  song version arr D.Edge, orch H.Carr & J.Clements
    in D   ∅ 2000/0000/hp/str   2'25"   Arranger   TO 1195
    arr F.Charrosin   PC 112.3sx.1/2230/perc/acdn/str   Bosworth   22035
    arr R.Douglas   ∅ 21+ca.22/4231/timp.perc/hp/str   Arranger   TO 1762
    arr G.Daines, in Db   ∅ 1020/0220/perc/hp/str   Arranger   LMG 4492
    arr S.Torch   ∅ 2121/2230/perc/hp/str   Arranger   24800
SOUVENIR DE YRADIER: fantasy of Mexican songs by Yradier
    arr Morena (op.46)   PC 1222/4230/timp.perc/str   Bosworth   6654

YSAŸE, Eugène (1858-1931)

CAPRICE, for violin & orch (d'après l'étude en forme de valse de Saint-Saëns, op.52, no.6)
                                  ∅ 2222/2200/timp.perc/str   (Durand)   Misc 5613
CHANT D'HIVER: poem no.3, op.15, for violin & orch
                                  ∅ 2222/2000/timp/str   Enoch,1902   Misc 858
EXIL: poem, op.25   ∅ vlns.vlas   8'30"-9'   BBC   Misc 330 C

YSAŸE, Théophile (1865-1918)

Le CYGNE: esquisse symphonique, op.15
                                  ∅ 42+ca.2+bcl.2/4331/timp/2hp/str   7'   Schirmer   15212
FANTAISIE SUR UN THÈME POPULAIRE, op.13
                                  ∅ 3(picc)2+ca.23/4431/timp.perc/hp/str 7'   G.Schirmer   6087
La FORÊT ET L'OISEAU: esquisse symphonique no.3, op.18
                                  ∅ 3(picc)2+ca.23/4431/timp.perc/str   Breitkopf   Misc 3806

YUASA, Joji (1929-

CHRONOPLASTIC (1972)   ∅ 3(picc,2afl)34(Ebcl)3(cbsn)/6431/5perc
                                     (timp.2sets bells.flex.leather belts.2mba.tamtam.
                                     2vib.wooden drum)/hp.2pf(cel)/str(14.14.12.10.8:2 cb
                                     players also play tamtam)   Schott,1972 Misc 9434
TIME OF ORCHESTRAL TIME (1975/76) ∅ 4(4picc.2afl)4(ca)4(Ebcl.bcl)4(2cbsn)/662.2btbn.1/
                                     5perc(timp.bells.cbells.cel.glock.mba.tamtam.vib.xyl)/
                                     hp.pf(cel)/str(12.12.12.10.8)   (Composer)   Misc 9433

YUN, Isang (1917-

CONCERTI
  Cello & orch (1976)   ∅ 2(2picc,afl)22(bcl)2(cbsn)/3220/timp.2perc.
                                     incl.cel.glock.gro.xyl/str(no vlc)   27'   Bote & B,1976 Misc 9178 B
  Flute(afl) & small orchestra (1977)
                                  ∅ 1222/2000/2[=1]perc(claves.glock.gongs.gro.
                                     Hyoshigi.sleighbells.vib.tomtoms.tplbl.wdbl)/
                                     str   21'-22'   Bote & B,1977 Misc 9673

YUN, Isang (cont)

CONCERTI (cont)
  Oboe, harp & small orchestra (1977)

	∅	2(2picc)122/2110/2perc(glock.gongs.tamtams. tomtoms.tplbl.xyl)/str	34'	Bote & B,1978	Misc 9674
FLUKTUATIONEN (1964)	∅	2(picc)22(bcl)2(cbsn)/4320/timp.perc/str	13'	Bote & B,1969	Misc 6928
MUAK: dance fantasy (1978)	∅	3(picc)333/4321/timp(tamb).2perc(glock.gro. mrc.tomtoms.xyl)/str	16'	Bote & B,1979	Misc 9939

ON MANI PADME HUM: cycle for Soprano & Baritone soli, chorus & orch (1964)
  1. Lotosblüte (Lotus)
  2. Gotamo, befragt (Gotamo,asked)
  3. Durst (Thirst)
  4. Entwerden (Nirvanishing)
  5. Zum Nirvana (To the Nirvana)

	∅	3(picc)2+ca.2(bcl)1+cbsn/2211/timp.perc.bells.vib/ cel.2hp/str	26'	Bote & B	Misc 8409

PIÈCE CONCERTANTE for chamber ensemble or small orchestra (1976)

	∅	1(afl)01/(bcl)0/0000/timp.perc(bells.gongs.mrc. tomtoms.tplbl.vib.wdbl.whip)/pf(tomtoms.wdbl)/ str	14'	Bote & B,1977	Misc 9564

YVAIN, Boris

COLETTE: waltz	PC	org/str		Weekes	6836

YVAIN, Maurice (1891-1965)

Un BON GARÇON: operetta

Selection	PC	1121/2230/perc/hp/str	10'	Salabert	8095

KADUBEC: operetta

Selection	PC	1121/2230/timp.perc/str	14'	Salabert	9250

PAS SUR LA BOUCHE: operetta

Selection	PC	1121/2230/timp.perc/str		Salabert	11260

YVOIRE, Claude

CANCANETTE	PC	2121/2210/perc/gtr.hp/str	2'50"	Ed Cadenza	21134 Avo
DERBY WINNER	PC	2121/2210/perc.vib/gtr.hp/str		Cadenza/Wright	MLO 1131
La RONDE DES BOIS: scherzo, op.57	∅	2222/1000/vib/hp/str	3'	Riccardo,1958	22610

ZABEL, Albert (1834-1910)

CONCERTO for harp & orch, op.35, in C min
   orch E.Reiche   φ 2222/2230/timp.perc.bells.tamtam/str   26'   Zimmermann,1905   Misc 1005

ZACH, Johann (18th cent)

CONCERTO for harpsichord & orch
   in C, arr W.Höckner   0000/2000/str   Pro Musica   20474
CONCERTO for harpsichord & orch
   in D min, ed A.B.Gottron   φ str   Nagel,1947   Misc 3804 B

ZACHAU (Zachow) Friedrich Wilhelm (1663-1712)

CANTATAS for soli, chorus, harpsichord, organ & orch
  1. Das ist das ewige Leben
     ed M.Seiffert,rev M.Moser   φ 0201/0000/str/cont(hpsd)   Breitkopf,1905.DDT 21-22   MRL
                                  φ 00.2ob-da.01/0000/str/cont   DDT   20384
  2. Herr, wenn ich nur dich habe
     ed M.Seiffert,rev M.Moser   φ hp/str/cont(hpsd)   Breitkopf,1905.DDT 21-22   MRL
  3. Ich will mich mit dir verloben
     ed M.Seiffert,rev M.Moser   φ 0000/00.2cln.00/org/str/cont(hpsd)   Breitkopf,1905.DDT 21-22   MRL
  4. Ruhe, Friede, Freud und wonne
     ed M.Seiffert,rev M.Moser   φ 0201/0000/org/str/cont(hpsd)   Breitkopf,1905.DDT 21-22   MRL
  5. Vom Himmel kam der Engel Schar
     ed M.Seiffert,rev M.Moser   φ 0001/00.4cln.00/timp/org/str/cont(hpsd) Breitkopf,1905.DDT 21-22   MRL
  6. Meine Seel' erhebt den Herren
     ed M.Seiffert,rev M.Moser   φ 2201/2000/str/cont(hpsd)   Breitkopf,1905.DDT 21-22   MRL
  7. Siehe, ich bin bei euch alle Tage
     ed M.Seiffert,rev H.J.Moser φ 0000/00.2cln.00/str/cont(hpsd)   Breitkopf,1905.DDT 21-22   MRL
  8. Lobe den Herrn meine Seele
     ed M.Seiffert,rev H.J.Moser φ 0201/2000/str/cont(hpsd)   Breitkopf,1905.DDT 21-22   MRL
  9. Es wird eine Rute aufgehen
     ed M.Seiffert,rev H.J.Moser φ 0201/2000/org/str/cont(hpsd)   Breitkopf,1905.DDT 21-22   MRL
 10. Dies ist der Tag
     ed M.Seiffert,rev H.J.Moser φ 0201/2000/str/cont(hpsd)   Breitkopf,1905.DDT 21-22   MRL
 11. Ich bin sicher und erfreut
     ed M.Seiffert,ref H.J.Moser φ str/cont(hpsd)   Breitkopf,1905.DDT 21-22   MRL
 12. Nun aber gibst du, Gott
     ed M.Seiffert,ref H.J.Moser φ 0201/2000/str   Breitkopf,1905.DDT 21-22   MRL
MISSA BREVIS: Missa super chorale: Christ lag in Todesbanden
   ed M.Seiffert, rev H.J.Moser   Breitkopf,1905.DDT 21-22   MRL

ZADOR, Jenö (Eugen) (1894-1977)

RONDO   φ 3(picc)222/3230/timp.perc/hp/str   15'   Universal,1934   Misc 2857
SINFONIA TECHNICA   φ 3(picc)2+ca.2+bcl.2+cbsn/444[=3]1/
                                perc/hp.pf/str   20'   Universal,1932   Misc 997
STUDIES FOR ORCHESTRA   φ 3(picc)222/4331/timp.perc.bells.mba.vib.xyl/
                                hp.pf/str   22'   MCA,1971   Misc 7596
SUITE for horn, strings and percussion
  1. Prelude   4. Elegie
  2. Fantasy   5. Rondo
  3. March
                            φ timp.2perc(gong.xyl)/str   (Composer)   Misc 9401
UNGARISCHES CAPRICCIO   φ 3(picc)222/4230/timp.perc.glock.xyl/str 9'-10' Eulenburg   13549

ZAFRED, Mario (1922-

SINFONIA BREVE   see   SYMPHONIES
SINFONIETTA (1953)   ∮   1111/2000/str   Ricordi,1957   Misc 9732
SYMPHONIES
    No.3 'Canto del carso (1949)' ∮   2(picc)222/4331/timp.perc.xyl/str   Zerboni,1953   Misc 4304
    No.4 'In onore della resistenza (1950)'
                                ∮   3(picc)2+ca.22/4331/timp.perc/str   24'   Ricordi,1952   Misc 3927
    No.7 (1969)   ∮   2+picc.2+ca.2+bcl.2+cbsn/4331/timp.perc/str 23' Ricordi,1969   Misc 7114
    for string orchestra (Sinfonia Breve)(1955)
                                ∮   str   15'   Ricordi,1956   Misc 5178

ZAKHAROV arr

WHY DOESN'T HE TELL HER: Ukrainian folksong
    in A: Soprano & Contralto, arr M.Seiber
                                ∮   2121/2230/perc/str   (W M A)   TO 1310
    in F: Soprano & Contralto, arr M.Seiber
                                ∮   2222/4320/perc/acdn/str   (W M A)   TO 2003

ZALVA, George L.

BAMBI: selection, arr   PC 112.3sx.1/2220/timp.perc.glock.xyl/str   6'   W.Disney   16878
                                                                                               Cp D E
BING CROSBY HITS: selection, arr PC 112.3sx.1/2220/timp.perc.vib(=glock)xyl/
                                    str   8'30"   Victoria Mus   15975 Atv CpD
CAVALCADE OF MARTIAL SONGS: selection, arr
                                ∮   1121/2220/perc/hp.pf/str   (L.Wright)   11827
COCKNEYANIA: selection, arr
    Part 1   ∮   1121/2220/perc/hp.pf/str   MS   8645
    Part 2   ∮   1121/2220/perc/hp.pf/str   MS   8646
DANNY BOY: song, arr
    in Eb   PC 212.4sx.1/2230/timp/str   Boosey   18768
GEMS OF IRISH SONG: new selection, arr
                                PC 2(picc)12.3sx.1/2230/timp.perc/str   11'30"   Chappell   14235
                                                                                               Cni
GEORGE GERSHWIN'S MELODIES: selection, arr
    arr H.Hall   PC 112.3sx.1/2220/timp.perc/str   10'   Chappell   15916 B
GUNG'L IN THE BALLROOM: selection, arr
                                PC 112.3sx.1/2230/timp.perc.glock/str   Boosey & H   12022
IRVING BERLIN CAVALCADE: selection including new numbers from film 'Alexander's ragtime band',arr
                                PC 112.3sx.1/2220/timp.perc.bells.glock.vib/
                                    str   Chappell   15443 B
IRVING BERLIN'S SONGS: selection, arr
                                ∮   1(picc)11.3sx.1/2220/timp.perc.glock.vib/
                                    str   8'30"   F D & H   15451
                                PC 111.3sx.1/2220/perc.vib/str   F D & H   13575 A
TRISTESSE 'So deep is the night' (song adapted from Chopin's study, op.10 no.3, in E) arr
    in Eb   PC 112.3sx.1/2220/timp/str   3'   K.Prowse   16296 B

ZÁMEČNÍK, Evžen (1939-

IN MEMORIAM IGOR STRAVINSKY (1971) ∮ 2(picc)2+ca.2+bcl.2/4331/timp.perc.bells.
                                    tamtam.2tomtom/hp/str   7'   Czech SM,1980 Misc 10298

ZAMECNIK, J.S.

ALL-AMERICA: march	PC	1(picc)121/2210/perc.xyl/str	Sam Fox	4741
CHANT DES BOULEVARDS	PC	1121/2210/timp.perc/str	Sam Fox	11545
JINGLES: intermezzo	PC	1121/2210/perc/str	Sam Fox	11865
MEN OF SPARTA: march	PC	1121/2210/timp.perc/str	Sam Fox	16965
POLLY: symphonic orchestration	PC	1121/2210/perc/str	Sam Fox	13340
SLAVONIC FANCIES	PC	2+picc.221/2210/timp.perc/str	Sam Fox	11578
VARSITY: one-step or two-step	PC	112.3sx.1/2210/perc/str	Sam Fox	11880

ZAMUDIO, Daniel   see   SILVA, Jesus Bermudez

ZANDONAI, Riccardo (1883-1944)

ARIA (Porporax) for cello and strings, arr					
	φ	str	3'30"	Ricordi	Misc 1167
BALLATA EROICA (1932)	φ	2+picc.2+ca.2+bcl.2+cbsn/4440/timp.perc. bells.glock.xyl/cel.hp.pf/str		Ricordi,1932	Misc 8812
COLOMBINA: overture on a popular Venetian theme					
	φ	2+picc.222/4310/timp.perc/cel.hp/str	7'30"	Ricordi,1936	Misc 1762
CONCERTO ANDALUSO for cello and small orch					
	φ	1011/1000/perc/pf/str	20'	Ricordi,1937	Misc 1932
CONCERTO ROMANTICO for violin and orch					
	φ	2+picc.222/4240/timp.perc/cel.hp/str	35'	Ricordi,1939	Misc 2052
CONCHITA: opera					
Complete	φ	2+picc.2+ca.2+bcl.2+cbsn/4330/timp.perc. bells.tamtam/hp/str		Ricordi,1921	Misc 84 C
Selection,arr E.Tavan	PC	2(picc)222/2231/timp.perc/str		Ricordi	6025
Extracts					
Intermezzo nella strada (Act I, Sc.2)					
	φ	3+picc.2+ca.2+bcl.2+cbsn/4340/timp.perc/ cel.hp/str	4'50"	(Ricordi)	TO 1360
La Cancellata for chorus & orch in Gb (orig)		32+ca.2+bcl.2+cbsn/4340/perc/cel.hp/str		(Ricordi)	TO 1359
La FARSA AMOROSA: opera					
Overture					
arr I.Culotta	φ	2(picc)222/2230/timp.perc/str	7'	Ricordi	14844
Intermezzo					
arr I.Culotta	PC	2+picc.222/4330/timp.perc/str	2'30"	Ricordi	18895
I1 FLAUTO NOTTURNO: poem for flute and small orch					
	φ	0010/2000/tamtam/hp.pf/str	10'30"	Ricordi	Misc 1651
FRANCESCA DA RIMINI: opera in 4 acts					
Complete (Act I: 33'; Act II: 26')					
	φ	2+picc.2+bcl.2+ca.2+cbsn/4340/timp.perc. bells/hp/str Offstage: 1+picc.01[=ob]0/0100/lute.vla		Ricordi,1926	Misc 975 B
Selection, arr E.Tavan	PC	2222/2231/timp.perc/str		Ricordi	1134
Extracts					
Closing scene Act I					
in D (orig) arr S.Robinson	φ	2121/2230/perc/cel.hp/str		(Ricordi)	MS 5572
GIULIETTA E ROMEO: opera					
Intermezzo arr de Cecco		1120/2210/perc/str		Ricordi	11480
Symphonic episode from the torch dance and cavalcade					
	φ	2+picc. 2+ca.2+bcl.2/6440/timp.perc.bells. tamtam/cel.hp.pf/str	10'30"	Ricordi,1928	Misc 66
I1 GRILLO DEL FOCOLARE: opera					
Selection arr E.Tavan	PC	2222/2231/timp.perc/str		Ricordi	1715

ZANDONAI, Riccardo (cont)

MENELIS: opera
   Selection, arr E.Tavan   PC 2(picc)222/2231/timp.perc/str   Ricordi   1154
QUADRI DI SEGANTINI (Segantini's pictures): symphonic poem (1911)
   1. L'Aratura (The Ploughing)
   2. Idillio (Idyll)
   3. Ritorno al paese natìo (Return to the native village)
   4. Meriggio (High noon)
                 ø 2+picc.2+ca.2+bcl.asx.2/4340/timp.perc.
                    bells.glock.wmc/cel.2hp.pf/str   Ricordi,1931   Misc 8810
SERENATA MEDIOEVALE for cello solo
                 0000/2000/hp/str   12'   Ricordi,1912   Misc 1224
TERRA NATIVA: symphonic impressions
   No.2 'Autunno fra i monti'
     1. Canti nostalgici   3. Vespro
     2. Colloqui rusticani   4. Mattino di caccia
              ø 2+picc.2+ca.2+bcl.2+cbsn/4340/timp.perc.
                 cel.2hp.org/pf/str   Ricordi,1921   Misc 3751
VERE NOVO: symphonic poem for Baritone & orch, in E
              ø 2+picc.2+ca.2+bcl.2+cbsn/4340/timp.perc/
                 cel.2hp/str   Ricordi,1913   21476

ZARDO, N.

VALSE NINON, arr Godin from song by Zardo
              PC 1+picc.122/2230/perc/str   A H & C   2886

ZARET

MY SISTER AND I: song by Zaret, Whitney & Kramer
   in A, arr B.Berlin   ø 2121/2230/timp.perc/hp/str   (C.Connelly) TO 902 ø only

ZARZYCKI, Alexander (1834-1895)

POLONAISE: suite, op.37
   1. À la polonaise   3. Intermezzo cantabile
   2. À la mazourka   4. À la cracovienne
         ø 2+picc.222/2230/timp.perc/str   Simrock   2454

ZAVERTAL, Ladislao (1849-1942)

LOYAL HEARTS: patriotic overture on national airs
              ø 2+picc.232/4430.euph/timp.perc/hp.org/str   Boosey,1897   Misc 2103

ZBINDEN, Julien-François (1917-

FANTASIE for flute & orch, op.22ø 1000/2000/pf/str   Breitkopf,1954 22218
SUITE FRANCAISE, op.23 (1954)
   1. Symphonie   3. Air   5. Gigue
   2. Gavotte   4. Menuet
         ø str   13'   Breitkopf,1955 24964

ZECCHI, Adone

TRATTENIMENTO MUSICALE   ø str(6.2.2.1)   14'15"   Ricordi,1970   Misc 8128

ZECHNER, Johann Georg (1716-1778)

CONCERTI
   Harpsichord & strings
     in D, ed G.Schmeiser   ø str (no vla)   Akad Druck u.Verl,1973 25754

ZECHNER, Johann Georg (cont)

CONCERTI (cont)
  Harpsichord & strings (cont)
    in F, ed G.Schmeiser   φ   str (no vla)   Akad Druck u.Verl,1973   25754
    in A, ed G.Schmeiser   φ   str (no vla)   Akad Druck u.Verl,1973   25755
    in Bb, ed G.Schmeiser   φ   str (no vla)   Akad Druck u.Verl,1973   25755

ZEHLE, W.

VISCOUNT NELSON: march   φ   3222/4231/timp.perc/hp/str   2'15"   Hawkes   230 Ap B
WELLINGTON: march   φ   2+picc.222/4231/timp.perc/hp/str   Hawkes   853

ZEHM, Friedrich (1923-

SCHWIERIGKEITEN & UNFÄLLE MIT I CHORAL for wind
                φ   2(picc)22(Ebcl)2(cbsn)/2000
                    (conductor & all players except bsns
                    also play toy instruments)   10'   Schott,1976   Misc 8861

ZELENKA, Jan Dismas (1679-1745)

BEATUS VIR (Psalm 111) for Alto solo, chorus & orch
  ed J.Racek rev V.Bělský   φ   0200/0000/str/cont(org)   Czech SM,1971   Misc 10090
CAPRICCIOS
  No.1, in D
    ed C.Schoenbaum   φ   0201/2000/str/cont   Artia,1963.MAB 61   Misc 5880 & MRL
  No.2, in G
    ed C.Schoenbaum   φ   0201/2000/str/cont   Artia,1963.MAB 61   Misc 5880 & MRL
  No.3, in F
    ed C.Schoenbaum   φ   0201/2000/str/cont   Artia,1963.MAB 61   Misc 5880 & MRL
  No.4, in A
    ed C.Schoenbaum   φ   0201/2000/str/cont   Artia,1963.MAB 61   Misc 5880 & MRL
  No.5, in G
    ed C.Schoenbaum   φ   0201/2000/str/cont   Artia,1963.MAB 61   Misc 5880 & MRL
      Last mvt (Il contento) only
        ed C.Schoenbaum   φ   0201/0000/str/cont   (Artia)   25838
CONFITEBOR (Psalm 110) for STB-soli, chorus & orch
  ed J.Racek, rev V.Bělský   φ   0200/0000/vln-solo.str/cont(org)   Czech SM,1971   Misc 10090
DE PROFUNDIS (Psalm 129) for AT.38-soli,chorus & orch
  ed J.Racek, rev V.Bělský   φ   0200/0030/str/cont(org)   Czech SM,1971   Misc 10090
HIPOCONDRIA (1723)
  ed C.Schoenbaum   φ   0201/0000/str/cont   Artia,1963.MAB 61   5880 PL 633 Ani
                                                                                      & MRL

IN EXITU ISRAEL (Psalm 113) for SATB-soli, chorus & orch
  ed J.Racek, rev V.Bělský   φ   0200/0000/str/cont(org)   Czech SM,1971   Misc 10090
LAMENTATIONES JEREMIAE PROPHETAE for ATB-soli & orch
                            φ   2201/0000/vln-solo.str/cont(org)   Czech SM,1969   Misc 10101
MAGNIFICAT for Soprano & Alto soli, chorus & orch, in D
  ed W.Horn   φ   0201/0000/str/cont(org)   Carus,1980   Misc 10091
  ed J.Racek, rev V.Bělský   φ   0201/0000/str/cont(org)   Czech SM,1971   Misc 10090
OUVERTURE à 7 concertanti: suite
  1. Overture   3. Menuetto I   5. Siciliano
  2. Aria   4. Menuetto II   6. Folia
    ed C.Schoenbaum   φ   0201/0000/str/cont   25'   Universal,1960   25766
SYMPHONIES
  in A minor (1723)
    ed C.Schoenbaum   φ   0201/0000/str/cont   Artia,1963.MAB.61   Misc 5880
      1st mvt (Allegro) only   0201/0000/str/cont   (Czech SM)   26778 + Ani
      2nd mvt (Capriccio) only
        ed O.Schoenbaum   φ   0201/0000/str/cont   Czech SM,1963   26182 +

ZELENKA, Jan Dismas (cont)

SYMPHONIES (cont)
   in A min (cont)
      Minuets 1 & 2 only   ∅   0201/0000/str/cont   (Artia)   25892 Ani
      3rd mvt only   ∅   0201/0000/str/cont   (Artia)   25891

ZELEŃSKI, Wladyslaw (1837-1921)

JANEK: aria
   in B♭ min, arr A.Franzel   ∅   1110/0000/perc/hp.pf/str   Arranger   LM A 617
NIGHTINGALE MINE: Polish song
   in F, arr A.Franzel   ∅   1110/0000/perc/acdn.hp.pf/str   Arranger   LM A 619
SUITE DE DANSES POLONAISES, op.47 ∅   2+picc.222/4231/timp.perc/str   Jurgenson   9899

ZELLER, Carl Friedrich (1842-1898)

The BIRD-SELLER see   Der VOGELHÄNDLER
DRY YOUR EYES: song
   in F, arr M.Mackie   ∅   2222/4000/timp/hp.pf/str   (Allan)   21955
Der OBERSTEIGER (The master miner): operetta
   Selection, arr L.Artok   PC 1121/2210/perc/str   Schott   478
   Extracts
      Sei nicht bös (Don't be cross): Martin-Walzer (Farewell Waltz)
         in F (orig), arr I.Sutherland
                                  ∅   2222/4000/hp/str   (Bosworth)   26879
         in E♭ & E   ∅   1122/4210/str   (Bosworth)   24884
         in E♭, arr F.Cramer   org.pf/str   (Bosworth)   LM G 7942
ROSES FROM TYROL: song see   Der VOGELHÄNDLER: Extracts - Roses from Tyrol
Der VAGABOND: operetta
   Selection, arr Lloyd   PC 1121/2210/timp.perc/str   Bosworth   12393
Der VOGELHÄNDLER (The Bird-seller): operetta (English version - The Bird-seller)
   Overture
      arr Bauckner   ∅   2(picc)22.3sx.2/4230/timp.perc/hp/str 5'30"-6'30" Bosworth 11143 B
   Selections
      arr A.Ischpold   PC 2+picc.222/4230/timp.perc/hp/str   10'   Bosworth   18921
      arr L.Weninger   PC 2(picc)222/4230/timp.perc/str   Benjamin   13690
   Extracts
      The Cherry tree: song
         in F   VS 2022/2000/str   Bosworth   26159
      The Nightingale: song
         in B♭   VS 2222/4230/str   Bosworth   26158
      Roses from Tyrol (Schenkt man sich Rosen in Tyrol): duet for Soprano & Tenor soli, chorus & orch
         in B♭, arr B.Hartmann   VS 2222/4230/timp.perc/str   Bosworth   26157
         in B♭, arr A.Bauckner, orch L.Weninger for Soprano solo & orch
                                  ∅PC 222.[2asx.tsx].2/42[=2cnt].[tpt-solo].3.[tbn-solo].0/
                                      timp.perc/hp/str   Bosworth   24880
         arr A.Bauckner, orch L.Weninger (non-vocal)
                                  PC 222.2asx.tsx.2/42[=2cnt]30/timp.carillon.vib/
                                      str   2'30"   Bosworth   15217
WALTZING WITH ZELLER, arr Schreider PC 2222/4230/timp.perc/acdn.hp/str   Weinberger,1952 20783

ZELTER, Karl Friedrich (1758-1832)

ABENDPHANTAISE: song
   arr G.Williams   str   Arranger MS:BBC MS 30061
CONCERTO for viola & orch
   arr Mlynarczyk & Kranz   PC 0000/2000/hpsd/str   16'   Grahl   19200

ZEMLINSKI, Aleksandr (1872-1942)

LYRIC SYMPHONY for Soprano & Baritone soli & orch, op.18 (1923)
                         ϕ   4(2picc)2+ca.3+bcl.2+cbsn/4331/timp.perc/   (Misc 8478 &
                             cel.hmn.hp/str   45'   Universal,1954   (PL 675
SINFONIETTA, op.23   ϕ   22(ca)22/4330/timp.perc/hp/str   25'   Universal,1935   Misc 455 B

ZENDER, Hans

SCHACHSPIEL (Chess game) for 2 orchestral groups (1969)
                         ϕ   Group 1: 1(picc)111/1111/bells.xyl/hp.pf/
                                       str(1.0.1.1.1)
                             Group 2: 1(picc)111(cbsn)/1111/glock.vib/
                                       gtr.hp/str(1.0.1.1.1)   9'36"   Bote & B,1971   Misc 8149
ZEITSTRÖME for orch (1974) ϕ 3330/433[=2+btuba]0/4xyl[=2xyl+2pf]/str   Bote & B,1976   Misc 9573

ZHITOMIRSKI, A   see JITOMIRSKY, A

ZIANI, Marc' Antonio (c.1653-1715)

ALMA REDEMPTORIS MATER: motet for Contralto solo & orch
    ed C.Schoenbaum   ϕ   0001/0000/str/cont   Universal,1962.DTÖ 101-2   MRL
JESU CORONA VIRGINUM: motet for Bass solo & orch
    ed C.Schoenbaum   ϕ   str/cont   Universal,1962.DTÖ 101-2   MRL

ZIANI, Pietro Andrea (c.1620-84)

Il TALAMO PRESERVATO DALLA FEDELTA D'EVDOSSA: opera (1683)[Reggio version of the opera produced in Venice
        under the title "L'Innocenza risorta, ovvero Etio"]
    Complete
        Facsimile of contemporary MS (I MOe MS Mus.F.1554)
                         ϕ   0000/0100/str/cont   Garland,1978   MRL facs

ZIEHRER, Carl Michael (1843-1922)

BACKFISCHERLN (Coquettes): waltz, op.432
                             2121/2230/perc.glock/str   Hawkes   331
BIEDERMEIER-WALZER (Old folks)   PC 1(picc)121/2210/timp.perc.bells/str   Cranz   8408
BOSHAFT (Bundle of mischief), op.424
                             PC 1+picc.222/2230/timp.perc/str   Hawkes   5429
CALL ME YOUR DEAREST ONE   PC 1+picc.121/2210/perc/str   C.Fischer   6718
DIESEN KÜSS DER GANZEN WELT (A kiss to all the world): waltz, op.442
                             PC 1121/2210/perc.glock/str   Cranz   12447
FASCHINGSKINDER (Carnaval des enfants): waltz, op.382
                             PC 2(picc)222/4230/timp.perc/hp/str   Doblinger   9842
    arr F.Salabert   PC 1121/2230/perc/str   Salabert   6783
FESCHE GEISTER (Jovial Spirit): operetta
    Overture
        ed M.Schönherr   PC only   Doblinger,1959   Misc 7411
JUGENDSTREICHE (Folle jeunesse): galop, op.461
                             PC 1121/2210/timp.perc/str   Cranz   10686
Die LANDSTREICHER: operetta
    Complete   PC 2(picc)222/4230/timp.perc/hp/str   Doblinger   10809
    Extracts
        Sei gepriesen, du lauschige Nacht!: waltz-song
                             PC 2([picc])222/42.flg.30/timp.perc/hp/str   Doblinger,1899   24494
NACHTSCHWÄRMER (Les noctambules): waltz, op.466
                             PC 1121/2210/timp.perc/str   Cranz   12289

ZIEHRER, Carl Michael (cont)

PARFUM-WALZER, op.469	PC	2(picc)222/4230/timp.perc/hp/str		Cranz	8438
RUTSCHERPETER, op.459	PC	1121/2210/perc/str		Cranz	12476

SCHÄTZMEISTER: operetta, op.518

Overture	∅	2(picc)222/4230/timp.perc.glock/hp/str		Doblinger	3026

Extracts
    Her einspaziert: waltz

arr H.Schneider	PC	2+picc.222/4230/timp.perc/acdn.hp/str		Doblinger	22913

SECOLO NUOVO, VITA NUOVA (New century, new life): waltz, op.498

arr Ferrari	PC	1+picc.222/4230/timp.perc/hp.mand/str	7'15"	Schmidl	12144

SINGEN, LÄCHEN, TANZEN: waltz, op.486

	PC	1+picc.122/4230/timp.perc.glock/hp/str		Doblinger	12408
Die TANZGELEHRTEN: waltz, op.405	PC	1+picc.222/4230.euph/timp.perc.glock/hp/str		Hawkes	5026

Ein TOLLES MÄDEL

Overture	∅	2(picc)222/4230/timp.perc.glock/hp/str		Weinberger	11467

VIENNA WALTZ, OUR HEART'S DELIGHT
    arr W.Schmidt-Gentner, orch F.Killer

	PC	112.3sx.1/2230/perc/acdn.gtr/str		Bosworth	20463

WIENER BÜRGER (Les enfants de Vienne): waltz, op.419

arr A.Winter	PC	1121/1220/timp.perc/str		Hawkes	926 +
arr H.Schneider	PC	2+picc.222/4230/timp.perc/hp/str		Weinberger	21514

WIENER LUFT, op.411

arr A.Winter	PC	2222/2230/perc/str		Hawkes	7626 B

WIENER MÄD'LN.(Girls of Vienna): waltz, op.388

	∅PC	3(picc)22.3sx.2/4231/timp.perc/hp/str	8'15"	Hawkes	927

ZIELENSKI, Mikolaj (c.1550-1615)

LAETENTUR COELI: offertory for double chorus & orch

	∅	0000/0440/timp/org/str	Polish SM,1955.	
			Music of the Polish Renaissance	MRL

ZIINO, Ottavio (1909-

THEME, 7 VARIATIONS & FUGUE	∅	2+picc.2+ca.2+bcl.2+cbsn/4331/timp.xyl/		
		cel.hp.pf/str	Curci,1967	Misc 8241

ZILCHER, Hermann (1881-1948)

TANZFANTASIE, op.71	∅	3(picc)222/4331/timp.perc.glock.xyl/			
		cel.hp/str	16'	Eulenburg	Misc 1961

Der WIDERSPENSTIGEN ZAHMUNG (The Taming of the Shrew), op.54b
  Suite

1. Einleitung	9. Sturm
2. Schlau's Erwachen	10. Bianca
3. Die Musikanten spielen auf	11. Die Widerspenstige
4. Petruchio	12. Ängstlicher Auftritt
5. Katharina	13. Stets Widerspruch
6. Hortnesio	14. Verwirrung
7. In Unruhe	16. Beschluss und Ausklang
8. Hochzeitsmusik	

	∅	1(picc)111/2100/str	Breitkopf	9725

ZILLIG, Winfried (1905-1963)

CONCERTO for cello & wind instruments (1934)

	∅	2(picc)2(ca)1+Ebcl+bcl.2(cbsn)/4221	42'35"	Bärenreiter,1960	Misc 5703 B

CONCERTO FOR ORCHESTRA in one movement

	∅	2+picc.2+ca.1+Ebcl+bcl.2+cbsn/4331/			
		timp.perc.bells.glock.tamtam.xyl/			
		cel.hp/str	10'35"	Bärenreiter,1958	Misc 5702 B

ZIMBALIST, Efrem (1889-1980)

LEGENDE by E.Zimbalist & V.S.Kalinikov
  arr L.Artok   PC 2222/2110/timp/str   2'   Schott   9315
SUITE OF DANCES
  arr L.Artok (op.98)
     1. Polish dance   2. Russian dance   3. Neapolitan dance
                         PC 1121/2210/timp/str   Schott   9315

ZIMMER, Carl

BACH & HANDEL: Selection from the works of J.S.Bach & G.F.Handel
                         PC 2222/4230/timp/hp/str   Huhn   1140

ZIMMER, Ján (1926-

SYMPHONY No.1, op.21 (1955)   ∅ 2+picc.2+ca.2+bcl.2+cbsn/4331/timp.perc/
                                      cel.hp.pf/str   Czech SM,1963   Misc 10387

ZIMMERMANN, B.A. (1918-1970)

CANTO DI SPERANZA: cantata for cello & small orch (1957)
                         ∅ 3(2picc)2+ca.3(bcl)sx.1/1200/timp.perc
                            glock.xyl/hp.pf(cel)/str(no vlns)   20'   Schott,1958   Misc 7559
CONCERTO en forme de "pas de trois" for cello & orch (1965/66)
                         ∅ 3(picc)3(2ob-d'a)3(bcl)sx.3(cbsn)/
                            22(cnt)2(cbtbn).0.cbtuba/timp.perc.glock.
                            vib/dulc.gtr(egtr).hp.mand.
                            musical glasses [=cel].pf(hpsd)/str   Schott,1972   Misc 7769
"ICH WANDTE MICH UND SAH AN ALLES UNRECHT, DAS GESCHAH UNTER DER SONNE" ("I turned and saw all the injustices
   that are committed under the sun"): Ecclesiastical Action for 2 speakers, Bass solo & orch (1970)
                         ∅ 3(3picc,afl)3(ca)33/5361/timp.perc.bells.
                            3cbells.3gongs.mba.3tamtam.vib.xyl/egtr.hp/
                            str   Schott,1972   Misc 8033
PHOTOPTOSIS: prelude for orch (1968)
                         ∅ 4(2picc)3(2ob-d'a,ca)4(2bthn,bcl)3(cbsn)/
                            5(tuba)4(btpt)4(cbtbn)1/timp.perc.glock/
                            hp.org.pf(cel)/str   13'   Schott,1970   Misc 7328
DIE SOLDATEN : opera   ∅ 4(4picc,afl)3(3ob-d'a,ca)4(Ebcl,bcl).asx.
                            2(2cbsn)/5(5ttuba,btuba)4(Bbtpt.Atpt.Ebbtpt)
                            4(btbn)1(cbtuba)/timp(picctimp)8or 9perc(bells.
                            cbells.crot.glock.mba.vib.xyl)/cel.gtr.2hp.hpsd.org-
                            duet.pf/str(14.12.10.10.8)
                            Onstage: 3perc - each playing timp.perc.
                            bells.cbells.
                            No.2 also plays crot
                            Nos.2 & 3 play acym.jazz combs(cl.tpt.gtr.ampcb)
                                                            Schott,1975   Misc 8725
STILLE UND UMKEHR (Stillness and Return): Sketches for orch (1970)
                         ∅ 43+ca.3(bcl)sx.0.cbsn/421+cbtbn.0/perc/acdn.hp/
                            vln.vla.3vlc.3cb   Schott,1971   Miss 7460

SINFONIE IN EINEM SATZ   ∅ 3(2picc)3(ca)3(bcl)3(cbsn)/4331/2timp.4perc.
                            mba.vib.xyl/2hp.pf(cel)/str(32vln.12vla.
                            10vlc.8)   Schott,1957   Misc 7996

ZIMMERMANN, C.A.

ANCHORS AWEIGH: song march
    rev D.Savino   PC   111.3sx.1/2210/perc/gtr/str   F D & H   23257 +

ZIMMERMANN, Udo (1943-

MUTATIONS for orchestra (1973)   φ   3(picc)333/4440/5timp.3perc(bells.bgos.crots.tambs.
                                      tomtoms.vib.wdbl)/hp/str(9.9.9.6.3)   12'   DVfM,1975   Misc 9612

ZINGARELLI, Niccolò Antonio (1752-1837)

see: LONGYEAR, Rey Morgan. Thematic index of the symphonies of Niccolo Zingarelli in the Symphony,
series A vol 8. New York: Garland, 1980   MRL

Numbers prefixed by 'L' refer to entries in this index.

LAUDATE PUERI DOMINUM (O Praise the Lord) for Tenor solo, chorus & orch
                                  VS   2202/2000/str   7'   Novello   25827
SYMPHONIES
    L.4, in D
      ed R.Longyear   φ   0200/2000/str   Garland,1980.The Symphony Vol 8   MRL &
                                                                                         Misc 10397
    L.8, in E   MRL &
      ed R.Longyear   φ   0200/2000/str   Garland,1980.The Symphony Vol 8   Misc 10398
    L.9, in D min   MRL &
      ed R.Longyear   φ   0200/2000/str   Garland,1980.The Symphony Vol 8   Misc 10399
    L.15, in D   MRL &
      ed R.Longyear   φ   2201/2000/str   Garland,1980.The Symphony Vol 8   Misc 10400
    L.18, in Eb
      ed R.Longyear   φ   2222/2000/str   Garland,1980.The Symphony Vol 8   MRL &
                                                                                         Misc 10401
    L.42, op.6
      ed R.Maione   φ   2222/2000/timp/str   6'   Curci,1961 Misc 9465
    L.51, op.22 no.3, in C
      rev R.Maione   φ   2222/2000/str   7'   Zanibon,1959   25777
    L.52, in E min   MRL &
      ed R.Longyear   φ   2222/2000/str   Garland,1980.The Symphony Vol 8   Misc 10402
    L.60, op.22 no.1, in G
      ed R.Maione   φ   2222/0000/str   Carisch,1961   26167
    L.69, in C min (Sinfonia funèbre)
      ed R.Longyear   φ   2222/2220/str   Garland,1980.The Symphony Vol 8   Misc 10403

ZINNEN, J.A.

ONS HÉMÉCHT (WÒ D'VOLZÉCHT DURÉCH D'WISEN ZÈT): national anthem of Luxembourg
                                  PC   2(picc)222/4230/timp.perc/str   Breitkopf   14305
                                  PC   2(picc)222/4231/timp.perc/str   Benjamin   16363 +
    arr G.Williams   φ   fl.cl/str   Arranger   8116
    arr J.Greenwood   φ   fl.cl/hp/str   Arranger   10534
    arr L.Salter for unison voices & orch
                              φ   1111/2110/str   Arranger   2032 +

ŽIVKOVIĆ, Mirjana (1902-

SYMPHONIC TORSO (1967)   φ   3(picc)222/4231/timp.perc.bells/str   Yugoslav SM Misc 8468

ZOGRAFSKI, Tomislav (1934-

FANTASIA CORALE   φ   2(picc)+2picc.2+ca.2+bcl.asx.tsx.barsx.2+cbsn/
                                  6331/timp.perc.bells.vib.xyl/cel.hp.2pf/str   Yugoslav SM Misc 8539

ZOGRAFSKI, Tomislav (cont)

9 MINIATURES | ∅ | 2+picc.22+bcl.sx.2/0200/timp.perc/cel.hp/
| | str | | Yugoslav SM,1961 | Misc 9799
SINFONIETTA in E♭ | ∅ | 1011/0000/pf/str | | Yugoslav SM,1962 | Misc 9800

ZÖLLNER, Heinrich (1854-1941)

La PATRIE: Swiss air
  arr A.Scassola | VS | 1221/2230/timp.perc/str | | Foetisch | 6425
UNTER DEM STERNENBANNER (Under the Star Spangled Banner): overture op.88
| ∅ | 3(picc)222/4331/timp.perc.glock/str | | Forberg | 8469
Die VERSUNKENE GLOCKE (The sunken bell) op.80
  Prelude to Act V | PC | 1120/0110/timp.perc/str | | Breitkopf | 6958

ZOLOTARYOV, Vasili Andreyevich (1873-1964)

FÊTE VILLAGEOISE: overture op.4 | ∅ | 2(picc)222/4231/timp.perc/str | 7' | Belaieff | 4759
RHAPSODIE HEBRAÏQUE op.7 | ∅ | 2+picc.222/4231/timp.perc/2hp/str | 10' | Belaieff | 5586 B
SYMPHONY No.1, op.8 | ∅ | 2+picc.222/4231/timp.perc/str | 28' | Belaieff | Misc 2110

ZOLTÁN, Aladár (1929-

SYMPHONY | ∅ | 3(picc)2+ca.2+bcl.3(cbsn)/4331/timp.perc.bells. | | Rumanian SM,1970 |
| | glock.3gong.tamtam.3tomtom.xyl/cel.hp.pf/str | | | Misc 9839

ZOZAYA, C.

NIOBE: ballet
  Suite | ∅ | 2+picc.2+ca.22/4331/timp.perc.glock/cel.2hp/
| | str | 40'45" | Composer | 9669

ZUCCA, Mana

I LOVE LIFE: song   see   MANA-ZUCCA

ZULUETA, Pedro de

AS YOU LIKE IT: incidental music to Shakespeare's play
   1. Foresters sound the cheerful horn (Act II, Sc.3)
   2. Under the greenwood tree: song in F (Act II, Sc.4)
   3. Blow, blow thou winter wind: song in A
   4. Breed it like a fool: song in E
   5. End of Act IV

| | 1122/2210/str | | MS(Siddell) | 18340
BIANCA: waltz arr Frisk | PC | 112.3sx.1/2210/perc/bells.bjo/str | | Chappell | 7719 B
The CARNATION (El clavel): tango | | 1(picc)121/2230.euph/perc.cast/pf/str | | Chappell | 5984 Ap
The CLOWN'S SERENADE: intermezzo two-step
  arr H.M.Higgs | PC | 1+picc.121/2230.euph/perc/str | | Chappell | 7793 B
LOVE'S WONDERFUL MUSIC: waltz
  arr H.M.Higgs | PC | 112.2sx.1/2210/timp.perc/bjo/str | | Chappell | 6250
STARLIGHT: intermezzo | PC | 1(picc)121/2230.euph/timp.perc/str | | Chappell | 2937
SUNRISE: waltz
  arr H.M.Higgs | PC | 1+picc.121/2230.euph/timp.perc/str | | Chappell | 3627
TAKE HANDS AND PART: song
  in D, arr Fletcher | | str | | K.Prowse | 17220

ZUSCHNEID, K.

LENZFAHRT (Away to the forest) for male choir and brass insts, op.22
                      φPS 0000/42.cnt.31/timp/str   Breitkopf,1895   Misc 2374

ZWAR, Charles

BET YOUR LIFE, by C.Zwar & K.Leslie-Smith
    Selection, arr F.Rapley   PC 2+picc.12.3sx.1/2230/perc/hp/str   8'   Chappell,1951   20479 C
MARIGOLD: musical play
    Selection, arr F.Rapley   PC 2(picc)12.3sx.1/2230/timp.perc/hp/str   6'30"   Chappell,1959   23098 Ap

ZWIERZCHOWSKI, Mateusz (c.1713-1768)

REQUIEM, for SATB soli, chorus & orch
    ed F.Dabrowski   φ   0000/0200/str(no vlas)/cont(real J.Jargon)   Polish SM,1968   Misc 7831

ZWYSSIG, Josef [Alberich] (1808-1854)

TRITTST IM MORGENROT DAHER (SCHWEIZERPSALM): national anthem of Switzerland
                                   φ   2(picc)222/4231/timp.perc/str   Benjamin   16363 +
                                       2+3picc.4+ca.4+bcl.4+cbsn/8561/timp.perc/
                                       2hp/str   BBC   13638
    arr A.Franzel   φ   2+picc.222/42.2cnt.31/timp.perc/str   Arranger   19522
    arr A.Scassola   VS 1221/2230/timp.perc/str   Foetisch   6425

ADESTE FIDELES   see   O COME ALL YE FAITHFUL
ALL POOR MEN AND HUMBLE: Welsh traditional carol
   in A, arr Stanton   str/⌈unison chorus⌉⌊acc to SATB chorus⌋   OUP   2852
AS WITH GLADNESS (Dix)(C.Kocher)
   arr H.Perry   PC 1121/2230/timp/pf/str   Hawkes   4970 B
AWAY IN A MANGER (W.J.Kirkpatrick)
   arr R.Docker for SBar soli, chorus & orch (1976)
                φ   2(picc)2(ca)2(bcl)2/42+tpt.31/timp.perc.bells.glock.vib/
                   hp.pf/str   (Arranger) 26187
   in A♭, arr S.Robinson (1952) φ 2222/2000/timp.perc/str   2'15"   (Arranger) 20776
BELLS ACROSS THE SNOW (C.Gounod)
   in D, arr O.Langley   PC 0020/0230/str   Lafleur   13520
BETHLEHEM
   in B♭, arr L.Isaacs   φ 2200/2220/perc/str   (Arranger) MS 8367
BETHLEHEM CALLS YOU: Hungarian carol
   arr G.Williams   φ 2222/2230/timp.perc/hp.pf/str   (Arranger) 21244 Awa
The BOAR'S HEAD CAROL: traditional English carol
   in C, arr G.Williams   1000/0000/str   (Arranger) MS 20034
CAROL FOR THE NATIVITY (H.H.Lumby)
                 φ str   3'15" Hinrichsen,1957 25522
CAROL OF SERVICE: old French tune
   in D min, arr G.Williams φ 2222/0000/hp/str   (Arranger) MS 8367
CAROL POTPOURRI by Peter Wishart (1953)
   1. Ding dong merrily on high   3. Good King Wenceslas
   2. Love came down at Christmas
                 φ 1010/0100/pf/str/chorus   OUP   MLO 988
5 CAROLS WITH FANFARES by Leonard Isaacs
   1. The first Nowell (in D)   4. Christ the Lord is born (in D)
   2. Good King Wenceslas (in A)   4a.Fanfares
   3. Bethlehem (Polish carol)(in B♭) 5. O come, all ye faithful (in A)
                 φ 2200/2220/timp/str/chorus   Arranger MS:BBC MS 8367
CAROLCADE: a collection of Christmas carols, arr G.Langford (1970)
                 φ 2(picc)222/4231/timp.perc.glock.vib.xyl/cel.hp/
                   str   12'30" (Arranger) 25124 +
CHRIST THE LORD IS BORN
   in D, arr L.Isaacs   φ 2200/2220/perc/str/chorus   (Arranger) MS 8367
CHRISTIANS AWAKE! SALUTE THIS HAPPY MORN (Yorkshire)(J.Wainwright)
                   1121/20.2cnt.30/perc/str   Boosey   20417
   in D, arr H.Perry   PC 1121/0000/timp.perc/org/str   Hawkes   4970 B
   in D, arr G.Williams   φ 1111/0000/perc/hp/str/chorus   (Arranger) MS 20312
A CHRISTMAS SONG: Gascon carol
   arr G.Williams   φ 2121/2230/timp.perc/hp/str   (Arranger) 19963 Awa
CHRISTMAS SONG (On this day earth shall ring)
   in F min, arr G.Holst   2222/2000/timp.perc/bells/org/str/chorus Curwen   20364
COME YE LOFTY: Breton carol
   arr G.Williams   φ 1+picc.111/0000/perc/hp/str   (Evans)   21242 Awa
COVENTRY CAROL
   in G min & A min (2 settings), arr F.Collinson
                 φ 1121/1000/perc/str   (Arranger) MS 31010
   arr P.Wishart   φ 1000/0000/str   Arranger MLO 1849
The CRADLE (Melody form 'Geistliche Nachtigal' by S.G.Corner)
   in G, arr W.Stanton & M.Shaw str/⌈unison chorus⌉⌊=acc to SATB chorus⌋ OUP 18981
The CRADLE: Austrian carol
   arr Grace Williams   φ 1+picc.111/0000/perc/hp/str   (OUP)   21242 Awa
CROWN OF ROSES (Tchaikovsky)
   in E min, arr W.Stanton   str/⌈unison chorus⌉⌊=acc to SATB chorus⌋ OUP   18982

DASHING THROUGH THE SNOW (Jingle bells): traditional carol
    in Ab, arr P.Wishart   φ 1+picc.222/4230/timp.perc.glock.sbell/str   (Arranger)   MLO 991
DING DONG MERRILY ON HIGH (French, 16th cent)
    in G, arr H.Carruthers   φ cel/str   (Arranger)   22448
    arr R.Docker for Soprano & Baritone soli, chorus & orch (1976)
                    φ 2(picc)2(ca)2(bcl)2/42+sitpt.31/timp.perc.bells.
                        glock.vib/hp.pf/str   (Arranger)   26187
    arr G.Williams   2222/4230/timp.perc/cel.hp/str   (Arranger)   19964 Awa
DOWN IN YON FOREST: traditional Derbyshire carol
    arr Grace Williams   φ 2121/2230/timp.perc/hp/str   (Arranger)   19962 Awa
FANTASIA ON CHRISTMAS CAROLS for Baritone solo, chorus & orch by R.Vaughan Williams
                    φ 2222/4231/perc/org/str   Stainer & B   11392
    arr P.Wishart   φ 11[=cl]00/1[1]00/str   (Arranger)   MLO 1852
5 FAVOURITE YULE-TIDE SONGS by G.Borch, arr with S.Wright)
    1. Cantique do Noël   4. Sacred night, holy night.
    2. O faithful pine (O Tannenbaum)   5. O come all ye faithful
    3. O Sanctissima
                  PC 112.2sx.1/2210/timp/str   C.Fischer   13302
The FIRST NOWELL
    arr R.Barsotti   PC 1+picc.12.4sx.2/4230/perc/str   Boosey & H   21039 B
    in Eb, arr S.Herbert   PC 1122/2330/perc/str   Boosey   8080 C
    in D, arr L.Isaacs for chorus & orch
                    φ 2200/2220/perc/str   (Arranger)   MS 8367
    in Eb, arr M.Lubbock   φ 2121/2220/timp.perc/hp.org/str   (Arranger)   MS 30164
    in D, arr H.Perry   PC 1121/0000/timp.perc/org/str   Hawkes   4970 B
    in D, arr M.Saunders for mv chorus & orch
                    φ 2222/4230/timp.perc/cel.hp/str   (Arranger)   17259
    arr W.E.Stanton   φ 1121/2210/timp/str   (Arranger)   MLO 509
    in D, arr W.Stanton and M.Shaw str/[unison chorus][=acc to SATB chorus]   OUP   16688
    in D, arr G.Williams for chorus & orch
                    φ 1111/0000/perc/hp/str   (Arranger)   MS 20311
FLEMISH CAROL
    arr G.Williams   2222/4230/timp perc/cel.hp/str   (Arranger)   19964 Awa
The GARDEN OF JESUS: Dutch melody (17th cent)
    in G, arr W.Stanton & M.Shaw str/[unison chorus][=acc to SATB chorus[OUP   18985
GLORIA IN EXCELSIS
    in F, arr G.Williams   1000/0000/str   (Arranger)   MS 20034
GOD REST YOU MERRY GENTLEMEN φ 2222/2220/timp.perc/str   Arranger   MLO 2508
    in E min, arr V.Hely Hutchinson for chorus & orch
                    φ 2122/4231/perc/str   (Arranger)   MS 1555
    in E min, arr S.Kendal (version 'Carols New and Old')
                    φ 2222/4230/perc/str   Boosey   MLO 2508
    in E min, arr G.Williams   φ 2222/4230/perc/str   (Arranger)   MS 20034
GOING THROUGH THE HILLS (Shepherd's Pipe Carol)(J.Rutter) for chorus & orch
                  φ 1(picc)101/2000/hp/str   OUP,1973   26753
GOLDEN CAROL   see NOW IS CHRISTMAS Y-COME
GOOD KING WENCESLAS
    arr R.Barsotti   PC 1+picc.12.4sx.2/4230/perc/str   Boosey & H   21039 B
    in Ab, arr S.Herbert   PC 1122/2330/perc/str   Boosey   2020 C
    in G, arr P.Hope for chorus [organ] & orch
                  φ 2222/4230/timp.perc/hp/str   (AH & C)   23755 +
    in A, arr L.Isaacs for chorus & orch
                  φ 2200/2220/perc/str   (Arranger)   MS 8367
    arr R.Jacques for chorus & orch
                  φ 2222/2200/timp.perc/str   OUP,1971   26752

```
GOOD KING WENCESLAS (cont)
    in A, arr G.Williams for chorus & orch
                        φ   1111/0000/perc/hp/str                          (Arranger)    MS 20310
HARK THE HERALD ANGELS SING (Mendelssohn)(F.Mendelssohn)
    in G, rev F.Bye     φ   2222/4230/timp/hp/str                          Arranger      MLO 2514
    in G, arr S.Robinson for chorus & orch (1959)
                        φ   2222/4231/timp.perc/str                        (Arranger)    23077 +
    in G, arr M.Saunders for mv chorus & orch
                        φ   2222/4230/timp.perc/cel.hp/str                 (Arranger)    17259
    in G, arr G.Williams for chorus & orch
                        φ   1111/0000/perc/hp/str                          (Arranger)    MS 20309
HERE WE COME A-WASSAILING
    in F min, arr M.Shaw, orch Bidgood for chorus & orch
                            1010/0100/str                                  (Arranger)    MS 5824
        arr Grace Williams (Wassail Song)
                            2222/4230/timp.perc/cel.hp/str                 (Arranger )   19964 Awa
                            2121/2230/timp.perc/hp/str                     (Arranger)    19962 Awa
    in G, arr P.Wishart for fv chorus (or soli) & orch
                        φ   1010/0100/timp.perc/pf/str         (OUP)(Oxford Carol Bk)    MLO 2535
The HOLLY AND THE IVY
    in G, arr W.Davies & J.Byfield  pf/str (to go with printed chorus parts)  (Novello)  LM G 7863
        arr W.Stanton & M.Shaw    str/[unison chorus][=acc to SATB chorus]       OUP    18984
        arr P.Wishart for chorus & orch
                        φ   1+picc.222/4000/hp/str             (OUP)(Oxford Carol Bk)    MLO 2507
I SAW THREE SHIPS
    in G, arr G.Holst for chorus & orch
                            2222/2200/timp.perc.bells/org/str              Curwen        20364
        arr P.Wishart for voices & orch
                        φ   1010/0100/perc/str                             Arranger      MLO 1850
        arr P.Wishart   φ   11[=ca]00/1[=tpt]000/perc/str                  Arranger      MLO 1851
IN DULCI JUBILO (German, 14th cent)
    in F, arr H.Carruthers  φ  cel/str                                     (Arranger)    22448
    in F, arr C.Mackerras for Soprano solo & orch
                        φ   2222/4330/timp.perc.glock.bells/hpsd.org/str   (Arranger)    23479 +
    in G, arr Stanton & Gesius   str/[unison chorus][=acc to SATB chorus]       OUP      15545
IN THE BLEAK MIDWINTER (G.Holst)
    IN F, arr G.Williams        1000/0000/str                             (Arranger)    MS 20034
INFANT HOLY: Polish carol
        arr Grace Williams  φ   1+picc.111/0000/perc/hp/str               (Evans)       21242 Awa
IT CAME UPON THE MIDNIGHT CLEAR
    in F, arr S.Herbert    PC   1122/2330/perc/str                         Boosey        8080 C
JESUS, JESUS REST YOUR HEAD
        arr Grace Williams  φ   1000/0100/perc/hp/str                      (Arranger)    20042
JINGLE BELLS   see   DASHING THROUGH THE SNOW
JOSEPH BEING AN OLD MAN
    in A min. arr R.Vaughan Williams for unison chorus & orch
                        φ   bells/str                                      OUP           MS 20495
JOSEPH DEAREST, JOSEPH MINE (German,14th cent)
    in Eb, arr W.Stanton & R.Vaughan Williams
                            str/[unison chorus][acc to SATB chorus]        OUP           13587
KING HEROD AND THE COCK: Worcestershire traditional
        arr Grace Williams  φ   1000/0100/hp/str                          (Arranger)    20042
The KINGDOM: Angevin carol
        arr Grace Williams  φ   2121/2230/timp.perc/hp/str                (Arranger)    19963
LINDEN TREE CAROL (Traditional)
    in F                    0110/0000/str/fv chorus                        [BBC]         MLO 2802
```

LITTLE JESUS, SWEETLY SLEEP (Rocking Carol): Czech Carol
   in F, arr S.Robinson to fit M.Shaw's SATB version
               φ 2222/0000/str   (Arranger)   20775
   in F, arr W.Stanton and M.Shaw for Soprano solo (or SATB[=unison] chorus) & orch
                        str   (Arranger)   18986
      arr Grace Williams   2222/4230/timp.perc/cel.hp/str   (Arranger)   19964 Awe
MASTERS IN THIS HALL: old French air
   in D min, arr G.Holst for choir & orch
                      2222/2200/timp.perc.bells/org/str   Curwen   20364
A MERRY CHRISTMAS   see   WE WISH YOU A MERRY CHRISTMAS
NOW IS CHRISTMAS Y-COME (Golden Carol)
   in C for Soprano & Tenor soli, unison chorus & orch
                      bells/str   OUP   MS 20495
NOWEL: three carols (1976), arr R.Docker
   1. Away in a manger   3. O come, all ye faithful
   2. Ding dong! Merrily on high
               φ 2(picc)2(ca)2(bcl)2/4.2+sitpt.31/timp.perc.bells.glock.vib/
                   hp.pf/str/S.Bar soli,chorus   (Arranger)   26187

O COME, ALL YE FAITHFUL
   in C, arr R.Docker (1976)   φ 2(picc)2(ca)2(bcl)2/42.sitpt.31/timp.perc.bells.glock.vib/
                   hp.pf/str   (Arranger)   26187
   in G, arr P.Hope   φ 2222/4230/perc/hp.[org]/str/chorus   OUP   23752 +
   in G & A, arr V.Hely-Hutchinson
               φ 2121/4231/timp/str/chorus   (Arranger)   MS 1556
   in A♭, arr R.Barsotti   PC 1+picc.12.4sx.1/4230/perc/str   Boosey & H 21039 B
   in A♭, arr S.Herbert   PC 1122/2330/perc/str   Boosey   8080 C
   in A   1121/2230/perc/str   Boosey   20417
   in A, arr A.Franzel   φ 2222/4230/timp/str   (Arranger)   19394 +
   in A, arr L.Isaacs   φ 2200/2220/perc/str/chorus   (Arranger)   MS 8367
   in A, arr V.Novello   PC 2222/4230/timp/str   Novello   16684
   in A, arr H.Perry   PC 1121/2230/timp/pf/str   Hawkes,1951 4970
   in A, arr S.Robinson   0002/4230/(to fit Novello version, with descant to v.3) (Arranger)   MS 30582 A
   in A, arr R.Vaughan Williams   bells/   (OUP)   MS 20495
   in A, arr G.Williams   φ 1111/0000/timp/hp/str/chorus   (Arranger)   MS 20308
   in A, arr P.Wishart   φ 1101/0100/pf/str   Arranger   MLO 1848
   arr D.Godfrey   PC 2222/40.2cnt.30/timp/str   Chappell   2867
O LITTLE ONE SWEET (Melody   Samuel Scheidt)
   in B♭, arr W.Stanton & M.Shaw   str/[unison chorus][acc to SATB chorus]   OUP   18987
   arr Grace Williams   φ 2121/2230/timp.perc/hp/str   (Arranger)   19963 Awa
O LITTLE TOWN OF BETHLEHEM
   arr R.Jaques (after R.Vaughan Williams) for chorus & orch
               φ 2222/2200/str   OUP,1971   26752
ON CHRISTMAS DAY WE FORTH DID GO: Herefordshire carol
   in G min, arr F.Collinson   φ 1121/2210/timp/hp/str   (Arranger)   MS 30886
ON CHRISTMAS NIGHT ALL CHRISTIANS SING
   in G, arr F.Collinson   φ 1121/2210/perc/hp/str   (Arranger)   MS 30876
   in G, arr F.Bye   φ 2222+cbsn/4030/perc/hp/str   OUP   MLO 2744
ON THE FIRST DAY OF CHRISTMAS (The twelve days of Christmas)
   arr F.Austin, orch F.Bye   1120/0000/hp[=pf]/str/voice   (Arranger)   MLO 2570
   arr Grace Williams   2222/4230/timp.perc/cel.hp/str   (Arranger)   19964 Awa
ONCE IN ROYAL DAVID'S CITY (H.J.Gauntlett)
   in G, arr H.Carruthers   φ cel/str   (Arranger)   22448
   in G, arr R.Docker for boy treble, SSTBar soli, chorus, military band & orch
            φ 2(picc)222/4330/timp.bell/hp[org]/str   2'30"   (Arranger)   25162 +
   in G, arr H.Perry   PC 1121/0000/timp.perc/org/str   Hawkes   4970
   in G, arr M.Saunders for mv chorus & orch
            φ 2222/4230/timp.perc/cel.hp/str   (Arranger)   17259

PATAPAN
    arr Grace Williams   2222/4230/timp.perc/cel.hp/str   (Arranger)   19964 Awa

QUELLE EST CET ODEUR AGRÉABLE: French Carol
    in F, arr D.Arundell   ϕ   1111/2130/timp/str   Arranger   TO 883

REJOICE AND BE MERRY: Dorset carol
    in G, arr W.Stanton & M.Shaw   str/[unison chorus][=acc to SATB chorus]   OUP   16457

ROCKING CAROL <u>see</u>   LITTLE JESUS SWEETLY SLEEP

SEE AMID THE WINTER'S SNOW (Goss)(J.Goss)
    arr D.Willcocks for chorus & orch
                  ϕ   2222/2200/timp/str   OUP,1791   26752

SHEPHERDS IN THE FIELDS ABIDING: French traditional
    arr Grace Williams   ϕ   2121/2231/timp.perc/hp/str   (Arranger)   19963 Awa

SHEPHERD'S PIPE CAROL <u>see</u>   GOING THROUGH THE HILLS

SILENT NIGHT, HOLY NIGHT (F.Grüber)
    in B♭, arr S.Herbert for solo (or cornet) & orch
                  PC 1121/2230/perc/str   Boosey   1650
    in C, arr V.Hely Hutchinson for chorus & orch
                  ϕ   2122/4231/timp.perc/str   (Arranger)   MS 1555
    in C, arr L.Lucas   ϕ   2222/2000/str   (Arranger)   19010
    in C, arr G.Stacey   pf/str   (Arranger)   LM G 3600

SLEDGING Russian folk-tune
    arr Grace Williams   ϕ   2121/2230/timp.perc/hp/str   (Arranger)   19963 Awa

SLEEP MY LITTLE SON: German carol
    arr G.Williams   ϕ   1121/0220/timp.perc/hp/str   (Arranger)   21038 Awa

SUSANNI: German carol
    arr Grace Williams   ϕ   2121/2230/timp.perc/hp/str   (Arranger)   19963 Awa

SUSSEX CAROL <u>see</u>   ON CHRISTMAS NIGHT

TODAY IN BETHLEHEM
    arr Grace Williams   ϕ   1000/0100/perc/hp/str   (Arranger)   20042

TRES MAGI DE GENTIBUS (C.S.Lang)
    in E♭, orch G.Williams   ϕ   2222/4231/timp.perc/str   (YBP)   MS 20482

The TWELVE DAYS OF CHRISTMAS <u>see</u>   ON THE FIRST DAY OF CHRISTMAS

WASSAIL
    in G, arr F.Collinson   ϕ   1121/2320/timp.perc/hp/str   (Arranger)   MS 30998

WE THREE KINGS (J.H.Hopkins)
    in A, arr S.Robinson   2222/4230/timp.perc/hp/str   (Arranger)   20774

WE WISH YOU A MERRY CHRISTMAS
    arr G.Williams   ϕ   1000/0100/perc/hp/str   Arranger   20042

WELCOME YULE: old English melody (1652)
    in F, arr Hogben, orch Bidgood, for chorus & orch
                  ϕ   1010/0100/pf/str   (Arranger)   MS 5826

WHILE SHEPHERDS WATCHED THEIR FLOCKS (Winchester Old)
                       1121/2230/perc/str   Boosey   20417
    arr R.Barsotti   PC 1+picc.12.4sx.2/4230/perc/str   Boosey & H 21039 B
    arr G.Williams   ϕ   2121/2230/timp.perc/hp/str   (Arranger)   19962 Awa
    in F, arr S.Herbert   PC 1122/2330/perc/str   Boosey   8080
    in F, arr H.Perry   PC 1121/0000/timp.perc/org/str   Hawkes   4970 B
    in F, arr S.Robinson for chorus & orch
                  ϕ   22(ca)22/4331/timp/str   (Arranger)   23362 +
    in F, arr R.Vaughan Williams for chorus & orch
                  ϕ   bells/str   (OUP)   MS 20495
    in F, arr H.Carruthers ϕ   cel/str   (Arranger)   22448
    in G, arr G.Williams for chorus & orch
                  ϕ   1111/0000/perc/hp/str   (Arranger)   MS 20313

ALPAERTS, Florent

FANFARE (Inhuldidingsfanfare/Fanfare d'inauguration) [1939]
           ø   0000/3230/[timp]   Metropolis,1952   26316

ARNOLD, Malcolm

FANFARE FOR A ROYAL OCCASION   0000/0330   (Composer)   22889

BACH, Carl Philipp Emanuel

MARCH (fanfare), W.188
   rev E.Simon   0000/0300/timp   E.B.Marks   CM 54268

BARSOTTI, Roger

2 FANFARES
   1. Declamatory   2. Occasional fanfare
                        0000/0330/perc   Boosey & H   21039 B
5 MILITARY FANFARES   . 0000/0420   Brit & Dom   MB 2768

BAX, Arnold

2 FANFARES (used in 'Show Business', 1951)
                       0000/3300/sdm   (Composer)   MS 55422 Ap

BENJAMIN, Arthur

FANFARE FOR A FESTIVE OCCASION   0000/0210   Boosey & H   15389
3 FANFARES
   1. For a state occasion   2. For a brilliant occasion   3. For a gala occasion
                    PC 0000/0530/timp   Hawkes,1953   20976

BLISS, Arthur

FANFARE (in '6 brilliant fanfares by various composers')
                         military band   Boosey & H   MB 3202
FANFARE FOR A DIGNIFIED OCCASION 0000/03+E♭tpt.30   Boosey & H   15389
FANFARE FOR HEROES (1930)   0000/0330/timp.cym   Novello,1970 Misc 7446
2 FANFARES FOR 'LET THE PEOPLE SING'
              ø 0000/0330/perc   (Composer)   23210
6 FANFARES FOR 'VICTORY PROGRAMME' (1945)
   arr F.Collinson   tpts & orch   (BBC)   MSS 20068
3 JUBILANT FANFARES   0000/0331   Novello   MB 3883 B
6 JUBILEE FANFARES   full military band   (BBC)   MB 2712
PEACE FANFARE for children (1944)
              ø 0000/0330/timp.bells   [Composer]   MS 20107
6 ROYAL FANFARES (composed for the wedding of HRH Princess Margaret in Westminster Abbey, 6th May 1960)
   1. The Sovereign's fanfare   4. Royal fanfare
   2. Fanfare for the bride   5. A Wedding fanfare
   3. Interlude   6. Royal fanfare
     Complete   0000/033[1]/perc   Novello,1965 Misc 6203
     Nos. 5 & 6 only   0000/033[1]   Novello,1960 23306 B
3 SOLEMN FANFARES   full military band   Novello   MB 3883 B

BONNEAU, Paul

FANFARE   0000/4321/timp.cym   Leduc,1951   20742

BRIAN, Havergal

FESTIVAL FANFARE (formerly 'Fanfare for the orchestral brass')(1967)
                             φ   0000/4432   1'30"   Musica Viva,1974   26179
FLOURISH FOR 4 TRUMPETS: from 'The Cerci' (1952)
                             φ   0000/0400   35"   Musica Viva

BRITTEN, Benjamin

FANFARE FOR ST.EDMONDSBURY (1950)
                             φ   0000/0300   Boosey & H,1969   24970 C

BUSCH, Carl

FANFARE   0000/0600   Fitz Simons   13213

BUSCH, Geofrey

FANFARE AND MARCH 'The Prince of Morocco'
                             φ   22[=1]3[=2]2[=1]/4[=2]231/timp.perc/[cb]   Novello 1965   Misc 6822

BUSH, Irving

4 FANFARES FOR ALL OCCASIONS
   1. Fanfare for the Peninsula Fair,1977   3. Out of the past
   2. Motion   4. Present tense
                             φ   4tpt   Wimbledon,1978   CM 56723

CALLAGHAN, T.

6 FANFARES   0000/0200   Boosey & H   MB 3201
25 FLOURISHES, MARCHES, etc   0000/0400   Boosey & H   MB 3201

CARTER, Elliot

BIRTHDAY FANFARE for Sir William Glock's 70th birthday (1978)
                             φ   3tpt/vib(bells)   Composer,1978   CM 56826 φ only

CATALINET, Philip Bramwell

4 CEREMONIAL FANFARES
   1. Royalty   2. Parliament   3. The Services   4. The Colours
                             0000/04[=cnt][E♭tpt.E♭cnt]00   Hinrichsen,1954 17011

CHAGRIN, Francis

2 FANFARES   φ   4 equal instruments/perc   Novello,1962   CM 55116

CHIGNELL, Robert

3 FANFARES   0000/4331/timp.perc   (Composer)   MSS 4939

CLIFFORD, Hubert

EPIC FANFARE FOR AUSTRALIA DAY   0000/2[+]2[+]11/timp.perc   (Composer)   MB 3512
ROYAL VISITOR: FANFARE, from 'The Cowes Suite'
                         ∅   0000/03+E♭tpt.30   (Composer)   23016

COPLAND, Aaron

CEREMONIAL FANFARE (1969)   ∅   0000/4331   Boosey & H,1974   26113
FANFARE FOR THE COMMON MAN   0000/4331/timp.perc   Boosey & H   Misc 2974
INAUGURAL FANFARE for wind & percussion (1969, rev 1975)
                         ∅   3(picc)220/4331/timp.4perc.glock.vib Boosey & H,1976   26264

COWELL, Henry

FANFARE TO THE FORCES OF OUR LATIN AMERICAN ALLIES
                             0000/4330/perc   Boosey & H   Misc 2974

CRESTON, Paul

FANFARE FOR PARATROOPERS   0000/4330/sdm.cym   Boosey & H   Misc 2974

CRUFT, Adrian

10 FANFARES, op.3 (1948)   ∅   0000/0600/[sdm]   Galliard,1964   24060

CURZON, Frederic

3 FANFARES (fanfares nos. 4, 5 & 6)
                             0000/02[+]10   Boosey & H   15389

DUNCAN, Trevor

3 FANFARES
    1. Royal command   2. Imperial solemnity   3. Chivalry
                        PC   0000/0530/timp   Boosey & H,1953   20976

EDGE, D.

FANFARE (General release)
    arr R.Burston   ∅   0000/2331/timp.perc/hp   (Composer)   TO 889

ELGAR, Edward

CIVIC FANFARE in B♭ (1927)(intended as a prelude to the National Anthem)
                    ∅   2+picc.2+ca.2+bcl.2+cbsn/4331/timp.perc/
                        org/str (no vlns)   1'30"   (K.Prowse)   26151

ENGLEMAN, Joseph

20 FANFARES for brass ensemble or orch
    Set 1 (nos. 1-10)
        1. Ceremonial   6. Weird fanfare
        2. Solemn ceremonial   7. A joyful fanfare
        3. Hunting scene   8. Heroic
        4. Comic fanfare   9. In ancient style
        5. Palace scene   10. Grand processional
                        PC brass ensemble: 0000/2210/dm
                        PC orch: 112.3sx.1/2210/perc/str   Bosworth   9346 Ap

ENGLEMAN, J. (cont)

20 FANFARES for brass ensemble or orch (cont)
   Set 2 (Nos. 11-20) (10 Movistone fanfares)
      11. Introduction   16. Valse fanfare
      12. Military fanfare   17. Rustic fanfare
      13. Oriental fanfare   18. Sad fanfare
      14. Festal fanfare   19. Consecration fanfare
      15. Dramatic fanfare   20. Jovial fanfare
                                PC brass ensemble: 0000/2210/dm
                                PC orch: 1121/2210/perc/str   Bosworth   10005

FERGUSON, Howard

2 FANFARES
   1. A Festive fanfare   2. A Solemn fanfare
                                0000/04[=4cnt].30/   Hawkes,1953   20975

FULEIHAN, A.

FANFARE FOR THE MEDICAL CORPS   0000/4331   Boosey & H   Misc 2974

GLAZUNOV, Aleksandr

Les FANFARES, exécutées au Jubilée de N.Rimsky-Korsakov, by A.Glazunov & A.Lyadov
                        ∅   0000/4331/timp.perc   Belaieff,1891 6312

GOOSSENS, Eugene

FANFARE FOR A CEREMONY, op.48, no.1
                            0000/0420   (Chester)   TO 974
FANFARE FOR THE MERCHANT MARINE   0000/4330/timp.perc   Boosey & H   Misc 2974

HANSON, Howard

FANFARE FOR THE SIGNAL CORPS   0000/4331/timp.sdm.tendm   Boosey & H   Misc 2974

HARASOWSKI, A.

FANFARE   military band   (BBC)   MB 3541

HARRISON, Julius

4 FANFARES FOR SHAKESPEARE'S TRAGEDIES
                        ∅   0000/0300/sdm   Composer MS:BBC MS 30233

HELY-HUTCHINSON, Victor

ADVANCE AUSTRALIA   ∅   0000/0430/timp.perc   (Composer)   MS 8473
EMPIRE DAY 1944   ∅   0000/0430/timp.perc   (Composer)   MS 8476
O CANADA   ∅   0000/0430/timp.perc   (Composer)   MS 8473
WAIATA POI   ∅   0000/0430/timp.perc   (Composer)   MS 8475

HODKISON, Sydney

2 FANFARES FOR A FESTIVAL   ∅   0000/0430/perc.3tomtom   1'10"   AMP,1978   26668

HOLLOWAY, Robin

2 FANFARES FOR BRISTOL CATHEDRAL (CONSECRATION FANFARES)(1973)
   1. Body   2. Blood
                  ϕ   0000/0430   (Composer)   CM 55806

HOWELLS, Herbert

FANFARE FOR SCHOOLS (1943)   0000/4331/timp.sdm   (BBC)   MS 1560

INGELBRECHT, Désiré-Émile

4 FANFARES

1. Pour une fête	0000/4220	1'	Senart	Misc 1653 B
2. Pour le Président	0000/4331	1'	Senart	Misc 1653 B
3. Funèbre	0000/4331/timp.tamb	1'45"	Senart	Misc 1653 B
4. Dédicatoire	0000/4331	0'50"	Senart	Misc 1653 B

JANACEK, Leos

SOKOL FANFARE (from Sinfonietta, 1926)
             ϕ 0000/09+2btpt.00.2ttuba/timp   3'35"   Universal,1975   26059

JOINER, A.E.

TRUMPET FANFARES
   1. Vive les Caribiniers   3. St Cyre   5. Scotland for ever
   2. Châlons   4. Ubique   6. Quis separabit
                      0000/0400   Boosey & H   MB 3200

JOLIVET, André

FANFARE POUR BRITANNICUS
   1. Prelude   3. Héron   5. Narcisse
   2. Burrhus   4. Agrippire   6. Postlude
              ϕ 0000/4441/timp.perc   Boosey & H,1962   Misc 5747

JOSQUIN DES PRÉS

FANFARE ROYALE (VIVE LE ROY), pour la cérémonie du Sacre de Louis XII (1498)
   rev F.Raugel   0000/0310   (or   0000/0220)   Schola Cant,1954   CM 54688

KETÈLBY, Albert William

FANFARE FOR A CEREMONIAL OCCASION
                  0000/0430/timp.sdm   Bosworth   12592

LEES, Benjamin

FANFARE FOR A CENTENNIAL (1966)
             ϕ 0000/4331/timp.3perc   Boosey & H,1973   26131

O'DONNELL, P.S.G.

EMPIRE FANFARE   0000/02.2cnt.20/timp   (Composer)   MB 3354

O'KEEFE, W.

CORONATION FANFARE (Delhi Durbar 1911)
                           0000/0800/timp   Potter   MB 3431
CORONATION FANFARES, nos. 5-7   0000/0800/timp   Potter   MB 2935

PISTON, Walter

FANFARE FOR THE FIGHTING FRENCH
                           0000/4331/timp.perc   Boosey & H   Misc 2974

RHODES, S.

OCCASIONAL FANFARES   cnts.tbn.basses/timp   N.Richardson BB 1123 B

SULLIVAN, Arthur

FANFARE from finale Act 2 of 'The Gondoliers'
                  PC 0000/0230   [BBC]   TO 738

TAYLOR, Deems

FANFARE FOR RUSSIA
   arr G.Turner   0000/4331/timp.perc   Boosey & H   Misc 2974

THOMSON, Virgil

FANFARE FOR FRANCE   0000/4330/sdm.fielddm   Boosey & H   Misc 2974

TIPPET, Michael

FANFARE FOR BRASS   φ   0000/4330   Schott,1971   26071

TOMASI, Henri

FANFARES LITURGIQUES
   1. Annonciation   3. Apocalypse (Scherzo)
   2. Evangrile   4. Procession du Vendredi-Saint
                 φ   0000/4341/timp.perc   Leduc,1952   21049

WAGENAAR, Bernard

FANFARE FOR AIRMEN   0000/4331/timp.sdm   Boosey & H   Misc 2974

WAGNER, Richard

3 FANFARES   φ   0000/00.4signal tp 1+00/timp   M.Hieber   11044

WALTON, William

HAMLET: FILM
   Fanfare, arr.M.Sargent   φ   0000/4331/timp.sdm   OUP,1965   24304
A QUEEN'S FANFARE (for NATO Parliamentarians' Conference, London,1959)
                 0000/084[=4tpt.3tbn]0   0'40"   OUP,1972   Misc 7780

WILLIAMS, Gerrard

3 FANFARES (used in programme 'Italian Surrender')
                 0000/3430/timp.perc   (BBC)   MS 30377

WOOD, Haydn

FANFARE   0000/01[+]1[+]0   Boosey & H   15389

WOOD, Thomas

2 FANFARES
   1. General salute: suggested by 'The Grenadiers'   2. C in C's salute
               1+picc.00.E♭cl.0/0330/cym.sdm   (Composer)   MS 1561

ZELENKA, Jan Dismas

6 REITERFANFAREN (CAVALRY FANFARES)
   ed K.Janetzky   ∅   0000/0400/timp   Hofmeister,1962   CM 53480

ABIDE WITH ME
   Eventide (Monk)   1121/20.2cnt.30/perc/str   Boosey   20417
       arr M.L. Lake   112.B♭sx.E♭sx.1/20.2cnt.10/timp.perc/str   C.Fischer   19720
       arr R.Barsotti   PC   1+picc.12.4sx.2/4230/perc/str   Boosey & H   21039 B
       arr D.Godfrey   PC   2222/40.2cnt.30/timp/str   Chappell   2867
ABOVE THE CLEAR BLUE SKY
   Children's voices
       arr H.Perry   PC   1121/2230/timp/pf/str   Hawkes,1957   4970
ABOVE THE STARY SPHERES
   St Michael   1121/20.2cnt.30/perc/str   Boosey   20417
The ADVENT OF OUR KING
   Franconia (J.B.König)   1121/20.2cnt.30/perc/str   Boosey   20417
ALL GLORY, LAUD AND HONOUR
   St Theodulph (M.Teschner)   1121/20.2cnt.30/perc/str   Boosey   20417
       arr H.Perry   PC   1121/2230/timp/pf/str   Hawkes,1957   4970
ALL HAIL THE POWER OF JESU'S NAME
   Miles Lane (W.Schrubsole)   1121/20.2cnt.30/perc/str   Boosey   20417
   St Leonard (H.Smart)   1121/20.2cnt.30/perc/str   Boosey   20417
       arr D.Godfrey   PC   2222/40.2cnt.30/timp/str   Chappell   2867
ALL PEOPLE THAT ON EARTH DO DWELL
   Old 100th (L.Bourgeois)   1121/20.2cnt.30/perc/str   Boosey   20417
                               112.B♭sx.E♭sx.1/20.2cnt.10/timp.perc/str   C.Fischer   19720
       arr A.Benoy & A.Bryce   ∅   11[=fl]21/1220/str   OUP,1962   25286
       arr R.Vaughan-Williams, re-scored R.Douglas for chorus, congregation & orch
                          ∅   0000/0300/[timp]/org   OUP,1969   25128
       arr D.Godfrey   PC   2222/40.2cnt.30/timp/str   Chappell   2867
       arr H.Perry   PC   1121/2230/timp/pf/str   Hawkes,1957   4970
ALL THINGS BRIGHT AND BEAUTIFUL
   All things bright and beautiful (W.Monk)
       arr H.Perry   PC   1121/2230/timp/pf/str   Hawkes,1957   4970
       arr G.Vinter   ∅   2222/4000/timp.perc/str   (BBC Hymn Bk)OUP,1951   22112 +
ALLELUYA SING TO JESUS
   Hyfrydol (R.Prichard)
       arr J.Patten   003[=3ob]0/3[=3tpt]000/pf   Arranger   24534
ALMIGHTY FATHER HEAR OUR . CRY
   Rockingham (E.Miller)
       arr H.Perry   PC   1121/2230/timp/pf/str   Hawkes,1957   4970
AND DID THOSE FEET
   Jerusalem (C.Parry)   ∅   2222/4230/timp/str   Curwen   5041 E
       arr R.Barsotti   PC   1+picc.12.4sx.2/4230/perc/str   Boosey & H   21039 B
ART THOU WEARY?
   Christus Consolator (J.Dykes)   1121/20.2cnt.30/perc/str   Boosey   20417
AS PANTS THE HART
   Martyrdom (H.Wilson)   1121/20.2cnt.30/perc/str   Boosey   20417
       arr A.Benoy & A.Bryce   ∅   11[=fl]21/1220/str   OUP,1962   25286
AS WITH GLADNESS MEN OF OLD
   Dix (C.Kocher)   1121/20.2cnt.30/perc/str   Boosey   20417
       arr H.Perry   PC   1121/2230/timp/pf/str   Hawkes,1957   4970
AT EVEN ERE THE SUN WAS SET
   Angelus   1121/20.2cnt.30/perc/str   Boosey   20417
AT THE NAME OF JESUS
   Evelyns (H.Monk)
       arr H.Perry   PC   1121/2230/timp/pf/str   Hawkes,1957   4970
AWAKE MY SOUL AND WITH THE SUN
   Commandments (L.Bourgeois)   1121/20.2cnt.30/perc/str   Boosey   20417

BE THOU MY GUARDIAN
   Abridge (I.Smith)
     arr A.Chatterley (1966)   2111/0000   (Arranger)   24534
BLESSED ARE THE PURE IN HEART
   Franconia (J.B.König)
     arr A.Benoy & A.Bryce   φ 11[=fl]21/1220/str   OUP,1962   25286
BREATHE ON ME, BREATH OF GOD
   Carlisle (C.Lockhart)
     arr A.Benoy & A.Bryce   φ 11[=fl]21/1220/str   OUP,1962   25286
BRIEF LIFE IS HERE OUR PORTION
   St Alphege (H.Gauntlett)   1121/20.2cnt.30/perc/str   Boosey   20417
BRIGHTLY GLEAMS OUR BANNER
   Vexillum (H.Smart)   1121/20.2cnt.30/perc/str   Boosey   20417
                          112.B♭sx.E♭sx.1/20.2cnt.10/timp.perc/str   C.Fischer   19720
CHILDREN OF THE HEAVENLY KING
   Innocents
     arr H.Perry   PC 1121/2230/timp/pf/str   Hawkes,1957   4970
CHRIST THE LORD IS RISEN AGAIN
   Würtemburg (J.Rosenmüller)   1121/20.2cnt.30/perc/str   Boosey   20417
CHRIST THE LORD IS RISEN TODAY
   Easter Hymn (W.Monk)   1121/20.2cnt.30/perc/str   Boosey   20417
CHRISTIANS AWAKE, SALUTE THE HAPPY MORN
   Yorkshire (J.Wainwright)   1121/20.2cnt.30/perc/str   Boosey   20417
     arr H.Perry   PC 1121/2230/timp/pf/str   Hawkes,1957   4970
The CHURCH'S ONE FOUNDATION
   Aurelia (S.Wesley)   1121/20.2cnt.30/perc/str   Boosey   4970
     arr H.Perry   PC 1121/2230/timp/pf/str   Hawkes,1957   4970
CITY OF GOD
   Richmond (T.Haweis)
     arr A.Benoy & A.Bryce   φ 11[=fl]21/1220/str   OUP,1962   25286
COME, LET US JOIN OUR CHEERFUL SONGS
   Nativity (H.Lahee)
     arr H.Perry   PC 1121/2230/timp/pf/str   Hawkes,1957   4970
COME UNTO ME YE WEARY
   Come unto me (J.Dykes)   1121/20.2cnt.30/perc/str   Boosey   20417
COME, YE DISCONSOLATE   112.B♭sc.E♭sx.1/20.2cnt.10/timp.perc/str   C.Fischer   19720
COME YE THANKFUL PEOPLE, COME
   St George (Windsor)(J.Elvey)
     arr H.Perry   PC 1121/2230/timp/pf/str   Hawkes,1957   4970
CONQUERING KINGS THEIR TITLES TAKE
   Innocents
     arr H.Perry   PC 1121/2230/timp/pf/str   Hawkes,1957   4970
CRIMOND   <u>see</u> The LORD'S MY SHEPHERD
CROWN HIM WITH MANY CROWNS
   Diademata (G.Elvey)   1121/20.2cnt.30/perc/str   Boosey   20417
DANKGEBET: prayer of thanksgiving   112.B♭sx.E♭sx.1/20.2cnt.10/timp.perc/str   C.Fischer   19720
The DAY THOU GAVEST LORD IS ENDED
   St Clement (C.Scholefield)   1121/202.cnt.30/perc/str   Boosey   20417
DAYS AND MOMENTS QUICKLY FLYING
   St Sylvester (J.Dykes)   1121/20.2cnt.30/perc/str   Boosey   20417
DEAR LORD AND FATHER OF MANKIND
   Repton (C.H.Parry)
     arr F.Cordell   φ 0100/0000/str   (BBC Hymn Bk)OUP,1951   20967

DISPOSER SUPREME, AND JUDGE OF THE EARTH
    Hanover (W.Croft)   1121/20.2cnt.30/perc/str   Boosey   20417
        arr H.Perry   PC 1121/2230/timp/pf/str   Hawkes,1957   4970
DO NO SINFUL ACTION
    Newland (J.Gauntlett)
        arr H.Perry   PC 1121/2230/timp/pf/str   Hawkes,1957   4970
DRAW NIGH, AND TAKE THE BODY OF THE LORD
    Coena Domini (A.Sullivan)   1121/20.2cnt.30/perc/str   Boosey   20417
ETERNAL FATHER, STRONG TO SAVE
    Melita (J.Dykes)   1121/20.2cnt.30/perc/str   Boosey   20417
        arr D.Godfrey   PC 2222/40.2cnt.30/timp/str   Chappell   2867
        arr H.Perry   PC 1121/2230/timp/pf/str   Hawkes,1957   4970
FAR FROM MY HEAVENLY HOME
    Lyte (J.Wilkes)   1121/20.2cnt.30/perc/str   Boosey   20417
A FEW MORE YEARS SHALL ROLL
  ' Chalvey (L.Hayne)   1121/20.2cnt.30/perc/str   Boosey   20417
FIERCE RAGED THE TEMPEST
    St Aёlred (W.Monk)   1121/20.2cnt.30/perc/str   Boosey   20417
        arr H.Perry   PC 1121/2230/timp/pf/str   Hawkes,1957   4970
FIGHT THE GOOD FIGHT
    Duke Street.(J.Hatton)
        arr A.Bryce & A.Benoy) φ 11[=fl]21/1220/str   OUP,1962   25286
    Pentecost (W.Byrd)   1121/20.2cnt.30/perc/str   Boosey   20417
FILL THOU MY LIFE
    Richmond (T.Haweis)
        arr H.Perry   PC 1121/2230/timp/pf/str   Hawkes,1957   4970
The FIRST NOWELL
        arr R.Barsotti   PC 1+picc.12.4sx.2/4230/perc/str   Boosey & H 21039 B
        arr H.Perry   PC 1121/2230/timp/pf/str   Hawkes,1957   4970
FOR EVER WITH THE LORD
    Nearer Home (J.Woodbury)   1121/20.2cnt.30/perc/str   Boosey   20417
FOR THEE, O DEAR, DEAR COUNTRY
    Jenner (Jenner)   1121/20.2cnt.30/perc/str   Boosey   20417
FOR THY MERCY AND⌒THY GRACE
    Culbach   1121/20.2cnt.30/perc/str   Boosey   20417
FORTY DAYS AND FORTY NIGHTS
    Heinlein (M.Herbst)   1121/20.2cnt.30/perc/str   Boosey   20417
FORWARD! BE OUR WATCHWORD
    St Boniface (H.Gadsby)   1121/20.2cnt.30/perc/str   Boosey   20417
FROM GREENLAND'S ICY MOUNTAINS
    Aurelia (S.Wesley)   1121/20.2cnt.30/perc/str   Boosey   20417
GENTLE JESUS, MEEK AND MILD
    Gentle Jesus (M.Shaw)
        arr H.Perry   PC 1121/2230/timp/pf/str   Hawkes,1957   4970
GLORIOUS THINGS OF THEE ARE SPOKEN
    Austria (J.Haydn)   112.B♭sx.E♭sx.1/20.2cnt.10/timp.perc/str   C.Fischer 19720
        arr A.Benoy & A.Bryce   φ 11[=fl]21/1220/str   OUP,1962   25286
        arr H.Perry   PC 1121/2230/timp/pf/str   Hawkes,1957   4970
GLORY BE TO JESUS
    Caswall (F.Filitz)   1121/20.2cnt.30/perc/str   Boosey   20417
GLORY TO THEE WHO SAFE HAST KEPT
    Tallis Canon (T.Tallis)   1121/20.2cnt.30/perc/str   Boosey   20417
GOD ETERNAL, MIGHTY KING
    Innocents
        arr H.Perry   PC 1121/2230/timp/pf/str   Hawkes,1957   4970

GOD MOVES IN A MYSTERIOUS WAY				
London New (harm Wesley)		1121/20.2cnt.30/perc/str	Boosey	20417
GOD THE ALL TERRIBLE				
arr D.Godfrey	PC	2222/40.2cnt.30/timp/str	Chappell	2867
GOOD KING WENCESLAS				
arr R.Barsotti	PC	1+picc.12.4sx.2/4230/perc/str	Boosey & H	20139 B
GRACIOUS SPIRIT, HOLY GHOST				
Capetown (F.Filitz)				
arr A.Benoy & A.Bryce	φ	11[=fl]21/1220/str	OUP,1962	25286
GREAT GOD, WHAT DO I SEE AND HEAR				
Luther (M.Luther)		1121/20.2cnt.30/perc/str	Boosey	20417
HAIL TO THE LORD'S ANNOINTED				
Crüger (J.Crüger)				
arr H.Perry	PC	1121/2230/timp/pf/str	Hawkes ,1957	4970
HARK! HARK! MY SOUL				
Pilgrims (H.Smart)		1121/20.2cnt.30/perc/str	Boosey	20417
HARK MY SOUL! IT IS THE LORD				
St Bees (J.Dykes)		1121/20.2cnt.30/perc/str	Boosey	20417
HARK THE GLAD SOUND!				
Bristol (harm T.Ravenscroft)		1121/20.2cnt.30/perc/str	Boosey	20417
HARK! THE SOUND OF HOLY VOICES				
Deerhurst (J.Langran)		1121/20.2cnt.30/perc/str	Boosey	20417
HAVE MERCY ON US, GOD SO HIGH				
St Flavian		1121/20.2cnt.30/perc/str	Boosey	20417
HE WHO WOULD VALIANT BE				
Monks Gate		1[=cl]001[=hn]/0220/perc	(Arranger)	24534
HILLS OF THE NORTH REJOICE				
Little Conrad (M.Shaw)		str	(Arranger)	MS 5677
HOLY FATHER, CHEER OUR WAY				
Vesper (J.Stainer)		1121/20.2cnt.30/perc/str	Boosey	20417
HOLY FATHER, IN THY MERCY				
Cairnbrook (E.Prout)				
arr D.Godfrey	PC	2222/40.2cnt.30/timp/str	Chappell	2867
HOLY, HOLY, HOLY, LORD GOD ALMIGHTY				
Nicaea (J.Dykes)		1121/20.2cnt.30/perc/str	Boosey	20417
arr H.Perry	PC	1121/2230/timp/pf/str	Hawkes,1957	4970
HOW SWEET THE NAME OF JESUS SOUNDS				
St Peter (R.Reinagle)		1121/20.2cnt.30/perc/str	Boosey	20417
A HYMN OF THE HOMELAND (Sullivan)		1121/20.2cnt.30/perc/str	Boosey	20417
IMMORTAL, INVISIBLE, GOD ONLY WISE				
St Denio				
arr A.Benoy & A.Bryce	φ	11[=fl]21/1220/str	OUP,1962	25286
IN THE LORD'S ATONING GRIEF				
St Prisca (R.Redhead)		1121/20.2cnt.30/perc/str	Boosey	20417
JERUSALEM THE GOLDEN				
Ewing (A.Ewing)		1121/20.2cnt.30/perc/str	Boosey	20417
arr D.Godfrey	PC	1121/2230/timp/pf/str	Hawke,1957	4970
JESU LOVER OF MY SOUL				
Hollingside (J.Dykes)		1121/20.2cnt.30/perc/str	Boosey	20417
JESU, MEEK AND GENTLE				
St Constantine (W.Monk)				
arr H.Perry	PC	1121/2230/timp/pf/str	Hawkes,1957	4970
JESU, THE VERY THOUGHT OF THEE				
St Agnes (J.Dykes)		1121/20.2cnt.30/perc/str	Boosey	20417

MINE EYES HAVE SEEN THE COMING OF THE GLORY OF THE LORD
   John Brown's Body   112.Bbsx.Ebsx.1/20.2cnt.10/timp.perc/str   C.Fischer   19720
      arr R.Barsotti   PC 1+picc.12.4sx.2/4230/perc/str   Boosey & H   21039
MORN OF MORNS, AND DAY OF DAYS
   Innocents
      arr H.Perry   PC 1121/2230/timp/pf/str   Hawkes,1957   4970
MY ANCHOR HOLDS
      arr F.Cordell   φ 1111/0000/pf/str   (Arranger)   20902
MY GOD, HOW WONDERFUL THOU ART
   Westminster (J.Turle)   1121/20.2cnt.30/perc/str   Boosey   20417
      arr A.Benoy & A.Bryce φ 11[≡fl]21/1220/str   OUP,1962   25286
MY GOD, MY FATHER WHILE I STRAY
   Troyte's chant no.1 (A.Dyke-Troyte)
                        1121/20.2cnt.30/perc/str   Boosey   20417
MY HUMBLE CRY
      arr M.Macdonald   φ 1111/0000/hp/str   (Arranger)   20921
MY SOUL, THERE IS A COUNTRY
   Christus der ist mein Leben (M.Vulpus)
      arr H.Perry   PC 1121/2230/timp/pf/str   Hawkes,1957   4970
NATIONAL ANTHEM
      arr D.Godfrey   PC 2222/40.2cnt.30/timp/str   Chappell   2867
NEARER MY GOD TO THEE
   Bethany (H.Smart)   112.Bbsx.Ebsx.1/20.2cnt.10/timp.perc/str   C.Fischer   19720
   Horbury (J.Dykes)
      arr D.Godfrey   PC 2222/40.2cnt.30/timp/str   Chappell   2867
   Liverpool (J.Roberts)
      arr M.Price   1222/4230/timp.perc/hp/str   (Arranger)   19330
NON NOBIS DOMINE: (R.Quilter)
   arr G.Williams for Soprano & Tenor soli, chorus & orch
                      φ 1121/2210/timp/hp/str   (Boosey & H) MLO 309
NOW I BELONG TO JESUS
      arr F.Cordell   φ 1111/0000/hp/str   (Arranger)   20922
NOW THANK WE ALL OUR GOD
   Nun danket (J.Crüger)   1121/20.2cnt.30/perc/str   Boosey   20417
      arr D.Godfrey   PC 2222/40.2cnt.30/timp/str   Chappell   2867
NOW THE LABOURER'S TASK IS O'ER
   Requiescat (J.Dykes)   1121/20.2cnt.30/perc/str   Boosey   20417
O COME, ALL YE FAITHFUL
   Adeste Fideles   1121/20.2cnt.30/perc/str   Boosey   20417
      arr R.Barsotti   PC 1+picc.12.4sx.2/4230/perc/str   Boosey & H   21039 B
      arr D.Godfrey   PC 2222/40.2cnt.30/timp/str   Chappell   2867
      arr P.Hope for chorus, organ & orch
                      φ   (OUP)   23752 +
      arr H.Perry   PC 1121/2230/timp/pf/str   Hawkes,1957   4970
O DAY OF REST AND GLADNESS
   Wordsworth (W.Monk)   1121/20.2cnt.30/perc/str   Boosey   20417
O FOR A CLOSER WALK WITH GOD
(Martyrdom (H.Wilson)   1121/20.2cnt.30/perc/str   Boosey   20417
O GOD, OUR HELP IN AGES PAST
   St Anne (W.Croft)   1121/20.2cnt.30/perc/str   Boosey   20417
      arr R.Barsotti   PC 1+picc.12.4sx.2/4230/perc/str   Boosey & H   21039 B
      arr A.Benoy & A.Bryce φ 11[=fl]21/1220/str   OUP,1962   25286
      arr H.Perry   PC 1121/2230/timp/pf/str   Hawkes,1957   4970
O GOD, WHO METEST IN THINE HAND
   Eisenach (J.Schein)   1121/20.2cnt.30/perc/str   Boosey   20417

O HAPPY BAND OF PILGRIMS
  Kocher (J.Knecht)
    arr H.Perry   PC 1121/2230/timp/pc/str   Hawkes,1957   4970
O HELP US LORD
  Bedford (W.Wheale)   1121/20.2cnt.30/perc/str   Boosey   20417
O JESU THOU ART STANDING
  St Catherine (R.Dale)   1121/20.2cnt.30/perc/str   Boosey   20417
O JESUS I HAVE PROMISED
  Day of rest (J.Elliot)   1121/20.2cnt.30/perc/str   Boosey   20417
    arr H.Perry   PC 1121/2230/timp/pf/str   Hawkes,1957   4970
O LORD BE WITH US WHEN WE SAIL
  Dundee
    arr D.Godfrey   PC 2222/40.2cnt.30/timp/str   Chappell   2867
O LORD OF HEAVEN
  Almsgiving (J.Dykes)   1121/20.2cnt.30/perc/str   Boosey   20417
O LOVE, HOW DEEP! HOW BROAD! HOW HIGH
  Leipsic (J.Schein)   1121/20.2cnt.30/perc/str   Boosey   20417
O LOVE THAT WILT NOT LET ME GO
  St Margaret (A.Peace)
    arr H.Perry   PC 1121/2230/timp/pf/str   Hawkes,1957   4970
O PARADISE, O PARADISE
  Paradise No 1 (H.Smart)   1121/20.2cnt.30/perc/str   Boosey   20417
O PRAISE YE THE LORD
  Laudate Dominum (C.H.Parry)
    arr A.H.Chatterly   φ 0101/0220/timp.sdm   (Arranger)   24483
O WORSHIP THE KING
  Hanover (W.Croft)
    arr A.Benoy & A.Bryce φ 11[=fl]21/1220/str   OUP,1962   25286
  Old 104th   1121/20.2cnt.30/perc/str   Boosey   20417
OFT IN DANGER, OFT IN WOE
  University College (H.Gauntlett) 1121/20.2cnt.30/perc/str   Boosey   20417
    arr A.Benoy & A.Bryce φ 11[=fl]21/1220/str   OUP,1962   25286
    arr R.Docker for boy treble, SSTBar soli, chorus, mil bd & orch
                  φ 2(picc)222/4330/timp.perc.bells/hp.[org]/str 2'30"   Arranger   25162
    arr D.Godfrey   PC 2222/40.2cnt.30/timp/str   Chappell   2867
OH, WHAT THE JOY AND THE GLORY MUST BE
  O Quanta qualia   1121/20.2cnt.30/perc/str   Boosey   20417
ON JORDAN'S BANK
  Winchester New   1121/20.2cnt.30/perc/str   Boosey   20417
    arr H.Perry   PC 1121/2230/timp/pf/str   Hawkes,1957   4970
ON THE WATERS DARK AND DREAR
  German Hymn (I.Pleyel)   1121/20.2cnt.30/perc/str   Boosey   20417
ONCE IN ROYAL DAVID'S CITY
  Irby (H.Gauntlett)
    arr H.Carruthers   φ cel/str   Arranger   22448
    arr H.Perry   PC 1121/2230/timp/pf/str   Hawkes,1957   4970
    arr M.Saunders   2222/4230/timp.perc/cel:hp/str   Arranger   17259
ONWARD CHRISTIAN SOLDIERS
  Gauntlett (H.Gauntlett)
    arr D.Godfrey   PC 2222/40.2cnt.30/timp/str   Chappell   2867
  Onward Christian Soldiers (H.Gauntlett)
                      1121/20.2cnt.30/perc/str   Boosey   20417
  St Gertrude (A.Sullivan)   112.Bbsx.Ebsx.1/20.2cnt.10/timp.perc/str C.Fischer   19720
    arr H.Perry   PC 1121/2230/timp/pf/str   Hawkes,1957   4970
OUR BLESSED REDEEMER
  St Cuthbert (J.Dykes)   1121/20.2cnt.30/perc/str   Boosey   20417

PEACE, PERFECT PEACE
   Pax Tecum (G.Caldbeck)   1121/20.2cnt.30/perc/str   Boosey   20417
PLEYEL'S HYMN   112.B♭sx.E♭sx.1/20.2cnt.10/timp.perc/str   C.Fischer   19720
PLEASANT ARE THY COURTS ABOVE
   Maidstone (W.Gilbert)   1121/20.2cnt.30/perc/str   Boosey   20417
PRAISE MY SOUL THE KING OF HEAVEN
   Alleluia Dulce Carmen   1121/20.2cnt.30/perc/str   Boosey   20417
PRAISE THE LORD, YE HEAVENS ADORE HIM
   Austria (J.Haydn)   1121/20.2cnt.30/perc/str   Boosey   20417
      arr H.Perry   1   1121/2230/timp/pf/str   Hawkes,1957   4970
PRAISE TO THE HOLIEST IN THEHIGHT
   Gerontius (J.Dykes)
      arr H.Perry   PC   1121/2230/timp/pf/str   Hawkes,1957   4970
   Helvellyn
      arr H.Perry   PC   1121/2230/timp/pf/str   Hawkes,1957   4970
   Montrose
      ed K.Parry, arr E.Griffiths for solo & chorus
                       org/str   (Independent Press,1951)   17974
   Richmond (T.Haweis)
      arr H.Perry   PC   1121/2230/timp/pf/str   Hawkes,1957   4970
PRAISE TO THE LORD
   Lobe den Herren
      arr A.Benoy & A.Bryce   φ   11[=fl]21/1220/str   OUP,1962   25286
      arr G.Vinter for solo, chorus & orch
                 φ   org/str   (OUP)   23313 +
PRAYER OF THANKSGIVING   <u>see</u>   DANKEGEBET
REJOICE THE LORD IS KING
   Gopsal (G.Handel)
      arr A.Benoy & A.Bryce   φ   11[=fl]21/1220/str   OUP,1962   25286
      arr H.Perry   PC   1121/2230/timp/pf/str   Hawkes,1957   4970
REJOICE TODAY WITH ONE ACCORD
   Ein feste Burg (M.Luther)   1121/20.2cnt.30/perc/str   Boosey   20417
RESTING FROM HIS WORK TODAY
   Redhead (R.Redhead)   1121/20.2cnt.30/perc/str   Boosey   20417
RIDE ON, RIDE ON IN MAJESTY
   St Drostane (J.Dykes)   1121/20.2cnt.30/perc/str   Boosey   20417
ROCK OF AGES
   Fine   112.B♭sx.E♭sx.1/20.2cnt.10/timp.perc/str   C.Fischer   19720
   Redhead (Petra)(R.Redhead)
      arr D.Godfrey   PC   2222/40.2cnt.30/timp/str   Chappell   2867
The ROSEATE HUES OF EARLY DAWN
   The Roseate Hues (J.Stainer)   1121/20.2cnt.30/perc/str   Boosey   20417
SAVIOUR, BLESS'D SAVIOUR
   Edina (H.Oakley)   1121/20.2cnt.30/perc/str   Boosey   20417
SAVIOUR, WHEN TO THEE IN DUST
   Aberystwyth (J.Parry)
      arr H.Perry   PC   1121/2230/timp/pf/str   Hawkes,1957   4970
SHEPHERD DIVINE, OUR WANTS RELIEVE
   St Etheldreda (T.Turton)   1121/20.2cnt.30/perc/str   Boosey   20417
SOLDIERS OF CHRIST ARISE
   St Ethelwald (W.Monk)
      arr A.Benoy & A.Bryce   φ   11[=fl]21/1220/str   OUP,1962   25286
                     PC   1121/2230/timp/pf/str   Hawkes,1957   4970
   St Oswald (J.Dykes)   1121/20.2cnt.30/perc/str   Boosey   20417
SOLDIERS OF CHRIST ARISE! GIRD WITH YOUR ARMOUR BRIGHT
   Crucis Milites (M.Foster)   1121/20.2cnt.30/perc/str   Boosey   20417

SOLDIERS, WHO ARE CHRIST'S BELOW
  Orientis Partibus (Pierre de Corbeil)

		1121/20.2cnt.30/perc/str	Boosey	20417

SPIRIT OF MERCY, TRUTH AND LOVE
  Melcombe (S.Webbe)

		1121/20.2cnt.30/perc/str	Boosey	20417

STAND UP, STAND UP FOR JESUS
  Stand Up (J.Barnby)

		1121/20.2cnt.30/perc/str	Boosey	20417

The STRAIN UPRAISE OF JOY AND PRAISE
  Troyte's chant No 2 (A.Dyke-Troyte)

		1121/20.2cnt.30/perc/str	Boosey	20417

The STRIFE IS O'ER, THE BATTLE DONE (with alleluias)
  Victory (P.Palestrina)

		1121/20.2cnt.30/perc/str	Boosey	24017

SUN OF MY SOUL
  Grosser Gott

arr D.Godfrey	PC	2222/40.2cnt.30/timp/str	Chappell	2867
Horsley		1121/20.2cnt.30/perc/str	Boosey	20417

The SUPREME SACRIFICE

arr R.Barsotti	PC	1+picc.12.4sx.2/4230/perc/str	Boosey & H	21039 B

SWEET SAVIOUR, BLESS US ERE WE GO
  St Matthias (W.Monk)

		1121/20.2cnt.30/perc/str	Boosey	20417

TAKE TIME TO PRAY

arr F.Cordell	φ	1111/0000/hp/str	(Arranger)	20923

TAKE UP THY CROSS
  Breslau

		1121/20.2cnt.30/perc/str	Boosey	20417

TEN THOUSAND TIMES TEN THOUSAND

arr D.Godfrey	PC	2222/40.2cnt.30/timp/str	Chappell	2867

THE... see the second word of the first line.

THERE IS A BOOK
  Tallis' Ordinal (T.Tallis)

arr A.Benoy & A.Bryce	φ	11[=fl]21/1220/str	OUP,1962	25286

THERE IS A GREEN HILL FAR AWAY
  Horsley (W.Horsley)

		1121/20.2cnt.30/perc/str	Boosey	20417

THERE'S A FRIEND FOR LITTLE CHILDREN
  In Memoriam

arr H.Perry	PC	1121/2230/timp/pf/str	Hawkes,1957	4970

THOU WHOSE ALMIGHTY WORD
  Fiat Lux (J.Dykes)

		1121/20.2cnt.30/perc/str	Boosey	20417

THROUGH ALL THE CHANGING SCENES OF LIFE
  Wiltshire (G.Smart)

		1121/20.2cnt.30/perc/str	Boosey	20417

THROUGH THE NIGHT OF DOUBT AND SORROW
  St Oswald (J.Dykes)

arr H.Perry	PC	1121/2230/timp/pf/str	Hawkes,1957	4970

TO CHRIST, THE PRINCE OF PEACE

St George (Gauntlett)(H.Gauntlett)		1121/20.2cnt.30/perc/str	Boosey	20417

TO THE NAME OF OUR SALVATION
  Oriel

		1121/20.2cnt.30/perc/str	Boosey	20417

TO THEE, O LORD, OUR HEARTS WE RAISE
  Golden Sheaves (A.Sullivan)

		1121/20.2cnt.30/perc/str	Boosey	20417

WE ARE BUT LITTLE CHILDREN WEAK
  Alstone (C.Willing)

	PC	1121/2230/timp/pf/str	Hawkes,1957	4970

WE ARE SOLDIERS OF CHRIST
  Milites (W.Monk)

		1121/20.2cnt.30/perc/str	Boosey	20417

WE PLOUGH THE FIELDS AND SCATTER
   Wir pflügen (J.A.P.Schulz)
      arr H.Perry   PC 1121/2230/timp/pf/str   Hawkes,1957   4970
WE WILL SING OF OUR REDEEMER
   arr F.Cordell for chorus & orch
                     φ 1111/0000/hp/str   (Arranger)   20924
WHEN I SURVEY THE WONDROUS CROSS
   Rockingham (E.Miller)   φ 1121/20.2cnt.30/perc/str   Boosey   20417
      arr H.Perry   PC 1121/2230/timp/pf/str   Hawkes,1957   4970
WHILE SHEPHERDS WATCHED THEIR FLOCKS BY NIGHT
   Winchester Old   1121/20.2cnt.30/perc/str   Boosey   20417
      arr R.Barsotti   PC 1+picc.12.4sx.2/4230/perc/str   Boosey & H   21039 B
      arr H.Perry   PC 1121/2230/timp/pf/str   Hawkes,1957   4970
WHO ARE THESE LIKE STARS APPEARING
   All Saints   1121/20.2cnt.30/perc/str   Boosey   20417
WHO WOULD TRUE VALOUR SEE
   Monks Gate
      arr H.Perry   PC 1121/2230/timp/pf/str   Hawkes,1957   4970
YE HOLY ANGELS BRIGHT
   Darwell's 148   (J.Darwell)
      arr A.Benoy & A.Bryce   φ 11[=fl]21/1220/str   OUP,1962   25286
The YEAR IS GONE BEYOND RECALL
   Tallis (T.Tallis)   1121/20.2cnt.30/perc/str   Boosey   20417

ABERYSTWYTH (J.Parry)					
arr H.Perry	PC	1121/2230/timp/pf/str		Hawkes,1957	4970
ADESTE FIDELES		1121/20.2cnt.30/perc/str		Boosey	20417
arr D.Godfrey	PC	2222/40.2cnt.30/timp/str		Chappell	2867
arr P.Hope	φ	2222/4230/perc/hp/str		(OUP)	23752 +
arr H.Perry	PC	1121/2230/timp/pf/str		Hawkes,1957	4970
ALFORD (J.Dykes)					
arr D.Godfrey	PC	2222/40.2cnt.30/timp/str		Chappell	2867
ALL SAINTS		1121/20.2cnt.30/perc/str		Boosey	20417
ALL THINGS BRIGHT AND BEAUTIFUL (W.Monk)					
arr H.Perry	PC	1121/2230/timp/pf/str		Hawkes,1957	4970
arr G.Vinter	φ	2222/4000/timp.perc/str		(OUP,1951;BBC Hymn Bk)	22112 +
ALLELUIA DULCE CARMEN		1121/20.2cnt.30/perc/str		Boosey	20417
arr H.Perry	PC	1121/2230/timp/pf/str		Hawkes,1957	4970
ALMSGIVING (J.Dykes)		1121/20.2cnt.30/perc/str		Boosey	20417
ALSTONE (C.Willing)					
arr H.Perry	PC	1121/2230/timp/pf/str		Hawkes,1957	4970
ANGELUS (G.Joseph)		1121/20.2cnt.30/perc/str		Boosey	20417
ANTIOCH		112.B♭sx.E♭sx.1/20.2cnt.10/timp.perc/str		C.Fischer	19720
AURELIA (S.Wesley)		1121/20.2cnt.30/perc/str		Boosey	20417
arr H.Perry	PC	1121/2330/timp/pf/str		Hawkes,1957	4970
AUSTRIA (J.Haydn)		1121/20.2cnt.30/perc/str		Boosey	20417
		112.B♭sx.E♭sx.1/20.2cnt.10/timp.perc/str		C.Fischer	19720
arr A.Benoy & A.Bryce	φ	11[=fl]21/1220/str		OUP,1962	25286
arr H.Perry	PC	1121/2230/timp/pf/str		Hawkes,1957	4970
BATTLE HYMN OF THE REPUBLIC		112.B♭sx.E♭sx.1/20.2cnt.10/timp.perc/str		C.Fischer	19720
BEDFORD (W.Wheale)		1121/20.2cnt.30/perc/str		Boosey	20417
BETHANY (H.Smart)		112.B♭sx.E♭sx.1/20.2cnt.10/timp.perc/str		C.Fischer	4970
BLAENWERN (W.P.Rowlands)					
arr M.Price		2222/4230/timp.perc/hp/str		(Arranger)	19330
BRESLAU		1121/20.2cnt.30/perc/str		Boosey	20417
BRISTOL (harmonized T.Ravenscroft)		1121/20.2cnt.30/perc/str		Boosey	20417
BUCKLAND (L.Hayne)					
arr H.Perry	PC	1121/2230/timp/pf/str		Hawkes,1957	4970
CAIRNBROOK (E.Prout)					
arr D.Godfrey	PC	2222/40.2cnt.30/timp/str		Chappell	2867
CAPETOWN (F.Filitz)					
arr A.Benoy & A.Bryce	φ	11[=fl]21/1220/str		OUP,1962	25286
CARLISLE (C.Lockhart)					
arr A.Benoy & A.Bryce	φ	11[=fl]21/1220/str		OUP,1962	25286
CASWALL (F.Filitz)		1121/20.2cnt.30/perc/str		Boosey	20417
CHALVEY (L.Hayne)		1121/20.2cnt.30/perc/str		Boosey	20417
CHILDREN'S VOICES					
arr H.Perry	PC	1121/2230/timp/pf/str		Hawkes,1959	4970
CHRISTUS CONSOLATOR (J.Dykes)		1121/20.2cnt.30/perc/str		Boosey	20417
CHRISTUS DER IST MEIN LEBEN (M.Vulpus)					
arr H.Perry	PC	1121/2230/timp/pf/str		Hawkes,1957	4970
CLOISTERS (J.Barnby)		1121/20.2cnt.30/perc/str		Boosey	20417
COENA DOMINI (A.Sullivan)		1121/20.2cnt.30/perc/str		Boosey	20417
COME UNTO ME (J.Dykes)		1121/20.2cnt.30/perc/str		Boosey	20417
COMMANDMENTS (L.Bourgeois)		1121/20.2cnt.30/perc/str		Boosey	20417
CRIMOND (J.Irvine)		0100/0000/str		(OUP,1951;BBC Hymn Bk)	20967
CRUCIS MILITES (M.Foster)		1121/20.2cnt.30/perc/str		Boosey	20417
CRÜGER (J.Crüger)					
arr H.Perry	PC	1121/2230/timp/pf/str		Hawkes,1957	4970
CULBACH		1121/20.2cnt.30/perc/str		Boosey	20417

DARWELL'S 148 (J.Darwell)				
arr A.Benoy & A.Bryce	φ	11[=fl]21/1220/str	OUP,1962	25286
DAY OF REST (J.Elliot)		1121/20.2cnt.30/perc/str	Boosey	20417
arr H.Perry	PC	1121/2230/timp/pf/str	Hawkes,1957	4970
DEERHURST (J.Langran)		1121/20.2cnt.30/perc/str	Boosey	20417
DIADEMATA (G.Elvey)				
		1121/20.2cnt.30/perc/str	Boosey	20417
DIX (C.Kocher)		1121/20.2cnt.30/perc/str	Boosey	20417
arr H.Perry	PC	1121/2230/timp/pf/str	Hawkes,1957	4970
DOMINUS REGIT ME (J.Dykes)		1121/20.2cnt.30/perc/str	Boosey	20417
arr A.Benoy & A.Bryce	φ	11[=fl]21/1220/str	OUP,1962	25286
DUKE STREET (J.Hatton)				
arr A.Benoy & A.Bryce	φ	11[=fl]21/1220/str	OUP,1962	25286
DUNDEE		1121/20.2cnt.30/perc/str	Boosey	20417
arr D.Godfrey	PC	2222/40.2cnt.30/timp/str	Chappell	2867
arr H.Perry	PC	1121/2230/timp/pf/str	Hawkes,1957	4970
EASTER HYMN (W.Monk)		1121/20.2cnt.30/perc/str	Boosey	20417
arr H.Perry	PC	1121/2230/timp/pf/str	Hawkes,1957	4970
EDINA (H.Oakely)		1121/20.2cnt.30/perc/str	Boosey	20417
EIN FESTE BURG (M.Luther)		1121/20.2cnt.30/perc/str	Boosey	20417
		112.B♭sx.E♭sx.1/20.2cnt.10/timp.perc/str	C.Fischer	19720
EISENACH (J.Schein)		1121/20.2cnt.30/perc/str	Boosey	20417
EVELYNS (W.Monk)				
arr H.Perry	PC	1121/2230/timp/pf/str	Hawkes,1957	4970
EVENTIDE		1121/20.2cnt.30/perc/str	Boosey	20417
		112.B♭sx.E♭sx.1/20.2cnt.10/timp.perc/str	C.Fischer	19720
arr R.Barsotti	PC	1+picc.12.4sx.2/4230/perc/str	Boosey & H	21039 B
arr D.Godfrey	PC	2222/40.2cnt.30/timp/str	Chappell	2867
EWING (A.Ewing)		1121/20.2cnt.30/perc/str	Boosey	20417
arr D.Godfrey	PC	2222/40.2cnt.30/timp/str	Chappell	2867
FIAT LUX (J.Dykes)		1121/20.2cnt.30/perc/str	Boosey	20417
FINE		112.B♭sx.E♭sx.1/20.2cnt.10/timp.perc/str	C.Fischer	19720
FIRST NOWELL				
arr H.Perry	PC	1121/2230/timp/pf/str	Hawkes,1957	4970
FRANCONIA		1121/20.2cnt.30/perc/str	Boosey	20417
arr A.Benoy & A.Bryce	φ	11[=fl]21/1220/str	OUP,1962	25286
arr H.Perry	PC	1121/2230/timp/pf/str	Hawkes,1957	4970
GAUNTLETT (H.Gauntlett)				
arr D.Godfrey	PC	2222/40.2cnt.30/timp/str	Chappell	2867
GENTLE JESUS (M.Shaw)				
arr H.Perry	PC	1121/2230/timp/pf/str	Hawkes,1957	4970
GERMAN HYMN (I.Pleyel)		1121/20.2cnt.30/perc/str	Boosey	20417
GERONTIUS (J.Dykes)				
arr H.Perry	PC	1121/2230/timp/pf/str	Hawkes,1957	4970
GOLDEN SHEAVES (A.Sullivan)		1121/20.2cnt.30/perc/str	Boosey	20417
GOPSAL (G.Handel)				
arr H.Perry	PC	1121/2230/timp/pf/str	Hawkes,1957	4970
arr A.Benoy & A.Bryce	φ	11[=fl]21/1220/str	OUP,1962	25286
GROSSER GOTT				
arr D.Godfrey	PC	2222/40.2cnt.30/timp/str	Chappell	2867
GWALCHMAI (J.Jones)				
arr J.Patten	φ	1[=cl]1[=cl]11/0000/gtr.pf	(Arranger)	24535
HANOVER (W.Croft)		1121/20.2cnt.30/perc/str	Boosey	20417
arr A.Benoy & A.Bryce	φ	11[=fl]21/1220/str	OUP,1962	25286
arr H.Perry	PC	1121/2230/timp/pf/str	Hawkes,1957	4970

HEINLEIN (M.Herbst)		1121/20.2cnt.30/perc/str	Boosey	20417
HELVELLYN				
arr H.Perry	PC	1121/2230/timp/pf/str	Hawkes,1957	4970
HOLLINGSIDE (J.Dykes)		1121/20.2cnt.30/perc/str	Boosey	20417
HORBURY (J.Dykes)				
in E♭, arr R.Chignell	φ	1121/2100/str	Arranger	MS 3303
arr D.Godfrey	PC	2222/40.2cnt.30/timp/str	Chappell	2867
HORSLEY (W.Horsley)		1121/20.2cnt.30/perc/str	Boosey	20417
HURSLEY		1121/20.2cnt.30/perc/str	Boosey	20417
HYFRYDOL (R.Prichard)				
arr J.Patten	φ	003[=3ob]0/3[=3tpt]000/pf	(Arranger)	24534
IN MEMORIAM				
arr H.Perry	PC	1121/2230/timp/pf/str	Hawkes,1957	4970
INNOCENTS				
arr H.Perry	PC	1121/2230/timp/pf/str	Hawkes,1957	4970
IRBY (H.Gauntlett)				
arr H.Perry	PC	1121/2230/timp/pf/str	Hawkes,1957	4970
JENNER (Jenner)		1121/20.2cnt.30/perc/str	Boosey	20417
JERUSALEM (C.Parry)	φ	2222/4230/timp/str	Curwen	5041 E
arr R.Barsotti	PC	1+picc.12.4sx.2/4230/perc/str	Boosey & H	21039 B
KOCHER (J.Knecht)				
arr H.Perry	PC	1121/2230/timp/pf/str	Hawkes,1957	4970
LAUDATE DOMINUM (C.H.Parry)				
arr A.H.Chatterley	φ	0101/0220/timp.sdm	(Arranger)	24483
LEIPSIC (J.Schein)		1121/20.2cnt.30/perc/str	Boosey	20417
LITTLE CONRAD (M.Shaw)				
arr.S.Robinson		str	(Arranger)	MS 5677
LIVERPOOL (J.Roberts)				
arr M.Price		1222/4230/timp.perc/hp/str	(Arranger)	19330
LOBE DEN HERREN				
arr H.Perry	PC	1121/2230/timp/pf/str	Hawkes,1957	4970
arr G.Vinter for solo, chorus & orch				
		org/str	(OUP)	23313 +
LONDON NEW		1121/20.2cnt.30/perc/str	Boosey	20417
LOVE DIVINE (J.Stainer)				
arr H.Perry	PC	1121/2230/timp/pf/str	Hawkes,1957	4970
LUTHER (M.Luther)		1121/20.2cnt.30/perc/str	Boosey	20417
LUX BENIGNA (J.Dykes)		1121/20.2cnt.30/perc/str	Boosey	20417
		112.B♭sx.E♭sx.1/20.2cnt.10/timp.perc/str	C.Fischer	19720
arr D.Godfrey	PC	2222/40.2cnt.30/timp/str	Chappell	2867
LYTE (J.Wilkes)		1121/20.2cnt.30/perc/str	Boosey	20417
MAIDSTONE (W.Gilbert)		1121/20.2cnt.30/perc/str	Boosey	20417
MANNHEIM				
arr A.Benoy & A.Bryce	φ	11[=fl]21/1220/str	OUP,1962	25286
MARTYRDOM (H.Wilson)		1121/20.2cnt.30/perc/str	Boosey	20417
arr A.Benoy & A.Bryce	φ	11[=fl]21/1220/str	OUP,1962	25286
arr H.Perry	PC	1121/2230/timp/pf/str	Hawkes,1957	4970
MELCOMBE (S.Webbe)		1121/20.2cnt.30/perc/str	Boosey	20417
MELITA (J.Dykes)		1121/20.2cnt.30/perc/str	Boosey	20417
arr R.Barsotti	PC	1+picc.12.4sx.2/4230/perc/str	Boosey & H	21039 B
arr D.Godfrey	PC	2222/40.2cnt.30/timp/str	Chappell	2867
arr H.Perry	PC	1121/2230/timp/pf/str	Hawkes,1957	4970
MENDELSSOHN (F.Mendelssohn)		1121/20.2cnt.30/perc/str	Boosey	20417
MILES LANE (W.Schrubsole)		1121/20.2cnt.30/perc/str	Boosey	20417

MILITES (W.Monk)		1121/20.2cnt.30/str	Boosey	20417
MONKS GATE				
arr J.Patten	φ	1[=c1]001[=hn]/0220/perc	(Arranger)	24534
arr H.Perry	PC	1121/2230/timp/pf/str	Hawkes,1957	4970
MONTROSE				
arr E.Griffiths	φ	hp/org/str	(Independent Press,1951)	17974
NATIVITY (H.Lahee)				
arr H.Perry	PC	1121/2230/timp/pf/str	Hawkes,1957	4970
NEARER HOME (J.Woodbury)				
arr A.Sullivan		1121/20.2cnt.30/perc/str	Boosey	20417
NEWLAND (J.Gauntlett)				
arr H.Perry	PC	1121/2230/timp/pf/str	Hawkes,1957	4970
NICAEA (J.Dykes)		1121/20.2cnt.30/perc/str	Boosey	20417
arr H.Perry	PC	1121/2230/timp/pf/str	Hawkes,1957	4970
NUN DANKET (J.Crüger)		1121/20.2cnt.30/perc/str	Boosey	20417
arr D.Godfrey	PC	2222/40.2cnt.30/timp/str	Chappell	2867
O QUANTA QUALIA		1121/20.2cnt.30/perc/str	Boosey	20417
OLD 100th (L.Bourgeois)		1121/20.2cnt.30/perc/str	Boosey	20417
		112.B♭sx.E♭sx.1/20.2cnt.10/timp.perc/str	C.Fischer	19720
arr A.Benoy & A.Bryce	φ	11[=f1]21/1220/str	OUP,1962	25286
arr D.Godfrey	PC	2222/40.2cnt.30/timp/str	Chappell	2867
orch G.Jacob for the opening of the Festival of Britain, 1951				
	φ	3332+cbsn/42.2cnt.31/timp.perc/str	[Arranger]	20220
arr H.Perry	PC	1121/2230/timp/pf/str	Hawkes,1957	4970
OLD 104th		1121/20.2cnt.30/perc/str	Boosey	20417
ONWARD CHRISTIAN SOLDIERS (H.Gauntlett)				
		1121/20.2cnt.30/perc/str	Boosey	20417
ORIEL		1121/20.2cnt.30/perc/str	Boosey	20417
ORIENTIS PARTIBUS		1121/20.2cnt.30/perc/str	Boosey	20417
PARADISE no.1 (H.Smart)		1121/20.2cnt.30/perc/str	Boosey	20417
PAX TECUM (G.Caldbeck)		1121/20.2cnt.30/perc/str	Boosey	20417
PENTECOST (W.Boyd)		1121/20.2cnt.30/perc/str	Boosey	20417
PETRA see REDHEAD				
PILGRIMS (H.Smart)		1121/20.2cnt.30/perc/str	Boosey	20417
QUEM PASTORES				
arr A.Benoy & A.Bryce	φ	11[=f1]21/1220/str	OUP,1962	25286
REDHEAD (also known as Petra)(R.Redhead)				
		1121/20.2cnt.30/perc/str	Boosey	20417
arr D.Godfrey	PC	2222/40.2cnt.30/timp/str	Chappell	2867
REPTON (C.Parry)				
arr F.Cordell		0100/0000/str	(OUP,1951:BBC Hymn Bk)	20967
REQUIESCAT (J.Dykes)		1121/20.2cnt.30/perc/str	Boosey	20417
RICHMOND (T.Haweis)				
arr A.Benoy & A.Bryce	φ	11[=f1]21/1220/str	OUP,1962	25286
arr H.Perry	PC	1121/2230/timp/pf/str	Hawkes,1957	4970
ROCKINGHAM		1121/20.2cnt.30/perc/str	Boosey	20417
arr H.Perry	PC	1121/2230/timp/pf/str	Hawkes,1957	4970
The ROSEATE HUES (J.Stainer)		1121/20.2cnt.30/perc/str	Boosey	20417
RUDDLAN				
arr A.Benoy & A.Bryce	φ	11[=f1]21/1220/str	OUP,1962	25286
St AELRED (J.Dykes)		1121/20.2cnt.30/perc/str	Boosey	20417
arr H.Perry	PC	1121/2230/timp/pf/str	Hawkes,1957	4970
St AGNES (J.Dykes)		1121/20.2cnt.30/perc/str	Boosey	20417
St ALBINUS (H.Gauntlett)		1121/20.2cnt.30/perc/str	Boosey	20417
St ALPHEGE (H.Gauntlett)		1121/20.2cnt.30/perc/str	Boosey	20417

St ANNE (W.Croft)		1121/20.2cnt.30/perc/str	Boosey	20417
arr A.Barsotti	PC	1+picc.12.4sx.2/4230/perc/str	Boosey & H	21039 B
arr A.Benoy & A.Bryce	φ	11[=fl]21/1220/str	OUP,1962	25286
arr D.Godfrey	PC	2222/40.2cnt.30/timp/str	Chappell	2867
arr H.Perry	PC	1121/2230/timp/pf/str	Hawkes,1957	4970
St BEES (J.Dykes)		1121/20.2cnt.30/perc/str	Boosey	20417
St BONIFACE (H.Gadsby)		1121/20.2cnt.30/perc/str	Boosey	20417
St CATHERINE (R.Dale)		1121/20.2cnt.30/perc/str	Boosey	20417
St CLEMENT (C.Scholefield)		1121/20.2cnt.30/perc/str	Boosey	20417
St COLUMBIA				
arr A.Benoy & A.Bryce	φ	11[=fl]21/1220/str	OUP,1962	25286
St CONSTANTINE				
arr H.Perry	PC	1121/2230/timp/pf/str	Hawkes,1957	4970
St CUTHBERT (J.Dykes)		1121/20.2cnt.30/perc/str	Boosey	20417
St DENIO				
arr A.Benoy & A.Bryce	φ	11[=fl]21/1220/str	OUP,1962	25286
St DROSTANE (J.Dykes)		1121/20.2cnt.30/perc/str	Boosey	20417
St ETHELDREDA (T.Turton)		1121/20.2cnt.30/perc/str	Boosey	20417
arr A.Benoy & A.Bryce	φ	11[=fl]21/1220/str	OUP,1962	25286
St ETHELWALD (W.Monk)		1121/20.2cnt.30/perc/str	Boosey	20417
arr H.Perry	PC	1121/2230/timp/pf/str	Hawkes,1957	4970
St FLAVIAN		1121/20.2cnt.30/perc/str	Boosey	20417
St GEORGE (Gauntlett)(H.Gauntlett)		1121/20.2cnt.30/perc/str	Boosey	20417
St GEORGE (Windsor)(J.Elvey)		1121/20.2cnt.30/perc/str	Boosey	20417
arr H.Perry	PC	1121/2230/timp/pf/str	Hawkes,1957	4970
St GERTRUDE (A.Sullivan)		112.B♭sx.E♭sx.1/20.2cnt.10/timp.perc/str	C.Fischer	19720
arr H.Perry	PC	1121/2230/timp/pf/str	Hawkes,1957	4970
St LEONARD (H.Smart)		1121/20.2cnt.30/perc/str	Boosey	20417
arr D.Godfrey	PC	2222/40.2cnt.30/timp/str	Chappell	2867
St MARGARET (A.Peace)				
arr H.Perry	PC	1121/2230/timp/pf/str	Hawkes,1957	4970
St MATTHIAS (W.Monk)		1121/20.2cnt.30/perc/str	Boosey	20417
St MICHAEL		1121/20.2cnt.30/perc/str	Boosey	20417
St OSWALD (J.Dykes)		1121/20.2cnt.30/perc/str	Boosey	20417
arr H.Perry	PC	1121/2230/timp/pf/str	Hawkes,1957	4970
St PETER (R.Reinagle)		1121/20.2cnt.30/perc/str	Boosey	20417
St PRISCA (R.Redhead)		1121/20.2cnt.30/perc/str	Boosey	20417
St SYLVESTER (J.Dykes)		1121/20.2cnt.30/perc/str	Boosey	20417
St THEODULPH (M.Teschner)		1121/20.2cnt.30/perc/str	Boosey	20417
arr H.Perry	PC	1121/2230/timp/pf/str	Hawkes,1957	4970
St THOMAS		1121/20.2cnt.30/perc/str	Boosey	20417
STAND UP (J.Barnby)		1121/20.2cnt.30/perc/str	Boosey	20417
TALLIS (T.Tallis)		1121/20.2cnt.30/perc/str	Boosey	20417
TALLIS' CANON (T.Tallis)		1121/20.2cnt.30/perc/str	Boosey	20417
TALLIS' ORDINAL (T.Tallis)				
arr A.Benoy & A.Bryce	φ	11[=fl]21/1220/str	OUP,1962	25286
TROYTE'S CHANT no.1 (A.Dyke-Troyte)		1121/20.2cnt.30/perc/str	Boosey	20417
TROYTE'S CHANT no.2 (A.Dyke-Troyte)		1121/20.2cnt.30/perc/str	Boosey	20417
TRURO				
arr A.Benoy & A.Bryce	φ	11[=fl]21/1220/str	OUP,1962	25286
UNIVERSITY COLLEGE (H.Gauntlett)		1121/20.2cnt.30/perc/str	Boosey	20417
arr A.Benoy & A.Bryce	φ	11[=fl]21/1220/str	OUP,1962	25286

arr R.Docker for boy treble, SSTBar soli, chorus .mil band, & orch

	φ	2(picc)222/4330/timp.perc.bells/hp/[org]			
		str	2'30"	Arranger	25162

UNIVERSITY COLLEGE (cont)				
arr D.Godfrey	PC	2222/40.2cnt.30/timp/str	Chappell	2867
VESPER (J.Stainer)		1121/20.2cnt.30/perc/str	Boosey	20417
VEXILLUM (H.Smart)		1121/20.2cnt.30/perc/str	Boosey	20417
VICTORY (With Alleluias)(P.Palestrina)				
		1121/20.2cnt.30/perc/str	Boosey	20417
WESTMINSTER (J.Turle)		1121/20.2cnt.30/perc/str	Boosey	20417
arr A.Benoy & A.Bryce	φ	11[=fl]21/1220/str	OUP,1962	25286
WILTSHIRE (G.Smart)		1121/20.2cnt.30/perc/str	Boosey	20417
WINCHESTER NEW		1121/20.2cnt.30/perc/str	Boosey	20417
arr H.Perry	PC	1121/2230/timp/pf/str	Hawkes,1957	4970
WINCHESTER OLD		1121/20.2cnt.30/perc/str	Boosey	20417
arr H.Perry	PC	1121/2230/timp/pf/str	Hawkes,1957	4970
WIR PFLÜGEN				
arr H.Perry	PC	1121/2230/timp/pf/str	Hawkes,1957	4970
WORDSWORTH (W.Monk)		1121/20.2cnt.30/perc/str	Boosey	20417
WÜRTEMBURG (J.Rosenmüller)		1121/20.2cnt.30/perc/str	Boosey	20417.
YORKSHIRE (J.Wainwright)		1121/20.2cnt.30/perc/str	Boosey	20417
YORKSHIRE				
arr H.Perry	PC	1121/2230/timp/str	Hawkes,1957	4970

The National Anthems listed here include superseded anthems as well as those current at the time of
writing, either of which may be required for broadcasting purposes.   For up-to-date information on
National Anthems, see the latest edition of NATIONAL ANTHEMS OF THE WORLD, ed M.Shaw, H.Coleman &
T.M.Cartledge.   4th edn, rev & enlarged.   Dorset: Blandford Press, 1975, referred to here as 'Blandford'.
For military and brass band arrangements, see appendix to Band Catalogue.   Works are arranged under the
appropriate country with National Anthems preceding National and Patriotic Airs.

ABYSSINA   see   ETHIOPIA

AFGHANISTAN

NATIONAL ANTHEM (M.Farukh), adopted 1943

	PC	2(picc)222/4230/timp.perc/str		Breitkopf	14305
orch N.Fulton	∅	2222/4330/timp/str		(Blandford)	24094 +

NATIONAL AIRS
  AMIRI MARCH & 3 SALUTES   PC 1121/2230.euph/timp/str   Boosey   2817

ALBANIA   see   BAND CATALOGUE

ALGERIA

NATIONAL AIRS
  YA MEN K'TA DJEBAL: air
    arr M.L.Lake   PC 112.2sx.1/2210/perc/str   C.Fischer   19720

ARABIA   see   SAUDI ARABIA

ARGENTINE

NATIONAL ANTHEM
  OID, MORTALES, EL GRITO SAGRADO LIBERTAD (José Blas Parera), adopted 11 May, 1813

	PC	2(picc)222/4220/str	Benjamin	16364
	PC	2(picc)222/4230/timp.perc/str	Breitkopf	14305
arr G.French	∅	2222/2230/timp.perc/str	(Blandford)	25214 +
arr M.L.Lake	PC	112.2sx.1/2210/perc/str	C.Fischer	19720
arr F.Salabert	PC	1(picc)221/223[1]/timp.perc/str	Salabert	3816

NATIONAL AIRS
  SAN LORENZO MARCH (C.A.Silva)
                        PC 2(picc)222/4220/str   Benjamin   16364

ARMENIA   see   UNION OF SOCIALIST SOVIET REPUBLICS - ARMENIA

AUSTRALIA

NATIONAL ANTHEM
  ADVANCE AUSTRALIA FAIR (Peter Dodds McCormick)
                  2+picc.222+cbsn/4331/timp.perc/hp/str   [Blandford]   20119
NATIONAL AIRS
  MAKER OF EARTH AND SEA (T.Summers)
                  PC 2(picc)222/4220/str   Benjamin   16364
  The SONG OF AUSTRALIA
    arr M.L.Lake PC 112.2sx.1/2210/perc/str   C.Fischer   19720

AUSTRIA

NATIONAL ANTHEM
   LAND DER BERGE, LAND AM STROME (Österrichische Bundeshymne)(attrib W.A.Mozart from
      Freimauerer-Kantate, K.623), adopted 25 February, 1947

	ø	1200/2000/str	Breitkopf	18716 (ø & cont)
arr M.Schönherr	ø	2(picc)222/4231/timp.perc/str	Bundesverlag,1947	23381

FORMER NATIONAL ANTHEMS
   DEUTSCH ÖSTERREICH, DU HERRLICHES LAND (Wilhelm Kienzl) (1920-29)

arr F.Eber	PC	1121/2210/perc/str	Universal	9061

   GOTT ERHALTE FRITZ DEN KAISER (Austrian hymn: Glorious things of thee are spoken), by F.J
      Haydn; H-XXVIa:43

	ø	str	Choudens	9736
arr H.Perry	PC	1121/0000/timp.perc/org/str	Hawkes	4970 B
arr Treibel (non-vocal)		str	André	452

NATIONAL AIRS
   ANDREAS HOFER: Tyrolean song

arr M.L.Lake	PC	122.2sx.1/2210/perc/str	C.Fischer	19720

   O, DU MEIN ÖSTREICH

arr M.L.Lake	PC	112.2sx.1/2210/perc/str	C.Fischer	19720
PRINZ EUGEN	PC	2(picc)222/4231/timp.perc/str	Benjamin	16363 +

BAHRAIN   see   BAND CATALOGUE

BANGLADESH

NATIONAL SONG (East Bengal)

arr H.Murrill	ø	12+ca.2+bcl.2+cbsn/4131/timp.perc/str	[Arranger]	19741

BELGIUM

NATIONAL ANTHEM
   La BRABANÇONNE (François van Campenhout)

	PC	2(picc)222/4230/timp.perc/str	Breitkopf	14305
	PC	1(picc)222/2230.euph/perc/str	Hawkes	1835
	PC	2(picc)222/4231/timp.perc/str	Benjamin	16363 +
arr A.Franzel	ø	2222/4331/timp.perc/hp/str	[Arranger]	19629
arr A.Franzel	ø	2121/2230/timp.perc/str	[Arranger]	19629
arr M.L.Lake	PC	112.2sx.1/2210/perc/str	[Arranger]	MS 20142
arr G.Williams		1+2picc.2+ca.2+bcl.2+cbsn/4331/timp.perc/hp/str	C.Fischer	19720
			[Arranger]	13701

BELIZE   see   BAND CATALOGUE

BOLIVIA

NATIONAL ANTHEM
   BOLIVIANOS, EL HADO PROPICIO (Benedetto Vincenti), adopted 1842

	PC	2(picc)222/4220/str	Benjamin	16364
	PC	2(picc)222/4230/timp.perc/str	Breitkopf	14305
arr G.French	ø	2222/2230/timp.perc/str	(Blandford)	25228 +
arr M.L.Lake	PC	112.2sx.1/2210/perc/str	C.Fischer	19720

BOTSWANA   see   BAND CATALOGUE

BRAZIL

NATIONAL ANTHEM
  OUVIRAM DO YPIRANGA (Francesco Manuel da Silva), adopted 1831 (words changed 1922)
	PC	2(picc)222/4220/str		Benjamin	16364
	PC	2(picc)222/4230/timp.perc/str		Breitkopf	14305
arr & orch L.Miquez	∅	2+picc.222/42.2cnt.31/timp.perc/str		Brazilian Consulate	Misc 2122
arr E.Pereira	∅	pf/str		Brazilian Embassy	16374 B
arr F.Salabert	PC	1(picc)221/223[1]/timp.perc/str		Salabert	3816
arr G.Williams	∅	2222/4231/timp.perc/str		[Arranger]	16232

FORMER NATIONAL ANTHEM
  HYMNO DA PROLAMAÇAO DA REPUBLICA (Seja um pallio de luz)(Léopold Mignez)
	PC	2(picc)222/4220/str		Benjamin	16364

NATIONAL AIRS
  HYMNO À BANDEIRA NACIONAL (F.Braga)
	PC	2(picc)222/4220/str		Benjamin	16364

BRUNEI   see   BAND CATALOGUE

BULGARIA

FORMER NATIONAL ANTHEMS
  BULGARIA MILA, ZEMYA NA GHEROI (Hail our republic)(1946-64)   see   BAND CATALOGUE
  SHOUMI MARITZA (Gabriel Šebek)(adopted 1885)
	PC	2(picc)222/4230/timp.perc/str		Breitkopf	14305
	PC	2(picc)222/4231/timp.perc/str		Benjamin	16363 +
arr M.L.Lake	PC	112.2sx.1/2210/perc/str		C.Fischer	19720

BURMA

NATIONAL ANTHEM
  GBA MAJAY, adopted 1948)
arr R.Barsotti	∅	2221+cbsn/4231/timp/str		[Arranger]	20112

CAMBODIA   see   BAND CATALOGUE

CAMEROON   see   BAND CATALOGUE

CANADA

NATIONAL ANTHEM
  O CANADA (Calixa Lavallée)
	PC	2(picc)222/4230/timp.perc/str	Breitkopf	14305
arr R.Barsotti	PC	1+picc.12.4sx.2/4230/perc/str	Boosey & H	21039 B
arr M.L.Lake	PC	112.2sx.1/2210/perc/str	C.Fischer	19720
arr F.Salabert	PC	1(picc)221/223[1]/timp.perc/str	Salabert	3816

NATIONAL SONGS
  The MAPLE LEAF FOR EVER (Alexander Muir)
	PC	2(picc)222/4220/str	Benjamin	16364
arr M.L.Lake	PC	112.2sx.1/2210/perc/str	C.Fischer	19720
NATIONAL SONG	PC	2(picc)222/4220/str	Benjamin	16364

  VIVE LA CANADIENNE (L.Streabbog)
arr M.L.Lake	PC	112.2sx.1/2210/perc/str	C.Fischer	19720

CENTRAL AFRICAN REPUBLIC   see   BAND CATALOGUE

CEYLON   see   SRI LANKA

CHILE

NATIONAL ANTHEM
  PURO CHILE (Dulce patria/Dear homeland)(Ramón Carnicer), music adopted 17 September, 1847; anthem
      officially recognised 27 June, 1941

	PC	2(picc)222/4220/str	Benjamin	16364
	PC	2(picc)222/4230/timp.perc/str	Breitkopf	14305
arr M.L.Lake	PC	112.2sx.1/2210/perc/str	C.Fischer	19720
arr F.Salabert	PC	1(picc)221/223[1]/timp.perc/str	Salabert	3816

NATIONAL AIRS
  HIMNO À LA VICTORIA DE YUNGAY

	PC	2(picc)222/4220/str	Benjamin	16364

CHINA

NATIONAL ANTHEM
  PEOPLE'S REPUBLIC   see   BAND CATALOGUE
FORMER NATIONAL ANTHEMS
  SONG OF KUOMINTANG (San-Min-Chu-I Wu Tang So Tsung)(Che'ng Mao-Yün,1928):   former National Anthem of
      the Republic (Taiwan)

	PC	2(picc)222/4230/timp.perc/str	Breitkopf	14305
arr T.Wood & Williams	∅	4443+cbsn/8461/timp.perc/hp.org/str	[Arrangers]	19652

  The WORLD'S DELIGHT (Twung-kuoh hiung li jüh dschon tiãn)

arr M.L.Lake	PC	112.2sx.1/2210/perc/str	C.Fischer	19720

COLOMBIA

NATIONAL ANTHEM
  O GLORIA INMARCESIBLE (Orestes Sindici), first perf c.1905

	∅	2+picc.222/4331/perc/str	(Colombian Ministry)	Misc 3743
	PC	2(picc)222/4220/str	Benjamin	16364
	PC	2(picc)222/4230/timp.perc/str	Breitkopf	14305
arr M.L.Lake	PC	112.2sx.1/2210/perc/str	C.Fischer	19720

COSTA RICA

NATIONAL ANTHEM
  NOBLE PATRIA, TU HERMOSA BANDER (Noble Country)(Manuel Maria Gutiérrez), adopted 1853, words 1900

	PC	2(picc)222/4220/str	Benjamin	16364
arr M.L.Lake	PC	112.2sx.1/2210/perc/str	C.Fischer	19720

      see also   BAND CATALOGUE

CUBA

NATIONAL ANTHEM
  La BAYAMESA (Himno Bayamés)(Pedro Figueredo), first perf 1868

	PC	2(picc)222/4230/timp.perc/str	Breitkopf	14305
arr M.L.Lake	PC	112.2sx.1/2210/perc/str	C.Fischer	19720

CZECHOSLVAKIA

NATIONAL ANTHEM (adopted 1919)
  Part 1: KDE DOMOV MUJ (Where is my home)(František Škroup)
  Part 2: NAD TATRÚ SA BLÝSKA (traditional melody)

	PC	2(picc)222/4230/timp.perc/str	Breitkopf	14305
arr J.Flegl	PC	1+picc.222/4230/timp.perc/str	Urbanek	9760
arr J.Flegl	PC	1121/2220/timp.perc/str/chorus	Urbanek	10812

CZECHOSLOVAKIA (cont)

NATIONAL ANTHEM (cont)
  arr A.Franzel   ø 2121/2230/timp.perc/hp/str   [Arranger] MS 20142 +
  arr A.Franzel   ø 2222/4331/timp.perc/hp/str   [Arranger] 19637
 Part 1 only
  arr M.L.Lake   PC 112.2sx.1/2210/perc/str   C.Fischer 19720
NATIONAL AIRS
 WAR SONG OF THE HUSSITES
  arr M.L.Lake   PC 112.2sx.1/2210/perc/str   C.Fischer 19720

DAHOMEY see BAND CATALOGUE

DENMARK

NATIONAL ANTHEM
 KONG KRISTIAN STOD VED HØJEN MAST (King Christian stood by the lofty mast)(attrib J.E.Hartmann or
  D.L.Rogart)
      PC 2(picc)222/4230/timp.perc/str   Breitkopf 14305
      PC 2(picc)222/4231/timp.perc/str   Benjamin 16363 +
  arr M.L.Lake PC 112.2sx.1/2210/perc/str   C.Fischer 19720
  arr G.Williams ø 2222/4331/timp.perc/hp/str   [Arranger] 19636
NATIONAL AIRS
 DER ER ET LAND, DETS STED ER HØJT MOD NORDEN (C.E.F.Weyse)
      PC 2(picc)222/423[1]/perc/str   Benjamin 16363
 ORLOGSMARCH (March for the Navy)
  arr R.Lindebro PC 1120/0220/perc/str   Nyt Dansk 18960
 DEN TAPPRE LANDSOLDAT (J.O.E.Horneman)
      PC 2(picc)222/4231/timp.perc/str   Benjamin 16363 +
 VIFT STOLT PAA CODANS BØLGE (The Dannebrog)(R.Bay)
      PC 2(picc)222/4231/timp.perc/str   Benjamin 16363 +

DOMENICAN REPUBLIC

NATIONAL ANTHEM
 QUISQUEYANOS VALIENTES, ALCEMOS (Valiant sons of Quisqueya)(José Reynes, 1883), first perf 1900
      PC 2(picc)222/4220/str   Benjamin 16364
  arr M.L.Lake PC 122.2sx.1/2210/perc/str   C.Fischer 19720

ECUADOR

NATIONAL ANTHEM
 SALVE, OH PATRIA (Antonio Neumane), adopted 1948 (in use previously)
      PC 2(picc)222/4230/timp.perc/str   Breitkopf 14305
      PC 2(picc)222/4220/str   Benjamin 16364
  arr M.L.Lake PC 112.2sx.1/2210/perc/str   C.Fischer 19720

EGYPT

NATIONAL ANTHEM see BAND CATALOGUE
FORMER NATIONAL ANTHEM
 AIR DU KHEDIVE (Song of the Khedive)(attrib G.Verdi)
      PC 2(picc)222/4230/timp.perc/str   Breitkopf 14305
      PC 2(picc)222/4220/str   Benjamin 16364
  arr M.L.Lake PC 112.2sx.1/2210/perc/str   C.Fischer 19720
  arr F.Salabert PC 1(picc)221/223[1]/timp.perc/str   Salabert 3816

EIRE (Republic of Ireland)(see also GREAT BRITAIN)

NATIONAL ANTHEM
   AMHRÁN NA BHFIANN (The Soldiers' song)(Seo dhibj/We'll sing a song)(P.Kearney & P.Heaney), adopted
      July 1926·

arr A.Franzel	φ	1+picc.222/42.2cnt.31/timp.perc/hp/str	[Arranger]	19520
arr & orch J.Larchet (with add pts ed & arr M.Sargent)				
	φ	2+picc.222/2231/timp.perc/str	Pigott (Dublin)	21526
arr L.Weninger	PC	2(picc)222/4230/timp.perc/str	Breitkopf	14305

      see also   BAND CATALOGUE
NATIONAL AIRS
   PRESIDENTIAL SALUTE
      arr J.Larchet (wit add pts ed & arr M.Sargent)

	φ	2+picc.222/2231/timp.perc/str	Pigott (Dublin)	21526

ESTONIA   see   UNION OF SOCIALIST SOVIET REPUBLICS

ETHIOPIA

NATIONAL ANTHEM   see   BAND CATALOGUE
NATIONAL AIRS
   NATIONAL SONG (not the National Anthem)

arr M.L.Lake	PC	112.2sx.1/2210/perc/str	C.Fischer	19720

EUROPE

The EUROPEAN ANTHEM (L'Inno Europeo)(part of Finale of Beethoven's 9th Symphony), adopted by the Council
    of Europe, 1972

arr H.von Karajan	φ	2222+cbsn/2230/timp/str	2'15"	Schott,1972	25692

FINLAND

NATIONAL ANTHEM
   MAAMME LAULU (Vart land)(Fredrik Pacius)

	PC	2(picc)222/4230/timp.perc/str	Breitkopf	14305
	PC	2(picc)222/4231/timp.perc/str	Benjamin	16363 +
arr M.L.Lake	PC	112.2sx.1/2210/perc/str	C.Fischer	19720
arr G.W.Williams	φ	2222/4331/timp.perc/str	[Arranger]	19634

NATIONAL AIRS
   BJÖRNEBORGARNES MARCH

	PC	2(picc)222/4231/timp.perc/str	Benjamin	16363 +

   HÖR, HUR, HÄRLIGT SANGEN: National Hymn (F.Pacius)

	PC	2(picc)222/4231/timp.perc/str	Benjamin	16363 +

FRANCE

NATIONAL ANTHEM
   La MARSEILLAISE(Claude-Joseph Rouget de L'Isle), adopted 15 July 1795

	PC	2(picc)222/4231/timp.perc/str	Benjamin	16363 +
	PC	2(picc)222/4230/timp.perc/str	Breitkopf	14305
		1+picc.22.3sx.2/4230/timp.perc/str	Hawkes	16841 Cp
arr G.Bantock	φ	2+picc.2+ca.2+bcl.2+cbsn/4331/timp.perc/hp/str	[Arranger]	19644
arr H.Berlioz	φ	0022/4631[=oph]/3timp.bdm/str/chorus	Brandus	23339
arr A.Franzel	φ	2121/2230/timp.perc/hp/str	[Arranger]	MS 20142
arr A.Franzel for BBC Symphony Orch				
	φ	2+picc.222/4230/timp.perc/hp/str	[Arranger]	Misc 2407
arr M.L.Lake	PC	112.2sx.1/2210/perc/str	C.Fischer	19720
arr M.Mackie	φ	cel/str-4tet	[Arranger]	MS 30651
arr G.Stacey		1110/0000/timp/acdn.hp/str	(Paxton)	3553
arr G.Williams		2+2picc.2+ca.2+bcl.2+cbsn/4331/timp.perc/2hp/str	[Arranger]	13637

FRANCE (cont)

NATIONAL AIRS

ÇA IRA (Bécourt)
   in C, arr F.Chagrin for Tenor & Baritone soli, chorus & orch

		2221/2230/timp.perc/hp/str		[Arranger]	TO 1286

La CARMAGNOLE
   arr F.M.Collinson   ∮   1+picc.221/2330/timp.perc/hp/str   [Arranger]   TO 1286
   arr G.Williams for Baritone solo, chorus & orch

	∮	2221/2230/timp.sdm/hp/str		[Arranger]	TO 1286

Le CHANT DU DÉPART (Méhul)   PC   2(picc)222/4231/timp.perc/str   Benjamin   16363 +
   arr F.M.Collinson   ∮   1+picc.221/2330/timp.perc/hp/str   [Arranger]   TO 1286
   arr G.Stacey   1110/0000/timp/acdn.hp/str   (Heugel)   3553

CHEVALIER DE LA TABLE RONDE
   in Bb, arr F.Chagrin for Tenor solo, chorus & orch

		2221/2230/perc/hp/str		[Arranger]	TO 1286

CHOEUR DES GIRONDINS (Mourir pour la patrie)(P.Varney)

PC   2(picc)222/4231/timp.perc/str   Benjamin   16363 +
   arr M.L.Lake   PC   112.2sx.1/2210/perc/str   C.Fischer   19720

Un CONTE BLEU (La Toussaint)(P.Lacome D'Estaleux)
   arr G.Stacey   1110/0000/timp.perc/acdn.hp/str   (Enoch)   3553

EN PASSANT PAR LA LORRAINE (Les Trois capitaines)(Tiersot)
   arr for solo voice, chorus & orch

	∮	1+picc.221/2330/timp.perc/hp/str		[BBC]	TO 1286
arr G.Stacey		1110/0000/timp/acdn.hp/str		(Heugel)	3553
		perc/vln.vlc		[BBC]	MS 2293

Le JOLI TAMBOUR (G.Weitz)
   arr G.Stacey   1110/0000/timp/acdn.hp/str   (Chester)   3553

MARCHE DES ZOUAVES
   arr F.M.Collinson   ∮   1+picc.221/2230/perc/str   [Arranger]   TO 1286

MARCHE LORRAINE (L.Ganne)   PC   1+picc.222/2231/perc/str   Enoch   744 E
   arr F.M.Collinson   ∮   2+picc.221/2330/perc/hp/str   4'30"   [Arranger]   TO 1286

MARLBROUK S'EN VA-T-EN GUERRE

PC   2(picc)222/4231/timp.perc/str   Benjamin   16363 +
   in F, arr F.M.Collinson for solo voices, chorus & orch
                  ∮   2(picc)222/2330/timp.perc/hp/str   [Arranger]   TO 1286

La PARISIENNE (D.F.Auber)   PC   2(picc)222/4231/timp.perc/str   Benjamin   16363 +

PARTANT POUR LA SYRIE (Hortense Eugenie de Beauharnais)

PC   2(picc)222/4231/timp.perc/str   Benjamin   16363 +
   arr M.L.Lake   PC   112.2sx.1/2210/perc/str   C.Fischer   19720

Le PAS ORDINAIRE
   arr F.M.Collinson   ∮   0000/0300/sdm/str   [Arranger]   TO 1286

QUAND MADELON (Camille Robert)
   in C, arr F.Chagrin for Baritone solo & orch
                  1+picc.221/2330/timp.perc/hp/str   [Arranger]   TO 1286

SONG OF THE MAQUIS
   in E min, arr F.M.Collinson for Baritone solo & orch
                  2222/2230/timp.perc/hp/str   [Arranger]   TO 1286

GABON   see   BAND CATALOGUE

GAMBIA   see   BAND CATALOGUE

GERMANY

NATIONAL ANTHEMS
  EAST GERMANY (Deutsche Demokratische Republik)
    AUF ERSTANDEN AUS RUINEN (Hanns Eisler), adopted 7 October, 1949

	φ 2222/3331/timp.perc/str		Hinrichsen	23735

  WEST GERMANY (Bundesrepublik Deutschland
    EINIGKEIT UND RECHT UND FREIHEIT (official words adopted 1950; formerly 'Deutschland, Deutschland
      über alles')(Tune 'Austria' by F.J.Haydn)

	PC 2(picc)222/4231/timp.perc/str		Benjamin	16363 +
	PC 2(picc)222/4230/timp.perc/str		Breitkopf	14305
	2+2[=3]picc.4+ca.4+bcl.4+cbsn/8561/timp.perc/1[=2]hp/ str		[BBC]	13640 C
arr M.L.Lake	PC 112.2sx.1/2210/perc/str		C.Fischer	19720

FORMER FEDERAL ANTHEM
  HYMNE AN DEUTSCHLAND (Land des Glaubens)(H.Reutter)

arr Lutz	PC 1110/0210/timp/str	3'	(Schott,1951)	20268

NATIONAL AIRS
  ABSCHIED: So leb' denn soh, du stilles Haus (W.Müller)

arr M.L.Lake	PC 112.2sx.1/2210/perc/str		C.Fischer	19720

  ACH DU LIEBER AUGUSTIN (traditional)

arr M.L.Lake	PC 112.2sx.1/2210/perc/str		C.Fischer	19720

  ACH, WIE IST'S MÖGLICH DANN? (F.Kücken)

arr M.L.Lake	PC 112.2sx.1/2210/perc/str		C.Fischer	19720

  Die AUSDRWÄHLTE: Mädele ruck, ruck, ruck (Swabian folk-song)

arr M.L.Lake	PC 112.2sx.1/2210/perc/str		C.Fischer	19720

  BEN BOLT (traditional)

arr M.L.Lake	PC 112.2sx.1/2210/perc/str		C.Fischer	19720

  DES JAHRES LETZTE STUNDE (The last hour of the year)(Am Sylvester-Abend)(J.A.P.Schulz)

arr M.L.Lake	PC 112.2sx.1/2210/perc/str		C.Fischer	19720

  DEUTSCHER FREIHEIT SCHLACHTRUF (A.Methfessel)

arr M.L.Lake	PC 112.2sx.1/2210/perc/str		C.Fischer	19720

  DEUTSCHES FLAGGENLIED (Richard Thiele)

	PC 2(picc)222/4231/timp.perc/str		Benjamin	16363 +
arr M.L.Lake	PC 112.2sx.1/2210/perc/str		C.Fischer	19720

  DU BIST SO NAH' UND DOCH SO FERN (Thou art so near and yet so far)(A.Reichardt)

arr M.L.Lake	PC 112.2sx.1/2210/perc/str		C.Fischer	19720

  DU, DU LIEGST MIR IN HERZEN (traditional)

arr M.L.Lake	PC 112.2sx.1/2210/perc/str		C.Fischer	19720

  EDELWEISS (traditional)

arr M.L.Lake	PC 112.2sx.1/2210/perc/str		C.Fischer	19720

  GAUDEAMUS: medieval students' song (traditional)

arr M.L.Lake	PC 112.2sx.1/2210/perc/str		C.Fischer	19720

  Der GUTE KAMERAD: Ich hatt' einen Kameraden (traditional)

arr M.L.Lake	PC 112.2sx.1/2210/perc/str		C.Fischer	19720

  HEIL, DIR IM SIEGERKRANZ <u>see</u> <u>GREAT BRITAIN</u>, NATIONAL ANTHEM
  HEIL, UNSERM KÖNIG, HEIL <u>see</u> <u>GREAT BRITAIN</u>, NATIONAL ANTHEM
  HORST WESSEL-LIED

	PC 2(picc)222/4230/timp.perc/str		Breitkopf	14305

  JAGERLEBEN: Im Wald und auf der Heide (traditional)

arr M.L.Lake	PC 112.2sx.1/2210/perc/str		C.Fischer	19720

  KRAMBAMBULI (traditional)

arr M.L.Lake	PC 112.2sx.1/2210/perc/str		C.Fischer	19720

  LAUTERBACH

arr M.L.Lake	PC 112.2sx.1/2210/perc/str		C.Fischer	19720

  Die LORELEY (F.Silcher)

arr E.Ascher	PC 1111/2210/perc/str		E.Ascher	8014
arr M.L.Lake	PC 112.2sx.1/2210/perc/str		C.Fischer	19720

GERMANY (cont)

NATIONAL AIRS (cont)

O SCHÖNE ZEIT, O SEL'GE ZEIT (Those happy days, those days of yore)(K.Götze)
arr M.L.Lake	PC 112.2sx.1/2210/perc/str	C.Fischer	19720

O TANNENBAUM (traditional)
arr M.L.Lake	PC 112.2sx.1/2210/perc/str	C.Fischer	19720

RITTERS ABSCHIED (J.Kinkel)
arr M.L.Lake	PC 112.2sx.1/2210/perc/str	C.Fischer	19720

VERLASSEN BIN I (Forsaken)(Koschat)
arr M.L.Lake	PC 112.2sx.1/2210/perc/str	C.Fischer	19720

Die WACHT AM RHEIN (Carl Wilhelm)
	PC 2(picc)222/4231/timp.perc/str	Benjamin	16363 +
arr M.L.Lake	PC 112.2sx.1/2210/perc/str	C.Fischer	19720

WANDERLIED (Wohlauf noch getrunken)(traditional)
arr M.L.Lake	PC 112.2sx.1/2210/perc/str	C.Fischer	19720

WAS IST DES DEUTSCHE VATERLAND? (G.Reichardt)
arr M.L.Lake	PC 112.2sx.1/2210/perc/str	C.Fischer	19720

WENN DIE SCHWALBEN HEIMWÄRTS ZIEH'N (When the swallows homeward fly)(F.Abt)
arr M.L.Lake	PC 112.2sx.1/2210/perc/str	C.Fischer	19720

Das ZERBROCHENE RINGLEIN: In einem kühlen Grunde (after a melody by C.Friedrich Glück)
arr M.L.Lake	PC 112.2sx.1/2210/perc/str	C.Fischer	19720

GERMANY - REGIONS

NATIONAL AIRS
  BADEN
NATIONAL SONG	PC 2(picc)222/4231/timp.perc/str	Benjamin	16363 +

  BAVARIA
    BAYERN, O HEIMATLAND (F.Lachner)
	PC 2(picc)222/4231/timp.perc/str	Benjamin	16363 +

  BRUNSWICK
    HOCH LEBE FRIEDRICH WILHELM
	PC 2(picc)222/4231/timp.perc/str	Benjamin	16363 +
LUSTIGE BRAUNSCHWEIGER	PC 2(picc)222/4231/timp.perc/str	Benjamin	16363 +

  HAMBURG
    STADT HAMBURG AN DER ELBE AUEN
	PC 2(picc)222/4231/timp.perc/str	Benjamin	16363 +

  HANOVER
LUSTIGE HANNOVERANER	PC 2(picc)222/4231/timp.perc/str	Benjamin	16363 +
SONG OF THE GUELPHS	PC 2(picc)222/4231/timp.perc/str	Benjamin	16363 +

  OLDENBURG
HEIL DIR, O OLDENBURG	PC 2(picc)222/4231/timp.perc/str	Benjamin	16363 +

  PRUSSIA
    ICH BETE AN DIE MACHT DER LIEBE
	PC 2(picc)222/4231/timp.perc/str	Benjamin	16363 +

    ICH BIN EIN PREUSSE (August Heinrich Neithardt): former National Anthem of Prussia
	PC 2(picc)222/4231/timp.perc/str	Benjamin	16363 +
arr M.L.Lake	PC 1+picc.12.2sx.1/2210/perc/str	C.Fischer	19720

  SAXONY
    GOTT SEI MIT DIR, MEIN SACHSENLAND (J.Otto)
	PC 2(picc)222/4231/timp.perc/str	Benjamin	16363 +

  SAXONY-MEININGEN
    BRÜDER, SINGT MIT LAUTEM FREUDENSCHALL
	PC 2(picc)222/4231/timp.perc/str	Benjamin	16363 +

  SCHLESWIG-HOLSTEIN
    SCHLESWIG-HOLSTEIN, MEERUMSCHLUNGEN
	PC 2(picc)222/4231/timp.perc/str	Benjamin	16363 +

GERMANY - REGIONS

NATIONAL AIRS (cont)

WALDECK

UNTER DIESER EICHE LASS EUCH NIEDER

PC	2(picc)222/4231/timp.perc/str	Benjamin	16363 +

WESTPHALIA

IHR MÖGT DEN RHEIN, DEN STOLZEN PREISEN

PC	2(picc)222/4231/timp.perc/str	Benjamin	16363 +

WÜRTEMBERG

PREISEND MIT VIEL SCHÖNEN REDEN

PC	2(picc)222/4231/timp.perc/str	Benjamin	16363 +

GHANA

NATIONAL ANTHEM

GOD BLESS OUR HOMELAND GHANA (Philip Gbeho), adopted 1957; new word, 1966

PC	2222/4230/timp.perc/str	Boosey & H, 1959	22910 B

GREAT BRITAIN

NATIONAL ANTHEM

GOD SAVE THE QUEEN (attrib T.Arne, J.Bull or H.Carey)

also known as 1. My Country 'tis of thee - United States of America
2. Heil, dir im Siegerkranz - Germany
3. Rufst du mein Vaterland - Switzerland
4. Heil, unserm König, heil - Germany
5. Oben am deutschen Rhein - Liechtenstein

PC	2(picc)222/4231/timp.perc/str	Benjamin	16363 +
PC	2+picc.2+ca.2+bcl.2sx.2+cbsn/4331/timp.perc/ hp.org/str	Boosey & H	16301 Ap
PC	2(picc)222/4230/timp.perc/str	Breitkopf	14305
	1+picc.22.3sx.2/4230/timp.perc/str	Hawkes	16841 Cp
arr T.Arne	∅ 0200/0000/str	(BBC)	26070 +
arr G.Bantock, in B♭	∅ 3+picc.3+ca.3+bcl.3+cbsn/63.3cnt.31/timp.perc.glock/ hp.org/str		
arr G.Bantock (1940)	∅ 2+picc.2+ca.2+bcl.2+cbsn/4331/timp.perc/str	Breitkopf	2385
arr B.Britten for chorus & orch		[Arranger]	19638

in B♭: can be used by orchestra and military band combined
in G: for orchestral and ceremonial purposes
in G: for general purposes (strings only, if required)

∅	2222/4231/timp.perc/str	Boosey & H(H)	PL 530 Amv
arr M.Costa	∅ 1+picc.222+cbsn/42.2cnt.30.oph.spt/timp.perc/ org/str		
arr M.Costa, rev G.Jacob		[BBC]	3516
∅	2222/42.2cnt.31/timp.perc/org/str	[Arranger]	19640
arr M.Costa, rev G.Williams			
∅	2222/4230/timp.perc/hp/str	[Arranger]	19641
arr M.Costa, orch H.Vowles			
∅	2222/42.2cnt.31/timp.perc/org/str	[Arranger]	19567 Amv

arr M.Costa, orch H.Vowles (each orchestra holds its own version on retention)
Midland Light Orchestra

∅	2222/2230/timp/str	[Arranger]	19695

Northern, Scottish Opera Orchestra (Welsh Orchestra and Midland Light Orchestra when
augmented)

∅	2222/4231/timp.perc/org/str	[Arranger]	19695
Symphony Orchestra ∅	2222/4000/str	[Arranger]	19695

West of England Light Orchestra

∅	2121/2220/timp/str	[Arranger]	19695
Welsh Orchestra ∅	2121/2230/timp/str	[Arranger]	19695

GREAT BRITAIN (cont)

NATIONAL ANTHEM (cont)

arr Desmond	PC	1222/2230.euph/perc/str	Hawkes	2682
arr E.Elgar	∅	2+picc.22+bcl.2+cbsn/42.2cnt.31/timp.perc/ org/str/[military band]	Siddell	8655 B
arr J.Fitz-Gerald	PC	1222/2230.euph/perc/str	Hawkes	1840
arr D.Godfrey	PC	2222/4230/timp.perc/str	Chappell	2867
arr V.Hely-Hutchinson	∅	1+picc.222/4231/timp.perc/str	[Arranger]	MS 8476
	∅	2+2picc.2+ca.2+bcl.2+cbsn/4231/timp.perc/str	[BBC]	23667 Amv Eh Gwe +
arr V.Hely-Hutchinson	∅	1+picc.222/4230/timp.perc/str	[Arranger]	19639
arr G.Jacob, in G	∅	2+picc.2+ca.2+bcl.2+cbsn/4331/timp/hp.org/str Fanfare: 0000/0430	Novello,1965(H)	PL 409
arr G.Jacob, in G	∅	2+picc.2+ca.32/4231/timp.perc/org/str (with military band material)	[Arranger]	MS 1800
arr G.Jacob, in G	∅	2+picc.2+ca.32/4231/timp.perc/org/str	[Arranger]	MS 1801
arr G.Jacobs & G.Williams				
	∅	2222/4231/timp.perc/hp/str/Soprano & Bass chorus pts	[Arranger]	MS 20142
arr Stanford	∅	2222+cbsn/4231/timp.perc/hp/str	Boosey	14280 Bs
arr H.Vowles	∅	3222/42.2cnt.31 (no str or perc)	[Arranger]	19696
arr W.Walton, in G (1965)				
	∅	2+picc.32+bcl.2+cbsn/4331/timp.perc/2hp/str	[Arranger]	24162 C +
arr G.Williams	∅	2+picc.2+ca.2+bcl.2+cbsn/4331/timp.perc/hp/str	[Arranger]	19643
arr G.Williams	∅	1131/2220/perc/str	[Arranger](H)	PL 36
arr H.J.Wood				
1st version	PC	2+picc.2+ca.2+bcl.2+cbsn/4431/timp.perc/2hp.org/str	Curwen	6630 Amv B +
2nd version	PC	3+picc.3+ca.3+bcl.3+cbsn/4431/timp.perc/2hp.org/str	Curwen	6630 Amb B +
[arr]		1222/2230/perc/str	Boosey	20417

Four part versions

in Eb, ed & transcr T.Dart (1955)

	∅	0000/2000/str	(GB-Lbm.Add 29466)	23346 +

c.1740 version, arr R.Leppard (as used by Royal Shakespeare Company)

	PC	hns.[tpt]	Gamut,1962	Misc 5808 B

arr V.Hely-Hutchinson, ed S.Robinson (1st six bars only: 'The Royal Salute')

	∅	1+picc.222/4231/timp.perc/str	[Arranger]	21304

NATIONAL AIRS

The ACCEPTED MASON

arr J.Desmond	PC	1222/2230.euph/perc/str	Hawkes	1682

The BRITISH GRENADIERS (traditional)

arr J.Desmond	PC	1222/2230.euph/perc/str	Hawkes	2682
arr J.Fitz-Gerald	PC	1222/2230.euph/perc/str	Hawkes	1840
arr M.L.Lake	PC	112.2sx.1/2210/perc/str	C.Fischer	19720
arr C.Richardson	PC	2(2picc)12.2sx.1/2230/perc/str	Prowse	11638 B
arr F.Salabert	PC	1(picc)221/223[1]/timp.perc/str	Salabert	3816
arr A.Winter	PC	1222/2230/perc/str	Hawkes	6100
arr L.O.de Witt for cornet, trombone or Baritone solo				
	PC	2(picc)121/2210/perc/str	C.Fischer	5924

COME LANDLORD, FILL THE FLOWING BOWL see LANDLORD, FILL THE FLOWING BOWL

A FINE OLD ENGLISH GENTLEMAN (C.H.Purday)

in Eb	∅	1121/2210/perc/str	(Siddell)	18080
arr R.Barsotti	PC	1+picc.12.4sx.2/4230/perc/str	Boosey & H	21039 B
arr J.Desmond	PC	1222/2230.euph/perc/str	Hawkes	2682

FISHER'S HORNPIPE (traditional)

arr.M.L.Lake	PC	112.2sx.1/2210/perc/str	C.Fischer	19720

FOR HE'S A JOLLY GOOD FELLOW (He won't go home until morning)(traditional)

arr J.Desmond	PC	1222/2230.euph/perc/str	Hawkes	2682
arr M.L.Lake	PC	112.2sx.1/2210/perc/str	C.Fischer	19720

GREAT BRITAIN (cont)

NATIONAL AIRS (cont)

HEART OF OAK (W.Boyce)

in C, arr S.Robinson	∅	1111/1120/timp.perc/str	[Arranger]	MS 6339
in B♭, arr A.Franzel	∅	2+picc.22+bcl.2+cbsn/4331/timp.perc/hp/str	[Arranger]	12701
in B♭, arr G.Stacey	∅	2222/4230/timp.perc/str	[Arranger]	MS 20392
in B♭, arr A.Winter	PC	1222/2230/perc/str	Hawkes	6100
in B♭, arr T.Wood for chorus & orch				
	∅	33(ca)3(bcl)2(cbsn)/6431/timp.perc/hp/str	[Arranger]	MS 1596
in B♭, arr T.Wood, orch C.Groves				
	∅	2(picc)121/2230/timp.perc/str	[Arranger]	TO 1126
arr R.Barsotti	PC	1+picc.12.4sx.2/4230/perc/str	Boosey & H	21039 B
arr J.Desmond	PC	1222/2230.euph/perc/str	Hawkes	2682
arr F.Dunn (March past of the Royal Navy)				
	PC	1121/20.2cnt.30/perc/str	Royal Marines	24552
arr M.L.Lake	PC	112.2sx.1/2210/perc/str	C.Fischer	19720

HERE'S A HEALTH TO ALL GOOD LASSES (traditional)

arr J.Desmond	PC	1222/2230.euph/perc/str	Hawkes	2682

HOME SWEET HOME (H.R.Bishop)

in E♭, arr G.Stacey		pf/str	[Arranger]	LM G 3431
in E		2122/2200/str	(Siddell)	17646
in E, arr S.Robinson		1121/2000/str	[Arranger]	LM G 5314
in F & G		1121/2000/str	[BBC]	TO 103
in F, arr G.Williams	∅	hp/str	[Arranger]	14486
in G	∅	1111/1220/timp.perc/hp/str	[BBC]	MS 4485
arr J.Desmond	PC	1222/2230.euph/perc/str	Hawkes	2682
arr M.L.Lake	PC	112.2sx.1/2210/perc/str	C.Fischer	19720

JOHN PEEL: old hunting song

arr J.Desmond	PC	1222/2230.euph/perc/str	Hawkes	2682

The KEEL ROW (traditional)

arr M.L.Lake	PC	112.2sx.1/2210/perc/str	C.Fischer	19720

LANDLORD, FILL THE FLOWING BOWL (traditional)

arr M.L.Lake	PC	112.2sx.1/2210/perc/str	C.Fischer	19720

The LEATHER BOTTÉL (When I survey the world around): air from 'Wit and Drollery'

arr J.Desmond	PC	1222/2230.euph/perc/str	Hawkes	2682

A LIFE ON THE OCEAN WAVE (H.Russell): regimental march of the Royal Marines

arr F.Dunn	PC	1121/20.2cnt.30/perc/str	Royal Marines	24552

MANY HAPPY RETURNS OF THE DAY (J.Blockley)

arr J.Desmond	PC	1222/2230.euph/perc/str	Hawkes	2682

NINETY-FIVE (traditional)

arr M.L.Lake	PC	112.2sx.1/2210/perc/str	C.Fischer	19720

NON NOBIS, DOMINE (attrib W.Byrd)

arr J.Desmond	PC	1222/2230.euph/perc/str	Hawkes	2682

The PLOUGH BOY: country dance (traditional)

arr M.L.Lake	PC	112.2sx.1/2210/perc/str	C.Fischer	19720

POP GOES THE WEASEL (traditional)

arr M.L.Lake	PC	112.2sx.1/2210/perc/str	C.Fischer	19720

RIFLEMEN FORM

arr J.Desmond	PC	1222/2230.euph/perc/str	Hawkes	2682

The ROAST BEEF OF OLD ENGLAND (R.Leveridge)

arr R.Barsotti	PC	1+picc.12.4sx.2/4230/perc/str	Boosey & H	21039 B
arr J.Desmond	PC	1222/2230.euph/perc/str	Hawkes	2682
arr M.L.Lake	PC	112.2sx.1/2210/perc/str	C.Fischer	19720
arr L.O.de Witt for cornet, trombone or Baritone solo				
	PC	1(picc)121/2210/perc/str	C.Fischer	5924

GREET BRITAIN (cont)

NATIONAL AIRS (cont)

The ROGUE'S MARCH (traditional)

arr M.L.Lake	PC	112.2sx.1/2210/perc/str	C.Fischer	19720

RULE BRITANNIA

in C, for voice & orch		2222/2230.euph/timp/str	Novello	17832
in C, arr A.Carse	φ	0201/0200/timp/str/solo.chorus	Augener	16481
in G, arr G.Jacob for Baritone solo, chorus & orch				
	φ	2(picc)222/4331/timp.perc/org/str	[Arranger]	22166
in A♭ & B♭, arr M.Sargent for Tenor solo, chorus & orch				
	φ	2+picc.2+ca.2+bcl.2+cbsn/4331/timp.perc/ org/str	OLP (H)	(PL 466 Amv (A♭) (Bmv (B♭)
in A, arr P.Hope for Soprano & Tenor soli, 2 pianos & orch				
	φ	3(picc)232/4330/timp.perc/hp/str	[Arranger]	25077 +
in A, arr S.Robinson	φ	1111/1120/timp/str/solo.chorus	[Arranger]	MS 7645
in B♭, arr C.Groves	φ	0100/2200/timp/str	[Arranger]	TO 1098
in B♭, arr T.Wood for chorus & orch				
	φ	3+picc.3+ca.3+bcl.3+cbsn/6441/timp.perc/str	[Arranger]	13978
arr R.Barsotti	PC	1+picc.12.4sx.2/4230/perc/str	Boosey & H	21039 B
arr J.Fitz-Gerald	PC	1222/2230.euph/perc/str	Hawkes	1840 B
arr A.Hohenstein	PC	2(picc)222/4231/timp.perc/str	Benjamin	16363 +
arr M.L.Lake	PC	112.2sx.1/2210/perc/str	C.Fischer	19720
arr F.Salabert	PC	1(picc)121/2231/timp.perc/str	Salabert	3816
arr A.Winter	PC	1222/2230/perc/str	Hawkes	6100
[arr]		1222/2210/perc/str	Boosey	20417

The SOLDIER'S JOY (traditional)

arr M.L.Lake	PC	112.2sx.1/2210/perc/str	C.Fischer	19720

TO ALL YOU LADIES

arr J.Desmond	PC	1222/2230.euph/perc/str	Hawkes	2682

The VICAR OF BRAY

arr J.Desmond	PC	1222/2230.euph/perc/str	Hawkes	2682
in C, arr L.O.de Witt for cornet, trombone or Baritone solo				
	PC	1(picc)121/2210/perc/str	C.Fischer	5924

WELCOME EVER WELCOME, FRIENDS

arr J.Desmond	PC	1222/2230.euph/perc/str	Hawkes	2682

GREAT BRITAIN - IRELAND

NATIONAL AIRS

The BATTLE OF BOYNE

arr G.Williams	φ	2+picc.2+ca.2+bcl.2+cbsn/4331/timp.perc/hp/str	[Arranger]	13699

BELIEVE ME IF ALL THOSE ENDEARING YOUNG CHARMS (My lodging is on the cold ground)

in D♭, arr L.O.de Witt for cornet, trombone or Baritone solo				
	PC	1(picc)121/2210/perc/str	C.Fischer	5924

CEAD MILE FAILTE (100,000 welcomes)(traditional)

in D, arr W.Davies	φ	2121/2220/timp.perc/hp.pf(cel)/str	[Arranger]	25083 Ani +

The CRUISKEEN LAWN (traditional)

arr M.L.Lake	PC	112.2sx.1/2210/perc/str	C.Fischer	19720
in F, arr L.O.de Witt for cornet, trombone or Baritone solo				
	PC	1(picc)121/2210/perc/str	C.Fischer	5924

GARRY OWEN (traditional)

arr M.L.Lake	PC	112.2sx.1/2210/perc/str	C.Fischer	19720

The HARP THAT ONCE THROUGH TARA'S HALLS

arr M.L.Lake	PC	112.2sx.1/2210/perc/str	C.Fischer	19720
in C, arr L.O.de Witt for cornet, trombone or Baritone solo				
	PC	1(picc)121/2210/perc/str	C.Fischer	5924

GREATBRITAIN - IRELAND (cont)

NATIONAL AIRS (cont)
  The IRISH WASHERWOMAN (traditional)
    arr M.L.Lake   PC 112.2sx.1/2210/perc/str   C.Fischer   19720
  KATE KEARNEY (traditional)
    arr M.L.Lake   PC 112.2sx.1/2210/perc/str   C.Fischer   19720
  LARRY O'GAFF (traditional)
    arr M.L.Lake   PC 112.2sx.1/2210/perc/str   C.Fischer   19720
  The LAST ROSE OF SUMMER
    in F, arr P.Hope   φ 2222/4000/timp/hp/str   [Arranger]   23672 +
    arr M.L.Lake   PC 112.2sx.1/2210/perc/str   C.Fischer   19720
    in D♭, arr L.O.de Witt for cornet, trombone or Baritone solo
                  PC 1(picc)121/2210/perc/str   C.Fischer   5924
    in F, arr W.Cooper, orch G.Stacey
                    pf/str   (Beal, Stattard)   LM G 5468
  LET ERIN REMEMBER THE DAYS OF OLD (traditional)
    arr A.Hohenstein   PC 2(picc)222/4231/timp.perc/str   Benjamin   16363 +
    arr M.L.Lake   PC 112.2sx.1/2210/perc/str   C.Fischer   19720
  LONDONDERRY AIR (Danny Boy)
    arr A.Wilkinson   φ hp/str   [Arranger]   24266
  The LOW BACK'D CAR (traditional)
    arr M.L.Lake   PC 112.2sx.1/2210/perc/str   C.Fischer   19720
  The MEETING OF THE WATERS (traditional)
    in F, arr L.O.de Witt for cornet, trombone or Baritone solo
                  PC 1(picc)121/2210/perc/str   C.Fischer   5924
  The MINSTREL BOY (traditional)
    arr M.L.Lake   PC 112.2sx.1/2210/perc/str   C.Fischer   19720
    arr A.Winter   PC 1(picc)222/2230/perc/str   Hawkes   8734
    in E♭, arr L.O.de Witt, for cornet, trombone or Baritone solo
                  PC 1(picc)121/2210/perc/str   C.Fischer   5924
  MISS MCLEOD'S REEL (traditional)
    arr M.L.Lake   PC 112.2sx.1/2210/perc/str   C.Fischer   19720
  MONEY MUSK (traditional)
    arr M.L.Lake   PC 112.2sx.1/2210/perc/str   C.Fischer   19720
  O'DONNELL ABOO (traditional)
    arr M.L.Lake   PC 112.2sx.1/2210/perc/str   C.Fischer   19720
    arr A.Winter   PC 1(picc)222/2230/perc/str   Hawkes   8734
  PADDY'S WEDDING (traditional)
    arr M.L.Lake   PC 112.2sx.1/2210/perc/str   C.Fischer   19720
  The PRETTY GIRL MILKING HER COW (traditional)
    arr M.L.Lake   PC 112.2sx.1/2210/perc/str   C.Fischer   19720
    in F min, arr L.O.de Witt for cornet, trombone or Baritone solo
                  PC 1(picc)121/2210/perc/str   C.Fischer   5924
  RAKES OF MALLOW (traditional)
    arr M.L.Lake   PC 112/2sx.1/2210/perc/str   C.Fischer   19720
  REMEMBER THE GLORIES OF BRIEN (traditional)
    arr A.Hohenstein   PC 2(picc)222/4231/timp.perc/str   Benjamin   16363 +
  RORY O'MORE (traditional)
    arr M.L.Lake   PC 112.2sx.1/2210/perc/str   C.Fischer   19720
  ST PATRICK'S DAY (traditional)
    arr M.L.Lake   PC 112.2sx.1/2210/perc/str   C.Fischer   19720
    arr A.Winter   PC 1(picc)222/2230/perc/str   Hawkes   8734
  SAVOURNEEN DELISH (traditional)
    in A♭, arr L.O.de Witt for cornet, trombone or Baritone solo
                  PC 1(picc)121/2210/perc/str   C.Fischer   5924
  The WEARING OF THE GREEN (traditional)
    arr M.L.Lake   PC 112.2sx.1/2210/perc/str   C.Fischer   19720
    arr L.O.de Witt for cornet, trombone or Baritone solo
                  PC 1(picc)121/2210/perc/str   C.Fischer   5924

IRELAND - ULSTER For special arrangements of Ulster folksongs & National Airs, contact BBC Music
             Library, Belfast

GREAT BRITAIN - ISLE OF MAN

NATIONAL ANTHEM
   ARRANE ASHOONAGH DY VANNIN (traditional Manx air)
     adapted W.H.Gill; orch S.Robinson
          φ   3222/4231/timp.perc/str   [Arranger]   22606 +

GREAT BRITAIN - SCOTLAND

NATIONAL AIRS
  AFTON WATER (Flow gently, sweet Afton)
    arr M.L.Lake   PC 112.2sx.1/2210/perc/str   C.Fischer   19720
    in Bb, arr L.O.de Witt for cornet, trombone or Baritone solo
                  PC 1(picc)121/2210/perc/str   C.Fischer   5922
  ARGYLE IS MY NAME (traditional)
    arr Fitz-Gerald   PC 2222/0130.euph/str   Hawkes   7854
  AULD LANG SYNE (traditional)
    in F, arr C.Thorpe Davie for Soprano solo, chorus & orch
                  φ 2+picc.332+cbsn/4331/timp.perc.xyl/hp/str   (Composer,1979)   26637
    in F, arr L.O.de Witt for cornet, trombone or Baritone solo
                  PC 1(picc)121/2210/perc/str   C.Fischer   5922
    in G, arr F.Bye   φ 1121/2200/timp/str   Arranger   MLO 853
    in G, arr S.Torch & A.Masters for 3 solo voices, chorus, orch & military band
                  φ 2222/4330/timp.perc/hp/str   [Arrangers]   23974 +
    arr J.Desmond   PC 1222/2230.euph/perc/str   C.Fischer   2682
    arr Fitz-Gerald   PC 2222/0130.euph/str   Hawkes   7854
    arr A.Hohenstein   PC 2(picc)222/4231/timp.perc/str   Benjamin   16363 +
    arr M.L.Lake   PC 112.2sx.1/2210/perc/str   C.Fischer   19720
  AULD ROBIN GRAY
    in C, arr L.O.de Witt for cornet, trombone or Baritone solo
                  PC 1(picc)121/2210/perc/str   C.Fischer   5922
  BONNIE DUNDEE (attrib C.Sainton-Dolby)
                  PC 1+picc.12.4sx.2/4230/perc/str Boosey & H   21039 B
    arr M.L.Lake   PC 112.2sx.1/2210/perc/str   C.Fischer   19720
  BONNIE, SWEET BESSIE (traditional)
    arr M.L.Lake   PC 112.2sx.1/2210/perc/str   C.Fischer   19720
  The CAMPBELLS ARE COMING (traditional)
    arr M.L.Lake   PC 112.2sx.1/2210/perc/str   C.Fischer   19720
  CHARLIE IS MY DARLING (traditional)
    arr M.L.Lake   PC 112.2sx.1/2210/perc/str   C.Fischer   19720
  COMIN' THRO' THE RYE
    in F, arr L.O.de Witt for cornet, trombone or Baritone solo
                  PC 1(picc)121/2210/perc/str   C.Fischer   5922
    arr M.L.Lake   PC 112.2sx.1/2210/perc/str   C.Fischer   19720
  The DREAM (I dreamed I lay)(traditional)
    in Eb, arr L.O.de Witt for cornet, trombone or Baritone solo
                  PC 1(picc)121/2210/perc/str   C.Fischer   5922
  HIGHLAND LADDIE (traditional)
    see   WHITE COCKADE
  KINLOCH OF KINLOCH (traditional)
    arr M.L.Lake   PC 112.2sx.1/2210/perc/str   C.Fischer   19720
  The LASS O'GOWRIE (traditional)
    arr M.L.Lake   PC 112.2sx.1/2210/perc/str   C.Fischer   19720
  LOCH LOMOND (traditional)
    arr M.L.Lake   PC 112.2sx.1/2210/perc/str   C.Fischer   19720
    arr A.Winter   PC 1222/2230/perc/str   Hawkes   7977
  LOCH-NA-GAR
    arr Fitz-Gerald   PC 2222/0130.euph/str   Hawkes   7854

GREAT BRITAIN - SCOTLAND (cont)

NATIONAL AIRS (cont)

LOGIE O'BUCHAN (traditional)
in Ab, arr L.O.de Witt for cornet, trombone or Baritone solo
PC 1(picc)121/2210/perc/str   C.Fischer   9522

MAID OF DUNDEE (traditional)
in F, arr L.O.de Witt for cornet, trombone or Baritone solo
PC 1(picc)121/2210/perc/str   C.Fischer   5922

OLD SCOTTISH DANCE TUNES: The Gleneagles' collection of Strathspeys, reels & country dances
PC 101.2sx.0/0210/perc/str   LMS   5974

PRINCE CHARLIE (traditional)
arr Fitz-Gerald   PC 2222/0130.euph/str   Hawkes   7854

ROBIN ADAIR
in Ab, arr L.O.de Witt for cornet, trombone or Baritone solo
PC 1(picc)121/2210/perc/str   C.Fischer   5922
arr M.L.Lake   PC 112.2sx.1/2210/perc/str   C.Fischer   19720

SCOTS WHA HAE WI' WALLACE BLED
in Ab, arr L.O.de Witt for cornet, trombone or Baritone solo
PC 1(picc)121/2210/perc/str   C.Fischer   5922
arr Fitz-Gerald   PC 2222/0130.euph/str   Hawkes   7854
arr A.Hohenstein   PC 2(picc)/222/4231/timp.perc/str   Benjamin   16363 +
arr M.L.Lake   PC 112.2sx.1/2210/perc/str   C.Fischer   19720

WHITE COCKADE (Highland Laddie)(traditional)
arr Fitz-Gerald   PC 2222/0130.euph/str   Hawkes   7854
arr M.L.Lake   PC 112.2sx.1/2210/perc/str   C.Fischer   19720

GREAT BRITAIN - WALES

NATIONAL AIRS

The ASH GROVE (Llwyn on)(traditional)
arr Fitz-Gerald   PC 2222/2230.euph/perc/str   Hawkes   2999 B
arr M.Mackie, orch G.Jacob φ 2222/4000/timp/hp/str   [Arranger]   20847

The BELLS OF ABERDOVEY (Clychau Aberdyfi)(C.Dibdin)
arr Fitz-Gerald   PC 2222/2230.euph/perc/str   Hawkes   2999 B

The CAMP
arr Fitz-Gerald   PC 2222/2230.euph/perc/str   Hawkes   2999 B

GOD BLESS THE PRINCE OF WALES (Brinley Richards)(1852)
PC 2+picc.2+ca.2+bcl.2sx.2+cbsn/4231/timp.perc/
hp.org/str   Boosey   16301 Ap
arr Fitz-Gerald   PC 1222/2230.euph/perc/str   Hawkes   1840 B
arr A.Hohenstein   PC 2(picc)222/4231/timp.perc/str   Benjamin   16363 +
[arr]   1222/2230/perc/str   Boosey   20417

LAND OF MY FATHERS (J.James)(regarded as National Anthem of Wales)
arr R.Barsotti   PC 1+picc.12.3sx.1/4230/perc/str   Boosey & H   21039 B
arr A.Franzel   φ 2222/4230/timp.perc/hp/str   [Arranger]   19630
in Eb, arr S.Herbert   PC 1(picc)13.2sx.2/4330/perc/str   Boosey   8081 C
arr R.M.Price   1222/4230/timp.perc/hp/str   [Arranger]   19330 Awa
arr G.Williams   2+3picc.4+ca.4+bcl.4+cbsn/8561/timp.perc/2hp/str [Arranger] 13116
arr A.Winter   PC 1(picc)222/2230/timp.perc/str   Hawkes   8735 B

LLANDOVER WELSH REEL
arr Gerrard Williams   φ 1121/220.btbn.0/timp.perc/str   [Arranger]   MS 31371

The MARCH OF THE MEN OF HARLECH (Rhyfelgyrch gwyr Harlech)(traditional)
in F, arr H.Carr   φ 1111/1120/timp.perc/hp/str   [Arranger]   MS 8237
in G, arr R.Chignell   φ 1111/1120/timp.perc/hp/str   [Arranger]   MS 5558
in Bb, arr H.Evans, orch G.Vinter for mv-chorus & orch
φ 2222/4230/timp.perc/str   (Ed Pub Co.,Wrexham) 22384 +

GREAT BRITAIN - WALES (cont)

NATIONAL AIRS (cont)
  The MARCH OF THE MEN OF HARLECH (cont)

arr A.Hohenstein	PC	2(picc)222/4231/timp.perc/str	Benjamin	16363 +
arr M.L.Lake	PC	112.2sx.1/2210/perc/str	C.Fischer	19720
arr R.M.Price		1222/4230/timp.perc/hp/str	[Arranger]	19330
arr G.Williams	⌀	2222/4231/timp.perc/str (each section of the orchestra is complete in itself & may be used together or separately)	[Arranger]	5293
arr A.Winter	PC	1(picc)222/2230/timp.perc/str	Hawkes	8735 B

GREECE

NATIONAL ANTHEM
  SEGNŌRIZŌ APO (Nicolaos Manzaros), adopted 1864

	PC	2(picc)222/4230/timp.perc/str	Breitkopf	14305
arr W.G.Chapman	PC	2+picc.22.4sx.2/4231/timp.perc/str	Hawkes,1944	20361
arr A.Franzel	⌀	2222/4331/timp.perc/hp/str	[Arranger]	19633
arr A.Hohenstein	PC	2(picc)222/4231/timp.perc/str	Benjamin	16363 +
arr M.L.Lake	PC	112.2sx.1/2210/perc/str	C.Fischer	19720
arr Seredy	PC	112.2sx.1/2210/perc/bjo/str	Apollo	19275

NATIONAL MARCH
  MAYP'EIN'H NYXTA (G.Sailer)

arr Seredy	PC	112.2sx.1/2210/perc/bjo/str	Apollo	19276

GUATEMALA

NATIONAL ANTHEM
  GUATEMALA FELIZ (Guatemala, blest land)(Rafael Alvarez), adopted 1896; modified 1934

	PC	2(picc)222/4220/str	Benjamin	16364
arr M.L.Lake	PC	112.2sx.1/2210/perc/str	C.Fischer	19720
see also BAND CATALOGUE				

GUINEA

NATIONAL ANTHEM
  LIBERTÉ (Alfa Yaya)[independence 2 October, 1958]

arr G.French	⌀	2222/2230/timp.perc/str	(Blandford)	25507 +

GUYANA   see   BAND CATALOGUE

HAITI

NATIONAL ANTHEM
  La DESSALINIENNE (Pour le pays/March on!)(Nicholas Geffrard, 1904)

	PC	2(picc)222/4230/timp.perc/str	Breitkopf	14305

HAWAII   see   UNITED STATES OF AMERICA - HAWAII

HOLLAND   see   The NETHERLANDS

HONDURAS

NATIONAL ANTHEM
  TU BANDERA (Compatriotas de Honduras los Fueros/As your standard)(Carlos Härtling), adopted 1915

	PC	2(picc)222/4220/str	Benjamin	16364
	PC	2(picc)222/4230/timp.perc/str	Breitkopf	14305
arr G.French	⌀	2222/2230/timp.perc/str	(Blandford)	25223 +

HONDURAS (cont)

NATIONAL AIRS
    DIOS SALVE A HONDURAS: patriotic song
        arr M.L.Lake   PC 112.2sx.1/2210/perc/str   C.Fischer   19720

HUNGARY

NATIONAL ANTHEMS
    ISTEN, ÁLDD MEG A MAGYART (Ferencz Erkel), adopted 1844

	PC	2(picc)222/4231/timp.perc/str	Breitkopf	14305
	∅	3+picc.2+ca.4+bcl.4+cbsn/6561/timp.perc/2hp/str	[BBC]	13639
in E♭	∅	2222/2230/timp/str	[BBC]	6578
arr A.Franzel	∅	2222/42.2cnt.31/timp.perc/str	[Arranger]	19519
arr A.Hohenstein	PC	2(picc)222/4231/timp.perc/str	Benjamin	16363 +
arr A.Kotasek	PC	2121/2210/perc/str	Nordska,1956	22100
arr G.Williams	∅	2222/4331/timp.perc/hp/str	[Arranger]	19632

    SZOZAT (Swear, Hungarian, by thy country)(Benjamin Egressy)

	PC	2(picc)222/4230/timp.perc/str	Breitkopf	14305
arr A.Hohenstein	PC	2(picc)222/4231/timp.perc/str	Benjamin	16363 +
arr M.L.Lake	PC	112.2sx.1/2210/perc/str	C.Fischer	19720

NATIONAL AIRS
    HUNGARIAN NATIONAL MARCH (J.Haydn, 1802 [H.VIII:4])
                    ∅ 0222/2100/(no str)   Doblinger,1959   23127
    RAKOCZY MARCH
        arr A.Hohenstein   PC 2(picc)222/4231/timp.perc/str   Benjamin   16363 +

ICELAND

NATIONAL ANTHEM
    O GUD VORS LANDS (Sveinbjörn Sveinbjörnsson, 1874)

		2222/4230/timp/str	[BBC]	Misc 510
	PC	2(picc)222/4230/timp.perc/str	Breitkopf	14305
arr A.Franzel	∅	2222/42.2cnt.31/timp.perc/str	[Arranger]	19518
arr G.French	∅	2222/2230/timp.perc/str	(Blandford)	25512 +

INDIA

NATIONAL ANTHEM
    JANĂ GANĂ MANĂ (Rabindranath Tagore), adopted 1950

arr G.French	∅	2222/2230/timp.perc/str	(Blandford)	25226 +
arr H.Murrill	∅	22+ca.2+bcl.2+cbsn/4231/timp.perc/str	[Arranger]	19805
arr S.Sharan	∅	2222/4230/timp.perc/hp[=pf]/str	Music Board, Calcutta	Misc 3224

NATIONAL AIRS
    BALAHARI SWAVAJATI: traditional song
        arr Redman   ∅ 1110/0000/perc/pf/str   [Arranger]   MS 20276

INDONESIA

NATIONAL ANTHEM   see BAND CATALOGUE
NATIONAL SONGS
    INDONESIA RAJA: patriotic song (Th.H.E.Loing)
        arr A.Franzel   ∅ 2+picc.222/4331/timp.perc/str   [Arranger]   19586

IRAN

NATIONAL ANTHEM
    SHAHHANSHAHEMAW ZENDE (Long live the Shah)(Lt. Najmi Moghaddam), adopted 1944
        orch W.G.Chapman   ∅ 222.4sx.2/4230/timp.perc/str   Hawkes,1944   22888

IRAN (cont)

FORMER NATIONAL ANTHEM
  SALAMATI SCHAH (General Lemaire)
                              PC 2(picc)222/4220/str   Benjamin   16364
        arr M.L.Lake   PC 112.2sx.1/2210/perc/str   C.Fischer   19720
NATIONAL AIRS
  PATRIOTIC SONG   PC 2(picc)222/4220/str   Benjamin   16364

IRAQ

NATIONAL ANTHEM   see   BAND CATALOGUE
NATIONAL AIRS
  ROYAL FANFARE (attrib Alan Murray or A.Chaffoo)
        orch M.Saunders   ∅ 2222/4230/timp.perc/hp/str   [Arranger]   21440

IRELAND   see   EIRE   and   GREAT BRITAIN - IRELAND

ISRAEL

NATIONAL ANTHEM
  HATIKVAH (Kol owd ba-lay-vov p'nee-moh)
        arr & orch B.Benas   ∅ 2222+cbsn/2231/timp/hp/str   R.Mazin   19738

ITALY

NATIONAL ANTHEM
  IL CANTO DEGLI ITALIANI (Inno di Mameli)(Fratelli d'Italia)(Michel Novaro), adopted 2 June, 1946
        arr A.Franzel   ∅ 2+picc.222/4331/timp.perc/str   [Arranger]   19587
        arr A.Hohenstein   PC 2(picc)222/4231/timp.perc/str   Benjamin   16363 +
        arr F.Salabert   PC 1(picc)221/223[1]/timp.perc/str   Salabert   3816
        arr M.Seiber   ∅ 212.sx.0/2230/perc/str   [Arranger]   19740
        see also   BAND CATALOGUE
FORMER NATIONAL ANTHEMS
  GARIBALDI'S HYMN (Inno di gierra)(attrib A.Olivieri)
        arr A.Hohenstein   PC 2(picc)222/4231/timp.perc/str   Benjamin   16363 +
        arr M.L.Lake   PC 112.2sx.1/2210/perc/str   C.Fischer   19720
        arr M.Seiber   ∅ 2120/2230/timp.perc/str   (Ricordi)   14996
  La GIOVINEZZA (Giuseppe Blanc & G.Castaldo)(suppressed in 1944)
                              PC 2(picc)222/4231/timp.perc/str   Breitkopf   14305

  MARCIA REALE (Royal march)(G.Gabetti)
                              PC 2(picc)222/4230/timp.perc/str   Breitkopf   14305
        arr A.Hohenstein   PC 2(picc)222/4231/timp.perc/str   Benjamin   16363 +
        arr M.L.Lake   PC 112.2sx.1/2210/perc/str   C.Fischer   19720
NATIONAL AIRS
  L'ADDIO DEL VOLUNTARIO (The Volunteer's farewell): Florentine traditional song
        arr M.L.Lake   PC 112.2sx.1/2210/perc/str   C.Fischer   19720
  HYMN TO PIUS IX
        arr A.Hohenstein   PC 2(picc)222/4231/timp.perc/str   Benjamin   16363 +
  NATIONAL MILITARY AIRS OF ITALY: selection, arr G.Marchisio
                                    1+picc.221/4230/perc/str   Ricordi   3016

  SANTA LUCIA: Neapolitan song
        arr M.L.Lake   PC 112.2sx.1/2210/perc/str   C.Fischer   19720

IVORY COAST   see   BAND CATALOGUE

JAMAICA

NATIONAL ANTHEM
 ETERNAL FATHER BLESS OUR LAND (Robert Lightbourne), adopted 19 July 1962
  arr T.Wade   φ 2222/4230/str   [Arranger,1976] 26079
   see also BAND CATALOGUE

JAPAN

NATIONAL ANTHEM
 KIMAGAYO (revised F.Eckert), adopted 12 August, 1893
        PC 2(picc)222/4220/str   Benjamin 16364
        PC 2(picc)222/4230/timp.perc/str   Breitkopf 14305
        PC 1+picc.222/2230.euph/perc/str Hawkes 1837
  arr G.Jacob   φ 2222/4331/timp.perc/str   [Arranger] 20733
  arr M.L.Lake   PC 112.2sx.1/2210/perc/str   C.Fischer 19720
NATIONAL AIRS
 FOU SO KA
  arr M.L.Lake   PC 112.2sx.1/2210/perc/str   C.Fischer 19720

JORDAN

NATIONAL ANTHEM
 'ASHAAL MALEEK (Abdulkadir At-Tannir), adopted 25 May, 1946
  orch M.Saunders   φ 2222/4230/timp.perc/hp/str   [Arranger] 21439

JUGOSLAVIA see YUGOSLAVIA

KUWAIT

NATIONAL ANTHEM, adopted 1951
 arr G.French   φ 1+picc.222/2230/timp.perc/str (Blandford) 25511 +

LAOS see BAND CATALOGUE

LATVIA see UNION OF SOCIALIST SOVIET REPUBLICS - LATVIA

LESOTHO

NATIONAL ANTHEM (L.Laur, 19th cent), adopted 2 May, 1967
 arr G.French   φ 2222/2230/timp.perc/str   (Blandford) 25510 +

LIBERIA

NATIONAL ANTHEM
 SALVE, LIBERIA, SALVE (All Hail, Liberia)(Olmstead Luca)
  arr M.L.Lake   PC 112.2sx.1/2210/perc/str   C.Fischer 19720

LIBYA see BAND CATALOGUE

LIECHTENSTEIN

NATIONAL ANTHEM
 OBEN AM DEUTSCHEN RHEIN (composer unknown)
  arr G.French   φ 1+picc.222/2230/timp.perc/str (Blandford) 25509
   see also GREAT BRITAIN, NATIONAL ANTHEM

LITHUANIA   see   BAND CATALOGUE, UNION OF SOCIALIST SOVIET REPUBLICS - LITHUANIA

LUXEMBOURG

NATIONAL ANTHEM
   ONS HÉMECHT (Wò d'Uolzécht duréch d'Wisen zĕt)(J.A.Zinnen), adopted 1895

	PC	2(picc)222/4230/timp.perc/str	Breitkopf	14305
arr J.Greenwood	φ	1010/0000/hp/str	[Arranger]	10534
arr A.Hohenstein	PC	2(picc)222/4231/timp.perc/str	Benjamin	16363 +
arr L.Salter for unison voices & orch				
	φ	1111/2110/str	[Arranger]	2032 +
arr G.Williams	φ	1010/0000/str	[Arranger]	8116

NATIONAL AIRS
   AN AMÉRIKA: Luxembourg song

in A, arr Williams	φ	1010/0000/hp/str	[Arranger]	14528

   6 LUXEMBOURG SONGS, arr J.Greenwood

1. de Withelmus   4. Drei Froen
2. Ons Hernecht   5. Hemechtsleft
3. Drei Farwen   6. Ons Freihet

	φ	1010/0000/hp/str	[Arranger]	10534

MADAGASCAR   see   BAND CATALOGUE

MALAWI

NATIONAL ANTHEM
   O GOD BLESS MALAWI (Mlungu dalitsani Malawi)(Michael-Fred P.Sauka), adopted 1964

arr G.French	φ	2222/2230/timp.perc/str	(Govt of Malawi)	25208 +

MALAYSIA   see   BAND CATALOGUE

MALI   see   BAND CATALOGUE

MALTA

NATIONAL ANTHEM
   INNU MALTI (Hymn of Malta)(Robert Sammut), adopted 1941

arr G.Frnech	φ	2222/2230/timp.perc/str	(Bladford)	25207 +

MEXICO

NATIONAL ANTHEM
   CIÑA, OH PATRIA (Jaime Nunó)

	PC	2(picc)222/4230/timp.perc/str	Breitkopf	14305
	PC	2(picc)222/4220/str	Benjamin	16364
arr W.Chapman	PC	2+picc.22.4sx.2/4231/timp.perc/str	Hawkes,1944	20361
arr M.L.Lake	PC	112.2sx.1/2210/perc/str	C.Fischer	19720

MONACO

NATIONAL ANTHEM
   PRINCIPAUTÉ MONACO MA PATRIE (Albrecht), 1st performed 1867

	PC	2(picc)222/4230/timp.perc/str	Breitkopf	14305
arr G.French	φ	2222/2230/timp.perc/str	(Blandford)	25506 +
arr L.Jehin	PC	1(picc)222/4231/timp.perc/str	Decourcelle	7274

MONTENEGRO   see   YUGOSLAVIA - MONTENEGRO

MOROCCO   see   BAND CATALOGUE

NAURU

NATIONAL ANTHEM
   SONG OF NAURU (L.H.Hicks), composed for independence 31 January, 1968

arr G.French	⌀ 2222/2230/timp.perc/str	[Arranger]	25521 +

The NETHERLANDS

NATIONAL ANTHEM
   WILHELMUS VAN NASSOUWE (anon)

	PC 2(picc)222/4230/timp.perc/str	Breitkopf	14305
arr A.Franzel	⌀ 2121/2230/timp.perc/hp/str	[Arranger]	MS 20142
arr A.Franzel	⌀ 2222/4331/timp.perc/hp/str	[Arranger]	19635
arr A.Hohenstein	PC 2(picc)222/4231/timp.perc/str	Benjamin	16363 +

ALTERNATIVE NATIONAL ANTHEM
   WIEN NEERLANDS BLOED IN D'ADEREN VLOEIT (Jan Wilms)

arr A.Hohenstein	PC 2(picc)222/4231/timp.perc/str	Benjamin	16363 +
arr M.L.Lake	PC 112.2sx.1/2210/perc/str	C.Fischer	19720

NATIONAL AIRS
   DANKGEBET (Prayer of Thanksgiving)(E.Kreuser)

arr A.Hohenstein	PC 2(picc)222/4231/timp.perc/str	Benjamin	16363 +

NEW ZEALAND

NATIONAL ANTHEM: British National Anthem is used by New Zealand   see   GREAT BRITAIN
NATIONAL SONG
   GOD DEFEND NEW ZEALAND (John J.Woods)

arr R.Chignell	⌀ 2222/4231/timp.perc/str	[Arranger]	13751
arr R.Chignell	⌀ 1121/2210/perc/hp/str	[Arranger]	13763
arr M.L.Lake	PC 112.2sx.1/2210/perc/str	C.Fischer	19720

NICARAGUA

NATIONAL ANTHEM
   SALVE A TÍ NICARAGUE (Hail Nicaragua)

	PC 2(picc)222/4230/timp.perc/str	Breitkopf	14305
arr M.L.Lake	PC 112.2sx.1/2210/perc/str	C.Fischer	19720

NATIONAL AIRS
   HERMOSA SOBERANA (A.Cousin)   PC   2(picc)222/4220/str

		Benjamin	16364

NIGERIA   see   BAND CATALOGUE

NORWAY

NATIONAL ANTHEM
   JA VI ELSKER DETTE LANDET (The Song of Norway)(Rikard Nordraak), adopted 1864

	PC 2(picc)222/4230/timp.perc/str	Breitkopf	14305
arr G.Bantock	⌀ 2+picc.2+ca.2+bcl.2+cbsn/4331/timp.perc/hp/str	[Arranger]	19631
arr A.Franzel	⌀ 2121/2230/perc/str	[Arranger]	19506
arr A.Hohenstein	PC 2(picc)222/4231/timp.perc/str	Benjamin	16363 +
arr H.Perry	PC 1+picc.22.3sx.2/4230/timp.perc/str	Hawkes	16841 Cp

NORWAY (cont)

ALTERNATIVE NATIONAL ANTHEM
    SØNNER AF NORGES DET AELDGAMLE RIGE (Chr. Blom)
        arr A.Hohenstein   PC 2(picc)222/4231/timp.perc/str   Benjamin   16363 +
        arr M.L.Lake   PC 112.2sx.1/2210/perc/str   C.Fischer   19720
NATIONAL SONGS
    BOER JEG PAA DET HØJE FJELD: traditional song
        arr A.Hohenstein   PC 2(picc)222/4231/timp.perc/str   Benjamin   16363 +

PAKISTAN see   BAND CATALOGUE

PANAMA

NATIONAL ANTHEM
    ALCANZAMOS POR FIN LA VICTORIA (Santos Jorgea), first used 4 November, 1903
                      PC 2(picc)222/4230/timp.perc/str   Breitkopf   14305
        arr M.L.Lake   PC 112.2sx.1/2210/perc/str   C.Fischer   19720

PARAGUAY

NATIONAL ANTHEM
    PARAGUAYOS, REPÚBLICA Ó MUERTE (A los pueblos de América infausto/Once the lands of America)(F.A.de
        Figueros), adopted 1846; official version arr R.Gimenez, 1934
                      PC 2(picc)222/4220/str   Benjamin   16364 +
        orch N.Fulton   φ 2222/2230/timp.perc/str   (Blandford) 24093 +
        arr M.L.Lake   PC 112.2sx.1/2210/perc/str   C.Fischer   19720

PERSIA see   IRAN

PERU

NATIONAL ANTHEM
    SIMOS LIBRES, SEAMOS LO SIEMPRE (José Bernardo Alzedo, rev C.Rebagliati, 1821)
                      PC 2(picc)222/4220/str   Benjamin   16364
                      PC 2(picc)222/4230/timp.perc/str   Breitkopf   14305
                      PC 112.2sx.1/2210/perc/str   C.Fischer   19720
        arr M.L.Lake
        see also   BAND CATALOGUE

The PHILIPPINES

NATIONAL ANTHEM
    TIERRA ADORADA (Julian Felipe)
                      PC 2(picc)222/4230/timp.perc/str   Breitkopf   14305
NATIONAL AIRS
    AUG PALIMOS: patriotic song
        arr M.L.Lake   PC 112.2sx.1/2210/perc/str   C.Fischer   19720

POLAND

NATIONAL ANTHEM
    JESZCZE POLSKA NIE ZGINEŁA (Dabrowski anthem)(Josef Wybicki), adopted 1927
        Orig version   PC 2(picc)222/4230/timp.perc/str   Breitkopf   14305
            arr G.Bantock   φ 2+picc.2+ca.2+bcl.2+cbsn/4331/timp.perc/str [Arranger] 19646
            arr A.Carse   φ 2222/4231/timp.perc/str   Augener   16092 B
            arr A.Franzel   φ 2222/4331/timp.perc/hp/str   [Arranger] 19647 +
            arr A.Hohenstein   PC 2(picc)222/4231/timp.perc/str   Benjamin   16363 +

POLAND (cont)

NATIONAL ANTHEM (cont)
    Orig version (cont)
        arr M.L.Lake   PC 112.2sx.1/2210/perc/str   C.Fischer   19720
        arr H.Perry   1+picc.22.3sx.2/4230/timp.perc/str   Hawkes   16841 Cp
        arr S.Robinson   str   [Arranger]   MS 5669
    Rev version (1948), arr Sikorsky
        orch Maklakeivicz   PC 2121/2210/timp.perc/str   Polish SM   21659 +
NATIONAL AIRS
    BOŻE COS POLSKE (K.Kurpinski)
        arr A.Hohenstein   PC 2(picc)222/4231/timp.perc/str   Benjamin   16363 +
    POLISH UNDERGROUND SONG
        arr C.H.Moore   1121/2230/str   [Arranger]   5389
    ZDYMEN POZARÓW (Józef Nikorowicz)
        arr A.Hohenstein   PC 2(picc)222/4231/timp.perc/str   Benjamin   16363 +

PORTUGAL

NATIONAL ANTHEM
    HEROIS DO MAR (Alfredo Keil), adopted 1910
                               PC 2(picc)222/4230/timp.perc/str   Breitkopf   14305
        arr F.Salabert   PC 1(picc)221/223[1]/timp.perc/str   Salabert   3816 +
        arr W.G.Chapman   PC 2+picc.22.4sx.2/4231/timp.perc/str   Hawkes,1944 20361
        see also   BAND CATALOGUE
FORMER NATIONAL ANTHEM
    O PATRIA, O REI, O POVO (King Pedro IV of Portugal)
        arr A.Hohenstein   PC 2(picc)222/4231/timp.perc/str   Benjamin   16363 +
        arr M.L.Lake   PC 112.2sx.1/2210/perc/str   C.Fischer   19720

PRUSSIA   see   GERMANY - REGIONS, PRUSSIA

QATAR

NATIONAL ANTHEM
    arr G.French   ∅   0.2picc.222/2230/timp.perc/str   (Blandford) 25508 +

ROMANIA (Rumania)

NATIONAL ANTHEM
    TE SLÁVIM, ROMÂNIE (We glorify thee, Romania)(Matel Socor), adopted 1953
        arr G.French   ∅   2222/2230/timp.perc/str   (Blandford) 25513 +
        arr N.Fulton   ∅   2222/4330/timp.perc/str   (Blandford) 24113 +
FORMER NATIONAL ANTHEM
    TRĂEASCĂ REGELE ÎN PACE SI ONOR (E.A.Hübsch)
                               PC 2(picc)222/4230/timp.perc/str   Breitkopf   14305
        arr A.Franzel   ∅   2222/4331/timp.perc/str   [Arranger]   19648
        arr A.Hohenstein   PC 2(picc)222/4231/timp.perc/str   Benjamin   16363 +
        arr M.L.Lake   PC 112.2sx.1/2210/perc/str   C.Fischer   19720
NATIONAL AIRS
    ROMANIAN ANTHEM (not the National Anthem)
        arr G.Walter   ∅   1120/2210/timp/hp/str   [Arranger]   19654

RUSSIA   see   UNION OF SOCIALIST SOVIET REPUBLICS

EL SALVADOR

NATIONAL ANTHEM
   SALUDEMOS LA PATRIA ORGUILLOSOS (Mother country, thy people salute thee!)(Jean Aberle), adopted 1953
                                  PC 2(picc)222/4220/str   Benjamin   16364
                                  PC 2(picc)222/4230/timp.perc/str   Breitkopf   14305
       arr M.L.Lake   PC 112.2sx.1/2210/perc/str   C.Fischer   19720
          see also   BAND CATALOGUE

SAN MARINO

NATIONAL ANTHEM
   ONORE A TE (Federico Consolo)
       arr G.French   ∅   2(picc)222/2230/timp.perc.glock.vib/str   (Blandford)   25519 +

SARAWAK   see   MALAYSIA

SAUDI ARABIA

NATIONAL ANTHEM (Abdur Rehman Al-Hatib), adopted 1950
       arr G.French   ∅   1+picc.222/2230/timp.perc/str   (Blandford)   25225 +
NATIONAL AIRS
   SONG
       arr M.L.Lake   PC   112.2sx.1/2210/perc/str   C.Fischer   19720

SCOTLAND   see   GREAT BRITAIN - SCOTLAND

SERBIA   see   YUGOSLAVIA

SIAM   see   THAILAND

SIERRA LEONE   see   BAND CATALOGUE

SINGAPORE   see   BAND CATALOGUE

SOMALIA   see   BAND CATALOGUE

SOUTH AFRICA

NATIONAL ANTHEM
   Die STEM VAN SUID-AFRIKA (M.L.de Villiers), adopted 1936
                                  PC 2(picc)222/4230/timp.perc/str   Breitkopf   14305
       arr A.Franzel   ∅   2+picc.222+cbsn/4331/timp.perc/str   [Arranger]   19651
       arr G.Jacob   ∅   2+picc.222/4331/timp.perc/str   [Arranger]   20734
NATIONAL AIRS
   SARIE MARAIS: popular song
       arr G.Jacob   ∅   2(picc)222/4331/timp.perc/str   [Arranger]   20731

SPAIN

NATIONAL ANTHEM
   MARCHA REAL, adopted July, 1942
       arr A.Franzel   ∅   1+picc.222/4331/timp.perc/hp/str   [Arranger]   19649
       arr A.Hohenstein   PC   2(picc)222/4231/timp.perc/str   Benjamin   16363 +
       arr M.L.Lake   PC   112.2sx.1/2210/perc/str   C.Fischer   19720

SPAIN (cont)

FORMER NATIONAL ANTHEM
   HIMNO DE RIEGO (Soldados la Pátria)(Herta)

	PC	2(picc)222/4230/timp.perc/str	Breitkopf	14305
arr A.Hohenstein	PC	2(picc)222/4231/timp.perc/str	Benjamin	16363 +

NATIONAL AIRS
   CONSTITUTION HYMN

arr A.Hohenstein	PC	2(picc)222/4231/timp.perc/str	Benjamin	16363 +

   JUANITA: Spanish air

arr M.L.Lake	PC	112.2sx.1/2210/perc/str	C.Fischer	19720

   REPUBLICAN HYMN (R.Torralba)

	PC	111.2sx.1/2210/perc/str	Garzon	12762

   ROYAL MARCH   see   NATIONAL ANTHEM

SRI LANKA

NATIONAL ANTHEM
   SRI LANKA MARTHA, adopted 1952 (first two words changed from 'Namo Namo' in 1973 - music retained)

arr G.French	ø	21+ca.22/2230/timp.perc/str	(Blandford)	25224 +
arr G.Jacob	ø	2+picc.222/4331/timp.perc/str	[Arranger]	20732

SUDAN   see   BAND CATALOGUE

SWAZILAND   see   BAND CATALOGUE

SWEDEN

NATIONAL ANTHEM
   DU GAMLA, DU FRIA (folk melody), adopted 1880-90)

	PC	2(picc)222/4230/timp.perc/str	Breitkopf	14305
arr A.Hohenstein	PC	2(picc)222/4231/timp.perc/str	Benjamin	16363 +
arr E.Kallstenius	ø	2222/4[=2]23[=1][1]/timp/str	[Arranger]	Misc 2582

ALTERNATIVE NATIONAL ANTHEM
   UR SVENSKA HJERTANS DJUP EN GANG (King's Anthem)(O.Lindblad)

arr H.Berens	ø	1+picc.222/4230/timp.perc/str	[Arranger]	Misc 1735
arr A.Franzel	ø	2222/4331/str	[Arranger]	19650
arr A.Hohenstein	PC	2(picc)222/4231/timp.perc/str	Benjamin	16363 +
arr M.L.Lake	PC	112.2sx.1/2210/perc/str	C.Fischer	19720

NATIONAL AIRS
   HELL DIG, DU HÖGA NORD (B.Crusell): patriotic song

arr A.Hohenstein	PC	2(picc)222/4231/timp.perc/str	Benjamin	16363 +

SWITZERLAND

NATIONAL ANTHEM
   SCHWEIZERPSALM (Trittst im Morgenrot daher)(Alberik Zwyssig), adopted September 1961 for a trial period

		2+3picc.4+ca.4+bcl.4+cbsn/8561/timp.perc/str	[BBC]	13638
arr A.Franzel	ø	2+picc.222/42.2cnt.31/timp.perc/str	[Arranger]	19522
arr A.Hohenstein	ø	2(picc)222/4231/timp.perc/str	Benjamin	16363 +
arr Scassola	VS	1221/2230/timp.perc/str	Foetsich	6425

FORMER NATIONAL ANTHEM
   RUFST DU, MEIN VATERLAND   see   GREAT BRITAIN: NATIONAL ANTHEM

NATIONAL AIRS
   BERNER-MARSCH: TRÄM, TRÄM, TRÄMDERIDI

arr A.Hohenstein	PC	2(picc)222/4231/timp.perc/str	Benjamin	16363 +

SYRIA

NATIONAL ANTHEM   see   BAND CATALOGUE
NATIONAL AIRS   C.Fischer   19720
   TYPICAL AIR, arr M.L.Lake   PC   112.2sx.1/2210/perc/str

TAIWAN   see   CHINA

TANGANYIKA   see   TANZANIA

TANZANIA

NATIONAL ANTHEM
   MUNGU IBARIKI AFRICA (former National Anthem of Tanganyika, retained on union with Zanzibar, 1964:
      17 bar arrangement of the anthem for the whole continent of Africa)(Enoch Sontonga)
                                                                   (Blandford)   25520 +
      arr G.French   ø   2222/2230/timp.perc/str
      arr N.Fulton   ø   2222/4230/timp/str   (Lovedale Press, South Africa)   23456 +
        see also   BAND CATALOGUE
FORMER NATIONAL ANTHEM OF ZANZIBAR
   The SULTAN'S HYMN (D.Tovey)   C.Fischer   19720
      arr M.L.Lake   PC   112.2sx.1/2210/perc/str

THAILAND

NATIONAL ANTHEM
   SANRASOEN PHRA BARAMI (Huvitzen, 1872), adopted 1934   Benjamin   16364
                PC   2(picc)222/4220/str   C.Fischer   19720
      arr M.L.Lake   PC   112.2sx.1/2210/perc/str

TOGO

NATIONAL ANTHEM
   MIEDO GBE NAWO, TOGUIWO! (Salut à Toi, pays de nos/Hail th thee, land of our forefathers)(Alex
      Casimir-Dossek), adopted on independence, 1960   (Blandford)   25505 +
      arr G.French   ø   1+picc.222/2230/timp.perc/str

TONGA   see   BAND CATALOGUE

TRANSJORDAN   see   JORDAN

TRINIDAD & TOBAGO   see   BAND CATALOGUE

TUNISIA

NATIONAL ANTHEM   see   BAND CATALOGUE
PATRIOTIC SONGS
   1. Ed ozil   2. El asbain   3. Rèsed el osil   Benjamin   16364
                  PC   2(picc)222/4220/str

TURKEY

NATIONAL ANTHEM
   KORKMA, SÖNMEZ BU SAFAK (Istiklâl Marsi/The March of independence)(Osman Zeki Üngör), adopted
      12 March 1921   Breitkopf   14305
                PC   2(picc)222/4230/timp.perc/str   (Blandford)   25209 +
      arr G.French   ø   2222/2230/timp.perc/str

TURKEY (cont)

FORMER NATIONAL ANTHEMS
   FORMER NATIONAL ANTHEM
      arr A.Hohenstein   PC 2(picc)222/4231/timp.perc/str   Benjamin   16363 +
   EI VATAN EI UMMI (Aug.G.Selvelli)
      arr A.Hohenstein   PC 2(picc)222/4231/timp.perc/str   Benjamin   16363 +
   OUR GOD, SAVE TO US OUR SULTAN (Nedjib-Pasha)
      arr M.L.Lake   PC 1+picc.12.2sx.1/2210/perc/str   C.Fischer   19720
NATIONAL AIRS
   MARCH OF THE SULTAN
      arr A.Hohenstein   PC 2(picc)222/4230/timp.perc/str   Benjamin   16363 +

UGANDA   see   BAND CATALOGUE

UNION OF SOCIALIST SOVIET REPUBLICS

NATIONAL ANTHEM
   GIMN SOVETSKOVO SOYUZA (A.V.Aleksandrov)(1944 edn)
                  ø 2+picc.222/4431/timp.perc/str   Russian SM 7338 +
                  ø 2+picc.222+cbsn/4331/timp.perc/hp/str   [BBC]   15567 B
FORMER NATIONAL ANTHEM
   GOD SAVE OUR NOBLE TSAR (A.Lvov)
      arr J.Fitz-Gerald   PC 2222/2230/timp.perc/str   Hawkes   1839
      arr D.Godfrey   PC 2222/4230/timp.perc/str   Chappell   2867
      arr A.Hohenstein   PC 2(picc)222/4231/timp.perc/str   Benjamin   16363 +
      arr Kasanli for chorus & orch
                  ø 2[1]2[1]/2210/perc/str   Chester   Misc 499
      arr M.L.Lake   PC 112.2sx.1/2210/perc/str   C.Fischer   19720
   The INTERNATIONAL (Debout, les damnés de la terre (Pierre Degeyter)
      arr G.Bantock   PC 2121/4230/timp.perc/str   Goodwin & T 433
      arr A.Franzel   ø 1+picc.222+cbsn/4331/timp.perc/str   [Arranger] 19616
      arr A.Franzel   ø 2+picc.2+ca.32+cbsn/4431/timp.perc/hp/str [Arranger] 5222
NATIONAL SONG
   The LAND OF FREEDOM: song by Isaac Dunayevsky (1900-)
      in G, arr Bishop   PC 112.4sx.1/2330/timp.perc/gtr/str   Boosey & H 16800
      in G, arr Isaacs   ø 3222/4331/timp.perc/str   [BBC]   4655
   The RED SARAFÀN
      arr J.Fritz-Gerald   PC 2222/2230/timp.perc/str   Hawkes   1839
   SCHÖNE MINKA
      arr J.Fritz-Gerald   PC 2222/2230/timp.perc/str   Hawkes   1839
   SONG OF THE VOLGA BOATMEN ø 1121/2210/timp/str   [BBC]   Misc 555
   SONG OF YOUTH (Salute to life)
      orch L.Isaacs   ø 3222/2100/perc/hp/str   [Arranger] 13006
   TROIKA SONG
      arr J.Fitz-Gerald   PC 2222/2230/timp.perc/str   Hawkes   1839
   VIELE JAHRE DEM KAISER
      arr A.Hohenstein   PC 2(picc)222/4231/timp.perc/str   Benjamin   16363 +

USSR - ARMENIA

NATIONAL AIRS
   NOR OGHCHIOON (Glad Tidings)(Bishop Minas)
      arr M.L.Lake   PC 112.2sx.1/2210/perc/str   C.Fischer   19720

USSR - ESTONIA

FORMER NATIONAL ANTHEM
    MU ISAMAA, MU ÕNN JA RÕÕM (Fredrik Pacius)
                            PC 2(picc)222/4230/timp.perc/str   Breitkopf   14305

USSR - LATVIA

FORMER NATIONAL ANTHEM
        DIEVS, SVETI LATVIJU (Karlis Baumanis, 1873)
                            PC 2(picc)222/4230/timp.perc/str   Breitkopf   14305

UNITED ARAB REPUBLIC   see   BAND CATALOGUE

UNITED STATES OF AMERICA

NATIONAL ANTHEM
    The STAR-SPANGLED BANNER (attrib John S.Smith; formerly attrib Samuel Arnold), adopted 3 March, 1931
                            PC 2(picc)222/4230/timp.perc/str   Breitkopf   14305
                            PC 2(picc)222/4220/str   Benjamin   16364
                            ø   2222/4231/timp.perc/str   [BBC]   19653
        in Bb, arr F.M.Collinson   ø 1121/2220/hp/str   [Arranger]   MS 30863
        in Bb, arr W.Walton (1965)
                            ø   2+picc.32+bcl.2+cbsn/4331/timp.perc/2hp/str   [Arranger]   24161 C +
        arr J.Fitz-Gerald   PC 1222/2230.euph/perc/str   Hawkes   1841
        arr M.L.Lake   PC 112.2sx.1/2210/perc/str   C.Fischer   19720
        arr F.Salabert   PC 1(picc)221/223[1]/timp.perc/str   Salabert   3816
NATIONAL AIRS
    ABRAHAM'S DAUGHTER (Raw Recruits)(traditional)
        arr M.L.Lake   PC 112.2sx.1/2210/perc/str   C.Fischer   19720
    The BATTLE-CRY OF FREEDOM (G.F.Root)
        arr M.L.Lake   PC 112.2sx.1/2210/perc/str   C.Fischer   19720
    BINGO (Old Nassau)(traditional)
        arr M.L.Lake   PC 112.2sx.1/2210/perc/str   C.Fischer   19720
    The BULL-DOG (traditional)
        arr M.L.Lake   PC 112.2sx.1/2210/perc/str   C.Fischer   19720
    CARRY THE NEWS (traditional)
        arr M.L.Lake   PC 112.2sx.1/2210/perc/str   C.Fischer   19720
    FAIR HARVARD: college song
        arr M.L.Lake   PC 112.2sx.1/2210/perc/str   C.Fischer   19720
    GLORY, GLORY, HALLELUJIA (John Brown's body)(arr W.Steffe)
        arr M.L.Lake   PC 112.2sx.1/2210/perc/str   C.Fischer   19720
    GOOD-NIGHT LADIES (Merrily we roll along)(traditional)
        arr M.L.Lake   PC 112.2sx.1/2210/perc/str   C.Fischer   19720
    HAIL COLUMBIA (P.Phile)   PC 2(picc)222/4220/str   Benjamin   16364
        arr arr J.Fitz-Gerald PC 1222/2230.euph/perc/str   Hawkes   1841
        arr M.L.Lake   PC 112.2sx.1/2210/perc/str   C.Fischer   19720
        arr F.Salabert   PC 1(picc)221/223[1]/timp.perc/str   Salabert   3816
    HOW CAN I LEAVE THEE?   see   GERMANY: NATIONAL AIRS - ACH, WIE IST'S MÖGLICH DANN
    LITORIA (Yale College is a jolly home): college song
        arr M.L.Lake   PC 112.2sx.1/2210/perc/str   C.Fischer   19720
    MARYLAND, MY MARYLAND see GERMANY: NATIONAL AIRS - O TANNENBAUM
    MY COUNTRY, 'TIS OF THEE see   GREAT BRITAIN: NATIONAL ANTHEM
    OLD ZIP COON (Turkey in the straw)(traditional)
        arr M.L.Lake   PC 112.2sx.1/2210/perc/str   C.Fischer   19720
    OUR FLAG IS THERE (traditional)
        arr J.Fitz-Gerald   PC 1222/2230.euph/perc/str   Hawkes   1841
        arr M.L.Lake   PC 112.2sx.1/2210/perc/str   C.Fischer   19720

UNITED STATES OF AMERICA (cont)

NATIONAL AIRS

The QUILTING PARTY (I was seeing Nellie home)(traditional)
    arr M.L.Lake   PC   112.2sx.1/2210/perc/str

The RED, WHITE AND BLUE (Columbia, the Gem of the Ocean)

The QUILTING PARTY (I was seeing Nellie home)(traditional)				
arr M.L.Lake	PC	112.2sx.1/2210/perc/str	C.Fischer	19720
The RED, WHITE AND BLUE (Columbia, the Gem of the Ocean)				
arr R.Barsotti	PC	1+picc.12.4sx.2/4230/perc/str	Boosey & H	21039 B
arr J.Desmond	PC	1222/2230.euph/perc/str	Hawkes	2682
arr M.L.Lake	PC	112.2sx.1/2210/perc/str	C.Fischer	19720
arr A.Winter	PC	1121/1210/perc/cel.hp/str/chorus	Hawkes	6102 Ap
UPIDEE (The Shades of Night were falling)(traditional)				
arr M.L.Lake	PC	112.2sx.1/2210/perc/str	C.Fischer	19720
YANKEE DOODLE (traditional)	PC	2(picc)222/4220/str	Benjamin	16364
arr J.Fitz-Gerald	PC	1222/2230.euph/perc/str	Hawkes	1841
arr M.L.Lake	PC	112.2sx.1/2210/perc/str	C.Fischer	19720
arr F.Salabert	PC	1(picc)221/223[1]/timp.perc/str	Salabert	3816
arr G.Williams	∅	1+picc.121/2230/timp.perc/str	[Arranger]	13227

USA - HAWAII

FORMER NATIONAL ANTHEM

HAWAII PONOI (Our Native Land)(attrib Kalakana, King of Hawaii)				
arr H.Berner	PC	2(picc)222/4220/str	Benjamin	16364
arr M.L.Lake	PC	112.2sx.1/2210/perc/str	C.Fischer	19720

NATIONAL AIRS

ALOHA OE: Hawaiian farewell song (Queen Lilinokalani)				
in A	PC	0020/0100/perc/gtr.pf/str	[BBC]	MS 5937
arr M.L.Lake	PC	112.2sx.1/2210/perc/str	C.Fischer	19720

UPPER VOLTA   see   BAND CATALOGUE

URUGUAY

NATIONAL ANTHEM

ORIENTALES, LA PATRIA Ó LA TUMBA (Juan Coppetti), adopted 18 July, 1845				
	PC	2(picc)222/4220/str	Benjamin	16364
	PC	2(picc)222/4230/timp.perc/str	Breitkopf	14305
arr D.T.Deballi		2+picc.222/2221/timp.perc/str	[Arranger]	19956
arr M.L.Lake	PC	112.2sx.1/2210/perc/str	C.Fischer	19720

VATICAN   see   BAND CATALOGUE

VENEZUELA

NATIONAL ANTHEM

GLORIA AL BRAVO PUEBLO (Juan José Landaeta), adopted 25 May, 1881				
	PC	2(picc)222/4220/str	Benjamin	16364
	PC	2(picc)222/4230/timp.perc/str	Breitkopf	14305
arr M.L.Lake	PC	112.2sx.1/2210/perc/str	C.Fischer	19720

VIETNAM   see   BAND CATALOGUE

WALES   see   GREAT BRITAIN - WALES

WESTERN SAMOA   see   BAND CATALOGUE

YEMEN

NATIONAL ANTHEM
    SALIMTA IMAMANLI 'ARSHIBI LADI (May you be safe)
                             ∅   str [=str-4tet]   [BBC]   Misc 4760

YUGOSLAVIA

NATIONAL ANTHEM
    HEJ SLAVENÍ (same tune as Polish National Anthem), adopted 1945)
        arr & orch P.Sainton   ∅   3222/4231/timp.perc/str   (Yugoslav Embassy, London)   20829
FORMER NATIONAL ANTHEM
    Part 1: BOŽE PRAVDE, TI ŠTO SPASE (from Serbian hymn - Davorin Jenko)
    Part 2: LIJEPA NAŠA DOMOVINO (from Croatian hymn - attrib Josip Runjanin or V.Lichtenegger)
    Part 3: NAPREJ ZASTAVA SLAV (from Slovene hymn - Davorin Jenko)
                             PC   2(picc)222/4230/timp.perc/str   Breitkopf   14305
        arr H.Carr & Williams   ∅   2121/2230/timp.perc/hp/str   [Arrangers]   MS 20142
        arr G.Williams   ∅   2222/4331/timp.perc/str   [Arranger]   19645
    Part 1: Serbian hymn complete
        arr A.Hohenstein   PC   2(picc)222/4231/timp.perc/str   Benjamin   16363 +
        arr M.L.Lake   PC   112.2sx.1/2210/perc/str   C.Fischer   19720

YUGOSLAVIA - MONTENEGRO

FORMER NATIONAL ANTHEM
    ONAM, ONAMO, ZA BRDA ONA
        arr A.Hohenstein   PC   2(picc)222/4231/timp.perc/str   Benjamin   16363 +
NATIONAL AIRS
    OHAMO, OHAMO ZA OPGA OHA: patriotic song (D.Jenko)
        arr M.L.Lake   PC   112.2sx.1/2210/perc/str   C.Fischer   19720

ZANZIBAR   see   TANZANIA

SCORES

The list of instruments is preceded by a symbol showing the type of score available, as follows:

ø	Full score
LS	Lead sheet, or control score, showing the main outlines of the music
OS	Open score (instrumentation not specified)
PA	Piano accompaniment (ie. piano part, without melody or indication of instrumentation)
PC	Piano conductor
PS	Piano score (ie. piano reduction, without indication of instrumentation)
SS	Short (condensed) score
VS	Vocal score

GENERAL ABBREVIATIONS

A	Alto (Voice)
a	prefix for alto instrument
	eg. asx = saxophone
acdn	accordian
acym	antique cymbals
add	additional
afl	alto flute
alphn	alpine horn
amp	amplified
aob	see ob'da
anv	anvil
asx	alto saxophone in E♭
asxhn	alto saxhorn in E♭
atbn	alto trombone
attrib	attributed
B	Bass (Voice)
b	prefix for bass instrument
	eg. bcl = bass clarinet
bal	balalaika
Bar	Baritone (Voice)
bar	baritone (instrument)
barsx	baritone saxophone in E♭
bary	baryton (viola di bardone)
Bbar	Bass baritone (Voice)
BB♭tuba	contrabass tuba (military bands)
bcl	bass clarinet
bdm	bass drum
bells	tubular bells
cbells	cow bells
hbells	hand bells
sbells	sleigh bells
bfl	bass flute
bgo	bongoes
bgtr	bass guitar (electric)
bjo	banjo
bmba	bass marimba
bob	bass oboe
Bp	Basso profondo (Voice)
br	brass

brec	bass recorder
bsn	bassoon
cbsn	contra bassoon
bsx	bass saxophone
bsxhn	bass saxhorn
btbn	bass trombone
bthn	basset horn
bv chorus	boy's voices
bvtbn	bass valve trombone
bwtuba	bass wagner tuba
bxyl	bass xylophone
ca	cor anglais
cab	cabaca
cast	castanets
cb	double bass (instrument)
cb	prefix for contrabass instrument
	eg. cbtbn = contrabass trombone
cbcl	contrabass clarinet
cbells	cow bells
cbsn	contra bassoon/double bassoon
cbsx	contrabass saxophone in E♭
cbsxhn	contrabass saxhorn in E♭
(Cbtpt)	bass trumpet in C, normally btpt
cbtuba	contrabass tuba
cel	celesta
cga	conga drum
chal	chalumeau
ch-chorus	chamber chorus
chit	chiterone
choc	chocalho
chorg	chamber organ
chorus	mixed voice chorus (SATB)
chp	celtic harp
cim	cimbalon
cl	clarinet(in A, B♭ or C)
bcl	bass clarinet
Dcl	clarinet in D
E♭cl	clarinet in E♭
cl-d'a	clarinet d'amour

cnt	cornet B♭ or A		hmn	harmonium
E♭cnt	soprano cornet in E♭		hn	horn
cntto	cornetto (cornett)		Horg	Hammond organ
Coll Ed	Collected Edition		hp	harp
conc	concertante, concertino		hpsd	harpsichord
congr	congregation		htpf	honky-tonk piano
cont	continuo			
cor-dc	cor di caccia.[hunting horn]			
ctna	concertina		inst	instrument
crot	crotales (antique finger cymbals)			
Ct	Counter-tenor (Voice)			
cv chorus	children's chorus		jhp	jew's harp
CW	Complete Works		jpf	jangle piano (multitone)
cym	cymbals			
			kbd	keyboard (unspecified)
dbl	double		kglock	keyed glockenspiel
Dcl	clarinet in D		kit	drum kit
dctne	dulcitone		kz	kazoo
disc	gramophone (phono) record			
dm	drum			
mildm	military drum		latin	latin-american percussion
drec	descant recorder			
Dtpt	trumpet in D			
dulc	dulcimer		Ma	Male alto
			mand	mandoline
			mba	marimba
ehpsd	electric harpsichord		mbn	marimbophone
egtr	electric guitar		mbula	marimbula
elec	electronic equipment (other than synthesizer or pre-recorded tape)		mbx	musical box
			mell	mellophone
eorg	electric (electronic) organ		mildm	military drum
epf	electric (electronic) piano		min	minor
euph	euphonium (tenor tuba)		mrc	maracas
			mtl	metallophone
			mv chorus	male voices
fftpt	fanfare trumpets		mvt	movement
fl	flute		Mz	Mezzo-soprano (Voice)
afl	alto flute			
bfl	bass flute			
flag	flageolet		narr	narrator
flex	flexatone		nat	national
flg	flügelhorn		nov	novochord
Ftpt	trumpet in F			
fv chorus	female chorus			
			ob	oboe
			bob	bass oboe
gbrec	great bass recorder		ca	cor anglais
glock	glockenspiel		heck	heckelphone (baritone oboe)
gro	guiro		obbl	obbligato
gtr	guitar		oc	ocarina
			ob-d'a	oboe d'amore
			ob-dc	oboe di caccia
hbells	handbells		om	ondes martenot
hca	harmonica		oph	ophicleide
heck	heckelphone		opt	optional
hht	hi-hat			

org	organ	sx	saxophone	
Horg	Hammond organ	asx	alto saxophone in E♭	
porg	portative organ	barsx	baritone saxophone in E♭	
posorg	positive organ	bsx	bass saxophone in E♭	
prorg	prepared organ	cbsx	contrabass saxophone in E♭	
		sisx	sopranino saxophone in E♭	
		ssx	soprano saxophone in B♭	
perc	percussion	tsx	tenor saxophone in B♭	
perf	performed	sxhn	saxhorn	
pf	piano	asxhn	alto saxhorn in E♭	
picc	piccolo	B♭sxhn	bass saxhorn in B♭	
porg	portative organ	cbsxhn	contrabass saxhorn in B♭	
posorg	positive organ	E♭bsxhn	bass saxhorn in E♭	
pr	prepared	sisxhn	sopranino saxhorn in E♭	
prfl	prepared flute	ssxhn	soprano saxhorn in B♭	
prorg	prepared organ	tsxhn	tenor saxhorn in B♭	
prpf	prepared piano	syn	synthesizer	
ptimp	pedal timp			
		T	Tenor (Voice)	
		t	prefix to tenor instruments	
rctr	reciter		eg. tdm = tenor drum	
real	realised	tamb	tambourine	
rec	recorder	tamtam	tam-tam	
brec	bass recorder	tape	tape recording (ie. pre-recording)	
drec	descant recorder	tnkp	tenor banjo	
sirec	sopranino recorder	tblrec	treble (alto) recorder	
tblrec	treble (alto) recorder	tbn	trombone	
trec	tenor recorder	btbn	bass trombone in G or F	
recit	recitative	E♭btbn	bass trombone in E♭	
reconstr	reconstructed	ttbn	tenor trombone in B♭	
redn	reduction	tbtbn	tenor-bass trombone	
		vtbn	valve trombone	
S	Soprano (Voice)	tdm	tenor drum	
s	prefix for soprano instrument	thn	tenor horn	
	eg. ssx = soprano saxophone	timb	timbales	
sarr	sarrusophone	timp	timpani	
saw	musical saw	tmc	thunder machine	
sbells	sleigh bells (jingles)	tpbell	temple bell	
scym	suspended cymbals	tpbl	temple blocks	
sdm	side (snare) drum	tomtom	tom-tom	
shm	shawm	toypf	toy piano	
si	prefix for sopranino instrument	tpt	trumpet in A, B♭ or C	
	eg. sirec = sopranino recorder	btpt	bass trumpet in C	
sirec	sopranino recorder	cbtpt	contrabass trumpet in C	
sisx	sopranino saxophone in E♭	Dtpt	trumpet in D	
sisxhn	sopranino saxhorn in E♭	E♭btpt	bass trumpet in E♭	
sitpt	sopranino trumpet in E♭	E♭ptpt	E♭ piccolo trumpet	
	(also called piccolo trumpet)	E♭tpt	soprano trumpet in E♭	
skbt	sackbut	fftpt	fanfare trumpet	
sous	sousaphone	Ftpt	trumpet in F	
spkr	speaker	sitpt	sopranino trumpet in B♭	
spt	serpent	transcr	transcribed	
ssx	soprano saxophone in B♭	transl	translated	
ssxhn	soprano saxhorn in B♭	transp	transposed	
stpt	soprano trumpet	trec	tenor recorder	
str	strings	tri	triangle	

tsh	thunder sheet	vltta	violetta
tsx	tenor saxophone in B♭	vtbn	valve trombone
tsxhn	tenor saxhorn in B♭		
ttbn	tenor trombone in B♭		
ttuba	tenor tuba (euphonium)	wdbl	woodblock
tuba	bass tuba (ie. normal orchestral	wddm	wooddrum
	tuba in F)	whip	whip
twtuba	tenor wagner tuba	wmc	windmachine
		wtuba	wagner tuba
		ww	woodwind
uke	ukelele		
		xba	xylorimba
vib	vibraphone	xyl	xylophone
vla	viola	xmba	xylomarimba
vla-d'a	viola d'amore	xmbn	xylomarimbaphone
vla-db	viola da braccia		
vla-dg	viola da gamba		
vlc	cello	4tet	quartet
vln	violin	5tet	quintet
vlne	violone	6tet	sextet

PUBLISHERS

Aff Mus Inc	Affiliated Musicians Incorporated
Akad Druck u Verl	Akademische Druck und Verlagsanstalt
AH & C	Ascherberg, Hopwood & Crewe
AIM	American Institute of Musicology
AMP	Associated Music Publishers
Boccaccini & S	Boccaccini & Spada
Boosey & H	Boosey & Hawkes
Bote & B	Bote & Bock
Box & C	Box & Cox
Breitkopf & H	Breitkopf & Härtel
Carisch & J	Carisch & Jänichen
CML	Central Music Library (Westminster Public Libraries)
CUP	Cambridge University Press
Czech SM	Czech State Music Publishers
Deiss & C	Deiss & Crepin
Dept Ed Chile	Departamento de Educación, Chile
DVfM	Deutscher Verlag für Musik
EFSDS	English Folk Song & Dance Society
Ed Bib Nat	Éditions Bibliothèques Nationales
Ed Mus Trans	Éditions Musicales Transatlantiques
Ed Musica	Edition Musica, Budapest
Enoch & C	Enoch & Costallat
Evette & S	Evette & Schaeffer
FD & H	Francis Day & Hunter
Gebethner & W	Gebethner & Wolff
Goodwin & T	Goodwin & Tabb
Gould & B	Gould & Bolttler
H-M Presse	Haydn-Mozart Presse
Hargail Mus	Hargail Music Press
IISM	Instituto Italiano per la Stria della Musica
IMC	International Music Corporation
Israel MI	Israel Music Institution
Kiesel & B	Kiesel & Böhme
Kistner & S	Kistner & Siegel
Longman & B	Longman & Broderip
Mackar & N	Mackar & Noël
MwV	Musikwissenschaftlicher Verlag
MV	Manheimer Music Verlag
OUP	Oxford University Press
Phillips & P	Phillips & Page
PMMS	Plainsong & Medieval Music Society
Polish SM	Polish State Music Company
Praeger & M	Praeger & Meier
Raabe & P	Raabe & Plothow
RAI	Reale Accademia d'Italia
Reinecke & B	Reinecke & Bland
Ries & E	Ries & Erler
RMA	Royal Musical Association
RSCM	Royal School of Church Music
Russian SM	Russian State Music Company
Rieter-B	Rieter-Biedermann
Rt Lerolle	Rouart Lerolle

S Zerboni	Suivini Zerboni
Schauer & M	Schauer & May
Schweers & H	Schweers & Haake
SMA	Scottish Music Archive
Stainer & B	Stainer & Bell
Tischer & J	Tischer & Jaegenberg
UME	Union Musical Española
UMF-E	Union Musical France - Espagnol
UMP	United Music Publishers
Victoria MP	Victoria Music Publishers
Wagner & L	Wagner & Levien
WMA	Workers' Music Association
YBP	Year Book Press
Yugoslav SM	Yugoslav State Music Publishers

PUBLISHED ANTHOLOGIES   For abbreviations of Complete Works of composers, see under relevant composer

CIDM   CLASSICI ITALIANI DELLA MUSICA.   Rome: Del Turco Editore, 1956-

DDT   DENKMÄLER DEUTSCHER TONKUNST.   Leipzig: Breitkopf & H, 1892-1931

DDT NS   DENKMÄLER DEUTSCHER TONKUNST - New Series.   Leipzig: Breitkopf & H, 1967-

DDTB   DENKMÄLER DEUTSCHER TONKUNST IN BAYERN

      Vols 1-31 - Leipzig: Breitkopf & H, 1900-1920

      Vols 32-36 - Augsburg: B.Filser, 1924-1931

Denk Rhein   DEMNKMÄLER RHEINISCHER MUSIK.   Düsseldorf: L.Schwann, 1951-

DTÖ   DEMNKMÄLER DER TONKUNST IN OSTERREICH.

      Vienna: Artaria, 1894-1919

      Vienna: Universal, 1920-

EDM   Das ERBE DEUTSCHER MUSIK.   Leipzig: Breitkopf & H, 1935

MAB   MUSICA ANTIQUA BOHEMICA.   Prague: Artia, 1949-

MB   MUSICA BRITANNICA.   London: Royal Musical Association/Stainer & B, 1951-

PAPTM   PUBLIKATIONEN ALTERER PRAKTISCHER UND THEORETISCHER MUSIKWERKE, ed

      R.Eitner.   Leipzig: Breitkopf & H, 1873-1905.   Reprinted

      Broude Bros

STIM   SOCIÉTÉ SUEDOISE DE COMPOSITEURS AUTEURS ET EDITEURS DE MUSIQUE

      TEGNÉRLUDDEN, 3.   Stockholm, Sweden

RISM Sigla

Where the library holds copies of manuscripts or of early printed editions specially obtained from
another library, the library of origin is listed using the sigla adopted by RISM (Répetoire Internationale
des Sources Musicales.   Kassel: Bärenreiter, 1971), eg. GB-Lbm = British Library - London

A

AFAS MUSIK VERLAG (HANS DUNNEBEIL)
   see BOTE & BOCK [Schirmer]

AFFILIATED MUSIC PUBLISHERS LTD
   Now EMI MUSIC

AHN & SIMROCK
   Widenmayerstr 6, 8000 Munich 22, West Germany

ALKOR EDITION
   [Bärenreiter]

ALSBACH & DEYER
   Postbus 338, Bussem, Netherlands

AMERICAN INSTITUTE OF MUSICOLOGY
   [Blackwells]

AMICI DELLA MUSICA DA CAMERA, GLI
   [Hinrichsen]

AMPHION EDITIONS MUSICALES
   [United Mus Publishers]

AM-RUS EDITION
   see LEEDS MUSIC CORP [Leeds Music]

ANDRAUD, ALBERT J.
   see SOUTHERN MUSIC CO TEXAS [Musica Rara]

ANDRE, JOHANN
   Frankfurterstr 28, Offenbach am Main

ANGLO-SOVIET MUSIC PRESS (LONDON) LTD
   [Boosey & Hawkes]

ARNOLD, EDWARD, (PUBLISHERS) LTD
   see NOVELLO

ARS VIVA
   see SCHOTT

ARTIA
   [Kalmus]

ASCHERBERG HOPWOOD & CREW LTD
   see CHAPPELL

ASHDOWN, EDWIN LTD
   275-81 Cricklewood Bdy, London NW2 6QR

ASSOCIATED BOARD OF THE ROYAL SCHOOLS OF MUSIC
   14 Bedford Sq, London WC1B 3JG

ASSOCIATED MUSIC PUBLISHERS INC
   [G.Schirmer]

AUGENER LTD
   see STAINER & BELL

AYRE, ALEX
   84 Bois Moor Rd, Chesham, Bucks

B

BANK, ANNIE, EDITIONS
   [Alex Ayre Music Services]

BÄRENREITER LTD
   17-18 Bucklersbury, Hitchin SG5 1BB

BARENREITER VERLAG
   [Bärenreiter Ltd]

BAYLEY & FERGUSON LTD
   65 Berkeley St, Glasgow G3 7DZ

BELAIEFF, EDITIONS
   [Peters Edition]

BENJAMIN, ANTON J. GMBH
   [Schauer]

BENOIT
   see SALABERT

BERLIN, IRVING, LTD
   [Chappell]

BESSEL, W & CO LTD
   [Boosey & Hawkes]

BILLAUDOT
   [A.A.Kalmus]

BIRCHARD C.C.
   see SUMMY-BIRCHARD [A.A.Kalmus]

BIRNBACH, RICHARD
   Dürerstr 28a, Berlin-Lichterfelde-West

BLACK, A & C
   [Chappell]

BOHM, ANTON UND SOHN
   Ludwigstr 15, Augsberg 2 [Direct only]

BOILEAU, CASA EDITORIAL DE MUSICA
   Provenza 285-287, Barcelona

BOMART MUSIC PUBLICATIONS INC
   [A.A.Kalmus]

BONGIOVANNI, FRANCESCO
   Via Rizzoli, 28E Bologna [Direct only]

BOOSEY & HAWKES LTD
   295 Regent Street, London W1

BORNEMANN EDITIONS
   [United Music Publishers]

BOSTON MUSIC COMPANY
   [Chappell]

BOSWORTH & CO LTD
   14-18 Heddon St, London W1

BOTE & BOCK
   [G.Schirmer]

BRANDUS ET CIE
   see JOUBERT [United Music Publishers]

BREITKOPF & HARTEL, WIESBADEN
   [A.A.Kalmus]

BREITKOPF & HARTEL, LEIPZIG
   [Fentone Music]

BRITISH & CONTINENTAL MUSIC AGENCIES LTD
   Now EMI

BROADCAST MUSIC INC
   320 W57th St, NY10019, U.S.A.

BROCKHAUS, MAX
   Oskar-Gretherstr 13, Lärrach-Tumringen, Baden

BROEKMANS & VAN POPPEL
   [A.A.Kalmus]

BROUDE BROS
    [Fentone Music]
BRUCKNERVERLAG
    [A.A.Kalmus]
BRUZZICHELLI
    [A.A.Kalmus]

C

CAMPBELL, CONNELLY & CO LTD
    37 Soho Sq, London W1
CARISCH S.P.A.
    [Peters/Boosey]
CARL FISCHER INC
    see FISCHER, CARL [Boosey]
CARY, L.J. & CO LTD
    [Chappell]
CASA EDITORIAL DE MUSICA BOILEAU
    see BOILEAU
CAVENDISH MUSIC CO LTD
    [Boosey]
CeBeDeM FOUNDATION
    [Lengnick]
CHANT DU MONDE, ÉDITIONS, LE
    [United Music Publishers]
CHAPPELL & CO LTD
    129 Park St, London W1A 3FA
CHESTER, J & W LTD
    7-9 Eagle Court, London EC1
CHOUDENS, ÉDITIONS
    [United Music Publishers]
CHURCH, JOHN, CO
    [Kalmus]
CINEPHONIC MUSIC PUBLICATIONS INC
    [Campbell]
CONCORDIA PUBLISHING HOUSE
    3558 S Jefferson Ave, St Louis, Missouri
COSTALLAT, ÉDITIONS
    [United Music Publishers]
CRAMER, J B & CO LTD
    99 St Martins Lane, WC2N 4AZ
CRANZ & CO LTD
    [United Music Publishers]
CRANZ, AUGUST, GMBH
    [United Music Publishers]
CRANZ, A, ÉDITIONS
    [United Music Publishers]
CURCI, EDIZIONI, SRL
    Galleria del Corso 4, Milan
CURWEN, J & SONS, LTD
    [Faber/Schirmer/Elkin, Norwich]
CZECH STATE MUSIC
    [A.A.Kalmus]

D

DANIA, EDITION
    [Chester]
DASH, IRWIN, MUSIC CO LTD
    [Campbell]
DE RING
    17 Laurierstraat, Antwerp
DE SANTIS
    [Peters]
DEISS
    see SALABERT [United Music Publishers]
DELRIEU & CIE
    14 Rue Trachel, 06000, Nice
DESCLÉE & CIE
    [Chester]
DEUTSCHER VERLAG FÜR MUSIK
    [Fentone Music]
DISNEY, WALT, MUSIC CO LTD
    68 Pall Mall, London SW1Y 5EX
DITSON, OLIVER
    [A.A.Kalmus]
DIX LTD
    [EMI]
DOBLINGER MUSIKVERLAG
    [A.A.Kalmus]
DONEMUS FOUNDATION
    [A.A.Kalmus]
DURAND & CIE
    [United Music Publishers]

E

EDITION: Firms beginning with this word are
entered under the words which follow, eg Russe
de musique, Edition

ELKAN-VOGEL CO INC
    [United Music Publishers]
ELKIN & CO LTD
    [Novello]
ELKIN, WILLIAM
    Deacon House, Brundill, Norwich
ENGSTRØM & SØDRING MUSIK-FORLAG
    [Hinrichsen]
ENOCH & CIE
    [Ashdown]
ESCHIG, MAX
    [Schott]
EULENBURG, EDITION, GMBH
    [Schott]
EULENBURG, EDITION, INC
    373 Park Av S, New York 16 NY
EULENBURG, ERNST, LTD
    [Schott]

F

FABER MUSIC LTD
   3 Queen Sq, London WC1N 3AU
FAITH PRESS LTD
   Wing Road, Leighton Buzzard, Beds LU7 7NG
FAZER MUUSIIKKIKAUPPA OY
   Aleksanterinkatu 11, Helsinki [Direct only]
FEIST, LEO, INC
   799 7th Ave, New York 19, NY
FELDMAN, B & CO LTD
   64 Dean St, London W1
FISCHER, CARL, INC
   [Boosey]
FISCHER, J & BRO
   Harristown Road, Glenrock, NJ
FOETISCH FRÈRES
   [Chester]
FORBERG, ROBERT
   [Peters Edition]
FORLIVESI, A CASA MUSICALE
   Via Rome 4, Firenze [Direct only]
FORSYTH BROS, LTD
   126-8 Deansgate, Manchester M3 2GR
FOX, SAM, PUBLISHING CO INC
   [EMI]
FRANÇAISES DE MUSIQUE, ÉDITIONS
   26 Rue Beaujon, Paris 8
FRANCIS, DAY & HUNTER LTD
   [EMI]
FREDERICK HARRIS MUSIC CO LTD
   see HARRIS, FREDERICK
FREEMAN, E H LTD
   [EMI]
FRENCH, SAMUEL, LTD
   26 Southampton St, St, London WC2
FÜRSTNER, ADOLPH
   [Boosey & Hawkes]

G

GALAXY MUSIC CORP
   2121 Broadway, New York 23, NY 10023, U.S.A.
GALLIARD, LTD
   [Stainer & Bell]
GAUDET, E EDITIONS
   see SALABERT
GAY, NOEL, MUSIC CO LTD
   24 Denmark St, London WC2
GEHRMANS, CARL, MUSIKFORLAG
   [Boosey & Hawkes (Orchestral only) (Hire)]
   [Chester (Sale)]
GILLES
   see SALABERT
GLOCKEN VERLAG LTD
   12 - 14 Mortimer St, London W1N 8EL

GRAHL, H.L.
   Güntersburger Allee 46, Frankfurt am Main
GRAY, H.W. CO INC
   [Belwin-Mills]
GRUS, L. & CIE
   65 bis, Rue de Miromesnil, Paris 8
GUTHEIL, A. GMBH
   [Boosey & Hawkes]
GWYNN PUBLISHING CO
   Llangollen, North Wales LL20 8SN

H

HAINAUER, JULIUS, LTD
   29 Cranbourne Gdns, London NW11
HAMELLE, J
   [United Music Publishers]
HANNSLER-VERLAG
   7303 Neuhausen, Stuttgart, Postfach 1220,
   West Germany
HANSEN'S MUSIKFORLAG, WILHELM
   [Chester]
HARGAIL MUSIC PRESS
   [Kalmus]
HARMS INC
   [Chappell]
HARMS, T.B. & CO
   [Chappell]
HARRIS, FREDERICK, MUSIC CO LTD
   [Lengnick]
HASLINGER, CARL
   Tuchlauben 16, Wien 1
HAWKES & SON LTD
   see BOOSEY & HAWKES
HAYDN INSTITUT
   [Kalmus]
HAYDN-MOZART PRESSE
   [Kalmus]
HEINRICHSHOFEN'S VERLAG
   [Peters Edition]
HENLE, VERLAG
   [Bärenreiter]
HENN EDITIONS
   [UMP]
HEUGEL & CIE (AU MENESTREL)
   [United Music Publishers]
HINNENTHAL, J.P.
   Königsbrügg 22, Bielefeld
HINRICHSEN EDITION LTD
   [Peters Edition]
HOFMEISTER, FRIEDRICH
   [A.A.Kalmus]
HUDEBNI MATICE
   see ARTIA [A.A.Kalmus]
HUG & CO
   [Peters]

HUNGARIAN STATE MUSIC
  [Boosey & Hawkes]

I

INTERNATIONAL MUSIC CO
  [Kalmus]
INTERNATIONALE MUSIKLEIHBIBLIOTHEK, DIE
  Brunnenstr 188/190, Berlin N54
IRVING BERLIN LTD
  see BERLIN, IRVING, LTD
IRWIN DASH MUSIC CO LTD
  see DASH, IRWIN
ISRAELI MUSIC INSTITUTE
  [A.A.Kalmus]
ISRAELI MUSIC PUBLICATIONS
  [Peters Edition]

J

JOBERT, JEAN, EDITIONS
  [United Music Publishers]
JOSEPH WILLIAMS LTD
  see WILLIAMS, JOSEPH
JOUBERT & CIE
  [Chappell]
JUNGNICKEL, ROSS
  165 E 35th St, New York NY
JUNNE, OTTO
  Mitterstrasse 1, München 15

K

KAHNT, C.F.
  [Novello]
KALLMEYER, GEORG, VERLAG
  [Novello]
KALMUS, ALFRED A LTD
  2-3 Fareham St, London W1
KALMUS, EDWIN F
  [Kalmus, A.][Belwin-Mills]
KEITH PROWSE MUSIC PUBLISHING CO LTD
  see PROWSE, KEITH
KERR, JAMES S.
  79 Berkeley St, Glasgow C3
KING, ROBERT, MUSIC CO
  7 Canton St, Nth Easton, Mass
KISTNER FR. SIEGAL, C.F. and Co
  [Novello]
KNEUSSLIN, VERLAG
  [Peters]
KRENN, LUDWIG
  [Bosworth]
KULTURA
  [Boosey & Hawkes]

L

LAFLEUR & SON
  see BOOSEY & HAWKES
LARWAY, J.H.
  [Ashdown]
LAUDY & CO
  see BOSWORTH
LAWRENCE WRIGHT MUSIC CO LTD
  see WRIGHT, LAWRENCE
LEDUC, ALPHONSE, & CIE
  [United Music Publishers]
LEEDS MUSIC LTD
  438 Piccadilly, London W1V 95H
LEEDS MUSIC CORPORATION
  [Leeds Music Ltd]
LEMOINE, HENRI & CIE
  [United Music Publishers]
LENGNICK, ALFRED & CO LTD
  Purley Oaks Studios, 421a Brighton Rd,
  South Croydon CR2 6YR
LEONARD, GOULD & BOLTTLER
  99 St Martins Lane, London WC2
LEUCKART, F.E.C.
  [Novello]
LIBER-SOUTHERN LTD
  8 Denmark St, London WC2
LIENAU, ROBERT
  [Peters]
LITOLFF, HENRY, VERLAG
  [Peters]
LUNDQUISTS, ABRAHAM MUSIKFORLAG
  Katarina Bangata 17, 116 25 Stockholm
LYCHE, HARALD
  3001 Drammen, Norway
LYREBIRD PRESS
  see OISEAU-LYRE, ÉDITIONS DE L'
  [United Music Publishers]

M

MANNHEIMER MUSIKVERLAG
  Richard Wagner Str 6, Mannheim 68
MARKS, EDWARD B∅ MUSIC CORPORATION
  [Intersong]
MATHOT
  see SALABERT
MAURICE, PETER, MUSIC CO LTD
  [EMI]
MERCURY MUSIC CORPORATION
  [A.A.Kalmus]
MERION MUSIC INC
  [A.A.Kalmus]
MERSEBURGER VERLAG
  [Peters]

MILLS MUSIC LTD
  [Belwin-Mills]
MODERN, EDITION
  [A.A.Kalmus]
MOECK, HERMANN, VERLAG
  [A.A.Kalmus]
MÜSELER VERLAG
  [Novello]
MOWBRAY, A.R. & CO LTD
  28 Margaret St, London W1
MUSICA RARA
  Le Traversier. Chemin de la Buire 84170, Monteux
MUSICALES TRANSATLANTIQUES, ÉDITIONS
  [United Music Publishers]
MUSICUS, EDITION
  333 W 52nd St, New York 19, NY
MUSIKWISSENSCHAFTLICHER VERLAG
  [A.A.Kalmus]

N

NAGELS VERLAG
  [Bärenreiter]
NEUE MUSIK VERLAG
  [Fentone]
NEW MUSIC EDITION
  see MERION MUSIC INC [A.A.Kalmus]
NEW WIND MUSIC CO
  23.Ivor Place NW1
NOEL GAY MUSIC CO LTD
  see GAY, NOEL
NOEL, PIERRE
  [United Music Publishers]
NORDISKA MUSIKFORLAGET
  [Chester]
NORSK MUSIKFORLAG
  [Chester]
NOVELLO & CO LTD
  Borough Green, Sevenoaks, Kent

O

OERTEL, L
  Ainmiller Str 42, D8000 Munich 40,
  West Germany
OISEAU-LYRE, ÉDITIONS DE L'
  [United Music Publishers]
OLIVAN PRESS
  [A.A.Kalmus]
OLSCHKI, LEO S.
  CP66, 50100 Florence
OXFORD UNIVERSITY PRESS (MUSIC DEPARTMENT)
  37 Dover St, London WIX 4AH

P

PATERSON'S PUBLICATIONS LTD
  38 Wigmore St, London W1H 0EX

PAXTON, W. & CO LTD
  [Novello]
PEER INTERNATIONAL
  [Southern Music]
PEER MUSIKVERLAG GMBH
  Muhlenkamp 43, 2 Hamburg 60
PETER MAURICE MUSIC CO LTD
  see MAURICE, PETER
PETERS, C.F. CORPORATION
  [Peters]
PETERS EDITION
  119-125 Wardour St, London W1V 4DN
POLSKIE WYDAWNICTWO MUZYCZNE
  [A.A.Kalmus]
PRESSER, THEODORE CO
  [A.A.Kalmus]
PRO MUSICA VERLAG
  [Fentone]
PROWSE, KEITH, MUSIC PUBLISHING CO LTD
  [EMI]

R

RAHTER, D
  [Schauer]
RICORDI, G. & CO LTD
  The Bury, Church St, Chesham (Hire only)
  [Novello (Sales)]
RIES & ERLER MUSIKVERLAG
  [Hinrichsen]
ROBBINS MUSIC CORP LTD
  [EMI]
ROUART LEROLLE & CIE
  , see SALABERT
ROZSAVOLGYI
  see KULTURA [Boosey & Hawkes]
RSMV
  see RUSSIAN STATE PUBLICATION CO
RUSSE DE MUSIQUE, EDITION
  [Boosey & Hawkes]
RUSSIAN STATE PUBLICATION CO (MUSIC)
  Russian State Edition, c/o Collet's Holdings
  Ltd, Dennington Estate, Wellingborough

S

SALABERT, FRANCIS, ÉDITIONS
  22 Rue Chauchat, Paris 9
SAMUEL FRENCH LTD
  see FRENCH, SAMUEL
SCHAUER, RICHARD
  67 Belsize Lane NW3 5AX
SCHIRMER, E.C. MUSIC CO
  [Schauer]
SCHIRMER, G. INC
  140 Strand, London WC2R 1HG

SCHOLA CANTORUM, ÉDITIONS
[United Music Publishers]
SCHOTT & CO LTD
48 Gt Marlborough St, W1V 2BN
SCHWANN, L. MUSIKVERLAG
[Peters]
SCOTUS MUSIC PUBLICATIONS LTD
28 Dalrymple Crescent, Edinburgh EH9 2NX
SENART MAURICE ÉDITIONS
see SALABERT
SIKORSKI, HANS, VERLAG
[Belwin-Mills]
SIMROCK, N
[Lengnick, Schauer]
SKANDINAVISK MUSIKFORLAG
[Chester]
SONZOGNO, CASA MUSICALE
[United Music Publishers]
SOUTHERN MUSIC CO
1100 Broadway, San Antonio 6, Texas
SOUTHERN MUSIC PUBLISHING CO LTD
8 Denmark St, London WC2
STAINER & BELL LTD
82 High Road N2 9PW
STEINGRÄBER VERLAG
[Bosworth]
STOCKHAUSEN VERLAG
5067 Kurten, W Germany
SUECIA, EDITION
see GEHRMANS MUSIKFORLAG
[Boosey & Hawkes, Francis Day & Hunter]
SUMMY-BIRCHARD PUBLISHING CO
[A.A.Kalmus]

T

TRANSATLANTIQUES, ÉDITIONS
[United Music Publishers]

U

UNIÓN MUSICAL ESPAÑOLA SA
[United Music Publishers]
UNITED MUSIC PUBLISHERS LTD
1 Montague St, London WC1

UNIVERSAL EDITION AG
[A.A.Kalmus]
UNIVERSAL EDITION (LONDON) LTD
2-3 Fareham St, London W1
URBANEK FR. A.
see ARTIA [A.A.Kalmus]

V

VIEWEG, C.F.
[Novello]
VIKING MUSIKFORLAG
Norrebrogade 34, Copenhagen N

W

WALT DISNEY MUSIC CO LTD
see DISNEY, WALT
WARNER BROS PUBLICATIONS INC
1230 Ave of the Americas, NY 10012, U.S.A.
WEEKES, A & CO LTD
[Stainer & Bell]
WEINBERGER, JOSEF, LTD
12-14 Mortimer St, W1N 8EL
WEINTRAUB MUSIC CO
33 W 60th St, NY 10023, U.S.A.
WILLIAMS, JOSEPH, LTD
[Stainer & Bell]
WILLIAMSON MUSIC INC
[Chappell]
WINTHROP ROGERS
see ROGERS, WINTHROP
WITMARK, M & SONS
[Warner Bros]
WRIGHT, LAWRENCE, MUSIC CO LTD
[ATV]

Z

ZANIBON, G.C.
[Peters]
ZERBONI, SUVINI, EDIZIONI
[Boosey]
ZIMMERMANN, WILHELM, MUSIKVERLAG
[Novello]